This book acts as a trusted guide in these uncertain times. The title *Media & Entertainment Law* does not do justice to the contribution that Ursula Smartt makes. Of course, on one level, this is a book for students of law. But it is much more than that; it puts law into its historical, political and social context. The breadth and depth of coverage is striking. Smartt is unafraid to reach strong conclusions and provides analyses of questions, such as, 'is trolling a criminal offence?' This book acts as a beacon. It helps readers to understand not only what the law is, but also why the law is what it is. In a fast-changing world, that is an invaluable contribution.

Sir Keir Starmer QC, MP

Ursula Smartt's *Media & Entertainment Law* is an invaluable and practical guide for working journalists and editors seeking legal guidance in pressured newsrooms. The clarity of content and signposting make it a reference work that is easy to search and practical to use. The chapters cover all aspects of law relevant to the media, from privacy to internet freedom. The book also serves as a broad primer on media and entertainment law of potential interest to media executives seeking context and history, as well as law students and lawyers outside this specialized sector.

Tom Thomson OBE, former Managing Editor, Reuters

The book is aimed primarily at students and lecturers of media law, although its erudition and clarity of presentation should attract a much wider readership. Key principles throughout are amply supported by reference to legislation and relevant cases, including a lot of famous ones involving celebrities. Since this is a dynamic and fast-moving area of law, this important and certainly readable book should inevitably attract the interest of media lawyers, not to mention [a] motley throng of advertising folk and journalists.

Elizabeth Robson Taylor and Phillip Taylor MBE of Richmond Green Chambers

From the perspective of students and lecturers in the media law and journalism area this versatile book is invaluable on many levels. It is accessible due to its jargon-free narrative and supports a range of pedagogies. This makes it attractive to undergraduate journalism students, including those on courses accredited by the NCTJ. Postgraduate journalism students benefit both from a robust introduction to media law and broader policies and regulations. The book's authoritative rigour and illuminating further reading sections make it the "go-to" title for law students, too. Finally, the author's inclusive approach to push the fourth edition firmly into the digital era and to make generous space for Scottish and Northern Irish angles in areas where the law differs from England and Wales in those jurisdictions adds much comprehensive and comparative value.

Thorsten Lauterbach, Law Lecturer, Robert Gordon University, Aberdeen

Media & Entertainment Law

The fourth edition of *Media & Entertainment Law* has been fully updated, analysing some of the most recent judgments in media law from across the United Kingdom, such as *Cliff Richard v the BBC*, *Max Schrems v Facebook and the Irish Information Commissioner*, developments on the 'right to be forgotten' (*NT1 and NT2*) and *ABC v Daily Telegraph* (Sir Philip Green).

The book's two main themes are freedom of expression and an individual's right to privacy. Regulation of the communication industries is covered extensively, including discussion of the print press and its online editions following Leveson, traditional broadcasting regulations for terrestrial TV and radio as well as media activities on converged devices such as tablets, iPads, mobile phone devices and 'on demand' services. Intellectual property law (specifically copyright) in the music and entertainment industries is also explored in the book's later chapters.

Also new to this edition are sections on:

- A focus on freedom of expression: its philosophical foundations; the struggles of those who have fought for it; and the varied ways in which the courts interpret freedom of expression regarding the taking and publishing of photographs.
- The 'right to be forgotten', data breaches, and the General Data Protection Regulation (GDPR).
- The media's increasing access to the courts, particularly when considering the privacy of those who are suspected of sexual offences.
- Press regulators, broadcasting and advertising regulations, and film and video regulations.
- Election and party-political broadcast regulations, with a focus on social media and recent election fraud.
- The emergence of online music distribution services, internet radio and free digital streaming music services, and their effect on the music industry.

The fourth edition also features a variety of pedagogical features to encourage critical analysis of case law and one's own beliefs.

Ursula Smartt lectures in law at New College of the Humanities – Northeastern University, Boston, USA, and London. She is a Researcher in Media and Entertainment Law at the University of Surrey, Guildford.

Ursula Smartt

Media &
Entertainment Law

FOURTH EDITION

Ursula Smartt

With a foreword by Baroness Helena Kennedy QC

Routledge
Taylor & Francis Group

LONDON AND NEW YORK

Fourth edition published 2020
by Routledge
2 Park Square, Milton Park, Abingdon, Oxon OX14 4RN

and by Routledge
52 Vanderbilt Avenue, New York, NY 10017

Routledge is an imprint of the Taylor & Francis Group, an informa business

First edition published by Routledge in 2011
Third edition published by Routledge in 2017

British Library Cataloguing-in-Publication Data
A catalogue record for this book is available from the British Library

Library of Congress Cataloging-in-Publication Data
Names: Smartt, Ursula, author.
Title: Media & entertainment law / Ursula Smartt.
Other titles: Media and entertainment law
Description: 4th edition. | Milton Park, Abingdon, Oxon; New York,
    NY : Routledge, 2020. | Includes bibliographical references and index.
Identifiers: LCCN 2019041317 (print) | LCCN 2019041318 (ebook) |
    ISBN 9781138479128 (hardback) | ISBN 9781138479135 (paperback) |
    ISBN 9781351066549 (ebook)
Subjects: LCSH: Mass media—Law and legislation—Great Britain. | Performing
    arts—Law and legislation—Great Britain. | Copyright—Great Britain.
Classification: LCC KD2870 .S53 2020 (print) | LCC KD2870 (ebook) |
    DDC 343.41/07830223—dc23
LC record available at https://lccn.loc.gov/2019041317
LC ebook record available at https://lccn.loc.gov/2019041318

ISBN: 978-1-138-47912-8 (hbk)
ISBN: 978-1-138-47913-5 (pbk)
ISBN: 978-1-351-06654-9 (ebk)

Typeset in Joanna
by Apex CoVantage, LLC

Contents

Foreword

In a remarkably short time, the Internet has revolutionized how people communicate and access news, information, entertainment and other media. It has created an increasingly converged market, with major companies – amongst them the world's biggest – now in the business of telecoms, content and online distribution. This has undoubtedly delivered important benefits to individuals and society. But there are enormous problems too as governments and lawmakers struggle to understand these developments and what to do about them. This book addresses such issues in a deep and analytical way.

As arguments rage, particularly online, about how and whether the Internet could or should be regulated, Ursula Smartt covers issues relating to harmful content and conduct; such as when British schoolgirl, Molly Russell, 14, took her own life in November 2017, after she had followed age-inappropriate content via social media. Smartt investigates how sites, that seem to encourage self-harm and suicide, should be better regulated. Should online destinations such as Instagram-Facebook, Pinterest and YouTube (Google) be left to police their own content or should the authorities try and step in? And in a digitally connected world without physical borders, is regulation actually possible effectively?

The regulators' chapters focus inter alia on misleading political advertising, 'fake news' and how to minimize possible harm from big on-demand TV-like services.

The depth of coverage in Ursula Smartt's 4th edition of *Media and Entertainment Law* is striking, focussing throughout on detailed case law analysis, the media's right to freedom of expression and the individual's right to privacy. Her style of writing is extremely readable and yet legally accurate, as every relevant case has been studied in detail from original court reports. It will be a highly informative resource not only for those who study media law but professional journalists as well. She brings many 'double gagging' orders (super injunctions) to life and illustrates how the law differs in parts of the UK by highlighting the 'outing' of some celebrities and sports personalities by the Press north of the border, where English injunctions were not applicable in the Scottish jurisdiction.

The public interest balancing test by the courts is reviewed at every stage and how the responsible journalism test has changed with different Strasbourg Human Rights Court rulings increasingly applied by the UK courts.

Since the last edition, Smartt has followed the law of online libel, harassment and harm with particular interest. She argues that libel tourism has now moved from London to the Edinburgh and Belfast high courts, whereby these jurisdictions have not yet adopted English defamation laws (The Defamation Act 2013).

She has kept abreast of European legal challenges in the 'right to be forgotten' arena, following the CJEU *Google Spain* ruling. She looks at the practical implication and applications by the UK courts, such as the NT1 and NT2 cases, and how some individuals are successful in being 'delinked' and 'delisted' online and others are not. She comes to the conclusion that complete privacy in the internet age seems to hardly exist for those who openly disclose and publish their private lives via social media.

She discusses the increasing use of 'secret courts' and 'closed hearings', whereby some terrorism cases are being held in private and where the media can only report the result at the end of such lengthy proceedings. She says courtroom secrecy is becoming more apparent, which could be seen to interfere with the open justice principle, so unique to the British justice system.

The data protection and freedom of access public information chapters act as a trusted guide to most recent legislation, such as the GDPR, and the increasing power and fines of the Information Commissioner. As social media and other online services become primary sources of information for many, and campaign advertising spend is moving decisively online, Smartt says that the current legal framework covering election and party political broadcasts, as well as advertising, has become inadequate; should there be stronger regulation and legislation to ensure that elections remain free and fair and not captured by a narrow range of interests, following the Cambridge Analytica scandal?

The breadth of coverage in this book — which is bang up to date — is astounding; including privacy, freedom of expression, technology, regulation, defamation, intellectual property and much more. The book contains the latest ruling in the *Kraftwerk* music copyright case which has taken over a decade in the German and European courts (*Pelham GmbH v Hütter*, CJEU July 2019).

Students of media law in England, Wales, Scotland and Northern Ireland can see this book as a trusted guide in these uncertain 'Brexit' times. It helps readers to understand not only what the law is, but also *why* the courts decide in privacy matters, for example, in the *Sir Cliff Richard v BBC* case. It is an invaluable contribution to modern legal education.

Helena Kennedy QC, London
5 October 2019

Preface

The fourth edition to this book is once again a completely new rewriting of all chapters and their contents. The two main themes are of course still freedom of speech and privacy, which run like a golden thread through all ten chapters of the text. Though the UK prides itself on having a free press, journalistic activities today are restricted by numerous pieces of legislation, the majority of which form the subject matter of this book. As common law has developed, particularly in the area of human rights, it will be demonstrated that the courts have attempted to strike a fine balance between the freedoms and responsibilities of the press, while safeguarding an individual's right to privacy.

Chapter 1 looks at the philosophical foundations and developments of freedom of expression and the struggle of individual writers who fought for such freedoms in their respective societies. The term 'freedom of expression' importantly includes any act of seeking, receiving and imparting information or ideas, regardless of the medium used. The right to freedom of expression has been interpreted to include the right to take and publish photographs of strangers in public areas without their permission or knowledge. Supported by Article 10 of the European Convention on Human Rights (ECHR), it is a principle that supports the freedom of an individual or community to articulate one's opinions and ideas without fear of retaliation, censorship or punishment.

Chapter 2 deals with the right of privacy, a topic that has led to considerable argument between the media and those individuals who believe that the media are abusing it. To this day, there is no UK statute which covers expressly an individual's right to privacy, as Judge Glidewell famously said in the *Gordon Kaye* case (1991)[1] – 'there is no tort of privacy known to English law' – though this may well have changed now with the ruling in the *Cliff Richard* case when reporting on criminal suspects.[2]

Chapter 2 discusses privacy and confidentiality in a wide range of topics including drone photography and the invasion of privacy by paparazzi. Do we still have a 'right to be let alone' – as so eloquently expressed in the seminal essay by US lawyers Samuel Warren and Louis Brandeis, who first defined 'privacy' in 1890?[3] Sadly, their view no longer captures the purpose of privacy in our modern society.

The Human Rights Act 1998 (HRA) has had a considerable impact on UK privacy law, introducing in the UK some of the principles which have long been in force in other European states, also followed by the Strasbourg Human Rights Court. Its jurisprudence is now firmly part of UK law, and the courts regularly apply its judgments.

Whilst France and Germany have strict privacy laws, the UK stands out as not providing an actionable right to privacy – that is, the ability to sue someone who has seriously

---

1   *Kaye v Robertson & Sport Newspapers Ltd.* [1991] FSR 62 (Glidewell J).
2   *Sir Cliff Richard OBE v (1) The British Broadcasting Corporation (2) The Chief Constable of South Yorkshire Police* [2018] EWHC 1837; [2018] All ER (D) 111 (Jul) (Ch).
3   Warren, S.D. and Brandeis, L.D. (1890), 193–220.

invaded the secrets of your private life.[4] Some newspaper editors, such as former editor of the *Daily Mail*, Paul Dacre, famously argued that common law judge-made development has created a privacy law 'via the back door'.[5] Other commentators (and indeed the courts) will adhere to Article 8 ECHR and the importance of an individual's right to privacy no matter how famous the person might be. The important concepts of confidentiality and privacy are at the heart of this chapter.

The 'right to be forgotten', as developed in *Google Spain* (2014),[6] paved the way for claims to be made for damages for distress caused by data breaches, which in turn led to the strengthening of the EU General Data Protection Regulation (GDPR). We will look at case development, such as NT1 and NT2 (2018),[7] and how courts have dealt with individuals asking search engines such a Google to 'delink' and 'delist' their names from their common algorithms. The question which has become all too common, 'is there still privacy in the digital age?' has become rhetorical.

Chapter 3 deals with defamation and provides a brief historical overview of common law cases but swiftly moves on to online libel and award of damages by courts, said to vindicate injury to reputation and the surrounding publicity of any false statements which have been published. This includes injury to business reputation.

Due to the 'serious harm' test introduced by section 1(1) Defamation Act 2013, libel actions have declined considerably in the English and Welsh courts whilst privacy injunctions have become increasingly fashionable as they can prevent damaging articles from ever seeing the light of day. Devolved nations, such as Scotland and Northern Ireland, have not yet incorporated the 2013 Act into their legislation, and it is argued that libel tourism has shifted to the Edinburgh and Belfast courts.

While print media may eventually fade in people's memories, online publications, social media posts and news archives can potentially remain in cyberspace indefinitely. As Tugendhat J remarked in *Clarke (t/a Elumina Iberica UK) v Bain & Another* (2008): 'what is to be found on the Internet may become like a tattoo'.[8]

Defamation lawyers mainly deal with reputation management today, and the law together with privacy injunctions (Chapter 2) becomes multifaceted, arguably only accessible to the rich and famous. An individual or company has a different reputation for different aspects of their life or activities, such as business success, honesty, legal compliance and so forth. As we know, the internet has no geographical legal borders, and articles can be read in foreign jurisdictions and can even appear in Scotland or the Republic of Ireland if privacy injunctions have not been sought in those devolved jurisdictions. For this purpose, harm to reputation is capable of occurring on each occasion when a false statement referring to a complainant is communicated to another or others — for it is then that they may be likely to think the worse of the complainant.

Chapter 4 looks at the important area of court reporting in conjunction with the uniquely British open justice principle — a phenomenon which regularly astounds my students who are not from the UK. As part of my Public Law and English Legal System

---

4   Markesinis, B. S. and Unberath, H. (2002).
5   Speech to the Society of Editors by Paul Dacre, *Press Gazette*, 9 November 2008, following the ruling in *Mosley v Newsgroup Newspapers Ltd* [2008] EWHC 1777 (QB).
6   *Google Spain SL v Agencia Española de Protección de Datos (AEPD)* (C-131/12) [2014] QB 1022.
7   *NT1 & NT2 v Google LLC and Information Commissioner* [2018] EWHC 799 (QB).
8   [2008] EWHC 2636 para. 55 (Tugendhat J).

teaching at various universities, I direct my law students to various courts for observational visits (Magistrates', Crown and County Courts, the UK Supreme Court and the Royal Courts of Justice). They cannot believe that 'you just walk in'. The chapter will highlight, however, when media access rights are restricted in order to ensure fair trials for the protection of those who are vulnerable, such as children and victims of sexual offences. In high-profile cases, such as historical child sex offences, media interest can be particularly acute, and the argument will be advanced whether suspects of sexual offences should receive initial media anonymity.

A subject of concern is that of 'secret courts' and 'closed hearings', whereby some terrorism cases are now increasingly held in private and where the state argues in favour of public interest immunity (PII) for witnesses from the UK security services, police informers and undercover agents. The then Lord Chief Justice, Lord Thomas of Cwmgiedd, commented in 2015, when courtroom secrecy became increasingly prominent, that this practice interfered with the open justice principle, and it was a matter of constitutional concern.[9]

Chapter 5 focuses on contempt of court, unique to court reporting in the UK. Common law and statutory provision for 'contempt' ensure that *any* court – be it civil or criminal jurisdiction – is free to decide on the matters before it, without undue influence from the media during *sub judice* proceedings.

The practical function of the law of contempt has the purpose of preserving the integrity of the legal process in order to provide a fair trial to all parties in court. It is particularly relevant in criminal proceedings, where the court is under a duty to ensure the accused a fair trial, covered by Article 6(1) ECHR.[10]

We will look at a number of prosecutions by the Attorney General of some 'tweeting' jurors who have disobeyed judges' orders not to use the internet or social media for research on cases they are hearing and deliberating.

Chapter 6 deals with the topic of freedom of information, one of the pillars upon which an open and democratic government should operate. There will be a brief historical overview of freedom of information legislation in the UK and other countries, followed by a detailed discussion of the Freedom of Information Act 2000 (FOIA), a rather complex though extremely useful piece of legislation, and the increasingly important role of the Information Commissioner. The impact of the General Data Protection Regulation (GDPR)[11] will be examined and how the Data Protection Act 2018 is having a positive impact on individuals in the UK.

It will be argued that the FOIA has been a resounding success. Some cases will be examined, such as *Guardian* journalist Rob Evans' tireless quest to reveal the Prince of Wales' 'spider letters' and memos to government department and ministers after a decade-long battle through the courts.[12]

The theme of internet privacy and whether one can still hide one's identity and personal details on the internet will be explored. Can an individual still demand the right to remain anonymous when internet security now appears to be in the hands of social media giants such as Facebook and Twitter rather than EU and global legislators? The Edward

---

9 Judicial College (2015), pp. 3–5 (Lord Thomas LCJ).
10 *R v Sang* [1980] AC 402.
11 Regulation (EU) 2016/679 (the General Data Protection Regulation – GDPR) which repealed the Data Protection Directive 95/46 EC.
12 *Evans (Rob) v Information Commissioner* [2012] UKUT 313.

Snowden revelations by the *Observer* newspaper in 2013 are highlighted with an exposé of leaked whistle-blower documents by a Cambridge Analytica analyst who confirmed that Facebook had harvested personal and private information from more than 87 million individuals. Christopher Wylie, who worked with a Cambridge University academic to obtain the data, told the *Observer*: 'We exploited Facebook to harvest millions of people's profiles. And built models to exploit what we knew about them and target their inner demons. That was the basis the entire company was built on'.[13] The theme will be picked up again in Chapter 8 (regulating online harmful content).

Chapter 7 looks at regulating the print media and their online editions. The chapter on regulators used to be quite short in previous editions of this book and has since expanded into two chapters (7 and 8) with increasing importance for those working in the media and communications industries.

The media landscape has changed dramatically. How many people still read a print edition of a newspaper? One of the main challenges faced by the press today is falling revenue. Like all industries, newspapers and magazines have had to adapt to the technological changes which are shaping the way we live and how we consume our media. As more and more of us go online and use our smartphones, fewer of us are relying on the printed press for our news and entertainment. Most newspaper websites are free to access (although some charge subscriptions, such as *The Times/Sunday Times, The Daily Telegraph, The Financial Times*), and revenue is raised through advertising. As more and more people are choosing to read their news online, this causes a drop in overall revenues, which in turn can potentially affect how a newspaper operates.

Relevant media content has been included in form of internet sources, traditional law reports and judgments. Non-traditional platforms such as Vice News and BuzzFeed have also been consulted, in addition to traditional accredited news organization, such as BBC News Online and Reuters. Due to the demise of the 'red top' *News of the World* (*NoW*) and the aftermath of the Leveson Report, the case load of scandalous cases has been considerably reduced – though there have been a large number of (out of court) privacy actions against the Murdoch press going through the courts.

High-quality journalism is now under threat from the rise of clickbait and fake news; from falling circulations and difficulties in generating revenue online; and from the dramatic and continued rise of largely unregulated social media. These overarching themes will be discussed in this chapter.

Chapter 8 continues the theme of regulators and looks at traditional broadcasting regulations for terrestrial TV and radio as well as media activities on so-called converged devices, such as tablets, iPads, mobile phone devices and 'on demand' services such as video-on-demand (VoD) service providers.

Catch-up TV services now offer around-the-clock media content, and potentially anyone can have access to these services, including children. Additionally, there are numerous podcasts, BBC Sounds and the iPlayer, Amazon Prime, Netflix and YouTube services. All of these need regulating in one form or other – but can they be regulated? Whilst Amazon UK can be regulated by British regulator Ofcom, Netflix and YouTube (being US-based

---

13 Source: 'Revealed: 50 million Facebook profiles harvested for Cambridge Analytica in major data breach', Carole Cadwalladr and Emma Graham-Harrison, *Guardian*, 17 March 2018.

services) cannot be regulated in the UK. Media convergence today means an overlap of communications and media activities which are difficult to regulate.

This chapter covers traditional broadcast regulations, paid-for services, advertising standards, regulating the film and video industries and party political and election broadcasts. A large part discusses the regulation of online harmful content with summaries of parliamentary and Ofcom consultations.

Chapter 9 deals with the basics of intellectual property (IP), which is to ensure that a work is not copied or used without permission and to protect the economic rewards ('royalties') of the creators and authors of the works. 'Intellectual property' is something unique which is physically created by the 'author', 'creator' or inventor and refers to creations of the mind, such as inventions, literary and artistic works, designs and symbols, names and images used in commerce. An idea alone is not IP. For example, an idea for a book does not count, but the words written down do count. IP rights are like any other property right; they allow creators or owners of patents, trade marks or copyrighted works to benefit from their own intellectual work in the form of royalties and earned recognition from what they have invented or created. Some IP rights are automatic, such as copyright; some have to be registered, such as patents and trade marks.

Chapter 10 puts copyright law into practice and focuses on the entertainment industries. We begin with the development of the phonogram (recording) industry and the technological developments of mechanical rights. We then look at some large-scale industrial copyright infringements, such as internet piracy, peer-to-peer (P2P) file-sharing and sampling. Some performance artists, such as Lily Allen and Shania Twain, have argued that their royalties have been dramatically reduced since music downloads and streaming services make artists' recordings freely available via the internet.

There has been some good news in the extension of music performance rights from 50 years to 70 years – so-called Cliff's Law, named after its most ardent campaigner, Sir Cliff Richard, who lobbied the European Commission in order to get performers' rights extended – as some of the most famous artists' and bands' songs were reaching the 50-year mark, and performances could be 'grabbed' by any label.

The chapter looks at performing rights' societies and collection agencies that act on behalf of artists and songwriters by collecting their royalties and promoting economic rights of creators in the music and entertainment industries and how licensing agreements should be sought by any artist or band in order to avoid later legal challenges in joint copyright claims.

We will have a look at a number of copyright challenges in the music industry, such as those of Led Zeppelin, Procol Harum and Kraftwerk, and also look at some pirated films: for example, there were blockbuster movies including *Aquaman*, *Bohemian Rhapsody*, *Green Book* and *Fantastic Beasts: The Crimes of Grindelwald* with more than 30 million illegal downloads in 2019.

The emergence of online music distribution services, such as Amazon's Cloud Player and iTunes, as well as internet radio and free digital streaming music services such as Spotify and Pandora, have created challenges for the music industry and the various royalty-collecting and performance rights societies.

I hope the readers enjoy this new edition.

Ursula Smartt
Godalming, Surrey
November 2019

Acknowledgements

Much has changed since the first, second and third editions of this book. Legal commentator Joshua Rozenberg (2011) wrote in his foreword to the first edition about the fast-moving news channels (e.g. BBC News Online) and the 'biggest challenges' to court reporting and contempt legislation being social networks. Prominent lawyer, Michael Mansfield QC (2014), in the foreword to the second edition, worried about the surveillance state in the post-Snowden world and that the boundaries of privacy had become blurred to non-existent. Sir Keir Starmer QC in his foreword to the third edition (2017) drew on his experience as Director of Public Prosecutions (2008–2013) and his work as an eminent human rights lawyer to fight miscarriages of justice.

This edition is supported by a foreword by Baroness Helena Kennedy QC, one of the UK's most distinguished lawyers. She is a member of the Doughty Street Chambers in London and has practised at the Bar for over 40 years in the field of criminal law. She has conducted many of the leading cases in those years, including the Balcombe Street Siege in London, where four IRA gunmen eventually freed their two hostages and gave themselves up to police in December 1975; the Brighton bombing trial, where the IRA had targeted the Conservative party conference at the Grand Hotel at 2.54am on 12 October 1984. Helena Kennedy also conducted the Guildford Four Appeal in 1989; the Michael Bettaney Espionage case, who was convicted under the Official Secrets Act in 1984 at the Old Bailey for photographing secret documents for the KGB; the car bomb attack of the Israeli Embassy in London in 1994, injuring 20 civilians; the Jihadist fertiliser bomb plot by al-Qaeda sympathisers (2003–2007) and the transatlantic bomb plot, where a large device containing a printer cartridge bomb was found aboard a UPS plane at East Midlands Airport following a Saudi intelligence tip off in 2006. Baroness Kennedy has championed law reform for women, especially relating to sexual and domestic violence and developed the defence of Battered Woman's syndrome in the British courts. She has chaired the British Council and the UK Human Genetics Commission. She has been a member of the House of Lords for over 20 years, where she chaired The European Union Sub-committee on justice issues. She is the President of Justice, the British arm of the International Commission of Jurists. She is the chair of the Booker Prize Foundation and a member of Microsoft Technology and Human Rights Advisory Council. She stepped down as Principal of Mansfield College, Oxford, and became the Chancellor of Sheffield Hallam University in 2018. In January 2019 Baroness Helena Kennedy QC became the Director of the International Bar Association's Human Rights Institute (IBAHRI). She is the IBAHRI's third Director since its foundation in 1995 under the Honorary Presidency of Nelson Mandela.

For the fourth edition of this book, there have once again been a large number of individuals and professionals who have given their support, time and advice to shape the contents of the book. I want to thank them all.

My first acknowledgement goes to my mother (**Mutti**), **Helga Hertel**, who in her 94th year has not been too well, and her health was my major concern during the writing of this edition. She is one of the last survivors of an era in Germany which saw war and destruction under the Hitler regime of the Third Reich, the German economic miracle during the 1960s and the fast advancement of the technological age. Though Mutti never quite forgave me for going to England (Hull) as an au pair aged 17 and marrying the enemy (Mike in 1977), she came to realize that I enjoyed life in Britain. She never learnt English but found out that there was loss and sadness on both sides during World War II.

My husband **Mike Smartt OBE** former editor in Chief of BBC News Interactive, continues to support my writing of this book – though each time another edition is published he says, 'surely, this is it?!' Mike is and always has been at the forefront of technology and the digital world, and it is thanks to him that some of the digital and technological advancements have been brought to the reader's attention. I thank him for his love and support and his professional journalistic advice.

Louise Berg, Head of Legal at GForces, Kent. After leaving Reed Smith, Louise became the first in-house lawyer for this leading provider of digital solutions, software and marketing services to the auto industry. Louise is a former pupil of mine (King Edward's School Witley, Surrey) and has become a prominent lawyer in the media and entertainment sector. She continues advising on the book and remains a good friend.

Jane Macaulay JP, chairman of the Surrey Magistrates, and all my fellow magistrates on the Surrey Bench and legal advisers, led by **Lise Buckingham**, for supporting me in this venture and for some legal advice, particularly in the area of court reporting and reporting restrictions (which have changed over and again, especially in the area of youth justice).

My gratitude goes to the anonymous reviewers, whom I only know as A, B and C. I want to thank **Thorsten Lauterbach** and **Tom Thomson** in particular for their tremendous contributions in form of scrupulous and painstaking reviews of each chapter: Thorsten for his painstaking legal scrutiny, particularly in the IP area of law, and Tom for his fresh ideas in the journalistic field. Both paid tremendous attention to detail and made the book what it is.

Fiona Clark of 8 New Square Chambers is a leading barrister in all aspects of intellectual property law. Her advice and pointing out new cases has moved the chapters forward, not only in IP law but also in respect of cases concerning 'the right to be forgotten'. Since I taught her German A-Level years ago at Wetherby High School, we have become very good friends.

Cheryl Grant, who has advised on all editions of this book with her vast experience of the music publishing and entertainment industry. Cheryl founded her own record label, White Label Productions, and is at the forefront of important strategic developments in the UK's entertainment industry with regard to copyright and branding. She is my close friend and keeps me entertained with her infectious laughter.

Rosalind McInnes, BBC Scotland's Legal Director and author of *Scots Law for Journalists*, provided great insight into some current issues in Scotland. She continues to fight the adoption of the Defamation Act 2013 into Scots law and has advised the Scottish Law Commission on the advancement of defamation laws. Together with other media lawyers, Rosalind was instrumental in persuading the Scottish courts in February 2019 to reveal the identity of the teenage boy who raped and murdered 6-year-old Alesha MacPhail. Judge Lord Matthews, who presided over the trial at the High Court in Glasgow, lifted a ban on naming 16-year-old Aaron Campbell. Rosalind made a case on behalf of the BBC for reversing the court order which had protected the killer's identity because he was under the age of 18. She argued that it would be 'naïve' to think the teenager's identity was not already known among members of the Bute community and the name of Campbell had been widely disseminated on Facebook and Twitter.

John McLellan, Director, Scottish Newspaper Society and Honorary Professor of Journalism, University of Stirling, advised on the development and adaptation of the IPSO arbitration system. This means there is a slightly different set of rules for the complaints process involving Scottish complainants and press publications.

Advocate General His Honour Judge Jeff Blackett, who advised on the court martial system and highlighted the complexities of the *Marine A* (Alexander Blackman) trial in 2013. The Royal Marine sergeant was found guilty by the court martial panel for killing a wounded Taliban fighter on 15 September 2011. He was acquitted of murder and his conviction reduced to manslaughter in 2017. Jeff Blackett is the author of *Rant on the Court Martial and Service Law*, the leading textbook on naval and military justice systems and the new court martial system as a single prosecuting authority. I value Jeff as a good (tennis) friend and thank him for inviting a number of my law students to both court martial and high court proceedings.

Emily Kindleysides, Senior Commissioning Editor of Law, championed this edition and together with **Chloe James**, Editorial Assistant, has supported me throughout the editorial process and progress of this book. I thank them both for their support and meticulous diligence in getting this edition to production stage.

Legal references in this book are accurate to the best of my knowledge as at 1 November 2019. Views and legal opinions and interpretations expressed in the text are mine. I have also consulted a large number of legal journals and scholarly opinion specifically related to the field of media, internet and IP law. No liability can be accepted by me or the publishers Routledge (Taylor & Francis) for anything done in reliance on the matters referred to in this book.

Ursula Smartt
Godalming, Surrey
October 2019

Glossary of acronyms and legal terms

A

ABC
: Audit Bureau of Circulations. The industry body for media measurement.

Acquis (communautaire)
: EU Law; this is a French term meaning, essentially, 'the EU as it is', i.e. the rights and obligations that EU countries share. The *acquis* includes all EU law, such as treaties, Directives, Regulations, declarations and resolutions, international agreements on EU affairs and the judgments given by the Court of Justice. Accepting the *acquis* means taking the EU as you find it. Candidate countries have to accept the *acquis* before they can join the EU, and make EU law part of their own national legislation.

Acte clair (EU Law)
: The idea that there is no need to refer a point of law, which is reasonably clear and free from doubt, to the European Court of Justice (ECJ), e.g. this court found the matter *acte clair* and declined to refer the interpretation of Article 5 to the ECJ.

Actio injuriarum (or: *iniuriarum*)
: Scots private law 'injuries to honour'; action covers affront-based delicts such as defamation, wrongful arrest, personal molestation and harassment, breaches of confidentiality and privacy.

Acts of Adjournal
: Scots law: regulations as to court procedure made by the High Court of Justiciary in criminal law.

Acts of Sederunt
: Scots law: Acts passed by the Lords of Council and Session relating to civil procedure.

Adduce
: Introduce.

Admissible evidence
: Evidence allowed in proceedings.

Advocate
: Scots law: a member of the Scottish Bar.

Advocate Depute	Scots law: an advocate appointed by the Lord Advocate to prosecute under his/her directions and paid by salary.
Advocate General (ECtHR)	The Court of Justice is composed of 27 judges and eight Advocates General. Advocates General are appointed by Governments of Member States for a term of six years (renewable) (see also: CJEU – Court of Justice of the European Union).
Advocate General (Scotland)	UK Government Minister and the UK government's chief legal adviser on Scots law.
Advocate, Lord	Scots law: Senior Scottish Law Officer responsible for the prosecution of crime and investigation of deaths in Scotland and the principal legal adviser to the Scottish Government.
Affidavit	A written, sworn statement of evidence.
AG	Attorney General. The AG is the Government's principal legal adviser. Usually a Member of Parliament, they provide advice on a range of legal matters. As well as carrying out various civil law functions, the AG has final responsibility for the criminal law. Their deputy is the Solicitor General.
Alternative dispute resolution (ADR)	Collective description of methods of resolving disputes otherwise than through the normal trial process.
A&R (Artists and Repertoire)	The division of a record label that is responsible for talent-scouting and the artistic development of a recording artist. A&R acts as liaison between artist and record label.
Anton Piller order	An *ex parte* court injunction that requires a defendant to allow the claimant to (a) enter the defendant's premises, (b) search for and take away any material evidence, and (c) force the defendant to answer questions (usually in copyright infringement actions). Its primary objective is to prevent destruction or removal of evidence. *Anton Piller* is not a search warrant. The defendant is in contempt of court if he refuses to comply. Named after the case of *Anton Piller KG v Manufacturing* (1976).

Arraign	To put charges to the defendant in open court in the Crown Court.
Arraignment	The formal process of putting charges to the defendant in the Crown Court which consists of three parts: (1) calling him to the bar by name; (2) putting the charges to him by reading from the indictment; and (3) asking him whether he pleads guilty or not guilty.
ASA	Advertising Standards Authority.
Assignment	The transfer of property or rights from one party to another (copyright).
Authorities	Judicial decisions or opinions of authors of repute used as grounds of statements of law.
Avizandum	Scots law: time taken for further consideration of a judgment.
AVMSD	Audio Visual Media Services Directive (Directive 2010/13/EU).

B

BBFC	British Board of Film Classification.
Bill of indictment	A written accusation of a crime against one or more persons – a criminal trial in the Crown Court cannot start without a valid indictment.
Bitcoin	A type of digital currency in which encryption techniques are used to regulate the generation of units of currency and verify the transfer of funds, operating independently of a central bank.
BitTorrent	BitTorrent tracker is a server that assists in the communication between peers using the BitTorrent protocol for peer-to-peer (P2P) file-sharing. These sites are typically used to upload music files.
BPI	British Phonographic Industry (originally 'The British Recorded Music Industry').
BSI	British Standards Institution.
BTOP	Broadband Technology Opportunities Program – a US government project.

C

CAA	Civil Aviation Authority.
Case stated	An appeal to the High Court against the decision of a magistrates' court on the basis that the decision was wrong in law or in excess of the magistrates' jurisdiction.
CDPA	Copyright, Designs and Patents Act 1988.
CFA	Conditional fee agreement (also known as 'no win, no fee' agreement) whereby fees and expenses only become payable in certain circumstances (most commonly used in personal injury claims but also in defamation cases). Until 1 April 2013, lawyers entered into CFAs at their own risk, and as a result of this a 'success fee' was usually charged in addition to the lawyer's standard fees if the case was won. If a success fee was also payable it was expressed as a percentage of the standard fee, although it could not be more than 100 per cent of those fees. Part 2 of the Legal Aid Sentencing and Punishment of Offenders Act 2012 (and associated Regulations and changes to the Civil Procedure Rules) abolished the recovery of success fees under CFAs and also abolished the recovery of ATE (after the event) insurance premiums from the losing side, with the exception of clinical negligence cases where some of the ATE premium was likely to be recoverable. From 1 April 2013, claimants are still able to use CFAs but will now have to pay their lawyer's success fee and any ATE insurance.
Champertous	A vexatious claim by a stranger in return for a share of the proceeds.
Community (EU)	In the 1950s, six European countries formed three organizations: the European Coal and Steel Community (ECSC), the European Atomic Energy Community (Euratom) and the European Economic Community (EEC). These three communities – collectively known as the 'European Communities' – formed the basis of what is now the European Union (EU). With the Lisbon Treaty in 2009 the word 'community' disappeared, replaced by the 'European Union'.

	Many texts still use the word 'community'; it means more or less the same as 'EU'.
Complainant	A person who makes a formal complaint. In relation to an offence of rape or other sexual offences, the complainant is the person against whom the offence is alleged to have been committed.
Contempt of court	Disobedience or wilful disregard of the judicial process (Contempt of Court Act 1981). 'Contempt' can also relate to any attempt to interfere with proceedings or to obstruct or threaten Members of Parliament in the performance of their parliamentary duties.
Contra mundum injunction	Order 'binding on the whole world'. Injunctions are usually made against named individuals (*in personam*). When made *contra mundum*, they are made against the entire world (i.e. no media organization is allowed to publish details of the case or person(s)).
Convention	This term has various meanings, including (in the EU context) a group of people representing the EU institutions, the national governments and parliaments, who come together to draw up an important document. Conventions of this sort have met to draw up the Charter of Fundamental Rights of the European Union or new EU treaties; the European Convention on Human Rights and Fundamental Freedoms is also meant by this term (see: Convention right).
Convention right	A right under the European Convention on Human Rights (see: ECHR).
Counsel	Barrister. In Scotland, a member of the Faculty of Advocates practising at the Bar.
Counterclaim	A claim brought by a defendant in response to the claimant's claim, which is included in the same proceedings as the claimant's claim.
CJEU	Court of Justice of the European Union (formerly: European Court of Justice – ECJ), based in Luxembourg. The CJEU ensures compliance with EU law and rules on the interpretation and application of the treaties establishing the European Union.

CPD	Criminal Practice Direction.
CPR	Civil Procedure Rules (or Criminal Procedure Rules).
Cross-examination	Questioning of a witness by a party other than the party who called the witness.
Cy-près	Scots law: approximation; as near as possible.

D

DAB	Digital Audio Broadcasting.
Damages	A sum of money awarded by the court as compensation to the claimant.
Declaration of incompatibility	A declaration by a court that a piece of UK legislation is incompatible with the provisions of the European Convention on Human Rights (see: ECHR).
De facto	According to the fact; in point of fact.
Defender	Scots law: defendant. A person who disputes the claim of the pursuer and lodges defences (see also: pursuer).
De jure	According to law, or in point of law.
De minimis	'Of minimum importance' or 'trifling'; de minimis doctrine means the law has no interest in trivial matters.
Deposition	Written record of a witness's written evidence.
Derivative work	A work that is based on (derived from) another work (copyright), e.g. a painting of a photograph. As the adaption of copyright work is a restricted act, unless covered under fair dealing rules, the artist will normally require the permission of the copyright owner before making a derivative work.
Devolution	The decentralization of governmental power, such as the Scottish Parliament, the National Assembly for Wales and the Northern Ireland Assembly.
Dictum (pl. dicta)	'Remark'; refers to a judge's comment in a ruling or decision which is not required to

	reach the decision, but may state the judge's interpretation of a related legal principle.
Diplock courts	Juryless courts in Northern Ireland from 1973 to 2007.
DMB	A Digital Multimedia Broadcasting – Audio.
DNS	Domain Name System.
DOCSIS	Data Over Cable Service Interface Specification – a technology for next generation broadband services over the cable network.
DPI	Digital Phone Interphase technology.
Draft bill	A bill that has not yet been formally introduced into Parliament and enables consultation and pre-legislative scrutiny before a bill is issued formally. This process is known as pre-legislative scrutiny.
DRM	Digital Rights Management.
DS	Developers' System.

E

ECHR	European Convention on Human Rights and Fundamental Freedoms ('The Convention').
ECJ	European Court of Justice (now: 'The Court of Justice of the European Union').
ECtHR	European Court of Human Rights: an international court set up in 1959 in Strasbourg; it rules on individual or state applications alleging the violations of civil, political or human rights set out in the European Convention on Human Rights (ECHR) (also known as 'the Strasbourg Court') (see also: Grand Chamber; HUDOC).
EPG	Electronic Programme Guides.
Estoppel	Equitable doctrine that may be used to prevent a person from relying upon certain rights or facts, e.g. words said or actions performed, which differ from an earlier set of facts.

Estreatment (of recognizance)	Forfeiture.
European Arrest Warrant (EAW)	The UK adopted the EAW in 2002, following the terrorism atrocities of 9/11. The EAW is widely used to secure the arrest and surrender of suspected criminals across the European Union.
Evidence-in-chief	The evidence given by a witness for the party who called him.
Exemplary damages	Or: punitive damages. Awarded by a court when the defendant's wilful acts were malicious, violent, oppressive, fraudulent, wanton or grossly reckless. They reward the claimant for his/her suffering, for example, damage to his/her reputation (defamation) or harassment. These damages go beyond compensating for actual loss and are awarded to show the court's disapproval of the defendant's behaviour.
Ex parte	A hearing where only one party is allowed to attend and make submissions, mainly in judicial review; now cited as, for example, R (on the application of Animal Defenders International) v Secretary of State for Culture, Media and Sport [2008] 1 AC 1312. Proceedings are ex parte when the party against whom they are brought is not heard.

F

Fair dealing (or 'fair use')	Acts which are allowable in relation to copyright works under statutory legislation. What constitutes 'fair use' may differ from country to country, but normally includes educational and private study and news reporting.
Fatal accident inquiry	Scotland. An inquiry before a sheriff into the circumstances of a death of a person. Such an inquiry must be held where the person died at work or in legal custody.
FOIA or FOI	Freedom of Information Act 2000.
Footprints	Deliberate mistakes or hidden elements that are only known to the author or creator of a work

(copyright), e.g. the software designer who includes redundant subroutines that identify the author in some way.

Forfeiture

A broad term used to describe any loss of property without compensation. In contract law, one party may be required to forfeit specified property if the party fails to fulfil its contractual obligations. In criminal procedures, it is the loss of a defendant's right to his property which has been confiscated by the police when used during the commission of a crime. For example, the seizure by police of a car which was used during a bank robbery; or the forfeiture of illegal narcotics (possession of class A drugs).

Forum (non) conveniens

As applied to a court which, although having jurisdiction, is not the appropriate court for the matter in issue. This doctrine is employed when the court chosen by the claimant is inconvenient for witnesses or poses an undue hardship on the defendants, who must petition the court for an order transferring the case to a more convenient court, e.g. a lawsuit arising from an accident involving a foreign resident who files the complaint in his home country when the witnesses and doctors who treated the claimant are in the country where the accident occurred, which makes the latter country the more convenient location for trial.

FTT

First Tier Tribunal (formerly: Information Tribunal). Appeals to the First Tier Tribunal are against the decisions from Government departments and other public bodies (see also: FOIA) (see also: Upper Tribunal (UT)).

G

General Court

Formerly Court of First Instance as part of the European Court of Justice.

Grand Chamber

(Of the European Court of Human Rights – ECtHR) The Grand Chamber is made up of 17 judges: the Court's President and Vice Presidents, the Section Presidents and the national judge, together with other judges selected by drawing of lots. The initiation of proceedings before the Grand Chamber takes two different forms: referral and relinquishment (see also: ECtHR).

Green Paper

A consultation document produced by the Government. The aim of this document is to allow people both inside and outside Parliament to debate the subject and give the department feedback on its suggestions.

H

Hansard

The official report of the proceedings of Parliament, published daily on everything that is said and done in both Houses of Parliament. In the House of Commons, the Hansard reporters sit in a gallery above the Speaker and take down every word that is said in the Chamber. In the Westminster Hall Chamber, they sit next to the Chairman. The Hansard reporters in the House of Lords sit below the Bar of the House, facing the Lord Speaker. The name 'Hansard' was officially adopted in 1943 after Luke Hansard (1752–1828), who was the printer of the *House of Commons Journal* from 1774. The first detailed official reports were published in 1803 in *William Cobbett's Political Register* by the political journalist of the same name.

Harmonization

This may mean bringing national laws into line with one another; in EU law this means removing national barriers that obstruct the free movement of workers, goods, services and capital. Harmonization can also mean coordinating national technical rules so that products and services can be traded freely throughout the EU (e.g. in copyright and IP law).

Her Majesty's Advocate

Scotland. The senior Law Officer responsible for the prosecution of crime and investigation of deaths and the principal legal adviser to the Scottish Government. Referred to as 'Her Majesty's Advocate' in criminal matters and the 'Lord Advocate' in civil matters.

High Court of Justiciary	Scotland. Usually referred to as 'the High Court' in Edinburgh. Consists of two appellate courts (the Court of Criminal Appeal and the Justiciary Appeal Court) and a court of first instance (i.e. a court trying persons on indictment with a jury). The judges of the High Court are formally called Lords Commissioners of Justiciary. The judges of the court are also the judges of the Court of Session.
HRA	Human Rights Act 1998.
HUDOC	A database which provides access to the case law of the European Court of Human Rights (Grand Chamber, Chamber and Committee judgments, decisions, communicated cases, advisory opinions and legal summaries from the Case Law Information Note), the European Commission of Human Rights (decisions and reports) and the Committee of Ministers (resolutions) (see also: ECtHR).

I

IAB	Internet Advertising Bureau.
IC	Information Commissioner (see also: FOIA).
ICANN	The Internet Corporation for Assigned Names and Numbers is a non-profit organization that is responsible for the coordination of maintenance and methodology of several databases of unique identifiers related to the namespaces of the internet and ensuring the network's stable and secure operation. ICANN performs the actual technical maintenance work of the central internet address pools and Domain Name System (DNS) registries pursuant to the Internet Assigned Numbers Authority (IANA) function contract. ICANN's main aim is to help preserve the operational stability of the global internet community.
ICT	Information and Communication Technology.
IFPI	International Federation of the Phonographic Industry; represents the recording industry worldwide. IFPI safeguards the rights of record

	producers and expands the commercial uses of recorded music (see: BPI).
In camera	Court proceedings in private where the public is not allowed access, though the media may be permitted access by special permission from the legal adviser or judge.
Indemnity	A right of someone to recover from a third party the whole amount which he himself is liable to pay.
Indictment	The document containing the formal charges against a defendant; a trial in the Crown Court cannot start without this.
Informant	Someone who lays information.
Infringement (copyright)	The act of copying, distributing or adapting a work without permission.
Injunction	An injunction is a court order which orders a person to stop (called a 'prohibitory injunction') or to do (a 'mandatory injunction') a particular act or thing. A breach of an injunction is generally punishable as a contempt of court and in some circumstances can lead to imprisonment. Interim injunctions are either obtained 'on notice' or 'without notice'. With an 'on notice' application, the other side is told that the application for an injunction is being made and when and where it will be heard (see also: *contra mundum* injunction; interim injunction).
Inner House	Scots law: the two appellate divisions of the Court of Session, so called originally on the simple topographical ground that their courts lie farther from the entrance to the courthouse than did the Outer House (see also: Outer House).
Intellectual property (IP)	A product of the intellect, including copyright works, trade marks and patents.
Inter alia	Among other things.
Interdict	Scots law: a judicial prohibition or court order preventing someone from doing something. It is comparable to the English (interim) injunction. This judicial prohibition is issued by the Court of Session or Sheriff Court. In an emergency, interim interdict

	can be obtained in the absence of the person against whom the order is sought (i.e. *ex parte*).
Interested party	A person or organization who is not the prosecutor or defendant, but who has some other legal interest in a case.
Interim injunction	The applicant applies for 'interim relief' from the court for the purposes of preserving evidence or assets (in intellectual property law) at the very outset of the proceedings. Interim injunctions are applied for at commencement of legal proceedings, without a full examination by the court of the facts said to justify a final injunction.
International Court of Justice (ICTJ)	Judicial organ of the United Nations, based in The Hague. Those who commit crimes on a large or systematic scale such as genocide are tried here. The Court has roots in international legal obligations dating back to the Nuremberg trials, the most recent trials being the International Criminal Tribunals for the former Yugoslavia (ICTY) and Rwanda (ICTR).
Inter partes	A hearing where both parties attend and can make submissions (see: *ex parte*).
IP	Intellectual property (or Internet Protocol).
IPO	Intellectual Property Office
IPSO	Independent Press Standards Organisation. Regulator for the newspaper and magazine industry (including online editions).
IPTV	Internet Protocol Television – television services delivered over the internet.
ISB	Independent Spectrum Broker.
ISDN	Integrated Services Digital Network – a data transfer technology using the copper wire phone network.
ISMN	International Standard Music Numbers (ISMNs) – an international system specifically for printed music publications. ISMNs are to printed music what ISBNs are to books.
ISP	An internet service provider (ISP) is an organization that provides services for accessing, using or participating in the internet. Internet

services typically provided by ISPs include internet access, internet transit, domain name registration or web hosting. Top ISPs in the UK are BT, Sky Broadband, Virgin Media, EE, Talk Talk and Kingston Communications.

J

Jigsaw identification	The ability to identify someone by using two or more different pieces of information from two or more sources. The media refers to the 'jigsaw effect' in *sub judice* proceedings, where a person's identity is to be kept anonymous for legal reasons (e.g. children and young persons under 18).
Judge Rapporteur	EU law: the Judge Rapporteur draws up the preliminary report of the general meeting of the judges and the Advocates General before the Court of Justice known as 'measures of inquiry' (see also: ECJ).
Judicial review	A remedy used by the Administrative Court (or the Court of Session in Scotland). If a public body (or authority) has made a decision in breach of any public law principle, then that decision may be challenged by an individual or group action. Court proceedings can be by judge-alone hearings where the lawfulness of a decision or action made by a public body is reviewed. For example, where the challenge is based on an allegation that the public body has taken a decision unlawfully (*ultra vires*) and usually where there is no adequate alternative remedy.

L

Laches	Equity: a defence to an equitable action that bars recovery by the plaintiff because of the plaintiff's undue delay in seeking relief.
Law Lords	Highly qualified, full-time judges, the Law Lords carried out the judicial work of the House of Lords until 30 July 2009. From 1 October 2009, the UK Supreme Court assumed jurisdiction

on points of law for all civil law cases in the UK and all criminal cases in England and Wales and Northern Ireland. The existing 12 Lords of Appeal in Ordinary (Law Lords) were appointed as Justices of the Supreme Court and were thereafter disqualified from sitting or voting in the House of Lords. When they retire from the Supreme Court they can return to the House of Lords as full members, but newly appointed Justices of the Supreme Court will not have seats in the House of Lords (see also: Supreme Court).

Leave to appeal	Permission granted to appeal the decision of a court.
Licence (Copyright)	An agreement in copyright that allows use of a work subject to conditions imposed by the copyright owner.
Limited right	Right by virtue of the HRA 1998 (see: HRA) — so that, within the scope of the limitation, the infringement of a guaranteed right may not contravene the Convention.
Lisbon Treaty	EU law: the treaty was signed on 13 December 2007 in Lisbon and entered into force on 1 December 2009. Technically, the Lisbon Treaty consists of several specific changes of articles compared to the previous treaties.
Litigation	Process by which a person or company begins a civil lawsuit. Full legal action tends to be avoided and dispute resolution is often used (e.g. libel actions). Most top law firms have specialist litigation and dispute resolution departments, whilst smaller or specialist firms concentrate all their resources on litigation.
Lord Chief Justice (LCJ)	The name given to the judge who presides over the Queen's Bench Division of the High Court (QBD). Since the passing of the Constitutional Reform Act 2005, the LCJ is now Head of the Judiciary of England and Wales, a role previously performed by the Lord Chancellor. In addition, he is President of the Courts of England and Wales and responsible for representing the views of the judiciary to Parliament and the Government.

Lucas Box meaning	Defamation: a defendant in a libel action must set out in his/her statement of case the defamatory meaning s/he seeks to prove to be essentially or substantially true ('justification').

M

Mandatory order (formerly: mandamus or 'writ of mandate')	Order from the divisional court of the Queen's Bench Division ordering a body (such as a magistrates' court) to do something (such as rehear a case). The writ can order a public agency or governmental body to perform an act required by law when it has neglected or refused to do so. Example: after petitions were filed with sufficient valid signatures to qualify a proposition for a ballot, a town council has refused to call an election, claiming it has a legal opinion that the proposal is unconstitutional.
Mareva order	*Mareva* injunctions (also known as 'asset-freezing orders') are court orders that negate the banker's duty to pay or transfer funds as per the instructions of the customer. A *Mareva* order is an interlocutory order (injunction), granted ancillary to a substantive claim involving money, that seeks to prevent a defendant from rendering a decree against him worthless by removing his assets from the jurisdiction of the court.
Master	Procedural judge for the majority of the civil business in the Chancery (Ch) and Queen's Bench Divisions (QBD). A Master at first instance deals with all aspects of an action from its issue until it is ready for trial by a trial judge – usually a High Court judge. After the trial the master resumes responsibility for the case.
Master of the Rolls (MR)	Title of an English judge ranking immediately below the Lord Chief Justice. He presides over the Court of Appeal and is responsible for the records or 'rolls' of the Chancery Court (see also: Lord Chief Justice).
MCPS	Mechanical Copyright Protection Society – licences mechanical (or reproduction)

copyrights on behalf of music publishers and composer members. Collects royalties whenever a piece of music is reproduced for broadcast or online.

Moral rights
Are concerned in copyright with the protection of the reputation of the author, in particular the right to be attributed with the creation of a work and the right to object to defamatory treatment.

MPA
Music Publishers Association.

N

NDPB
Non-departmental public body which has a role in the process of national government but is not a government department or part of one and therefore operates to a greater or lesser extent at arm's length from ministers (see also: Quango).

Nobile officium
Scots law: 'The noble office or duty of the Court of Session' is an equitable jurisdiction in the High Court of Justiciary or the Inner House of the Court of Session which can provide a remedy where none other would be available or soften the effect of the law in a particular circumstance.

Nolle prosequi
'Will not prosecute'; formal entry in the records of the case in the court by the prosecutor in a criminal case that they are not willing to go any further in the case. This means that the CPS withdraws the charge(s) against the defendant(s).

Norwich Pharmacal order (NPO)
A Norwich Pharmacal order requires a respondent to disclose certain documents or information to the applicant. The respondent must be involved in a wrongdoing (whether innocently or not) and is unlikely to be a party to the potential proceedings. An NPO will only be granted where 'necessary' in the interests of justice. Orders are commonly used to identify the proper defendant to an action or to obtain information to plead a claim. An NPO can be obtained pre-action, during the course of an action and post-judgment. An NPO can be made in one jurisdiction to identify a defendant for the

	purpose of proceedings in another jurisdiction. For a third party to be liable to present the information requested by the claimant, they must have been involved, innocently or not, in the wrongdoing against the claimant. It must also be clear that justice will be served by the revelation of this information.
Notice of transfer	Procedure used in cases of serious and complex fraud, and in certain cases involving child witnesses, whereby the prosecution can, without seeking judicial approval, have the case sent directly to the Crown Court without the need to have the accused committed for trial.

O

Obiter dictum ('obiter')	Opinion given incidentally.
ODPS	On-demand programme services.
OECD	Organisation for Economic Co-operation and Development.
Ofcom	Office for Communications. Independent regulator and competition authority for the UK communications industries.
Offence triable either way ('either-way-offence')	A statutory criminal offence, which may be tried either in the magistrates' or Crown Court.
Offence triable only on indictment	An offence which can be tried only in the Crown Court.
Offence triable only summarily	An offence which can be tried only in a magistrates' court.
OFT	Office of Fair Trading. The organization promotes and protects consumer interests in the UK.
Ombudsman	Now 'Parliamentary and Health Service Ombudsman', which combines the two statutory roles of Parliamentary Commissioner for Administration (the Parliamentary Ombudsman) and Health Service Commissioner for England (Health Service Ombudsman). Investigates complaints from members of the public about government departments; has wide powers to obtain evidence; makes recommendations about cases s/he hears.

Open court	In a courtroom which is open to the public (see also: open justice principle; in *camera*).
Open justice principle	The public (and media) has the statutory right to attend most court proceedings – unless held in *camera* (see: in *camera*; open court).
Operators of Websites	Section 5 Defamation Act 2013 provides website operators with a defence to defamation provided they follow the procedure set out in the Defamation (Operators of Websites) Regulations 2013.
Ordinary, Lords	Scots law: the judges who try cases at first instance in the Court of Session.
Outer House	Scots law: the part of the Court of Session which exercises a first instance jurisdiction (i.e. Inner House). The Supreme Court is split into these two Houses. The Judges in the Outer House deal with 'first instance' (new work), which has not been before a 'Court' but may have been before a tribunal or panel (see also: Inner House).

P

PACT	Producers Alliance of Cinema and Television.
Parliament Acts	The Parliament Act of 1911 was introduced to reform Parliament, and the House of Lords (HL) in particular. It deprived the HL of any power over Money Bills and gave the Speaker the power to decide what was a Money Bill. It allowed Bills that had been passed by the Commons in three successive sessions, but rejected by the Lords in all three, to become law. The Parliament Act 1949 reduced the powers that the HL had to delay a bill from becoming law if the House of Commons approved it. Since the Parliament Act 1911 the HL had been able to delay legislation for two years. The 1949 Act reduced this to one year.
Passing off (copyright)	Using the work or name of an organization or individual without consent to promote a competing product or service.
Patent	A grant made by a government that confers upon the creator of an invention the sole right

	to make, use and sell that invention for a set period of time.
PCC	Press Complaints Commission.
Per incuriam	Through negligence, mistake or error.
Perjury	Offence committed by a witness in court proceedings involving the affirmation of a deliberate falsehood on oath or on an affirmation equivalent to an oath.
Petition	A document by which court proceedings are initiated, like a summons but used for specific types of case. Can have various meanings. An indictment is originally called a petition until the Crown is in a position to indict the accused on the charges. In civil business the term also relates to certain types of applications to the court.
Phonogram (Copyright)	The symbol 'P' in a circle is a distinct right applied to an individual sound recording, which will operate separately from rights existing in the underlying musical composition.
PII	Public interest immunity certificate, where the prosecution contends that it is not in the public interest to disclose any sensitive material (secret courts) (see also: in camera).
PLR	Public Lending Right.
PMLL	Printed Music Licensing Ltd; represents music publishers to allow UK schools to make copies of printed music.
PPL	Phonographic Performance Ltd; licenses sound recordings and music videos for use in broadcast, public performance and new media.
Practice direction	Direction relating to the practice and procedure of the courts.
Precedent	The decision of a court regarded as a source of law or authority in the decision of a later case.
Preliminary ruling	EU Law: to ensure effective and uniform application of EU law, national courts can refer to the Court of Justice (or ECJ) and ask it to clarify a point in EU law; reference for a preliminary ruling can also seek the review of the validity of an act of EU law (Treaty provision).

President, Lord	Scots law: the highest civil Judge in Scotland, who presides over the First Division of the Court of Session.
Prima facie case	A prosecution case which is strong enough to require the defendant to answer it.
Primary legislation	Acts of Parliament.
Privilege	The right of a party to refuse to disclose a document or produce a document or to refuse to answer questions on the ground of some special interest recognized by law.
Privy Council	Privy Councillors are members of the Queen's own Council: the 'Privy Council'. There are about 500 members who have reached high public office. Membership includes all members of the Cabinet, past and present, the Speaker, the leaders of all major political parties, archbishops and various senior judges as well as other senior public figures. Their role is to advise the Queen in carrying out her duties as monarch. Privy Counsellors are referred to as 'The Right Honourable Member'. The Judicial Committee of the Privy Council, situated in the Supreme Court building, is the court of final appeal for the UK overseas territories and Crown dependencies, and for those Commonwealth countries that have retained the appeal to Her Majesty in Council or, in the case of Republics, to the Judicial Committee.
Procurator Fiscal	Scots law: literally, the procurator for the fiscal or treasury; now the style of the public prosecutor in the sheriff court.
PRP	Press Recognition Panel. An independent body set up by Royal Charter to ensure that regulators of the UK press are independent, properly funded and able to protect the public.
PRS	The Performing Right Society. Body which represents music publishers (see also: MCPS).
PSB	Public Service Broadcasting.
PSN	Public Sector Network.
Pursuer	Scots law: the party initiating a lawsuit (English law: plaintiff or claimant).

Q

Qualified right	Right by virtue of the HRA 1998 so that, in certain circumstances and under certain conditions, it can be interfered with (see: HRA).
Quango	Quasi-autonomous non-governmental organization; also known as non-departmental public bodies (NDPBs). Quangos are organizations funded by taxpayers, but not controlled directly by central government. For example, ACAS (Advisory, Conciliation and Arbitration Service); the Big Lottery Fund; the Boundary Commission for Wales; UK Anti Doping (see: NDPB).

R

Remand	A criminal court sends a person away when a case is adjourned until another date; the person may be remanded on bail (when he can leave, subject to conditions) or in custody.
Reporter	Scots law: a person appointed to hold a public inquiry or to whom the court may remit some aspect of a case for investigation or advice (such as the Children's Hearings in Scotland).
Representation order	An order authorizing payment of legal aid for a defendant.
Resident Sheriff	Scots law: the Sheriff who holds the commission to sit at a particular court (as opposed to a Sheriff sitting part time) (see also: Sheriff).
Res noviter veniens ad notitiam	Scots law: things newly come to light, which may warrant the admission of further evidence or even a new trial.
Respondent	The party in a civil action defending on appeal.
Restraining order	Criminal law: a restraining order can be a significant part in managing the risks to a victim in preventing further harassment or harm. Conditions on the perpetrator can include no contact with the victim; not to go near the victim's address and so forth (under s 12 Domestic Violence, Crime and Victims Act 2004; or s 2 Protection from Harassment Act 1997).

Restraint order – Civil Restraint Order (CRO)	Civil law: a CRO is an order issued against people who have had more than one court claim or application dismissed or struck out for being totally without merit. The order prevents that person from issuing further claims or making applications in some or all of the county courts in England and Wales and also in the High Court, without first getting the permission of the judge named in the order.
RIPA	Regulation of Investigatory Powers Act 2000.
Royal Assent	The monarch's agreement to make a bill into an Act of Parliament.
Royal Commission	A selected group of people appointed by the Government to investigate a matter of important public concern and to make recommendations on any actions to be taken.
Royalties	A share paid to an author or a composer out of the proceeds resulting from the sale or performance of his or her work (copyright).
RPAS	Remotely Piloted Air Systems ('drones').
RRO	Reporting Restriction Order.

S

Safe harbour	Privacy agreement of 2000 ('pact') between the EU and USA regarding online privacy. The pact allows firms to transfer data from the EU to the USA if they provide safeguards equivalent to those required by the EU data-protection directive ('safe-harbour').
Security money	Deposited to ensure that the defendant attends court (also known as 'surety').
Secretary of State	The title held by some of the more important Government ministers, for example the Secretary of State for Foreign Affairs. Usually a member of the Cabinet (the Executive).
Sending for trial	Procedure whereby indictable offences are transferred to the Crown Court (or 'sent') without the need for a committal hearing in the magistrates' court.

Set aside	Cancelling a judgment or order or a step taken by a party in the proceedings.
Sheriff	Scots law: legally qualified person who sits in judgment at the sheriff court.
SI	Statutory Instrument. SIs are a form of legislation which allow the provisions of an Act of Parliament to be subsequently brought into force or altered without Parliament having to pass a new Act. They are also referred to as secondary, delegated or subordinate legislation.
Sine qua non	Latin for '[a condition] without which it could not be' or 'but for. . .' or 'without which [there is] nothing that can be effectively done'. The term refers to an indispensable and essential action, condition or ingredient; a necessary condition without which something is not possible.
Sist	Scots law: court order stopping or suspending legal proceedings.
Skeleton argument	A document prepared by a party or their legal representative setting out the basis of the party's argument, including any arguments based on law; the court may require such documents to be served on the court and on the other party prior to a trial.
Slander	Defamation: spoken words which have a damaging effect on a person's reputation.
SOCA	Serious Organised Crime Agency. SOCA tackles serious organized crime that affects UK citizens.
Solatium	Scots law: extra damages allowed in certain delict cases in addition to actual loss – for 'injury to feelings' or 'wounded feelings' (see also: actio injuriarum).
Special measures	Measures which can be put in place to provide protection and/or anonymity to a witness (e.g. a screen separating witness from the accused or hearing child witnesses on a live link).
SSI	Scots law: Scottish Statutory Instrument. The form in which Scottish orders, rules and instruments, regulations or other subordinate legislation are made.

Stay	A stay imposes a halt on court proceedings (e.g. in contempt of court actions). Proceedings can be continued if a stay is lifted.
Strict liability	Not all offences require proof of *mens rea*. By a crime of strict liability is meant an offence of which a person may be convicted without proof of intention (*mens rea*), recklessness or even negligence. The prosecution is only obliged to prove the commission of the *actus reus* and the absence of any recognized defence (see *R v Adomako* (1994)).
Strike out	Striking out means the court ordering written material to be deleted so that it may no longer be relied upon (e.g. a police interview transcript).
SUA	Small Unmanned Aircraft
Sub judice	A rule that prevents any journalist or Member of Parliament to refer to a current or impending court case (see: contempt of court).
Subpoena	A summons issued to a person directing their attendance in court to give evidence (see: summons).
Summons	A document signed by a magistrate after information is laid before him/her which sets out the basis of the accusation against the accused and the time and place at which they must appear.
Supreme Court	The Supreme Court of Justice is the final court of appeal in the UK for civil cases. It hears appeals in criminal cases from England, Wales and Northern Ireland.
Surety	A person who guarantees that a defendant will attend court, usually linked to a bail hearing.
SVOD	Subscription video-on-demand services.

T

TEFU	Treaty on European Union (as amended by the Treaty of Lisbon).
Territorial Authority	A national authority which has power to do certain things in connection with co-operation

	with other countries and international organizations in relation to the collection of the hearing of evidence.
Time-shifting	A person is allowed to make a copy of a broadcast for private and domestic use to watch or listen to at a more convenient time, or for educational purposes, using methods such as video recording or the BBC iPlayer.
Trade mark (™ or ®)	A name, symbol or other device identifying a product or company. Trade marks are registered via national trade mark or patent offices and legally restrict the use of the device to the owner; it is illegal to use the ® symbol or state that the trade mark is registered until the trade mark has in fact been registered.
Tribunal	There are tribunals in England, Wales, Scotland and Northern Ireland covering a wide range of areas affecting day-to-day life. HM Courts and Tribunals administers many of them, although some are the responsibility of the devolved governments in Scotland, Wales and Northern Ireland, for example, employment tribunals or immigration and asylum tribunals. Tribunal judges are legally qualified; they usually sit with two tribunal members who are specialist non-legal members of the panel and include doctors, chartered surveyors, ex-service personnel or accountants.
Troll(s)	Internet slang: a 'troll' is someone who posts inflammatory or off-topic messages in an online social networking community, such as a forum, chat room, or blog, with the primary intent of provoking readers into an emotional response.
TSI	Trading Standards Institute.

U

UAS	Unmanned Aerial Systems.
UAVs	Unmanned Aerial Vehicles ('drones').
Universal Declaration of Human Rights	Text adopted by the United Nations in 1948 in order to strengthen human rights protection at the international level.

Upper Tribunal (UT)

The Upper Tribunal hears appeals from the First Tier Tribunal (FTT) on points of law (i.e. an appeal made over the interpretation of a legal principle or statute). Further appeals may be made, with permission, to the Court of Appeal (see also: FTT).

V

VSC

Video Standards Council – regulator of the video industry.

Venire de novo

A Queen's Bench Division (QBD) order requiring a new trial following a verdict given in an inferior court. In criminal matters the court of trial may, before verdict, discharge the jury and direct a fresh jury to be summoned and even after verdict, if the findings are so imperfect as amount to no verdict at all.

Vlogging

Video blog or video blogger; a form of blog for which the medium is video. Vlog entries often combine embedded video (or a video link) with supporting text, advertisements, images and other metadata.

W

Warrant of distress

Court order to arrest a person (distress warrant).

Wash-up period

Refers to the last few days of a Parliament, after a General Election has been announced but before dissolution. All the unfinished business of the session must be dealt with swiftly and the Government seeks the co-operation of the Opposition in passing legislation that is still in progress. Some Bills might be lost completely; others might be progressed quickly but in a much-shortened form (e.g. Digital Economy Act 2010).

Wasted costs order

An order that a barrister or solicitor is not to be paid fees that they would normally be paid by the Legal Services Commission.

White Paper

A document produced by the Government setting out details of future policy on a

	particular subject. A White Paper will often be the basis for a bill to be put before Parliament. The White Paper allows the Government an opportunity to gather feedback before it formally presents the policies as a bill.
WIPO	World Intellectual Property Organization.
Without prejudice	Negotiations with a view to a settlement are usually conducted 'without prejudice', which means that the circumstances in which the content of those negotiations may be revealed to the court are very restricted.

Table of cases

R App

Table of UK legislation

Legislation for England, Wales, Northern Ireland and Scotland
Unless otherwise stated, the following statutes cover the jurisdiction of Great Britain. Please note that certain enactments may not extend to Scotland, Northern Ireland and the Channel Islands where different legislation may apply.

Statutes

Table of treaties and international legislation

International legislation/ instruments

Austria

Belgium

Denmark

Chapter 1

Freedom of expression

Key points

This chapter will cover the following questions:

- ○ What are the philosophical arguments and reasons behind the idea of freedom of expression?
- ○ How has freedom of speech developed over time?
- ○ Should freedom of expression be fundamental in a democratic society?
- ○ Should freedom of expression be limited by the state?
- ○ How has press freedom developed over time?
- ○ How has Article 10 ECHR manifested itself in Strasbourg jurisprudence and common law?
- ○ How far can freedom of expression be permitted on the internet?
- ○ Should journalistic sources be protected?
- ○ How do we know what amounts to 'fake news'?

1.1 Overview

This first chapter deals with concepts of freedom of expression and press freedom. From the start it is important that the reader appreciates the principles and fine nuances between these. Arguably, freedom of speech is an older, more grounded concept, and freedom of expression was made more 'popular' with definitions as part of Article 10 of the European Convention on Human Rights (ECHR).

The chapter examines how governments can limit some forms of free expression by banning books, plays, films and so forth by either introducing laws or changing existing legislation and how outspoken writers and journalists have been punished after they have spoken out.

Examples will be provided from social media and internet hate speech, causing people harassment, alarm and distress in their daily lives; we will ask whether these forms of expression should be limited or censored on the internet and whether more laws should be introduced to limit trolls, extreme pornography and racial hatred.

We will then move on to the question of whether journalists should ever reveal their sources. Some journalists have gone to prison for not revealing their sources before a court. There is no state privilege to protect a journalist's confidential sources. For a journalist, it is an essential means of enabling the media to perform its important function of public watchdog and should not be interfered with unless in exceptional circumstances where vital public or individual interests are at stake. But in the era of fake news, why should the public trust journalists and news sources in print and online who offer so much information without any meaningful indication of where the information came from? Some anonymous source may not be a whistle-blower but rather a manipulating spin doctor working for the rich and powerful and hiding behind a journalist's promise of anonymity.

1.2 Philosophical foundations of freedom of expression

Freedom of speech possibly dates back to the Greek philosopher Socrates (470 BCE – c.399 BCE). Socrates argued that democracy established in Athens was designed to be impartial and create better citizens; one of the main principles of a democratic society was freedom of speech.[1] This right to freedom of expression is a natural right that everyone should have. It is a right that confirms one's value as a human being. Throughout history, the discussion has centred on the balance between the individual and the state and which of the two should have precedence. Freedom of speech is an acknowledgement of the individual's *value* as a human being in a democratic society. How should the balance between the two be maintained?

During the late seventeenth and eighteenth centuries, the Age of the Enlightenment movement in Europe focused on the use of 'reason'. Some outstanding philosophical writers, such as John Locke, Immanuel Kant, Benedict de Spinoza, Voltaire and Charles de Secondat, the Baron de Montesquieu produced key themes, including the belief in progress, tolerance, faith in reason and freedom of expression. The only grounds for imposing any limitations on these individual freedoms, they argued, should be considerations for the right of others to the same freedoms.

Central to Kant's critical philosophy was the metaphysical assertion of 'reason' (*Kritik der reinen Vernunft*, 1787), based on the earlier more 'rationalist' philosophers including Leibniz and Descartes. Most important for Kant was 'communication' by way of reason (*Vernunft*), in that a member of 'the society of citizens of the world' would be able to freely express his thoughts: 'for the enlightenment of this kind, all that is needed is freedom. And the freedom in question in the most innocuous form of all – freedom to make public use of one's reason in all matters', as he famously pointed out in his essay 'What Is Enlightenment?' (1784).[2] Importantly, according to Kant, citizens must be able to reason freely, offering critical scrutiny of government policies and religious teachings.

Many philosophers of the Enlightenment were trying to share their ideas by publishing their works. However, there existed strict censorship from both religious and governmental institutions at the time. Censorship of free speech and press freedom became key topics at the time, as Jonathan Israel points out, because 'press freedom . . . is the foremost instrument of human enlightenment' and 'the root of all political and social evil . . . was lack of freedom of expression and the press'.[3]

This led to Enlightenment thinkers writing on a wide variety of subjects including religious tolerance, freedom of speech, freedom of the press and freedom to criticize the government. The Enlightenment impacted and influenced both the American (1765–1783) and French (1789) Revolutions, resulting in arguments and foundations for a constitution and the American Bill of Rights (1791). The First Amendment of the US Constitution reflects some of these ideas and guarantees freedom of religion, speech and the press and the right to free assembly.[4]

---

1 Isocrates (Norton, G.) (1980).
2 Immanuel Kant, 'What Is Enlightenment?' Königsberg, Prussia, 30 September, 1784.
3 Israel, J. (2006) pp. 338–339.
4 The first ten amendments to the US Constitution are collectively known as the 'Bill of Rights'; there are five freedoms guaranteed by the First Amendment, the fifth being the right 'to petition the government for a redress of grievances'.

When Edmund Burke, an intellectual Protestant and Whig in the English Parliament, published his criticism of the French Revolution in his *Reflections* (1790), he repudiated the belief in divinely appointed monarchic authority and the idea that the people had no right to depose an oppressive government. Burke advocated that citizens should have a stake in their nation's social order which would aid constitutional reform (rather than by revolution, as in France). Burke advocated specific individual rights such as freedom of speech, including writing and printing – a form of freedom of expression against oppression by government. Burke famously detested injustice and abuse of power.

English philosopher John Stuart Mill fought for freedom of speech in Parliament and in his writings. In his essay *On Liberty* (1859) he argued in favour of tolerance, individuality and freedom of expression.[5] Mill also fought for 'liberty of the press' as the paramount safeguard against 'corrupt or tyrannical government'.[6]

1.2.1 Foundations of freedom of speech in Britain

Magna Carta of 1215 ('Great Charter of Freedoms'), signed into law by King John I of England, remains one of the most important statutes that limited the power of the monarch. Though Magna Carta did not specifically guarantee freedom of speech, it began a tradition of civil rights in Britain that laid the foundation for the first Bill of Rights some 400 years later which allowed for freedom of speech as a legal right granted by Parliament in 1688.

One of the key issues of the English Civil War (1642–1649) was freedom of speech. One of the first great proponents of free speech was Cromwell's secretary, John Milton, who in his *Areopagitica* (1644) vehemently opposed literary censorship, after Parliament had issued the 'Licensing Order of 16 June 1643' which was designed to bring publishing (and therein copyright) under the crown's control by creating a number of official censors.[7] *Areopagitica* remains the most influential and eloquent philosophical work defending the principle of the right to freedom of speech and embodies the cornerstone of press freedom. Crown licensing eventually ended in 1695 when the House of Commons refused to renew the licensing legislation.

See
Chapter 3

The Bill of Rights 1688/1689 significantly established freedom of speech in the Westminster Parliament relating to debates and proceedings in that they ought not to be questioned in any a court of law. This in essence established parliamentary privilege as a means of stopping a monarch from interfering with the workings of Parliament. To this day, parliamentary privilege means that all parliamentarians have the right to say whatever they like in Parliament without fear of being sued in defamation.

1.2.2 Limitations to freedom of expression

There will be times when the state must legislate for limitations and restrictions on our freedom of expression – in times of war, for instance, where the media cannot and should not freely report everything they witness in order to protect armed forces and civilians on

---

5   Mill, J.S. (1859), Introduction, p. 26.
6   For further discussion see: Wragg, P. (2013b).
7   Milton, J. (1644) at p. 41.

the ground. Such limitations may be expressed by moral standards in a community or by rules of law established by governmental power.

One such example is the Defence of the Realm Act 1914 (DORA), enacted by the British Government at the start of World War I. This enabled the government to impose all kinds of controls and restrictions on the British population in the interests of maintaining security (and ultimately winning the war). The measure included restrictions and control of the press and what could and could not be published from the war front by news reporters – potentially interfering with press freedom.

The Emergency Powers (Defence) Act 1939 was then passed by Parliament which effectively re-implemented parts of DORA. This 1939 act in conjunction with secondary-delegated legislation, such as Regulation 2D, was a measure to stop subversive newspaper propaganda which would impede the war effort. Under Regulation 2D two communist papers were closed down, and the editors of the *Daily Mirror* and the *Sunday Pictorial* were told to cease publishing anti-government war propaganda. Following mass rallies in response, the ban was lifted.

Press censorship by governments continues being a topic of intense discussion. UNESCO's Director-General, Audrey Azoulay, held a World Press Freedom Day in May 2019 in Addis Ababa. The event provided a platform for journalistic exchange including threats to freedom of the press.[8]

1.2.3 Obscenity and blasphemy laws in the UK

The Obscene Publications Act of 1959 put an end to aspects of 'obscene' or 'seditious' libel in English common law and therein ended these criminal offences. The offences of blasphemy and blasphemous libel were eventually abolished by section 79 of the Criminal Justice and Immigration Act of 2008. 'Blasphemy' consisted of words that tended to vilify Christianity or the Bible.

The definition of 'obscene' still exists in English law and thereby limits freedom of expression in various (art) forms. The Obscene Publications Act of 1959 is still used by police and prosecution authorities when works of art, literature, drama or photography are seen to adversely affect the morality and sensibilities of the ordinary 'decent' citizen. Some prominent cases have been heard before criminal juries who have to decide whether words or statements used, paintings, plays, films or photographs in public galleries are likely to deprave and corrupt public morals.

There were the famous 'saucy seaside postcards' painted by Donald McGill (1875–1962) that fell foul of Britain's obscenity laws (Obscene Publications Act 1857 and Obscene Publications Act 1959). McGill had produced about 12,000 postcard designs between 1904 and 1962, and local 'policing' groups and 'friendship societies' took it upon themselves to remove these 'obscene' postcards from shops. On 15 July 1954 a jury at Lincoln Crown Court found Donald McGill guilty of obscene publications. He was fined £50 plus £25 court costs and all existing postcards and their templates were ordered to be destroyed. McGill went bankrupt.

---

8   The 26th celebration of World Press Freedom Day was jointly organized by UNESCO, the African Union Commission and the Government of the Federal Democratic Republic of Ethiopia. Addis Ababa, 1–3 May 2019 at the African Union Headquarters. The theme was 'Media for Democracy: Journalism and Elections in Times of Disinformation'.

Penguin Publishers were charged under section 1(1) of the Obscene Publications Act 1959 for the 'unacceptable' erotic portrayals in D.H. Lawrence's novel *Lady Chatterley's Lover*.[9] The indictment was based on the premise that the novel put promiscuity on a pedestal and that the majority of the book was merely 'padding' between graphic scenes of sexual intercourse and filthy language. Lawyers for Penguin's defence at the notorious 'Lady C's trial' called upon a string of expert witnesses to defend the book's literary merit, including several members of the clergy, one of whom remarked that the work 'was a novel and novels deal with life as it is'. On 10 November 1960, the jury acquitted Penguin of all charges. As soon as the verdict was pronounced, London's largest bookstore, W&G Foyle Ltd, reported a run on their bookshop with 300 copies sold in just 15 minutes and orders for 3,000 more copies. The case marked a famous turning point, with a victory for more liberal publishing houses, making literary prosecutions more difficult.

Ten years after the 'Lady C' trial, the *Trial of Oz* in 1971 became the longest obscenity trial in English legal history, held at the Old Bailey under the auspices of Judge Michael Argyle QC.[10] Issue 28 of May 1970, *Schoolkids Oz*, led to the convictions of editors Richard Neville, Felix Dennis and Jim Anderson (all later overturned on appeal). Central to the obscenity allegations was the notoriously explicit cartoon by Robert Crumb, depicting Rupert Bear in a sexual position ravishing a gypsy granny. What made it worse was that the editors had invited young readers, aged between 15 and 18, to edit Issue 28. The 'Schoolkids' issue, with its French erotic cover design ('Desseins Erotiques'), contained 48 pages of content on homosexuality, lesbianism and sadism.[11]

John Mortimer QC (late author of the famous *Rumpole of the Bailey* short stories and TV series) acted for Oz's defence. He called a number of witnesses, such as DJ (the late) John Peel, the late jazz musician George Melly (who at one point explained a Latin sexual term in detail to the jury) and comedy writer Marty Feldman, who called the judge a 'boring old fart'. The three editor defendants turned up at court dressed as schoolgirls, a judicial hint at the *Hicklin* 'innocent schoolgirl' test.[12] All three Oz editors were found guilty by the jury, and Judge Argyle set out a prison term of 15 months for the editor, Richard Neville, and 12 months and 9 months respectively for his associates.

On appeal, Lord Widgery LCJ revoked the sentences by recognizing 14 errors of law. The CA ruling was appealed, and the House of Lords dismissed the (counter) appeal, stating that the offence could be committed by encouraging 'obscene' conduct, which although not itself illegal might be calculated to corrupt public morals (applying *Shaw v DPP* (1962)[13]). Oz ceased publication not long after the trial due to bankruptcy.

So what about pornographic websites? Do they fall under the current obscenity laws too? A legal row broke out in 2017 about 'Roxxxy', the world's first sex robot, invented by 'True Companion', a US-based artificial intelligence company. Roxxxy is an inflatable sex doll, digitally engineered to look, act and communicate like a human being. It also enables

See below
1.6

---

9 R v *Penguin Books Ltd* [1961] Crim LR 176.
10 The controversial underground magazine Oz was first published in Sydney, Australia, in 1963.
11 Palmer, T. (1971; new ed. 2014).
12 R v *Hicklin* (1868) LR 3 QB 360 established the 'innocent schoolgirl' test in common law as 'obscene' or 'immoral'. The test was whether the publication had a tendency to deprave and corrupt 'upright' members of society, particularly 'innocent schoolgirls', should the publication fall into their hands.
13 [1962] AC 220.

users to simulate rape, explained in detail in its website, thereby normalizing extreme violence – illegal in UK law.

It is not an offence to own a Roxxxy in the UK, albeit the importation of 'indecent or obscene articles' is illegal under section 42 of the Customs Consolidation Act 1876, deployed against individuals importing child sex dolls from abroad (see: *Henn and Darby* (1979)).[14]

Under the Obscene Publications Act 1959 it is a criminal offence for pornography sites to publish content which is 'deemed to be obscene if its effect . . . taken as a whole, [is intended] to deprave and corrupt persons' (s 1(1) OPA). This means that pornographic website operators can find themselves facing criminal proceedings for platforming content that is 'explicit and/or lingering' if it 'indicate[s] to the viewer approval or encouragement . . . thereby normalising the depraving or corrupting behaviours'.

It is also an offence to possess non-photographic child pornography under section 62 of the Coroners and Justice Act 2009 ('Possession of prohibited images of children'), even where no children were harmed in its making. Plainly, this is designed to prevent non-photographic pornography triggering a sexual interest in young people that manifests itself in more traditionally criminal ways (for example, possessing pornography involving actual children or committing a sexual offence against a child). If the net of criminal liability is cast wide enough to encompass this content, there is a compelling argument to criminalize Roxxxy the sexbot too.

 FOR THOUGHT

> The law on obscenity in the UK centres on the notion that a publication – a book, play, film or photograph – has to have a tendency to 'deprave and corrupt' those who are likely to view it. Are the UK's obscenity laws still valid in the digital age, or should the 1959 Act be repealed?

1.2.4 Constitutional rights of freedom of expression

Most democratic societies enshrine freedom of expression in their constitutions such as the German Basic Constitution (*Grundgesetz*). Article 5 *Grundgesetz* states that

> every person shall have the right freely to express and disseminate his opinions in speech, writing and pictures, and to inform himself from generally accessible sources. Freedom of the press and freedom of reporting by means of broadcasts and films shall be guaranteed. There shall be no censorship.

The *Grundgesetz* was formulated in 1949 largely by the allied forces after Germany's defeat in World War II when the Holocaust and the spectre of Hitler's Germany were fresh in public memory. The second paragraph of Article 5 restricts freedom of expression 'in the provisions of general laws, in provisions for the protection of young persons and in the right to personal honor'.

---

14 *R v Henn (Maurice Donald), R v Darby (John Frederick Ernest)* (Case 34/79) [1979] ECR 3795 (CJEU).

The German Government has made use of this measure, limiting free speech when hate or racist speech is used publicly: for example, when Holocaust denier Ernst Zündel was convicted in 2007. German prosecutors regularly resort to the 'incitement to hatred' clause under § 130 of the German Criminal Code (*Strafgetzbuch*, or *StGB*) to convict right-wing leaders using hate speech against refugees in Germany.

Lutz Bachmann, founder of the German right-wing anti-Islamist organization PEGIDA (Patriotic Europeans against the Islamization of the West) has led several outspoken anti-immigrant marches in Dresden since 2014. He has criminal convictions and fines concerning racial hate speech in Germany.[15] In March 2018, Bachmann was refused entry into the UK by the Home Office and subsequently deported from Stansted airport, as he was about to lead an anti-immigration march in Birmingham. The Home Office told *The Independent* that Bachmann was refused entry on grounds his presence in Britain was 'not in the interest of the public good'.[16]

German satirical TV show host and comedian Jan Böhmermann recited a satirical poem on his live TV show in 2016, accusing Turkish President Recep Tayyip Erdoğan of suppressing Kurds and targeting Christians 'while watching child pornography', among other things. He was charged under § 103 StGB for insulting a foreign head of state. For many months Böhmermann faced up to five years' imprisonment for the alleged offence; the charge was later dropped. In June 2017 the German Parliament abolished § 103.

See below
1.4

Since the United Kingdom does not have a written constitution, it has to rely on Article 10 ECHR for 'freedom of expression', now enshrined in the HRA 1998 Schedule 1 part 1.[17] Worth noting is that Article 10(1) ECHR is a protection for individual rather than corporate freedom of expression and does not expressly refer to media or journalistic (press) freedom.

In *Centro Europa* (2012),[18] the Grand Chamber of the European Court of Human Rights (ECtHR) re-affirmed the importance of media plurality under Article 10 of the Convention. The case concerned an Italian TV company's inability to broadcast for nearly ten years, despite having a broadcasting licence, due to lack of television frequencies allocated to it.

The Court concluded that the Italian legislative framework had lacked clarity and precision and that the authorities had not observed the deadlines set in the licence, thereby frustrating Centro Europa's expectations. These shortcomings had resulted in reduced competition in the audiovisual sector. The Italian state had failed to put in place an appropriate legislative and administrative framework to guarantee effective media pluralism.

The ECtHR held that this amounted to a serious breach of Article 10(1) (and of Article 1 of the First Protocol), noting that

> there can be no democracy without pluralism. Democracy thrives on freedom of expression. It is of the essence of democracy to allow diverse political programmes

15 Source: 'Die nächste Verurteilung des Lutz Bachmann' ('The next verdict for Lutz Bachmann'), by Stefan Locke, *Frankfurter Allgemeine*, 23 March 2018.

16 Source: 'Border Force has the power to refuse entry to an individual if it is considered that his or her presence in the UK is not conducive to the public good', by Maya Oppenheim, *Independent*, 18 March 2018 at www.independent.co.uk/news/uk/home-news/lutz-bachmann-pegida-detained-stansted-deported-a8262131.html.

17 For further discussion see: Stein, E. (2000), p. 347.

18 *Centro Europa 7 S.R.L. and Di Stefano v Italy* (*Application No* 38433/09), [2012] ECHR 974 (ECtHR). Grand Chamber judgment of 7 June 2012. The applicants were Centro Europa 7 S.R.L., an Italian analog TV company based in Rome, and Francescantonio Di Stefano, its statutory representative.

to be proposed and debated, even those that call into question the way a State is currently organised, provided that they do not harm democracy itself.[19]

The Italian state was not allowed to justify their actions under Article 10(2) ECHR and were ordered to pay the TV company €10,000,000 and €100,000 to Mr di Stefano in respect of costs and expenses, plus any tax that may be chargeable in respect of pecuniary and non-pecuniary damage – a substantial fine in 2012.[20]

1.3 Theoretical foundations of free speech rights

Freedom of speech is an integral part of democracy. In a democracy, the opinions of the people are the basis for the government's exercise of power. The opinions and ideas freely expressed by individual citizens ought to be the final authority in a democratic society. Some have argued that the democratic process ought to be limited to decisions that are not incompatible with the proper functioning of the democratic process. At times it may be necessary as part of the democratic process to limit freedom of association or freedom of speech as long as these limitations do not extend beyond the requirements for proper democratic functioning.

In Europe, after the twentieth-century dictatorships of Adolf Hitler[21] in Germany, Benito Mussolini[22] in Italy and Francisco Franco in Spain,[23] freedom of expression was formally identified as a human right under Article 19 of the Universal Declaration of Human Rights of 1948 (UDHR).[24] Article 19 of the UDHR states:

> Everyone has the right to freedom of opinion and expression; this right includes freedom to hold opinions without interference and to seek, receive and impart information and ideas through any media and regardless of frontiers.

The idea that citizens can receive free and objective information and engage in free debate and critical reflection was adopted in the twentieth century by the German philosopher Jürgen Habermas. He believed that the emancipation of the informed citizen could be brought about only by 'critical communication and analysis of modern institutions'. The only way such informed criticism could take shape was, in his opinion, through a free and uncensored press, which he included in his 'three normative models of democracy'.[25] During the 1960s Habermas also developed the concept of 'private and public spheres'.[26] His definition of the 'public sphere' later had a great impact on privacy

---

19 Ibid. at para. 129 (Françoise Tulkens, President, Grand Chamber, ECtHR).
20 Ibid. at paras 214–227.
21 Chancellor of Nazi Germany, 1933–1945.
22 Italian Fascist dictator and founder of the Organizzazione per la Vigilanza e la Repressione dell'Antifascismo (OVRA) (Organization for Vigilance and Repression of Anti-Fascism), 1927–1945.
23 The military head of Spain from 1936 to 1975.
24 The Universal Declaration of Human Rights (UDHR) was drafted by representatives with different legal and cultural backgrounds from all regions of the world. The Declaration was proclaimed by the United Nations General Assembly in Paris on 10 December 1948 (Resolution 217 A III).
25 Habermas, J. (1994).
26 Habermas, J. (1962, translation 1989).

See
Chapter 2

and media freedom in relation to the reporting on celebrities, such as Caroline von Hannover (see: *von Hannover v Germany (No 1) (2005)*[27]).

Freedom of speech was also recognized as an international human right in the International Covenant on Civil and Political Rights (ICCPR), which amended the version of Article 19 UDHR by stating that the exercise of these rights carries 'special duties and responsibilities' and may 'therefore be subject to certain restrictions' when necessary '[f]or respect of the rights or reputation of others or '[f]or the protection of national security or of public order (order public), or of public health or morals'.

Similar to Articles 10(1) and 10(2) of the European Convention, freedom of speech and expression are therefore not absolute in this international instrument. Governments of various states may place common limitations on these freedoms. In the UK these include laws relating to defamation (libel and slander), obscenity, child pornography, incitement to hatred, terrorism, extreme pornography on the internet, copyright breaches and matters of national security – to name but a few. John Stuart Mill called this the 'harm principle'.

At the beginning of Chapter II of *On Liberty*, Mill makes a strong and bold defence of free speech. Mill tells us that *any* doctrine should be allowed the light of day no matter *how* immoral it may seem to everyone else. Such liberty should exist with every subject matter so that every citizen has 'absolute freedom of opinion and sentiment on all subjects, practical or speculative, scientific, moral or theological'.[28] The 'Millian Principle' – as Harvard scholar and philosopher Thomas Scanlon calls it – allows us, even in 'normal [peace] times', to consider whether the publication of certain information might present serious hazards to public safety by giving people the capacity to inflict certain harms. Mill argues that these risks are worth taking in times of peace in order to allow full discussion of certain delicate or problematic questions, which might well be intolerable in wartime.

T. M. Scanlon offers three distinguishable elements of the Millian Principle, which is absolute but serves only to rule out certain justifications for legal restrictions on acts of expression: first, on grounds of whether they reflect an appropriate balancing of the value of certain kinds of expression relative to other social goods; second, whether they insure equitable distribution of access to means of expression throughout the society; and third, whether they are compatible with the recognition of certain special rights, particularly political rights. Within the Millian limits governmental policies can then be set by legislation which can affect or restrict opportunities for expression, positively intervene in free speech and thereby justify governmental actions and interventions on these grounds.[29]

1.3.1 Freedom of speech fighters

The fight for freedom of speech continues around the world, and there are numerous examples of writers and journalists who either had to go into exile, went to prison or died for their courage. Here are just a few.

The Russian dissident, Aleksandr Solzhenitsyn, experienced a Siberian labour camp ('the Gulag') during the Stalinist era in Russia, for publishing his famous autobiographical

---

27 (2005) 40 EHRR 1.
28 Mill, J.S. (1859), *On Liberty*, Chapter II, p. 15.
29 Scanlon, T. (1972), pp. 204–226.

account *One Day in the Life of Ivan Denisovich*.[30] Solzhenitsyn was imprisoned for eight years after 1945 for writing derogatory comments about Joseph Stalin when serving in the Red Army during the Second World War.

On 14 February 1989, British Indian author Salman Rushdie was telephoned by a BBC journalist and told that he had been 'sentenced to death' by the Ayatollah Khomeini. For the first time he heard the word *fatwa*. His crime? To have written a novel called *The Satanic Verses* (1988),[31] which was accused of being 'against Islam, the Prophet and the Qur'an'. Sir Salman Rushdie became another dissident who had to live in exile for his writings. In his memoirs, *Joseph Anton* (2012),[32] Rushdie describes the extraordinary story of his life in exile, forced underground, living with the constant presence of an armed police protection team. He was asked to choose an alias that the police could call him by. He thought of writers he loved and combinations of their names; then it came to him: the first names of Conrad and Chekhov – Joseph Anton. His story is of one of the crucial battles for freedom of speech. In April 1989, two London bookshops – Dillons and Collets – were firebombed for stocking the Rushdie novel. There followed explosions in High Wycombe and London's King's Road and a bomb in Liberty's department store, which had a Penguin bookshop – because Penguin had published *Satanic Verses*. Rushdie lived in secretly guarded exile for ten years until 1998 when the *fatwa* was withdrawn.

In November 2002, Nigerian journalist Isioma Daniel incensed Muslims in her country by writing about the Prophet Mohammed in a newspaper article. In her fashion column for a Lagos newspaper, she commented about the Miss World pageant which was about to be held in Nigeria:

> the Muslims thought it was immoral to bring 92 women to Nigeria and ask them to revel in vanity. What would Mohammed think? In all honesty, he would probably have chosen a wife from one of them.[33]

A *fatwa* was issued on Isioma Daniel by the deputy governor of Zamfara state because her article had incited major religious riots for being held a 'blasphemous' publication. Information Minister Umar Dangaladima reiterated Zamfara state policy by his public announcement:

> it's a fact that Islam prescribes the death penalty on anybody, no matter his faith, who insults the Prophet.[34]

In August 2012 Russian judge Marina Syrova sentenced three members of the punk band Pussy Riot to two years in a prison labour camp for staging a 40-second punk feminist 'flash mob' inside Moscow's official church as they performed a 'punk prayer'. One Pussy Riot member, Yekaterina Samutsevich, was set free by a Moscow appeals court in

---

30 Aleksandr Solzhenitsyn, *One Day in the Life of Ivan Denisovich* (first published in the Soviet literary magazine *Noviy Mir* (New World) in November 1962).

31 The title refers to a group of Qur'anic verses that allow for prayers of intercession to be made to three pagan goddesses in Mecca. See: Rushdie, S. (1989; new edition 1998).

32 Rushdie, S. (2012).

33 Source: Thisday press office release, Kaduna, 27 November 2002.

34 Source: 'Fatwa is issued against Nigerian journalist', by James Astill and Owen Bowcott, *Guardian*, 27 November 2002.

October 2012, leaving Maria Alyokhina and Nadezhda Tolokonnikova – found guilty of hooliganism and blasphemous religious rioting – to serve two years in a Russian labour colony. No doubt the punk band members had offended many Russian Orthodox believers by screaming lyrics such as 'Shit, shit, the Lord's shit' inside the Cathedral of Christ the Saviour, but the trial itself became an old-fashioned Soviet show trial, one of the first criminal crackdowns of President Vladimir Putin's campaign against political activists.

The Russian opposition figurehead and anti-Putin blogger Alexei Navalny and 15 other protesters were arrested in Moscow in January 2018 after Navalny attempted to lead a protest in advance of the Russian presidential election in March 2018, which expected the unchallenged return of Vladimir Putin to power for another six years. On 29 January, 41-year-old Navalny was wrestled to the ground by officers amid chaotic scenes with police wielding truncheons to fight off Navalny supporters. Navalny tweeted from a police van: 'I have been detained. This means nothing. You are not rallying for me, but for yourselves and your future'. On 18 March, Putin cruised to victory, elected to a fourth term as Russian President until 2024, making him the first Kremlin leader to serve two decades in power since Josef Stalin.

1.3.2 Should freedom of expression be curtailed by the state?

Although we have freedom of expression, we also have a duty to respect other people's rights, as Locke and Kant pointed out; Montesquieu stressed that we also have duty to behave responsibly. Public authorities (such as the police) may restrict this right if they can show that their action is lawful, necessary and proportionate in order to protect national security, territorial integrity (i.e. the state) or public safety.

There are various laws, such as the Public Order Act 1986 which created new offences relating to public order such as s 1 'riot', s 3 'affray' and the later added s 4A, causing 'intentional harassment, alarm or distress' in a public place. The act confers substantial powers on the police in order to control public processions and assemblies in the UK.

The UK Parliament has passed several 'terrorism' related laws, granting extensive powers to police and security services and therein limiting freedom of expression which now includes digital hate speech online and social media. Whilst the legislation of the 1970s and 1980s was primarily aimed at the 'Troubles' in Northern Ireland and related IRA (Irish Republican Army) terrorism attacks on the UK mainland, later acts of Parliament from 2000 onwards had wider aims to curtail and combat global terrorism.

The Prevention of Terrorism (Temporary Provisions) Acts of 1974 and 1989 (later repealed) conferred emergency powers upon police forces. It had been Prime Minister Margaret Thatcher's unrelenting aim from 1979 onwards to stop violence in Northern Ireland. Her Conservative Government policies included limiting freedom of speech of members of the republican political party Sinn Féin (the political wing of the IRA) and several other paramilitary organizations. A decree of 19 October 1988 banned 11 loyalist and republican organizations and their leaders from speaking about the conflict in media broadcasts. Thatcher claimed this would deny terrorists 'the oxygen of publicity'.

Instead of hearing Gerry Adams[35] or Martin McGuinness,[36] BBC viewers and radio listeners would hear an actor's voice reading a transcript of the individuals' words. Sanders

---

35 Gerard ('Gerry') Adams (born 1948), an Irish republican politician and former leader of Sinn Féin from 1983 to 2018.
36 Martin McGuinness (1970–2017) was an Irish republican and Sinn Féin politician who was the deputy First Minister of Northern Ireland from May 2007 to January 2017.

highlights journalistic coverage of terrorism as being particularly difficult in terms of free speech and media ethics.[37] She specifically examined broadcast reporting during the Troubles from 1989 to the Belfast (Northern Ireland) Agreement in 1998, looking particularly at interviews with IRA and INLA (Irish National Liberation Army) members, concluding that these were difficult times for press and media freedom.

A BBC documentary by Paul Hamann featuring an extensive interview with Martin McGuinness was banned by the government until the start of the peace talks in 1994 when media restrictions in Northern Ireland were gradually lifted. Hamann's documentary, *Real Lives: At the Edge of the Union*, could finally be shown.

Since the atrocities of 9/11 (2001) in New York and the London bombings in July 2005, the UK Parliament has passed a number of 'terrorism' statutes. In the context of heightened threats from the so-called Islamic State and several terrorist attacks on the UK mainland and mainland Europe, the Westminster Parliament has passed, *inter alia*, the Counter-Terrorism Act 2008, the Counter-Terrorism and Security Act 2015 and the Investigatory Powers Act 2016. The overarching aim is to strengthen the legal powers and capabilities of public authorities, law enforcement and intelligence services to disrupt terrorism and prevent individuals from being radicalized in the first instance.

The Guardian and *The Observer* newspapers published excerpts from former MI5 spy Peter Wright's book *Spycatcher*, a memoir that included allegations that the security services had acted unlawfully. The book was published outside the UK in Australia and later in Canada. The Attorney General on behalf of the UK government succeeded in obtaining a court order (interim injunction), preventing the newspapers from printing further material until proceedings relating to a breach of confidence had finished. The newspapers eventually took their complaint to the Strasbourg Human Rights Court alleging that the continuation of the court order had breached their right to freedom of expression in Article 10(1) ECHR.[38]

The ECtHR held that, although the court order was lawful as it was in the interest of national security, there was insufficient reason for continuing the newspaper publication ban once the book had been published (abroad). The court order should have ended once the information was no longer confidential.[39] That said, the Convention had not yet passed into UK law; the Human Rights Act 1998 (HRA) was still some six years away, though this judgment may well have persuaded Parliament.

Public authorities in the UK now have extensive legislation to restrict freedom of expression if, for example, an individual expresses their views that encourage racial or religious hatred or incites terrorism offences on the internet. However, the relevant public authority must show that the restriction is 'proportionate', in other words that it is appropriate and no more than necessary to address the issue concerned. Article 10(2) ECHR enshrines such restrictions and state powers:

> The exercise of these freedoms, since it carries with it duties and responsibilities, may be subject to such formalities, conditions, restrictions or penalties as are prescribed by law and are necessary in a democratic society, in the interests of national security, territorial disorder or crime, for the protection of health or morals, for

---

37 Sanders, K. (2003), p. 71.
38 *A-G v Guardian Newspapers Ltd* (No 2) [1990] 1 AC 109 (sub nom. *Spycatcher No 2*).
39 *Observer and Guardian v UK* (1992) 14 EHRR 153 (sub nom. *the Spycatcher action*) (ECtHR).

the protection of the reputation or rights of others, for preventing the disclosure of information received in confidence, or for maintaining the authority and impartiality of the judiciary.

1.4 Freedom of expression and Article 10 ECHR

The right to freedom of expression is crucial in a democracy, helps to inform political debate and is essential to the media to report on government transparency and the checks and balances imposed by Parliament on the executive.

In 1948, the Universal Declaration of Human Rights was adopted by the UN General Assembly. Its main aim was to promote human, civil, economic and social rights, including freedom of expression and religion, among all its subscribing nations. There followed the European Convention on Human Rights and Fundamental Freedoms (ECHR), adopted in 1950. The subsequent International Covenant on Civil and Political Rights 1966 (ICCPR) recognized the right to freedom of speech as 'the right to hold opinions without interference'.[40]

Article 10(1) ECHR gives everyone the right to freedom of expression, which includes the freedom to hold opinions and to receive and impart information and ideas without state interference. The type of expression protected includes:

- political expression (including comment on matters of general public interest);
- artistic expression; and
- commercial expression, particularly when it also raises matters of legitimate public debate and concern.

See
Chapter 2.6

To ensure that free expression and debate are possible, there must be protection for elements of a free press, including protection of journalistic sources (see below 1.8). Interferences with press freedom usually involve restrictions on publication (injunctions or super injunctions).

Article 10 is a qualified right, and as such the right to freedom of expression may be limited by the state and public authorities under Article 10(2) ECHR, which provides that freedom of expression 'carries with it duties and responsibilities' and may be limited as long as the limitation:

- is prescribed by law;
- is necessary and proportionate; and
- pursues a legitimate aim.

Such 'legitimate aim' might include the interests of national security, territorial integrity or public safety, but can also include the prevention of disorder or crime, the protection

---

40 International Covenant on Civil and Political Rights (ICCPR), United Nations Treaty, New York, 16 December 1966. UN Treaty Series, vol. 999, p. 171 and vol. 1057, p. 407 (procès-verbal of rectification of the authentic Spanish text); depositary notification C.N. 782.2001.

of public health or morals, the protection of a person's reputation or preventing the disclosure of information received in confidence (confidentiality).

Freedom of speech must at times yield to other cogent social interests, such as national security when a state may well derogate under Art 10(2) ECHR or limit freedom of speech under domestic laws. This was recognized in the *Spycatcher*[41] action well before the European Convention entered into UK domestic law. In *Derbyshire County Council v Times Newspapers Ltd*,[42] Lord Keith of Kinkel, speaking for a unanimous House, observed about Article 10:

> As regards the words 'necessary in a democratic society' in connection with the restrictions on the right to freedom of expression which may properly be prescribed by law, the jurisprudence of the European Court of Human Rights has established that 'necessary' requires the existence of a pressing social need, and that the restrictions should be no more than is proportionate.[43]

1.4.1 Freedom of expression and the digital age

If we then translate the Millian Principle into the digital age, the application of freedom of expression becomes rather controversial. Mill argued that those citizens who exhibit cruelty, malice, envy, insincerity, resentment and crass egotism would be open to greater sanctions by the state and forms of punishment should be admonished because these faults are 'wicked and other-regarding'.[44] We could then translate some people's actions on the internet, social media or via mobile phone messages as acting with malice, harassment, libel, envy or resentment which violates the rights of others. This is what Mill called the 'harm principle' as the only legitimate ground for interference with freedom of expression and free speech.

It could then be argued that restricting means of communication on the internet amounts to a legitimate action by a state in order to prevent harm to its citizens. One such example is China's *Golden Shield Project* (Chinese: 金盾工程; pinyin: *jīndùn gōngchéng*), also named *National Public Security Work Informational Project* (全国公安工作信息化工程), the Chinese nationwide network-security e-government project of the People's Republic of China. This project includes the security management information system (治安管理信息系统), the criminal information system (刑事案件信息系统), the exit and entry administration information system (出入境管理信息系统), the supervisor information system (监管人员信息系统) and the traffic management information system (交通管理信息系统). The *Golden Shield Project* is a means by which the Chinese Government (the Ministry of Public Security) filters potentially unfavourable data from foreign countries, and is seen as one of the causes for the Hong Kong riots in 2019.

---

41 *AG v Guardian Newspapers Ltd (No 1)*; *AG v Observer Ltd*; *AG v Times Newspapers Ltd* [1987] 1 WLR 1248 (Spycatcher case); also: *AG v Guardian Newspapers Ltd (No 2)* [1990] 1 AC 109 (Spycatcher No 2).
42 *Derbyshire County Council v Times Newspapers Ltd and Others* [1993] AC 534.
43 Ibid. at 550H–551A.
44 Mill, J.S. (1859), On Liberty, p. 55.

1.5 Conceptual differences between freedom of expression and media freedom

Freedom of expression can include a number of objectives, such as the power or right to express one's opinions without censorship, restraint or legal penalty. Article 10 ECHR has enshrined these concepts in law, protecting an individual's right to hold their own opinions and to express them freely without government interference. This includes the right to express one's views aloud (for example at London's Speakers' Corner, through public protest and demonstrations) and through published articles, books or leaflets. The European Convention also protects an individual's freedom to *receive* information from other people by, for example, being part of a social media audience or via the internet.

1.5.1 Media freedom and the law

Media freedom can be defined as the ability and opportunity for journalists to say and write what they want without restriction or interference from the state and elsewhere. Media or press freedom is not expressly defined or mentioned in Article 10 ECHR, and it is therefore important to read the phrasing of Articles 10(1) and (2) ECHR in detail.

For daily practical journalistic and investigative purposes, we need to place our trust in the media and broadcasting institutions. Today press freedom accepts certain restrictions on providing information, such as war reporting,[45] contempt, extreme hate speech, the protection of minors, racial discrimination and national security. Frost argues that it can be rather confusing that many people in Britain and other Western European countries appear to support media freedom on the one hand while supporting censorship on specific matters on the other, such as the coverage of terrorism or sexually explicit material.[46] Ultimately, there are ethical and moral issues that govern newsgathering, investigative journalism and war reporting. These are usually left to broadcasting organizations' policy, such as the BBC's editorial code and the IPSO editors' code.

See

Chapter 7

1.5.2 Cartoons and the boundaries of press freedom

Cartoonists and caricaturists can often say a great deal more than a journalist can through their visual medium. In Britain, caricatures and satires are generally dealt with by the tort law of defamation.[47] In *Charleston v News Group Newspapers Ltd* (1995),[48] the House of Lords considered the digitally enhanced photomontage that showed the faces of two famous Australian actors, Anne Charleston ('Madge') and Ian Smith ('Harold'), of the popular TV series *Neighbours*, superimposed on the nearly naked bodies of others in pornographic poses, and agreed with Blofeld J's order to strike out the libel action against the publishers of the *News of the World*. Their Lordships, applying the 'bane and antidote' defence, declined to find defamation in *Charleston*. They further commented if the readers who did not take 'the trouble to discover what the article was all about, carried away the impression that

---

45 For further discussion see: Burchill, R., White N.D. and Morris, J. (2005).
46 Frost, C. (2011).
47 Rogers, W.V.H. and Parkes, R. (2010) *Gatley on Libel and Slander*, first supplement to the eleventh edition, para. 3.4. For further detail see *Gatley on Libel and Slander* (2013).
48 [1995] 2 AC 65.

⊙ **FOR THOUGHT**

German, French and British lawmakers are pushing for social media firms, such as Facebook and Twitter, to set up an independent body for EU Member States to review and respond to reports of offensive content from the public, rather than the individual companies doing that themselves. Should private social media companies decide themselves what is right and what is wrong on their platforms? Would this mean a limiting of free expression?

two well-known actors in legitimate television were also involved in making pornographic films, they could hardly be described as ordinary, reasonable, fair-minded readers'.[49]

See
Chapter 3

1.5.3 Prophet Mohammed cartoons controversy

This sections looks at how the cartoons row developed from the Danish newspaper *Jyllands-Posten*'s cartoons depicting the Prophet Mohammed as a terrorist with a bomb in 2005 to the *Charlie Hebdo* killings in Paris. In many Islamic and Roman Catholic countries, blasphemy laws remain rigorous and are strictly enforced, often with austere penalties – even potentially the death penalty. This demonstrates that the extent and scope of national laws protecting religious beliefs remain very culture-specific.

When the Danish newspaper *Jyllands-Posten* published 12 editorial cartoons of the Prophet Mohammed on 30 September 2005, accompanied by an article titled 'The Face of Mohammed', it caused outrage in the Muslim world, with violent protests erupting across the Middle East. The introduction to the article was headed 'Freedom of Expression', making the point that Denmark was not afraid of criticizing Islam, and that 'some Muslims reject modern, secular society' and they demand 'a special position' in Western society with 'special consideration for their religious beliefs'.

On 15 March 2006, the Danish Director of Public Prosecutions (DPP) decided there was no basis for commencing criminal proceedings against the newspaper *Jyllands-Posten* and its editor in chief for publishing the article. The criminal legal issue was whether the article and the cartoons fell within the provisions of sections 140 and/or 266b of the Danish Criminal Code.[50] The Danish DPP decided not to prosecute, also citing the right to freedom of expression as laid down in Article 77 of the Danish Constitution and Article 10(1) ECHR. He further argued that the right to freedom of expression also includes statements which may shock, offend or disturb and that this right might be curtailed by Danish law as is necessary in a democratic society (i.e. proportionate to the legitimate aim pursued).

---

49 Ibid. at 76 (Lord Bridge of Harwich).
50 S. 140 of the Danish Criminal Code provides that any person who mocks or scorns religious doctrines or acts of worship of any lawfully existing religious community in public shall be liable to imprisonment for any term not exceeding four months. S. 266b(1) states that any person publicly or with the intention of wider dissemination makes a statement or imparts other information by which a group of people are threatened, scorned or degraded on account of their race, colour, nationality or ethnic origin, religion or sexual orientation shall be liable to a fine or imprisonment for any term not exceeding two years.

Newspapers and magazines around the world subsequently reprinted the Mohammed cartoons, leading to a global wave of protests and riots by Muslims who claimed that the caricatures were just another expression of Western colonialism. On 6 February 2006, hundreds of Iranians attacked the Danish and Norwegian embassies in Tehran, and Saudi Arabia recalled its ambassador to Denmark, while Libya closed its embassy in Copenhagen, and Lebanese demonstrators set the Danish embassy in Beirut on fire. The violence further escalated as newspapers in France, Germany, Spain and Italy reprinted the cartoons.

The offices of *Jyllands-Posten* had to be evacuated several times after security threats, and in early 2010 Kurt Westergaard, one of the Danish cartoonists, became the subject of an attempted attack at his home. Eleven Danish newspapers were contacted by the Saudi lawyer Faisal Yamani, representing eight Muslim organizations and some 94,923 descendants of Prophet Mohammed, demanding that *Jyllands-Posten* and the other newspapers remove the cartoons from their websites and print apologies.

On 26 February 2010, Danish newspaper *Politiken* published an apology for reprinting the caricatures. Though this was welcomed by the Danish prime minister, he also stressed the importance of freedom of expression and press freedom. The cultural and foreign affairs editor of *Jyllands-Posten*, Flemming Rose, who had originally commissioned the Mohammed cartoons, said that its sister paper had failed in the fight for freedom of speech and called it a 'sad day' for the Danish press.

On 7 January 2015, gunmen shot dead 12 people at the Paris office of French satirical newspaper *Charlie Hebdo* in an apparent militant Islamist attack with the gunmen shouting, 'We have avenged the Prophet Mohammed' and 'God is the Greatest' in Arabic ('*Allahu Akbar*'). The attack took place during the magazine's daily editorial meeting. Cartoonist Philippe Honoré was amongst those killed. He had drawn the last cartoon for the magazine, showing the leader of the self-styled Islamic State, Abu Bakr al-Baghdadi, presenting his New Year message, saying 'and especially good health!' Nine months later, French opinion was deeply divided about the controversial Mohammed cartoons in *Charlie Hebdo*. Its senior cartoonist, Luz – the man who designed the famous green cover of the first edition after the attacks – announced his resignation in October 2015; columnist Patrick Pelloux announced the same.

A month later, on Friday 13 November 2015, gunmen and suicide bombers hit the Bataclan Concert Hall, the Stade de France and restaurants and bars almost simultaneously in Paris, leaving 130 people dead and hundreds wounded. The attacks were described by President François Hollande as an 'act of war' organized by the Islamic State (IS) militant group. The man suspected of killing a policewoman in a shooting in Montrouge was a member of the same jihadist group as the two suspects in the attack on *Charlie Hebdo*.

 FOR THOUGHT

Should an editor of a magazine (and its online edition) apologize for a satirical poem which has offended a leader of state? Or does this attack the artist's freedom of expression? Discuss with reference to leading authorities.

1.5.4 Strasbourg jurisprudence in relation to obscenity and blasphemy laws

Various obscenity and blasphemy laws in mainly Roman Catholic European countries prohibit film and video game releases. Strasbourg jurisprudence remains non-committal in this area of law and generally applies only to anything which might encourage public indecency or glorify criminal activity by those engaging in internet activity, such as watching or uploading extreme sexual violence or torture on YouTube.

When examining human rights law, it could be argued that the European Court of Human Rights (ECtHR) has – in general – not interfered with a country's freedom of religion under Article 9 ECHR in favour of Article 10 ('freedom of expression') (see: Murphy v Ireland (2000)[51]).

The controversial case of Otto-Preminger[52]-Institut v Austria (1994)[53] concerned the banning and forfeiture of the film Council of Love (Das Liebeskonzil), based on a nineteenth-century play in which the Eucharist is ridiculed, and God the Father is presented as a senile, impotent idiot, the Virgin Mary as a wanton woman who displays erotic interest in the devil and Jesus Christ as a low-grade mental defective given to fondling his mother's breasts.

Das Liebeskonzil was to be screened at a private film club before an informed adult audience in the Tyrol in 1987, but the Innsbruck district court injuncted the film because of its blasphemous content which, the court reasoned, would shock the predominantly Roman Catholic audience in Tyrol.[54] Preminger opposed the injunction, citing Article 10(1) ECHR as 'freedom of [artistic] expression'. On appeal, the Austrian Constitutional Court in Vienna held the film to be blasphemous because it contained provocative and offensive portrayals of objects of veneration of the Roman Catholic religion. The Austrian court cited Article 10(2) of the Convention as a reason for derogating against 'freedom of expression' and confirmed the injunction as permanent: the court ruled that the Innsbruck court had not overstepped the 'margin of appreciation'.[55]

Jens Olaf Jersild is a prominent Danish journalist, well-known for his investigative and critical reportage. In 1985 Jersild investigated a group of right-wing racists, called 'The Greenjackets' (grønjakkerne). He was convicted under the Danish Criminal Code for repeating and using highly racist comments by three members of the Greenjackets, including 'a nigger is not a human being – it's an animal'. After a number of unsuccessful appeals, including the regional court (the Østre Landsret) and the Danish Supreme Court, Jersild successfully claimed that the Danish state had breached his Article 10(1) ECHR right. The Human Rights Court in Strasbourg (ECtHR) ruled that he did not intend to spread racist language but merely depicted society as a journalist and public watchdog.

---

51 (2000) 38 EHRR 13 (ECtHR).
52 Otto Ludwig Preminger (1905–1986) was a famous Austro-Hungarian film director. Living mostly in the United States, he directed over 35 Hollywood movies which tended to be of the film noir genre. Topics were intentionally blasphemous and provocative, e.g. Fallen Angel (1945), The Moon is Blue (1953), The Man with the Golden Arm (1955), Anatomy of a Murder (1959) and Advise and Consent (1962).
53 (1995) 19 EHRR 34 (Case No 13470/87) 20 September 1994 (ECtHR).
54 Contrary to s 188 ('insult') of the Austrian Criminal Code as promulgated on 13 November 1998 (Federal Law Gazette I, p. 945, p. 3322) (Strafgesetzbuch).
55 Judgment by the ECtHR of 20 September 1994 with the result of the immediate withdrawal of the movie by the Austrian Constitutional Court (Urteil vom 20. September 1994, A/295-A EGMR Einziehung des Films 'Das Liebeskonzil', verstößt nicht gegen Art 10(1) EMRK).

> ❖ KEY CASE   *Jersild v Denmark* (1994) 19 EHRR 1

Precedent
- ❖ A publication or broadcast is justified under Article 10(1) ECHR if – given the margin of appreciation of that country – the article (or broadcast) contributes discussions of matters of public interest.
- ❖ A state should not derogate from the freedom of expression and ban a publication or broadcast under Article 10(2) ECHR if the public interest test is satisfied.

Facts
On 31 May 1985 the Danish *Sunday News Magazine* (*Søndagsavisen*) published an article describing the racist attitudes of members of a group of young people, calling themselves 'The Greenjackets' at Østerbro in Copenhagen. In the light of this article, the editors of the *Sunday News Magazine* decided to produce a documentary on the Greenjackets. The applicant, Mr Jens Olaf Jersild, a Danish journalist, contacted representatives of the group, inviting three of them, together with Mr Per Axholt, a social worker, to take part in a TV interview. During the interview, the three Greenjackets made abusive and derogatory remarks about immigrants and ethnic groups in Denmark. The edited film – lasting only a few minutes – was broadcast by Danmarks Radio on 21 July 1985 as part of the Sunday news magazine programme. The documentary feature included avowed racist views.

In their statements the youths described black people as belonging to an inferior subhuman race:

> the niggers . . . are not human beings. . . . Just take a picture of a gorilla . . . and then look at a nigger, it's the same body structure. . . . A nigger is not a human being, it's an animal, that goes for all the other foreign workers as well, Turks, Yugoslavs and whatever they are called.

Following the programme, no complaints were made to the Radio Council or to Danmarks Radio, but the Bishop of Ålborg complained to the Minister of Justice. Subsequently, the three youths were convicted for making racist statements and Mr Jersild for aiding and abetting them in making racist comments in a public place.[56] Mr Jersild, but not the three Greenjackets, appealed against the City Court's judgment to the High Court of Eastern Denmark (*Østre Landsret*), but his appeal was rejected, and his conviction was upheld by the Danish Supreme Court.

Decision
The ECtHR jointly dissented with the opinion and judgment of the Danish Supreme Court. Judges Gölcüklü, Russo and Valticos stated, 'We cannot share

---

56 Under Article 266(b) of the Danish Penal Code.

the opinion of the majority of the Court in the Jersild case'. The ECtHR held that Mr Jersild's Article 10 right to freedom of expression had been violated and that he was not a racist. He had a valid defence in making the programme. The reasons given by the Danish court in support of Jersild's conviction and sentence (and derogation under Article 10(2) ECHR) were not sufficient to justify interference with a journalist's right of free expression in a democratic society.

Analysis

It is interesting that the Strasbourg Court in *Jersild* did not show any concern or sensibility towards vulnerable groups in the face of racial abuse compared with its judgment in the *Otto Preminger* case, where the Catholic population of the tiny Tyrol region was very much taken into consideration over the offending film. Were the religious sensibilities so fundamentally different in character in the satirical film by Otto Preminger to the 'nigger' quote in the Danish documentary by Jersild? Why did the ECtHR not apply the 'margin of appreciation' in the *Jersild* case?[57] The Strasbourg Court found it particularly important in *Jersild* to send a message to combat racial discrimination. This, in fact, had been Mr Jersild's intention when making the Danish TV documentary. The ECtHR stressed that freedom of expression at times constitutes publications (or broadcasts) which may shock or offend but that this is one of the essential underpinnings of a democracy, and the media plays an important role in the duty to inform.

The ECtHR ruling in *Jersild* provides journalists and media outlets with the protection needed to disseminate controversial opinions; however, it does caution against the dissemination of unbalanced and overly obscene or blasphemous communication.[58]

 FOR THOUGHT

> Would you agree with some proponents of internet free speech that any proposed regulations would choke new innovations and freedom of expression? Discuss.

1.6 Revenge porn, sextortion, trolling and extreme hate speech: online media and internet censorship

There are now millions of amateurs who blog or tweet, share photos via Instagram or Snapchat or upload some of their most intimate details on Facebook or YouTube. Most of these individuals will be ignorant of the law in this area, such as defamation, mental abuse and harassment. Growing numbers of people are falling victim to organized gangs

---

57 For further discussion see: Mahoney, P. (1997), pp. 364–379.
58 For further discussion see: Council of Europe (2010) 'Blasphemy, insult and hatred: Finding answers in a democratic society', *Science and Technique of Democracy* 47. Brussels: Council of Europe Publication.

who lure them into sending sexually explicit images and then threaten to post the pictures online unless they get payment. There has also been a sharp rise in webcam blackmail, also known as sextortion. The National Crime Agency (NCA) recorded 1,250 cases reported to the police between 2015 and 2016, though stated that unreported cases are probably more than 700 (and rising) per year.

Iulian Enache, a 31-year-old from Romania, shared intimate photos belonging to 17-year-old Ronan Hughes from Northern Ireland, after the schoolboy failed to pay a ransom. The teenager killed himself hours afterwards. Enache subsequently received a four-year prison sentence in August 2017 from a Romanian court after Europol and the NCA together with the Police Service of Northern Ireland tracked him down. Enache had masked his identity by setting up a complicated network of proxy internet servers to cover his tracks.

Sextortion can be committed by individuals or international organized crime groups, all demanding ransoms. The NCA suggested that criminal groups operate in the Philippines, Ivory Coast and Morocco. The phenomenon has grown with the use of social media and can affect anyone, though the most targeted group is teenage and young men between 14 and 24. These rising figures mirror revenge pornography – and the NCA predicted a 51 per cent increase from 2017 to 2018.

In the absence of any privacy laws in the UK, there exists no restraint or protection for an individual other than resorting to court restraining orders against an internet service provider (ISP) or operators of a website – most of these being located in the United States or outside the European Union.

1.6.1 Which laws protect individuals against online abuse in the UK?

In February 2018 then Prime Minister Theresa May ordered a review of British laws governing online communications and abuse. Speaking in Manchester in celebration of 100 years of the British women's suffrage movement and the birthplace of Emmeline Pankhurst, the prime minister warned that 'intimidation and aggression' on social media was 'coarsening public debate', deterring people from participating in politics and threatening the UK's democracy.

Mrs May said that online abuse was disproportionately targeted at political candidates who were female, black, minority ethnic or LGBT, which was damaging equal representation in politics. She placed the task of addressing such abuse squarely at the door of firms like Facebook and Google and said that social media companies 'must now step up' to safeguard public life. She called for a Law Commission review of current legislation relating to offensive online communications, 'to ensure that the criminal law, which was drafted long before the creation of social media platforms, is appropriate to meet the challenges posed by this new technology'. The prime minister also referred to the need for a social media code of practice, setting out clearly the minimum standards expected of social media platforms.[59]

---

59 Source: 10 Downing Street Press Release, 6 February 2018, 'PM speech on public life to mark the centenary of women's suffrage'.

Let's have a look at the legislation which can presently be invoked in instances relating to online harassment and sexual and racial abuse, providing relevant measures to law enforcement agencies:

- Obscene Publications Act 1959 and 1965;
- Protection of Children Act 1978 (England and Wales);
- Civic Government (Scotland) Act 1982;
- Malicious Communications Act 1988;
- Protection from Harassment Act 1997;
- Sexual Offences Act 2003;
- Communications Act 2003 (sections 125–130[60]);
- Police and Justice Act 2006 (sections 35–40[61]);
- Criminal Justice and Immigration Act 2008 (section 63[62]);
- Coroner's and Justice Act 2009 (section 62;[63] section 69[64]);
- Sexual Offences (Scotland) Act 2009;
- Criminal Justice and Licensing (Scotland) Act 2010 (sections 40–44);
- Criminal Justice and Courts Act 2015 (section 33[65] – see below).

1.6.2 Revenge porn

Revenge porn or 'image-based sexual abuse' is the act of sharing sexually explicit images or videos of another person, online or offline, without their consent for the purpose of coercion or causing embarrassment and distress. About 54,000 revenge porn cases are reported to Facebook each month, with the company disabling 14,130 accounts as a result.

A typical case of revenge porn might involve an ex-partner uploading an intimate image of the victim (which she has previously sent him) to the internet or sending it to their friends and family on Facebook.

Julie Howard, 38, was found guilty of 'revenge pornography' at Worcester Magistrates' Court in January 2017 under s 33 of the Criminal Justice and Courts Act 2015. She was sentenced to a six-week suspended prison sentence. Howard had sold topless photos of her friend, Susanne Hinte, to *The Sun* for £750 because she was 'broke'. After Howard and Hinte had fallen out, Howard copied indecent photographs from Hinte's mobile phone via a cloud storage service. *The Sun* published the photographs on its website and in print on Sunday 3 April 2016.

Susanne Hinte had made the headlines in early 2016 when she tried to claim a £33m lottery prize with a ticket that she said had been damaged in the wash. Camelot had rejected her claim, but Hinte became a brief favourite with the tabloids, who gave her the nickname 'Lotto Gran'. Hinte died suddenly of a heart attack in August 2017, aged 49.

---

60 'Offences relating to networks and services'.
61 'Computer misuse' and 'indecent images of children'.
62 'Possession of extreme pornographic images'.
63 'Possession of prohibited images of children'.
64 'Indecent pseudo-photographs of children: marriage etc'.
65 'Disclosing private sexual photographs and films with intent to cause distress', 'revenge pornography' or 'revenge porn'.

Following her mother's death, Ms Hinte's daughter, Natasha Douglas, pursued a claim against the newspaper company, News Group Newspapers (NGN), for the misuse of private information. She also sued NGN for breach of confidence, copyright and data protection law, as well as for the distress the article caused to her mother and to her family at the time. NGN settled for a five-figure sum but did not admit liability. The settlement was read out in open court on 14 June 2018 – it was the first time a statement of this kind was read out in open court in a privacy case for a deceased person.[66]

American YouTube star Chrissy Chambers, 26, was not successful in pursuing criminal charges against her British ex-boyfriend for revenge porn (who cannot be named for legal reasons). Since the accused owned the copyright to the video clips, Ms Chambers was unable to force the free-to-watch pornographic site Redtube to remove them. The sexually explicit video clips had been copied and shared to dozens more sites.

She had to crowdfund her own civil action against the aggressor ($36,900 (£26,750)) and won her case in the London High Court in January 2018. The court heard that the perpetrator had filmed their sexual activity on 3 September 2009 at Ms Chambers' home in Atlanta, Georgia, and had subsequently uploaded six videos to the porn site between December 2009 and January 2012, after they had split up. He admitted the wrongdoing and agreed to pay a 'substantial' undisclosed sum as well as to cover Ms Chambers' legal costs.

Section 33 of the Criminal Justice and Courts Act 2015 created the new criminal offence of revenge pornography, making it a criminal offence to disclose private sexual photographs and films without the consent of an individual who appears in them and with the intent to cause that individual distress. Section 33 created the offence of disclosing private sexual photographs and films with intent to cause distress:

> (1) It is an offence for a person to disclose a private sexual photograph or film if the disclosure is made –
>
> (a) without the consent of an individual who appears in the photograph or film, and
> (b) with the intention of causing that individual distress.

Crucial to the offence are (a) the lack of consent of the individual appearing in the photograph or video; and (b) the intent to cause that individual distress. The offence carries a maximum two-year prison sentence. The offence applies both online and offline (including caching) and to images which are shared electronically or in a more traditional way, so it includes the uploading of images on the internet, sharing by text and email or showing someone a physical or electronic image.

Sexual material not only covers images that show the genitals but also anything that a reasonable person would consider to be sexual, so this could be a picture of someone who is engaged in sexual behaviour or posing in a sexually provocative way.[67]

For a successful prosecution under 'revenge porn' legislation there have to be two incidents. Prosecutors would then consider that a course of conduct has to include a

---

66 Source: 'The Sun pays damages over revenge porn images of lottery claimant', by Jenny Kleeman, *Guardian*, 14 June 2018; see also: 'The Sun pays over Worcester 'Lotto Gran' topless pics', *BBC News Online*, 14 June 2018.
67 Section 33(9) Criminal Justice and Courts Act 2015.

range of unwanted behaviours towards the complainant, and a communication sent via social media has to be one manifestation of this. Where an individual receives unwanted communications from another person via social media in addition to other unwanted behaviour, all the behaviour is then considered together ('in totality') by the prosecutor when determining whether or not a course of conduct was made out.[68]

Brown (2018)[69] argues that the law is not equipped to deal with the modern phenomenon of 'revenge porn'. He offers a remedy in Scots law which might assist a victim in pursuing a civil action because they are likely to suffer from severe emotional distress but, Brown argues, the problem is that these injuries are non-patrimonial, making it difficult to frame an action for damages. The author introduces the idea of *delict iniuria* which might offer appropriate remedy in instances of revenge porn. In Roman law, the *actio iniuriarum* was a delict which served to protect the non-patrimonial aspects of a person's existence – 'who a person is rather than what a person has'. As the propagation of sexually explicit images of an individual without their consent is clearly an affront to the esteem of that individual, Brown argues that instances of revenge porn ought to be considered actionable as *iniuria* in modern Scottish law.

1.6.3 Trolls and hate speech

What is 'trolling'? A 'troll' is a person who sows discord via the internet by starting arguments or upsetting people by posting inflammatory messages and hate speech. This is usually done under a false identity or pseudonym. Trolling has become an online phenomenon which sees users of social media, forums and microblogging sites post offensive or inflammatory comments where they can be seen publicly. The term can also be applied to those who post opinions and comments, which they may not actually believe, to online discussions in order to throw the debate into disarray. Trolls have become an increasing threat to a person's reputation and can destroy businesses.

In August 2013, internet troll Oliver Rawlings, 20, was made to apologize to academic classicist Professor Mary Beard, after sending hundreds of anonymous abusive messages to her. Nottingham University student Rawlings had used his Twitter account to call the Cambridge University professor a 'filthy old slut', making highly offensive sexual comments about her online. But Professor Beard retweeted the remarks to all her followers, saying she would not be 'terrorized' by online abuse. It was by this method that Rawlings was 'outed' and Professor Beard could therefore discover the troll's identity.[70]

The term 'troll' or 'trolling' has become a catch-all term for everything from minor disagreements through to annoying incivility through to criminal behaviour such as death threats. So, is trolling a criminal offence? Yes and no. It is a criminal offence under section 127 of the Communications Act 2003 if a profile is created under the name of the victim with fake information uploaded which, if believed, could damage their reputation and humiliate them. This piece of legislation creates an offence of 'sending', or 'causing to be sent, by means of a public electronic communications network, a message or other matter that is grossly offensive or of an indecent, obscene or menacing character'.

---

68 For further discussion see: Ledward, J. and Agate, J. (2017), pp. 40–42.
69 Brown, J. (2018) at pp. 396–410.
70 Source: 'Internet troll who abused Mary Beard apologises after threat to tell his mother', by Sam Marsden, *Daily Telegraph*, 29 July 2013.

Since the introduction of the offence, there have been a number of high-profile prosecutions of 'trolls'. Feminist Caroline Criado-Perez became the subject of numerous trolls after her successful campaign to feature Jane Austen on the new £10 note. The first conviction for trolling abusive, life-threatening and hate speech came in January 2014 when Isabella Sorley, 23, from Newcastle-upon-Tyne, and her co-defendant John Nimmo, 25, from South Shields, Tyne and Wear, received 12-week and 8-week prison sentences, respectively, at Westminster Magistrates' Court. Sorley's Twitter trolls included:

> Fuck off and die . . . you should have jumped in front of horses, go die; I will find you and you don't want to know what I will do when I do . . . kill yourself before I do; rape is the last of your worries. I've just got out of prison and would happily do more time to see you berried [*sic*]; seriously go kill yourself! I will get less time for that; rape?! I'd do a lot worse things than rape you.

Nimmo had used five different Twitter accounts, saying:

> Ya not that gd looking to rape u be fine; I will find you; come to geordieland [Newcastle] bitch; just think it could be somebody that knows you personally; the police will do nothing; rape her nice ass; could I help with that lol; the things I cud do to u; dumb blond bitch.

Sentencing judge Howard Riddle J had referred to the trolls as 'life threatening' and 'extreme' as they were read out in court.

In October 2014 Brenda Leyland was accused of 'trolling' the parents of Madeleine McCann, Kate and Gerry McCann, after she was identified by Sky News as being one of a number of people posting hate messages aimed at the couple online. Using the Twitter ID @sweepyface, Leyland had tweeted or retweeted 2,210 posts, of which 424 mentioned the McCanns between November 2013 and September 2014.

Sky News crime reporter Martin Brunt had tracked down the 63-year-old to her home in Burton Overy, Leicestershire, and confronted her about her online activities and exposed Mrs Leyland as one of the internet trolls responsible for the hate messages directed at the McCanns. On 4 October 2014, Brenda Leyland was found dead in her Marriott Hotel room in Enderby, Leicester. An inquest found subsequently that she had committed suicide.[71]

Communications which constitute 'credible threats' of violence to the person or damage to property are also regularly prosecuted under section 2A(3) of the Protection from Harassment Act 1997, often falling under the label of 'stalking'. Threats must 'specifically target an individual or individuals'. Section 7(3) of the 1997 'stalking' Act makes clear that a 'course of conduct' must involve conduct on at least two occasions.

Communications via social networking sites or mobile phones (i.e. text messages) that are considered grossly offensive, indecent or obscene are treated particularly seriously by the prosecution authorities and tend to attract a custodial sentence (under the public interest test). Credible threats to kill are prosecuted under section 16 Offences Against the Person Act 1861.

Furthermore, sections 32–35 of the Criminal Justice and Courts Act 2015 ('Offences involving intent to cause distress etc.') together with CPS social media guidelines provide

---

71 Source: 'Brenda Leyland inquest: McCann "Twitter troll" overdosed on helium after Sky News confrontation', by Yasmin Duffin, *Leicester Mercury*, 20 March 2015.

further criminal legislation for online abuse on social media platforms. The CPS prosecutors' guidelines provide the following charging standards:

> - *Category 1*: when online activity results in a credible threat to an individual;
> - *Category 2*: when someone is specifically targeted for harassment, stalking, revenge porn or coercive behaviour to former partners or family members;
> - *Category 3*: cases resulting in breaches of a court order.

Context and circumstances are highly relevant in these cases, though the accused may always raise an Article 10(1) ECHR defence, relying on the precedent set in *Handyside v UK* (1976),[72] where the court held that 'freedom of expression' also included the right to 'offend, shock or disturb'.

So, what are leading internet companies doing about trolls? Both Facebook and Twitter have rules on what can and cannot be posted on their sites, and the social media giants will now take down postings and videos that violate them. Clearly internet users are bound by existing criminal legislation against inciting hatred on the basis of race, religion, transgender or sexual orientation or disability. But the lack of a coherent, standalone legislation addressing online hate crime inevitably makes the process of investigating which legislation exactly has been breached harder for the authorities to pursue and prosecute. A prosecution can be avoided if the communication 'was not intended for a wide audience, nor was the obvious consequence of sending the communication' or did not go beyond 'what could conceivably be tolerable or acceptable in an open and diverse society which upholds and respects freedom of expression'.

Hate speech and trolling via social media have increased enormously embracing nationality, race or religion – aimed to shock, offend or disturb, often hiding behind 'freedom of expression'. The UN International Covenant on Civil and Political Rights (ICCPR)[73] not only permits signatory states to prohibit hate speech but actually requires them to do so. Article 2(1) ICCPR reads:

> Each State Party to the present Covenant undertakes to respect and to ensure to all individuals within its territory and subject to its jurisdiction the rights recognized in the present Covenant, without distinction of any kind, such as race, colour, sex, language, religion, political or other opinion, national or social origin, property, birth or other status.

In addition, one particular form of hate speech – incitement to genocide – is one of only a few types of acts recognized as a crime under international law, akin to war crimes and crimes against humanity. Article 20(2) ICCPR reads:

> Any advocacy of national, racial or religious hatred that constitutes incitement to discrimination, hostility or violence shall be prohibited by law.

---

72 1 EHRR 737 (ECtHR). A prosecution was brought against the publisher based on the Obscene Publications Act 1959.

73 Adopted and opened for signature, ratification and accession by General Assembly resolution 2200A (XXI) of 16 December 1966, entry into force 23 March 1976, in accordance with Article 49.

1.6.4 Possession of extreme pornography on the internet

Section 63 Criminal Justice and Immigration Act 2008 ('Possession of extreme porno-graphic images') makes it an offence to *possess* a limited range of extreme pornographic material on the internet[74] – that is mere *possession* rather than publication.

Section 63(10) of the 2008 Act defines such acts as 'life-threatening acts' or those which would cause serious injury, such as depictions of necrophilia and bestiality. Section 63(6) defines an 'extreme' image as one which is grossly offensive, disgusting or otherwise of an obscene character and portrays the activity in an *explicit and realistic way*.

What then are the practicalities of prosecuting a section 63 offence? Since the legis-lation is not articulated clearly and convincingly and contains elements of the Obscene Publications Act 1959, the prosecution needs to evidence a clear link between *possession* and *harm*. For possession of an 'extreme pornographic' image to be proved, it is necessary to establish some knowledge of its existence, also evidenced in common law (see: *Atkins v DPP; Goodland v DPP* (2000)[75] – see below).

The image then has to be both pornographic and constitute an *extreme* image.[76] An extreme act is one which threatens a person's life; which results or is likely to result in serious injury to a person's anus, breasts or genitals; which involves sexual interference with a human corpse or which involves a person performing intercourse or oral sex with an animal. But 'life-threatening' is not defined in the 2008 Act.[77]

'Serious injury' is also not defined in the Act, and this will be a question of fact for the magistrates or jury. The intention is that 'serious injury' should be given its ordinary Eng-lish meaning. The reference to 'serious injury' was not intended to expressly link into the case law with respect to 'grievous bodily harm' under sections 18 and 20 of the Offences Against the Person Act 1861, which has been interpreted as being capable of including psychological harm.

Taking an example which was raised during parliamentary debates on the Criminal Justice and Immigration Bill, the anal sex scene in *Last Tango in Paris*, even if it were to be considered pornographic and of an obscene nature, would not be caught by the offence, because it is not explicit and does not portray an act resulting or likely to result in serious injury to a person's anus.

The complex legislation involving 'possession' and 'making' of extreme pornogra-phy and/or indecent images (of children) was put to the test in the conjoined cases of *Atkins* and *Goodland*.[78] The CA held that indecent images stored without the defendant's, Dr Antony Rowan Atkins', knowledge by browser software in a hidden cache, of which he was also unaware, did *not* amount to knowledge of possession. The situation was akin to a person having a holdall in which, unknown to him, was a gun. Knowledge of the bag was enough, but ignorance of the bag itself made it no crime. Though both cases concerned internet child pornography prosecutions (pseudo photographs of child images), the rul-ing can be applied to the section 63 offence of the 2008 Act. Atkins was convicted at the

---

74 Section 71 of the Act amends the Obscene Publications Act 1959 by increasing the maximum penalty for offences under that Act from three years' imprisonment to five years' imprisonment.
75 [2000] 2 Cr App R 248.
76 Section 63(2) Criminal Justice and Immigration Act 2008.
77 Section 63(3).
78 *Atkins v DPP; Goodlands v DPP* [2000] 2 Cr App R 248 (CA).

Bristol Magistrates' Court on 27 May 1999 of ten offences of having in his possession indecent photographs of children contrary to section 160(1) CJA 1988.

Dr Atkins had held a lectureship in the Department of English at Bristol University since October 1997. He had available to him there both a Viglen computer set up in his office and also a departmental computer mostly used by others in the department's main office. On 16 October 1997, another member of the department logged into the departmental computer and was immediately concerned by the menu of internet addresses recently called up. The IT department checked the computer's cache files and found there pictures of naked young girls in crude postures with the PC's history pointing to Dr Atkins. Similar pictures were found in the Viglen cache. The court found that Dr Atkins had deliberately chosen to store the material on the hard drives of the computers, which amounted to 'possession'.

Dr Atkins raised the defence under section 160(2) CJA 1988, namely that he had a legitimate reason for having the photographs in his possession, for the purpose of 'legitimate academic research'. Dr Atkins appealed against his conviction on the ten possession counts; the prosecutor appealed against Dr Atkins' acquittal on 21 of the 'making' counts.

In addressing the issue of 'making' contrary to section 1(1)(a) of the Protection of Children Act 1978, Simon Brown LJ found that Dr Atkins had made a directory (named 'J') for the specific purpose of storing the material, thereby agreeing with the prosecution that this would 'call for a conviction'. For possession of an indecent image (of a child) to be proved, it is necessary to establish some knowledge of its existence.

It was by sheer coincidence that both cases of *Atkins* and *Goodland* appeared before the Bristol District Judge. Mr Peter John Goodland was also convicted at Bristol Magistrates' Court (on 21 April 1999) on one count of having in his possession an indecent pseudo-photograph of a ten-year-old girl. The cross-appeal by the Director of Public Prosecutions was allowed, and Mr Goodland was duly convicted. Since the 'sellotaped' copied images of the little girl were so 'pitifully crude' – according to Blofeld J's summing-up in the Court of Appeal – Mr Goodland was sentenced to a two-year conditional discharge with an order to pay £50 costs. He was, however, placed on the Sex Offenders Register (Sex Offenders Act 1997) for a period of five years.

What about deleting the images on one's computer? Case law suggests that deleting images held on a computer is sufficient to get rid of them (i.e. this would get rid of the 'possession' element of the offence). An exception would be where a person is shown to have intended to remain in control of an image even though he has deleted it – that will entail him having the capacity (through skill or software) to retrieve the image.

Foster argues the section 63 offence of the Criminal Justice and Immigration Act 2008 ('possession of extreme pornographic images') may well conflict with Article 10(1) ECHR and also intrudes into an (adult) individuals' private life under Article 8(1).[79] He claims that section 63 fails both in regulating truly harmful images that glorify sexual violence and in imposing necessary and proportionate restrictions on free speech and the right to access those images in private.[80]

---

79 Foster, S. (2010), pp. 21–27.
80 For further discussion see: Akdeniz, Y. (2008).

1.7 Global internet censorship and governance

Can cyberspace be regulated and governed? Should we leave it to the internet companies and social media magnates to control their own violence and hate speech online? We know that there are no physical or legal barriers concerning the World Wide Web to prevent access of information from geographically remote places. We also know that in many cases we do not know the physical location of either an ISP or the server or indeed the author of a defamatory or hate message on Twitter or any other social media site.

What should be done with gangs who post 'drill' music videos on YouTube – a dark form of urban dance music featuring violent lyrics, open references to drug dealing, misogynistic content and extreme violence? Metropolitan Police Commissioner Cressida Dick has blamed some YouTube videos for fuelling a surge in murders and violent crime in London – and has singled out drill music. Following recent convictions, she asked YouTube to delete content which glamorizes violence. YouTube responded by a statement that it takes down between 50 and 60 music videos annually because they were deemed to incite violence.

In June 2018 five gang members who made drill music videos, glorifying violence, were sentenced at Kingston Crown Court after being caught with machetes and baseball bats. They were members of the Ladbroke Grove gang, '1011', arch-rivals of the '12 Worlds' gang from Shepherds Bush. Micah Bedeau, 19; Yonas Girma, 21; Isaac Marshall, 18; Jordan Bedeau, 17; and Rhys Herbert, 17, were convicted for conspiracy to commit violent disorder in Notting Hill. The court heard that the attack was in retaliation to the drill video on YouTube posted by '12 Worlds' of the grandmother of the Bedeau brothers being harassed. The jury was shown the drill music videos made by the gang members and were told that these had been watched more than 15 million times online and that they had earned thousands of pounds from music streaming sites. Police also applied to Judge Recorder Ann Mulligan for a court order to stop the group making drill music.

YouTube (owned by Alphabet Inc.'s Google) states on its 'privacy' settings that it does not permit terrorist organizations to use its service for any purpose, including recruitment. YouTube also strictly prohibits content related to terrorism, such as content that promotes terrorist acts, incites violence or celebrates terrorist attacks. YouTube is a popular media site for firearms enthusiasts. The service introduced tighter restrictions on videos involving weapons in March 2018. It also regularly bans videos that promote or link to websites selling firearms and accessories, including bump stocks, which allow a semi-automatic rifle to fire faster. Additionally, YouTube said it will prohibit videos with instructions on how to assemble firearms.

Twitter has similar policies against hate speech, pornographic videos, extreme violence, terrorism and guns.

In the Virginia news crew shooting incident in August 2015, Twitter took down the gunman's account within ten minutes of its being posted. The trouble with most PC or tablet settings is that imbedded video footage plays automatically as soon as people access a news site. The gruesome footage in the Virginia item was that gunman Vester Flanagan (alias 'Bryce Williams') had filmed his shooting of WDBJ reporter Alison Parker and cameraman Adam Ward at close range and had uploaded the video footage on his own Facebook page. All videos about the shooting were removed by YouTube (Google) and Facebook.

There is as yet no universally agreed-upon definition of internet governance, especially in areas such as intellectual property, privacy, law enforcement, internet free speech and cybersecurity.

1.7.1 Who governs the internet?

The short answer is that the internet is basically not governed. The United States has undeniably regulated the World Wide Web since its inception in 1991.[81] The not-for-profit public benefit corporation ICANN (Internet Corporation for Assigned Names and Numbers), headquartered in Los Angeles, and IANA (Internet Assigned Numbers Authority) allocate and supervise domain names and run a joint internet stewardship. ICANN/IANA internet policy decisions intersect with national laws, particularly in areas such as intellectual property, privacy, law enforcement and cybersecurity.

This means that policing any international legislation across cyber borders is very difficult to impossible and has to be left to individual states. Some governments – such as the United Kingdom, Germany and France – have advocated increased intergovernmental influence over the way the internet is governed. Most protective schemes and attempts to restrict the flow of information on the internet, based on geographical locations, have proved futile so far, though there have been some attempts made.

The French courts ruled in 2014, for instance, that Yahoo! Inc. must block French users from its sites auctioning Nazi artefacts. Yahoo! argued that it could not possibly limit access to certain geographical regions; alternatively, it could comply with French legislation and block everyone from bidding for the artefacts.

Russia has engaged in selective internet filtration for at least a decade. The Kremlin enforces various censorship laws via the Russian Federal Service for Supervision in the Sphere of Telecom, Information Technologies and Mass Communications (Roskomnadzor), sending frequent 'cease and desist' letters to Google, Twitter and Facebook, warning them against violating Russian internet laws. Roskomnadzor has kept a centralized blacklist (known as the 'single register') of individual URLs, domain names and IP addresses. But the single register also blocks materials advocating drug abuse and production, child pornography and suicide methods. There are also laws prohibiting 'abuse of mass media freedom', and websites criticizing the Kremlin or President Putin are frequently shut down by state prosecutors.

The Indian Government practises selective internet censorship, for example, by periodically blocking internet pornography sites such as www.indianpornvideos.com and www.pornhub.com.[82]

Facebook has been blocked in China since 2009, following a series of riots in the western capital of Xinjiang province, Urumqi. Facebook and other Western social networks are perceived as a threat that could undermine Communist Party rule in China. In 2018 Facebook planned to launch a $30m subsidiary called Facebook Technology (*Hangzhou*)

---

81 On 6 August 1991, the World Wide Web became publicly available. Its creator, Tim Berners-Lee, posted a short summary of the project on the alt.hypertext newsgroup and gave birth to a new technology which would fundamentally change the world.

82 See: The Order Notice by the Government of India Ministry of Communication and IT of 31.6.2015. No 813–7/25/2011 – DS (Vol-V).

and run a startup incubator that would have made small investments and given advice to local businesses, but it was immediately blocked and never really got off the ground.[83]

However, Germany relaxed its legislation on Nazi symbols in August 2018. In games like the Wolfenstein series, German editions would until then have to change Hitler's name, remove his moustache, and replace swastikas with another shape. These can now appear in video games in Germany, ending a long-running and frequently ridiculed censorship. The ban on extremist symbols is still in place, but rating body USK (Unterhaltungssoftware Selbstkontrolle) – Germany's Entertainment Software Self-Regulator – now applies its rules to video games in the same way they are used for films on a case-by-case basis. A game can now get past the rating procedure if an artistic or dramatic use is justified.[84]

See
Chapters 8.6
and 8.8

1.7.2 EU net neutrality law: the digital single market and the open internet

Contrary to Golden-Shield-type government initiatives in China or India, the European Parliament and the Council introduced groundbreaking legislation on 25 November 2015 with Regulation (EU) 2015/2120.[85] The regulation on net neutrality (or 'open internet') provided for the digital single market within the EU and came into force on 30 April 2016.

This means that every European now has access to the open internet and all content across Member States. Under the Regulation, blocking, throttling and discrimination of internet traffic by internet service providers (ISPs) is not allowed in the EU, save for three exhaustive exceptions:

1   compliance with legal obligations;
2   integrity of the network;
3   congestion management in exceptional and temporary situations, and users are free to use their favourite apps and services.

Now all EU internet traffic has to be treated equally. This means, for example, that there can be no prioritization of traffic in the internet access service. Common rules and 'equal internet treatment' mean that internet access providers cannot pick winners or losers on the internet or decide which content and services are available.

This regulation is seen as a major and rather progressive achievement for the 'Digital Single Market'. Regulation 2015/2120 created the individual and enforceable right for end users with the EU Member States to access and distribute internet content and services of their choice. Net neutrality, then, means in practice that all filters that prevent people from viewing, for example, online pornography can be removed. EU net neutrality rules allow *reasonable* traffic management and, with the necessary safeguards, 'specialised

---

83 Source: 'Facebook plans innovation hub in China despite tightening censorship', by Cate Cadell, *Reuters*, 24 July 2018.

84 Unterhaltungssoftware Selbstkontrolle (USK) at: www.usk.de/.

85 Regulation (EU) 2015/2120 of the European Parliament and of the Council of 25 November 2015, laying down measures concerning open internet access and amending Directive 2002/22/EC on universal service and users' rights relating to electronic communications networks and services and Regulation (EU) No 531/2012 on roaming on public mobile communications networks within the Union (EU Regulation on net neutrality).

services'; those are services which assure a specific quality level, required for instance for connected cars or certain 5G applications.

The UK had already introduced adult content filters in July 2013, championed by the then Conservative Prime Minister David Cameron. This meant that internet users were required to 'opt in' in order to view pornographic material or content showing gratuitous violence; otherwise such sites were automatically blocked. This type of net neutrality has now been rolled out across all EU Member States whereby internet traffic is treated equally.

EU Net Neutrality

- no discriminatory blocking and throttling (e.g. of Skype by telecom companies);
- EU Regulation 2015/2120 on net neutrality sets out clear rules for internet traffic management which must be non-discriminatory, proportionate and transparent;
- all internet traffic has to be treated equally in all EU Member States.

1.7.3 Regulating hate crime on social media in the EU

On 25 May 2017 the European Commission adopted a proposal amending the Audiovisual Media Services Directive (AMSD) and aligning it with the Council Framework Decision 2008/913 on racism and xenophobia. This brings the Europe-wide framework into line with German legislation to fine social media platforms up to €50m if they fail to remove hate speech postings immediately. The Commission also proposes a 'Good Samaritan' rule, which means that social media organizations that actively track and shut down hate speech will have a defence. This represents the start of an EU-wide regulation of social media with a code of conduct regarding hate speech. Such a code includes blocking of videos which promote terrorism or incite hatred, the main targets being Facebook, YouTube and Twitter. Bryden and Salter suggest that this marked a major shift with primary responsibility on content providers to actively take steps to remove hate speech and support for terrorism.[86]

1.8 Protecting journalistic rights and sources

Daphne Caruana Galizia, a prominent investigative journalist and blogger, was assassinated on 16 October 2017 near her house in Bidnija, Malta, in a targeted car bomb attack. Galizia spent much of her work in recent years exposing government corruption and having reported extensively on the Panama Papers, which exposed the offshore activities of powerful officials and companies around the world. Her blog, 'Running Commentary',[87] which included investigative reports on Maltese politicians, was one of the most widely read websites in Malta and abroad At the time of her killing, Galizia was fighting 47

---

86 Bryden, C. and Salter, M. (2017) at p. 11.
87 See: https://daphnecaruanagalizia.com.

civil and criminal defamation lawsuits from an array of business people and politicians, brought by multiple law firms. In the months before her death, the anti-corruption journalist received letters from the law firm Mishcon de Reya, which had been hired to defend the reputation of a client doing business in Malta. The killing has triggered a debate at English PEN, whose mission it is to defend writers and freedom of speech. The British law firm Mishcon was representing the 'golden passport' agency Henley & Partners, a 'global leader in residence and citizenship planning'.[88]

Increasingly some of the top media law firms have gained a reputation for muscling in on journalists and silencing critics and pressure groups with the threat of ruinous court action; this is known in the business as SLAPP, which stands for 'Strategic Lawsuit Against Public Participation', a term for often baseless claims which aim to silence free speech and debate about issues of public interest by forcing critics to spend money defending themselves or revealing their sources.

MEP David Casa wrote to the Vice President of the European Commission, Frans Timmermans, in April 2018 urging the Commission to pass anti-SLAPP legislation. In his letter he noted that several Maltese journalists had been victims of SLAPP procedures by entities such as leading London law firms the Pilatus Bank and similar institutions in foreign jurisdictions, such as the United States. In his letter, Mr Casa said that such practices are abusive, pose a threat to media freedom and have no place in the European Union.[89]

Protection of journalistic sources is one of the basic conditions for press freedom, as is reflected in the laws and the professional codes of conduct in a number of contracting states to the European Convention on Human Rights (ECHR) and is affirmed in several international instruments on journalistic freedoms. For example the comprehensive groundbreaking resolution regarding the safety of journalists by the UN Human Rights Council adopted on 29 September 2016, or the Resolution on Journalistic Freedoms and Human Rights,[90] and the Council of Europe Conference of Ministers Responsible for Media and Information Society in Belgrade in 2013,[91] regarding 'Freedom of Expression and Democracy in the Digital Age – Opportunities, Rights, Responsibilities', and again at the Council of Europe European Ministerial Conferences on Mass Media Policy on 'Media and Internet Directorate General of Human Rights and Rule of Law' in Strasbourg 2016[92] and Resolution on the Confidentiality of Journalists' Sources by the European Parliament, 1994[93].

Without such international protection for journalists, sources may be deterred from assisting the media in informing the public on matters of public interest. As a result the vital public watchdog role of the media may be undermined and the ability of the press

---

88 Henley and Partners at www.henleyglobal.com.
89 Source: Letter from David Casa MEP to Frans Timmermans, Vice President of the European Commission, Brussels, Belgium, 10 April 2018.
90 Human Rights Council Resolution (A/HRC/RES/33/2) on the Safety of Journalists.
91 Council of Europe (2013) Conference of Ministers Responsible for Media and Information Society on 'Freedom of Expression and Democracy in the Digital Age – Opportunities, Rights, Responsibilities', Belgrade, 7–8 November 2013.
92 Council of Europe (2016) European Ministerial Conferences on Mass Media Policy and Council of Europe Conferences of Ministers Responsible for Media and New Communication Services, 'Media and Internet Directorate General of Human Rights and Rule of Law', Strasbourg 2016: https://rm.coe.int/16806461fb.
93 Resolution on the Confidentiality of Journalists' Sources by the European Parliament, 18 January 1994, Official Journal of the European Communities No. C 44/34.

to provide accurate and reliable information may be adversely affected. Having regard to the importance of the protection of journalistic sources for press freedom in a democratic society and the potentially chilling effect a court order of source disclosure has on the exercise of that freedom, the courts have held that such a measure cannot be compatible with Article 10 ECHR unless it is justified by an overriding requirement in the public interest. This was held by the Strasbourg Human Rights Court in the case of *Goodwin v UK* (1996)[94] (see below).

However, alongside these international instruments and ethical considerations, British counter-terrorism legislation now places legal obligations on journalists and the media to disclose certain information to the police and the courts as soon as 'reasonably practicable'. There have been a number of events where a journalist has been ordered by a court to reveal his sources of information.[95] There then exists the potential for conflict between a judicial order either prohibiting the publication of details relating to a matter before the courts in the form of super injunctions or a journalist having to disclose his vital source of information in the absence of any privacy law protection in the UK (confirmed in *Kaye v Robertson* (1991)[96] and *Wainwright v The Home Office* (2003)[97]).

Reporters need to be aware that their broadcasts or online publications need to be aware of ethical issues when reporting from war zones because matters reported will involve loss of life, human suffering or distress.[98] Each media organization will have its own policy on this matter. In the UK such regulation is mostly covered by the Ofcom Broadcasting Code.

See
Chapter 8.4

Section 10 of the Contempt of Court Act 1981 deals with the protection of journalistic sources. Section 10 provides:

> No court may require a person to disclose, nor is a person guilty of contempt of court for refusing to disclose the source of information contained in the publication for which he is responsible, unless it be established to the satisfaction of the court that disclosure is necessary in the interests of justice or national security or for the prevention of disorder or crime.

See
Chapter 5.3

This was put to the test in the *William Goodwin* case.

❖ **KEY CASE** ***Goodwin (William) v United Kingdom* (1996) 22 EHRR 123 (ECtHR).**

Precedent

❖ No journalist should have to disclose his sources of information unless disclosure is necessary in the interests of justice (s 10 Contempt of Court Act 1981 – CCA).

❖ Section 10 CCA is not an absolute mandate to the judiciary to order

94 *Goodwin (William) v United Kingdom* (1996) 22 EHRR 123 (ECtHR).
95 For further discussion see: Geddis, A. (2010).
96 [1991] FSR 62.
97 [2003] UKHL 53 (HL).
98 For further discussion see: Allan, S. and Zelizer, B. (eds) (2004) *Reporting War: Journalism in Wartime.*

journalists to disclose their sources purely on a complaint by an aggrieved private party.

❖ Courts should balance the journalist's confidentiality of his sources with the interests and administration of justice whether disclosure of the source is 'necessary'.

❖ Limitations on the confidentiality of journalistic sources call for careful scrutiny by the courts.

Facts

William Goodwin joined *The Engineer* magazine as a trainee journalist on 3 August 1989. The magazine was published by Morgan-Grampian Ltd. On 2 November 1989 Mr Goodwin was telephoned by a bona fide source, giving him information about 'Tetra Ltd' and that the company was in financial difficulties: Tetra was trying to obtain a £5m loan as a result of an expected loss of £2.1m for 1989 on a turnover of £20.3m. Mr Goodwin had received no payment, and it was the strict understanding that his source was to remain confidential. Intending to write an article, Mr Goodwin telephoned Tetra to check the facts and seek its comments on the information (7 November). The same day, Tetra applied for an *ex parte* interim injunction to restrain the publishers of *The Engineer* from publishing any information derived from the corporate plan which had come into the possession of Mr Goodwin. Mr Justice Hoffmann granted the injunction (Chancery Div of the High Court). Tetra's reasons were, if the company's financial plan was to be made public, it could result in a complete loss of confidence in the company on the part of its actual and potential creditors, its customers and in particular its suppliers, with a risk of loss of orders and of a refusal to supply the company with goods and services. This would inevitably lead to problems with Tetra's refinancing negotiations. If the company went into liquidation, there would be approximately 400 redundancies.

Between 14 and 22 November 1989, Hoffmann J ordered the publishers (and therein Mr Goodman) to disclose all the journalist's notes and to identify his source on the grounds that it was necessary 'in the interests of justice' under section 10 of the Contempt of Court Act 1981 (CCA). Tetra could then bring proceedings against the source to recover the documents and to obtain an injunction preventing further publication. Following Mr Goodman's appeal, the CA rejected his appeal on 12 December 1989. The CA referred to the balancing exercise it had to undertake regarding the interests of justice test: on the one hand maintaining the confidentiality of journalistic sources (the reason why section 10 CCA was enacted), and on the other whereby disclosure was necessary in the general interests of the administration of justice (i.e. if information disclosed about a public company where shareholders were unjustifiably being kept in ignorance of information vital to their making a sensible decision on whether or not to sell their shares). The CA held that publication of the article on Tetra would amount to an unjustified intrusion into the company's privacy and that the balance would be in favour of disclosure of the journalist's sources. The House of Lords upheld the CA's decision on 4 April 1990. A *Norwich Pharmacal* order[99] was applied for, seizing all information and therein the source from Mr Goodwin's property. Mr Goodwin had been served with contempt of court proceedings for disobeying the court orders to disclose his source (an offence punishable by an unlimited fine or up to two years' imprisonment under s 14 CCA). Following the HL's dismissal of his appeal, Mr Goodwin was fined £5,000 for contempt of court at the High Court on 10 April 1990. He applied to the Strasbourg Human Rights Court (ECtHR) arguing that the *Norwich Pharmacal* disclosure order requiring him to reveal the identity of a source violated his right to freedom of expression under Article 10 ECHR.[100]

Decision (ECtHR)

The court opined that Mr Goodwin's Article 10 right had been breached by the UK (courts). Furthermore, that the disclosure order (*Norwich Pharmacal*) was an interference with prescribed law and that the section 10 Contempt of Court Act 1984 (CCA) had failed to satisfy the interests-of-justice exception to the protection of journalistic sources.[101]

Analysis

The *Goodwin* case is fundamentally important to the issue of disclosure of journalistic sources. The Strasbourg Human Rights Court ruling criticized the UK Contempt of Court Act 1984 (CCA) in that Parliament had not sufficiently and precisely worded section 10: the legislator had not foreseen the circumstances in which such a disclosure order could be made against journalists in order to protect a private company. Therefore, the foreseeability requirement which flows from the expression prescribed by law had failed. Regarding the balancing exercise in relation to 'the interests of justice', introduced by Lord Bridge in the HL in this case, had amounted to 'subjective judicial assessment' of factors based on retrospective evidence presented by the party seeking to discover the identity of the source (Tetra). The ECtHR opined that the journalist Mr Goodwin could not possibly have known whether Tetra's 'livelihood' was at stake at the time his source had provided the information; he certainly believed that the information about the company's demise was in the public interest and therefore publishable in the magazine. The ECtHR commented that s 10 CCA was not an absolute mandate for the judiciary to order journalists to disclose their sources purely on a complaint of an aggrieved private party. The court noted, however, that there is a general public interest in the free flow of information to journalists; both sources and journalists must recognize that a journalist's express promise of confidentiality or his implicit undertaking of non-attributability may have to yield to a greater public interest and the administration of justice if ordered by a court.

---

99 *Norwich Pharmacal Co v Customs and Excise Commissioners* [1974] AC 133.
100 Application no. 17488/90.
101 See: Opinion of 7 September 1993, Commission Report of 1 March 1994 (art. 31), violation of Article 10 by 11 votes to 6 (re: *Goodwin v UK*).

As a matter of general principle, the 'necessity' for any restriction on freedom of expression must be convincingly established (see: *Sunday Times v UK (no. 2)* (1991).[102] The ECtHR stated that national authorities (including the courts) must assess whether there is a 'pressing social need' for applying any derogation under national law (here s 10 CCA and applying Art 10(2) ECHR). In making their assessment, the courts then enjoy a certain margin of appreciation. In the present context, the national margin of appreciation is circumscribed by the interest of democratic society in ensuring and maintaining a free press and the confidentiality of journalistic sources. Courts should decide whether the restriction is proportionate to the legitimate aim pursued. Limitations on the confidentiality of journalistic sources call for the most careful scrutiny by the courts.

1.8.1 The *David Miranda* case: freedom of journalistic expression

Linked to *The Guardian's* investigation and revelations concerning whistle-blower Edward Snowden, David Miranda, a Brazilian citizen and spouse of former *Guardian* journalist Glenn Greenwald, had been part of a professional operation involving the leaking of classified information from the US National Security Agency (NSA) in 2013. Edward Snowden, a former contractor at the NSA, had leaked details of extensive internet and phone surveillance by American intelligence services by downloading some 1.5 million NSA security files which he had then handed over to journalists Glenn Greenwald and Laura Poitras in a Hong Kong hotel.

To assist Greenwald's journalistic activities, Miranda had travelled from Rio to Berlin, while carrying related encrypted material, to collect computer drives containing further material. The UK Security Service asked the police to stop Miranda at Heathrow Airport when he was transferring flights on 18 August 2013. Miranda was subsequently detained for nine hours at Heathrow – permitted under anti-terrorism legislation.[103] Miranda challenged the legality of his detention.

The High Court ruled Mr Miranda's detention was lawful, saying it was a 'proportionate measure in the circumstances'. Lord Justice Laws, sitting with Mr Justice Ouseley and Mr Justice Openshaw, ruled there was 'compelling evidence' that stopping David Miranda was 'imperative in the interests of national security' and that the Schedule 7 stop was a 'proportionate measure'.[104] Furthermore, Schedule 7 of the Terrorism Act 2000 was not overbroad or arbitrary and was prescribed by law, in compliance with Article 10 ECHR (applying *Beghal v DPP* (2013)[105]).

In his ruling, Lord Justice Laws said: 'The claimant was not a journalist; the stolen GCHQ intelligence material he was carrying was not "journalistic material", or if it was,

---

102 *Sunday Times v United Kingdom (No. 2)* (13166/87) (1991) [1991] ECHR 26 pp. 28–29, para. 50.
103 Specifically, para. 2(1) of Schedule 7 of the Terrorism Act 2000 ('Port and Border Control') deals with stop and search.
104 *R (on the application of Miranda [David]) v Secretary of State for the Home Department* [2014] EWHC 255 (Admin) at paras 46, 65, 71 (Laws LJ).
105 [2013] EWHC 2573 (Admin).

only in the weakest sense'. The court held that journalists have a professional responsibility to take care, so far as they are able, to see that the public interest, including state security and the lives of other people, is not endangered by what they publish. However, that was not an adequate safeguard for lives and security.[106] Miranda appealed.

The Court of Appeal ruling in the David Miranda[107] case came on 19 January 2016, hailed as a (partial) victory for Miranda because the CA noted that Schedule 7 of the Terrorism Act 2000 did not include sufficient protection for journalists carrying sensitive information. However, the CA ruled that Miranda's detention at Heathrow under Schedule 7 had been lawful.[108]

Lord Dyson in his leading judgment held that the publication of material did amount to an act of terrorism if the material endangered life and the person publishing the material intended it to have that effect, provided that it was designed to influence the government or an international governmental organization or to intimidate the public or a section of the public, and it was for the purpose of advancing inter alia a political or ideological cause.[109]

Most importantly, however, was the judicial interpretation of interference with the appellant's Article 10 rights where a journalist is required to reveal his sources. There was no reason in principle for drawing a distinction between disclosure of journalistic material simpliciter and disclosure of journalistic material which might identify a confidential source (applying Sanoma Uitgevers BV v Netherlands (2011)[110]).

The CA criticized Laws LJ who had relied on the ruling in Beghal (2013), a case which predominantly concerned Article 8 ECHR rather than Article 10 concerning freedom of journalistic expression. Lord Dyson said that the constraints on the exercise of the Schedule 7 stop power identified by Laws LJ in the High Court did not afford effective protection of journalists' Article 10 rights. If journalists and their sources could have no expectation of confidentiality, they might decide against providing information on sensitive matters of public interest. For this reason, the Schedule 7 stop power was incompatible with Article 10 of the Convention in relation to journalistic material in that it was not subject to adequate safeguards against its arbitrary exercise. The natural and obvious safeguard would be prior, or immediate post factum, judicial or other independent and impartial oversight.[111]

The CA held that the stop power under the counter-terrorism legislation of 2000, if used in respect of journalistic information or material, was incompatible with Article 10 ECHR because it was not 'prescribed by law' as required by Article 10(2) ECHR – that is, the power was not subject to sufficient legal safeguards to avoid the risk that it would be exercised arbitrarily. The court therefore granted a certificate of incompatibility, and it would be a matter for Parliament to decide how to provide such a safeguard.[112]

---

106 Miranda [2014] EWHC 255 at para. 73.
107 R (on the application of Miranda [David]) v (1) Secretary of State for the Home Department (2) Commissioner of Police of the Metropolis [2016] EWCA Civ 6 (CA Civ Div).
108 Ibid. at paras 25–31 (Lord Dyson).
109 Ibid. at paras 38 to 56.
110 (Application No 38224/03) [2011] E.M.L.R. 4 (ECtHR).
111 Miranda [2016] EWCA Civ 6 at paras 98–119 (Lord Dyson).
112 Ibid. at paras 94 to 117.

From December 2013 onwards the *Guardian* and Germany's political magazine, *Der Spiegel*, began to report on the leaked material how America's top secret National Security Agency was hacking into and infiltrating national government computer systems around the world and breaking into the toughest data targets. Snowden had revealed how the Tailored Access Operations (TAO) were stealing data and inserting invisible 'back door' spying devices into national computer systems. Edward Snowden was subsequently granted asylum in Russia where he still resides.

1.8.2 Fake news: true or false?

How did the term 'fake news' evolve – and what's next in the world of disinformation? One definition is the deliberate making up of news stories to fool or entertain.

When Donald Trump beat Hillary Clinton in November 2016 to become the 45th US president, 'fake news' became his buzzword. In record time, the phrase morphed from a description of a social media phenomenon into a journalistic cliché and an angry political slur.

Of course, fake news has always been around, as Mark Twain (or Jonathan Swift or possibly Winston Churchill) allegedly said, 'a lie gets half the way round the world before the truth gets its shoes on'. And even that quote is disputed and might be fake news.

With the arrival of social media and the majority of citizens now obtaining their news from Facebook as opposed to bona fide news sources, such as the BBC or Reuters, this has meant real and fictional stories are now presented in such a similar way that it can sometimes be difficult to tell the two apart.

During the Trump election campaign in 2016, BuzzFeed News identified more than a hundred pro-Trump websites being run from a single town in the former Yugoslav Republic of Macedonia. BuzzFeed's Craig Silverman, who heads a team looking into the effects of fake news, explains just how easily fake news can end up being reported as true by the mainstream media:

> A fake news website might publish a hoax, then because it's getting social attention another site might pick it up, write that story as though it's true and may not link back to the original fake news website. From there it's a chain reaction until at some point a journalist at a largely credible outlet might see it and quickly write something up, because many journalists are trying to write as many stories as possible and write stories that get traffic and social attention. The incentive is towards producing more and checking less.[113]

How impartial should the media be? What is the difference between comment, conjecture, fact or fiction, and what are the boundaries of a free press? One of the few certainties in the world of journalism and editorial policy is that the age-old tension between freedom of expression and the right to robust and occasionally rude debate will, from time to time, come into conflict with the sensibilities of those who feel insulted or abused and

---

113 Source: 'How Teens in the Balkans Are Duping Trump Supporters With Fake News', *BuzzFeed*, Craig Silverman and Lawrence Alexander, 3 November 2016: www.buzzfeed.com/craigsilverman/how-macedonia-became-a-global-hub-for-pro-trump-misinfo?utm_term=.qy63MvBjr#.keonr16Pk.

minorities who can feel oppressed by the slights, real or imagined, of the majority. Populist politics and shifts in media consumption via social networking sites such as Facebook and Twitter mean that it is harder than ever to be sure about the quality of the news and information we consume. Coupled with citizen journalism and increasing public debate via social media, it is difficult to discern what is deliberate misinformation (for advertising, commercial or political reasons) and what amounts to 'the truth' in media reporting.

1.8.3 Propaganda and untruths: what impact does fake news have on public understanding of the world?

Over the last few years, there have been rising concerns about the perceived trend for the public to distrust traditional sources of news, such as newspapers and broadcasters, and instead to turn to the internet and social media (such as Facebook or Google News), despite the fact that the source of the stories is often unclear, and it is not known whether the reports are factually accurate. The fear that this might lead to the public being fed propaganda and untruths has been increased by the suggestions that electors in the 2016 US presidential election were subjected to possibly unprecedented amounts of 'fake news' and concerns that this may have had a significant impact on democratic processes.

In January 2017, the House of Commons Select Committee on Culture, Media and Sport launched an inquiry into 'Fake news: the growing phenomenon of widespread dissemination, through social media and the internet, and acceptance as fact of stories of uncertain provenance or accuracy'. Damian Collins MP, Chair of the Committee, said:

> The growing phenomenon of fake news is a threat to democracy and undermines confidence in the media in general. Just as major tech companies have accepted they have a social responsibility to combat piracy online and the illegal sharing of content, they also need to help address the spreading of fake news on social media platforms. Consumers should also be given new tools to help them assess the origin and likely veracity of news stories they read online. The Committee will be investigating these issues, as well as looking into the sources of fake news, what motivates people to spread it, and how it has been used around elections and other important political debates.

Following the Cambridge Analytica scandal in March 2018, the House of Commons Digital, Culture, Media and Sport Committee (DCMS) had requested that Mark Zuckerberg appear before the Committee's 'Fake News inquiry' on 20 March 2018, but the CEO had declined to give evidence. Representatives from Facebook had previously given evidence to members of the DCMS inquiry in Washington, DC, on 8 February.

Facebook's CEO eventually broke his silence and admitted in a US press conference on 5 April 2018 that the personal data of up to 87 million people had been improperly shared by the political consultancy Cambridge Analytica by harvesting the data from Facebook users. About 1.1 million of these users were UK based.[114] Zuckerberg told the

---

114 Source: Interview with Mark Zuckerberg, 'Facebook: "Malicious actors" abused its search tools to collect data on most of its two billion users', *Independent*, 5 April 2018, by Craig Timberg, Tony Romm, Elizabeth Dwoskin:

press conference that 'malicious actors' had been abusing a feature that let users search for one another by typing email addresses or phone numbers into Facebook's search box. As a result, many people's public profile information had been 'scraped' and matched to the contact details, which had been obtained from elsewhere. He had previously said if Facebook gave people privacy tools, it was largely their responsibility to decide how to use them. He now apologized and said that this assumption was 'wrong in retrospect' to have had such a limited view.

Mark Zuckerberg testified before the US House Commerce Committee regarding the firm's use and protection of user data and the fact that Facebook knew for many years that Cambridge Analytica had harvested data from about 50 million of its users.

1.8.4 What's the best way to tame the beast?

Whilst traditional journalism has been based on researching the facts, evidence and reliance on journalistic sources, the complexities of communicating objective news have become scarce, particularly with the decline of newspapers. Richard Sambrook, former director of BBC News, now Professor of Journalism at Cardiff University, believes that the term 'fake news' has been rendered 'meaningless' by overuse (and not just by President Trump). He believes misinformation or disinformation will be with us for a long time to come. Sambrook warns that it could even get worse because the technology now exists to combine video and audio to make people appear convincingly to say things they never said. News organizations increasingly realize that they should be more open and clear with the public on the difference between opinion and evidence-based reporting. Sambrook hopes that the rise in traditional media will gradually increase and that 'people will come around to recognizing what they can trust and can't trust'.[115]

Since 2016 Facebook and Google say they use technology to prevent the spread of fake news online through algorithms that promote 'trusted news' rather than dubious sources. In March 2017, Google began to employ an army of human 'quality raters' whereby some 10,000 'evaluators' now flag up 'offensive or upsetting' content online. The quality raters use 200-page instruction manuals providing them with guidelines to assess website quality and whether the results they review meet the needs of those who might search for particular queries, such as 'holocaust denial'. The Google guidelines typically include the following:

- content that promotes hate or violence against a group of people based on criteria including (but not limited to) race or ethnicity, religion, gender, nationality or citizenship, disability, age, sexual orientation or veteran status;
- content with racial slurs or extremely offensive terminology;
- graphic violence, including animal cruelty or child abuse;
- explicit how to information about harmful activities (e.g. how to commit human trafficking or violent assault);

www.independent.co.uk/news/world/americas/facebook-hackers-personal-data-collection-users-cambridge-analytica-trump-mark-zuckerberg-latest-a8289816.html.
115 Source: 'Professor Richard Sambrook – Fake news', blog by Susie Bailey, 3 May 2017: http://blogs.cardiff.ac.uk/alumni/2017/05/03/professor-richard-sambrook-fake-news/.

- other types of content which users in your locale would find extremely upsetting or offensive.[116]

Freedom of expression and freedom of the press do not always go hand in hand: there can be abuses by powerful media moguls which threaten media pluralism, as the Leveson Inquiry has shown.

See Chapter 7.5

There are increasing challenges facing the use of new technologies, and there is an urgent need for more stringent compliance with international legislation that protects both freedom of expression and an individual's right to privacy. Certainly, there needs to be clarification as to how human rights are to be protected if there is to be freedom of expression in electronic media.

 ## 1.9 Further reading

Barendt, E. (2016) *Anonymous Speech: Literature, Law and Politics*. Oxford: Hart.
Eric Barendt raises the question in this thought-provoking book: should rights of free expression include anonymous speech? He discusses topical questions such as 'fake news' and internet trolls and engages in the general discussion about free speech. Barendt discusses forms and degrees of anonymity ranging from the non-disclosure of one's officially registered name to unnamed sources only known to journalists or whistle-blowers who operate under fake names, where anonymity merges with confidentiality. Barendt sees a stronger case for anonymity when a third party can be held responsible. Authors, whistle-blowers, journalists' sources, and even internet trolls can more credibly claim legal protection once publishers, human resources officials, journalists or website managers assume vicarious liability. The author accepts compulsory disclosure when, for example, defamatory material or hate speech are published on websites that assume no responsibility for their content. For Barendt, content-based restrictions may impede the expression of ideas and information; bans on anonymity do not. As new electronic media continue to confront legislatures and courts with difficult problems of anonymity, this book looks to the future with great concern for democratic legitimacy.

Frosio, G. F. (2018) 'Why keep a dog and bark yourself? From intermediary liability to responsibility', *International Journal of Law and Information Technology*, 26(1), 1.
Giancarlo Frosio contextualizes the recent developments in intermediary liability theory and policy within a broader move towards privacy online. The author argues that online intermediaries' governance could move away from a well-established utilitarian approach and towards a moral approach by rejecting negligence-based intermediary liability arrangements. He examines various policy tools, such as monitoring and filtering obligations, blocking orders, graduated response, payment blockades and follow-the-money strategies, private domain name system content regulation, online search manipulation or administrative enforcement – in particular, intellectual property rights holders who are trying to coerce online intermediaries into implementing these policy strategies through voluntary measures and self-regulation,

---

116 See: Google Search Quality Ratings Manual, March 2017: https://static.googleusercontent.com/media/www.google.com/en//insidesearch/howsearchworks/assets/searchqualityevaluatorguidelines.pdf.

in addition to validly enacted obligations. The author argues that the intermediary liability discourse is shifting towards an intermediary responsibility discourse. Frosio proposes that by enlisting online intermediaries as watchdogs, governments would de facto delegate online enforcement to algorithmic tools. Due process and fundamental guarantees get mauled by technological enforcement, curbing fair uses of content online and silencing speech according to the mainstream ethical discourse.

Nelson, L. S. (2018) *Social Media and Morality: Losing Our Self Control*. **Cambridge: Cambridge University Press.**
This book is intended for anyone seeking to understand the moral significance of social media and provides an explanation of how our current legal and policy approach is lacking and in need of modification. Lisa Nelson lays bare a new space for reflection and critique in our digital culture. The author suggests a new methodological approach to understanding social networking cultures and technologies as well as new moral frameworks. She takes the current discussion on digital technologies beyond issues of privacy and control. The book presents an ethical discussion of our digital society.

Sanders, K. (2003) *Ethics and Journalism*. **London: Sage.**
This book provides readers with a summary of philosophical perspectives relevant to the topic in relation to the print press and broadcast journalism. There are also relevant references to film and literature.

Scanlon, T. (1972) 'A theory of freedom of expression', *Philosophy and Public Affairs*, **1(2), 204–226.**
This essay on 'freedom of expression' will never date. Harvard philosopher T. M. (Tim) Scanlon explains the doctrine of freedom of expression in general terms, thought of as a class of 'protected acts' which it holds to be immune from restrictions to which other acts are subject. He argues by singling out the 'harm principle' of John Stuart Mill's theory expressed in *On Liberty* that governments may have to justify coercive or punitive authority by limiting or curtailing free speech in times of extreme peril or war. The 'Millian Principle' is then a necessary limitation or even undermining of freedom of expression whereby governments may rule by virtue of complete authority, controlling their citizens in the ways that the Millian Principle was intended to exclude. Such actions, Scanlon argues, would have to be justified on some other ground (e.g. utilitarian), and the claim of their agents to be obeyed would not be that of a legitimate government in 'the usual (democratic) sense'. In those circumstances, he argues, citizens will normally obey the laws.

Spencer, J. R. (1989) *Jackson's Machinery of Justice* **(8th ed.) (Original publication by Professor R. M. Jackson in 1903). Cambridge: Cambridge University Press.**
This is a classic text. First published in 1903, R. M. Jackson's *Machinery of Justice* has long been an established text on the subject of 'justice' in England and Wales. For this edition, J. R. Spencer has undertaken a full-scale revision, incorporating major topical issues such as PACE (Police and Criminal Evidence Act of 1984) and the Prosecution of Offences Act 1985.

Wragg, P. (2013b) 'Mill's dead dogma: the value of truth to free speech jurisprudence', *Public Law*, **April, 363–385.**
The purpose of this article is not so much to articulate fresh insights into John Stuart Mill and his famous work *On Liberty* but to scrutinize the role of Mill's argument in the UK in relation to Article 10 ECHR jurisprudence. Paul Wragg argues that Mill's theory

is sometimes misrepresented in the academic literature as chiefly concerned with 'the truth' about uninhibited discussion. The author looks at the complexity of Mill's argument on free speech which, Wragg argues, has at times been oversimplified. The author argues that, given certain societal conditions, absolute freedom of thought and 'almost' absolute freedom of expression represent the optimal conditions by which 'truth' may be discovered.

Chapter 2

Confidentiality and privacy

> **Key points**
>
> This chapter will cover the following questions:
>
> ○ How did confidentiality develop in common law?
> ○ Has a tort of privacy developed after the Human Rights Act 1998?
> ○ What is the meaning of the 'public interest test'?
> ○ How do you distinguish between injunctions, super injunctions and anonymity orders?
> ○ Does a child have its own right to privacy, independent of that of his/her parents?
> ○ What is the meaning of the 'right to be forgotten' in relation to search engines?
> ○ Can there be complete privacy in the digital age?

2.1 Overview

This chapter deals with the concepts of confidentiality at common law and how the notion of a possible tort of privacy has developed since the coming into force of the Human Rights Act 1998 in the UK (1 October 2000).

Once the concepts of confidentiality and privacy have been explained, this chapter focuses on the difference between injunctions, super injunctions and anonymity orders and how the courts have made use of 'double gagging' orders to restrain publication in the media in order to grant certain celebrities complete anonymity with a view to keeping confidential information, such as an illicit affair, from the public eye. The public interest balancing test by the courts will be reviewed by looking at specific cases developed since the HRA came into force.

The chapter then examines the *Google Spain*, NT1 and NT2 cases and how the 'right to be forgotten' has entered domestic laws of the EU Member States by individuals asking search engines such a Google to 'delink' and 'delist' their names from their common algorithms. We discuss the wide-ranging repercussions of these rulings and whether there actually still exists complete privacy in the internet age.

It will be argued that persistent surveillance by overhead drone cameras, capturing our personal data, such as photographs of our home locations, undermines our privacy and can amount to harassment. This is because pervasive drone surveillance (by video or aerial photography) tends to shape the actions, thoughts and personalities of those being observed. Such actions happen gradually, even imperceptibly.

We will examine the *Cliff Richard* (2018) ruling and analyze what this means for freedom of expression, media freedom and the open justice principle. Arguably Mr Justice Mann has set a not altogether helpful precedent which may well have eroded press freedom when it comes to reporting historic child sex abuses and generally on criminal suspects for a very long time until Parliament may change the law in this respect. The famous singer brought his privacy action against the BBC (and the South Yorkshire Police), and the court made clear that the BBC failed to follow high editorial standards with its use of a helicopter to report on the raid of Sir Cliff's apartment in Berkshire in a sensational way. Whilst Richard was granted the right to privacy under Article 8(1) ECHR, the judge did not rule that his data protection rights had been breached.

Has this case encouraged Parliament to change the law, possibly granting suspects of (historical) sexual offences anonymity with the media? Not yet. This never-ending debate of whether defendants should be named and 'shamed' prior to being officially charged has started afresh, championed by Sir Cliff Richard and other prominent celebrities and will be discussed further in Chapter 4. Suffice it to say that under current legislation – the Sexual Offences (Amendment) Act 1992 – lifetime anonymity remains in place for complainants of rape and other sexual offences, and despite frequent debate in the Lords and the Commons, plus research and opportunity to do so, Parliament has not legislated again on this specific issue.

Lastly the question will be asked how the courts balance an individual's right to privacy (Article 8 ECHR) and the media's freedom of expression (Article 10 ECHR), coupled with the public interest argument which is often misunderstood. All too often courts are presented with justifications by certain media organizations' lawyers that intrusions into privacy are the public's right to know. The judges' answer is then that this intrusion into a person's private life amounts to nothing more than a desire to publish salacious material in order to sell newspapers, and that this does not amount to freedom of expression and press freedom.

2.2 Confidentiality: historic developments, legal conventions and common law remedies

John Stuart Mill in his writings *On Liberty* argued that privacy allows people to engage in 'experiments in living'.[1]

The concept of 'privacy' was first mentioned in relation to press freedom during the late 1880s by two American lawyers and partners in a Boston law firm, Samuel D. Warren (1852–1910) and Louis D. Brandeis (1856–1941) in their seminal 1890 article, 'The Right to Privacy' in the *Harvard Law Review*.[2] Their privacy theory was based on natural rights, responding to privacy threats from new sources such as the telephone and paparazzi photography and sensationalist journalism in the 'yellow press'[3] (see: *Midler (Bette) v Ford Motor Co. and Young & Rubicam* (1988)[4]).

See below
2.10.1

Raymond picked up Warren and Brandeis' discourse almost 100 years later, when he argued that the emergence of newspapers and the mass media brought freedom of expression into the public domain but to the detriment of a person's privacy.[5]

---

1 Mill, J.S. (1859).
2 Warren, S.D. and Brandeis, L.D. (1890) at pp. 193–220.
3 'Yellow press' or 'yellow journalism' is an American term, akin to 'tabloid' journalism in the UK, meaning 'exaggeration', 'scandal mongering' and 'sensationalism'. See: Campbell, W.J. (2001).
4 [1988] 849 F.2d 460 (Case No: 87–6168) United States Court of Appeal for the Ninth Circuit on 22 June 1988. The case centred on the protectability of the voice of the celebrated chanteuse from commercial exploitation without her consent (2005) 40 EHRR 1.
5 Raymond, J. (1998), pp. 109–136

English common law of confidence developed towards generally concerned obligations to control confidential information, such as collective cabinet confidentiality in the *Crossman Diaries* case.[6]

Wacks claims that the lines between privacy and media freedom have become rather blurred. He points out that 'we cannot have it all': people want to have the 'right to be left alone' on one hand whilst openly disclosing all their personal likes, dislikes and secrets on the social networking 'psychiatrist's couch'.[7]

2.2.1 Common law of confidentiality

One of the first legal cases involving a breach of confidential information and the Royal Household was that of *Prince Albert v Strange* (1849).[8] His Royal Highness, the Prince Consort, Prince Albert, had to ask the courts for an order to restrain the printer William Strange and publishers Jasper Tomsett Judge & Son from reproducing private royal family drawings and etchings for 'mass' publication and to exhibit these 'sketches' in public.

Her Majesty Queen Victoria and her husband Prince Albert had occasionally, for their own amusement, made drawings and etchings principally of subjects of the Royal Household at Windsor and Osborne House on the Isle of Wight. These were not meant for general publication; however, limited copies had been made by a private press (Strange), and the plates were kept by Her Majesty under lock and key at her private apartments at Windsor. The defendants Strange, J.A.F. Judge and his son had in some manner obtained some of these impressions, which had been surreptitiously taken from some of such plates. Copies of these etchings had then been exhibited at a private gallery collection in Windsor without the permission of Her Majesty and Prince Albert. The defendants had also compiled and printed a catalogue, comprising 63 etchings, costing sixpence.[9]

On 8 February 1849 the Lord Chancellor (Cottenham) granted a permanent injunction restraining the defendants from publishing any 'work being or pretending to be a catalogue of the etchings'. The defendants were also asked to 'deliver up' all the etchings and prints which had been made for the catalogue, and large costs were awarded against the defendants which subsequently bankrupted the publishers.

See
Chapter 9.2

The *Prince Albert* case set the precedent for confidentiality (and indeed copyright) in relation to private material, kept under lock and key, for Her Majesty's private use or pleasure and that such information should be kept from public knowledge.

Some 157 years later, HRH Prince Charles found himself in the same predicament as his royal ancestor when his private travel journals had fallen into the wrong hands, namely the *Mail on Sunday*, and some extracts of his journals were published. In *HRH Prince of Wales v Associated Newspapers*,[10] Prince Charles asked the courts to restrain 'mass' publication of his private thoughts in his diaries which had fallen into the hands of a journalist. The Prince of Wales successfully gained a court order (by way of an injunction), restraining any further publications of the other seven journals, citing breach of confidence and copyright as well as his right to privacy under Article 8(1) ECHR. The *Mail* had used the

---

6 *Attorney General v Jonathan Cape Ltd* [1976] 1 QB 752 (sub nom. *The Crossman Diaries case*).
7 Wacks, R. (2013) pp. 12–14.
8 *Albert (Prince) v Strange* [1849] 1 Macnaghten & Gordon 25 (1849) 41 ER 1171.
9 Ibid. at 1173.
10 [2006] EWHC 522 (Ch).

See
Chapter 6

'public interest test' defence which later became prominent in the 'Prince Charles spider letter' case (see: *R (on the application of Evans) v Attorney General* (2015)[11]).

One thing is clear in both the *Prince Albert* and *Prince Charles* cases: the courts will interfere by way of an injunction with any party who avails themselves of unauthorized material in violation of any right or breach of confidence which is of contractual nature (see: *Ashdown v Telegraph Group Ltd* (2001)[12]).

2.2.2 When does a duty of confidence arise?

From the 1960s onwards, we can observe two branches of 'confidentiality' developing in common law: one in relation to trade and business secrets (i.e. *Coco* or *Campbell Engineering* type cases) and the second in relation to misuse of private information in the form of 'kiss and tell' stories involving celebrities.

Let us firstly have a look at the *Coco* case,[13] which set the precedent for 'confidential information': a person who receives valuable or sensitive secret information in confidence owes a duty known as 'a duty of confidence' neither to disclose nor make use of that information for any purpose other than that for which the disclosure was made without consent. Should the receiver of such information ('the confidant') threaten to do so, the person who imparted it to him is entitled to an injunction to restrain such unauthorized use or disclosure.

The *Coco* case concerned the protection of a trade secret – namely the 'Coco Moped' with an Italian-designed two-stroke engine. Sadly, Mr Coco, the Italian inventor, and the UK engineering company A.N. Clark (Engineers) Ltd had not sealed the 'deal' in the form of a contract, though the defendant engineering company had given an oral undertaking to pay a royalty of five shillings per engine. Mr Coco sought a court order by way of an interlocutory injunction to stop Mr Clark from manufacturing a copy, named the 'Scamp Moped'. Mr Coco could only rely on the duty of confidentiality in common law, which he argued had arisen between himself and Mr Clark as he had imparted his moped engine to Mr Clark 'in confidence'.

In the end, the trial never took place since British intellectual property laws were weak at the time. The 'Coco engine' was subsequently discontinued after a short production run estimated at 3,000, and A.N. Clark (Engineers) Ltd went into administration.[14] This meant that inventions and trade secrets could easily be stolen or copied, and the inventor would not have any redress.[15]

The *Coco* case is important because it established fundamental principles of law in the definition and precedent of duty of confidence. Megarry J in the High Court Chancery Division had to decide firstly what amounted to a breach of confidence and secondly whether the case was one where an injunction could be granted. He noted that the equitable jurisdiction in cases of breach of confidence was 'ancient' (referring to *Prince Albert v Strange*). Megarry J said that there was no breach of contract in the *Coco* case, for no contract

---

11 [2015] UKSC 21.
12 [2001] Ch 685 (Ch D).
13 *Coco v AN Clarke (Engineers) Ltd* [1969] RPC 41, [1968] FSR 415.
14 For further discussion see: Richardson, M. and Thomas, J. (2012).
15 For further discussion see: Carty, H. (2008) at pp. 416–455.

had ever come into existence. Accordingly, he could only consider the pure equitable doctrine of confidence in the realms of commerce (referring to *Saltman Engineering Co. Ltd v Campbell Engineering Co. Ltd* (1948)[16]).

2.2.3 What is a breach of confidence?

The common law or, more precisely, the courts of equity, have long afforded protection to the wrongful use of private information by means of the cause of action which became known as breach of confidence. A breach of confidence has been defined in equity as a form of unconscionable conduct, akin to a breach of trust. A breach of confidence goes back to the time when the cause of action was based on improper use of information disclosed by one person to another in confidence. To attract protection, the information had to be of a confidential nature. The cause of action in confidence then is that information of this nature has been disclosed by one person to another in circumstances 'importing an obligation of confidence' (see the *Coco* case above).

Mr Justice Megarry in *Coco* named three elements which set the precedent for a breach of confidence action to succeed:

1   the information itself must have the necessary quality of confidence about it;
2   the claimant must have disclosed the information to the defendant in circumstances which created an obligation of confidence; and
3   the information must have been used to the detriment of the claimant without authorization.[17]

Confidential information includes:

- *Trade secrets*: formulae, recipes, production methods, source codes, test results and other information obtained by research or other work;
- *Business secrets*: budgets, customer lists, marketing plans and other information the release of which would be advantageous to a competitor and injurious to the claimant;
- *Personal information*: diaries, photographs, private information about public figures the disclosure of which could be profoundly embarrassing ('kiss and tell' stories);
- *Professional information*: information supplied to a solicitor, accountant or other professional advisor in the course of his or her professional duties.

---

16 [1948] 65 RPC 203.
17 *Coco* [1969] RPC 41 at 47 (Megarry J).

The modern law of breach of confidence is summarized in Mr Justice Warby's judgment of the Court of Appeal in *ABC v Telegraph Media Group Ltd* (2018)[18] – involving billionaire businessman Sir Philip Green, owner of Topshop and other retail companies.[19]

The fundamental principles established in the *Coco* case, were applied in ABC, plus the intended threats by a whistle-blower to 'go public' with the information they had on the claimant.

In *ABC*, the Topshop boss, Sir Philip Green, had 'gagged' the *Daily Telegraph* from publishing misconduct allegations, including sexual and racial abuse and bullying, against five employees. From the CA judgment, lifting the privacy order, we learnt that on 16 July 2018 a journalist, Daniel Foggo, had sent Sir Philip and Neil Bennett of Arcadia's advisers, Maitland, an email giving notice that the *Daily Telegraph* was preparing for publication an article containing allegations of misconduct of Sir Philip, which had been the subject of non-disclosure agreements (NDAs). Sir Philip then applied for an interim injunction to restrain disclosure of the information pending trial, asserting rights of confidentiality by virtue of the NDAs. At first instance, relief was refused. But the Court of Appeal reversed that decision.

The first application was heard by Haddon-Cave J on 23 July in the High Court in *camera*, because if it had been heard in open court, the information whose confidentiality the claimant was seeking to protect would have been lost irrespective of the outcome of the application. Section 12 HRA 1998 and Article 10(1) ECHR were directly engaged, and the court also had the necessary regard to Article 8(1) ECHR of the individual in question who featured in the intended publication. Haddon-Cave J pointed out that these were not unqualified rights, thus asking the media's lawyers to take into account the respective Articles 10(2) and 8(2) of the Convention.[20]

Whilst the injunction was in place, in October 2018, former Labour Cabinet Minister, Lord Hain, used parliamentary privilege to name Sir Philip as the businessman accused by the *Daily Telegraph* of sexual and racial harassment, after the newspaper was prevented by the injunction from doing this. On 24 October 2018, the *Daily Telegraph* ran a front-page article prominently headed:

The BRITISH #MeToo SCANDAL WHICH CANNOT BE REVEALED. Leading businessman facing allegations of sexual harassment and racial abuse gags the *Telegraph* from publishing detail.

At the end of January 2019, Sir Philip dropped his legal action against the newspaper. He denied any allegations that he behaved wrongly and maintained that the *Daily Telegraph* had pursued a 'vendetta' against him. Green said the legal action and injunction were now 'pointless' after he was named in Parliament as the businessman behind the

---

18 [2018] EWCA Civ 2329.
19 Sir Philip Nigel Ross Green was chairman of Arcadia Group at the time, a retail company that included Topshop, Topman, Wallis, Evans, Burton, Miss Selfridge, Dorothy Perkins and Outfit. The defunct BHS chain had also been part of the group.
20 *ABC v Telegraph Media Group Ltd* [2018] EWHC 2177 (QB) (Haddon-Cave J).

injunction.[21] The claimants (Sir Philip and the Arcadia Group) sought various specific orders: including continued confidentiality for documents generated by the claim and departures from the default position in relation to costs on discontinuance, which is that the discontinuing claimant paid the defendant's costs up to the time of discontinuance.[22]

In April the House of Lords Commissioner for Standard, Lucy Scott-Moncrieff, dismissed a complaint against Lord Hain for using parliamentary privilege to name Sir Philip Green as the businessman at the centre of harassment allegations and the ABC injunction. The HL Commissioner accepted that Hain had decided to take the action on moral grounds, without close examination of the legal circumstances.

Whenever a person threatens or intends to publish information, the Convention right to freedom of expression must be considered by the courts. An injunction which restrains publication is an interference with that right, which can only be justified if it pursues one of the legitimate aims identified in Article 10(2) ECHR and is *necessary* to and *proportionate* for the pursuit of such aim(s).

The method by which the courts then strike the balance between competing considerations in this field is discussed in the ABC case, which emphasizes the weight to be given to obligations of confidence which are assumed under a contract, freely entered into, for good consideration. There is, as the CA emphasized in ABC, an important public interest in upholding contractual bargains (here by way of NDAs) which cannot be impeached for fraud, undue influence or any other vitiating factor.

This aspect was highlighted in *Mionis v Democratic Press SA* (2018),[23] a case in which the CA drew heavily on ABC. The authorities indicate that the right approach for the court to take, when faced with a contest between public interest considerations and a contractual duty of confidence, is to ask itself not just whether the information is matter of public interest but 'whether in all the circumstances it is in the public interest that the duty of confidence should be breached'.[24]

In the ABC case, the court had to take account of the Convention rights of third parties involved, that is those of ex-employees with complaints and grievances against their employer (Sir Philip Green). The matters they brought forward plainly engaged their rights to respect for their private lives, and their correspondence, protected by Article 8 of the Convention.

The court must be persuaded that the threat or risk is sufficient to justify the intervention of the court. The applicant must then satisfy the court that it is 'likely to establish that publication should *not* be allowed' under section 12(3) HRA. This requirement looks forward to the time of a trial and to what would happen then. 'Likely' in this context normally means 'more likely than not', though a lesser prospect of success may suffice where the court needs a short time to consider evidence/argument or where the adverse consequences of publication might be extremely serious (see: *Cream Holdings Ltd v Banerjee* (2005)[25]).

---

21 *Arcadia Group Limited* (1) *Topshop/Topman Limited* (2) *Sir Philip Green* (3) *v Telegraph Media Group Limited* [2019] EWHC 223 (QB) judgment of 8 February 2019 (Warby J).
22 Under Civil Procedure Rules r 38.6(1).
23 [2018] QB 662.
24 *HRH Prince of Wales v Associated Newspapers Ltd* [2006] EWCA Civ 1776 at para. 68.
25 [2005] 1 AC 253.

2.2.4 Equitable remedies for breach of confidence

Once a breach of confidence has been established, an equitable remedy for such a breach comes into existence, including:

1 injunctions;
2 compensatory damages;
3 exemplary damages;
4 account of profits;
5 delivery-up;
6 proportion of costs.

How then are damages awarded by the courts for breach of confidence? Ten years after the *Coco* judgment, Sir Robert Megarry VC commented in *Malone* on the unsatisfactory state of the law of equity, in that

> the right of confidentiality is an equitable right which is still in the course of development, and is usually protected by the grant of an injunction to prevent disclosure of the confidence. . . . In such a case, where there is no breach of contract or other orthodox foundation for damages at common law, it seems doubtful whether there is any right to damages, as distinct from an account of profits.[26]

With no relationship between confider and confidant, the obligation of confidence is not established, and a claimant will not succeed in a confidentiality action.

2.2.5 'Kiss and tell' stories: confidentiality in the domestic settings

See
Chapter 4.2

When people kiss and later one of them tells, the person who does so is almost certainly breaking a confidential arrangement. Common law has long advanced the principle that private communication between couples in whatever modern form should be free from distribution to the media. However, in the notorious divorce case, *Scott v Scott* (1913),[27] the courts gave a carte blanche approach to the disclosure of confidential information and therein established the 'open justice' principle which still exists today in all British courts.

The principle of open justice in conflict with the law of confidence in personal relationships was further developed in another sensational divorce, concerning the *Duchess and Duke of Argyll*[28] (see also: *Stephens v Avery* (1988)[29]).

The *Argyll* divorce case was the scandal that rocked the nation during the 1980s. During the lengthy divorce proceedings, the Duchess' husband, Ian Campbell, the 11th Duke of Argyll, produced sexually explicit Polaroid photos found in his wife's possession as evidence at their divorce trial. The photos revealed a couple of 'headless' men in sexually

---

26 *Malone v Metropolitan Police Commissioner* [1979] 1 Ch 344 (Sir Robert Megarry VC).
27 [1913] AC 417.
28 *Argyll v Argyll and Others* [1967] Ch 301.
29 [1988] 1 Ch 449.

explicit poses with the Duchess. Controversy and speculation about the male subjects' identities continue to this day.

At the trial in the Scottish court, the pursuer, the Duchess, sought to invoke 'confidentiality' in the photos and private diaries in order to obtain an injunction against publication in the press. Lord Reid held:

> The effect, and indeed the purpose, of the law of confidentiality is to prevent the court from ascertaining the truth so far as regards those matters which the law holds to be confidential.[30]

Whenever a former partner goes to the press to sell their story on a 'kiss and tell' basis, their former partners are not always successful in relying on the *Argyll* precedent in relation to confidentiality actions against former partners or lovers. John Lennon of the Beatles (1940–1980) could not rely on *Argyll*.[31] When Lennon tried to 'injunct' his former wife Cynthia Lennon's memoirs, *A Twist of Lennon*,[32] also selling her story to the *News of the World* following a bitter divorce, the London High Court ruled that John Lennon could not rely on *Argyll* because:

1   John Lennon himself had publicized the most intimate details of their marriage;
2   the 'dirty linen' had already been washed in public, and there was nothing left which was confidential; and
3   all the information was already in the public domain.

Courts have made clear that it matters not that both partners are subjects of public and media attention (without which the issue would hardly arise or come to court) – the fact is that their private sexual conduct might interest the public and help sell newspapers or copy. This, the courts have repeatedly pointed out since the early confidentiality cases, does not necessarily amount to the 'public interest' test (see 2.9 below). Lord Lester of Herne Hill later referred to this in his book, *Five Ideas to Fight For*:

> News is a business and not only a profession. Commercial pressures push papers to publish salacious gossip and invasive stories. It is essential to ensure that those pressures do not drive newspapers to violate proper standards of journalism.[33]

So, what about unmarried couples? Confidentiality injunctions were difficult to obtain under *Argyll*, particularly involving same-sex couples (this of course changed with the Civil Partnership Act 2004). In *Stephens v Avery*[34] the court granted an injunction restraining publication concerning a lesbian relationship. Sir Nicholas Browne-Wilkinson VC made clear that the law of confidence is capable of protecting relationships outside that of husband and wife, though possibly only where the confidence was 'express' (i.e. made by a form of contract). Though the court stressed that gross sexual immorality might not be

---

30 Ibid. at para. 93 (Lord Reid).
31 *Lennon v News Group Newspapers* [1978] FSR 573.
32 Lennon, C. (1978).
33 Lester, A. (Lord Lester of Herne Hill) (2016) at p. 152.
34 [1988] 1 Ch 449.

protected from disclosure, information about sexual activities could be protected under a legally enforceable duty of confidence, where it would be unconscionable for someone who had received information on an expressly confidential basis to disclose it.

The ruling in the *Michael Barrymore* case[35] is significant in this respect. On 17 March 1997, *The Sun* outed TV personality Michael Barrymore, 44 as homosexual. No one, including his wife of 19 years, Cheryl, knew at that time that he was gay. He sought an *ex parte* injunction against his lover Paul Wincott, 22, who had gone to the press, claiming breach of confidence in relation to a 'Trust and Confidence Agreement' made by deed between him and his lover in 1995. The agreement included the obligation not to disclose or make use of any confidential business or personal information. The High Court granted the injunction to restrain any further publications, citing Lord Wheatley's judgment in *Argyll* and extending the principle of confidentiality in correspondence between married couples to that of 'close relationships'. Jacob J said:

> The fact is that when people kiss and later one of them tells, that second person is almost certainly breaking a confidential arrangement.[36]

However, it was impossible for Michael Barrymore to sue the newspapers for compensatory and exemplary damages. The damage had been done, and Barrymore's career was effectively over.

The media's lawyers will always oppose injunctions since the publication of a juicy 'kiss and tell' story clearly increases revenue, especially in times of sharply declining newspaper sales.

In the *Jamie Theakston* case,[37] the popular broadcaster tried unsuccessfully to 'gag' a story which had been leaked by a prostitute to the *Sunday People* and *News of the World*. Theakston (now presenting on Heart FM) was best known at the time as a presenter on BBC Radio 1 and hosted the BBC's *Top of the Pops* and *Live and Kicking*. The headlined articles showed Theakston coming out of a Mayfair brothel. Ouseley J granted an interim injunction in January 2002, banning the newspapers from using any photographs of the young presenter taken inside the brothel because the prostitute had used threatening text messages, demanding 'ransom' money from Theakston.[38]

The order was subsequently discharged because the story was seen as having a 'public interest' element which the court said the law of confidence should not protect. The fact that the popular presenter had behaved in the manner he did was in the public interest, given his public role as perceived by young people as a role model and respectable figure. However, the photos were permanently injuncted because they had been taken by the prostitute without Theakston's consent and passed to the papers. Ouseley J granted a privacy injunction in the photos. Phillipson argues that Ouseley J appreciated the need for proportionality in his decision in that the photographs taken of the

---

35 *Barrymore v Newsgroup Newspapers Ltd and Another* [1997] FSR 600 (Ch D).

36 Ibid. at 602 (Jacobs J).

37 *Theakston (Jamie) v MGN* [2002] EWHC 137 (QB).

38 Ibid. at 69 (Ouseley J).

claimant at the brothel had a lower level of public interest than the disclosure of the actual brothel visit.[39]

This leaves the concept of breach of confidentiality rather open-ended and perhaps too flexible. In 'privacy' cases before the HRA 1998 came into force, those individuals seeking injunctions had to exhaust the UK courts' hierarchy first before they could seek redress at the Strasbourg Human Rights Court. This made for a rather uneasy relationship, as demonstrated in the *Earl Spencer* case.[40] In his privacy action before the Strasbourg Court, the ninth Earl Spencer, brother of the late Diana, Princess of Wales, submitted that the UK had failed to comply with its obligations to protect his and his wife's right to respect for their private life under Article 8(1) ECHR.

Earl Spencer claimed before the ECtHR that the UK courts had failed to prohibit the publication and dissemination of information relating to his wife Victoria,[41] Countess Spencer's private affairs and therein failed to provide a legal remedy. He argued that the domestic courts ought to have prevented the release of private and confidential information concerning Victoria's eating disorders and drug and alcohol abuse during their marriage. Reasons for the media frenzy were that both Earl Spencer's wife Victoria and his sister, Diana, had been suffering from eating disorders and unhappy marriages.

❖ **KEY CASE** *Earl Spencer and Countess Spencer v United Kingdom (1998) 25 EHRR CD 105 (ECtHR)*

Precedent

❖ Citizens should exhaust domestic court remedies first before applying to the European Court of Human Rights in Strasbourg (ECtHR) for breach of Convention rights.

❖ In the UK there exist adequate remedies in common law for breach of confidence.

Facts

The *News of the World* (*NoW*) published an article on 2 April 1995, titled 'Di's Sister-in-Law in Booze and Bulimia Clinic'. This detailed some of the personal problems of Countess Spencer and included a photograph taken with a tele-photo lens while she walked in the grounds of a private clinic. Earl Spencer complained to the Press Complaints Commission, which concluded there was a clear breach of Code 3 ('privacy') vis-à-vis his wife. The second publication was an article in the *People* on the same day, referring to the Countess' admission to a private clinic for an eating disorder. The third article was published in the *Sunday Mirror*, on the same day, alleging that the Countess had a drink problem.

---

39 Phillipson, G. (2003) at pp. 54–72.
40 *Earl Spencer and Countess Spencer v UK* (1998) 25 EHRR CD 105 (App Nos 28851/95, 28852/95) of 16 January 1998 (ECtHR).
41 Victoria Lockwood had married Earl Spencer in 1989, with Prince Harry as a pageboy. The couple divorced in 1997.

Instead of suing the newspapers, complaining to press regulators or filing a confidentiality claim in the UK courts, the Earl and Countess applied to the European Commission on Human Rights (and therein the ECtHR), complaining that English law had failed to provide adequate respect for their privacy, violating their Article 8 right. Apart from arguing the breach of confidence action, the Spencers complained that the UK had no effective remedy in the common law of confidence for the invasion of their privacy by the press.

Decision
The ECtHR declared inadmissible an application by Earl and Lady Spencer on the basis that they had not exhausted their domestic remedies, rejecting the Spencers' complaints under Article 8 on the basis that the couple had not completely exhausted the domestic remedies available to them for breach of confidence as outlined in *Spycatcher No 2* and *Barrymore*.

Analysis
The Strasbourg Court found that the UK's common law provisions in the law of confidence were 'adequate and reasonable' to remedy the Spencers' complaint. However, since the Spencers had chosen not to avail themselves of any domestic court action in the first place, and therein not following the hierarchy of the courts, they were not entitled to seek redress in the Human Rights Court.

In summary, supposed infidelity cannot be a guise under which the media can disclose kiss and tell stories in order to sell newspapers (or online editions). In a legal sense, this has been confirmed by a series of European Court of Human Rights (ECtHR) judgments. In the UK the watershed was yet to come following the introduction of the Human Rights Act 1998 in the United Kingdom (see below 2.4).

 FOR THOUGHT

Discuss the remedies available in the UK courts for breach of confidence for an unauthorized disclosure of personal information accompanied by unsolicited photographs of a famous claimant.

2.3 Official secrets

Classified information is protected because its disclosure might harm national security or damage international relations. If such information is misused, serious damage can be caused, which is why the unauthorized disclosure of such information is criminalized by the Official Secrets Acts of 1911 and 1989. In addition, there is a multitude of other offences contained in numerous statutory provisions that protect different categories of information. The balancing of the right of the public to receive information – for example under Freedom of Information requests (FOIA 2000) – and the interests of a state in withholding it is not an easy task. The material often relates to matters of public interest. Some whistle-blowers who leak classified information are either hailed as heroes or, like former MI5 officer David Shayler, are imprisoned for breach of the Official Secrets Acts because classified information could damage national security if it gets into the wrong hands.

See below 2.3.1

There is limited case law in this area, and the few cases recorded largely involve whistle-blowing. Some cases are brought by the Attorney General under the doctrine of cabinet confidentiality; others are formally prosecuted under the provisions of the Official Secrets Acts (largely the 1911 Act).

2.3.1 Does Official Secrets Act legislation chill media freedom?

The Crossman Diaries case[42] presented the first court action that tested the constitutional convention of Collective Cabinet Confidentiality (and therein the Minister's individual Cabinet responsibility), a paradigm of restraining government ministers from any publication of Cabinet 'secrets'. In this case, the government had applied via the Attorney General to restrain the publication of Cabinet Minister Richard Crossman's posthumous diaries covering the period of Harold Wilson's government between 1964 and 1970. Following Crossman's death in April 1974, volume one of the book, Diaries of a Cabinet Minister, which covered the years 1964–1966, had been sent to the Secretary of the Cabinet for his approval but was rejected on the ground that publication was against the public interest, in that the doctrine of Collective Cabinet Responsibility would be harmed by the disclosure of details of Cabinet discussions. In July 1974 Crossman's literary executors gave an undertaking not to publish the book without giving prior notice to the Treasury Solicitor, but, in January 1975, the first extracts from the book were published in the Sunday Times without the consent of the Cabinet Secretary.

On 18 June 1975, the Attorney General issued a writ against the first defendants, the publishers Jonathan Cape Ltd and Hamish Hamilton Ltd, and against the second group of defendants, Crossman's literary estate, namely his wife Anne Patricia Crossman, writer Graham Greene and Labour Party leader Michael Foot, seeking an injunction to restrain the defendants from printing, publishing, distributing, selling or otherwise disclosing in any manner, the contents of the book Diaries of a Cabinet Minister or any extracts from it. The Attorney General also applied for an injunction against the Sunday Times to restrain publication of any extracts of the three volumes of the book.

The Court of Appeal dismissed the actions and lifted all injunctions on the grounds of public interest. The court ruled that volume one of the Diaries could be published immediately since it was dealing with events ten years previously and that Cabinet discussions should no longer remain confidential.[43] Lord Widgery CJ made it abundantly clear that the convention of Joint Cabinet Responsibility was in the public interest:

It is unacceptable in our democratic society that there should be a restraint on the publication of information relating to Government when the only vice of that

---

42 *AG v Jonathan Cape Ltd; AG v Times Newspapers Ltd* [1976] QB 752 (Crossman Diaries case).
43 [1976] QB 752 at pp. 765D–E, 769H–770A, 770B–D, 770G–771H, 772A–C.

information is that it enables the public to discuss, review and criticise Government action. Accordingly, the court will determine the Government's claim to confidentiality by reference to the public interest. Unless disclosure is likely to injure the public interest, it will not be protected.[44]

The British secret services, particularly MI5, have always been the object of conspiracy theories, according to Cambridge professor Christopher Andrew, author of the first official history of MI5.[45] Layers of official secrecy were exposed by former spy Peter Wright's sensational publication of *Spycatcher: The Candid Autobiography of a Senior Intelligence Officer*, which had come onto the Australian market. The former MI5 officer – by now retired in Tasmania – described in detail how 'we bugged and burgled our way across London at the State's behest, while pompous, bowler-hatted civil servants in Whitehall pretended to look the other way'.[46]

The *Spycatcher* (No 1)[47] and (No 2)[48] actions are best known for their numerous injunctions. The Attorney General, on behalf of the British government, attempted to restrain prior publication of Wright's memoirs in order to preserve the confidentiality of government and secret service material. Wright had, of course, signed the Official Secrets Act 1911 and was bound by this beyond his employment.[49] The question arose whether the Crown (via the AG) could ask the High Court to permanently injunct a publication outside the United Kingdom. The short answer was 'no', and the book was published outside the UK and serialized in the *Sunday Times*.[50] The restraining order was directed at the *Guardian* and the *Sunday Times* (and thereby *contra mundum*), and the *Sunday Times* editor at the time, Andrew Neil, was severely criticized by Lord Keith of Kinkel, who referred in his judgment in *Spycatcher No 2* to Mr Neil's blatantly ignoring the interim injunction as employing 'peculiarly sneaky methods'.[51]

Had Peter Wright returned to the UK he would, no doubt, have been arrested and charged with offences contrary to the Official Secrets Act 1911.

In May 2007, David Keogh,[52] a civil servant working in Whitehall's communication centre, was convicted and sentenced to three months' imprisonment for breaching sections 3 and 5 of the Official Secrets Act 1989. He had leaked a secret memo about a meeting on Iraq between Tony Blair and George Bush, revealing that the then US President had contemplated bombing the broadcaster Al Jazeera. Keogh's defence argument at the time was that the information would have been in the public interest, in that two of the most powerful men in the world were contemplating committing war crimes.

The Government in the *Keogh* case argued that the contents of the leaked document could be heard only by the crown court jury with no press or public present. The judge agreed and also made it clear he regarded the contents of the document as sensitive

---

44 Ibid. at 735 (Lord Widgery).
45 Andrew, C. (2009).
46 Wright, P. (1987), pp. 104–106.
47 *Attorney General v Guardian Newspapers Ltd and Ors (No 1)* [1987] 1 WLR 1248 ('Spycatcher').
48 *Attorney General v Guardian Newspapers Ltd (No 2)* [1990] 1 AC 109.
49 For further discussion see: Barendt, E. (1989), p. 204; also: Bindman, G. (1989), p. 94.
50 For further discussion see: Lee, S. (1987), p. 506; see also: Leigh, I. (1992), p. 200.
51 *AG v Guardian Newspapers (No 2)* [1990] 1 AC 109 at 261 (Lord Keith of Kinkel).
52 *R v Keogh (David)* [2007] 1 WLR 1500.

enough that the press could not report what Mr Keogh said when he was asked in open court about what preyed on his mind when he first saw the document.

The judge, Mr Justice Aikens, said Keogh's reckless and irresponsible' actions could have cost British lives:

> You decided that you did not like what you saw. Without consulting anyone, you decided on your own that it was in the best interest of the UK that this letter should be disclosed. Your reckless and irresponsible action in disclosing this letter when you had no right to could have cost the lives of British citizens. This disclosure was a gross breach of trust of your position as a crown servant.[53]

Another seminal case was that of whistle-blower David Shayler.[54] He was found guilty of passing secret MI5 documents to *The Mail on Sunday*, alleging that MI5 was paranoid about 'socialists' ('reds under the bed') and that it had previously investigated Labour Party Ministers Peter Mandelson, Jack Straw and Harriet Harman. The *Mail* had then run a front-page story on 24 August 1997, headlined 'MI5 Bugged Mandelson', with the claim that Tony Blair's favourite Cabinet Minister had his phone tapped for three years during the late 1970s. On 19 July 1998, Mr Shayler published further revelations on his own website, www.shayler.com, such as an MI5 plot to kill the Libyan leader, Colonel Muammar Gaddafi.

Shayler was arrested in a Paris hotel by French police and extradited to the UK and charged under the Official Secrets Act 1989. He unsuccessfully used the Article 10 ECHR defence, and the public interest, both of which were rejected at appeal. Shayler's six-month prison sentence was upheld by the HL.[55]

2.3.2 Protecting classified information in the modern world

The Official Secrets Act 1911 still provides the principal legal protection in the United Kingdom against espionage, despite the fact it was enacted in the run-up to the First World War. Since its implementation over 100 years ago, this legislation has been subject to very little independent scrutiny. As a result, the British Cabinet Office, on behalf of the government, asked the Law Commission to review the effectiveness of the laws that protect Government information from unauthorized disclosure in 2017. The Law Commission subsequently published suggested improvements and amendments to existing legislation that would ensure the protection of classified information in the digital age, including:

- clarifying the scope of espionage-type offences and those related to making unauthorized disclosures;
- proposed increased maximum sentences to reflect the seriousness of some conduct;
- new measures to ensure sites are protected if necessary to safeguard national security;

53 Quoted in 'Gagging order as two are jailed for leaking Blair-Bush memo', *Guardian*, 11 May 2007.
54 *R v Shayler (David Michael)* [2003] 1 AC 247.
55 For further discussion see: Hollingsworth, M. and Fielding, N. (1999).

- making clear that the criminal offences protecting sensitive information apply whether the conduct takes place at home or abroad;
- simplifying and modernizing the language to remove anachronistic terms like 'code words' and 'enemy' and replacing them with language that will future-proof the legislation;
- providing a process for concerns about illegality and impropriety to be investigated in an independent and rigorous way which is compliant with the European Convention on Human Rights.

The last point made by the Law Commission is worth exploring further. Whilst free speech is now well enshrined in Article 10(1) ECHR, we also know that this is a qualified right in that Article 10(2) prescribes that Member States to the Convention can lawfully interfere with freedom of expression which requires interference prescribed by law in pursuit of a legitimate aim and necessary in a democratic society. The legitimate aim generally furthered is national security. Strasbourg jurisprudence has adopted a 'proportionality' test, with the interference being balanced against the aim being pursued.

In *Giniewski v France* (2007),[56] the applicant Paul Giniewski, a journalist, sociologist and historian, found himself being criminally charged with racial defamation, following the publication of an article in 1994 in the newspaper *Le quotidien de Paris*, headlined 'The Obscurity of Error'. The article contained a critical analysis of the particular doctrine developed by the Roman Catholic Church and its possible links with the origins of the Holocaust. The journalist, the newspaper's editor and publishers were convicted under French law. The Orléans Court of Appeal ordered that Giniewski pay damages to the 'General Alliance against Racism and for Respect for the French and Christian Identity' (AGRIF) and that the court's decision was to be published at his expense in a national newspaper. After an unsuccessful appeal in the Paris Supreme Court, Monsieur Giniewski filed a claim for breach of his Article 10(1) right with the Strasbourg Human Rights Court.

The ECtHR in its judgment of 31 January 2006 held in the applicant's favour. While the article may have shocked and offended, the article in question had contributed to a debate on the various possible reasons behind the extermination of Jews in Europe – a question of indisputable public interest in a democratic society. The article had not been 'gratuitously offensive' or insulting and had not incited disrespect or hatred, nor had it cast doubt in any way on clearly established historical facts. His conviction breached his Article 10(1) right.

In contrast, the Strasbourg Court did not rule in the applicant's favour in *Norwood v UK* (2004).[57] The applicant, Mark Anthony Norwood, a parish councillor of Gobowen in Shropshire, had been found guilty of a religiously aggravated offence contrary to s 5(1)(b) Public Order Act 1986 at Oswestry Magistrates' Court. He was fined £300. The 41-year-old, a regional organizer for the BNP, had displayed a large poster in his bedroom window in the wake of the 9/11 attacks. The poster contained a photograph of the New York City Twin Towers in flames, the words 'Islam out of Britain – Protect the British People' and a symbol of a crescent and star in a prohibition sign. On appeal at London's

---

56 *Giniewski v France* (2007) (App no 64016/00, 2006-I), (2007) 45 EHRR 23, Strasbourg 31 January 2006 (ECtHR).
57 *Norwood v United Kingdom* (2004) 40 EHRR SE 111; [2004] ECHR 730 (ECtHR).

High Court in June 2003, Norwood relied on Articles 10 and 14 of the Convention, but Lord Justice Auld disagreed. Before the Strasbourg Human Rights Court Norwood submitted that free speech included not only the inoffensive but also the irritating, contentious, eccentric, heretical, unwelcome and provocative, provided that it did not tend to provoke violence. In reply, the ECtHR referred to Article 17 of the Convention which states:

> Nothing in [the] Convention may be interpreted as implying for any State, group or person any right to engage in any activity or perform any act aimed at the destruction of any of the rights and freedoms set forth herein or at their limitation to a greater extent than is provided for in the Convention.

The general purpose of Article 17 is to prevent individuals or groups with totalitarian aims from exploiting in their own interests the principles enunciated by the Convention. The ECtHR, found in particular that the freedom of expression guaranteed under Article 10(1) of the Convention may not be invoked in a sense contrary to Article 17. The ECtHR held that the poster in the applicant's window constituted an act within the meaning of Article 17 ECHR, which did not enjoy the protection of Articles 10 or 14 ECHR.

Media response to the Law Commission's proposals has been largely negative. It has focused on the proposed changes to the 1989 Act, particularly with comment on possible implications for public interest disclosures ('leaking') and journalism. Much of the press comments have concerned the inclusion of those who 'obtain or gather' secrets in any redrafted offence, despite this being true of the current law.[58]

In a February 2017 editorial, The Guardian said that the new official secrets proposals 'threaten democracy', particularly highlighting that reporters publishing stories based on a leak could be subject to criminal charges. The Guardian also opposed the increase of sentences to up to 14 years.[59]

2.4 Privacy: legal developments since the Human Rights Act 1998

Whilst German, French and Scandinavian lawmakers have enshrined the right to privacy into domestic legislation and the constitutions, there is no such right in English law. This was expressed in the now famous dictum by Glidewell LJ in Kaye v Robertson:

> It is well known that in English law there is no right to privacy, and accordingly there is no right of action for breach of a person's privacy.[60]

In this case, the editor and publishers of the Sunday Sport had published 'lurid and sensational style' photographs accompanied by an interview with the actor Gordon Kaye, who was lying in hospital on life support. The actor, best known for his role as René in the popular BBC TV series (1982–1992), 'Allo 'Allo!, had sustained severe head injuries on

---

58 For further discussion see: House of Commons (2017).
59 Source: 'The Guardian view on official secrets: new proposals threaten democracy', Guardian, 12 February 2017.
60 Kaye (Gordon) v Robertson [1991] FSR 62 at 66 (Glidewell LJ).

25 January 1990 when, as he was driving in London during a gale, a piece of wood from an advertisement hoarding smashed through his windscreen and struck him on the head.

Kaye established that 'hospital beds' are out of bounds for the media. It is worth noting that subsequent authorities demonstrate that Lord Glidewell's *dicta* in *Kaye v Robertson* have been superseded, although courts continue to use and perhaps distort the action for breach of confidence instead of recognizing they have created a tort of 'misuse of private information' – though this principle may well have changed now after the *Cliff Richard* judgment.

See below
2.8.1

Until the Human Rights Act 1998 (HRA) came into force on 1 October 2000, the law of equity included the protection of personal information with the remedy for breach of confidence, and it is argued here that out of this doctrine and with development of Strasbourg jurisprudence the new cause of action, namely that of 'privacy', was born. We have seen in the earlier parts of this chapter that there was a requirement that the defendant owed the claimant a duty of confidence which we called the *Coco* principle.

See above
2.2.4

Privacy rights serve to protect a personal and private state of affairs, preventing information that the individual has chosen not to convey from being disclosed. The common law of confidentiality developed obligations to control confidential information (generally when there was no contract to prevent such information from being disclosed). Should privacy injunctions be treated differently by the courts for celebrities than for ordinary citizens? Article 8(1) ECHR makes it clear that the concept of privacy is not limited to isolated individuals, but includes the general 'zone' of the family, the home, correspondence with others, telephone conversations and a person's well-being. Article 8(1), 'Right to respect for private and family life', reads:

> Everyone has the right to respect for his private and family life, his home and his correspondence.

However, Article 8 is not an absolute right and may be 'qualified', which means a Member State to the Convention[61] may derogate under Article 8(2) ECHR:

> There shall be no interference by a public authority with the exercise of this right *except* such as is in accordance with the law and is necessary in a democratic society in the interests of national security, public safety or the economic well-being of the country, for the prevention of disorder or crime, for the protection of health or morals, or for the protection of the rights and freedoms of others.

2.4.1 What is 'privacy'?

The protection of someone's privacy is frequently seen as a way of drawing the line as to how far society can intrude into an individual's private affairs. To define 'privacy' is perhaps most difficult, as the notion of privacy differs from country to country and from culture to culture. Individual states have defined their constitutional laws and substantive case law as the notion of privacy has developed.[62]

---

61 There are 47 subscribing Member States to the Convention and members of the Council of Europe.
62 Hixson, R. (1987).

Witzleb expresses concern that the lack of a substantive privacy law in the UK has led to insufficient legal remedies for invasions of privacy.[63] Bennett disagrees and maintains that this is negated somewhat by the courts' flexibility in interpreting the equitable action for breach of confidence and in how they assess breaches of privacy and the fact that it is considered on a case-by-case basis.[64] However, the flexible nature of privacy in English common law has meant that a person's privacy right does not sit comfortably with press freedom, particularly when the opposing rights of confidential information and freedom of expression coincide (see: *Spencer v UK* (1998)[65]).

But privacy is not just about celebrities, as the Leveson Inquiry showed.[66] The inquiry into phone hacking by the *News of the World* (*NoW*) and other unethical media practices was told in May 2012, for example, how the then missing teenager Milly Dowler's mobile phone was hacked into by reporters and private detectives of *NoW*, and how the police knew about it.

Before we examine definitions in common law let us consider how some scholars have defined 'privacy' before we look at leading authorities. Barber argues that privacy prevents others from learning everything about our activities.[67] American sociologist Barrington Moore defines 'privacy' within the following categories:

See Chapter 7.5

- Information privacy involves the establishment of rules governing the collection and handling of personal data such as credit information and medical records;
- Bodily privacy concerns the protection of people's physical selves against invasive procedures such as drug testing;
- Privacy of communications covers the security and privacy of mail, telephones, email and other forms of communication;
- Territorial privacy concerns the setting of limits on intrusion into the domestic environment such as the workplace or public sphere; to control the channels through which one's image is distributed.[68]

Rachels contends that privacy is valuable in that it allows us to limit the information that others know about us: that there are different sorts of social relationships that bring different levels of intimacy. Some information remains confidential to us.[69]

Wacks discusses the controversy and uncertainty surrounding the right to personal privacy in the digital age, extending the notion to 'personal information', sensitive and intimate facts, which individuals are now sharing via social media (Twitter, Facebook, etc.).[70] Wacks acknowledges that there is no 'natural right' to privacy and that it would be inconceivable – at least in American law – that there is a legal right to privacy.[71]

---

63 Witzleb, N. (2009).
64 Bennett, T.D.C. (2010).
65 (1998) (28851/95, 28852/95) 25 EHRR CD 105.
66 Leveson, Lord, LJ (2012).
67 Barber, N.W. (2003).
68 Source: Moore, B. (1984), p. 5.
69 Rachels, J. (1975), p. 323.
70 Wacks, R. (2013) at pp. 1–6.
71 For further discussion see: Hixson, R. (1987) at p. 98.

2.4.2 Celebrities and their privacy: the 'red carpet rule'

So far Parliament has not found it necessary to enact any privacy laws, relying mainly on Article 8 ECHR which has not changed substantive law in this respect. As the law of confidence developed by way of common law jurisprudence in the UK courts, the notion of 'privacy' developed alongside, arguably changing from the law of confidence to privacy with the inception of HRA 1998.

Patten J argued in the *J.K. Rowling (David Murray)* case that there is a clear difference between celebrities' and private individuals' private lives, what this author has referred to as 'the red carpet rule':

See below 2.5

> If a simple walk down the street qualifies for protection then it is difficult to see what would not. For most people who are not public figures in the sense of being politicians or the like, there will be virtually no aspect of their life which cannot be characterized as private. Similarly, even celebrities would be able to confine unauthorized photography to the occasions on which they were at a concert, film premiere or some similar occasion. . . . Even after *von Hannover [No 1]* there remains, I believe, an area of routine activity which when conducted in a public place carries no guarantee of privacy.[72]

The first case which tested the notion of privacy in relation to a celebrity couple in the English courts was that of *Douglas v Hello! Ltd*.[73] This was the first legal challenge after the Human Rights Act 1998 (HRA) had come into force on 1 October 2000. What mattered in this case was the question whether Catherine Zeta-Jones and Michael Douglas had a reasonable expectation of privacy in their wedding photographs taken at the high-profile event at the Plaza Hotel in New York in November 2000. And would the notion of privacy under Article 8(1) ECHR include the exclusivity of their commercial wedding photographs which the celebrity couple had sold for £1m to OK magazine? Whilst the couple recovered damages against *Hello!* magazine in the Chancery Division of the High Court some five years later,[74] the main issue in the 2001 action was their claim under Article 8 ECHR. They did not succeed in their privacy claim, and on 8 January 2000, Sedley LJ stated:

> We have reached a point at which it can be said with confidence that the law recognises and will appropriately protect a right of personal privacy.[75]

The judge gave two reasons for his comment. Firstly, that equity and the common law had to respond to an increasingly invasive social environment. Secondly, that such recognition was now required by the HRA and in particular Article 8 ECHR. Sedley LJ went on to

---

72 *Murray (David) v Big Pictures* [2008] EWCA Civ 446 at 65–66 (Patten J).
73 [2001] EMLR 563 (QB).
74 *OBG Ltd and Others v Allan and Others, Douglas and Another and Others v Hello! Ltd and Others, Mainstream Properties Ltd v Young and Others and Another* [2007] UKHL 21 (on appeal from: [2005] EWCA Civ 106, [2005] EWCA Civ 595, [2005] EWCA Civ 861 (sub nom. *Douglas v Hello! No 7*) – judgment of 2 May 2007 (HL)).
75 *Douglas v Hello! Ltd (No 1)* [2001] at para. 115 (Sedley LJ).

say that since *Kaye v Robertson* had been decided, 'the legal landscape has altered' and that the right of privacy was grounded in the equitable doctrine of breach of confidence. Sedley LJ's observations in the *Douglas* case in respect of balancing the Douglases' right to privacy and the media's freedom of expression (Article 10(1) ECHR) are highly relevant when he said:

> the Convention right, when one turns to it, is qualified in favour of the reputation and rights of others and the protection of information received in confidence. In other words, you cannot have particular regard to Article 10 without having equally particular regard at the very least to Article 8.[76]

Following the revelation that six unauthorized photographs were going to be published a day after their wedding at the Plaza Hotel in New York, on Monday 20 November, in the *Hello!* issue No. 639, the Douglases obtained an *ex parte* injunction to restrain publication. This was opposed by the publishers of *Hello!* (the Sánchez family[77]) and eventually discharged by the Court of Appeal on Thursday 23 November.

Issue 639 of *Hello!* went on sale on Friday 24 November, on the same day as issue No. 241 of *OK* also went on sale, with its 'exclusive' coverage of the Douglases' wedding. Clearly, there was no longer exclusivity in the wedding photos. Sales figures for *Hello!* issue 639 rose to 523,000 that week (150,000 above sales average).

Commenting that the Douglases' right to privacy had not been breached, the CA ruled that a wedding is essentially a public affair, that the famous couple's lives were already in the public domain and that they had sold their photographs for financial gain. For these reasons there was no breach of Article 8(1) ECHR, and the court ruled in favour of freedom of expression under Article 10(1).

Photographs can have a special intrusive effect, as was held in the *Beckham*[78] case conveying visual information which words alone could not achieve. The claimants, David and Victoria Beckham, had purchased a house in the Hertfordshire town of Sawbridgeworth for £2.5m in 2001. As their marital home and arranged for extensive refurbishment and alteration works to be carried out. They were particularly concerned about security arrangements, being a high-profile celebrity couple (footballer and former Spice Girl). According to their lawyers, the Beckhams had received a number of threats, including a threat of kidnap their Son Brooklyn, aged 2. The building works were carried out under tight security, and all those involved in the works were required to sign a confidentiality agreement. Despite those precautions, an unidentified paparazzi photographer managed to obtain photographs of the interior of the house via a builder, which he then sold to the Mirror newspaper group (MGN).

When the claimants were notified of that, they contacted the paper, which confirmed that it intended to publish the photographs in its next *Sunday People* edition. The claimants thereupon applied for an injunction against the defendant newspaper publishers, preventing the publication of *any* photographs of their house, other than those taken from outside

---

76 Ibid. at para. 138.
77 Eduardo Sánchez Junco, journalist and publisher of the Spanish gossip magazine ¡Hola! and 14 different national editions in ten languages, selling overall some 10m copies a week, died 14 July 2010.
78 *Beckham v Mirror Group Newspapers Ltd* [2001] All ER (D) 307.

the boundary of the claimants' property. They contended that publication would infringe their right to privacy under Article 8 of the Convention and would also potentially compromise their security arrangements, since they might reveal the nature of those arrangements or show certain valuable items, giving rise to attempted break-ins.

Worth noting is that the Beckhams had previously entered into negotiations with a glossy magazine about the possibility of publishing exclusive pictures of the interior of their new home but had been deterred from agreeing to a deal for similar reasons of security. They were adamant that they would not contemplate any such publication unless they had absolute control over which photographs were included.

The High Court granted an interim injunction on the condition that the claimants undertook not to publish or permit publication of any photographs of the subject matter covered by the injunction. That undertaking was intended to maintain the status quo between the parties pending the full hearing of the injunction application. At that hearing, the defendant sought to retain the undertaking in the final injunction, on the basis that any such publication would place the subject matter in the public domain, within the meaning of section 12(4)(a)(i) of the Human Rights Act 1998 (whenever Article 10(1) ECHR is being challenged). The newspaper wanted to retain the right to make submissions to the court before such publication in relation to the injunction against it.

Mr Justice Eady upheld the interim injunction in favour of the Beckhams, preventing the *Sunday People* from publishing photographs of their matrimonial home and protecting the claimants from unwarranted intrusions into their privacy. A week after winning their legal action in June 2001 Victoria Beckham launched a website featuring a virtual tour of "Beckingham Palace".[79]

How does the *Beckham* case differ from that of *Douglas*? Both decisions fell in the same year immediately after the HRA 1998 had come into force. There is only a fine nuance in contract: the Beckhams had not yet made a commercial contract with a glossy magazine, featuring the interior design of their new home. The Douglases had made a £1m contract with OK magazine for the exclusive publishing rights of their wedding photos. The Mirror Group publishers in the *Beckham* privacy injunction were keen to gain first-hand commercial advantage by publishing their own paparazzi photos of the Beckhams' home before anyone else could. It is clear that the Beckhams themselves wanted control of their own commercial advantage over the release of their own photos. Once they would do so, the publication of the photographs would be in the public domain and – as Eady J pointed out – there was nothing to stop MGN and others from publishing these images.

See below
2.10

More or less at the same time the *Douglas* and *Beckham* actions were going through the High Court, famous international fashion model Naomi Campbell began her action by suing the publishers and editor of the *Daily Mirror*. Her action in the first instance did not rely on privacy but on the common law of breach of confidence for the wrongful publication of highly personal and confidential information (in conjunction with an action in defamation).[80] Ms Campbell had courted publicity since the early 1990s and had frequently, but untruthfully, told the media that she did not take drugs.

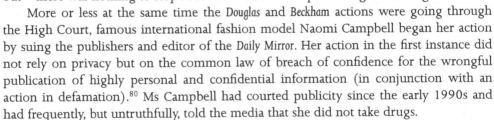

---

79 Ibid. at 9, line C (Eady J).
80 *Campbell v Mirror Group Newspapers Ltd* [2002] EWHC 499 (QB).

> ❖ KEY CASE

Campbell (Naomi) v Mirror Group Newspapers [2004] 2 AC 457 (HL)

Precedent

- ❖ Private information, such as medical or rehabilitative treatment, amounts to a duty of confidence and must be protected.
- ❖ The private nature of rehabilitation (here: Narcotics Anonymous meetings) encourage addicts to attend them in the belief that they can do so anonymously. The assurance of privacy is an essential part of rehabilitative treatment.
- ❖ The courts have to balance an individual's right to privacy under Article 8(1) and the media's right to inform the public under Article 10(1) EHCR.
- ❖ Though celebrities who seek the public limelight have their Article 8 right to privacy severely curtailed, those undergoing rehabilitative or hospital treatment will be protected under the common law of confidentiality and the right to privacy (see: Lord Nicholls' and Lord Hope's dissenting judgments).

Facts

In February 2001, the *Daily Mirror* published photographs and details of rehabilitative group drug meetings attended by the supermodel Naomi Campbell. One of the photographs was captioned 'Hugs: Naomi . . . arrives for a lunchtime group meeting this week'. It showed the claimant in the street on the doorstep of a building as the central figure in a small group. She was being embraced by two people whose faces had been pixelated. The article did not name the venue of the meeting, but anyone who knew the district well would have been able to identify the place shown in the photograph. Ms Campbell actioned in privacy and confidentiality in the High Court, and Morland J awarded her £2,500 damages, plus £1,000 aggravated damages in respect of further articles published by the newspaper.[81] The *Mirror* cross-appealed, arguing that the photos and details about Miss Campbell's drug treatment exposed her lies, demonstrating that the newspaper had done an excellent piece of investigative journalism. The CA reversed the original decision in favour of the *Mirror*.[82] Miss Campbell appealed to the House of Lords on 23 February 2003.

Decision (House of Lords)

Allowing the appeal (Lord Nicholls of Birkenhead and Lord Hoffmann dissenting), the House of Lords set the threshold test as to whether information was private: whether a reasonable person of ordinary sensibilities, placed in the same situation as the subject of the disclosure (rather than its recipient), would find the disclosure offensive. The HL argued that it depends how the information was obtained and by what means, such as by covert or surreptitious long-lens photography by paparazzi or phone hacking, without the subject's consent or in a private

---

81 Ibid. at 502 (Morland J).
82 *Campbell v MGN* [2002] EWCA Civ 1373 (CA).

place (referring to Wainwright v Home Office (2004);[83] Fressoz and Roire v France (1999);[84] Jersild v Denmark (1994);[85] Peck v UK (2003)[86]). Despite the weight that had to be given to the right to freedom of expression under Article 10(1) ECHR that the press needed if it were to play its role effectively, there had been an infringement of the claimant's right to privacy under Article 8(1) which could not be justified. The details about the therapy which the appellant (Campbell) had been receiving from Narcotics Anonymous were analogous to details about a medical condition or its treatment and amounted to private information which imported a duty of confidence. Attending rehabilitative treatment deserves privacy and anonymity. Their Lordships stated that, in deciding the degree of confidentiality that was to be attached to a therapy for drug addiction, one had to assume the reasonable person test, also in need of such treatment, and disclosure of the details of rehabilitative therapy would disrupt any success of treatment.

When striking the balance between Articles 8 and 10 ECHR, it was the duty of the courts to consider the public interest test in favour of open media reporting (to impart information and ideas of public interest which the public had a right to receive) on the other hand and the degree of privacy to which the appellant was entitled under the law of confidence as to the details of her therapy. The court had to take account of the newspaper's wish to put forward a story that was credible and to present Ms Campbell in a way that commended her for her efforts to overcome her addiction. It also had to be recognized, however, that the right of the public to receive information about the details of her treatment was of a much lower order than the undoubted right to know that she had misled the public when she had said that she did not take drugs. The HL ruled in Ms Campbell's favour. The potential for the disclosure of the information to cause harm was an important factor here to which their Lordships (by majority) attached considerable weight. For this reason there was a pressing need to protect the appellant's right to privacy, thereby restoring the original privacy orders which the High Court judge had ordered.

Analysis

The HL judgment in *Campbell* set a new precedent (threshold) test as to whether information is private or not: whether a reasonable person of ordinary sensibilities, placed in the same situation as the subject of the disclosure (rather than its recipient) would find the disclosure of private and confidential information (drug rehabilitation) offensive. Miss Campbell's drug rehabilitation treatment certainly amounted to confidential information contained in her medical records, and the publication clearly breached that confidentiality and her right to privacy. It is worth looking at the dissenting judgments by Lords Nicholls and Hope, commenting the famous model's denial of her drug addiction to her large fan base and that she had

---

83 [2004] 2 AC 406.
84 (1999) 31 EHRR 28.
85 (1994) 19 EHRR 1.
86 (2003) 36 EHRR 719.

sought enormous publicity for many years. Now the fact that the disclosure of rather unattractive and highly personal photographs, leaving a drug rehabilitation clinic, did not suit Ms Campbell's public image was of great interest to the media. The *Mirror* wanted to publish a legitimate story where they felt Ms Campbell had deceived the public. The majority of the HL however looked at the margin of appreciation, the balancing test between press freedom and Ms Campbell's right to privacy. In this context the HL found an unnecessary intrusion into Ms Campbell's private life. Accordingly, the publication of the *Mirror* articles and the accompanying photos constituted an unjustified infringement of Ms Campbell's right to privacy whilst undergoing treatment; therefore she was entitled to damages.

After the HL ruling in *Campbell*, then editor Piers Morgan immediately voiced his opinion, saying that it was 'a good day for lying, drug-abusing prima donnas who want to have their cake with the media and the right to then shamelessly guzzle with their Cristal champagne'.

He added: 'Five senior judges found for the Mirror throughout the various hearings in this case, four for Naomi Campbell, yet she wins. If ever there was a less deserving case for what is effectively a back door privacy law it would be Miss Campbell's. But that's showbiz'.[87]

2.5 A child's right to privacy

Increasingly we see children participate in reality TV shows where parents have clearly waived the child's privacy right by way of contract with the broadcaster. The main motivation for the parent or guardian is often financial gain. While reality shows, such as *Britain's Got Talent*, featuring children, may cause television ratings to go up, children participating in these shows can face immense pressure.

A child's welfare is of paramount importance, a principle enshrined in the United Nations Convention on the Rights of the Child 1989 which provides in Article 3:

1   In all actions concerning children, whether undertaken by public or private social welfare institutions, courts of law, administrative authorities or legislative bodies, the best interests of the child shall be a primary consideration.

and Article 16:

1   No child shall be subjected to arbitrary or unlawful interference with his or her privacy, family, home or correspondence, nor to unlawful attacks on his or her honour or reputation.

2   The child has the right to the protection of the law against such interference or attacks.

---

87 Source: 'Campbell wins privacy case against Mirror', by Owen Gibson, *Guardian*, 6 May 2004.

Article 24 of the Charter of Fundamental Rights of the European Union 2000 provides:

> (2) In all actions relating to children, whether taken by public authorities or private institutions, the child's best interests must be a primary consideration.

In English law, the Children and Young Persons Act 1933[88] and the Children Act 1989 protect the upbringing and – if necessary – anonymity of a child going through family court proceedings in England and Wales. The Victims and Witnesses (Scotland) Act 2014 introduced the same reporting restrictions in Scotland in September 2015.[89] These principles ensure that all decisions made in respect of children must be in their best interest and must be respected by all persons, including a child's parents or guardians and all private and public bodies. Any interference with a child's right to privacy will ultimately be decided by the courts who have the welfare of the child in mind.

See
Chapter 4.4

See below
2.5.2

There have been decisions made by the courts which conflict with parental interests, separate to those of the relevant child. Where there exists such conflict with the parents' interests, the courts tend to rule in the child's best interest and welfare, though relief will not always be granted under Article 8(1) ECHR, according to the ruling in the *AAA*[90] case.

2.5.1 Are parents seeking privacy via their children?

There is now a tendency by celebrities to include their children in lifestyle magazines or reality programmes which enhance their parents' celebrity status as 'yummy mummy' or 'superdad'. When we see the Beckhams' children Brooklyn, Romeo, Cruz and Harper Seven, or Kim Kardashian and Kanye West's daughter North, or Tamara Ecclestone breastfeeding baby Sophia in glamour magazines, we can be sure that the celebrities will have allowed publication of the children's images for financial gain by lucrative commercial contracts. Otherwise we would see celebrity children's photographs pixelated.

In *Re Z* (1996)[91] the CA granted an injunction to prevent publicity and identification of a child who attended a special school. The mother had consented to a TV company filming the child's particular treatment, and the TV programme was to show the results of the child's institutional care as well as the child's treatment in which the child and mother would play active roles. The CA held that the parent's right to waive a child's privacy rights is strictly limited, reiterating Lord Oliver's judgment in *Re KD (A Minor) (Ward: Termination of Access)*.[92]

---

88 The Criminal Justice and Courts Act 2015 inserted s 39A into the 1933 Act including 'Prohibition on publication of certain matters: providers of information society services' extending publication beyond the realm of 'newspapers'.

89 Section 15 Victims and Witnesses (Scotland) Act 2014 ('Reporting of proceedings involving children') amended restrictions on reporting proceedings involving children in s 47 Children (Scotland) Act 1995 so that they apply to a person under 18, rather than under 16. Section 47 of the 1995 Act puts certain restrictions on newspapers to prevent them revealing the identity of persons under 16 who are involved in criminal proceedings (as the person against or in respect of whom the proceedings are taken, or as a witness). However, the court has discretion to dispense with these requirements if it is satisfied that it is in the public interest to do so. The provisions also apply to sound and television programmes.

90 *AAA (by her litigation friend BBB) v Associated Newspapers* [2013] EWCA Civ 554; [2012] EWHC 2103 (QB).

91 *Re Z (A Minor) (Identification: Restrictions on Publication)* [1996] 2 FCR 164 CA.

92 *Re KD (A Minor) (Ward: Termination of Access)* [1988] FCR 657 (HL).

The leading case in relation to a permanent injunction regarding identification of a child is that of *Re S* (2004).[93] On 19 February 2003 a judge in the Family Division of the High Court (Hedley J) had dismissed an application for an injunction restraining the publication by newspapers of the identity of a defendant in a murder trial which had been intended to protect the privacy of her eight-year-old son (CS), who was not involved in the criminal proceedings. It is worth noting that this application for an injunction extended beyond the scope of section 39 Children and Young Persons Act 1933, the usual remedy provided by Parliament to protect juveniles directly affected by criminal proceedings.

See
Chapter 4.4

On 20 August 2001, CS's older brother DS, then aged nine, had died of acute salt poisoning in Great Ormond Street Hospital where he was a patient. Press reports about the death appeared soon afterwards, namely in the *Evening Standard* (22 August; also 28 August), headlined 'Poison Theory over Mystery Death of Boy, 9'; in a local newspaper, *The Recorder* (24 August), headlined, 'Police Probe into Boy's Death; in *The Independent* (29 August), headlined, 'Poisoning Suspected after Heart Attack Kills Boy Aged Nine' and many other newspapers. All these reports named the dead child and where he lived. Local papers also named his parents, his younger brother and his school. CS had been taken into care by the London Borough of Havering. The Court of Appeal then granted the injunction, and the various newspapers appealed, citing Article 10(1) of the Convention and the public interest test.

Through his guardian, the child subsequently challenged the majority decision of the Court of Appeal. Counsel for the child submitted that the majority misapplied the principle of proportionality in a case of competing rights under the ECHR (namely Articles 8 and 10) and in doing so exposed a vulnerable child to interference with his private and family rights. The child's counsel argued further that CS had a right to protection from publicity which could damage his health and well-being and risk emotional and psychiatric harm. Recognizing that the subject matter of the mother's trial was a matter of public interest, counsel for the child submitted that a proportionate response would be to permit only newspaper reports which did not refer to the family name or incorporate photographs of family members or the deceased boy.

Their Lordships carefully balanced the public interest test: publishing the name of the mother, accused of murdering her child by salt poisoning, against the welfare interests of her surviving child CS. Their Lordships commented that the public interest, in the legal sense, in publication was very strong. However, there was also strong expert evidence regarding the welfare interests of the surviving child CS.

The HL stated where the values of both Articles 8 and 10 ECHR are in conflict, an intense focus on the comparative importance of the specific rights being claimed in the individual case is necessary. Lord Bingham stated that the justifications for interfering with or restricting each right must be taken into account, and the proportionality test had to be applied to each. He called this 'the ultimate balancing test'.

Dismissing the appeal, the HL agreed with the original approach by Hedley J in the High Court. Lord Bingham said that granting an injunction on a child not directly

---

93 *S (FC) (A Child)* (Identification: Restrictions on Publication) [2004] UKHL 47 (HL); [2005] 1 AC 593 (on appeal from [2003] EWCA Civ 963) (also known as '*Re S*').

involved in criminal proceedings (of his mother) would be seen as a 'step too far'.[94] Their Lordships said that in future similar privacy applications (for adults or children) should follow the HL's decision in Campbell.

The HL judgment in Re S has been seen as a true triumph for the media.

Another leading case is that of David Murray,[95] concerning the then 19-month-old son David Murray, whose mother is the famous author of the Harry Potter series. The child was photographed covertly with a long lens by paparazzi from the Big Pictures agency in a buggy as the author was strolling in a public street in Edinburgh in November 2004. Big Pictures is a well-known celebrity photo agency which licenses its photos in the UK and internationally. The child's photograph was published in April 2005 (without the parents' permission) in the Sunday Express magazine, accompanying an article on Joanne Rowling's attitude to motherhood. J.K. Rowling and her husband Dr Murray sought an injunction to stop publication on behalf of their son David.

The question before the Court of Appeal was whether a small child being pushed in a buggy down the high street was 'private'. The CA found that it depends on the circumstances in which the photograph was taken which would determine if Article 8 ECHR can be engaged.

The CA stated that the circumstances in which a child has a legitimate expectation of privacy are wider than those in which an adult has such expectations: adults can expect a greater degree of intrusion as part of their daily lives, whilst a young child may be unaware of media hype. Furthermore, the court ruled that a child's right to privacy is distinct from that of each of its parents owing to its vulnerability and youth.

The court ruling in the David Murray case made it clear that a child's right to privacy is not entirely separate from that of his parents. Rather the court posed the question as to whether the child's right to privacy is engaged should not be determined by reference to the parents' own interest and actions.[96] The court made reference to parental conduct and motive when assessing whether an interference with the child's privacy is justifiable. The court recognized that parents can, in limited circumstances, waive a child's right to privacy – which many celebrities have done, such as the Beckhams with their children – but for financial gain.

The CA in Murray pointed out that children, unlike adults, are very unlikely to derive any benefit from publication of information. This does not mean that children should never be photographed in public, as long as it is not detrimental to the child at the time of publication or in the future. In any case, this should be in line with normal parental responsibility and the statutory duty to protect the child's well-being.

July 2011 involved another celebrity High Court action, namely Hugh Grant and Ms Ting Lang Hong. Paparazzi from the picture agency Splash News had constantly 'door-stepped' and harassed the mother of the actor's child, Ms Hong, until she sought a permanent undertaking from the High Court to be left alone and for the child's identity to be protected until at least his or her 18th birthday.[97] An illustrated article had appeared in

---

94 Ibid. at para. 17 (Lord Bingham of Cornhill).
95 Murray (David) v Express Newspapers and Others [2008] EWCA Civ 446 (CA) (also known as: 'Murray v Big Pictures'; also: 'J.K. Rowling case').
96 For further discussion see: Carter-Silk, A. and Cartwright-Hignett, C. (2009) pp. 212–217.
97 Ting Lang Hong and Child KLM v XYZ and Others [2011] EWHC 2995 (QB).

the *News of the World*, dated 8 April 2011, headlined 'Hugh's Secret Girl'. At the time of the publication Ms Hong had no idea that she was being followed and photographed.

The order was granted under section 1(1)(a) of the Protection from Harassment Act 1997, a ruling by Tugendhat J which has been used by celebrities in subsequent actions, providing enhanced measures of protection against paparazzi and media intrusion.

Also in 2011, the then still existing *News of the World* (*NoW*) was prevented by a privacy injunction from publishing salacious gossip about a well-known married male TV actor and his on-screen mistress (X). The source of *NoW*'s information suggested that this relationship became obvious to those with whom ETK and X were working, and more than 100,000 users of Twitter had already outed the identities of ETK and X. Towards the end of April 2010, ETK's wife had confronted him with her belief that he was having an affair. He admitted it. This was deeply distressing for the wife, but she and her husband determined, not least for the sake of their two teenage children, to rebuild her trust and their marriage. To that end ETK accepted that he would end his sexual relationship with X and he so informed her.

Nevertheless, ETK (by then known as 'K') sought an injunction under Article 8(1) ECHR giving the main reason that finding out about their father's affair would lead to 'distressing experiences in the playground' for his children. But was the main reason not to prevent *NoW* from reporting that X had been sacked from her job after a previous affair with another colleague? After successful cross-appeal from the newspaper, the case proceeded to the Court of Appeal.

Balancing Articles 8 and 10 ECHR, the CA held that that ETK's right to privacy and that of his family and children wholly outweighed *NoW*'s right to freedom of expression, since the harm that would be done to his family life would be 'detrimental'. Ward LJ held that ETK and X's sexual relationship was essentially a private matter, and the mere knowledge of their work colleagues did not put the information into the public domain (citing *Re S*;[98] *Browne v Associated Newspapers Ltd* (2007)[99] and *X v Persons Unknown* (2006)[100]). Weight had to be given not only to ETK's Article 8 rights but also to those of his wife, children and X.

The precedent set in ETK has since been widely used by celebrities and public figures, most notably (and unsuccessfully) by Andy Coulson and Rebekah Brooks (themselves former editors of *NoW*) in their attempts to prevent their own extramarital affair from being reported during the phone-hacking trial.

See Chapter 7.5

ETK was also cited in *Rocknroll v News Group Newspapers Ltd* (2013),[101] where actress Kate Winslet's new husband Edward (or 'Ned') had asked the High Court for an interim injunction prohibiting *The Sun* from printing semi-naked photographs of him taken in 2010.[102] Briggs J granted an interim injunction under Article 8(1) ECHR, establishing that Mr Rocknroll's right to respect for his family life – and that of Kate Winslet's children – should prevail over the newspaper's Article 10(1) right to freedom of expression. However, the order was lifted at trial, though the interest of Ms Winslet's children continued to be protected by a new anonymity order.

---

98 *Re. S (FC) (A Child)* (Identification: Restrictions on Publication) [2005] 1 AC 593.
99 [2007] EWCA Civ 295.
100 [2006] EWHC 2783 (QB).
101 [2013] EWHC 24 (Ch).
102 The then 34-year-old businessman was born Abel Smith but changed his name by deed poll to Edward Rocknroll in 2008. He is Richard Branson's nephew and ex-husband to socialite Eliza Pearson.

Lady Hale's judgment in *PJS* is worth noting regarding the interests of children when their celebrity parents seek privacy injunctions 'via the back door', using their children as 'a trump card':

> It is simply not good enough to dismiss the interests of any children who are likely to be affected by the publication of private information about their parents with the bland statement that 'these cannot be a trump card'. Of course they cannot always rule the day. But they deserve closer attention than they have so far received in this case, for two main reasons. . . . Not only are the children's interests likely to be affected by a breach of the privacy interests of their parents, but the children have independent privacy interests of their own. They also have a right to respect for their family life with their parents.[103]

These UK court rulings demonstrate that the courts will have to consider carefully the nature and extent of the likely harm to children's interests, which will result in the short, medium and longer terms from the publication of this kind of information about their parents. Lady Hale in *PJS* expressed the hope that privacy injunctions would make it possible that children could be protected from any risk of being damaged by media reporting about their parents and that media editors ought to exercise a degree of voluntary restraint in order to protect the paramount interest of children.

2.5.2 What price a child's privacy?

Until she turned 18, Flora Keays (born 31 December 1983 in Merton, Greater London) did not officially exist. She had been subject of a super injunction involving Flora's father, the late Cecil Parkinson, one-time right-hand man of Margaret Thatcher and rising star of the Conservative Party in the 1980s. His 12-year affair with Flora's mother Sara Keays – at the time his personal secretary – was exposed on 14 October 1983, after the papers revealed that Keays was bearing his child.

Suffering from physical and learning difficulties, Flora was subjected to a draconian court order, which forbade anyone from doing anything that could lead to her identity being revealed. It meant she could not appear in school photographs and was banned from class theatrical productions and that even her mother – could not talk about her life. After Flora's physical and mental health issues, including Asperger's, became an increasing burden, Sara sued Parkinson for maintenance, but it was granted only on condition of Parkinson's demanding the draconian injunction would continue until Flora turned 18 in 2002. On Flora's 18th birthday, the reporting restrictions and super injunction were finally lifted, and Flora herself revealed her heartbreak at being cut off from her own father – simply, it seems, because she was a political inconvenience. After Parkinson's death in 2016, Flora's name was not included in the death notice his family placed in the press, despite it mentioning his other children, grandchildren and even his two stepgrandsons.[104]

---

103 *PJS v News Group Newspapers Ltd* [2016] UKSC 26 at para. 72 (Lady Hale).
104 Source: 'Cecil Parkinson is still punishing his love child daughter from beyond the grave', by Dominic Utton, *Daily Express*, 10 May 2018.

Sara Keays published her own book about the controversy, *A Question of Judgement*,[105] in 1985. In January 2002, Channel 4 broadcast a documentary film on Sara and Flora Keays.[106]

Another controversial case involving a high-profile politician and a love child was that of *AAA* (2013).[107] The claimant baby and her mother brought an action before the High Court for breach of their privacy right under Art 8(1) ECHR and under the Protection from Harassment Act 1997 against the *Daily Mail* for the publication of an article and photographs during the summer of 2010. The *Daily Mail* argued that the publication of the photo was necessary in order to permit readers to see whether or not there was any family resemblance as between the baby and her supposed father (later known as former London Mayor and subsequently Conservative Foreign Secretary, and Prime Minister, Boris Johnson).[108]

AAA claimed damages for the behaviour of the journalists and photographers, who it was claimed had 'laid siege' to her family home as well as for the publication of her photograph and the articles, which contained speculation that on the identity of her famous philandering politician father AAA had been forced to stay with her maternal grandparents in Kent. The court heard about persistent ringing of her mother's doorbell, calling her mother's mobile telephone and shouting outside the home of Helen Macintyre (the child's mother, subsequently known).

AAA sought an injunction to restrain further publication of details reasonably likely to lead to her identification (in conjunction with information concerning her paternity) and her photograph. Further articles followed, and her photograph was republished despite assurances given by the publishers of the rail.

A year later, during June 2011, the claimant served proceedings on the defendant newspaper. Judge Nicola Davies ruled that AAA's privacy right had been breached and at the end of the six-day trial ordered the *Mail*'s publishers, Associated Newspapers, to pay £15,000 in damages for publishing photographs of the baby, though the judge pointed out that much of the information was already in the public domain, citing the CA in *Douglas v Hello!* (2006):

> Once intimate personal information about a celebrity's private life has been widely published it may serve no useful purpose to prohibit further publication.[109]

The court had evidence of Miss Macintyre AAA's mother's numerous conversations with friends and that she had told a gossip magazine executive at a party that Boris Johnson was the father of Stephanie (AAA). These facts had clearly compromised the claimant child's reasonable expectation of privacy. For these reasons, Davies J ordered AAA's legal representatives to pay 80 per cent of the newspaper's legal costs – an estimated £200,000. Miss Macintyre appealed against the cost order, but the Court of Appeal rejected her application.

---

105 Keays, S. (1985).

106 Source: 'Parkinson's daughter in a touching family drama with a sub-plot of revenge', by Simon Hoggart, *Guardian*, 10 January 2002.

107 *AAA v Associated Newspapers Ltd* [2013] EWCA Civ 554 (CA).

108 [2012] EWHC 2103 (QB) at 121–122.

109 [2006] QB 125 at 105.

At the appeal hearing the CA balanced the defendant newspaper's Article 10 rights with the claimant's Article 8 rights and justified publication as a high one of 'exceptional public interest', due to the baby's father's professional and private family life as a high-profile politician, married man and father of four children and his notoriety for extramarital adulterous liaisons. The claimant baby AAA was alleged to be the second such child conceived as a result of an extramarital affair of the supposed father.[110] Master of the Rolls Dyson LJ said: 'It is not in dispute that the legitimate public interest in the father's character is an important factor to be weighed in the balance against the child's expectation of privacy'.[111]

The CA also rejected any further privacy injunctions since much of the information had already been put in the public domain by Miss Macintyre, so that an injunction to prevent any further publication about this topic would have served no real purpose.

The ruling in *AAA* is clearly different from that of Murray: the CA in *AAA* found that the conduct of the child's mother had demonstrated ambivalence towards the baby's genuine privacy interest. There had been inconsistencies in her approach during the court proceedings, and the court questioned the mother's genuine interest and concern for the child's privacy. Most importantly, the paternity of *AAA* was already in the public domain, mostly advanced by the child's mother's own gossip at parties. The core information was that AAA's father (Boris Johnson) had had an adulterous affair with the mother (Miss Macintyre), deceiving both his own wife and the mother's partner.[112]

Mrs Justice Nicola Davies commented in *AAA* that when David Murray had actioned in privacy against *Express Newspapers* he had sued both the publishers and the paparazzi agency Big Pictures. This course of action had been open to the claimant in the *AAA* case but had not been taken.

The claimant child in *AAA* had relied on the privacy aspect in *Reklos and Davourlis v Greece* (2009).[113] But Davies J pointed out that in this case the Strasbourg Human Rights Court had stated that neither the child's lack of awareness of the taking or the existence of photographs, nor the fact that they revealed no private information (other than what the baby looked like), nor anything potentially embarrassing, had prevented there being an infringement of the child's right of privacy. The CA went even further in *AAA* when commenting that the information put 'out there' about the baby's father amounted to recklessness. For these reasons the CA held that the claimant's reasonable expectation of privacy under Article 8 was to be given less weight than would have been the position had the claimant's mother said or done nothing (as was the case with David Murray and his mother J. K. Rowling). As Davies J had concluded: 'This was a story which was going to be published. If the defendant had not done it, another newspaper would'.[114]

In the matter of M (Children) (2015),[115] Sir James Munby, then President of the Family Division, ordered complete anonymity and reporting restrictions on the four children of Asif Malik and Sara Kiran, aged between 20 months and seven years, all British citizens. The story broke with extensive newspaper reporting on Sunday 19 April 2015 about the family having suddenly left home without telling the wider family, who had reported

110 [2013] EWCA Civ 554 (CA).
111 Ibid. at 39 (Master of the Rolls, Dyson LJ).
112 For full coverage of the story see: 'Boris's secret lovechild and a victory for the public's right to know: Judge rejects lover's attempts to keep daughter's birth quiet', by Michael Seamark, *Daily Mail*, 20 May 2013.
113 (2009) (Application No 1234/05) (ECtHR).
114 [2012] EWHC 2103 (QB) at 129 (Davies J).
115 [2015] EWHC 1433 (Fam).

them missing. They had been caught on CCTV going through customs at the Port of Dover on 7 April 2015 at midnight. The acting Deputy Chief Constable of the Thames Valley Police had voiced concern that the family might be travelling to Syria. It transpired that the family was detained by Turkish authorities in Ankara. The UK Counter Terrorism Unit provided the court with intelligence that the parents had intended to cross into Syria with their children in order to join Islamic State.

After the family was deported from Turkey to Moldova, they eventually returned to the UK. The children were made wards of court, and a super injunction was granted under the application and extensive collaboration between the local authority, Slough Borough Council, Thames Valley Police and the Foreign and Commonwealth Office (FCO).

The super injunction in the case of the M-children was necessary so that the investigation into the abducting parents could be carried out without any information being leaked to the media. These applications were made *ex parte* and without notice.[116]

Whilst super injunctions must be deemed 'necessary' by the presiding judge they are, in their strictest form, a derogation from the *open justice principle* in that they seek:

1   a private hearing (*in camera*);
2   anonymity for the applicant (and other persons involved in the 'relationship');
3   that the entire court file should be sealed;[117] and
4   that the court order should prohibit publication of the existence of the proceed-
     ings, usually until after the conclusion of any trial.

See
Chapter 4.2

 FOR THOUGHT

Is it right for media companies to rely on parental consent where it is clear that publication is not in the interest of the child's welfare? Discuss with reference to the legal rights of a child.

2.6 Privacy orders and super injunctions

Not a month goes by when we don't learn that yet another top celebrity has taken out a so-called super injunction to prevent the press from reporting a story on their personal and professional life. This type of extreme 'gagging order' prevents any information which could lead to the identity of the celebrity involved, including their sex, the reason they are famous and information relating to the story. The order is usually cited against 'persons unknown', usually a newspaper, and forms a *contra mundum* injunction. This legal measure, granted a High Court is also called an 'anonymised privacy injunction' and has largely been used by rich and famous individuals, such as footballers, to cover up sexual infidelity. Though it is called a *contra mundum* 'banning' order, preventing publication of information across England and Wales, the injunction cannot stop media organizations from the rest of the world from printing details. Lawyers would have to seek an *interdict* in the Scottish High Court, separate from the super injunctions in the London High Court,

---

116 Ibid. at para. 37 (Munby P).
117 CPR 5.4 C (7).

if details of their client should not be leaked in the Scottish press. Users of social media have frequently circumvented a super injunction when details of the alleged infidelity or impropriety have been published online on servers outside England and Wales, such as Twitter, Facebook or Google. Any contempt of court punishment is then beyond the reach of English and Welsh judges.

There has been a steady rise in super injunctions to stop reporting of potentially embarrassing revelations of celebrities since 2000. Super injunctions that were sought – but not granted or subsequently lifted – involved, for instance, Garry Flitcroft, the then Blackburn Rovers football captain, millionaire and father of a seven-month-old daughter, who spent £200,000 trying to stop the *Sunday People* naming him in a story about him having extramarital affairs with a lap dancer and nursery nurse. The super injunction ended in 2002 when the Lord Chief Justice, Lord Woolf, turned down a final plea from the player's lawyers for his anonymity to be continued after learning that Flitcroft himself had negotiated with another newspaper to sell his version of events.

A couple of David Beckham's super injunctions failed. The first was in 2004, against Sky Broadcasting, when his former lover and personal assistant, Rebecca Loos, gave an interview about their four-month affair. Beckham's lawyers claimed that Loos had broken a confidentiality agreement.

In February 2017 a High Court super injunction failed to suppress a story about David Beckham's alleged foul-mouthed response to being snubbed for a knighthood. Beckham's lawyers had sought the injunction in December 2016, when the High Court accepted that emails written by Beckham and his PR advisers were stolen from a Portuguese company associated with Beckham's spokesman, Simon Oliveira. The injunction was to prevent the *Sunday Times* from publishing the emails.

However, the interim 'gagging order' was rendered worthless after a consortium of European media outlets from Romania to France published the contents of leaked emails which were part of a cache of 18.6m documents leaked to the German political magazine *Der Spiegel* via an individual called 'John' and his Football Leaks website. Several media organizations, including Germany's *Der Spiegel* and France's *L'Equipe*, published details of the cache. They reported how Beckham was angry at not being granted a knighthood in 2013, that the honours committee was concerned about his tax affairs and that he was annoyed to be asked for a major cash donation to Unicef, of which he was a global ambassador. In an email he had described the honours committee as 'a bunch of c**ts after he was overlooked for a Queen's honour.[118]

TV personality Andrew Marr used a gagging order to hush up a five-year extramarital affair with a BBC colleague in January 2008 and was subsequently the first public figure voluntarily to admit trying to conceal his infidelity. At the time, he believed he had fathered a child with the woman. He also made maintenance payments – until he discovered in 2011 through a DNA test that he was not the girl's father. Mr Marr told the *Daily Mail*: 'I did not come into journalism to go around gagging journalists. Am I embarrassed by it? Yes. Am I uneasy about it? Yes'.[119]

118 Source: 'Publication of hacked David Beckham emails renders injunction worthless', by Robert Booth and Jamie Grierson, *Guardian*, 6 February 2017; see also: 'Football Leaks: Legal gag on Times titles lifted after Sun and others reveal David Beckham 'c*nts' response to knighthood snub', by Dominic Ponsford, *Press Gazette*, 7 February 2017.
119 'Gagging orders are out of control, says Andrew Marr as he abandons High Court injunction over his extramarital affair', by Sam Greenhill, *Daily Mail*, 26 April 2011.

Other super injunctions included the then Chelsea football captain John Terry, England striker Wayne Rooney and Manchester United and Wales footballer Ryan Giggs, all of whom had had extramarital affairs and had the financial means to use expensive lawyers to exercise legal rights denied to ordinary members of the public.

2.6.1 Reporting restriction orders and anti-tipping-off orders

The general rule is that all court hearings be heard in public ('the open justice principle'). In special circumstance, mostly in the Family Court, the court will be asked to grant a reporting restriction order (RRO)[120]. The question before the judge is then what form those restrictions should take and what information is already in the public domain, say by previous media or social media publication. A pro-*contra mundum* order in the form of an RRO which has long been familiar in the Family Court Division of the High Court must be deemed appropriate and effective to achieve the desired result of anonymity, usually that of a child. An interim RRO is usually made to prohibit publication of a particular story in the press and for court proceedings to continue anonymously rather than being frustrated.

See
Chapter 4.4

Such non-disclosure orders – in whatever form (be they anonymity, *contra mundum* or super injunctions) – have also been referred to as anti-tipping-off orders; they prohibit the publication or disclosure of the fact of the proceedings and any order made for a short period to ensure that the purpose of the order is not frustrated through publicity. Such an order contains what can be characterized as the super-injunction element.

Examples of such orders in the context of civil proceedings are, for instance, search orders and freezing injunctions (*Anton Piller* order[121]). In such cases, temporary secrecy is essential in order to ensure that alleged wrongdoers are not tipped off to the order's existence, which would then enable them to frustrate its primary purpose.

In the context of family justice, non-disclosure orders are a well-established means to prevent tipping off in proceedings concerning the location of missing children, for example. Again, tipping off in such cases would frustrate the purpose of such proceedings. Temporary secrecy via non-disclosure is thus an essential feature of the proper administration of justice in such cases.

An anti-tipping-off order is usually be drafted in the following terms:

> **Example of a privacy ('anti-tipping-off') order**
>
> Judge X considers that it is strictly necessary, pursuant to CPR r 39.2(3)(a), (c) and (g), to order that the hearing of the application be in private, and there shall be no reporting of the same.

Plainly, such a privacy order should only be granted in an exceptional case where hearing the application in private is strictly necessary and where reporting on the matter would interfere with the course of justice.

---

120 Civil Procedure Rules (CPR) 39.2 (1) and (2).
121 See: *Anton Piller KG v Manufacturing Processes Ltd and Bernard Preston Wallace and Alfred Henry Stephen Baker* [1976] Ch 55.

> **Civil Procedure Rules 39.2**
>
> (3) A hearing, or any part of it, may be in private if –
>
> (a) publicity would defeat the object of the hearing;
>
> (b) it involves matters relating to national security;
>
> (c) it involves confidential information (including information relating to personal financial matters) and publicity would damage that confidentiality;
>
> (d) a private hearing is necessary to protect the interests of any child or protected party;
>
> (e) it is a hearing of an application made without notice and it would be unjust to any respondent for there to be a public hearing;
>
> (f) it involves uncontentious matters arising in the administration of trusts or in the administration of a deceased person's estate; or
>
> (g) the court considers this to be necessary, in the interests of justice.
>
> (4) The court may order that the identity of any party or witness must not be disclosed if it considers non-disclosure necessary in order to protect the interests of that party or witness.

2.6.2 What are super injunctions?

A super injunction (also referred to by the media as a 'double gagging order') is a term commonly given to an order restraining disclosure and publication of the claimant's identity and the fact the claim has been brought. These are usually interim court orders (injunctions) which prevent news organizations from revealing the identities of those involved in legal disputes or even reporting the existence of the injunction at all.

The subjects of a super injunction are initially only named in court proceedings by computer-generated acronyms, such as LNS (John Terry) or CTB (Ryan Giggs). Such anonymized privacy injunctions were in the past exclusively used in the family courts to protect the identity of juveniles and children in care, adoption or divorce proceedings. In their simplest form, super injunctions prevent the media from reporting what happens in court, usually on the basis that doing so could prejudice a trial or someone's right to privacy.[122]

See
Chapter 5.3

At a hearing which started on 8 December 2017, Warby J granted an interim super injunction, sought by claimant 'a famous entertainer', only known as LJY,[123]

---

122 Tugendhat and Christie (2016).
123 *LJY v Persons Unknown* [2017] EWHC 3230 (QB).

who was being black mailed. The anti-tipping-off order restrained the defendant(s) from publishing allegations of serious criminal misconduct by LJY. His representative, Jacob Dean (instructed by Taylor Wessing), had received a letter from a 'highly discreet organization', alleging that LJY had committed a very serious criminal offence against an unnamed female client. The letter did not disclose her identity or the details of the alleged offence. Payment of £50,000 was sought as 'financial recompense' for the client, payable within 96 hours of receipt of the letter. Part of the letter read:

> In the current political and social environment we feel sure you will understand that this will have lasting damage to your career, your reputation and your personal life. This would in turn almost certainly hurt you more than the modest financial settlement we are seeking.[124]

A reduced settlement figure was offered if he made contact within 48 hours. If payment was not made, the details of the case were to be released to several news agencies and online resources. An unregistered and untraceable phone number was provided for the claimant to communicate with the organization. The letter warned him not to advise anyone of its existence or the details would be disclosed. The claimant contacted the police and his solicitors. The police considered that the letter was a clear blackmail attempt and part of a scam due to its generic content. The police were aware of six letters in the same form.[125]

The hearing was in public, subject only to a temporary reporting restriction under s 4(2) of the Contempt of Court Act 1981. Although the defendants were not present at the hearing, at which they were accused of blackmail, they chose the cloak of anonymity, so there was no unfairness to them in a public hearing.

The reporting restriction was designed to protect the rights asserted by the claimant, by ensuring that the defendants could not know of the application until they were served with the injunction in accordance with the terms of the order. The defendants had threatened to publish the information at issue if the claimant went to the authorities. For this reason the judge accepted that the claimant was justified in applying to the High Court *without notice* to the defendants, despite the provisions of s 12(2) HRA (whenever Article 10(1) ECHR is at issue). Warby J stressed that he had no power to grant an injunction *unless* he was satisfied that LJY was likely to establish at trial that publication should not be allowed (in this context, the word 'likely' generally means more likely than not, as held in *Cream Holdings Ltd v Banerjee* (2004)[126]). In this case the issues concerned misuse of private information and harassment (including blackmail), which were sufficient proof that success at trial was likely.[127] This was the case, and Mr Justice Nicklin confirmed a permanent injunction at the High Court in January 2018.

---

124 Ibid. at para. 13.
125 Ibid. at paras 1–5 (Warby J).
126 [2005] AC 253.
127 Section 1(3) Protection from Harassment Act 1997.

In March 2018 Nicklin J granted another anti-tipping-off order in form of a super injunction on the grounds of blackmail and harassment, similar to LJY. In *NPV v QEL and ZED* (2018),[128] an interim non-disclosure and anti-harassment injunction was granted against the defendants. Nicklin J said that the evidence showed that the defendants had demanded, and continued to demand, payments of large sums of money from NPV, 'a successful, married businessman', under the threat of exposing NPV's adulterous relationship with QEL.

QEL was an employee of a business. She held a customer service role and consequently met members of the public during her work. In early 2017, she had met NPV in the course of her employment, subsequently meeting him socially for a drink. By doing so, QEL broke rules prohibiting contact between employees and customers. She was suspended and became subject to a disciplinary process. NPV supported QEL through this process, and a sexual relationship developed between them. Whilst the disciplinary process was still ongoing, QEL resigned as an employee, and NPV gave her some financial support. Increasingly, QEL became more demanding and asked NPV for money. He refused. NPV then received a telephone call from ZED, the second defendant, in which ZED said that he worked for a media agency and that he was working on an article about powerful people who abused their positions and that he intended to cite NPV as an example. ZED told NPV that for £75,000 the matter 'would go away'. NPV applied to the court, without notice to QEL and ZED, for an interim injunction for misuse of private information and harassment. Nicklin J granted the interim injunction and served the order on ZED by text message (at that point QEL and ZED were still expecting the blackmail ransom). It is worth noting that at this point, the judge only had NPV's evidence to go on in making his decision. The defendants did not have the chance to prove their side of the story.

In *GYH v Persons Unknown* (2018),[129] an interim super injunction was granted by Warby J (without notice at a hearing held on 14 December 2017). The injunction was made permanent by Knowles J at a later hearing, restraining the defendant newspaper from publishing information of various items of the claimant's personal information in what was described as a campaign of harassment and defamation. GHY was described in the judgment as a transgender woman who works as an escort providing sexual and companionship services to her clients under a work name. She actively manages this work through the use of social media, specifically Facebook, YouTube and a blogging channel.

On or around 4 December 2015, GHY received a text message from an unknown person requesting to meet with her personally, but without paying for the usual services she gave as part of her work. GHY declined the request to meet, and the conversation then deteriorated into abuse. What followed was a wide-ranging campaign of online harassment which involved posting information on a number of websites using both GHY's legal and work names.

The content of these websites was said to contain a number of oppressive and unpleasant features which included:

---

128 [2018] EWHC 703 (QB) (28 March 2018).
129 [2018] EWHC 121 (QB).

- purported private information that GHY was mentally ill, anorexic, practised unsafe sex with her partner and had HIV;
- allegations that the claimant offered services in the knowledge that she had STDs and/or HIV, and that she practised unsafe sex during the course of her work; and
- a number of images, some of which had been altered, which graphically detailed intimate and private information which exacerbated the above allegations.

It is a long-standing principle that (super) injunctions are not generally granted in defamation actions. In the case of GHY, the court granted the injunction only in conjunction with the harassment claim with a real prospect that the claim was going to succeed at trial. The applicant cited defamation and harassment. For this reason the court is required to consider the defamation rule if it suspects 'cause of action shopping' (i.e. where the court determines that the claimant's objective is to prevent damage to reputation). As Buxton LJ said in *McKennitt v Ash* (2006):[130]

> If it could be shown that a claim in breach of confidence was brought where the nub of the case was a complaint of the falsity of the allegations, and that that was done in order to avoid the rules of the tort of defamation, then objections could be raised in terms of abuse of process.[131]

See
Chapter 3

If such an order (including an interim injunction) is disclosed, say by a newspaper, this can amount to contempt of court – but only if the publication is in breach of an *express* prohibition: for example, where the court order expressly prohibits the publication of certain information relating to the hearing or the proceedings, to third parties with knowledge of such an order.

GYH demonstrates that the courts are increasingly using super injunctions to protect the subject from harassment and possible damage to reputation.

2.6.3 Notorious privacy injunctions

Let us have a look at some famous (super) injunctions – or '(double) gagging orders' as the media call them – and ask the question: do privacy injunctions actually work, or are they meaningless in the social media age? Because of the randomly selected alphabet acronyms by the High Court computer, these anonymity orders are notoriously difficult to

---

130 [2006] EWCA Civ 1714 (Buxton, Latham and Longmore LJJ). Loreena McKennitt (M), a Canadian citizen and a well-known folk music recording artist, had claimed that a substantial part of the book written by Niema Ash (N), her former friend, revealed personal and private details about her that she was entitled to keep private (*Travels with Loreena McKennitt: My Life as a Friend*, 2005). Their Lordships concluded that M was very protective of her privacy, that M and N had had a very close friendship during which N had acquired confidential information about M and that N realized that substantial parts of the book would fall within the scope of a reasonable expectation of privacy or a duty of confidence. The judge granted protection in relation to information about M's personal and sexual relationships, her personal feelings and in particular in relation to her deceased fiancé and the circumstances of his death, her health and emotional vulnerability, the terms of a recording contract and a legal dispute between M and N that had been settled. The original judge (Eady J) had been correct to conclude that M had a reasonable expectation of privacy in the information that she was granted her Article 8 ECHR right.

131 Ibid. at para. 79 (Buxton LJ).

find via legal databases such as Westlaw or Lexis, for example *G and G v Wikimedia Foundation Inc.* (2009).[132] It is only when such injunctions are lifted that we find out the applicants' identities.

One of the first super injunctions was that of 'Trafigura'. The United Nations 'Minton Report',[133] commissioned in September 2006, based on 'limited' information, had exposed that a toxic waste-dumping incident had taken place at locations around Abidjan in Ivory Coast in August 2006, involving the multinational Dutch oil company Trafigura. The Minton Report revealed that truckloads and shiploads of chemical toxic waste from a Trafigura cargo ship, the *Probo Koala*, had been illegally fly-tipped. The Ivorian authorities claimed that tens of thousands of people in Abidjan had been affected by fumes, reporting serious breathing problems, sickness and diarrhoea, and that 15 people had died.

On 12 October 2009, Labour MP Paul Farrelly tabled a question in the House of Commons (HC) for then Justice Secretary Jack Straw to answer questions in relation to Trafigura's alleged dumping of toxic oil and the UN Minton Report. The second part of Mr Farrelly's question was of greater interest to freedom of speech in Parliament, as it concerned the super injunction obtained by solicitors Carter-Ruck, acting on behalf of Trafigura at the time. Strictly speaking, the 'Trafigura' injunction of 11 September 2009 had prevented the *Guardian* (and therefore all other UK media outlets) from identifying the MP, what the question in Parliament was, which minister might answer it and where the question was to be found.[134] All that could be reported was that the case involved the London libel lawyers Carter-Ruck.

The *Guardian* had requested disclosure of the Minton Report under a freedom of information access request in December 2009,[135] but all matters concerning the report and the spilling of toxic waste off Ivory Coast had been 'gagged' under the injunction against the newspaper. The Twitterati revealed that Trafigura lawyers Carter-Ruck had attempted to prevent the issue being raised in Parliament, relying on the *sub judice* rule. Nevertheless, Mr Farrelly still referred to the 'Trafigura' super injunction in Parliament, thereby breaching the *sub judice* rule of the injunction, relying on his defence of parliamentary privilege.

Numerous tweets called into question the privilege which guarantees free speech in Parliament, and Peter Bottomley, Tory MP for Worthing West, threatened to report the law firm Carter-Ruck to the Law Society. Within 12 hours of the parliamentary debate, millions of people around the world knew of the Minton Report, and Trafigura had become one of the most searched-for internet terms.

The 'Trafigura' injunction was subsequently lifted, and senior managers at Trafigura and their lawyers admitted that their approach may have been a little 'heavy-handed', insisting it had not been their intention to try to silence Parliament. Trafigura agreed to

---

132 [2009] EWHC 3148 (QB).
133 The United Nations 'Minton Report' (September 2009) had exposed a toxic waste-dumping incident in August 2006 in Ivory Coast, involving the multinational Dutch oil company Trafigura.
134 *RJW and SJW v Guardian News and Media Limited* [2009] EWHC 2540 (QB); [2011] 1 WLR 294 ('Trafigura injunction').
135 The author of this initial draft study, John Minton, of consultants Minton, Treharne and Davies, said dumping the waste would have been illegal in Europe, and the proper method of disposal should have been a specialist chemical treatment called wet air oxidation. Source: 'Minton Report: Carter-Ruck give up bid to keep Trafigura study secret', by David Leigh, *Guardian*, 17 October 2009.

pay out more than £30m to some 30,000 Abidjan inhabitants who had been affected by the toxic waste. But all was not over yet.

Trafigura subsequently sued the BBC's *Newsnight* for libel after the company was criticized on the programme on 13 May 2009.[136] Trafigura's lawyers claimed that the oil traders had been wrongly accused of causing deaths and not just sickness in Ivory Coast. The BBC's defence was that it had merely focused on the gasoline waste dumped by Trafigura in Abidjan in August 2006, with *Newsnight* reporting that Trafigura's actions had caused deaths, miscarriages, serious injuries and sickness with long-term chronic effects.

After lengthy negotiations with Trafigura's director, Eric de Turckheim, the BBC agreed to settle on 17 December 2009, by apologizing for the investigatory programme and paying £25,000 to a charity. As part of the 'offer of amends', the public broadcaster had to withdraw any allegation that Trafigura's toxic waste dumped in West Africa had caused deaths. The BBC still issued a separate combative statement, pointing out that the dumping of Trafigura's hazardous waste had led to the British-based oil trader being forced to pay out £30m in compensation to victims. The BBC's decision to settle caused dismay in journalistic circles because the public broadcaster was penalized for trying to report what had been factually raised in Parliament and by the United Nations.

Since the disclosure of the *Trafigura* oil scandal in 2009 by way of parliamentary privilege, MPs have repeatedly broken several (super) injunctions by naming public figures and celebrity footballers, such as Ryan Giggs or John Terry.

On 22 January 2010, lawyers acting for the then England football captain, John Terry, asked the High Court for a prohibition in the form of an interim super injunction on publishing details of a 'specific personal relationship' between their client and 'another person'. The LNS 'double gagging order' (2010)[137] sought complete privacy, stating that any publication of any information, including photographs, evidencing the extramarital relationship could lead to harming the private family life of the applicant.

John Terry's lawyers argued that the intended publication in the *News of the World* (*NoW*) would amount to a breach of confidence and misuse of private information in that £1m had been promised to an informant to keep the story quiet. The newspaper was about to publish their scoop on the footballer's adulterous affair with French underwear model Vanessa Perroncel, who happened to be the former girlfriend of Terry's friend and teammate Wayne Bridge. The story was to be the front-page headline on Sunday 24 January 2010.

Opposing the injunction at the hearing on 29 January 2010, lawyers for Rupert Murdoch's News Group Newspapers made a strong submission before Tugendhat J, supporting freedom of expression under Article 10(1) ECHR, thereby invoking s 12 HRA and the public's 'right to know' (i.e. that John Terry as England football captain was a role model to many young people and prided himself on being a family man).

See below 2.6.5

The problem in the *John Terry* super injunction[138] was that the famous Chelsea footballer claimed not to know the name of the newspaper that had a specific interest in his story. In Terry's case, Tugendhat J did not accept that explanation since it had become quite clear that the *News of the World* intended to publish on Sunday 24 January 2010 the story about Terry's affair

---

136 *Trafigura Limited v British Broadcasting Corporation* [2009] QBD 15 May 2009. Claim No: HQ09X02050. Unreported.
137 *LNS v Persons Unknown* [2010] EWHC 119 ('John Terry super injunction').
138 John Terry (LNS) [2010] EWHC 119 (QB).

with the lingerie model, Vanessa Perroncel. The public interest lay in the fact that Terry was England football captain at the time and had portrayed himself as a 'clean-living' family man.

Tugendhat J considered Articles 6, 8 and 10 of the Convention in turn, giving additional consideration to the open justice principle. Balancing one right against the other, he considered the right to speak freely, the right to private life and reputation and the right to a fair hearing. The judge noted that there was no evidence before the court and no personal representation from the applicant of proof to convince him to apply the right to privacy under Article 8(1) ECHR, nor was there proof that any confidentiality had been breached: Terry had produced no relevant photographs, nor did he evidence any confidential or private information. For this reason Tugendhat J lifted the interim order, stating *inter alia* that privacy law was not there to protect someone's reputation, which in this case included the footballer's commercial interests (e.g. sponsorship by Daddies Sauce, Umbro, Samsung and Nationwide).

After *John Terry* the press – particularly in Scotland – became increasingly daring and aggressive in their revelations about other infidelities and indiscretions of celebrities, often completely ignoring any super injunctions which might have been in place at the time, particularly where the celebrities' lawyers had not sought an interdict at the High Court in Scotland.

One of these was the *Ryan Giggs* super injunction.[139] Despite the court anonymity order, the extramarital affair of the then married Manchester United and Wales football star – referred to only as 'CTB' in the order – with lingerie model Imogen Thomas was widely exposed on Twitter and other social networking sites in May 2011. Mr Giggs' lawyers also hoped that a High Court order would force Twitter to hand over the names and email and IP addresses of those persons behind the Twitter accounts of UK individuals who had disclosed Giggs' identity and that they would be prosecuted for breaches of a court order (i.e. contempt of court). This resulted in a warning by the then Lord Chief Justice, Lord Judge, that 'modern technology was totally out of control'. He granted a *Norwich Pharmacal* search order against the US-based Twitter site on Friday 20 May 2011 in an attempt to compel the social media site provider to identify those responsible for naming the footballer.

The Ryan Giggs 'gagging order'[140] made sensational headlines in the Glasgow-based *Sunday Herald* because the Scottish newspaper named the footballer in spite of the (English) court privacy order (super injunction). The Herald's front-page 'splash' featured the footballer with a thin black band across his eyes and the word 'censored' in capital letters. Ryan Giggs was easily recognizable, and the caption below the photograph read:

> Everyone knows that this is the footballer accused of using the courts to keep allegations of a sexual affair secret. But we weren't supposed to tell you that.[141]

Richard Walker, then editor of Glasgow's *Sunday Herald*,[142] had taken the courageous decision to name the England footballer on the front page on Sunday 22 May 2011. In an

---

139 *CTB (Ryan Giggs)* [2011] EWHC 1326 (QB).
140 *CTB v News Group Newspapers* [2011] EWHC 1326 (QB) ('Ryan Giggs super injunction').
141 Source: *Sunday Herald*, front page, 22 May 2011.
142 The *Sunday Herald* was axed after 19 years, with its final edition published on 2 September 2018. Owners Newsquest published two new titles from 9 September 2018, the *Herald on Sunday* and *The Sunday National*.

accompanying editorial, Richard Walker commented[143] that he had taken the decision to identify the footballer just hours before the paper went to press (on Saturday), following legal advice from Paul McBride QC[144] and media lawyer David McKie[145] that the English privacy injunction did not apply in Scotland. In an interview with the author of this book, Richard Walker said:

> Our piece, naming Ryan Giggs, was not so much about his sexual infidelities but about the principle of privacy and super injunctions taken out by famous celebrities having been exposed on Twitter and that the internet was now exposing stories about Strauss-Kahn's alleged past sexual behaviour and that of others, such as (Sir) Fred Goodwin and his super injunction trying to suppress an affair with a senior colleague at Royal Bank of Scotland. Initially we were looking to portray Ryan Giggs as a pixelated front page photo but then it occurred to me that the injunction would not be in force in Scotland so I took legal advice and the advice was that that was indeed the case.[146]

Two days after Ryan Giggs had been named in the Glasgow *Sunday Herald*, the footballer was identified by the Liberal Democrat MP, John Hemming, in the House of Commons, using parliamentary privilege. Ultimately, the injunction was compromised between Mr Giggs and the woman he had had an affair with, supermodel Imogen Thomas. On 15 December 2011, Ms Thomas issued a public statement categorically denying that she was the source of the *Sun* article and that she had not blackmailed Giggs (as he had alleged when applying for the super injunction on 14 April 2011). Ultimately Tugendhat J struck out the injunction (*Giggs No 2*)[147], a full six months *after* the world had learnt of Mr Giggs' identity. In his March 2012 judgment, Tugendhat J said that there was 'no purpose' in allowing the super injunction to continue:

> There can be few people in England and Wales who have not heard of this litigation. The initials CTB have been chanted at football matches when Mr Giggs has been playing for Manchester United. And Mr Giggs has been named in Parliament, raising questions as to the proper relationship between Parliament and the judiciary.[148]

Evidently the *Ryan Giggs* No 1 and No 2 privacy orders did not achieve their purpose. Had Mr Giggs known in April 2011, at the time the principal injunction was sought, that Imogen Thomas was not the source of the *Sun* article, it may well have been that the footballer would not have sought an order against NGN to gag the press. But Mr Giggs' lawyers thought otherwise. In *Giggs No 2* (March 2012) his lawyers asked for aggravated

---

143 Source: 'Sex, lies and private laws'. Analysis by Richard Walker. *Sunday Herald*, 22 May 2011, pp. 12–16.
144 Paul McBride (1964–2012) was a leading Scottish criminal lawyer. He died suddenly on a trip to Pakistan, aged 47.
145 David McKie, partner in the Glasgow law firm Levy & McRae. In an interview with the author on 2 July 2015, Mr McKie recounted the complex legal background to the Ryan Giggs' publication in the *Sunday Herald*.
146 Source: Richard Walker in an interview with the author on 2 July 2015 at the *Glasgow Herald* headquarters.
147 *Ryan Giggs (No 2)* [2012] EWHC 431 (QB).
148 Ibid. at para. 1 (Tugendhat J).

damages, seemingly only directed against Imogen Thomas; Tugendhat J dismissed the application.

Another prominent figure was also named in Parliament during the existence of a (super) injunction, namely the former Royal Bank of Scotland (RBS) Chief Executive, (then Sir) Fred Goodwin.[149] The Liberal Democrat Peer, Lord Stoneham, revealed during a debate in the House of Lords in May 2011 that Sir Fred had obtained a super injunction to stop press reports that he was having a sexual relationship with a colleague.

Sir Fred's application for an injunction in March 2011 before Mrs Justice Sharp alleged that the tabloid newspaper *News of the World* (NoW) was threatening his right to privacy by intending to publish details of his secret relationship with an RBS colleague. The injunction sought, known as MNB,[150] also prevented the publication of the identity of the woman.

At a subsequent hearing on application by NGN, Mr Justice Tugendhat lifted the injunction in parts, with a lifelong ban on the identity of the woman and details of the affair.[151] *News of the World* were content in keeping the name of the woman super-injuncted. Sir Fred was stripped of his knighthood in 2012.

In October 2011, former BBC *Top Gear* presenter Jeremy Clarkson 'outed' his own super injunction by stating that these 'gagging orders' are 'pointless'. Clarkson told the *Daily Mail*:

> Super injunctions don't work. You take out an injunction against somebody or some organization and immediately news of that injunction and the people involved and the story behind the injunction is in a legal free world on Twitter and the internet.[152]

In the aptly named *AMM* ('Aston Martin Man') v *HXW* ('His ex-wife'), Super injunction[153] Mr Clarkson had applied for a 'gagging' order in September 2010 to restrain his former wife, Alex Hall, from publishing a book about their extramarital affair, *after the* couple had divorced and Clarkson had remarried. Edwards-Stuart J granted the injunction after hearing that Ms Hall (HXW) had blackmailed Mr Clarkson by threatening to expose their relationship to the media unless he paid a 'very substantial sum' of hush money. As soon as the order was served on the *Daily Mail* (Associated Newspapers Ltd) on 30 September 2010, the 'Jeremy Clarkson super injunction' story reached the Twittersphere, with the 'red tops' freely reporting on it.[154]

---

149 Former CEO of the Royal Bank of Scotland (RBS), Fred Goodwin oversaw the multibillion-pound deal to buy Dutch rival ABN Amro at the height of the financial crisis in 2007, which led to RBS having to be bailed out to the tune of £45bn by taxpayers.

150 *MNB v News Group Newspapers Ltd* [2011] EWHC 528 (QB) (Sharp J).

151 *Goodwin (Sir Fred) v News Group Newspapers* [2011] EWHC 1309 (QB) (Tugendhat J).

152 Source: 'Jeremy Clarkson lifts the gag on his ex-wife: She claims she had an affair with Top Gear star after he remarried', by Michael Seamark, *Daily Mail*, 27 October 2011.

153 [2010] EWHC 2457 (QB); [2010] All ER (D) 48 (Oct) ('Jeremy Clarkson super injunction').

154 Smartt, U. (2011), pp. 135–140.

In May 2011 the Neuberger Report[155] established the framework in which future applications for super injunctions ('anonymized injunctions') should be made. Master of the Rolls, Lord Neuberger's Committee had been formed in April 2010 following a report of the Culture, Media and Sport House of Commons Select Committee and in the light of growing public concerns about the use and effect of super injunctions and the impact they were having on open justice. The report stresses the fundamental principles of open justice and freedom of speech and that 'secrecy orders' should only be made if they are 'strictly necessary' in the interests of justice; a fair balance should be struck by the courts in making such orders between the principles of freedom of expression and an individual's right to privacy.

As common law and ECtHR jurisprudence have developed, the courts have stressed that the 'necessity' for any restriction on freedom of expression must be convincingly established as a matter of general principle. Mindell argues that there are two forms of privacy that are protected in English law: the torts of trespass (to the person and to land) and protection under the Human Rights Act 1998.[156] The author further argues that there exist 'secondary forms of privacy': the first being 'the informational realm' and the other 'territorial information', depicted in *Peck v UK*[157] (personal information).

 FOR THOUGHT

With social media's widespread dissemination of protected information about celebrities' private lives, would you agree that the main objective of a super injunction is now largely unachievable? Discuss.

2.6.4 PJS: the 'celebrity threesome' super injunction

In January 2016, a celebrity only named as PJS applied to the London High Court for an interim injunction to prevent the *Sun on Sunday* publishing a story on a 'celebrity three-some' and further preventing *The Sun* (and other newspapers) from printing details of PJS' extramarital affairs. Interestingly, this was not a super injunction (since the newspaper was named). This resulted in the fact that – by March 2016 – every British editor knew the true identity of PSJ and YMA, and everyone who really wanted to find out about the marital commitment of the two men and their two small children could either find their names via social media or *Scottish Mail on Sunday* which released the names and photos of the 'celebrity couple' on 10 April 2016 in their print edition (on the front page and page 6). Lawyers for PJS later regretted not taking out a 'double gagging' order; they also had not sought an interdict in the Scottish courts. American and Canadian newspapers (and

155 Master of the Rolls (2011) Report of the Committee on Super-Injunctions: Super-Injunctions, Anonymised Injunctions and Open Justice ('the Neuberger Report'): www.judiciary.gov.uk/Resources/JCO/Documents/Reports/super-injunctionreport – 20052011.pdf.
156 Mindell, R. (2012), pp. 52–58.
157 (2003) 36 EHRR 719.

their online editions) also reported about the 'celebrity couple' and that the 'betrayal by a cheating husband' would result in a '$450m divorce'.

The Sun and Guardian newspapers appealed the injunction, arguing that such a 'gagging order' had become meaningless in the internet and social media age. The Court of Appeal duly dismissed the interim injunction with the proviso that PJS had a couple of days in which to appeal to the Supreme Court.[158] This meant that the 'well-known' celebrity who reportedly had a 'three-way sexual encounter' between 2009–2011 and his husband were still to be kept anonymized.

A new ground for the application of an interim injunction had been sought, namely, 'in the interest of children'. Lord Jackson stressed, however, that children should not be used 'as a trump card'. He also said that the two children would, in due course, learn about these matters from their mates in the playground and via social media. Clearly reasons for privacy injunctions had shifted: there were no longer claims of blackmail or threats to PJS' other family members, as had been the reason given in the John Terry[159] or Jeremy Clarkson[160] super injunctions.

The UK Supreme Court gave one if its speediest rulings in legal history (within one month) in May 2016 in PJS,[161] upholding the interim injunction by a majority in the light of extensive media interest. The judgment was streamed on live TV and was available via YouTube. The grounds cited by the Supreme Court justices centred on the privacy interests of the appellant (PJS), his partner (YMA) and their two young children (pending a trial). Their Lordships commented that the forthcoming trial against the newspaper was likely to involve further tortious invasion of privacy of the appellant and his partner as well as of their children, who had of course no conceivable involvement in the conduct in question.

The court observed that those interested in a prurient story could, if they so wished, easily read about the identities of those involved in the Scottish and American media and find in great detail all the unpleasant details about PJS' conduct with another couple.

The UKSC found no evidence of 'public interest' in any legal sense in the story involving PJS, though the respondent newspapers (mainly The Sun) hoped during the interim injunction that further evidence would emerge at trial. The court ruled that the media storm which would ensue had their Lordships discharged the injunction would have unleashed more enduring media and social networking attention with an even more damaging and everlasting invasion of privacy particularly of the children.[162]

See below
2.6.5

The celebrity couple eventually settled out of court, and the injunction regarding PJS' and YMA's identities and those of their children were permanently protected by a final injunction granted at the Queen's Bench Division on 4 November 2016. Other ciphers

158 PJS v News Group Newspapers Ltd [2016] EWCA Civ 100 (Jackson and King LJJ).
159 John Terry (LNS) v Persons Unknown [2010] EWHC 119 (QB).
160 AMM v HXW [2010] EWHC 2457 (Jeremy Clarkson super injunction).
161 PJS [2016] UKSC 26 (Lord Mance, Lord Neuberger, Lady Hale and Lord Reed; Lord Toulson dissenting).
162 Ibid. at paras 44–45.

for three persons – AB, CD and EF – with whom PJS had had a relationship and/or sexual encounter were also permanently protected by the order and Art 8 ECHR.[163]

Louise Berg and Michael Skrein of the media law firm Reed Smith commented on the company's website that PJS 'will have fought tooth and nail to preserve the injunction' and that 'maybe he just didn't like to lose'.[164] The lawyers accused the UKSC however of failing to acknowledge the realities of a connected and globalized media landscape, echoing the dissenting judge, Lord Toulson, who warned, 'the court must live in the world as it is and not as it would like it to be'.[165]

2.6.5 The importance of section 12 HRA 1998

Whenever an application for an injunction concerning a celebrity, royal or public figure is made, the media will invoke their Article 10(1) ECHR right to freedom of expression. A claimant who applies for an interim restraining order (or interim injunction) against a publisher is obliged to give advance notice of the application under section 12 HRA, especially where the publisher or media organization relies on their Article 10(1) ECHR right to 'freedom of expression'. In Scotland such an order would be called an *interdict* and would have to be applied for separately at the High Court in Edinburgh.

In considering the application, the high court judge will then weigh up the applicant's privacy right (Article 8(1) ECHR) – as well as consider the 'public interest' test and the media's Article 10(1) right. As soon as the legal representatives of the media organization apply for the injunction to be discharged, the court will invoke section 12 HRA.

It has become clear that a claimant's privacy right weighs less against the media's freedom of expression when the facts are already generally known about the celebrity claimant's indiscretions. Greater protection is usually extended by the courts to privacy rights than to rights in relation to confidential material (see: *OBG Ltd v Allan* (2007);[166] *ETK v News Group Newspapers Ltd* (2011)[167]). That said, the claimant may still have a damages claim for misuse of private information.

It is important to consider section 12 HRA 1998 in its entirety; it reads:

1   This section applies if a court is considering whether to grant any relief which, if granted, might affect the exercise of the Convention right to freedom of expression.

2   If the person against whom the application for relief is made ('the respondent') is neither present nor represented, no such relief is to be granted unless the court is satisfied:

---

163   *PJS v News Group Newspapers Ltd* [2016] EWHC 2770 (QB); [2016] All ER (D) 29, 4 November 2016.
164   Source: 'Privacy in a Connected World: The Celebrity Threesome Injunction', by Louise Berg and Michael Skrein, 20 May 2016 at www.reedsmith.com/Privacy-in-a-Connected-World-The-Celebrity-Threesome-Injunction-05–20–2016.
165   Ibid. at para. 86 (Lord Toulson dissenting).
166   [2007] UKHL 21.
167   [2011] EWCA Civ 439.

(a) that the applicant has taken all practicable steps to notify the respondent; or

(b) that there are compelling reasons why the respondent should not be notified.

3 No such relief is to be granted so as to restrain publication before trial unless the court is satisfied that the applicant is likely to establish that publication should not be allowed.

4 The court must have particular regard to the importance of the Convention right to freedom of expression and, where the proceedings relate to material which the respondent claims, or which appears to the court, to be journalistic, literary or artistic material (or to conduct connected with such material), to:

(a) the extent to which (i) the material has, or is about to, become available to the public; or (ii) it is, or would be, in the public interest for the material to be published;

(b) any relevant privacy code.

The effect of section 12(3) HRA is that a court is not to make an interim restraining order unless satisfied that the applicant's prospects of success at trial are sufficiently favourable to justify such an order being made in the particular circumstances of the case and taking into account the relevant jurisprudence under Article 10 ECHR. If there is any public interest, Article 10(1) will triumph over the individual's right to privacy. According to section 12(3), an injunction before trial is not granted unless the court is satisfied that the applicant is likely to establish that publication should not be allowed.

If granted, the order is then binding on the party against whom injunctive relief is sought (and binding *contra mundum*) by application of the *Spycatcher* principle, unless:

1 the claimant has no reason to believe that the non-party has or may have an existing specific interest in the outcome of the application;

2 the claimant is unable to notify the non-party having taken all practicable steps to do so; or

3 there are compelling reasons why the non-party should not be notified.

See above 2.2

Looking at the judgment by Tugendhat J in *LNS* (John Terry), it appears that the general approach by the courts in the granting (or continuation) of (super)injunctions tends to be 'exceedingly slow', by making an interim restraining order where the applicant has not satisfied the court that he would probably succeed at trial.[168] However, where the potentially adverse consequences of disclosure are particularly grave – say, in family cases involving children or where a short-lived injunction is needed to enable the court to hear and give proper consideration to an application for interim relief pending trial (see PJS) or any relevant appeal – the courts have granted such restraining orders under section 12 HRA with great expediency (see: *X (a woman formerly known as Mary Bell) and another v O'Brien and others* (2003)[169]).

See Chapter 4.4

168 Ibid. at 120 (Tugendhat J).
169 [2003] EWHC 1101 (QB).

Once a court has considered section 12(3) HRA, the court is obliged to have regard to the public interest in the matter before the court and subject matter of the (super) injunction. The test is set out in section 12(4) HRA. Under section 12(4)(b), the court must have particular regard to any relevant press or broadcasting privacy code.[170]

Section 12(4)(a)(ii) provides guidance on how the evidence available to the court must be approached and whether there is effectively (no) public interest in a legal sense in further disclosure or publication. As to the factor in section 12(4)(a)(i), the requirement is to have particular regard to the extent to which journalistic material (or conduct connected with such material) 'has, or is about to, become available to the public'. And the question whether material has, or is about to, become available to the public will then be considered by the court with reference to, inter alia, the medium and form in relation to which injunctive relief is sought.

The Supreme Court in PJS specifically considered section 12(4) HRA and the effect of the social media and internet disclosures already in the public domain (Scotland and United States) and how these would – in future – impact on the children of the celebrity couple.[171] The court said that there had been too much focus on those disclosures and not enough emphasis on the 'qualitative difference in intrusiveness and distress' that was likely to be involved if there was unrestricted publication by the English media in hard copy, as well as on their own internet sites.[172] Lord Mance said:

> There is little doubt that there would be a media storm. It would involve not merely disclosure of names and generalised description of the nature of the sexual activities involved, but the most intimate details. This would be likely to add greatly and on a potentially enduring basis to the intrusiveness and distress felt by the appellant, his partner and, by way of increased media attention now and/or in the future, their children.[173]

The interpretation of 'public interest' in PJS became a specific issue where the Supreme Court disagreed with the Court of Appeal ruling. The CA had argued that there was only a 'limited public interest' in publishing the details of someone's extramarital sexual relations (e.g. 'Gay couple alleged to have had a threesome'[174]).

Once the case had reached the Supreme Court the justices gave particular regard to section 12(4)(a) HRA, stressing the importance of the media's right of freedom of expression. The UKSC considered two factors:

1   the extent to which the material had, or was about to, become available to the public; and
2   the extent to which it was, or would be, in the public interest for the material to be published.

The court ruled that the material was not in the public interest, applying a fact-sensitive assessment of all matters before the court and taking the couple's children's privacy into

---

170 For example, the IPSO Editors' Code Clause 3, 'Privacy'.
171 PJS [2016] UKSC 26 at paras 33–34.
172 Ibid. at para. 35.
173 Ibid. at para. 35 (Lord Mance).
174 PJS [2016] EWCA Civ 393 at para. 47(ii).

account. The court held that the 'celebrity couple' was most likely to succeed at trial. And a lifelong injunction and anonymity order was subsequently granted.

Recent authorities have shown that section 12 HRA does not provide any defence to the tort of misusing private information, but it enhances the weight which Article 10 rights carry in the balancing exercise, and it has raised the hurdle which the claimant has to overcome to obtain an interim (super) injunction.

2.6.6 The scope of the tort of intentionally causing physical or psychological harm: the Rhodes case

See
Chapter 3

The tort of intentionally causing physical or psychological harm was first established in 1897 in the case of *Wilkinson v Downton* (1897).[175] Mr Downton told Mrs Wilkinson (the wife of his pub landlord) that her husband had fractured his legs and had sent for help to get home. She suffered severe shock despite no previously known predisposition to this condition. Mrs Wilkinson was awarded damages on the basis that:

> 1 she had a legal right to personal safety;
> 2 Mr Downton had committed a wilful act;
> 3 that act was 'calculated' to cause physical harm to Mrs Wilkinson;
> 4 there was no justification for the act; and
> 5 although there was no desire to cause the harm, the act was imputed in law as malicious (akin to 'malicious falsehood' in the tort of defamation).

In the case of James *Rhodes* (2015),[176] the Supreme Court considered the scope of the *Wilkinson v Downton* tort and whether it could ever be used to prevent a person from publishing true information about themselves.

The *Rhodes* case relates to a book written by classical pianist, writer and television film maker James Rhodes, titled *Instrumental*. The book includes vivid autobiographical accounts of the physical and sexual abuse and rape inflicted on him from the age of six by the boxing coach at his school. It goes on to chart his subsequent resorting to drink, drugs, self-harm and attempts at suicide as well as his time in psychiatric hospital culminating in his redemption through learning, listening to and playing music.

The book also refers to his first marriage, to an American novelist then living in London, and the son they had together, to whom the book is dedicated. During their divorce, they made a residence and child contact order in London on 15 June 2009. The son was diagnosed with Asperger's syndrome, attention deficit hyperactivity order, dyspraxia and dysgraphia.

The *Rhodes* case concerns the mother's claim to stop the autobiography being published in June 2014. The claim was brought by the son by way of the mother and another litigation friend, his godfather. Both mother and son lived in the United States. There was expert evidence that the publication of the book would be likely to cause the son psychological harm, the tort recognized in *Wilkinson v Downton*. The CA justified the injunction of the book publication by using this tort.

---

175 [1897] 2 QB 57.
176 *Rhodes (James) v OPO (by His Litigation Friend BHM) and Another* [2015] UKSC 32.

The Supreme Court reversed this judgment and unanimously allowed James Rhodes' appeal. The justices noted that such an injunction could lead to interference with the right to freedom of speech, ruling that the CA had made an error in regarding the publication of that book as conduct towards the claimant boy and his litigation friends, whereas it had been directed towards a larger audience. Lady Hale and Lord Toulson considered the domestic case law in relation to the tort in *Wilkinson v Downton*. It consists of three elements:

1   a conduct element;
2   a mental element; and,
3   a consequence element.

They noted that only (1) and (2) were at issue in this case.[177] The conduct element requires words or conduct directed towards the claimant for which there was no justification or reasonable excuse, and the burden of proof is on the claimant. They held that in this case, there was every justification for the publication: 'the father has the right to tell the world about his story'. Lady Hale stated that the law places a very high value on freedom of speech, and it is hard to envisage any case where words which are not deceptive, threatening or (possibly) abusive could be actionable under the tort recognized in *Wilkinson v Downton*.[178]

> Freedom to report the truth is a basic right to which the law gives a very high level of protection. . . . The right to report the truth is justification in itself.[179]

The justices on reviewing all aspects of the tort elements concluded that the father, James Rhodes, did not have any intention of causing psychiatric, mental or emotional harm to his son. They further concluded that the book publication would not constitute the two elements of conduct and mental harm that Lady Hale and Lord Toulson had identified from their consideration of the tort in *Wilkinson v Downton* as being necessary for the tort to be proven. Neither element could be found to be present. Lord Neuberger, with whom Lord Wilson agreed, also gave his agreement to the appeal being allowed for the reasons set out by Lady Hale and Lord Toulson.[180] In granting the appeal, the Supreme Court restated that the freedom to report the truth is a basic right to which the law gives a very high level of protection.

2.7 Internet privacy: the 'right to be forgotten'

We are all experienced in using search engines via Google Chrome, Firefox, Safari, Bing and other browsers to trawl the web to find stored data about other people (or even ourselves). Whilst the Google browser 'autocomplete' function undeniably helps us locate data and information more quickly, it can have the negative effect of spreading rumours which, in turn, can lead to false information and seriously harming someone's reputation. The interference with a person's rights (known as the 'data subject') can be very serious.

---

177 Ibid. at paras 31–73 (Lady Hale and Lord Toulson).
178 Ibid. at paras 75–77 (Lady Hale).
179 Ibid. at para. 77.
180 Ibid. at paras 101–121.

At the same time, the economic interest of a browser in processing the data has to be borne in mind (for nothing ever comes free of charge).

See Chapter 1.7

2.7.1 Can the internet be regulated?

We have already established in Chapter 1 that there is no such thing as 'internet law', and what we have been looking at so far is the invasion of privacy by those who use social networking sites and by search engines such as Google or Bing who look into and pass on personal data of subscribers (most of whom will not have read the lengthy privacy policies of ISPs and social media sites which include the collection of personal information of individuals). And we have established that there are no privacy laws in the UK. Yet, we can look at the European Court in Luxembourg (CJEU). Europe's regulatory approach was once criticized as unfairly focusing on technology companies from the United States but is now viewed as a potential global model as governments question the influence of Silicon Valley. The EU is now seen as passing legislation at the forefront of a broad debate about the role of tech platforms such as Apple, Amazon, Facebook and Google, and whether their size and power hurt competition.

In March 2019, the CJEU fined Google €1.5bn ($1.7bn) for antitrust violations in the online advertising market, continuing its efforts to rein in the world's biggest technology companies.[181] Article 102 of the Treaty on the Functioning of the European Union (TFEU) and Article 54 of the EEA Agreement prohibit abuse of a dominant position (antitrust rules). The fine was the third against Google by the European Union since 2017, reinforcing the CJEU's position as the world's most aggressive watchdog of an industry with an increasingly powerful role in society and the global economy.[182] Google was found to have violated antitrust rules by imposing unfair terms on companies that used its search bar on their websites in Europe. Spotify also complained to the EU about Apple's alleged antitrust abuses.[183] The EU is now pioneering a distinct tech doctrine that aims to give individuals control over their own information and the profits from it and to prise open tech firms to competition. If the doctrine works, it could benefit millions of users, boost the economy and constrain tech giants that have gathered immense power without a commensurate sense of responsibility.

See Chapter 8.7

The CJEU in *Google Spain*[184] and the subsequent UK courts' ruling in NT1 and NT2 (2018)[185] now provide for data subjects the possibility to ask an ISP, operator of a website or search engine to 'delist' or 'delink' them from a specific searches establishing an individual's 'right to be forgotten'.

---

181 Source: European Commission Press Release: 'Antitrust Commission fines Google €1.49 billion for abusive practices in online advertising'. Brussels, 20 March 2019.

182 In April 2015 the EU Commission commenced proceedings against Google LLC (previously Google Inc.) and Alphabet Inc., Google's parent company, concerning Google's conduct as regards the Android operating system and applications and sent a Statement of Objections to Google in April 2016. In June 2017, the Commission fined Google €2.42bn for abusing its dominance as a search engine by giving an illegal advantage to Google's own comparison shopping service. The Commission continued to monitor Google's compliance with that decision. The Commission also continued to investigate restrictions that Google had placed on the ability of certain third party websites to display search advertisements from Google's competitors ('the AdSense case'). In July 2016, the Commission came to the preliminary conclusion that Google had abused its dominant position in a case concerning AdSense. See: *Commission v Google Inc* No 40099 July 2018.

183 Source: 'Google Fined $1.7 Billion by E.U. for Unfair Advertising Rules', by Adam Satariano, *New York Times*, 20 March 2019.

184 *Google Spain SL v Agencia Española de Protección de Datos (AEPD)* (C-131/12) [2014] QB 1022.

185 *NT1 & NT2 v Google LLC and Information Commissioner* [2018] EWHC 799 (QB).

2.7.2 The right to be forgotten: *Google Spain*

On 13 May 2014, the Court of Justice of the European Union (CJEU) published its ruling on *Google Spain SL v Agencia Española de Protección de Datos* (AEPD).[186] The case became known as the 'right to be forgotten' ruling. The CJEU considered whether EU citizens have a right to request that personal data published on search engine results be removed. The Luxembourg court clarified that search engines are controllers of personal data within the meaning of EU law, namely Directive 95/46/EC. The General Data Protection Regulation 2016 (GDPR)[187] now incorporates a consolidation of the principles set out in *Google*, confirming the 'right to be forgotten' as a focal point of European data protection legislation. The GDPR replaced the Data Protection Directive 95/46/EC and thereby harmonized all data privacy laws across the EU to protect and empower all EU citizens' data privacy and to reshape the way organizations across the Member States approach data privacy.

See Chapter 6.7

The request to the Court of Justice arose in the context of proceedings between Google Spain SL and Google Inc. on the one side and the Agencia Española de Protección de Datos (AEPD) (the Spanish National Data Protection Agency) and Mr Mario Costeja González on the other side, concerning the application of the Data Protection Directive to an internet search engine that Google operated as service provider in Spain.

❖ KEY CASE

Google Spain SL v Agencia Española de Protección de Datos (AEPD) – European Court of Justice (Grand Chamber) (CJEU) 13 May 2014[188]

Precedent (CJEU)

❖ Search engines are data controllers within the meaning of Directive 95/46 (now superseded by the GDPR).

❖ EU law applies to search engines even where they process data *outside* the EU if they have a branch or subsidiary in a Member State which promotes the selling of advertising space offered by the search engine.

❖ The data subject (individual) can ask the search engine for their name and personal details to be 'delisted' or 'delinked' from relevant web pages published by third parties.

❖ Article 10(1) ECHR includes the right of internet users to receive information (via internet search engines).

❖ The 'right to be forgotten' is a qualified right, and courts or regulators have to balance the data subject's right to privacy and the economic interests of the data controller (search engine).

❖ Individuals playing a role in public life may not benefit from the right to be delisted ('the right to be forgotten').

Facts

In March 2010, Spanish citizen Mario Costeja González complained that search results on Google (Spain) included an article from Spanish newspaper *La*

---

186 (C-131/12) [2014] QB.
187 Regulation (EU) 2016/679 of the European Parliament and of the Council of 27 April 2016 on the protection of natural persons with regard to the processing of personal data and on the free movement of such data, and repealing Directive 95/46/EC (General Data Protection Regulation – GDPR) (OJ L 119, 4.5.2016, p. 1).
188 *Google Spain* (C-131/12) [2014] QB 1022 (CJEU).

Vanguardia of 19 January and 9 March 1998 about a home repossession which had been resolved years previously and was no longer relevant. González requested from the newspaper that the articles be altered or removed and that Google Spain or Google Inc. (USA) remove their listings so that his personal data no longer appeared in the search results. When all his requests remained unsuccessful, he complained to the Spanish National Data Protection Agency (Agencia Española de Protección de Datos) (AEPD). The AEPD rejected his claim against *La Vanguardia* (the information in the paper had been lawfully published) but upheld the complaint against both Google entities and requested that they 'delisted' any personal data from their indexes and links on their search engine. Google Spain and Google Inc. counterclaimed and brought actions before the Spanish High Court seeking to have the AEPD decision annulled. The national court referred the case to the CJEU to clarify the territorial scope of application of EU data protection rules, the legal position of internet search engines and the 'right to be forgotten'. Specifically, the CJEU was asked to consider whether the Data Protection Directive 95/46/EC applied to Google and other search engines, whether Google Spain was subject to the Directive given that their servers were based outside the European Union and whether an individual has a right to request that their personal data be erased from the results of a search engine.

The main issues before the CJEU in Luxembourg were as follows:

1   Do the activities Google carries out in compiling its search engine results constitute activities covered by the Data Protection Directive?
2   Is Google a data controller?
3   Is the Data Protection Directive territorially applicable to Google's activities?
4   Do the rights of a data subject (e.g. Mr González) extend to requesting search engines providers to 'delist' personal data (i.e. 'the right to be forgotten')?

Decision (Preliminary ruling of 13 May 2014 by Judge Skouris, President)
The CJEU noted that:

1   *Data collection*: by searching automatically, constantly and systematically for information published on the internet, the operator of a search engine 'collected' data within the meaning of Article 2(b) Directive 95/46.
2   *Data controller*: the operator (Google), within the framework of its indexing programs, 'retrieved', 'recorded' and 'organized' the data in question, which it then 'stored' on its servers and 'disclosed' and 'made available' to its users in the form of lists of results. Those operations were to be classified as 'processing', regardless of the fact that the operator of the search engine also carried out the same operations in respect of other types of information and did not distinguish between the latter and the personal data; this made Google a 'data controller' within the meaning of the Article 2(d) of the Directive.
3   *The territorial scope of the Data Protection Directive*: the Court observed that Google Spain was a subsidiary of Google Inc. on Spanish territory and, therefore, an 'establishment' within the meaning of the Directive. Where

personal data were processed for the purposes of a search engine operated by an undertaking which, although it had its seat in a non-Member State, had an establishment in a Member State, the processing was carried out 'in the context of the activities' of that establishment (i.e. within the meaning of Article 4(1)(a) Directive 95/46) if the establishment was intended to promote and sell, in the Member State in question, advertising space offered by the search engine in order to make the service offered by the engine profitable.

4   *'The right to be forgotten' (delisting of personal data)*: the operator was, in certain circumstances, obliged to remove links to web pages that were published by third parties and contained information relating to a person from the list of results displayed following a search made on the basis of that person's name. Such an obligation may also exist in a case where that name or information was not erased beforehand or simultaneously from those web pages, and even, as the case may be, when its publication in itself on those pages was lawful.

Analysis

The *Google Spain* ruling means that citizens of EU Member States have a *qualified* 'right to be forgotten' and can request that search engines remove personal data that is inaccurate, inadequate, irrelevant or excessive for the purposes of data processing. The CJEU confirmed that search engines are data controllers for the purposes of Directive 95/46/EC as they are responsible for determining the purpose and means of processing personal data that appears on third party web pages and must observe the principles laid out under EU law. It was further held that EU law applies to search engines even where they process data *outside* the EU, if they have a branch or subsidiary in a Member State which 'promotes the selling of advertising space offered by the search engine'.

The Court stressed that the 'right to be forgotten' is a qualified right depending on the nature of the information in question, its sensitivity for the data subject's private life and on the interest of the public in having that information, particularly if that person played a major role in *public life*. The Advocate General expressed the view that search engines should not be unduly saddled with the obligation of having to assess an unmanageable number of requests on a case-by-case and day-to-day basis.[189] When appraising such a request operators of search engines are entitled to retain the information on their websites if the data subject is in the public interest. Where the data controller (search engine) refuses a 'delinking' or 'delisting' request from an individual, that person may bring the matter before the national 'supervisory authority' (i.e. the regulator) or the relevant court so that the search engine may be ordered to take specific action (or not).

---

189 Advocate General's Opinion in Google Spain [2014] QB 1022 at paras 60–68.

Building on the foundations laid by the Data Protection Directive and the *Google Spain* ruling, the General Data Protection Regulation 2016 (GDPR) now allows the data subject to request the erasure of personal data from a search engine relating to them where specified grounds apply. The ruling confirmed that the physical location of the servers that process personal data is not relevant, focusing instead on whether services are provided to European consumers, and imposes heavy fines for breaches of the legislation.

The *Google Spain* ruling is important in relation to the protection of EU data subjects. The CJEU noted that personal data on any subject's private life was easily available and accessible online via aggregation on search engines, meaning that private information was open to the world at large (see also: *Hegglin v Persons Unknown* (2014);[190] *Schrems v Data Protection Commissioner* (2015)[191]). The ruling (and in turn the GDPR) means that operators of search engines should not retain personal data for longer than necessary for processing purposes, and this in effect gives data subjects (like Mr Costeja González) a 'right to be forgotten' and a 'right to be delinked' (or delisted).

The *Google Spain* 'right to be forgotten' ruling (RTBF) vindicates individual data protection and safeguards privacy interests. Arguably the ruling unduly burdens freedom of expression and information retrieval via search engines and weblinks. Many think it depends on the facts, and there is a general feeling amongst privacy lawyers that the implementation of the RTBF rule should be more transparent for these reasons:

1   the public should be able to find out how social networking sites, operators of websites and search engine providers exercise their power over readily accessible information and the processing of that information; and
2   implementation of the ruling affects global efforts to accommodate privacy rights with other interests in data flows, such as international law enforcement in relation to terrorism-linked offences.

The RTBF ruling was brought into question by the Hungarian *Weltimmo* case (2015).[192]

Following the *Google Spain* ruling, six EU authorities individually initiated enforcement proceedings against Google Inc. One case was that of Dan Shefet, a Danish lawyer working in France. He brought an action against Google.fr via the French data protection authority (CNIL);[193] Google rejected that request by Mr Shefet to be delisted. The CNIL's Sanctions Committee subsequently issued a monetary penalty of €150,000 to Google Inc. and Google.fr for noncompliance with the provisions of the French Data Protection Act. In its decision, the Sanctions Committee ruled that French law applies to the processing of personal data relating to internet users established in France, contrary to Google's claim.[194]

By October 2014 some 18,304 requests had been made from UK individuals, wanting links to their name removed on www.google.co.uk. Google Inc. confirmed

---

190 [2014] EWHC 2808 (QB) 31 July 2014.
191 (*Case* C-362/14) [2015] All ER 34 (CJEU).
192 *Weltimmo s.r.o. v Nemzeti Adatvédelmi és Információszabadság Hatóság* (2015) (Case C-230/14) (CJEU –Third Chamber), Luxembourg, 1 October 2015 (the Weltimmo case).
193 Commission nationale de l'informatique et des libertés (CNIL) at www.cnil.fr.
194 Source: Deliberation No 2013–420 of the Sanctions Committee of CNIL imposing a financial penalty against Google Inc. Paris, 3 January 2014.

that it had removed 35 per cent (18,459) of unwanted links to web pages from its UK service by December 2015; UK citizens had made the third-highest number of requests behind French and German citizens, with 29,010 and 25,078, respectively.[195] There were nearly 220,000 requests in 2015 in the UK, most of which came from high-profile clients, including criminals, politicians and public figures; fewer than half of the requests were granted.

Max Mosley was engaged in an EU-wide campaign asking various search engines (mainly Google) to remove the 'Nazi Orgy' images from the web pages. The facts are well known that Mr Mosley asked the High Court in London to grant him interim injunctive relief against News Group Newspapers (the *News of the World*) for misuse of private information in the publication of images of his sadomasochistic encounters with prostitutes dressed in Nazi uniforms.[196] In January 2015 Mr Justice Mitting dismissed Max Mosley's action against the Google search engine at London's High Court under sections 10, 13 and 14 of the Data Protection Act 1998.[197]

In 2018, Mr Mosley began a new action against the Mirror Group, Associated Newspapers (*Daily Mail*) and *The Times*, claiming they were breaching the Data Protection Act 1998 because they continued to refer to 'an infamous sadomasochistic orgy', involving him when he was the Formula 1 boss over a decade ago, which was secretly filmed by the now defunct Rupert Murdoch-owned *News of the World* and published on the front page of the tabloid with video footage on its website. Mosley also wanted the newspaper groups to stop saying he had control or influence over IMPRESS, due to the fact that the press regulator was largely funded by him.

See Chapter 7.6

Mr Mosley claimed that data protection and privacy laws required the press to stop disseminating information about him that was not in the public interest, but media lawyers as well as the newspaper owners said his demand was an attempt to rewrite the historical record. The *Daily Mail* investigation revealed in February 2018 that Mr Mosley handed more than £500,000 to Labour Party Deputy Leader Tom Watson. The newspaper was trying to prove that Max Mosley lied at the 'Nazi Orgy' privacy trial in 2008. At that time Mr Mosley had categorically denied under oath that a Nazi-themed pamphlet written in 1961 by him had existed. The hateful pamphlet had now come into the hands of the *Daily Mail*, in 2018 'published by Max Mosley' and written for a 1961 by-election at which young Max Mosley, son of Sir Oswald Mosley, leader of the pre-war British Union of Fascists, was the agent for his father's post-war political party, the Union Movement (UM).[198]

See below 2.9

2.7.3 *NT1 and NT2*: right to delist criminal convictions

It took four years since the CJEU ruling in *Google Spain* before a legal action was commenced by two individual businessmen (known only as NT1 and NT2[199]) against Google

---

195 The top five countries by October 2015 were France (14,086), Germany (12,678), the UK (8,497), Spain (6,176) and Italy (5,934).
196 *Mosley v Newsgroup Newspapers Ltd* [2008] EWHC 1777 (QB).
197 *Mosley v Google Inc Ltd and Google UK* [2015] EWHC 59 (QB) at para. 55 (Mitting J).
198 Source: 'The Daily Mail accuses F1 tycoon who bankrolls Labour deputy leader Tom Watson of racist thuggery and asks . . . Did Max Mosley lie to orgy trial?' by Sam Greenhill, Stephen Wright and Bill Akass, *Daily Mail*, 28 February 2018: www.dailymail.co.uk/news/article-5441827/Did-F1-tycoon-Max-Mosley-lie-orgy-trial. html?ito=email_share_article-factbox#mol-5368d3c0-1bf0-11e8-a4b3-efb343085dbb.
199 *NT1 & NT2 v Google LLC and Information Commissioner* [2018] EWHC 799 (QB).

and the UK Information Commissioner to remove search results about criminal convictions. The two trials took place sequentially in February and March 2018, both before Mr Justice Warby and with the claimants sharing the same legal team. Both claimants were granted anonymity (cited only as NT1 and NT2) so as to avoid undermining the purpose of their claims. Third parties and businesses were also anonymized in the public judgment to try and prevent jigsaw identification. Date references in the judgment are vague, making it difficult to impossible to identify the claimants.

Google right from the start argued abuse of process. The Information Commissioner's Office (ICO) suggested that the court should disapply the provision of the First Data Protection Principle, which requires a condition in Schedule 3 of the DPA 1998 to be met before there can be any lawful processing of *sensitive* personal data (which includes allegations of criminality and reporting of criminal proceedings). This was because if none of the conditions applied, all such data processing (i.e. returning search results about any criminal proceedings/allegations) would automatically be unlawful.

The landmark ruling by Mr Justice Warby on 13 April 2018 on the 'right to be forgotten' (RTBF) has wide-ranging repercussions. The CJEU had ruled in *Google Spain* 2014 that irrelevant and outdated data should be erased from a search engine on request.

The first claimant, NT1, lost his application; he had been convicted of conspiracy to account falsely in the late 1990s and was described as a 'public figure with a limited role in public life'. At the time of his prosecution, conviction and sentence, Article 8 ECHR was not engaged, and the claimant had no reasonable expectation of privacy. Warby J was scathing about NT1's position since leaving prison:

> He claims to have 'accepted' the findings of the jury but his statement nowhere admits his guilt, and in the witness box he appeared reluctant to concede that the Court's decision in this, and in other respects, was correct. However, the conviction is evidence that NT1 was guilty (Civil Evidence Act 1968, s 11(2)). . . . He has not accepted his guilt, has misled the public and this court, and shows no remorse over any of these matters. He remains in business, and the information serves the purpose of minimising the risk that he will continue to mislead, as he has in the past. Delisting would not erase the information from the record altogether, but it would make it much harder to find.[200]

The claimant who won, known as NT2, was convicted more than ten years ago of conspiracy to intercept communications. NT1 was sentenced to four years' imprisonment, while NT2 received a six-month prison sentence. NT1 was granted an appeal. Both men demanded that Google remove search results mentioning the cases for which they were convicted. These include links to web pages published by a national newspaper and other media. Google UK and Inc. had refused their request. The decision in NT2's favour may well have implications for other convicted criminals and those who want embarrassing stories about them erased from the World Wide Web. No damages were awarded under s 13 DPA 1998.[201]

---

200 Ibid. at paras 68–70.
201 Ibid. at para. 173.

When addressing the Data Protection Act 1998, Warby J found that Condition 5 of Schedule 3 DPA was met ('Conditions relevant for purposes of the first principle: processing of sensitive personal data'): the information had been made public as a result of steps deliberately taken by the data subject. Warby J held that a consequence of the open justice system is that in committing a criminal offence one is deliberately taking steps to make information about that offence public. In order for *any* personal data to be processed, one of the conditions in Schedule 2 must be met.

Condition 6(1) of Schedule 2 ('Conditions relevant for purposes of the first principle: processing of any personal data') allows data processing where it is *necessary* in pursuance of legitimate interests by the data controller or by third parties to whom the data is disclosed. Processing for such 'legitimate interests' is prevented only where it is unwarranted by virtue of prejudice caused to the rights, freedoms or legitimate interests of the data subject.

Warby J stated that there was no doubt that Google had a legitimate interest in processing personal data in pursuit of its business as a search engine operator and that third parties (i.e. the general public) have a legitimate interest in being able to receive information from Google (as well as other search engines).

The question was whether in the cases of NT1 and NT2 such processing was 'necessary', in pursuance of those legitimate interests, or 'unwarranted', considering any prejudice caused to the claimants. The balancing and proportionality test before the court in these two cases was essentially that of Article 8(1) and Art 10(1) ECHR, applied in all privacy cases and as rule in the *Google Spain* case.

Warby J then carried out a detailed analysis of the nature of the (spent) convictions of NT1 and NT2, the surrounding circumstances and events and the claimants' behaviour since the offences took place. In short: had each claimant been 'rehabilitated'? (Rehabilitation of Offenders Act 1974).

Whereas NT1 had shown no remorse, NT2 had shown remorse. The judge also took into account the submission that NT2's conviction did not concern actions taken by him in relation to 'consumers, customers or investors', but rather in relation to the invasion of privacy of third parties:

> There is no plausible suggestion, nor is there any sold basis for an inference, that there is a risk that this wrongdoing will be repeated by the claimant. The information is of scant if any apparent relevance to any business activities that he seems likely to engage in.[202]

Warby J concluded in relation to NT2:

> the crime and punishment information has become out of date, irrelevant and of no sufficient legitimate interest to users of Google search to justify its continued availability.[203]

---

202 Ibid. at para. 222(4) (Warby J).
203 Ibid. at para. 140.

> ❖ **KEY CASE**
>
> ***NT1 & NT2 v Google LLC and Information Commissioner* [2018] EWHC 799 (QB)**

Precedent set in NT1 and NT2

Individuals who are thinking of submitting a delisting ('right to be forgotten') (RTBF) application to a search engine regarding their (spent) criminal convictions should note the following:

❖ The fact that a conviction is spent is substantial, but not decisive. The applicant (data subject) may think criminal convictions should be 'forgotten' and delisted, but Google (or any other search engine) may disagree;

❖ The Information Commissioner's Office (ICO) has published its own guidelines for data controllers' and data processors' handling and storing of criminal convictions of data subjects (see below);

❖ The case for delisting and RTBF applications to a search engine will be stronger if the data subject can demonstrate genuine remorse for the past criminal conduct; the behaviour after a spent conviction is also relevant, demonstrating that the individual has either 'made good' to society and/or 'turned over a new leaf' (as was the case with NT2);

❖ The individual should demonstrate honesty and sincerity in the witness stand ('I found the witness [NT2] to be an honest and generally reliable witness who listened carefully to the questions put to him, and gave clear and relevant answers'[204]);

❖ It is relevant how a professional body has dealt with the individual *after* the conviction (e.g. a solicitor being struck off by the Law Society; an accountant being struck off by a professional body such as the ACCA, etc.; a doctor being struck off by the GMC, etc.);

❖ The case *against* delisting is stronger if the applicant is a 'public figure' (with a degree of media exposure) or a regulated business professional (e.g. financial adviser or solicitor who has been convicted of fraud); the prospect of being delisted is lower if the offence was dishonesty-related;

❖ The prospect of delisting an unspent conviction is remote;

❖ Where criminal proceedings resulted in acquittal or discontinuance it could be argued by the search engine (data controller/processor) that *none* of the conditions in Schedule 3 DPA 1998 are met ('Conditions relevant for purposes of the first principle: processing of sensitive personal data'); strictly speaking, the data subject has *not* committed a criminal offence; however, Google may argue that an acquittal or discontinuance is not a finding of innocence and can therefore make a case against delisting; the data subject has to provide evidence to the contrary;

❖ The data subject should set out the damage and distress suffered and provide specific examples of the search results affecting his/her personal life (loss of partner or job, etc.; distress caused to children being bullied;

---

204 Ibid. at para. 176 (Warby J).

impact on elderly parents, etc.;[205] 'he has been treated as a pariah in his social life');[206]

❖ No reference can be made to loss of business or financial impact since data protection legislation only refers to living individuals (DPA 1998; DPA 2018; GDPR).

The ruling caused the Information Commissioner's Office (ICO) to reassess its own approach to a review of delisting requests. The ICO states as follows on criminal offence data:

See
Chapter 6.4

- To process personal data about criminal convictions or offences, data processors and data controllers ('organizations') must have both a lawful basis under Article 6 ECHR and either legal authority or official authority for the processing under Article 10 ECHR;
- The Data Protection Act 2018 deals with this type of data in a similar way to special category data, and sets out specific conditions providing lawful authority for processing it (ss 2(1) and 2(2)) – in line with the GDPR;
- Organizations *cannot* keep a comprehensive register of criminal convictions unless they do so in an official capacity; conditions for lawful processing of offence data (or identify your official authority for the processing) must be documented.

In a subsequent ruling by the UK Supreme Court in January 2019, the Supreme Court Justices dismissed the Government's (Home Office) appeals in the conjoined cases of *Lorraine Gallagher, P, G and W* (2019).[207] The judges allowed the government's appeal in relation to W, who had a conviction for assault as a juvenile for which he was given a two-year conditional discharge.

The four appellants claimed their lives had been unfairly haunted by minor criminal offences, reprimands and cautions by the police. The five Supreme Court Justices found that minor historical convictions and cautions given to children (as in the case of P) may no longer have to be disclosed during criminal record checks when they seek work with children. In all four cases, the actions concerned job offers or applications which had been withdrawn after the Enhanced Criminal Record Certificate disclosed all previous convictions and cautions.

The majority of the judges found that the way criminal records are disclosed is disproportionate and infringes human rights under Article 8 ECHR. The justices found that the revised criminal records disclosure scheme – governing disclosure by the Disclosure and Barring Service in England and Wales or Access NI in Northern Ireland – was 'disproportionate' in two respects – the requirement that *all* previous convictions should be disclosed, however minor, where the person has more than one conviction, and in the

205 NT2 judgment at paras 148–149.
206 Ibid. at para. 154.
207 R (on the Application of Lorraine Gallagher, P, G and W) v Secretary of State for the Home Department and Another [2019] UKSC 3.

case of warnings and reprimands issued to young offenders. A majority of the court (Lord Sumption, Lord Carnwath, Lord Hughes and Lady Hale) reached that result based on a partial breach of the proportionality test. Lord Sumption (with whom Lord Carnwath and Lord Hughes agreed) gave the leading judgment. Lady Hale (with whom Lord Carnwath also agreed) gave a concurring judgment.

One of the four cases was of a woman, referred to as P, who, while suffering from undiagnosed schizophrenia in 1999, received a caution for theft of a sandwich and was in the same year convicted of shoplifting a 99p book and of failing to answer bail. She had committed no further offences, but she had been unable to get work as a teaching assistant. Another case was of G, who was arrested at the age of thirteen in 2006 two years after sexually assaulting two younger boys, aged eight and nine. The activity was consensual and appeared to be a form of dares. He received two police reprimands after the Crown Prosecution Service decided it was not in the public interest to prosecute him. He had not offended since.

This case – similar to NT1 and NT2 (above) questioned the complexity and legality (with regard to compatibility with Article 8 ECHR) concerning the disclosure by the ex-offenders under the Rehabilitation of Offenders Act 1974 in England and Wales, and in these four appellants' cases, also the corresponding provisions of the Rehabilitation of Offenders (Northern Ireland) Order 1978 in Northern Ireland (materially the same as the English provision). By section 4(2)–(3) of the 1974 Act, where a question is put to an ex-offender about previous convictions (and indeed cautions) – there is no duty of disclosure. However, for any of 13 specified purposes in the Rehabilitation of Offenders Act 1974 (Exceptions) Order and the Rehabilitation of Offenders (Exceptions) Order (Northern Ireland), there is a duty of disclosure. The second scheme, governing disclosure by the Disclosure and Barring Service in England and Wales or Access NI in Northern Ireland, is governed by Part V of the Police Act 1997 (as amended). Sections 113A and 113B deal with Criminal Record Certificates and Enhanced Criminal Record Certificates. These provisions create a system of mandatory disclosure of all convictions and cautions on a person's record if the conditions for the issue of a certificate were satisfied.

Lord Kerr disagreed with the majority on compliance with the legality test and the proportionality test.[208] He suggested two potential modifications: (1) a provision which linked the relevance of the data to be disclosed to the nature of the employment sought,[209] and (2) an individual review mechanism in some cases, such as that introduced in Northern Ireland in 2016.[210]

2.8 The privacy ruling in *Cliff Richard*

In July 2018, Conservative MP, Anna Soubry, used Prime Minister's Questions in Parliament to ask former Prime Minister Theresa May to bring in a new law, called 'Cliff's Law', following Sir Cliff Richard's privacy case against the BBC. Sir Cliff was

---

208 Ibid. at paras 80–100; 101–146 (Lord Kerr).
209 Ibid. at paras 165–173.
210 Ibid. at paras 174–175.

awarded £210,000 in damages by the High Court over the BBC News coverage of a police raid on his home in August 2014, following allegations of historical child sexual assault. Former regional broadcast journalist for 14 years and barrister, the MP for Broxtowe in Nottinghamshire since 2010, Ms Soubry[211] proposed a blanket ban on identifying people questioned by police as suspects, particularly concerning sexual offences.

The *Cliff Richard* (2018) case[212] set a precedent posing a new legal conundrum for journalists: what can and cannot be reported in respect of the pre-charge stage of a police investigation? Until Mr Justice Mann's judgment in *Richard*, this was an unresolved area — made all the more difficult by a range of conflicting opinions, conventions and 'contempt' laws in the UK.

See Chapter 5.3

Until the High Court ruling in *Richard*, all celebrity suspects in historical child sex abuse cases had been named at 'investigation' and 'suspect' stages (prior to charge), such as Rolf Harris or Max Clifford. Both were convicted with lengthy prison sentences. Publicist Max Clifford subsequently died, aged 74, on 10 December 2017 whilst serving an eight-year prison sentence for indecent assault. He denied until his death that he had sexually assaulted young women. His daughter Louise continued his appeal challenge. However, Clifford's conviction for sex offences was upheld by the Court of Appeal in April 2019.

BBC Radio 2 DJ Paul Gambaccini won damages against the Surrey Police in November 2018 over unfounded historical sexual abuse allegations. Gambaccini had been a fixture on UK radio for decades before the allegations were made. The American-born broadcaster had been arrested in October 2013 under Met Police Operation Yewtree as part of the inquiry into alleged sexual offences by former BBC TV and radio personality Jimmy Savile (deceased), over a claim he sexually assaulted two teenage boys. Four personalities had already been charged under Operation Yewtree, including the Australian entertainer Rolf Harris, celebrity publicist Max Clifford, DJ Dave Lee Travis and David Smith (deceased), a former BBC driver. Gambaccini (then 69) spent a year on bail before the case against him was dropped in what he labelled a 'completely fictitious' affair. Gambaccini's legal dispute against the Crown Prosecution Service (CPS) centred on a press statement issued by Baljit Ubhey, Chief Crown Prosecutor for London, in October 2014, which stated:

> Having carefully reviewed this case, we have decided that there is *insufficient evidence* to prosecute in relation to allegations of sexual offences made by two males believed to be aged between 14 and 15 at the time of the alleged offending.

Gambaccini won his action against the CPS and settled for an undisclosed amount out of court. But the damage to his reputation was done. Comedians Jim Davidson and Freddie Starr also had their lives ruined when false allegations were made against them.

---

211 Anna Soubry left the Conservative Party over the Brexit debacle in February 2019 and joined the Independent Group.
212 *Sir Cliff Richard OBE v (1) The British Broadcasting Corporation (2) The Chief Constable of South Yorkshire Police* [2018] EWHC 1837; [2018] All ER (D) 111 (Jul) (Ch).

2.8.1 The *Cliff Richard* case

Sir Cliff Richard, the famous pop singer, was also investigated as part of Operation Yewtree by the South Yorkshire Police, after allegations of historical sexual abuse were revealed (by a member of the police) to the BBC.

In a high profile legal action against the BBC, Sir Cliff claimed the sensational *News at One* TV report in August 2014 was a 'serious invasion' of his privacy. The BBC had used a helicopter to get footage of the South Yorkshire Police raid and search through the windows of Sir Cliff's flat in Sunningdale, Berkshire. Sir Cliff was never arrested or charged with historical child sex abuse.

Four years later, on 18 July 2018, Sir Cliff won his privacy case against the BBC. The Chancery Division awarded the then 77-year-old singer general damages of £210,000 and aggravated damages, for which the BBC would be 65 per cent liable with the South Yorkshire Police for damages for which they were jointly responsible, as it had been the more potent causer of damage, and its breach had been more significant. The BBC was also ordered to pay an additional £850,000 at a cost hearing on 26 July. The BBC subsequently decided not to appeal.

Mister Justice Mann held that the BBC coverage was a serious breach of the singer's privacy. The judge commented on the tone of the broadcast which seemed more appropriate to an embassy siege than to the investigation of a suspect not even arrested or charged. Sir Cliff had told the High Court in London how the broadcast and accusations had had an impact on his physical and mental health and how his name had been smeared across the world's media and how his reputation had been 'tainted' forever.

Whilst the court believed that the BBC's reporter, Dan Johnson, sniffing a scoop, had seized the opportunity to make up some ground in advance of rival coverage by ITN and tabloid newspapers, he and senior editorial staff forgot about privacy issues and editorial codes of practice. Mann J concluded that although the BBC reported the facts accurately, it did so 'with a significant degree of breathless sensationalism'.

Mann J was rather derisive about evidence given at trial by some senior BBC staff, such as Jonathan Munro, head of newsgathering at the time, criticizing him for 'almost wilfully failing to acknowledge inconsistencies' between the BBC's defence statement and the evidence provided in court (including a large email trail about the issue).[213] Most unsatisfactory, however, according to the judge's summing up, was Gary Smith's evidence, the then UK news editor, who infamously sent an email reading 'congratulations and jubilations' when he heard that Cliff Richard was being investigated by the police. Mann J said: 'Mr Smith was unduly defensive, and to a degree evasive, in much of his evidence. . . . I regret that I felt I could not always rely on him as a reliable witness'.[214]

 **❖ KEY CASE**   ***Sir Cliff Richard OBE v (1) The British Broadcasting Corporation (2) The Chief Constable of South Yorkshire Police* [2018] EWHC 1837 (Ch)**

Precedent

❖   The protection of reputation is a part of the function of privacy law (Art 8(1) ECHR).

---

213 *Sir Cliff Richard OBE v (1) The British Broadcasting Corporation (2) The Chief Constable of South Yorkshire Police* [2018] EWHC 1837 (Hc) at para. 26 (Mann J).
214 Ibid. at paras 22–23.

❖ **Individuals who are subject to police investigation have a reasonable expectation of privacy.**

Facts

The claimant, Sir Cliff Richard, is a well-known entertainer who has enjoyed a worldwide reputation since the late 1950s. In 2014, and unknown to him, he became the subject of an investigation by the South Yorkshire Police (SYP) in relation to allegations of an historic sex offence. Until the events of this case Sir Cliff was still pursuing his career even though he was by then in his mid-seventies. In the period leading up to June 2014 the Metropolitan Police were conducting various investigations of historic child sex abuse under the umbrella Operation Yewtree. There were several high-profile arrests, charges and convictions of public figures. Operation Yewtree became aware of an allegation made against Sir Cliff about an incident in the 1980s, at a Billy Graham evangelist rally in Sheffield, involving an adolescent boy under the age of 16. Because it was a single incident within a particular police area it was proposed to hand the investigation over to SYP, in whose area the incident allegedly took place. Supt Fenwick briefed Assistant Chief Constable Jo Byrne because of the high-profile nature of the subject of the investigation. BBC reporter Daniel (Dan) Johnson (J) had found out about the investigation from a confidential source and approached SYP (in the form of a media officer, Miss Carrie Goodwin) about it. That led to a meeting at which J was told about an intended search warrant of Sir Cliff's English flat in Sunningdale. The search took place on 14 August 2014, and the BBC immediately gave prominent and extensive television coverage to it, as it was happening and thereafter. In June 2016, it was announced by SYP that there would be no charges brought against Sir Cliff. Sir Cliff issued proceedings, claiming that both the BBC and the SYP violated his rights both in privacy and under the DPA 1998. The BBC contended that, in so far as Sir Cliff's claim was based on damage to reputation, that could not be the subject of a privacy claim – he should have taken out a defamation action against the BBC for loss of reputation. In May 2017, Sir Cliff reached a settlement with SYP and was paid damages of £400,000 and costs. The BBC continued to trial. There were 19 witnesses who gave evidence, mainly senior editorial members of the BBC, the BBC reporter Dan Johnson and senior members of the SYP. The BBC had also entered the broadcast news coverage for an award at the Royal Television Society Awards as the 'Scoop of the Year' (which, incidentally, it did not win).[215]

Legal issues

(1) Whether the SYP had co-operated with the BBC because it had actively wanted publicity for its search and investigation, as contended by the BBC, or because it had felt it had to give J some co-operation to discourage him from publishing before the search and prejudicing the investigation, as contended by SYP. The SYP not have offered J anything, or at least nothing

---

215 Ibid. at para. 365.

worthwhile, and would not have provided details of the search. J and the SYP representatives had agreed that he would not publish his story, and, in exchange, he would be given advance notice of the search. In so agreeing, J had been aware that the SYP representatives had thought there was a risk of publication and had been buying him off.[216]

(2) Whether Sir Cliff had had a legitimate expectation of privacy in the published information and, if so, whether his Article 8(1) ECHR privacy right had been infringed. Whether as a matter of general principle, a suspect had a reasonable expectation of privacy in relation to a police investigation. The fact of an investigation would, of itself, carry some stigma, no matter how often one said it should not.[217]

(3) Whether Sir Cliff's privacy rights had been outweighed by the BBC's freedom of expression rights under Article 10(1) ECHR.

(4) Whether an award of general, aggravated and special damages should be made.

(5) Whether the BBC could be subject to the contribution claim made by SYP and whether it had a full claim against SYP.

Decision (High Court Chancery Division)

Mr Justice Mann ruled that Article 8(1) ECHR was engaged vis-à-vis both SYP and the BBC.[218] He held that Sir Cliff's privacy rights had *not* been outweighed by the BBC's rights to freedom of expression, particularly since the style of reporting and the way in which film footage of the police raid was obtained (the helicopter) was 'sensationalist'. The judge suggested that a low-key report of the search and investigation would have been advisable. The reporter's degree of drama and sensationalism by the very nature of the coverage had materially impacted on the invasion of privacy of the famous singer.[219] Mann J noted that the consequences of a disclosure for a person such as Sir Cliff were capable of being, and had been, very serious. The failure of the BBC to keep the presumption of innocence in mind at all times meant that there was inevitably going to be stigma attached to the revelation, which was magnified by the nature of the allegations against Sir Cliff, which had been allegations of extreme seriousness. There was a very significant public interest in the fact of the SYP's investigations into historic child sex abuse, including the fact that those investigations were pursued against those in public life. However, Mann J held that the public interest in identifying those persons did not exist in the present case.[220] Sensational BBC reporting on the investigation by using helicopter footage of the police raid on his flat had amounted to a serious invasion of privacy (coupled with

---

216 Ibid. at para. 224.
217 Ibid. at paras 248 and 251.
218 Ibid. at para. 263.
219 Ibid. at para. 318.
220 Ibid. at para. 317.

BBC coverage of Sir Cliff's residences in Portugal and Barbados).[221] The BBC was liable for infringing Sir Cliff's privacy rights when it had disclosed, by broadcasting, the fact that Sir Cliff had been the subject of an investigation for historic child sexual abuse and that his property was being searched in connection with that investigation. The judge ruled that the DPA 1998 claim added nothing to the privacy claim.[222] The BBC had been the more potent causer of Sir Cliff's damage, and its breach had been more significant than SYP's. For this reason the court ordered the BBC to bear a greater share of the damages than SYP. The split was 20 per cent as to SYP and 80 per cent awarded against the BBC.[223]

Analysis

The ruling in *Richard* presents a tension between the media's freedom of expression – *inter alia* 'freedom to report' – and a suspect's right to reasonable expectation of privacy. Since Sir Cliff Richard had not been charged with a criminal offence at the time the information was in the hands of the BBC reporter, the matter required complete editorial judgment and consideration of the suspect's Article 8 ECHR right. Mann J ruled that the protection of reputation was part of the function of the law of privacy as well as the function of the law of defamation. This demonstrates that privacy and defamation claims might be fusing into one since reputational harm can arise from matters of fact which are true, but within the scope of a privacy right. The fact that Sir Cliff was a public figure, and one who had promoted his Christian beliefs in his writing and his public appearances, should not have detracted from his reasonable expectation of privacy (*Axel Springer* (2012)[224] and *Rocknroll* applied (2013)[225]). It might be that a given public figure waives, at least, a degree of privacy by courting publicity or adopting a public stance which would be at odds with the privacy rights claimed, but nothing like that applied in the present case (*Douglas v Hello! Ltd* (2001) applied).[226] The court held that Sir Cliff's public status emphasized the need for privacy in the given circumstances, and the matter was *not* in the public interest (*Max Mosley* (2008) applied).[227]

The ruling in Richard marks a significant shift against press freedom and an important principle around the public's right to know regarding suspects in police investigations. Mann J's judgment means that – save in exceptional circumstances – suspects of a

---

221 Ibid. at paras 315–316.
222 Ibid. at paras 226 and 323.
223 Ibid. at paras 446–448.
224 *Axel Springer AG v Germany* (*Application No 39954/08*) (2012) 32 BHRC 493.
225 *Rocknroll (Edward) v News Group Newspapers Ltd* [2013] EWHC 24 (Ch).
226 *Douglas v Hello! Ltd* [2001] QB 967.
227 *Mosley (Max) v Newsgroup Newspapers Ltd* [2008] EWHC 1777.

crime are entitled to reasonably expect the matter is being kept private and not covered by the media.

In his ITV interview post the court hearing, Sir Cliff paraphrased the eighteenth-century jurist William Blackstone, who set out how courts should err on the side of innocence. 'I'd rather ten guilty people get away with it than one innocent person suffer, there is no reason for that', the singer said. He added: 'I will fight to the death against the abuse of the freedom of speech. What the BBC did was an abuse. Freedom without responsibility is anarchy. To me this was an anarchic thing to do'.[228]

Paedophilia carries with it a particular stigma, and Sir Cliff is probably right when he said that the public will remember him for this exposition, and his reputation will be forever tainted.

2.8.2 A new precedent in police suspect anonymity?

What does the ruling in *Richard* mean for the open justice principle and media freedom? Following Mr Justice Mann's ruling in the case, the media has become rather uncertain: must they now wait with naming a police suspect until someone is arrested and charged? Arguably, Mann J's ruling in *Richard* extends privacy law because it bans journalists from naming the subjects of police investigations before they are charged. It then seems that suspects are now able to block the media from reporting their arrests. The principle, which is already being called 'Cliff's Law', could make convictions harder to secure. In several past cases, other victims have come forward after a suspect's arrest was reported in the press.

Richard has dramatically changed the privacy landscape from that of *Kaye v Robertson* (1991),[229] where Glidewell LJ famously ruled that the well-known actor Gordon Kaye had no right to privacy when he was hoodwinked by a *Sunday Sport* reporter dressed as a medic as he lay in Charing Cross Hospital, recovering from brain surgery in 1990.[230]

Some 30 years later, the world has been transformed by the internet and 24-hour news where the rich and famous are trying to achieve privacy through the courts or via their children (see the *David Murray* case (2008)[231] or *PJS v News Group Newspapers Ltd* (2016)[232]), arguing that their right to privacy trumps that of the public's right to know.

See
Chapter 4.2

The *Richard* case is not only about freedom of expression and media freedom but also about the open justice principle. It challenges the notion that justice must be seen to be done. In the words of social reformer Jeremy Bentham, 'publicity is the very soul of justice'. The ruling in *Richard* by Mr Justice Mann leaves unresolved issues such as principles of open justice and freedom of expression under Article 10(1) ECHR.

---

228 Source: 'ITV News exclusive: Emotional Sir Cliff Richard speaks of his 'most wonderful relief' after privacy case win over BBC', Video report by ITV News Correspondent Paul Davies, 18 July 2018: www.itv.com/news/2018-07-18/sir-cliff-richards-bbc-court-battle-verdict.

229 *Kaye (Gordon) v Robertson & Sport Newspapers Ltd* [1991] FSR 62.

230 A copy of a recent edition of *Sunday Sport* had been put before the judge at the time showing that many of the advertisements contained in it showed various forms of pornographic material which indicated to his Lordship 'the readership it seeks to attract'.

231 *Murray v Express Newspapers* [2008] EWCA Civ 446.

232 [2016] UKSC 26.

FOR THOUGHT

Does the *Sir Cliff Richard* judgment present a disproportionate shift from media freedom to privacy for police suspects? Discuss.

2.9 What is 'the public interest test'?

As common law developed post-HRA 1998 we can observe that the public interest defence advanced by newspapers and media organizations can be successful. The case which specifically examined the distinction between the public interest and what the public is interested in, was undoubtedly that of *Max Mosley*.[233]

Case law informs us that the public interest defence now tends to be limited to matters of genuine political, legal, constitutional, social or economic relevance and importance, and whether the publication is capable of contributing to a debate in a democratic society. The Strasbourg Human Rights Court held in *von Hannover* (No 1)[234] that the individual claiming privacy and confidentiality (e.g. in photographs) must carry out public functions.

If not in statute, the term 'public interest' is defined in the Editors' Code of the Independent Press Standards Organisation (IPSO), one of the UK press regulators. IPSO's definition includes detecting or exposing crime or serious impropriety, protecting public health and safety and preventing the public from being misled by an action or statement of an individual or organization. IPSO's public interest definition is deliberately loose in order to allow the adjudicators to judge each complaint fully on its merits.

2.9.1 Privacy and 'social utility': the *Campbell* and *Mosley* judgments

As the line between public and private blurs on the internet, can the courts truly protect what they regard as 'private' and 'confidential' in an attempt to protect a person's reputation, including personal images and photographs? In recent years, English law has adapted the action for breach of confidence to provide a remedy for the unauthorized disclosure of personal information, such as in the *Naomi Campbell* case. This development has been mediated by the analogy of the right to privacy conferred by Article 8(1) ECHR and has required a balancing of that right against the right to freedom of expression conferred by Article 10(1) of the Convention. More recently, the Strasbourg Court confirmed in the *Axel Springer* case[235] that Articles 8 and 10 ECHR are of equal value, as long as the 'balancing exercise' is genuinely conducted by domestic courts, following the margin of appreciation.

Their Lordships said in *Campbell* (2004) that the law of confidence does not protect useless information or trivia.

---

233 *Mosley (Max) v Newsgroup Newspapers Ltd* [2008] EWHC 1777 (QB).
234 *von Hannover v Germany* (No 1) (2005) 40 EHRR 1.
235 *Axel Springer v Germany* (2012) (Application No 3995/08) Strasbourg judgment of 7 February 2012 (ECtHR).

In *Mosley*,[236] Eady J extended the confidentiality notion to what amounts to personal conduct and what would be regarded as 'socially harmful'. He then applied the terms 'social utility' and 'pressing social need',[237] first coined in *Francome*[238] by Sir John Donaldson MR, where he explained that:

the 'media', to use a term which comprises not only the newspapers, but also television and radio, are an essential foundation of any democracy. In exposing crime, anti-social behaviour and hypocrisy and in campaigning for reform and propagating the view of minorities, they perform an invaluable function.[239]

Max Mosley[240] sued the *News of the World* (News Group Newspapers Ltd), complaining about a number of articles relating to clandestine videos taken by a prostitute, known from the law reports only as 'Woman E'. On 28 March 2008, she had taken video footage of the claimant on a concealed camera provided to her by a *NoW* journalist while Max Mosley was engaged in a private sexual orgy in a flat in Chelsea. Still images from the footage were published prominently in the newspaper on 30 March 2008, and edited footage was displayed on the *NoW* website on 30 and 31 March 2008. The newspaper and website were viewed by millions of people.

Neville Thurlbeck,[241] at the time the chief reporter for *NoW*, headlined the 'exclusive' on 30 March 2008: 'F1 Boss Has Sick Nazi Orgy With 5 Hookers', with the subheading: 'Son of Hitler-loving fascist in sex shame'.

Of 'public interest' – the newspaper argued – was that Mr Mosley, the youngest son of the right-wing fascist leader Sir Oswald Mosley[242] and Diana Mitford, had engaged not only in an orgy with call girls, but in a 'Nazi orgy'. Mr Mosley knew nothing of the article before publication nor of the clandestine video footage which had been taken by an undercover reporter posing as a prostitute. The first he knew of the scoop was on the very same Sunday that millions of people were reading the article and watching the accompanying footage on the *NoW* website.

Mosley's cause of action centred on both a breach of confidence (i.e. the unauthorized disclosure of personal information) and an infringement of his privacy under Article 8(1) ECHR. Eady J referred to the principle of 'pressing social need', where revealing someone's identity in court and therefore in the media was useful to society and 'of social utility', for the purpose of revealing criminal misconduct and antisocial behaviour (see: *X*

---

236 *Mosley v NGN* [2008] EWHC 1777 (QB).
237 Ibid. at 173.
238 *Francome v MGN* [1984] 1 WLR 892.
239 Ibid. at 989 (Sir John Donaldson MR).
240 Mr Mosley was at the time president of the Fédération Internationale de l'Automobile (FIA) – Formula 1's governing body (1993–2009).
241 Thurlbeck became one of the most notorious figures of the phone-hacking scandal. His name was literally written on the smoking gun, the 'For Neville' email of voicemail transcripts that left little alternative for him (and others) but to plead guilty to the intimidation of a witness contrary to s 51 of the Criminal Justice and Public Order Act 1994 and assisting an offence contrary to s 46 of the Serious Crime Act 2007 in May 2012 as part of the Met Police's Operation Weeting ('phone hacking'). He went to prison for 37 days (of a six-month sentence). Thurlbeck's book *Tabloid Secrets* (2015) describes a series of scoops and how luck, determination and a perversely admirable talent for sabotaging his opposition led to countless *NotW* exclusives, lurid revelations about celebrities, politicians, murderers and victims.
242 Sir Oswald Ernald Mosley, 6th Baronet (1896–1980) was an English politician, known principally as the founder of the British Union of Fascists (BUF) in 1932.

v *Persons Unknown* (2006)[243]). Clearly, it was not alleged that the Formula 1 boss had engaged in unlawful sexual activity. Eady J stressed that Mr Mosley's conduct was in private and not socially harmful. He drew the analogy between the law on consumption of alcohol with that of other intoxicating substances: was such conduct in private and by consenting adults in the public interest and of social utility?

Eady J ruled that that the photographs of and articles on the Formula 1 chief's sado-masochistic activities with hired call girls were of *no social utility* at all. They rather amounted to 'old-fashioned breach of confidence' by way of conduct inconsistent with a pre-existing relationship, rather than simply of the 'purloining of private information'. The judge stressed that the content of the published material was inherently private in nature, consisting of S&M sexual practices. Moreover, there had been a pre-existing relationship of confidentiality between the participants, who had all known each other for some time and took part in such activities on the understanding that they would be private and that none of them would reveal what had taken place. Clearly 'Woman E' had breached that trust by recording her fellow participants.[244]

In his judgment handed down on 24 July 2008, Eady J found that the claimant had a reasonable expectation of privacy in relation to sexual activities which had been infringed by publication of the images and footage, and awarded Max Mosley £60,000 compensatory damages and a permanent injunction restraining NGN Limited, publishers of the *News of the World*, from republishing them. No injunction was made against persons who were not parties to the action.

Max Mosley had chosen not to sue the newspaper in defamation. Though he was successful in the privacy claim it still meant that the offending articles and video footage of the 'Nazi Orgy' available on the *NoW* website were already in the public domain, and the damage to Mr Mosley's reputation had been done. Mr Mosley had hoped that the successful outcome of his litigation and the deterrent effect which it would have on persons minded to republish the images or footage would lead to a gradual loss of interest in these events. To a degree, this did happen; but persons other than NGN still maintained posts of the images on websites accessible by search engines on the internet.

On 29 September 2008, Max Mosley filed an application before the European Court of Human Rights (ECtHR) heard on 11 January 2011 in Strasbourg. Mr Mosley had asked the court to rule in favour of 'prior notification', which would compel the British (and EU) press to notify the subject of a story before publication.[245] He lost his claim. The ECtHR ruled against any pre-notification regimes concerning the media which would require powerful civil or criminal sanctions. The ruling stated that such a measure would have an adverse impact on media freedom beyond the limits of 'entertainment journalism' and the trade in the private lives of celebrities. The Strasbourg Court concluded:

> The limited scope under Article 10 for restrictions on the freedom of the press to publish material which contributes to debate on matters of general public interest must be borne in mind. Thus, having regard to the chilling effect to which a

---

243 [2006] EWHC 2783 (QB).
244 *Mosley v NGN* [2008] EWHC 1777 QB at 2–6 (Eady J).
245 *Mosley v UK* (2011) 53 EHRR 30 (ECtHR).

pre-notification requirement risks giving rise, to the significant doubts as to the effectiveness of any pre-notification requirement and to the wide margin of appreciation in this area, the Court is of the view that Article 8 does not require a legally binding pre-notification requirement.[246]

See
Chapter 7.5

During his testimony at the Leveson Inquiry on 24 November 2011, Max Mosley disclosed that he was suing the Google search engine in France and Germany in a libel action, in an attempt to force the internet company to monitor and censor search results about his alleged sadomasochistic orgy and the *NoW* video.[247]

His action was superseded by the *Google Spain* case (C-131/12)[248] resulting in the 'right to be forgotten' ruling.

See above 2.7

We have seen in *Mosley* (2008) that the courts protect the individual when the intrusion into a claimant's life has been 'highly offensive' and when the objective 'sober and reasonable man' would agree that intrusion has been unacceptable.

 FOR THOUGHT

In what circumstances will the courts grant privacy protection in the absence of 'Max Mosley–style' pre-notification regulation to editors?

2.9.2 Genuine public interest or mere 'tittle-tattle'? The *von Hannover Nos 1–3* and *Axel Springer* actions

The German weekly 'gossip' magazines such as *Bunte* or *Neues Blatt* have always been interested in the private lives of European royalty, focusing particularly on Princess Caroline of Monaco[249] during her various marriages, the last being to Ernst August von Hannover. The applicant, Princess Caroline von Hannover, a Monegasque national who was born in 1957. The German media interest focused on the royal family in Monaco, started with the marriage of Prince Rainier III (1923–2005) to the Hollywood and Oscar-winning actress Grace Kelly (1929–1982) in 1956 and their children Princess Caroline, Prince Albert II and Princess Stephanie.

Princess Caroline made repeated attempts to prevent the publication of photographs portraying her private life, often by taking legal action in the German courts. Two series of photographs, published in 1993 and 1997, were the subject of three sets of proceedings. Those proceedings were the subject of the judgment of 24 June 2004 in *von*

---

246 Ibid. at 132.
247 Source: Witness statement by Max Rufus Mosley to the Leveson Inquiry at MOD100023418 and MOD100023425 signed and dated 31 October 2011: www.levesoninquiry.org.uk/wp-content/uploads/2011/11/Witness-Statement-of-Max-Mosley.pdf.
248 *Google Spain SL, Google Inc. v Agencia Española de Protección de Datos, Mario Costeja González* ('right to be forgotten' Case C-131/12) Court of Justice of the European Union, Luxembourg, 13 May 2014.
249 Her official title is Princess Caroline Louise Marguerite, Prinzessin von Hannover, Herzogin zu Braunschweig und Lüneburg. She married Ernst August Prinz von Hannover on 23 January 1999, her second marriage, after Caroline of Monaco had married Philippe Junot on 28 June 1978; their marriage was annulled on 9 October 1980.

Hannover v Germany (No 1)[250] in which the European Court of Human Rights (ECtHR) held that the court decisions in question had infringed the applicant's right to respect for her private life under Article 8(1) ECHR.

In a joint action, Caroline and her husband, Ernst August von Hannover,[251] subsequently brought several sets of proceedings seeking injunctions against the publication of further photographs in German glossy and gossip magazines between 2002 and 2004. The German Federal Court of Justice dismissed their claims in part, and the Federal Constitutional Court rejected a constitutional complaint by the applicants. Those proceedings were the subject of the Grand Chamber judgment of 7 February 2012 in the case of von Hannover v Germany (No 2),[252] in which the Court held that the court decisions at issue had not infringed the right of Princess Caroline von Hannover and her husband to respect for their private life.

Noteworthy in von Hannover (No 1) was the judgment by presiding Judge Zupani, who made the distinctions between the different levels of 'privacy' which were rather confusing in German copyright law and constitutional jurisprudence (Begriffsjurisprudenz). The CJEU criticized Germany's Constitutional Court for allowing publication of the pictures four and a half years earlier and said there had been no 'legitimate interest' in Princess Caroline's private life and that the general public did not have a legitimate interest in knowing her whereabouts or how she behaved generally in her private life. The ECtHR raised the standard of protection of private life to a level higher than in Germany, similar to the privacy laws of France. Zupani's ruling set the precedent for the 'balancing test' in human rights legislation between the public's right to know and freedom of the media to report under Article 10 ECHR and the celebrity's right to privacy:

> he who willingly steps upon the public stage cannot claim to be a private person entitled to anonymity. Royalty, actors, academics, politicians etc. perform whatever they perform publicly. They may not seek publicity, yet, by definition, their image is to some extent public property.[253]

The ruling in von Hannover (No 1) significantly impacted on media practices throughout Europe at the time. Paparazzi had to make sure when taking a celebrity photo: was it taken in a clandestine and secret long-lens way by peeping over a fence into a private garden, or was the celebrity individual undertaking an official duty in public? Von Hannover (No 1) set the scene for the 'public' or 'private sphere'. And if the picture was of public interest it could safely be published, irrespective of consent.

The ruling in von Hannover (No 2) was different. The ECtHR did not really reverse the ruling in the No 1 action but did not grant the Article 8(1) 'privacy' right to Princess Caroline von Hannover for different reasons. The action concerned the publication of photographs in the 'gossip' magazine Frau im Spiegel in 2002, showing the Princess and

---

250 von Hannover (No 1) (2005) 40 EHRR 1.
251 Born 1954 and of particular interest since he is a member of the royal House of Hannover as Ernst August, Prince of Hanover, Duke of Brunswick and Lüneburg (Ernst August Albert Paul Otto Rupprecht Oskar Berthold Friedrich-Ferdinand Christian-Ludwig Prinz von Hannover Herzog zu Braunschweig und Lüneburg Königlicher Prinz von Großbritannien und Irland).
252 von Hannover v Germany (No 2) (2012) (Application Nos – 40660/08, 60641/08) (unreported) Judgment of 7 February 2012.
253 von Hannover (No 1) (2005) 40 EHRR 1 at 32 (Judge Zupani).

her husband, Prince Ernst August von Hannover (joint applicants), on a skiing holiday in St Moritz. The accompanying article reported on the deteriorating health of the Princess' father, Prince Rainier III of Monaco, and that the Princess should have been at his bedside as he was dying. The ECtHR ruled that the publication of the said photo and the accompanying article did not breach the applicants' privacy rights because the subject matter (the poor health of the reigning Prince of Monaco) was of general public interest. The Strasbourg Court also confirmed that the link between the photographs and the subject matter of the accompanying article was sufficiently close so as to render their publication justifiable. The case was jointly heard with the *Axel Springer* case (see below).

❖ KEY CASE

Axel Springer v Germany (2012) (joint application No 3995/08 with *von Hannover No 2*) Strasbourg judgment of 7 February 2012 (ECtHR)

Precedents (in both actions: *Axel Springer* and *von Hannover No 2*)

- ❖ **Contribution to a debate of general interest** – this covers not only political issues or crimes but sporting issues or performing artists.[254]
- ❖ **How well known the person was and the subject of the report** – a distinction has to be made between private individuals and persons acting in a public context, as political or public figures.[255]
- ❖ **Prior conduct of the person concerned: the conduct of the person prior to the publication is a relevant factor** – although the mere fact of having co-operated with the press cannot be an argument for depriving a person of all protection.[256]
- ❖ **Method of obtaining the information and its veracity** – these are important factors; the protection of Article 10(1) ECHR is subject to the proviso that journalists are acting in good faith, on an accurate factual basis, providing reliable and precise information in accordance with the ethics of journalism.[257]
- ❖ **Content, form and consequences of the publication** – the way in which the photo or report is obtained and the way in which the individual is represented are factors to take into account.[258]
- ❖ **Severity of the sanction imposed.**[259]
- ❖ **Courts should balance Articles 8 and 10 ECHR equally depending on the facts and circumstances (the proportionality test).**
- ❖ **Article 8(1) ECHR does not create an 'image right', nor does it create a 'right to reputation'.**
- ❖ **Individuals who seek the public limelight have their Article 8(1) right to privacy severely curtailed.**

---

254 *Axel Springer v Germany* (2012) at para. 90.
255 Ibid. at para. 91.
256 Ibid. at para. 92.
257 Ibid. at para. 93.
258 Ibid. at para. 94.
259 Ibid. at para. 95.

Facts

The applicant, Axel Springer-Verlag, is the publisher of the daily German tabloid *Bild-Zeitung* ('*Bild*'), registered in Hamburg since 1952, with a circulation of about 2.6 million per day (in 2004). *Bild* is famous for its salacious gossip and sensational journalistic headlines.

The case concerned two articles about X, a well-known TV actor.[260] X had been the subject of two stories and photos in *Bild* in 2004 and 2005, after he was arrested in a beer tent at the Munich Oktoberfest for possessing cocaine. The story made the headlines: 'Cocaine! Superintendent Caught at Munich Beer Festival', with a photo of X. The second article was published some ten months later and reported details of X pleading guilty to the drug possession offence and how he was sentenced to a €18,000 fine. Axel Springer claimed that prior to publication the journalist had confirmed the arrest with the police sergeant present at the scene; the public prosecutor had also verified the charges.

Whilst the Hamburg regional court had granted X an injunction, restraining *Bild* (and other publications) from publishing the story, *Bild* went ahead and published the story and photos. The Hamburg court found Axel Springer guilty of contempt by disobeying the existing court order. The applicant publishers petitioned the ECtHR relying on their Article 10(1) right.

Decision: *Axel Springer*

The Grand Chamber (of the ECtHR) disagreed with the German courts' reasoning for granting the injunction to the actor. Judges of the Grand Chamber opined that X's arrest and conviction were of general public interest, particularly since the public prosecutor had confirmed the criminal charges of possession of class A drugs. It was also in the public interest and therefore of importance to uphold the law, since X had been a role model for young people, playing the character of a police superintendent (*der Kommissar*) whose job it was to combat crime. The Court noted that X had regularly contacted the press himself or via his PR company and that he had previously revealed detailed information about his private life in a number of media interviews. The Court reasoned that X's 'legitimate expectation' of protection for his private life was reduced by virtue of the fact that he had 'actively sought the limelight'. Because 'TV cop' X was a well-known actor, known particularly as a law enforcement officer on screen, the ECtHR held:

> he was sufficiently well known to qualify as a public figure. That consideration . . . reinforces the public's interest in being informed of X's arrest and of the criminal proceedings against him.[261]

---

260 The German left-wing daily newspaper *TAZ* (*Tageszeitung*) disclosed X's identity, that of Bruno Eyron, well-known for playing a RTL-TV cop, 'Kommissar Balko'. Source: 'Caroline von Monaco zu Recht geknipst. Ein europäisches Gericht stärkt die deutsche Pressefreiheit: Ein Foto von Caroline von Monaco durfte gedruckt werden. Ebenso das Bild eines koksenden Schauspielers', by Christian Rath, *TAZ*, 7 February 2012.

261 Ibid. at para. 99.

The Grand Chamber found by 12 votes to 5 that the German courts had violated the publishers' Article 10(1) rights by their overzealous injunctive sanctions imposed on the tabloid newspaper. The restraining order had been too severe, and accordingly there had been a violation of the publishers' Article 10 right. The newspaper publishers were awarded damages and costs in the domestic proceedings and in the Strasbourg action.

Analysis of *Axel Springer* and *von Hannover (No 2)*

The difficulty with both the conjoined cases was compounded by a series of appeals and cross-appeals by the applicants and various publishers, including complaints in respect of publications and photographs elsewhere. Nevertheless, the ECtHR's decision in both cases is an important win for the media, particularly as media practices were severely criticized at the Leveson Inquiry in London's High Court of Justice. The *Axel Springer* and *von Hannover (No 2)* judgments remind us of the important role played by a free and uncensored press in a pluralistic democracy where the Human Rights Court undertook a careful balancing exercise between freedom of expression and the individuals' privacy rights. In both cases the Grand Chamber of the ECtHR explained the criteria, based on existing human rights law, which are to be applied when balancing the competing Article 8 and 10 rights in the public interest. Both the ECtHR decisions in *Axel Springer* and *von Hannover (No 2)* can be seen as important victories for the media and for press freedom in general. With the Leveson Inquiry into media ethics and phone hacking dominating the headlines at the same time as the Grand Chamber judgment in 2012, the judgment provides suitable encouragement and support for the media across Europe in relation to the publication of stories and photographs about the private lives of celebrities.[262]

The von Hannover (No 3) (2013)[263] action concerned a complaint lodged by Princess Caroline von Hannover relating to the refusal of the German courts to grant an injunction prohibiting any further publication of a photograph of her and her husband Ernst August taken without their knowledge while on holiday in their villa on an island off the Kenyan coast. In its judgments in *Axel Springer AG* and von Hannover (No 2) (see above) the ECtHR had set out the relevant criteria for balancing the right to respect for private life against the right to freedom of expression. These were contribution to a debate of general interest; how well known the person concerned was; the subject of the report; the prior conduct of the person concerned; the content, form and consequences of the publication; and, in the case of photographs, the circumstances in which they were taken.

In von Hannover (No 3), the Strasbourg Court noted that the German Federal Constitutional Court had taken the view that, while the photograph in question had not contributed to a debate of general interest, the same was not true of the article accompanying it, which reported on the current trend among celebrities towards letting out their holiday

---

262 For a detailed discussion see: Pillans, B. (2012).
263 *von Hannover v Germany* (No 3) (2013) (Application No 8772/10) ECHR 264.

homes. The Federal Constitutional Court and, subsequently, the Federal Court of Justice had observed that the article was designed to report on that trend and that this conduct was apt to contribute to a debate of general interest. The Court also noted that the article itself did not contain information concerning the private life of the applicant or her husband, but focused on practical aspects relating to the villa and its letting. It could not therefore be asserted that the article had merely been a pretext for publishing the photograph in question or that the connection between the article and the photograph had been purely contrived. The characterization of the subject of the article as an event of general interest, first by the Federal Constitutional Court and then by the Federal Court of Justice, could not be considered unreasonable. The Human Rights Court could therefore accept that the photograph in question had made a contribution to a debate of general interest.

The Strasbourg Court reiterated that on several occasions the applicant and her husband were to be regarded as public figures who could not claim protection of their private lives in the same way as individuals unknown to the public. Noting that the German courts had taken into consideration the essential criteria and Strasbourg jurisprudence in balancing the various interests at stake, the court concluded that they had not failed to comply with their positive obligations and that there had been no violation of Article 8(1) of the Convention.

The Strasbourg Human Rights Court messages sent out in *von Hannover* (No 2) and *Axel Springer* (2012) and *von Hannover* (No 3) are helpful, making a distinction between what is of genuine public interest and what is not. In *von Hannover* (No 2), the article did not centre on Princess Caroline. Instead, its main focus was her father, Prince Rainier of Monaco, and his deteriorating health, which was a matter of public interest given his official role as reigning head of state. In *von Hannover* (No 1) the photographs at issue depicted Princess Caroline's personal relationships and day-to-day life and activities, such as horse riding, skiing and playing tennis, which the ECtHR decided were purely private. What is clear from the three *von Hannover* judgments is that where an article and accompanying photo can be shown to contribute to a debate of genuine public interest, it can be justified and be published. Let us call this the 'red carpet' rule, where the ECtHR defined what is meant by 'public' and 'private sphere' more clearly in relation to celebrities and public figures.

Nicol J did not grant the claimant David Axon 'a reasonable expectation of privacy' because of his 'very public position' as the Commanding Officer of a Royal Navy frigate, HMS *Somerset*. Complaints that Axon had bullied junior officers on the ship had been published in *The Sun* in December 2004. The judge concluded that the fact of Axon's removal from command was a public fact, and his role was that of a 'very public position'.[264]

2.9.3 Privacy and harassment claims and the public interest defence

It is worth noting how the Strasbourg Human Rights Court (ECtHR) has developed the public interest test in relation to privacy (and more recently harassment) claims. This was highlighted in *Armonienė v Lithuania* (2009),[265] where in 2002 a major Lithuanian

---

264 See *Axon v Ministry of Defence* [2016] EWHC 883; [2016] 3 Costs L.O. 401 (QBD) 19 April 2016.
265 [2009] EMLR 7 (Application no 36919/02) (ECtHR). Judges Popović and Tsotsoria expressed a partly dissenting opinion and Judge Zagrebelsky expressed a dissenting opinion.

newspaper had disclosed information that the applicant's husband, Mr Laimutis Armonas, was HIV positive and that he had two children with another woman, whom he was not married to and who had AIDS.

The Lithuanian courts awarded Mr Armonas €2,896 for breach of privacy (at the time the maximum sum for non-pecuniary damage). Mr Armonas' wife, Judita Armoniené, appealed, arguing that the adjudged sum of money was inappropriate and that there was a violation of her husband's right to an effective domestic remedy; furthermore, the Lithuanian state had not granted her husband effective protection of the right to private and family life under Article 8(1) ECHR. Ms Armoniené contended that it was the state's obligation to penalize acts which were damaging an individual's privacy and loss of reputation.

The ECtHR in *Armoniené* emphasized the duty of the media to impart information and ideas on matters of public interest, but noted that:

> a fundamental distinction needs to be made between reporting facts – even if controversial – capable of contributing to a debate in a democratic society and making tawdry allegations about an individual's private life.[266]

The ECtHR found that Lithuanian law did not provide sufficient protection for breach of Article 8(1) ECHR and awarded Ms Armoniené €6,500. The court noted that the publication of the newspaper article about the HIV status of her husband and the information that he was the father of two children by another woman who was suffering from AIDS 'cannot be deemed to contribute to any debate of general interest to society'.

The court emphasized that the family lived in a village rather than a big city; therefore such information could lead to public shaming and a high risk of ostracism. The court commented that the publication in a national daily newspaper with a large circulation could have a negative impact on the willingness of others to take voluntary HIV tests.

Whilst the court noted that each Member State enjoys a degree of margin of appreciation in deciding how to interpret 'respect' for private life, in particular domestic legal circumstances, the court also found that there should be adequate and commensurate compensation by the state when determining a breach of convention right.

Importantly, the ECtHR in *Armoniené* extended the applicant's Article 8 right *beyond* the private family circle to include a social dimension (here the protection of confidentiality relating to another person's HIV status). For these reasons the court ruled that there was no public interest in publishing the information.

The court observed that this was a case of 'outrageous abuse of press freedom' and further criticized the domestic courts' limitations on judicial discretion in relation to awarding damages for breach of privacy. The court stated that the sole purpose of publication had been 'to satisfy the prurient curiosity' of a particular readership.

The public interest defence was advanced by the publishers of the *Daily Mail*, Associated Newspapers, in the *Carina Trimingham* case[267] (see below). The journalist and former press officer to and lover of Chris Huhne MP applied for a privacy injunction under Article 8(1) ECHR in August 2010 against the *Daily Mail* and *Mail on Sunday* in respect of

---

266 Ibid. at para. 39.
267 *Trimingham v Associated Newspapers Ltd* [2012] EWHC 1296.

a series of articles and photographs published about her having an affair with the MP.[268] At the time of the affair Mr Huhne was married to Vicky Pryce for almost 25 years; the couple had five children, three together and two from Ms Pryce's first marriage.[269]. The comments about Ms Trimingham in the newspapers focused on her appearance, referring to her as 'bisexual' and a 'lesbian' and that she had previously lived in a civil partnership with another woman. Whilst Ms Trimingham did not action in defamation (because the allegations were substantially true), her legal complaint focused on repeated 'pejorative' references to her sexuality and appearance in eight articles. She actioned in harassment, privacy and breach of copyright in respect of the photographs.

❖ KEY CASE — *Trimingham v Associated Newspapers Ltd* [2012] EWHC 1296 (QB)

Precedent

❖ Claimants cannot rely on their Article 8(1) ECHR privacy rights if they are not private individuals; in the case of a public figure performing a public function the expectation of privacy is limited.

❖ The public interest defence (for the media) exists where the conduct and behaviour of the claimant in his or her personal life is likely to affect the business of government.

❖ A reasonable person with the same characteristics as the claimant would not think it unreasonable to disclose matters of genuine public interest (here Ms T was a press officer and journalist and had the knowledge of media practices).

❖ It would be a serious interference with freedom of expression (Article 10(1) ECHR) to silence the views of the press by subjective claims of harassment.

❖ There is no 'privacy' in photos if the claimant publishes personal photos on social media (e.g. Facebook).

Facts

Carina Trimingham (T) had worked as a press officer in three political campaigns and had been the campaign director for the Electoral Reform Society. She began to have an affair with married MP, Chris Huhne (Lib Dem) (H), in 2010, then a leading figure in the Coalition government and for whom Ms T had worked as a press officer. At the time Ms T was in a civil partnership with another woman, and both she and Mr H's wife were unaware of the affair. Numerous articles appeared in the *Mail Online* and the print editions of the *Daily*

---

268 Mr Christopher Huhne MP had been re-elected as the Member of Parliament for Eastleigh in Hampshire at the General Election held in May 2010. He became Secretary of State for Energy in the Coalition government. He was one of the leading figures in the government and in the Liberal Democrat Party at the time.

269 Mr Huhne and his by now ex-wife Vicky Pryce, a prominent economist, were convicted of perverting the course of justice after she took speeding points for him following an incident on the M11 in 2003. Pryce had claimed the defence of marital coercion. Both were found guilty at Southwark Crown Court in March 2013 and each was given an eight-month prison sentence.

Mail and the *Mail on Sunday*, calling T 'bisexual' and 'lesbian' and making comments about her appearance, for example:

'Chris Huhne's bisexual lover: Life and very different loves of the PR girl in Doc Martens' by Barbara Davies, *Daily Mail* 21 June 2010.

'First picture of Chris Huhne's lover and the lesbian civil partner she has left broken-hearted' by Barbara Davies, *Daily Mail* 22 June 2010.

'It's Chris Huhne's hypocrisy and lies that matter, not his sex life' by Richard Littlejohn, *Daily Mail* 22 June 2010.

Photographs which had been taken by a professional photographer and personal friend of T at her home prior to her going to her civil partnership ceremony and at the ceremony were published in the *Daily Mail* and the *Mail on Sunday* (eight articles in August 2011 and other newspapers such as *The People*). T submitted that the *Mail* had:

1 pursued a course of conduct amounting to harassment under section 1(3)(c) Protection from Harassment Act 1997;
2 misused private information under Article 8(1) ECHR and breach of confidentiality; and
3 breached copyright contrary to section 85 Copyright, Designs and Patents Act 1988 (CDPA) by publishing the photographs.

Ms T sought aggravated damages and a privacy injunction at trial.

Decision
The claim was dismissed with an order for costs against Ms Trimingham. Tugendhat J gave the following reasons:

1 *The harassment claim*
The judge considered that repeated publication in the media of offensive or insulting words about a person's appearance, sexuality, or any other characteristic *did not* amount to harassment.[270] Reasons advanced were:

(a) Ms T was *not* a private figure and in her private capacity she had conducted a sexual relationship with H which she knew would be likely to lead to a political scandal.[271] The scope of her protected private life was therefore limited (see: *Saaristo v Finland* (2010)).[272]

(b) T claimed that the defendant newspaper *ought* to have known that their conduct by publication amounted to harassment. Tugendhat J applied the 'reasonable person' test and pointed out: 'she was tough, a woman of strong character, not likely to be upset by comments or offensive language, a woman who was known to give as good as

---

270 *Trimingham* [2012] EWHC 1296 at para. 70 (Tugendhat J).
271 Ibid. at para. 249.
272 [2010] ECHR 1497.

she got'[273] (applying *Banks v Ablex Ltd* (2005)[274]). The judge found that the newspaper's hostility was directed towards her conduct, not her appearance. The words 'bisexual' and 'lesbian' were not normally understood to be pejorative and no reasonable reader of the words complained of would understand them in a pejorative sense[275] (applying *Jeynes v News Magazines Ltd* (2007)[276]).

(c) The reasonableness of the course of conduct. The judge found that it is not unreasonable for a newspaper to refer to these facts and if a journalist is criticizing a person for deceitful, unprofessional or immoral behaviour in a sexual and public context, it is not unreasonable to refer to that person as 'lesbian' or 'homosexual' given the newsworthiness of events.[277]

2   *The Article 8 privacy and breach of confidentiality claims*

Tugendhat J said these were rather limited since Ms T was not a purely private figure. She had openly and publicly declared her sexuality and previous sexual relationships[278] (applying: *Murray v Express Newspapers plc* (2007)[279]). The judge said it would be a serious interference with freedom of expression (Article 10(1) ECHR) if members of the media, wishing to express their own views, could be silenced by, or threatened with, claims for harassment based on subjective claims by individuals that they felt offended or insulted.

3   *The breach of copyright claim*

Section 85 CDPA affords rights to a person who 'commissions' the taking of a photograph. The photographs published in the newspapers had been commissioned by Ms T for her civil partnership ceremony; and Ms T had given these pictures to the *Evening Standard* in 2008 and posted them on her Facebook page. She only removed them from the site after the 'Huhne' story had broken. Tugendhat J held that the publication of the 'wedding' photographs disclosed no significant information and that T had no reasonable expectation of privacy in respect of these photos[280] (applying: *Ultraframe (UK) Ltd v Fielding* (2005)[281]).

Analysis

The *Trimingham* case touches on several areas of law: protection from harassment, copyright, privacy under Article 8(1) ECHR and confidentiality. Like *Max Mosley*, Ms Trimingham decided not to sue in defamation. She chose the Protection from Harassment Act 1997, which obliges the state to prevent interference with an individual's right to privacy and the protection of their private lives under Article 8(1) ECHR. Was Carina Trimingham a public or

---

273 Trimingham [2012] EWHC 1296 at para. 252.
274 [2005] EWCA Civ 173.
275 Trimingham [2012] EWHC 1296 at para. 255.
276 [2007] EWCA Civ 1270.
277 Trimingham [2012] EWHC 1296 at para. 261.
278 Ibid. at para. 263.
279 [2007] EWHC 1908 (Ch).
280 Trimingham [2012] EWHC 1296 at paras 328, 337, 338.
281 [2005] EWHC 679 (Ch).

private figure? The judge determined that T was *not* a private individual because of her association with a politician. She also had a high-profile career as PA to Mr Huhne. She could not claim privacy in the photographs because she had herself disclosed photos and matters about her private life on Facebook.

The case is a good example where the courts are balancing 'privacy' and 'freedom of expression' – Tugendhat J decided in favour of the latter. He also dismissed Ms Trimingham's harassment claim (s 1(3)(c) PHA 1997) because the conduct of the newspaper was held to be not so unreasonable in the particular circumstances and there was a 'pressing social need' to publish the story. This means that the privacy rights of the individual came second to the right of press freedom.

2.9.4 Do privacy injunctions interfere with the right to freedom of expression?

The media's defence of 'public interest' in privacy actions will be considered by the courts in respect of a 'pressing social need'. This test is based on the ruling in *Max Mosley*.[282] Where a litigant intends to serve a prohibitory injunction upon a publication, the courts rely on the *Spycatcher* principle, in that the individual author, journalist or publisher should be given a realistic opportunity to be heard on the appropriateness of granting the injunction and the scope of its terms, mirrored closely by the provisions contained in section 12 HRA 1998. As the Strasbourg Court observed in *von Hannover* (No 1):

> the court considers that a fundamental distinction needs to be made between reporting facts – even controversial ones – capable of contributing to a debate in a democratic society relating to politicians in the exercise of their functions, for example, and reporting details of the private life of an individual who, moreover, as in this case, does not exercise official functions. While in the former case the press exercises its vital role of 'watchdog' in a democracy by contributing to 'impart[ing] information and ideas on matters of public interest' it does not do so in the latter case.[283]

What should be borne in mind is that if an individual is properly entitled to a privacy injunction, the whole purpose of that injunction may in some situations be undermined by disclosure of the fact that an injunction has been obtained by that individual. In such circumstances the alternative to justice being done behind closed doors is that justice will not be done at all.

Where the potential adverse consequences of disclosure are particularly grave – say, in family cases – the courts have granted restraining orders under section 12 HRA with great expediency.

A media organization may well be in contempt if they disclose the information that the court has ordered not to be disclosed. In *Re H (A Healthcare Worker)* (2002)[284] the claimant

---

282 *Mosley v NGN* [2008] EMLR 679.
283 *von Hannover v Germany* (No 1) (2005) 40 EHRR 1 at 63.
284 *H (A Healthcare Worker) v Associated Newspapers Ltd* [2002] EMLR 425.

was seeking to prevent the disclosure by N, a health authority, of confidential information that he was HIV positive. Kennedy LJ held that the court could properly make an order in the proceedings, restraining the publication of information made available in the course of the proceedings which, if disclosed, would pre-empt the decision of the court on the issues before it.

See Chapters 4 and 5

The UK courts increasingly regard personal information as 'private' and 'confidential' when a reasonable person of ordinary sensibilities who finds themselves in the same position as the claimant would have had a reasonable expectation of privacy in all the given circumstances. Such was the case in AMP,[285] where the judge granted a super injunction against 'Persons Unknown' to prevent the transmission of sensitive, personal photos belonging to the claimant who had lost her mobile phone. When some of her naked photos were uploaded to Facebook, the court order not only protected her and the images (which were subsequently removed) but also stopped the threats which not only endangered her reputation but also that of her father's business; her father had allegedly been blackmailed over some of his daughter's images.

There is now a basic framework within Articles 8 and 10 ECHR that provides for a social equilibrium between individuals, the media and society (see: *Fressoz and Roire v France* (1999)[286]).

2.10 Paparazzi, drones and privacy

British tabloid journalism is well-known for its intrusion into the private lives of celebrities. Photographs are a record of a frozen moment in time and therefore have a permanence and presentational power which the human eye and words alone cannot capture. Paparazzi photographs taken on a public beach will not normally be considered private, while those taken in a private location will. Celebrities whose behaviour is seen as 'discreditable' and those who mislead the media about the truth are unlikely to have their secrets preserved.

In determining whether photographs taken in a public place are capable of protection the courts have taken account of the context in which the photographs are taken and published, and whether the person photographed had a reasonable expectation of privacy in relation to their subject matter, and whether the photographs were taken surreptitiously (e.g. by drone paparazzi). Additionally, the information conveyed by photographs has to be judged by reference to the captions and surrounding text as part of the publication.

In November 2016 Kensington Palace issued an unprecedented statement to the media about the harassment being experienced by Meghan Markle and her family as the US *Suits* actress was starting to date Prince Harry. Whilst the statement from the Royal Household confirmed the couple's relationship for the first time, Prince Harry voiced his concern about Miss Markle's safety and accused the press and social media trolls of sexist and racial abuse. The Prince complained about *The Sun's* front page smear 'Harry's Girls on Porn Hub' (4 November 2016) publishing intimate clips of Miss Markle in network television drama *Suits* appearing on Pornhub. *The Sun* strongly denied any smear and said it made clear that the 'steamy sex scenes' it had referred to appearing on the adult site were

285 *AMP v Persons Unknown* [2012] All ER (D) 178.
286 (1999) 31 EHRR 28.

from her appearances in the US drama series. Paparazzi were not only doorstepping the US actress, but also invasive drone photographers were beginning to access Harry and Meghan's private get-togethers.

Similarly in August 2015 Kensington Palace had issued a letter to leaders of international media industry bodies, providing an overview of the challenges facing the Duke and Duchess of Cambridge (Prince William and his wife Katherine), seeking to protect their children Prince George and Princess Charlotte from harassment and surveillance by paparazzi and drone photographers. Communications Secretary Jason Knauf urged the media to uphold standards on the protection of children in a rapidly changing media landscape.

In recent years, the royal family has come down hard on invasions of privacy or inaccuracy by attempting to go straight to the public via social media, as Prince Harry (now the Duke of Sussex following his marriage to Miss Markle in May 2018) has repeatedly done via the royal family's Facebook posts. Prince Harry has repeatedly accused the media and paparazzi of hounding Meghan in the way they hounded his mother, Princess Diana, but with 'racial undertones', too.

In September 2017 royal superfan Louise Chantry, 40, described by The Sun as an 'unemployed holistic healer', was released with a police caution, accused of stalking Prince George. Police had arrested her after she turned up twice at, revealing the location of the Duke and Duchess of Cambridge's firstborn and third in line to the British throne. Ms Chantry had triggered a major security alert after gaining access to the co-educational private primary school in South London shortly after the four-year-old prince had started school on September 6. As a future king, Prince George is one of the best protected members of the royal family.

It is clear that long-lens paparazzi photography is being superseded by 'drone journalism' with photojournalists obtaining Civil Aviation Authority (CAA) licences in the UK to fly RPAS and UAVs with a camera strapped to the device, for commercial purposes. There is as yet no case for 'responsible journalism' or any media regulation apart from data protection regulation and complex CAA rules. Will we be seeing the next picture of a junior royal or a topless princess by obtaining a picture for publication through privacy intrusion?

2.10.1 The Streisand effect: drones, trespass and privacy laws

Drones, the common term for 'Remotely Piloted Aircraft Systems' (RPAS) or 'Unmanned Aircraft Systems' (UAS), are no longer the preserve of the military in that they can be used by private detective agencies and undercover reporters for the purpose of surveillance. Media organizations are making routine use of drone photography to cover stories in remote or disaster areas, and they provide a powerful tool for paparazzi to invade an individual's privacy.

An early homemade 'drone' was used to take aerial photos over the wall of Manchester Strangeways Prison during the riots in 1990 when a UK broadcast company strapped a camera to a model airplane. Now drones deliver illegal drugs to prison cell windows.

The main issue with drones is the height they are permitted to fly amounting to possible trespass; the law and regulations differ from country to country. Few reported cases in the UK concern aircraft which fly at a height which — the owners argue — in no way affects the use of the land. One of the earliest cases was that of *Pickering v Rudd* [1815],[287] where it was held as 'not trespass' to pass over a man's property in a balloon.

In the case of *Bernstein* in the 1970s concerning aerial kite photography, it was again held to be no trespass, establishing that a property owner does not have unqualified rights over the airspace above his land. Additionally there is no authority stating that a land-owner's right in the airspace over land extends to an unlimited height.

❖ KEY CASE   *Bernstein of Leigh (Baron) v Skyviews & General Ltd* [1978] 1 QB 479

Precedent

- ❖ The rights of a landowner in the airspace above his land are restricted to such a height necessary for the ordinary use and enjoyment of his land and the structures upon it.
- ❖ Above that height, the landowner has no greater rights than the general public.
- ❖ Adjoining landowners have no right to erect structures overhanging their neighbour's land.

Facts

Lord Bernstein (B) complained when he was offered an aerial photograph of his country home, Coppings Farm, in Kent that the photo was taken without his consent and was a gross invasion of his privacy. He demanded that the prints and negative should be handed over to him or destroyed. Defendant, Mr Arthur Ashley, managing director of Skyviews (S), said if he had known of this request he would have undertaken to destroy the photograph and negative and not to take another similar photograph in the future. However, B's letter was answered by an 18-year-old secretary, who offered to sell him the negative for £15.

B started proceedings claiming that S wrongfully entered the airspace above his premises (trespass) in order to take the photograph of his house and also claiming an invasion of his right to privacy. B relied on the old Latin maxim *Cujus est solum ejus est usque ad coelum et ad inferos* ('whose is the soil his is also that which is above and below it').[288] B claimed the right to exclude any entry into airspace above his property. S argued in their defence that the photo was taken while the aircraft was flying over adjoining land. The issue before the court was: does flying over a person's private property constitute trespass of airspace?

Decision

The CA held that S's aircraft did not infringe any rights of B's airspace – thus no trespass. Applying this test to the facts of this case, Griffiths J found that, even

---

287 [1815] 171 ER 70.
288 The maxim, first coined in the thirteenth century in Bologna, had been used by English judges in a number cases concerned with structures attached to adjoining land – overhanging buildings, signs, telegraph poles and the like.

though Skyviews' aircraft had flown over Lord Bernstein's property, it did not infringe any of B's rights to airspace, and thus no trespass was committed. B had complained, not that the aircraft had interfered with his use of his land, but that a photograph was taken. His Lordship stated that there was no law against taking a photograph.

Analysis

Lord Bernstein relied on a Latin maxim which meant that an owner of land is the owner of everything up to the heavens above, and everything down to the hell beneath – which the court held inappropriate. S's aircraft flew at such a height which in no way affected the use of the land and could therefore not amount to trespass. There was no law against taking a photograph in public and no authority stating that a landowner's right in the airspace over land extends to an unlimited height. The position is similar in the United States and has been since about 1948 when the US Supreme Court memorably declared that 'The air is a public highway' and that, if it were not, 'every transcontinental flight would subject the operator to countless trespass suits. Common sense revolts at the idea'.

In 2003 Barbara Streisand sued aerial photographer Kenneth Adelman and the California Coastal Records Project (CCRP) for invasion of her privacy, namely publishing and permanently displaying aerial shots of her house in Malibu, California. CCRP had published a series of photos of the California coastline as part of an aerial photographic survey. As part of its public service, DDRP host extensive pictures within their search engine on its website, which happens to include shots of Ms Streisand's mansion in Malibu. However, Ms Streisand's lawsuit backfired when it emerged that the famous singer had inadvertently given her details to CCRP. Social media admonished her for this frivolous suit, stating it was harmful to freedom of speech. As the links proliferated, thousands of people saw the pictures of Ms Streisand's house — far more than would otherwise ever have bothered to browse through the CCRP's archives. By the time a judge eventually dismissed the lawsuit, Ms Streisand's privacy had been far more thoroughly compromised than it would have been had she and her lawyers left the CCRP alone.[289]

On 6 April 2013 Wikimedia France, the local chapter of the Wikimedia movement that runs Wikipedia, released a press statement that it allegedly been contacted by the Direction Centrale du Renseignement Intérieur (DCRI), France's domestic spy and security agency, which was unhappy with an article about Pierre-sur-Haute, a military radio base run by the French Air Force. The spooks wanted the article amended to remove what they claimed was classified information. When the Wikipedians refused, the DRCI ordered a French Wikipedia editor to delete the entire article or face immediate arrest for espionage. The article "Station hertzienne militaire de Pierre-sur-Haute" became the most mad page during the weekend of 6–7 April 2013 with more than 120,000 page views. The article is still on Wikipedia France. This was a textbook example of what internet aficionados call the 'Streisand effect', named after the American singer and actress Barbra Streisand.

---

289 Source: 'What is the Streisand effect?' *Economist*, 16 April 2013.

The Streisand effect now describes an online phenomenon in which an attempt to hide or remove information – a photo, video, story and so forth – results in the greater spread of the information in question.

2.10.2 How can drone cameras impact on privacy?

The current state of the law in the UK remains convoluted and confusing (to the police and the courts) in relation to recreational drone use and paparazzi journalism. Some drones fitted with cameras can loiter overhead for long stretches, engaging in 'persistent surveillance'.

UK privacy laws remain weak to non-existent, as we have seen in this chapter, and questions remain whether one is flying a drone camera in public – an open field for example – or in a space where one has a 'reasonable expectation of privacy' (see: *von Hannover* (No 1)).

John Moreland, spokesman for the UAV Systems Association, argues that in this era of 'big data' the line between public and private can no longer be delimited by physical boundaries, as he told BBC News online:

> Hundreds of these UAVs are being used commercially these days, typically flying below 400ft (120m) and with a range of about 500m (0.3 miles). Most are engaged in aerial photography and 3D surveying, but applications are expanding all the time.[290]

Regulations in form of secondary legislation exist for recreational drone flights, contained within the Air Navigation Orders of 2016 and 2009 (ANO). CAA guidelines in simplified form have also been issued in form of the 'Dronecode'[291] by the UK Civil Aviation Authority (CAA). The Dronecode states that the drone must:

- be flown below 400 ft (122 m)
- stay away from people and property by 150 ft (50 m)
- never fly near aircraft.

In April 2014, Robert Knowles from Cumbria was the first person in the UK to be successfully prosecuted by the CAA for the dangerous and illegal flying of a UAV ('the drone').

He was found to have flown the drone in restricted airspace over a nuclear submarine facility. Analysis by the police of video footage taken from a camera fitted to the drone revealed that during its flight it had skimmed over the busy Jubilee Bridge over Walney Channel, well within the legally permitted 50-metre separation distance required. Both offences breached the UK's Air Navigation Order.

Knowles was found guilty of 'flying a small unmanned surveillance aircraft' within 50 metres of a structure (contra s 167 of the Air Navigation Order 2009) and flying

---

290 Source: 'Sky high thinking: Could we all soon own a drone?', by Matthew Wall, *BBC News Online*, 19 February 2013.
291 The Dronecode, Civil Aviation Authority, 30 July 2018: http://dronesafe.uk/wp-content/uploads/2018/06/Dronecode_2018-07-30.pdf.

over a nuclear installation (contra reg. 3(2) of the Air Navigation (Restriction of Flying) (Nuclear Installations) Regulations 2007). Mr Knowles was fined £800 and with costs to the CAA of £3,500 at Furness and District Magistrates' Court. The Robert Knowles case has raised important safety issues concerning recreational flying of unmanned aircraft with cameras attached.

Some UK police forces are more 'keen' than others and have issued a number of cautions to photographers for using drones for commercial purposes without permission when trespassing on owners' land without asking for permission.

In December 2014a freelance photojournalist, Brighton-based Eddie Mitchell, carrying out aerial photography with a drone camera, was arrested by police officers for 'dangerous behaviour'. Mitchell had a CAA licence to fly drones professionally. On 30 December 2014, Mitchell had been taking aerial photos of a fatal fire at a caravan site in Newchapel, Surrey, in which a mother and two children died. Mitchell had flown his 1.2 kg drone in order to get a general view picture of the caravan site whilst staying some distance away from the scene of the actual fire. Three Surrey police officers subsequently arrested Mitchell, placing him in handcuffs, and used the remote control to attempt to land the drone themselves. Eventually Mitchell had to land it for them still in handcuffs. He was held in a Surrey police cell for some five hours for breach of the peace and eventually freed after the intervention of a BBC lawyer. Mitchell claimed the 'debacle' came about because police were unaware of the CAA regulations governing drone use.[292] Mitchell urged the Association of Chief Police Officers (ACPO) to issue new guidance after the officers arrested him whilst the drone was airborne, rather than allowing him to land it safely.

Following sightings of drones at Gatwick Airport in December 2018, where the airport had to be shut down for two days for fears of security risks, the law was changed. From March 2019 it is illegal to fly a drone within 5 km of an airport (up from 1 km). From 30 November 2019, owners of drones weighing 250 grams or more have to register with the CAA, and drone pilots must take an online safety test to ensure the UK's skies are safe from irresponsible flyers. Smaller toy drones are still exempt, but serious models like the DJI Phantom 4 are covered by the new legislation. The new drone awareness tests cover topics such as safety, security and privacy. Anyone who fails to register or sit the competency tests faces fines of up to £1,000.[293]

2.10.3 The 'topless Kate' photos

In 2012 the Duke and Duchess of Cambridge launched legal proceedings against the UK publication of *Closer* preventing the magazine from printing any further images of topless photographs of Kate Middleton, taken in the private gardens of a French chateau. Separate legal action was taken in a Paris court for invasion of privacy and complicity.

---

292 Source: 'Licensed drone operator arrested by "dangerous and idiotic" police officers while filming near Gatwick', by Jamie Merrill, *Independent*, 31 December 2014: www.independent.co.uk/news/uk/home-news/licensed-bbc-drone-operatorarrested-by-dangerous-and-idiotic-police-officers-while-filming-near-gatwick-9951784.html.

293 Source: House of Commons, Department of Transport (2019) 'Taking Flight: The Future of Drones in the UK Government Response Moving Britain Ahead'. 17 January 2019 (CP7) at https://assets.publishing.service.gov.uk/government/uploads/system/uploads/attachment_data/file/771673/future-of-drones-in-uk-consultation-response-web.pdf.

Images of the Duchess sunbathing topless whilst the Royal couple were holidaying in Provence in 2012 had been published in *Closer* magazine in France. The Italian version of the magazine had also published the photographs and regional newspaper *La Provence* had printed swimwear pictures of Katherine. The royal couple had been staying at a chateau in Provence owned by Viscount David Linley, nephew of Queen Elizabeth II.

The trial against six people linked to *Closer* magazine began in May 2017. On 5 September 2017 presiding judge Florence Lasserre-Jeannin at the Tribunal de Grande Instance in Nanterre, near Paris, convicted all six defendants of charges relating to the taking and publication of the images. Ernesto Mauri, 70, chief executive of publishing group Mondadori, which produces *Closer*, and Laurence Pieau, 51, editor of the magazine in France, were fined for their conspiracy role in the invasion of privacy. They were both ordered to pay the maximum penalty of €45,000 (£41,000).

Paparazzi agency photographers Cyril Moreau and Dominique Jacovides, who had denied taking the topless photos at the centre of the controversy, were told to each pay €10,000 (£9,200). They were found guilty of taking long-lens shots of the royals, including the topless pictures of the Duchess of Cambridge, from a public road.

Also convicted were the photographers and editor of *La Provence*. Marc Auburtin, 57, La Provence's publishing director at the time, was fined €1,500 (£1,380), and the paper's photographer, Valerie Suau, 53, was fined €1,000 (£920) (suspended).[294] The Duke and Duchess did not attend court; a written statement had been read out at the trial by Prince William's lawyer Jean Veil:

> My wife and I thought that we could go to France for a few days in a secluded villa owned by a member of my family, and thus enjoy our privacy. We know France and the French, and we know that they are, in principle, respectful of private life, including that of their guests. The clandestine way in which these photographs were taken was particularly shocking to us as it breached our privacy.

Prince William had stated that the images were 'all the more painful' given the experience of his mother, Diana, Princess of Wales, who died in a car crash in Paris in 1997 as she was being pursued by photographers.

The court also heard evidence of mobile phone data which had placed paparazzi photographers Moreau, 32, and Jacovides, 59, in the area between 4 and 6 September 2012, when the topless images had been taken. Paul-Albert Iweins, representing *Closer* magazine, had argued in the magazine's defence that the couple had been the subject of much media attention – including the broadcast of their wedding on 29 November 2011 – and that the photos did not constitute a breach of privacy and cast them in a positive light.

2.11 A tort of privacy?

We know by now that there is no UK law that protects an individual's right to privacy. The absence of any general cause of action for invasion of privacy was acknowledged by the

---

294 Source: 'Duke and Duchess of Cambridge awarded more than €100K in damages over topless photographs', by Sally Wardle, PA, *Cambridgeshire Live News*, 5 September 2017.

Court of Appeal in *Kaye v Robertson* (1991),[295] in which a newspaper reporter and photographer invaded the actor Gordon Kaye's hospital bedroom, purported to interview him and took photographs. The law of trespass provided no remedy because the claimant was not owner or occupier of the room and his body had not been touched. Publication of the interview was restrained by interlocutory injunction on the ground that it was arguably a malicious falsehood to represent that the plaintiff had consented to it. But no other remedy was available. Glidewell LJ said:

> The facts of the present case are a graphic illustration of the desirability of Parliament considering whether and in what circumstances statutory provision can be made to protect the privacy of individuals.[296]

Bingham LJ likewise said:

> The problems of defining and limiting a tort of privacy are formidable but the present case strengthens my hope that the review now in progress may prove fruitful.[297]

However, there is nothing in the opinions of the judges in *Kaye v Robertson* which suggests that the members of the court would have held any view, one way or the other, about a general tort of privacy.

One could argue that a 'tort' of privacy was created by Parliament when it introduced the HRA by way of Article 8(1) ECHR ('right to privacy'). This would then echo what former editor in chief of *The Daily Mail* Paul Dacre so publicly stated when he criticized Mr Justice Eady following the Max Mosley judgment in 2008. Dacre said:

> This [privacy] law is not coming from parliament. No, that would smack of democracy, but from the arrogant and amoral judgments, words I use very deliberately, of one man. I am referring, of course, to Justice David Eady who has, again and again, under the privacy clause of the Human Rights Act, found against newspapers and their age-old freedom to expose the moral shortcomings of those in high places.[298]

An 'informal' tort was first expressed by Lord Nicholls (dissenting) in the *Naomi Campbell* case (2004) that 'protects the right to control the dissemination of information about one's private life'.[299] Both Lords Hoffmann and Nicholls dissented in this case on the ground that as *The Daily Mirror* was allowed to publish the fact that the famous supermodel had been a drug addict for some time and that she was receiving treatment for her addiction, and that printing the pictures of her leaving her Narcotics Anonymous meeting was within the margin of appreciation of the editor as he was allowed to state that she was an addict and receiving treatment for her addiction. Lord Nicholls observed that 'confidence' was an artificial term for what could more naturally be termed 'privacy'.

See above
2.4.2

---

295 [1991] FSR 62.
296 Ibid. at para. 66.
297 Ibid. at para. 70.
298 Source: 'Daily Mail chief Paul Dacre criticises BBC growth and privacy rulings', *Guardian*, 10 November 2008: www.theguardian.com/media/2008/nov/10/pauldacre-dailymail.
299 *Campbell v MGN Ltd* [2004] 2 AC 457 at 51.

In the same year, Lord Hoffmann was unequivocal in *Wainwright v The Home Office* (2003) when he said that English law recognizes *no* common law tort of invasion or breach of privacy in relation to Art 8(1) ECHR:

> Although Article 8 guarantees a right of privacy, I do not think that it treats that right as having been invaded and requiring a remedy in damages, irrespective of whether the defendant acted intentionally, negligently or accidentally. . . .

> Article 8 may justify a monetary remedy for an intentional invasion of privacy by a public authority, even if no damage is suffered other than distress for which damages are not ordinarily recoverable. It does not follow that a merely negligent act should, contrary to general principle, give rise to a claim for damages for distress because it affects privacy rather than some other interest like bodily safety. . . .

> Be that as it may, a finding that there was a breach of Article 8 will only demonstrate that there was a gap in the English remedies for invasion of privacy which has since been filled by sections 6 and 7 of the 1998 Act [HRA]. It does not require that the courts should provide an alternative remedy which distorts the principles of the common law.[300]

The claimants in the case of *Wainwright*, a mother and son, had been strip-searched for drugs during a visit to Armley Jail in Leeds when visiting Mrs Wainwright's son Patrick O'Neill on 15 August 1996. The claimants argued that this breached the Prison Rules 1964 (consolidated 1998) in that they had been humiliated and distressed. The judge awarded basic and aggravated damages of £2,600 to the first claimant (the mother) and £4,500 to the second claimant (her son Alan). The Court of Appeal allowed the Home Office's appeal against the finding of trespass, dismissed the first claimant's claim and reduced the award of damages to the second claimant. The main questions before the HL were whether English common law recognizes a cause of action for invasion of privacy and/or for intentional infliction of emotional harm.

The HL held in *Wainwright* that there was no common law tort of invasion of privacy; that creation of such a tort required a detailed approach which could only be achieved by legislation rather than the broad brush of common law principle; that adoption of a right to privacy as a principle of law in itself was not necessary to comply with Article 8(1) ECHR; and that any gaps in existing remedies for breaches of Article 8 by public authorities had been filled by sections 6 and 7 of the Human Rights Act 1998. That insofar as there might be a tort of intention to cause harm under which damages for distress which did not amount to recognized psychiatric injury might be recoverable, the necessary intention was not established on the facts of the case.

Counsel for the Wainwrights relied on Peck's[301] as demonstrating the need for a general tort of invasion of privacy. As explained by Sir Robert Megarry in *Malone*, this is an area of law which requires a detailed approach which can be achieved only by legislation rather than the broad brush of common law principle.[302]

---

300 *Wainwright v The Home Office* [2003] UKHL 53 at 51–52 (HL) (Lord Hoffmann).
301 Peck v UK [2003] EHRR 287.
302 *Malone v Commissioner of Police of the Metropolis (No 2)* [1979] Ch 344.

2.11.1 The tort of privacy: developments in common law jurisdictions

Since the celebrated article by US attorneys Warren and Brandeis, 'The Right to Privacy' in the Harvard Law Journal in 1890,[303] the question of whether such a tort of privacy exists, or should exist, has been much debated in various common law jurisdictions.

Warren and Brandeis suggested that one could generalize certain cases on defamation, breach of copyright in unpublished letters, trade secrets and breach of confidence as all are based upon the protection of a common value which they called privacy or, following Judge Cooley's now famous saying: 'the right to be let alone'.[304] Warren and Brandeis said that identifying this common element should enable the courts to declare the existence of a general principle which protected a person's appearance, sayings, acts and personal relations from being exposed in public.[305]

There are a number of common law countries where the tort of invasion of privacy has been found in jurisprudence, such as the United States and Canada since the 1970s. New Zealand and Australian courts have long recognized the existence of a common law tort of privacy (see: *Australian Broadcasting Corporation v Lenah Game Meats Pty Ltd* (2001)[306]). The UK courts do not recognize such a tort by that very name, and presently there is only the equitable action for breach of confidence which addresses the misuse of private information.

See above
2.2.3

The privacy laws of the United States deal with several different legal concepts, one being the tort of invasion of privacy. This means that an aggrieved individual can file a lawsuit in common law against an individual or media company who unlawfully intrudes into their private affairs, discloses their private information, publicizes them in a false light or appropriates their name for personal gain.

The essence of the law derives from a right to privacy, defined broadly as 'the right to be let alone'. It usually excludes personal matters or activities which may reasonably be of public interest, like those of celebrities or participants in newsworthy events.

Most importantly, the individual has the right to claim damages against the person or entity violating the right to privacy (also enshrined in the Fourth Amendment, the right to be free of unwarranted search or seizure; the First Amendment, the right to free assembly; and the Fourteenth Amendment, the right to due process, including the right to privacy within family, marriage, motherhood, procreation and child-rearing).

Courts in the United States have always been receptive to this proposal, and a jurisprudence of privacy began to develop during the early 1900s. It became apparent, however, that the developments could not be contained within a single principle – not, at any rate, one with greater explanatory power than the proposition that it was based upon the protection of a value which could be described as privacy.

William Lloyd ('Bill') Prosser (1898–1972), Dean of the College of Law at the University of California, Berkeley, became concerned with the various and differing aspects of 'privacy' in tort law. In his work *The Law of Torts* ('Prosser on Torts'), Dean Prosser said that:

---

303 Warren, S.D. and Brandeis, L.D. (1890) pp. 193–220.
304 *Cooley on Torts* (1888) at p. 29.
305 For further discussion see: Hauch, J.M. (1994) at p. 1219.
306 (2001) 208 CLR 199.

> What has emerged is no very simple matter . . . it is not one tort, but a complex of four. To date the law of privacy comprises four distinct kinds of invasion of four different interests of the plaintiff, which are tied together by the common name, but otherwise have almost nothing in common except that each represents an interference with the right of the plaintiff 'to be let alone'.[307]

What he meant by these 'four different interests' was:

1. intrusion upon the claimant's (plaintiff) physical solitude or seclusion, including unlawful searches, telephone tapping, long-distance photography and telephone harassment;
2. public disclosure of private facts (i.e. confidentiality);
3. publicity putting the claimant in a false light, and
4. appropriation, for the defendant's advantage, of the claimant's name or likeness.

These, Prosser said, had different elements and were subject to different defences.[308]

The need in the United States to break down the concept of 'invasion of privacy' into a number of loosely linked torts casts doubt on the value of any high-level generalization which can perform a useful function in enabling one to deduce the rule to be applied in a concrete case.

English law has so far been unwilling, perhaps unable, to formulate any such high-level principle as a common tort of privacy. We have seen above that there are a number of common law and statutory remedies in other jurisdictions of which it may be said that one (at least) of the underlying values they protect is a right of privacy.

See above 2.2

As far back as 1973, the Younger Committee advised against enactment of any general tort of invasion of privacy, recommending that the then regulator the Press Council should deal with the continued regulation of the print press and that any breaches of privacy be dealt with on a case-by-case basis.[309]

At the time of the Gordon Kaye judgment (16 March 1990), a Committee under the chairmanship of Sir David Calcutt QC was considering whether individual privacy required statutory protection against intrusion by the press. The committee referred to Prosser's analysis (see above) of the development of the law of privacy in the United States and suggested that similar rights could be created in England only by statute.

When the Calcutt Committee reported in June 1990, they recommend that 'entering private property, without the consent of the lawful occupant, with intent to obtain personal information with a view to its publication' should be made a criminal offence.[310] Calcutt also recommended that certain other forms of intrusion, like the use of surveillance devices on private property and long-distance photography and sound recording,

---

307 Prosser, W. L. (1971) at p. 804.
308 Ibid. at p. 814.
309 House of Commons (1973) The Younger Report on Privacy.
310 House of Commons (1990) The Calcutt Report at para. 6.33.

should be made offences. But the Calcutt Committee did not recommend the creation of a generalized tort of infringement of privacy.[311] This was not because they thought that the definitional problems were insuperable. They said that if one confined the tort to 'publication of personal information to the world at large', it should be possible to produce an adequate definition.

The Committee made some suggestions about how such a statutory tort might be defined and what the defences should be. But they considered that the problem could be tackled more effectively by a combination of the more sharply focused remedies which they recommended. As for a 'general wrong of infringement of privacy', they accepted that it would, even in statutory form, give rise to 'an unacceptable degree of uncertainty.[312]

Sir Brian Neill's article 'Privacy: A Challenge for the Next Century'[313] discusses that common law torts include trespass, nuisance, defamation and malicious falsehood. He then refers to the equitable action for breach of confidence and statutory remedies under the Protection from Harassment Act 1997 and the Data Protection Act 1998. There are also extralegal remedies under Codes of Practice applicable to broadcasters and newspapers. But he also notes that there are gaps in the law – cases in which the courts have considered that an invasion of privacy deserves a remedy which the existing law does not offer. Sometimes, Neill argues, the perceived gap can be filled by judicious development of an existing principle. The law of breach of confidence has undergone such a process as noted above, particular in the judgment of Lord Phillips of Worth Matravers MR in Campbell v MGN Ltd.[314]

On the other hand, an attempt to create a tort of telephone harassment by a radical change in the basis of the action for private nuisance in Khorasandjian v Bush (1993)[315] was held by the House of Lords in Hunter v Canary Wharf Ltd (1997)[316] to be a step too far. The gap was filled by the Protection from Harassment Act 1997 (formerly known as the 'stalking bill').

For a long time the UK courts refused to formulate a general principle of 'invasion of privacy' from which the conditions of liability in any particular case could be deduced – reasons were discussed by Sir Robert Megarry VC in Malone v Metropolitan Police Commissioner (1974).[317] In this case the question was whether the claimant, an antiques dealer from Dorking, suspected of handling stolen goods, had a cause of action for having his telephone tapped by the police and his mail intercepted without any trespass upon his land. This was (as the ECtHR subsequently held in Malone v UK (1984)[318]) an infringement by a public authority of his right to privacy under Article 8(1) of the Convention, but because there had been no trespass, it gave rise to no identifiable cause of action in English law.

---

311 Ibid. at para. 12.5.
312 Ibid. at paras 12.12–12.32.
313 Neill, B. (1999) Chapter 1, 'Privacy'.
314 [2003] QB 633 (Lord Phillips).
315 [1993] QB 727.
316 [1997] AC 655.
317 Malone v Commissioner of Police of the Metropolis [1979] Ch 344 at 372–381 (Megarry VC).
318 (1984) 7 EHRR 14.

Sir Robert Megarry VC was invited to declare that invasion of privacy, at any rate in respect of telephone conversations, was in itself a cause of action. He said:

> I am not unduly troubled by the absence of English authority: there has to be a first time for everything, and if the principles of English law, and not least analogies from the existing rules, together with the requirements of justice and common sense, pointed firmly to such a right existing, then I think the court should not be deterred from recognising the right. On the other hand, it is no function of the courts to legislate in a new field. The extension of the existing laws and principles is one thing, the creation of an altogether new right is another.[319]

As for the analogy of construing statutes in accordance with the Convention, which appealed to the judge in the *Malone* case, Sir Robert said:

> I readily accept that if the question before me were one of construing a statute enacted with the purpose of giving effect to obligations imposed by the Convention, the court would readily seek to construe the legislation in a way that would effectuate the Convention rather than frustrate it. However, no relevant legislation of that sort is in existence. It seems to me that where Parliament has abstained from legislating on a point that is plainly suitable for legislation, it is indeed difficult for the court to lay down new rules of common law or equity that will carry out the Crown's treaty obligations, or to discover for the first time that such rules have always existed.[320]

Parliament eventually provided a remedy in form of the Interception of Communications Act 1985 (see also: R v Khan (Sultan) (1997)[321] and Khan v UK (1997),[322] regarding the electronic bugging of a private home).

Sedley LJ in *Douglas v Hello! Ltd* (2001)[323] drew particular attention to the way in which the development of the law of confidence had weakened the need for a relationship of confidence between the recipient of the confidential information and the person from whom it was obtained.

The ECtHR in *Earl Spencer v UK* (1998)[324] stated that English law of confidence provided an adequate remedy to restrain the publication of private information about the applicants' marriage and medical condition and photographs taken with a telephoto lens of Princess Diana's brother, Earl Spencer, and his then bulimic wife, Victoria, undergoing rehabilitative treatment. These developments showed that the basic value protected by the law in such cases was privacy.

As common law developed post the HRA 1998, we saw an increase in truth-telling and 'kiss and tell' stories as well as an increase in media applications for freedom of

---

319 Ibid. at para. 372.
320 Ibid. at para. 379.
321 [1997] AC 558.
322 [2000] ECHR 194.
323 [2001] QB 967 (Seley LJ).
324 (1998) 25 EHRR CD 105.

expression under Article 10(1) ECHR and the defence of the public interest, advanced when newspapers had reported on a celebrity's indiscretions.

In the seminal case of *Vidal-Hall v Google Inc.* (2015),[325] Master of the Rolls McFarlane LJ ruled in the Court of Appeal that misuse of private information is distinct from breach of confidence and should now be recognized as a tort.

In this case, three claimants (respondents to the appeal) pursued Google for claims that Google (the 'data controller'), through its use of internet 'cookies', had misused their private information and breached their confidence and that Google had infringed section 13(2) of the Data Protection Act 1998 (DPA). All three individuals had used Apple computers and Safari browsers, between summer 2011 and 17 February 2012, to access the internet. They sued Google (situated in California, USA) in the London High Court. Google then applied for permission to appeal to the Supreme Court which granted permission to appeal in part. The Court ordered that permission to appeal be refused on ground 1 (the issue whether the claim is in tort) because this ground does not raise an arguable point of law. The Court ordered that permission to appeal be granted on all other grounds.

The issues in *Vidal-Hall v Google Inc.* before the Court of Appeal were as follows:

1   whether the cause of action for misuse of private information is a tort; and
2   whether there can be a claim for compensation without pecuniary loss within the meaning of damage in section 13(2) of the Data Protection Act 1998.

The CA ruled that:

1   the misuse of private information constitutes a tort for the purposes of the rules providing for service of proceedings out of the jurisdiction;
2   the claimants could recover damages for non-material loss;[326] and
3   that section 13(2) DPA should be disapplied on the grounds that it conflicts with the rights guaranteed by Articles 7 ('right to private and family life') and 8 ('right to protection of personal data') of the EU Charter of Fundamental Rights.

Vidal-Hall v Google Inc. is a landmark decision, not only for the confirmation that misuse of private information is a tort but also for the disapplication of primary domestic legislation on the basis of incompatibility with an EU Directive and provisions of Articles 7, 8 and 47 of the EU Charter of Fundamental Rights (see also: *Benkharbouche v Embassy of the Republic of Sudan* (2015)[327]). This means that claims for compensation for breach of the Data

---

325 Judith Vidal-Hall, Robert Hann and Marc Bradshaw and the Information Commissioner v Google Inc. [2015] EWCA Civ 311 (CA).
326 The issue of compensation for a contravention by a data controller is dealt with in Article 23 of the Directive (95/46/EC). The CA found it was not possible to interpret s 13(2) DPA in a way that was compatible with Article 23.
327 [2015] EWCA Civ 33.

Protection Act can be made for damages for distress even though one has not suffered any pecuniary loss; moreover, this case was not related to purposes of journalism, the arts or literature.

2.11.2 Analysis and discussion: have the courts developed a general tort of invasion of privacy?

So where does this leave us with the development of a tort of privacy in the United Kingdom? Is there a development of a tort of privacy by the back door via the courts' jurisprudence?

Looking at the cases discussed in this chapter we are left with piecemeal and fragmented privacy protection where some judges, such as Eady J, are prepared to take an active role in the development of the tort and others, such as Tugendhat J, await further guidance from the UK Supreme Court, the Strasbourg Human Rights Court or even the Court of Justice of the European Union when protecting the 'right to be left alone' or the digital right to be forgotten. This leaves privacy protection in tort law problematic and without any real legal damages which can be awarded by the courts with no real apportioning of liability. Some UK courts have adopted the 'breach of confidence' approach in common law, though the results are inconsistent and the damage is already done. There seems to be a great difference between identifying privacy as a value which underlies the existence of the rule of law and privacy as a principle of law in itself.

There is nothing in the jurisprudence of the ECtHR which suggests that the adoption of some high-level principle of privacy is necessary to comply with Article 8 of the Convention. The Strasbourg Human Rights Court is only concerned with whether domestic law provides an adequate remedy in a specific case in which it considers that there has been an invasion of privacy contrary to Article 8(1) and not justifiable under Article 8(2) ECHR.

In the *Earl Spencer* case (1998),[328] for example, the ECtHR was satisfied that the action for breach of confidence provided an adequate remedy in the UK courts for the Spencers' breach of confidentiality complaint and looked no further into the rest of the range of remedies available to the victims of other invasions of privacy.

Likewise, in *Peck v UK* (2003),[329] the Strasbourg Court expressed some impatience at being given a tour of the remedies provided by English law to deal with every imaginable kind of invasion of privacy. Did Mr Peck have an adequate remedy when he was filmed by a CCTV camera operated by Brentwood Borough Council in a public street, moments after he had attempted to commit suicide by slashing his wrists with a kitchen knife? The court held that the CCTV film footage widely published by the media was a considerable invasion of his privacy and breached his Article 8 right. The ECtHR concluded that Mr Peck was not afforded adequate remedies in UK law, however that there were no available remedies in spite of having his Article 8 rights violated.[330]

Arguably, the coming into force of the Human Rights Act 1998 has weakened the argument that a general tort of invasion of privacy is needed to fill gaps in the existing

---

328 *Earl Spencer and Countess Spencer v UK* (1998) 25 EHRR CD 105 (ECtHR).
329 *Peck v UK* (2003) 36 EHRR 719 (Case No 44647/98) (ECtHR).
330 Ibid. at para. 103.

remedies. Sections 6 and 7 HRA are in themselves substantial gap fillers. If a person's rights under Article 8 ECHR have been infringed by a public authority, the claimant will have a statutory remedy.

Following the ECtHR's conflicting judgments in *von Hannover No 1*[331] and *von Hannover No 2*[332] and *No 3*,[333] one could possibly begin to define 'breach of confidence' as a tort that protects private information. However, it is important to note that in *von Hannover No 1* the ECtHR ruled that a celebrity has a 'public' and a 'private sphere', the latter being strictly protected by privacy with no invasion by paparazzi or the media.

In the *Beckham* case[334] the ruling was similar, in that famous couples like Victoria and David Beckham and their children have a right to privacy in the comfort and circumference of their own home.

Although Article 8(1) ECHR guarantees a right of privacy, it does not automatically provide a remedy in damages, irrespective of whether the defendant acted intentionally, negligently or accidentally. An Article 8 breach then demonstrates that there is, at present, a gap in the English common law remedies for invasion of privacy (unless the breach was caused by a public authority). It does not require that the courts should provide an alternative remedy which distorts the principles of the common law – as we learnt from the judgment in NT 1 & NT2 (2018),[335] where two businessmen actioned against the search engine Google to have their criminal convictions removed. This landmark ruling made by Mr Justice Warby meant that NT 2 was successful in his claim to have his name and criminal convictions from the late 1990s delisted, whereas NT1 was not successful in his claim for the reasons cited above.

See above
2.7.3

There now exists a wide interpretation by the UK courts of the concept of privacy and what amounts to 'confidential information'. The argument advanced in *Spycatcher* was that the second *Coco* requirement, the need for a confidential relationship, would justify equity's interference with freedom of speech, as it served as the link between the recipient's conscience in not revealing the confidential information and the doctrine itself. This meant that the maintenance of confidential relationships was thereby sidelined.

This standpoint was challenged by the press in the *Rio Ferdinand*[336] super injunction case, and subsequently clarified by the Strasbourg Court in Princess Caroline's second privacy action, *von Hannover (No 2)*.[337] Neither Rio Ferdinand nor Princess Caroline von Hannover in her second action were awarded Article 8 rights to privacy, because the court held that the matters in question were in the public interest. More recent jurisprudence has given greater weight to the public interest test by allowing the media their Article 10(1) right.

Legal uncertainty continues to exist, creating ambiguity for both the claimant in the level of 'tortious' protection in their privacy rights and for the media on the other hand, whose editors have to make decisions on such common law considerations.

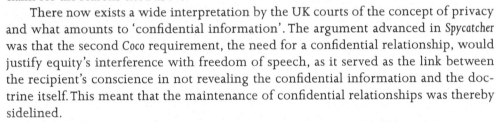

---

331 *von Hannover v Germany (No 1)* [2005] 40 EHRR 1.
332 *von Hannover v Germany (No 2)* [2012] ECHR 228.
333 *von Hannover v Germany (No 3)* [2013] ECHR 835
334 *Beckham v MGN Ltd* (28 June 2001; unreported).
335 *NT1 & NT2 v Google LLC and Information Commissioner* [2018] EWHC 799 (QB).
336 *Ferdinand (Rio) v Mirror Group Newspapers Ltd* [2011] EWHC 2454 (QB).
337 *von Hannover v Germany (No 2)* (2012) (Application Nos – 40660/08, 60641/08) Judgment of 7 February 2012.

If we then accept that there now exists a tort of privacy in relation to 'misuse of private information', it follows that we can safely assume that this law now affords protection to information in respect of which there is a reasonable expectation of privacy, even in circumstances where there is no pre-existing relationship. This in itself will then give rise to an enforceable duty of confidence. The law now seems to be concerned with the prevention of the violation of a person's autonomy, dignity and self-esteem taking into account Convention rights as well as common law development since the coming into force of the HRA 1998 and the *Douglas* case in 2001.

So, should Parliament now address a statutory tort of privacy, particularly in the digital age of social networking? Mindell has long argued that 'proper' privacy legislation could acknowledge breaches of privacy 'in both primary and secondary forms and understanding the remedial possibilities of each', so that the law could ultimately protect private information because it is 'private' and undisclosed rather than because it is 'confidential information'.[338]

Clearly there are misunderstandings and social differences in what some deem 'private' and some regard or even misuse as 'confidential' information. The law in this area could then provide objective criteria for the courts to apply when misuse of another's private information has taken place.

 FOR THOUGHT

> Why do you think the UK Parliament has been so reluctant to formulate a specific law relating to the invasion of privacy? Discuss with reference to leading authorities and scholarly debate.

2.12 Analysis and discussion: balancing individual rights to privacy and the media's freedom of expression

In (super) injunction applications and general privacy orders, the court applies the test for a 'reasonable expectation of privacy' – which is an objective one, depending on all the circumstances (see: *Murray v Express Newspapers Ltd* (2008)[339]). The methodology by which the necessary balance should be struck was explained by Lord Steyn in *Re S (A Child)* (2004).[340]

Where the values protected by Articles 8 and 10 of the Convention are in conflict, an intense focus on the comparative importance of the specific rights being claimed in the individual case is necessary and the justifications for interfering with or restricting each right must be taken into account and balanced against each other. This is known as the proportionality test.

Strasbourg jurisprudence encourages domestic courts to apply the balancing test between Articles 8 ('privacy') and 10 ECHR ('freedom of expression'). This has led to a more nuanced approach to freedom of expression in Europe compared with the more

---

338 Mindell, R. (2012) at pp. 52–58.
339 [2008] EWCA Civ 446.
340 *S (FC) (A Child)* (Identification: Restrictions on Publication) [2004] UKHL 47 at 17 (HL) (Lord Steyn).

absolutist approach in the United States, where freedom of expression is a rather dominant right compared with privacy and other rights.

We have seen that the ECtHR pronounced very different judgments in the three *von Hannover* actions. The first action granted Princess Caroline of Monaco privacy.[341] In the conjoined judgments of *von Hannover* (No 2)[342] and *Axel Springer*,[343] the Grand Chamber carefully balanced Articles 8 and 10 ECHR and ruled in favour of 'freedom of expression', thereby granting the publications the right to contribute to a debate of general and genuine public interest. *Von Hannover* (No 3)[344] repeated that message.

It is only when a fine balance has been struck by the courts between the competing privacy rights of the individual and the right to free speech that the issue of whether a matter is in the public interest can be decided. Publication at all costs, merely designed to satisfy the public's curiosity and to increase newspaper sales, should be avoided. The ECtHR has stressed, however, that Article 8 should not extend to the protection of someone's reputation or commercial interest (*Karakó v Hungary* (2009)[345]).

❖ KEY CASE	*Karakó v Hungary* (2009) (Application No 39311/05) Strasbourg, 28 April 2009 (ECtHR)

Precedent
- ❖ Article 8(1) ECHR does not extend to 'reputation'.
- ❖ Member States to the Convention have their own legislation to deal with a person's reputation (e.g. defamation laws).

Facts
During the Hungarian parliamentary elections of 2002, Mr László Karakó (K), Member of Parliament for the Fidesz Party ('the Civic Union') and a candidate in one of the electoral districts of Szabolcs-Szatmár-Bereg County, complained that the respondent state (Hungary) had breached his Article 8 rights. K had pressed criminal charges and brought a private prosecution for libel against 'LH', chairman of the county regional assembly (Szabolcs-Szatmár-Bereg). LH had accused K of regularly voting against the interests of the county. The prosecuting authorities decided not to pursue K's libel charges, also dismissing his private prosecution. K argued before the Strasbourg Court that the Hungarian authorities had failed to assist him to pursue his libel actions against his political opponent, claiming that this had violated his right to reputation which he argued breached his Article 8 right.

Decision
As K claimed a violation of Article 8(1) ECHR by way of 'injury to his reputation', the Strasbourg Court had to determine whether Article 8(1) included 'reputation'

---

341 *von Hannover v Germany* (No 1) (2005) 40 EHRR 1 (Application No 59320/00) (ECtHR).
342 *von Hannover v Germany* (No 2) (2012) (Application Nos – 40660/08, 60641/08). Strasbourg judgment of 7 February 2012 (ECtHR).
343 *Axel Springer v Germany* (2012) (Application No 39954/08) Strasbourg judgment of 7 February 2012 (ECtHR).
344 *von Hannover v Germany* (No 3) (2013) (Application No 8772/10) ECHR 264 (ECtHR).
345 (2009) (Application No 39311/05) Strasbourg, 28 April 2009 (ECtHR).

as part of the privacy right. The Court found that the impugned statement was a value judgment, dismissing K's complaint on the grounds that the 'right to privacy' under Article 8 did not imply a right to reputation. The judgment referred to the principle established in *von Hannover (No 1)*,[346] where the ECtHR had extended the protection of private life to the protection of personal integrity which did not extend to 'reputation'.

This meant that the complainant's allegation that his reputation as a politician had been harmed by an allegedly libellous statement was not a sustainable claim regarding the protection of his right to respect for personal integrity under Article 8 ECHR.

Analysis

In *Karakó* the ECtHR held that there was sufficient legislation in several Member States to the Convention (such as the UK), whereby reputation had traditionally been protected by the law of defamation.[347] A limitation on freedom of expression for the sake of Karakó's (K's) reputation would have been disproportionate under Article 10(1) ECHR. Consequently, there had been *no* violation of K's Article 8(1) right.

The Strasbourg Court decision in *Karakó* is an important one and impacts on many other cases thereafter (such as *LNS – John Terry*). In this case K had not shown that the publication constituted such a serious interference with his private life as to undermine his personal integrity. Accordingly, it was K's reputation alone which was at stake in the context of an expression made to his alleged detriment.[348]

In summary, the ECtHR decision in *Karakó* conformed with Convention rights and standards in carefully balancing Articles 8 and 10 ECHR. The Court concluded that national laws of Member States were adequate enough to deal with claims of defamation[349] or other causes of action, such as 'harassment' (see: Protection from Harassment Act 1997).

Unfortunately the Strasbourg Court has not always sent out the same message and can conflict in its own jurisprudence. In *Lindon v France* (2007)[350] the ECtHR determined that the right to reputation should always be considered as safeguarded by Article 8(1) ECHR. This case arose from a novel published in France titled *Jean-Marie Le Pen on Trial* (*Le Procès de Jean-Marie Le Pen*) in respect of which Monsieur Le Pen and his right-wing National Front

---

346 *von Hannover v Germany* (2004) EMLR 21.
347 Paras 21–29 of the judgment.
348 For further discussion see: Milo, D. (2008), pp. 15–43.
349 *Gatley on Libel and Slander* 11th edn, §27.17 and the cases there cited.
350 *Lindon, Otchakovsky-Laurens and July v France* (2007) (Applications Nos 21279/02 and 36448/02) judgment of 22 October 2007 (ECtHR).

party brought defamation proceedings in France against the writer and publisher of the book.[351]

The serious and murderous allegations against Monsieur Le Pen and the National Front were found to be factually incorrect, defamatory and unproven, and the Paris court upheld the defamation claims. The three applicants (Lindon, Otchakovsky-Laurens and July – respectively, the author, the chairman of the board of directors of the publishing company P.O.L. and the publication director of the newspaper Libération) were found guilty of defamation.

The three applicants claimed that their Article 10 right had been breached, that any exceptions to freedom of expression should be 'construed strictly' and that politicians ought to 'display a great degree of tolerance'. The ECtHR ruled that the French appeal court had made a reasonable assessment of the facts in finding that to liken Monsieur Le Pen to a 'chief of a gang of killers' overstepped the permissible limits of freedom of expression. The Lindon case was in stark contrast to the UK Reynolds[352] jurisprudence, whereby Judge Loucaides in the ECtHR particularly emphasized both the importance of truth and of media organizations being accountable to those against whom they make false or defamatory allegations.

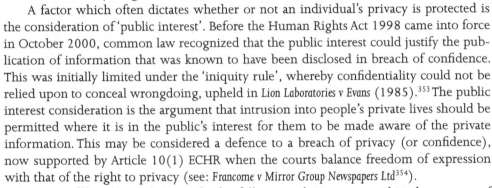

See
Chapter 3

A factor which often dictates whether or not an individual's privacy is protected is the consideration of 'public interest'. Before the Human Rights Act 1998 came into force in October 2000, common law recognized that the public interest could justify the publication of information that was known to have been disclosed in breach of confidence. This was initially limited under the 'iniquity rule', whereby confidentiality could not be relied upon to conceal wrongdoing, upheld in Lion Laboratories v Evans (1985).[353] The public interest consideration is the argument that intrusion into people's private lives should be permitted where it is in the public's interest for them to be made aware of the private information. This may be considered a defence to a breach of privacy (or confidence), now supported by Article 10(1) ECHR when the courts balance freedom of expression with that of the right to privacy (see: Francome v Mirror Group Newspapers Ltd[354]).

In Jameel,[355] Lord Bingham made the following observations within the context of confidentiality and the public interest:

> the necessary precondition of reliance on qualified privilege in this context is that the matter published should be one of public interest. In the present case the subject matter of the article complained of was of undoubted public interest. But that is not always, perhaps not usually, so. It has been repeatedly and rightly said that what engages the interest of the public may not be material which engages the public interest.[356]

At a trial for a claim for misuse of private and confidential information, a claimant must first establish that he has a reasonable expectation of privacy in relation to the confidential

351 Lindon, M. (1998).
352 Reynolds v Times Newspapers Ltd [2001] 2 AC 127.
353 [1985] QB 526.
354 [1984] 1 WLR 892.
355 Jameel (Mohammed) v Wall Street Journal [2007] 1 AC 359.
356 Ibid. at 31–33 (Lord Bingham).

information of which disclosure is threatened, as established in *Murray v Express Newspapers* (2008):[357]

> whether a reasonable person of ordinary sensibilities would feel if he or she was placed in the same position as the claimant and faced the same publicity.[358]

That case concerned photographs of a young child (David, son of J. K. Rowling) in a public place taken covertly and published without the parents' permission.

The *Max Mosley*[359] privacy ruling made it clear that matters concerning the 'extramarital bed', 'death bed' or 'hospital bed' are out of bounds as far as freedom of expression and media reporting are concerned.

In *AMP*,[360] a British university student used her mobile phone to take explicit naked photos of herself at her home; the mobile phone was subsequently stolen while she was on a tram in Nottingham in 2008. After the phone was found, her photos were uploaded to the BitTorrent network and circulated under the name 'Sexy Rich Chick Mobile Phone Found By IRC Nerdz'. Her application for an interim (super) injunction to prevent transmission, storage and indexing of any part or parts of these photographic images was granted by Ramsey J in December 2011 to protect the claimant's rights to privacy under Article 8 ECHR and to prevent harassment under section 3 Protection from Harassment Act 1997.

Until *von Hannover (No 1)*[361] there existed some confusion as to the meaning of 'public' and 'private' domain' as to what would be regarded in the 'public interest' in relation to an individual's right to privacy. This was perhaps better defined in *Spycatcher (No 2)*,[362] where the ECtHR ruled that the public interest test does not always amount to a justification for publication of confidential information. Since *Spycatcher (No 2)* the law imposes a 'duty of confidence' in common law whenever a person receives information which he knows or ought to know is fairly and reasonably to be regarded as confidential. Nevertheless, the law remains awkward and bewildering, caused partly by confusing case law relating to trade secrets with misuse of private personal information, which may require different parameters and treatment. This has given rise to ever greater legal actions. As common law has developed, 'public interest' is now the most common justification for publishing information which is either confidential or which has been challenged in the tort of defamation.

If we consider recent judgments relating to privacy rights and the 'right to be forgotten' we first look at the CJEU's balancing exercise in the *Google Spain* case. Here the CJEU held that the validity of a delisting request had to be determined by striking a fair balance between the legitimate interests of internet users in having access to the information and the data subject's Article 8 rights.

Those interests were of *equal* weight, and *Google Spain* was not to be read as saying that the public's interest in access to information was inherently of lesser value than the individual's privacy rights. Moreover, although guidelines published by the 'Working Party on

---

357 [2008] EWCA Civ 446.
358 Ibid. at 24.
359 *Mosley v NGN* [2008] EWHC 1777 (QB).
360 *AMP v Persons Unknown* [2012] All ER (D) 178.
361 *von Hannover v Germany (No 1)* [2004] EMLR 21.
362 *AG v Guardian Newspapers Ltd (No 2)* [1990] 1 AC 109 (Spycatcher).

the Protection of Individuals with regard to the Processing of Personal Data' established under Directive 95/46 art.29 set out criteria to be used in the balancing exercise, those criteria were non-exhaustive and liable to evolve over time.[363]

The right to rehabilitation – as was claimed by businessmen NT1 and NT2[364] – was an aspect of the law of personal privacy, and it included the right to reputation and the right to respect for family and private life. However, it was not unqualified (as in the case of NT1) and would inevitably come into conflict with the rights of others to freedom of information and expression.

While it was helpful for Parliament to prescribe the point at which a given conviction would be treated as spent under s 1 of the Rehabilitation of Offenders Act 1974, this had to be read down as expressing a legal policy or principle. A person would not enjoy a reasonable expectation of privacy in respect of information disclosed in legal proceedings held in public. Once the conviction was spent, Article 8 ECHR would be engaged, and the fact that the conviction was spent would normally weigh heavily against the further use or disclosure of the information. However, the data subject's Article 8 rights still had to be weighed against competing considerations. If the claim relied to a significant extent upon harm to reputation, the court had to have regard to s 8 of the 1974 Act: that section could not be disregarded merely because the claim was not framed in defamation.[365]

For these reasons neither NT1 nor NT2 were entitled to compensation because Google had taken such care as was reasonably required to comply with the relevant requirements.[366]

2.13 Further reading

Bingham, T. (1996) 'Should there be a law to protect rights of personal privacy?' *European Human Rights Law Review*, 5, 455–462.
Lord (Tom) Bingham discusses the protection of breach of confidence and whether there should be law to protect personal privacy following the *Gordon Kaye* case (where he was one of the judges). Bingham argues that the expansion and distortion of any confidence action cannot serve as an adequate substitute for a full privacy action and a 'proper' privacy law, unless, by either judicial sleight of hand or the bold grasping of the privacy nettle, a free-standing tort of privacy emerges fully from any confidence action.

Blythe, A. (2017) 'Website blocking orders post-*Cartier v BSkyB*: an analysis of the legal basis for these injunctions and the potential scope of this remedy against other tortious acts', *European Intellectual Property Review*, 39(12), 770–777.
Alice Blythe examines the full implications and the extent to which the CA judgment in *Cartier v BSkyB* (2016) has impacted on the liabilities of internet service providers (ISP). The CA had ordered ISPs BSkyB, BT, EE, TalkTalk and Virgin Media (together providing 95 per cent of the UK broadband market) to block the access by their users to six target websites which were infringing the claimant's trade marks by selling counterfeit goods. The author argues that the *Cartier* case marked a change of tactic by the courts. Furthermore, Blythe notes that the way in which Kitchin LJ upheld the website blocking injunctions

---

363 *Google Spain SL v Agencia Española de Protección de Datos AEPD* [2014] Q.B. 1022 at paras 124, 128, 131–135.
364 *NT1 & NT2 v Google LLC and Information Commissioner* [2018] EWHC 799 (QB).
365 Ibid. at paras 163, 166 (Warby J).
366 Ibid. at paras 173, 227–228 (Warby J).

poses important questions regarding the possible future scope of this remedy for other tortious acts beyond the sale of counterfeits and possibly beyond the bounds of intellectual property law. She points to the CJEU judgment and remedies ordered in *Google Spain* and raises important issues in relation to striking the correct balance between the exemptions and liabilities placed on ISPs. She argues that this remedy could be used for a multitude of other torts. The ability to seek a blocking injunction against offending and fraudulent websites might be a useful weapon for authorities to deploy, especially if they seek to tighten regulations and introduce an industry watchdog that could use website blocking as a sanction against the worst offenders.

Carter-Silk, A. and Cartwright-Hignett, C. (2009) 'A child's right to privacy: "out of a parent's hands"', *Entertainment Law Review*, 20(6), 212–217.
This article discusses whether children have a fundamental right to privacy separate from that of their parents and what happens if the parents 'waive' their children's rights in order to gain financially. The authors argue that some celebrities use their children to obtain privacy via the back door. The authors ask whether any purported waiver of that privacy right is void unless it is in the child's best interest.

Foster, S. (2015) 'Reclaiming the public interest defence in the conflict between privacy rights and free speech', *Coventry Law Journal*, 19(2), 1–23.
Steve Foster discusses some of the leading authorities regarding privacy applications and the press defence of 'public interest'. Foster argues that the distinction between what is in the public interest and what is mere 'tittle-tattle' has become blurred when dealing with revelations about the private lives of public figures.

Lester, A. (Lord Lester of Herne Hill) (2016) *Five Ideas to Fight For: How Our Freedom Is Under Threat and Why It Matters*. Bloomsbury, London: One World Publications.
Human rights, equality, freedom of expression, privacy, the rule of law. Lord Lester presents these five ideas in his wonderful book which he regards as vitally important to the way of life we enjoy today. He describes the hard-fought legal battle to establish these principles by illustrating a number of difficult cases, such as when some 200,000 British Asians were almost stripped of their British citizenship as a result of racist legislation in the 1970s. The book is autobiographical in parts, charting Anthony Lester's political and judicial 60 years from his early Jewish upbringing to his active involvement in the pursuit of justice, recounting events during the troubles in Northern Ireland, where he was legally involved, to suggesting the UK should move towards an explicitly federal constitution. His very readable writing style covers key cases as well as political involvement in bringing the European Convention into UK law via the HRA 1998.

Markesinis, B.S. (ed) (1999) *Protecting Privacy*. Oxford: Oxford University Press.
Professor Basil Markesinis has persuaded some of the most eminent international scholars to contribute on the topic of the 'right to privacy' in this wonderful edition since the right to privacy is a much debated topic, starting in the 1990s and still topical today. The essay contributions explore the reasons why the UK media find the right to privacy more threatening than their counterparts in other countries, such as Germany, the United States, Italy and France. The contributors to this book examine political, economic and social situations – such as the *von Hannover* case – where celebrities did and did not receive privacy protection from the state for invasion of privacy.

Mindell, R. (2012) 'Rewriting privacy: the impact of online social networks', *Entertainment Law Review*, 23(3), 52–58.
This article discusses the meaning of 'privacy' in English common law in relation to technological innovations, such as Twitter and Facebook, which have put privacy at risk. He argues that the force of social media remains uncontrolled.

Phillipson, G. (2003) 'Breach of confidence, celebrities, freedom of expression, legal reasoning, newspapers, privacy, public interest, right to respect for private and family life', *European Human Rights Law Review* **(Special Issue on 'Privacy'), 54–72.**
The article criticizes the legal reasoning applied by the Court of Appeal in *A v B plc* in respect of two key issues: (1) the horizontal application of Article 8(1) ECHR in cases concerning media intrusion, and (2) the circumstances in which there is a public interest justification for publication. The author questions the meaning of public interest in relation to 'public figures'.

Pillans, B. (2012) 'Private lives in St Moritz: *von Hannover v Germany (No 2)***',** *Communications Law,* **17(2), 63–67.**
Brian Pillans discusses the judgments in *Axel Springer* and *von Hannover (No 2)*. He looks at the nature of the individuals involved and the publications and examines the ECtHR's balancing test in respect of the right to freedom of expression and the individual's right to privacy.

Scaife, L. (2013) 'Social media and injunctions: can *contra mundum* **apply when stories develop wings?'** *Communications Law,* **18(2), 42–44.**
Laura Scaife argues in this article that super injunction cases cannot keep pace with the viral quality of social media. She suggests a complete overhaul of the current regime of privacy orders. In addition the CPS should lead the way with guidance designed to raise public consciousness as to the potential sanctions for using online mediums to express themselves. The article identifies perpetrators of online criminal activity in the aftermath of *Tamiz*. Scaife uses the example of the Bulger killers, Venables and Thomson, and how frequent online photographs and locations identify the killers, in spite of there being a lifelong anonymity order (contra mundum injunction) on the identity of V and T. She further argues that the Attorney General's office ought to be more proactive in punishing those who frequently disobey super injunctions and anonymity orders.

Smartt, U. (2011) 'Twitter undermines super injunctions', *Communications Law,* **16(4), 135–140.**
The article discusses common law in respect of personal privacy, grounded in the equitable doctrine of breach of confidence and relevant case law with specific discussion of *Douglas v Hello! Ltd* (2001) and the development of super injunctions (*CTB v NGN* (2011) and *DFT v TFD* (2010)). Smartt examines the remedies available in an action for breach of confidence and asks whether super injunctions have become meaningless in the age of social media.

Wacks, R. (2013) *Privacy and Media Freedom.* **Oxford: Oxford University Press.**
Raymond Wacks' book is both eminently readable and also extremely detailed in its legal and philosophical discourse on privacy (the book also mentions defamation). American Professor Wacks discusses the notion of privacy in great detail as well as examining rights-based theories of free speech in the US First Amendment. He compares French and German privacy laws and their constitutional 'right to personality' and refers to the individual's right to privacy as a 'mixed blessing'.

Warren, S. D. and Brandeis, L. D. (1890) 'The right to privacy', *Harvard Law Review,* **4(5) (15 December), 193–220.**
This classic publication by Warren and Brandeis developed the concept of an individual's right to privacy at the time when this was absent in US law and is often cited in scholarly research.

Chapter 3

Defamation

3.1 Overview

The tort of defamation exists to afford redress for unjustified injury to reputation. By a successful action the injured reputation is vindicated. Though it used to be the case pre-Defamation Act 2013 that individual claimants were not required to prove that they had suffered financial loss, they now have to pass the 'serious harm' test, introduced under section 1(1) of 2013 Act.

This area of law has been profoundly affected by technological change. Most English 'cases' are now unreported because they tend to be settled out of court. Contrary to a general belief that emotional, rude or defamatory social media posts on Twitter or Facebook about an individual are exempt from libel laws because they are fleeting, perhaps made as a joke, and are transient, defamation laws can apply to the internet in the same way as to newspapers, magazines, books, films and other similar publications. Such stories can easily 'go viral', and a defamatory meaning can be shared over a thousand times, causing damage to a person's reputation or business acumen.

Devolved nations, such as Scotland and Northern Ireland, have not yet incorporated the 2013 Act into their legislation, and for this reason some of the common law areas, such as republication and the *Reynolds*[1] qualified privilege defence, are still included in this chapter.

The law needs to keep up with a changing world – particularly since most libel actions now involve the internet and social media. Defamation cases still relied on in the courts can come from a different era. When deciding on liability for repetition of defamatory material (e.g. via retweeting), modern courts can be faced with common law cases dating back to the nineteenth century. But there is new case law, and many older cases have now been enshrined in statute in form of the Defamation Act 2013.

---

1   *Reynolds v Times Newspapers Ltd* [2001] 2 AC 127.

3.1.1 Defamation and reputation

People have been fascinated by high-profile defamation cases for more than 300 years, and tabloid journalism has been thriving on libel actions – as well as being regularly sued by the rich and famous.

The starting point is that the law of defamation is there to protect a person's reputation. As stated by Cave J in *Scott v Sampson* (1882):[2]

> The law recognises in every man a right to have the estimation in which he stands in the opinion of others unaffected by false statements to his discredit.

Reputation is intangible, yet of immense value, personally and commercially. Jeff Bezos, the American technology entrepreneur, philanthropist and the founder and CEO of Amazon defines 'reputation' as 'what people say about you once you've left the room'. The impact of the internet and social media can have a disastrous or positive effect on one's reputation. Online information and allegations have been described as 'tattoos – extremely difficult to get rid of' (see: *Clarke (t/a Elumina Iberica UK) v Bain* (2008).[3] With the decline in newspapers the old saying: 'today's newspapers are tomorrow's fish and chip wrapping' is no longer true. Online editions and social media postings remain online and in archives forever. The internet search engines are then the first port of call when investigating an individual, a company or their reputations.

The law of defamation is at times concerned with conflicting issues of great sensitivity, involving both the protection of good reputation and the maintenance of the principle of free speech. The terms 'libel' and 'slander' are often used interchangeably to define defamation. But there is a distinct difference. In *Brent Walker Group plc v Time Out Ltd*[4] Parker LJ commented on the absurdity of the 'tangled web of the law of defamation'.

Defamation is the generic term for two torts, libel and slander, and occurs when a person communicates material to a third party, in words or any other form, containing an untrue imputation against the reputation of a claimant.[5]

Libel is a wrongful act that concerns the *publication* of material in writing or some other permanent form. In defending a libel action the difference between a statement of verifiable fact and one of honest opinion can be crucial. As Lord Atkin defined it:

> Defamation is a publication of an untrue statement about a person that tends to lower his reputation in the opinion of 'right-thinking members of the community'.
>
> *(Sim v Stretch* (1936)[6])

In relation to statements made on the internet or via social media, it is now generally accepted that defamatory statements are to be regarded as libel that is publication (see: *Smith (Nigel) v ADVFN Plc* (2010)[7]).

---

2   [1882] 8 QBD 491.
3   [2008] EWHC 2636 (QB).
4   [1991] 2 QB 33.
5   For further discussion see: Descheemaeker, E. (2009) at pp. 603–641.
6   [1936] 2 All ER 1237 (Lord Atkin).
7   [2010] EWHC 3255 (QB).

If it is *spoken* or in some sort of other transient form, it is a slander. In *Westcott v Westcott* (2009),[8] Richard Westcott sought damages for slander and libel as well as an injunction to restrain further publication against his daughter-in-law, the defendant Sarah Westcott, over allegations which she had made about him during an interview with the police. After a heated family argument, Mrs Westcott had telephoned the police and claimed in an oral and written statement that Mr Westcott, her father-in-law, had assaulted her and her baby. But the police decided to take no further action.

Clement Gatley famously said in his textbook on *Libel and Slander* in the 1930s that 'everyone has a reputation'.[9]

Defamation cases tend to 'lift the carpet' on things people want kept out of public view. It is fair to say that the media thrives on gossip stories about celebrities, trying to find any given opportunity to expose their lives. Here just some recent examples.

In 2018, the estranged husband of an award-winning comedian sued Louise Beamont (stage name Reay) for defamation over material in her standup show. Beamont's show, 'Hard Mode', was billed as 'hard core' at that year's Edinburgh Fringe Festival, featuring material from the breakup of her marriage. Apart from defamation, Thomas Reay also sued his wife for breach of privacy and data protection, seeking £30,000 in damages plus legal costs and a permanent injunction to prevent her publishing statements about him. The case raised concerns that if Beamont – who faced bankruptcy – lost, it could prevent comedians from using material about their loved – or unloved – ones in standup shows. Mr Reay dropped the legal action in December 2018.

Leading media lawyer, Mark Stephens CBE, had described the lawsuit as a 'test case', commenting that, had the case come to court, the judgment would rest on the judge's sense of humour. Stephens further argued that since the introduction of the 'serious harm' test under section 1 of the Defamation Act 2013, defences for the likes of comedians, academics and scientists were rather 'beefed up'.[10]

In March 2017 writer and food blogger Jack Monroe won a libel action against *Daily Mail* columnist Katie Hopkins and was awarded £24,000 damages in a row over tweets suggesting Monroe approved of defacing a war memorial during an anti-austerity demonstration in Whitehall.

Mr Justice Warby found there had been 'harm' to Monroe's reputation, which was serious, albeit not 'very serious' or 'grave'. A finding of serious harm is necessary for a successful libel claim under s 1 DA 2013.

The case centred on a Twitter exchange in May 2015, in which Hopkins confused two well-known anti-austerity commentators: Monroe and Laurie Penny, a columnist for the *New Statesman*. Penny had tweeted about a memorial to the women of the Second World War in Whitehall having been vandalized with the words, 'Fuck Tory scum'. Commenting on the graffiti, Penny tweeted from her account @PennyRed that she '[didn't] have a problem' with the vandalism as a form of protest, as 'the bravery of past generations does not oblige us to be cowed today'. Hopkins attributed the opinion to Monroe and tweeted

---

8 [2009] QB 407; [2009] 2 WLR 838.
9 *Gatley on Libel and Slander*, now edited by Milmo, P., Rogers, W.V.H., Parkes, R., Walker, C. and Busuttil, G., in its 12th edition (2017).
10 Source: 'Standup comedian's husband sues for defamation over 'provocative' show', by Haroon Sidique, *Guardian*, 19 February 2018.

to her then account @MsJackMonroe: 'Scrawled on any memorials recently? Vandalized the memory of those who fought for your freedom. Grandma got any more medals?'

Katie Hopkins got her break by being loud and rude on the UK reality TV show *The Apprentice*, then gradually found a niche as a pundit by tapping into fears about immigration and the perceived 'dilution' of traditional British and Western values.

After Hopkins was successfully sued in Monroe's defamation action, Hopkins' contract as *Daily Mail* columnist was not renewed 'by mutual consent' in November 2017 after a number of complaints over her comments on terror attacks and other controversies, such as libel allegations.[11]

In 1997, the *Daily Mail* printed a controversial front page referring to the killing of Stephen Lawrence in 1993 in south-east London. The tabloid subsequently embarked on a campaign to bring five young male racist suspects to justice. On the 14 February 1997, the *Mail* took the unprecedented step of naming them, showing large photographs and the caption 'Murderers' and 'If we are wrong, let them sue us'. The paper named Gary Dobson, David Norris, Neil and Jamie Acourt and Luke Knight as Stephen's killers and challenged the gang to sue the newspaper in a libel action. They never did.

The paper reprinted the same front page in July 2006 after new evidence emerged in the Stephen Lawrence killing. Gary Dobson and David Norris were eventually convicted of Stephen's racist murder. Gary Dobson was sentenced at the Old Bailey to a minimum of 15 years and two months' imprisonment and David Norris to 14 years and three months' imprisonment because both had been under 18 at the time of the killing.

3.2 History of defamation in common law

English libel law was invented by the judges of the Queen's Bench as an alternative to duelling, and conceived for the protection of gentlemen, whose reputations were seen as worthy of the kind of high-class litigation offered by the High Court.

Until the coming into force of the Defamation Act 2013 in January 2014, the tort of defamation was substantially governed by common law plus some statutory intervention, namely the Defamation Acts of 1952 and 1996. The 'offer of amends' to speed up matters in the courts and to encourage the parties to settle was introduced with the 1996 Act by way of an apology and damages.[12]

3.2.1 The tort of defamation

The tort of defamation developed through the common law tradition over hundreds of years, periodically being supplemented by statute. Over 50 years ago Diplock LJ referred to 'the artificial and archaic character of the tort of libel' in *Slim v Daily Telegraph Ltd*.[13]

The basis of the tort of defamation is injury to reputation, so it must be proved that the statement was communicated to someone other than the person defamed – a third party – because it can reasonably be assumed that a third party may well communicate the

---

11 Source: 'Katie Hopkins leaves Mail Online by 'mutual consent' as column dropped after two years', by Lizzie Dearden, *Independent*, 27 November 2017.
12 For further discussion see: Gibbons, T. (1996).
13 [1968] 2 QB 157.

information independently of the author of it. If the statement is not obviously defamatory, the claimant must show that it would be understood in a defamatory sense, such as by some innuendo[14] or inference.[15] It is not necessary to prove that the defendant intended to refer to the claimant. The test is whether reasonable people would think the statement referred to him. Professor Winfield gave the widely accepted definition of a defamatory statement:

> [one which] tends to lower a person in the estimation of right thinking members of society generally; or which tends to make them shun or avoid that person.[16]

The main tests established by the courts in deciding whether material is defamatory are whether the words used 'tend to lower the claimant in the estimation of right-thinking members of society generally',[17] 'without justification or lawful excuse [are] calculated to injure the reputation of another, by exposing him to hatred, contempt, or ridicule',[18] or tend to make the claimant 'be shunned and avoided and that without any moral discredit on [the claimant's] part'.[19] An insult or vulgar abuse is not considered to be defamatory because generally it is not considered likely to lower the reputation of the claimant in the estimation of right-thinking members of society (see: *Skuse v Granada Television Ltd* (1996)[20]).

The standard definition of 'defamation' in common law is:

- an imputation which is likely to lower the person in the estimation of right-thinking people;
- an imputation which injures a person's reputation, by exposing them to hatred, contempt or ridicule;
- an imputation which intends to make a person be shunned or avoided.

The tort of defamation recognizes two types of meaning:

- *Natural and ordinary meaning of the words*: this is not limited to the literal and obvious meaning but includes any inference which the ordinary, reasonable reader would draw from the words.
- *Innuendo meaning*: there are two types of innuendo meaning:

    (a) *false innuendo*: an alternative meaning which the ordinary reasonable person can read between the lines or infer from the words;
    (b) *true innuendo*: where the words appear to be innocent to some people but appear to be defamatory to others because they have special knowledge or extra information. An example of this would be the *Lord McAlpine* case.[21]

---

14 An allusive or oblique remark or hint, typically a suggestive or disparaging one.
15 By suggestion or implication.
16 Winfield, P.H. (1937), p. 256.
17 *Sim v Stretch* [1936] 2 All ER 1237 (Lord Atkin).
18 *Parmiter v Coupland* [1840] 6 M & W 105 at 108 (Lord Wensleydale; then Parke B).
19 *Youssoupoff v MGM Pictures Ltd* [1934] 50 TLR 581 at 587 (Slesser LJ).
20 [1996] EMLR 278 at 286 (Sir Thomas Bingham MR).
21 *Lord McAlpine of West Green v Sally Bercow* [2013] EWHC 1342 (QB); (Lord Alistair McAlpine of West Green 1942–2014).

The claimant must show that the defamatory statement referred to him, which is normally not too difficult. If the claimant is not identified by name, then he has to show that the words complained of are understood by some reasonable readers to be referring to him.

Defamation actions also include where the claimant has been the subject of a comical or satirical portrayal which then tended to subject him or her to ridicule or contempt (see: *Dunlop Rubber Co. Ltd v Dunlop* (1921);[22] *Hulton v Jones* (1910)[23]).

A typical example arose in *Gillick v BBC* (1996).[24] Serial litigant Mrs Victoria Gillick, well-known anti-abortionist and mother of ten children, asserted that she would be 'ridiculed, shunned and avoided' during her anti-contraceptive campaign in the 1980s when she claimed being defamed on a live BBC TV chat show (*The Garden Party* on 27 July 1989). It was implied that Gillick was morally responsible for the suicide of pregnant girls, following her campaign to prevent doctors from giving contraceptive advice to under 16-year-old girls without their parents' consent. The words, 'but after you won that battle . . . there were at least two reported cases of suicide by girls who were pregnant', were held by the CA as bearing the defamatory meaning that Mrs Gillick was morally responsible for two girls' deaths.

3.2.2 The meaning of 'publication'

Words need to be published to a third party. The law of defamation has become highly complex in the digital age where libel and slander after often blurred when statements are published online or via social media. The details are invariably highly fact-specific. A defamatory publication is usually in words, but can also be pictures, gestures and other acts also count. Even relatively transient publications such as tweets can constitute libel provided they have caused or are likely to cause serious harm to reputation – as the Lord McAlpine[25] case proved.

See
below 3.5.1

Any person or company involved in publishing the defamatory material can be sued in libel or slander. This includes the author, any editor or any publishing company. Sometimes distributors of defamatory material can also be sued, including website owners and ISPs.

Section 5 Defamation Act 2013 (DA) provides a defence to persons who are not authors, editors or commercial publishers of websites if they took reasonable care in the publication and did not know nor had any reason to believe that they had inadvertently contributed to the publication (online) of a defamatory statement. This covers printers, distributors, online device providers and so forth.

A defamation claim must start within one year of the date of publication. In the case of material which continues to be published online, the time will start to run from the date the material was first published.

---

22 [1921] 1 AC 367 (HL).
23 *Hulton (E) & Co. v Jones* [1910] AC 20 (HL), [1910] AC 20 (HL).
24 [1996] EMLR 267 (CA); see also: *Gillick v Department of Health and Social Security* [1986] AC 112 (HL).
25 *Lord McAlpine of West Green v Sally Bercow* [2013] EWHC 1342 (QB).

3.2.3 On whom lies the burden of proof?

It is common that a claimant in civil law has to prove his case to succeed at trial. Not so in a defamation action: here the claimant alleges that a publication is false, and the defendant has to prove the statement at the heart of the case is true. It seems ironic that the defendant's burden of proof was originally established to protect a person's honour and that this ancient common law principle has since been used in favour of libel claimants in the British courts.

Before changes were brought about by the 'serious harm' test under s 1(1) Defamation Act 2013, the tort of defamation lent itself to misuse by unscrupulous claimants.

One such example is the Dr Simon Singh case,[26] where the British Chiropractic Association (BCA) brought a claim for libel against academic science writer Dr Simon Singh over an article he wrote in The Guardian in April 2008.[27] Singh's article carried the following criticism that the BCA

> claims that their members can help treat children with colic, sleeping and feeding problems, frequent ear infections, asthma and prolonged crying, even though there is not a jot of evidence. This organization is the respectable face of the chiropractic profession and yet it happily promotes bogus treatments.[28]

When Singh was made aware of the BCA's action, The Guardian immediately offered them to put the record straight with a 'right to reply', published by the newspaper, but the BCA refused, also refusing the Guardian's offer to make amends. The BCA continued with their libel action against Simon Singh.

During the preliminary hearing, Eady J acknowledged that that the BCA had been technically correct in claiming they had been defamed. The judge's final ruling in favour of the BCA meant that Singh's article constituted fact and not comment. In terms of the burden of proof, it meant that Dr Singh had to prove not only that there was no evidence to support chiropractic as an effective treatment for children's colic, but also that the BCA knew this to be the case (see: Lingens v Austria (1986)[29]).

Dr Singh eventually won his long-drawn-out 'libel' action in the Court of Appeal, relying on the defence of 'fair comment' which led to the case against him being dropped by the BCA. The case cost Singh more than £200,000 which he never managed to fully recover. His two-year battle marked a landmark case in the libel reform campaign and formed the basis for the Defamation Bill and is now enshrined in section 6 DA 2013 ('Peer-reviewed statement in scientific or academic journal etc').

3.2.4 Juxtaposition

Although a statement may be quite innocent, it can become defamatory in relation to the article if read as a whole or if placed next to a picture, as was the issue in the Petters[30] case,

---

26 British Chiropractic Association (BCA) v Singh [2010] EWCA Civ 350.
27 Source: Simon Singh, 'Beware the spinal trap', Guardian, 19 April 2008. The original was subsequently withdrawn from the online version by the Guardian.
28 Ibid.
29 (1986) 8 EHRR 407 (ECtHR).
30 Petters (Leigh) v BBC, 22 October 2007 (unreported).

where solicitor Leigh Petters appeared in a Channel 5 quiz show called *Brainteaser*, filmed in Bristol. Mr Petters had beaten the other three contestants to get through to the final round, which he then won together with prize money. On 8 March 2007, Channel 5 disclosed that there had been irregularities in the way in which *Brainteaser* had been run. In particular, it was revealed that on five occasions, when no member of the public had phoned in, the production company had put up the names of fictional winners, and in one case a member of the production team went on air pretending to be the winner. Channel 5 suspended the programme and issued a statement apologizing unreservedly to viewers. In June 2009, Ofcom fined Channel 5 £300,000 for the irregularities on *Brainteaser* and the show was axed.

The discovery of these irregularities on *Brainteaser* formed the subject of reports on news bulletins on BBC *One News* at 6pm and 10pm and BBC *News* 24 at 6pm, 7pm, 8pm, 9pm, 10pm, 11pm and midnight on 8 March 2007. The story also featured prominently on *Newsnight* on BBC Two that evening and was again referred to in a subsequent edition of *Newsnight* on 14 March. These news reports all featured library footage of *Brainteaser* which showed Mr Petters taking part in the quiz.

Mr Petters claimed that the juxtaposition of these pictures of him with the reports of the quiz irregularities were defamatory of him. He sued the BBC in libel, claiming that viewers would have understood that he was in fact involved in the *Brainteaser* scam. This allegation was untrue. Mr Petters had taken part in the *Brainteaser* quiz show in good faith, and he had won it fairly. The juxtaposition of pictures coupled with the report were deemed defamatory, and Mr Petters won damages of £60,000 from the BBC and Channel 5.

The libel trial between the multi-millionaire financier Nat Rothschild[31] and the *Daily Mail* offers an intimate glimpse into the lives of the politically powerful and super-rich, such as the billionaire Russian industrialist Oleg Deripaska, Rothschild and the then EU Trade Commissioner Lord Mandelson (pre-2013 Act).

 KEY CASE — *Rothschild (the Hon Nathaniel Philip Victor James) v Associated Newspapers Ltd* [2012] EWHC 177 (QB)

Precedent

- ❖ It is a complete defence to a defamatory action that the words complained of are true.
- ❖ The meaning of a defamatory statement must be understood as such by a hypothetical reasonable reader.

Facts

Mr Rothschild sued the *Daily Mail* publishers, Associated Newspapers Ltd (ANL), for libel for a 'special investigation' article headed: 'EXCLUSIVE: Mandelson, an oligarch and a £500m deal', published on Saturday 22 May 2010. The article extended over pages 2, 8 and 9. The headline on page 9 read: 'Revealed: the astonishing story of the night Lord Mandelson was flown to Moscow by private jet to join a billionaire friend desperate to strike a deal that cost British jobs'. The paper alleged that Lord Mandelson had broken the EU Commissioners'

---

31 [2012] EWHC 177 (QB).

Code of Conduct and that Mr Rothschild's conduct had been 'inappropriate' – thereby alleging corruption of politicians.

Decision

In deciding whether the words complained of bore a defamatory meaning, Tugendhat J stated that the court was not concerned with what the writer or publisher intended, nor with what any actual reasonable reader may have understood. The judge said that there must be a single meaning, 'that is a meaning which the court finds would be understood by the hypothetical reasonable reader' (applying *Slim v Daily Telegraph* (1968)[32]).

The judge cited the test applied by Sir Anthony Clarke MR in *Jeynes v News Magazines Ltd* (2008),[33] as to the meaning of 'defamatory':

1 The governing principle is reasonableness.
2 The hypothetical reasonable reader is not naïve, but he is not unduly suspicious. He can read between the lines. He can read in an implication more readily than a lawyer and may indulge in a certain amount of loose thinking, but he must be treated as being a man who is not avid for scandal and someone who does not, and should not, select one bad meaning where other non-defamatory meanings are available.
3 Over-elaborate analysis is best avoided.
4 The intention of the publisher is irrelevant.
5 The article must be read as a whole, and any 'bane and antidote' taken together.
6 The hypothetical reader is taken to be representative of those who would read the publication in question.
7 The court should rule out any meaning which 'can only emerge as the produce of some strained, or forced, or utterly unreasonable interpretation'.
8 It follows that it is not enough to say that by some person or another the words might be understood in a defamatory sense.

The court held that ANL had established that the words complained of by Mr Rothschild were substantially true (notwithstanding the admitted inaccuracies); that the allegation – that the purpose of the visit to Moscow was for Lord Mandelson to assist in the closing of the Alcoa deal by discussing tariffs – was so serious that it precluded the finding that the court made, namely that the facts surrounding the trip to Siberia for the joint venture proved that the meaning of the article was substantially true.

Analysis

It is then a complete defence to an action for libel (here against a newspaper) that the words complained of are substantially and materially true – known as

---

32 [1968] 2 QB 157.
33 [2008] EWCA Civ 130 (Sir Anthony Clarke MR).

'justification' or 'fair comment'.[34] Though ANL were able to prove only part of the defamatory allegations made against Mr Rothschild, the law is clear in that a defendant may nevertheless succeed if he can prove, on the balance of probabilities, that what he has alleged is *substantially* true (see: *Sutherland v Stopes* (1925);[35] *Maisel v Financial Times Ltd* (1915)[36]).

It is important to note that a preliminary ruling can be sought from the judge, who has to decide whether the words are legally capable of being defamatory, to avoid the expense of a full trial.[37]

3.2.5 *Reynolds* privilege

Section 4 of the Defamation Act 2013 (DA) replaced what was commonly known as the *Reynolds defence* (or *Reynolds privilege*). Section 4 created a new defence to an action for defamation of publication on a matter of public interest. It is based on the existing common law defence established in *Reynolds v Times Newspapers* (2001)[38] and was intended to reflect the principles established in that case and in subsequent case law.

Section 4(1) DA provides for the defence to be available in circumstances where the defendant can show that the statement complained of was, or formed part of, a statement on a matter of public interest and that he reasonably believed that publishing the statement complained of was in the public interest.

The intention in this provision is to reflect the existing common law as set out by the UKSC in *Flood v Times Newspapers* (2011).[39] It reflects the fact that the common law test contained both a subjective element — what the defendant believed was in the public interest at the time of publication — and an objective element — whether the belief was a reasonable one for the defendant to hold in all the circumstances.

See
below 3.3

Scotland and Northern Ireland still use the *Reynolds* defence in common law since the DA 2013 has not been adopted in those devolved legislations. This means the *Reynolds* defence can be raised where it is clear that a journalist (or 'author' generally), accused of defamation, has a duty to meet the 'ten-point' Lord Nicholls' criteria test in order to claim the defence (as affirmed in *Jameel v Wall Street Journal* (2007)[40]).

If and when *Reynolds* is advanced the court is required to interpret and apply this defence in a way that is compatible with Article 10(1) ECHR and Strasbourg jurisprudence on the importance of free speech and consider at the same time whether Article 8(1) ECHR is engaged (such was the case in the Tim Yeo libel action[41]).

See
below 3.6.6

---

34 Sections 5 ('Justification') and 6 ('Fair Comment') Defamation Act 1952.
35 [1925] AC 47.
36 [1915] 84 LJKB 2145.
37 Section 2 Defamation Act 1996 ('offer to make amends').
38 [2001] 2 AC 127.
39 [2011] UKSC 11.
40 [2007] 1 AC 359.
41 *Yeo (Tim) v Times Newspapers Ltd* [2015] EWHC 3375 (QB).

3.2.6 *Reynolds v Times*

The background to the *Reynolds* case itself dates back to 1994. In his libel action against *The Times*, the former Irish Taoiseach, Albert Reynolds,[42] found himself embroiled in a political crisis, when the Irish section of *The Times* alleged that Mr Reynolds had misled the Irish Parliament (Dáil Éireann). The English version of the newspaper had omitted the Taoiseach's 'right of reply'. After a number of cross-appeals, the House of Lords set the precedent for the now famous *Reynolds* qualified privilege defence, which set the tone for future media cases in defamation.

During the series of allegations and cross-appeals it emerged that Reynolds had appointed a new President of the High Court, Harry Whelehan, whom Mr Reynolds had elevated to that post from Attorney General. It emerged that AG Whelehan had delayed the extradition of a couple of Irish priests who were wanted in the Belfast court for alleged child sex abuse, and the newspaper alleged that both Reynolds and Whelehan had deliberately procrastinated in signing the extradition warrants. Mr Reynolds' government fell shortly afterwards, partly as a result of the controversial piece in *The Times*.

During the ensuing defamation action with a jury, Lord Nicholls gave the leading judgment, providing the now legendary ten-point list of factors to take into account when deciding whether the qualified privilege defence ('in the public interest') should be available to journalists. The ten-point *Reynolds* test comprises:[43]

1 *The seriousness of the allegation.* The more serious the charge, the more the public is misinformed and the individual harmed if the allegation is not true.
2 *The nature of the information,* and the extent to which the subject matter is a matter of public concern.
3 *The source of the information.* Some informants have no direct knowledge of the events. Some have their own axes to grind, or are being paid for their stories.
4 *The steps taken to verify the information.*
5 *The status of the information.* The allegation may have already been the subject of an investigation which commands respect.
6 *The urgency of the matter.* News is often a perishable commodity.
7 *Whether comment was sought from the claimant.* He may have information others do not possess or have not disclosed. An approach to the claimant will not always be necessary.
8 *Whether the article contained the gist of the claimant's side of the story.*
9 *The tone of the article.* A newspaper can raise queries or call for an investigation. It need not adopt allegations as statements of fact.
10 *The circumstances of the publication,* including the timing.

---

42 Albert Reynolds (1932–2014) was an Irish politician who was Taoiseach (Prime Minister) of Ireland, serving from February 1992 to December 1994. He is credited, along with his British counterpart Conservative Prime Minister John Major, with a crucial role in energizing the long-drawn-out peace process in Northern Ireland.

43 [2001] 2 AC at para. 205 (Lord Nicholls of Birkenhead).

3.2.7 *Reynolds* defence applied in common law

The *Reynolds* ten-point test was (unsuccessfully) applied by the *Daily Telegraph* in the *George Galloway* case,[44] where the former Glasgow MP sued the newspaper and its journalists for publishing libellous articles during April 2003, which claimed that Mr Galloway had 'received money from the Iraqi ruler Saddam Hussein's regime, taking a slice of oil earnings worth £375,000 a year', and that the Scottish MP had asked for 'a greater cut of Iraq's exports' and 'was profiting from food contracts'. A further article had stated that, according to the claimant's Iraqi intelligence profile, the claimant 'had a family history of loyalty to Saddam Hussein's Ba'ath Party', and referred to him as a 'sympathiser with Iraq'.

The High Court (affirmed by the CA) ruled in *Galloway* that the defendant newspaper could not rely on *Reynolds* qualified privilege, because not all of the ten-point criteria had been satisfied. Though the court said that the subject matter was 'undoubtedly of public concern', the sources of information could not be regarded as 'inherently reliable', and the *Telegraph*'s publishers, the editor and journalist had not taken sufficient steps to verify the information. The court, presiding without a jury, ruled in favour of Mr Galloway, who was awarded £150,000 in damages.

What can be concluded from *Galloway* is that a newspaper which obtains critical material from an anonymous or slightly dubious source will not be able to rely on the qualified privilege defence unless the source material passes the *Reynolds* – qualified privilege – test. George Galloway's success against the *Telegraph* effectively meant that by breaching any one of the ten-point *Reynolds* criteria the newspaper's defence had been lost.

Shortly after the Supreme Court ruling in *Flood*,[45] the *David Hunt*[46] libel action made legal headlines. This lengthy and complex action arose from a publication of an article in the *Sunday Times* by investigative journalist, Michael Gillard, about David Hunt in May 2010, headlined 'Underworld Kings Cash in on Taxpayer Land Fund'.[47] It was accompanied by a photograph of the claimant. The article referred to a £20m fund run by the London Development Authority which sought to acquire land for regeneration. It said that potential beneficiaries of the fund had been implicated in murder, drug-trafficking and fraud, and that these included Hunt, described as a man 'whose criminal network is allegedly so vast that Scotland Yard regards him as "too big" to take on'. The article alleged that the claimant (1) controlled a criminal network involved in murder, drug trafficking and fraud; (2) in criminal proceedings against him in 1999, assaulted the main prosecution witness; and (3) in order to obtain a financial benefit from the sale of land to the London Development

---

44 *Galloway v Telegraph* [2004] EWHC 2786 (QB).

45 *Flood* [2012] UKSC 11.

46 *Hunt (David) v Times Newspapers Ltd (No 1)* [2012] EWHC 110 (QB); see also: *Hunt (David) v Evening Standard Limited* [2011] EWHC 272 (QB).

47 The procedural history of the Hunt claims is complex. On 2 December 2010, 49 sub-paragraphs of the original plea of justification were struck out following a hearing before Tugendhat J. A separate action had been brought by the Commissioner of Police for the Metropolis and SOCA against the *Sunday Times* and Mr Gillard to restrain them from relying on and disclosing documents said to have been handed to Mr Gillard in breach of confidence (see: *Commissioner of Police of the Metropolis & Anor v Times Newspapers Ltd & Anor* [2011] EWHC 1566 (QB)). Two judgments were handed down which restricted the use the defendant/s could make of leaked documents in this action. The defendants then served an amended defence, and Hunt again applied to strike out the pleading, Eady J permitting the defendants to rely on some of the particulars of justification and the Reynolds defence (see: *Hunt v Times Newspapers Ltd (No 1)* [2012] EWHC 110 QB). Some of D's reformulated defence was then allowed by Eady J (*Hunt v Times Newspapers Ltd (No 2)* [2012] EWHC 1220 (QB)). On the first day of trial the Times was allowed to add new particulars to the plea of justification (*Hunt v Times Newspapers Ltd (No 3)* [2013] EWHC 1090 (QB)).

Agency, attacked and threatened to kill a property developer at a court hearing, and then avoided prosecution by intimidating witnesses.[48]

The defendant newspaper and journalist pleaded defences of 'justification' and *Reynolds* privilege. Mr Hunt argued that the entire justification defence should be struck out, because no particulars survived in the evidential disclosed material to support the most serious defamatory meaning.[49]

In his fifth action (Hunt No 5)[50] in July 2013, Simon J finally dismissed the case, saying that journalist Michael Gillard was highly experienced and gave evidence that was both lucid and entirely credible, allowing the *Reynolds* public interest defence, though noted that a plea of *Reynolds* privilege should not be a longstop for a failed or inadequate plea of justification. The mere fact of existing allegations or rumours could not be found by the defence; rather the court had to focus on proportionality and the quality of the research undertaken by *The Times* journalist. Hunt's barrister, Hugh Tomlinson QC, was also Chairman of the 'Hacked Off' campaign and attempted to discredit *Times* reporter Michael Gillard during the action. Mr Gillard had been investigating Hunt and his associates for about 11 years and during that time had obtained a significant amount of information which led him honestly to believe that Hunt was a violent and dangerous criminal at the head of a family-based network.[51]

The *Reynolds* qualified privilege defence was newly formulated regarding the 'public interest' test by Lord Phillips in the *Gary Flood* action,[52] when he said:

[it] protects publication of defamatory matter to the world at large where

(i)   it was in the *public interest* that the information should be published and
(ii)   the publisher has acted responsibly in publishing the information, a test usually referred to as 'responsible journalism'.[53]

Flood also set the precedent for the 'responsible journalism test' (see also: *Hughes v Rusbridger* (2010)[54]). In summary, the *Reynolds* defence could protect defamatory factual statements which were not or could not be proved to be true.

Some legal critics have commented on *Reynolds* qualified privilege as being divisive, and it remains a controversial issue particularly in Scotland and Northern Ireland. Clayton and Tomlinson (2009) argue that *Reynolds* privilege left the law of defamation in a state of uncertainty when it came to investigative journalism and matters of opinion.[55] Whether it could protect comment remains a moot point.

The *Flood* ruling in 2011 had marked the end of a six-year legal battle that began with an article by Michael Gillard on 2 June 2006 in *The Times* (and its online edition) headed 'Detective accused of taking bribes from Russian exiles'. The newspaper alleged that DS

---

48 Ibid. at para. 2.
49 Ibid. at para. 106.
50 Hunt (David) v Times Newspapers Ltd (No 5) [2013] EWHC 1868 (QB).
51 Source: 'Britain's newest "underworld king" unmasked after he loses libel claim against Sunday newspaper that labelled him violent and dangerous', by Simon Tomlinson, *Daily Mail*, 5 July 2013.
52 *Flood v Times Newspapers Ltd* [2012] UKSC 11.
53 Ibid. at para. 2 (Lord Phillips.)
54 [2010] EWHC 491 (QB).
55 Clayton, R. and Tomlinson, H. (2009) at para. 15.249.

Flood had accepted bribes from a private security company that was acting for a Russian oligarch. The legal dispute centred on the *Reynolds* defence whereby Tugendhat J had initially ruled in the High Court in 2009 that the newspaper *could* use *Reynolds* qualified privilege; however, the CA allowed Mr Flood's appeal in 2010 and overturned the High Court ruling.

The Supreme Court (UKSC) ruling in *Flood* (2011)[56] allowed the *Reynolds* defence 'in the public interest'. This ruling was significant in that the media regained their right to freedom of expression. This crucially meant that the truth of the allegations did not have to be proved as long as the matter was of 'serious public concern'. The case also set the precedent for the 'responsible journalism test' (also applied in *Spiller and Another v Joseph and Others* (2010)[57]).

The Times' reporting serious police corruption in the DS Gary Flood case was seen as being of considerable public interest. What could finally be reported was that Flood had abused his position as a police officer with the Metropolitan Police's Extradition Unit by corruptly accepting £20,000 in bribes from some of Russia's most wanted suspected criminals in return for selling to them highly confidential Home Office and police intelligence about attempts to extradite them to Russia to face criminal charges. DS Flood had 'committed an appalling breach of duty and betrayal of trust' and 'had thereby also committed a very serious criminal offence'.[58]

Since the *Jameel* (2007) and *Flood* (2012)[59] actions we can see a shift towards the (libel) courts' accepting that responsible investigative journalism is embraced by Article 10(1) ECHR as well as being covered by the *Reynolds* qualified privilege defence, particularly where a story is of genuine public interest. *Reynolds* privilege is not exclusively reserved for the media, but it is the media who are most likely to take advantage of it, for it is usually the media that publish to the world at large. The privilege has enlarged the protection enjoyed by the media against liability in defamation (see also: *AB Ltd v Facebook Ireland Ltd* (2013)[60]).

 FOR THOUGHT

Consider the rulings in *Flood v Times Newspapers Ltd* (2012) and *Jameel (Mohammed) v Wall Street Journal Europe Sprl* (2007). Would you agree that the law of privacy is moving ever closer to defamation law? Discuss.

3.2.8 Justification

It is important to note that the defence of justification is now replaced by 'truth' under section 2(1) DA (England and Wales). We will however look at the defence historically in common law since it is still used in Northern Ireland and Scotland.

---

56 *Flood v Times Newspapers Ltd* [2012] UKSC 11.
57 [2010] UKSC 53.
58 *Flood v Times Newspapers Ltd* [2009] EWHC 4075 (QB) at para. 12 (Nicola Davies J).
59 *Flood v Times Newspapers Ltd* [2012] UKSC 11.
60 [2013] NIQB 14 (QB (Northern Ireland)).

For a plea of 'justification' to succeed, there must be a final finding on the merits by a court on admissible evidence that the defamatory 'sting' of the allegation complained of (the 'sting of the libel') is objectively true as a matter of fact. The defendant does not have to prove that every word he published was true. He has to establish the 'essential' or 'substantial' truth of the sting of the libel. To prove the truth of some lesser defamatory meaning does not provide a complete defence.

Under modern libel practice a defendant must set out in his statement that the defamatory meaning he seeks to prove is essentially or substantially true. This is called the 'Lucas Box meaning'. The Lucas Box principle was formulated by the Court of Appeal in *Lucas Box v News Group Newspapers Ltd* (1986).[61] It was held that, in a defamation action, a defendant who does not agree with the meaning of the words complained of by the claimant is entitled to give an *alternative meaning* and give particulars to justify that meaning ('the *Lucas Box* meaning').

Whether 'justification' is permitted as a defence depends on the answer to three questions:

1   Is the defence meaning capable of arising from the publication?
2   Does the defence meaning arise from a separate and distinct allegation in the publication, about which the claimant does not complain?
3   Has the defendant provided proper particulars of fact that are capable of supporting the defence?

The *Lucas Box* meaning was applied in the *Elaine Chase* case (2002).[62] Ms Chase, a qualified state registered children's nurse – formerly employed as a paediatric community sister by the South Essex Mental Health and Community Care NHS Trust – alleged that she was being 'fingered' (i.e. exposed) by *The Sun* for a front-page article on 22 June 2002. The headline read: 'NURSE IS PROBED OVER 18 DEATHS: WORLD EXCLUSIVE'. The article did not directly name her but alleged that Ms Chase was suspected of overdosing terminally ill youngsters with painkillers. The tabloid identified the children concerned as nine boys and nine girls, aged between eight weeks and 17 years. Ms Chase argued that a significant number of readers would identify her by way of jigsaw identification. *The Sun* made references to mercy killers, such as Dr Harold Shipman and nurse Beverley Allitt. Ms Chase argued that the implication of such juxtaposition was unmistakable and referred to her. A subsequent edition of *The Sun* published a photograph of the claimant on the front page, although her face was pixelated following an injunction obtained earlier against the newspaper.

The defendant newspaper sought to rely on the fact that allegations were made by largely unidentified third parties in broad terms about the claimant, irrespective of whether those allegations were true or false. This meant a defence of justification based on reasonable grounds for suspicion focusing on some conduct of the individual so as to give rise to the suspicion ('the conduct rule'). The judge rejected the newspaper's defence of justification and entered judgment in favour of Elaine Chase. The newspaper appealed. The

---

61 *Lucas Box v News Group Newspapers Ltd; Lucas Box v Associated Newspapers Group plc and Others; Polly Peck (Holdings) plc v Trelford, Viscount de L'Isle v Times Newspapers Ltd* [1986] 1 WLR 147 (CA) (as per Ackner LJ).
62 *Chase (Elaine) v News Group Newspapers Ltd* [2002] EWCA Civ 1772 (CA).

court held that the defence of justification based on 'reasonable grounds for suspicion' must focus on conduct of the claimant that gave rise to the suspicion. It was not permissible to rely on hearsay. The appeal was dismissed.

3.2.9 Unintentional libel and lookalike publications

Some journalists have learned, to the financial detriment of their newspapers, that a sense of humour or, worse still, a joke, finds no favour in the libel courts. The problem arises frequently when a wrong caption to a photo or the wrong TV footage has been added in a newspaper or online edition. Or journalists have got it wrong when their intention was to be either funny or witty in satirical sketches by using innuendo.

The common law rule for 'lookalike' libel dates back to an early twentieth-century case, that of *Artemus Jones* (see: *Hulton v Jones* (1910)[63]). A seemingly simple joke misfired when, in 1910, the *Sunday Chronicle* published a satirical sketch about a certain 'Artemus Jones', said to be a fictional Peckham church warden, who had gone to France with a woman 'who was not his wife'. A Welsh barrister called Thomas Artemus Jones (who was not from Peckham and was not a church warden) complained to the defamation courts and received the then enormous sum of £1,750 in libel damages. He satisfied the House of Lords that reasonable people might conclude that the defamatory words referred to him. The newspaper's assertion that its Artemus Jones was completely imaginary was somewhat undermined by the fact that Thomas Artemus Jones had been a subeditor on the paper seven years earlier. The *Artemus Jones* case remains the precedent for strict liability in defamation law, placing the burden on the publisher, editor and/or author to ensure – as a matter of principle – that no individual has to put up with a damaged reputation as a result of that publication, even if the person concerned suffers damage wholly independently of any fault on the part of the publisher.

The *Artemus Jones* rule was applied in *Dwek v Macmillan Publishers Ltd* (1999),[64] where a book published a photograph – taken some 20 years earlier – showing the claimant Norman Dwek sitting next to a woman who was (correctly) described as a prostitute. The photo in question showed a young woman sitting between two men on a sofa, published in an unauthorized biography of then Harrods owner Mohammed Al Fayed. It was the caption which dramatically transformed the meaning of the image. It read: 'Fantasies: Louise "Michaels" was a prostitute who befriended Dodi (left in photograph)'. But the man on the left in the photo was not Dodi Al Fayed,[65] but Norman Dwek, a family dentist from Richmond. The same photograph (with the other man cropped out of the picture) was reprinted in both the *Mail on Sunday* and the *Evening Standard*, with the respective captions: 'Shared: Dodi with high-class prostitute Louise Dyrbusz, who also saw his uncle'.

Mr Dwek successfully sued the book publishers and the newspapers for defamation. The Court of Appeal agreed with Mr Dwek that readers would look at the photograph in the context of the caption and believe that the man in the photo had sex with prostitutes. Mr Dwek rightly argued that many readers would recognize him as being that man, even

---

63 [1910] AC 20 (HL).
64 *Dwek v Macmillan Publishers Ltd & Others* [1999] EWCA Civ 2002.
65 Emad El-Din Mohamed Abdel Moneim Fayed, better known as Dodi Fayed, was the son of Egyptian billionaire Mohamed Al-Fayed. He was the lover of Diana, Princess of Wales, with whom he died in a car crash in Paris on 31 August 1997.

though it was said to be a photograph of Dodi Al Fayed. The CA held that the photographic juxtaposition was defamatory.

The addition of a caption to a photograph may render it defamatory, so care should be taken when choosing appropriate captions or TV footage, particularly when the subject matter is controversial. The media publisher may seek to defend the libel action on the basis that any reader who identified the person in the photograph would know that the allegation was untrue.

With digital photo imaging and the ease with which images can now be changed or enhanced, there are additional potential dangers highlighted in the now famous defamation action brought by the *Neighbours* actors Anne Charleston and Ian Smith.[66] The actors, best known as the respectable married couple Harold and Madge Bishop in the soap, sued the publisher and editor of the *News of the World* over photographs showing their faces superimposed on to the bodies of pornographic models. The headlines read: 'Strewth! What's Harold up to with our Madge?' and 'Porn Shocker for Neighbours stars'. The accompanying article made clear that the photographs were from a pornographic computer game and produced by superimposing the actors' faces on the bodies without their knowledge. The argument advanced by Ms Charleston and Mr Smith was that many readers simply scan headlines and 'eye-catching' images without bothering to read the whole of the article. However, the House of Lords decreed that, when determining whether the photograph and text were defamatory, the *whole* of the accompanying article must be taken into account (for example 'bane (poison) and antidote (remedy)' as per *Charleston v News Group Newspapers Ltd* (1995)[67]).

Another case involving Harrods owner Mohammed Al Fayed demonstrates how the *Artemus Jones* case[68] is still applied in 'lookalike' situations. On 31 March 2002 Harrods issued a press release headed 'Al Fayed reveals plan to "float" Harrods', inviting the media to contact someone called Loof Lirpa[69] as there was to be an important announcement on the morning of the following day (i.e. 1 April): the launch of a floating shop on a canal boat.[70] The *Wall Street Journal* picked up the story on 5 April under the headline, 'The Enron of Britain?' reporting that 'if Harrods, the British luxury retailer, ever goes public, investors would be wise to question its every disclosure'. Eady J determined that the resulting libel action should be heard in the UK, rather than the US, stating that the words could mean that every corporate disclosure of Harrods should be distrusted, and even that 'it is reasonably suspected that if the claimant [Harrods] were to become a public company it would prove itself to be Britain's Enron by deceiving and defrauding its investors on a huge scale'. The case was settled out of court (under the 'offer to make amends') with Harrods demanding an apology and damages to be paid to charity. The journal's defence stated that it was 'meant to be a humorous comment on the bogus press release'.[71] The April fool joke had badly backfired. The history of the 'joke' defence is therefore not a happy one. Words are defamatory and intention is irrelevant.

---

66 *Charleston v News Group Newspapers Ltd* [1995] 2 AC 65 (HL).
67 [1995] 2 AC 65 (HL).
68 *Hulton v Jones* [1910] AC 20 (HL).
69 Note: 'April fool' – spelt backwards!
70 The statement was only available until noon on the chairman's personal website, www.alfayed.com.
71 See also: *Dow Jones & Company, Inc. v Harrods Ltd, and Mohamed Al Fayed* (2003) (Docket No 02–9364). United States Court of Appeals, Second Circuit. Argued: 23 September 2003. Decided: 10 October 2003.

In *O'Shea v MGN* (2001)[72] Morland J endeavoured to strike a balance between freedom of expression and an individual's right to privacy under Article 8(1) ECHR when considering strict liability libel. The judge had to decide whether a photograph (of Miss E) would be recognized by those who knew the claimant and would identify her – albeit wrongly – as being the person in the photograph, which would give her the cause of action in libel. Miss E had appeared in an advertisement for a pornographic internet service provider (the second defendant), who in turn had advertised in the *Sunday Mirror*. In this case the claimant bore a striking resemblance to a 'Miss E', though the photograph in question did not name or identify the claimant, other than by virtue of the strong resemblance between her and Miss E. Referring to *Hulton v Jones*, Morland J concluded:

> The test in law is objective. Would the ordinary reader of the advertisement, having regard to the words complained of and the photograph in the context of the advertisement as a whole and clothed with the special knowledge of the publishers, that is that the photograph was the 'spit and image' of the claimant, have reasonably concluded that the woman speaking into the telephone [in the photograph] was the claimant?[73]

Morland J ruled that the strict liability principle should not cover the 'lookalike' situation in this case, and to allow it to do so would be an unjustifiable interference with the vital right of freedom of expression and the democratic principle of a free press. Consequently, Miss O'Shea may well have suffered some embarrassment, but the court held that she was not protected under Article 8 ECHR, nor did she win her libel action.

 FOR THOUGHT: CASE EXAMPLE

You are a lawyer for a mainstream UK TV channel. Advise the producer of the 10 o'clock news who has incorrectly and accidentally used the photograph of an individual in connection with a recent terrorist attack in Manchester story. The individual in question is now suing the TV channel and the news producer in a libel action and is asking for substantial damages. The individual claims that the juxtaposition of her picture next to a piece of sync and news footage commentary have libelled her.

3.2.10 What are the cost implications of a libel action?

Legal aid is not generally available for defamation cases, so the cost of proceedings will generally have to be paid personally by the defendant – as in the case of *Dr Simon Singh*.[74]

Prior to the introduction of Conditional Fee Agreements (or CFAs – commonly known as 'no win no fee deals'), with recoverable success fees and ATE ('after the event') insurance premiums, claimants could not realistically bring defamation claims, however meritorious, against newspapers because they could not afford the legal fees.

See above 3.2.3

---

72 [2001] EMLR 40 (QBD).
73 *Hulton v Jones* [1910] AC at 84 (Morland J in O'Shea v MGN).
74 *British Chiropractic Association (BCA) v Singh* [2010] EWCA Civ 350.

The Access to Justice Act 1999 (ss 27–31), which came into force in April 2000, dramatically increased the attractiveness of 'no win no fee' deals as judges could make the losing side shoulder the extra costs associated with conditional fee cases. These were the 'uplift' fees charged by solicitors, an increase on normal fees to compensate for the possibility of loss and therefore no fee, and the ATE insurance premiums paid to protect against the other side's legal costs in the event of defeat.

Increasingly CFAs were used in defamation cases, such as that of Naomi Campbell in her action against the Daily Mirror.[75] Lawyers would typically charge an uplift of up to 100 per cent in 'success fees', which encouraged them to accept cases with a 50/50 chance of success. Newspapers and media organizations would regularly and deliberately outspend claimants in order to force them into submission.

Since CFAs were readily available via the 'access to justice' route, this meant that newspapers and other media groups were increasingly subject to numerous 'libel' claims from individuals who had until then been unable to enforce their legal rights against them. A CFA agreement then enabled a defamation litigant to engage a lawyer on a total or partial 'no win no fee' basis with an agreement that the lawyer would be paid up to twice their fee if they were successful. New rules on CFAs, following the Jackson[76] reforms, came into force on 1 April 2013.[77]

It is relatively rare for individuals to defend a libel case successfully against a big corporation as the McLibel case in 2005 demonstrated.[78] Gardener Helen Steel and postman David Morris were found 'guilty' in 1997 of libelling the world's largest hamburger corporation, McDonald's, in a leaflet campaign issued by London Greenpeace.

The 'McLibel Two' (Steel and Morris) spent 314 days in the High Court defending themselves because – as stated above – defamation actions generally do not warrant legal aid. McDonald's were awarded £60,000 in damages (later reduced to £40,000 on appeal).

In Steel and Morris v UK (2005),[79] the ECtHR ruled that the two defendants did not have a fair trial under Article 6 ECHR, because of the lack of legal aid available to libel defendants in the UK, and that their freedom of expression under Article 10 ECHR had been violated by the 1997 High Court judgment. The human rights court recommended that the UK Parliament change the law in relation to legal aid for libel actions.

Sometimes claimants are disappointed with damages and cost awards by the courts – in spite of their victory. Coronation Street actor Bill (William) Roache won his libel action against The Sun over a claim in November 1990 that he was as boring as his screen character Ken Barlow and hated by his television colleagues.[80] The defendant newspaper, its editor Kelvin Mackenzie and freelance journalist Ken Irwin pleaded 'fair comment' and, to a limited extent, justification. They paid at first £25,000 and then a further £25,000 into court, but Mr Roache did not accept the amount of damages, arguing that £50,000 would not cover his six-figure court costs. He had expected at least £100,000.

---

75 Campbell v Mirror Group Newspapers Ltd [2002] EWHC 499 (QB) – initially a defamation action; her privacy action was successful in the House of Lords, see: Campbell v Mirror Group Newspapers Ltd [2004] UKHL 22.
76 Ministry of Justice (2010b) Review of Civil Litigation Costs. Final Report by Rupert Jackson J, December 2009 ('The Jackson Report').
77 These changes were brought about by ss 44 and 46 Legal Aid, Sentencing and Punishment of Offenders Act 2012 (LAPSO) and the Conditional Fee Agreements Order 2013.
78 McDonalds Corporation v Steel and Morris [1995] 3 All ER 615.
79 Steel and Morris v United Kingdom [2005] (Application No 68416/01); judgment of 15 February 2005 (ECHR).
80 Roache v Newsgroup Newspapers Ltd [1998] EMLR 161.

Roache then sued his famous libel lawyer, Peter Carter-Ruck, for negligence over his handling of his libel action against the *Sun* – which Roache duly lost. He had to declare himself bankrupt in 1999 with debts of around £300,000.

Another litigant who was virtually bankrupted through his libel action was self-professed 'Third Reich' specialist David Irving, who has consistently denied the Holocaust. In *Irving v Penguin Books Ltd and Deborah Lipstadt* (1996),[81] David Irving lost his lengthy libel action against American academic Deborah Lipstadt and her publishers Penguin.[82] Lipstadt said in her 1994 book that Irving had misinterpreted historical evidence to minimize Hitler's culpability in the Holocaust.[83] Gray J – sitting without a jury (because the bulk of evidential material produced by Mr Irving was in German) – ruled that Mr Irving was 'an active Holocaust denier, anti-Semitic and racist' who had 'distorted historical data to suit his own ideological agenda'.[84]

3.2.11 Malicious falsehood: the role of malice

There may be occasions when the claimant is entitled to legal aid if he pursues a 'malicious' or 'injurious falsehood' claim. He must then prove actual economic loss rather than purely non-economic damage to his reputation.

In *Joyce v Sengupta* (1993),[85] the CA allowed an appeal by Linda Joyce, the Princess Royal's maid, when claiming malicious falsehood. The case of Ms Joyce had attracted considerable public and media attention where Linda Joyce had been accused of stealing intimate love letters written to Princess Anne by Commander Timothy Lawrence which, in turn, had sparked rumours about the Princess Royal's troubled 15-year marriage to Captain Mark Phillips. Kim Sengupta, Chief Crime Correspondent of the *Today* newspaper, had published the offending article and allegations on 25 April 1989, headlined 'Royal Maid Stole Letters'. Though the article appeared grossly defamatory, Ms Joyce did not have the money 'up front' to sue in libel, and legal aid was clearly not available to her. Ms Joyce argued 'injurious falsehood' (also referred to as 'trade libel') and that the article had caused her financial loss by loss of reputation, loss of employment and by not obtaining references from her former employer, the Royal Household. Ms Joyce's claim of malicious falsehood was successful, in that the article contained serious untruths about her, that it had been published maliciously and the defendants were recklessly indifferent about the falsity of the allegations.

What is important in such a claim is that damages and economic loss have to be quantified as illustrated in the *Stéphane Grappelli*[86] case. Internationally famous jazz violinist Stéphane Grappelli (1908–1997) and guitarist William Charles Disley ('Diz' Disley, 1931–2010) sued their concert and tour promoters, Derek Block (Holdings) Ltd, in malicious falsehood. Derek Block had arranged 'gigs' for the Grappelli Jazz Trio at Tameside on 26 November 1976 and Milton Keynes on 4 December 1976.

---

81 *Irving (David John Caldwell) v Penguin Books Ltd and Deborah Lipstadt* (1996) (No. 1996-I-1113) [2000] WL 362478 (Q.B. Apr. 11, 2000) (unreported).
82 For a detailed discussion of the case see: Mulvihill, D. (2000).
83 Lipstadt, D.E. (1994).
84 Lipstadt, D.E. (2006), quoting Gray J at p. 214.
85 [1993] 1 WLR 337.
86 *Grappelli v Derek Block (Holdings) Ltd* [1981] 1 WLR 822.

On 21 September 1976 tour promoters cancelled the Tameside and Milton Keynes concerts, with the explanation that Mr Grappelli was 'very seriously ill' in Paris, adding that it would be surprising 'if he [Grappelli] ever toured again'. Lord Denning MR dismissed the original defamation action on the grounds that the statement itself was not defamatory. The claimants filed a new action relying on injurious falsehood and maliciousness, since the announcement was clearly damaging to Mr Grappelli's and the Trio's future success. The claimants were successful in their malicious falsehood action after they had provided the court with evidence of financial losses by way of a statement of quantum of damages.[87]

In *Tse Wai Chun Paul v Albert Cheng* (2001)[88] Lord Nicholls of Birkenhead was concerned with the ingredients of 'malice', which could defeat the defence of 'fair comment', when he said:

> First, the comment must be on a matter of public interest. Public interest is not to be confined within narrow limits today. Second, the comment must be recognisable as comment, as distinct from an imputation of fact. If the imputation is one of fact, a ground of defence must be sought elsewhere, for example, justification or privilege. . . . Third, the comment must be based on facts which are true or protected by privilege . . . the comment must be one which could have been made by an honest person, however prejudiced he might be, and however exaggerated or obstinate his views.[89]

Here follow two examples which demonstrate that companies can sue for defamation and claim malicious falsehood.

In *Tesco Stores v Guardian* (2008)[90] the supermarket giant sued for 'maliciousness' after the newspaper and its editor, Alan Rusbridger, had claimed the company was avoiding corporation tax through complex offshore property deals. It turned out that Tesco's dealings did aim to avoid tax, but a different one – stamp duty land tax – and for far less than alleged. Before the article was published, Tesco declined to meet the reporters and gave limited written responses. In the circumstances, the newspaper misunderstood the purpose behind the deals, but the story's thrust – regarding tax avoidance – was correct. In May, the *Guardian* nonetheless issued an extensive apology and explanation of its inaccuracies. Tesco, advised by Carter-Ruck, carried on its action in spite of an 'offer of amends' from the *Guardian*.[91] Subsequent investigations by *Private Eye* found that Tesco had offshore schemes to reduce corporation tax too.

At a pre-trial hearing before Eady J, lawyers for Tesco tried to exclude the *Private Eye* evidence and keep the 'offer of amends' on the table, while it pursued the action. The judge ruled against the corporation and struck out the action for 'malicious falsehood'. Two months later, Tesco agreed to a further correction and apology, and a settlement was reached out of court. By then, the costs had become enormous, dwarfing any damages.[92]

---

87 Referring *inter alia* to *Wright v Woodgate* [1835] 2 CR M & R 573 at 577.
88 [2001] EMLR 777 (Lord Nicholls of Birkenhead, sitting in the Court of Final Appeal of Hong Kong).
89 Ibid., paras 16–21.
90 *Tesco Stores Ltd v Guardian News & Media Ltd and Rusbridger* [2008] EWHC 14 (QB).
91 Source: 'Corrections and clarifications', *Guardian*, 3 May 2008.
92 *Tesco* [2008] at para. 860.

After the settlement, Mr Rusbridger argued in his defence that the *Guardian* was guilty of 'erroneous statements honestly made', but was not afforded the same protections as in the United States, quoting the landmark judgment in *New York Times Co. v Sullivan* (1964).[93] The court held that the correct approach to the proposed amendment and apology was to err on the side of generosity, thereby apologize and publish a correction.[94]

'Malicious falsehood' was also advanced in the *Tesla Motors* (2013)[95] case, an action against the BBC's popular programme *Top Gear* in 2008 and its then host, Jeremy Clarkson. Electric sports car maker Tesla Motors Inc., best known for its luxury electric cars and based in Palo Alto, California, claimed that *Top Gear* had faked a scene that appeared to show a Tesla Roadster running out of power, which Tesla claimed led to lower sales. Clarkson had ridiculed the Tesla Roadster running out of battery power after only 55 miles, far short of the 200 miles that Tesla had claimed.

In its ruling in 2013, the CA dismissed the Tesla Motors malicious falsehood claim. Moore-Bick LJ agreed with the first instance judge that the comments made by Clarkson regarding the car's range and reliability whilst testing them on the *Top Gear* test track could not bear the defamatory meaning, specifically that Tesla had intentionally and significantly misled potential customers. With respect to the malicious falsehood claim, the judge held that Tesla had failed sufficiently to particularize any damage the allegedly false statements were calculated to cause. While the court did not go so far as to say Tesla's claim was an abuse of process, it did not consider Tesla's prospect of recovering a substantial sum by way of damages sufficient to justify continuing the proceedings. Moore-Bick LJ found it difficult to believe that Tesla claimed to have suffered loss in revenue in the region of $4m. The company had not been able to show any 'special damage' right from the outset of its claim in 2008.

In summary, an action in malicious falsehood for a publication or statement in fact must be injurious to the character of another and requires proof of economic loss. It is only then that the law will consider the publication 'malicious', and the courts will interpret the meaning of 'malice' narrowly.

3.3 Defamation Act 2013

It took three years to pass the Defamation Act 2013 (DA) in Parliament, following an initial promise by then Labour Justice Minister and Lord Chancellor Jack Straw in 2009 to reform the libel laws after a series of revelations that libel threats had silenced scientists, doctors, biographers, community lawyers, consumer groups and human rights activists. Additionally, the cases of *Singh*[96] and *Flood*[97] had demonstrated the complexities of modern

---

93 (1964) 376 US 254 (United States Supreme Court). The case established the actual malice test which has to be met before press reports about public officials can be considered to be defamatory, and hence allowed free reporting of the civil rights campaigns in the southern United States. It is one of the key decisions supporting the freedom of the press. The actual malice standard requires that the claimant has to prove that the publisher of the statement in question knew that the statement was false or acted in reckless disregard of its truth or falsity. Because of the extremely high burden of proof on the claimant, and the difficulty of proving the defendant's knowledge and intentions, such cases – when they involve public figures – rarely prevail.
94 *Tesco* [2008] at para. 868.
95 *Tesla Motors Ltd v British Broadcasting Corporation* [2013] EWCA 152 (CA Civ Div).
96 *BCA v Singh* [2010] EWCA Civ 350.
97 *Flood v Times Newspapers Ltd* [2012] UKSC 11.

English libel laws with a multifaceted substantive overburdened common law and a costly procedure affordable only to celebrities and rich foreigners.

To reduce the chilling effect on freedom of expression resulting particularly from the *Simon Singh* case, Lord Lester of Herne Hill proposed a private member's Defamation Bill in the House of Lords in July 2010.[98] This was then followed by the government's own bill,[99] championed by Lord McNally, the Liberal Democrat leader in the Lords and Secretary of State for Justice at the time. One of the aims was to reduce foreign defamation actions in the UK which had made London the 'libel capital of the world'.

See
Chapter 7.5

The legislative fallout from the Leveson Report in 2012,[100] with its proposed Royal Charter, became inextricably linked with the draft Defamation Bill which had been nearing its completion in February 2013. Leveson LJ had recommended that members of the print press who declined to co-operate with a new regulator should be liable for all costs in libel and privacy cases, even when they won, and that politicians and officials should be entitled to curb media reporting, provided 'it is for a legitimate purpose and is necessary in a democratic society'.[101]

The 'Leveson clause' was introduced by film producer and Labour Peer, Lord Puttnam, in early February 2013, and looked set to sabotage the Defamation Bill, with Prime Minister David Cameron arguing that this was press regulation by the back door. For Labour, which favoured statutory regulation of the press, this was a way to kill two 'media' birds with one legislative stone. In fact, for a while it looked as if the Defamation Bill was totally dead. In a last-minute attempt to quell the revolt in the House of Lords,[102] Lord McNally promised the much-discussed government proposal for a Royal Charter to oversee press regulation in order to save the long-awaited defamation legislation.

The Defamation Act 2013 was enacted on 25 April 2013. The most significant changes included the introduction of a requirement to show 'serious harm' (to reputation of individual(s) or profit loss for profit-making organizations), the reformulation of the defences of truth in the form of 'honest opinion' and publication on matters of public interest (putting *Reynolds* on a statutory footing), and the introduction of greater protection for operators of websites. The 2013 Act was not adopted by either Scotland or Northern Ireland.

It is important to note that the Defamation Act 2013 reforms aspects of the law of defamation which means that common law continues to coexist alongside statute (i.e. the Defamation Acts of 1952 and 1996) as well as in common law (particularly in Scotland and Northern Ireland).

3.3.1 Defamation Act 2013: key areas

The DA 2013 comprises 17 sections, with a mixture of codification, revision and general provisions. Here is a summary of the main areas of law.

---

98 [2010–12] First Report: Draft Defamation Bill (HL Paper 203/HC 930).
99 Ministry of Justice (2012c).
100 Leveson, Lord LJ (2012).
101 Ibid., vol. 4, Part K, 'Regulatory Models for the Future', at para. 15.3, pp. 1703–1704. For a full set of recommendations see: ibid., pp. 1584–1594.
102 The rebellion in the House of Lords included prominent Tories such as Lord Fowler, Lord Hurd and Lord Ashcroft, as well as more than 60 crossbenchers including Baroness O'Neill (the chair of the Equalities and Human Rights Commission) and former Speaker of the House of Commons Baroness Boothroyd.

Section 1 introduces the 'serious harm' test which now serves as the threshold test to the bringing of a claim. Sections 2 to 7 concern defences. The main common law defences are abolished and replaced. Section 2 restates the 'justification' defence under the label of 'truth', section 3 recasts the honest comment defence as 'honest opinion' and section 4 replaces Reynolds privilege with a new defence of 'publication on a matter of public interest'. Section 4(3) restates the reportage variant of the defence, for 'the defendant to believe that publishing the statement was in the public interest'. Section 5 provides a new defence for the operators of websites. Sections 6 and 7 deal with aspects of privilege, including the provision of a qualified privilege for statements made in peer-reviewed scientific or academic journals.

The latter part of the statute concerns publication, jurisdiction, the trial process and remedies. In a revision of particular importance to online publishers, section 8 introduces a 'single publication rule' that limits the period for claims to run from the date of 'first publication', thereby abolishing the Duke of Brunswick multiple-publication rule. Section 9 addresses the phenomenon of 'libel tourism', and now compels the court to refuse jurisdiction unless it is satisfied that England and Wales are 'clearly the most appropriate place' for the action to be brought for claimants outside the UK and the EU.

See below 3.8.3

Section 10 provides that an action cannot be brought against persons who are involved in, but not primarily responsible for, publication unless 'it is not reasonably practicable for an action to be brought against the author, editor or publisher'. Section 11 ends the presumption of trial by jury in defamation actions (unless specifically ordered by a judge in exceptional cases). Sections 12 and 13 address the question of remedies. They provide the court with power to order publication of summaries of judgments and to compel the 'take-down' of impugned publications. The final substantive provision, section 14, concerns aspects of the law of slander and special damage.[103]

Summary of substantial contents of the Defamation Act 2013

Section 1 DA: the effect of the 'serious harm test' and the Jameel principle

Section 1(1) DA provides the serious harm test: that a statement is not defamatory unless its publication has caused or is likely to cause serious harm to the reputation of the claimant. The serious harm test and level of seriousness was first introduced in its current meaning by Tugendhat J in Thornton[104] which caused there to be a significant development in the law for this purpose.

The Sarah Thornton litigation arose out of a book review by well-known journalist Lynn Barber of Thornton's book Seven Days in the Art World.[105] Dr Thornton was successful in her action against the Telegraph after a number of cross-appeals. The case made headlines because the defendant's 'offer of amends' was overturned by a finding of 'malice' (on the journalist's behalf), and the court awarded general damages for malicious falsehood. The precedent for the 'serious harm' test in common law was set.

In that case, Tugendhat J, basing himself on the judgment of Neill LJ in Berkoff v Burchill (1996),[106] listed some of the proposed definitions of the word 'defamatory'. Tugendhat J

---

103 Section 14(1) repeals the Slander of Women Act 1891.
104 Thornton (Sarah) v Telegraph Media Group Limited [2010] EWHC 1414 (QB) (Tugendhat J).
105 Thornton, S. (2009).
106 [1996] 4 All ER 1008 (Neill LJ).

was plainly concerned, particularly in the context of Article 10 ECHR and proportionality considerations, about the need to exclude trivial claims. He concluded, after considering authorities such as Sim v Stretch (1936),[107] that there was a requirement for a 'threshold of seriousness'.[108] On that basis, Tugendhat J concluded:

> *the fact that in law damage is presumed is itself an argument why an imputation should not be held to be defamatory unless it has a tendency to have adverse effects upon the claimant. It is difficult to justify why there should be a presumption of damage if words can be defamatory while having no likely adverse consequence for the claimant.[109]*

The precedent set in Thornton raised the threshold from one of 'substantiality' to one of 'seriousness'; this was then subsumed in statute which now reads:

> Section 1(1) DA 2013:
>
> A statement is not defamatory unless its publication has caused or is likely to cause serious harm to the reputation of the claimant.

So what, then, are the meaning and effect of s 1(1)? Unfortunately, the section conspicuously does not purport to offer a definition of a defamatory statement. It does not tell you what a defamatory statement is. It tells you what it is not. The second point to be made is that s 1(1) focuses solely on the harm to the reputation of the individual claimant. It does not focus, as s 1(2) does, on whether that harm to reputation has caused or is likely to cause serious financial loss. It does not focus on whether, for example, the published statement has caused injury to feelings. Likewise, in contrast to cases of slander under s 14 DA, s 1(1) imposes no requirement of special damage. Thus the distinction between harm to reputation on the one hand and the consequences of that harm on the other hand is maintained in s 1(1).

The Jameel principle[110] requires the court to consider whether a 'real and substantial tort' has been committed. If this question is answered in the negative, the claim is liable to be struck out on the basis that to allow it to proceed would amount to an abuse of the court's process because so little is at stake. A defendant disputing the existence of serious harm may still, if the circumstances and facts so warrant, issue a Jameel application.

Section 1(1) DA was first put to the test in the Bruno Lachaux case (2017)[111] (see below), where the CA unanimously dismissed the appeals of the defendants (The Independent and Evening Standard newspapers) against the decision of the High Court (2015)[112] that the claimant had established 'serious harm' within the meaning of section 1 of the Defamation Act 2013. The High Court had found serious harm in relation to four of the five articles complained of by the French aerospace engineer in his libel actions against three newspapers and the Huffington Post online.

---

107 [1936] 2 All ER 1237.
108 Thornton (2010) at paras 90 and 92 (Tugendhat J).
109 Ibid. at para. 94.
110 Jameel (Yousef) v Dow Jones & Co. Inc. [2005] EWCA Civ 75.
111 Lachaux (Bruno) v Independent Print Ltd; Lachaux v Evening Standard Ltd. [2017] EWCA Civ 1334 (CA).
112 [2015] EWHC 2242 (QB) (Warby J).

❖ KEY CASE	*Lachaux (Bruno) v Independent Print Ltd; Lachaux v Evening Standard Ltd.* [2017] EWCA Civ 1334 (CA)

Precedent

❖ The 'serious harm' test under section 1(1) DA is that a statement is *not* defamatory of a person *unless* it has caused or will probably cause *serious harm* to that person's reputation.

❖ It is enough for a judge to *infer* that the words complained about are likely to cause serious harm without requiring specific evidence of this.

❖ Section 1(1) DA 2013 raised the threshold for libel claims from 'substantial harm' to 'serious harm'.

Facts

The claimant, Bruno Lachaux, a French national and aerospace engineer living in the United Arab Emirates (UAE), brought a defamation action against three different news publishers in respect of five articles first published between 20 January and 10 February 2014. Two of the five articles were published online in the *Huffington Post* by AOL (UK) Ltd. Two were published in hard copy in *The Independent* newspaper and its sister paper *i* by Independent Print Ltd (IPL). The *Independent* article was also published online. The fifth article was published in the *Evening Standard* newspaper and online.

Each of the articles complained of by Mr Lachaux contained an account of events in the UAE, including proceedings against the claimant's ex-wife, Afsana Lachaux (a British citizen and ex-civil servant), for 'kidnapping' the couple's son. The articles reported allegations against the claimant – said to have been made by Afsana – who was described in the first *Huffington Post* article as a 'British victim of domestic abuse'. The claimant was accused of domestic violence and abuse (alleging criminal acts of assault), child abduction, fabricating false allegations against Afsana with a view to having her imprisoned (alleging perverting the course of justice), manipulating the Emirate Sharia system so as to discriminate against Afsana and to deprive her of access to her son. The inference was therefore of serious reputational harm by these publications.

The readership figures for the two *Post* articles online were some 4,800; for the *Independent* around 154,370–231,555 and 523,518–785,277 for the *i*. The *Independent* article had 5,655 unique visitors online. The *Evening Standard* readership was around 1.67–2.5 million for the print edition and 1,955 unique visitors online at the time.

The main issue for the CA was whether the publications (in print and online) had caused or were likely to cause sufficient harm to the claimant's reputation to justify the bringing of these claims and would meet the 'serious harm' test under s 1(1) DA. The defendant newspapers and online publishers relied on *Cooke v Mirror Group Newspapers Ltd* (2014)[113] – asking for proof of *actual* damage caused to Mr Lachaux's business reputation.

---

113 *Cooke v Mirror Group Newspapers Ltd* [2014] EWHC 2831 (QB). In Cooke, Bean J accepted that evidence is admissible and may be necessary on the issue of whether serious harm to reputation has been or is likely to be caused, at paras 37–39.

Decision (CA)

The judgment from Lord Justice Davis states that it is not necessary for a libel claimant to provide concrete evidence of harm to their reputation. From the fact that Mr Lachaux was known by or to a substantial number of people who, it could be inferred, read the publications complained of in one of the relevant places and from the fact that his reputation amongst those readers in those places to whom he was not yet known was a matter of real significance to him (referring to *Knupffer v London Express* (1944)[114]). Regarding the serious harm test under section 1(1)DA, the CA agreed with the High Court judge Warby J who concluded that on the balance of probabilities there were 'tens of people and possibly more than 100 who knew or knew of the claimant and read one or more of the articles and identified him, and who thought the worse of him as a result'.[115] In addition, there were people to whom the sting of the libel was passed via the 'grapevine', including social media (citing *Jameel*[116]). The CA ruled the defamatory meanings as 'serious', especially since the publishers were reputable. All the articles but one had caused serious harm to the claimants' reputation.

Analysis

This seminal judgment in *Lachaux* is a welcome one in that it provides a common law definition of section 1(1) 'serious harm'. The CA simplified matters and produced a sound definition of 'serious harm' which has further discouraged costly litigation in this area of law. Serious harm may be proved by inference, but the evidence may or may not justify such an inference (applied in *Ames (Craig) and McGee (Robert) v The Spamhaus Project Ltd and Stephen Linford* (2015)[117]).

The Supreme Court unanimously dismissed the newspaper's appeal agreeing with the CA on 'serious harm'.[118]

The *Jameel* principle and its importance were reconsidered in the light of s 1(1) DA 2013 in (1) Rob McGee (2) Craig Ames v (1) Spamhaus Project Ltd (2) Stephen Linford (2015).[119] The claimants were two California residents, Rob McGee and Craig Ames, who had founded a bulk email marketing services business. The first defendant (which was founded by the second defendant) was Spamhaus Project Ltd, a UK organization that investigates, collates data on and reports internet spam. Between December 2013 and May 2014, Spamhaus published documents on its website alleging that the claimants were known

---

114 [1944] AC 116 at para. 120.
115 *Lachaux* [2015] at para. 138 (Warby J).
116 *Jameel (Yousef) v Dow Jones & Co. Inc.* [2005] EWCA Civ 75.
117 *Ames (Craig) and McGee (Robert) v The Spamhaus Project Ltd and Stephen Linford* [2015] EWHC 127 (QB) 21 January 2015 (Warby J).
118 *Lachaux v Independent Print Ltd. and another* [2019] UKSC 27.
119 [2015] EWHC 3408 (QB).

spammers, calling their business a '*massive snowshoe operation*' (a technique used by spammers to spread spam output across many ISPs and domains), and placing them on their 'ROKSO' (Register of Known Spam Operations) list and at the top of their list of the world's worst spammers.

The claimants asserted that they had substantial reputations in England and Wales, and that Spamhaus also enjoyed substantial influence across these locations. They alleged that the material published by the defendants bore defamatory meanings and had caused serious damage to their business reputations.

The defendants applied to strike out the libel claim as an abuse of process pursuant to the *Jameel* principle. The defendants argued that the claimants in fact had no significant reputation in the jurisdiction, that the extent of publication was minimal and had now ceased, and that the publication had not, and would not, cause substantial or serious harm. As an alternative, the defendants sought summary judgment by the court, arguing that the claimants could not satisfy the serious harm test under s 1(1) DA, in that the publication had not caused serious harm to the reputation of the claimants, nor was it likely to do so.

The London High Court dismissed the application to strike out the libel claim. Mr Justice Warby found that the claimants had a real prospect of demonstrating that the publications may be read by people whose opinions could affect the reputation and future prospects of the business. The judge explained that the *Jameel* principle was not abolished by the 2013 Defamation Act, but the requirement that serious harm had been, or was likely to be inflicted took precedence over the requirement that a 'substantial or serious tort' had occurred. Warby J also held that it was preferable to deal with issues of serious harm by means of preliminary issue rather than a strike out or summary judgment application.

This was the first case to consider the serious harm test alongside the *Jameel* abuse jurisdiction. The judgment indicates that where the serious harm test is satisfied, it will be unusual for that claim to fall foul of the principle in *Jameel*. Taking these factors into account, Warby J dismissed the defendants' application to strike out as the claimants could conceivably establish that serious harm had been caused to their reputation.

In determining whether serious harm has occurred or is likely to occur, the court must now base its decision on a variety of factors including:

- the nature of the defamatory statement itself;
- the gravity of its meaning;
- the nature and extent of libellous publication;
- the identity of the publishees;
- the nature and extent of the claimant's existing connections in the jurisdiction; and
- the claimant's reputation among those who are likely to have read the statement.

Section 2 DA: *the defence of 'truth'*
Section 2 replaces the common law defence of 'justification' with a new statutory defence of truth.[120]

2(1)   It is a defence to an action for defamation for the defendant to show that the imputation conveyed by the statement complained of is substantially true.

Section 2(1) DA focuses on the imputation conveyed by the defamatory statement and raises two questions:

1   What imputation is actually conveyed by the statement?
2   Is the imputation conveyed substantially true?

The 'truth' defence was first raised in the case of *Chase v News Group Newspapers Ltd* (2002),[121] where the CA indicated that in order for the defence of 'justification' to be available the defendant does not have to prove that every word he published was true. All he has to establish is the 'essential' or 'substantial' truth of the sting of the libel. The new section 2 defence of truth of the 2013 Act applies where the defendant can show that the imputation conveyed by the defamatory statement complained of is substantially true. The defence of 'truth' applies where the imputation is one of fact.

Section 3 DA: *the defence of 'honest opinion'*
Section 3 replaces the common law defence of 'fair comment' with a new defence of 'honest opinion'. This section broadly simplifies and clarifies certain defence elements, but does not include the previous requirement for the opinion to be on a matter of public interest.

3(1)   It is a defence to an action for defamation for the defendant to show that the following conditions are met.
(2)   The first condition is that the statement complained of was a statement of opinion.
(3)   The second condition is that the statement complained of indicated, whether in general or specific terms, the basis of the opinion.
(4)   The third condition is that an honest person could have held the opinion on the basis of –

    (a)   any fact which existed at the time the statement complained of was published;
    (b)   anything asserted to be a fact in a privileged statement published before the statement complained of.

Subsections (1) to (4) provide for the defence to apply where the defendant can show that three conditions are met. These are:

---

120 Section 2(2) and (3) of the 2013 Act replaced and repealed s 5 of the Defamation Act 1952 ('justification').
121 [2002] EWCA Civ 1772.

- *Condition 1*: that the statement complained of was a statement of opinion;
- *Condition 2*: that the statement complained of indicated, whether in general or specific terms, the basis of the opinion; and
- *Condition 3*: that an honest person could have held the opinion on the basis of any fact which existed at the time the statement complained of was published or anything asserted to be a fact in a privileged statement published before the statement complained of.

See
below 3.6.5

Section 4 DA: *the defence of publication on a matter of public interest*

Section 4(1) provides for the defence to be available in circumstances where the defendant can show that the statement complained of was, or formed part of, a statement on a matter of public interest and that he reasonably believed that publishing the statement complained of was in the public interest.

4(1)   It is a defence to an action for defamation for the defendant to show that –

(a)   the statement complained of was, or formed part of, a statement on a matter of public interest; and

(b)   the defendant reasonably believed that publishing the statement complained of was in the public interest.

The public interest at the time of publication is an objective test. This section effectively abolishes the *Reynolds* defence[122] (though not in Scotland and Northern Ireland).

See
above 3.2.5

Section 5 DA: *operators of websites*

Section 5 creates a new defence for the operators of websites where a defamation action is brought against them in respect of a statement posted on the website.

5(1)   This section applies where an action for defamation is brought against the operator of a website in respect of a statement posted on the website.

(2)   It is a defence for the operator to show that it was not the operator who posted the statement on the website.

(3)   The defence is defeated if the claimant shows that –

(a)   it was not possible for the claimant to identify the person who posted the statement,

(b)   the claimant gave the operator a notice of complaint in relation to the statement, and

(c)   the operator failed to respond to the notice of complaint in accordance with any provision contained in regulations.

See
below 3.7

---

122 *Reynolds v Times Newspapers* [2001] 2 AC 127 (HL).

See
above 3.2.3

*Section 6 DA: defence of qualified privilege for peer-reviewed statements in
scientific or academic journals*

There have been a number of high-profile libel actions over the past decade involving scientists who have commented on and criticized corporations and conglomerates in academic journals. We have already noted the action of the British Chiropractic Association against Dr Simon Singh.[123] In defending the actions, he was in danger of losing his home.

A three-year long defamation trial in London's High Court eventually collapsed in 2011 when the US company NMT Medical Inc., based in Boston, went into liquidation. NMT had sued British cardiologist Dr Peter Wilmshurst for libel after he publicly criticized the company's research at a US cardiology conference in 2007. Additionally, NMT claimed that by discussing the details of the case on national radio (BBC Radio 4's *Today* programme in 2011), Dr Wilmshurst defamed the company's reputation further.

Wilmshurst's remarks concerned a medical trial which he himself designed, called MIST, to find out whether closing small holes in the heart with one of NMT's medical devices could stop migraines ('the STARFlex septal repair implant').[124] The trial did not succeed. One of Dr Wilmshurst's allegations was that doctors in the medical trials were paid large consultancy fees by NMT and even owned shares in the company.[125] The company argued that the payment of such fees was normal and acceptable, and the shareholdings were below the 'significant' $50,000 (£30,000) level that would have caused concern.

NMT did not sue the American specialist online cardiology journal, *Heartwire*, which had published a version of Dr Wilmshurst's remarks; instead, the company sued Dr Wilmshurst personally in the English High Court. Wilmshurst paid in excess of £100,000 of his own money to defend himself against NMT in three defamation claims, each time for both libel and slander (the radio broadcast).

Many academics and scientists have been put off by the *Wilmshurst* and *Singh* actions from voicing their concerns about research results in academic, scientific or medical journals. Such fears were also expressed in a report on 'Press standards, privacy and libel' (2010) by the House of Commons Culture, Media and Sport Committee. The report expressed strong concerns about the country's present libel laws in the internet age, in particular the defence of fair comment when challenged in the libel courts over academic and peer-reviewed publications.[126]

Section 6 DA 2013 now provides for the defence of 'qualified privilege' relating to peer-reviewed material in scientific or academic journals (whether published in electronic form or otherwise).[127] This has been welcome news for the academic community.

6(1)   The publication of a statement in a scientific or academic journal (whether published in electronic form or otherwise) is privileged if the following conditions are met.

---

123 *BCA v Singh* [2010] EWCA Civ 350.
124 Migraine Intervention with STARFlex Technology trials were carried out in the UK from 2004 to 2006.
125 Wilmshurst, P. (2011), pp. 1093–1094.
126 House of Commons (2010a) at para. 142.
127 The term 'scientific journal' includes medical and engineering journals.

(2)   The first condition is that the statement relates to a scientific or academic matter.

(3)   The second condition is that before the statement was published in the journal an independent review of the statement's scientific or academic merit was carried out by –

   (a)   the editor of the journal, and
   (b)   one or more persons with expertise in the scientific or academic matter concerned.

Sections 6(1) to (3) provide for the defence to apply where two conditions are met; firstly, that the statement relates to a scientific or academic matter; and, secondly, that before the statement was published in the journal an independent review of the statement's scientific or academic merit was carried out.

- *Condition 1*: that the statement relates to a scientific or academic matter; and
- *Condition 2*: that before the statement was published in the journal an independent review of the statement's scientific or academic merit was carried out by the editor of the journal and one or more persons with expertise in the scientific or academic matter concerned.

The requirements in Condition 2 are intended to reflect the core aspects of a responsible peer-review process.

Section 6(4) DA extends the protection offered by the defence to publications in the same journal of any assessment of the scientific or academic merit of a peer-reviewed statement, provided the assessment was written by one or more of the persons who carried out the independent review of the statement, and the assessment was written in the course of that review. This is intended to ensure that the privilege is available not only to the author of the peer-reviewed statement, but also to those who have conducted the independent review who will need to assess, for example, the papers originally submitted by the author and may need to comment.

Section 6(5) DA provides that the privilege given by the section to peer-reviewed statements and related assessments also extends to the publication of a fair and accurate copy of, extract from or summary of the statement or assessment concerned.

Section 6(6) DA states that the privilege given by the section is lost if the publication is shown to be made with malice. This reflects the condition attaching to other forms of qualified privilege.

Section 6(7)(b) DA has been included to ensure that the new section is not read as preventing a person who publishes a statement in a scientific or academic journal from relying on other forms of privilege, such as the privilege conferred under section 7(9) to fair and accurate reports and so forth of proceedings at a scientific or academic conference.

Section 6(8) provides that the reference to 'the editor of the journal' is to be read, in the case of a journal with more than one editor, as a reference to the editor or editors who were responsible for deciding to publish the statement concerned. This may be relevant where a board of editors is responsible for decision-making (such as the *Entertainment Law Review* or the *Communications Law Review*).

Section 7 DA: *reports etc. protected by privilege*

Section 7 extends the defences of 'absolute' and 'qualified privilege' to proceedings in any court of the UK (or territory outside the UK), and any international court or tribunal established by the Security Council of the United Nations or by an international agreement.[128]

Section 8 DA: *the single publication rule*

Section 8 introduced a *single publication rule* to prevent an action being brought in relation to publication of the same material by the same publisher after a one-year limitation period from the date of the first publication of that material to the public or a section of the public. This replaces the 'multiple publication rule' (Re Brunswick).[129]

8(1)   This section applies if a person –

    (a)   publishes a statement to the public ('the first publication'), and

    (b)   subsequently publishes (whether or not to the public) that statement or a statement which is substantially the same.

This measure also underpins freedom of expression under Article 10 ECHR by providing far greater protection to publishers. It equally safeguards the right to reputation since the court has discretion to extend the one-year time period whenever it is just to do so. Section 8 DA only applies to material that is 'substantially the same' as the original publication.

Specifically, section 8(1) indicates that the provisions apply where a person publishes a statement to the public (defined in subsection (2) as including publication to a section of the public), and subsequently publishes that statement or a statement which is substantially the same. The definition in subsection (2) is intended to ensure that publications to a limited number of people are covered (for example where a blog has a small group of subscribers or followers).

Section 8(3) has the effect of ensuring that the limitation period in relation to any cause of action brought in respect of a subsequent publication within the scope of this section is treated as having started to run on the date of the first publication. It specifically will not apply to material that is published in a 'materially different manner', taking into account the level of prominence and extent of the subsequent republication.

Section 8(4) provides that the single publication rule does not apply where the manner of the subsequent publication of the statement is 'materially different' from the manner of the first publication.

Section 8(5) provides that in deciding this issue the matters to which the court may have regard include the level of prominence given to the statement and the extent of the subsequent publication. A possible example of this could be where a story has first

---

128 Section 7(1) of the 2013 Act replaces and repeals s 14(3) of the Defamation Act 1996, which concerns the absolute privilege applying to fair and accurate contemporaneous reports of court proceedings.
129 *Brunswick v Harmer* [1849] 14 QB 185.

appeared relatively obscurely in a section of a website where several clicks need to be made to access it, but has subsequently been promoted to a position where it can be directly accessed from the home page of the site, thereby increasing considerably the number of hits it receives (see: *Budu v BBC* (2010)[130]).

Section 8(6) confirms that the section does not affect the court's discretion under section 32A Limitation Act 1980 to allow a defamation action to proceed outside the one-year limitation period where it is equitable to do so. It also ensures that the reference in subsection (1)(a) of section 32A to the operation of section 4A of the 1980 Act is interpreted as a reference to the operation of section 4A together with section 8 of the Defamation Act 2013.[131] Section 32A provides a broad discretion which requires the court to have regard to all the circumstances of the case, and it is envisaged that this will provide a safeguard against injustice in relation to the application of any limitation issue arising under this section.

Arguably, the single publication rule under section 8 may have been drafted too narrowly. While it protects the individual who originally published the material once the one-year period has expired, it does not protect anyone else who republishes the same material in a similar manner later. For instance, an online archive that publishes material written by someone else could be sued successfully, even though the original author could no longer be pursued for continuing to make the material available to readers. A publisher who republishes material previously published by a different person will similarly be exposed. It is argued further that the single publication rule should protect anyone who republishes the same material in a similar manner after it has been in the public domain for more than one year. The law is also not clear on merely transferring a paper-based publication onto the internet, or vice versa; does this amount to republication which is in a 'materially different' manner? Would this undermine the usefulness of the single publication rule? The answer will lie in the courts' interpretation of section 8 of the 2013 Act.

Section 9 DA: *jurisdiction: action against a person not domiciled in the UK or a Member State*

Section 9 addresses the issue of 'libel tourism' and focuses the provision on cases where an action is brought against a person who is not domiciled in the UK, an EU Member State or a state which is a party to the Lugano Convention.[132]

9   This section applies to an action for defamation against a person who is not domiciled —

   (a)   in the United Kingdom;

   (b)   in another Member State; or

   (c)   in a state which is for the time being a contracting party to the Lugano Convention.

---

130 [2010] EWHC 616 of 23 March 2010 (QB).

131 Section 4A concerns the time limit applicable for defamation actions.

132 Convention on jurisdiction and the enforcement of judgments in civil and commercial matters signed in Lugano on 30 October 2007. See: Official Journal on 21 December 2007 (L339/3). Lugano governs issues of jurisdiction and enforcement of judgments between the EU Member States and the European Free Trade Association countries other than Liechtenstein (namely Iceland, Switzerland and Norway).

Subsection (2) provides that a court does not have jurisdiction to hear and determine an action to which the section applies unless it is satisfied that, of all the places in which the statement complained of has been published, England and Wales is clearly the most appropriate place in which to bring an action in respect of the statement.

This means that in cases where a statement has been published in a British jurisdiction and also abroad, the court will be required to consider the overall global picture to consider where it would be most appropriate for a claim to be heard. It is intended that this will overcome the problem of courts readily accepting jurisdiction simply because a claimant frames their claim so as to focus on damage which has occurred in the UK jurisdiction only. Section 9 then limits the circumstances in which an action for defamation can be brought against someone who is not the primary publisher of an allegedly defamatory statement. This may well be affected now that Britain has voted to leave the EU.

Section 10 DA: *action against a person who was not the author, editor, etc.*

Section 10 limits the circumstances in which an action for defamation can be brought against someone who is not the primary publisher of an allegedly defamatory statement.

10(1) A court does not have jurisdiction to hear and determine an action for defamation brought against a person who was not the author, editor or publisher of the statement complained of unless the court is satisfied that it is not reasonably practicable for an action to be brought against the author, editor or publisher.

Section 11 DA: *trial without a jury*

Section 11 removes the presumption in favour of jury trial in defamation cases.[133]

11(1) In section 69(1) of the Senior Courts Act 1981 (certain actions in the Queen's Bench Division to be tried with a jury unless the trial requires prolonged examination of documents etc.) in paragraph (b) omit 'libel, slander'.

(2) In section 66 (3) of the County Courts Act 1984 (certain actions in the county court to be tried with a jury unless the trial requires prolonged examination of documents etc.) in paragraph (b) omit 'libel, slander'.[134]

The reality is that defamation cases are now tried without a jury unless a court orders otherwise (except in Northern Ireland and Scotland).

Section 12 DA: *summary of court judgment*

Section 12 gives the court power to order a summary of its judgment to be published in defamation proceedings more generally.

Subsection (2) provides that the wording of any summary and the time, manner, form and place of its publication are matters for the parties to agree. Where the parties are unable to agree, subsections (3) and (4) respectively provide for the court to settle the wording, and enable it to give such directions in relation to the time, manner, form or place of publication as it considers reasonable and practicable.

---

133 Provided under s 69 Senior Courts Act 1981 and s 66 County Courts Act 1984 in certain civil proceedings, such as malicious prosecution, false imprisonment, fraud, libel and slander.

134 Subsections (1) and (2) amended the 1981 and 1984 Acts to remove libel and slander from the list of proceedings where a right to jury trial exists.

That said, section 8 Defamation Act 1996 still grants the power to a court to order an unsuccessful defendant to publish a summary of its judgment where the parties cannot agree the content of any correction or apology.

Section 13 DA: *removal of statements*

Section 13 relates to situations where an author may not always be in a position to remove or prevent further dissemination of material which has been found to be defamatory. This section is particularly relevant to publications online. Section 13 enables the 'author' or operator of a website to remove an alleged defamatory posting during or shortly after the conclusion of proceedings.

Section 14 DA: *special damage in actions for slander*

Section 14 repeals the Slander of Women Act 1891 and overturns a common law rule relating to special damage. The 1891 Act provided that 'words spoken and published . . . which impute unchastity or adultery to any woman or girl shall not require special damage to render them actionable'.

In relation to slander, some special damage must be proved now to flow from the (oral) statement complained of (unless the publication falls into certain specific categories specified in the Act).

Section 15 DA: *general provisions: the meaning of 'publish' and 'statement'*

Section 15 sets out definitions of the terms 'publish', 'publication' and 'statement'. Broad definitions cover a wide range of publications in any medium, including pictures, visual images and gestures.

3.4 Injury to business reputation

Many people tend to think of defamation law in connection with someone's conduct or character in their personal life, the focus being on individual litigants. Corporate reputations are formed and reformed by the near-constant barrage of information available to us every day both in the business sections of newspapers, their online editions and social media. The ability to sue for defamation offers particular advantages in protecting a business reputation. The basic principle remains: the tort of defamation exists to protect against blatantly untrue damaging statements which can potentially ruin a company's business acumen and international standing. As John Disley said when he and Chris Brasher won their libel action in 1995, 'Take away my good name and you take away my life'.[135]

A damaging libel may lower a company's standing in the eyes of the public and even its own staff, and make people less ready to deal with it or less willing and less proud to work for it. If this were not so, corporations would not go to the lengths they do to protect and burnish their corporate images. In his leading judgment in *Jameel*,[136] Lord

---

135 Source: The Reunion: The First London Marathon, BBC Radio 4, 4 April 2010. Brasher and Disley, original founders and organizers of the London Marathon, accepted more than £380,000 in libel damages in an out-of-court settlement on 23 May 1995 over magazine and TV allegations that they used the London Marathon to enrich themselves.

136 *Jameel (Mohammed) v Wall Street Journal Europe Sprl (No 3)* [2007] 1 AC 359.

Bingham found nothing repugnant in the notion that this is a value which the law should protect. He did not accept that a publication, if truly damaging to a corporation's commercial reputation, would result in provable financial loss, since the more prompt and public a company's issue of proceedings, and the more diligent its pursuit of a claim, the less the chance that financial loss would actually accrue.

3.4.1 Can a corporation sue for harm to reputation?

In the *South Hetton Coal* case (1894),[137] *The Times* publishers argued that a corporation could have no personal character, and that the offending article had not related to the business of the company. Lawyers for the newspaper further argued that defamation laws did not apply to trading companies.[138] *The Times* had published an article strongly critical of the way in which the claimant (old: plaintiff), a colliery owner, housed his workers, and the company had not pleaded or proved any actual damage. However, the Court of Appeal unanimously rejected this argument. Lord Esher MR held the law of libel to be one and the same for *all* plaintiffs.[139] While he referred to obvious differences between individuals and companies, his conclusion was clear:

> Then, if the case be one of libel – whether on a person, a firm, or a company – the law is that damages are at large. It is not necessary to prove any particular damage; the jury may give such damages as they think fit, having regard to the conduct of the parties respectively, and all the circumstances of the case.[140]

This case established that trading companies that have reputations could sue for defamation and recover general damages. Since 1993, however, following the case of *Derbyshire County Council v Times Newspaper Ltd* (1993),[141] local authorities, trade unions and unincorporated bodies cannot sue for defamation. Increasingly the UK courts were asked to deal with attacks on international business reputation which – generally – the courts held as defamatory. This became known as the 'Derbyshire Principle'.

The *Derbyshire* Principle was applied three years later in *Shevill v Presse Alliance SA* (1996),[142] where a differently constituted committee of the HL decided that a trading company with a trading reputation in the UK may recover general damages without pleading or proving special damage if the publication complained of had a tendency to damage it in the way of its business.

3.4.2 Corporate defamation: the *Jameel v Wall Street* action

There are many defamatory things which can be said about individuals (for example, about their sexual appetite) which cannot be said about corporations. But some statements may well be seriously injurious to the general commercial reputation of trading and charitable corporations: for example, that an arms company has routinely bribed

---

137 *South Hetton Company Limited v North-Eastern News Association Limited* [1894] 1 QB 133.
138 Ibid., paras 134, 137.
139 Ibid., para. 138 (Lord Esher MR).
140 Ibid., paras 138–139.
141 *Derbyshire County Council v Times Newspapers Ltd and Others* [1993] AC 534.
142 [1996] AC 959.

officials of foreign governments to secure contracts; that an oil company has wilfully and unnecessarily damaged the environment; that an international humanitarian agency has wrongfully succumbed to government pressure; that a retailer has knowingly exploited child labour; and so on. Should the corporation be entitled to sue in its own right only if it can prove financial loss? The House of Lords in *Jameel v Wall Street* (No 3) (2007)[143] did not think so.

The contextual circumstances to the *Jameel* case were the 9/11 terrorism atrocities, when, on 11 September 2001, terrorists destroyed the World Trade Center in New York.[144] Shortly afterwards, the *Wall Street Journal* alleged that 15 of the terrorists had been financed by Saudi Arabia. The journal headlined 'Saudi Officials Monitor Certain Bank Accounts' on 6 February 2002, claiming that the Saudi Arabian Monetary Authority (SAMA)[145] was watching the accounts of certain named Saudi companies at the request of the US Treasury. These included accounts of Mr Jameel, principal director of the holding company named in the article, to trace whether any payments were finding their way to terrorist organizations.[146] The article was written by James Dorsey, the journal's special correspondent in Riyadh, and had been checked by financial journalist Glenn R. Simpson for accuracy.

The claimants brought their proceedings in the UK against the publishers of the European edition of the *Wall Street Journal*, where the article had also appeared. Eady J rejected the *Journal's* claim to *Reynolds* privilege, and the libel jury in the High Court found that the article was defamatory of both claimants, Mr Jameel and the Jameel Corporation, culminating in awards of £30,000 and £10,000, respectively.[147] There followed a number of appeals and cross-appeals by the *Wall Street Journal* with the eventual HL judgment in favour of the Jameel corporation.[148]

By a majority of 3 to 2, the Law Lords agreed that reputation is a thing of value and applies equally to companies as to individuals. This meant that a corporation could sue for defamation on its reputation and could recover damages without proof of special damage (i.e. economic loss). Lord Hope explained:

> this does not mean . . . that it [a company] can only be injured in a way that gives rise to loss which, because it can be calculated, has the character of special damage. What it means is that it must show that it is liable to be damaged in a way that affects its business as a trading company.[149]

---

143 *Jameel (Mohammed) v Wall Street Journal Europe Sprl (No 3)* [2007] 1 AC 359.
144 Four passenger airliners (operated by United Airlines and American Airlines) coordinated by Islamic terrorist group Al Qaeda crashed into the North and South Towers of the World Trade Center complex, killing 2,996 people and injuring 6,000 others. Within an hour and 42 minutes, both 110-storey towers collapsed.
145 On 28 September 2001 the UN Security Council had passed Resolution 1373, which required all states to prevent and suppress the financing of terrorist acts, with the United States making diplomatic efforts to secure the co-operation of the Saudi Arabian Monetary Authority (SAMA).
146 The Abdul Latif Jameel Company Ltd (the second claimant in the lawsuit) was well-known as a substantial Saudi Arabian trading company with interests in a number of businesses, including the distribution of Toyota vehicles, and was part of an international group owned by the Jameel family. The company also included Hartwell plc, a company which distributes vehicles in the UK. Mr Mohammed Abdul Latif Jameel (the first claimant) was General Manager and President at the time.
147 *Jameel (Mohammed)* [2003] EWHC 2322 (Eady J).
148 *Jameel (No 3)* [2007] 1 AC 359.
149 Ibid. at para. 95 (Lord Hope).

Their Lordships also re-qualified the *Reynolds* defence in relation to the meaning of 'responsible journalism' which became known as the *Jameel-Reynolds* tests:

1   Is the publication in the public interest in the context of the work as a whole?
2   Will the work or article pass the 'fairness test'?
3   How much weight is attached to the professional judgment of the journalist and his reliable sources?

Given the reaffirmation by the HL in *Jameel* (No 3) (2007) of the rights of companies to sue in defamation, it was then argued that the law could only be changed by statute if it was desirable to address potential abuses of libel laws by big corporations. During its debate of the Defamation Bill Parliament considered introducing a new category of tort called 'corporate defamation' which would require a corporation to prove actual damage to its business before an action could be brought. The *Jameel* actions (2006 and 2007) formed part of the discussions when the Defamation Bill 'ping-ponged' through Parliament in 2012–2013.

Eventually the Defamation Act 2013 made no mention of 'corporations', and case law in this area prevails.

Section 2(1) DA 2013 ('truth') indirectly addresses the area of 'corporate' law in respect of defamation claims. What this means in practice is that a for-profit company must now specify in its defamation claim under 'particulars of claim' that the defamatory statement:

1   has caused or is likely to cause the body financial loss;
2   specify the type of loss; and
3   that the loss is serious.

3.5 Internet libel: cyberbullies, bloggers, tweeters and emoticons

There is now a sufficient body of case law which tells us that a tweet or blog post can amount to a defamatory publication. So, when does an individual have a claim when faced with a particular libellous comment? Eady J suggested in *Thompson v James* (2013)[150] that the claimant must prove some sort of financial loss and that words in a tweet, blog or message board must always be interpreted in their context which may then give rise to a different interpretation.

What if a tweet on Facebook comment is combined with an emoticon (*McAlpine*) or additional text (*Jack Monroe v Katie Hopkins*)? This may well produce a stronger presumption that the poster is publishing defamatory content, depending on the facts.

---

150 [2013] EWHC 515 (QB).

When dealing with the Katie Hopkins libel case in March 2017, Mr Justice Warby defined 'how Twitter works' in a four-page appendix. Retweeting or sharing content at the click of a button means that defendants may well find themselves liable for damage caused by the online dissemination of libellous material, even if they originally shared this content with a relatively small group. While Monroe's reputation had not suffered 'gravely', the publication complained of caused 'serious' harm to it, and therefore met the threshold set by the act. Here follow some recent examples where claimants settled out of court following the introduction of the Defamation Act 2013.

In 2018 the consumer advice and money-saving expert, Martin Lewis, founder of consumer website MoneySavingExpert.com, sued Facebook for defamation. Lewis alleged that the social media site published more than 50 fake adverts featuring Martin Lewis. In a statement, Facebook said it had been 'working with Martin Lewis' team for some time' and had removed 'fraudulent ads that falsely featured him'. Lewis sought to draw a distinction between Facebook as a message board and the adverts it publishes in order to find a way to stop Facebook making profits at the expense of vulnerable people. This case aroused large media interest since it was about one individual suing the large media conglomerate to save his reputation.[151] In January 2019, Lewis and Facebook settled out of court. Part of the agreement was that Facebook made a binding commitment to donate £3 million to set up the Citizens Advice Scams Action (CASA) service, to provide one-to-one support. Facebook also agreed to create a 'scam ads' reporting tool, unique to Facebook in the UK, which started in July 2019.

The real problem of internet defamation is anonymity. In *Smith (Nigel) v ADVFN Plc* (2010),[152] the High Court classified chat on an internet bulletin board as more akin to slander than to libel as the posts were like contributions to a casual conversation (the analogy sometimes being drawn with people chatting in a bar) which people simply note before moving on; they are often uninhibited, casual and ill thought-out; those who participate know this and expect a certain amount of repartee or 'give and take'.

Additionally, Tugendhat J described the defamatory statements about Nigel Smith as cyberbullying which had appeared on an internet bulletin board, a hate campaign which had been set up under different pseudonyms, published about Smith via bulletin boards on a financial information website of a company whose website was named ADVFN.com. Some 267 defamatory statements had been made by 71 offenders (though some may have been the same person using different pseudonyms).

Mr Smith, the appellant, had set up an action group website ('The Langbar Action Group') in 2005 to recover compensation for investors in some fraudulently conducted companies. Nigel Smith sought an order from the court to block or delete the alleged defamatory posts.

The court, however, struck out all of Mr Smith's claims because they had no real prospect of success: the words complained of were not defamatory but amounted to abuse, and there were defences of qualified privilege and fair comment (this being before the coming into force of the Defamation Act 2013).

---

151 Source: Martin Lewis's blog post of 2 May 2018: https://blog.moneysavingexpert.com/2018/04/
martin-lewis-to-sue-facebook/.
152 [2010] EWHC 3255 (QB).

Tugendhat J said that Mr Smith's claim had no real prospect of success because he would not be able to prove that the publication complained of caused, or was likely to cause, any material damage to him. In short, Mr Smith's claim was wholly without merit.[153]

In the two conjoined cases, decided by the CA on the same day – *Cairns v Modi; C v MGN Ltd* (2012)[154] – the issue concerned Twitter messages and reputational harm.

In the first action, former New Zealand cricket captain Chris Cairns sued Lalit Modi, former chairman of the Indian Premier League (IPL) in the UK High Court for libel over an accusation on Twitter that Cairns was involved in match-fixing. Both litigants were well-known in the cricketing world.

The claimant, Mr Cairns, argued that the Twitter comments had tainted his entire cricket career. He was successful in his action and was awarded £90,000 damages against the defendant, who never made an apology for the libel. Mr Modi appealed against the award of damages on the ground, *inter alia*, that a more analytical reasoning process should be adopted in assessing damages in such cases.

Chris Cairns won further libel damages in 2016 when London's Marylebone Cricket Club (MCC) paid him substantial damages for wrongly linking him to match-fixing, in addition to making a public apology. Cairns settled with the MCC out of court for a five-figure sum.

In the second case – C v MGN – the claimant C was the father of a Baby P, Peter Connelly, who died of neglect in Tottenham on 3 August 2007. The child's mother, Tracey Connelly, was convicted of causing and permitting the 17-month-old son's death. Peter was tortured to death by her lover. Tracey Connelly was sentenced to prison along with her boyfriend Steven Barker and his brother Jason Owen, who were convicted at trial of the same offence.

The claimant was a man of good character and not in any way responsible for the ill-treatment of Baby Peter. *The People* (MGN) published a story which falsely alleged that C was a sex offender and had been convicted of raping a 14-year-old girl in the 1970s. This was untrue. He successfully sued for libel and was awarded £75,000 damages against the defendant, representing a 50 per cent discount for an early apology and offer of amends under s 2 DA 1996.

Similar to the *Cairns* case, the defendant newspaper appealed against the award of damages on the ground, *inter alia*, that the judge, in his assessment of compensation and his determination of an appropriate starting point, had attached too much importance to the large circulation and readership figures for the relevant newspaper, linking the circulation and readership of the newspaper to his assessment of the appropriate starting point, and failing to give sufficient focus on the very limited nature and extent of publication where the claimant had been and remained anonymous pursuant to an order of the court.

The CA dismissed the appeal in the first case (*Cairns*), that there was a very wide latitude in the assessment of damages in libel actions, where regard would be had to all the circumstances of the case as well as the constraints of necessity and proportionality. The court stressed that assessing compensation in defamation cases was 'multi-layered', including elements of hurt feelings, injury to reputation and the need for vindication, involved consideration of enormously variable combinations of circumstances and different features which did not lend themselves to straightforward categorization. The

---

153 Ibid. at paras 35–37 (Tugendhat J).
154 [2012] EWCA Civ 1382.

court was unwilling to set 'libel bands' of damages. It was held appropriate in defamation actions that the judge would normally arrive at a global figure by way of an award which is proportionate to the seriousness of the allegation and its direct impact on the claimant and would serve to vindicate his reputation.

In the second case, Re. C, the CA was influenced by the seriousness of the false allegation of rape rather than by the newspaper's argument that the claimant was not named, not famous and identifiable to relatively few readers. Dismissing the MGN's appeal, the court took into consideration the newspaper's circulation and readership figures of 500,000 (in print) and 1.2 million (online) and stated the starting point figure was £150,000.

3.5.1 Determining the words and meaning of a tweet or emoticon

Determining the meaning of words, especially in space-constrained postings or tweets (in 280 characters) can amount to a libel action. Throwaway tweets or posts on Facebook can amount to innuendo and can even amount to a criminal offence, as Paul Chambers, 28, of Northern Ireland, found out. He was found guilty in May 2010 of sending a 'menacing electronic communication' when he tweeted that he would blow up Robin Hood Airport in Doncaster when it closed after heavy snow. After a hearing at the High Court in London, his conviction was quashed.[155]

Words of 'gestures' in form of emoticons can also have an inference or a meaning that can be read between the lines without any specialist knowledge, amounting to an innuendo meaning that can be attributed to the words by readers who have a specialist knowledge. This can give rise to a great deal of uncertainty in a libel action. The reason for this is that it is not only the superficial meaning that may be defamatory, but also 'hidden' meaning that can be inferred.

A leading judgment in this respect is that of Lord McAlpine[156] where the wife of the Speaker of the House of Commons, Sally Bercow's tweet was found seriously defamatory in its natural and ordinary meaning. The case was brought just before the DA 2013 came into force. Sally Bercow's tweet on 4 November 2012 was accompanied by an emoticon:

'Why is Lord McAlpine trending?' [followed by the emoticon '*Innocent face*'][157]

The background to this unhappy case was that a BBC 2 Newsnight programme on 2 November 2012 had featured a special investigation into child sexual abuse in North Wales care homes in the 1970s and 1980s. The report claimed that two victims had been abused by 'a leading Conservative politician from the Thatcher years'. The alleged perpetrator was not identified. By the time the Newsnight report was broadcast, there had been 12 hours of speculation on social media regarding the identity of the alleged perpetrator.

Since Sally Bercow refused to apologize, Lord McAlpine began defamation actions by asking Twitter to disclose the names of 'twitterers' by way of a High Court order to the US ISP. Mrs Bercow's and other names were disclosed.

---

155 *Chambers (Paul) v Director of Public Prosecutions* [2012] EWHC 2157 (Admin) (sub nom. 'The Twitter joke trial').
156 *Lord McAlpine of West Green v Sally Bercow* [2013] EWHC 1342 (QB).
157 Ibid. at para. 3.

The High Court in *McAlpine* considered two new terms as part of the meaning of 'innuendo': 'trending' and the use of an emoticon. The court stated that the defendant, Mrs Bercow, was telling her followers that the claimant was 'trending' on Twitter and that there was no alternative explanation for why this particular peer was being named in the tweets which produced the 'trend', and then it is reasonable to infer that he is trending because he fits the description of the unnamed abuser. The reader would therefore reasonably infer that the defendant had provided the last piece in the jigsaw.[158]

As a result, taking into account the so-called repetition rule (or republication rule – the rule that a defendant who repeats a defamatory allegation made by another is treated as if he had made the allegation himself), the defendant was to be treated as if she had made, with the addition of the claimant's name, the allegation on the BBC 2 *Newsnight* television programme rather than on Twitter.[159]

Tugendhat J found that Sally Bercow's tweet coupled with the emoticon ('*innocent face*') on 4 November 2012 amounted to innuendo, alleging that Conservative Peer, Lord McAlpine, was a paedophile who was guilty of sexually abusing boys living in care. The judge explained that the emoticon was to be read as a stage direction and was part of the defamatory sting of the libel. Readers of the tweet were to imagine that they could see an expression of innocence on Sally Bercow's face (though Mrs Bercow claimed in her defence it was a deadpan look).

Lord McAlpine argued on the other hand that Mrs Bercow was using irony – that '*innocent face*' was meant to be read as the opposite of its literal meaning. Tugendhat J decided the reasonable tweeter would understand Bercow's words as insincere and ironical. The court held that a tweet suffixed with an emoticon could be defamatory,[160] and furthermore that emoticons may be especially relevant when considering if there has been an element of malice.[161] Mrs Bercow did not avail herself of a public interest defence (*Reynolds* privilege or reportage).

Tugendhat J ruled that the tweet was defamatory not only in its 'natural and ordinary meaning' but also through innuendo and the use of the emoticon to Mrs Bercow's 56,000 followers on Twitter at the time. Mrs Bercow settled out of court with an offer to make amends of £150,000, which Lord McAlpine donated to charity.

At the time the judgment was pronounced in May 2013, other twitterers were identified, such as the *Guardian* columnist George Monbiot, who subsequently apologized to Lord McAlpine, thereby avoiding further costly legal action. The comedian Alan Davies was ordered to pay £15,000 after retweeting an internet post linking Lord McAlpine to the paedophile allegations.[162]

McAlpine demonstrates that Twitter (and other social media sites) are no different from people chatting in the pub. They are a public platform, and tweets can seriously harm people's reputation and can amount to a defamatory statement.

In the context of postings made via social media sites, the advent of new technologies has meant that individuals can express themselves in different ways, such as by posting

---

158 Ibid. at para. 85.
159 Ibid. at para. 155.
160 Ibid. at para. 33 (Tugendhat J).
161 Ibid. at para. 163.
162 Source: 'Lord McAlpine row: George Monbiot reaches "unprecedented" settlement', by Josh Halliday, *Guardian*, 12 March 2013.

funny pictures or using emoticons in addition to the text that they post. Posters should be aware that the use of emoticons or similar graphics can be considered by courts when determining if a statement is defamatory.

This unhappy case concluded when the former principal adviser to Mrs Thatcher and successful businessman, Lord McAlpine of West Green, died shortly after his libel action against Sally Bercow. On his death on 17 January 2014, one obituary – written by his long-standing friend, Simon Heffer, in the *Daily Mail* – commented that Sally Bercow's tweet and refusal to apologize to Lord McAlpine had added to 'Alastair's utter distress'.[163]

3.6 General defences

A person who publishes a defamatory statement may be able to rely on the defences of 'absolute' and 'qualified' privilege in a wide variety of circumstances. The defence of absolute privilege, as its name suggests, protects the publisher whatever their motive for publication. The defence of qualified privilege is defeated if the publisher was malicious in the sense that the dominant motive for publication was improper. There are other defences available in statute. This section is particularly relevant to Scotland and Northern Ireland where the Defamation Act 2013 has not been enacted.

3.6.1 Summary of defences available

The defences available in a defamation action cut across a number of statutes:

- *justification* that the material is true (section 5 Defamation Act 1952);
- *fair comment (now repealed)*[164] – this in the past protected statements of opinion or comment on matters of public interest (with no malice) (section 6 Defamation Act 1952);
- *absolute privilege*, which guarantees immunity from liability in certain situations such as in parliamentary and court proceedings (section 14 Defamation Act 1996);
- *qualified privilege*, which grants limited protection on public policy grounds to statements in the media provided that certain requirements are met (section 15(1) Defamation Act 1996 – 'no malice');
- *honest opinion* replaces common law defence of 'fair comment' (see above) (section 3 Defamation Act 2013);
- *Reynolds privilege*;
- *publication on matter of public interest* (section 4 Defamation Act 2013);
- *peer-reviewed statement in scientific or academic journal etc.* (section 6 Defamation Act 2013).

---

163 Source: 'I believe this ghastly woman hastened my friend's death: As libel-storm Tory Lord McAlpine dies, an impassioned Simon Heffer pays tribute', by Simon Heffer, *Daily Mail*, 20 January 2014.

164 Section 3(8) Defamation Act 2013 abolished the common law defence of 'fair comment' and also repealed s 6 Defamation Act 1952.

3.6.2 Absolute privilege

The defence of *absolute privilege* gives the author of a 'defamatory' statement utter freedom in the communication of views and information. This privilege of free speech, dating back to Article 9 of the Bill of Rights 1688, is extended to all Members of Parliament and to statements made during judicial or tribunal proceedings. However, absolute privilege does not protect ministers or peers *outside* the Houses of Parliament (such as on College Green) or outside the courthouse (see: *Church of Scientology of California v Johnson-Smith* (1972)[165]).

Examples of absolute privilege include testimony by a witness in court and contemporaneous reports of proceedings in open court (e.g. written statements of witnesses). Although often classified as 'parliamentary privilege', Members of Parliament participating in parliamentary proceedings are similarly protected. This category of privilege reflects a particularly strong public interest in there being no inhibition on being able to speak or write freely even if there is an adverse impact on the other person's reputation. The defence is central to the proper functioning of an orderly and democratic society.[166]

3.6.3 Offer to make amends

Section 2 of the Defamation Act 1996 provides a procedure by which a defendant can make an 'offer to make amends' to enable valid claims to be settled without the need for court proceedings. Section 2(2) Defamation Act 1996 reads:

> the offer may be in relation to the statement generally or in relation to a specific defamatory meaning which the person making the offer accepts that the statement conveys ('a qualified offer').

In the offer to make amends, under section 4 of the 1996 Act: the defendant must:

(a) make a suitable correction of the statement complained of and a sufficient apology to the aggrieved party;

(b) publish the correction and apology in a manner that is' reasonable'; and

(c) pay to the aggrieved party (the claimant) compensation (if any) and costs.

Johnson (2008b) argues that the substantive defences in a defamatory action, such as absolute and qualified privilege, are going 'quite strongly in favour of the publisher of the material' and that the courts and Human Rights Court rulings have been in favour of freedom of expression.[167] But if the basic elements of responsible journalism, such as accuracy and reliable sources, are ignored, the courts will take a dim view of journalists if they put basic economics to sell newspapers or promote their websites before truthful reporting.

---

165 [1972] 1 QB 522.
166 Smartt, U. (2014).
167 Johnson, H. (2008b), pp. 126–131.

3.6.4 Qualified privilege

The defence of qualified privilege can protect private communications that contain defamatory material where there is a shared duty and interest between the publisher and the recipient. Qualified privilege also applies by statute[168] to a wide range of reports of public proceedings and notices, provided the relevant material is on a matter of public concern and for the public good.

Section 15 DA 1996 unfortunately does not define 'qualified privilege'; it just states that the publication must not be made with malice. Otherwise 'there is no defence'. There are a number of situations defined in Schedule 1 of the 1996 Act which detail 'qualified privilege' scenarios.

This defence arises where media freedom warrants some additional protection from the threat of litigation, particularly relevant to newspaper reports of public meetings or court proceedings.

'Qualified' means it is not 'absolute', and there will be certain conditions put on the author of the statement. A statement made in the performance of a duty may attract the defence of qualified privilege under common law,[169] provided that the person making the statement has a legal, moral or social duty to make the statement, and the person receiving it has an interest in doing so in that it allows such person to make a quality decision.

The prima facie defence of qualified privilege is lost if the claimant can prove that the defendant was motivated by 'actual' or 'express malice', though there is no sufficient definition in common law as to the meaning of 'malice'. A defendant establishes a prima facie defence of qualified privilege in common law if he can show that the publication was made by him in pursuance of a duty or in protection of an interest to a person who had a duty or interest in having the matter published.[170]

3.6.5 Honest opinion

Section 3 DA 2013 Act broadly reflects and simplifies elements of the common law – replacing the defence of 'fair comment' – but no longer includes the requirement for the opinion to be on a matter of public interest. Subsections (1) to (4) provide for the defence to apply where the defendant can show that three conditions are met.

Condition 1 ('that the statement complained of was a statement of opinion') embraces the requirement for 'fair comment', established by Lord Nicholls of Birkenhead in the Hong Kong case of *Tse Wai Chun Paul v Albert Cheng* (2001)[171] that the statement must be recognizable as comment as distinct from an imputation of fact. Nicholls LJ said:

> A comment which falls within the objective limits of the defence of fair comment can lose its immunity only by proof that the defendant did not genuinely hold the view he expressed. Honesty of belief is the touchstone. Actuation by spite, animosity, intent

---

168 Originally contained in the Defamation Act 1952, now part of the Defamation Act 1996, s 15 and Sch. 1.
169 Common law is recognized by s 15(4) Defamation Act 1996.
170 *Hebditch v MacIlwaine* [1894] 2 QB 54.
171 [2001] EMLR 777.

to injure, intent to arouse controversy or other motivation, whatever it may be, even if it is the dominant or sole motive, does not of itself defeat the defence. However, proof of such motivation may be evidence, sometimes compelling evidence, from which lack of genuine belief in the view expressed may be inferred.[172]

The judgment in *Cheng* is implicit in Condition 1 of s 3(1) DA 2013 that the assessment is on the basis of how the ordinary person would understand it. As an inference of fact is a form of opinion, this would be encompassed by the defence.

Condition 2 ('that the statement complained of indicated, whether in general or specific terms, the basis of the opinion') reflects the test approved by the Supreme Court in *Spiller v Joseph* (2010)[173] that 'the comment must explicitly or implicitly indicate, at least in general terms, the facts on which it is based'.[174] In *Spiller*, the Supreme Court unanimously allowed the appeal and held that the defence of fair comment should be open to the appellants.

Condition 3 ('that an honest person could have held the opinion') is based on any fact which existed at the time the statement complained of was published or anything asserted to be a fact in a privileged statement published before the statement complained of. This condition is an *objective* test and consists of two elements. It is enough for one to be satisfied.

The first element of Condition 3 is whether an honest person could have held the opinion on the basis of any fact which existed at the time the statement was published.[175] The second element of Condition 3 is whether an honest person could have formed the opinion on the basis of anything asserted to be a fact in a 'privileged statement' which was published before the statement complained of.[176]

The honest opinion defence is defeated if the claimant shows that the defendant did not hold the opinion 'honestly'.[177] This is a *subjective* test which means the defence of 'honest opinion' will fail if the claimant can show that the statement was actuated by malice.

Section 3(6) makes provision for situations where the defendant is not the author of the statement. For example, where an action is brought against a newspaper editor in respect of a comment piece rather than against the person who wrote it. In these circumstances the defence is defeated if the claimant can show that the defendant knew or ought to have known that the author did not hold the opinion.

Section 3(8) abolishes the common law defence of 'fair comment'. Although this means that the defendant can no longer rely on the common law defence (except in Scotland and Northern Ireland), in cases where uncertainty arises in the interpretation of section 3, case law continues to provide a helpful but not binding guide to interpreting how the new statutory defence should be applied.

172 Ibid. at paras 70–99 (Lord Nicholls of Birkenhead).
173 [2010] UKSC 53 (The substantive judgment was given by Lord Phillips (President), with some additional comments from Lord Walker).
174 Ibid. at para. 124.
175 Section 3(4)(a) DA 2013.
176 Section 3(4)(b) DA 2013.
177 Section 3(5) DA 2013.

What does this mean practically? The defence of honest comment has five requirements. The statement must:

> 1   be on a matter of public interest;
> 2   be recognizable as comment, as distinct from imputation of fact;
> 3   be based on facts which are true or protected by privilege;
> 4   explicitly or implicitly indicate those facts, at least in general terms; and
> 5   be a comment which could have been made by an honest person.[178]

Requirement (3) does not demand proof that all the facts indicated as the basis for the comment are true.

Requirement (5) is generously known as 'the objective test' of honest comment. It protects *any* comment which could have been made honestly, even if only by a person who is prejudiced or holds exaggerated or obstinate views.[179]

A defence of honest comment will fail even though the objective test is satisfied, if the claimant establishes that in fact the defendant was malicious (i.e. did not believe the comment).

3.6.6 The public interest test

Much has been said already in previous chapters about the various common law definitions of 'public interest'. The same applies to defences in defamatory actions.

Whether an opinion expressed by a journalist or author firstly passes the 'honest opinion' test (as per section 3 DA 2013) and was published in the public interest, thereby passing the 'responsible journalism' test, was first raised in *Jameel v Wall Street*.[180] Lord Hoffmann explained that it requires a two-stage approach:

See

Chapter 2.9

> The first question is whether the subject matter of the articles [as a whole] was a matter of public interest. In answering that question . . . one should consider the article as a whole and not isolate the defamatory statement . . .
>
> If the article as a whole concerned a matter of public interest, the next question is whether the inclusion of the defamatory statement was justifiable. The . . . allegations . . . must be part of the story. And . . . make a real contribution to the public interest element in the article.[181]

This defence is best illustrated by the Tim Yeo case.[182] The articles complained of were written by Jonathan Calvert, *The Sunday Times* 'Insight Editor', and his then deputy, Heidi

---

178   As per Lord Nicholls in *Tse Wai Chun v Cheng* [2001] EMLR 777 at paras 16–21 as endorsed by Lord Phillips (with one modification) in *Joseph v Spiller* [2011] 1 AC 852 at para. 105.

179   *Turner v Metro-Goldwyn-Mayer Pictures Ltd* [1950] 1 All ER 449, 461 (Lord Porter), commenting on an observation in *Merivale v Carson* [1888] 20 QBD 275, 281 (Lord Esher).

180   *Jameel (Mohammed) v Wall Street Journal Europe Sprl* [2007] 1 AC 359.

181   Ibid. at paras 48–51 (Lord Hoffmann).

182   *Yeo (Tim) v Times Newspapers Ltd* [2015] EWHC 3375 (QB).

Blake, in June 2013, resulting from their undercover investigation of the former South Suffolk MP's lobbying practices. Mr Yeo had represented his constituency for more than 30 years until May 2015 and had been chairman of the Energy and Climate Change Select Committee.

The 'sting' by the two *Times* journalists involved one of them posing as 'Robyn Fox' of a fictitious consultancy firm called 'Coulton & Goldie Global', and during a 'business' lunch discussions had taken place ostensibly with the purpose of providing Mr Yeo with consultancy for a couple of days per month with 'an extremely generous remuneration package'. The work was to relate to a European launch strategy for a leading edge solar technology developer in the Far East. The ensuing articles were headlined 'Top Tory in new Lobbygate row' and sub-headlined 'MP coached client before committee grilling', suggesting that Mr Yeo was prepared to, and had offered to, act in a way that was in breach of the House of Commons Code of Conduct by acting as a paid parliamentary advocate who would push for new laws to benefit the business of a client for a daily fee of £7,000 and approach ministers, civil servants and other MPs to promote a client's private agenda in return for cash. The articles also expressed the journalists' opinion, to the effect that Mr Yeo had acted scandalously and shown willingness to abuse his position as an MP.

Mr Yeo then sued the *Sunday Times* for libel over the three 'cash-for-advocacy' stories. Times Newspapers' defence was that its factual allegations were substantially true and made in the public interest. On 9 June 2014, Warby J held that the articles contained a defamatory factual imputation and a defamatory comment.[183] Shortly before that ruling Mr Yeo was cleared by the Parliamentary Commission for Standards of breaking lobbying rules.

The watchdog claimed the newspaper had used 'subterfuge, misrepresentation and selective quotation' in the reporting of the undercover sting.

Times Newspapers Ltd cross-appealed, citing as its defence 'justification', 'honest comment' and '*Reynolds* privilege' in respect of those meanings. At the appeal hearing Warby J dismissed Mr Yeo's claim as 'utterly implausible' and that the former MP did not present his action 'convincingly'. Celebrating the successful 'public interest' and 'responsible journalism' defence, Martin Ivens, editor of *The Sunday Times*, said the decision was 'a victory for investigative journalism'. The *Yeo* case vindicated the role of the press in exposing the clandestine advocacy by some MPs of undisclosed interests.[184]

3.7 Operators of websites

Following conflicting case law — such as *Godfrey* (2011),[185] *Tamiz* (2012)[186] and *Davison v Habeeb* (2011)[187] — the government introduced section 5 DA 2013 to clarify the law in relation to operators of websites (which were called 'online intermediaries' in some

---

183 *Yeo v Times* [2014] EWHC 2853 (QB) at paras 121–122, 136 and 138 (Warby J); Warby J also held that the online versions of the articles bore the same meanings as the printed versions, at para. 126.
184 For further discussion see: Bedat, A. (2015) at pp. 31–33.
185 *Godfrey v Demon Internet Ltd* [2001] QB 201.
186 *Tamiz v Google Inc.* [2012] EWHC 449 (QB).
187 [2011] EWHC 3031 (QB).

authorities). The question was whether operators of websites were merely a 'host' or liaison point between the defamed person and the author of the material and against whom the claimant could bring an action. Could he sue the intermediary? US law has always been very clear on this: website operators are merely 'hosts'.

The first landmark judgment in the UK courts was that of *Godfrey v Demon Internet Ltd* (2011),[188] where the court took into account the liability of an internet service provider (ISP) under section 1 Defamation Act 1996. And though *Demon* could have (and should have) removed the defamatory posting about Dr Godfrey from its news server once given notice by the complainant on 17 January 1997, the posting remained on the ISP's server and website for another 15 days. Dr Godfrey was awarded damages in the High Court by Morland J with the result that operators of websites would thereafter routinely take down any newsgroup postings and web pages which were allegedly defamatory.

In *Davison v Habeeb* (2011),[189] HHJ Parkes QC noted that it was arguable that Google was liable for publication of the articles at common law, on the basis that it had not merely acted as a passive conduit but could be seen as a publisher, hosting material on its servers and responding to requests for downloads, like the defendant in *Godfrey v Demon Internet Ltd* (2001).[190] Therefore, Google provided an almost infinitely huge electronic 'notice board' which was within its control, so it became liable once it refused to take the defamatory statements and postings down.[191]

Eady J's decision in *Tamiz v Google Inc.* (2012)[192] somewhat contradicted *Godfrey*, when he ruled that Google (in this case as host of blogger.com) was *not* a publisher at common law, regardless of notification.

Website operators now have a complete defence against liability in the UK for defamatory content posted by third parties under section 5 DA 2013, provided that the complainant is able to identify the poster of the defamatory statement.

This section has to be read in conjunction with the Defamation (Operators of Websites) Regulations 2013 ('the Regulations') (see below), which are complex and not altogether helpful. They attempt to define a complete procedure for responding to formal complaints. In a nutshell, the operator must forward the notice to the poster within 48 hours. The poster then has five calendar days to respond.

Section 5 seeks to prevent actions in relation to publications online outside the one-year limitation period for the initial publication, unless the publisher refused or neglected to update the electronic version, on request, with a reasonable letter or statement by the claimant by way of explanation or contradiction. This then reflected the ECtHR ruling in *Times Newspapers v UK* (2009),[193] which recognized the important role played by online archives in preserving and making available news and information as a public service and as an important educational research tool in our information society.

---

188 [2001] QB 201.

189 *Davison v Habeeb* [2011] EWHC 3031 (QB) (HHJ Parkes QC).

190 [2001] QB 201.

191 For further discussion see: McEvedy, V. (2013), pp. 108–112.

192 [2012] EWHC 449 (QB) (Eady J).

193 *Times Newspapers Ltd (Nos 1 and 2) v United Kingdom* [2009] EMLR 14 (Applications 3002/03 and 23676/03) 10 March 2009 (ECtHR).

3.7.1 The Defamation (Operators of Websites) Regulations 2013

Though the Ministry of Justice intended for the section 5 procedure to be 'as straightforward as possible', there are at least 20 cross-references linked to the Regulations 2013 which provide further guidance, and it takes a great deal of patience and mental agility to make sense of the section 5 Regulations.

Section 5(2) provides for the defence to apply if the operator of a website can show that they did not post the statement on the website.

Section 5(3) provides for the defence to be defeated if the claimant can show that it was not possible for him to identify the person who posted the statement; that he gave the operator a notice of complaint in relation to the statement; and that the operator failed to respond to that notice in accordance with provisions contained in regulations to be made by the Secretary of State.

Section 5(4) interprets section 5(3)(a) which states:

> The defence is defeated if the claimant shows that –
>
> (a)   it was not possible for the claimant to identify the person who posted the statement

and explains that it is possible for a claimant to 'identify' a person for the purposes of that subsection only if the claimant has sufficient information to bring proceedings against the person. This means that the complainant must have sufficient information to be able to bring court proceedings against the poster. By contrast, anonymous (or pseudonymous) content is subject to what amounts to a non-mandatory notice-and-takedown scheme.

Section 5(5) includes provisions for the operators of websites to remove a posting and provisions for time limits for the taking of any action and for conferring a discretion on the court to treat action taken *after* the expiry of a time limit as having been taken before that expiry.

Section 5(6) sets out certain specific information which must be included in a notice of complaint. The notice must:

1   specify the complainant's name;
2   explain why the statement is defamatory of the complainant;
3   specify where on the website the statement was posted; and
4   contain other information as may be specified in regulations. Regulations may specify what other information must be included in a notice of complaint.

Sections 5(7) to (10) further provide for regulations and secondary legislation (statutory instruments) including notice periods for complaints in different circumstances.

It is important to note: where the poster of a defamatory statement can be identified the website operator may not need to consider section 5. Then section 10 of the 2013 Act comes into play.

Section 10 ('Action against a person who was not the author, editor etc.') provides that:

> A court does not have jurisdiction to hear and determine an action for defamation brought against a person who was not the author, editor or publisher of the statement complained of unless the court is satisfied that it is *not reasonably practicable* for an action to be brought against the author, editor or publisher.

This section then limits the circumstances in which an action for defamation can be brought against someone who is not the primary publisher of an allegedly defamatory statement. Section 10(1) provides that a court does not have jurisdiction to hear and determine an action for defamation brought against a person who was not the author, editor or publisher of the statement complained of unless it is satisfied that it is not reasonably practicable for an action to be brought against the author, editor or publisher. For example, if a claimant wishes to bring an action against a poster based in Canada, it might then not be 'reasonably practicable' to bring an action against that poster. If the poster can be identified, he can easily be served notice by email.

3.7.2 Section 5 notice to website operators

Under the section 5 procedure a complainant is required to send a notice to the website operator containing information prescribed by the 2013 Act and the accompanying Regulations (known as a 'section 5 notice'). Section 5 of the 2013 Act should additionally be read in conjunction with Directive 2000/31/EC ('E-Commerce Directive'),[194] the implementing Regulations of 2013 and the Electronic Commerce Regulations 2002 ('e-Commerce Regs'),[195] which already provide immunities for operators of websites.

A section 5 notice is only valid if these seven 'boxes' are 'ticked' and the complainant has provided the following:

1. the name and email address of the complainant;
2. the URL or location of the statement complained of;
3. an explanation of what the statement says and why it is defamatory of the complainant;
4. the meaning the complainant attributes to the statement complained of;
5. the aspects of the statement which the complainant believes are factually incorrect or opinions not supported by fact;
6. confirmation that the complainant does not have sufficient information about the author to bring proceedings against them; and
7. confirmation of whether the complainant consents to his name and email address being provided to the poster.

---

194 Directive 2000/31/EC On 'Liability of Intermediary Service Providers' on Electronic Commerce of 8 June 2000 ('E-Commerce Directive').
195 Electronic Commerce (EC) Regulations 2002 (S.I. 2002/2013).

The complainant need not be correct either in law or in fact, for example in identifying words as fact rather than comments or as defamatory as opposed to mere abuse; he simply needs to satisfy the seven 'boxes' (above). If the section 5 notice is missing *any* of these elements, the website operator can reject it, provided that it does so within 48 hours of receipt and sets out in its response the requirements of a valid notice. The operator need not explain why the notice received was deficient.

Once the notice has been received, the website operator has to communicate the position to the poster (if it has the means to do so), who then has a chance to reply and provide their contact details. Having complied with the process, the website operator can avail itself of the defence under section 5, regardless of the position as between the complainant and the poster. It is then a complete defence for the operator to show that it was not the operator who posted the statement on the website (section 5(2)). This defence can be defeated if the claimant can show that it was not possible for him to identify the person posting the statement, the claimant gave the operator a notice of complaint in relation to that statement and the operator did not respond to the notice of complaint in accordance with these regulations.

Once the website operator has received a section 5 notice, the 'abuse team' has to check whether it complies with the requirements of both section 5(6) of the 2013 Act and regulation 2 of the 2013 Regulations ('Notice of complaint: specified information').

In cases where the poster cannot be identified *and* the posting is not obviously unlawful or otherwise in breach of the website operator's terms of use, that website operator will have to decide whether to rely on the section 5 procedure, simply take the posting down, or rely on the other defences to defamation, including the important hosting defence provided by regulation 19 of the E-Commerce Regulations 2002 (known as 'the Regulation 19 defence'). If the website operator elects to follow the section 5 procedure, they will need to look carefully at their online complaints procedure, provide training to those responsible for dealing with complaints, and perhaps develop some software to monitor the numerous deadlines included in the procedure.

Section 5(11) provides for the defence to be defeated if the claimant shows that the website operator has acted with malice in relation to the posting of the statement concerned. This might arise where, for example, the website operator had incited the poster to make the posting or had otherwise colluded with the poster of the statement.

Section 5(12) explains that the defence available to a website operator is not defeated by reason only of the fact that the operator moderates the statements posted on it by others. To avoid liability, the operator must remove the allegedly defamatory statement unless the original poster provides a response within that period stating that the poster does not wish for the statement to be removed and including the poster's full name and postal address. However, the poster is entitled to refuse to consent to the disclosure of that information to the complainant.

The Regulations provide for a tight timeline. If the operator has no means of contacting the poster, the allegedly defamatory content must be removed within 48 hours of receiving the complaint. If the operator sends the notice to the poster and receives no reply, the content must be removed within seven days of the operator sending the notice. On its face, there is no provision for the operator to reject a complaint as unfounded, and, under regulation 4 ('Defective notices to be treated as notice of complaint'), operators are required to respond even to formally defective complaints, albeit only by informing the complainant of the applicable requirements.

In summary, though complex, section 5 DA 2013 provides an extremely useful defence for website operators in circumstances where the poster of the defamatory statement can be identified and served with legal proceedings (as was the case in Lord McAlpine). In such circumstances, there is actually no need for the website operator to follow any procedure, or even respond to a notice of complaint at all.

3.7.3 Website operators' defence: what is publication?

There is now a substantial body of case law which involves social media tweets which can amount to defamation and/or harassment. The question which has been central to each legal challenge: is the ISP, social media platform or website operator a publisher? Most problems of defamatory or harassing posts online are associated with social networking sites' inability to identify the real identity of its posters who have uploaded defamatory or hurtful content on their platform without disclosing their real identity.

We have seen above that there are conflicting judgments (e.g. Godfrey or Tamiz). If the court decides that the ISP or social media platform is a publisher in relation to s 5 DA 2013 they may still be potentially liable for statements made by their users.

In Bunt v Tilley (2006)[196] the High Court held that an ISP that merely passively facilitated postings on the internet could not be deemed to be a 'publisher' at all. The claimant sued three individuals for libel and harassment over allegedly defamatory postings made on internet chatrooms. He also sued the ISP of each individual (AOL, Tiscali and BT), on the basis that having each provided their respective customer with a connection to the internet they too were responsible for the postings complained of. The ISP defendants applied to have the claim struck out and/or for summary judgment on it; they argued that they were protected from an action in defamation by the Electronic Commerce (EC Directive) Regulations 2002. Bunt argued that the ISPs fell afoul of the provisions under s 1(1) (c) DA 1996 as a consequence of his email notifications.

Eady J held that the ISPs were not publishers. There was no prospect of the claimant establishing that the ISPs had knowingly participated in the relevant publications and that they fell within the definition of an 'information society service for the purpose of the 2002 Regulations'. Bunt's claims were therefore struck out as there was no realistic prospect of success.

But, if the operator of website company decides to exert some form of editorial control by editing the articles or providing summary extracts, it may become a primary publisher (such as BBC Online, Mail Online, etc.). There will then be the question before the courts as to the distinction between primary and secondary publishers.

Generally, the section 5 defence ('website operators' defence') has been seen by website operators and ISPs as a welcome safeguard against actions brought in respect of third-party content on their websites.

An operator of an online forum, blog site or any site that encourages user-generated content (such as readers' letters or comments online, e.g. Guardian or Times) in respect of a statement posted on that operator's website, it will be a defence for the operator to show that it did not post that statement itself (see s 5(2) DA 2013). The new defence does not affect any of the pre-existing common law or statutory defences available to website operators.

---

196 [2006] EWHC 407 (QB).

It is therefore important for social networking sites that they can demonstrate the ability to identify their account holders that are operating the account or page (even though most of the social networking sites are US-based). Operators of websites should also ensure SNS users link their real names to their accounts.[197]

3.8 Defamation in Scotland and Northern Ireland

Scotland's defamation laws have remained largely untouched since 1996. While the law south of the border has clarified key defences of truth, fair comment and publication on an issue of public interest with the Defamation Act 2013, in Scotland these defences still rely on a patchwork of case law going back many years. Scottish lawyers such as Rosalind McInnes, Principal Solicitor for BBC Scotland, have long argued that this is most unsatisfactory. It allows the exact meaning of the law to be shrouded in confusion. McInnes' experience has consistently revealed the holes in Scottish defamation law, which, she argues, leaves everyone vulnerable. She stated at a Scottish PEN meeting in 2017: 'If you don't think defamation is important, you don't think freedom of expression is important'.[198]

Cases which have concerned lawyers include Andy Wightman, the Green MSP, who was sued for £750,000 over an article published on his personal blog. The moderator of a Facebook page, a community volunteer, also faced defamation action over posts made by other people about the sale of a local property.

Scots defamation law compensates the wronged party who has suffered 'injury to hurt feelings': this generally means a person's reputation (or honour) has been damaged. The greater the circulation of the publication (including online) by the original defamer the greater the sum of damages awarded by the courts. This includes republication (for example of a forwarded email or SMS) – since the multiple publication rule still exists in Scots defamation law. In cases where publication has been with malice, aggravated damages will be awarded if the case is proved. Even if the statement is truthful but designed to injure the claimant out of malice, an action can be brought when a statement is communicated, but only to the person defamed. This action includes injury to the feelings of the person defamed as well as injury to reputation. The pursuer of such a 'personal injury' claim cannot take advantage of the Court of Session procedure afforded to accident cases, for example.

In Northern Ireland, defamation actions are heard either in the county courts, situated all over Northern Ireland, or the High Court in Belfast. County court defamation cases carry a monetary jurisdiction of £3,000, and legal costs are significantly higher where jurisdiction is attached to the High Court.

---

197 SNS or social networking service is an online vehicle for creating relationships with other people who share an interest, background or real relationship. Social networking service users create a profile with personal information, photos and so forth and form connections with other profiles. These users then use their connection to grow relationships through sharing, emailing, instant messaging and commenting.

198 Source: 'Defamation Scotland: Making noise, calling for reform'. Debate in the Scottish Parliament by Scottish PEN, 30 June 2017: https://scottishpen.org/defamationscot-making-noise-calling-reform.

3.8.1 Defamation law in Scotland

Scots civil law on defamation has developed largely from the civil Roman law tradition (or Canon law), periodically supplemented by statute – similar to what happened in England and Wales.[199] The main difference between 'English' and Scots defamation law is that in Scottish law we look at the *delict* (or civil wrongdoing) with the award of damages for 'injurious feelings'. The seventeenth-century institutional writer Viscount Stair contributed much information in this area of Scots law.

The main difference between English and Scots defamation law is that an offending statement may not necessarily be defamatory and forms part of *delict*. Scots law then refers to 'hurtful words', and is similar to German or French law in this respect, being essentially harmful to the character, honour or reputation of the affected person ('the pursuer') because it is 'derogatory' or 'disparaging' or 'demeaning' or 'calumnious' in the eyes of the reasonable person. It is then more akin to 'malicious falsehood' (or 'malice') in English law or a slander of title.

Whilst English law makes the distinction between libel and slander, Scots law does not make this distinction, making a 'defamatory communication' a separate delict amounting to 'verbal injury' or *convicium*. Present Scottish law centres on the ('defamatory') statement which must be false and must lower the defamed in the estimation of right thinking members of society (see: Lord Atkin's definition in Sim v Stretch (1936)[200]). A Scottish court will ask what that standard is today, as it is within this context that the court will look at the allegedly offending statement. It is important to note when accusing someone of 'libel' that that accusation may, in itself, be defamatory.

A pursuer's libel claim bears the nature of *solatium* for hurt feelings, and if proved there will be an award of damages for the loss proved or presumed from a reputation unjustly attacked. Since there has been little precedent set to put a precise figure on 'injured reputation' or 'hurt feelings', Scottish judges can at times find it problematic to assess the seriousness of an account for damages in relation to the defender. Allegations of drunkenness made about a minister or of dishonesty made about a solicitor would be treated more seriously than if the same statement were made about an ordinary member of the public.

There is also a separate delict of 'invasion of privacy' linked to Article 8 ECHR, in which the making of a statement may give rise to liability for an attack on someone's reputation.[201] Neither of these delicts comes under the general heading of 'defamation'.

For a successful defamation action in the Scottish courts, it must be shown that there was a disparaging statement made by one person about another, which is communicated, and for which there is no defence; 'communication' includes internet posts via blogs or other social media channels such as Facebook or Twitter. But in Scots law a communication need not be to a third party in order to be actionable: communication solely to the victim of a defamatory statement may result in that person suffering relevant insult or affront. Whether material is defamatory (i.e. harmful to reputation) is a matter for the courts to determine. The burden of proof in this regard rests with the pursuer. However, the pursuer is

---

199 For an historical overview see: Normand, the Right Hon Lord (1938), pp. 327–338.
200 [1936] 2 All ER 1237 at para. 1240 (Lord Atkin).
201 Sections 29 and 57 Scotland Act 1998 also provide that the Scottish Parliament and Scottish ministers must not contravene certain Convention Rights, as defined in the Human Rights Act 1998, including Article 10 of the ECHR.

not required to show that the material is false; there is a rebuttable presumption that defamatory material is also false material, and it is for the defender to prove otherwise.

3.8.2 Defamation actions in Scotland involving *inter alia* Tommy Sheridan

Similar to its English counterpart, the development of Scots common law in defamation, coupled with 'privacy' challenges, is in a state of flux in that even relatively recent decisions can soon become out of date, best illustrated with reference to cases involving photographs, as was highlighted in the *Frances Curran* case (2011)[202] (below). The case was linked to a well-known Scottish 'celebrity', former parliamentarian (MSP) and then leader of the SSP, Tommy (Thomas) Sheridan.

Scottish courts have frequently referred to the *von Hannover* (Nos 1–3) decisions in relation to the invasion of someone's privacy when defamatory actions are being considered. When the court considered privacy in the *Ewing*[203] action it referred, *inter alia*, to *Reklos v Greece* (2009) in relation to reputation and defamation.[204]

❖ KEY CASE	*Curran (Frances) v Scottish Daily Record and Sunday Mail Ltd* [2011] CSIH 86 (A952/08) Extra Division, Inner House, Court of Session, 29 December 2011

Facts

The pursuer was Frances Curran;[205] the defenders the publishers of the *Daily Record* and *Sunday Mail*. On 7 August 2006 the defenders published a four-page article based on an interview with Tommy Sheridan,[206] in which certain remarks were made about the pursuer and three other MSPs, Colin Fox, Rosie Kane and Carolyn Leckie, accompanied by photographs. The front-page headline read: 'I'll destroy the scabs who tried to ruin me: Tommy vows to win back leadership of Scottish Socialists'. The defenders sought dismissal of the action on the basis that no relevant case of defamation was made out in the pursuer's pleadings and an *esto* position that, were the action to proceed to proof before answer, deletions would be required to be made.

The defenders submitted that criticism by an MSP of another MSP did not amount to defamation because of the permitted latitude in criticizing those who

---

202 *Curran (Frances) v Scottish Daily Record and Sunday Mail Ltd* [2011] CSIH 86 (A952/08) Extra Division, Inner House, Court of Session, 29 December 2011.

203 *Ewing (Terence Patrick) v Times Newspapers Ltd* [2010] CSIH 67 Outer House, Court of Session, Edinburgh.

204 (2009) (Application No 1234/05) ECtHR of 15 January 2009.

205 Frances Curran (born 21 May 1961, Glasgow) is a former co-chair of the Scottish Socialist Party (SSP) and a former Member of the Scottish Parliament (MSP) for the West of Scotland region during 2003–2007.

206 Tommy Sheridan (born 7 March 1964, Glasgow) then an MSP and leader of the SSP. In a civil jury trial in 2006 Sheridan sought damages for defamation against News Group Newspapers Limited (*News of the World* (NoW)). He alleged that articles in NoW (e.g. 31 October 2004 an article by Anvar Khan) had falsely accused him of having visited a swingers' club, committed sexual indiscretions, and been unfaithful to his wife. On 4 August 2006 the jury found in his favour and awarded £200,000 in damages. In December 2010 Sheridan was convicted of perjury following the libel trial against NoW in 2006. His wife Gail was acquitted after the Crown withdrew charges against her (see: *Her Majesty's Advocate against Thomas Sheridan and Gail Sheridan* [2011] ScotHC HCJ 001).

hold public office. Further, it was submitted that the comments made in the article were protected by the *Reynolds* qualified privilege defence. The pursuer would have to prove malice for the defence to fail. This she had not done. The defenders further submitted that the article be looked at as a whole, representing an attack on the public as well as the political activities of the pursuer(s), and that the term 'scab' in the article referred to her being a 'political scab'. Counsel for Ms Curran submitted that the case should be sent to proof and submitted that the tenor of the article was that she was guilty of dishonest conduct with base motives and that it went beyond fair criticism of a holder of a public office.

Opinion

Temporary Judge Mrs Morag Wise QC dismissed the action. She considered whether the article, taken as a whole, would tend to lower the pursuer in the estimation of right-thinking members of society generally, or be likely to affect her adversely in the estimation of reasonable people generally. She ruled:

> I do not consider that it would have that effect. Right-thinking members of society are well able to read an article of this sort and see it as no more than a robust criticism of the pursuer as a former colleague and ally of Mr Sheridan. The reference to the pursuer as a 'scab' simply has no context without the detail given of the political plot alleged by Mr Sheridan and the references to collaboration with 'the enemy' namely Newsgroup Newspapers Limited.[207]

Wise also ruled, 'In relation to the photograph this should not be seen in isolation but as part of the whole article, as demonstrated in *Charleston v News Group Newspapers Ltd* (1995)', i.e. the defence of 'bane and antidote'.[208]

Analysis

The Edinburgh court held that the photo of the Scottish MPs amounted to neither defamation nor an infringement of their privacy under Article 8(1) ECHR, citing the *Reklos* judgment. Wise J's opinion focused on the 'eye-catching' photograph in particular and stated that the matter was in the public interest, thereby allowing the qualified privilege defence under *Reynolds* (where all the ten-point criteria had been met by the newspaper). She stated that it was of particular public interest – and therein protected by Article 10(1) ECHR – that the leadership of a political party was explained and the (in this case) inability of some of its members to work with each other. Accordingly, she did not consider that this was an attack on the private character of the main pursuer, Frances Curran, but rather on her political decisions and political loyalties (also applied: *McLeod v News Quest (Sunday Herald) Ltd* (2007)[209]).

---

207 Curran (Frances) v Scottish Daily Record and Sunday Mail Ltd [2011] CSIH 86 at para. 29 (Judge Morag Wise QC).
208 [1995] 2 AC 65 (HL).
209 [2007] SCLR 555.

The Tommy (Thomas) Sheridan defamation actions against the now defunct *News of the World* (*NoW*) (News Group Newspapers) go back to 2004. Sheridan (the pursuer) was then a prominent member of the Scottish Parliament and leader of the Scottish Socialist Party (SSP). His claim related to an article published by *NoW* on 14 November 2004, containing a number of allegations concerning his private life, alleging sexual practices involving bondage, spiked heels, and whipping. There were also allegations of adultery, participating in orgies and drinking champagne (when he was a teetotaller). All of this Sheridan claimed was false.

On 23 November 2004, the pursuer raised an action of defamation and sought libel damages against the defenders. At his trial the pursuer brought 13 witnesses, including his wife Gail Sheridan. On 4 August 2006, after a trial which lasted five weeks, the 'libel' jury returned a verdict in the Sheridans' favour and assessed damages at £200,000.

The defender newspaper then enrolled a motion for a new trial under section 29(1) of the Court of Session Act 1988. That had the effect of postponing any further procedure at first instance, including the motion for application of the jury's verdict, until the appellate proceedings were determined. Meantime, the defenders came across material which suggested that the pursuer may have committed perjury at the trial. This prompted an averring *res noviter*.[210] The alleged perjury was reported to the police. On 25 September 2007, the Summar Roll[211] was discharged, and the cause was sisted pending criminal investigation.

The sist had been requested by the Lord Advocate, who had intervened in the process, on the grounds that further inquiries in the civil process could prejudice that investigation. The pursuer had opposed the sist, but the defenders had been content with it. On 23 December 2010, after a 12-week trial at the High Court in Glasgow, Tommy Sheridan was convicted of perjury. Leave to appeal was eventually refused at second sist on 3 August 2011.[212] Worth noting here that Andy Coulson's perjury trial – former editor of *NoW* – arose from the Sheridan perjury trial. Coulson had given evidence at Sheridan's perjury trial on 10 and 11 December 2010 as a defence witness. The perjured evidence was said to have been related to Mr Coulson's knowledge of 'phone hacking' by employees of the newspaper or people acting for *NoW* and of payments to them. Andy Coulson was cleared of all charges.

See
Chapter 7.5

Tommy Sheridan subsequently applied to the Scottish Criminal Cases Review Commission (SCCRC) for his case to be referred to the appellate jurisdiction of the High Court. On 14 February 2012, the pursuer resisted a motion by the defenders to recall the sist on the basis that he was attempting to have his conviction quashed. In May 2015 the SCCRC declined to refer the case. That decision, and another dated 27 May 2016, were the subject of an unsuccessful judicial review,[213] which subsequently became the subject of a reclaiming motion (appeal).[214]

On 17 September 2015 the sist was recalled. A new Summar Roll hearing, before an Extra Division, was fixed for 10 May 2016 for three days. On 12 May 2016, the

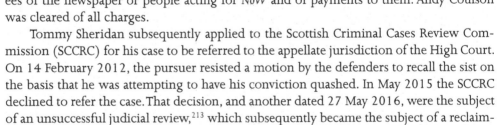

---

210 *Res noviter veniens ad notitiam* – things newly come to light, which may warrant the admission of further evidence or even a new trial.
211 The list of appeals and other business conducted by the Inner House of the Court of Session.
212 *Her Majesty's Advocate against Thomas Sheridan and Gail Sheridan* [2011] ScotHC HCJ 001.
213 [2018] CSOH 69.
214 *Sheridan (Thomas) v News Group Newspapers* [2018] CSIH 76.

court made *avizandum*. By interlocutor dated 19 August 2016, the motion for a new trial was refused. An application for permission to appeal to the UK Court followed. This was refused on 3 November 2016.

The pursuer eventually claimed interest on the jury's verdict and award of damages of £200,000, backdated to 14 November 2004. On 8 March 2018, the Lord Ordinary, Lord Turnbull, refused to award any interest on the damages which the jury had assessed almost ten years previously. He criticized the 'utterly reprehensible' conduct of the *News of the World* and refused to grant the extra payment to Sheridan.[215]

In December 2018 the Court of Session judges Lord Carloway, Lord Menzies and Lord Brodie concluded that their colleague, Lord Turnbull, had misinterpreted the law surrounding payments. Their Lordships ruled that annual interest of 8 per cent should be applied to the £200,000 damages award from its initial award in August 2006. This meant that former MSP, Tommy Sheridan, won his legal battle to secure an extra £173,159 payment from the publishers of the now defunct *News of the World*. In the reclaiming motion statement the Court of Session concluded:

> There is no difficulty at all in understanding that a person who is defamed and to whom a jury awarded £200,000 as damages for the effect on his reputation such as it may have been entitled to interest on that sum from on or about the date of the award until payment as compensation for the loss of use of that money.[216]

Another high profile defamation action in the Scots courts included *McAnulty v McCulloch* (without a jury).[217] In December 2018 former SNP councillor, Julie McAnulty, won £40,000 in damages from Sheena McCulloch, then an assistant to SNP MSP Richard Lyle. The court case centred on an email sent by Ms McCulloch to senior party figures. She claimed that Ms McAnulty — then a North Lanarkshire councillor — had made a racist remark while the pair were out campaigning ahead of a council by-election in 2015. McCulloch had claimed that McAnulty had referred to 'Pakis' in the SNP party. The email later appeared in the *Daily Record*, and Ms McAnulty was suspended from the party and dropped as a potential candidate for Holyrood elections. She was later deselected as a council candidate and stood unsuccessfully as an independent in the 2017 local elections after resigning from the SNP. The concluding opinion of Lord Uist included in summary:

> The false allegation of racism against the pursuer was extremely serious in nature and caused her great distress. The defender must be held liable for direct publication to the recipients of the complaint. Counsel for the pursuer submitted that the defender must also be held liable for all further publications of the allegation as these would not have occurred but for her complaint. She was actually aware, or at least a reasonable person in her position should have been aware, that there was a significant risk that what she said would be repeated in whole or in part in the media and that would increase the damage caused to her, particularly in light of the

---

215 Ibid. at para. 5.
216 Ibid. at para. 50.
217 *McAnulty (Julie) v McCulloch (Sheena)* [2018] CSOH 121. Outer House Court of Session, 19 December 2018.

previous articles concerning the pursuer having been leaked to the Daily Record. The conclusion that there was actual awareness was consistent with the proposition that the defender was actually engaged in seeking to damage the pursuer.[218]

The libel in question, which made an unfounded allegation of racism, was an outrageous one which has had a serious effect on the pursuer's personal reputation and effectively ended her political career.[219]

It is then worth noting that the republication rule still exists in Scotland. For this reason, Lord Uist reminded counsel for Ms McCulloch that she will be held liable for all further publications of the allegation.

The *Campbell v Dugdale* (2019)[220] £25,000 libel action was brought by pro-Scottish independence blogger, Stuart Campbell, against former Scottish Labour leader, Kezia Dugdale. Campbell lost his defamation action against her in April 2019. The action commenced in 2018 when Campbell, who runs the blog 'Wings Over Scotland', sued Ms Dugdale in defamation after she accused him of writing 'homophobic tweets'.

The sting of the libel centred on a tweet posted by Mr Campbell during the Scottish Conservative conference on 3 March 2017. The tweet said 'Oliver Mundell is the sort of public speaker that makes you wish his dad had embraced his homosexuality sooner'.

The reference concerned Conservative MSP, Oliver Mundell, whose father, Scottish Secretary David Mundell, had announced in January 2016 that he was gay. Writing in her *Daily Record* column, Ms Dugdale had responded that she was 'shocked and appalled to see a pro-independence blogger's homophobic tweets'. Campbell argued that her article was defamatory and implied he was homophobic. The defender's argument before Sheriff McGowan at Edinburgh Sheriff Court (2018) was that the article complained of constituted fair comment on a matter of public interest.[221]

Ms Dugdale also argued that that honest comment was made, on the basis of the pursuer's own averments, in direct response to the original comment in the pursuer's tweet. Ms Dugdale requested to have the action struck out, but the Sheriff McGowan refused her request, relying on the objective 'honesty' test in *Telnikoff v Matusevitch* (1992),[222] where proof of malice has to be determined. The judge concluded:

I am not saying that the defender defamed the pursuer. I am simply saying that as a matter of law, the words used *may* carry the defamatory meaning complained of by the pursuer. Accordingly, on this issue the pursuer is entitled to an evidential hearing to establish the facts. It will be a matter for whoever hears the evidence to determine whether the words used did as a matter of fact bear that defamatory meaning, taking account of the circumstances and the other lines of defence taken.[223]

---

218 Ibid. at para. 33 (Lord Uist).
219 Ibid. at para. 37.
220 *Campbell (Stuart) v Dugdale (Kezia)* [2019] SC EDIN 32 Sheriffdom of Lothian and Borders at Edinburgh 16 April 2019.
221 *Campbell (Stuart) v Dugdale (Kezia)* [2018] SC EDIN 49.
222 [1992] AC 343.
223 *Campbell (Stuart) v Dugdale (Kezia)* [2018] SC EDIN 49 Sheriffdom of Lothian and Borders at Edinburgh 17 August 2018. *Campbell v Dugdale* [2018] at para. 156 (Sheriff Kenneth J McGowan).

Ms Dugdale argued that a 'healthy democracy' should have a range of views, but that Mr Campbell's tweet crossed the line into discrimination as it 'considered gay people to be lesser because they can't have children' – something which she said was not the case. She maintained an honest belief that Mr Campbell was homophobic.

In his final judgment Sheriff N.A. Ross found no malice in Ms Dugdale's comment piece and granted her the defence of fair comment. The judge did not allow the Reynolds qualified privilege defence because it did not apply in this case because the article did not reveal anything not already in the public domain. The article in the *Record* was simply a comment piece which contained already known facts, analysis and opinion. The public was already aware of Mr Campbell's tweet and was capable of forming its own view.[224] The judge concluded that Ms Dugdale's comment had been 'fair':

> A comment can be fair even though it is wrong (referring to the *Dr Simon Singh* case).[225] As long as it is a comment which can be rationally justified from the correct facts, the defence will apply. It is an objective test, but it is necessary to recognise that what is rational will differ from person to person. Depending on the facts, it may be possible to justify different and conflicting views arising out of the same facts. Conflicting comments, even though diametrically opposite, might be 'fair'.[226]

3.8.3 General defences in Scots law

The defences available in Scotland are broadly the same as in the English jurisdiction (see above 3.6), the most common one being *veritas* (truth or justification); this being equivalent to the English defence of 'truth' (section 2 Defamation Act 2013). The defence of 'fair comment' provides for freedom of expression and protects the inherent public interest in expressing opinions on public figures, political and legal decision makers. An alleged defamer may also offer to make an apology in a reasonable manner as well as offer to pay compensation ('offer to make amends'), and this will provide a defence to an action of defamation as long as the defamer did not know, or have reason to believe, that the statement complained of was false and defamatory. If the offer is accepted, the wronged party accepting the offer may not bring, or continue with, defamation proceedings in respect of the defamatory statement. Defences of qualified privilege and absolute privilege apply similarly north and south of the border. Remedies can take the form of *interdict* (injunction) to prevent further publication of the defamatory statement or damages, which seek to compensate the pursuer for injury to feelings or to reputation. The wider the audience which receives the defamatory statement, the greater damages are likely to be.

3.8.4 The multiple publication rule in Scots and Northern Irish law

One historical relic in defamation law was the long-standing principle that each republication of a defamatory statement or broadcast gave rise to a separate cause of action which was subject to its own limitation period. This was known as the 'multiple publication

---

224 *Campbell (Stuart) v Dugdale (Kezia)* [2019] SC EDIN 32 at paras 89–90 (Sheriff N.A. Ross).
225 *British Chiropractic Association v Singh* [2011] 1 WLR.
226 *Campbell v Dugdale* [2019] SC EDIN 32 at para. (Sheriff N.A. Ross).

rule', based on a Victorian-era doctrine known as the 'Duke of Brunswick' principle (see: *Brunswick v Harmer* (1849)[227]). This rule still exists in Scotland and Northern Ireland.

The central character in the *Brunswick* case was an exiled German ruler, Karl II.[228] In 1848, the Duke sent a servant to procure a copy of an article which had been published in 1830, containing an alleged defamatory statement about the Duke. The statement had been known to him since its original publication. Clearly, the then six-year limitation period for bringing an action for defamation had expired, but still the Duke sent his servant to procure copies of the offending article and brought defamation proceedings for injury to his reputation. After obtaining a fresh copy of the article from the London publishers, the Duke promptly sued on the basis that he had the original copy and a fresh copy of the article, thereby suing for republication. The Queen's Bench held that the act of procuring the 'fresh' article by the Duke amounted to a new publication of a libel, giving rise to a fresh cause of action in respect of each article, and that was in spite of the fact that there was a statute in place which limited the bringing of such a civil action to six years. The court held that publisher Harmer's back issue of the offending publication in 1848 constituted a separate act of publication and was therefore within the statutory time limit. The new action commenced at the point in time when the publication was received, rather than the date of its original printing and distribution 17 years previously.

The effect of the *Brunswick* doctrine was that each individual access to an allegedly libellous publication could potentially give rise to a separate cause of action, with a separate limitation period attached to it – particularly acute in actions concerning internet archives. The limitation period is now *one year* in which an action can be brought (see also: section 8(6) Defamation Act 2013).

Kirby J criticized the doctrine in *Dow Jones & Co. Inc. v Gutnick* (2002),[229] where he said that the open-ended liability for publishers made the limitation period pointless in the internet (archive) age. He said that every time the defamatory material was accessed online, the 'stopwatch runs anew from zero'.[230] Each separate publication was then subject to the one-year limitation period.

The old Duke of Brunswick principle of republication was upheld in a range of 'online libel' cases, such as the HL ruling in *Berezovsky v Michaels* (2000).[231]

The controversial judgments in the *Loutchansky*[232] actions (Nos 1–5) highlighted the serious restrictions on press freedom under Article 10 ECHR, implied in the multiple publication rule, and unsuccessfully claimed the necessity of applying the approach taken in the United States where the single publication rule limitation period runs from the first internet posting.[233]

International businessman, Dr Grigori Loutchansky, began libel action against *The Times* publishers in 1999. *The Times* magazine had portrayed Loutchansky as the head of a Russian criminal organization, involved in smuggling nuclear weapons and money laundering. The

---

227 [1849] 14 QB 185.
228 Official title: Herzog zu Braunschweig-Lüneburg-Wolfenbüttel.
229 [2002] CLR 575.
230 Ibid. at para. 92 (Kirby J).
231 [2000] 1 WLR 1004.
232 *Loutchansky v Times Newspapers Ltd* (*Nos 1–5*) [2001] EWCA Civ 1805.
233 [2002] 1 All ER at p. 312. The first action was brought on 6 December 1999 in respect of two articles published in *The Times* respectively on 8 September 1999 (the first article) and 14 October 1999 (the second article); the second action was brought on 6 December 2000 in respect of the continued internet publication of the same two articles on *The Times* website after 21 February 2000.

actions concerned allegations of defamation in the print editions as well as online editions. The defendants claimed qualified privilege under Reynolds[234] on the ground that they had a duty to publish and that the public had a right to know the allegations, but were unable to identify sources of their information ('public interest test'). The appellants also invoked Article 10(1) ECHR before the ECtHR in Strasbourg in 2009.

The High Court ruled in favour of the claimant in April 2001, and The Times publishers cross-appealed. The CA dismissed the print and online appeals. In doing so the court considered the 'responsible journalism' test and established unless the journalists had acted 'responsibly' he (and the publishers) could not claim qualified privilege.

This involved inter alia that the newspaper had a duty to publish the information (whether true or false): whether the publisher would have been open to legitimate criticism had he not published (applying: Al-Fagih v H.H. Saudi Research and Marketing (UK) Limited (2001)[235]).

The CA also considered the Brunswick republication rule. The Times claimed that limitation ran from the date when the issue was put on the paper's website, and the claimant that limitation began afresh, each time the site was accessed and transmitted to a reader. The CA dismissed The Times' libel defence of 'archive privilege'.

The Master of the Rolls, Simon Brown LJ, held:

> The Times' website could not possibly be described as responsible journalism. We do not believe that it can be convincingly argued that the appellants had a Reynolds duty to publish those articles in that way without qualification. It follows that we consider that the Judge was right to strike out the qualified privilege defence in the second action although not for the primary reason that he gave for so doing. For these reasons the Internet Single Publication appeal is also dismissed.

3.8.5 Libel juries, judge-alone trials and damages in Northern Irish and Scottish courts

Northern Ireland did not adopt the Defamation Act 2013 and still operates under the Defamation Act (Northern Ireland) 1955 which is an identical Act to the English Defamation Act 1952. There are two sections of the Defamation Act 1955 which are still in force in Northern Ireland: section 5 – failure to prove every allegation of fact in the defences of justification – and section 6 – fair comment (a defence to a libel action in which the defendant does not have to show the words were fair but s/he must show that they were honest and published without malice.)

Although English courts have now abolished 'libel jury' trials, Scottish courts had already abandoned jury trials in defamation actions. In the past 'libel juries' awarded punitive damages in England and Wales (see: Elton John[236] and Esther Rantzen[237]).

Though the Tommy Sheridan libel action in August 2006 was held with a jury, judge-alone trials are more common in Scottish libel actions; the Evidence (Scotland) Act of 1866 (still in force) makes judge-alone trials possible if 'special cause' can be shown.[238]

See above 3.8.2

---

234 Reynolds v Times Newspapers Ltd [2001] 2 AC 127.
235 Unreported, 5 November 2001 (Simon Brown LJ's judgment).
236 John v Mirror Group Newspapers Ltd [1997] QB 586.
237 Rantzen v Mirror Group Newspapers (1986) Ltd [1994] QB 670.
238 Chapter 37 Court of Session Rules, r. 37(1) 'Jury Trials'.

Though 'special cause' is not defined in either common law or statute, it is generally assumed that it means 'special circumstances' depending on each individual case. Once a Scottish court holds the words to be capable of bearing a defamatory meaning, the following are presumed:

1   that the words are false;
2   that the words are spoken with intent to injure; and
3   that the pursuer has suffered some form of material injury which must result in financial compensation being due from the defender.

The Scottish courts regard money damages as the remedy for a wrong done. However, damages are always to compensate, never to punish. In 1908, Lord President Dunedin reviewed the question of punitive or exemplary damages and could find no authority for them in the law of Scotland. In fact, he felt that the heading of 'reparation' under which the matter is treated in the textbooks excluded the very idea of exemplary damages. When the argument was again raised in a defamation case 60 years later, Grant LJC held that the fact that a libel was actuated by malice was not enough to entitle the pursuer to greater damages. The 'offer to make amends' relates to the Defamation Act 1996 (the same as in England and Wales).[239]

In *Baigent v BBC* (1999),[240] temporary Judge Coutts QC awarded exceptionally high damages. The case concerned a TV programme which alleged that the owners of a nursing home were operating 'a callous and uncaring regime'. Mrs Baigent was awarded £60,000, Mr Baigent £50,000 and each of the three Baigent children £20,000 (upheld on appeal). The Baigent case probably marked the turning point when the Scottish courts began to award similarly high damages to the English courts. Coutts J stressed that damages in Scottish libel actions are compensatory rather than punitive. Similarly high awards, each of £60,000, were made in *Clinton v News Group Newspapers Ltd* (1999)[241] and *Wray v Associated Newspapers Ltd* (2000).[242]

Another major difference is the limitation period afforded to a pursuer, which makes litigation in the Scottish courts more attractive to litigants. Section 17 of the Prescription and Limitation Act (Scotland) 1973 grants a litigant three years in which to raise proceedings (compared to the one-year time limit in England and Wales). While Article 6 ECHR permits access to a court, that right is not absolute, and the granting of an award of caution is a permissible limitation to that right (see: *Monarch Energy Ltd v Powergen Retail Ltd* (2006)[243]).

'Serial litigant' Terence Patrick Ewing (the pursuer and reclaimer) had sued for 'unlimited damages – *solatium* including *actio iniuriarum*' in respect of an article published by the defender and respondent on 11 February 2007 in the *Sunday Times Scotland* edition, and on two related websites. Ewing had a long history of civil litigation, with the High Court of England and Wales declaring him to be a vexatious litigant on 21 December 1989. But Ewing then took advantage of Scottish and later Northern Irish jurisdictions when he sued in both the delicts of 'personal injury' and 'injury to privacy'. Pursuer Mr Ewing,

239 Rule 54 (1) Rules of the Court of Session.
240 [1999] SCLR 787.
241 [1999] SC 367.
242 [2000] SLT 869.
243 [2006] SLT 743.

co-founder of the Euston Trust, whose members travel around the UK to make objections to planning applications, filed a libel action against the Scottish edition of the *Sunday Times* in respect of an online article of 11 February 2007, titled 'Heritage Fakers Hold Builders to Ransom', in which investigative journalists Daniel Foggo and Robert Booth had claimed to have exposed Mr Ewing as a fraudster and also of having considerable debts from statutory demands for non-payment of fines.

On 19 June 2008, the pursuer and reclaimer Mr Ewing applied to the High Court for leave to initiate his action against the defender and respondent in the English courts. This application was refused. Around this time, the Inner House noted the pursuer and reclaimer had travelled to Scotland, where he downloaded the internet version of the article concerned and also read a hard copy of the article at a public library. The publication in question had been downloaded by Mr Ewing's companion at the Edinburgh City Library.[244]

Mr Ewing sued for defamation, claiming, *inter alia*, breach of data protection, invasion of his privacy and harassment as well as breach of confidence. The court held that there was a 'stateable case' on his pleadings and confined the pursuer's damages to a claim that would not be 'substantial' because his case did not have 'serious merits' and was an 'artificial litigation',[245] based on Lord Donaldson's ruling in *Henry J Garratt & Co. v Ewing* (1991).[246] One crucial factor for the court's decision was that the pursuer had made 'at least 25 vexatious claims . . . none of this bodes well for the manner in which he is likely to conduct this action in a jurisdiction'[247] (see also: *Rush v Fife Regional Council* (1985)[248])

From the outset, the defender and respondent newspaper moved the Scottish court to ordain caution in the sum of £50,000 as a condition precedent to continuing the action. This motion was granted by the Lord Ordinary, Lord Brodie, in December 2008. Lord Brodie then took the unprecedented step at the Edinburgh High Court of Sessions in January 2009 and merely granted Mr Ewing a motion for caution in the sum of £15,000, additionally refusing Mr Ewing leave to reclaim any damages at a later hearing. The court granted decree of absolvitor. The pursuer reclaimed against these decisions (see: *Ewing v Times Newspapers Ltd* (2008)[249]).

In considering the pursuer and reclaimer's first submission, the Inner House considered that the Article 6 ECHR right to access to justice was not unqualified, nor absolute. The court noted it was subject to the rights of the other party to be protected against being put to irrevocable expense by an impecunious and irresponsible litigant. The court added that such protection was a legitimate aim, to which a requirement to find caution was properly directed. In relation to the pursuer and reclaimer's second submission, the Inner House noted that the distinction drawn on the timing of the order for caution was of no significance, noting that if the action was unlikely to succeed in any event, it was right that the court should grant caution at an early stage of proceedings; otherwise, the purpose of the caution itself would be defeated. Finally, the Inner House opined that the proper test to be applied when considering the pursuer's reputation was whether the

244 Ibid. at paras 3 and 21.
245 Ibid. at para. 25.
246 [1991] 1 WLR 1356 at 1357E (Lord Donaldson MR).
247 [2008] CSOH at para. 29 (Lord Brodie).
248 [1985] SLT 451 (Lord Wheatley).
249 [2008] CSOH 169, Outer House, Court of Session, Edinburgh.

Lord Ordinary exercised his discretion as no Lord Ordinary could reasonably have done. Lord Justice-Clerk Gill, in delivering the opinion of the court, noted that Lord Brodie had given a careful account of his reasons for ordering caution and that he could see no reasons to suggest that his decision was unreasonable. The reclaiming motion was refused, and the defender's motion for expenses was granted.[250] Mr Ewing then took his libel actions to the High Court of Justice in Northern Ireland, Queen's Bench Division, Belfast in 2011[251] and subsequently to the courts in Gibraltar.

Henderson (2009) argued that it would be wrong to presume that the finding in the Ewing claim (including privacy) was not stateable, as disclosing any emerging principle of the approach that the Scots courts would take to such actions.[252] First there was an absence of any expectation of privacy on the part of the pursuer, and second the context of the libel complaint had to be taken into account in that Mr Ewing had simply supplied a photocopy of the cases cited, where the court held that the pursuer 'did not set out in any comprehensive way in his pleadings the basis upon which he avers that delictual liability has been incurred'.[253]

Despite the differences noted above, it is likely that in many Scottish cases English authorities in defamation will continue to be relied upon, as there are relatively few Scottish decisions reported.

Northern Ireland's High Court in Belfast cites English cases, demonstrating the close links between the jurisdictions between the English and Welsh and Northern Irish systems. In terms of civil and criminal cases in Northern Ireland, the Supreme Court is the final and authoritative court of appeal. Some defamation cases have in the past still been heard by a 'libel' jury. Northern Ireland still uses the term 'plaintiff' (claimant).

The Northern Irish courts award damages in line with those from personal injury claims, and it was noted in O'Rawe v William Trimble Ltd. (2010)[254] that disproportionate awards of damages could constitute a violation of the Article 10 ECHR right to freedom of expression. In this case the defendant pleaded justification and qualified privilege and that publication was in the public interest and the words constituted fair comment. In addition to this it pleaded mitigation pursuant to the Bernstein principle.[255]

The Court held that in relation to the mitigation, a defendant seeking to reduce damages should not be restricted to adducing evidence, which is directly relevant to a claimant's conduct or reputation. Applying the Bernstein principle, the defendant in this action

---

250 Ewing (Terence Patrick) v Times Newspapers Ltd [2010] CSIH 6.
251 Ewing (Terence Patrick) v Times Newspapers Ltd [2011] NIQB 63.
252 Henderson, G. (2009), pp. 116–118.
253 [1985] SLT 451 (Lord Wheatley).
254 [2010] NIQB 124 (29 June 2010).
255 Bernstein v Times Newspapers Limited (2001) 1 WLR 579. Composer Leonard Bernstein sued The Times on a diary piece, alleging that he 'used to organise bands of hecklers to go about wrecking performances of modern atonal music, particularly anything by Harrison Birtwhistle'. At trial Bernstein applied to strike out various particulars pleaded in mitigation of damages relating to his activities as co-founder of 'The Hecklers', which included a notorious occasion of booing at the end of a performance of Birtwhistle's 'Gawain' at the Royal Opera House. The defendant newspaper applied for summary disposal of the claim under s 8 DA 1996 Act on the ground that the damages should be limited to £10,000. The judge acceded to the claimant's application and refused the defendants'. The jury awarded £8,000. The Times appealed, arguing that the judge should not have struck out the particulars in purported mitigation of damages. It was held that some of the particulars should not have been struck out. However, the jury's award would stand as the Court was not persuaded that it would have been any lower if the material had not been excluded. Nor was the judge's decision not to order a summary disposal wrong. The Bernstein principle was a landmark case in libel awards of damages.

was permitted to adduce evidence of facts which were relevant to the case which started with a 'libel' jury but proceeded by judge alone. An award was given by the trial judge in the sum of £44,000 in favour of the plaintiff.

The judgment also mentioned how the request for expenses followed a failed bid by the publishers of *NoW* to have a new defamation trial.

3.8.6 The future of Scottish and Northern Irish defamation laws

In the light of the significant changes made by the Defamation Act 2013 in England and Wales, the Scottish Law Commission published a Discussion Paper in March 2016,[256] covering key areas of defamation law, including the defences of public interest, fair comment and truth. The Commission asked whether there should be a mechanism for filtering out claims where little was at stake and liability for publication of defamatory material online.[257]

In a letter to Professor Hector MacQueen, Chairman of the Scottish Law Commission, Rosalind McInnes, Principal Solicitor for BBC Scotland, expressed her concern regarding the multiple publication rule and the *Reynolds* defence. Ms McInnes said that the restriction on jurisdiction in Scotland, the extension of the defences of qualified and absolute privilege internationally and a shorter time bar period may all combine to encourage 'forum shopping' in favour of Scotland, thereby transferring libel tourism to the High Courts of Justiciary in Edinburgh or Glasgow.[258]

After a number of unsuccessful defamation claims in the English, Welsh and Scottish courts, serial litigant Mr Ewing tried his luck in the Belfast High Court. The previous UK jurisdictions had already expressed concern about Mr Ewing's 'forum shopping' as a serial 'libel tourist', calling his claims 'vexatious' and an abuse of process against the Times Newspaper Group.

Gillen J confirmed two mechanisms for dismissing Mr Ewing's claim in the Northern Irish court under the Rules of the Court of Judicature (Northern Ireland) 2009, recognizing the practical hardships that defamation actions could create. Under the Rules the judge set the precedent for a 'new climate' supportive of judges exercising discretion in dismissing such vexatious cases.

Proponents of the status quo in Northern Irish defamation law have argued that the *Ewing (Northern Ireland)* judgment shows how the common law and procedural rules provide ample means for identifying and disposing of unmeritorious uses of defamation law before the courts.

However, not deterred by previous rulings across the UK jurisdictions, Mr Ewing then took the matter to the Supreme Court of Gibraltar in relation to copies of the *Sunday Times* international Madrid edition of 11 February 2007. Puisne Judge, Jack J, pointed out that the claimant had no connection to Gibraltar whatsoever, nor would anyone have known

256 Scottish Law Commission (2016) 'Defamation Law: Time for change?' A Discussion Paper, issued on behalf of the Scottish Law Commission on 17 March 2016.
257 For further discussion see: Lord Pentland, Chairman of the Scottish Law Commission (2017) 'The Scottish Law Commission's recent report contains radical proposals in this area of law. Its chairman outlines the need for reform and explains the thinking behind some key recommendations'. *Journal of the Law Society of Scotland*, 19 February 2018: www.journalonline.co.uk/Magazine/63-2/1024387.aspx.
258 Source: Letter by Rosalind McInnes to the Scottish Law Commission of 18 July 2014.

that the offending article in *The Times*, dating back some seven years, referred to him on the British Overseas Territory. Mr Ewing was subsequently remanded in custody for criminal contempt for abuse of process in bringing his vexatious claim again in Gibraltar courts when the courts in England/Wales, Scotland and Northern Ireland had already sufficiently dealt with the matter by way of abuse of process.[259]

Jack J alerted Mr Ewing (as always representing himself) that the maximum punishment for criminal contempt of court in Gibraltar was two years' imprisonment. The judge also said that – to that date – Mr Ewing had never paid any legal costs ordered in the other jurisdictions and that present costs – including Gibraltar – amounted to £30,000. Striking down both claims in defamation and privacy, the judge cited the leading judgment by the Northern Irish High Court by Sir Declan Morgan JC – the only difference being that that claim concerned the Ulster edition of the *Sunday Times* and this claim the Madrid edition.[260]

Whilst in England and Wales a company can sue for defamation, the present argument in Northern Ireland tends to be against adoption of this rule, one reason being that the concept of 'serious financial loss' does not capture the range of harms that might be caused to corporate reputations; alternatively, harm to corporate reputation may not manifest itself obviously or clearly in specific, identifiable financial losses, and it might be difficult for a trading company to show loss of profit linked to harm caused by a false publication.

 FOR THOUGHT

> A defendant Ulster newspaper has archived materials that are or may be defamatory. Would an appropriate notice warning against treating it as the truth remove the sting of the libel from the material, or will the Belfast High Court regard this publication as equally important to the dissemination of contemporary material? Discuss.

The Northern Ireland Law Commission launched a consultation on reform of defamation law in October 2014.[261] Current law provides that a libel claim can be summarily dismissed where it discloses no 'real or substantial tort' that has occurred in Northern Ireland. Such an order was affirmed by the Northern Irish Court of Appeal, having been made by the High Court in *Ewing v Times* (2013).[262]

In spite of some interesting comparisons and efforts to reform the defamation laws of Northern Ireland, the Law Commission for Northern Ireland was disbanded in 2015 'due to budgetary constraints'. The libel laws in Northern Ireland remain unchanged.

---

259 Rule 81.16 CPR.
260 *Ewing (Terence Patrick) v Times Newspapers Ltd* (2014) Claim No 2013-E-42 – In the Supreme Court of Gibraltar, Judgment of 17 November 2014 at para. 5 (Adrian Jack J Puisne Judge).
261 Northern Ireland Law Commission (2014).
262 *Ewing (Terence Patrick) v Times Newspapers Ltd* [2013] NICA (Sir Declan Morgan JC).

FOR THOUGHT

Has libel tourism shifted from the English to the Scottish and Northern Irish High Courts? Discuss your reasons by comparing and contrasting existing libel laws.

3.8.7 Defamation law reform in Scotland

The Defamation Act 2013 was not adopted by Scottish and Northern Irish jurisdictions. This means that common law tradition prevails. For example, website operators based in Scotland or Northern Ireland have no general shield from liability for defamation claims over third-party content under the section 5 defence of the (English) 2013 Act. This also means that the 'innocent dissemination' defence prevails. This defence will only be defeated where the website operator has actual knowledge of the defamatory content, or even merely had reason to suspect its presence or had been negligent in failing to detect it (as was the case in *Godfrey v Demon*).

See above 3.7

In other words, defamation laws in Scotland, largely common law based, continue to prioritize pursuers, offering an easy way to silence journalists, campaigners, academics, scientists, activists and people across the country.

In December 2017, the Scottish Law Commission published its final report and draft bill for reforming defamation law. This has been seen as a step in the right direction by legal practitioners, members of the media and authors to change the law to better protect free expression in Scotland.

In March 2018 more than 150 Scottish writers and academics, including Ian Rankin, Karen Campbell and Christopher Brookmyre, called on the Scottish government to bring forward the Defamation Bill (Scotland). Prompted by the writers' organization the Scottish PEN, the open letter to Annabelle Ewing, the legal affairs minister, read:

> A vibrant democracy is a loud one; an environment that supports the diverse, divergent and contradictory voices that shape Scotland. By reforming defamation law we are defending the principle that everyone, irrespective of wealth, influence or access to legal representation, has a right to be heard. By advocating reform, the Scottish government will be demonstrating a clear and bold commitment to free expression in Scotland. Without reform these laws will continue to threaten civic debate and journalistic endeavour through the continued risk of legal action.[263]

The Scottish Law Commission in its report has advocated a serious harm threshold, a statutory public interest defence, a single publication rule, outlawing public authorities from bringing actions and free expression protections — very similar to what has already been in law in England and Wales in form of the Defamation Act 2013.[264]

The Defamation and Malicious Publication (Scotland) Bill 2017 marks a significant step towards defamation law reform. The bill is in three parts and contains 36 sections and a schedule.

---

263 Source: Scottish PEN defamation law reform: https://scottishpen.org/
help-us-call-scottish-government-back-defamation-reform.
264 Scottish Law Commission (2017).

Part 1 deals with defamation and covers amendments to the law of defamation. It makes provision in relation to actionability of defamatory statements and restrictions on bringing proceedings, defences, absolute and qualified privilege, offers to make amends, jurisdiction and the removal of the presumption that defamation proceedings are to be tried by jury.

Part 2 deals with verbal injury (i.e. slander) and makes provision to replace common law verbal injuries with three new statutory actions relating to malicious publications causing harm.

Part 3 makes provision as to remedies and limitation of defamation actions and actions under Part 2 as well as miscellaneous provisions dealing with matters such as interpretation and commencement.

Defamation law reforms in Scotland propose:

- the *implementation of a single publication rule* to ensure that liability remains with the original publication and does not extend the time within which an action can be brought if the content is shared or retweeted;
- an *honest opinion defence* that protects the free and open sharing of opinion and expression, both online and off;
- requiring the defamatory statement to be a *communicated to a third party*; and
- the inclusion of a *serious harm test* to ensure vanity cases and those brought solely to silence others cannot make it to court.

In January 2019 the Scottish Government published its document 'Defamation in Scots Law: A Consultation'. Ms Ash Denham, Minister for Community Safety, sought the opportunity via this consultation document to ensure that any reform to defamation law was fully tested, stating that

> we want our law of defamation to be fit for 21st century Scotland, with a clear and accessible framework that balances freedom of expression and protection of reputation. . . . Reputation is a component of the right to private life, and it forms the basis of the law of defamation. It is an integral and important part of the dignity of the individual, and helps to inform many decisions in a democratic society which are fundamental to its well-being.[265]

At the time of going to print Scotland's libel laws remained unchanged.

3.9 Libel tourism and forum shopping

So-called libel tourism or forum shopping was certainly one of the primary drivers of the libel reform campaign in England and Wales and one of the main reasons the Westminster

---

265 Scottish Government (2019) 'Defamation in Scots law: consultation at p. 4.

Parliament changed the defamation laws in 2013 after growing concern that London had become the 'libel capital of the world' – particularly for foreign litigants. So, has the introduction of the 'serious harm' test under s 1(1) DA 2013 put a stop to libel tourism in the English and Welsh courts? Has forum shopping been transferred to the Edinburgh and Belfast high courts since those jurisdictions still adhere to the old libel laws? Do most claimants now settle out of court?

One such example is the US first lady, Melania Trump, who settled her libel claim against *The Daily Mail* and *Mail Online* in April 2017. An agreed statement was read out to Mr Justice Nicol in court 14 of the Royal Courts of Justice, London on 12 April on behalf of both parties. It is understood that Mrs Trump received damages and legal costs in the region of $3m (£2.4m). The precise amount was not disclosed in the hearing.

The original *Daily Mail* story, alleging that Melania had formerly worked as a model, was published on 20 August 2016 under the headline: 'Racy photos and troubling questions about his wife's past that could derail Trump'. The double-page spread had included 'false and defamatory claims about [Mrs Trump] which questioned the nature of her work as a professional model and republished allegations that she provided services beyond simply modelling'.[266]

This was one of the highest libel damage settlements since Elton John reportedly received £1m from *The Sun* in a 1988 out-of-court settlement.

3.9.1 *Forum conveniens*

Kennedy v National Trust for Scotland (2017),[267] a defamation case, dealt with the issue of forum *conveniensis* where a multinational case should be heard. The case provides a complex yet rare insight into intra-UK jurisdiction and conflicts of laws. The case deals with two important issues of procedural law. Firstly, it confirmed a trend in the London High Court in favour of separating the CPR r. 7.5(1) and (2) rules on claim form validity periods from the r. 6.14 deemed service provisions. Secondly, that *Kennedy* applied the *Shevill v Presse Alliance SA* (1995)[268] rule from Brussels I Regulation jurisprudence to part of the question of whether a claim in England should be stayed in favour of Scotland under the forum *conveniens* rules preserved under the Civil Judgments and Jurisdiction Act 1982 and how *Kennedy* deals with damages suffered outside the UK.

The dispute arose when Howard Kennedy, a photographer domiciled in Scotland, took photographs, for commercial use, of a naked model on the grounds of Craigievar Castle in 2012. The castle, located in Aberdeenshire, Scotland, was a gift by Lord Sempill to the National Trust for Scotland (NTS). According to Mr Kennedy, permission for the shoot had been orally obtained by a representative of the NTS, and a payment of £200 was made for the use of the building. The specific nature of the shoot was known to the NTS, something evidenced by the fact that the session was supervised by at least one female member of staff, either in person or through CCTV.

In 2016, the daughter of Lord Sempill, the castle's previous owner, became aware of the situation and subsequently objected to the fact that the grounds of the castle had been

---

266 Source: Statement read out by Mrs Trump's solicitor John Kelly, of the law firm Harbottle and Lewis, outside the Royal Courts of Justice on 12 April 2017.
267 *Kennedy (Howard) v National Trust for Scotland* [2017] EWHC 3368 (QB).
268 *Shevill v Presse Alliance SA* (C-68/93) EU:C:1995:61; [1996] AC 959 (CJEU).

used for the purpose of taking nude photographs. What followed was a statement by the NTS denying that the photo shoot had been authorized. The statement in question was published online and offline in various media outlets in both England and Scotland and online in Italy, France and Brazil (in the respective languages of those countries) on 24 February 2016.

The claimant sought damages for defamation, characterizing the defendant's statement as an allegation that the claimant had taken the photos without permission. Kennedy issued proceedings at the High Court in London, for libel, negligent misstatement and breach of the Data Protection Act 1998, including the 8th data protection principle (transfer of data outside of the European Economic Area, namely Brazil). The claim form was issued on 24 February 2017, posted on 23 August 2017 and received on 24 August 2017. Service in Scotland is as-of-right (no need for the Court's permission), and a claim form is valid for six months.

The defendant trust applied under CPR Part 11 (challenge to jurisdiction) for (a) a declaration that the claim form had expired and had not been served within its period of validity because of the deemed data provision in CPR rule 6.14; (b) a stay under s 49 of the Civil Jurisdiction and Judgments Act 1982; alternatively (c) to strike out C's claim in respect of publication outside of England and Wales. Kennedy cross-applied for (a) a declaration that the claim form was served within its period of validity; and (b) alternatively, a retrospective extension of time for the service of the claim form of one day under CPR rules 7.6, 6.15, 3.9 and/or 3.10.

The defendant additionally sought a stay of the English action on the basis that Scotland would be the more appropriate forum. The claimant resisted this on two main grounds. Firstly, he argued that the Brussel I Regulation applied to the dispute; under *Owusu v Jackson* (2005)[269] the English court had no jurisdiction to stay on *forum non conveniens* grounds. Secondly, if that failed, he argued that England was the more appropriate jurisdiction to hear the claim under s 49 CJJA 1982, because damage had been suffered in England, and because certain juridical and personal advantages accrued to him in England. Eady J rejected both of the claimant's arguments and therefore found that the action should be stayed.

Eady J found that r. 6.14 did not modify the operation of r. 7.5(2), so the claim form had been served in time. The Judge concluded that Scotland was the more appropriate forum for the trial, deciding several important points regarding intra-UK jurisdiction. The Brussels I Regulation 2015 did not apply to cases where both defendants were domiciled in the same Member State, even if damage was suffered in another Member State. Applying the *Shevill v Presse Alliance SA*[270] doctrine under s 16 and Sch. 4 of the Civil Jurisdiction and Judgments Act 1982, this principle states that in defamation cases, the defendant can be either sued for the global damages at their domicile or in each individual jurisdiction where some damage occurred, but only up to the value of the damage that happened in that particular jurisdiction. This meant that the claimant's claims for damages located outside England would have to be struck out if the case was heard there.

---

269 *Owusu v Jackson (t/a Villa Holidays Bal Inn Villas)* (C-281/02) EU:C:2005:120 [2005] Q.B. 801 (CJEU).
270 *Shevill v Presse Alliance SA* (C-68/93) EU:C:1995:61 [1996] AC 959 (CJEU).

❖ **KEY CASE**   *Kennedy (Howard) v National Trust for Scotland* [2017] EWHC 3368 (QB).

Main legal issues

The issues of interest from a conflict of laws point of view arising from this case were:

1 whether the *forum non conveniens* discretion was precluded as per *Owusu v Jackson* (2005);[271]
2 if that was not the case, whether a stay could be granted on the basis that Scotland was the 'clearly more appropriate' forum; and
3 if the case was to be heard in England and Wales, whether the English court would have jurisdiction to award global damages.

Legal issues in detail

1 Was the Claim Form served within its period of validity (six months)?
   Held: Yes. The deemed service provision in CPR r. 6.14 was not applicable for the purposes of determining the validity of the claim form.
2 If not, should the Court grant a retrospective extension of time?
   Held: No – had the claim form not been served within its period of validity, the judge would not have granted discretionary relief.
3 Was the *forum non conveniens* discretion precluded by the rule in *Owusu v Jackson*?
   Held: No – both the claimant and the defendant were domiciled in the UK, and the rival fora preferred by the parties were England and Scotland. There were no 'international elements', and the case was 'purely domestic'.
4 If not, should a stay be granted on the basis that Scotland was the 'clearly more appropriate' forum for trial of the action?
   Held: Yes – the factual dispute, including most likely witnesses and documents, were in Scotland. The Scottish courts could per Eady J's ruling on issue (5) consider global damage, whereas the English court could not.
5 If to be heard in England and Wales, did the English court have jurisdiction to award global damages?
   Held: No – the CJEU's ruling in *Shevill v Press Alliance* should be applied by analogy into Schedule 4 of the Civil Jurisdiction and Judgments Act 1982. Accordingly, to recover global damages, the defendants had to be sued not only in the UK (the Member State of its domicile) but in the part of the UK of its domicile (Scotland) which alone had general (not special) jurisdiction.

Judgment

At the handing-down of the judgment on 17 January 2017, Eady J gave the claimant permission to appeal on issues (3), (4) and (5), and gave the defendant permission to appeal issue.

---

271 *Owusu v Jackson (t/a Villa Holidays Bal Inn Villas)* (C-281/02) EU:C:2005:120 [2005] Q.B. 801 (CJEU).

Analysis

This decision provides an interesting insight into the thinking of the High Court in London when it comes to the consideration of the application of the Brussels Regulation in defamation cases, where there is online publication in a number of jurisdictions. Third-party publications in jurisdictions outside of the UK do not introduce an international element and are, as such, insufficient for the purposes of bringing the Brussels Regulation into play. Stukalina (2018) argues that on balance, Sir David Eady's decision in this case is correct to hold that r. 6.14 is no longer a 'general rule' for deemed service in the CPR, and that *Kennedy* demonstrates the limitations of judicial decisions in making sense of statutory provisions whose wording does not fit harmoniously together; it also considers further implications of holding that r. 7.5(2) does not have a fixed 'due date'.[272]

3.9.3 Defamation cases involving foreign nationals

One of the main reasons why foreign nationals have in the past preferred UK courts in their defamation actions is that the law has been perceived as loaded against the defendant and rather claimant-friendly. All too often both litigants are foreign nationals or a company or newspaper organization abroad, such as *Al-Fagih v HH Saudi Research & Marketing (UK) Ltd* (2001).[273]

This case concerned a publication in a Saudi Arabian newspaper, *Asharq Al-Awsat*,[274] of allegations made by one prominent Saudi dissident against another in the context of a political dispute. The words complained of comprised an allegation made by Dr Mohammed Al-Mas'aari (AM) about the claimant (AF) in the course of a dispute between the two men. Both were prominent members of a Saudi Arabian dissident political organization known as the 'Committee for Defense of Legitimate Rights' (CDLR).[275] The defendant's newspaper supported the Saudi Arabian government and was in part owned by the Saudi Arabian royal family. It sold about 1,500 copies a day in London at the time, mainly to persons from the Saudi Arabian community.

The particular report complained of stated that AM had told the defendant's journalist, Mr Al-Khamees (AK), that AF had spread malicious rumours about him (AM) and had said that AM's mother had procured women to have sexual intercourse with him at his home. It was common ground that AM had made that allegation to AK and that it was in fact untrue. Although there was a defence of justification, this was based not upon the truth of that allegation, but rather upon a particular letter allegedly written by AF to AM's

---

272 Stukalina, J. (2018) at pp. 332–343.
273 [2001] EWCA Civ 1634.
274 Asharq al-Awsat (Arabic: الشرق الأوسط, meaning 'The Middle East') is an Arabic international newspaper headquartered in London. The paper is noted for its distinctive green-tinted pages.
275 The Committee for the Defense of Legitimate Rights (CDLR; Arabic: لجنة الدفاع عن الحقوق الشرعية) was a Saudi dissident group created in 1993 which opposed the Saudi government as un-Islamic. The CDLR was the first opposition organization in the Saudi Arabian Kingdom openly challenging the monarchy, accusing the government and senior ulama of not doing enough to protect the legitimate Islamic rights of the Muslims. They sought to bring about human rights by non-violent means.

Dow Jones v Gutnick (2002).[286] In response to this, the SPEECH Act[287] was introduced in the United States in 2010, specifically to prevent foreign libel judgments from being enforceable there.[288]

 FOR THOUGHT

Forum shopping in defamation actions are on the increase. Discuss relevant cases since *Jameel v Dow Jones*, explaining the way in which damages are now awarded.

3.9.3 Has the Defamation Act 2013 made a difference to libel tourism?

Arguably, the 2013 Act has shifted the balance between free speech and the right to reputation, in favour of free speech. In some areas this shift has been significant, particularly where companies who in the past sued for libel now have to prove actual economic harm under s 1(1) DA 2013. What is clear is that the law now prevents a court from hearing an action in defamation in England and Wales *unless* it is satisfied that the UK jurisdiction is the 'most appropriate place for a defamation action to be brought'. Recent cases which settled out of court provided the following reasons at preliminary hearing stage:

- The claimant had a bad reputation anyway, and there was reasonable doubt that his reputation would be seriously harmed over and above his existing (suspect) reputation.
- The claimant needed to prove an innuendo identification, and the people (with the special knowledge) who could possibly have identified the claimant would not believe the words would seriously harm the claimant's reputation (under the previous law, this would generally not prevent the meaning being defamatory).
- There was only limited publication in the jurisdiction and/or the claimant was not known in that jurisdiction.
- The meaning was borderline vulgar abuse, 'pub talk' or a mere criticism of the claimant (or his goods or services).
- Any damage was transient or short-lived due to a quick retraction, clarification or apology from the publisher.
- There was a *Jameel* abuse-type argument being deployed by the defendant, and a 'serious harm' requirement led to an early strike-out application by the defendants on both grounds.

---

286 [2002] CLR 575.
287 The SPEECH Act (Seeking the Protection of [US] Enduring and Established Constitutional Heritage) was passed in the United States in 2010.
288 For further discussion see: Watson, R., Roldan, R. and Faza, A. (2017).

Hooper et al. (2013)[289] predicted in advance of the 2013 Act's coming into force that the new legislation would ultimately restrict libel tourism, commenting *inter alia* favourably on the abolition of libel juries and the hurdle of the 'serious harm' threshold.

 FOR THOUGHT

Codifying libel law into statute is very fact-sensitive to account for many different scenarios. Has the Defamation Act 2013 simplified this area of law to account for the finer points such as fact and honest opinion? Discuss.

 ## 3.10 Further reading

Klazmer, E. (2012) 'The uncertainties of libel tourism, is diplomacy the answer?' *Entertainment Law Review*, **23(6), 164–168.**
Erica Klazmer compares US libel laws with UK authorities and specifically analyzes the approach in the New York court's decision in *Ehrenfeld*.[290] The case concerned a book by Dr Rachel Ehrenfeld, published in 2003 in Chicago titled *Funding Evil: How Terrorism Is Financed – and How to Stop It*. In the book, Dr Ehrenfeld stated that Saudi Arabian businessman, Khalid Salim Bin Mahfouz, provided monetary support to Al Qaeda and other terrorist organizations. Mahfouz sued Ehrenfeld in an English court and received a default judgment. Ehrenfeld then retaliated by filing a lawsuit in the US District Court for the Southern District of New York seeking a declaratory judgment that Mahfouz could not prevail on his libel claim. The author also discusses the US Speech Protection Act of 2009 which allows parties to protect assets abroad.

O'Leary, S. (2018) 'Balancing rights in a digital age', *Irish Jurist*, **59, 59–92.**
Siofra O'Leary wrote this article in memory and honour of Mr Justice Brian Walsh (1918–1998), an Irish Supreme Court and European Court of Human Rights justice and barrister. She examines some of the judgments in the human rights field, and how one of Ireland's 'greatest judges' and outstanding legal reformists sat on key cases such as *Byrne (Kathleen) v Ireland* (1969)[291] – abolished the immunity of the state in tort, *McGee v Attorney General* (1974)[292] – the right to marital privacy and contraceptives and *Crotty (Raymond) v An Taoiseach and others* (1987)[293] – on the ratification of EU treaties. The author examines a wealth of case law in the area of defamation and the right to reputation, the right to privacy and the right to be forgotten, freedom of expression – and how the ECtHR and the CJEU have balanced some of those rights in the courts.

Parkes, R., Mullis, A., Busuttil, G., Speker, A., Scott, A. and Strong, C. (eds) (2017) *Gatley on Libel and Slander* **12th ed. London: Sweet & Maxwell.**
This essential work for those involved in libel litigation has a high reputation in a number of common law countries. Originally written by Clement Gatley, this mighty tome is the classic reference text and procedural guidance for litigation practitioners

---

289 Hooper, D., Waite, K. and Murphy, O. (2013), pp. 199–206.
290 *Ehrenfeld v Mahfouz* (2007) 9 N.Y.3d 501.
291 I.R. (1967. No. 936 P.).
292 [1974] IR 284.
293 [1987] 1 I.R. [1986 No. 12036P].

in this field. *Gatley on Libel and Slander* is a comprehensive guide to the law of defamation, including significant changes brought about by the Defamation Act 2013, including expert commentary and analysis of substantive defamation law and recent cases, including decisions from Australia, New Zealand, Canada and Hong Kong. The eminent authors discuss the jurisprudence of the European Court of Human Rights and the impact of the Human Rights Act 1998 on defamation law and privacy.

Watson, R., Roldan, R. and Faza, A. (2017) 'Toward Normalization of Defamation Law: The U.K. Defamation Act of 2013 and the U.S. SPEECH Act of 2010 as Responses to the Issue of Libel Tourism', *Communication Law and Policy,* **1.**
In the wake of several high-profile libel actions brought by US celebrities and foreign businessmen in London because of more favorable defamation laws there, London was dubbed the 'libel tourism capital of the world'. The US response in 2010 was the passage of the SPEECH Act, preventing courts from enforcing libel judgments from foreign jurisdictions not providing the same level of protection as the United States. The UK then responded to international and national criticism with Parliament passing the Defamation Act 2013 to address the loophole in its system that caused the abuse. Both acts have been criticized, the first for its aggressiveness, and the second for its conservative nature. This article examines the development of the law of defamation in the two jurisdictions and analyzes the content of both statutes, along with their criticisms, proposing international co-operation to address the issue of libel tourism.

Whitty, N. R. and Zimmermann, R. (eds) (2009) *Rights of Personality in Scots Law: A Comparative Perspective.* **Dundee: Dundee University Press.**
This book considers, in a comparative perspective, important issues affecting the law on rights of personality in jurisdictions drawn from the families of common law, civil law and mixed legal systems. The main focus is on the private law of personality rights, including the defamation delict in Scots law, taking into account the impact of freedom of expression under Article 10 ECHR as well as constitutional legislation and Scots law conventions.

Chapter 4

Reporting legal proceedings

4.1 Overview

This chapter examines the open justice principle, which makes the UK courts unique in that *all* courts (except for youth courts and certain family court proceedings) are open to the public and members of the media. The openness of judicial proceedings is a fundamental principle also enshrined in Article 6(1) ECHR ('right to a fair trial').

There are however times when the court orders reporting restrictions or allows complete anonymity orders; this is then enshrined in statute, such as the protection of children under the age of 18 in criminal proceedings.

As more and more members of the British armed forces face court martial charges of desertion, war crime offences or misdemeanours in the armed forces, including rape, we will focus on court martial proceedings, the role of the Judge Advocate General and why reporting restrictions are at times necessary, as in the case of Sergeant Blackman, better known as Marine A. (2017).

A subject of concern is that of 'secret courts' and 'closed hearings', which are increasingly held in private (*in camera*) in terrorism or complex drug trials where the state applies for public interest immunity (PII) for witnesses from the UK security services, police informers and undercover agents. The Secretary of State or the Director of Public Prosecutions (DPP) will usually argue for PII when scientific or operational techniques (such as surveillance) should not be disclosed and reported on to avoid exposing individuals to the risk of personal injury or death, thereby jeopardizing the success of future operations.

4.2 The open justice principle

The open justice principle and judicial independence are fundamental to the rule of law, and the integrity of the UK court system depends upon a fair and public hearing by an independent and impartial tribunal. The open justice principle, as clearly recognized by Parliament and the courts in *Scott v Scott*,[1] grants the public and media statutory and common law rights to attend all court proceedings in UK courts and tribunals. Open justice helps to ensure that trials are properly conducted. It puts pressure on witnesses to tell the truth. It can result in new witnesses coming forward, such as in historic child sex offences. It provides public scrutiny of the trial process, maintains the public's confidence in the administration of justice and makes inaccurate and uninformed comment about proceedings less likely. Open court proceedings and the publicity given to criminal trials are vital to the deterrent purpose behind criminal justice.

See
below 4.7

It is then generally unacceptable that advocates have discussions with the judge in chambers about matters which could and should be dealt with in open court, for example, concerning the acceptability of pleas in a criminal trial. This practice does not serve the best interests of open and transparent justice, being in the absence of the defendant, the jury, the public and the media. Such discussions should not take place, save for truly exceptional cases where some particular sensitivity requires it. An example might be where there are public interest immunity (PII) issues involved which cannot be canvassed in open court. If there is an exceptional need for matters to be discussed in chambers, then those conversations must be properly recorded.

If there are circumstances where the court may justify hearing a case *in camera*, it must be stated in open court why such secrecy is necessary in the interest of justice. The test is one of 'necessity', and an application to proceed *in camera* must be supported by relevant evidence. All submissions must be made orally in open court (see: *Attorney General's Reference (No 80 of 2005)*[2]). To summarise:

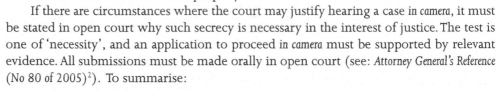

The open justice principle

- The general rule is that the administration of justice must be done in public.
- The public and the media have the right to attend all court hearings, and the media is able to report those proceedings fully and contemporaneously.
- Any restriction on these usual rules will be exceptional. It must be based on necessity.
- The burden is on the party seeking the restriction to establish it is necessary on the basis of clear and cogent evidence.
- The terms of any order must be proportionate – going no further than is necessary to meet the relevant objective.

---

1 *Scott (Morgan) and another v Scott* [1913] AC 417 of 5 May 1913 (as per Lord Atkinson) (HL).
2 [2005] EWCA Crim 3367.

4.2.1 Hearings from which the public are excluded: trials in private

The important role of the media as a public watchdog has been recognized under the right to freedom of expression guaranteed by Article 10 ECHR. As public authorities under s 6 of the Human Rights Act 1998, courts must act compatibly with Convention rights, including the right to freedom of expression and the right to a public hearing under Article 6 ECHR, though it has to be recognized that both Articles 10 and 6 are qualified rights, and the law therefore permits exceptions to the open justice principle.

In some cases, the right to privacy under Article 8 may be engaged and needs to be weighed in the balance. However, any restriction on the public's right to attend court proceedings and the media's ability to report them must fulfil a legitimate aim under these provisions and be necessary, proportionate and convincingly established. It is for the party seeking to derogate from the principle of open justice to produce clear and cogent evidence in support of the derogation. The common law attaches a very high degree of importance to the hearing of cases in open court, and under Article 6 ECHR the right to a public hearing and to public pronouncement of judgment is protected as part of a defendant's right to a fair trial.

Each court has an inherent power to regulate its own proceedings and may hear a trial or part of a trial in private in exceptional circumstances. The only exception to the open justice principle at common law justifying hearings in private is where the hearing of the case in public would frustrate or render impractical the administration of justice (see: *AG v Leveller Magazine* (1979)[3]; *R v Times Newspapers* (2007)[4]. The test is one of necessity. The fact, for example, that hearing evidence in open court will cause embarrassment to witnesses does not meet the test for necessity (*Scott v Scott* (1913)). Neither is it a sufficient basis for a hearing in private that allegations will be aired which will be damaging to the reputation of individuals (see: *Global Torch v Apex Global Management Ltd* (2013)[5]). In this case the court held that hearings in public were integral to open justice and that open justice in line with Articles 10 and 6 ECHR would generally trump the Article 8 rights to reputation of parties and witnesses in a civil case. The same considerations in favour of open justice would carry even greater weight in a criminal case. Furthermore, the interests of justice can never justify excluding the media and public if the consequence would be that a trial might be unfair (see: *R v Wang Yam* (2008)[6]). This was reiterated by the then Lord Chief Justice, Lord Thomas, who said that

> open justice is a hallmark of the rule of law. It is an essential requisite of the criminal justice system that it should be administered in public and subject to public scrutiny. The media play a vital role in representing the public and reflecting the public interest. However, as is well known, there are some exceptions to these principles. Difficulties and uncertainty can sometimes arise in ensuring they are correctly applied and observed.[7]

---

3   [1979] AC 440 per Lord Diplock at para. 450.
4   [2007] 1 WLR 1015.
5   [2013] 1 WLR 2993 (CA).
6   [2008] EWCA Crim 269.
7   Judicial College (2015 – updated in 2016) Reporting Restrictions in the Criminal Courts.

That said, the law is complex in this area, and several pieces of legislation come into play – not helped by recent changes in youth justice legislation. One thing to remember, however: all courts in the UK are open to the public and the media, *unless* there are exceptional circumstances, laid down by statute or common law, that the court proceedings are to be held in private. This means in general terms, the court must not:

- order or allow the exclusion of the press or public from court for any part of the proceedings;
- permit the withholding of information from the open court proceedings;
- impose permanent or temporary bans on reporting of the proceedings or any part of them including anything that prevents the proper identification, by name and address, of those appearing or mentioned in the course of proceedings.

Like 'without notice' (formerly *ex parte*) hearings, hearings in *camera* raise concerns about fairness, particularly in light of the principle that, 'not only must justice be done, it must also be seen to be done'.[8] Before imposing any reporting restriction or restriction on public access to proceedings the court is required to ensure that each party and any other person directly affected is present or has had an opportunity to attend or to make representations.[9]

4.3 Automatic reporting restrictions and anonymity orders

Where a court departs from the open justice principle and Article 6 ECHR, a judge must find exceptional circumstances where a hearing or trial is held in private.[10] Such hearings must be justified by the court in either statute or common law (see: *AG v Leveller Magazine* (1979);[11] *R v Times Newspapers* (2007)[12]). The test is one of necessity.[13] It is not a sufficient basis for a hearing in private that allegations will be aired which will be damaging to the reputation of individuals (e.g. *Global Torch v Apex Global Management Ltd* (2013)[14]). Criminal hearings carry even greater weight to justify public and media presence (see: *R v Wang Yam* (2008)[15]).

Automatic reporting restrictions and, at times, lifelong anonymity orders, apply as follows:

---

8 *Hobbs v Tinling and Company Limited* [1929] 2 KB 1 at 33 per Lord Sankey LC; also: *R v Sussex Justices ex parte McCarthy* [1924].
9 Criminal Procedure Rules 2016, r. 16.
10 CPR 2016, r. 16(8) governs procedure 'where a court can order a trial in private'. (as amended 2019).
11 [1979] AC 440 at 450.
12 [2007] 1 WLR 1015.
13 Scott v Scott [1913] AC 417.
14 [2013] 1 WLR 2993 (CA).
15 [2008] EWCA Crim 269.

- reporting restrictions for children and young people in criminal proceedings (under 18);[16]
- reporting restrictions for children and young people in non-criminal proceedings (e.g. family court);[17]
- lifetime reporting ban for victims and witnesses under age 18;[18]
- lifetime reporting ban on victims of sexual offences;[19]
- vulnerable adult witnesses;[20]
- withholding information from the public in the interest of the administration of justice;[21]
- reporting restrictions (or postponement) during trial;[22]
- appeals;[23]
- prosecution appeals.[24]

When a party makes an application for anonymity or reporting restrictions (or both), the court must be satisfied that the quality of evidence or level of co-operation by the witness is likely to be diminished by reason of fear or distress in being identified by the public.

On appeal, automatic reporting restrictions apply from the moment the prosecution indicates its intention to appeal to prevent the publication of anything other than certain specified factual information.[25] However, in the digital age, it is virtually impossible to delete all the information which was present at trial and verdict stage. Once an appeal has started (particularly acute in criminal matters), the CA will usually invite representations from the media and encourage open debate in advance of a court hearing (see: R v Teesdale and Wear Valley Justices ex parte M (2000)[26]).

4.3.1 Lifetime anonymity for victims of sexual offences

Anonymity is granted by law to a wide range of people in the UK justice system, including victims of sex crime, people under 18 facing criminal charges and those in family court cases. However, these rules can be undermined if people can search for names on the internet and publish them via social media.

Victims of a wide range of sexual offences are given lifetime anonymity under the Sexual Offences (Amendment) Act 1992. The prohibition imposed by section 1 of the 1992 Act applies to 'any publication' and therefore includes traditional media as well as

---

16 s 45 Youth Justice and Criminal Evidence Act 1999.
17 s 39 Children and Young Persons Act 1933.
18 s 45A Youth Justice and Criminal Evidence Act 1999.
19 s 1 Sexual Offences (Amendment) Act 1992 (as amended by Sch. 2 of the Youth Justice and Criminal Evidence Act 1999).
20 s 46 Youth Justice and Criminal Evidence Act 1999.
21 s 11 Contempt of Court Act 1981.
22 s 4(2) Contempt of Court Act 1981.
23 s 35 Criminal Procedure and Investigations Act 1996; s 9(11) Criminal Justice Act 1987.
24 ss 58 and 82 Criminal Justice Act 2003.
25 ss 71 and 82 Criminal Justice Act 2003.
26 (2000) of 7 February 2000 (unreported).

online media and individual users of social media websites, who have been prosecuted and convicted under this provision. The offences to which the prohibition applies are set out in s 2 of the 1992 Act and include rape, indecent assault, indecency towards children and the vast majority of other sexual offences.

There are three main exceptions to the anonymity rule. First, a complainant (victim) may waive the entitlement to anonymity by giving written consent to being identified (if they are 16 or older).[27]

Secondly, the media is free to report the victim's identity in the event of criminal proceedings other than the actual trial or appeal in relation to the sexual offence. This exception caters for the situation where a complainant in a sexual offences case is subsequently prosecuted for perjury or wasting police time in separate proceedings. The complainant retains anonymity if, during the course of proceedings, sexual offences charges are dropped and other non-sexual offence charges continue to be prosecuted.[28]

Thirdly, the court may lift the anonymity order to persuade defence witnesses to come forward, or where the court is satisfied that it is a substantial and unreasonable restriction on the reporting of the trial and that it is in the public interest for it to be lifted.[29] This last condition cannot be satisfied simply because the defendant has been acquitted or other outcome of the trial.[30]

The main problem is that the search engine Google's algorithms facilitate searches for attackers and alleged attackers in a few easy clicks. By entering the name of a victim or complainant in the site's search engine Google's automated 'related search' and 'autocomplete' functions direct users to uncover the identity of rape victims whose anonymity is protected by law and often also the identity of their abuser or alleged abuser. Several prominent sexual assault cases automatically revealed the names of women and their accused or convicted abuser.

There have been a number of prosecutions commenced by the Attorney General against individuals who posted on social media sites, revealing the identity of rape victims, such as in the high-profile rape trial in 2012 of the then Sheffield United and Welsh international footballer, Ched Evans. After a jury at Carnarvon Crown Court found him guilty and he was sentenced to five years' imprisonment on 20 April 2012, the Twitter mob almost immediately began to reveal the identity of the 19-year-old rape victim more than a thousand of times. The woman was forced to relocate from her hometown of Rhyl and change her identity. The hashtag '#ChedEvans' appeared on Twitter, and later, #JusticeForChed. Some tweets questioned why one defendant was found guilty and the other not (Evans' co-accused, Port Vale footballer Clayton McDonald, was found not guilty).[31] Others blamed and named the victim, focusing on her being drunk.

The then Attorney General, Dominic Grieve QC, commenced criminal proceedings against those who had contravened section 5 of the Sexual Offences (Amendment) Act 1992. In November 2012 nine people pleaded guilty at Prestatyn Magistrates Court in

---

27 It is a defence to an offence of publishing identifying matter under s 5(2) of the Sexual Offences (Amendment) Act 1992 to show that the complainant gave written consent to the publication.
28 Ibid., s 1(4).
29 Ibid., s 3.
30 Ibid., s 3(3).
31 Four years later, on 21 April 2016, Evans won his appeal against his rape conviction. Hallett LJ announced that there would be a retrial. On 14 October 2016 Ched Evans was found not guilty at retrial.

North Wales to publishing material likely to lead members of the public to identify the complainant in a rape case. Among the accused were Evans' cousin, Gemma Thomas from Rhyl, the footballer's friend Craig McDonald, 26, from Prestatyn and 25-year-old biology schoolteacher Holly Price from Prestatyn.[32] Each were fined £624 at Prestatyn Magistrates' Court.

Google and other search engine technologies have turned rape and sexual assault victims into clickbait, and it is of great concern how Google et al. facilitate easy access to the names of victims and complainants. Police and the senior judiciary have proposed to assist Google by informing it of cases where a victim's anonymity is at risk. Is it not about time that Google and other search engines operate within the law of the UK?

4.3.2 Anonymity for defendants of sexual offences

Whilst the law provides lifetime anonymity for rape victims, such anonymity has not been available to rape defendants. The law is now rather unclear regarding suspects involved in historic sexual allegations (and generally suspects of a crime who have come to the attention of the police) since Mr Justice Mann's ruling in the *Sir Cliff Richard* (2018) case.[33] Mann J ruled that it may sometimes be appropriate to name a suspect, and other times it would not be 'lawful'; each case should be decided on its merits. Since that ruling the media and the police simply do not know whether they can name a criminal suspect. Rather than issue guidance or recommend that Parliament should intervene, the BBC has since decided not to appeal the *Cliff Richard* ruling and the Prime Minister, Theresa May, indicated that she is unlikely to persuade Parliament to change the law. However, the case for anonymity legislation in the area of naming suspects in historic child sexual offence cases has got stronger.

See
Chapter 2.8

Since there is no power under the 1992 Act to restrict the naming of a defendant in a sex case, the defendant may apply for the restriction to be lifted if that is required to induce potential witnesses to come forward and the conduct of the defence is likely to be substantially prejudiced if no such direction is given. Once an allegation of a sexual offence has been made, nothing can be published which is likely to lead members of the public to identify the alleged victim.

The question of the anonymity of the accused has been a long-standing subject of public and parliamentary debate, for two reasons: the first is the number of well-known people arrested as part of the Metropolitan Police's 'Operation Yewtree', and the second is the advent of social media which has amplified the problem, causing reputational damage by naming a suspect. Operation Yewtree found at least 589 alleged victims linked to the Jimmy Savile abuses following his death on 29 October 2011. The Met also investigated allegations of historical child sexual abuse going back to the Thatcher years. Those linked to historical child sex offences included the late Sir Leon (Lord) Brittan, former EU Commissioner, and the BBC Radio 2 DJ Paul Gambaccini. Allegations were subsequently dropped by the police. but those implicated suffered months of incredible stress.

---

32 Source: 'Ched Evans rape case: nine fined over naming of footballer's victim: Woman's name was circulated on social networking sites including Twitter and Facebook', *Press Association and Guardian*, 5 November 2012: www.theguardian.com/uk/2012/nov/05/ched-evans-rape-naming-woman.

33 *Sir Cliff Richard OBE v (1) The British Broadcasting Corporation (2) The Chief Constable of South Yorkshire Police* [2018] EWHC 1837 (Mann J).

In Gambaccini's case, the BBC even suspended him without pay, the result of which was lost income and legal fees of around £200,000.[34] In July 2019 CarlBeech, 51, from Gloucester, was found guilty of 12 counts of perverting the course of justice, accusing Senior Politicians of sexual abuse in the 1970s and 80s. He was sentenced to 18 years in prison.

Should suspects accused of sex crimes have their identities protected until they are convicted? Under current legislation, people who complain they have been a victim of sexual offences automatically receive anonymity, but suspects do not.

The Sexual Offences (Amendment) Act 1976 initially only offered anonymity to rape victims, but subsequently extended a lifetime reporting ban to other sex offences. The provisions granting anonymity to suspects and accused were repealed in the Criminal Justice Act 1988.

The Heilbron[35] Committee (1975), a Home Office Advisory Committee, recommended that the identity of rape complainants should be kept secret. Whilst they initially considered anonymity for rape defendants, they did eventually not recommend anonymity for rape defendants because the Committee felt complainants and defendants were not comparable in principle, and that in cases of other serious crimes where the complainant was often anonymous, defendants were not granted anonymity.[36]

What followed was the Sexual Offences (Amendment) Bill in 1976, where Parliament adopted the recommendations of Heilbron granting lifelong anonymity for rape victims and providing anonymity for rape defendants as well. The main reason for this was to guard against the possibility of reputational damage for those acquitted of rape and to provide equality between complainants and defendants in rape cases.[37]

With increasing social media and modern technology being allowed in court by the media, an issue arose in R (Press Association) v Cambridge Crown Court (2012),[38] whereby the Press Association (PA) appealed against a lifelong 'rape' anonymity order on the defendant, imposed by His Honour Judge Hawksworth at Cambridge Crown Court on 16 April 2012, following the defendant's conviction of five counts of rape and four counts of breaching a restraining order in February 2012.[39] The trial had taken place in open court, listed under the defendant's full name. The CA overturned that order and held that the courts do not have power to protect victims of sexual crime by anonymizing defendants who have been named in open court. The judgment highlights the thorny issues that arise whenever anonymity is sought in criminal cases. It also contains an interesting discussion about the role of judicial guidance and journalistic responsibility in relation to media reporting on court proceedings.

The issue of rape defendants' anonymity has arisen frequently in Parliament and was last debated during the passage of the Sexual Offences Bill in the 2002–2003 session. In a hearing before the Home Affairs Committee in March 2015, the Commissioner of the Metropolitan Police, Sir Bernard Hogan-Howe, supported the proposal for granting accused suspects of sexual offences anonymity until charge.[40] However, the law has not changed in this respect.

---

34 House of Commons (2014), p. 6.
35 Dame Rose Heilbron DBE QC (1914–2005) was the first woman to be appointed King's Counsel and first female judge to sit at the Old Bailey. She chaired the committee on rape laws in 1975.
36 Home Office (1975) at pp. 27–31.
37 Ministry of Justice (2010c) at p. 2; see also: Criminal Law Revision Committee (1984).
38 Re Press Association [2012] EWCA Crim 2434 (CA).
39 Ibid. at para. 2(ii).
40 House of Commons (2015).

4.4 Reporting on children and young persons

The freedom of a child to grow up and make mistakes, to act badly and not to have this permanently recorded is an essential human right recorded in the UN Convention on the Rights of the Child 1989.[41] Article 40 of the UN Convention guarantees the right of a child defendant 'to have his or her privacy fully respected at all stages of the proceedings'. Where the welfare and interest of a child are concerned, the Strasbourg Human Rights Court has sought to protect the privacy of a child under Article 8 ECHR, and any court can now make an order prohibiting the identification of the child. That said, human rights jurisprudence equally states that this power must be used *proportionately*, balancing other interests protected by Articles 6 and 10 of the Convention (see: *McKerry v Teesdale and Wear Valley Justices* (2000)).[42]

4.4.1 Changes in reporting restrictions for under-18s

From 13 April 2015 substantial statutory changes were made regarding reporting restrictions for under-18s (including Scotland – see below 4.4.2). Under s 45 of the Youth Justice and Criminal Evidence Act 1999 (YJCEA), a criminal court can grant anonymity to a juvenile defendant, victim or witness in adult criminal proceedings. Such anonymity will last until that person reaches the age of 18. This power is not available to Youth Courts, since s 49 CPYA provides *automatic* anonymity in those proceedings.

In addition, under s 45A of the YJCEA, criminal courts including Youth Courts are given a new power to grant *lifelong anonymity* to juvenile victims and witnesses, bringing the law for under-18s into line with the law for adult victims and witnesses. Consistently with the law in relation to adult defendants, there is no power under s 45A to grant lifelong anonymity to juvenile defendants.

This change in the law follows the criticisms made by Sir Brian Leveson in *JC and RT v Central Criminal Court* (2014),[43] where he called for urgent reform to address the anomaly that a child or young person who was the subject of a section 39 order (Children and Young Persons Act 1933 – CYPA) lost anonymity when they reached the age of 18, while adults who obtained orders under s 46 of the Youth Justice and Criminal Evidence Act 1999 could be granted lifelong anonymity.[44]

Section 45 YJCEA replaces s 39 CYPA in relation to all criminal proceedings.[45] However, section 39 continues to apply to *civil and family proceedings* and to Criminal Behaviour Injunctions and Criminal Behaviour Orders. Section 39 has been amended so that reporting restrictions made under section 39 now apply to online publications as well as the print and broadcast media.

This change follows the judgment of Mr Justice Tugendhat in *MXB v East Sussex Hospitals Trust* (2012),[46] where he held that s 39 CYPA only applied to reports of court proceedings

---

41 Document A/RES/44/25 of 12 December 1989.
42 [2000] 164 JP 355 (DC).
43 [2014] EWHC 2041.
44 For further discussion see: Smartt, U. (2015b) at pp. 5–13.
45 Note: It has to be pointed out that 'old' criminal cases involving youths will still cite a section 39 order relating to defendant children involved in criminal proceedings.
46 [2012] EWHC 3279 (QB).

in newspapers and broadcast services and did not cover online publications. The same finding was made by Sir Brian Leveson in *JC & RT v Central Criminal Court* (2014)[47] This deficiency was remedied by an amendment to s 39 CYPA in s 79(7) of the Criminal Justice and Courts Act 2015, widening the definition of publication in section 39.[48]

The intention of Parliament in enacting these provisions was to widen the scope of protection applying specifically to under-18s. Although the new powers are of broader application than s 39 CYPA 1933, they give rise to similar issues, and it has been held that the section 39 case law provides appropriate guidance to the principles and practice to be followed concerning applications under section 45 (see: *R v H* (2015)[49]).

The prohibition on publication also extends to proceedings on appeal from a youth court (including by way of case stated); proceedings in a magistrates' court for breach, revocation or amendment of a youth rehabilitation order (YRO); and on appeal from such proceedings in a Magistrates' Court (including by way of case stated).[50]

Hearings from which the public may be excluded

- The general rule is that all court proceedings must be held in open court to which the public and the media have access ('open justice principle');
- The court may hear trials in private in exceptional circumstances where doing so is necessary to prevent the administration of justice from being frustrated or rendered impractical;
- Where lesser measures such as discretionary reporting restrictions would prevent prejudice to the administration of justice, those measures should be adopted;
- Where is it necessary to hear parts of a case in private the court should adjourn to open court as soon as it is no longer necessary for the public to be excluded;
- The embarrassment caused to witnesses from giving evidence in open court does not meet the necessity test;
- There is statutory exception to the open justice principle for proceedings in the Youth Courts, which members of the public are prohibited from attending.

4.4.2 Reporting on children *not* involved in criminal proceedings: section 39 order

Section 39 CYPA used to apply to reporting restrictions for children involved in criminal proceedings. This is no longer the case. An order under section 39 can be made by the court in respect of a child or young person (under 18) appearing in non-criminal proceedings as witness or complainant. Unlike an order in respect of a criminal young defendant,

---

47 [2014] EWHC at para. 1041 (Sir Brian Leveson).
48 For further discussion see: Benaim, G. and Oakley, J. (2014) at pp. 221–223.
49 [2015] EWCA Crim 1579 at para. 8 (Treacy LJ).
50 s 49(2) Children and Young Persons Act 1933 (CYPA).

the section 39 order is not automatic. There must be good reason to make the order, and generally the open justice principle prevails. This includes orders such as criminal behaviour injunctions or criminal behaviour orders.[51] All parties, including the media, are invited to make representations to the court. A party seeking a section 39 order, preventing the publication of the name, address and other details relating to the child, may not wish the media (and therein the neighbourhood) to know that a girl of 14 is on a Criminal Behaviour Injunction or has indeed breached it.

The child or young person will be 'concerned' in criminal proceedings if s/he is a victim, defendant or witness in the case, but not merely because s/he is 'concerned' in the sense of being 'affected' (see: R v Jolleys (2013)[52] or a case brought 'in respect of' a child, which may be sufficient for section 39 order as per R(A) v Lowestoft Magistrates' Court (2013)[53]).

The court has no power to prohibit the publication of the names of adults involved in the proceedings or other children or young persons not involved in the same (civil) proceedings as witnesses, defendants or victims.

The CA held in ex parte Godwin (1992)[54] that a section 39 order — originally imposed by Judge Laurie at Southwark Crown Court — was only available where the terms of section 39(1) CYPA related to a relevant child. In this case the newspapers had previously reported the abusing stepfather's (S) name, referring to the victim as 'an 11-year-old schoolgirl'. There was a serious risk of jigsaw identification in that the composite picture would present the identification of that child.

The appellants, Caroline Godwin, the Daily Telegraph, Mirror Group Newspapers and Associated Newspapers Ltd, appealed against the section 39 order, arguing that the judge had wrongly interpreted section 39.[55] They further argued that there was no evidence that the naming of the defendant (S) would lead to the identification of the child. The CA subsequently quashed the order in its entirety. After the conclusion of the trial S's child continued to be protected by a lifelong anonymity order provided under s 1 Sexual Offences (Amendment) Act 1992 ('Anonymity of victims in certain offences') (see above).

The so-called Godwin direction means that a section 39 order does not empower a court to prevent the naming of adult defendants in general; section 39 orders, are, by their very nature, specifically related to children and young persons under 18. The court may, however, give guidance to the media if it considers that the naming of an adult defendant would be likely to identify a child ('jigsaw identification'); however, such guidance is not legally binding. The media may, for instance, be able to name a defendant without infringing the order if the relationship of the victim to the defendant is omitted or the nature of the offence is blurred (e.g. 'a sexual offence' rather than incest).

In Re Gazette Media Co. Ltd (2005),[56] the CA considered the scope of a section 39 order where two men, S and L, were being prosecuted (and eventually convicted) for offences contrary to section 1 of the Protection of Children Act 1978 and for conspiracy to rape. S was charged with offences of making or distributing indecent photographs of his daughter and with the offence of conspiracy to rape. L was charged with conspiracy to rape and

---

51 s 1 Anti-social Behaviour, Crime and Policing Act 2014.
52 [2013] EWCA Crim 1135, paras 12–13.
53 [2013] EWHC 659 (Admin), paras 8–9.
54 R v Southwark Crown Court ex parte Godwin and Others [1992] QB 190 (CA (Civ Div).
55 Under s 159 Criminal Justice Act 1988.
56 Gazette Media Company Ltd & Ors, R (on the application of) v Teeside Crown Court [2005] EWCA Crim 1983 (CA (Crim Div).

also with offences of making and distributing indecent photographs of a child. In this case, the Middlesbrough Recorder had made the section 39 order by stating:

> no reporting of any proceedings in respect of R v S and L. No identification of the defendant S by name or otherwise the nature of the case against him, the identification of the alleged victim [S's daughter], her age place of abode or any circumstances that may lead to her identification in connection with these proceedings.[57]

Solicitors acting for *Gazette Media* wrote to the Recorder complaining about the wording of the section 39 order, citing *Godwin*: that — as a matter of law — the order did not empower a court to prevent the names of (adult) defendants from being published. Maurice Kay LJ in *Re Gazette* remarked that it was clear beyond doubt that the order made by the Recorder 'flew in the face of *Godwin*' in that a section 39 order could not add specifics beyond the words of section 39(1). Therefore, a departure from *Godwin* could not be justified. It was not enough to delete the restriction against the reporting of any proceedings in relation to the defendants and the victim; it was also necessary to delete the express restriction on the identification of S and L and the nature of the case against them.

The additional problem in *Re Gazette* was that the restriction provided by section 1 Sexual Offences (Amendment) Act 1992 ('Anonymity of victims in certain offences') was not sufficient to protect the identity of the victim during the proceedings and could be interpreted by the media as 'freedom to report'. While conspiracy to rape was an offence to which section 1 of the 1992 Act applied, other linked offences were not. The order was quashed in its entirety, and a new order in conventional *Godwin* terms was substituted. Additionally, it was submitted by the Attorney General that, while a total embargo on the reporting of the proceedings remained unlawful, the prohibition of the naming of a defendant — so as to protect the interests of a child — was now possible within the remit of the human rights provision of Article 8 ECHR and section 3 Human Rights Act 1998, which requires primary legislation to be compatible with Convention rights.

Any order made must comply with Article 10 ECHR.[58]

- it must be necessary;
- it must be proportionate; and
- there must be a pressing social need for it.

New definitions of 'publication' were introduced in 2015 and are included in s 39(3) CYPA.[59] Publication covers print, broadcast and online media (including social media) as well as photographs. That a child's identity is already known to people in the community is not necessarily a good reason for allowing publication of that identity.[60]

---

57 Ibid. at 138.
58 *Briffett v CPS* [2002] EMLR 12.
59 Section 39(3) was introduced by s 79(7) of the Criminal Justice and Courts Act 2015.
60 *R (Y) v Aylesbury Crown Court* [2012] EWHC 1140 (Admin).

The relationship between Articles 8 and 10 ECHR was put to the test in child proceedings in *Re S (A Child) (Identification: Restrictions on Publication)* (2004).[61] The House of Lords did not consider that there was scope for extending the restrictions on freedom of expression beyond the *Godwin* direction. In *Re S* all the facts were then reported except for the identity of the parties to avoid jigsaw identification of the child. The decision in *Re S* underlines the considerable difficulties confronting a court when carrying out a balancing exercise between a child's right to private life under Article 8 and the right of the press to freely report.

In *Re S* a child's nine-year-old older brother, DS, had died of acute salt poisoning in the Great Ormond Street Hospital. At a hearing in July 2002, Hedley J found that the salt poisoning had been administered by the child's mother. As a result of this finding, the mother was charged with murder, with a trial set for November 2004. In the pre-trial proceedings, the trial judge was asked in the interests of the child (a five-year-old boy) to ban normal reporting of the trial of his mother for the murder of his nine-year-old brother. Since this terrible situation was going to be known to the boy's school, his neighbours and friends, his guardian applied to the High Court for an injunction to prevent publication of any information which might lead to the child's identification under section 39 CYPA, including his name, address, school or any picture of him and his parents. Hedley J declined to do so.

Balancing Articles 8 and 10 of the Convention, Hedley J decided that the order should contain a proviso such that the newspapers were not prevented from publishing the identity of the defendant mother or the deceased child DS or photographs of them in reports of the criminal trial. The appeal to the Court of Appeal was dismissed, and the child's guardian appealed to the House of Lords. Both the CA and the HL upheld the trial judge's decision. The appellate courts have emphasized that Parliament intended to preserve the distinction between juveniles in youth court proceedings and in the adult courts (see: *R v Central Criminal Court ex parte W, B and C* (2001)[62]). In *R v Central Independent Television* (1994),[63] a wife failed to secure an injunction preventing the broadcasting of a programme identifying her husband as a convicted molester of small boys. She argued that a broadcast would be prejudicial to the welfare of her five-year-old daughter. The identity of the boys was covered by a section 39 order, but the girl was regarded as too remote from the proceedings, and the programme had nothing to do with her care or upbringing. More precisely, the little girl was not within the specific categories covered by section 39.

In *Ex parte Crook* (1995),[64] the appellant journalists challenged a section 39 order which stated that nothing should be published which would lead to the identification of children who were alive and named on the indictment. The indictment included a count of manslaughter of another child of the defendant, whose surviving children were in local authority care. The three young children in this case, for whom the protective order was made, were the alleged victims of cruelty by both parents, charges which were heard together with the allegation of manslaughter in respect of their sibling. The CA, dismissing the appeal, stated that a judge (or magistrate), in making the section 39 order,

---

61 [2004] UKHL 47 (HL).
62 [2001] 1 Cr App R 7.
63 (1994) 9 February 1994, (CA) (unreported).
64 *R v Central Criminal Court ex parte Crook* [1995] 1 WLR 139 (CA (Crim Div)).

has complete discretion to allow representatives from the media – who have a legitimate interest – to make representations *before* the order is made. The CA ruled that the original judge had been completely correct in making the section 39 order on receipt of the borough council's report and that any publication would have had an otherwise damaging effect on the surviving children. In making the order, the judge had correctly weighed the children's interest against the freedom of the press to report and had reached the conclusion that the likely harm to the children outweighed the restriction of freedom to publish.

A court may lift a section 39 order, a principle established in *Lee* (1993).[65] This case concerned a 14-year-old boy convicted of 'grave crimes' (including rape). After conviction and on sentencing, the judge lifted the section 39 order. An interim injunction was made prohibiting identification by another judge, though too late to prevent publication in some newspapers. Lee's lawyers made an application to the sentencing judge to reimpose the section 39 order. The CA upheld the refusal of the judge to ban the media from identifying the 14-year-old convicted of robbery and rape because it would involve 'no real harm to the applicant, and [have] a powerful deterrent effect on his contemporaries if the applicant's name and photograph were published'.

This was the first case where the 'naming and shaming' of a young offender was made possible while court proceedings were still active, although Lord Bingham stressed that publicity should not be used as an 'additional punishment' – contrary to the views of successive Home Secretaries (Michael Howard, Conservative, at the time of the case) and ministers of justice (e.g. Jack Straw, Labour; Michael Gove, Conservative).

The *Lee* direction has been used frequently by judges to lift reporting restrictions post sentence of a young offender. In April 2012, Flaux J lifted the anonymity order on 14-year-old Daniel Bartlam, naming the young killer for murdering his mother Jacqueline Bartlam, 47. Nottingham Crown Court heard how Bartlam had been 'obsessed' with *Coronation Street*'s killer character John Stape, who had battered a woman with a hammer before leaving her body in the wreckage of a tram crash to cover up his crime. Bartlam had copied the *modus operandi* and had beaten his mother to death with a claw hammer, then padded her body with paper, doused it in petrol and set fire to it to destroy the evidence. Flaux J sentenced the 14-year-old to life imprisonment,[66] with a minimum tariff of 16 years.

The most notorious case of open court reporting post sentence is that of child killers Jon(athan) Venables and Robert Thompson. The then ten-year-old boys killed 18-month-old James ('Jamie') Bulger on 12 February 1993 after they had snatched the toddler during a shopping trip with his mother at the Strand shopping centre in Bootle. They took Jamie to a disused freight railway line where they brutally tortured him and left him to die. A jury at the (adult) Crown Court in Preston found Venables and Thompson guilty of murder on 24 November. Morland J then lifted the section 39 order 'in the public interest'. A media frenzy ensued, resulting in shocking and distressing facts being openly reported by naming the two (by now) 11-year-olds and their dysfunctional family backgrounds. They were sentenced to be detained for a maximum tariff of eight years in secure youth accommodation.

---

65 R v Lee (*Anthony William*) (*a Minor*) [1993] 1 WLR 103 (CA (Crim Div)).
66 s 53(1) Children and Young Persons Act 1933.

Following public outrage over the 'short' tariff, the editor of the *Sun* handed a petition bearing nearly 280,000 signatures to the then Conservative Home Secretary, Michael Howard, in a bid to increase the time spent by both boys in custody where life should mean life. In July 1994 Mr Howard announced that the boys would be kept in custody for a minimum of 15 years; Venables and Thompson challenged this decision under judicial review, arguing the Home Secretary had acted *ultra vires*.[67]

They were successful and, in his judgment, Lord Donaldson criticized the Home Secretary's intervention as *ultra vires*, describing the increased custodial tariff as 'institutionalised vengeance . . . [by] a politician playing to the gallery'. The increased minimum term was overturned by the House of Lords.

The increase of the sentencing term was further criticized by the European Court of Human Rights in *V v UK; T v UK* (1999).[68] The ECtHR stated that the Bulger killers had not received a fair trial and that the UK courts had breached Article 6 ECHR. Not only because proceedings were held in an adult court but also because of the intense media coverage prior to the trial which had put the boys' parents and other siblings' lives at risk. The ECtHR did not rule that youth trials in the UK in the Crown Court were unfair per se.

Following on from the Strasbourg ruling in *V v UK; T v UK*, the Westminster Parliament enacted the Youth Justice and Criminal Evidence Act 1999 (YJCEA). This Act deals with proceedings in the youth court, lifting of reporting restrictions and intimidation, humiliation or distress in court proceedings and the general protection of vulnerable witnesses. Lord Woolf LCJ reinforced the new legislation by a Practice Direction, stating that:

> all possible steps should be taken to assist the young defendant to understand and participate in the proceedings. The ordinary trial process should, so far as necessary, be adapted to meet those ends.[69]

B, aged 14, had been convicted of a grave sexual offence. He applied for judicial review of the Winchester trial judge's decision in *R v Winchester Crown Court ex parte B* (*A Minor*) (1999),[70] to discharge reporting restrictions after sentence on the basis that open justice was essential in a civilized society. Judges Simon Brown LJ and Astill J in the Administrative Court dismissed B's application and reiterated that it was well within the Crown Court's powers to discharge a section 39 order in relation to proceedings on indictment after conviction.

A section 39 order automatically lapses when the person reaches the age of 18 and cannot extend to reports of the proceedings after that point (see: *JC & RT v Central Criminal Court* (2014)[71]). Any journalist who publishes any matter in contravention of any child anonymity order is liable on summary conviction under section 39(2) of the 1933 Act, to a maximum level 5 fine.[72]

---

67 *Secretary of State for the Home Department ex parte Venables; R v Secretary of State for the Home Department ex parte Thompson* [1998] AC 407.

68 (1999) 30 EHRR 121 (ECtHR).

69 Source: Practice Direction by the Lord Chief Justice of England and Wales (Woolf LCJ): Trial of Children and Young Persons in the Crown Court of 16 February 2000.

70 [1999] 1 WLR 788. B had been sentenced to three years' detention for an offence contrary to s 1 Criminal Attempts Act 1981.

71 [2014] EWHC (1041) (Divisional Court).

72 Upper limits for a level 5 fine (£5,000) were abolished under s 85 Legal Aid, Sentencing and Punishment of Offenders Act 2012 (LASPO).

4.4.2 Reporting on children in Scotland: Children's Hearings

The Social Work (Scotland) Act 1968 abolished youth courts in Scotland and replaced these with the Children's Hearing System (CHS), following the recommendations of the Kilbrandon Report of 1961.[73] The CHS began operation on 15 April 1971. Children were referred to the Children's Reporter in ever-increasing numbers with hearings taking place across Scotland. By 1996, when the 12 regional local authorities were reorganized into 32 single-tier authorities, there were approximately 2,000 panel members serving throughout Scotland and this number continued to increase. The Children's Hearings (Scotland) Act 2011 created the new agency, Children's Hearings Scotland (CHS), and established a single national Children's Hearings panel for Scotland, which oversees 32 panels.[74]

Section 46 of the Children and Young Persons (Scotland) Act 1937 applies to civil proceedings and allows the court to make an order prohibiting publication of details calculated to lead to the identification of a person under 17 years of age concerned in the proceedings. Section 44 of the Children (Scotland) Act 1995 *prohibits* the publication of information that identifies or is likely to identify a child concerned in proceedings before a children's hearing.

Section 57(3) Children and Young Persons Act 1963 extended section 39 CYPA 1933 to Scotland. There was however until recently a discrepancy between reporting restrictions in England and Wales and Scotland: young persons under the age of 16 involved in Scottish criminal or Children's Hearing proceedings, or linked with adult offenders, would normally never be named or identified in the Scottish media. Further confusion arises in the age of criminal responsibility: unlike in England and Wales – where the age of criminal responsibility is ten – in Scotland it is twelve years old.[75]

Now reporting restrictions have been brought in line, and generally reporting on a child or young person across the UK is not permitted under the age of 18 (though there are still reported cases where the age was 16 prior to 2015).

Section 47 of the Criminal Procedure (Scotland) Act 1995 *prohibits* the publication of the name, address, school or any particulars calculated to lead to the identification of any person under the age of 18 who is an accused, victim or witness in criminal proceedings.[76] Where a person under the age of 18 years is concerned in the proceedings as a witness only, and no one against whom the proceedings are taken is under the age of 18 years, the requirements shall not apply unless the court so directs. This applies *even when such details are revealed in open court*. The media may apply to have this restriction lifted through a formal court motion.

 FOR THOUGHT

In April 2016, 39-year-old British citizen Angela Wrightson was brutally killed by two teenage girls aged 13 and 14. They excitedly shared their ruthlessness on Snapchat to update their friends about their brutality. Should children be tried as adults? Discuss with reference to leading authorities.

---

73 Kilbrandon, Lord (1964) Report of the Committee on Children and Young Persons, Scotland; see also: Kilbrandon, Lord (1971) at p. 128.
74 Children's Hearings Scotland: www.chscotland.gov.uk.
75 s 52 Criminal Justice and Licensing (Scotland Act) 2010 (changed from aged 8).
76 Formerly the Act covered children under the age of 16. This change came into effect from 1 September 2015.

4.4.3 Reporting on children involved in criminal proceedings: section 45 order

The general power to impose a *discretionary* reporting restriction in relation to a person under aged 18 is now contained in s 45 of the Youth Justice and Criminal Evidence Act 1999 (YJCEA). This discretionary power applies to under-18 victims, witnesses and defendants in a *criminal* court.

Section 45 YJCEA permits a criminal court to prevent any information being included in a publication which is likely to lead members of the public to identify the under-18 victim, witness or defendant as a person concerned in the proceedings. When deciding whether to make a section 45 order, the court must have regard to the welfare of that person.

As with any departure from open justice there must be a good reason for imposing an order under section 45. The court must be satisfied that, on the facts of the case before it, the welfare of the child outweighs the strong public interest in open justice (see: *R v Central Criminal Court ex parte W, B and C* (2001)[77]).

Section 45(8) YJCEA identifies particular examples of information that a section 45 reporting restriction may contain, such as:

1   her or his name;
2   her or his address;
3   the identity of any school or other educational establishment attended by her/him;
4   the identity of any place of work; and
5   any still or moving picture of her/him.

This list is not exhaustive.

When deciding whether to make an order under section 45 the court must have regard to the welfare of that person. As this restriction is a departure from 'open justice', there must be a good reason for imposing it (see: *R v Inner London Crown Court ex parte B* (1996)[78]). Furthermore, the court must be satisfied that, on the facts of the case, the welfare of the child outweighs the strong public interest in open justice.

The court, or an appellate court, may dispense with a section 45 reporting restriction if it is satisfied that doing so is in the interests of justice or that the restrictions impose a substantial and unreasonable restriction on the reporting of the proceedings and it is in the public interest to remove or relax the restriction. When considering the 'public interest' the court should have regard, in particular, to the matters identified in section 52 YJCEA:

- the open reporting of crime;
- the open reporting of matters relating to health and safety;
- the prevention and exposure of miscarriages of justice;
- the welfare of the child or young person and the views of the child or young person.

---

77   [2001] 1 Cr App R 7 (and the cases cited therein).
78   [1996] COD 17 (DC).

In *McKerry v Teesdale and Wear Valley Justices* (2000),[79] a 16-year-old boy, with a long record of offending, pleaded guilty at the youth court to a 'TWOCing' offence.[80] Upon request by a local newspaper, the magistrates lifted the reporting restrictions and permitted his identity to be revealed under section 49 of the 1933 Act, giving as reasons that the young offender posed a serious danger to the public and had shown a complete disregard for the law. The Divisional Court held that the magistrates' reasons were completely acceptable because 'no doubt the justices had in mind that members of the public, if they knew the appellant's name, would enjoy a measure of protection if they had cause to encounter him'. The court further added that the power to dispense with anonymity 'must be exercised with very great circumspection' and that the public interest criterion must be met.

In the conjoined cases of *R (on the application of T) v St Albans Crown Court; Chief Constable of Surrey v JHG* (2002),[81] it was held that antisocial behaviour orders (ASBOs) were very much in the general public interest and that reporting restrictions would not be granted. In the first case, the court had refused to grant anonymity under section 39 Children and Young Persons' Act 1933 to an 11-year-old boy (T) in respect of whom an ASBO[82] had been made. T sought a judicial review of that decision. In the second case, the court had granted anonymity to 17-year-old twins (J and D) when making an ASBO, with the Chief Constable of Surrey appealing against that decision. The allegations against T included abuse, minor criminal damage and two assaults, and those against J and D included assault, nuisance, trespass, criminal damage, threatening behaviour and intimidation. T, J and D submitted that, given that ASBOs were civil in character, they were less serious than many of the offences in respect of which section 39 applications were commonly refused in Crown Court proceedings. T submitted that the court had failed to consider relevant matters, including his age and improvement in his behaviour, and in J and D's case the Chief Constable submitted that the court had considered irrelevant matters, including the impact on members of J and D's families.

Applying the *Lee* balancing exercise, that of the public interest test in disclosure of the name versus the welfare of the young person in question, the public interest test weighed in favour of disclosure in T and JHG, where it could be reported that the individuals were on an ASBO, and the neighbourhood could learn about the orders, assisting the police in making the orders effective to prevent future antisocial behaviour (see also: *R v Winchester ex parte B (A Minor)* (1999).[83]

In summary, the protection of under-18s under a section 45 YJCEA order includes the following:

- A criminal court may make an order preventing the publication of information that identifies a child or young person as being a victim, witness or defendant in the proceedings.
- This restriction applies to traditional print and broadcast media as well as online publications.
- The court must have regard to the welfare of the child or young person.

---

79 [2000] 164 JP 355 (DC).
80 s 12 Theft Act 1968 ('taking a vehicle without the owner's consent').
81 [2002] EWHC 1129 (Admin) of 20 May 2002 (QBD (Admin).
82 s 1 Crime and Disorder Act 1998.
83 [1999] 1 WLR 788.

- The court may remove or relax the section 45 reporting restriction if satisfied that it imposes a substantial and unreasonable restriction on reporting and that it is in the public interest.

Just as with a section 39 order, a section 45 reporting restriction order ceases to apply when the young person reaches the age of 18. In these circumstances, the court has the power to impose lifelong anonymity under section 45A YJCEA if the relevant conditions are met (see below 4.4.3).

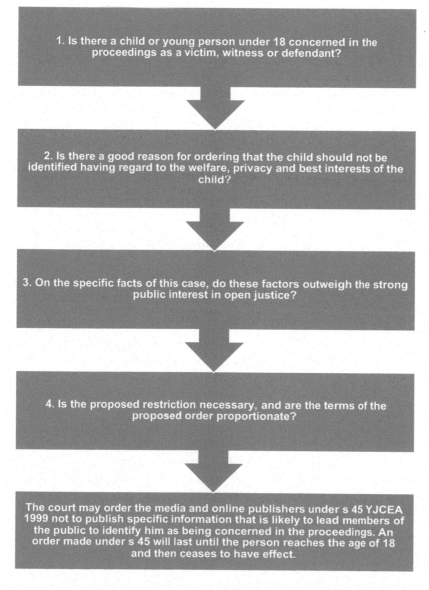

Figure 4.1 Protecting the welfare of under-18 witnesses, victims and vulnerable defendants: discretionary reporting procedures

4.4.3 Lifelong anonymity orders: section 45A Youth Justice and Criminal Evidence Act 1999

Section 45A YJCEA[84] contains the power for the court to impose a lifelong reporting restriction in the case of an under-18 victim or witness. This provision has long been used for young murderers and means there must be no publication about them during their lifetime.

When Coulson J lifted the reporting restrictions on Ann Maguire's teenage killer, identifying 16-year-old William (Will) Cornick at Leeds Crown Court in November 2014, the media's interest was as intense as in 1993 when Morland J lifted the section 39 anonymity order on Venables and Thompson. After Cornick's guilty plea, Coulson J reasoned that 'there is a public interest in naming young defendants who are convicted of murder'. He sentenced the young killer to a minimum of 20 years.[85]

The test for making a section 45A order is that the court must be satisfied that fear or distress on the part of the victim or witness in connection with being identified as a person concerned in the proceedings is likely to diminish the quality of that person's evidence or the level of co-operation they give to any party to the proceedings in connection with that party's presentation of its case. When applying the test the court is required to take into account certain particular matters:

- the nature and alleged circumstances of the offence to which the proceedings relate;
- the age of the victim or witness;
- their social and cultural background and ethnic origins;
- their domestic, educational and employment circumstances;
- any religious and political beliefs;
- the views expressed by the victim or witness (victim impact statement).

In summary, under section 45A of YJCEA a criminal court may make a lifetime anonymity order, preventing any publication of information that identifies a child or young person as being a victim or witness in court proceedings. The court must also take Article 10 ECHR into account, the effect that such an order will have on the media's ability to report the proceedings. The court can remove or relax the order and reporting restrictions at any time if reporting is in the public interest.

The issue of a lifelong anonymity order was raised in common law in the 'Mary Bell' case (Re X (1985)[86]), where a lifelong injunction was sought on behalf of the claimant – notorious child killer 'Mary Bell' (not her real name) – and her daughter. This is now known as a 'Mary Bell order'. (See below 4.4.5). Cusack J described Mary as 'dangerous' and sentenced her to be detained in secure accommodation at Her Majesty's Pleasure.

---

84 Inserted by s 78(2) Criminal Justice and Courts Act 2015 'lifetime reporting restrictions in criminal proceedings for witnesses and victims under 18'.
85 Sentencing remarks by Coulson J in R v William Cornick, Leeds Crown Court, 3 November 2014.
86 X CC v A [1985] 1 All ER 53 (sub nom. Re X (a minor) (wardship injunction – a woman formerly known as Mary Bell).

There were three major periods when X's identity and whereabouts were either discovered or at risk of discovery by the media. The first was after she formed a settled relationship with a man (the second defendant in Re X) and gave birth to Y on 25 May 1984. Child Y was made a ward of court five days later and granted anonymity until her 18th birthday. In July 1984, the News of the World became aware of the birth, and an injunction was granted by Balcombe J in Re X (1985).[87] It is believed that Bell's daughter did not know her mother's identity until it was revealed by reporters (for full background details of the case see: Re X (a Woman Formerly Known as Mary Bell) and Others v O'Brien and Others (2003)[88]).

A 'Mary Bell order' was also made on child killers Jon Venables and Robert Thompson by Dame Elizabeth Butler-Sloss in 2001,[89] granting the 'Bulger killers' lifelong anonymity. When the mother of the murdered James Bulger, Denise Fergus, asked the court in 2010 to lift the lifelong anonymity order on Venables, the then Justice Secretary, Jack Straw, intervened and reiterated the Mary Bell order and the order made by the President of the Family Division in 2001. Appearing via video link at the Old Bailey, 27-year-old Jon Venables pleaded guilty on 23 July 2010, to the offences of downloading and distributing indecent images of children. Bean J partially lifted reporting restrictions to reveal Venables had been living in Cheshire at the time of the offences.[90] (see below 4.4.5).

4.4.4 Reporting restrictions on adult witnesses: section 46 Youth Justice and Criminal Evidence Act 1999

Section 46 YJCEA gives the court power to restrict reporting about certain adult witnesses (other than the accused) in criminal proceedings on the application of any party to those proceedings. Again, publication of the name, address, educational establishment, workplace, photo and so forth of the witness, likely to lead to his or her identification as a witness by the public in any criminal proceedings, is not permitted. A section 46 order may also restrict the identification of children where it would lead to the identification of the adult in question.

Such anonymity orders are not granted often by courts since it is a long established principle that the defendant in a criminal trial is entitled to be confronted by his accuser in open court.[91] Media organizations have a right of appeal against section 46 orders, even where the restriction on reporting is confined to photographs or film (see: ITN News v R (2013)[92]).

The court can further exercise its powers to allow a name or any other matter to be withheld from the public in criminal proceedings under section 11 of the Contempt of Court Act 1981 (CCA), prohibiting the publication of that name or matter in connection with the proceedings if any evidence in open court would frustrate or render impractical the

---

87 [1985] All ER 53.
88 Re X [2003] EWHC 1101.
89 Venables v NGN [2001] Fam 430.
90 Source: 'Bulger killer Venables jailed over child abuse images', BBC News Online, 23 July 2010.
91 s 88 Coroners and Justice Act 2009.
92 [2013] 2 Cr App R 22 at para. 26.

See
Chapter 5

administration of justice (see: *AG v Leveller Magazine* (1979)[93]). In *Re Trinity Mirror* (2008),[94] the Court of Appeal overturned a Crown Court order under section 11 CCA which, in the interests of the defendant's children, prevented the naming of a defendant who had downloaded paedophile images.

In *A Local Authority and Others v News Group Newspapers Ltd* (2011),[95] Baker J declined to make an order restricting the publication of the names of a surviving child's adult family members, including that of a very vulnerable mother who had been charged with the murder of another child (referring to *Re Evesham Justices* (1988)).[96]

4.4.5 Protecting the right to life: lifelong anonymity orders for child killers

Strasbourg jurisprudence has enabled the protection of a citizen's right to life (under Article 2 ECHR) and not to be subjected to torture or to inhuman or degrading treatment or punishment (under Article 3 ECHR).

This issue has been repeatedly raised in the family court division of the High Court when lifelong anonymity orders in respect of child killers involved in murder convictions are applied for. The issue becomes critical when they turn 18 and the media claims the right to report on them.

The leading case is that of *Mary Bell* (not her real name) when, in 1968, ten-year-old Mary was convicted at Newcastle Crown Court of the murder of two little boys, aged three and four, by strangulation. After conviction, Mary Bell spent 12 years at Red Bank Approved School near Newton-le-Willows in Lancashire and was released on licence in 1980 with a new identity. There followed a number of applications to the courts for the anonymity order to continue beyond her coming of age. The first application on 25 May 1984 concerned an injunction to conceal the identity of her baby daughter (Y) and the baby's father after the *News of the World* had tracked down Mary Bell and her child (*Re X* (1985)[97]). Balcombe J granted a restraining order lasting until Y's 18th birthday, preventing identification of Mary's daughter as well as the child's father, and continuing the order on Mary (X) indefinitely. In 1988 the identities of X and Y (then aged four) had been revealed to the press by villagers where the mother and daughter lived at the time.

The third period was in 1998 after the publication of Gitta Sereny's book on the story of Mary Bell, *Cries Unheard*, whereby Sereny had paid Mary a 'substantial sum of money' to co-author the book.[98] Home Secretary Jack Straw did not succeed in injuncting the publication of the book and condemned the payment to Bell in an open letter to the *Sun*, stating that, by collaboration on the book, Mary Bell should forfeit her right to anonymity. Prime Minister Tony Blair criticized the payments to the former child killer as 'inherently repugnant'.

---

93 [1979] AC 440.
94 [2008] 2 Cr App R 1 (CA).
95 [2011] EWHC 1764 (Fam) (Baker J).
96 *R v Evesham Justices ex parte McDonagh* [1988] QB 553.
97 *Re X (a woman formerly known as Mary Bell) and CC v A* [1985] 1 All ER 53.
98 Sereny, G. (1998).

The fourth period began in December 2002 when Mary's acquitted co-accused 'Norma' demanded in the *Sunday Sun* on 15 December that it was 'time to unmask Mary Bell'. The *Newcastle Evening Chronicle* published a lead article on 11 April 2003, 'Still Haunted', in which family members of the two killed boys demanded that Mary Bell's identity be disclosed.[99]

The waiver of a child's privacy may not be permanent, though the (family) court can reimpose anonymity at any time (over the age of 18) even if it has previously been waived.

One of the most notorious cases involved two ten-year-old child murderers, Jon(athan) Venables and Robert Thompson, who killed 18-month-old James (Jamie) Bulger in February 1993. The horrific murder of toddler *James Bulger* in Bootle, Merseyside shocked the nation, and Venables and Thompson continued to be the object of death threats after their release from youth custody. They were given new identities to assist in their reintegration into the community.

In advance of their 18th birthday and release from the secure unit they applied to the Family Court (High Court Division) before the President, Dame Elizabeth Butler-Sloss, for a lifelong anonymity order, citing, *inter alia*, Article 2 ECHR ('right to life').[100]

Butler-Sloss P held that, as the court was a public authority under section 6(3) HRA, the Family Court had to act compatibly with Convention rights, having regard to Strasbourg jurisprudence. The President recognized that any restriction on freedom of the press had to fall within one of the exceptions in Article 10(2) ECHR, which should be construed narrowly and the onus of proof of which was on the claimants.[101]

Taking into account Articles 2, 3 and 8 ECHR, and the real possibility that the claimants, V and T, may be the objects of future revenge attacks, Butler-Sloss P stated that:

> the court does have the jurisdiction, in exceptional cases, to extend the protection of confidentiality of information, even to impose restrictions on the press, where not to do so would be likely to lead to serious physical injury, and there is no other way to protect the applicants.[102]

Butler-Sloss P granted the injunctions as they satisfied the requirements of Article 10(2), namely:

1   they were in accordance with the law, namely the law of confidence;
2   they would be imposed to prevent the disclosure of information received in confidence;
3   there was a very strong possibility, if not probability, that on the release of the claimants there would be serious efforts to find them, and if that information became public they would be pursued by those intent on revenge. Their rights under Articles 2 and 3 gave a strong and pressing social need in a democratic society for their confidentiality to be protected; and

---

99 *Re X: A Woman Formerly Known as 'Mary Bell' and another v O'Brien and Others* [2003] EWHC 1101 (QB).
100 *Venables and Thompson v News Group Newspapers Ltd* [2001] Fam 430.
101 Ibid. at 268, para. 25.
102 Ibid. at 288, para. 82 (Butler-Sloss P).

4   the injunctions were proportionate to the legitimate aim pursued, namely protecting the claimants from the real and serious risk of death or physical harm.[103]

The defendant newspapers (*The Daily Mail*, *The Sun*, *The Daily Mirror*, etc.) had argued that the
young killers' rehabilitation process and education whilst in youth custody were matters
of genuine public interest, and for that reason Venables' and Thompson's identities should
be revealed, citing – *inter alia* – freedom of expression. Butler-Sloss P granted the permanent injunctions 'against the world' (*contra mundum*), stating that:

> in the light of the implementation of the Human Rights Act, we are entering a new
> era, and the requirement that the courts act in a way compatible with the Conven-
> tion, and have regard to European jurisprudence, adds a new dimension to those
> principles.[104]

For these reasons the court had a duty of care to grant lifelong anonymity orders on the
young men (also known as *contra mundum* injunction) (see also: *Davies v Taylor* (1974);[105] *Re H
(Minors) (Sexual Abuse: Standard of Proof)* (1996)[106]).

A *contra mundum* injunction stipulates that the prohibited information includes no publication of the person's new name, address or any details of their whereabouts, any photograph or picture of any place they attend or any details of psychiatric care or treatment.
This extends to social media and the internet. Soliciting this information and even asking
questions with regard to it is also banned, and the penalties for breaching the order are
considerable, namely imprisonment or sequestration of assets (largely covered by the
Contempt of Court Act 1981).

See
Chapter 5.3

In January 2018, Jon Venables, one of the killers of toddler James Bulger, was
charged over indecent images of children. This was the second time during his release
on life licence that the by now 35-year-old, was recalled to prison for serious sexual
child pornography offences on the internet. The last time he pleaded guilty to such
offences was in March 2010. *Daily Mail* and *The Sun* campaigns together with James
Bulger's mother Denise Fergus have repeatedly asked the courts to lift the lifelong anonymity order on Venables, but the courts have not done so. The Butler-Sloss order from
2001 remains in place.

On 9 March 2010, Baroness Butler-Sloss addressed the House of Lords, giving reasons why the *contra mundum* anonymity order must never be lifted on the Bulger killers.
She told the House that the risk of harm to Jon Venables in particular would be too great,
and the court had a duty of care to protect even the most dangerous offenders (citing the
ruling in *Osman v UK* (1998)[107]).

On 7 February 2018 the person formerly known as Jon Venables was sentenced for
the second time since his release from prison in 2001 for the murder of toddler James
Bulger, having pleaded guilty to the possession of online child pornography. He received
a 40-month prison sentence. During these secret court proceedings an application had

---

103 Ibid. at 286–290, paras 77–87.
104 Ibid. at 295, para. 101.
105 [1974] AC 207.
106 [1996] AC 563.
107 (1998) 29 EHRR 245.

been made to the Family Court on 26 January 2018 by Ralph Stephen Bulger and James Patrick ('Jimmy') Bulger, James Bulger's father and paternal uncle, seeking a variation of the 'Venables and Thompson' lifelong anonymity order, made by Dame Elizabeth Butler-Sloss in 2001. James Bulger's mother (Denise Fergus) was not a party to this application.

The application was to discharge or vary the injunction regarding reporting restrictions on the 'person formerly known as Jon Venables' but not in respect of 'the person formerly known as Robert Thompson'.[108] The applicants contended that over 17 years since Venables' release from youth detention he had continued with serious offending involving the uploading and downloading of child pornography, that the 'anonymising' Jon Venables had not worked and that the original intention of the Family Court was on the premise that he was rehabilitated and could live a law-abiding life. They further argued that it was no longer necessarily the situation that Venables' right to life required anonymity, and the evidence appeared to suggest that he could not cope with 'living a lie', that the authorities (such as the Probation Service) had not been able to manage him in the community and that he appeared to have reverted to committing child sex offences.[109] Sir James Munby, President of the Family Division, adjourned the hearing, asking the applicants to submit further evidence by 4 July 2018 why they thought the variation or lifting of the Venables anonymity order was necessary. The anonymity order remained in place.

Media interest remains high as to the whereabouts and identity of the child killers. Irish film director Vincent Lambe's *Detainment* (2018) caused further distress to James Bulger's mother, Denise Fergus, when it was nominated for an Oscar in January 2019. Based on real police interviews with child killers Jon Venables and Robert Thompson, Lambe told TV viewers on *Good Morning Britain* that he tried to 'humanize' the two child killers' story and family background. The director admitted that he had not contacted Mrs Fergus about the film.[110]

Rarely are such lifelong anonymity orders granted for adults. A unique *contra mundum* injunction was granted by Mr Justice Eady on 24 February 2005 in relation to the woman formerly known as Maxine Carr, then aged 27 and girlfriend of the Soham murderer, Ian Huntley. She had been convicted of conspiring to pervert the course of justice with Huntley in December 2003, not in itself such a serious offence, which would not normally attract a lifelong anonymity injunction. Yet, the order emphasized the importance of Carr's perceived fragile psychological state as such a new criterion for granting contra mundum applications.

The reason for Carr's application was that on the eve of her release from prison her solicitors had applied without notice for an injunction to restrain the media from publishing any information about Carr's new identity and whereabouts. She had received death threats which the police believed to be credible. The injunction was sought on the basis of breach of confidence and *contra mundum* on the basis of the threats she had received.

At the first hearing on 13 May 2004, neither the claimant Carr nor the Home Secretary (who supported the application) made any reference to s 12 HRA 1998. News Group

---

108 *Venables, Re.* Also known as: *Application by Bulger* [2018] EWHC 1037 (Fam) (also cited as: *Venables, Re.* 'In the matter of the person previously known as Jon Venables'. *Application by Ralph Stephen Bulger and James Patrick Bulger before Sir James Munby President of the Family Division in the High Court of Justice* [2018] EWHC 1037 (Fam) (in open court) 3 May 2018) (Sir James Munby PFD).
109 Ibid. at paras 4–6.
110 Source: 'Controversial film on James Bulger's killers makes Oscars shortlist', *Good Morning Britain*, ITV, 4 January 2019: www.itv.com/goodmorningbritain/news/film-on-jamie-bulger-killers-makes-oscars-shortlist.

Newspapers and the Mirror Group applied to have the order set aside on the basis that s 12 had been breached. Further, they contended that the prohibition on soliciting information was disproportionate given the ban on publication and therein a breach of their Article 10(1) ECHR right.[111] The 'Maxine Carr' *contra mundum* protective order was eventually granted at a full hearing before Eady J. The order broadened the scope in relation to adults not only to safeguard her new identity but also her 'life and limb' and 'fragile psychological state' on the application of her advocate, Edward Fitzgerald QC.

Ian Huntley was convicted of the 'Soham killings' in 2005, namely the 10-year-old schoolgirls, Holly Wells and Jessica Chapman, whom the then school caretaker killed in August 2002. He was given a 40-year life sentence tariff for the killings and is not due for parole until 2042.

 FOR THOUGHT

Do lifelong anonymity orders (*contra mundum* injunctions) contravene the media's right to freedom of expression? Discuss with reference to legislation and leading authorities.

4.5 Family courts and the Court of Protection

Thousands of sensitive court decisions affecting vulnerable people in the Court of Protection and the family courts are made each year. Since 2016 the public and media have theoretically been granted greater though still statutorily limited access to these otherwise closed courts. The Court of Protection (COP)[112] was set up under the Mental Capacity Act 2005[113] to deal specifically with decisions involving people who are unable to make them (known as 'lack of mental capacity').

The starting point for consideration of publicity in the family courts and COP is the open justice principle as in *Scott v Scott* (1913).[114] Open justice promotes the rule of law as reiterated by Lord Judge CJ in the *Binyam Mohamed* case.[115] It also promotes public confidence in the legal system:[116] The principle of open justice has two aspects: proceedings should be held in open court to which the public and the media are admitted; and secondly, nothing should be done to discourage the publication to the wider public of fair and accurate reports of proceedings that have taken place in court as stated by Lord Diplock in *AG v Leveller Magazine* (1979).[117]

---

111 *Carr (Maxine) v News Group Newspapers Ltd and Others* [2005] EWHC 971 (QB).
112 Court of Protection: www.gov.uk/courts-tribunals/court-of-protection.
113 Part 2 ss 45–56 of the 2005 Act.
114 [1913] AC 417 (HL).
115 *R (Binyam Mohamed) v Secretary of State for Foreign and Commonwealth Affairs* [2010] EWCA Civ 65; [2011] QB 218 at paras 38–42 (as per Lord Judge CJ for a wide-ranging statement of the role of open justice and the principles it promotes).
116 *Re. Webster (A Child)* [2006] EWHC 2733; [2007] EMLR 7; [2007] 1 FLR 1146 at paras 24–25.
117 [1979] AC 440 at para. 450 (Lord Diplock).

But rising numbers of care applications and legal aid cuts have put the open justice system in these courts under strain. Judgments which could be legally disclosed remain largely anonymized. However, it is fair to say that in most cases dealing with difficult and complex decisions, the judgment will always remain anonymized for the lifetime of the victim or applicant, such as in the matter of *Re. M* (2018).[118] In this case, Mr Justice Baker was invited to make a declaration of non-marriage in relation to an Islamic marriage and to consider whether it was necessary to make a Forced Marriage Protection Order.[119] Reporting restrictions in forced marriages or female genital mutilation cases are always automatic and grant the victim lifelong anonymity.[120]

When reporting on such proceedings, responsible and ethical journalism must be at the forefront of every media organization when dealing with very difficult issues, such as 'doorstepping' bereaved families, taking photographs in hospitals or care homes, or invading the privacy of those who are giving their evidence in family courts. In addition to statutory legislation, there will also be editors' broadcast and press codes and regulations that should be adhered to by journalists. However, it is important that the courts balance the individual's privacy against the public's right to know what is going on in these courts.

See Chapters 7.6 and 8.2

4.5.1 Family courts

Family courts make far-reaching decisions, such as whether children should be taken into care or put up for adoption or given contact with parents who are divorcing. They also decide on custody and how finances should be split. Under youth court rules, it is unlawful to publish anything that would identify a minor (under 18) involved in a case, but it is possible to identify adults such as social workers and doctors.

The crisis in the family justice system, brought about by record numbers of applications to take children into care, means that long-standing arguments about openness versus privacy in the family courts took on a new urgency. The new President of the High Court's Family Division, The Rt Hon Sir Andrew McFarlane, speaking at the Bloomsbury Family Law Centre in May 2018, said that there was a £2bn shortfall in council budgets for children's services, with 73,000 children in care, up from 60,000 a decade ago. He called the situation 'untenable'. The president told the meeting that he wanted to put on record his concerns about the impact of the legal aid cuts and therein disappearance of new talented lawyers into publicly funded family work. Judicial recruitment and morale in family law was one of the 'most pressing challenges'.[121] The government was reviewing the impact of legal aid cuts at that time which had led to a growing number of litigants without representation, including in domestic violence cases.

---

118 *AB v (1) HT, (2) London Borough of Hammersmith and Fulham; (3) M (by her litigation friend, the Official Solicitor) and (4) MS (Case No: 11721504)* [2018] EWCOP 2 (also known as 'in the matter of M').

119 The Anti-social Behaviour, Crime and Policing Act 2014 made forced marriage a specific criminal offence. Three years later, the Policing and Crime Act 2017 inserted provisions into the 2014 Act to provide victims of forced marriage with lifelong anonymity, which brings the law relating to forced marriage in line with the law relating to female genital mutilation and the law relating to sexual offences.

120 Section 173 of the Policing and Crime Act 2017 inserted s 122A and Schedule 6A into the Anti-social Behaviour, Crime and Policing Act 2014 which provides for the automatic anonymity of victims of forced marriage. The provisions of Sch. 6A are modelled on Sch 1 of the Female Genital Mutilation Act 2003 (as amended by the Serious Crime Act 2015), which provides automatic, lifelong anonymity for the victims of FGM, which was, in turn, based on the Sexual Offences (Amendment) Act 1992, which provides automatic, lifelong anonymity to the victims of sexual offences, such as rape and sexual assault.

121 Source: 'Broken family', by Grania Langdon-Down, *Law Society Gazette*, 30 July 2018.

Arguably some statutory provisions have expanded the scope of the derogations from open justice. In addition to the specific class of cases involving children and cases of mental incapacity, ancillary relief proceedings, in which the parties' financial affairs are scrutinized, are also considered to concern private matters. Access to hearings is governed by a variety of statutory provisions and rules of court depending on the court. Additionally, courts have to adhere to the European Convention, specifically Articles 6, 8 and 10 ECHR. Under section 6 HRA 1998, the courts have an obligation to give effect to Convention rights. This has particular significance in respect of those Convention rights which impose a positive obligation on the Convention States to give effect to them.[122]

However, since changes in the law with the 2010 and 2014 statutes, duly accredited members of the media are entitled to attend hearings of family proceedings held in private in the Family Division, the County Court and Family Proceedings Courts, subject to the power to exclude them on specified grounds.[123] Neither media representatives nor members of the public may attend hearings which take place in *camera*. At common law a hearing may be held in *camera* where the hearing of the case in public would frustrate or render impracticable the administration of justice. The test is one of necessity. In cases of abduction (of a child or a vulnerable adult), the Court will sit in *camera* when determining issues which are directed towards locating the abducted person (despite the fact that the orders being made are likely to be draconian, such as freezing orders or orders compelling disclosure from anyone who may have knowledge of the person's whereabouts). To do otherwise would defeat the object of the hearing by alerting the abductor to the measures being taken.

The landmark case of *Clayton v Clayton* (2006)[124] raised in acute form the purpose and function of long-term injunctions under section 8 of the Children Act 1989 and the circumstances in which a litigant finds himself when restrained by such an injunction (known as a 'section 8 order') sought open reporting and publication of Simon Clayton's book. In a landmark (reversed) ruling, the CA ruled in Mr Clayton's favour. The then President of the Family Division, Sir Mark Potter, subsequently set out new practice guidelines on reporting restrictions proceedings involving a child:

> If, for example, the Appellant wishes to put photographs of himself and C on his website, in order to impart the information that they have had a very happy holiday together, this, to my mind, is not different in substance from the activities of many families which operate a 'blog' and exchange information and news about the progress of themselves and their children on a web-site. Against such activities there seems to me to be little point in having a blanket injunction which then exempts social and domestic purposes.[125]

The background to *Clayton v Clayton* concerned Simon Clayton, a 47-year-old bookseller from Hay-on-Wye in 2003, who abducted his seven-year-old daughter shortly before

---

122 *Marckx v Belgium* (1979) 2 EHRR 330 or *McKennitt v Ash* [2006] EWCA Civ 1714 – in respect of Article 8 ECHR.
123 FPR 2010 r. 27.11(2)(f) (re-enacting the provisions introduced by the Family Proceedings (Amendment) (No.2) Rules 2009/85); see also: Practice Direction (Family Proceedings: Media Representatives) [2009] 1 WLR 1111 on the previous provision in FPR 1991 r. 10.28 in the same terms as FPR 2010 r. 27.11(2); s 32 of the Matrimonial and Family Proceedings Act 1984; s 61 Senior Courts Act 1981.
124 [2006] EWCA Civ 878.
125 Ibid. at para. 137 (Sir Mark Potter P).

his divorce hearing, fearing he would lose custody to his wife. He was tracked down to Portugal and brought home under arrest, after which he fought a lengthy custody battle. Mr Clayton found he was legally barred from publishing a book about his case because it would disclose the identity of his daughter.[126] Mr Clayton had become a 'fathers for justice' pressure group spokesman and had asked the courts for the child anonymity and reporting restrictions orders to be lifted. The Court allowed Mr. Clayton's appeal to publish the book. The court took account of the Article 8 right of the child but ruled in favour at Article 10 ECHR.

In family proceedings, if a media representative applies to the judge to see documents referred to during proceedings, the judge may exercise the disclosure jurisdiction to grant the application. The position is to be contrasted with that in civil proceedings governed by the Civil Procedure Rules (CPR), which do not apply to most family proceedings. In such cases, where hearings take place in open court, there is what may be described as a presumption in favour of providing to third parties documents which were relied upon by the court in reaching its decision, though not the entire court file. This is not so in most ward proceedings and where the death of a child by neglect is involved.

In Re J (Children) (2012)[127] – Sitting in the Court of Appeal – Lord Justice McFarlane had said that unjustifiable delays in the lower courts meant it was too late, in the interests of the children of the family, for any investigation into claims and counterclaims going back eight years.[128] The case concerned the horrifying death of a three-week-old baby T-L, found to be dead in the bed of her parents in hostel accommodation in South Wales on 29 March 2004. Post-mortem examination showed that during her short life this baby had sustained some 17 fractures to her ribs a week or more prior to her death, together with bruising to her face, a shoulder and arm. She was also suffering from serious untreated nappy rash. The cause of death was asphyxia by obstruction of her airways, the precise mechanism being unascertained. JJ was T-L's mother and SW her father.

This appeal (by the local authority) was concerned with the 'possibility of perpetrator or perpetrators' who could be found – on the balance of probabilities – to have caused 'significant harm' to the child (with view towards criminal charges). The CA was dealing with the concept of a 'pool of possible perpetrators', where the evidence at the family court hearing before HHJ Masterman had been insufficient to identify one or other possible perpetrator as being 'the' perpetrator. After the CA dismissed the appeal, the case was heard before the Supreme Court in 2013. Lady Hale in her leading judgment found that the fact that an individual is in the pool of potential perpetrators of harm to a child is one of the many facts which may be relevant to the exercise of prediction of future harm to another child. She said that a possibility that a parent had harmed a child in the past is not, by itself, sufficient to establish the likelihood that s/he will cause harm to another child in the future.[129] The appeal was again dismissed. It then followed that should SW start a new family, any children in his care also could not be removed solely on the basis of his inclusion in the pool of possible perpetrators of the harm caused to T-L.

---

126 Section 97(2) Children Act 1989 prohibits publication of material likely to identify 'any child as being involved in any proceedings'.
127 Re: J (Children) [2012] EWCA Civ 380 at para. 142 (Lord Justice McFarlane).
128 Ibid. at paras 136–138.
129 Re J (Children) [2013] UKSC 9 (Lady Hale).

4.5.2 Reporting on divorce proceedings

Have high-profile divorce proceedings been granted greater access to open media report-ing since the introduction of Part 2 of the Children, Schools and Families Act 2010? Or do the rich and famous still manage to resort to privacy orders in order to keep their divorces and potential settlements out of the public eye by resorting to *in camera* proceedings? The intention of the 2010 Act was to create a more open and visible justice system in the previously closed family courts by allowing the media access to ensure accountability through professional and public scrutiny of court decisions and thereby increase public confidence in the way the family courts work.[130]

Divorce cases do not attract automatic anonymity as we know from the famous ruling in *Scott v Scott*.[131] At the divorce proceedings of Sir Paul McCartney and Heather Mills, Bennett J ruled against their lawyers' application for *in camera* proceedings. The open court judgment of 18 March 2008 was the first to be made available online, reported widely in the media that the former Beatle had to pay a lump sum settlement of £16.5m to his ex-wife whom he had been married to for seven years.[132] However, the ward proceedings concerning their child Beatrice were held in private (referring to: *Re KD (A Minor) (Ward: Termination of Access)* (1988);[133] *Re W (A Minor) (Wardship: Restrictions on Publication)* (1992);[134] *Re M & N (Minors) (Wardship: Publication of Information)* (1990),[135] *Re Z (A Minor) (Identification: Restrictions on Publication)* (1996)[136]).

The Children and Families Act 2014 aimed to further reform and improve the family justice system, in particular reducing delays in proceedings and encouraging families and divorcing couples to use the courts as a last resort to resolve disputes.[137]

The acrimonious divorce proceeding of rock star Liam Gallagher and All Saints singer Nicole Appleton took only 68 seconds. Their undefended petition for a 'quickie divorce' at the Principal Registry of the High Court in London in April 2014 was widely reported as their substantial assets were read out in open court.[138] The court had refused the couple's application for reporting restrictions.

However, in 2015 lawyers for the billionaire oligarch and Russian friend of President Putin, Arkady Rotenberg, managed to persuade Mr Justice Moor to grant the Rotenbergs ano-nymity during their divorce dispute.[139] Natalia and Arkady Rotenberg were divorced in Rus-sia in 2013, but, after the English court gave her permission to, the wife claimed financial provision from the husband in England under the jurisdiction provided by the Matrimonial Causes Act 1973, Part III. At a hearing at the High Court, London, in 2015, Mr Rotenberg

---

130 Part 2 s 13 Children, Schools and Families Act 2010 ('Authorised news publication').
131 [1913] AC 417.
132 Source: 'Sir Paul McCartney and Heather Mills divorce: Judge's full ruling to be made public', by Caroline Gammell and Matthew Moore, *Daily Telegraph*, 18 March 2008.
133 [1988] FCR 657.
134 [1992] 1 WLR 100.
135 [1990] Fam 211, in which a local newspaper intended to publish a story concerning the removal by a local authority of two wards from a long-term foster home without explanation. The CA accepted that there was a clear public interest in knowing more of why the decision to remove had been taken and implemented in this manner. But the welfare of the children dictated that the identity of the children, their previous foster parents, the new foster parents, the parents, the schools and any relevant addresses should not be published.
136 [1996] 2 FCR 164 (CA).
137 Section 17(3) of the Crime and Courts Act 2013 also created a single Family Court for England and Wales which operates more efficiently for court users in a single court centre.
138 *Appleton (Nicole) and Gallagher (Liam) v (1) News Group Newspapers Ltd (2) The Press Association* [2015] EWHC 2689 (FAM).
139 R v R [2016] EWHC 2073 (Fam) (Moor J).

successfully argued that he could not be ordered to make a divorce payout to the 37-year-old socialite because his EU assets had been frozen. He also asked the first-instance judge to make reporting restrictions which permitted very limited publication of the judgment in the proceedings in a manner which identified the parties' names and where the wife was living (in Surrey). The anonymity order prevented anyone from reporting the divorce dispute and also banned any mention that Mrs Rotenberg lived in Britain, even though she was broadcasting her socialite lifestyle, including trips to Royal Ascot and charity galas, on Twitter and Instagram. The Russian media, however, freely reported on the couple.

The anonymity order was opposed by The Times, arguing that the Russian couple were seeking protection afforded to almost no British citizen, and it was a matter of public interest that one of Mr Putin's closest allies was litigating his affairs in the British courts.[140] After a number of cross-appeals, the order was eventually discharged by the trial judge, but Mr Rotenberg appealed to the Court of Appeal in a bid to retain it. Although that court dismissed his appeal, it continued to protect his anonymity while he tried to pursue a further appeal to the Supreme Court.[141]

The CA cited the issue of anonymity in matrimonial financial provision proceedings on appeal in Norman v Norman (2017),[142] where the principal judgment was given by Gloster LJ in February 2017. The CA concluded in Norman that the principles and approach to anonymization which are applicable to the Court of Appeal in general apply in like manner to cases relating to matrimonial financial provision and that it will be very rare for the court to order anonymization in such a case. Whilst the balance under Article 8 and the right to freedom of expression under Article 10 still fails to be struck, on appeal the principle of open justice and its importance, together with the normal principle in favour of openness, will only be curtailed in exceptional circumstances.[143]

The CA in R v R and Times (2017) dismissed Mr Rotenberg's appeal, and on 23 February 2018 the Supreme Court gave brief reasons for rejecting Mr Rotenberg's appeal against the lifting of the reporting restriction. Technically, the three Justices of the Supreme Court were simply refusing his application for permission to appeal. Mr Rotenberg had come to the end of the road.[144]

So, have the family court reforms gone far enough in terms of open justice and media reporting? After the Clayton victory it could be argued that the opening up of the family courts has been a positive development, though the 2010 Act itself still poses many exemptions and procedural complications, often too complex and time consuming to allow media presence in family courts (see: Re Child X (Residence and Contact — Rights of media attendance) (2009);[145] Re A (a child) and B (a child) (Contact) (No 4) (2015)[146]).[147]

---

140 Source: 'Putin crony Arkady Rotenberg loses right to secrecy in Britain', Sean O'Neill, The Times, 24 February 2018.

141 R v R (1) and Times Newspapers Ltd. (2) [2017] EWCA Civ 1588 (CA) (sub nom. Arkady Rotenberg divorce case).

142 [2017] EWCA Civ 49.

143 Ibid. at para. 56 (Gloster LJ).

144 Rotenberg v Times Newspapers Ltd UKSC (2017/0192) 23 February 2018 (Lady Hale Lord Sumption Lord Hughes).

145 [2009] EWHC 1728 of 14 Jul 2009 (Fam).

146 [2015] EWHC 2839 (Fam) (Case No: FD08P01237) Judgment 14 October 2015 (Cobb J); following on from F1 and F2 (father 1 and father 2) v (1) M1 and M2 (mother 1 and mother 2); (2) A (a child) and B (a child) (by their Guardian) [2013] EWHC 2305 (Fam) 31 July 2013. All judgments were handed down in private and published in a redacted form (removing identifying features of the family).

147 For further discussion see: Bessant, B. (2018) pp. 7–24.

FOR THOUGHT

'Secrecy in the court system is a growing concern. The press has a duty to uphold the principle of open justice and act as the eyes and ears of the public in the courts. *The Times* will resist any attempts to erode those principles' (Pia Sarma, Editorial Legal Director for Times Newspapers, in 'Putin crony Arkady Rotenberg loses right to secrecy in Britain', *Times*, 24 February 2018). Discuss this statement with reference to leading authorities.

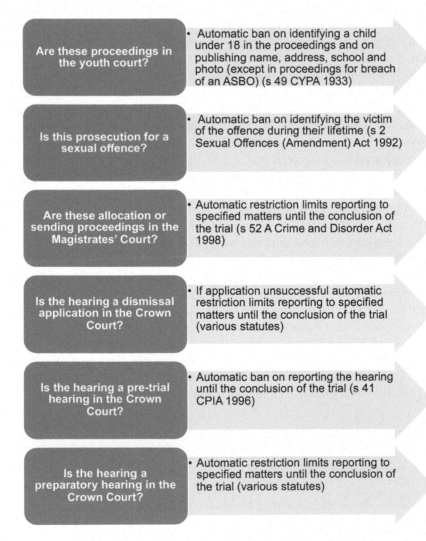

Figure 4.2 Reference guide to automatic reporting restrictions

4.5.3 The Court of Protection (COP)

The COP deals with 'capacity' (i.e. mental health) cases and the right to refuse treatment. The general rule is that the COP sits in private (in camera) (see: *Independent News and Media Ltd v A* (2010);[148] also: *Sugar v BBC* (2010)[149]).

In rare cases the media (or any person) may be permitted to attend a private hearing or part of it. More recently the COP has ordered a hearing or part of a hearing to take place in open court; if it does so, the court retains wide statutory powers to order reporting restrictions to protect identities and/or restrict publication of information. On an application to admit the media the court must state 'good reason' for permitting the media's attendance. The balance lies between the competing Convention rights engaged – namely the Article 8 rights of the individual who is the subject of the proceedings and, where relevant, the Article 8 rights of his family and the Article 10 rights of the media (see: *London Borough of Hillingdon v Neary* (2011)[150]).

In *Re Press Association* (PA) (2014) Jackson J lifted a COP anonymity order on 63-year-old Linda in June 2014. Ms McKenzie, a Jehovah's Witness, had rejected a blood transfusion and any treatment with blood products and had died on 26 February 2014. This followed an earlier hearing where Jackson J ruled it was lawful to refuse treatment.[151] The PA argued that the dead woman could be named since she could no longer be 'injured' by publicity and did not have relatives who might be distressed by reading about her in the press.

Although published judgments may be read by anyone on the internet, the media has a vital role in bringing COP proceedings to wider public awareness, such as *Re V* (2016);[152] or *Re T* (*Adult: Refusal of Treatment*) (1993)[153]) (see also: *An NHS Trust and others v Y* (*by his litigation friend, the Official Solicitor*) *and another* (2018);[154] also: *Re F* (*Mental Patient: Sterilisation*) (1990);[155] also: *Airedale NHS Trust v Bland* (1993)[156]).

Re V (with specific reference to an earlier hearing in *Re C*[157]) made tabloid headlines in January 2016. The *Daily Mail* (and other newspapers) had referred to C as a 'woman who had lost her sparkle'. Upon being diagnosed with breast cancer in December 2014 aged 49, C had refused to take medication prescribed for the disease because 'it made her fat'. Kings College NHS hospital trust had argued she did not have the mental capacity to make the decision to die. MacDonald J decided that C did have the capacity to make that decision and therefore dismissed the application of the Trust.[158] C was therefore entitled to refuse the treatment and died on 28 November 2015.

---

148 [2010] EWCA Civ 343.
149 [2010] EWCA Civ 715.
150 [2011] EWHC 413.
151 *Press Association v Newcastle upon Tyne Hospitals Foundation Trust* [2014] EWCOP 6 (Jackson J).
152 *V v Associated Newspapers Ltd, Times Newspapers Ltd, Independent News and Media Ltd, Telegraph Media Group Ltd and Associated Press* [2016] EWCOP 21 (Case No COP1278226) in the matter of proceedings brought by Kings College NHS Foundation Trust concerning C who died on 28 November 2015 COP, 24 April 2016.
153 [1993] Fam 95 at 102 (Lord Donaldson).
154 [2018] UKSC 46 (On appeal from: [2017] EWHC 2866 (QB)).
155 [1990] 2 AC 1.
156 [1993] AC 789.
157 See: *Kings College Hospital NHS Foundation Trust v C and V* [2015] EWCOP 80.
158 Ibid. at paras 98–100 (MacDonald J).

MacDonald J had given permission for the judgment to be published and expressly pointed out that there were strict anonymity orders in place provided by a schedule available to the media (known as the 'Pilot Order').[159] The media had then 'cherry-picked' some sections from the judgment in the 'Pilot Order' which they then sensationalized, such as C's lifestyle, reported as 'impulsive and self-centred', the fact that C had four marriages and a number of affairs and spent her husbands' money on lovers. The Daily Mail called her 'reckless', focusing on her 'excessive' consumption of alcohol, her material possessions and 'living the high life'.[160] Lawyers for the dead woman argued for a posthumous anonymity order to protect her daughters and a grandchild and the newspapers appealed. Charles J stated that the order must remain in place until all her children and the grandchild were 18.[161]

4.6 Military courts and inquests

The conduct of English soldiers was for many centuries regulated by the Court of the High Constable and Earl Marshal. From 1521 onwards, it was the 'Court of the Marshal', and after the standing army had been brought into being in Cromwellian times the office of Judge Advocate General was created in 1666 to supervise 'Courts-martial'. Court martial proceedings have been held in continuous succession ever since and were expanded to cover the United Kingdom, that is the Royal Air Force, the Royal Navy, and all British land, air and naval forces overseas. The Court Martial has global jurisdiction over all service personnel and civilians subject to service discipline (e.g. family members, civilian contractors, teachers, administrative staff when serving abroad) and hears all types of criminal cases including murder and serious sexual offences.

Historically the responsibilities of the Judge Advocate General (JAG) were very wide and included oversight of both prosecution and defence arrangements as well as the court. Since 1948, the role has concerned the court martial process.[162] The Armed Forces Act 2006 established a single system of service law and created the Court Martial as a standing court. It came into effect on 31 October 2009. The JAG is Head of the Service Justice System. There is also a Vice-Judge Advocate General (V-JAG) and several Assistant Judge Advocates General (A-JAGs). All the judges are civilians, appointed from the ranks of experienced barristers or solicitors in the same way as circuit judges. In court the judges wear legal costume, comprising a bench wig and black gown, with a tippet (sash) in army red with navy blue and air-force blue edges.

A coroner's inquest is a formal legal inquiry into the medical cause and circumstances of a sudden or unexplained death. Coroner's courts are held in public and follow the open justice principle.

---

159 The 'Transparency Pilot Order' provided reporting restrictions in serious medical treatment cases.
160 Source: 'Woman, 50, who lived for "looks, money and men" wins right to refuse life-saving kidney treatment because she doesn't want to be poor, old or ugly', by Keiligh Baker, Daily Mail, 1 December 2015.
161 ReV [2016] EWCOP 21 at para. 177 (Charles J).
162 The current JAG is Jeff Blackett J who is also a circuit judge and who formerly served in the Royal Navy.

4.6.1 The court martial

A Court Martial is a public court with similar powers to a Crown Court. It can impose prison sentences, fines or other forms of justice depending upon the nature of the crime. A court martial hearing is presided over by a Judge Advocate and a board of up to seven military members, individuals with no legal training much like a jury in civilian courts. In line with the government's 'transparency and open data initiative', the Military Court Service now publishes all court martial results in respect of the military court centres.

Charges are brought by the Service Prosecuting Authority (SPA), an independent prosecuting authority dealing with all criminal cases and offences contrary to military discipline. The SPA fulfils its functions in support of the operational effectiveness of the British Armed Forces throughout the world. The role of the SPA is to review cases referred to it by the Service Police or Chain of Command and prosecute that case at Court Martial or Service Civilian Court where appropriate. The SPA will also act as respondent in the Summary Appeal Court and represent the Crown at the Court Martial Appeal Court. A Judge Advocate arraigns each defendant and conducts the trial which is broadly similar to a civilian Crown Court trial in all cases, even when dealing with a minor disciplinary or criminal offence.

The jury, known as 'the board', comprises between three and seven commissioned officers or warrant officers depending on the seriousness of the case. Having listened to the Judge Advocate's directions on the law and summary of the evidence, they are responsible for finding defendants guilty or not guilty.

Serious matters – such as war crimes – including both offences against the civilian criminal law and specifically military disciplinary offences – *may* be tried in the Court Martial, which is a standing court.

4.6.2 The trial of *Marine A*

One of the most high-profile court martials was that of *Marines A–E*. Reporting restrictions and complete anonymity orders on the (initially) five accused were strict, since Judge Advocate General, His Honour Judge Jeff Blackett, had ordered a complete anonymity and reporting ban on 13 October 2012 on all five marines.[163]

The background to *Marines A–E* was the murder of an injured Taliban fighter in Afghanistan on 15 September 2011, when Royal Marine 3 Commando Brigade was based in Helmand. After the initial arrest of nine Marines by the Service Police in Helmand province video footage was found on a Marine's laptop that showed members of 3 Commando Brigade discussing what to do with a wounded gunman caught inside a compound in Helmand. Four Marines were later released without charge. The remaining three Marines could have been tried in a civilian court (as had happened in at least one case arising from the operations of HM Armed Forces in Iraq). However the decision was made by the SPA that the Marines should be prosecuted under the court martial system.

---

163 The order was made under r. 153 Armed Forces (Court Martial) Rules and s 11 Contempt of Court Act 1981.

This was the first time UK servicemen had been charged with a war crime in modern military history, and media interest was heightened, following the *Baha Mousa* atrocity. The death and torture of hotel receptionist Baha Mousa in Basra by British troops in 2003 had cast a dark shadow over the British army's reputation. Mousa had been arrested by British soldiers looking for insurgents, taken into custody for questioning and 36 hours later ended up dead. The shameful circumstances were revealed in Sir William Gage's public inquiry report and only increased the media's interest in reporting on court martial proceedings.[164] Mousa suffered at least 93 injuries prior to his death, and seven British soldiers were charged in connection with the case. Six were found not guilty. Corporal Donald Payne pleaded guilty to inhumane treatment of a prisoner and was sentenced to a year in prison and dismissed from the army.[165]

On Friday 8 March 2013, three Marines (A, B and C) were arraigned by Blackett HHJ and pleaded not guilty to a joint charge of murder of an Afghan insurgent in September 2011.[166] The trial commenced on 23 October 2013 at Bulford Military Court Centre, and the Ministry of Defence (MOD) advanced reasons for the complete anonymity orders on all Marines. One was that the Taliban's killing would be used for their own propaganda purposes. Another concern was the impact on the wider mission: British troops needed to remain in Afghanistan for another two years. The Press Association (PA) appealed against the complete reporting ban.[167] However, the anonymity orders stayed in place on all five defendant Marines.

In the end, Marine A was found guilty of murdering the Afghan insurgent on 5 December 2013, and Blackett J lifted all reporting restrictions so Sergeant Alexander Wayne Blackman, 39, could be named. The other two Marines, found not guilty, were also named as Corporal Christopher Watson and Marine Jack Hammond. The Judge Advocate General sentenced Blackman to serve a life sentence of at least ten years in a civilian prison. Blackman was also dismissed with disgrace from Her Majesty's Service.

The Court Martial found that Blackman's suggestion that he thought the insurgent was dead when he discharged the firearms was made up after he had been charged with murder. Although the insurgent may have died from his wounds sustained in the engagement by the Apache, Blackman gave him no chance of survival. The board found that Sergeant Blackman intended to kill the Afghan soldier and that Blackman's shooting had hastened his death. The video transcript revealed Blackman saying:

> Shuffle off this mortal coil, you c**t,

and instructing his fellow Marines:

> Obviously this doesn't go anywhere, fellas . . . I've just broken the Geneva convention.[168]

---

164 Baha Mousa Public Inquiry Report 2011 – all three volumes at: www.gov.uk/government/publications/the-baha-mousapublic-inquiry-report.

165 For further discussion see: Williams, A.T. (2012).

166 s 42 Armed Forces Act 2006.

167 R v Marines A–E (2012) Case Number 2012 CM 00442 (Court Martial – before the Judge Advocate General) 6 November 2012.

168 Quotation taken from Sergeant Blackman's appeal against sentence in R v Marines A, B, C, D & E [2013] EWCA Crim 2367 (CA) at para. 32.

Following Sergeant Blackman's conviction, the *Daily Mail* launched an appeal to 'free' the Marine with more than 30,000 supporters donating more than £750,000 by October 2015. Author Frederick Forsyth was spearheading the 'campaign for justice' for Sergeant Blackman.[169]

On 6 December 2016 the Criminal Cases Review Commission referred the murder conviction and sentence of former Royal Marine Alexander Blackman to the Courts Martial Appeal Court.

On 15 March 2017 the Court Martial Appeal Court quashed Blackman's murder conviction and replaced it by a verdict of manslaughter by reason of diminished responsibility.[170]

4.6.3 The coroners' system and inquests

The number of registered deaths in England and Wales has been relatively static over the last few years and has been around 500,000 Per annum. Most of these deaths are from natural causes, certified as such by a general practitioner or hospital doctor. But in every case where it is not clear that the death is from natural causes, it must be reported to the coroner. The Coroners and Justice Act 2009 reformed the coroners' inquiry system with new rules on 1 February 2010.[171]

All coroner's inquests are open to the public and the media (unless otherwise ordered). A coroner can exclude the public and the media from an inquest where issues of national security are involved (see below Litvinenko Inquest). An inquest into a death can be held with or without a jury. In 2016–2017 there were 576 inquests held with juries, a downward trend compared with previous years. The number of jury inquests is approximately 1 per cent of all inquests.[172]

The Chief Coroner's Report for England and Wales (2017) stated that 229,700 deaths were reported to coroners in 2017, the lowest level since 2014 – down 5 per cent (11,500) compared to 2016. There were 574 deaths in state detention.[173] In 2017, 31,500 inquests were opened – down 18 per cent compared to 2016.[174]

The Chief Coroner also supervises arrangements for major cases involving deaths overseas, such as the inquests arising out of the deaths of 30 British holidaymakers in Sousse, Tunisia, in a terrorist attack on 27 June 2015. These inquests were conducted by His Honour Judge Nicholas Loraine-Smith and took place at the Royal Courts of Justice in London with the proceedings made available through various satellite courtrooms in England and Wales to enable families living a distance from London more fully to participate. The inquest concluded on Tuesday 28 February 2017 with conclusions of unlawful killing in relation to each death.

---

169 Source: 'Fighting fund for jailed Marine tops £750,000: More than 30,000 generous readers help his battle for justice', by Sam Greenhill, *Daily Mail*, 5 October 2015.

170 *R v Blackman (AlexanderWayne* [2017] EWCA Crim 190.

171 Ministry of Justice (2013).

172 Source: Ministry of Justice (2017) Report of the Chief Coroner at paras 42–45.

173 Deaths comprised 298 in prisons, 10 in police stations, 1 in immigration removal centres, 252 Mental Heath Act detention cases, 1 in probation approved premises, 2 whilst on temporary release on licence for medical reasons, and 10 where released from custody within the last seven days in 2016–2017. Coroner's Report at para. 45. See the inquest into prisoner Stephen Chambers, who committed suicide in his cell at Preston Prison: *Chambers (Miss Rebecca) (by her mother and litigation friend Mrs Deborah Chambers) v HM Coroner for Preston and (1) West Lancashire and National Offender Management Service for HM Prisons and (2) Mrs Pauline Chambers* [2015] EWHC 31 (Admin).

174 Ministry of Justice (2017) Report of the Chief Coroner.

In exceptionally high-profile cases such as the inquests into the deaths in 1997 of Diana, Princess of Wales and Emad El-Din Mohamed Abdel Moneim Fayed (Mr Dodi Al Fayed), a senior member of the judiciary is appointed. Lord Justice Scott Baker was appointed in 2007 as Assistant Deputy Coroner for Inner West London for the purposes of the 'Diana and Dodi Al Fayed' inquests. Lady Justice Hallett was appointed Assistant Deputy Coroner for the Inner West London District of Greater London in order to conduct the inquests into the so-called 7/7 London terrorist bombings in which 56 people were killed on 7 July 2005.

Coroners' inquiries (or inquests) deal with:

- violent or unnatural deaths;
- deaths in prison or police custody;
- unexplained deaths after post-mortem;
- deaths abroad where the body is repatriated to the UK.

A high-profile inquest concerned the *Hillsborough Inquests* (2014–2016).[175] The background was the Hillsborough Football Stadium disaster on 15 April 1989 when over 50,000 people had travelled to Hillsborough (home of Sheffield Wednesday Football Club) to watch the FA Cup semifinal between Liverpool and Nottingham Forest. Ninety-six people died as a consequence of the crush in the stands, hundreds more were injured and thousands traumatized.

Over the two years the jury of six men and three women heard evidence from more than 600 witnesses about the design of the Hillsborough Football Stadium, the disorganized South Yorkshire Police operation and the delayed emergency response. There had been an inquiry led by Taylor LJ in 1989, resulting in the blaming of the Liverpool fans and a finding of accidental deaths of the victims.[176] *The Sun*, under the editorship of Kelvin MacKenzie, became famous for its hostile coverage at the time, blaming Liverpool fans under the banner headline 'THE TRUTH'; it read:

Drunken Liverpool fans viciously attacked rescue workers as they tried to revive victims of the Hillsborough soccer disaster, it was revealed last night.

Police officers, firemen and ambulance crew were punched, kicked and urinated upon by a hooligan element in the crowd.

Some thugs rifled the pockets of injured fans as they were stretched out unconscious on the pitch.[177]

A new inquest was ordered by Parliament in 2012 to be held before a jury, following the tireless efforts by the 'Hillsborough Family Support Group'.[178] The original verdict of accidental death was quashed in December 2012. The Rt Hon Sir John (now Lord)

---

175 The inquests (for there were a number of these) began on 31 March 2014 at a purpose-built coroner's courthouse in Warrington, Cheshire, with a verdict by nine members of the jury on 26 April 2016.

176 The Rt Hon Lord Justice Taylor (1989) The Hillsborough Stadium Disaster, 15 April 1989, Interim Report.

177 Source: *The Sun*, 19 April 1989, pp. 1–2.

178 *Attorney General v (1) HM Coroner of South Yorkshire (East) (2) HM Coroner of West Yorkshire (West)* [2012] EWHC 3783 (Admin) (sub nom. 'Hillsborough Inquest No 2').

Goldring was appointed as Assistant Coroner for South Yorkshire (East) and West Yorkshire (West) to conduct the new inquests.[179]

The *Hillsborough Inquests* jury's verdict on 26 April 2016 was that the 96 football fans had been 'unlawfully killed'. Reasons given were grave police error, causing the dangerous situation at the turnstiles, and failures by commanding police officers to prevent the crush in the stands. Chief Superintendent David Duckenfield was found to be responsible for opening the gates during the Hillsborough disaster and was one of the key figures facing criminal charges. Mr Duckenfield was match commander at the 1989 FA Cup semifinal. Under the law at the time, there could be no prosecution for the death of the 96th victim, Tony Bland, because he died more than a year and a day after his injuries were caused.[180]

The inquest jury also found that Sheffield Wednesday Football Club failed to approve the plans for dedicated turnstiles for each pen, with inadequate signage at the club and misleading information on match tickets. Following the jury verdict, *The Sun* headlined:

> *Hillsborough: The real truth.* Cops smeared Liverpool fans to deflect blame, new probe says 41 lives could have been saved. The Sun says: We are profoundly sorry for false reports and families of 96 victims call for prosecutions.[181]

Following the *Hillsborough Inquest* jury's findings, the Chief Constable of the South Yorkshire Police, David Crompton,[182] sought to judicially review the decision making of the Commissioner for South Yorkshire and the Police and Crime Commissioner for South Yorkshire (PCC) to suspend him on 27 April 2016. The Chief Constable argued on the grounds that those decisions were irrational, disproportionate, took account of irrelevant considerations and breached his rights under Article 8 ECHR.[183] Mr Crompton was successful in his claim, and the decisions of the police bodies were regarded as 'wholly disproportionate'. All decisions by the police bodies were quashed by the Administrative Court at Judicial Review, and the Chief Constable was duly reinstated.[184]

On 10 September 2018, former match commander at Hillsborough, Chief Superintendent David Duckenfield, 74, pleaded not guilty to the manslaughter by gross negligence of 95 Liverpool supporters at Preston Crown Court. At the subsequent ten-week trial at Preston Crown Court of Hillsborough match commander David Duckenfield, the jury was unable to reach a verdict in April 2019. Jurors heard that 96 men, women and children died as a result of a fatal crush on the Leppings Lane terrace at the Hillsborough Stadium on 15 April 1989. Lawyers for Mr Duckenfield said they opposed any application

---

179 House of Commons (2012b).
180 *Airedale N.H.S. Trust v Bland* [1993] AC 789. Tony Bland was an 18-year-old Liverpool FC supporter who travelled with two friends to Sheffield Wednesday's Hillsborough football ground for the FA Cup semi-final match on 15 April 1989. He was caught in the stadium crush which reduced him to a persistent vegetative state (PVS). He had been in this state for three years and was being kept alive on life support machines. Medical professionals declared that Bland had no hope of recovery. The hospital with the consent of his parents applied for a declaration to the High Court that it might lawfully discontinue all life-sustaining treatment and medical support measures designed to keep him alive in that state, including the termination of ventilation, nutrition and hydration by artificial means. The court (affirmed by the HL) granted the declaration.
181 Source: *The Sun*, 26 April 2016.
182 The Claimant, David Crompton, was appointed Chief Constable of South Yorkshire on 24 January 2012. Prior to the conclusion of the Hillsborough Inquest, Mr Crompton had indicated an intention to retire from the post of Chief Constable in November 2016. He had had no involvement in South Yorkshire Police at the time of the Hillsborough disaster.
183 See: *R (on the Application of David Crompton) v Police and Crime Commissioner for South Yorkshire and HM Chief Inspector of Constabulary and South Yorkshire Police and Crime Panel* [2017] EWHC 1349 (Admin) (before Lady Justice Sharp and Mr Justice Garnham).
184 Ibid. at paras 176–178 (Graham J).

from prosecutors for a retrial. Ex-Sheffield Wednesday club secretary Graham Mackrell, 69, was convicted of failing to discharge his duty under the Health and Safety at Work Act 1974, by a majority of 10 to 2.

The *Litvinenko Inquest* became a high profile and highly secretive investigation, ordered by the then Home Secretary, the Rt Hon Theresa May MP, on 22 July 2014. Former High Court Judge, Sir Robert Owen, chaired the inquiry into the death of Alexander Litvinenko.

Mr Litvinenko's death was a deeply shocking event. The inquest was eventually set up after the widow of the former KGB spy, Marina Litvinenko, had fought for more than seven years to persuade the courts to order the inquest. Marina Litvinenko told the High Court that only a public inquiry would uncover the Russian state's alleged role in her husband Alexander's death on 23 November 2006 from radiation poisoning by polonium-210.[185] Police, national security and counter-terrorism investigations, involving the assistance of 17 countries and frequent visits by police officers to Russia, resulted in highly confidential reports to the investigating coroner at the time (2006–2007).

Sir Robert Owen's report was published (with large sections redacted because evidence had been given under public interest immunity [PII]) on 21 January 2016.[186] Although an inquest (or 'inquiry') cannot assign civil or criminal liability, the report established that the fatal dose of polonium-210 was probably consumed by Mr Litvinenko on 1 November 2006 when he was in the company of Andrey Lugovoy and Dmitry Kovtun at a hotel in London. Sir Robert Owen was unequivocal in his finding that Lugovoy and Kovtun killed him. In spite of sustained efforts to extradite both suspects from Russia to the UK, the Russian authorities have refused on the ground that the Russian constitution prohibits the extradition of its own nationals.[187]

4.6.3 Fatal Accidents Inquiry in Scotland

There is no system of coroners' inquests in Scotland. Fatal accidents; deaths of persons in legal custody; sudden, suspicious and unexplained deaths and deaths occurring in circumstances giving rise to serious public concern are overseen by the Procurator Fiscal who decides whether a Fatal Accident Inquiry (FAI) should be held in accordance with s 1(1) of the Fatal Accidents and Sudden Deaths etc. (Scotland) Act 2016. Such a FAI is conducted by a Sheriff.[188] The purpose of a FAI is to:

1   establish the circumstances of the death; and
2   consider what steps (if any) might be taken to prevent other deaths in similar circumstances.[189]

---

185   See: R (on the application of Marina Litvinenko) v Secretary of State for the Home Department and (1) Assistant Coroner for Inner North London (2) Commissioner of Police of the Metropolis (3) Investigative Committee of the Russian Federation [2014] EWHC 194 (Admin) (sub nom. 'the Litvinenko Inquest').
186   See: Litvinenko Inquiry, The (2016) Report into the death of Alexander Litvinenko, by Sir Robert Owen: https://assets.publishing.service.gov.uk/government/uploads/system/uploads/attachment_data/file/493860/The-Litvinenko-Inquiry-H-C-695-web.pdf.
187   Ibid. at paras 2.17–2.21.
188   For a list of Fatal Accident Inquiries (FAI) see: www.scotcourts.gov.uk/search-judgments/fatal-accident-inquiries.
189   s 1(3) Fatal Accidents and Sudden Deaths etc (Scotland) Act 2016.

It is not purpose of an inquiry to establish civil or criminal liability. After hearing and considering all the evidence the Sheriff makes a determination as to the circumstances, namely:

1   when and where the death occurred;
2   when and where any accident resulting in the death occurred;
3   the cause or causes of the death;
4   the cause or causes of any accident resulting in the death;
5   any precautions that could reasonably have been taken, and
6   any other facts which are relevant to the circumstances of the death.[190]

For example, the death in custody at Glenochil Prison of Stanley Sandison on 17 December 2016 at 12:04pm in his cell (born on 24 February 1947), where Sheriff David Mackie determined in August 2018 that Mr Sandison's death was caused by ischaemic heart disease, a coronary artery atheroma and obesity.[191]

4.7 Secret courts and public interest immunity

Historically, there has always been a certain amount of collaboration between the UK government and the media that has offered a compromise between national security and press freedom. Introduced in advance of World War I, the 'D notice' system became a peculiarly British arrangement between government and the press, in order to ensure that journalists did not endanger national security. It was described as 'a gentleman's agreement', an appropriately quaint term which recalls the most famous news blackout of all — the affair between Edward VIII and the American divorcee, Wallis Simpson, in 1936. A 'DA notice' (Defence Advisory Notice), later called a 'Defence Notice' (D notice), remains an official request to news editors not to publish or broadcast items on specified subjects for reasons of national security.[192] Today, the government D notice system is still intended for stories deemed to affect national security.

The accountability of MI5 and MI6 and the question of whether they are fully subject to the rule of law lie at the heart of attempts by the media to sweep away the secrecy surrounding terrorism trials since the 9/11 (2001) attacks in the United States and 7/7 (2005) bombings in London.

It is fair to say, until the revelations by America's former contractor to the National Security Agency (NSA) and whistle-blower Edward Snowden, most people had no idea of the extensive legislative powers of Britain's digital spy agency, the Government Communications Headquarters (GCHQ) and how close its ties were with NSA. Snowden had copied and leaked top-secret classified information from the NSA without authorization to the British newspaper the *Guardian* and Germany's *Der Spiegel* in 2013 that both GCHQ and the NSA were spying on all international government executives.

---

190 s 26 of the 2016 Act.
191 *Sheriffdom of Tayside Central and Fife at Alloa* [2018] FAI 34 ALO-B51/18. Determination by Sheriff David Mackie under the Inquiries into Fatal Accidents and Sudden Deaths etc. (Scotland) Act 2016 into the death of Stanley Sandison.
192 For a detailed discussion see: Wilkinson, N. (2015).

The protection of the UK intelligence and security services in relation to terrorism legislation became even more apparent in the *David Miranda* case (2016).[193] Miranda, the partner of the then *Guardian* journalist Glenn Greenwald, had been detained by security forces at Heathrow Airport in 2013 for carrying secret information by Edward Snowden. The Court of Appeal held Miranda's detention lawful but the clause under which he was held as incompatible with the European Convention on Human Rights. Lord Dyson, who made the ruling with Richards and Floyd LJJ, said the powers contained in Schedule 7 of the Terrorism Act 2000 were flawed.

The *Miranda* ruling was seen as an indisputable victory for press freedom. The CA balanced the needs of security and the rights of journalists, that police anti-terror powers to stop and question travellers in and out of the UK were incompatible with Article 10 rights; furthermore, Mr Miranda should have had the protection of a public interest defence against his detention.

4.7.1 Public interest immunity

The UK legislation on 'Crown Privilege' – which later became public interest immunity (or PII) – was largely developed in civil cases, dating back to both world wars (see: *Conway v Rimmer* (1968);[194] *Burmah Oil v Bank of England* (1980);[195] *Air Canada v Secretary of State for Trade* (No 2) (1983)[196]).

PII is a common law rule of evidence, meaning that documents may be withheld from parties to legal proceedings when their disclosure would be injurious to the public interest (i.e. national security). PII applications are routinely made and authorized by a Minister of State – such as the Home Secretary or Secretary of State for Justice and Lord Chancellor (a combined position).

In the World War II case of *Duncan v Cammell Laird*,[197] involving the *Thetis* submarine disaster, documents were requested, including blueprints of the submarine. The HL unanimously agreed that a court could never question a claim of 'Crown Privilege' made in the proper form regardless of the nature of the documents to which it referred. It was held that ministers of the Crown were to be the sole arbiters of the public interest. The case attracted considerable criticism in Parliament at the time (see also: *Glasgow Corporation v Central Land Board* (1956)[198] and the *Burmah Oil* case (1980)[199]).

In highly sensitive cases the prosecution will apply for a PII certificate where the prosecution contends that it is not in the public interest to disclose any sensitive material. The PII application must state why the material should be withheld (i.e. why the public interest in withholding it outweighs the public interest in disclosure).

The courts' current view of PII claims remains complex. Ministers have claimed on a number of occasions that where disclosure is imperative in the interests of justice, claims that

---

193 R (on the application of Miranda [David]) v (1) *Secretary of State for the Home Department* (2) *Commissioner of Police of the Metropolis* [2016] EWCA Civ 6 (CA Civ Div) 19 January 2016.
194 [1968] AC 910.
195 [1980] AC 1090.
196 [1983] 2 AC 394.
197 [1942] AC 624.
198 [1956] SC 1 (HL) – when the HL held that the Scottish courts could go behind a minister's certificate and, after weighing private interests against public ones, decide for themselves whether or not a particular item of evidence should attract immunity on public interest grounds.
199 [1980] AC 1090.

documents be withheld on the ground that their disclosure would inhibit candour of communication are unlikely to succeed. Well-supported claims for immunity on class grounds are likely to be respected, but no class of document is automatically immune from disclosure.

The shortcomings of this unsatisfactory regime were vividly exposed by the CA's groundbreaking decision in the Judith Ward case.[200] The effect of Ward's miscarriage of justice was to require the prosecution, who sought to claim PII for documents helpful to the defence, to give notice of the claim to the defence so that, if necessary, the court could be asked to rule on the legitimacy of the prosecution's asserted claim.[201]

The procedural implications of PII applications for non-disclosure were re-defined by Lord Taylor of Gosforth CJ in R v Davis (1993)[202] and R v Keane (1994).[203] The court identified three types of cases. In the first and most frequent case, the prosecution must notify the defence of the application and indicate at least the category of material held and the broad ground of the PII claim. In the second class of cases, the prosecution contend that the public interest would be injured if disclosure were made even of the category of the material. In this category, the prosecution must still notify the defence that an application to the court is to be made, but the category of the material need not be specified: the defence will still have an opportunity to address the court on the procedure to be adopted, but the application will be made to the court in the absence of the defendant or anyone representing him. The third class comprises 'highly exceptional' cases where the public interest would be injured even by disclosure that an ex parte application is to be made. This application would be without notice to the defence. This procedure was enshrined in statute in the Criminal Procedure and Investigations Act 1996 ('the CPIA regime').

Part 5 of the Criminal Justice Act 2003 amended the above CPIA regime and came into force on 4 April 2005 which means that the prosecution now has to disclose material 'which might reasonably be considered capable of undermining the case for the prosecution . . . or of assisting the case for the defence'.[204]

In the case of Edwards and Lewis v UK (2004)[205] the European Court considered the ex parte PII procedures adopted in those cases violated the applicants' right to a fair trial (Article 6 ECHR). The defence cases involved allegations of entrapment by the police, and the ECtHR held that the ex parte (without notice) process was not a fair way to deal with the issues as the courts had to make findings of fact before deciding on disclosure. Those findings of fact were reached after hearing only one side – the prosecution. The Strasbourg Court suggested the appointment of a 'special' or 'independent' counsel (now 'Special Advocat') to argue the defendant's case which is now used by the UK courts in closed material proceedings (see below).

---

200 R v Ward (Judith) [1993] 1 WLR 619. Ward (25) was convicted to life imprisonment for killing 12 people aboard an army coach which exploded on the M62 motorway in February 1973. Judith Ward spent 18 years in prison before her conviction was quashed in 1992. For a detailed discussion see: Walker, C. and Starmer, K. (1999); see also: Mansfield, M. (2010).
201 Ward, J. (1993).
202 [1993] 1 WLR 613.
203 [1994] 1 WLR 746.
204 s 32 CJA 2003.
205 Edwards and Lewis v United Kingdom (App no 39647/98, App no 40461/98) ECHR 2004-X (2004) 40 EHRR 593 (ECtHR).

4.7.2 Secret trials, closed material proceedings and the role of the Special Advocat

R v H & C (2004)[206] was the first British case that successfully relied on the argument of Special (or Intermediary) Counsel. The House of Lords laid down further guidelines for judges considering disclosure and PII, thereby limiting the use of Special Counsel to exceptional cases only.

Powers to hold secret court hearings were introduced in July 2013 under section 61 of the Justice and Security Act 2013 (JSA) (known commonly as the 'the Secret Courts Act') so that trials could take place in civil courts without damaging national security.

Part 1 of the Act provides for oversight of the UK security services, the Secret Intelligence Service, the Government Communications Headquarters (GCHQ) and other activities relating to intelligence or security matters, including the parliamentary 'Intelligence and Security Committee'. Part 2 – the most controversial provision of the 2013 Act – makes provision for the 'closed material procedure' (CMP) involving the (non-)disclosure of sensitive material in trial proceedings.

An application for CMP proceedings is usually made by the Secretary of State in civil proceedings.[207] The High Court (or Court of Session Outer House in Scotland) then makes a declaration – an 'in principle' decision – whether or not a CMP should be available in the case. An application for a declaration is usually supported by some (but not necessarily all) of the relevant sensitive material.[208] A Special Advocat is appointed by the court to represent the interests of the claimant.[209] But the advocate cannot reveal precise details of the evidence held against the claimant; the advocate can only provide the 'gist' of the allegations against the claimant, which means, once the matter comes to criminal proceedings, the claimant may not be aware of all the allegations made against him. Although relatively small in number, the cases include some of the most politically sensitive cases heard in UK courts.

One such CMP application involved 'IRA mole' Martin McGartland[210] (now under new identity) who, together with his partner and carer Joanne Asher, was suing MI5 for breach of contract and negligence in his aftercare following a shooting by the IRA which left him unable to work. The then Home Secretary, Theresa May, had applied for a declaration under CMP that her lawyers should be allowed to give evidence in secret to defend the damages claim in the High Court. The former undercover agent of the Royal Ulster Constabulary (RUC) Special Branch (1987 and 1991) claimed the MI5 security service failed to provide care for his post-traumatic stress disorder and access to disability benefits.[211]

Three CA justices unanimously agreed that secret hearings are lawful, provided they are 'scrutinised with care' and discontinued if they become 'no longer in the interests of the fair and effective administration of justice'.[212] A second application, heard at the

---

206 [2004] 2 AC 134.
207 s 6 Justice and Security Act 2013 (JSA).
208 s 12(1) JSA.
209 s 11 (4) JSA.
210 *McGartland (Martin) and Asher (Joanne) v Secretary of State for the Home Department* [2015] EWCA Civ 686, 14 July 2015 (CA).
211 McGartland, M. (2009).
212 *McGartland* [2015] EWCA Civ 686 at para. 10 (Richards LJ, Lewison LJ and McCombe LJ).

same time, was that of *Ahmad Sarkandi*[213] and four other Iranians, subject to asset-freezing orders, who sued Foreign Secretary Philip Hammond for damages under the HRA 1998. The *McGartland* ruling enabled government ministers to defend themselves against damages claims (under CMP) while using secret hearings to prevent sensitive material being revealed in evidence in open court. Critics have condemned the ruling as a serious aberration from the tradition of open justice (see also: *Al Rawi v Security Service* (2012)[214]).

IRA and Al Qaeda related terrorism cases are now regularly heard in secret. PII and CMP hearings usually cite the safeguarding of national security as a precautionary approach. In the deportation case, *Secretary of State for the Home Department v Rehman* (2001),[215] Lord Slynn held that such decisions are primarily ones for the discretion of the Secretary of State.[216]

The leading case in common law in advance of security and terrorism legislation was that of *Chahal* (1996).[217] It involved the deportation of a Sikh separatist, Karamjit Singh Chahal (born 1948), back to India for national security reasons; he had entered the UK illegally in 1971 (the Home Office granted him leave to remain in 1974). Chahal was held in Bedford Prison from 1990 for deportation. He argued violation of his Article 3 ECHR right, that he would face torture at the hands of the Indian authorities. Though there was no question of secret evidence being used against him, the High Court simply could not look at the material that the Home Secretary had used as the basis for his deportation order before the 'three wise men' – Special Immigration Appeals Commission ('SIAC').[218] The Strasbourg Human Rights Court unanimously upheld Mr Chahal's complaint; not only was there a real risk of torture once he was returned to India, but also a breach of procedure under Article 5(4) ECHR because he could not challenge the secret evidence against him[219] (see also: *A and others v Secretary of State for the Home Department* (2004)[220]).

Closed 'secret court' hearings are now widespread. They are both *ex parte* and *in camera*, where the court considers closed or secret evidence laid by the security services. Closed hearings involve the exclusion of one party, as well as members of the public and the press. It is known that defendants in terrorism trials have been convicted on the basis of 'secret evidence': that is, evidence from anonymous witnesses. Secret evidence can now be used in a wide range of cases, including deportation hearings, parole board cases, asset-freezing applications, pre-charge detention hearings in terrorism cases, employment tribunals and even planning tribunals. The essential test of whether a case involves secret evidence or not is whether both parties have seen and had an equal opportunity to challenge all the evidence

---

213 R (*on the application of Sarkandi and Others*) v *Secretary of State for Foreign and Commonwealth Affairs* (Case No T3/2014/2545) EWCA Civ 686, 14 July 2015 (CA).
214 [2012] 1 AC 53 (HL).
215 [2001] UKHL 47 (HL).
216 Ibid. at para. 8 (Lord Slynn).
217 *Chahal and Others v UK* (1996) 23 EHRR 413 (ECtHR). The second applicant, Darshan Kaur Chahal (born 1956), living in Luton, came to England on 12 September 1975, following her marriage to the first applicant in India. The applicant couple had two children, Kiranpreet Kaur Chahal (born in 1977) and Bikaramjit Singh Chahal (born in 1978), who were the third and fourth applicants. By virtue of their birth in the UK, the two children had British nationality.
218 Under s 15 Immigration Act 1971.
219 *Chahal* (1996) 23 EHRR 413 at paras 130–131.
220 [2004] UKHL 56 (HL) ('Belmarsh case').

that is considered by the court in making its decision.[221] So long as the defendant has disclosure of all the evidence that is used by the court, then no question of the use of secret
evidence arises.[222]

In *Re Guardian News and Media Ltd* (2010),[223] the press and other media organizations
made an application for open reporting on appeals involving five individuals. Four of
them, A, K, M and G, were appellants; the fifth, HAY, was the respondent and cross-appel-
lant in an appeal by the Treasury. The Supreme Court set aside the anonymity order in the
case of G, naming him as Mohammed al-Ghabra (his identity was already in the public
domain). A, K and M, all brothers, had been informed on 2 August 2007 that they were
all subject to an asset-freezing order.[224]

HAY was concerned that his identification would lead to the jigsaw identification of his
wife and children, who would suffer adverse consequences from the Egyptian authorities.
The Guardian argued that articles about him had appeared in the press and Al-Jazeera broadcasts since 1999 (referring to *Youssef v Home Office* (2004),[225] which contained details about
him). M's identity was kept anonymized. Lord Rodger, in delivering the Supreme Court
judgment, concluded that there was no justification for making an anonymity order in
HAY's case and he was duly named as Mr Hani El Sayed Sabaei Youssef (or Hani al-Seba'i).

The approach in *Re Guardian News and Media Ltd* was encouraging: it meant that open
reporting in sensitive terrorism trials, including asset-freezing orders, could inform the
public regarding the complexity of terrorism trials. It would also encourage a wider debate
about state funding of terrorism. M was eventually named as Michael Marteen (formerly
known as Mohammed Tunveer Ahmed) (see also: *A v UK* (2009);[226] *Secretary of State for the
Home Department v AF and others* (2009);[227] *Secretary of State for the Home Department v AHK* (2009)[228]).

In 2009 the UK Treasury passed secondary legislation under the Counter-Terrorism
Act 2008, namely the Financial Restrictions (Iran) Order 2009. The main purpose of the
order was to shut down the UK operations of *Bank Mellat*[229] and its subsidiaries. Bank Mellat applied to the High Court in London to set the order aside.[230] Some of the evidence
in court was heard 'in secret' because the UK government had suspected that the Tehran-
based bank had financed firms involved in Iran's nuclear programme since 2009.

In *Bank Mellat*,[231] the appeal before the Supreme Court was primarily concerned with
the use of a closed material procedure (CMP) where the Treasury argued that the evidential

221 Section 3(1)(a) Criminal Procedure and Investigations Act 1996 (as amended by s 32 Criminal Justice Act
2003): the prosecution must disclose any material 'which might reasonably be considered capable of undermining the case for the prosecution against the accused or of assisting the case for the accused'.
222 *Secretary of State for the Home Department v AHK and others* [2009] EWCA Civ 287 (as per Clarke MR).
223 *Guardian News and Media Ltd and others in Her Majesty's Treasury v Mohammed Jabar Ahmed and others* (FC); also cited as: *HM Treasury v
Mohammed al-Ghabra* (FC); *R (on the application of Hani El Sayed Sabaei Youssef) v HM Treasury* [2010] UKSC 1 of 27 January 2010.
224 Under Article 4 Terrorism (United Nations Measures) Order 2006.
225 [2004] EWHC 1884 (QB).
226 [2009] Application No 3455/05 [GC], judgment of 19 February 2009 (ECHR).
227 [2009] UKHL 28.
228 [2009] EWCA Civ 287.
229 Bank Mellat (بانک ملت, lit. People's Bank) is a private Iranian bank, established in 1980, with a paid capital
of Rials 33.5bn as a merger of ten pre-revolution private banks, comprising Tehran, Dariush, Pars, Etebarat
Taavoni & Tozie, Iran & Arab, Bein-almelalie-Iran, Omran, Bimeh Iran, Tejarat Khareji Iran and Farhangian.
The bank's capital amounted to Rials 13,100bn (July 2016), one of the largest commercial banks in the
Islamic Republic of Iran, ranking among the top 1,000 banks of the world.
230 Under s 63 Counter-Terrorism Act 2008.
231 *Bank Mellat v Her Majesty's Treasury (No 1)* [2013] UKSC 38 (on appeal from: [2011] EWCA Civ 1).

material was so sensitive that it required the court to sit in a closed hearing. The Supreme Court allowed the bank's appeal and thereby quashed the Iran bank sanctions. The court criticized the secret hearings. Lord Neuberger commented on the use of closed material procedures:

> A [closed hearing] should be resorted to only where it has been convincingly dem-
> onstrated to be genuinely necessary in the interests of justice. If the court strongly
> suspects that nothing in the closed material is likely to affect the outcome of the
> appeal, it should not order a closed hearing.[232]

The ruling in *Bank Mellat* was seen as a severe setback for the government's enthusiasm for secret courts.

One of the most secret trials in UK legal history was that of London law student Erol Incedal (2016),[233] a British citizen also holding a Turkish residency permit. Known initially only as 'AB', he and his friend, Mounir Rarmoul-Bouhadjar ('CD'), were charged with planning terrorism offences.[234] Nicol J ruled on 19 May 2014 that the entirety of the criminal trial of both defendants should be in private and the publication of reports of the trial be prohibited.[235] But following a partly successful appeal by *The Guardian* and other media organizations to lift the injunctions and anonymity orders, the CA allowed for limited reporting of proceedings and the identification of both defendants.

Incedal and Rarmoul-Bouhadjar's trial went ahead at the Old Bailey ('Central Crimi-nal Court', London). Only accredited journalists were allowed to hear some of the secret evidence in locked sessions; their notebooks were retained by the court, and they could not write about the trial. More than a third of the prosecution case was held in complete secrecy with the jury told they could face imprisonment under 'contempt' legislation if they ever revealed what they had heard. Part of the evidence alleged that Incedal had planned an attack on Tony or Cherie Blair and that he had been involved in the terrorism attack on the Taj Hotel in Mumbai on 28 November 2008. The jury failed to reach a ver-dict on Incedal. After a retrial in October 2015, a second jury acquitted him of all charges. Rarmoul-Bouhadjar pleaded guilty to possessing a 'terrorism' manual – identical to that found on Incedal. He was sentenced to three years' imprisonment.[236]

The CA in *Incedal* (2016) set the precedent for a fundamental departure from the principle of open justice, whereby secret courts and CMP were held as 'strictly necessary' in terrorism cases. This meant that any public accountability for matters relating to the prosecution could not be achieved through the media in its function as 'watchdog' of the public interest.

Following a number of applications by the media to reveal the identity of the accused and trying to expose courtroom secrecy to protect MI5 and MI6, a practice direction was

---

232 Ibid., judgment at paras 119, 126, 133, 173 (Lord Neuberger).
233 *Guardian News and Media Ltd and Ors v R and Erol Incedal* [2016] EWCA Crim 11 (CA Crim Div) 9 February 2016 ('Erol Incedal' case) (on appeal from: *Guardian News and Media Ltd; Associated Newspapers Ltd; BBC; BSkyB Ltd; Express Newspapers; Independent Print Ltd; ITN; Mirror Group Newspapers Ltd; News Group Newspapers Ltd; Telegraph Media Group; Times Newspapers Ltd; Press Association v Erol Incedal and Mounir Rarmoul-Bouhadjar* [2014] EWCA Crim 1861 (Case No T2013/7502) 24 Sep-tember 2014 (formerly known as *R v AB and CD*) (Gross LJ, Simon and Burnett JJ).
234 Charged under s 5 Terrorism Act 2006 ('preparation of terrorist acts') and an offence contrary to s 58 Terror-ism Act 2000 ('collection of information').
235 *Erol Incedal* [2014] EWCA Crim 1861.
236 *Guardian News and Media Ltd v Incedal* [2016] EWCA Crim 11 eleven.

issued on 14 January 2019 by the Lord Chief Justice, The Rt Hon The Lord Burnett of Maldon on 'Closed Judgments' (CMP):

1 This Practice Direction applied to any Court of Tribunal giving a 'closed' judgment following a closed material procedure, whether pursuant to the provisions of Part 1 of the Justice and Security Act 2013, in the High Court, the Divisional Court or the Court of Appeal; in proceedings in relation to Terrorism Prevention and Investigation Measures (TPIMs); in any Tribunal established under the Tribunals, Courts and Enforcements Act 2007 and in any appeals therefrom.

2 A single printed copy and an electronic copy of each closed judgment and any related open judgment must be lodged with the RCJ Senior Information Officer within 14 days of being delivered or handed down, for consideration for inclusion in the library of closed judgments now established in the Royal Courts of Justice.

3 If it is decided to retain the judgment in the library, the relevant judge(s) or tribunal judge(s) will be informed. If the judgment is *not* to be retained, it will be disposed of securely.

4 Both printed and electronic judgments must at all times be maintained under secure handling provisions as set down in *Closed Judgments Library* – Security Guidance of 2017, a copy of which can be obtained from the RCJ Senior Information Officer.[237]

We can then conclude that any issues relating to terrorism offences will usually be tried in secret courts, leaving the evidence by the intelligence and security services unchallenged and unreported.

FOR THOUGHT

You are representing an Indian citizen with residency in the UK. Your client supports the campaign for an independent Sikh state in the Punjab. The Home Secretary wishes to deport Mr Ravinder Singh to India because the Secretary of State claims that Singh's support for Sikh independence and his past known activities mean that he is a serious threat to national security in the UK, particularly given the current concerns over terrorist activity. Mr Singh tells you that he will be tortured if returned to India. He also fears for his wife and two children who live with him in Wembley. On his last return to India some six years ago, he was arrested and detained by the Punjab police for 21 days and allegedly tortured. Later on, he was released without charge. Make an application to the High Court opposing your client's deportation and for a hearing in open court.

---

237 This Practice Direction is set out in Part 1 of Schedule 2 to the Constitutional Reform Act 2005 and under s 5 Civil Procedure Act 1997, ss 74 and 81 Courts Act 2003 in respect of the Courts of England and Wales. It is made under the procedure set out in s 23 Tribunals, Courts and Enforcement Act 2007 in respect of the First-tier and Upper Tribunals. Made by the Lord Chief Justice on 14 January 2019.

4.7.3 Investigatory powers and data retention legislation

The Data Retention and Investigatory Powers Act 2014 (DRIPA) – introduced by then Home Secretary, Theresa May, in July 2014 – required internet and phone companies to keep their communications data for a year, thereby granting access to police and intelligence agencies to personal data if necessary. DRIPA consolidated interception powers that existed under the Regulation of Investigatory Powers Act 2000 (RIPA) and Wireless Telegraphy Act 2006.[238] The new legislation followed the recommendations in the David Anderson Report of Britain's anti-terrorist legislation.[239]

In July 2015 Tom Watson MP (Labour) and David Davis MP (Conservative) success-fully challenged the lawfulness of DRIPA in that it was inconsistent with EU law.[240] They had argued that the legislation was incompatible with Article 8 ECHR ('right to privacy') and Articles 7 and 8 of the EU Charter of Fundamental Rights ('respect for private and family life' and 'protection of personal data'). Davis and Watson said that DRIPA had allowed the police and security services to 'snoop' on citizens without sufficient privacy safeguards.

The High Court ruling declared section 1(a) and (b) of DRIPA inconsistent with EU law.[241] The unlawful sections remained in force until the end of March 2016. DRIPA remained in force until December 2016.

Following the *Davis and Watson* ruling Theresa May introduced the Investigatory Powers Bill (known as 'the Snoopers' Charter') (now the Investigatory Powers Act 2016). The Act provides the framework to govern the use and oversight of investigatory powers by law enforcement and the security and intelligence agencies. A controversial measure of the Act is that internet service providers (ISPs) are forced to store personal browsing records for 12 months and allow bulk collection of internet traffic.

There are three main measures in the Investigatory Powers Act 2016:

1   The powers already available to law enforcement, security and intelligence agencies are brought together in the Act to facilitate data collection and personal commu-nications data in bulk form.
2   It introduces a 'double-lock' safeguard for interception warrants: the warrant has to have the Secretary of State's authorization as well as a judge's approval.
3   Provision for the retention of internet connection records for law enforcement to identify the communications service to which a device has connected.

The biggest objection to the 2016 Act is that it provides GCHQ with unlimited pow-ers to 'investigate' without adequate control mechanisms for the executive. Arguably,

---

238   The Act also provided for secondary legislation to replace the Data Retention (EC Directive) Regulations 2009 while providing additional safeguards. This was in response to the ECJ judgment of 8 April 2014 (Grand Cham-ber) in joined cases *Digital Rights Ireland Ltd v Minister for Communications, Marine and Natural Resources, Minister for Justice, Equality and Law Reform, The Commissioner of the Garda Síochána, Ireland and the Attorney General* (C-293/12) and *Kärntner Landes-regierung, Michael Seitlinger, Christof Tschohl and Others* (C-594/12) ('Digital Rights Ireland' case), which declared the Data Retention Directive (2006/24/EC) invalid.

239   Independent review of British Terrorism Legislation by David Anderson QC at: https://terrorismlegislationre-viewer.independent.gov.uk.

240   *R (on the application of (1) David Davis MP (2) Tom Watson MP (3) Peter Brice (4) Geoffrey Lewis) v Secretary of State for the Home Department and Open Rights Group; Privacy International; The Law Society of England and Wales* [2015] EWHC 2092 (Admin) High Court of Justice, 17 July 2015 (QB).

241   *Davis and Watson* [2015] EWHC 2092 (Admin) at para. 114 (Bean LJ and Collins J).

increasing terrorism-type legislation imposes growing reporting restrictions on court proceedings as secret courts and closed material applications infringe the open justice principle and contravene the media's freedom of expression under Article 10 ECHR. While the British legislature has historically been reluctant to interfere with the freedom of the press, reporting restrictions have been brought in by stealth via counter-terrorism legislation passed since 9/11 and the London bombings in July 2005. Not only broadcasting and print regulations have been affected but also online media coverage.

An independent review, commissioned by the then Prime Minister Theresa May in January 2018, was tasked with looking at ways to safeguard the future of the UK's free, independent and high-quality news in the digital age. The review led by academic and former economics journalist, Dame Frances Cairncross, called for evidence and views from both consumers and the media industry on current issues, including how to create and support the conditions that would enable high-quality See Chap journalism to continue and flourish in the digital age (The Cairncross Review 2018).

 FOR THOUGHT

> Does the public interest in reporting proceedings in a terrorism trial at a Crown Court outweigh the privacy and anonymity of the defendant who has not yet been found guilty? Discuss with reference to legislation and leading authorities.

4.8 Further reading

Bessant, C. (2018) 'Sharenting: balancing the conflicting rights of parents and children', *Communications Law*, 23(1), 7–24.
Claire Bessant closely examines children's rights to privacy by international law, including a right to privacy against their parents. The author looks at the long-lasting impact of parents now sharing information about their children on social media with friends, family and colleagues and what impact these online disclosures may have on the youngsters and the possible significance in law. She questions how the English courts and the ECtHR have responded to this recent phenomenon of 'sharenting', and the challenges it poses to children's privacy. Bessant looks at existing legal remedies available to anyone who objects to the online dissemination of people's personal, private or confidential information. She argues that in practice, where a child's privacy has been violated by their parents, their ability to obtain a remedy is, in some regards, potentially more limited than that of an adult whose privacy has been violated by a stranger. She finds that ECtHR jurisprudence and the English judiciary view parents as guardians of their children's privacy rather than as privacy threats, concluding that a court applying a 'reasonable expectation of privacy' test remains problematic for the child.

Blom-Cooper, L. (2008) 'Press freedom: constitutional right or cultural assumption?' *Public Law*, Summer, 260–276.
Fearless and trailblazing lawyer Sir Louis Blom-Cooper (1926–2018), who died in September 2018, was amongst other things the chairman of the Press Council (1989–1990). He supported the principle that there should be a requirement that newspapers accord a right of reply to those they attacked. He also called for a law against the

invasion of privacy, introduced changes to give complainants a better hearing and speed up adjudications and also introduced a code of practice for newspapers. In 1983, Blom-Cooper represented Stephen Raymond in the landmark case of *Raymond v Honey*,[242] where the HL established the right of convicted prisoners to have access to the courts and sue the prison authorities without first seeking the authorities' permission. This is one of his classic articles where Blom-Cooper explores the notion of press freedom by stating that the open justice system should prevail and that it is a citizen's right to freely and publicly criticize the executive and legislature. Sir Louis then develops the argument whether it is right that any court proceedings should be kept secret, wondering whether it is not the journalist's careful reporting on such proceedings which opens up the justice system to the public. The author also discusses the Leveson Report.

Smartt, U. (2015b) '"Why I was right to name the teachers' teen killer": naming teenagers in criminal trials and law reform in the internet age', *Communications Law,* **20(1), 5–13.**
The author of this book discusses existing (and at times confusing) legislation regarding reporting restrictions on children and young persons in criminal court proceedings. She compares the media coverage on Will Cornick with that of the Jamie Bulger killers, Venables and Thompson, and asks whether the public interest test is now overriding youth anonymity orders.

Smartt, U. (2018) 'The three Rs: Remorse, Rehabilitation, Right to be forgotten: how de-listing is left up to the courts in *NT1 & NT2* **and** *AR v Chief Constable of Greater Manchester'*, *European Intellectual Property Review,* **804–811.**
The author re-examines the *Google Spain* (2014) ruling – the 'right to be forgotten' (RTBF) – in the light of spent criminal convictions and acquittal at a rape trial and how it is left up to the courts to decide when an order for delisting or de-indexing can be made on operators of internet search engines. Smartt highlights the complexities of the Rehabilitation of Offenders Act 1974 (ROA) (in conjunction with changes made by the Legal Aid, Sentencing and Punishment of Offenders Act 2012 (LASPO)) and how legislation may conflict with the RTBF principle and interfere with an individual's privacy right under Article 8(1) ECHR. The author examines three privacy cases, all decided in 2018. and how the courts interpreted 'rehabilitation' and 'remorse' differently in the light of who can and cannot be 'delisted' (in the case of *NT2*) or not (in the case of *NT1*). In the case of AR, how an Enhanced Criminal Record Certificate (ECRC) can now show a rape acquittal (AR). Smartt argues that the courts have once again become moral rather than legal arbitrators in deciding an individual's right to privacy when it comes to delinking and delisting applications. Smartt argues that the ROA 1974 is not fit for the digital age and is too complex to interpret (for police forces) for delisting purposes and completion of an ECRC and a delisting order.

Wilkinson, N. (2015) *Secrecy and the Media: The Official History of the United Kingdom's D-Notice System.* **Abingdon, Oxon: Routledge.**
In his important and very readable book about the official history of the D notice system, retired Rear Admiral Nicholas Wilkinson explains that the Defence-notice system 'emerged amorphously across three decades of increasing concern about army and navy operations being compromised by reports in the British (and sometimes

---

242 [1982] AC 1.

foreign) press' (preface, xxi). It is rather ironic that Wilkinson book was itself subject to censorship by MI5, MI6 and GCHQ; the Foreign, Cabinet, and Home Offices; the Treasury Solicitor; and the Attorney General. The book was eventually published in 2009 without five chapters covering the period after Labour's return to power in 1997. Wilkinson provides an historical overview of spying, intelligence, secrecy and government – news media interaction over the course of almost the entirety of the twentieth century, starting with the Boer Wars – the conflicts between Britain and Afrikaaner settlers that determined the fate of Southern Africa.

Chapter 5

Contempt of court

> **Key points**
>
> This chapter will cover the following questions:
>
> o   What is the nature of contempt in UK law?
> o   What is common law contempt of court?
> o   What is statutory contempt?
> o   What is meant by active and *sub judice* proceedings?
> o   What are the general defences for the media when 'contempt' is alleged?
> o   What is the role of the Attorney General in contempt proceedings?
> o   What are the benefits of courtroom TV?

5.1 Overview

This chapter continues the theme of the open justice principle, already discussed in the previous chapter, and we now know that there are times when the court orders reporting restrictions, issues complete anonymity orders and can hold proceedings in private. This chapter discusses the strict liability offence of 'contempt of court' and the seriousness if members of the media (and indeed tweeting jurors) breach any such court orders. The Attorney General's role is then to bring 'contempt' proceedings against those who breach court privacy injunctions or lifelong anonymity orders (for rape for instance). The AG has recently taken a tough stance against those committing contempt by way of courts ordering high fines or even imprisonment for 'tweeting' jurors.

The debate whether suspects of historic child sexual abuse should be named in the media (prior to charge) is being considered, following the Jimmy Savile atrocities. Important (and at times rather confusing) reporting restrictions for juveniles and anonymity orders in criminal and non-criminal court proceedings are explained with plenty of case examples.

Finally, we will have a look at some innovative courtroom TV developments in the UK senior court system, possibly the most advanced open justice broadcasting system in Europe.

5.2 History: the common law of contempt

Contempt of court ('contempt') is the improper interference with the administration of justice. British contempt laws are possibly the strictest in the Western world. The American criminal justice system, for example, permits a whole genre of journalism to flourish during pre-trial periods (what we call the *sub judice* or 'active' period) when British reporters are constrained to remain silent by way of the strict liability rule under the Contempt of Court Act 1981 (CCA 1981). Coverage of the sexual assault charge against the French politician, Dominique Strauss-Kahn, for example, was permitted in graphic detail in advance of his trial in 2012 at a New York courthouse in Bronx Supreme Court. The former IMF chief subsequently settled the action and claims by Nafissatou Diallo, a 33-year-old former housekeeper, who had claimed that Strauss-Kahn sexually attacked her on 14 May 2011 at the Sofitel Hotel in Manhattan.

5.2.1 Contempt at common law

The concept of contempt was established at common law as 'an act or omission calculated to interfere with the administration of justice'.[1] The common law is still the starting point for determining what constitutes 'contempt', and case law has established the powers of courts to deal with contempt. Common law and statutory provisions ensure that any court – be it civil or criminal jurisdiction and certain tribunals, such as employment tribunals – is free to decide on the matters before it, without undue influence from the media.

Geoffrey Robertson QC defended the New Statesman magazine during the legal fallout of the sensational trial of Jeremy Thorpe MP. Thorpe, the leader of the Liberal Party between 1967 and 1976, was acquitted at the Old Bailey in May 1979 on charges of conspiracy and incitement to murder, arising from an earlier relationship with Norman Scott, a former model.[2] At that time there was no contempt legislation. Robertson argued later that Thorpe was acquitted because of the 'dirtiest deal in media history',[3] the significance of this deal was revealed by a jury member in the New Statesman. Shortly after the Thorpe trial and the 'Thalidomide' action (see below), Parliament passed the Contempt of Court Act 1981.

The publishers of the New Statesman were subsequently prosecuted by the Attorney General of the Thatcher government, Sir Michael Havers. The AG sought an order of contempt of court at common law following the publication in the New Statesman of a juror's account of significant parts of the jury's deliberations in the course of arriving at their verdict in the trial of the prominent politician. The application failed. Lord Widgery CJ held that the contents of the article did not justify the title of contempt of court. There were no special circumstances, other than publication of some of the secrets of the jury room, that called for condemnation. Robertson argued later that this victory was a 'victory for free speech' and freedom of the press (see also: Attorney General v Seckerson and Times Newspapers Ltd (2009)[4]).

See
below 5.5

The courts' jurisdiction to deal with contempt is divided into two broad categories: criminal contempt and civil contempt. In essence, a criminal contempt, such as contempt in the face of the court (see below 5.2.4), is an act which threatens the administration of

---

1   Fox, J.C. (1927), p. 394.
2   *Attorney General v New Statesman and National Publishing Company Ltd* [1981] QB 1 (sub nom. 'the Jeremy Thorpe trial').
3   Source: 'Here's another Jeremy Thorpe scandal – its chilling legacy in law', by Geoffrey Robertson QC, *Guardian*, 2 June 2018 (following the BBC TV dramatization of the Jeremy Thorpe trial, 'A Very English Scandal', starring Hugh Grant).
4   [2009] EMLR 371 (Admin).

justice. Courts are empowered to protect the administration of justice by acting on their own initiative, punishing those guilty of such contempt with detention in custody or a fine. Civil contempt involves disobedience of a court order or undertaking by a party who is bound by it. The court's sanction in civil contempt has been seen primarily as coercive or remedial. Civil contempt has largely arisen in respect of an order or undertaking made in civil litigation (see R v M (2008)[5]).

One of the leading authorities regarding 'contempt' can be found in Lord Diplock's words in the 'Thalidomide' case, AG v Times,[6] when he said:

> [contempt covers] particular conduct in court proceedings which tends to undermine that system or to inhibit citizens from availing themselves of it for the settlement of their disputes.[7]

This case involved decades of civil court actions by 'Thalidomiders' against the manufacturers and distributors of the drug thalidomide, Distillers Co. (Biochemicals) Ltd. The Sunday Times and its then editor Harold ('Harry') Evans (now 'Sir') had begun investigatory reporting on thalidomide victims and the 'atrocious' settlements offered to parents of the seriously malformed young children and babies born between 1958 and 1972.[8]

Five Law Lords overruled the CA and granted a contra mundum injunction to the Attorney General against the publishers of The Times, thereby restraining the newspaper and all other media organizations from publishing any matter which might prejudice present any future court proceedings.

After the Times publishers and Harry Evans lost their case in the House of Lords, they filed an application with the European Commission of Human Rights in 1978, claiming that the injunction infringed their right to freedom of expression guaranteed by Article 10 of the Convention.[9] The ECtHR held – by 11 votes to 9 – that the interference with the applicants' freedom of expression was not justified under Article 10(2) ECHR as a 'pressing social need' and could not therefore be regarded as 'necessary'. In the Thalidomide No 1 action, the Strasbourg Court extended the scope of Article 10(1) as conferring not only the right to 'impart' information and ideas but also the right to 'receive' them. The ECtHR also specifically identified Article 10(2) as 'maintaining the authority and impartiality of the judiciary' as a legitimate aim which may justify interference with freedom of expression.

In the Thalidomide No 2 action (1991)[10] the ECtHR reasoned that injunctions can be rendered useless due to publications in other countries, where the jurisdiction does not extend to cover their publications. Furthermore, injunctions granted to a single publisher can also cover other publishers, as it would frustrate the reason for the injunction, and

---

5 [2008] EWCA Crim 1901.
6 AG v Times Newspapers [1974] AC 273 ('Thalidomide').
7 Ibid. at para. 298 (Lord Diplock).
8 The original action concerned 466 victims, born between 1958 and 1961 to mothers who had taken the drug Distaval (first manufactured in Germany under the name Contergan by Chemie Grünenthal GmbH) for morning sickness in the early months of pregnancy. The first cases were settled out of court, but parents found that the ex gratia payments were not sufficient and not flexible enough to meet the young people's changing needs.
9 Sunday Times v UK (No 1) (1980) 2 EHRR 245 (ECHR) ('Thalidomide No 1') (ECtHR).
10 Sunday Times v UK (No. 2) (13166/87) (1991) ECHR 26 ('Thalidomide No 2') (ECtHR).

they could be in contempt of court for their actions. Ultimately, the Strasbourg Court held that the injunction in this case violated Article 10 (1) ECHR.

Following the *Sunday Times* ECtHR ruling in Thalidomide No 1, the UK Parliament rushed legislation through Parliament resulting in the Contempt of Court Act 1981.[11] On 23 December 2009, some 50 years after one of the worst disasters in medical history, the Thalidomiders finally received an apology from the UK government, followed by a £20m compensation package.[12]

At the same time as the thalidomide action in the UK courts, the Attorney General attempted to stop another publication, namely Peter Wright's autobiographical account of his time being a member of the British Security Service (MI5): *Spycatcher: The Candid Autobiography of a Secret Intelligence Officer*, published in Australia.[13] The AG of England and Wales attempted to prevent the book's publication and began litigation proceedings in the Australian courts arguing that the material of the book concerned allegations of improper, criminal and unconstitutional conduct on the part of MI5 officers and should be prohibited.[14]

The outcome of these proceedings was the court held that the material in *Spycatcher* was not entirely confidential since there had been other allegations made from other officers; thus, the publication of the book 'would not be detrimental to the British Government or the Security Service'.[15] Because of the worldwide availability of the book and the information contained within it, the CA reversed its earlier judgment and held that the injunctions were no longer necessary. In light of this, the *Sunday Times* and *Guardian* published the second serialization of the book.[16]

5.2.2 Civil contempt

Examples of civil contempt include disobedience of a court or undertaking by someone involved in litigation, and proceedings will normally be commenced by the other party aggrieved by it.

Civil contempt refers to conduct which is not in itself a crime, but which is punishable by the court in order to ensure that its orders are observed. Civil contempt is usually raised by one of the parties to the proceedings. Although the penalty for a civil contempt contains a punitive element, its primary purpose is coercion of compliance. A person who commits that type of contempt does not acquire a criminal record, and it is not a criminal offence, even if committed in connection with a criminal case (see: *Cobra Golf Inc v Rata* (1998)[17]; also *CTB v (1) News Group Newspapers Ltd and (2) Imogen Thomas* (2011)[18]).

---

11 Hansard, The Phillimore Report on 'Contempt', HC Deb 25 April 1978, vol. 948, cc 1340–1350.
12 Source: '50 years on, an apology to thalidomide scandal survivors', by Sarah Boseley, *Guardian*, 15 January 2010.
13 Wright, P. (1987).
14 *AG v Guardian Newspapers Ltd (No 1), AG v Observer Ltd, AG v Times Newspapers Ltd* [1987] 1 WLR 1248 ('*Spycatcher No 1*') at para. 14.
15 Ibid. at para. 21.
16 *AG v Guardian Newspapers Ltd., AG v Times Newspapers Ltd (No 2)* [1990] 1 AC 109 ('*Spycatcher No 2*').
17 [1998] Ch 109.
18 [2011] EWHC 1326 (QB) (later known as 'Ryan Giggs superinjunction' (2012)). The claimant (now known as footballer Ryan Giggs) had obtained a privacy injunction, but the name of the claimant had nevertheless been widey distributed on the internet and by the Scottish press. The defendant newspaper now sought to vary the terms. The second defendant did not oppose the injunction.

The only type of civil contempt the magistrates' court can deal with is the unauthorized use of disclosed prosecution material under s 17 of the Criminal Procedure and Investigations Act 1996 (CPIA). The maximum penalty the magistrates' court can impose for this is six months' imprisonment or a fine up to £5,000.

5.2.3 Criminal contempt

The procedure for criminal courts dealing with civil contempt (see above), which is less likely to occur in the face of the court, is set out in Rule 48.9 CrimPR. Contempt by breach of an undertaking is rarer in criminal proceedings than civil ones. Examples include failure to comply with restraint orders or Terrorism Act investigation orders in the Crown Court, or unauthorized use of disclosed prosecution material in the Magistrates' or Crown Court.[19] A further example would be where a sentence was mitigated on the basis of an undertaking made by someone to repay money stolen by the defendant. This could possibly also be a criminal offence such as perjury (where the undertaking is given on oath) or perverting the course of justice. Where the conduct may amount to a distinct criminal offence (particularly where it could amount to perjury, where the defendant has the right to jury trial) it would normally be appropriate to refer the matter to be investigated by the police, unless the maximum sentence available for the offence would not properly reflect the conduct in question.

In the Crown Court it applies where a party or other person directly affected alleges or the court deals on its own initiative with unauthorized use of disclosed prosecution material under s 17 CPIA, a failure to comply with a compliance order, restraint order, ancillary order or certain investigation orders under the Terrorism Act 2000 or the Proceeds of Crime Act 2002 and any other conduct with which that court can deal as a civil contempt of court. The Crown Court has an inherent power to imprison for a maximum of two years and/or impose a fine, and the same powers under s 18 CPIA 1996.

5.2.4 Contempt in the face of the court

This offence covers courtroom behaviour, such as being disrespectful to a bench of magistrates, wearing inappropriate clothing in the public gallery, the use of mobile phones and cameras in the courtroom (see: *DPP v Channel Four Television Co. Ltd* (1993)[20]).

The first published opinion on criminal contempt 'in the face of the court' was that of Wilmot J in *Rex v Almon* (1765)[21] He said:

> it is a necessary incident to every court of justice to fine and imprison for a contempt to the court, acted in the face of it.[22]

The issue of taking a mobile phone photograph in a courtroom was first addressed in R v D (*Vincent*) (2004),[23] still today prosecuted under the old legislation of section 41

---

19 See: CrimPR 15.8 and CrimPR Part 48.
20 [1993] 2 All ER 517.
21 (1765) Wilm. 243.
22 Ibid. at 254 (Wilmot J).
23 [2004] EWCA Crim 1271.

Criminal Justice Act 1925. The Act creates a contempt to take any photograph, make or attempt to make any portrait or sketch of a justice or a witness in, or a party to, any proceedings before a court (either in the courtroom or its precinct, such as the waiting room outside the courtroom or in the immediate circumference of the courthouse).

In this case, the juvenile appellant had taken three mobile phone photos at Liverpool Crown Court: one in the court canteen; one from the public gallery towards the witness box; and the third of his brother in the secure dock, also showing one of the security officers. The trial judge seized the appellant's mobile phone and charged him with the summary offence of criminal contempt. D was convicted and sentenced to 12 months' imprisonment; he appealed against sentence. The CA dismissed his appeal and Lord Aikens noted:

> a person could use photographs of members of the jury or a witness or advocates or even a judge in order to try to intimidate them or to take other reprisals. Witnesses who are only seen on a screen or who are meant to be known only by an initial could possibly be identified. The anonymity of dock officers or policemen who are involved in a case could be compromised if a photograph is taken and is used to identify them.[24]

Section 12 Contempt of Court Act 1981 (CCA) created two further statutory contempts:

- wilfully interrupting the proceedings; and
- otherwise misbehaving in court.

The Crown Court can issue proceedings for contempt 'in the face of the court' in the following circumstances:

- any contempt seen by the judge; or
- disobedience of a court order; or
- breach of an undertaking to the court.[25]

See
below 5.3.3

5.3 The Contempt of Court Act 1981: strict liability

The Contempt of Court Act 1981 (CCA) redefined and codified the strict liability offence of contempt of court in statute, which requires court proceedings to be 'active'.

Section 1 CCA provides for strict liability from the point a case becomes active. This is known as the period of *sub judice*, as set out in section 1 CCA:

> the strict liability rule means the rule of law whereby conduct may be treated as a contempt of court as tending to interfere with the course of justice in particular legal proceedings regardless of intent to do so.

The 'strict liability' rule is defined, whereby conduct may be treated as a 'contempt of court' if it tends to interfere with the course of justice in particular legal proceedings,

---

24 Ibid. at para. 15 (Lord Aikens).
25 DPP v Channel Four Television Co. Ltd [1993] 2 All ER 517.

regardless of intent to do so. This means even the most experienced journalist can fall foul of the law of contempt, even if he just wants to write a background piece to a forthcoming trial – it may well be that the publication is deemed to interfere with the course of justice. It is for this reason that every journalist, editor and publisher ought to be familiar with current contempt legislation.

Section 2(1) and (2) CCA ('Limitation of scope of strict liability') limits the scope of the strict liability rule, stating that it only applies to 'publications' including 'speech, writing and other communication in whatever form' which is addressed to the public at large. Only a publication which creates a 'substantial risk' of prejudice will be treated as 'strict liability' contempt. This is governed by case law.

A journalist, editor, broadcaster or publisher is not guilty of strict liability contempt if the publication amounts to fair and accurate reporting of legal proceedings held in public and published 'in good faith' (s 4(1) CCA).

Here are some examples of cases which are likely to attract national media interest and where strict liability contempt is particularly acute:

- *The defendant is famous* (e.g. when BBC broadcaster Stuart Hall admitted in May 2013 that he had indecently assaulted 13 girls during the 1960s, '70s and '80s).
- *The complainant is famous* (e.g. when ex-TV 'weathergirl' and TV presenter, Ulrika Jonsson, accused an ex-*Blue Peter* presenter of rape in 1988 in her autobiography, serialized in the *Daily Mail*).
- *The case is one of a serial rapist* (e.g. black cab driver John Worboys, who was convicted as a serial rapist in March 2009 for attacks on 12 women).
- *A high-profile cold case solved because of DNA advances* (e.g. the murder of BBC newsreader and presenter, Jill Dando, by gunshot outside her home in Fulham, West London, on 26 April 1999; Barry George was wrongly convicted of Dando's murder and spent eight years in prison; he lost his legal battle for compensation as a 'victim of a miscarriage of justice' in July 2013. Ms Dando's murder remains an unsolved crime).
- *Criminal appeal cases* (e.g. '*Marine A* case – see: *R v Blackman (Alexander Wayne) and Secretary of State for Defence* (2014);[26] the *Airline Bombers* case – see: *R v Abdulla Ahmed Ali and Others*) (2011).[27]

The main areas of the Contempt of Court Act 1981 are summarized below:[28]

- limits liability for contempt under the 'strict liability rule' (sections 1–7);
- deems jury interference as contempt (section 8);
- prohibits the use of tape recorders in court or bringing sound recording equipment into court without leave of the court and deems publication of a sound recording as a contempt (section 9);

26 [2014] EWCA Crim 1029 (CA Crim Div).
27 [2011] EWCA Crim 1260 (CA Crim Div).
28 Section 31(2) Crime and Courts Act 2013 inserted a new subsection (1A) into s 9 CCA.

- provides limited protection against contempt for a person refusing to disclose the source of information contained in a publication for which he is responsible (section 10);
- empowers magistrates' courts to deal with contempt in the face of the court by imposition of a fine or committal to custody for a maximum of one month or both (section 12);
- restricts the period of committal to prison for contempt where there is no express limitation to two years for a superior court and one month for an inferior court (section 14).

5.3.1 Active proceedings: *sub judice*

The risk of 'contempt' is most prevalent in criminal proceedings. The *sub judice* (or 'active') period starts when a summons has been issued or a defendant has been arrested without warrant (for serious indictable offences). Proceedings cease to be active where they conclude by either an acquittal or sentence or discontinuance of the charge.[29] During the *sub judice* period, the media can publish the following:

- the name of the accused;
- his or her address;
- the offence he or she is charged with.

In *Re B* (2006)[30] the CA had to decide whether publication of the defendant's name would create a serious risk of substantial prejudice to the fair trials of his remaining co-defendants. Could the media be trusted with fair and accurate reporting on the defendant's sentencing? This case concerned reporting restrictions post-conviction on Dhiren Barot on 12 October 2006, after he had pleaded guilty to conspiracy to murder. Indian-born Barot admitted in November 2006 at Woolwich Crown Court that he had planned to detonate a radioactive 'dirty bomb' and launch an attack on London's Underground and the Heathrow Express. Reporting restrictions were in place until the conclusion of the trial of his co-defendants. The judge was concerned that reports of Barot's sentencing would cause a risk of substantial prejudice to the trial of the co-defendants, as his reasons for sentence would give rise to a great deal of legitimate public interest and discussion. The CA ruled in favour of media reporting applying the principle in *Re Press Association*.

See Chapter 4.3

In July 2011, the *Daily Mirror* was fined £50,000 and the *Sun* £18,000 for contempt of court for articles published about a suspect arrested on suspicion of murdering Joanna

---

29 Schedule 1 paras 5 and 6 CCA; s 1 Powers of Criminal Courts (Sentencing) Act 2000; s 219 or 432 Criminal Procedure (Scotland) Act 1975; Article 14 Treatment of Offenders (Northern Ireland) Order 1976.
30 R v B [2006] EWCA Crim 2692 (CA) (sub nom. 'Re B').

Yeates.[31] The court ruled that the tabloid newspapers had seriously breached contempt laws with their reporting of the arrest of Christopher Jefferies, Yeates' landlord, who was later released without charge and was entirely innocent of any involvement.

The disappearance and tragic death of Miss Yeates during the Christmas period in 2010 had commanded enormous public interest and concern. Her body was discovered on 25 December, and much of the initial criminal investigation had focused on Yeates' landlord Christopher Jefferies. He was arrested on suspicion of her murder on 30 December. The front page of the Mirror of 31 December was headlined: 'Jo suspect is peeping Tom: Arrested landlord spied on flat couple', positively asserting that Mr Jefferies was a voyeur.[32] The Sun of 1 January 2011 carried the front-page headline 'Obsessed by death', alleging that Mr Jefferies 'scared kids' by a macabre fascination with Victorian murder novels. There were reports that Mr Jefferies might be gay, referring to him as a 'freak'. Further reports described him as 'Hannibal Lecter' and 'a little creepy'.[33] Both papers alleged that Mr Jefferies might be a paedophile. The court held that the material in the two tabloid publications was extreme and prejudicial and that the journalists and editors were guilty of 'strict liability' contempt under section 2(2) CCA.

Had Mr Jefferies been charged with Ms Yeates' murder, these articles would have provided Mr Jefferies with a serious argument that a fair trial would have been impossible. If he had been convicted, he would have argued on appeal that the trial was unfair because of the adverse publicity.[34]

Vincent Tabak, a 33-year-old Dutch engineer, was convicted of murdering his next-door neighbour Joanna Yeates and jailed for a minimum of 20 years in October 2011 at Bristol Crown Court.

We can find parallels with the Joanna Yeates murder coverage where trial by media has taken place, such as in the cases of Peter Sutcliffe (the 'Yorkshire Ripper' trial), Tom Stephens (the 'Suffolk Ripper' story), Colin Stagg,[35] Robert Murat[36] and Barry George.[37] In each case there were either contempt warnings by the Attorney General (or Solicitor General) to the media, or the newspapers were found guilty of contempt.

Once appeal proceedings have started, a journalist, broadcaster or publisher must adhere to the contempt legislation in the usual way.[38] Civil appellate proceedings are active from the time when arraignments for the hearing are made or from the time the hearing begins, until the proceedings are disposed of or discontinued or withdrawn.[39]

---

31 *AG v Mirror Group Newspapers Ltd and News Group Newspapers Ltd* [2011] EWHC 2074 (Admin) 29 July 2011 (Lord Judge LCJ, Thomas LJ and Owen J).
32 Ibid. at paras 5 and 6.
33 Ibid. at para. 8.
34 Though Lord Judge LCJ anticipated that any such appeal would have failed on the 'fade factor'.
35 Colin Stagg was wrongly accused of the killing Rachel Nickell in 1992. Robert Napper, a paranoid schizophrenic, confessed to Rachel Nickell's killing in December 2008.
36 Murat was accused by newspapers of killing or being involved in the disappearance of Madeleine McCann in Praia da Luz, Algarve on 3 May 2007. The Mirror Group Newspapers, Express Newspapers and Associated Newspapers were found guilty of contempt in 2008.
37 Barry George had been found guilty of the murder of TV presenter Jill Dando in 2001. He successfully appealed and was acquitted in November 2007.
38 Schedule 1 para. 12 CCA 1981.
39 Schedule 1 paras 11 and 15 CCA 1981.

5.3.2 When will a judge stay a trial?

A stay of proceedings is a ruling by the court in civil and criminal procedure, halting further legal process in a trial or other legal proceeding. When a court decides that an action constitutes contempt of court, it can issue a court order that in the context of a court trial or hearing declares a person or organization to have disobeyed or been disrespectful of the court's authority, called 'found' or 'held' in contempt. The court can subsequently lift the stay and resume proceedings based on events taking place after the stay is ordered.[40] In the *Kray* (1969)[41] and *Poulson* (1974)[42] cases, for example, the respective trial judges said that they could not see how the press could report the evidence without running the risk of being in contempt of other criminal proceedings which had already begun against co-defendants.

Whilst the courts are very reluctant to stay proceedings, there will be applications from defence lawyers for a stay when there has been frequent media coverage and background material on the defendants during or at the start of a trial. The taking of photographs in court can be particularly serious when identification at trial is an evidential issue ('it wasn't me'), as the CA indicated in *R v Bieber* (2006).[43] Once a photo has been published there is greater risk of jury prejudice – especially when the media publish a photo of the accused close to trial proceedings. In such cases a judge may well stay ('halt') 'active' trial proceedings.

See below 5.3.3

Footballers Lee Bowyer and Jonathan Woodgate (then still playing for Leeds) were standing trial at Hull Crown Court in 2000 for allegedly seriously wounding 21-year-old student Sarfraz Najeib outside the Majestyk nightclub in Leeds in January 2000.[44] For fear of 'contempt' during the 'active' trial period, the BBC's *Match of the Day* coverage on 26 November 2000 broadcast a cup match between Leeds United and Arsenal with Woodgate and Bowyer's heads pixelated, running as 'headless' players on the pitch.

During the jury's deliberation in April 2001, the *Sunday Mirror* published an interview with the victim's father, Muhammed Najeib, alleging a racist attack. On application by the defence, Poole J stayed the proceedings, citing contempt of court, and ordered a retrial. He made it clear that the newspaper had seriously prejudiced the jury verdict by its publication, stating that the editor, Colin Myler, should know his 'contempt' legislation better.[45]

At their retrial a year later at Leeds Crown Court in 2002, Woodgate and Bowyer were acquitted of sections 18 and 20 wounding charges (Offences Against the Person Act 1861). Woodgate pleaded guilty to affray and was sentenced to 100 hours' 'community service' and ordered to pay eight weeks' wages as a fine. Bowyer also pleaded guilty to affray and was fined four weeks' wages. Sarfraz Najeib told the court at the retrial that he

---

40 Part 81 Civil Procedure Rules.
41 R v Kray [1969] 53 Cr App R 412. Ronald Kray (of the Kray twins) had been convicted of murder on 4 March 1969, and on 15 April 1969 he and a number of others were facing a second indictment charging them with murder and other offences. His counsel sought to challenge prospective jurors for cause on the ground that the previous trial had been extensively reported and that prejudice to Kray resulting from press reporting would be likely to influence the minds of the jurors in the second trial.
42 R v Poulson and Pottinger [1974] Crim LR 141. The 'Poulson' trials through the 1970s were the most high-profile tax evasion cases brought by the Inland Revenue, resulting in the resignation of the Conservative Home Secretary Reginald Maudling, who had formerly been chairman of two of John Poulson's companies.
43 [2006] EWCA Crim 2776.
44 R v Bowyer (Lee) and Woodgate (Jonathan) (No 1) (2000) (unreported).
45 R v Bowyer (Lee), R v Woodgate (Jonathan) [2001] EWCA Crim 1853.

was still struggling to rebuild his life almost two years after he was attacked in Leeds city centre. The 21-year-old victim still had the physical scars of the attack as well as suffering psychologically.

After the conclusion of the second trial, the Attorney General issued contempt proceedings against the Trinity Mirror Group and the *Sunday Mirror*'s editor, Colin Myler. They were found guilty of contempt and subsequently fined a total of £175,000. Colin Myler resigned. Kennedy LJ and Rafferty J contended that the offending article had seriously impeded justice during a lengthy, expensive, high-profile case at a crucially difficult time (see also: 'the Rosemary West' trial – R v West (Rosemary) (1996)[46]).

A murder charge is always serious and an editorial error by a broadcaster or media outlet can seriously impede the course of justice; that includes not granting the accused a fair trial. In the *AG v ITV* case (below), the court upheld the strict liability contempt against the broadcaster, pointing out that the news bulletin had resulted in additional delay and distress to all parties involved in the proceedings. However, the court rejected the application by the defence in an earlier hearing that the proceedings should be stayed.

❖ KEY CASE	*Attorney General v ITV Central Ltd* [2008] EWHC 1984 (Admin)

Precedent

❖ A broadcaster (or other media organization) is guilty of strict liability contempt if he broadcasts or publishes information during 'active' court proceedings or broadcasts any other extraneous information about the case.

❖ Where the contemner has offered an immediate apology and offered to pay third-party costs, the court must take this into account in assessing the appropriate amount that the broadcaster should be fined.

Facts

A regional television breakfast news bulletin of 23 seconds by Central TV (ITV) in relation to the trial of five men for murder later that day referred to the fact that one of the men had been convicted of and was currently serving a sentence for murder. Defence counsel brought the ITV broadcast to the attention of the trial judge and the trial was stayed. The broadcaster offered an immediate and unreserved apology to the court, agreeing to pay all third-party costs to cover the postponement of the trial. Subsequently, all five defendants were convicted with court costs amounting to £37,014, which ITV paid.

After the trial, the Attorney General applied for an order for committal for contempt of court against the broadcaster ITV Central.

Decision

The Divisional Court took the view that the ITV Central news broadcast was a 'serious and basic error' which had caused disturbance to the court and delays

---

and further distress to third parties. However, in mitigation wasted costs had been voluntarily paid, and allowing for that it would be appropriate to impose a fine of £25,000.

Analysis

The case is a harsh reminder to media editors that there is no scope for honest error in contempt of court offences. The judgment in *AG v ITV* suggests that the courts take the strict liability offence under section 1 CCA 1981 seriously. The AG's application was granted for the reasons that the 'publication' (the broadcast) had amounted to a 'serious and basic error', creating a substantial risk of prejudice that the news bulletin might be seen by members of the jury due to hear the impending trial.

The trial of Levi Bellfield attracted enormous media attention. He had been found guilty in June 2011 of the murder of 13-year-old schoolgirl Milly Dowler, who had gone missing nearly 10 years previously on 21 March 2002. Bellfield's lawyers attempted several times to stay his trial for fear of a prejudiced jury due to extensive media coverage. In a separate trial brought by the Attorney General, the *Daily Mail* and the *Daily Mirror* were found guilty of contempt of court over their extensive pre-trial coverage of Bellfield during the *sub judice* period.[47] Sir John Thomas, President of the Queen's Bench Division, fined each newspaper £10,000.

In the *Dale Cregan* case,[48] His Honour Judge Gilbart QC imposed strict reporting restrictions under section 4(2) CCA 1981 at Manchester Crown Court on 24 September 2012, on the ground of 'very real risk of prejudice' because the case had attracted high-profile media and public attention. One-eyed Cregan, 30, was charged with the murders of police officers Fiona Bone, 32, and Nicola Hughes, 23, on 18 September 2012 by luring them to their deaths by dialling 999 to report a bogus burglary, then using a Glock handgun and a military grenade to murder the two women in Hattersley, Greater Manchester. This blanket reporting ban meant that there was no further reporting until the jury was sworn in. Any reports of preparatory hearings were limited to basic facts such as the name of the accused and the offences he was charged with.

The *Cregan* case was additionally complex since he was also jointly charged for other offences with his co-defendants Wilkinson and Ward with murdering father and son David and Mark Short on 9 August 2012 by causing an explosion at a property in Luke Road, Droylsden by using a hand grenade;[49] and additionally with Gorman, Livesey, Hadfield and others for the attempted murders of John Collins, Michael Belcher and Ryan Pridding on 25 May 2012 and Sharon Hark on 10 August 2012[50] and for the possession of illegal firearms with the intent to endanger life.[51]

---

47 *AG v Associated Newspapers Ltd and Mirror Group Newspapers Ltd* [2012] EWHC 2029 (Admin) of 18 July 2012 (Levi Bellfield contempt case).

48 *R v Cregan (Dale Christopher); Gorman (Damian); Livesey (Luke); Hadfield (Ryan);Ward (Matthew Gary James) and Wilkinson (Anthony)* 24 September 2012 (unreported).

49 s 2 Explosive Substances Act 1883.

50 s 1(1) Criminal Attempts Act 1981.

51 s 16 Firearms Act 1968.

See
below 5.4.2

Dale Cregan admitted the murders of the two policewomen as well as the other offences in May 2013 at Preston Crown Court.[52] He was sentenced to a whole-life tariff by Holroyde J at the end of the four-month trial that laid bare the brutality of Manchester's underworld.

 FOR THOUGHT

In high-profile criminal cases such as Dale Cregan (murder of two female police officers and others in Greater Manchester) or Vincent Tabak (murder of Joanna Yeates), where there is intense public and media interest, and the suspect is awaiting trial, is it right that a judge can impose total reporting restrictions under section 4(2) CCA 1981? Or do these restrictions not interfere with the open justice principle and Article 10 ECHR? Are newsworthiness and public interest sufficient reasons to impose reporting restrictions? Discuss.

5.3.3 Contempt by publication

Contempt covers media reporting by 'publication' which asserts or assumes, expressly or implicitly, the guilt of the defendant or possible negligence on behalf of the respondent in civil cases. In newspaper reporting terms this can be just a single headline (including online publication), or in broadcasting terms it can be a biased commentary or news item on the radio before or during a trial. It is doubtful that journalists have short memories and simply do not remember the strict liability rule which is inherent in contempt of court legislation. It is probably fair to say that many of the 'red tops' have taken the risk in order to increase their newspaper and online sales by printing popular background stories or even the accused's photograph, when the subject matter was *sub judice*, writing off possible legal costs against the benefit of extra sales. 'Publication' then refers to:

See
below 5.3.4

- the print media (including photographs);
- broadcasts;
- websites and other online or text-based communication (including Twitter, Facebook, Instagram, etc.).

The element of 'substantial risk' is judged at the time of publication and applies only to legal proceedings that are 'active' at the time of the publication. The longer the gap between publication and the trial, the less substantial the risk of serious prejudice is likely to be. This is known as the 'fade factor'.

In the *Geoffrey Knights* case[53] at Harrow Crown Court in October 1995, eight newspapers were referred to the Attorney General, Sir Nicholas Lyell, by trial judge Roger Sanders

---

52 Source: 'Police killer Dale Cregan pleads guilty to murders of father and son in gun and grenade attacks', by Rob Cooper, *Daily Mail*, 22 May 2013.
53 *R v Knights (Geoffrey)* (unreported, 1995) Harrow Crown Court 6 October 1995.

for 'contempt', for publishing stories and background about Mr Knights during *sub judice* proceedings.[54] Knights had been charged with wounding with intent on a cab driver, and the trial was stayed on the request of Knights' lawyers, stating that their client would not receive a fair trial. The *Daily Mirror* had published stories about Knights' 'stormy' relationship with *EastEnders* actress and later his wife, Gillian Taylforth.[55]

In November 2015, the US publisher of *GQ* magazine, Condé Nast, was found guilty of contempt over a 'very seriously prejudicial' article about the phone-hacking trial of Rebekah Brooks and Andy Coulson.[56] The article by Michael Wolff – published during the 'phone-hacking trial' in April 2014 – was accompanied by sketches and photos of the court proceedings. The feature also included claims that had not been put before the trial jury, including that Brooks had received a £10.8m settlement from Rupert Murdoch. Furthermore, the publication contained allegations that Rupert Murdoch, owner of the (now defunct) *News of the World* (*NoW*) was implicated in phone hacking. The front cover trailed the headline by court reporter, Michael Wolff: 'Hacking exclusive! The Trial of the Century'.[57]

The court heard that at the time of the offending article, *GQ* had total sales of 90,573, comprising 38,305 newsstand sales, 24,199 subscriber sales, 6,137 digital edition sales and 21,898 multiple copy sales (sales to airline companies, hotels, waiting rooms and the like).[58] What aggravated the 'contempt' by publication was that the article was available to read online during the evidence of some of the defendants: Rebekah Brooks (whose evidence began in February 2014, until 12 March 2014); Clive Goodman (13 March to 20 March 2014, when he became ill); Cheryl Carter (25 March to 27 March 2014); and Charlie Brooks (Mrs Brooks' husband – 28 March to 1 April 2014). The Lord Chief Justice, Lord Thomas, ruled that the article created 'a substantial risk' that the trial of Brooks, Coulson and other employees of *NoW* 'would be seriously impeded or prejudiced'.[59]

See Chapter 7.5

5.3.4 Photographs and contempt

Photographs are a major concern as a source of contempt by publication. This becomes particularly serious in criminal cases where a police suspect has not yet been positively identified by a witness in an ID parade. Since publication via social media, the criminal courts have been especially troubled by the dangers to the integrity and fairness of a criminal trial, where juries can obtain easy access to the internet and to other forms of instant communication in order to undertake background 'research' on the accused. Once information is published on the internet, it is difficult if not impossible to remove it completely. However, there will be jurors who disobey the judge's directions regarding the prohibition not to search the internet.

---

54 Source: 'Trial by media: watching for prejudice. After the Geoff Knights fiasco, can we trust the press to allow the accused a fair hearing?', by Grania Langdon-Down, *Independent*, 11 October 1995.
55 Taylforth was married to the late Geoff Knights for 23 years and had two children, Harrison and Jessica, before they separated in 2009. Geoff Knights died in 2013. Source: '"She was broken and devastated": Gillian Taylforth's children recall their mother's split from abusive husband Geoff Knights', by Rebecca Lawrence, *Daily Mail*, 27 March 2016.
56 *Attorney General v The Condé Nast Publications Ltd* [2015] EWHC 3322 (Admin), 18 November 2015 (Lord Thomas of Cwmgiedd LCJ and Nicola Davies J).
57 Ibid. at paras 1–3.
58 Ibid. at paras 10–11.
59 Ibid. at paras 39–41.

In *R v McLeod (Callum Iain)* (2001),[60] the Court of Appeal held there was no reason why a trial judge could not be considered to be an independent and impartial tribunal for proceedings for contempt of court. The CA further stated that Article 6 ECHR does not add to, or alter, the normal requirement that proceedings should be conducted fairly before an independent and impartial tribunal. Therefore, the trial judge in *McLeod* was entitled to deal with the intimidation of a witness, which had occurred in a corridor outside the courtroom.

In the 'footballer rape', publishing a photograph of the alleged footballer assailant by the *Daily Star* on 23 October 2003 amounted to strict liability contempt by publication. A 17-year-old girl had alleged that she had been raped by up to eight footballers at the Grosvenor House Hotel in London on 27 September 2003. The suspects were arrested and s 1 CCA 'strict liability' applied thereafter. There was surging media interest and speculation as to the identity of the footballers. Identification was the main defence issue, however, because no ID parade had been held. The Attorney General and police had warned the media not to name suspects or publish photographs or likenesses of them. *The Daily Star* then named Titus Bramble and Carlton Cole, identified their clubs and included a partially pixelated photo of Bramble. This resulted in no criminal charges being brought against any suspects. However, the AG issued contempt proceedings against the newspaper, and the *Daily Star* was found guilty of contempt and fined £60,000. This means that justice in this case was not seen to be done either for the complainant or the footballers to clear their names.[61]

The *Ryan Ward* case[62] demonstrates the need to recognize that instant online news requires instant and effective protection for the integrity of a criminal trial. Though the jury in the *Ward* case had been warned not to use the internet, the court could not be completely satisfied that a juror might not have accessed Ward's 'gun' photograph either via the internet or through Twitter. At the start of Ward's trial, *Mail Online* published an article with the caption: 'DRINK-FUELLED ATTACK: Ryan Ward was seen boasting about the incident on CCTV'. The article was accompanied by a photo showing Ward holding a pistol in his right hand with his index finger on the trigger while he indicated firing a handgun with his left hand. The picture remained online for four hours and 54 minutes, until it was removed at 9.58pm.

The *Daily Mail* and the *Sun* were found guilty of contempt in November 2009 for publishing an online photo of the murder trial defendant posing with a gun on their websites. Ward was about to stand trial for the murder of car mechanic Craig Wass at Sheffield Crown Court when the publication appeared in print and in the respective online editions. Angus McCullough QC, acting for the Attorney General in the contempt proceedings at London's High Court, told the court that the publication of the online photograph (in both *The Sun* and the *Mail*) had created a 'substantial risk' of prejudicing the forthcoming jury trial. Both newspaper publishers were found guilty of strict liability contempt under section 1 CCA.

60 [2001] Crim LR 589, 29 November 2000 (CA).
61 *AG v Express Newspapers* [2004] EWHC 2859 (Admin) ('footballer rape case').
62 *Attorney General v Associated Newspapers Ltd and Newsgroup Newspapers Ltd* [2011] EWHC 418 (Admin) (Ryan Ward case).

5.4 General defences

Once a newspaper or media organization has been charged with 'contempt', the Attorney General will commence proceedings after the original trial has been concluded. The court will then decide whether the publication has created a 'substantial risk'. Case law tells us that 'substantial risk' does not mean a 'large' or 'great' risk but a risk which is not remote, and the risk must be a practical rather than a theoretical risk.[63] The publication of noticeable prejudicial material during a trial is likely to create a much more substantial risk than the same publication which takes place a year before.

5.4.1 The section 5 defence

Section 5 CCA 1981 provides a statutory defence concerning 'discussion of public affairs', and further general defences can be found under section 3 and Schedule 1 CCA.

Section 5 can save a publication that would otherwise fall foul of the 'strict liability' rule if it is made a 'discussion of public affairs' and generally passes the public interest test (not defined by statute).

The test of whether the section 5 defence can be successfully applied is left to the Attorney General or the Divisional Court and usually comprises:

1   the size of the risk (of serious prejudice); and
2   the severity of impact of the publication.

Neither a remote risk of serious impediment nor a substantial risk of minor impediment will suffice. Arguably the terms used in section 5 CCA may well form part of the *actus reus* of contempt. But the terms are separately defined in section 2(2) CCA ('limitation of scope of strict liability') in the interests, presumably, of clarity and emphasis. This makes parts of the 1981 Act unclear and confusing: to judge whether an element forms part of the *actus reus* of the strict liability crime or is a defence as strictly defined has of course a bearing on who carries the burden of proof (see: R v Hunt (1987);[64] R v Lambert (2001)[65]).

This means that the section 5 defence is not altogether satisfactory, particularly where the restraint imposed would interfere with the journalist or publisher's freedom of expression as being 'necessary in a democratic society'.

In *AG v English* (1982),[66] the House of Lords ruled that the section 5 defence was available to the publishers of the *Daily Mail* and its columnist Malcolm Muggeridge,[67] because his comment piece had been written in 'good faith' and the piece was held to be 'in the public interest'. The opinion piece had been written by Muggeridge in support of a pro-life candidate running for Parliament. Though no actual mention was made of the 'Dr Arthur Trial'[68] at the time, the journalist made reference in general to

---

63 *AG v Guardian Newspapers (No 3)* [1992] 1 WLR 784 at 881.
64 [1987] AC 352 (HL).
65 [2001] UKHL 37 (HL).
66 [1982] 2 All ER 903 (HL).
67 Thomas Malcolm Muggeridge (1903–1990) was an English journalist and satirist.
68 Sheffield paediatrician, Dr Arthur, was standing trial at the time for murdering a prematurely born, severely disabled baby boy, by not operating on the child or giving life-sustaining treatment. Dr Arthur was later acquitted by the jury.

medical practices of failing to keep deformed children alive after birth. Lord Diplock opined that section 5 CCA provided the exception to the strict liability rule.[69]

5.4.2 The fade factor

What is the 'fade factor'? The court decides whether the offending publication appeared shortly before an impending trial and whether this may have influenced the decision-making of that trial. If the publication was a long time ago (common law stipulates that this usually amounts to six to nine months prior to the trial) the court will then conclude that the jurors' recollection of adverse publication in the media may well have faded. This will then make the alleged prejudicial reporting no longer contemptuous. In the (cricketer) *Ian Botham* case (1987),[70] the court took a robust view of the ability of jurors to decide cases uninfluenced by outside pressures, especially if the trial took place many months after any potentially prejudicial publicity had occurred.

Just in advance of a high-profile fraud trial involving the Maxwell brothers, Kevin and Ian, sons of the deceased Mirror newspaper tycoon Robert Maxwell, the BBC broadcast its popular news programme *Have I Got News For You* (then on BBC 2).[71] The trial was set down for 31 October 1994 and was scheduled to last for many months with a jury in this complex fraud and conspiracy trial involving the trustees and beneficiaries of the Mirror Group Pension Fund. Auld LJ held that the mere mention of the case on a television programme amounted to a contempt of court, despite the humorous context given to the remarks in the broadcast.

 ❖ KEY CASE | **Attorney General v BBC and Hat Trick Productions Ltd [1997] EMLR 76 (sub nom. Have I Got News For You case)**

Precedent
❖ A section 5 CCA 1981 defence is not available if the broadcast poses a *substantial* risk of prejudice to an impending or ongoing trial if the matter is not deemed in the public interest.
❖ The 'fade factor' is not a permissible defence if the trial is imminent (usually amounting to six months).

Facts
News quiz *Have I Got News For You*, chaired by Angus Deayton, on Friday 29 April 1994 on BBC Two, was broadcast between 22.00 and 22.30. When team leaders Ian Hislop, editor of *Private Eye*, and actor-comedian Paul Merton played the 'odd one out' round, the fourth photo showed some *Mirror* pensioners. The team members' repeated banter centred on the pensioners being 'allegedly' defrauded by Robert Maxwell, implying the 'guilt' of the Maxwell brothers. The programme was repeated the following night unedited.

69 *AG v English* [1982] 2 All ER 903 at paras 918 f–g (Lord Diplock).
70 *AG v News Group Newspapers* [1987] QB 1 (cricketer Ian Botham case).
71 *AG v BBC and Hat Trick Productions Ltd* [1997] EMLR 76.

At the start of the Maxwell sons' trial, their lawyers applied for proceedings to be stayed, arguing that the BBC news quiz had contravened contempt legislation and that Kevin and Ian Maxwell would not receive a fair trial due to adverse media coverage. Though the trial went ahead, and the Maxwell brothers were acquitted, the AG commenced contempt proceedings against the programme makers Hat Trick Productions and the BBC immediately after the conclusion of the fraud trial.

Decision

The court found both parties guilty of strict liability contempt for the reasons that the programme makers and the BBC should not have broadcast any material in connection with the forthcoming Maxwell trial during the *sub judice* period. The court further held that the public broadcaster had made no attempt to edit out the 'irrelevant' and 'rude' comments, particularly in its repeat programme. Auld LJ said:

> The degree of risk of impact of a publication on a trial and the extent of that impact may both be affected, in differing degrees according to the circumstances, by the nature and form of the publication and how long it occurred before trial. Much depends on the combination of circumstances in the case in question and the court's own assessment of their likely effect at the time of publication. This is essentially a value judgment for the court, albeit that it must be sure of its judgment before it can find that there has been contempt. There is little value in making detailed comparisons with the facts of other cases.[72]

Hat Trick and the BBC were each fined £10,000.

Analysis

It was clear in this case that the BBC broadcast alluded to the possible 'guilt' of the Maxwell brothers, amounting to strict liability contempt. It did not matter that the panel members of the satirical TV show did not intend the broadcast to interfere with the impending fraud trial or that the comments were said in jest. The 'fade factor' was not allowed, since the trial was imminent; neither was there a section 5 CCA defence because criminal proceedings were clearly 'active' at the time of the 'publication'.

At times the Attorney General has shown more leniency in commencing contempt proceedings against the media. Following the atrocities of the 7/7 London bombings in 2005 and the attempted terrorism attacks of 21 July of the same year, the CPS issued new practice guidelines allowing the media to make more extensive use of publishing police intelligence during active proceedings (following pre-trial proceedings), such as photos, CCTV footage and previous convictions of suspects – in this case Hussain Osman, 27, Ibrahim Muktar Said, 27, Yassin Hussan Omar, 26, and Ramzi Mohamed, 23. Their trial

---

72 Ibid. at para. 83 (Auld LJ).

took two years to come to Woolwich Crown Court. Each accused received a life sentence in July 2007.

In December 2011, the Lord Chief Justice for England and Wales, Lord Judge, allowed the use of 'live text-based communication' (e.g. Twitter) in court for the first time by way of a practice direction. A year later, Lord Judge further relaxed the rules, which meant that journalists no longer had to ask for permission to tweet in court, paving the way for more live coverage of court proceedings.[73] Thereafter members of the public could receive instant court reports via Twitter, such as the first extradition proceedings against WikiLeaks founder Julian Assange at City of Westminster Magistrates' Court, the trial of Vincent Tabak who was found guilty of Jo Yeates' murder in October 2011 and the trial of Gary Dobson and David Norris who were found guilty of murdering teenager Stephen Lawrence in 1993 at the Old Bailey in January 2012.

 FOR THOUGHT

You are representing a 19-year old terrorist defendant accused of plotting a pressure-cooker bomb attack on a famous London nightclub. She is standing trial at the Old Bailey in three months' time. The 'red tops' (and their online editions) continue with their sensational and inflammatory press coverage of your client in spite of *sub judice* and active proceedings. Media coverage includes the accused's family and schooling background in Surrey, a slur on her faith and reporting on her previous police cautions. Produce a skeleton argument for the court for an application to stay the trial, using 'contempt' and human rights legislation and leading authorities to persuade the judge.

5.4.3 Contempt proceedings in Scotland

The Contempt of Court Act 1981 covers the whole jurisdiction of the United Kingdom. Scottish contempt proceedings are usually dealt with by a Sheriff Court and are known as 'breach of interdict'.[74] There are some leading authorities in common law, such as *Johnson v Grant* (1923)[75]or *Johnston v Johnston* (1996).[76] Similar to English, Welsh and Northern Irish jurisdictions, Scottish courts treat the taking of photographs in court or recording proceedings during *sub judice* extremely punitively.[77] In fact, Scottish courts traditionally punish contempt more harshly than English courts. A different approach was however taken with the coming into force of the Human Rights Act 1998.

---

73 Practice Direction: The use of live text-based forms of communication (including Twitter) from court for the purposes of fair and accurate reporting. Lord Judge The Lord Chief Justice of England and Wales, 14 December 2011.

74 Section 15 CCA 1981, 'Penalties for contempt of court in Scottish proceedings' (incorporated by Criminal Procedure (Scotland) Act 1995).

75 [1923] SC 789.

76 [1996] SLT 499.

77 *Haney v HM Advocate* [2003] Appeal Court, High Court of Justiciary; also: *HM Advocate v McGee* [2005] High Court of Justiciary of 12 October 2005 (Lord Abernethy) (unreported); also: *HM Advocate v Cowan* [2007], 27 February 2007 (Sheriff Sinclair) (unreported).

The landmark case was *Cox and Griffiths* (1998)[78] where Peter Cox, editor of the Glasgow-based *Daily Record*, challenged a contempt allegation, arguing that the 1981 Contempt of Court Act contravened Article 10(1) ECHR and therein press freedom. Lord Prosser allowed the petition by stating that 'juries are healthy bodies' and that they do not need a 'germ-free' media atmosphere. The finding of contempt was quashed.

The ruling by the Scottish Court of Appeal in *Cox and Griffiths* was seen as rather liberal at the time compared with editorial leadership 'south of the border'. Some Scottish editors worried that Lord Prosser's approach in *Cox and Griffiths* may be misinterpreted, leading to greater liberties when reporting during a *sub judice* period. Rosalind McInnes undertook a research study in 2009, whereby she examined court reporting and possible contempt situations. She concluded that there was at that time a discrepancy between the Scottish and the English courts' contempt proceedings, arguing that such proceedings 'south of the border' had become 'increasingly rare' compared with Scotland.[79]

The *Aamer Anwar* case[80] demonstrates contempt proceedings involving a Scottish solicitor. Anwar had launched a bitter attack about the trial process following his client's (Mohammed Atif Siddique) conviction of terrorism offences on 17 September 2007. Siddique was the first person convicted of Islamist terrorism offences in Scotland. Following the actual court proceedings, trial judge, Lord Carloway, referred Mr Anwar to the High Court for contempt of court.[81]

 KEY CASE　　　*Aamer Anwar (Respondent in contempt proceedings)* [2008] HCJAC (case no 36 IN932/06)

Precedent

- Members of the public will not be deterred from performing their public duty as jurors, when called upon to do so, even though they may have heard a potentially contemptuous comment.
- Comments and opinions expressed post-trial outside the court do not amount to contempt.

Facts

The background was that on 17 September 2007, at the High Court in Glasgow, Mohammed Atif Siddique was found guilty after trial on several charges under the Terrorism Acts 2000 and 2006. He was sentenced to a total of eight years' imprisonment. Mr Siddique's solicitor was Aamer Anwar.

On the day when the jury's verdict was delivered, Mr Anwar read a statement outside the court building in the presence of members of the public and journalists, which was televised. The statement included the observation that Mr Siddique

> was found guilty of doing what millions of young people do every day, looking for answers on the internet. . . . It is farcical that part of the evidence

---

78 *Cox (Petitioner) and another* [1998] SCCR 561.
79 McInnes (2009b).
80 *Anwar (Aamer) (Respondent)* [2008] HCJAC (case no 36 IN932/06).
81 For further detail on Scots law see: Green, W. (2018).

against Atif was that he grew a beard, had documents in Arabic which he could not even read and downloaded material from a legitimate Israeli website run by Dr Reuven Paz, ex Mossad.[82]

On 23 October 2007, Mr Anwar was charged with contempt of court by the Advocate Depute.

Opinion

The opinion was delivered by The Right Honourable Lord Osborne. The court acquitted Mr Anwar of contempt, stating that Mr Anwar's comments contained 'angry and petulant criticism of the outcome of the trial process' and 'a range of political comments concerning the position of Muslims in our society' – but this was 'comment' and did not amount to contempt.[83]

But the court added a postscript criticizing the behaviour of a professional 'officer of the court'. Lord Osborne said: 'Any solicitor practising in the High Court of Justiciary owes a duty to the court, a fact recognized in paragraph (I) of the Preamble to the Code of Conduct for Scottish Solicitors of 2002' and 'that a court is entitled to expect better of those who practice before it'.[84]

Analysis

Though solicitor Mr Anwar was acquitted of contempt of court, it is worth noting the *obiter* opinion of Lord Osborne in relation to Mr Anwar's professional duty and obligations as a solicitor. Though the court accepted that Mr Anwar's comments outside the courthouse and on TV did not amount to contempt, their Lordships implied that the Law Society of Scotland ought to deal with Mr Anwar's behaviour in a professional capacity.

Two years after his conviction in February 2010, Mohammed Atif Siddique, 24, won his appeal on the grounds that his conviction was unsafe and amounted to a miscarriage of justice. One of the appeal judges, Lord Osborne, said some directions given to the jury by the trial judge, Lord Carloway, when explaining the main counter-terrorism legislation provisions faced by Siddique had been a 'material misdirection'.[85]

The Appeal Court did not quash all of Siddique's convictions, and he remains convicted of breach of the peace for showing gruesome images of terrorist beheadings to fellow students at Glasgow Metropolitan College and boasting that he planned to carry

---

82 Source: 'Press Release – Monday 17 September 2007 – HMA v Mohammed Atif Siddique – Guilty Verdict', statement read on the steps of the High Court by Mr Siddique's solicitor – Aamer Anwar.

83 Aamer Anwar (Respondent in contempt proceedings) [2008] HCJAC at para. 44 (Lord Osborne).

84 Ibid. at para. 45.

85 The charges were: s 54 Terrorism Act 2000: setting up websites providing links to documents providing instructions on how to operate weaponry and make explosives; s 2 Terrorism Act 2006: circulating terrorist publications by means of websites to encourage, induce or assist the commission, preparation or instigation of acts of terrorism; breach of the peace: showing images of suicide bombers, murders and beheadings to fellow students, threatening to be a suicide bomber and to carry out terrorism in Glasgow or elsewhere.

out a suicide bombing in the city. Siddique also remains convicted of setting up websites with links to instructions on bomb-making and weapons use and of distributing terror publications through the websites.[86]

5.5 The role of the Attorney General in contempt proceedings

The Attorney General (AG) is the government's chief legal adviser on domestic and international law, and the Solicitor General is his or her deputy. It is the AG's role to commence contempt proceedings against an offending publication or broadcaster, publisher and/or editor, usually after the (original) trial has concluded. Contempt proceedings are public law proceedings and are dealt with in the administrative court.[87] The financial penalties for contempt offences can be substantial and unlimited with an additional threat of up to two years' imprisonment for the editor. Fines can be unlimited at the Crown Court.[88] However, the last time an editor was imprisoned was in 1949 (see: R v Bolam, Ex parte Haigh[89]).

The rules when 'contempt' actually starts in criminal cases are not quite clear. Some newspapers argue they can still fully report on a suspect before he or she has been charged (i.e. at the point of arrest).[90] This area remains a grey area of the law, and the media has habitually ignored contempt legislation in high-profile cases. The AG's office issues frequent media warnings in high-profile cases that editors should not be complacent and rely on the 'fade factor'.

See above 5.4.2

Does the Attorney General always issue contempt proceedings when the media has breached the strict liability rule? Some AGs have been more proactive in taking out contempt proceedings than others. One example is the reporting during the 'Yorkshire Ripper', just at the time the Contempt of Court Act 1981 came into force.

When Peter Sutcliffe ('the Yorkshire Ripper') was arrested on 2 January 1981 by West Yorkshire police, it marked the sub judice period – according to the new legislation. On 5 January 1981, 35-year-old Peter Sutcliffe of 6 Garden Lane, Bradford, was charged at Dewsbury Magistrates' Court with the murder of Leeds University student, Jacqueline Hill, aged 20.[91] Sutcliffe was charged in total with the murder of 13 women, most of them prostitutes, over a five-year period.

The government's Solicitor General, Sir Ian Percival, issued a press warning in line with the new contempt legislation, intimating that the media would be liable to prosecution if their stories impeded a fair trial for Sutcliffe. But long before the 'Ripper Trial',

---

86 Source: 'Scot freed after his terror sentence was quashed insists: 'I'm not a terrorist, I'm more of a numpty', by Tom Hamilton, *Daily Record*, 10 February 2010.
87 Rules of the Supreme Court Ord. 52 (RSC Ord. 52); also: R v M [2008] EWCA Crim 1901.
88 Section 14 CCA 1981. If proceedings are brought by the AG for Northern Ireland under s 18 CCA 1981; s 35 Criminal Justice Act (Northern Ireland) 1945 applies to fines imposed for contempt of court by any superior court other than the Crown Court as it applies to fines imposed by the Crown Court.
89 (1949) 93 Solicitors Journal 220.
90 R v Richardson [2004] EWCA Crim 758.
91 Jacqueline Hill, from Middlesbrough, a third year English student, was found battered to death on 17 November 1980, on waste ground in Leeds.

there was extensive newspaper coverage when the 'red tops' together with Jacqueline Hill's mother alleged that the Ripper's last murder victim could have been saved.[92]

After a two-week trial at the Old Bailey, Peter Sutcliffe was found guilty of 13 counts of murder and sentenced on Friday 22 May 1981 to 30 years behind bars. Attorney General Sir Michael Havers QC did not prosecute any newspaper publishers or indeed any broadcaster for contempt.[93]

See Chapter 3

However, *Private Eye* was sued in defamation by Peter Sutcliffe's wife, Sonia. The satirical magazine had alleged that she had 'done a deal with the *Daily Mail*' worth £250,000, for telling her story ('My Life with the Yorkshire Ripper'). On 24 May 1989, Mrs Sutcliffe won her libel action against the *Eye* and its editor, Ian Hislop.[94] A High Court libel jury awarded Mrs Sutcliffe £600,000 damages, at that time the highest award in the UK. Mr Hislop commented afterwards: 'If this is justice, I'm a banana'. The sum was reduced to £60,000 on appeal.

See Chapter 7

The Byford Report (1981) – released under the Freedom of Information Act 2000 on 1 June 2006 – exposed details of 'systematic failure' by the West Yorkshire Police in the 'Ripper' inquiry and the handling of the press. Sir Lawrence Byford concluded that Peter Sutcliffe never stood a chance of a fair trial.[95]

5.6 Juries: social media and the internet

Juries are expected to decide their verdicts based only on the evidence put before them in court rather than on any other content published elsewhere, and this includes the internet and social media. Public discussion of an ongoing case, beyond contemporaneous reports of the evidence, risks swaying jurors and making a fair trial impossible.

Dominic Grieve QC was most probably the most enthusiastic Attorney General as far as contempt proceedings against 'tweeting' and internet-using jurors in criminal trials were concerned and advancing changes in the law.

On 20 February 2013 the jury at Southwark Crown Court in London in the Vicky Pryce trial had to be discharged when Mr Justice Sweeney concluded that the jury had a 'fundamental deficit in understanding' the trial process in spite of warnings issued by the judge not to use any digital communication or the internet. Ms Pryce, an economist, was charged with perverting the course of justice. She had taken speeding points on behalf of her (ex-)husband Chris Huhne, the former energy secretary and Liberal Democrat MP. At a second trial in March 2013, Vicky Pryce was found guilty. Chris Huhne (who had pleaded guilty) and Pryce were each imprisoned for eight months for perverting the course of justice.

In February 2018 two live broadcasts appeared on former English Defence League (EDL) leader Tommy Robinson's Facebook page, with footage he had taken during the high-profile trial of Darren Osborne at Woolwich Crown Court. Osborne was charged

---

92 Hill v Chief Constable of West Yorkshire Police [1989] AC 53 where the claimant, Mrs Hill, mother of the deceased Jacqueline Hill, the last of the 'Yorkshire Ripper' victims, sued the police in negligence alleging that the police conduct and investigations relating to the earlier 'Ripper' murders in West Yorkshire could have prevented her daughter's killing.

93 House of Lords Debate; HL Deb 20 July 1983 vol. 443 cc 1159–1170.

94 *Sutcliffe (Sonia) v Pressdram Ltd* [1991] 1 QB 153.

95 Home Office (1987), paras 466–482 ('The Byford Report').

and found guilty of the murder of one man and attempted murder of nine other victims of the Muslim community by driving a van into the individuals outside Finsbury Park Mosque on 19 June 2017.

Robinson, whose real name is Stephen Yaxley-Lennon, used 'Facebook Live' to broadcast details about the ongoing trial. He was charged with contempt of court and convicted in May 2018 at Leeds Crown Court for potentially derailing the long-running Osborne trial by live-streaming his commentary and publishing video footage on his website.

In May 2017 Judge Marson QC at Robinson's contempt trial had ordered reporting restrictions under s 4(2) CCA for fear of prejudicing the Leeds jury. The media 'gag' was successfully challenged by the news website Leeds Live and the Independent (online). Once the reporting ban was lifted all news websites and print editions were able to report that Tommy Robinson had received a 13-month prison sentence (suspended for 18 months).

Robinson had a previous 'contempt' conviction from Canterbury Crown Court for trying to film four men who were on trial for raping a girl. In the footage, which was broadcast while the trial was still going on, Robinson referred to the men as 'paedophiles'. He was convicted under s 41 of the Criminal Justice Act 1925, which prohibits taking or publishing pictures of people involved in trials (citing HM Solicitor General v Cox (2016) EWHC 1241).[96] When sentencing Robinson, Her Honour Judge Heather Norton also reminded the defendant of the meaning of 'contempt of court':

> This contempt hearing is not about free speech. This is not about the freedom of the press. This is not about legitimate journalism, this is not about political correctness, this is not about whether one political viewpoint is right or another. It is about justice and it is about ensuring that a trial can be carried out justly and fairly. It is about ensuring that a jury are not in any way inhibited from carrying out their important function. It is about being innocent until proven guilty. It is not about people prejudging a situation and going round to that court and publishing material, whether in print or online, referring to defendants as 'Muslim paedophile rapists'. A legitimate journalist would not be able to do that and under the strict liability rule there would be no defence to publication in those terms. It is pejorative language which prejudges the case, and it is language and reporting – if reporting indeed is what it is – that could have had the effect of substantially derailing the trial.[97]

In August 2018 Tommy Robinson won his appeal against both convictions (Canterbury and Leeds Crown Courts). Both convictions were quashed following the leading judgment by the Lord Chief Justice, Lord Burnett. The CA found that the legal process had not been properly followed.[98]

Robinson was originally given a 13-month prison sentence but was released two months into his sentence after winning an appeal. The case was then referred back to

---

96 [2016] EWHC 1241.

97 R v Stephen Yaxley-Lennon (case no S20170102) Canterbury Crown Court, 22 May 2017 (Her Honour Judge Norton, Honorary Recorder) (unreported).

98 Re. Stephen Yaxley-Lennon (aka Tommy Robinson) [2018] EWCA Crim 1856 (CA Crim Div. on appeal from the Crown Court at Canterbury and the Crown Court at Leeds, S20170102 & S20180448) 1 August 2018 (The Rt Hon The Lord Burnett of Maldon, LCJ, the Hon Mr Justice Turner and the Hon Mrs Justice McGowan).

Attorney General Geoffrey Cox, who announced in March 2019 that it was in the public interest to bring fresh proceedings. New contempt proceedings were brought against Robinson (Stephen Yaxley-Lennon) by the Attorney General in July 2019 before Mr Justice Warby, President of the Queen's Bench Division, and Dame Victoria Sharp, sitting at the Old Bailey. The court found that Tommy Robinson's (the respondent) conduct amounted to three 'contempts' on 25 May 2018 outside Leeds Crown Court when the jury was in retirement at the end of R v Akhtar, a long trial in which a number of men were accused of sexual offences against women and girls. The main focus of these new contempt proceedings was on Robinson's live-streaming of video of what he did and said to an online audience via his Facebook page, which had been liked or followed by some 1.2 million people at the time.

The court held that first, there was the online publication amounting to a breach of a reporting restriction order that had been imposed under s 4(2) of the Contempt of Court Act 1981, and which prohibited any reporting of the Akhtar trial until after the conclusion of that trial and all related trials. Secondly, a contempt was found in that the content of what was published gave rise to a substantial risk that the course of justice in the Akhtar case would be seriously impeded, thereby amounting to a breach of the rule of contempt law known as 'the strict liability rule'. Thirdly, that by confronting some of the defendants as they arrived at court, doing so aggressively and openly filming the process, Robinson had interfered with the due administration of justice. The court found that the respondent's conduct did give rise to a real risk that the defendants he confronted would arrive at court in an upset and agitated state, unsuitable for participation in the serious proceedings in which they were due to take part. Dame Victoria Sharp commented on the intimidating nature of the video which he called 'aggressive and provocative'. Therefore, the court agreed with all submissions made on behalf of the Attorney General.[99] The court further ruled that Robinson's claim for freedom of expression under Article 10(1) ECHR could not be justified.

Judge Dame Victoria told Robinson that the time he previously spent in prison for contempt would be taken into account, reducing his sentence to 19 weeks – of which he would serve half before being released. Robinson's barrister Richard Furlong raised the possibility of an appeal against the court's decision and was told he had 28 days to apply.

The Tommy Robinson case raised important issues about how the law of contempt applies to those who seek to report and comment on criminal proceedings and, in particular, how they conduct themselves in and near the courts. Contempt of court laws exist to ensure that defendants receive a fair trial no matter how serious the charge. The idea is that juries must not be influenced by anything but the evidence they hear in court. The contempt laws apply to everyone from journalists to people posting comments on social media, and even jurors. The maximum sentence for contempt of court is two years in prison, but it can also be punished with an unlimited fine.

5.6.1 Juror misconduct

Whilst the law of contempt by publication is intended to prevent any legal tribunal from becoming partial, the focus of the law has increasingly been on preventing bias amongst the jury. Therefore, contempt by publication is committed where a publication creates a

---

99 *Attorney General v Stephen Yaxley-Lennon (aka: Tommy Robinson)* [2019] EWHC 1791 (Admin) at paras 78–89 (Dame Victoria Sharp).

'substantial risk that the course of justice in the proceedings in question will be seriously impeded or prejudiced' regardless of whether the publisher or distributor of the publication intended it to have that effect or was aware that it might do (s 1 CCA).

Generally juror misconduct has been punished under s 8 CCA for the use of extraneous material, and the general principle remains that investigation and media reporting of what takes place in a jury room is entirely forbidden by law.

An appeal was allowed in R v Young (1995),[100] where some of the jurors had consulted a ouija board to consult with the deceased during their overnight stay in a hotel after retiring to consider their verdict. Having believed that contact had been made with the deceased victim, a jury member disclosed the fact that the deceased had named the accused as the murderer. At appeal the Lord Chief Justice, Lord Taylor of Gosforth, concluded:

> Having considered all the circumstances, we concluded there was a real danger that what occurred during this misguided ouija session may have influenced some jurors and may thereby have prejudiced the appellant. For those reasons we allowed the appeal but ordered a retrial.[101]

The position in relation to extraneous material has been the subject of considerable discussion in the authorities. In R v McDonnell (Michael William) (2010),[102] Lord Justice Moore-Brick stated:

> Just as it would in any other instance where it was satisfied that extraneous material had been introduced, the approach of this court is to make inquiries into the material. If, on examination, this material strikes at the fairness of the trial, because the jury has considered material adverse to the defendant with which he has had no or no proper opportunity to deal, the conviction is likely to be unsafe. . . . If the material does not affect the safety of the conviction, the appeal will fail.[103]

That case was followed in R v Deny (2013),[104] in which it was made clear by Mitting J:

> [We wish to emphasise] there is no rule that because material has been introduced to the jury after retirement a conviction must be quashed as unsafe.[105]

Since the arrival of the internet and social media, there have been a number of examples where jurors in criminal trials have been tweeting about or researching cases online whilst deliberating. All of whom were – until recent changes in the law – prosecuted by the Attorney General for breaching section 8 CCA ('juror contempt').

A prominent example was that of jury foreman, Michael Seckerson, who published an article in The Times on 29 January 2008, expressing his strong disagreement with the majority jury verdict of 10:2 in the case of childminder Keran Henderson. He believed she had

---

100 [1995] 2 Cr App R 379.
101 Ibid. at paras 332B-D (Lord Taylor of Gosforth CJ).
102 [2010] EWCA Crim 235.
103 Ibid. at para. 11 (Lord Justice Moore-Brick).
104 [2013] EWCA Crim 481.
105 Ibid. at para. 45 (Mitting J).

been wrongly convicted of manslaughter at Reading Crown Court for shaking 11-month-old Maeve Sheppard from Slough to death.[106] Following Mr Seckerson's controversial publication, Labour Attorney General at the time, Baroness Scotland QC, instigated criminal proceedings against The Times and Mr Seckerson for breaching contempt legislation. Both The Times publishers and Mr Seckerson argued 'freedom of expression' in their defence but were found guilty on 13 May 2009. The Times was fined £15,000 and Michael Seckerson £500 plus costs of £27,426 (paid by the newspaper). Section 8 CCA does not permit the public interest defence. Otherwise Mr Seckerson might have had a strong basis for arguing that alleged child cruelty (in the Keran Henderson case) was in the public interest.[107]

In July 2010, 19-year-old juror Danielle Robinson was found guilty of contempt of court for sending text messages to another woman sitting in a second trial at Hull Crown Court. She had passed on 'gossip' from the jury room, such as: 'Hi, it's Danielle from court. Are you doing the kid's case?' and 'He's been in prison before and is a paedo, and when he broke into the pub he took all the kids underwear xx'. Though both women were subsequently dismissed from sitting on the juries, it was touch and go whether the cases would be allowed to continue. Judge Roger Thorn QC called Robinson's texts a blatant attempt to influence a jury and said that her ignorance was no excuse for such contemptuous behaviour. She received an eight-month suspended sentence.[108]

In June 2011, juror Joanne Fraill,[109] 40, from Blackley, Manchester, revealed highly sensitive details about jury room discussions when she swapped online messages with Jamie Sewart, 34, who had been acquitted at the trial. Fraill had used Facebook to contact the defendant in a multimillion-pound drugs trial when the jury was still considering charges against the other defendants. Fraill admitted breaching s 8 CCA by using Facebook and also conducting an internet search into Sewart's boyfriend, Gary Knox, a co-defendant, while the jury was still deliberating in his case. Fraill's contemptuous actions led to the collapse of that trial, contributing to a £6m legal bill. The Lord Chief Justice, Lord Judge, and two other senior judges sentenced Ms Fraill to eight months' imprisonment for contempt of court.

Following the Joanne Fraill contempt conviction in 2011, the Lord Chief Justice, Lord Judge, issued a general warning over the need to preserve the integrity of jury trials.[110] Lord Judge referred to three separate criminal appeals where appellants were successful because of unsafe jury verdicts in the light of jury irregularities including the dangers of social networking in relation to jury tampering (see: R v Twomey and Others;[111] R v Guthrie & Others[112]).

In the Paul Chambers case[113] – also known as the 'Twitter Joke trial' – the administration and finance supervisor, Paul Chambers, 26, found himself convicted of tweeting his frustration when being delayed in a snowstorm at Robin Hood Airport in South Yorkshire on 6 January 2010. He had posted a message on Twitter: 'Crap! Robin Hood airport is

---

106 Source: 'Juror speaks out' by Mike Seckerson, Times, 29 January 2008.
107 Attorney General v Seckerson and Times Newspapers Ltd [2009] EMLR 371 (Admin).
108 Source: 'Teenager who jeopardised trials with texts to juror escapes jail', by Jo Adetunji, Guardian, 14 July 2010.
109 AG v Fraill and another; see also: R v Knox [2011] All ER 103.
110 Source: Press Release by the Judiciary of England and Wales on 9 December 2011: 'The Lord Chief Justice Issues Warning over Jurors Judicial Office news release'.
111 R v Twomey (John) & Blake (Peter) & Hibberd (Barry) & Cameron (Glen) [2011] EWCA Crim 8.
112 R v Guthrie (Riccardo) & Guthrie (Bianca) & Guthrie (Cosimo) & Campbell (Courtney) [2011] EWCA Crim 1338.
113 Chambers (Paul) v DPP [2012] EWHC 2157 (Admin) ('the Twitter Joke trial').

closed. You've got a week and a bit to get your shit together otherwise I'm blowing the airport sky high!!' Chambers used his own name for this purpose and was registered as '@PaulJChambers', with a personal photograph as his account picture. The message was later found by an off-duty manager at the airport during an unrelated computer search, and the matter was duly reported to the local police.

Chambers was arrested by anti-terror police, his house was searched and his mobile phone, laptop and desktop hard drive were confiscated. He was charged with 'sending a public electronic message that was grossly offensive or of an indecent, obscene or menacing character' contrary to section 127(1)(b) of the Communications Act 2003 and section 1 of the Malicious Communications Act 1988. On 10 May, he was found guilty at Doncaster Magistrates' Court and fined £385 and ordered to pay £600 costs. Chambers lost his appeal against his conviction in February 2012. In his second appeal against the DPP, the Lord Chief Justice, Lord Judge, announced a reserved judgment on 22 June 2012. Chambers' conviction was quashed on 27 July 2012. The approved judgment concluded that a 'tweet' does not constitute a criminal office if the message is not of a menacing character (i.e. he did not have the necessary *mens rea* for the Communications Act offence).[114]

In advance of the John Terry trial in February 2012, Newcastle United footballer Joey Barton sent some robust tweets with plain views on Terry and his opinion about the alleged racism charge. Terry had been charged with racially aggravated (verbal) offences against QPR defender Anton Ferdinand (including use of the word 'black') on 23 October 2011. Terry was cleared of the charge in July 2012. In respect of Joey Barton's tweets, the Attorney General, Dominic Grieve QC, decided to take no 'contempt' action, which was good news for Barton. Seemingly, the AG took the view that the tweets did not cause a serious impediment to John Terry's case by influencing any witnesses or the presiding magistrate who heard the case.

Following a number of social media offences by jurors, AG Dominic Grieve QC championed a new criminal offence of 'misconduct by a juror', a measure which would give clarity to jurors about what is and is not permissible.

This was subsequently recognized by Parliament when amending the Juries Act 1974 by way of ss 69–77 of the Criminal Justice and Courts Act 2015, making certain misconduct by jurors a criminal offence, as opposed to a contempt of court. Section 77 of the 2015 Act makes clear that the creation of the new offences does not affect what constitutes contempt of court at common law. Section 75 and Schedule 13 of the 2015 Act amended the Coroners and Justice Act 2015 to make similar provision for jurors at inquests during their deliberations, including provision for surrender of electronic devices by jurors and provision creating offences of juror misconduct.

The 2015 offences are now used to prosecute jurors where their misconduct falls within the proscribed behaviour and can amount to *indictable* offences.

Perhaps confusingly, there are now several offences for 'juror misconduct' which can be prosecuted under different pieces of legislation. Section 8 CCA relates specifically to proceedings for contempt regarding breaches of confidentiality of *jury deliberations* in criminal trials. Sections 20A–G of the Juries Act 1974 make certain misconduct by jurors a criminal offence, as opposed to a contempt of court.[115]

---

114 Ibid. at paras 35–38 (the Lord Chief Justice of England and Wales, Lord Judge).
115 ss 69–77 of the Criminal Justice and Courts Act 2015 amended the Juries Act 1974.

Indictable offences

It is an offence for a member of the jury to:

- research the case he or she is trying during the trial period for reasons connected to that case (s 20A Juries Act 1974);
- intentionally disclose information to another member of the jury that had been obtained by research in contravention of the previous section (s 20A) and the information has not been provided by the court (s 20B Juries Act 1974);
- intentionally engage in conduct, during the trial period, from which it may reasonably be concluded that the person intends to try the issue otherwise than on the basis of the evidence presented in the proceedings on the issue (s 20C Juries Act 1974). This is 'prohibited conduct';
- intentionally disclose information about statements made, opinions expressed, arguments advanced, or votes cast by members of a jury in the course of their deliberations in proceedings before a court, or to solicit or obtain such information (ss 20D, 20E, 20F and 20G Juries Act 1974).

The above offences are indictable only, and the maximum penalty is two years' imprisonment and/or a fine.

Under sections 20F(1)–(2) Juries Act 1974, *after* the jury has been discharged, it is not an offence for a person to disclose jury deliberations to the police or to designated court officers, if he or she reasonably believes that jury misconduct or a contempt of court has occurred, or where s/he reasonably believes that conduct of a juror in those proceedings may provide grounds for an appeal against conviction or sentence. Under sections 20F(3)–(9), disclosures made in the course of obtaining any information in the course of an investigation or in any subsequent proceedings for jury misconduct or contempt are also exempt from prosecution.

Present-day jury directions include a warning by the judge not to consult the internet or any other form of text-based or social networking communication until the full conclusion of the trial. Section 69 of the Criminal Justice and Courts Act 2015 inserted a new s 15A into the Juries Act 1974 ('Surrender of electronic communications devices'). This provision gives judges the discretionary power to order jurors to surrender their electronic communications devices for a period of time while on jury service. It will be a contempt of court to fail to surrender their devices in accordance with a direction to do so. Section 70 inserts a new s 54A into the Courts Act 2003 and gives a court security officer the power to search a juror (if ordered to do so by a judge) and seize such a device.

On 22 December 2016 in the Crown Court at Manchester before the Recorder of Manchester, HHJ Stockdale QC, and a jury, Piotr Olejarczyk, 30, was convicted of murder by majority verdict (11:1). On the following day he was sentenced to imprisonment for life, with the period specified as a minimum term of 21 years less time spent on remand.[116] Olejarczyk and his deceased victim, Jakub Gorski, were both Polish nationals,

---

116 s 269(2) Criminal Justice Act 2003.

were known to one another and both worked as builders. On 10 June 2016, following a confrontation, Olejarczyk stabbed the victim with a single stab wound to the chest which fatally penetrated his heart.

His appeal was heard in March 2018, where Olejarczyk argued that his trial was unfair – because the jury foreman had disobeyed the trial judge's warnings and had undertaken his own research online. A note to the trial judge had raised concerns that jury foreman Lionel Tweed had ignored the judge's strict rules issued to the jurors in advance of the trial, preventing jurors from making internet searches during a trial. A police investigation revealed that Tweed had searched the internet for information about compulsory military service in Poland during Olejarczyk's trial. The foreman was spoken to by police and his mobile phone, laptop and iPad were seized; Tweed was later sentenced to four months' imprisonment after pleading guilty to two charges involving research by a juror and sharing that research with other jurors.

The CA dismissed Olejarczyk's appeal after the judges found that Tweed's actions had not affected the 'safety' of the murderer's conviction. Sir Brian Leveson, President of the Queen's Bench Division, said that whether or not national service had been abolished in Poland was not an issue at the trial. His application for a retrial was refused.[117]

Assessing whether a juror's use of new media constitutes a communication to the public or a section of it will vary significantly both between the various (social) media available and depending on how the particular service is used. Email, for example, would generally seem analogous to private correspondence. Social networking sites, such as Facebook and Twitter, can involve communications to the world at large or to a limited number of 'friends' or 'followers' by the use of privacy settings. In such cases, it appears that whether a communication was to the public or a section of it would need to be decided on a case-by-case basis (see: *AG v Harkins and AG v Liddle* (2013)[118]).

5.6.2 Do British contempt laws interfere with freedom of expression?

We can refer to some Strasbourg jurisprudence in relation to the right to a fair trial under Article 6(1) ECHR. Whilst the ECtHR does not specifically refer to 'contempt of court' (for this will be different in domestic legislation of subscribing countries to the Convention) we can find some cases which involve juror misconduct. In *Remli v France* (1996)[119] the trial judge had failed to react to an allegation that an identifiable juror had been overheard to say that he was a racist.

In *Gregory v UK* (1997),[120] the decision of a judge, faced with an allegation of racial bias in a jury trying a black defendant, to give the jury a forceful redirection instructing them to put all thoughts of prejudice out of their minds and to consider the case on the evidence alone, was sufficient to ensure the jury's impartiality and to dispel any doubts as to the fairness of the defendant's trial. The ECtHR ruled by a majority of eight to one that there had been no infringement of the right to a fair hearing by an independent and impartial tribunal established by law under Article 6(1) ECHR.

---

117 R v *Olejarczyk (Piotr)* [2018] EWCA Crim 788 at para. 21 (CA Crim Div) (Sir Brian Leveson).
118 [2013] EWHC 1455 (Admin).
119 (1996) 22 EHRR 253.
120 (1997) 25 EHRR 577.

The applicant, David Gregory, who was black, had been tried for robbery before a jury at Manchester Crown Court in November 1991. The jury retired at 10.46am on 28 November to consider their verdict but returned at 12.28 and handed to the trial judge a note stating: 'Jury showing racial overtones. One member to be excused'. In the jury's absence, the judge consulted counsel for the prosecution and defence about a suitable response to the note. Defence counsel recollected asking the judge to discharge the jury, but in the judge's recollection both counsel agreed to his proposal to issue a redirection. The jury was recalled, and the judge instructed them to put out of their minds any thoughts of prejudice and to consider the case on the evidence alone. After a further direction in which the judge told the jury that he could accept a majority verdict, the defendant was found guilty by a 10–2 majority. The applicant was sentenced to six years' imprisonment. His applications for leave to appeal against conviction were refused. The Strasbourg Court stressed that the impartiality of a tribunal including a jury had to be determined on the basis of both a subjective and an objective test.

In *Sander v UK* (2000),[121] the Strasbourg Human Rights Court held that there had been a violation of Article 6(1) ECHR on the ground that the trial judge had failed to provide sufficient guarantees to exclude any objectively justified or legitimate doubts about the impartiality of the court towards an Asian accused. The ECtHR reviewed its decision in *Gregory* regarding the fundamental importance of public confidence in the courts and the rule governing the secrecy of jury deliberations and any outside influences jurors may use.

The same question was addressed by the House of Lords in the two conjoined appeals in *Mirza* and *Connor* (2004):[122] whether evidence about jury deliberations that revealed a lack of impartiality was always inadmissible under the common law secrecy rule. The issue in *Mirza* concerned a juror who had revealed after the verdict that some jury members were associated with a neo-Nazi group, and that, during jury deliberations, they strongly influenced the conviction of the accused because he was a black immigrant. In *Connor*, a juror had revealed after the verdict that a majority of the jury refused to deliberate at all and had made up its mind virtually at the start of the trial; that jury ultimately arrived at a guilty verdict by spinning a coin. Dismissing both appeals, the House of Lords stated that common and statutory provision of contempt of court was well established in the area of jury deliberations under section 8 CCA.

In *Re B* (2006),[123] the BBC and other media organizations appealed against a High Court ruling that had ordered a complete reporting ban under section 4(2) CCA until the conclusion of the trial proceedings. B and D were indicted for 23 offences, including conspiracy to commit murder and acts of terrorism. B had already pleaded guilty to some offences. B and D contended that the extraneous comments made by the media on B's previous sentencing hearing were potentially disastrous to a fair hearing in the present case and D's trial. The defendants argued that the media coverage would seriously prejudice a (yet unselected) jury, arguing, *inter alia*, Article 6(1) ECHR and their right to a fair trial. Allowing the appeal by the BBC, Sir Igor Judge ruled that media editors ought to be trusted to fulfil their responsibilities and exercise sensible judgment in the publication of such information – reasoning that the media would be familiar with contempt legislation.

---

121 (2000) 31 EHRR 1003.
122 *R v Connor and another; R v Mirza* [2004] (conjoined appeals) UKHL 2 (HL).
123 *R v B* [2006] EWCA Crim 2692 ('Re B').

To date the law of contempt has not been changed, and it appears that Parliament feels that the law still serves the interests of justice where defendants receive a fair (criminal) trial on one hand and the general public learn via the media about the court proceedings. Where the requisite risk of serious prejudice and section 1 'contempt' have been made out, editors and journalists respectively have faced a range of penalties including substantial fines, and jurors have faced up to two years' imprisonment. The law has also been enhanced making it an indictable offence for criminal jurors to consult the internet or any other form of text-based or social networking communication under new provisions of the Juries Act 1974.

Additionally, as we have seen in the previous chapter, UK legislation continues to provide a wealth of prior restraints and automatic reporting restrictions that can be deployed to restrict what may be published about trials, victims and witnesses involved in civil and criminal proceedings.

See
Chapter 4

 FOR THOUGHT

In November 2013 a blogger posts material that is highly prejudicial about D, knowing that D is under arrest. The blogger is unidentifiable. The blogging platform is contacted by the defence team representing D with information of the fact that proceedings are active and identifying material on the blog which created a substantial risk of serious prejudice. Discuss whether an internet intermediary could be liable for contempt.

5.6.3 The impact of social media on the administration of justice

We have seen above that a number of cases have been stayed ('halted') by trial judges in recent years after the judge decided that prejudicial comments online or via social media meant that the defendants could not have a fair trial. In each case the judge concluded that it would have been impossible for jurors to deliver a verdict based on the evidence heard in court alone. A retrial was ordered (usually at a different court) with significant reporting restrictions in place.

One such high-profile case was that of two schoolgirls accused of murdering Angela Wrightson, 39, in Hartlepool on 8 December 2014. The first trial of the teenagers, who were 13 and 14 at the time of the killing, was held at Teeside Crown Court in July 2015, overseen by Sir Henry Globe QC, an experienced High Court judge who served as a junior prosecutor in the case of James Bulger's murderers Jon Venables and Robert Thompson.

See
Chapter 4.3

On the third day of the trial on 3 July 2015, Mr Justice Globe was alerted to what he called 'an avalanche of prejudicial comment' on social media including more than 500 comments. The trial judge ordered the media to remove every comment about the trial from any news article and social media post and to disable every hyperlink. He also required the media to refrain from issuing or forwarding tweets relating to the trial.[124] The BBC and eight media organizations appealed against the order on the principle of

---

124 The orders were made under s 45(4) of the Senior Courts Act 1981.

open justice in British courts, and the fact that many modern web browsers allow instant sharing to social media.[125]

But both the prosecution and defence argued there was now a real risk that the defendants could no longer have a fair trial. Mr Justice Globe agreed, rejected the appeal and stayed the trial, and a retrial, ordering a complete reporting ban on the case until verdicts were returned at the new trial. The judge made it clear he was not objecting to the media's reporting. He did, however, make the point that the chilling Facebook comments by some members of the public went 'far beyond what may be described as abuse and angry bluster'.[126]

In January 2016, the Court of Appeal heard the case of R v F and D (2016)[127] and the application by the media to lift reporting restrictions on the case and during the new trial of the two teenage girls. The CA ordered total reporting restrictions under s 4(2) CCA until the end of the second trial.[128] Sir Brian Leveson, President of the Queen's Bench Division, commented that:

> We are conscious that although we have received comprehensive submissions from the media organisations, the DPP and the individual defendants, there is no doubt that there are wider issues involved than encompassed by this particular litigation. We have no doubt that the Attorney General (as guardian of the public interest in this area) should be involved in a general analysis of the overall position in order that a wider consultation can take place and appropriate guidance issued.[129]

The girls' second trial was held many miles away at Leeds Crown Court in July 2016. The court heard that Angela Wrightson, described as vulnerable, had befriended the two young girls, buying them alcohol and sweets from the local shop. The girls made Wrightson plead for her life as they forcibly restrained her and subjected her to a sustained and brutal attack in her home in Hartlepool, then posting mocking images on Snapchat. The girls, 15 at the time of the trial, were given a sentence for life under Her Majesty's Pleasure for a minimum of 15 years.

Following F and D's trial (above), the then Attorney General, Jeremy Wright QC MP, ordered a consultation and called for evidence on 'The Impact of Social Media on the Administration of Justice' on 15 September 2017.

In R v Sarker (Sudip) (2018),[130] the CA allowed an appeal by the BBC[131] against a reporting restriction order. The judgment, given by the Lord Chief Justice, The Rt Hon The Lord Burnett of Maldon, contains important guidance on the appropriate approach to applications for restrictions on reporting in criminal proceedings, specifically in relation to

---

125 These media organization included the BBC, Guardian News and Media Ltd, Associated Newspapers Ltd., Times Newspapers Ltd, Express Newspapers Ltd, Independent Print Ltd, The Telegraph Media Group Ltd, Mirror Group Newspapers and Sky News.

126 Source: 'Angela Wrightson murder: How the media fought to report the case', BBC Online, 7 April 2016.

127 R (on the application of British Broadcasting Corporation and eight other media organisations) v F and D [2016] EWCA Crim 12 (CA) (Sir Brian Leveson, President of the Queen's Bench Division, Lady Justice Hallett, the Vice President of the Court of Appeal Crim Div and Lady Justice Sharp).

128 Ibid. at para. 44.

129 Ibid. at para. 40 (Sir Brian Leveson).

130 [2018] EWCA Crim 1341.

131 Supported by Associated Newspapers, Guardian News and Media, Mirror Group Newspapers, News Group Newspapers, the Press Association and Times Newspapers.

online articles, and a clear restatement of the significance of *open justice* principles in such applications.

The defendant, Sudip Sarker, was a surgeon. He was charged with a single count of fraud contrary to s 1 of the Fraud Act 2006. The prosecution alleged that, between 9 May 2011 and 1 September 2011, he had dishonestly exaggerated his professional experience in order to obtain an appointment as a consultant surgeon at the Alexandra Hospital in Redditch (part of the Worcestershire Acute Hospital Trust), a post he took up in August 2011. The work he undertook included bowel surgery and the use of keyhole surgical techniques. After his appointment, serious concerns were raised about the defendant's competence, which resulted in various investigations that were the subject of media reporting. Those investigations did not form part of the evidence before the jury.

At trial, the judge ordered that there should be no reports of the trial until the verdict. The basis for the order was the judge's concern that jurors would be exposed to online reports concerning the investigations into the defendant, for instance in links contained in reports of the proceedings, and that prejudice would thereby ensue.

The CA allowed the BBC's appeal against this order, holding that fair and accurate contemporaneous reporting of the trial would not have given rise to any risk of prejudice. There was no reason to assume that media reports would contain links to other articles about the defendant, and in any event such a risk could not properly justify an order restricting reports of the trial. It was important that judges should take a structured approach to reporting restriction applications, that they give proper weight to open justice principles. They should also recognize that juries can be expected to follow the court direction to give their verdict solely on the evidence given at trial and that the media can be expected to act responsibly in its reporting of criminal proceedings.[132] Sudip Sarker was sentenced to six years' imprisonment for fraud.

Recent cases have shown that social media is having some negative impact on the administration of justice particularly during criminal trials. Whilst journalists are well aware of the traditional restrictions before and during court proceedings, most of the public posting comments on social media sites are unaware of such limits.

We noted above that the Contempt of Court Act 1981 provides the framework for what can be published in order to ensure that legal proceedings are fair and that the rights of those involved in them are properly protected. Sections 1 and 2 create the strict liability rule, which makes it a contempt of court to publish anything that creates a substantial risk that the course of justice in the proceedings in question will be seriously impeded or prejudiced, even if there is no intent to cause such prejudice. We have also noted that the strict liability rule applies to *all* publications, and there is now sufficient evidence including leading authorities that this includes all types of modern forms of communication. Section 2(1) CCA defines very widely what is meant by 'publication', as including 'any speech, writing, programme included in a programme service or other communication in whatever form, which is addressed to the public at large'.

Social media platforms allow individuals to reach thousands of people via a single post, making their views readily accessible to a potentially vast audience. Anyone posting a comment on a publicly available website which creates a substantial risk of causing serious prejudice in active proceedings faces the potential prospect of proceedings for

---

132 Ibid. at para. 34 (Lord Burnett CJ).

contempt of court. Whilst the traditional mainstream media are well aware of the boundaries set out in the 1981 Act and the consequences of stepping outside them, social media presents new challenges to these fair trial protections, and the criminal justice system must ensure that it keeps pace with the information age.

5.7 Courtroom TV

The argument in favour of courtroom broadcasts is that television has long been the principal source of information for the majority of people. Just as parliamentary broadcasts and UK Supreme Court live streams are freely accessible, it is argued that public broadcasting should now include the full criminal and civil justice system (except youth and family courts).

There have been a number of high-profile cases which were broadcast all over the world, for example the trial of former Paralympian athlete, Oscar Pistorius, who shot dead his model girlfriend, Reeva Steenkamp, on Valentine's Day in 2013 in Pretoria. Parts of the trial and sentencing were broadcast live during 2014 from the South African court and in December 2015 from South Africa's Supreme Court of Appeal in Pretoria after the original verdict of culpable homicide was changed to murder. The SA Supreme Court (SCA) found Pistorius guilty of murder in December 2015. He was sentenced to 13 years and 5 months imprisonment. The SA Supreme Court rejected his appeal in 2016.

The O. J. Simpson murder trial,[133] broadcast live for nine months from the Los Angeles County Superior Court (November 1994–October 1995), made courtroom TV history. The former national American football star was acquitted of murdering his ex-wife Nicole Brown Simpson and waiter Ron Goldman in June 1994.[134]

British courtroom TV history was made in November 2004 when TV cameras were allowed to film and record a pilot project in the Court of Appeal at the Royal Courts of Justice in the *Speechley* appeal.[135] This concerned the former Lincolnshire County Council leader, Jim Speechley, after he had been convicted at Sheffield Crown Court in April 2003 of 'misconduct in public office' and sentenced to 18 months' imprisonment. During the appeal hearing, robotic cameras were focused on Kennedy LJ (presiding), Bell and Hughes JJ. William Harbage QC and Catarina Sjolin appeared for the appellant; neither the dock nor the witness box was filmed. Both Mr Speechley's conviction and his sentence were upheld, though Kennedy LJ reduced £25,000 court costs to £10,000.

In April 2012, permission was granted by Lord Hamilton, the Lord President and Lord Justice General for Scotland, to record Judge Lord Bracadale's sentencing of David Gilroy, 49, at the High Court in Edinburgh for the murder of (missing) bookkeeper Suzanne Pilley. Gilroy, from Edinburgh, was found guilty on 15 March 2012 of murdering 38-year-old Miss Pilley. Broadcaster Scottish Television (STV) focused only on the judge as the sentence of life imprisonment (with a minimum custodial part of 18 years) was read out. Gilroy was not filmed, and neither was anyone else in the courtroom TV footage (except for the macer (mace bearer) and the legal clerk).[136]

---

133 People of the State of California v Orenthal James Simpson, January 24, 1995 (unreported).

134 For further discussion see: Hodes, W.W. (1996) pp. 1075–1108.

135 R v *Speechley* [2004] (unreported) (CA).

136 Source: TV footage: 'David Gilroy jailed for life for the murder of missing bookkeeper Suzanne Pilley', *STV*, 18 April 2012.

The Nat Fraser trial, filmed in the Edinburgh High Court in 2012, was shown on British TV in full in July 2013. The documentary *The Murder Trial* was made by Windfall Films as a Channel 4 production, following the full trial for six weeks as the jury returned a guilty verdict against Fraser on the charge of murdering his wife. The programme provided a rare insight into proceedings in Scottish courts. Television viewers heard and saw the same evidence as the jury of the retrial of a man who was found guilty, in 2003, of the murder of his wife Arlene in 1998, but whose conviction had been quashed. They heard the opening statement by prosecutor Alex Prentice QC and his introductory description of the case as 'tricky', since neither Arlene Fraser's body nor a murder weapon was ever found. Additionally, Fraser had accounted for his movements on the day of the murder. Ultimately, Fraser was found guilty by a majority verdict, and the film's biggest shock emerged – a history of domestic abuse that had been inadmissible at the trial.

5.7.1 The law regarding filming and photographing in courts

The UK has an open justice system, and courtroom TV could bring public benefits especially in high profile trials and appeals. In March 2016 the then Lord Chief Justice, Lord Thomas of Cwmgiedd, announced that Crown Court sentencing remarks could be broadcast from selected 'pilot' courts in England and Wales, including the Old Bailey (Central Criminal Court, London), Bristol, Manchester, Liverpool and Cardiff.[137] Lord Thomas pointed out that judicial discretion should always allow or disallow filming built into contempt of court legislation.[138]

Filming and recording have been banned in the UK since the early twentieth century. The deliberate taking of photographs in court remains a contempt of court as well as an offence under s 41 of the Criminal Justice Act 1925.

It was held in *Solicitor General v Cox* (2016)[139] that a specific intent to interfere with the administration of justice was not required before such a contempt could be proven. It was sufficient that the act was deliberate and in breach of the criminal law or a court order of which the contemner was aware. In this case the three teenage respondents had attended the sentencing hearing of a friend convicted of murder. They were all very familiar with court procedures, having been convicted of 70 offences between them. While waiting for the friend's hearing, despite notices at every courtroom entrance prohibiting the use of mobile phones, the respondents took photos with their phones of the courtroom. During the hearing, at which the victim's family were present, the second respondent took photos and video footage. Some of the images contained parts of the notices prohibiting the use of mobile phones. The respondents put some of the images on social media with derogatory comments about the judiciary.

The Solicitor General submitted that summary proceedings would inadequately reflect the gravity of the respondents' conduct and applied for the committal to prison of two respondents for contempt of court. The first respondent pleaded guilty to contempt, but the second respondent argued that it was wrong to extend the ambit of contempt of court when section 41 dealt with illegal photography. He further argued that contempt required a specific intention to impede or prejudice the course of justice, and he had not had the requisite intent.

---

137 Source: Message from the Lord Chief Justice: 'Broadcasting in the Crown Court', *Judicial News*, 24 March 2016.
138 ss 4(2) and 11 CCA 1981.
139 [2016] EWHC 1241 (QB).

The Divisional Court held that the taking and subsequent publication of the photos on social media each constituted the *actus reus* of contempt. The real and specific risk of serious interference with the proper administration of justice was evident. The photos taken prior to the sentencing hearing had created the real risk of interference through disruption of the proceedings in those courtrooms. The publication of illegally taken images was itself a serious contempt and risked diminishing the court's necessary authority over the conduct of its proceedings and its role in upholding the rule of law. The instant case clearly required the Solicitor General to bring proceedings for contempt given its gravity.[140]

As the law stands, broadcasting images of the witness box does not comply with victim protection legislation such as the Crime and Disorder Act 1998, the Protection from Harassment Act 1997 or the Vulnerable Witness (Scotland) Act 2004.[141] Arguably, there is a public interest argument in allowing filming of a prosecution or defence opening to a jury and of mitigation and sentence – a powerful teaching tool in law schools and an educational element for the public in general.

One danger of courtroom TV is that it might be seen as sensationalist and have a potential effect in high-profile trials, as already witnessed in the media circus which surrounded the 'Soham trial' of Ian Huntley in December 2003 or the eight-week historical child sex abuse trial of Rolf Harris in June 2014, when the 84-year-old iconic children's entertainer and veteran TV star was convicted at Southwark Crown Court of indecent assault on four girls aged between 7 and 19 over three decades ago.[142]

5.7.2 Arguments for and against courtroom TV

Legal experts are conflicted over whether the opening of English and Welsh courtrooms to television cameras would have positive or negative implications for the national justice system. The argument against courtroom TV rests on the belief that the camera's presence might intimidate witnesses and affect their testimony, thereby creating an O. J. Simpson–style media circus. But equally, as the Lockerbie trial and Speechley appeal have shown, there is a strong case for courtroom broadcasting, not just for public interest concerns but also for educational reasons, such as law school training and introducing the open justice principle to schools and colleges.

It is perhaps worth looking at a reality TV show, the Channel 5 TV series and reality show *Can't Pay? We'll Take It Away*, which demonstrates how an intrusive broadcast can impact on a family's right to privacy. The legal challenge concerned Shakir Ali and Shahida Aslam,[143] featuring their eviction from their home they had been renting at 137 Fanshawe Avenue, Barking, Essex on 2 April 2015. The eviction was executed by bailiffs ('High Court Enforcement Agents') enforcing a warrant and right of entry obtained by their landlord Rashid Ahmed. The TV programme showed shots of Mr. Ali having just woken up, wearing pyjama bottoms and a vest, and shots of the couple's bedroom and their two children's rooms and of family possessions stored in bags. It also showed the landlord's son humiliating the couple and revealed details including that the couple were

---

140 Ibid. at paras 23–24, 26, 28–31 (Ouseley J with whom Lord Thomas of Cwmgiedd CJ agreed in his judgment).
141 The Vulnerable Witness (Scotland) Act 2004 is aimed at making it easier for child and adult vulnerable witnesses to give their best evidence by formalizing existing special measures for giving evidence and introducing new measures, such as locations outside the courthouse known as 'remote sites'.
142 See also: Heistie, R. and Pennington, N. (1996) pp. 957–976.
143 *Shakir Ali and Shahida Aslam v Channel 5 Broadcast Ltd* [2018] EWHC 298 (Ch) (before Arnold on 22.2.2018).

unemployed and receiving housing benefit. The programme was watched 9.6m times on Channel 5 over an 18-month period and resulted, *inter alia*, the couple's daughter being bullied at school.

Mr Justice Arnold allowed the claim by the couple and awarded £20,000 in damages (£10,000 each). Arnold J referred to the 'ultimate balancing test' between the individuals' right to privacy and the general public interest when he said:

> I consider that the Claimants did have a reasonable expectation of privacy in respect of the information included in the Programme about which they complain. The justification relied upon by Channel 5 for interfering with the Claimants' Article 8 rights is that the Programme contributed to a debate of general interest. As I have explained, I accept that the Programme did contribute to a debate of general interest, but I consider the inclusion of the Claimants' private information went beyond what was justified for that purpose.[144]

Arguably, there are clear positive arguments in favour of open justice and justice being seen to be done by televising court proceedings. For example, had the trial of Tommy Robinson been seen on television, the conspiracy theory that he was punished for exercising a right to free speech could hardly have taken hold worldwide. Viewers could have observed and appreciated a degree of procedural unfairness in this case.[145]

See
above 5.6

The televising of criminal trials should have stringent protocols – unlike the US O.J. Simpson trial: the faces of the jury should never be shown, and defendants would not be pictured from the dock unless they protested from it or went into the witness box to give evidence. The trial judge would have wide discretion to bar coverage of vulnerable witnesses under current legislation. The former Victims' Commissioner, Baroness Helen Newlove, declared in August 2018 that courtroom TV could improve the open justice system and give victims a voice as their statements are read out in open court.

Geoffrey Robertson QC also advocates courtroom TV. He commented in the *Guardian* that televising trials meant that lawyers and barristers would be better prepared, the judges better behaved, and the public better informed. Robertson comments that courts are public occasions, but there will always be applications for privacy. and judges can avail themselves of ample legislation allowing either the media or the individual applicant their respective freedom of expression (and to receive information) and the right to privacy.[146]

Lord Burnett of Maldon LCJ announced on 10 September 2018 that judges should publish more judgments online and that they should engage more with the media, stating that:

> We cannot complain that the public does not understand what we do, and its importance, if we do not take steps to lift the veil a little and explain what we do.[147]

---

144 Ibid. at para. 210 (Arnold J).

145 *Re. Stephen Yaxley-Lennon (aka Tommy Robinson)* [2018] EWCA Crim 1856.

146 Source: 'Put cameras in British courtrooms, and make justice truly transparent', by Geoffrey Robertson QC, *Guardian*, 24 August 2018.

147 Lord Chief Justice of England and Wales (2018) The Right Hon. The Lord Burnett of Maldon, 'Becoming Stronger Together'. Speech given to the Commonwealth Judges and Magistrates' Association Annual Conference, Brisbane, Australia, 10 September 2018.

The legal scope for filming in courts has been expanding in recent years, with Lord Burnett LCJ informing the House of Lords constitution committee in early 2018 that plans are underway to live-stream selected cased from the Court of Appeal's civil division.

The Supreme Court's 2017–2018 annual report indicates that over 137,800 people watched proceedings in the court live, and a further 75,000 viewed archived cases on demand on YouTube. The most watched Supreme Court case remains Gina Miller's 2016 appeal regarding the legality of the government's power to trigger Brexit under Article 50 of the Treaty on the European Union.[148]

5.7.3 Open justice and court reporting: artificial intelligence

One way the open justice principle is upheld is the attendance and reporting by media representatives on court proceedings. An increasing number of journalists now represent online news platforms while some are freelance and either publish stories themselves or provide them to others. Some work for newspapers, national, regional or local; others work for broadcast media such as radio and TV. Others work for press agencies like the Press Association (PA) which provide stories to established media organizations. It is hoped that most journalists covering court and tribunal hearings will have had training in media law and should be familiar with legal issues relating to reporting proceedings.

In November 2018 former Justice Minister Lucy Frazer QC MP held roundtable discussions with representatives from the media how access to the courts could be maintained and enhanced as part of the Ministry of Justice (MOJ) modernization initiative. She announced:

> Open justice is a fundamental part of our legal system and impartial court reporting is crucial in maintaining public confidence. As we continue to reform our courts and tribunals, it is important that we work with the media to ensure access is maintained and, where possible, enhanced.[149]

The roundtable was attended by representatives of a range of large and small news organizations from across England and Wales, including editors and reporters, to help support and promote the principle of open justice. The UK government has invested £1bn in reforming and modernizing courts and tribunals, and artificial intelligence (AI) is now used in the majority of all summary and small claims proceedings. During the pilot run in courts from September 2018 onwards, some 1,500 guilty pleas were taken online in motoring offences, over 3,000 small claims were handled online in civil actions, about 40 per cent of divorce petitions were dealt with online and probate applications following

---

148 R (on the application of Miller and another) v Secretary of State for Exiting the European Union [2017] UKSC 5 ('the Gina Miller case').

149 Source: Ministry of Justice press release 15 November 2018, 'Justice Minister chairs roundtable on media access to courts. Newspapers, broadcasters and online platforms will today discuss open justice and access to courts at a roundtable hosted by Justice Minister Lucy Frazer QC MP'. Amongst those in attendance were Press Association; ITN; BBC; Evening Standard; News Media Association; Huffpost UK; Johnston Press; Express and Star (Wolverhampton); Coventry Evening Telegraph; News UK; Associated Newspapers; The Sun; Guardian Media Group; Manchester Evening News; Newsquest; Daily Telegraph; Buzzfeed; Society of Editors.

the death of a parent or loved were successfully dealt with. The MOJ argues that this use of AI has saved people time and trouble, cut errors by 90 per cent and reduced court delays.[150]

Increasingly the courts are conducting their work in private, online or via AI, and generally the British mainstream media comply with reporting restrictions and internet take-down orders. All of this is in stark contrast to the United States, where the First Amendment allows completely open media reporting of court proceedings, including publication of interviews with prosecutors, defence counsel, the families of the accused and the victims and even the jurors − all while the trial is in progress, as we have seen in the O.J. Simpson trial and other high-profile cases. The UK government's plans to achieve 'speedy' justice have largely been achieved, and it remains questionable whether transparency in the court system is suffering in the process. For this reason, it is important that courtroom TV is advanced so that broadcasts become more widespread in bringing local justice to the communities.

See
Chapter 4.7

 FOR THOUGHT

> Some legal commentators suggest that a wider use of cameras in British courts would lead to more openness in the English justice system and improve the public's understanding of and engagement with the law. However, others cite concerns with a move towards televised proceedings, including that this would promote sensationalism in the way trials are carried out and reduce the justice system to consumer entertainment. Discuss with reference to legislation and leading authorities.

 ## 5.8 Further reading

Erdunast, P. (2018) 'The multiple legal sources of the common law right of access to the courts', *Public Law*, July, 427–443.
Paul Erdunast's article uncovers and explains the multiple strands of authority behind the development of the open justice principle and access to the courts in the UK. He undertakes an exploration of sources of common and statutory provisions. The author examines how the courts have developed common law right over the past decade or so including a discussion on contempt of court. These rights are likely to survive the repeal of the HRA should this occur. This article critiques the predominant ways in which the development of human rights have previously been misunderstood, proposing a more nuanced and holistic assessment involving several distinct lines of case law. It concludes that open justice principle three main sources: firstly, and originally, the principle that justice is not to be denied; secondly, the principle that impeding access to court constitutes contempt of court; and finally, the case law of the European Court of Human Rights (ECtHR).

---

150 Ibid.

Hastie, R. and Pennington, N. (1996) 'The O. J. Simpson stories: Behavioral scientists' reflections on the *People of the State of California v. Orenthal James Simpson*', *University of Colorado Law Review*, 67(4), 957–976.
Reid Hastie and Nancy Pennington vividly describe and comment on the O. J. Simpson trial in 1994–1995, which captured the United States as it was fully televised for months. The authors call this the 'worst example of the American adversarial jury trial process' where the public saw this as a 'big money' trial, with prominent attorneys performing nine months of trial tactics and courtroom manoeuvres. The authors comment on a wide range of evidence, including heart-rending testimonials, horrifying photographs of the victims' bodies, intellectually challenging scientific analysis and mind-boggling statistics – all publicly aired on TV. The *Simpson* trial became the most widely observed legal event of all time, where this became a trial by the media. Reactions to the verdict were also dramatic, revealing a wide gap between the attitudes of majority white and minority African American citizens. The authors comment on jury behaviour and define the cognitive psychological model of the juror decision-making process in this fascinating essay.

Wood, H. (2018) 'From *Judge Judy* to *Judge Rinder* and *Judge Geordie*: humour, emotion and "televisual legal consciousness"', *International Journal of Law in Context*, 14(4), 581–595.
Helen Wood's paper looks at popular courtroom TV drama, such as the British shows – *Judge Rinder* (ITV) and *Judge Geordie* (MTV) – and America's *Judge Judy* (CBS) and reflects on whether the general public thinks that this form of courtroom TV reflects 'real' courts. Whilst media studies tend to focus on questions of representation, demonstrating how judge shows fit an ideological neoliberal agenda of educating audiences in lessons of self-responsibility, the author argues that the representation of 'the law' is missing from this form of legal representation. Will the general public be able to distinguish daytime reality courtroom TV from actual civil and legal courtroom procedure? Wood concludes that the key question about whether these shows offer a 'true' representation of a court is redundant; rather that these shows 'matter' in terms of a broader 'legal consciousness'. She surmizes that these reality courtroom TV shows offer 'televisual legal consciousness' that intervenes within the broader cultural moment of prolific adjudication in advanced capitalism, but not always in the most predictable and prescriptive of ways.

Chapter 6

Freedom of public information and data protection

> **Key points**
>
> This chapter will cover the following questions:
>
> o   What constitutes freedom of information?
> o   What type of information can be accessed and released under the FOIA?
> o   What is the role of the Information Commissioner?
> o   What is the legal route once an FOIA access request has been refused?
> o   What is the role of data controllers?
> o   What is the significance of the GDPR and the Data Protection Act 2018?
> o   Can an individual still demand the right to remain anonymous in the internet?
> o   Has the FOIA made a difference to public life?

6.1 Overview

This chapter looks at the changing landscape of data protection legislation in the EU and the UK and the impact of the General Data Protection Regulation (GDPR)[1] by way of the Data Protection Act 2018, and furthermore, how data controllers now have to safeguard personal data and the disclosing and sharing of personal data with third parties.

The increasingly important role as law enforcer of the Information Commissioner and her office (ICO) is explored in line with FOIA and data protection legislation. The Northern Irish and Scottish counterparts are also discussed.

Some legal challenges involving FOIA access requests are highlighted, such as the *Guardian's* Rob Evans' repeated requests to gain sight of the Prince of Wales, Prince Charles' correspondence with government departments and Ministers, known as the 'Prince Charles spider letters' case. This legal challenge took more than a decade until the Supreme Court eventually allowed insight into the future King's correspondence and views. Case law in this chapter will focus on FOIA appeals at the Upper Tribunal and UKSC levels, including the lengthy case of *BBC v Sugar* (2012).[2]

6.2 Historical overview and lessons from abroad

The public's 'right to know' has existed in Sweden since the eighteenth century, in the United States since 1966; in France since 1978;[3] in Canada, Australia and New Zealand since 1982 and in the Netherlands since 1991.

---

1   Regulation (EU) 2016/679 (the General Data Protection Regulation – GDPR) which repealed the Data Protection Directive 95/46 EC.
2   *BBC v Sugar (deceased) (No 2)* [2012] UKSC 4.
3   Two pieces of French legislation provide the right to access government records: (1) Loi no 78–753 du 17 juillet 1978 de la liberté d'accès au documents administratifs and (2) Loi no 79–587 du juillet 1979 relative à la motivation des actes administratifs et à l'amélioration des relations entre l'administration et le public.

The legislative struggle in Britain for freedom of information is inextricably linked to freedom of speech and press freedom. Until it was reformed in 1989, section 2 of the Official Secrets Act 1911 made it an offence for any civil servant or public contractor to reveal any information he had obtained in the course of his work, no matter how insignificant, an offence which successive governments continued to prosecute well into the 1990s, despite recommendations published in 1972 by the Franks Committee calling for reform.[4]

6.2.1 The legislative path to freedom of information in the UK

The Labour Party first pledged itself to a Freedom of Information Bill in its 1974 election manifesto, but the uncertain positions of the Wilson and Callaghan governments made progress impossible. In 1978, Liberal MP, journalist and humourist Clement Freud (1924–2009) introduced an Official Information Bill as a Private Member's Bill. The bill would have repealed the controversial catch-all section 2 of the Official Secrets Act 1911 and would have established the right of freedom of information two decades before the FOIA 2000. Freud secured a second reading of the bill despite entrenched opposition in Whitehall; it was some way through its committee stage when the Callaghan government collapsed in 1979. Two years later, Sheffield Labour MP Frank Hooley introduced another Freedom of Information Bill, which was opposed by the Conservative government and defeated at second reading. Another attempt was introduced by Liberal leader David Steel MP, which was eventually converted into the Data Protection Act passed in 1984. At the same time, Conservative MP Robin Squire promoted the 'Community Rights Project', which led to the Local Government (Access to Information) Act 1985; this Act granted the public wider rights in respect of public authorities, such as public access to council meetings, reports and papers. The Access to Personal Files Act 1987, introduced by Liberal MP Archy Kirkwood (now Lord Kirkwood of Kirkhope), gave citizens the right to see manually held social work and housing records about themselves as well as providing public access to school records.

The Access to Medical Reports Act 1988[5] resulted from another Private Member's Bill by Archy Kirkwood MP. The Act gave people the right to see any report produced by their own doctor for an employer or insurance company. In the same year, the Environment and Safety Information Act 1988 was passed, introduced as a Private Member's Bill by Chris Smith MP, which granted individuals the right to request information from a large number of organizations who had responsibilities for the environment. The Act includes public as well as private authorities and defines these as bodies that are 'under the control of' a public authority.

In 1991–1992 an amended version of the Freedom of Information Bill was reintroduced by Archy Kirkwood and backed by shadow Home Secretary Roy Hattersley MP, promising a 'Freedom of Information Act' should Labour win the 1992 general election. The bill lasted only 45 minutes in Parliament and did not receive a second reading. At the same time, the Labour front bench published the Right to Information Bill, which

---

4   Official Secrets Act debate in Parliament between Prime Minister Edward Heath and opposition leader Harold Wilson, Hansard, HC Deb 12 December 1972 vol. 848 cc 231–234.
5   As amended by the Access to Health Records Act 1990.

was partly based on the Kirkwood Bill, but also included proposals to reform the Official Secrets Act. But the Conservatives won their fourth general election on 9 April that year, defeating Neil Kinnock and his Labour Party.

Though the Conservative government under Prime Minister John Major (1990–1997) did not support any freedom of information legislation, Cabinet Minister William Waldegrave was given responsibility for implementing a policy of more open-style government. John Major introduced the White Paper on 'Open Government' and the 'Right to Know Bill' in July 1993, which proposed two new legal rights to information: public access to manually held personal files and to health and safety information. The bill also proposed to reform the Official Secrets Act 1989.[6] The 'Code of Practice' which was subsequently introduced relating to government openness and access to public official information was established in April 1994, supervised by the Parliamentary Ombudsman (the Parliamentary Commissioner for Administration[7]), who, when publishing his first report in 1996, recommended the introduction of a Freedom of Information Act.

When New Labour won the general election in 1997 under Tony Blair, they were immediately reminded of their earlier party manifesto promise to introduce freedom of information legislation. The White Paper 'Your Right to Know' in 1997 proposed wider public access to information from public bodies such as law enforcement agencies.[8] But first, the new Labour Home Secretary, Jack Straw, prioritized bringing European human rights legislation 'back home',[9] resulting in the Human Rights Act 1998.

The Freedom of Information Bill was introduced by Labour MP Andrew Mackinlay under the ten-minute rule in November 1998 in the House of Commons. It was backed by a slightly amended version in the House of Lords by the Conservative peer Lord Lucas of Crudwell, receiving its second reading in February 1999. The Macpherson Inquiry Report of 1999 into the Stephen Lawrence killing coincided with the second reading of the bill. Apart from the damning declaration that the Metropolitan Police were institutionally racist, Macpherson recommended that the police should be fully and openly accountable to public scrutiny; and the only way this could succeed would be by way of freedom of information legislation.

When the Freedom of Information Act 2000 was ultimately passed, many saw it as a disappointment, with great curtailment of the original proposals in the 'Your Right to Know' White Paper. The range of exemptions and the breadth of grounds on which information could legally be withheld has remained controversial. Tony Blair famously said in his memoirs that he regretted introducing the Freedom of Information Act at all:

> Freedom of Information. Three harmless words. I look at those words as I write them, and feel like shaking my head till it drops off my shoulders. You idiot. You

---

6 Debates in Parliament, Mr William Waldegrave and Mrs Marjorie (Mo) Mowlam, Labour MP for Redcar, Hansard, HC Deb 15 July 1993 vol. 228 cc 1113–1126.
7 The creation of the post of the Parliamentary Ombudsman was spurred on by the Crichel Down affair in 1954 and by the activism of pressure groups, including the Society for Individual Freedom. The position was created by, and his or her powers are documented in, the Parliamentary Commissioner Act 1967. Today the office also covers the NHS in England under the office of the Parliamentary and Health Service Ombudsman (created under the Health Service Commissioners Act 1993). The first Ombudsman was Sir Edmund Compton, and Dame Julie Mellor DBE has held the post since January 2012.
8 White Paper, 'Your Right to Know' (Cm. 3818), January 1998.
9 Based on the Labour Party Consultation Paper of 1996 headed 'Bringing Rights Home' which set out Labour's plans to incorporate the European Convention if it won the next election.

naive, foolish, irresponsible nincompoop. There is really no description of stupidity, no matter how vivid, that is adequate. I quake at the imbecility of it. Once I appreciated the full enormity of the blunder, I used to say – more than a little unfairly – to any civil servant who would listen: Where was Sir Humphrey when I needed him? We had legislated in the first throes of power. How could you, knowing what you know, have allowed us to do such a thing so utterly undermining of sensible government?[10]

The former Labour prime minister claimed that the FOIA was primarily used by the media, calling the Act 'dangerous' because it had deprived government of 'a reasonable level of confidentiality'. FOIA was used to address the invasion of Iraq by UK forces under the Chilcot Inquiry.[11]

6.3 The Freedom of Information Act, Environmental Information Regulations and INSPIRE Regulations

The Freedom of Information Act 2000 (FOIA) covers *any* recorded information that is held by a public authority in England, Wales and Northern Ireland, and by UK-wide public authorities based in Scotland.

The Environmental Information Regulations 2004 (EIR[12]) came into force at the same time as the FOIA 2000, generally referred to as the 'big bang approach'. Regulation 5 EIR enables public access to all documents containing 'environmental information'.

The INSPIRE ('Infrastructure for Spatial Information in the European Community') Regulations 2009[13] require public authorities that hold spatial or geographic information to make it available so that one can search it in particular ways. Spatial data is any data with a direct or indirect reference to a specific location or geographical area. Spatial data is often referred to as 'geospatial data' or 'geographic information', defined in Regulation 2 of the INSPIRE Regulations as:

> any data with a direct or indirect reference to a specific location or geographical area.

Regulation 7 INSPIRE is about network and telecommunication services, search criteria and ease of access in relation to spatial data sets and spatial data services. Regulation 7(4) relates to the discovery services, view services and download services.

Regulation 9 INSPIRE relates to the public interest test and allows public authorities to limit access to spatial data sets or spatial data services in certain circumstances.

---

10 Blair (2010).
11 House of Commons (2016) Chilcot Inquiry Report.
12 S.I. 2004/3391. The EIR 2004 are intended to give effect to the United Kingdom's obligation to implement the 2003 Directive.
13 This Instrument transposed the INSPIRE Directive 2007/2/EC ('Infrastructure for Spatial Information in the European Community') into UK law (see: Directive 2007/2/EC of the European Parliament and of the Council of 14 March 2007 establishing an Infrastructure for Spatial Information in the European Community (INSPIRE)).

Regulation 9 has a number of exceptions and limitations and is subject to consideration of the public interest test, similar to that in both the FOIA and the EIR.

Under the FOIA and EIR, individuals have a right to request any recorded information held by a public authority, such as a government department, local council or state schools. Environmental information requests can also be made to certain non-public bodies carrying out a public function, such as private universities. The right only covers *recorded* information which includes information held on computers, in emails and in printed or handwritten documents as well as images, video and audio recordings. When making a request you do not have to cite specific legislation; it is up to the public authority to decide which legislation they need to follow, such as INSPIRE, FOIA or EIR.

6.3.1 The FOIA 2000: legal purpose and exemptions

As soon as the statute came into force on 1 January 2005, journalists began to avail themselves of the new provision, making subject access requests to reveal government and ministerial secrets. Parliamentarians too have made great use of the Act. The Liberal Democrat peer, Lord Avebury,[14] for instance, made repeated FOIA requests to No 10 Downing Street for the dates of meetings or calls between Blair and Murdoch. The Cabinet Office eventually released the dates to Lord Avebury at the point he was appealing to the Information Tribunal. There were six contact dates between Blair and Murdoch between September 2002 and April 2005. In the days leading up to the start of the Iraq War in March 2003, Tony Blair had three telephone conversations with Rupert Murdoch. One of these was 'official' and minuted by civil servants. The other two were marked 'personal' or 'party political' and could not be released.

The main purpose behind Parliament passing the FOIA was that people now had a right to know about the activities of public authorities, unless there was a good reason for them not to. This is described as a presumption or assumption in favour of disclosure. The FOIA covers more than 100,000 public bodies including local councils, police forces, primary schools and GP surgeries. The Act grants general rights of access in relation to recorded information held by public authorities.

Part I of the Act is concerned with 'access to information held by public authorities'.[15] Section 1(1) states that:

Any person making a request for information to a public authority is entitled –

(a) to be informed in writing by the public authority whether it holds information of the description specified in the request, and
(b) if that is the case, to have that information communicated to him.

Schedule 1 of the Act contains a list of the bodies that are classed as public authorities in this context. Some of these bodies are listed by name, such as the Health and Safety

---

14 Eric Lubbock, 4th Baron Avebury, (1928–2016) was a Liberal MP and human rights campaigner. He won the Orpington by-election in 1962. From 1971 he served in the House of Lords, having inherited the title of Baron Avebury, until his death. In 1999, when most hereditary peers were removed from the HL, he was elected by his fellow Liberal Democrats to remain. When he died, he was the longest serving Liberal Democrat peer.
15 An extensive list is provided in Schedule 1 FOIA of the meaning of 'public authorities', covering England, Wales, Scotland and Northern Ireland.

Executive or the National Gallery. Others are listed by type, for example government departments, parish councils, or maintained schools. Executive agencies are classed as part of their parent government department; for example, the DVLA is covered by the act because it is part of the Department for Transport. However, arm's-length bodies are not considered part of the department sponsoring them, and they are listed individually in Part VI of Schedule 1.

The statute has a large number of exemptions and qualifications.[16] Exempt information need not be disclosed by the authority. The rights conferred under the FOIA are subject to 'procedural' and 'substantive limitations'. Where access is denied, the public authority has a duty to give reasons. In broad terms the FOIA established that a public authority is *not* required to publish or disclose information where to do so would put the public authority in contravention of its obligations under the Data Protection Act 1998 (DPA) – in other words, where the disclosure of the information would have a detrimental impact on an individual's expectation of privacy.

The 'class exemptions' sections of the FOIA generally fall within two categories:

Class Exemptions

- absolute exemptions;
- public interest exemptions.[17]

Section 40 contains an absolute exemption in relation to 'personal information', subject to the data protection principles set out in the Data Protection Act 1998. Section 41 exempts information which, if disclosed, 'would constitute an actionable breach of confidence'. Although that is an absolute exemption, public interest in disclosure is normally a defence to a claim for breach of confidence, and it appears to be accepted that it could, in principle, operate as an effective answer to reliance on section 41.

Section 32 FOIA exemptions remain the most legally challenged. This section covers the following *absolute exemptions* on public information:

Section 32 Exemptions

- court or tribunal reports of proceedings;
- inquests and post-mortem examinations and records;
- prison custody records.

---

16 Under Sch. I, Part VI FOIA.
17 Part II s 21 FOIA 'Exempt information accessible to applicant by other means'.

All exemptions are time-limited, expiring after 30 years when documents containing previously exempt information become historical records, unless the information is specifically exempted from the 30-year disclosure rule, such as sensitive information relating to correspondence by members of the royal family. For example, the abdication of Edward VIII in 1936 to marry American divorcee Mrs Simpson, which was sealed for 100 years.

Some *qualified information* that would (not) be in the public interest includes (*inter alia* exemptions under):

- national security (section 23 FOIA);
- defence (section 26 FOIA);
- international relations (section 27 FOIA);
- the economy (section 29 FOIA);
- domestic relationships (section 28 FOIA);
- law enforcement (section 31 FOIA);
- court records (section 32 FOIA);
- formulation of government policy (section 35 FOIA);
- communications with the monarch or any member of the royal family or household) (section 37 FOIA);
- health and safety (section 38 FOIA);
- legal professional privilege (section 42 FOIA);
- commercial interests (section 43 FOIA).

Here follows a brief summary of *standard class exemptions* of procedural access to 'public interest information':

Standard Class Exemptions

- *Section 1(3) FOIA* provides that a public authority may refuse to provide information if it is unable to understand what is being asked for. For example, if an inadequately particularized request is made, where the public authority reasonably requires further particulars in order to identify and locate the information requested. The public authority is then not obliged to provide the information until 'further particulars' have been received.
- *Section 9 FOIA* ('fees') allows the public authority to charge a fee before section 1(1) FOIA is complied with; the fees notice must be in writing and, once served, the public authority is not obliged to comply with the request for a period of three months.
- *Section 12 FOIA* allows a public authority not to comply with a request for information if the cost of compliance exceeds the 'appropriate' limit.
- *Section 14 FOIA* provides an exemption if the request for information is vexatious.

The Code of Practice provides guidance to public authorities on the discharge of their functions and responsibilities under Part I (Access to information held by public authorities) FOIA, issued under section 45 of the Act.[18]

 FOR THOUGHT – COMPANIES WHOLLY OWNED BY THE WIDER PUBLIC SECTOR

Exercise in statutory interpretation
If a company meets the definition of a publicly owned company under FOIA, it is a public authority in its own right and has the same responsibilities as any other public authority in complying with the act.

Read section 6 of the Freedom of Information Act 2000 ('publicly owned companies'). This is the only category of public authority that is not specifically referenced in the Schedules. Cite some examples of companies 'wholly owned by a single government'. Then find examples of companies 'wholly owned by the Crown'. Then provide some examples of companies 'wholly owned by the wider public sector' (s 6(2)(b) FOIA).

Is the Manchester Airports Group (MAG) a publicly owned company under FOIA? (See www.manchesterairport.co.uk/manweb.nsf/Content/AboutUsAndOurGroup). And what about the BBC? Have a look at Schedule 1 FOIA.

And what about universities? Are these subject to FOIA? What about Cambridge Enterprise Limited (the University of Cambridge) or University of Manchester Intellectual Property Limited (the University of Manchester)?

6.4 The role of the Information Commissioner's Office

The Information Commissioner's Office (ICO) is the UK's independent authority under the FOIA to uphold information rights in the 'public interest' and promote openness by public bodies and data privacy for individuals. The ICO handles data protection and freedom of information requests and is therefore covered by data protection and FOIA legislation. The General Data Protection Regulation (GDPR)[19] forms part of the data protection regime in the UK, together with the Data Protection Act 2018.

The Commissioner's role in relation to the INSPIRE Regulations 2009 is limited insofar as the enforcement and appeal provisions of the FOIA apply for the purposes of

---

18 Cabinet Office (2018) Freedom of Information Code of Practice. 4 July 2018 (minor amendments): https://assets.publishing.service.gov.uk/government/uploads/system/uploads/attachment_data/file/744071/CoP_FOI_Code_of_Practice_-_Minor_Amendments_20180926_.pdf.

19 Regulation (EU) 2016/679 of the European Parliament and of the Council of 27 April 2016 on the protection of natural persons with regard to the processing of personal data and on the free movement of such data, and repealing Directive 95/46/EC (General Data Protection Regulation – GDPR).

Regulations 7(4)(c) and 9. In effect the enforcement and appeal provisions of the FOIA are imported into the INSPIRE Regulations 2009 by virtue of Regulation 11. This means the ICO's role is limited to the consideration of complaints concerning the application of the exceptions/limitations set out in Regulation 9, including the personal data exception and the balancing of the relevant public interest test. The exceptions/limitations mirror, very closely, the exceptions in the EIR, and the INSPIRE regulations also require that a public authority has in place a complaints procedure and carries out a review of its initial decision when requested in writing.

In April 2016, the House of Commons Culture, Media and Sport Select Committee approved Elizabeth Denham as the new Information Commissioner; having previously held the position of Information and Privacy Commissioner for British Columbia, Canada and Assistant Privacy Commissioner of Canada, Ms Denham has led high-profile investigations into Yahoo!, Camelot, WhatsApp and Facebook.

What type of information can be obtained is ultimately the decision of the Information Commissioner (IC), who also decides whether the information requested might be exempt because of the risk – for instance – of prejudicing international relations.

6.4.1 The ICO's law enforcement powers

The Information Commissioner and her office (ICO) have extensive statutory law enforcement powers under FOIA and data protection legislation (DPA 2018 and GDPR), including criminal prosecution and non-criminal enforcement by way of substantial fines, audits and actions. The Commissioner has the power to serve a 'Monetary Penalty Notice' on a data controller, such as in the Bupa health insurance action in 2018. Bupa Insurance Services Limited (Bupa) was fined £175,000 by the ICO for failing to have effective security measures in place to protect customers' personal information.

The ICO established in its action that between 6 January and 11 March 2017, a Bupa employee had been able to extract the personal information of 547,000 Bupa Global customers and offered it for sale on the Dark Web. The employee accessed the information via Bupa's customer relationship management system, known as SWAN. The ICO's investigation found that, at the time, Bupa did not routinely monitor SWAN's activity log. Bupa was unaware of a defect in the system and was unable to detect unusual activity, such as bulk extractions of data. ICO Director of Investigations, Steve Eckersley, called this a serious breach, and Bupa failed to keep personal data secure. This amounted to a breach of the Data Protection Act 1998,[20] a systemic failure in Bupa's technical and organizational measures which left 1.5 million records at risk for a long time. The amount of the monetary penalty was £175,000.[21]

---

20 Due to the timing of this case, it was dealt with under the provisions and maximum penalties of the DPA 1998, and not the GDPR and DPA 2018.

21 Source: Data Protection Act 1998 Supervisory Powers of the Information Commissioner Monetary Penalty Notice to Bupa Insurance Services Ltd. of 1 Angel Court, London EC2R 7HI. Served by Stephen Eckersley, Director of Investigations Information Commissioner's Office on 26 September 2018: https://ico.org.uk/media/action-weve-taken/mpns/2259871/bupa-mpn-20180928.pdf.

A 'breach of privacy' order and fines notice was served by the ICO on 'Cold Call' under regulation 21 of the Privacy and Electronic Communications Regulations 2003 (PECR).[22] Regulation 21 applies to the making of unsolicited calls for direct marketing purposes.[23] In September 2015, the ICO fined Chichester-based company 'Cold Call Eliminations Ltd'[24] £75,000 for making unsolicited marketing calls to sell cold call–blocking devices. In 2013, 'Cold Call' had been telephoning elderly and vulnerable customers in particular to sell a call-blocking service to stop unsolicited calls, the same type of calls the company itself was making. One complainant reported to the ICO that a sales person from the company had implied they were calling from the statutory Telephone Preference Service (TPS).[25]

6.5 Data protection legislation

The Data Protection Act 2018 implemented the General Data Protection Regulation (GDPR)[26] and replaced the UK Data Protection Act 1998. The DPA 2018 is the UK's third generation of data protection law and commenced on 25 May 2018. The 2018 Act also transposed the EU Data Protection Directive 2016/680 (the Law Enforcement Directive) into domestic UK law.[27] The Directive complements GDPR and Part 3 of the DPA 2018 sets out the requirements for the processing of personal data for criminal 'law enforcement purposes', thereby enhancing the role of the Information Commissioner.

See above 6.4

This means that every EU Member State's public authority as a 'data controller' must provide access to requested information within reasonable time intervals (usually interpreted as once a year), without charge and without excessive delay, meaning usually within three months (see also: *Gillberg v Sweden* (2012)[28]).

6.5.1 The General Data Protection Regulation (GDPR)

The European Union's General Data Protection Regulation (GDPR) came into force in the UK on 25 May 2018, providing an EU-wide 'privacy shield', making the Data Protection Act 1998 effectively redundant. The GDPR provisions are included in the Data Protection Act 2018. This Act also includes measures related to wider data protection reforms in areas

---

22 As amended by the Privacy and Electronic Communications (EC Directive) (Amendment) Regulations 2004 and by the Privacy and Electronic Communications (EC Directive) (Amendment) Regulations 2011 (PECR 2011). PECR came into force on 11 December 2003 and revoked the Telecommunications (Data Protection and Privacy) Regulations 1999. PECR adopted Part V titled 'Enforcement' and Schs 6 and 9 of the DPA. By virtue of reg. 31(2) of PECR the Commissioner was made responsible for the enforcement functions under PECR.
23 PECR implemented European legislation (Directive 2002/58/EC) aimed at the protection of the individual's fundamental right to privacy in the electronic communications sector. PECR were amended for the purpose of giving effect to Directive 2009/136/EC which amended and strengthened the 2002 provisions. The ICO approaches the PECR so as to give effect to the Directives.
24 Source: Data Protection Act 1998, Supervisory Powers of the Information Commissioner Monetary Penalty Notice to Cold Call Eliminations Ltd, Suite 1 Metro House, Northgate, Chichester, West Sussex, PO19 1BE.
25 For further discussion see: Grant, H. and Round, N. (2012) pp. 8–12.
26 Also replacing the Data Protection Directive 95/46 EC from 25 May 2018. Part 3 of GDPR enhances requirements for obtaining data subject consent.
27 Directive 2016/680/EU of the European Parliament and of the Council of 27 April 2016 on the protection of natural persons with regard to the processing of personal data by competent authorities for the purposes of the prevention, investigation, detection or prosecution of criminal offences or the execution of criminal penalties, and on the free movement of such data, and repealing Council Framework Decision 2008/977/JHA (EU Law Enforcement Directive).
28 (2012) (App No 41723/06) of 3 April 2012 (ECtHR).

not covered by GDPR, such as law enforcement and security. The UK's decision to leave the EU does not affect the GDPR.

The ICO's law enforcement role is hereby substantially enhanced, which means the Information Commissioner can take action against organizations and individuals that collect, use and keep personal information. The ICO now has the power under the DPA 2018 to impose a civil monetary penalty on a data controller of up to £17million (€20m) or 4 per cent of global turnover (under the DPA 1998, the maximum financial penalty was £500,000).

Under the GDPR, the data protection principles set out the main responsibilities for organizations. The GDPR (and therein the Data Protection Act 1998) regulates the processing by an individual, a company or an organization of personal data relating to individuals in the EU. It does not apply to the processing of personal data of deceased persons or of legal entities. The legislation does not apply to data processed by an individual for purely personal reasons or for activities carried out in one's home, provided there is no connection to a professional or commercial activity. When an individual uses personal data outside the personal sphere, for socio-cultural or financial activities, for example, then the data protection law has to be respected.

Article 5 GDPR provides the key rules, including:

- *Lawfulness, fairness and transparency*: personal data must be processed in a *lawful and transparent manner*, ensuring fairness towards the individuals whose personal data is being processed.
- *Purpose limitation*: there must be a *specific purpose* for processing the data; the data controller must indicate those purposes to individuals when collecting their personal data. Data controllers cannot simply collect personal data for undefined purposes.
- *Data minimization*: data controllers must collect and process *only the personal data that is necessary to fulfil that purpose*.
- *Accuracy*: controllers must ensure the personal data is accurate and up to date, having regard to the purposes for which it is processed, and correct it if not.
- Personal data cannot be used for other purposes that are not *compatible* with the original purpose of collection.
- *Storage limitation*: data controllers must ensure that personal data is *stored for no longer than necessary* for the purposes for which it was collected.
- *Integrity and confidentiality*: organizations must install appropriate *technical and organizational safeguards* that ensure the security of the personal data, including protection against unauthorized or unlawful processing and against accidental loss, destruction or damage, using appropriate technology.

So what type of data can be processed and under what conditions? The type and amount of personal data that may be processed depends on the (legal) reason for processing it and what can be legally done with the data.

Examples

When the GDPR regulation applies
A company with an establishment in the EU provides travel services to customers based in the Baltic countries and in that context processes personal data of natural persons.

When the GDPR regulation does *not* apply
An individual uses their own private address book to invite friends via email to a party that they are organizing (household exception).

6.5.2 Adequacy provision under Article 45 GDPR: free flow of data

The UK's services-oriented economy is heavily reliant on data. Digitally intensive sectors, such as telecommunications and financial services, account for about 16 per cent of UK output and 24 per cent of total exports. Volumes of data entering and leaving the country increased 28 times between 2005 and 2015, and three-quarters of these data transfers are with EU countries. Any restriction placed on data flows would act as a barrier to trade, putting UK businesses at a competitive disadvantage. Free flow of data has become increasingly important for police and prosecutors trying to tackle cross-border crime. EU Member States have developed a range of tools to enable greater collaboration between them, many of which are dependent on the ability to transfer data freely.

The EU has very high standards for the protection of personal data. It only allows data to flow freely to a third country if the European Commission decides that the country offers a level of protection for personal data comparable to the EU's own. This is known as an 'adequacy decision'. Any transfer of personal data which is undergoing processing or intended for processing after transfer to a third country or to an international organization can only take place if the conditions laid down in the GDPR[29] are complied with by the controller and processor, including for onward transfers of personal data from the third country or an international organization to another third country or to another international organization. This is known as an 'adequacy provision'.

Article 45 GDPR deals with such transfers to third countries (particularly outside the EU) on the basis of an adequacy decision. The European Commission monitors such data transfers to third countries on an ongoing basis, pursuant to Paragraph 3 of Article 45 GDPR and decisions adopted on the basis of Article 25(6) of Directive 95/46/EC.[30]

This means the Commission has the power to determine, on the basis of Article 45, whether a country *outside* the EU offers an adequate level of data protection, whether by its

29 Regulation (EU) 2016/679.
30 Directive 95/46/EC On the Protection of Individuals with Regards to the Processing of Personal Data and on the Free Movement of Such Data (Data Protection Directive).

domestic legislation or the international commitments it has entered into. The adoption of an adequacy decision involves:

- a proposal from the European Commission;
- an opinion of the European Data Protection Board;
- an approval from representatives of EU countries;
- the adoption of the decision by the European Commissioners.

See below
6.5.3

At any time, the European Parliament and the Council may request the European Commission to maintain, amend or withdraw the adequacy decision on the grounds that its act exceeds the implementing powers provided for in the Regulation. The effect of such a decision is that personal data can flow from the EU (and Norway, Liechtenstein and Iceland) to that third country without any further safeguard being necessary. In other words, transfers to the country in question will be assimilated to intra-EU transmissions of data.

The European Commission has so far recognized 11 countries or territories as providing full adequacy provisions in data protection, including Andorra, Argentina, the Faroe Islands, Guernsey, Israel, the Isle of Man, Jersey, New Zealand, Switzerland, Uruguay and the United States (limited to the Privacy Shield framework). Adequacy talks are ongoing with South Korea. These adequacy decisions do not cover data exchanges in the law enforcement sector which are governed by the EU Law Enforcement Directive (Article 36 of Directive 2016/680/EU[31] deals with policing).

See below 6.7

The United States and Canada have been deemed to provide only partially adequate protection. In Canada, only private organizations that use the data for commercial activities have free access to EU data. Data transfers between the United States and EU were covered by the Safe Harbour Agreement, until the European Court of Justice (ECJ) found this agreement invalid in 2015 in light of the *Max Schrems* ruling in 2015.[32]

On 12 July 2016, the EU-US 'Privacy Shield' was adopted by the European Commission. The Privacy Shield entered into force immediately in all EU Member States (including the UK at that time). The Privacy Shield replaced the 'Safe Harbour' framework (post *Max Schrems*) and provides one of the lawful routes for transferring personal data from the EU to those US organizations that have publicly self-certified compliance with the Shield's rules, by providing 'adequate protection' for EU personal data transfer. The Privacy Shield framework became operational on 1 August 2016. This framework protects the fundamental rights of anyone in the EU whose personal data is transferred to the United States for commercial purposes. The

---

31 Directive 2016/680/EU of the European Parliament and of the Council of 27 April 2016 on the protection of natural persons with regard to the processing of personal data by competent authorities for the purposes of the prevention, investigation, detection or prosecution of criminal offences or the execution of criminal penalties, and on the free movement of such data, and repealing Council Framework Decision 2008/977/JHA (EU Law Enforcement Directive).

32 *Schrems (Maximilian) v Data Protection Commissioner* (Case C-362/14) [2015] All ER 34 (CJEU, Luxembourg, 6 October 2015) ('*Max Schrems No 1*').

framework also brings legal clarity for businesses relying on transatlantic data transfers. These arrangements include:

- strong data protection obligations on companies receiving personal data from the EU;
- safeguards on US government access to data;
- effective protection and redress for individuals;
- an annual joint review by EU and US to monitor the correct application of the arrangement.

6.5.3 UK data protection post-Brexit

While one of the main goals of the EU General Data Protection Regulation (GDPR) is harmonizing data protection rules throughout Europe, it does provide for certain areas where EU Member States 'shall' and 'may' pass their own legislation within the articles and exceptions of the regulation. Personal data can be transferred freely between European Economic Area (EEA) Member States, which includes all EU countries. As a third country, the UK will no longer automatically benefit from this free flow of data after Brexit.

In November 2018 the UK government published a draft text of the withdrawal agreement[33] concerning the UK's exit from – and future relationship with – the European Union. The withdrawal agreement confirmed that once Britain leaves the EU there will be a transition period lasting until 31 December 2020.[34] The EU has an option to extend this transition period. As a general rule, EU law will apply in the UK during the transition period, although the withdrawal agreement does provide for some exceptions. During the transition period, the institutions, bodies, offices and agencies of the EU will continue to have jurisdiction, as will the Court of Justice of the European Union (CJEU) in Luxembourg.

The withdrawal agreement sets out the UK's position regarding data protection during the transition period. In particular, it provides that:

- The General Data Protection Regulation 2016/679 (GDPR)[35] and the Privacy and Electronic Communications Directive 2002/58/EC (ePrivacy Directive)[36] will continue to apply to the UK in relation to personal data processed before or during the transition period, and to personal data processed

---

33 HM Government (2018).
34 The European Union (Withdrawal Agreement) Bill 2017–19 proposes to enshrine any Withdrawal Agreement between the UK and the EU in domestic law. The Withdrawal Agreement is the subject of ongoing and future Brexit negotiations and will not be detailed until the negotiations are completed.
35 Regulation (EU) 2016/679 of the European Parliament and of the Council of 27 April 2016 on the protection of natural persons with regard to the processing of personal data and on the free movement of such data, and repealing Directive 95/46/EC (General Data Protection Regulation – GDPR).
36 Directive 2002/58/EC of the European Parliament and of the Council of 12 July 2002 concerning the processing of personal data and the protection of privacy in the electronic communications sector (Directive on privacy and electronic communications – 'ePrivacy Directive').

- after the end of the transition period but on the basis of the withdrawal agreement.
- After the end of the transition period the UK is theoretically free to protect only the personal data of British citizens. The UK agrees, however, to ensure that the data of non-UK citizens will continue to be protected in accordance with GDPR standards, provided the data was being processed prior to the end of the transition period.
- The EU agrees not to treat data received from the UK during the transition period differently than data received from EU Member States solely on the basis that the UK has left the EU.

The withdrawal agreement permits the UK to 'negotiate, sign and ratify international agreements entered into in its own capacity in the areas of exclusive competence of the Union, provided those agreements do not enter into force or apply during the transition period, unless so authorized by the Union'.[37] This enables the UK to develop adequacy decisions during the transition period to support the future free flow of data outside Great Britain post-transition. This is likely to result in the recognition of the EU-US Privacy Shield as providing adequacy and to permit those with binding corporate rules approved by the Information Commissioner's Office (ICO) to still transfer data.

The UK's commitment to the European Convention on Human Rights and the Charter of Fundamental Rights of the Union will remain unchanged. This means that the UK remains a part of the Convention for the Protection of Individuals with regard to Automatic Processing of Personal Data (known as Convention 108), and transfers of data under this treaty mechanism will be deemed adequate. However, it should be noted that such transfers are limited to automatically processed data.

There is no guarantee in the withdrawal agreement that the UK will benefit from a future EU adequacy decision. Further, the withdrawal agreement does not mention the assessment to be undertaken in order to determine adequacy for the UK. The only mention of a UK adequacy decision assessment is in the political declaration outline, which states that the European Commission will commence its assessment and endeavour to adopt decisions by the end of 2020.[38] This means that in terms of international data transfer adequacy will need to be negotiated separately by the UK alongside other future trading positions. As yet, there is no transparency or clarity where data transfers is concerned after the transition period.

Many questions are left unanswered in respect how British organizations are going to undertake personal data transfer to and from the EU in the absence of an adequacy post brexit agreement.

---

37 HM Government (2018) at para. 50.
38 Ibid. at para. 39.

6.6 Legal challenges and actions

The Freedom of Information Act 2000 (FOIA) provides a statutory framework within which there are rights to be informed, on request, about the existence of, and to have communicated, information held by any public authority. The right of access to such information is a right that is applicable to everybody, and not merely those who have an interest in the information, such as the media. The duties imposed on public authorities are set out in section 1(1) FOIA and are essentially twofold:

- a duty to communicate that information; and
- a duty to 'confirm or deny' that the requested information exists.[39]

But the FOIA framework is not all-embracing. First, these rights do not apply in cases which are described as *absolute exemptions*[40] and are subject to a large number of other carefully developed qualifications. Secondly, section 78 FOIA specifies that nothing in it 'is to be taken to limit the powers of a public authority to disclose information held by it'.

See above 6.3

The ability of media organizations to hold personal data on individuals with a view to publication was under the legal spotlight in a high-profile case, namely *Stunt v Associated Newspapers* (2018).[41] James Stunt, a wealthy businessman, then married to the younger daughter of the Formula 1 tycoon Bernie Ecclestone,[42] complained about 27 articles in the *Daily Mail* titles, published between March 2014 and November 2015, including publications about his business activities and photographs of him in public enjoying a flashy lifestyle.

In the High Court proceedings he had asked Popplewell J for an injunction on the publication of any future unpublished material and photographs. Mr Stunt alleged misuse of private information under s 7 Data Protection Act 1998 (DPA). He asked for an order under ss 10 and 14 DPA to cease further publication. Associated Newspapers applied for a stay of the proceedings under s 32(4) DPA. Mr Stunt argued that this section was incompatible with EU law. The court had dismissed his argument and held that the measures in ss 32(4) and (5) DPA constituted a proper balance of the competing rights, applying the *Marleasing* principle.[43] The High Court determined that s 32(4) DPA 1998 (since superseded by the DPA 2018) was not incompatible with EU law. The High Court judge then stayed only the DPA claims relating to unpublished material.

In the CA Mr Stunt argued that the stay mechanism itself was incompatible with EU law, namely Article 9 of Directive 95/46/EC (rights to freedom of expression) and Article 22 (rights to an effective remedy). The question has become particularly relevant given that the mechanism has effectively been preserved within the 'new' Data Protection Act 2018.

---

39 s 1(6) FOIA.
40 s 2(1)(a) and (b) FOIA.
41 *Stunt (James) v Associated Newspapers Ltd and the Information Commissioner* [2018] EWCA Civ 1780 (CA).
42 Mr Stunt's marriage to Formula 1 heiress, Petra Ecclestone, ended in a bitter £5.5 billion divorce battle in 2017.
43 *Marleasing SA v La Comercial Internacional de Alimentación SA* (1990) (C-106/89) ECJ 13 NOV 1990 (1992) 1 CMLR 305; ECR I-4135. This decision by the European Court of Justice concerned the indirect effect of EU law. It established that the courts of European Union Member States have a duty to interpret national legislation in light of unimplemented EU Directives.

A data controller such as a newspaper facing proceedings under certain parts of the 'old' DPA 1998 can seek a stay of those proceedings where it claims that the personal data it holds is unpublished material being processed for journalistic purposes with a view to publication. Under s 32(4) and (5) of the 'old' Act, the court must stay the proceedings until either the claim is withdrawn or the Information Commissioner determines that the data are not being processed for the claimed purpose. The data subject cannot compel the IC to make a determination, which means that a stay will often become lengthy or permanent. In practice, the provision has acted as a considerable bar to bringing DPA proceedings against the press.

The CA judgment in *Stunt* has taken us not much further forward, as the court was split on the issue of compatibility. The majority view was that the UK, like all EU Member States, had a wide margin of appreciation in implementing the Directive and was entitled – having consulted widely with the media – to guard against the 'chilling effect' of pre-publication restrictions. The minority view was that compliance with the Directive was 'far from clear': a stay can be imposed without judicial scrutiny, and depends wholly and exclusively on the self-interested claim of the data controller.

The CA provided a unanimous interpretation of the scope of s 32(4) DPA. It favoured a narrow, purposive reading, which restricts the stay to journalistic material containing *unpublished* personal data at the pre-publication or disclosure stage, over a wider, literal interpretation, which would allow for a stay irrespective of whether the data had already been published or relied upon for publication. This interpretation was, the CA held, in line with the equivalent provisions under s 176 of the new DPA 2018.[44]

Ultimately, the CA referred the issue to the CJEU for a preliminary ruling. That ruling may prompt a new approach to the special purposes stay, but the DPA 2018 has largely answered these questions in statute.

6.6.1 Appeals before the First Tier Tribunal: section 32 exemptions

The First Tier Tribunal (FTT) hears appeals on information rights from appeal notices issued by the Information Commissioner (IC) under the following legislation:

- Data Protection Act 2018 (and formerly under DPA 1998);
- Freedom of Information Act 2000 (FOIA);
- Privacy and Electronic Communications Regulations 2003;
- Environmental Information Regulations 2004 (see: *Ofcom v The Information Commissioner* (2010)[45]).

Section 32 FOIA deals with information held by courts and persons conducting an inquiry or arbitration. The Supreme Court held in *Kennedy* (2014)[46] that its intention was not that such information should not be disclosed.[47] Its intention was to take such information outside the FOIA.

See below
6.6.3

---

44 *Stunt* [2018] EWCA Civ 1780 at para. 99 (by majority Sir Terence Etherton MR and McFarlane LJ).
45 [2010] UKSC 3; on appeal from: [2009] EWCA Civ 90.
46 *Kennedy v Charity Commission* [2014] UKSC 20.
47 Ibid. at para. 6.

6.6.2 Reports predominantly for the purpose of journalism: *Sugar v BBC*

The background to the *Sugar* case involved a BBC inquiry into news coverage of the Israeli-Palestinian conflict, resulting in the 'Balen Report', compiled by senior BBC journalist Malcolm Balen in 2004.[48] The inquiry was set up following allegations of anti-Israeli bias during the BBC's coverage of the Israeli-Palestinian conflict in 2003–2004. Hundreds of viewers and listeners had complained to the Corporation in 2003–2004, when the Middle East correspondent Barbara Plett revealed that she had cried at the death of Yasser Arafat. There were also allegations of pro-Jewish bias. The Balen Report was presented to the BBC's Journalism Board for consideration in 2004.

Following the Hutton Report[49] in January 2004, there were several changes in the top management of the BBC. The BBC governors had sacked Director General Greg Dyke within 24 hours of the report's publication, and Gavyn Davies, the BBC's chairman, had resigned. Mark Byford became Deputy Director-General of the BBC, and in August 2004, Richard Sambrook became Director of Global News and Helen Boaden took over Mr Sambrook's place as Director of News. Mark Thompson, the new Director-General, set up three new boards, including a Journalism Board of which Mr Byford was the chair and Mr Sambrook, Ms Boaden and other senior managers were members. The Board was to be responsible for setting the strategy which would direct, and for defining the values which would inform, journalism across all areas of the BBC's output. The Balen Inquiry then became of an equally sensitive nature as the Hutton Report, alleging the BBC's systematic and anti-Semitic bias against Israel.

On 8 January 2005, a commercial lawyer, Steven Sugar, asked to see the Balen Report and made a request to the BBC under FOIA. The BBC governors refused, reasoning that the Balen Report was an internal document aimed at checking its own standards of journalism. This meant that information held by the BBC for the purposes of journalism was effectively exempt from production under the FOIA, even if it was held for other, possibly more important purposes.[50] Mr Sugar complained to the Information Commissioner (IC), stating that the BBC – as a public body – was under a duty to disclose the requested information under FOIA.

On 24 October 2005, the IC ruled in favour of the BBC. Mr Sugar subsequently appealed to the Information Tribunal, which ruled in favour of Mr Sugar on 29 August 2006. This meant the BBC should disclose the report and could not derogate under FOIA.[51]

The BBC appealed against the tribunal's decision. The grounds of appeal before the High Court were as follows: that the tribunal did not have jurisdiction to hear an appeal from the IC; and, even if it did, the IC's decision had been flawed as a matter of law. On 27 April 2007, Davies J backed the IC's decision and held that the Balen Report was 'for the purpose of journalism'. Additionally, the judge imposed restrictions on potential appeals to the Information Tribunal in the future, stating, *inter alia*, that the tribunal

---

48 Mr Balen had at one time been editor of the BBC's *Nine O'Clock News*. By 2003 he was working as Head of News for a commercial television channel. On 1 November 2003, the then Director of BBC News, Richard Sambrook, had asked Mr Balen to re-join the BBC under a one-year contract to lead the inquiry.
49 'Report of the Inquiry into the Circumstances Surrounding the Death of Dr David Kelly CMG' ('the Hutton Report'), HC 247.
50 'For the purposes of journalism, art or literature' within the meaning of Sch. 1, Part VI FOIA.
51 *Sugar v BBC* [2007] EWHC 905.

lacked jurisdiction. The Court of Appeal rejected Mr Sugar's appeal,[52] ruling that the Balen Report was to be prohibited and exempt under section 44 FOIA.[53]

Eventually the case reached the UK Supreme Court with a judgment in February 2012.[54] Sadly the appellant, Mr Steven Sugar, had died during the proceedings in January 2011, and the court appointed his wife Fiona Paveley to represent his estate in the appeal.

The Supreme Court justices held that the CA had been correct in stating that once it is established that the information sought from the BBC is held 'for the purposes of journalism', it is effectively *exempt* from production under the FOIA. The Supreme Court Justices ruled that the BBC, as a public service broadcaster, should be free to gather, edit and publish news and comment on current affairs without the inhibition of an obligation to make public disclosure of or about their work under FOIA.[55] Lord Brown held that the Balen Report was held *predominantly* for purposes of journalism and accordingly fell within the exemption of the Act.[56] Their Lordships also commented that Article 10(1) of the Convention created no general right to receive freedom of information.[57]

The Supreme Court's decision in *Sugar* disappointed the Jewish community, which wanted to know whether the Balen inquiry found any evidence of anti-Israeli and anti-Jewish bias in news programming and reporting at the BBC. It had taken seven years from Steven Sugar's first submission of his request to the BBC under the FOIA in January 2005 to the final decision by the UK Supreme Court in 2012, with Mr Sugar dying in the meantime and his wife Fiona Paveley continuing the legal battle on his behalf. We will therefore never know whether the BBC's coverage of the Middle East conflict was biased either way. The Balen Report was never published made public.

6.6.3 Absolute exemptions under section 32 FOIA: *Kennedy v Charity Commission*

Another lengthy case concerning the disclosure of a report under FOIA was that of Dominic Kennedy,[58] an experienced *Times* journalist who had long expressed unease in his investigatory reports about the inquiries conducted by the Charity Commission into the 'Mariam Appeal'[59] and its founder, former Glasgow Kelvinside MP, George Galloway. There had been three inquiries by the Charities Commission into the Mariam Appeal. The results of the first two inquiries were published in June 2004 in a 'Statement of Results of the Inquiry' (SORI). At the same time, Mr Galloway had been accused by the *Daily Telegraph* of having received hundreds of thousands of pounds from Saddam

---

52 [2008] EWCA Civ 191.
53 For further discussion see: Johnson, H. (2008a), pp. 174–176.
54 *BBC and another v Sugar (deceased) (No 2)* [2012] UKSC 4.
55 Ibid. at para. 61 (as per Lord Walker with Lord Phillips, Lord Brown, Lord Mance agreeing).
56 Ibid. at paras 57, 60 (as per Lord Brown).
57 Ibid. at paras 94 and 98.
58 *Kennedy v Charity Commission* [2014] UKSC 20. On appeal from *Kennedy (Dominic) v Information Commissioner & Charity Commissioners* [2012] EWCA Civ 317; [2011] EWCA Civ 367; [2011] UKFTT EA/2008/0083; [2010] EWHC 475 (Admin) (QBD) (original IC application EA/2008/0083).
59 The 'Mariam Appeal' was set up to help an Iraqi girl suffering from leukaemia. The fund's known income was nearly £1.5m until its closure in 2003. The fund's three main backers were Saudi Arabia, the United Arab Emirates and Jordanian businessman Fawaz Zureikat, the Mariam Appeal's chairman.

Hussein. He successfully sued the *Daily Telegraph* in a libel action (see: *Galloway v Daily Telegraph* (2004)).[60]

See Chapter 3

In his reports in *The Times*, Kennedy had commented that the Charity Commission's two brief inquiries into the Mariam Appeal left significant questions unanswered. For this reason, he made an FOIA request on 8 June 2007 for disclosure of documentation relating to 'Mariam' from the Charity Commission.[61] His request was refused under the absolute exemption of section 32(2) FOIA ('court records etc' and 'Information held by a public authority'). The Charity Commission further argued that the exemption would last until any document regarding 'Mariam' was destroyed (or to be kept secret for 30 years under section 3 Public Records Act 1958).

When the case reached the Court of Appeal in 2012, Calvert-Smith J held that the Information Tribunal had been correct in its ruling that the wording of section 32(2) FOIA had a very wide scope.[62] The CA ruled that there was no absolute right under FOIA to disclosure of documents held by public authorities which had been placed in the custody of or created by a person conducting an inquiry. The judge held that the documents of the Charity Commission fell under the absolute exemptions set out under section 32 FOIA, regardless of their content and the consequences of their disclosure, and notwithstanding the public interest in their disclosure. The case reached the Supreme Court in 2013.

❖ KEY CASE — *Kennedy v The Charity Commission* (UK Supreme Court) [2014] UKSC 20[63]

Precedent

❖ Section 32 FOIA is compatible with Article 10 ECHR ('there is no automatic right to receive information').

❖ Section 62(1) FOIA provides that a record (court, inquiry, inquest, etc.) becomes an 'historical record' at the end of (now) 20 years.[64]

❖ Section 78 FOIA makes it clear that that nothing in the legislation is to limit the powers of a public authority to disclose information held by it.

Facts

The *Dominic Kennedy* appeal reached the Supreme Court more than six years after the *Times* journalist's initial request, after detailed consideration by the Information Commissioner, the Information Tribunal (twice), the High Court and the Court of Appeal (twice).[65] Kennedy had argued that the exemption under section 32(2) FOIA only subsisted for the duration of the inquiry by the Charity Commission; if a natural construction of section 32(2) did not produce that result, Article 10 ECHR required it to be read down to produce that result.

---

60 [2004] EWHC 2786 (QB).
61 The Charity Commission's relevant schemes and mechanisms were at that time to be found in the Charities Act 1993, as amended by the Charities Act 2006 (since replaced by the Charities Act 2011).
62 *Kennedy (Dominic) v Information Commissioner & Charity Commissioners* [2012] EWCA Civ 317 (as per Calvert-Smith J).
63 [2014] UKSC 20.
64 Amended by s 45(1) Constitutional Reform and Governance Act 2010 (which was 30 years).
65 *Kennedy v Information Commissioner & Charity Commissioners* [2012] EWCA Civ 317.

Key issues before the Supreme Court

1   Whether section 32(2) FOIA contained an *absolute exception* which continued *after* the end of the Charity Commissioners' inquiry.

2   If so, whether section 32(2) FOIA ('absolute exception') was compatible with Mr Kennedy's Article 10 rights (arguing that Article 10 ECHR included the right to *receive* information).

3   In the event of incompatibility, should section 32 FOIA be read in conjunction with section 3 HRA 1998, as either:

    (i)   ceasing to operate at the end of the inquiry; or
    (ii) being a *qualified exception* that requires a general balancing of the competing public interests?

4   Should the court make a declaration of incompatibility if it was not possible to interpret section 32(2) FOIA in a manner that was compatible with the Convention?

Decision

Their Lordships[66] dismissed the appeal, by a 5 to 2 majority (Lords Wilson and Carnwarth dissenting). It was held that:

1   *Section 32(2) was intended to provide an absolute exemption which would not cease at the end of inquiry proceedings.*
    The majority of the Supreme Court interpreted the critical phrase 'for the purposes of' in section 32(2) FOIA which qualified the immediately preceding words in that section and referred to the original purpose for which the relevant documents were placed in the custody of, or were created by, a person conducting an inquiry. Their Lordships interpreted section 62(1) in that a record would become an 'historical record' at the end of 20 years.

2   *Section 32 FOIA was compatible with Article 10 ECHR.*
    The majority's view was that the effect of section 32 was to take information falling within the absolute exemption outside the scope of the FOIA regime. The FOIA was never intended to determine whether or not such information should be disclosed. Section 78 specified that nothing in the FOIA was to be taken to limit the powers of a public authority to disclose information held by it. Any statutory or common law powers to order disclosure continued to apply alongside the FOIA.

3   *In the event of section 32(2) being incompatible with Article 10 ECHR, section 3 HRA did not require the provision to be 'read down'.*
    This point was considered *obiter* due to the majority decision. Lord Mance rejected the applicant's 'radical analysis' that a right to receive information could arise under Article 10, without any domestic right to the information. Lord Toulson agreed and Lords Wilson and Carnwarth dissented on this

---

66 Lord Neuberger, President, Lord Mance, Lord Clarke, Lord Wilson, Lord Sumption, Lord Carnwath and Lord Toulson. Lord Mance and Lord Toulson gave the leading judgments with which a majority of the court agreed. Lord Sumption gave a concurring judgment. Lord Wilson and Lord Carnwath gave dissenting judgments. The appeal was heard on 29 and 31 October 2013. The judgment was given on 26 March 2014.

point; they stated that ECtHR's case law was unsatisfactory (see: *Társaság a Szabadságjogokért v Hungary* (2011)[67]).

4   *No declaration of incompatibility was necessary as section 32 was compatible with the applicant's Article 10 rights.*

Their Lordships stated that Dominic Kennedy had misunderstood the statutory scheme of the FOIA: he had omitted to take into account the statutory and common law position to which, in the light of ss 32 and 78 FOIA, attention should have been given:

> Nothing in this Act is to be taken to limit the powers of a public authority to disclose information held by it.

They concluded that section 32(2) FOIA imposes an *absolute exemption* on disclosure of information and that this continues *after* the end of the relevant inquiry or court hearing. They made it clear that the FOIA was never intended to determine whether or not such information should be disclosed. Instead, any question as to its disclosure would be governed by other rules of statute and common law.

Lord Toulson concluded that Mr Kennedy could have availed himself of the provision of judicial review since the disclosure of the Mariam Appeal Charities' Commission investigations was of genuine public interest and would have had standing (*locus standi*).

Analysis

The *Kennedy* decision is an important ruling by the Supreme Court, particularly for those who seek FOIA disclosure of published documents from public bodies of inquiries or court records. It had been Dominic Kennedy's argument that the FOIA was an exhaustive scheme and that he had a *prima facie* right to disclosure, also advancing his Article 10 ECHR right to 'receive' information. But the majority of the Supreme Court refused to apply Article 10 and instead focused on the capacity of common law principles. The court referred to recent developments in Strasbourg jurisprudence which the UKSC held was not sufficient to justify a departure from the principle for which Article 10 was intended, namely freedom of expression (see: *Leander v Sweden* (1987),[68] *Gaskin v UK* (1989),[69] *Guerra v Italy* (1998)[70] and *Roche v UK* (2005)[71]).

---

67 (2011) 53 EHRR 3 (Application No 37374/05) (ECtHR). In Társaság the ECtHR had advanced a broader interpretation of the notion of 'freedom to receive information'; this was weakly based, clearly aspirational and tentative and not part of the essential reasoning of the Court's decision.
68 (1987) 9 EHRR 433 (A/116) (ECtHR).
69 (1989) 12 EHRR 36 (ECtHR).
70 (1998) 26 EHRR 357 (ECtHR).
71 (2005) 42 EHRR 599 (ECtHR).

The effect of the *Kennedy* judgment by the Supreme Court was not to achieve the openness, transparency and accountability of public bodies in domestic law that we had expected from the FOIA. Varuhas (2015) advances an interesting argument following the *Kennedy* decision and at the same time the UK Supreme Court's decision in *R (on the application of Moseley) v Haringey LBC* (2014)[72] – that there are two legal pathways to obtaining information and disclosure. Since the access to freedom of information regarding public authorities failed in Kennedy, there is still the route of judicial review to ensure public power is exercised properly, according to precepts of good administration and the duty to consult.

Varuhas argues that common law in this area of administrative law has developed dynamically in line with contemporary ideas of open and democratic governance under the requirements of natural justice (see: *R (on the application of Osborn) v Parole Board* (2015)[73]).[74]

6.6.4 The *Prince Charles 'black spider' letters* case

When a Minister of the Crown issues a certificate on national security exemption grounds (i.e. a public interest immunity or 'PII' notice), the appeal must be transferred to the Administrative Appeals Chamber of the Upper Tribunal (AAC-UT) once the application is received by the FTT. This was the case with the Attorney General's ruling in the *'Rob Evans – Prince Charles letters'* case.[75]

This long-running FOIA challenge became known as the 'black spider' letters case, so nicknamed by the media after Prince Charles' distinctive handwriting, with its abundant underlining and exclamation marks.

It all began in April 2005 with a simple one-line email from the editor of the *Guardian*, Alan Rusbridger, asking whether journalist Rob (Robert) Evans could submit freedom of information requests to ministers to see what letters they had received, and on what subjects, from Prince Charles. Rob(ert) Evans, who had worked for the newspaper since 1999, knew from the start that asking to have insight into correspondence between the future King and ministers in seven Whitehall departments would be a sensitive issue. Evans had already tracked some of Prince Charles' correspondence back to 1969, the year Charles Windsor was created Prince of Wales at a ceremony at Caernarfon Castle. That memo concerned the overfishing of Atlantic salmon. Rob Evans formally requested disclosure under FOIA of communications sent by HRH the Prince of Wales to various government departments between September 2004 and April 2005. The Freedom of Information request also included the Environmental Information Regulations 2004 (EIR) and concerned some 27 letters and memos.

Throughout the long-running legal dispute, Evans contended that disclosure of the Prince of Wales' correspondence would be in the public interest, at least to the extent that the correspondence involved 'advocacy correspondence' on the part of Prince Charles. By this the journalist meant correspondence with ministers and government departments in which Prince Charles advocated certain causes which were of particular interest to him, including causes which related to the environment.

It was well known that the prince had regularly lobbied ministers advocating his environmental policies. Some 'black spider' memos and letters had been leaked to the press in

---

72 [2014] UKSC 56; [2014] 1 WLR 3947 (SC).
73 [2015] AC 1115.
74 Varuhas, J.N.E. (2015), pp. 215–218.
75 *R (on the application of Evans) v Attorney General* [2015] UKSC 21 (on appeal from [2014] EWCA Civ 254).

the past, for example in June 2001 when the prince had sent a letter to the then Labour Lord Chancellor, Lord Irvine, on the subject of the Human Rights Act 1998. The prince had complained that the UK was 'sliding inexorably down the slope of ever-increasing petty-minded litigiousness' and 'too little is being done to stem the remorseless obsession with rights'.[76] Tony Blair's diaries and the former Labour spin doctor Alastair Campbell's diaries and subsequently published memoirs had commented on Prince Charles' leaked letters to the *Mail on Sunday*, from his objection to the government's 'absurd' Hunting Bill in 2004 to his allegiance with the farming lobby. The former editor of the *Daily Telegraph*, Max Hastings, revealed in the *Spectator* magazine that he had seen a copy of a letter where the prince had lobbied 'for some NHS funds to be diverted from conventional medicine to homeopathy'.[77]

The government departments refused Mr Evans' FOIA requests, and he subsequently complained to the Information Commissioner (IC), who upheld the departments' refusal. Evans then appealed to the Information Tribunal (IT), and eventually matters were transferred to the Upper Tribunal (UT[78]) (Administrative Appeals Chamber), which determined in September 2012 that the letters should be disclosed.[79] The UT did not order the release of genuinely private correspondence but specifically 27 'advocacy' letters about the prince's lobbying the executive.

The UT's decision was significant and subsequently highlighted by the Supreme Court in its judgment in March 2015. The UT had pointed out that the Prince of Wales had 'strongly held views' on a number of matters, including politically controversial issues and proposed legislation; that his communication of those views to government ministers was well known (not least because he, ministers and others had mentioned this publicly); that he had a 'selfperceived role' which was 'representational' and involved expressing 'views in danger of not being heard'; that some of the letters had been published; and that 'a high degree of publicity' had not stopped his correspondence with ministers.[80] The UT gave some examples, such as letters to the British Bankers' Association and to the trade union UNISON. In some letters the prince had reportedly availed himself of access to ministers in order to 'drive forward charities and promote views'.[81]

But the letters and memos were not released following the UT's ruling for, shortly afterwards, on 16 October 2012 the Attorney General (AG), Dominic Grieve QC, issued a statutory veto certificate under section 53(2) FOIA 2000 and regulation 18(6) EIR 2004, stating that he had, on 'reasonable grounds', formed the opinion that the departments had been entitled to refuse disclosure of the letters. Reasons given for the Attorney General's section 53 order which warranted 'exceptionality' were:

- the fact that the information in question consisted of private and confidential letters between the Prince of Wales and ministers;

---

76 Source: 'Too much information: Charles's letters wouldn't tell us anything we didn't already know', by Steve Richards, the i, 18 October 2012.

77 Source: 'Max Hastings's diary: The joys of middle age, and Prince Charles's strange letters', *Spectator*, 2 April 2015.

78 The UT is of equal status to the High Court.

79 *Evans v Information Commissioner* [2012] UKUT 313 (Administrative Appeals Chamber [AAC] (before Walker J, Judge John Angel and Ms Suzanne Cosgrave).

80 *Evans* [2012] UKUT 313 (AAC) at 21.

81 Ibid. at 156–158.

- the fact that the request in this case was for recent correspondence;
- Preparation for kingship;
- the potential damage that disclosure would do to the principle of the Prince of Wales' political neutrality, which could seriously undermine the prince's ability to fulfil his duties when he becomes King;
- the ability of the monarch to engage with the government of the day, whatever its political colour, and maintain political neutrality as a cornerstone of the UK's constitution;
- the fact that the letters in this case formed part of the Prince of Wales' preparation for constitutional framework.

The proposition that a member of the executive – in this case the Attorney General (AG) – can actually overrule a decision of the judiciary because he does not agree with that decision is remarkable, though of course judicially reviewable. The constitutional importance of the principle that a decision of the executive should be reviewable by the judiciary lay behind the majority judgment in *Anisminic*.[82]

Arguably, by overruling the UT's decision the AG had breached FOIA legislation and its main purpose, that of free access to public information. Rob Evans sought judicial review to quash the AG's certificate, arguing that it was invalid on two grounds. First, in domestic law, he contended that section 53 FOIA did not permit a certificate to be issued simply because the accountable person took a different view of the public interest from the Upper Tribunal when it came to the issue of disclosure.[83] Secondly, in EU law, because the advocacy correspondence included environmental information and Evans contended that, once the UT had issued its determination, it was contrary to the provisions of Article 6, supported by the EU Charter, for anyone, especially a member of the executive, to overrule that determination.[84]

The Divisional Court dismissed his claim. However, the Court of Appeal allowed Evans' appeal on both grounds and gave the AG permission to appeal to the Supreme Court.[85] In July 2013, the Administrative Court granted leave for Mr Evans and the *Guardian* for an appeal against the Attorney General's decision to veto any disclosure of the royal letters.[86] The Lord Chief Justice said in his judgment that Prince Charles' correspondence had a 'constitutional function and significance' and that – for this reason – a right to appeal had been allowed. Lord Judge CJ considered the 'extensive public interest'[87] (originally identified by the Information Tribunal), commenting that the Prince of Wales was in no different position from any other lobbyist when making representations to ministers.

The UK Supreme Court (UKSC) in March 2015 dismissed the Attorney General's appeal by a majority of 5 to 2 and held that the AG was not entitled to issue a certificate

---

82 *Anisminic Ltd v Foreign Compensation Commission* [1969] 2 AC 147 (HL).
83 Rob Evans argued that reasons given by the AG were not capable of constituting 'reasonable grounds' within the meaning of s 53(2) FOIA.
84 Because the advocacy correspondence was concerned with environmental issues, the certificate was incompatible with Directive 2003/4 on public access to environmental information and/or Article 47 of the EU Charter of Fundamental Rights (the EU Charter).
85 *R (on the application of Evans) v Attorney General* [2013] EWHC 1960 (Admin) (Lord Judge CJ, Davis LJ and Globe J).
86 *R (on the application of Evans) v Attorney General* [2014] EWCA Civ 254 (Lord Dyson MR and Richards and Pitchford LJJ).
87 *Evans* [2013] EWHC 1960 at paras 4–6; 21–22 (Lord Judge CJ).

under section 53 FOIA in the manner that he had done; therefore the certificate was invalid. The court held that the AG had impermissibly undertaken his own redetermination of the relevant factual background, including certain constitutional conventions on which the Upper Tribunal (UT) had heard detailed evidence, which he was not entitled to do. The certificate had proceeded on the basis of findings which differed radically from those made by the UT without real or adequate explanation. By a majority of 6 to 1, the court held that regulation 18(6) was incompatible with Directive 2003/4 on public access to environmental information and should be treated as invalid.[88]

Lord Neuberger, President of the Supreme Court (with whom Lord Kerr and Lord Reed agreed), concluded that section 53 FOIA did not permit the AG to override a decision of a judicial tribunal (the UT) by issuing a certificate merely because he, a member of the executive, took a different view. The AG's decision had cut across two constitutional principles: firstly, the rule of law, namely that a decision of a court is binding between the parties and could not be set aside; and, secondly, that decisions and actions of the executive were reviewable by the courts, and not vice versa.[89]

Lord Wilson, dissenting, accused his fellow justices of rewriting the Freedom of Information Act 2000 (FOIA). He argued that the justices' majority view undermined parliamentary sovereignty.[90] He said his colleagues should have resisted the temptation to uphold the decision of the Upper Tribunal (UT) against the AG's veto, even though the government had never appealed against the tribunal's decision. But Lord Neuberger explained when a court scrutinized the grounds relied upon for a section 53 FOIA certificate, it must do so against the background of the relevant circumstances (in this case in the light of the decision at which the certificate in *Evans* was aimed). Neuberger explained that the UT had adhered to the rule of law in that it heard evidence, called and cross-examined, as well as submissions on both sides, in public. In contrast, the AG had not done so. He had consulted in private, had taken into account the views of cabinet, former ministers and the IC, and had formed his own view without inter partes representations.

While the Supreme Court did not find it necessary to make a value judgment as to the desirability of Prince Charles encouraging or warning the government as to what to do, the justices did not think that the department's fear of disclosing the 27 letters was justified and that the consequences of disclosure would not be detrimental. In broad terms the Supreme Court ruling favoured disclosure of the 'advocacy correspondence' in the public interest.[91]

6.6.5 Why is the ruling in the *Rob Evans* case of constitutional importance?

The Supreme Court's ruling in the *Rob Evans* case signified a victory for freedom of information in the same year that the Magna Carta celebrated its 800th anniversary, heralding freedom of speech.

---

88 *Evans* [2015] UKSC 21 at 100 (Lord Neuberger and Lord Mance).
89 Ibid. at 52 (Lord Neuberger).
90 Ibid. at 172 (Lord Wilson dissenting).
91 For further discussion see: Smartt, U. (2015a) pp. 529–538.

On 13 May 2015 Clarence House released Prince Charles' 'spider' letters and memos (2004–2005), and the public could finally have an insight into the future King's views and personal concerns. The prince's lobbying topics covered an array of issues, including beef farming and dairy quotas, badger culling and the fate of sea birds, albatrosses and the Patagonian toothfish, the power of supermarkets, Lynx helicopters, derelict hospitals, listed buildings, Scott and Shackleton's Antarctic huts, summer schools, old-fashioned teaching methods and herbal medicines.

The public interest aspect of the *Evans* case is of undeniable importance in that the release of Prince Charles' letters under FOIA revealed the breadth and depth of the future King's lobbying of the executive, which stretched from Downing Street to Northern Ireland, covering topics such as defence (e.g. the performance of airborne surveillance aircraft in Iraq), the environment, architecture, organic farming, alternative medicine and education. Moreover, as the Supreme Court pointed out, the letters revealed a 'disturbing absence of proportion and self-awareness'. It is presumably for this reason that the former Attorney General, Dominic Grieve QC, fought so hard to stop publication.

The 'black spider' letters may well have engendered a contrary perception of the future monarch which might be difficult to dispel and which therefore might seriously compromise the future role of 'Charles III'. The constitutional implications are about the future King's judgment and the belief that the monarchy ought to be politically neutral. That said, the prince's letters show concern and were considered as fairly 'harmless' by most of the media commentators following publication. What would have been of greater public interest is the ministers' and Whitehall's response to the prince's lobbying memos. That might then have revealed some of the government's policies, openness and transparency in response to the future monarch's private concerns.

6.6.6 Data protection and the *Weltimmo* case

Before declaring the *Safe Harbour* decision invalid in the *Max Schrems* case (2015)[92] the CJEU released an important decision in favour of the Hungarian National Authority for Data Protection and Freedom of Information (Nemzeti Adatvédelmi és Információszabadság Hatóság (NAIH)), concerning the interpretation of the applicable law provisions of the EU Data Protection Directive 95/46/EC. The CJEU in *Weltimmo* handed down this landmark judgment on data protection legislation, tackling the issue of jurisdiction when a company is headquartered in one EU country and operates its business in another. The ruling extended the meaning of 'established' as Directive 95/46/EC to include 'real and effective activity' in a Member State through 'stable arrangements'. The decision had significant implications for companies operating across multiple EU countries.

See below 6.7

The case was brought by the Hungarian Data Protection Authority against Weltimmo which ran property-selling websites, 'www.ingatlandepo.com' and 'www.ingatlanbazar.com', concerning Hungarian real estate. However, the company was based in Slovakia. The Hungarian regulator fined Weltimmo for infringement of Hungarian Law CXII of 2011 on the 'right to self-determination', regarding information and freedom of information which it had passed on to a debt collection agency.[93] The CJEU found that the Slovakian

---

92 *Schrems (Maximilian) v Data Protection Commissioner* (2015) (Case C-362/14) [2015] All ER 34.
93 In the Hungarian original: 'Az információs önrendelkezési jogról és az információszabadságról szóló 2011. évi CXII. Törvény'. The law on information which transposed Directive 95/46 into Hungarian law.

company pursued real and effective activity in Hungary through stable arrangements. On the question of jurisdiction, the CJEU distinguished between investigative and sanctioning powers. It held that NAIH had the power to investigate the complaint irrespective of the applicable law. However, NAIH only had powers to impose penalties if the applicable law was Hungarian law. To the extent the applicable law is that of a Member State other than Hungary, NAIH would need to request the other Member State's supervisory authority to interfere and impose sanctions. The Court ruling for breach of the EU Directive by Weltimmo meant that the property agency was potentially liable for the 10 million Hungarian forint (£23,650) fine levied by the Hungarian regulator. The CJEU's findings on the applicability of national data protection laws potentially significantly affect the activities of online operators providing services across multiple EU Member States.

Before the *Weltimmo* judgment, companies such as Facebook or Google who chose to headquarter their European operations in one country and operate in another were thought to be subject to regulation only within that country. These companies could then operate in any EU Member State without having to gain regulatory approval in each country. The *Weltimmo* ruling is pivotal as it allows data protection legislation of a Member State to be applied to a foreign company that has representatives in that country and operates a service in the native language of that country, despite being headquartered in a different country.

The implications for the likes of Facebook, Google and others found dramatically increased compliance costs following the Weltimmo ruling, particularly where a website was targeted at multiple Member States, making the company subject to multiple data protection authorities.

Until the CJEU ruling in *Weltimmo*, little was known about the kind and quantity of information which was apparently being delisted from search results, what sources were being delisted and on what scale. We had no idea what kind of requests failed and in what proportion (i.e. who were the 'public figures' that were being refused) and what were Google's guidelines in striking the right balance between individual privacy and freedom to access information. The practical consequences following the *Weltimmo* decision for online business operators providing cross-border services in Europe can now be challenged. If an online business operator provides services in several languages, has local representatives in different countries and pursues the enforcement of claims in other Member States, such operator might now be compelled to comply with those Member States' data protection laws – including notification, registration and record-keeping requirements – and can also expect audits and sanctions from competent national data protection agencies and regulators.

6.7 The surveillance state: *Max Schrems* and Facebook

The Edward Snowden revelations in 2013 disclosed large-scale spying by America's National Security Agency (NSA), but also that data privacy in Western Europe varied markedly between countries. Snowden, an American computer specialist and former Central Intelligence Agency (CIA) employee, had leaked classified NSA information to *The Guardian*, *The Washington Post* and *Der Spiegel* in Germany. Thanks to Snowden's disclosures, we now know that each government sets different rules for what spies or 'spooks' may look at and access in an international context. The Snowden exposés showed the extent of government surveillance, highlighting the symbiotic relationship between the US National Security Agency (NSA) and Britain's GCHQ as well as the relationship of giant internet companies (Google, MSN, etc.) with each other and the data sharing across borders.

The archive of whistle-blower Edward Snowden revealed that not all encryption technologies live up to what they promise. Encryption – a mathematical process of converting messages, information or data into a form unreadable by anyone except the intended recipient – protects the confidentiality and integrity of content against third-party access or manipulation. Strong encryption, once the sole province of militaries and intelligence services,[94] is now publicly accessible and often freely available to secure email, voice communication, images, hard drives and website browsers. With 'public key encryption', the dominant form of end-to-end security for data in transit, the sender uses the recipient's public key to encrypt the message and its attachments, and the recipient uses her or his own private key to decrypt them. Encryption is also being used to create digital signatures to ensure that a document and its sender are authentic, to authenticate and verify the identity of a server and to protect the integrity of communications between clients against tampering or manipulation of traffic by third parties. Some online practices have since moved away from the traditional system towards 'forward secrecy' or 'off-the-record' technology such as the Dark Web, in which keys are held ephemerally, particularly for uses such as instant messaging.

See
Chapter 1.7

6.7.1 Facebook and Cambridge Analytica

The California-headquartered company Cambridge Analytica was involved in the acquisition of commercial data from multiple vendors, its amalgamation and analysis (including 'psychographic profiling' using models developed by academics at the University of Cambridge) and the use of the product of that analysis to facilitate targeted advertising and messaging ('micro-targeting') for clients. Amongst those clients were political parties and campaign groups who used the services of Cambridge Analytica to seek to influence voting behaviour. This business model involved the creation of vast databases. Cambridge Analytica said publicly that it held up to 5,000 data points on each of over 230 million American voters.

Critics of Cambridge Analytica, including the UK Information Commissioner, said that some of these data points were created through the misuse of data provided by 87 million Facebook users (some of whom had completed online surveys which afforded access to data on Facebook 'friends').

At the Chancery court hearing before Mr Justice Norris, it was said that Cambridge Analytica companies in the UK had access to some 700 terabytes of data (the equivalent of 52 billion pages of information).[95]

---

94 SANS Institute (2001) 'The Weakest Link: The Human Factor Lessons Learned from the German WWII Enigma Cryptosystem', InfoSec Reading Room at: www.sans.org/reading-room/whitepapers/vpns/weakest-link-human-factor-lessons-learned-german-wwii-enigma-cryptosystem-738.

95 (1) *Vincent John Green Petitioners* (2) *Mark Newman (as joint Administrators of each of the Respondent Companies) v (1) SCL Group Limited Respondents (2) SCL Analytics Limited (3) SCL Commercial Limited (4) SCL Social Limited (5) SCL Elections Limited (6)*

Public disquiet about the sourcing, aggregation and analysis of such vast quantities of data and its use for micro-targeting (not simply by Cambridge Analytica but also by others such as Facebook) dated back to newspaper articles published in December 2015, and it remained a matter of concern during the US presidential elections in 2016. One American voter was Professor David Carroll, an associate professor of media design at the Parsons School of Design in New York. His area of interest was online behavioural advertising techniques. His expertise included an examination of how within vast databases 'de-anonymization' techniques could be used to re-identify an individual from anonymous information. Academic curiosity and a general desire to ensure that his personal data was not used for purposes which he regarded as unsettling led him on 10 January 2017 to submit a Subject Access Request to SCL Group Limited (one of the UK Cambridge Analytica companies) seeking to find out whether it (or any associated company) held any of his personal data, what was the legal basis for any processing of that data and 'for each data point, full information as to its source'. He did not receive a satisfactory reply and instructed solicitors to write 'a letter before action' requesting a full response and outlining a claim for compensation for distress caused by breach of the Data Protection Act 1998, for tortious misuse of private information and for breach of confidence. According to the evidence of Prof. Carroll's solicitor, 'no response that can be put before the Court was received' [96] In the end prof. Carroll did not pursue his Claim for pre-action disclosure.

Facebook founder and CEO, Mark Zuckerberg, rejected two invitations to give evidence before the UK Parliamentary Select Committee in the House of Commons in 2018 with the explanation that he had spoken personally to three legislatures during that year: the US Congress, US Senate and European Parliament. In October 2018, the UK Information Commissioner's Office (ICO) issued a fines notice to Facebook Ireland Ltd. for £500,000 for serious breaches of data protection law (then the maximum fine under the now defunct Data Protection Act 1998 (DPA)[97]). In the end, Zuckerberg acknowledged that about 87 million people were affected by Facebook's data instrution.

See
Chapter 8.9

6.7.2 Investigatory powers and surveillance in the UK

We know by now that there is no dedicated privacy statute in the UK and that relevant legal provisions in this respect need to be extracted from either common law or a number of domestic or international legal instruments as well as the jurisprudence of the European Court of Human Rights (ECtHR); these include *inter alia* the International Covenant on Civil and Political Rights 1966, the European Convention on Human Rights 1950 (ECHR), the Human Rights Act 1998 (HRA), the Data Protection Act 2018 (incorporating the GDPR), the Regulation of Investigatory Powers Act 2000 and the Investigatory Powers Act 2016 (also known as the 'Snoopers' Charter'). While these instruments are meant to give us the ability to invoke our rights against undue interference and significant power imbalances in the context of privacy, they still do not provide a definition of privacy in

---

Cambridge Analytica (UK) Limited [2019] EWHC 954 at paras 1–5 (Norris J) (Ch) (*sub nom.* 'Cambridge Analytica case'). At that hearing, the judge appointing Joint Administrators to be liquidators of the company.

96 Ibid. at paras 6–7.

97 ICO Monetary Penalty Notice to Facebook Ireland Ltd. of 24 October 2018: https://ico.org.uk/media/action-weve-taken/mpns/2260051/r-facebook-mpn-20181024.pdf.

UK law. The Investigatory Powers Act 2016 allows bulk collection of metadata and permits a public authority to eavesdrop on the content of communications of a specific person or group under surveillance.[98]

In Liberty (2018),[99] the human rights organization challenged the compatibility of Part 4 of the 2016 Act with both the European Union Charter of Fundamental Rights 2000 and the European Convention on Human Rights (ECHR) of 1950. The judicial review held that Part 4 of the Investigatory Powers Act 2016 was incompatible with fundamental rights under EU law, on the grounds that access to retained data was not limited to combating serious crime and was not subject to prior review by a court or an independent administrative body.

In September 2017, Lord Justice Fulford was appointed to the new post of Investigatory Powers Commissioner, a position created under Part 8 of the 2016 Act. Furthermore, some 13 judicial commissioners were also appointed, supporting the Investigatory Powers Commissioner's Office (IPCO) which took over the responsibility for oversight of investigatory powers from the Interception of Communications Commissioner's Office, the Office of Surveillance Commissioners and the Intelligence Services Commissioner in September 2017.

The commissioner and the judicial commissioners are responsible for overseeing the use of investigatory powers by public authorities which include law enforcement, the intelligence agencies, prisons, local authorities and other government agencies (e.g. regulators). The more intrusive powers such as interception, equipment interference and the use of surveillance in sensitive environments will be subject to the prior approval of a judicial commissioner. Use of these and other surveillance powers, including the acquisition of communications data and the use of covert human intelligence sources, are also overseen by a programme of retrospective inspection and audit by judicial commissioners and IPCO's inspectors.

Following the CJEU's ruling in Tele2 Sverige AB v Post-och telestyrelsen (2017),[100] the UK government commenced a consultation in response to the ruling regarding the retention of, and access to, communications data and how the Investigatory Powers Act 2016 may have to be amended to align itself with Directive 2002/58 (ePrivacy Directive).

One thing is certain: the intelligence agencies and the information technology companies are in the same business, namely surveillance. Interestingly, both groups provide similar justification for what they do: that their surveillance is both necessary, for national security in the case of governments and for economic viability in the case of the companies (ISPs) – all of which is conducted 'within the law'. For this reason, the Max Schrems actions are of such importance and may lead the way to the furtherance of codification and legislation in cyberspace.

6.7.3 The Max Schrems actions

The focus on privacy rights has grown immensely since 2013, following the revelations about US surveillance by former NSA security contractor Edward Snowden. At its core,

---

98 For further discussion see: Benson, V. and Turksen, U. (2017) pp. 124–131.
99 R (on the application of National Council for Civil Liberties (Liberty)) v Secretary of State for the Home Department [2018] EWHC 975 (Admin).
100 Tele2 Sverige AB v Post-och telestyrelsen (C-203/15) EU (Case no: 2016:970) [2017] QB 771; [2016] 12 WLUK 618 (CJEU Grand Chamber).

the *Maximillian Schrems* actions involve a number of complex legal challenges on privacy grounds to the various methods by which social media companies, such as Facebook, Google, MSN or Twitter, transfer the personal data of EU citizens to countries outside the European Economic Area (EEA), mainly the United States.

The *Schrems* cases raise issues of fundamental concern to millions of people within the European Union and beyond. Firstly, the various actions in the Irish and CJEU courts are relevant to the data protection rights of millions of EU residents. Secondly, the actions have implications for billions of euros' worth of trade between the EU and the United States and, potentially, the EU and other non-EU countries. Lastly, and probably most importantly, the *Schrems* actions have potentially extremely significant implications for the safety and security of residents within the EU. Since proceedings are still ongoing, there is then considerable interest in the outcome of the latest proceedings by any parties having a very real interest in the issues at stake.

The background is as follows: whilst Austrian law student Maximillian (Max) Schrems was studying in the United States for a term at the Santa Clara University in the heart of Silicon Valley in 2010, he attended a talk by a Facebook privacy lawyer, allegedly downplaying Europe's privacy laws in relation to internet data security. Inspired and worried by the Edward Snowden revelations in *Der Spiegel* and *The Guardian*, Schrems (then 24) and some 22 fellow lawyers from Vienna University complained to Facebook European headquarters in Dublin, asking what happened to their personal data and records when going online and signing up to Facebook? When the social networking site did not respond, Schrems requested assistance from the Irish regulator, the Data Protection Commissioner, in December 2010. This had some success. The Irish regulator forced Facebook into a number of concessions, such as greater privacy controls for users and the ability to turn off Facebook's facial recognition feature. But Max Schrems did not stop there. Schrems' 'first round' litigation was heard before the High Court in Dublin,[101] where the law student argued that his privacy and personal data should have been safeguarded by the Irish regulator.

Schrems also established that US law did not offer sufficient protection against surveillance by public authorities of any data transferred to the United States from, say, Europe – and that this was known as the 'Safe Harbour Scheme'. The scheme included a series of principles concerning the protection of personal data to which US undertakings could subscribe voluntarily. The European Commission decided in July 2000 on 'safe harbour' that US companies complying with the principles were allowed to transfer data from the EU to the United States.

Mr Schrems' claim – which is ongoing – is such (written in the present tense for this reason): Facebook (Ireland) forwards his personal data to Facebook Inc. in the United States, where his data is processed. Facebook Inc. is subject to a number of known and secret laws, rules, court decisions and executive orders that oblige it to make his personal data available and/or oblige it to disclose it to US authorities, such as, for example, the National Security Agency (NSA) and the Federal Bureau of Investigation (FBI).

Schrems alleges that US law targets data rather than people and that there is no judicial remedy that would allow the data subject to take appropriate action. He asserts that

---

101 *Schrems (Maximillian) v Data Protection Commissioner* (2014) (Case C-362/14) High Court of Ireland 25 July 2014.

non-US persons are not covered by constitutional protections in the United States. Schrems also claims that Facebook Inc. is subject to 'gagging orders' that order it to deny and/ or not to disclose any facts about government surveillance systems to which it is subject. He argues that the US authorities have access to data held by Facebook Inc., among other US-based companies. He claims that there is clear evidence that leads him to believe that his personal data, controlled by Facebook and processed by Facebook Inc., is at the very least 'made available' to US government authorities under various known and unknown legal provisions and spy programmes such as the 'PRISM' programme. He also believes that there is a likelihood that his personal data has been accessed under these provisions, as he was prevented from boarding a transatlantic flight on 16 March 2012 to the United States for reasons of 'national security'.

He further argues that under Article 2(b) of the Directive, making data available is a form of processing, so that even if his personal data was never accessed by any US government agency, the mere fact that Facebook Inc. was obliged to make this data available to various government agencies in accordance with US law engaged the provisions not only of the Directive but also of Article 8 of the Charter of Fundamental Rights of the European Union (namely 'protection of personal data'). Article 8 of the Charter reads:

1   Everyone has the right to the protection of personal data concerning him or her.
2   Such data must be processed fairly for specified purposes and on the basis of the consent of the person concerned or some other legitimate basis laid down by law. Everyone has the right of access to data which has been collected concerning him or her, and the right to have it rectified.

In short: Mr Schrems' ongoing complaint before the CJEU and Irish courts relates to two operations: firstly, the transfer and/or disclosure of his personal data from Facebook (Ireland) to Facebook Inc. (USA) and secondly the subsequent processing. He argues that the operation of the 'mass surveillance' systems in the United States is only a secondary matter that has to be taken into account when assessing the legality of the relevant processing operation – which is the transfer from Facebook Ireland Ltd to Facebook Inc.[102]

The High Court in Dublin made a reference for a preliminary ruling in July 2014 to the Court of Justice of the European Union (CJEU). The question asked before the CJEU concerned the 'Data Protection Directive' (Directive 95/46/EC),[103] which at that time provided that the transfer of personal data to a third country (here the United States) may, in principle, take place only if that third country ensures an adequate level of protection of the data (the 'Safe Harbour Scheme'). The essence of the *Schrems No 1* (2015)[104] ruling concerned the legal basis for the transfer of personal data to businesses that were members of the 'US Safe Harbour Scheme'.

The CJEU held that the 'Safe Harbour Scheme' was unsafe and fundamentally interfered with an individual's right to respect for private life (Article 8(1) ECHR). The CJEU

---

102 For further discussion see: Fischer, P. (2018) pp. 143–153.
103 Directive 95/46/EC of the European Parliament and of the Council of 24 October 1995 on the protection of individuals with regard to the processing of personal data and on the free movement of such data ('the Data Protection Directive') (OJ 1995 L 281, p. 31).
104 *Schrems (Maximilian) v Data Protection Commissioner* (2015) (Case C-362/14) Luxembourg, 6 October 2015 (CJEU); [2015] All ER (D) 34 (Oct) (Schrems No 1).

also found that the 'Safe Harbour Scheme' denied the national supervisory authorities (here the Irish Data Protection Commissioner) their powers where a person called into question whether the scheme was compatible with the protection of the privacy and of the fundamental rights and freedoms of individuals.[105]

The CJEU's preliminary ruling in *Schrems* is important on many levels. Firstly, it confirms Edward Snowden's courageous whistle-blower action as an important service to civil society. His revelations prompted a wide-ranging reassessment of where our dependence on networking technology has taken us and stimulated some long-overdue thinking about how we might reassert some measure of democratic control over that technology. Snowden has forced all courts – including the CJEU – to rethink the way we share data across borders. Secondly, it makes a domestic regulator (such as the Irish Data Commissioner or the Information Commissioner in the UK) responsible for ensuring that a data subject receives an adequate level of protection of his or her personal data.

European reaction to the *Max Schrems No 1* case in 2015 was mixed, on the one hand praising the brave young litigant but on the other concerned about the ensuing legal conundrums following the collapse of the safe harbour regime and transatlantic data transfer. The *Max Schrems No 1* ruling revealed that European and American views about personal data protection and surveillance were (and still are) radically different. At the time of the Schrems judgment some 1,700 companies had been using the US privacy shield ('safe harbour') framework agreed between the United States and the EU. Although a major victory at the time, Max Schrems continued his actions and so did the Irish Data Protection Commissioner and Facebook (Ireland).[106]

After the ruling of the CJEU in *Schrems No 1* (2015) the judicial review proceedings came back before the Irish High Court.[107] In the *Data Protection Commissioner (Ireland) v Facebook Ireland and Schrems* (2017), a number of parties joined the proceedings as *amici curiae*; these were the United States, the Business Software Alliance (BSA), Digital Europe and the Electronic Privacy Information Centre (EPIC). Each of these parties made submissions at the hearing but were not permitted to adduce evidence before the High Court Commercial in Dublin. Facebook and the US government argued that electronic surveillance in the United States was consistent with European legal safeguards, as it was overseen by FISA (Foreign Intelligence Surveillance Act) courts and that the US Freedom Act 2015 also outlawed bulk surveillance. The US government admitted that intercepts made under a US presidential executive order (EO 12333) – which authorizes the tapping of undersea cables – 'are not governed by statute, are not subject to judicial review' and have no limits on data collected on foreign citizens. No evidence of data collection under EOs was presented.[108] Ms Justice Costello concluded that data collected under PRISM and Upstream (also two of Snowden's revelations) showed evidence of 'mass indiscriminate processing of data by the Unites States government agencies, whether this is described as mass or targeted surveillance.'[109]

---

105 For further discussion see: Mulligan, A. (2016) pp. 199–208.
106 For further discussion see: Varotto, S. (2016) pp. 78–87.
107 *Data Protection Commissioner (Ireland) v Facebook Ireland Ltd. and Maximillian Schrems* [2017] IEHC 545 (case 2016 No. 4809P.) The High Court Commercial, Dublin, 3 October 2017.
108 Ibid. at paras 177–180.
109 Ibid. at para. 192 (Ms Justice Costello).

Costello J pronounced that she was going to refer the case to the Irish Supreme Court since the High Court had identified 'the true controversy raised by the complaint and the point which requires to be determined in order properly to conclude the investigation into Mr Schrems' complaint'.[110]

In July 2018 the Irish Supreme Court heard Facebook's appeal in its long-running legal battle with privacy activist Max Schrems.[111] Five Supreme Court Justices granted Facebook's appeal acknowledging the complexity of the case which had by then taken five years concerning the issue of transatlantic data transfer mechanisms which, the court held, was of major national and international significance.[112] The Chief Justice, Mr Justice Clarke, also noted that the case had already been referred for the second time (by Max Schrems) to the CJEU (see below).

As part of its appeal to the Irish Supreme Court, Facebook questioned the validity and necessity of the Irish High Court's (original) reference to the CJEU and the content of the reference. The social media giant also alleged errors in the High Court's assessment of US law – including on its finding that there was mass indiscriminate processing of data and surveillance by US agencies. Despite this, Mr Justice Clarke said Facebook had a 'legitimate interest' in asking the Supreme Court to review the facts found by the High Court, as they 'have the potential to influence the assessment by the CJEU of the validity question which has been referred to it'.[113]

At the same time as the actions were going through the Irish courts, Max Schrems petitioned the Court of Justice of the European Union (CJEU) one more time. In *Schrems No 2*[114] the Court of Justice addressed the decisions first made under the then (and expiring) Data Protection Directive and the General Data Protection Regulation which allowed data protection authorities and the European Commission to fashion model clauses (including 'safe harbour' and 'privacy shield' protection). Furthermore, Max Schrems asked the CJEU for a preliminary ruling whether he could bring an individual and joint action in Austria against Facebook Ireland (since he is resident in Austria). His continued claim was that Facebook had infringed several data-protection provisions in relation to his private Facebook account,[115] and to the accounts of seven other users who had assigned to him their claims for the purposes of these proceedings.[116]

Facebook argued before the European Court in *Schrems No 2* (2018) that the Austrian courts did not have international jurisdiction, and accordingly that Mr Schrems could not rely on the rule of EU law that allowed consumers to sue a foreign contracting partner in

---

110 Ibid. at paras 331–332.
111 *Data Protection Commissioner (Ireland) v Facebook Ireland Ltd. and Maximillian Schrems* (2018) (Record No. 2018/68) The Supreme Court of Irland, Judgment of Mr Justice Clarke, Chief Justice, Dublin, 31 July 2018.
112 Ibid. at para. 8.5 (Mr Justice Clarke, Chief Justice).
113 Ibid. at paras 10.1–10.2.
114 *Schrems (Maximilian) v Facebook Ireland Limited* (2016) (Case C-498/16). Request for a preliminary ruling under Article 267 TFEU from the Oberster Gerichtshof (Supreme Court, Austria), made by decision of 20 July 2016, received at the Court (Third Chamber) on 19 September 2016, in the proceedings. Mr Schrems brought an appeal against the order at first instance before the Oberlandesgericht Wien (Higher Regional Court, Vienna, Austria).
115 Since 2010, Max Schrems had been using a Facebook account solely for his private activities. In addition, in 2011, he also opened a Facebook page (i) to inform internet users of the steps he is taking against Facebook, of his lectures, his participation in panel debates and his media appearances, (ii) to fundraise and (iii) to publicize his books.
116 Mr Schrems has also had assigned to him, by more than 25,000 people worldwide, claims for enforcement. Those other consumers were living in Austria, Germany and India.

their own place of domicile (the so-called Consumer Forum).[117] Facebook further contended that Mr Schrems, by using Facebook also for professional purposes, could not be regarded as a consumer. The Austrian Supreme Court in Vienna (Oberster Gerichtshof) then asked the CJEU for clarification under which the Consumer Forum might be invoked.

The Court of Justice held in January 2018 that Mr Schrems could bring an individual (private) action in Austria against Facebook Ireland. However, as an assignee of other consumers' claims, he could not benefit from the Consumer Forum for the purposes of a collective action.[118]

In May 2019 the Irish Supreme Court dismissed Facebook's final attempt to block Schems and the Irish Information Commissioner's reference to the CJEu.[119]

6.8 Freedom of information: Scotland and Northern Ireland

The Scottish Information Commissioner (SIC) is a public official appointed by Her Majesty the Queen (or the King) on the nomination of the Scottish Parliament. Much the same as his English counterpart, the Scottish Commissioner promotes and enforces both the public's right to ask for the information held by Scottish public authorities and good practice by authorities.[120] The SIC has a team of 23 people based in St Andrews, Fife. There are three departments: Corporate Services, Enforcement and Policy and Information. The Senior Management Team (SMT) is led by the Commissioner and is made up of the Commissioner and the three Heads of Department. The Corporate Services Team provides assurance to the Commissioner as Accountable Officer and a range of corporate services, including governance, finance, information management, human resources, procurement and contracts, risk and records management. The SIC is responsible for enforcing and promoting three pieces of devolved legislation:

- Freedom of Information (Scotland) Act 2002 (FOISA) – very similar to the English/ Welsh Act, it gives everyone the right to ask for any information held by a Scottish public authority.
- Environmental Information (Scotland) Regulations 2004 (the EIRs) – gives everyone the right to ask for environmental information held by a Scottish public authority.
- The INSPIRE (Scotland) Regulations 2009 – create a right to discover and view spatial datasets (e.g. metadata or map data) held by Scottish public authorities.

---

117 Council Regulation (EC) No 44/2001 of 22 December 2000 on jurisdiction and the recognition and enforcement of judgments in civil and commercial matters (OJ 2001 L 12, p. 1; 'the Brussels I Regulation'). According to that Regulation, defendants must, in principle, be sued in the courts of the Member State in which they are resident or have their registered office. It is only in cases mentioned in an exhaustive list that defendants may or must be sued before the courts of another Member State.

118 Source: Press release by the Court of Justice of the European Union, No 07/18 Luxembourg, 25 January 2018 in the case of *Maximilian Schrems v Facebook Ireland Limited* (Case C-498/16).

119 Data Protection Commissioner v Facebook Ireland Ltd. and Maximilian Schrems (2019) Irish Supreme Court. Appeal No: 2018/68.

120 Daren Fitzhenry took up his post as the Scottish Information Commissioner on 16 October 2017: www. itspublicknowledge.info/home/ScottishInformationCommissioner.aspx.

6.8.1 Interventions by the Scottish Information Commissioner

The Commissioner, Daren Fitzhenry's, Annual Report (2018) reported on the SIC's increasing appellate role in relation to specific requests for information. There has also been more direct intervention by the Scottish Information Commissioner, resulting in over 230 direct interventions in 2017–2018.[121]

There are four levels of intervention procedures under the SIC's enforcement procedures, including:

Level	Procedures
1: Minor failure to follow good practice	Staff alert the authority to the issue and may suggest remedial action, potentially with follow up action.
2: Ongoing practice failure	Senior staff raise the issue with authority and propose remedial action, with follow up.
3: Serious or systemic practice failings	Authority required to put in place an action plan to address the failure.
4: Consistent failure to comply with FOI law and guidance	The Commissioner will use statutory powers to address the problem.

The most frequent concerns raised with authorities at Level 1 in 2017–2018 were:

- compliance with timescales at review and request (45);
- review process (31);
- handling of initial request (21).

Level 2 interventions included:

- Aberdeen City Council: access to published information and charging;
- East Dunbartonshire Council: compliance with timescales. The SIC expressed concern that the council was failing to respond to requests and requests for review on time. There were continuing significant delays in the council responding to the Commissioner's investigations into the Court of Session's failing to comply with a Decision Notice (2016–2017);
- Glasgow Prestwick Airport Ltd: access to published information and charging. Requests were frequently refused on grounds of excessive cost;[122]
- Scottish Further and Higher Education Council (SFC): compliance with timescales.
- City of Edinburgh Council: responding under appropriate legislation.

---

121 Scottish Information Commissioner (2018).
122 SIC Decision 105/2017: Mr Andrew Picken and Glasgow Prestwick Airport Limited. Board meeting minutes. Reference No: 201700441. Decision Date: 5 July 2017.

Level 3 interventions included:

- *Scottish Government*: compliance with timescales (ongoing);
- *Police Scotland*: searching for and locating information.

Level 4 interventions:

- *Sycamore School Dunfermline, Fife and Eden Park Academy Muirkirk, East Ayrshire*: failed to adopt a publication scheme. Both authorities have now complied.

In 2017–2018 the Scottish Commissioner issued 205 decisions on appeals. One of the most significant decisions included the decision into the management of Hazlehead Crematorium during the 'baby ashes' scandal.[123] The SIC ruled that an internal report into 'abhorrent practices' at the crematorium in Aberdeen must be published. Aberdeen City Council had been asked by Kevin Keane of BBC Scotland for a copy of an independent report into the management of Hazlehead Crematorium. It refused the request, considering the report to be exempt under section 30(c) FOISA ('Prejudice to effective conduct of public affairs'). The SIC ordered the Council to make report public; it revealed that babies were being cremated with unrelated adults. The director, Pete Leonard, responsible for the crematorium subsequently resigned after he was quoted in the report as 'slow cooking' babies.[124]

Other significant decisions included:

- 139/2017: The Deputy First Minister's engagement on the 'Named Person' policy under the Children and Young People (Scotland) Act 2014.[125]

In this FOIA request 'NO2NP' ('No to the Named Persons') campaigner, Lesley Scott, had made a request for information to the Scottish Ministers on 12 January 2017, requesting all minutes of all meetings, or the information contained in the minutes, relating to the Deputy First Minister for Scotland, Mr John Swinney's 'No Named Person policy'. Mrs Scott alleged that the information suggested the Scottish government was intent on 'railroading' the proposals through Parliament without political support. The Scottish Deputy First Minister had refused several access requests reasoning that it would cost more than £600 to provide the information. NO2NP had fought the proposals all the way to the UK Supreme Court, which declared the original Holyrood legislation unlawful in 2016.[126]

Mrs Scott sought disclosure of the records of meetings which addressed the Scottish government's response to the UKSC ruling with possible amendments to the legislation.

---

123 SIC Decision 112/2017: Mr Kevin Keane and Aberdeen City Council. Hazlehead Crematorium – management investigation report. Reference No: 201601724. Decision Date: 18 July 2017.
124 Source: 'Hazlehead Crematorium report 'must be published', by Kevin Keane BBC Scotland's environment correspondent, BBC online, 20 July 2017.
125 SIC Decision 139/2017: Mrs Lesley Scott and the Scottish Ministers. Meetings about the Named Person policy. Reference No: 201700324. Decision Date: 29 August 2017.
126 Children and Young People (Scotland) Act 2014 Part 4.

The Commissioner found that the various Ministers had generally complied with Part 1 of FOISA in responding to the information request made by Mrs Scott. The Commissioner found that the Ministers had failed to respond to Mrs Scott's request within the timescale required by section 10(1) of FOISA.

- Decision 019/2018: where the Commissioner ordered disclosure of the name of a councillor in council tax arrears and provided a list of criteria for local authorities to consider when dealing with similar requests;[127]
- Decision 191/2017: about the environmental impact of sea lice medication used in salmon farming. For the first time, the Commissioner found that the requested environmental information related to 'emissions', meaning that the exception relied on to withhold the information could not apply.[128]

6.8.2 Differences and similarities between FOIA in England/ Wales and Scotland

The Freedom of Information (Scotland) Act 2002 (FOISA) contains much the same terms as its English and Welsh equivalent, though it is much broader in scope. There are several laws dealing with access to information which apply in Scotland.

Whilst the two Acts (FOIA 2000 and FOISA 2002) are broadly similar in many respects, some of the provisions of the Scottish Act are more rigorous. Some of the main differences between the two regimes are:

- The Scottish Act provides a straightforward right of access to information held, whereas the UK Act provides a right to be told whether or not information is held and to be provided with that information.
- The tests for exempt material are different. The Scottish Act requires public authorities claiming an exemption to exercise the public interest test, where applicable, within the 20 working day response period. The UK Act does not give a time limit.
- The harm test in the Scottish Act requires that disclosure would 'substantially prejudice' the effective conduct of public affairs, the commercial interests of an individual and so forth. The UK Act stipulates only 'prejudice'.
- Both Acts allow public authorities to recoup a proportion of the costs involved in providing information to individual requests (usually 10 per cent of search costs). In Scotland the first £100 is waived.
- The publication scheme requirements are different. The Scottish Act requires public authorities to take into account the public interest in information relating to the provision of services, including the cost of provision and the standards of those services, and major decisions made by the public authority, including facts and analyses on which the decisions are based. The UK Act only requires public authorities to have regard for the public interest in allowing public access to the information held by the authority and in the reasons for major decisions made by the authority.

---

127 SIC Decision 019/2018: Mr Tom Taylor and East Renfrewshire Council. Names of Councillors with Council Tax Arrears. Reference No: 201701113. Decision Date: 19 February 2018.
128 Decision 191/2017: Salmon and Trout Conservation Scotland and the Scottish Ministers. Report on the environmental impact of sea lice medicine. Reference No: 201701293. Decision Date: 20 November 2017.

- The UK Act allows information which is due to be published at some future date to be withheld until its publication (where it is reasonable to do so). The Scottish Act limits the withholding of information that is to be published to a maximum of 12 weeks, unless the information relates to a programme of research.
- The UK Act is enforced by the UK Information Commissioner (ICO),[129] the Scottish Act by the Scottish Information Commissioner.

TABLE 6.1 Freedom of Information Act 2000 (FOIA) and Freedom of Information (Scotland) Act 2002 (FOISA) Comparative Table

	FOI UK (England, Wales & Northern Ireland)	FOI Scotland
Jurisdiction of Commissioner	Commissioner responsible for both FOI (except Scotland) and Data Protection (whole UK). But note responsibility for FOI extends to UK-wide public authorities.	Commissioner responsible for FOI in Scotland. But see overlap with section 38 Data Protection Act 1998.
Duty to inform that the applicant PA[1] has the information requested	UK Act provides for dual rights: • to be informed that PA has information; and if so • to have that information communicated. The UK Act refers to first right as duty to confirm or deny (section 1(6) FOIA). Duty referred to throughout the Act. Arguably goes further than Scottish Act; application can be set aside for virtually every exemption (subject to public interest).	Scottish Act does not structure duty of authority in this way. Provides for one right: to be given the information requested. But does address issue via section 18 FOISA. The duty to confirm whether info exists or not is subject to public interest test. Slightly narrower than UK Act in that it only applies to certain exemptions (sections 28–35, 39(1) or 41).
Destruction of information	Destruction of material not specifically addressed in UK Act. Section 77 FOIA makes it an offence to alter, deface, block, erase, destroy or conceal info with intention of preventing disclosure by authority.	Specific section 1(5) FOISA prevents destruction of documents unless not reasonably practicable. Section 65 makes it an offence to destroy material with intention of preventing disclosure.

(Continued)

---

129 The UK Information Commissioner also covers the Data Protection Acts 1998 and 2018.

TABLE 6.1 (Continued)

	FOI UK (England, Wales & Northern Ireland)	FOI Scotland
Harm test	Authorities must show disclosure would prejudice or harm specified interest.	PA must show disclosure would substantially prejudice or harm. Higher standard than UK Act.
Public interest test	Does the public interest in maintaining the exemption outweigh the public interest in disclosing information (section 2(1)(b) FOIA)?	Is the public interest in disclosing the information requested outweighed by the public interest in maintaining exemption (section 2(1)(b) FOISA)?
Information received from UK government 'in confidence'	No reciprocal arrangement in relation to information from Scotland.	Section 3(2)(a)(ii) FOISA provides that information supplied by Minister or Departments of the UK government is held in confidence but not held by Scottish authority; therefore cannot be accessed under FOISA. In such cases UK FOIA will be used.
Disability rights	No specific mention of rights of disabled in relation to applying or receiving information requested.	Specific sections regarding disability rights (section 8; section 11(5) FOISA). Explicit reference to Disability Discrimination Act 1995.
Refusal of request on public interest	Section 17(2) FOIA allows PA more time where authority has not reached decision on the application of section 2(1)(a) or (2)(b) (whether the public interest in relation to duty or confirm or deny or in relation to exempt information applies). PA can issue applicant a notice estimating time within which decision will be reached (PA should aim to reach decision within 40 days).	Section 16 FOISA imposes strict time limits on authority (20 to 30 days) as soon as information is transferred to the 'Keeper of Records' even where public interest needs to be considered.

	FOI UK (England, Wales & Northern Ireland)	FOI Scotland
Information not held by PA	UK Act does not specifically address responsibility of authority when PA does not have info requested.	This issue is specifically addressed in section 17 FOISA. Formal notice must be issued to say that information is not held.
PA review of refusal to disclose	No provision in Act for internal review by authority. Must also refer to right of appeal to Information Commissioner (section 17(7) FOISA). Section 50(2) FOIA states that IC can refuse to entertain application when applicant has not exhausted all remedies.	Scottish authorities have 20 working days (30 days if information held by 'Keeper' and another PA has to carry out review) (section 21) to review their decision if they receive a requirement for review of refusal.
Publication schemes	The UK Act does not specify the type of information that authorities should consider providing access to via its publication scheme (section 19(3)) but simply refers to need to have regard to public interest.	When adopting publication scheme, an authority must have regard to public interest in allowing access to info relating to costs, standards, facts or analyses (section 23(3)(a)).
National Security Certificates – system of appeal	Section 60 FOIA provides for an appeal by IC or applicant against a certificate issued under section 23 or section 24 (relating to information supplied by security services and national security respectively). Under section 23 (where information is absolutely exempt) tribunal possesses power to quash a certificate where it finds that information is not exempt. Final point of Appeal to UT. Under section 24 (where information is subject to public interest test), the Tribunal can apply principles by court on application for judicial review.	Appeals from national security certificates (issued under section 31) not addressed in Scottish Act. Scottish Information Commissioner cannot challenge on public interest if certificate is conclusive of that fact. Certificate could be challenged via judicial review.

(Continued)

TABLE 6.1 (Continued)

	FOI UK (England, Wales & Northern Ireland)	FOI Scotland
Information intended for future publication	Section 22 FOIA refers to information to be published at some future date.	Section 27 FOISA specifies future date must be not later than 12 weeks from request.
Research	No specific section addressing research.	Detailed provision in relation to programme of research (section 27(2)).
Parliamentary privilege	Information that falls under parliamentary privilege can be exempt. Certificate can be provided to that effect (section 34). The IC cannot challenge the application of this exemption where it is supported by appropriate certificate. However, if no certificate is provided, the claim to this exemption can be challenged by the Commissioner.	The Scottish Act contains no corresponding provision. There is no concept of parliamentary privilege in relation to the Scottish Parliament or its members in the sense understood by Westminster. The Scotland Act 1998 has a number of provisions designed to give protection to Parliament so that it can conduct its business.
'Prejudice to public affairs'	Under section 36 FOIA it is left to the reasonable opinion of a qualified person to decide whether disclosure of the information would prejudice the effective conduct of public affairs (subjective test). Exemption becomes absolute in relation to information of both Houses of Parliament.	Opinion of individual is irrelevant in Scottish Act (section 30 FOISA). Applies an objective test.
'Legal professional privilege'	Exemption only applies to lawyer/client relations in England and Wales (s 42). Same section refers to situation in Scotland and uses phrase 'confidentiality of communications'. Wider application when dealing with Scottish public authorities covered by UK Act than other authorities.	Section 36(1) FOISA refers to 'confidentiality of communications' in legal proceedings. This is broader and could include doctor/patient, journalist/sources and possibly priests/penitent.

	FOI UK (England, Wales & Northern Ireland)	FOI Scotland
Commissioner review: time limit	UK Act provides no statutory time limit to review by IC (s 50 FOIA).	Commissioner must report to Parliament annually on number of decisions made outside four-month period (section 46(2) FOISA).
Judicial review	Equivalent law officers in UK do not have protection accorded to Scottish law officers.	Scottish Commissioner has no power to review refusals to disclose by Lord Advocate and procurators fiscal (s 48) in relation to role as head of criminal investigations.
Appointment of Commissioner	Information Commissioner (IC) appointed by monarch on nomination of government (section 6 Data Protection Act 1998).	Scottish Commissioner appointed by monarch on nomination of Parliament (section 42(1) FOISA).
Information tribunal	FOIA provides for both an Information Commissioner and an Information Tribunal. PA or applicant can appeal to the Tribunal against decision of Commissioner (section 57) whether decision, information or enforcement notice. Section 58 provides two grounds on which Tribunal can allow appeal: (a) notice not in accordance with law; (b) if it considers that Commissioner ought to have exercised discretion differently. Tribunal may review any finding of fact on which the notice is based. Further appeal possible to High Court on point of law.	FOISA provides only for an Information Commissioner. Scotland rejected need for Tribunal as introducing unnecessary extra appellate tier. PA/applicant can appeal to Court of Session against decision, information or enforcement notice issued by the Commissioner on point of law.
Commissioner settlement	No provision for settlement by IC contained in FOIA.	FOISA provides for Commissioner to attempt to effect a settlement before reaching decision (section 49(4)).

(Continued)

TABLE 6.1 (Continued)

	FOI UK (England, Wales & Northern Ireland)	FOI Scotland
Potential to override Commissioner	A Minister of the Crown or the Attorney General can issue a certificate in relation to exempt information (see Rob Evans case (2015) UKSC). Certificate can only be issued in relation to notice served on government department or PA designated by the order.	Scottish Executive can only issue certificate in relation to certain exemptions: sections 29, 31(1), 32(1)(b), 34, 36(1) and 41(b) (almost all class exemptions). Also information must be of 'exceptional sensitivity' (section 52). Only First Minister can give Commissioner the Certificate and following consultation with other members of the Scottish Executive. Certificate can only be issued in relation to notice served on Scottish Administration (i.e. ministers, junior ministers, non-ministerial office holders and their staff).
Exercise of rights of children	Unlike Scots law, capacity of **children under 16** is largely governed by common law. Guidance from the IC in relation to DPA makes it clear that there is **no minimum age** requirement for applicants. Children can apply for their own records provided they are capable of understanding the nature of the request. A parent or guardian can only apply on the child's behalf if (a) the child has given consent or (b) the child is too young to have the understanding to make an application.	Section 69 FOISA expressly entitles children to exercise their rights under the Act (similar provision exists in relation to Scotland only in section 66 DPA). See also: Age of Legal Capacity (Scotland) Act 1991; children can consent to certain activities (medical treatment/instructing solicitor) if have sufficient understanding. Presumed to have sufficient understanding if 12 or over.

[1] PA = Public Authority

6.8.3 The Northern Ireland Information Commissioner

The right to request information on public bodies under the Freedom of Information Act 2000 (FOIA) is not confined to citizens on the UK mainland. The Information Commissioner's Office in Belfast provides a local point of contact for members of the public and organizations based in Northern Ireland. The IC for Northern Ireland also influences policy and works closely with the departments of the NI Civil Service and the wider public sector.

Legislation in Northern Ireland is much the same as in England and Wales, and the FOIA and Data Protection Act 2018 both cover Northern Ireland.

Individuals could, for example, expect the Northern Ireland Assembly to provide current information on the role of the Assembly Commission or the Secretariat Management Group of the Assembly. The Assembly should be providing both outline and detailed information about its roles and responsibilities and the roles and responsibilities of those working there, such as roles, identities and biographical detail of the Speaker, First Minister and Deputy First Minister. Information relating to the legislation relevant to functions of the Assembly and its senior executives could also be requested under FOIA.

 FOR THOUGHT

> The INSPIRE (Scotland) Regulations 2009 apply to 'Scottish public authorities', as defined in the Freedom of Information (Scotland) Act 2002. In the absence of a definition of 'public task' in the Regulations, the University of Edinburgh concluded that, while it may be possible for a University to have a 'public task' for the purposes of INSPIRE, the University of Edinburgh did not have one. Discuss with reference to EU and Scottish legislation whether this statement is correct.

6.8.4 Has the freedom of information regime been a success?

Critics of the FOIA regime, such as WikiLeaks founder Julian Assange, have long argued that the FOIA regime is too complex with its class exemptions and long waiting times. However, freedom of information campaigner Heather Brooke would argue the opposite.[130] The British American journalist helped to expose the parliamentary expenses scandal, which culminated in the resignation of several House of Commons and some House of Lords parliamentarians. Several members or former members of the House of Commons, and members of the House of Lords, were prosecuted and sentenced to terms of imprisonment. With the assistance of the FOIA, the *Daily Telegraph* and Brooke were able to access and reveal parliamentary expenses 'abuses' in 2009–2010 which were of genuine public interest.

Similarly, *Guardian* journalist Rob Evans' access request regarding the disclosure of the Prince Charles letters – though the FOIA requests took nearly a decade for the letters to be released. Though the Prince Charles 'black spider' letters were not earth-shattering, they still revealed an insight into the future King's views, such as his support for proportional

---

130 Brooke, H. (2011).

representation in Westminster elections and his opposition to the Human Rights Act 1998. Most would agree that Rob Evans' immense efforts to access some 27 letters and memos written by the Prince of Wales to ministerial departments was a significant and important legal triumph to gain information which the public had a right to know.

There have been many other revelations, such as the naming of paedophile MPs and senior civil servants of the Thatcher government operating in the House of Commons at the time, suggesting a plot to cover up certain MPs' 'penchant for small boys'.

The downside is that appeals to the Information Commissioner's Office (ICO) tend to be lengthy, given that the Commissioner has to balance state, individual, corporate and media interests when making an effective decision as to whether to disclose sensitive information or not under the many exemption clauses of the Act.

6.9 Further reading

Cobbe, J. (2018) 'Casting the dragnet: communications data retention under the Investigatory Powers Act', *Public Law*, January, 10–22.
Jennifer Cobbe examines the Investigatory Powers Act 2016, specifically Parts 3 and 4 which, she argues, amount to an unjustifiable interference with Article 15(1) of the ePrivacy Directive,[131] read alongside Articles 7 and 8 of the EU Charter of Fundamental Rights 2000. The author found that there are serious issues with the communications data retention and disclosure framework under the Investigatory Powers Act 2016. She argues further while retention does appear to be limited to metadata, Parts 3 and 4 of the 2016 Act do not meet other requirements established by the CJEU. The author also argues that measures under the Act do not require a particularly high level of protection to be applied to retained data or that it be kept in the EU. The author points out that currently retention notices can be issued in pursuit of a range of purposes other than those permitted, and that retention is indiscriminate and is the rule rather than the exception. Furthermore, the length of the retention period is not objectively determined and limited to what is strictly necessary. Cobbe contends that the Act does not provide clear and precise rules governing the scope and application of retention. Communications data can be accessed for a variety of purposes other than those permitted. Access is not limited to data of individuals suspected of serious criminality. Finally, she claims that the oversight regulatory regime does not provide for independent prior review or for individuals whose data has been accessed to be notified when appropriate.

Crespi, S. (2018) 'The applicability of Schrems principles to the Member States: national security and data protection within the EU context', *European Law Review*, 43(5), 669–686.
Serena Crespi examines whether the principles set out in the Schrems (2015) judgment apply only in the specific context of an adequacy decision concerning the international transfer of data or also to access to data by EU Member State intelligence authorities. This article analyzes Article 4(2) TEU and Article 8 of the Charter, the GDPR (Data Protection Regulation 2016/679), along with the relevant

---

131 Directive 2002/58/EC of the European Parliament and of the Council of 12 July 2002 concerning the processing of personal data and the protection of privacy in the electronic communications sector (Directive on privacy and electronic communications – 'ePrivacy Directive').

case law of the CJEU (e.g. Digital Rights Ireland , Tele2) in order to assess whether, and if so, to what extent, EU law requirements may affect the activities of Member States in the area of national security, particularly at a time where Member States must deal with heightened internal and external security risks. The author advocates that the development of a clear and coherent legislative framework in this regard should not be seen as an obstacle to efficient intelligence activities but rather as an essential condition for their social acceptance, legitimacy and thus ultimately their effectiveness.

Smartt, U. (2015a) 'Prince Charles's "black spider memos": how a *Guardian* journalist succeeded in his 10-year quest under the Freedom of Information Act 2000', *European Intellectual Property Review*, 37(8), 529–538.
This article is an extended case comment on the *Rob Evans* case and the UK Supreme Court's ruling which signifies a victory for freedom of information and the Freedom of Information Act 2001 (FOIA).

Spurrier, M. (2012) '*Gillberg v Sweden*: towards a right of access to information under Article 10?' *European Human Rights Law Review*, 5, 551–558.
Spurrier discusses the ECtHR ruling in *Gillberg v Sweden* (App No 41723/06) of 3 April 2012, where the Human Rights Court recognized and developed a positive right of access to information. The author argues that the Strasbourg Court should take a more principled approach to the development of this right and observes that the changing landscape is provoking much debate in the domestic courts.

Varotto, S. (2016) 'The Schrems decision, the EU-US Privacy Shield and the necessity to rethink how to approach cross border personal data transfers at global level', *Communications Law*, 21(3), 78–87.
Stefano Varotto's article focuses on the *Schrems No 1* decision by the CJEU, arguing that the ruling is of 'seminal importance' since it posed to governments and businesses significant challenges regarding information privacy in an international context. The Schrems decision invalidated the safe harbour framework which, to that date (2015-2016) formed the legal basis for data transfer between the European Economic Area (EEA) and the United States in the context of transatlantic trade. The decision, per Varotto's argument, produced uncertain effects on the trade between the European Union and the United States, stimulating at the same time the urgent adoption of alternative legal solutions in relation to transatlantic data transfer. The author examines the safe harbour framework and possible solutions, particularly in the area of law enforcement regarding cross-border money laundering and cross-border data control outside the EEA.

Chapter 7

Regulating the print media

Key points

This chapter will cover the following questions:

- ○ What are the purpose and function of regulators?
- ○ How do we distinguish between statutory and self-regulation?
- ○ What was the background to the phone-hacking scandal?
- ○ Why was the Leveson Inquiry set up, and what was the outcome?
- ○ How is the print press (and their online editions) regulated in Britain?
- ○ What is the difference between IPSO and IMPRESS and press regulation in the UK?
- ○ Has the Leveson Inquiry had an impact on the future of UK press regulation?
- ○ How do we recognize fake news, and how can this be regulated?

7.1 Overview

We begin by looking at the advantages and disadvantages of regulatory bodies – statutory and non-statutory – and whether voluntary regulatory powers are sufficient to deal with wrongdoers and fake news. The chapter provides a summary and reflective overview of the 'phone-hacking' scandal at the *News of the World* (published by Rupert Murdoch's News International) which spread to other tabloids and looks at various police operations and criminal convictions which followed, starting around 2003.

The chapter examines the setting up of the Leveson Inquiry by then Conservative Prime Minister David Cameron, into the culture, practices and ethics of the British press, following the News International phone-hacking scandal. The public judicial inquiry, chaired by Lord Justice Leveson, comprised a series of public hearings, most of them broadcast live throughout 2011 and 2012. We reflect on Part 1 of the published Leveson Report of 29 November 2012 and explain why Part 2 of the inquiry was never commenced, which was supposed to shine a light on police malpractice, including their hacking of journalists' phones.

The chapter then provides a detailed look at current press regulation by IPSO and its rival organization IMPRESS, the IPSO Code and some adjudications by the press regulator. While IPSO has been backed by the vast majority of the UK press industry – except the *Guardian*, *Independent*, the *Financial Times* and *Private Eye* – IMPRESS has so far only attracted independent and small publications.

The chapter closes with some reflections on the meaning of 'fake news' and a few suggestions how to spot and possibly stop the fake news phenomenon.

7.2 What is the function of regulators and quangos?

Scottish moral philosopher and pioneer of political economy, Adam Smith (1723–1790), wrote in his *Wealth of Nations* (1776) that monopolies are inherently harmful and would cause a misallocation of scarce resources, with prices rising well above competitive prices. He recommended regulatory authorities that should closely monitor mergers and competitive behaviour of such monopolies.[1]

From the 1930s onwards most of the public utilities in the UK – gas, water and electricity – were nationalized to ensure economic survival and efficiency in the face of war and post-war reconstruction. Prime Minister Margaret Thatcher's Conservative policy from 1979 onwards was to privatize these utilities: gas in 1986, electricity in 1990 and water between 1985 and 1989. Her policy led to more than 50 companies being either sold off or privatized. Some of these natural monopolies required regulation and the 'quangos' were formed (quasi-autonomous non-governmental organizations).

The Nolan Committee, chaired by Lord Nolan, was set up in 1994 under the then Conservative Government, at the request of Prime Minister John Major, to examine, *inter alia*, standards of public life in the wake of allegations that MPs were asking parliamentary questions for cash. The Committee concentrated on Members of Parliament, ministers and civil servants, executive quangos and NHS bodies. Nolan recommended that all public appointments should be subject to independent scrutiny, that merit should be the overriding principle governing appointments and that all public bodies should follow a code of conduct. The post of Commissioner for Public Appointments was created in the wake of the Nolan Report and first held by Dame (now Baroness) Rennie Fritchie. Her role was to regulate, monitor and report on the public appointments process. However, only 12,500 of the total 35,000 public body appointments came under her remit at the time.[2]

Quangos were born, public bodies operating at arm's length from government, but for which ministers were ultimately accountable. In the case of Ofcom it is the Department for Digital, Culture, Media and Sport. Ministers are usually responsible for appointments, subject to scrutiny by an appointments review body under a Code of Practice, to avoid such things as conflicts of interest. Major players in the UK regulatory field include Transport for London, the Environment Agency and pay review bodies, such as the Office of Manpower Economics, an independent secretariat, incorporating eight pay review bodies, impacting 2.5 million workers in the UK (i.e. around 45 per cent of public sector staff) with an annual pay bill of around £100bn. There are the Armed Forces Pay Review Body (AFPRB), the Prison Service Pay Review Body (PSPRB), the National Crime Agency Remuneration Review Body (NCARRB) and the School Teachers' Review Body (STRB), to name just a few.

See
Chapter 8.4

When the Conservative-Liberal coalition came to power in May 2010 under the leadership of the then Prime Minister David Cameron he set out to overhaul the 'quango' system. In his pre-election pledge in July 2009, David Cameron chiefly declared war on Ofcom (Office of Communications), the broadcasting and communications regulator. At the time, Ofcom had 873 staff, a budget of £142m and was paying its chief executive nearly £400,000. Suffice it to say, Ofcom was not abolished and is now a most powerful regulator for the whole of the communications industry.

---

1   Smith, A. (1776 – new edition 2008 with explanatory notes by Kathryn Sutherland).
2   House of Commons (1994) First Report of the Committee on Standards in Public Life: The Nolan Report.

Some regulators have come and gone, depending on governmental preference and policy issues. The regulation of the film, games and commercial video industry is covered by the British Board of Film Classification (BBFC), a self-regulatory body with some statutory recognition such as the Video Recordings Act 1984. The impact of new media in general, and the internet in particular, continues to dominate the thoughts of those involved in the regulation of online audiovisual material.

See
Chapter 8.8

One of the best-known regulators was the non-statutory Press Complaints Commission (PCC), regulating the print press and their online content. The PCC ceased to exist and was replaced by the Independent Press Standards Organisation (IPSO) in September 2014. There is a crucial problem for the new press regulator IPSO: public perception. Is the new regulator entirely free from interference from publishing paymasters and editors such as its long-standing member and former chairman of the PCC, Paul Dacre, former editor in chief of the *Daily Mail* and still editor-in-chief of DMG Media, which publishes the *Daily Mail*, *The Mail on Sunday*, the free daily tabloid *Metro*, the *Mail Online* website and other titles? And what about those editors and journalists responsible for allowing the phone-hacking scandal at the now defunct *News of the World*, which led to the Leveson Inquiry? How many readers know about IPSO or the second press regulator IMPRESS? How does one know the difference? It could well be argued that the *Guardian's* self-regulation system, administered by an independent readers' editor with an appeals panel backup, is not working just as well without formal membership of a press regulator.

See below 7.6

Today the best-known regulators in the UK are Ofcom, the Charity Commission, the Environment Agency, the Law Society and Civil Aviation Authority. Lesser known agencies are PhonepayPlus, the regulator for all premium rate phone-paid services in the United Kingdom; the Internet Watch Foundation, which seeks to minimize the availability of potentially criminal internet content, specifically images of child sexual abuse hosted anywhere, and criminally extremely obscene adult content online; or the Office for Nuclear Regulation, also known as Ofnuke, the safety regulator for the civil nuclear industry in Britain.

7.2.1 Regulatory models in the UK

While all regulators have elaborate websites, are freely accessible and offer free advice, it is arguably not well-known by ordinary citizens that these authorities exist and offer free alternative redress to going to court in areas of privacy, defamation, harassment, obscenity, violence or child pornography.

There are three models of regulation, statutory, self-regulation and co-regulation, a hybrid version of the two. In the UK self- or co-regulation is primarily achieved by way of codes of practice, drawn up by a variety of professional bodies such as the Ofcom Broadcasting Code, the CAP Advertising Code (non-broadcast) or the BCAP Code (the UK Code of Broadcast Advertising). Such regulators are largely independent and generally involve public consultation when code changes are proposed. There now exists a mix of regulation and public funding which brings together commercial enterprise and public service broadcasting for consumers.

> **Three models of regulation**
>
> - *statutory regulation,* control by a statutory body, such as Ofcom, in relation to, for example, complaints about taste and decency, privacy and unfairness in relation to broadcasters;
> - *self-regulation,* where the industry regulates itself, paid for by members of a particular industry, such as the print press and online editions, for example, the Independent Press Standards Organisation (IPSO) or the Advertising Standards Authority (ASA), the independent regulator of advertising across all media and online services;
> - *co-regulation,* a combination of industry self-regulation with oversight by a statutory body (e.g. PhonepayPlus).

7.3 Models of self-regulation, co-regulation and statutory regulation

Statutory regulation has the same aims and functions as good quality self-regulation, which means the desirable features of statutory regulation are similar to those achieved under self-regulation. The difference is that statutory regulation has the force of the law to ensure that its aims are met; therefore enforcement and monetary fines can be a powerful means of compliance (such as applies to Ofcom). It is usually carried out by an independent body, accountable to the Westminster Parliament and subject to scrutiny by the National Audit Office. It is usually the most effective model where there is a clear divergence between commercial interests and the wider public interest.

7.3.1 Statutory regulators

See below 7.6

There are several ways to achieve statutory regulation. One is for a profession or body to pursue its own Act of Parliament which establishes a statutory regulating body. Regulatory bodies can be set up by order or Royal Charter (e.g. press regulation), subject to affirmative resolution in both Houses of Parliament or the Privy Council.

The advantages of statutory regulation include that the regulator is then derived from statute which means there is the legal underpinning of a body's disciplinary procedures. For example, a practitioner might be struck off due to misconduct in his or her office, such as the 'Sachsgate' affair about the Jonathan Ross and Russell Brand Radio 2 broadcast in October 2008, where comedian Russell Brand and presenter Jonathan Ross made prank calls to actor Andrew Sachs that led to controversy in the BBC and their ultimate dismissal (or rather resignations).

See Chapter 8.4

Another advantage is that the relevant statutory regulatory body can legally use a particular title (such as Ofcom) and enforce its standards by way of statute. This provision then makes it very easy for the public to determine who is and who is not a properly recognized regulator.

7.3.2 Self-regulation

Self-regulatory models are industry designed and led, allowing the industry to define an approach best suited to achieving its desired outcomes. Self-regulatory systems rely on a strong alignment between the incentives of participants and the wider public interest. Membership is voluntary and there is no statutory legal scheme.

The advantages of self-regulators are generally speed and dealing with public complaints out of court; the downside of self-regulation is that these authorities tend not to have legal powers in the form of injunctions, fines or damages (such as does Ofcom).

Traditionally, non-statutory regulatory authorities could not be challenged in the administrative courts by way of judicial review, though Lord Woolf stated in the *Ian Brady* case,[3] when the moors murderer challenged an adjudication by the Press Complaints Commission (PCC), that any exercise of jurisdiction over the PCC 'would be reserved for cases where it would clearly be desirable for this court to intervene'. Newsreader Anna Ford also tried to seek judicial review in a PCC decision, but the courts could see no justifiable basis for interfering with a self-regulatory body.[4]

Another negative aspect of self-regulatory regimes is that they are unlikely to prove effective when confronted by circumstances which present a tension between the public interest and the corporate interests of industry players. Critics argue that self-regulation is unlikely to provide sufficient incentive for firms to behave responsibly. If the actions of a voluntary regulator impinge on the rights of the subjects of the decision, particularly their human rights such as freedom of expression or privacy rights, then it is likely that the courts will intervene, which could mean that the strict demarcation between non statutory (self or voluntary) and statutory regulators is breaking down. This became the subject of the Leveson Inquiry.

See below 7.5

7.3.3 Co-regulation

Co-regulatory models typically provide more industry involvement than statutory regulation and can be particularly effective when there is widespread industry support for the objectives of regulation. They require periodic monitoring by a backstop body to ensure effectiveness and can require the backstop body to carry out enforcement activity.

The Authority for Television On Demand (ATVOD) is such a co-regulator. It co-regulates UK video-on-demand and TV-like services with Ofcom (known as 'on-demand programme services' or ODPS). Examples are catch-up TV such as ITV and Channel 4 'iplayers' (but not the BBC) and Amazon Prime (but not Netflix, which comes from the United States). ATVOD generally covers 'harm' issues in advertising, sponsorship and children's access to pornography. But it does not cover 'taste and decency', nor does it regulate fairness or privacy. If a complaint to ATVOD is upheld the regulator will publish a 'determination' on its website citing the breach of its rules. To demonstrate the complexity of co-regulation in converged media services and the overlap of regulation it is worth having a look at the Ofcom 'determination' in the Vice News 'case'.

See Chapter 8.4

We have seen that the model of co-regulation can, like self-regulation, struggle where there are pronounced tensions between commercial interests and the wider public interest, but usually less so than self-regulatory models. This is because the existence of the backstop body obliges the participants to find a way of resolving the inherent problems, or else face some kind of sanction from the backstop body.

---

3   R v PCC ex parte Stewart-Brady [1997] EMLR 185.
4   R v PCC ex parte Anna Ford [2002] EMLR 5.

7.4 Historic development of British print press regulation

The origins of regulation of the British print press can be traced back to the post – Second World War period when the Labour government established a Royal Commission in 1947 under the chairmanship of Sir David Ross to review and advise Parliament on the finance, control, management and ownership of the press. When the Commission reported on its findings it recommended the establishment of a self-regulatory press, and the Press Council was set up in 1953: a voluntary body that aimed to maintain high ethical standards of journalism and to promote press freedom.

During the 1980s a small number of publications failed in the view of many to observe the basic ethics of journalism. This in turn reinforced a belief among many Members of Parliament that the Press Council, which had lost the confidence of some in the press, was not a sufficiently effective body. Some believed that it would be preferable to enact a law of privacy and right of reply as well as to set up a statutory press council wielding enforceable legal sanctions.[5] Given the serious implications of such a course of action, the Conservative Home Secretary Douglas Hurd appointed a Departmental Committee in 1989 under (later Sir) David Calcutt QC to consider the matter.

The Calcutt Report on 'Privacy and Related Matters' (1990)[6] did not suggest new statutory controls but recommended that a 'Press Complaints Commission' ought to replace the Press Council.

7.4.1 The Press Complaints Commission

The Press Complaints Commission (PCC) was established in 1991 as an independent self-regulatory body for the print press, including magazines and, later, online editions. The main role of the PCC was to handle readers' complaints, by administering and upholding the Editors' Code of Practice. Until 2013, Paul Dacre, editor of the *Daily Mail* and editor in chief of Associated Newspapers (until 2018), was Code Committee Chairman.

The PCC Code was regarded as the cornerstone of press self-regulation, to which the industry and its editors had made a binding commitment. The funding of the PCC was via annual membership of newspaper editors and substantial fees paid to the regulator. Nearly all members of the press who had signed up to the PCC and its Code had a duty to maintain the highest professional standards. It was then the responsibility of editors and publishers to apply the Code to editorial material in both printed and online versions of publications. *Private Eye* editor Ian Hislop (since 1986) never signed up to the PCC nor to any press regulation to this day.

Periodically, Parliament discussed whether there should be some form of statutory press regulation and privacy legislation to curtail media intrusion into private lives. In July 1995, the Conservative Secretary of State for National Heritage, Virginia Bottomley, reported the findings of the Select Committee on 'Privacy and Media Intrusion' to the House of Commons, that a case had not been made out to enact a privacy law. The Labour MP for Islington and Finsbury, Chris Smith, asked Mrs Bottomley why a criminal offence had not been

---

5   For further discussion see: Rampal, K.R. (1981).
6   House of Commons (1990).

introduced specifically designed to prevent physical intrusion from bugging devices planted by the press which seriously invaded a person's private property.[7] The Secretary of State's response was non-committal, stating that it was up to the press regulator, the PCC, to keep its journalists in check by way of adherence to their Code of Practice.

In 2003, the House of Commons Parliamentary Select Committee for Culture, Media and Sport considered once again whether some form of statutory regulation of the print press ought to be introduced since there were increasing calls for the abolition of the PCC. Liberal Democrat peer Lord McNally launched a scathing attack on the press regulator in June 2003, saying it had 'all the power of a toothless poodle'. He called in the House of Lords for the PCC to be brought under the control of the then new media regulator Ofcom.

Defending the PCC, Mr Justice Tugendhat told the Media Select Committee that 'no new laws are necessary because recent changes in the law have already cured the defect in English law. I agree with the PCC that there is no need to introduce new legislation at the present time'.[8] Tugendhat J based his views on the statutory provisions of the Human Rights Act 1998, the Data Protection Act 1998 and the Protection from Harassment Act 1997, as well as common law decisions in *Campbell* (2002),[9] *A v B* (2002)[10] and the Strasbourg Court's ruling in *Peck* (2003).[11] Did the senior judge actually say at the time that no changes in the law were necessary because the HRA and DPA had 'cured' the defect in English privacy law?

7.4.2 The PCC: a 'toothless poodle'

One question remained: how could the PCC realistically punish its journalistic miscreants when it had no real power to sanction an editor or photographer by imposing a large fine (as does Ofcom)? All the PCC could do was to demand that an offending publication print an apology, publish a relatively small summary of the outcome of its adjudications or present editors with 'cease and desist' notifications which were repeatedly not followed – though *Daily Mail* editor Paul Dacre strongly denied that editors took no notice of the PCC. How effective was the press regulator really in dealing with serious media intrusion into people's private lives?

There was relentless press coverage with extensive media intrusion into the lives of Gerry and Kate McCann following the disappearance of their daughter Madeleine while on holiday in Portugal in May 2007. There was harassment and defamation of a prime suspect, Robert Murat. Neither the McCanns nor Mr Murat were helped by the PCC, so they sought legal redress via the High Court in the tort of defamation, with the result that four national newspaper groups had to apologize to Robert Murat in July 2008 for publishing false allegations about him over claims that he was involved in the abduction of Madeleine McCann. Murat received £600,000 in libel damages from News International,

---

7 House of Commons (1995) at para. 1326.
8 House of Commons – Department of Culture, Media and Sport (2003). Supplementary memorandum submitted by Mr Michael Tugendhat QC. Comment on the Supplementary Memorandum submitted by the PCC, 16 June 2003, at para. 501.
9 [2004] 2 AC 457 (HL).
10 [2002] EWCA 337 (QB).
11 *Peck v UK* (2003) 36 EHRR 719 (ECHR).

See
Chapter 3

Mirror Group Newspapers, Express Newspapers and Associated Newspapers.[12] The Express Newspapers' titles, including the *Daily Express*, *Daily Star* and *Sunday Express*, were made to apologize to Kate and Gerry McCann for wrongly suggesting that the couple were responsible for Madeleine's death, by printing front-page apologies and paying a settlement of £550,000 damages.[13]

When the House of Commons Committee for Culture, Media and Sport launched another inquiry into the possible discontinuation of press self-regulation in 2007, its report concluded that the PCC should continue, since there were now sufficient safeguards in statutory and common law to support private individuals if they could not be granted satisfactory redress by the regulator.

Leading media lawyer Geoffrey Robertson QC disagreed. He had frequently attacked the existence of the PCC, saying that 'the most satisfactory reform of the PCC would be its abolition', and questioning whether its 'lay' members really were 'lay' and truly represented ordinary members of society. In a *Guardian* blog debating the continued existence of the press regulator, Mr Robertson wrote in November 2009:

> the PCC tries to function as a poor person's libel court, but why should the vilified poor have to resort to an amateur set of adjudicators who can award them no compensation or damages – not even their bus fare home – and cannot direct newspapers to publish any correction prominently? The PCC's worst feature has been its propagandistic claim that it has raised standards of journalism – which it has not, other than perhaps the reporting of the Royal Family, over whom it is obsessively protective. It goes to extravagant lengths to deter people from asserting their legal rights.[14]

During a February 2010 debate in the House of Commons on 'Press Standards, Privacy and Libel', the PCC was again criticized for being ineffective and 'toothless' on the issue of use of phone-tapping and clandestine recording devices, particularly by the *News of the World*.[15] At the same time, Justice Secretary Jack Straw and Lord Lester proposed that the libel laws and press regulation ought to be reformed at the same time by way of a Defamation Bill. During another parliamentary debate the then Labour opposition leader, Ed Miliband, called the PCC a 'toothless poodle' and asked for an urgent replacement of the press self-regulatory watchdog (House of Commons, 7 July 2011).

The PCC ceased to exist in September 2014.

7.4.3 Some high-profile PCC adjudications

In 2008, Professor Sir Roy Meadow[16] complained that a comment piece in *The Times*, headlined 'A moving response to our family justice campaign', was inaccurate and misleading.[17] His complaint centred on Clause 1 ('Accuracy') of the Code. The journalist's point

---

12 Source: 'Madeleine McCann: Newspapers pay out £600,000 to Robert Murat', by Oliver Luft and John Pluckett, *Guardian*, 17 July 2008.
13 Source: 'Papers paying damages to McCanns', *BBC News Online*, 19 March 2008.
14 Source: 'What should be done with the PCC?', by Geoffrey Robertson QC, *Guardian*, 23 November 2009.
15 House of Commons (2010a) at para. 58.
16 *Professor Sir Roy Meadow v The Times*. PCC adjudication of 17 July 2008.
17 Source: 'A moving response to our family justice campaign', by Camilla Cavendish, *The Times*, 17 July 2008.

was that the complainant's submission of statistics-based evidence in the *Sally Clark*[18] case, when he was not a statistician, was an example of his going beyond his remit, and that other women had won their appeals against similar 'cot death' murder convictions also based on the misleading statistical evidence of Sir Roy on 'Sudden Infant Death Syndrome' – simply, that he had misled the jury in the *Sally Clark* case. As a means of resolving the complaint by Sir Roy, *The Times* invited the professor to submit a letter for publication outlining his concerns, but the complainant rejected the offer. The PCC did not uphold Professor Meadow's complaint, stating that *The Times* piece was an opinion piece and that the columnist's interpretation of the 'cot death' cases was accurately based on the appeal judgments, including those in other cases.[19] Above all, they held that the piece had been in the public interest.

Following the untimely death of 33-year-old singer Stephen Gately of pop band Boyzone on 10 October 2009 in Mallorca, the PCC received more than 23,000 complaints from the public about an opinion piece written by the *Daily Mail* columnist Jan Moir on 13 October. The article was published the day before Gately's funeral in Dublin with the original head-line on the *Mail*'s website: 'Why there was nothing "natural" about Stephen Gately's death'. This was later amended in the printed edition and online to: 'A strange, lonely and troubling death'. Moir told her readers that Gately's death after a drunken night out in Mallorca 'strikes another blow to the happy-ever-after myth of civil partnerships'.

The public outcry about Moir's article was fuelled by widespread discussions on social networking sites like Twitter and resulted in the highest number of complaints the PCC had ever received about a single article. Justifying its public interest responsibility, the Commission got in touch with Gately's family. The Commission also asked the *Daily Mail* editor, Paul Dacre – a member of the PCC's editorial board – to supply a response. In a new *Daily Mail* piece on 23 October 2009, Jan Moir expressed regret over her original column, though she stood by her earlier assertion that the circumstances surrounding the pop star's sudden death were 'more than a little sleazy' and that there was 'nothing natural' about Gately's death. The PCC's decision not to uphold the public complaint against the *Daily Mail* over its publication of Jan Moir's article caused great controversy. The adjudication made the point that one of the primary functions of a self-regulatory system was to defend freedom of speech. The PCC endorsed the newspaper's view that it must allow its journalists freedom of speech, which includes offensive views by its columnists. The PCC's director at the time, Stephen Abell, said the article contained flaws, but the Commission had decided 'it would not be proportionate to rule against the columnist's right to offer freely expressed views about something that was the focus of public attention'.[20]

---

18 Solicitor Mrs Sally Clark was convicted in 1999 of killing her 11-week-old son Christopher in December 1996 and 8-week-old Harry in January 1998 (the 'cot death' case). Her first appeal against the convictions failed in 2000, but the second succeeded and she was acquitted in 2003, when three Appeal Court judges ruled that Mrs Clark's conviction was 'unsafe', based on Professor Sir Roy Meadow's evidence during her trial. Expert witness Professor Meadow (for the prosecution) told the jury that the probability of two natural unexplained cot deaths in a family was 73 million to 1. At appeal, the Royal Statistical Society and other medical experts disputed that figure, stating that the odds of a second cot death in a family were around 200 to 1. The GMC found Sir Roy guilty of serious professional misconduct in July 2005; he was struck off the medical register. Sally Clark died on 16 March 2007, aged 42.

19 Angela Cannings served 18 months after being wrongly convicted of killing her two sons. Donna Anthony served six years after being wrongly convicted of killing her son and daughter. Trupti Patel was cleared of killing three of her children.

20 Press release by the PCC on 17 February 2010.

The PCC remained under constant criticism for performing inadequately amid claims that the search for an alternative system had become urgent. The Jan Moir decision may not have weighed in the press regulator's favour.

 FOR THOUGHT

Can press self-regulation be effective? Discuss with reference to regulation in some Western European, Asian and Middle Eastern countries.

7.5 The phone-hacking scandal and the Leveson Inquiry

The Leveson Inquiry was set up in 2011 by the then Prime Minister David Cameron when evidence emerged of phone hacking by the (now defunct) *News of the World* (*NoW*).[21] For the sixth time in less than 70 years, a report had been commissioned by the government which was to deal with concerns about press regulation.[22]

The public Leveson Inquiry was ordered, following revelations that someone working for the tabloid had, in 2002, illegally accessed the voicemail messages of the missing schoolgirl, Milly Dowler – who was later found murdered.

The Leveson Inquiry commenced its hearings on 14 November 2011 and ended on 24 July 2012. Leveson LJ was assisted by a panel of six independent assessors with expertise in the key issues that were considered. The inquiry was approached in four modules:

- *Module* 1: The relationship between the press and the public; phone hacking and other potentially illegal behaviour.
- *Module* 2: The relationships between the press and police and the extent to which that had operated in the public interest.
- *Module* 3: The relationship between the press and politicians.
- *Module* 4: Recommendations for a more effective policy and regulation that supports the integrity and freedom of the press while encouraging the highest ethical standards.

The Leveson Report was published in 2012,[23] and it can be said that most of the objectives of Part 1 of the Leveson Inquiry have been acted upon: an investigation into the culture, practices and ethics of the press with recommendations for a more effective regulatory regime of the print press (and their online editions).

The terms of reference for Part 2 were drafted before Part 1 had started. They included a requirement to examine the extent of unlawful or improper conduct within News

---

21 *NoW* was eventually closed down by Rupert Murdoch, the last edition being on 10 July 2011 headlined: 'Thank You & Good Bye'.
22 There were Royal Commissions in 1947, 1962 and 1973, the Younger Commission on Privacy and the Calcutt Report.
23 Leveson, Lord, LJ (2012) The Leveson Report in 4 Volumes.

International (publishers of *NoW*) and other newspaper organizations; to inquire into how police investigated allegations or evidence of such unlawful conduct; to inquire into the extent to which police received corrupt payments or other inducements; to inquire into the extent of corporate governance and management failures at News International; and in the light of these inquiries to consider the implications for the relationships between newspaper organizations and the police, prosecuting authorities and relevant regulatory bodies.

Leveson Report (2012): Main findings and key recommendations

- *Newspapers recklessly pursued sensational stories* – Leveson made no findings on any individual but stated that he was not convinced hacking was confined to one or two people. There had been a recklessness in prioritizing sensational stories by the press, almost irrespective of the harm the stories may cause and the rights of those who would be affected.
- *Covert surveillance* – Leveson found that there was a willingness to deploy covert surveillance, blagging and deception in circumstances where stories are difficult to get.
- *Families of actors and footballers also have rights to privacy* – Leveson found that some families of famous people had their lives destroyed by the relentless pursuit of the press. Actors, footballers, writers and pop stars were 'fair game' and 'public property' with little entitlement to any private life or respect for dignity.
- *The police* – Senior Met officers were 'too close' to News International. The hospitality police received from the media, including lavish restaurant meals and champagne, did not enhance the Met's reputation, leaving a 'defensive' mindset.

Key recommendations
- *New regulatory framework for the press* – a system of voluntary self-regulation, overseen by a recognition body established by Royal Charter.
- *An independent self-regulatory body* underpinned by statute, 'free of any influence from industry and government'.
- *Powers, remedies and sanctions by the regulator* with fines of 1 per cent of turnover, with a maximum of £1m. The watchdog should have 'sufficient powers to carry out investigations both into suspected serious or systemic breaches of the code'.
- *A libel resolution unit* – the new regulator should have an arbitration process in relation to civil legal claims against subscribers.
- *Membership* – though this would not be legally obligatory, and editors could *opt out* of the regulatory body.

Leveson LJ spent nearly 18 months gathering evidence from editors, politicians and victims of press intrusion. At the same time there were three police operations into criminal conduct by journalists and private investigators covering a wide range of offences at a cost of over £43m. Given the extent of these criminal investigations and the implementation of recommendations from Part 1 of the Leveson Inquiry, the government declared in March 2018 that Part 2 of the inquiry would most likely not take place. The then Secretary of State for Digital, Culture, Media and Sport, Matt Hancock, announced that the government would not continue with the Leveson Inquiry (Part 2) and declared that section 40 of the Crime and Courts Act 2013 would be repealed in the public interest.[24]

7.5.1 Phone hacking, blagging, pinging and informants

To understand the background and full impact of Leveson, we need to look back to events which led up to the inquiry. For many years, there had been complaints that certain parts of the tabloid press were riding roughshod over private individuals, celebrities and the royals. Rumours about the phone-hacking prevalence at NoW were rife, but the press regulator, the PCC, did nothing to investigate in order to expose the unethical conduct tolerated at Rupert Murdoch's News International. Phone hacking was only one of a range of methods of clandestine and intrusive information gathering; others included blagging,[25] pinging,[26] paying informants and tailing them.

See
Chapter 6.4

A report by the Information Commissioner's Office (ICO) – 'What Price Privacy' (2006) had also suggested that NoW journalists were increasingly contravening section 55 of the Data Protection Act 1998 by obtaining personal information via illicit means, such as phone tapping or using private detectives in order to dig up stories at any price.[27]

In the six years since the Leveson Inquiry published its report, following the three detailed police investigations into the activities of the media, there were 40 convictions. From February to August 2013, over 100 arrests were made as part of Scotland Yard's 'Operation Weeting' (investigation into phone hacking). 'Operation Elveden' investigated alleged corrupt payments to public officials such as police and prison officers by journalists, and 'Operation Tuleta' concentrated on computer hacking. By mid-2013, the Met had 185 officers and civilian staff working on the investigations: 96 on Weeting, 70 on Elveden and 19 on Tuleta. Police estimated that around 5,500 people had been victims of NoW phone hacking.

Clive Goodman, former NoW Royal Correspondent, pleaded guilty to the interception of phone messages from Prince William's voicemails; he was sentenced to four months' imprisonment in January 2007. His co-conspirator, private investigator Glenn Mulcaire, also pleaded guilty to five counts of unlawful interception of communication.[28] Mulcaire, former striker at AFC Wimbledon, had been providing the Sunday tabloid with the mobile phone details of celebrities and royals, including supermodel Elle Macpherson, publicist Max Clifford, football agent Skylet Andrew and Gordon Taylor, Chief Executive of the Professional Footballers' Association.

---

24 Department of Digital, Culture, Media and Sport (2018).
25 Obtaining something by using persuasion or guile.
26 Monitoring a user's mobile phone and tracking its location. This should only be used legally by police and security services.
27 Information Commissioner's Office (2006a) at paras 5.1–5.4.
28 s 1 Regulation of Investigatory Powers Act 2000 (RIPA) ('unlawful interception').

A complex Court of Appeal action – known as *Re Phillips*[29] – involving some 50 claimants, provides some insight into Glenn Mulcaire's phone-hacking activities at *NoW*. In this action, actor-comedian Steve Coogan sought disclosure of information from Glenn Mulcaire in this long-running civil action about his intercepting celebrities' voicemails at the time. Mulcaire was afraid that he would further incriminate himself by this disclosure and sought assurance from the courts that this would not take place.

In October 2013 the 'phone-hacking trial' at the Old Bailey, Central Criminal Court in London made for sensational headlines. Former News International Chief Executive Rebekah Brooks (née Wade), her racehorse trainer husband Charlie, Prime Minister David Cameron's former Director of Communications Andy Coulson[30] and seven other defendants faced a number of charges linked to phone hacking at the by now defunct *NoW*.[31] All pleaded not guilty to the charges of conspiring to pervert the course of justice.

The trial, which was one of the longest and most expensive in British criminal history, heard allegations of how journalists working at the *NoW* and *The Sun*, under the stewardship of Mrs Brooks and Mr Coulson, routinely broke the law in pursuit of exclusive stories. Jurors were told how reporters at *NoW* hacked mobile phones of hundreds of public and private figures, including celebrities, politicians, even victims of crime: they included Prince William, Prince Harry's ex-girlfriend Chelsy Davy, former Attorney General Lord Goldsmith, former Labour Home Secretary Charles Clarke, the actor Jude Law, football manager José Mourinho, football pundit Gary Lineker, the parents of *Harry Potter* actor Daniel Radcliffe, London Mayor Boris Johnson, Angelina Jolie, Simon Cowell, Sir Paul McCartney, former Liberal Democrat leader Charles Kennedy, David Miliband, Elle Macpherson and Heather Mills.

On 24 June 2014, former spin doctor for Prime Minister David Cameron at No 10 Downing Street in 2010 and former editor of *NoW* (2003–2007), Andy Coulson,[32] was found guilty and sentenced to 18 months' imprisonment for plotting to hack phones while he was editor of *NoW*. Saunders J said that Coulson had to take the major share of the blame for the tabloid's delay in telling police about hacking the voicemail of the missing Surrey schoolgirl Milly Dowler in 2002, the major motivation being to sell the maximum number of newspapers.[33]

On the same day, Rebekah Brooks was cleared of all charges, including conspiracy to hack phones, conspiracy to corrupt public officials and conspiracy to pervert the course of justice. Mrs Brooks' former personal assistant Cheryl Carter was cleared of conspiracy to pervert the course of justice; also cleared was former managing editor of *NoW*, Stuart

---

29 *Phillips v News Group Newspapers Ltd* (1) *News Group Newspapers Ltd* (2) *Glenn Mulcaire; Coogan v* (1) *News Group Newspapers Ltd* (2) *Glenn Mulcaire* [2012] EWCA Civ 48 (also cited as '*Steve Coogan v News Group Newspapers Ltd and Glenn Mulcaire; Nicola Phillips v News Group Newspapers Ltd and Glenn Mulcaire*').

30 Andy Coulson was the News of the World 's deputy editor between 2000 and 2003 and editor between 2003 and 2007. He resigned his post on the day of Clive Goodman's conviction in 2007.

31 The other defendants were Stuart Kuttner, former managing editor of *NoW*, Ian Edmondson, former *NoW* Head of News, Cheryl Carter, Rebekah Brooks's former secretary, and Mark Hanna, Head of Security for News International.

32 Andy Coulson, David Cameron's Communications Director, resigned from his post in January 2011, blaming the continuing row over phone hacking which made his job difficult.

33 *R v Coulson (Andrew) and others* (2014) (unreported). Sentencing remarks of Saunders J Central Criminal Court 4 July 2014 at: www.judiciary.gov.uk/wp-content/uploads/2014/07/sentencing-remarks-mr-j-saunders-r-v-coulson-others.pdf.

Kuttner. Mrs Brooks' husband Charlie and News International Director of Security Mark Hanna were also cleared of all charges.

Coulson faced further criminal charges, namely perjury, in May 2015 at the Edinburgh High Court. These charges concerned alleged lying under oath at the 2010 trial of ex-MSP Scottish Socialist party leader Tommy Sheridan.[34] In July 2015, Mr Coulson was cleared of the perjury charges after the case against him collapsed. His lawyers had successfully argued that there was no case to answer. Also in July 2015, former *NoW* features editor, Jules Stenson, pleaded guilty to overseeing widespread phone hacking. He received a four-month suspended prison sentence with 200 hours of unpaid work in the community, was fined £5,000 and was ordered to pay £18,059.61 in court costs.[35]

See
Chapter 3.8

Several civil proceedings were brought by those whose identity as victims of phone hacking had been exposed by the prosecution of Goodman and Mulcaire. These claims stretched beyond *NoW* and by June 2015 included defendant newspapers *Daily Mirror*, *The Sunday People* and *The Sunday Mirror*. Out-of-court settlements ranged from £72,500 to £260,250 in respect of eight celebrity claimants for phone hacking.[36]

By January 2019, Rupert Murdoch's News Corp. settled some 377 privacy claims out of court amounting to £332m, some individual celebrity claimants being paid more than £1m, including Cherie Blair, Jude Law and former cabinet ministers David Blunkett and Tessa Jowell as well as former boxer Frank Bruno.[37] (see also: *AAA v Associated Newspapers Ltd* (2012);[38] *Weller (Paul) v Associated Newspapers Ltd* (2014)[39]).

The latest claims, settled in January 2019, included Elizabeth Hurley, Elton John and the ex-wife of Paul McCartney, Heather Mills, who settled their phone-hacking claims against *The Sun* at the last minute, avoiding a potentially embarrassing trial for Rupert Murdoch's media empire over claims that the practice was widespread not only at the *News of the World* but also *The Sun*.

The decision meant that leading executives at News Group Newspapers would not be called to give evidence in the trial, which was due to start at the High Court in February 2019, involving claims by John's husband, David Furnish, and Mills' sister, Fiona Mills.

Following her acquittal in June 2014 at the Old Bailey, Rebekah Brooks returned as Chief Executive of Rupert Murdoch's UK newspaper operations in September 2015.[40]

In September 2014, the Met's investigation report on 'Operation Alice' was published, concluding that police officers had obtained phone records from *The Sun* journalists involved in the 'Plebgate' scandal.[41] Plebgate concerned an altercation between Conservative MP, Andrew Mitchell, then Government Chief Whip (who later resigned because of the incident) and the police, which took place on 19 September 2012, when police

---

34 For further information on the long running court action concerning Tommy Sheridan see: *Sheridan (Thomas) v News Group Newspapers* [2016] CSIH 67. Extra Division, Inner House, Court of Session, 19 August 2016.

35 *R v Stenson (Jules)* (2015) (unreported). Sentencing remarks of Saunders J Central Criminal Court 6 July 2015 at: www.judiciary.gov.uk/wp-content/uploads/2015/07/r-v-stenson-sentencing-remarks1.pdf.

36 *Representative Claimant Respondents v MGN Ltd* [2015] EWCA Civ 1291 (Ch) 17 December 2015 (Arden, Rafferty and Kitchin LJJ).

37 Ibid., Schedule to judgment and individual settlement pay-outs to claimants can be found here.

38 [2012] EWHC 2103 (QB).

39 [2014] EMLR 24.

40 Brooks had resigned in 2011 in the wake of the phone-hacking scandal and was given a £16m payoff by News Corp.

41 Metropolitan Police 'Operation Alice' Report, September 2014.

officers would not allow Mitchell to take his cycle through Downing Street's main gate. The Sun had published the story on 20 September 2012 alleging that Mitchell swore at the officers, calling them 'plebs'.

The Operation Alice Report found that a senior police officer rather than a judge had authorized the 'phone tapping' of Sun journalists and that the Met had (mis)used their powers under section 1 RIPA, thereby circumventing their powers under PACE (Police and Criminal Evidence Act 1984).[42]

In February 2016 Scotland Yard closed Operation Elveden after nearly five years of investigations into phone hacking.

7.6 Press regulation in the United Kingdom post Leveson

How has press regulation changed since the Leveson Inquiry? Leveson had recommended statutory regulation of the print press, akin to the Irish Press Council model.

From July 2013, the newspaper and magazine industry pushed ahead with the establishment of a new press regulator. Leading publishers and editors announced that the new regulator would be called the 'Independent Press Standards Organisation' (IPSO). Important policy makers championing the news IPSO regulator included Rupert Murdoch's News UK (formerly News International), the Daily Mail publishers Associated Newspapers, the Telegraph Media Group, the Newspaper Society (representing regional and local papers), the Newspaper Publishers Association (national papers), the Scottish Newspaper Society and PPA (magazine publishers).

In September 2014 the PCC was shut down – it had been found not fit for purpose by Leveson. At the same time IPSO, the new regulator, supported by the majority of the print press, came into existence with wider powers in its complaints handling and investigations (see below).

However, some of the most influential editors announced that they would not (ever) sign up to any statutory scheme. Fraser Nelson, editor of The Spectator magazine, was one of the first who vowed he would never support statutory press regulation.[43] Guardian publisher Guardian News and Media and the publishers of the Financial Times, Independent and Evening Standard made clear they would not sign up to the new regulator, and Ian Hislop, long-standing editor of Private Eye, had made his anti-statutory stance clear a long time ago and was not going to change his mind now.

Confusingly, another self-regulator – IMPRESS – also emerged at the same time, being the first to be recognized by the Press Recognition Panel (PRP) in October 2016.

7.6.1 How many Royal Charters on press regulation?

A Royal Charter is a formal document issued by a monarch as letters patent, granting a right or power to an individual or a body corporate. Royal Charters are, used to establish significant organizations such as the BBC, cities or universities. They are approved by the

---

42 Ibid. at paras 5.115–5.118.
43 Source: 'Why The Spectator won't sign the Royal Charter', by Fraser Nelson, Spectator, 23 March 2013.

Privy Council, a formal body of advisers to the sovereign, which is mostly made up of current or former Members of Parliament.

One draft Royal Charter was proposed by the pressure group, Hacked Off,[44] drafted by Hugh Tomlinson QC and Parliamentary Counsel Daniel Greenberg. Actor Hugh Grant, a director of the 'Hacked Off campaign', told the BBC's *Andrew Marr Show* that the draft 'Hacked-Off Bill' proposed to set up an appointments commission mainly involving the judiciary which, in turn, would appoint a recognition body that in turn would oversee the body established by the press to regulate itself.[45]

See
Chapter 3

Then there was the government's draft Royal Charter Bill of 15 May 2013; it contained very few Leveson recommendations (such as incorporating the new proposed defamation legislation).

In a last-minute attempt to stop the Privy Council introducing a Royal Charter on press regulation, a group of newspaper and magazine publishers sought a High Court injunction. Industry bodies representing the publishers were granted an emergency High Court hearing just hours before the government's Press Regulation Royal Charter – backed by the three main parties and Hacked Off campaigners – was set to go before the Privy Council for sealing by the Queen. However, the injunction was not granted by Richards LJ and Sales J. The applicant newspaper publishers immediately declared their intention to take their case to the Court of Appeal. They sought a ruling that any decision to seal the cross-party Charter could be overturned by way of judicial review.

On 30 October 2013, the Royal Charter on Press Self-Regulation was granted by Queen Elizabeth II[46] which set out an independent body, the Press Recognition Panel (PRP). The idea being that the PRP would receive applications from press regulators that would meet the criteria wishing to apply for recognition in line with that recommended in the Leveson Report. Dr David Wolfe became the first Chair of the PRP.

7.6.1 Section 40 Crime and Courts Act 2013: exemplary damages – a system of carrots and sticks

A crucial part of Leveson relied on persuading the press to join a recognized regulator. Lord Justice Leveson knew this would not be easy, and the Royal Charter on Self-Regulation of the Press 2013 was to introduce a system that hinged on costs and incentives, trying to balance two key objectives: providing access to justice for ordinary people wronged by the press without the risk of enormous legal costs and protecting news publishers from wealthy litigants threatening them with financially ruinous court proceedings.

A contentious part of the Charter was then legislation requiring publishers to pay both sides' costs in a privacy or libel action, even if they won – unless they signed up to a

44 Established in 2011, Hacked Off campaigns for a free and accountable press. See: http://hackinginquiry.org.
45 Source: 'Leveson: Hugh Grant slams Cameron's press reform plan', *The Andrew Marr Show*, BBC TV, 17 March 2013.
46 Royal Charter on Self-Regulation of the Press. Granted by Elizabeth the Second by the Grace of God of the United Kingdom of Great Britain and Northern Ireland and of Our other Realms and Territories Queen, Head of the Commonwealth, Defender of the Faith, 30 October 2013: https://assets.publishing.service.gov.uk/government/uploads/system/uploads/attachment_data/file/254116/Final_Royal_Charter_25_October_2013_clean__Final_.pdf.

regulator (e.g. IPSO or IMPRESS). This was inherent in section 40 of the Crime and Courts Act 2013 ('Awards of costs'). Section 40 reads in part:

(1) This section applies where –

(a) a relevant claim is made against a person ('the defendant'),
(b) the defendant was a relevant publisher at the material time, and
(c) the claim is related to the publication of news-related material.

(2) If the defendant was a member of an approved regulator at the time when the claim was commenced (or was unable to be a member at that time for reasons beyond the defendant's control or it would have been unreasonable in the circumstances for the defendant to have been a member at that time), the court must not award costs against the defendant unless satisfied that –

(a) the issues raised by the claim could not have been resolved by using an arbitration scheme of the approved regulator, or
(b) it is just and equitable in all the circumstances of the case to award costs against the defendant.

(3) If the defendant was not a member of an approved regulator at the time when the claim was commenced (but would have been able to be a member at that time and it would have been reasonable in the circumstances for the defendant to have been a member at that time), the court must award costs against the defendant unless satisfied that –

(a) the issues raised by the claim could not have been resolved by using an arbitration scheme of the approved regulator (had the defendant been a member), or
(b) it is just and equitable in all the circumstances of the case to make a different award of costs or make no award of costs . . .

. . .

(6) This section does not apply until such time as a body is first recognised as an approved regulator.

Section 40 of the 2013 Act had not yet come into force, and there were a number of parliamentary debates as to whether it should come into force at all, and if so, when. In general, the section precluded the award of costs against a defendant newspaper, if it were a member of a regulator when the claim began, unless the issues were incapable of resolution by arbitration or it was just and equitable to award costs. If the defendant were not a member of a regulator, the court would generally have to award costs against it even if the claim was unsuccessful, unless the issues would have been incapable of resolution by arbitration or it was just and equitable to make a different or no award.

An arbitration scheme – recommended by Leveson – was to be introduced at the same time by way of sections 34 to 42 and Schedule 15 of the Crime and Courts Act 2013 to cover 'publishers of newsrelated material: damages and costs'. These measures set out a new system for 'exemplary damages and costs', as well as defining those who met the definition of a 'relevant publisher' to whom the new system of exemplary damages was to apply.[47]

Section 34 of the 2013 Act ('awards of exemplary damages') reads in part:

(1)   This section applies where –

    (a)   a relevant claim is made against a person ('the defendant'),

    (b)   the defendant was a relevant publisher at the material time,

    (c)   the claim is related to the publication of news-related material, and

    (d)   the defendant is found liable in respect of the claim.

(2)   Exemplary damages may not be awarded against the defendant in respect of the claim if the defendant was a member of an approved regulator at the material time.

(3)   But the court may disregard subsection (2) if –

    (a)   the approved regulator imposed a penalty on the defendant in respect of the defendant's conduct or decided not to do so,

    (b)   the court considers, in light of the information available to the approved regulator when imposing the penalty or deciding not to impose one, that the regulator was manifestly irrational in imposing the penalty or deciding not to impose one, and

    (c)   the court is satisfied that, but for subsection (2), it would have made an award of exemplary damages under this section against the defendant.

(4)   Where the court is not prevented from making an award of exemplary damages by subsection (2) (whether because that subsection does not apply or the court is permitted to disregard that subsection as a result of subsection (3)), the court –

    (a)   may make an award of exemplary damages if it considers it appropriate to do so in all the circumstances of the case, but

    (b)   may do so only under this section.

(5)   Exemplary damages may be awarded under this section only if they are claimed.

(6)   Exemplary damages may be awarded under this section only if the court is satisfied that –

    (a)   the defendant's conduct has shown a deliberate or reckless disregard of an outrageous nature for the claimant's rights,

    (b)   the conduct is such that the court should punish the defendant for it, and

    (c)   other remedies would not be adequate to punish that conduct.

Section 34 (once in force) precludes exemplary damages after a claim against a relevant publisher in relation to news-related material if the defendant were a member of an approved regulator, unless that regulator acted irrationally. 'Approved regulator' means a body recognized by the PRP (see below); 'relevant claim' is for libel, slander,

---

47   The sanctions under Part 36 of the Civil Procedure Rules ('offers to settle') were reformed to encourage early settlement. This was intended to encourage claimants to make, and defendants to accept, reasonable early offers which, in turn, would help reduce the time taken for cases to settle and consequently help to lower overall costs.

breach of confidence, misuse of private information, malicious falsehood or harassment; 'relevant publisher' means a body which in the course of business publishes news-related material written by different authors editorially controlled.

These measures proposed in the 2013 Act introduced a system of carrots and sticks: if a news publisher joined a recognized regulator then access to low-cost arbitration would become mandatory. At the same time this would remove the threat of potentially vast costs for both ordinary citizens who may be the victims of illegal journalistic behaviour and for publishers who may be threatened by a wealthy litigant who does not like what the tabloids printed about them. Only claimants with a genuine legal case would be offered arbitration, thereby avoiding trivial and malicious claims being brought. If a newspaper, on the other hand, decided not to join a recognized regulator and thereby refused to offer affordable access to justice, then they would be liable to pay all costs of court action against them (section 40).

Section 40 became a highly controversial issue, and the then Secretary of State for Culture, Media and Sport, Karen Bradley, came under increasing pressure from both sides of the debate and eventually put the commencement of section 40 out to public consultation, which closed on 10 January 2017.

On 14 June 2018 the House of Commons voted against forcing the government to hold Part 2 of the Leveson Inquiry. The then Culture Secretary, Matt Hancock, hailed 'a great day for a free and fair press', after the government narrowly defeated a Labour bid to force it to launch a second phase of the Leveson Inquiry. Former Labour Leader, Ed Miliband, had tabled an amendment to the government's Data Protection Bill, aimed at reopening the Leveson Inquiry, which was initially conceived when it was launched in 2011 as a two-stage investigation into the behaviour of the press. The government won the vote by 304 votes to 295, a majority of 9 after apparently making concessions to the Democratic Unionist party (DUP). One Labour MP, John Grogan, voted with the government, while up to 18 more appeared to have stayed away.

To date, section 40 has not been repeated nor has it been implemented.

7.6.2 Press regulation: the current system

Presently, there appear to be two coexisting press regulators, the Independent Press Standards Organisation (IPSO) and the Press Recognition Panel (PRP), set up by Royal Charter. At the same time, a 'third way' of press self-regulation exists alongside in the form of the 'IMPRESS Project' ('IMPRESS'). Its founding donors include Sir Harold Evans (former editor of the Sunday Times), actors Michael Frayn and Terry Gilliam, playwright and theatre director David Hare, novelist Ian McEwan, Harry Potter author J.K. Rowling, publisher and philanthropist William Sieghart and Guardian journalist Polly Toynbee.

7.6.3 IPSO: the Independent Press Standards Organisation

IPSO started the moment the PCC closed down on 8 September 2014. It is fair to say that the new regulator was not dissimilar to the just disbanded one: IPSO was established and designed by the press industry on lines closely modelled on the failed PCC lines that had been explicitly rejected by the Leveson Inquiry as tending to put the interests of the industry before those of the public. IPSO's first chairman was Sir Alan Moses, a former Lord Justice of Appeal. Lord Edward Faulk QC will take up the role from, January 2020.

By 2018, IPSO was regulating some 85 publishers, with more than 1,500 printed publications and over 2,500 online titles – the majority of the UK's newspaper and magazine industry. Major publications include the Trinity Mirror group (*Daily Mirror, Sunday Mirror, Sunday People*), the Telegraph Media Group, Northern and Shell (*Daily and Sunday Express, Daily Star, New!, OK!, Star Magazine*), News UK (*The Sun, The Times, The Sunday Times, The Times Literary Supplement*) and Associated Newspapers (*Daily Mail, The Mail on Sunday, Metro*).[48]

In August 2018 IPSO introduced a compulsory arbitration scheme for all its participating members. It is a process designed specifically to rule on media law disputes. An expert media law barrister impartially rules on the claim still trying to keep fee costs low at around £100, so that a ruling can be made more quickly than going through the courts. Complainants can win damages of up to £60,000 and recover costs of up to £25,000.

7.6.4 The IPSO Editors' Code[49]

IPSO is a non-profit Community Interest Company which regulates those publishers who have agreed to be subject to its regulation. The publisher has submitted to the jurisdiction of IPSO pursuant to a set of contractual arrangements. The constitution, remit, functions and procedures of IPSO are governed by its Articles of Association (and in particular Articles 5, 7 and 8.1) and by Regulations. One function which the Articles and the Regulations confer on IPSO is the provision of a 'complaints handling' service. This involves ruling on complaints against regulated publishers that they have infringed the Editors' Code of Practice which IPSO has adopted. By Regulation 8, IPSO is given power to consider complaints in three categories:

- from those personally and directly affected by the alleged breach;
- from a representative group;
- from a third party seeking to correct a significant inaccuracy of published information.

Regulations 14 to 31 and 37 provide for the investigation, mediation and determination of complaints that the Code has been infringed, to be carried out by IPSO's Complaints Committee. This consists of 12 members, chaired by the Chair of IPSO's Board. Six of the 12 members (in addition to the chair) must be independent as defined in the Regulator's Articles.

IPSO introduced its Editors' Code of Practice in 2014 which deals with issues such as accuracy, invasion of privacy, intrusion into grief or shock and harassment – in fact it is strikingly similar to the PCC's former Code.

IPSO has the power, where necessary, to require the publication of prominent corrections and critical adjudications and can now also fine publications in cases where failings are particularly serious and systemic, following arbitration.

IPSO regards its Code as the cornerstone of the system of voluntary self-regulation to which all members of the magazine, print and online press have a binding contractual commitment. The Code sets out the framework for the highest professional journalistic

---

48 IPSO Annual Report 2017.
49 The latest version of the Editors' Code of Practice came into effect on 1 January 2018.

standards that members of the press subscribing to IPSO have undertaken to maintain. It balances both the rights of the individual and the public's right to know (similar to Articles 8 and 10 ECHR).

Members are invited to interpret the Code neither so narrowly as to compromise its commitment to respect the rights of the individual, nor so broadly that it infringes the fundamental right to freedom of expression – such as to inform, to be partisan, to challenge, shock, be satirical and to entertain – or prevents publication in the public interest.

It is then the responsibility of editors and publishers to apply the Code to editorial material in both printed and online versions of their publications. They should take care to ensure it is observed rigorously by all editorial staff and external contributors, including non-journalists.[50]

Once a complaint is upheld, the IPSO Complaints Committee considers what remedial action should be required. The Committee has the power to require the publication of a correction and/or adjudication; the nature, extent and placement is determined by IPSO. It may also inform the publication that further remedial action is required to ensure that the requirements of the Editors' Code are met. Here follow the clauses of the Code:

The IPSO Editors' Code of Practice

1. Accuracy

i) The Press must take care not to publish inaccurate, misleading or distorted information or images, including headlines not supported by the text.

ii) A significant inaccuracy, misleading statement or distortion must be corrected, promptly and with due prominence, and – where appropriate – an apology published. In cases involving IPSO, due prominence should be as required by the regulator.

iii) A fair opportunity to reply to significant inaccuracies should be given, when reasonably called for.

iv) The Press, while free to editorialise and campaign, must distinguish clearly between comment, conjecture and fact.

v) A publication must report fairly and accurately the outcome of an action for defamation to which it has been a party, unless an agreed settlement states otherwise, or an agreed statement is published.

2. *Privacy[51]

i) Everyone is entitled to respect for his or her private and family life, home, health and correspondence, including digital communications.

ii) Editors will be expected to justify intrusions into any individual's private life without consent. In considering an individual's reasonable expectation of privacy, account will be taken of the complainant's own public disclosures of

---

50 For further discussion see: Carney, D. (2017) at pp. 112–123.
51 There may be exceptions to the clauses marked * where they can be demonstrated to be in the public interest.

information and the extent to which the material complained about is already in the public domain or will become so.

iii) It is unacceptable to photograph individuals, without their consent, in public or private places where there is a reasonable expectation of privacy.

3. *Harassment

i) Journalists must not engage in intimidation, harassment or persistent pursuit.

ii) They must not persist in questioning, telephoning, pursuing or photographing individuals once asked to desist; nor remain on property when asked to leave and must not follow them. If requested, they must identify themselves and whom they represent.

iii) Editors must ensure these principles are observed by those working for them and take care not to use non-compliant material from other sources.

4. Intrusion into grief or shock

In cases involving personal grief or shock, enquiries and approaches must be made with sympathy and discretion and publication handled sensitively. These provisions should not restrict the right to report legal proceedings.

5. *Reporting suicide

When reporting suicide, to prevent simulative acts care should be taken to avoid excessive detail of the method used, while taking into account the media's right to report legal proceedings.

6. *Children

i) All pupils should be free to complete their time at school without unnecessary intrusion.

ii) They must not be approached or photographed at school without permission of the school authorities.

iii) Children under 16 must not be interviewed or photographed on issues involving their own or another child's welfare unless a custodial parent or similarly responsible adult consents.

iv) Children under 16 must not be paid for material involving their welfare, nor parents or guardians for material about their children or wards, unless it is clearly in the child's interest.

v) Editors must not use the fame, notoriety or position of a parent or guardian as sole justification for publishing details of a child's private life.

7. *Children in sex cases

The press must not, even if legally free to do so, identify children under 16 who are victims or witnesses in cases involving sex offences.

In any press report of a case involving a sexual offence against a child –

i) The child must not be identified.

ii) The adult may be identified.

iii) The word 'incest' must not be used where a child victim might be identified.

iv) Care must be taken that nothing in the report implies the relationship between the accused and the child.

8. *Hospitals

i) Journalists must identify themselves and obtain permission from a responsible executive before entering non-public areas of hospitals or similar institutions to pursue enquiries.

ii) The restrictions on intruding into privacy are particularly relevant to enquiries about individuals in hospitals or similar institutions.

9. *Reporting of crime

i) Relatives or friends of persons convicted or accused of crime should not generally be identified without their consent, unless they are genuinely relevant to the story.

ii) Particular regard should be paid to the potentially vulnerable position of children under the age of 18 who witness, or are victims of, crime. This should not restrict the right to report legal proceedings.

iii) Editors should generally avoid naming children under the age of 18 after arrest for a criminal offence but before they appear in a youth court unless they can show that the individual's name is already in the public domain, or that the individual (or, if they are under 16, a custodial parent or similarly responsible adult) has given their consent. This does not restrict the right to name juveniles who appear in a crown court, or whose anonymity is lifted.

10. *Clandestine devices and subterfuge

i) The press must not seek to obtain or publish material acquired by using hidden cameras or clandestine listening devices; or by intercepting private or mobile telephone calls, messages or emails; or by the unauthorised removal of documents or photographs; or by accessing digitally-held information without consent.

ii) Engaging in misrepresentation or subterfuge, including by agents or intermediaries, can generally be justified only in the public interest and then only when the material cannot be obtained by other means.

11. Victims of sexual assault

The press must not identify or publish material likely to lead to the identification of a victim of sexual assault unless there is adequate justification and they are legally free to do so. Journalists are entitled to make enquiries but must take care and exercise discretion to avoid the unjustified disclosure of the identity of a victim of sexual assault.

12. Discrimination

i) The press must avoid prejudicial or pejorative reference to an individual's, race, colour, religion, sex, gender identity, sexual orientation or to any physical or mental illness or disability.

ii) Details of an individual's race, colour, religion, gender identity, sexual orientation, physical or mental illness or disability must be avoided unless genuinely relevant to the story.

13. Financial journalism

i) Even where the law does not prohibit it, journalists must not use for their own profit financial information they receive in advance of its general publication, nor should they pass such information to others.

ii) They must not write about shares or securities in whose performance they know that they or their close families have a significant financial interest without disclosing the interest to the editor or financial editor.

iii) They must not buy or sell, either directly or through nominees or agents, shares or securities about which they have written recently or about which they intend to write in the near future.

14. Confidential sources

Journalists have a moral obligation to protect confidential sources of information.

15. Witness payments in criminal trials

i) No payment or offer of payment to a witness – or any person who may reasonably be expected to be called as a witness – should be made in any case once proceedings are active as defined by the Contempt of Court Act 1981. This prohibition lasts until the suspect has been freed unconditionally by police without charge or bail or the proceedings are otherwise discontinued; or has entered a guilty plea to the court; or, in the event of a not guilty plea, the court has announced its verdict.

*ii) Where proceedings are not yet active but are likely and foreseeable, editors must not make or offer payment to any person who may reasonably be expected to be called as a witness, unless the information concerned ought demonstrably to be published in the public interest and there is an over-riding need to make or promise payment for this to be done; and all reasonable steps have been taken to ensure no financial dealings influence the evidence those witnesses give. In no circumstances should such payment be conditional on the outcome of a trial.

*iii) Any payment or offer of payment made to a person later cited to give evidence in proceedings must be disclosed to the prosecution and defence. The witness must be advised of this requirement.

16. *Payment to criminals

i) Payment or offers of payment for stories, pictures or information, which seek to exploit a particular crime or to glorify or glamorise crime in general, must not be made directly or via agents to convicted or confessed criminals or to their associates – who may include family, friends and colleagues.

ii) Editors invoking the public interest to justify payment or offers would need to demonstrate that there was good reason to believe the public interest would be served. If, despite payment, no public interest emerged, then the material should not be published.

The Public Interest

1   The public interest includes, but is not confined to:

- Detecting or exposing crime, or the threat of crime, or serious impropriety.
- Protecting public health or safety.
- Protecting the public from being misled by an action or statement of an individual or organization.
- Disclosing a person or organization's failure or likely failure to comply with any obligation to which they are subject.
- Disclosing a miscarriage of justice.
- Raising or contributing to a matter of public debate, including serious cases of impropriety, unethical conduct or incompetence concerning the public.
- Disclosing concealment, or likely concealment, of any of the above.

2   There is a public interest in freedom of expression itself.
3   The regulator will consider the extent to which material is already in the public domain or will become so.
4   Editors invoking the public interest will need to demonstrate that they reasonably believed publication – or journalistic activity taken with a view to publication – would both serve, and be proportionate to, the public interest and explain how they reached that decision at the time.
5   An exceptional public interest would need to be demonstrated to over-ride the normally paramount interests of children under 16.

From time to time IPSO also publishes new guidelines on important and sensitive issues which are to assist journalists and help to understand how to cover issues such as reporting on suicides[52] or historic child sex abuse cases.[53] All rulings and decisions are published on the regulator's website.

7.6.5 Press regulation and judicial review

Similar to the PCC, the new press regulator may be subject to legal challenges under judicial review. Judicial review is a public law jurisdiction, governed by Part 54 of the

---

52 IPSO press release 'Reporting on Suicides' of 17 December 2018: www.ipso.co.uk/news-press-releases/press-releases/press-watchdog-publishes-guidance-on-reporting-suicide-for-editors-and-journalists/.
53 Press release 'Guidance on reporting of sexual offences for journalists and information for survivors' 15 October 2018: www.ipso.co.uk/news-press-releases/press-releases/press-watchdog-publishes-guidance-on-reporting-of-sexual-offences-for-journalists-and-information-for-survivors/.

Civil Procedure Rules which provide, so far as relevant, that judicial review is available in respect of 'a decision, action or failure to act in the exercise of a public function'.[54]

Where a court carries out judicial review, it is not determining the merits of the decision under challenge or conducting an appeal. It does not reach a decision of its own on the issue that was before the decision-maker and substitute that for the original decision. It only assesses whether the decision-maker has acted lawfully. If not, the remedies available include declaratory orders, orders quashing the decision and orders requiring the person or body concerned to re-make the decision.

In Ex parte Stewart-Brady (1997)[55] and Ex parte Anna Ford (2002),[56] the High Court decided that it was arguable that the PCC was amenable to judicial review, but dismissed the claim at the permission stage as having no real prospect of success. As a form of judicial precedent, these two PCC cases are of relatively little value on the jurisdiction issue in any future cases, such as Coulter v IPSO (2018)[57] because time has moved on and, with it, the legal and factual context have changed. IPSO's set-up is different from that of the PCC.

Jonathan Coulter claimed in judicial review that IPSO had mishandled his and some other 30 complaints where The Times and The Sunday Times had reported on a campaign by the Palestinian Return Centre (PRC), held at the House of Lords, chaired by Baroness Tonge. Mr Coulter had complained about the accuracy of the newspapers' reporting, that they were misleading and inaccurate (Clause 1 of the Code).

The background to the Coulter case is as follows: During the First World War, on 2 November 1917, the British government issued a public statement announcing that it 'view[ed] with favour the establishment in Palestine of a national home for the Jewish people', and would use its best endeavours to facilitate the achievement of this objective. The declaration was made in an open letter written to Lord Rothschild, one of the leaders of the British Jewish community, by the then Foreign Secretary, Arthur Balfour. It has become known as the Balfour Declaration. On Monday 25 October 2016, a meeting was organized at the House of Lords by the Palestinian Return Centre (PRC), chaired by Baroness Jenny Tonge. The aim of the meeting was the launch of the second phase of the 'Balfour Apology Campaign', relating to the Balfour Declaration. It was attended by the claimant, Jonathan Coulter, among others. This claim arises from reporting of the meeting in The Times.

> ❖ **KEY CASE**   *Coulter v IPSO* **[2018] EWHC 919 (QB)**
>
> **Precedent**
> ❖ IPSO's decisions are amenable to judicial review.
>
> **Facts**
> Jonathan Coulter complained on behalf of the Palestinian Return Centre, in addition to 10 other complainants, that *The Sunday Times* breached Clause 1

---

54 R. 54.1(2)(a)(ii) Civil Procedure Rules.
55 R v Press Complaints Commission, ex parte Stewart-Brady [1997] EMLR 185.
56 R v Press Complaints Commission ex parte Anna Ford [2002] EMLR 5 (QBD).
57 [2018] EWHC 919 (QB).

(Accuracy) of the Editors' Code of Practice in an article headlined 'Peace be upon Israel – the Lib Dems have cut off their Tonge', published in print and online on 30 October 2016. The article described a meeting in the House of Lords which had been organized by the Palestinian Return Centre, chaired by Baroness Tonge. The article claimed that Baroness Tonge 'cheerfully clapped and cheered along as they spouted the stuff you might have heard in Berlin in 1936, or Tehran in 2012'. One attendee had said that Israel would not have been founded were it not for the Balfour Declaration; he then called for Britain to apologize. Referring to the meeting, the article claimed:

> Off they went: the UK should apologise for having created Israel; that country should be wiped from the map – that's for starters. Then: Jews caused the Holocaust because they pushed Hitler too far; Israel is comparable to ISIS; and – my favourite, since you ask – if any country in the world is anti-semitic, it's Israel.

IPSO had declined to deal with the claimant's complaint which had related to the reporting of Baroness Tonge's conduct at the meeting, on the basis that he was a third party in respect of those complaints. Since Baroness Tonge had not made a complaint to the press regulator herself, the IPSO Complaints Committee did not think it appropriate for it to consider those matters in the absence of a complaint from her.

For this reason, the IPSO Committee ruled that the article did *not* breach Clause 1 ('Accuracy'), that the article was a comment piece and that the author of the article was entitled to characterize the position as believing that Israel 'should be wiped from the map'. The article's claim that the meeting had heard that 'the UK should apologise for having created Israel' was not misleading. A participant had drawn a comparison between Israel and the Islamic State, and it was not misleading to claim that the meeting had heard that they were comparable. These aspects of the complaint did not raise a breach of Clause 1.[58]

Legal issues

Mr Coulter's challenge before the court was advanced on three grounds:

1   that it was unlawful for IPSO to decline to deal with his third party complaints relating to the reporting of Baroness Tonge's behaviour at the meeting;
2   that IPSO was in breach of a duty of sufficient inquiry, by failing to take account of a report of the House of Lords Committee for Privileges and Conduct into the conduct of Baroness Tonge at the meeting ('The Report'); and,
3   that IPSO had acted unlawfully by applying an incorrect and irrational standard of review to the complaints of inaccuracy.[59]

---

58 *Coulter v The Sunday Times*. Decision of the IPSO Complaints Committee No. 14095–16, 21 April 2017: www.ipso.co.uk/rulings-and-resolution-statements/ruling/?id=14095-16.
59 See: *Coulter v IPSO* [2018] EWHC 919 at para. 26.

The remedy sought was an order quashing the IPSO decision.

Decision (Administrative Court – High Court)

Mr Justice Warby dismissed the claim and held that the IPSO decision not to adjudicate on the claimant's complaint was a rational decision and that the decision had been reached within the scope of the discretion given to IPSO by the Regulations. Its approach to the inaccuracy complaints did not involve errors of principle, nor did they 'betray confusion over what can and cannot count as opinion'.[60] Its approach to inaccuracy was not wrong in principle.

Analysis

The *Coulter* judicial review challenged the way that the press regulator 'filters out' complaints without considering their merits. The complainant argued that some complaints were not brought by 'the right person'. Firstly, the case is important because it set the precedent that IPSO's Complaints Committee's decision are amenable to judicial review. The decision of Stanley Burnton J in the *Jockey Club case* (2005)[61] was considered, where it was held that 'a body which would otherwise exercise only private functions could not assume public functions by its own action alone' and that some governmental intervention was required. In Warby J's view in *Coulter*, 'it might be said that the argument against IPSO decisions being amenable to judicial review is stronger that it was in the case of the jockey club'.[62] It will be interesting to see what approach IPSO takes in future. It is worth noting Mr Justice Warby's confirmation of Lord Woolf MR's observation in the *Stewart-Brady* case, a judicial review concerning the adjudications of the PCC, IPSO's predecessor, that 'it is very important where you have a body such as the Press Complaints Commission that if the court has any jurisdiction over them, it is reserved for cases where it would be clearly desirable for this court to intervene'.[63] In this case IPSO refused to rule on whether Baroness Tonge had been misrepresented, because she herself did not bring the complaint.

7.6.6 IPSO rulings

The Annual Report 2017 detailed a large number of 'multiple' complaints, where more than one similar complaint was made about the same article. In his introductory remarks, Sir Alan Moses, Chairman of IPSO, said that the regulator ensured that editors and journalists operate to the highest standards, helping publications distinguish themselves from the 'babble on the web'. He said that it is the press regulator's duty to make sure editors adhere to the code and to provide guidance to avoid breaches in the future: 'IPSO stands at

---

60 Ibid. at para. 68 (Warby J).
61 R (Mullins) v *Appeal Board of the Jockey Club* [2005] EWHC 2197.
62 *Coulter v IPSO* [2018] EWHC 919 at para. 33 (Warby J).
63 R v *Press Complaints Commission ex parte Stewart-Brady* [1997] EMLR 185 at para. 37 (Lord Woolf MR).

the boundary between protection of the public and freedom of speech; it preserves both by striking a balance'.[64]

During 2017, *The Sun* topped the list of most complaints received with 4,847 complaints, followed by the *Daily Mail* (4,176), *Mail Online* (3,536), *Metro* (1,500) and *The Mail on Sunday* (1,452). In 2017 *The Sun's* publisher News UK had 12 complaints upheld and 30 not upheld. Associated Newspapers (*Daily Mail, Mail Online, Mail on Sunday, Metro*) had 10 complaints upheld and 24 complaints not upheld.

The regulator also issued 57 Private Advisory Notices in 2017, bringing the total number it has issued since it was founded in 2014 to 150. IPSO, which regulates over 90 per cent of national newspapers, has the power to issue these notices where there are concerns about potential press intrusion. Such notices are issued by the Readers' Advisory Panel, made up of people who are not employed by a publisher that is or could be regulated by IPSO. The panel meets three times a year and issues the following to the IPSO board:

- provides advice and observations to IPSO on its work and wider industry issues from the perspective of readers and citizens;
- acts as a focal point for the public or representative groups to feedback on their experience of IPSO;
- provides a readers' and citizens' view to any external review or audit of IPSO;
- provides comment to IPSO on any issues on which it consults, including the annual review of the Editors' Code and any guidance.

A key feature, other than introducing its advisory and arbitration service, the regulator introduced the 'IPSO Crystal Mark', demonstrating how newspapers, magazines and their websites embrace responsible journalism and high editorial standards and public accountability in an era of 'fake news'.

One of the earliest rulings by the new press watchdog concerned the row over the *Sun's* headline, 'Queen Backs Brexit', published on 9 March 2016 in the run-up to UK referendum on leaving the European Union on 23 June 2016. In *Buckingham Palace v The Sun*,[65] the IPSO Complaints Committee ruled that the headline was significantly misleading and represented a failure to take care not to publish inaccurate, misleading or distorted information – a clear breach of Clause 1 (Accuracy) of the Code. The Committee ordered that the adjudication be published in full and on 18 May 2016 the headline 'IPSO RULES AGAINST SUN – QUEEN HEADLINE' was 'splashed' across *The Sun's* front page.

Following the terror attack which took place at the Ariana Grande pop concert in the Manchester Arena on 22 May 2017, many concertgoers were still missing, most of them children. It later emerged that 23 people were killed, including the attacker Salman Abedi, and 139 were wounded. Reporting on this terrible event was clearly a sensitive issue.

---

64 Annual Report 2017 Independent Press Standards Organisation, at p. 8; www.ipso.co.uk/media/1569/ipso_annual_report_2017e.pdf.
65 *Buckingham Palace v The Sun, Decision of the Complaints Committee* 01584–16, 18 May 2016 at: www.ipso.co.uk/rulings-and-resolution-statements/ruling/?id=01584-16.

❖ **IPSO RULING**   *Gorman v The Daily Star* (2017)[66]

Complaint upheld – relevant Code provisions breached
❖   Clause 2 (Privacy)
❖   Clause 6 (Children)

Facts

On its front page, *The Daily Star* had published a number of photographs of individuals who had died or were missing (24 May 2017) following the Ariana Grande Concert at Manchester Arena. One of the photos was of the complainant Pauline Gorman's daughter, accompanied with the caption: 'MISSING: Lucy Cross'. The photograph and the caption were also published on page 4, in an article which reported on the attack.

Pauline Gorman complained to IPSO stating that her 13-year-old daughter was *not* missing: her daughter, *not* called Lucy Cross, had in fact been at home at the time of the attack. The publication of her daughter's photograph alongside individuals who were missing or dead had been traumatic and had intruded into her daughter's private and family life, as well as her time at school. She claimed that the *Star* had breached Clause 1 (Accuracy), Clause 2 (Privacy), Clause 4 (Intrusion into grief or shock) and Clause 6 (Children) of the Editors' Code of Practice.

The tabloid responded to the complaint that, when notified of the inaccuracy by the complainant, it had immediately offered a prominent apology: the following day, 25 May, it had published a front-page reference, in a box, to an apology on page 2.

The newspaper said that the article had been published in exceptional circumstances, in the aftermath of a terror attack involving numerous children. The paper had obtained the story from a trusted source (an agency), after a Twitter account named '@_maddisonallen' had posted a photograph of the complainant's daughter and had falsely claimed that her name was 'Lucy Hannah Cross' and that she was missing following the attack. The newspaper said that at the time of publication, it had no reason to believe that the information was false.

Findings of the Committee

On receipt of this information by the 'trusted agency', the newspaper had taken no further steps to establish the accuracy of the claims that had been circulated on the Twitter account. The newspaper did not, for example, attempt to contact the Twitter account holder or the family of the individual pictured. Given the fact that the story claimed that 'Lucy Cross' was missing following a terror attack, and particularly where the photograph clearly showed a child, greater

---

66 *Gorman v The Daily Star, Decision of the Complaints Committee* 12629–17, 10 August 2017: www.ipso.co.uk/ rulings-and-resolution-statements/ruling/?id=12629-17.

care should have been taken. This represented a failure to take over the accuracy of the article, in breach of Clause 1(i) (Accuracy). However, the Committee noted favourably that in the following day's edition, the *Star* had published a front-page reference to an apology on page 2. This had identified the inaccuracy and had been illustrated with the photograph of the complainant's daughter, to make readers aware of the correct position. This meant that the publication had met the requirements of Clause 1(ii) by publishing a prompt and prominent apology. Therefore, there was no breach of Clause 1 in relation to the remedial action taken.

In publishing this material concerning a child on its front page, without consent, alongside photographs of those who were missing or dead in the attack, the newspaper had published information which had intruded into the complainant's daughter's private life and into her time at school. Therefore the complaint under Clauses 2 (privacy) and 6 (children) were upheld.

The Committee acknowledged that the publication of her daughter's photograph had caused the complainant and her family significant upset. However, in circumstances where the complainant's daughter was not missing, this was not a case which involved the personal grief or shock of the complainant or her daughter. The terms of Clause 4 (intrusion into grief or shock) were *not* breached (or indeed engaged).

Remedial action required
Since the *Star* had promptly published a correction in print which identified the inaccuracy as well as a prominent apology, the Committee considered this appropriate in the circumstances (sufficient to remedy the breach of Clause 1(i)).

However, having upheld the complaint under Clauses 2 and 6, the Committee considered what further remedial action should be required. Given that the breach of Clause 1(i) had resulted in the publication of material which had related to the welfare of a child, in an article that identified individuals who were missing or dead following the attack, the Committee considered that the publication of an adjudication was an appropriate remedy.

The headline of the adjudication must make clear that IPSO has upheld the complaint, and refer to its subject matter; it must be agreed in advance. The photograph of the complainant's daughter had been published on its front page as well as on page 4. However in considering the placement of the adjudication, the Committee had regard to the fact that the newspaper had already published a front page reference to an apology, identifying to its readers the correct position. As such, the adjudication should appear on page 4 or further forward.

Analysis
Newspapers play an important role in reporting on the aftermath of a terror attack and raising awareness of the real impact of such incidents on members of the public. In this instance, however, there was no public interest in

publishing the inaccurate claim that the complainant's daughter was missing. The newspaper had relied upon information obtained from a 'trusted agency', and in doing so, the newspaper had published material which had inaccurately claimed that the complainant's daughter was missing. This had resulted in the publication of inaccurate material relating to the complainant's daughter, without consent, which had intruded into her private life and her time at school.

Though these were exceptional circumstances of reporting on the aftermath of a terror attack, the newspaper was ultimately responsible for the inaccuracy in publishing the article and photographs of missing children. Instead the editor had relied on information gained from a 'trusted' agency. The IPSO Complaints Committee considered it vitally important that sufficient care must be taken by editorial staff to ensure the accuracy of any claims, particularly in such horrendous circumstances.

First-person journalism in the form of editorial comment has a long history in the UK and means the free expression of opinion and the exercise of the right to freedom of expression. Lynn Barber is such a journalist and has written for many well-known publications, including the Sunday Times, for many years. She is best known for her honest profiles and hard-hitting stories.

The article in question – an opinion piece – was published in the Sunday Times magazine and ran over six pages on 28 May 2017, a year after Barber and Ahmed (the complainant) had last encountered each other. It gave the journalist's first-person account of her experience hosting a migrant refugee in her own home. She described her experience as 'a story of two parts, without a happy ending'.[67]

The article included various details about Mohammed Ahmed's background, including that he was Sudanese, that he was married, and that he had told the writer's daughter that he was 'one of eighteen siblings' and that his father 'married four times'. It reported that Ahmed had registered with the Home Office as an official asylum seeker and had an identity card, which stated that he was not allowed to find employment but instead 'got a weekly £35 living allowance while waiting for his asylum hearing'.

The article reported Lynn Barber's recollection of various conversations that she had with the complainant, including an occasion when Ahmed said that he planned to treat her like his mother. The journalist said that she did not want to be treated like a Sudanese mother as this might include 'a lot of cooking, cleaning and washing'.

Barber had shown Ahmed an early draft copy of the article, and he was furious, protesting, 'I am not a refugee! I am a political leader! My family are very rich! We could buy you up like that!' After a vehement row in which he claimed, 'You Christians are all racist', they parted company. Ultimately, Ms Barber wrote a very different article about her house guest after discovering all was not as it seemed.[68]

---

67 For a full version of the article and commentary see: www.thetimes.co.uk/article/
lynn-barber-i-took-an-asylum-seeker-into-my-home-it-didn-t-end-well-xtzn7gw99.
68 Source: 'Press watchdog gets it wrong', Sunday Times leading editorial, 4 February 2018: www.thetimes.co.uk/
article/press-watchdog-gets-it-wrong-80glp5chc.

❖ IPSO RULING   *Ahmed v The Sunday Times (Lynn Barber)* (2018)[69]

Complaint upheld – relevant Code provisions breached
- Clause 1 (Accuracy)
- Clause 2 (Privacy)

Facts

Following an article published in *The Sunday Times* on 28 May 2017 headlined 'I'm not altruistic, I'm pretty selfish, but I had to do something, so I took in a refugee', Mohammed Ahmed complained to IPSO that *The Sunday Times* had breached Clause 1 (Accuracy), Clause 2 (Privacy), Clause 3 (Harassment) and Clause 12 (Discrimination) of the Editors' Code of Practice.

The article, which included the complainant's first name and an unpixellated photograph, was the journalist's first-person account of her experience hosting the complainant, at the time an asylum seeker, in her home. The article included various details about the complainant's background and personal life and reported the journalist's recollection of various conversations that she had with the complainant. It also included the text of a letter of apology that the complainant had written to the journalist after they had argued over the central heating.

The journalist recalled that, while living with her, the complainant had suffered from an illness, and the article included details of the illness. She also said that the complainant had left pornographic images on her computer, and she described the content of these images.

The complainant was concerned that his life and experiences had been the focus of a story in a national newspaper, which he considered to be an intrusion into his privacy. He was not a public figure and had not expected to be the subject of an article. He had not consented to its publication.

The Sunday Times in its response said that the article was a first-hand piece on a challenging topic written by a widely acclaimed journalist of great experience and integrity. In sharing her story, the journalist was exercising her right to freedom of expression. She was entitled to report her experiences and opinions and was contributing to a topic of general discussion and debate. The newspaper did not accept that the article had intruded into the complainant's privacy. It said that the complainant did not have a reasonable expectation of privacy in relation to his behaviour, or conversations with the journalist, while staying at her home. It noted that he was a non-paying guest in the house, and that he had shared most of the information in the article with his host

---

69 *Ahmed v The Sunday Times (Lynn Barber), Decision of the Complaints Committee* 16237–17, 5 February 2018: www.ipso.co.uk/rulings-and-resolution-statements/ruling/?id=16237-17.

voluntarily, in the knowledge that she was a journalist working for a major newspaper.

Findings of the Committee

IPSO's Complaints Committee emphasized that first-person journalism has a long history as a means to exercise the right to freedom of expression. Clause 2 of the Code makes clear that everyone is entitled to respect for his or her private and family life, home, health and correspondence. This reflects the enhanced privacy rights that people have in their own homes. The Committee rejected the newspaper's position that, as the complainant was not paying rent, these rights were forfeited. It also did not accept that, as his host was a journalist, the complainant should have presumed that any information he shared with her might be published without his consent.

The article included extensive information about the complainant, relating to his family and personal relationships; his domestic arrangements; his financial circumstances; his journey to the UK; his asylum application; his relationships and interactions with the journalist, including an argument they had had, and a letter he had written to her, expressing his feelings about the disagreement; his psychological and physical health; his drug use; and allegations about the possession of private, sexual material. These details were used to create a detailed and intimate portrait of the complainant and his life. The Committee held that the complainant was not a public figure and had not publicly disclosed the information about his experiences contained in the article or consented to the article's publication. The extent of this detail, published without his consent, and where no steps were taken to obscure his identity, represented an intrusion into his private life. There was a breach of Clause 2.

The Committee then turned to consider the issues raised under Clause 1 (Accuracy). The complainant had not been receiving the £35 living allowance, as reported in the article. The newspaper had argued that it had been unable to verify this information with the complainant, as the journalist did not have his contact details. However, the journalist had not attempted to contact friends of the complainant with whom she had previously been in touch, to obtain his contact details or to ask them to verify the claim that the complainant, who came from a wealthy family, was receiving this allowance while living rent-free with the journalist. This was used as evidence to support the journalist's general contention that the complainant was untrustworthy. This was therefore a significant inaccuracy, and the failure to seek to verify this claim represented a failure to take care over the accuracy of the article, in breach of Clause 1(i). The newspaper had offered to publish a clarification, setting out the complainant's position that he had not received this allowance.

Remedial action required

The Committee required that the clarification (see above) should be published to avoid a breach of Clause 1(ii). In relation to the breach of Clause 2, the IPSO adjudication was to be published on or before page 16 of the magazine section of *The Sunday Times* (with the wording of the headline and article to be agreed by IPSO). The adjudication should also be published on the newspaper's website, with a link to the full adjudication (including the headline) appearing on the homepage for 24 hours, followed by archiving.

Analysis

There were a large number of different views expressed, following the IPSO ruling in *Ahmed v Sunday Times (Lynn Barber)*. Some, like the then editor of the *Daily Mail*, Paul Dacre, agreed with the ruling, saying that the journalist was entitled to publish her story, and the IPSO Committee recognized that the matters discussed in the article were of significant public interest. However, this was not sufficient to justify the extent of the information about the complainant and the resulting intrusion into his private life. In short, the journalist's right to freedom of expression did not outweigh the complainant's right to privacy in this instance.

The Sunday Times editor, Eleanor Mills, disagreed and published an editorial which immediately followed the publication of the IPSO ruling on 4 February 2018. In spite of its very prominent publication of the IPSO adjudication in *The Sunday Times* magazine, its editor said that the IPSO ruling was 'a cruel blow to Ms Barber's freedom of expression and the press freedom that sustains the quality of *The Sunday Times'* journalism'.[70] Ironically, the newspaper and its magazine had submitted to the new self-regulatory rules of the press and had stated over and again that *The Times* and *Sunday Times* would not succumb to state press regulation by statute. The newspaper did however question whether the *Ahmed* ruling had gone too far and had now set a 'precedent' preventing an acclaimed journalist such as Lynn Barber from keeping loyalty with her readers. Ian Hislop, editor of *Private Eye*, also disagreed with the IPSO ruling. He said the regulator's rebuke forbids similar first-person and opinion writers from telling a story without the approval of their subjects.[71] And if this stance were to be repeated, there would be no more memoirs or eyewitness accounts in the press. *The Times* editors saw the ruling as an attempt to silence journalists' first-hand experiences and may well drive controversial narratives to the unregulated internet.

---

70 Source: 'Press watchdog gets it wrong', *Sunday Times* leading editorial, 4 February 2018: www.thetimes.co.uk/article/press-watchdog-gets-it-wrong-80glp5chc.

71 *Private Eye* Issue 1464 at p. 9, 'The private life of Brian'.

In July 2018 former Liberal Democrat MP, Lembit Opik,[72] won a privacy complaint against *The Sun* after it published snaps of him 'nuzzling' a woman's 'boobs' while on holiday and labelled him a 'rat' in an article.

❖ **IPSO RULING**   *Opik v The Sun* (2018)[73]

Complaint upheld – relevant Code provisions breached
❖   Clause 2 (Privacy)

Facts
The Sun reported that Lembit Opik had sent the images to his former partner 'accidentally' in a story headlined: 'RAT OPIK NUZZLES LOVER'S LEMBITS', published on 18 November 2017. The piece was based on an interview with Opik's former partner, with whom he has a young child, about the breakdown of their relationship. She claimed he sent the pictures to her in August 2016. *The Sun* described the photos as a 'saucy snap' and said Opik 'accidentally sent her pictures of him nuzzling [named woman's] boobs as she lay on a sun lounger in a bikini'. The article said Opik's former partner had told the *Sun* journalist: 'This picture shows their friendship has crossed a line'. It reported that Opik had been unavailable for comment.

Mr Opik complained to IPSO that the images were a breach of Clause 1 (accuracy), Clause 2 (privacy), Clause 6 (children) and Clause 10 (clandestine devices and subterfuge) of the Editors' Code. He said the images had been taken while he was on a private holiday with the woman and where they could not be seen by the general public. He said there was no public interest justification for publishing the photograph, which had caused 'severe intrusion' into his life and his relationships with his former partner and their child.

Opik said the story was inaccurate because the woman pictured was not his 'lover', as *The Sun* had claimed, and he was not a 'rat'. He said characterizing him in this way was misleading, because it implied he was in a sexual relationship with the woman while still with his former partner. He said he had not consented to publishing the pictures, so it was inaccurate for the paper to report that he had been unavailable for comment. Mr Opik further claimed he did not send the pictures to his former partner and did not know how they had come to be sent, possibly by a third party.

---

72 Lembit Opik (Öpik) served as a Member of Parliament, representing Montgomeryshire, Wales, from 1997 until he lost his seat in the 2010 General Election. Opik has been in the public eye as a result of his personal relationships with TV weather presenter Siân Lloyd and with pop star Gabriela Irimia of The Cheeky Girls.
73 *Opik v The Sun*. Decision of the Complaints Committee 20850–17, 10 July 2018: www.ipso.co.uk/rulings-and-resolution-statements/ruling/?id=20850-17.

The Sun in response said the location and being on holiday with someone was not private, that the image did not show any sexual activity and that it had been taken by an acquaintance. The tabloid's editor did not accept publication of the photograph was intrusive. *The Sun*'s response also said that Opik's former partner was entitled to talk about the breakdown of her relationship with him given he had previously spoken publicly about it. *The Sun* said its journalist had attempted to contact the complainant several times and that they received two emails from Mr Opik after the newspaper had gone to print with the story.

Findings of the Committee

The questions for the Committee were whether the article, including the photographs, was intrusive into the complainant's private life such that justification for its publication was required under the terms of Clause 2 – and whether, if so, it had provided a sufficient justification. The Committee upheld Mr Opik's complaint on privacy grounds only (Clause 2 of the Code).

The Committee reasoned that *The Sun* newspaper had been aware at the time of publication that the complainant had not consented to the sharing of the photographs either with his former partner or with a wider audience; this was apparent from the fact that it had reported that he had forwarded the photographs 'accidentally', notwithstanding the complaint's position that he had not in fact done so. He had not placed the photographs in the public domain. The complainant was entitled to expect that photographs showing an intimate moment with a close friend in a private place would not be published without his consent. The publication of the photographs clearly had the potential to intrude into his private life.

The Committee did not uphold Mr Opik's complaint under Clause 1. It was accurate to report that the complainant had been unavailable to comment on the allegations contained in the article under complaint in circumstances where the newspaper had only received communications from him *after* the newspaper had gone to print. The Committee also did not uphold his complaint under Clause 10. The email chain provided by the newspaper had shown that an email which enclosed the photograph had been sent from the complainant's email address to his former partner. The Committee did not find any grounds to establish that the newspaper had engaged in subterfuge in order to obtain this material.

Remedial action required

As the photograph had appeared on page 7 of the print edition, the Committee decided that the adjudication should be published on page 7. The headline to the adjudication should make clear that IPSO upheld the complaint (breach of Clause 2 'privacy'), give the title of the newspaper, and refer to the complaint's subject matter. The headline of the adjudication was to be agreed with IPSO in advance. The adjudication should also be published on the newspaper's website, with a link to the full adjudication appearing on the top half of the homepage for 24 hours; it should then be archived.

Analysis

The photographs in question had captured a moment which would have only been seen by a small number of people and had been taken while the complainant had been enjoying a private holiday. Notwithstanding the complainant's position that he was joking around with a friend and the fact that the photographs had been taken by a third party, they showed an intimate moment with a close friend, which had taken place in a closed courtyard within a private hotel with limited access to the wider public. The newspaper had suggested in the article that the photographs provided grounds to question the complainant's position that they were 'just good friends', speculating about aspects of his private life.

Whilst the newspaper advanced its right to exercise freedom of expression the IPSO Committee found that the story and the accompanying photograph were inherently private and not in the public interest. Simply put: Mr Opik had not consented to the photographs being printed, and the publication of photos had the potential to be particularly intrusive. *The Sun* had not identified a public interest that would justify the publication of a photograph of the complainant sharing an intimate moment with a friend, and the extensive speculation and discussion of this moment deserved privacy.

 FOR THOUGHT

Is self-regulation still the best way to regulate the UK print press (and their online editions) or should statutory regulation take over, similar to the Irish Press Council? Discuss.

7.6.7 IMPRESS

We have learnt above that most national newspapers have, by now, signed up to the Independent Press Standards Organisation (IPSO), the voluntary independent body not backed by the government (i.e. non-statutory).

IMPRESS is the other press regulator in the UK. It was the first – and to date, only – regulator recognized by the Press Recognition Panel (PRP). Unlike IPSO, IMPRESS calls itself 'fully compliant with the recommendations of the Leveson Inquiry'. It is fair to say that fewer newspaper publications have signed up to this regulator. By August 2018 it regulated 64 publishers and a total of 111 titles.[74] It also has an arbitration scheme, operated in partnership with the Chartered Institute of Arbitrators (CIArb) and provides an 'affordable

---

74 IMPRESS regulated publications as at 25 December 2018: www.impress.press/complaints/regulated-publishers. html.

and speedy means' by which members of the public can seek redress if they have an action-able legal claim against a publisher regulated by IMPRESS. In 2017–2018 IMPRESS handled a total of 83 complaints about 56 separate issues, of which 55 per cent were upheld.[75]

It appears from its annual report and adjudication website that most of the complaints concern online publications, such as The Canary[76] or Skwawkbox.[77]

IMPRESS relies overwhelmingly on funding from the Independent Press Regulation Trust (IPRT) and will for the next few years. IPRT was set up so to allow IMPRESS to receive funds from the Alexander Mosley Charitable Trust (AMCT),[78] whose trustees are ex-Formula 1 Boss, Max Mosley, his son Max Patrick, his wife Emma and Horatio Mortimer. The AMCT donated £3.8m in 2015 to IMPRESS, and the regulator subsequently secured a further £3m in 2018 from the charity which seeks to sustain the press regulator until at least 2022.

Mr Mosley has since 2008 campaigned to strengthen regulation of the press after the *News of the World* printed photographs of him involved in a sex orgy. He won £60,000 in damages in his privacy dispute from the Rupert Murdoch newspaper.[79] He unsuccessfully argued in the European Court of Human Rights for an obligation on newspapers to notify in advance anyone whose privacy would be compromised by publication, thus allowing an opportunity to seek injunctive relief.[80] In 2016 Max Mosley gave £200,000 to Tom Watson, Deputy Leader of the Labour Party, linked to the pressure group 'Hacked Off' and a critic of Rupert Murdoch and of some of his businesses.

See Chapter 2.7.2 and 2.9

Newspapers that signed up to IPSO have feared that the recognition of IMPRESS might trigger legislation forcing newspapers to pay the costs of libel or privacy actions against them, even if they win their cases. The independent left-wing website, Skwawkbox, was considering leaving IMPRESS at the end of 2018 together with some other online publishers because they felt uneasy about Max Mosley's continued funding of the regulator. This came after the revelation by the *Daily Mail* that Mosley's name was found on a 'racist' political pamphlet from 1961.

In October 2017, IMPRESS fought off a High Court legal challenge in London over its status.[81] The News Media Association (NMA), which represents publishers, argued that the Press Recognition Panel (PRP), established by the Royal Charter on Self-Regulation of the Press after the Leveson Inquiry in 2013, should not have given IMPRESS formal approval at the start. The Leveson Report, published on 29 November 2012, recommended the establishment of an independent self-regulatory regime which determines applications from regulators for recognition. The Charter defines 'Regulator' as 'an independent body formed by or on behalf of relevant publishers for the purpose of conducting regulatory activities in relation to their publications'.[82] It defines 'relevant publisher', as does the 2013 Act, in terms set out in section 41 of that Act and Schedule 15.

---

75 IMPRESS Annual Report 2017–18: www.impress.press/downloads/file/annual_report_2017-18.pdf.
76 Mr Jamie Thunder and The Canary, Case No 087/2017.
77 Mr Graham Hindson and The SKWAWKBOX, Case No. 106/2017.
78 The AMCT is named after Max Mosley's eldest son who died of a suspected heroin overdose in 2009.
79 Mosley v Newsgroup Newspapers Ltd [2008] EWHC 1777 (QB).
80 Mosley v UK (2011) 53 EHRR 30 (ECtHR).
81 R (on the application of News Media Association) v Press Recognition Panel and IMPRESS: The Independent Monitor for the Press CIC [2017] EWHC 2527 (Admin) 12 October 2017.
82 Royal Charter on Self-Regulation of the Press 2013 Schedule 4 para. 1(a).

See above
7.6.1

NMA sought judicial review of the PRP's decision of 25 October 2016 to grant recognition to IMPRESS. NMA argued that the PRP misinterpreted and misapplied the Charter and invited the court to quash its decision and to declare that IMPRESS failed to meet the Charter's Recognition Criteria (set out in Schedule 3). The PRP opposed the application. The PRP argued it must grant recognition if the applicant meets 23 criteria listed in Schedule 3 of the Charter, and must consider effectiveness, fairness and objectivity of standards, independence and transparency of enforcement and compliance, credible powers and remedies, reliable funding and effective accountability.[83] The NMA argued that the PRP had misinterpreted and misapplied the Charter, but Lady Justice Rafferty and Mr Justice Popplewell rejected the claim.

Giving effect to the plain language of the Charter, the court held that it is not contrary to Leveson whether a regulator and therein the Press Recognition Panel are publicly or privately funded by a third private party. In other words, money put up by private parties 'does not constitute a problem'.[84]

The Chairman of IMPRESS, Walter Merricks, told the Guardian: 'This judgment shows that the system of externally verified self-regulation, recommended by Sir Brian Leveson, is fully functional'. In response to the judgment, the NMA said: 'We are deeply disappointed by the court's decision but maintain that the PRP's decision to recognise IMPRESS was deeply flawed'.[85]

It could be argued that IMPRESS is not truly 'independent' as a press regulator and the Press Recognition Panel is a statutory body,[86] because the Royal Charter established the PRP with a set of detailed rules for who can be a member, how they are to be appointed and how the panel is to operate, and similarly detailed rules for how any regulator must operate in order to be 'recognized'.[87] Moreover, the panel is entirely government-funded, and its decisions have the force of law, since any newspaper that does not sign up to an approved regulator may face punishment in the courts. Is this not 'independence' in name only? And does this system not amount to state regulation of the press in all but name?

The other side of the argument could be that misbehaving newspapers can simply refuse to accept arbitration, since the published IPSO rules say: 'Both parties must voluntarily agree to arbitrate. Without agreement, the arbitration process will not be available for your claim'.

There now exist three forms of press regulation: IPSO, IMPRESS and the third way, whereby The Guardian along with the Financial Times and Private Eye have decided to pursue their own model of oversight, accountable to readers and the public.

---

83 Part K, Chapter 7, Section 4 of Leveson.
84 R (on the application of News Media Association) v Press Recognition Panel and IMPRESS: The Independent Monitor for the Press CIC [2017] EWHC 2527 at para. 46 (Lady Justice Rafferty and The Hon Mr Justice Popplewell).
85 Source: 'High court rejects challenge to status of UK press regulator', Guardian, 12 October 2017: www.theguardian.com/media/2017/oct/12/high-court-rejects-challenge-to-status-of-impress-uk-press-regulator?CMP=Share_iOSApp_Other.
86 PRP Annual Report 2017: https://pressrecognitionpanel.org.uk/wp-content/uploads/2017/11/State-of-Recognition-Report_2017_web.pdf.
87 The Press Recognition Panel recognizes IMPRESS: https://pressrecognitionpanel.org.uk/impress-2/.

FOR THOUGHT

> Should IMPRESS and IPSO be allowed to continue to coexist to administer their own forms of self-regulation? What redress is open to ordinary people who have been libelled in the press or whose privacy has been invaded in a newspaper and its online edition? Discuss.

7.7 Analysis and discussion: regulating fake news?

The term 'fake news' is bandied around with no clear idea of what it means. 'Fake news' became widely used by US presidential candidate Donald Trump, in 2016 – though he was not the originator of this term.

Fake news is not new. One historical example is the 'Great Moon Hoax' of 1835, in which the *New York Sun* published a series of six long articles about the discovery of life on the moon made by a famous astronomer, Sir John Herschel. The public was entranced by stories of how Herschel had built a powerful new telescope and how he had observed fantastic living creatures on the moon from the Cape of Good Hope. *The Sun* reported on plants and animals, including herds of bison, blue unicorn, birds, other horned animals and what looked like sheep. Herschel's most interesting discovery was furry bat people 'with short and flossy copper-colored hair and wings composed of a thin membrane'. *The Sun* admitted, soon after the six articles were published, that it was a hoax.[88] Fake news has since taken on a variety of meanings, including a description of any statement that is not liked or agreed with by the reader.[89]

'Fake news' has become a force of enormous reach and influence within the news media environment. There is now substantial research in this area – for example, there is said to be clear evidence of Russian state-sponsored attempts to influence elections in the US (Donald Trump versus Hilary Clinton in November 2016) and the UK's EU (Brexit) Referendum in June 2016 by using social media and spreading rumours and fake news.[90] It is evident that social network sites play an enormous role in generating traffic to fake news, and the democratic implications of fake news have been described by many as a 'news crisis'.

See
Chapter 8.9

In December 2018, Germany's most famous political magazine, *Der Spiegel*, was faced with the biggest fake news scandal in its 70-year history. Claas Relotius, 33, a high-flying journalist, acclaimed for writing very readable personal news reportage from across the world, having won a string of awards, was uncovered as to having invented most of his stories.

In a special edition *Der Spiegel* apologized for not detecting 'the case of Relotius', telling its loyal readership that its entire editorial team was 'devastated'.[91] Usually Relotius worked alone, but this time he had been paired on a story in Mexico with a fellow reporter, Juan

---

88 Source: 'Remembering the Great Moon Hoax of 1835', by Gabe Pressman, NBC *News*, 20 August 2012: www.nbcnewyork.com/news/local/moon-hoax-166810096.html.
89 For further discussion see: Gelfert, A. (2018) 'Fake News: A Definition', *Informal Logic*, Vol. 38, No. 1, pp. 84–117.
90 For further discussion see: Allcott, H. and Gentzkow, M. (2017) pp. 211–236.
91 Source: *Der Spiegel*, Nr 52 of 22 December 2018: 'We're saying it how it is: how one of our own reporters faked his stories and why he got away with it' ('Sagen was ist: Wie einer unserer Reporter seine Geschichten fälschte und warum er damit durchkam').

Moreno. Moreno, 46, had reported for the magazine from across the world since 2007; he became the whistle-blower, since he had long felt that the Relotius stories had become more and more colourful, reading like a fairy story (ein Märchen).[92] Moreno thought the stories were just a little too brilliant, and, after discreet complaints to his bosses at Spiegel, he was met with disbelief – and with veiled threats his own job might be on the line. He took the extraordinary step of travelling back to Arizona at his own expense to retrace his colleague's steps. He found two sources quoted extensively by Relotius in the article, both of whom denied having met him.

Confronted with the evidence by one of his editorial managers, Ozlem Gezer, Deputy Head of the Gesellschaft (society) section, Relotius came clean. He admitted making up large parts not only of the Arizona-Mexico story (Jaegers Grenze – 'how a mother from Honduras walked with her 5-year old daughter Alice through Mexico into Arizona in order to escape'), but also of many of the other 55 pieces he had written for Der Spiegel – including one about an imaginary 'Mexicans keep out' sign outside Fergus Falls, a Minnesota town that voted for Trump, another about a Yemeni prisoner in Guantanamo, and an award-winning piece about a Syrian boy convinced he had contributed to the country's civil war through a piece of graffiti he had daubed onto a wall.

'It has now become clear', Der Spiegel wrote as part of its 23-page apology and account of the whole Relotius saga, that he 'is neither a reporter nor a journalist. Rather, he produces beautifully narrated fiction'. Der Spiegel further alleged that the journalist had emailed readers from a private account encouraging them to send money to help orphaned children in Turkey – which then ended up in Relotius' private account.

Comparisons have been drawn with the case of Jayson Blair, a then 27-year-old reporter with Time magazine, who resigned in 2003 over claims he had plagiarized and made up stories, and with Janet Cooke, a reporter for The Washington Post who won a Pulitzer Prize in 1981 for an article later found to be fabricated.

Spiegelgate is embarrassing for the hard-hitting, left-leaning German magazine with a print circulation of more than 800,000 copies a week. Some readers praised the magazine for its honesty and commendable speed in which it investigated Relotius' fabrications and printed its honest account and apology immediately. Others demanded to know how so many falsehoods and fake news stories could have found their way through the army of fact checkers meant to go through every piece it publishes.[93] Richard Grenell, the US Ambassador to Berlin, also weighed in, demanding the magazine hold an independent inquiry. Grenell, a controversial figure in Germany, has been repeatedly criticized in Der Spiegel for his right-wing stance. Grenell said that some of Relotius' fabrications and fake stories had focused on US policies and certain segments of the American people, ridiculing them. Dirk Kurbjuweit, one of Der Spiegel's deputy editors in chief, apologized to all Americans 'who have been insulted and denigrated by these reports', though he rejected Grenell's accusations of anti-US bias.[94]

---

92 Ibid., 'It was just a feeling'. Spiegel reporter Juan Moreno describes how he uncovered the deceit by his colleague Claas Relotius. ('Es war ein Gefühl', Spiegel Mitarbeiter Juan Moreno beschreibt, wie er den Betrug seines Kollegen Claas Relotius aufdecken konnte) at pp. 47–48.
93 Ibid., 'The fake news stories at Spiegel have resulted in substantial debates in other media sources and amongst its readership' ('Die Fälschungen beim Spiegel haben heftige Diskissionen in den Medien und unter den Lesern ausgelöst') at pp. 52–55.
94 Ibid., Der Spiegel editorial at p. 3.

So how do readers and consumers know to distinguish between accurate and fake content? Between quality and trusted content and harmful fake news? What are the possible solutions? In its 5th Report (2018), 'Disinformation and "fake news"', the House of Commons Digital, Culture, Media and Sport Committee recommended that the term 'fake news' should be replaced by the terms 'misinformation' and 'disinformation'. Furthermore, that the government should provide clear guidelines for companies and media organizations on these definitions, underpinned by regulation and enforcement.[95]

There is no regulatory body that oversees social media platforms and written content including printed news content, online, as a whole. However, in the UK, under the Communications Act 2003, Ofcom sets and enforces content standards for television and radio broadcasters, including rules relating to accuracy and impartiality. In July 2018, Ofcom's then Chief Executive, Sharon White, called for greater regulation of social media and announced plans to release an outline of how such regulation could work in the autumn of that year.[96]

Arguably, the potential of fake news can pose a threat to democracy and social values. Deliberately distorted facts can now be easily disseminated through state-sponsored programmes by groups with a particular political agenda, including the desire to affect political elections.

IPSO proposes an external set of standards, such as the IPSO Editors' Code, which can assist readers and consumers to identify truth from fiction. It is important to educate children and young people making them aware of the impact of fake news.

Both Facebook and Google are now removing fake news sites from their advertising platforms on the grounds that they violate policies against misleading content. Furthermore, Facebook has taken steps to identify fake news articles, flag false articles as 'disputed by 3rd party fact-checkers', show fewer potentially false articles in users' news feeds and help users avoid accidentally sharing false articles by notifying them that a story is 'disputed by 3rd parties' before they share it.[97] These actions by the main social network providers may increase social welfare, but identifying fake news sites and articles also raises important questions about who becomes the arbiter of truth.

In March 2018 Microsoft launched its software tool 'NewsGuard' for users of Microsoft Edge mobile apps on iOS and Android. NewsGuard checks websites for online 'fake news' content based on journalistic credibility and transparency criteria and can be applied to all news websites. The idea came from entrepreneur Steven Brill and former *Wall Street Journal* publisher Gordon Crovitz. The checks are conducted by trained analysts with diverse backgrounds who review thousands of news websites daily. In January 2019 the NewsGuard plug-in brought up a warning, stating that the online *Daily Mail* service www.dailymail.co.uk 'generally fails to maintain basic standards of accuracy and accountability'. The New York–based service is planning to include its tool in further products from the Windows developer as well as other tech firms. It can be used as an add-on extension in the desktop version of web browsers including Edge, Google's Chrome, Mozilla's Firefox and Apple's Safari.

---

95 House of Commons (2018).
96 Source: 'It's time to regulate social media sites that publish news', by Sharon White, *The Times*, 13 July 2018.
97 Source: 'Working to Stop Misinformation and False News', by Adam Mosseri, *Facebook News Feed*, 7 April 2017: www.facebook.com/facebookmedia/blog/working-to-stop-misinformation-and-false-news.

Waisbord (2018) argues that the phenomenon 'fake news' is indicative of the contested position of news and the dynamics of belief formation in contemporary societies. It is symptomatic of the collapse of the old news order and the chaos of contemporary public communication. This new 'communication chaos' makes it necessary to revisit normative arguments about journalism, democracy and truth, and journalistic practices and standards are now harder to achieve and to maintain amid the destabilization through fake news.[98]

A number of EU Member States have recently adopted legislation to counter hate speech and fake news, such as Germany's Network Enforcement Act 2017 (*Netzwerkdurchsetzungsgesetz* – NetzDG). Section 1(1) NetzDG provides that the NetzDG applies to 'telemedia service providers which operate a platform over the internet, with the intention of generating profit from it, which follows the purpose to enable its users to share any content with other users or to make it accessible to the public (social network)'.

Section 1(2) NetzDG qualifies this broad definition and sets out an exemption from the review and reporting requirements if the social network has fewer than two million registered users in Germany. The German legislation takes a unique approach in that it shifts the responsibility to assess and determine any unlawful or 'fake' content to the social media provider.

The European Commission has also addressed issues such as tackling fake news as part of its Digital Single Market initiative. Currently the approach to combating online hate speech and fake news is based on voluntary self-regulation by way of a code of conduct, established in 2016.[99] In its report on 'Fake news and disinformation' and 'media plurality and media freedom' the European Parliament recommended the continuation of a self-regulatory approach.[100] Interestingly, this report commissioned by the EU Commission avoids the term 'fake news', describing the term as inadequate to capture the complex problems of disinformation, which may encompass content that blends fabricated information with facts. Recommendations in the report include promoting media literacy to counter disinformation, and the development of tools for empowering users and journalists to tackle disinformation. The report also stresses the importance of safeguarding the diversity and sustainability of the European news media in this context and recommends further research regarding the impact of disinformation in Europe, advocating a 'Code of Principles' that online platforms and social networks should commit to. Among the ten key principles in the report is the suggestion that online platforms should ensure transparency by explaining how algorithms select news items.

---

98 Waisbord, S. (2018) pp. 1866–1878.

99 Code of Conduct on countering illegal hate speech online, 2016, based on the EU Framework Decision 2008/913/JHA of 28 November 2008: https://ec.europa.eu/info/files/code-conduct-countering-illegal-hate-speech-online_en.

100 Source: European Parliament Report 'On media pluralism and media freedom in the European Union (2017/2209(INI)) 12 April 2018: www.europarl.europa.eu/sides/getDoc.do?pubRef=-//EP//TEXT+REPORT+A8-2018-0144+0+DOC+XML+V0//EN.

7.8 Further reading

Allcott, H. and Gentzkow, M. (2017) 'Social Media and Fake News in the 2016 Election', *Journal of Economic Perspectives*, 31(2), 211–236.
Hunt Allcott and Matthew Gentzkow, both eminent professor of economics at US universities, examined the exposure of persuasive fake news of the ordinary citizen during the Trump-Clinton US presidential election campaign in 2016 providing some statistical evidence on the changing attitudes and an assessment on the way people voted. The authors measured the number of news stories read and remembered compared with fake news stories, building up a database of pro-Trump fake news and the impact on the voters. As economists they then calculated the social costs fake news might have and suggested what could and should be done in relation to social media platforms and consumer advertising.

O'Brien, P. (2017) '"Enemies of the people": judges, the media, and the mythic Lord Chancellor', *Public Law,* (Nov Supp, (Brexit Special Extra Issue), 135–149.
Patrick O'Brien examines the long history of robust criticism of judges in the UK. He makes the important distinction between criticism that emanates from politicians and criticisms made by the media, such as the reaction to the *Gina Miller*[101] judgment (High Court 2016) by the *Daily Mail* in particular. The author notes that media criticism can be an important aspect of judicial accountability, but certain media criticism of the judiciary can constitute a genuine threat to judicial independence and impartiality. Whilst the Lord Chancellor ought to 'fight the judiciary's corner' as 'special guardian of judicial independence', O'Brien calls the modern existence of this office 'a myth'. The article criticizes the post-2005 Lord Chancellors for failing to perform a guardianship role and the core function of defending judicial independence and impartiality.

Schwiddessen, S., Clark, B., Defaux, T. and Groom, J. (2018) 'Germany's Network Enforcement Act – closing the net on fake news?' *European Intellectual Property Review*, 40(8), 539–546.
The authors examine Germany's latest legislation, the Network Enforcement Act 2017 (*Netzwerkdurchsetzungsgesetz* – NetzDG), which aims to combat hate speech and fake news, which came into force on 1 January 2018. It embodies a new legislative concept which transfers the responsibility of enforcing criminal offences in the digital sphere to social media providers while at the same time making them subject to significant fines in the case of failures in performing this task. This article provides an overview of the provisions under the NetzDG, outlines some of the main points of criticism raised against it and explores some of the other initiatives aimed at tackling fake news in the EU.

Wragg, P. (2015) 'The legitimacy of press regulation', *Public Law*, April, 290–307.
Professor Paul Wragg charts the post-Leveson reform of print press regulation and discusses the industry-backed Independent Press Standards Organisation (IPSO) and its refusal to engage with the Royal Charter for the Self-Regulation of the Press. Wragg has been a long-standing commentator in this field. The author examines press freedom and whether it has been curtailed by the Leveson recommendations.

---

101 R (on the application of Miller) v Secretary of State for Exiting the European Union [2016] EWHC 2768 (Admin); [2017] 1 All ER 158.

Chapter 8

Regulating the communications industry

Chapter contents

> **Key points**
>
> This chapter will cover the following questions:
>
> o How is the communications industry regulated in the UK?
> o What is the full remit and purpose of Ofcom?
> o What are the broadcasting regulations in relation to public service broadcasting?
> o How are paid-for and streaming services regulated − if at all?
> o Is there any way to regulate online harmful content?
> o How is advertising regulated on various UK and international media platforms?
> o How is the film and online video industry regulated?
> o What are the laws concerning elections and party political broadcasts in the UK?

8.1 Overview

This chapter follows on from the previous one, looking at statutory, self- and co-regulation of the communications, advertising, video and movie industries. We will also ask whether online harmful content can be regulated.

A free media should be − by definition − decentralized and self-regulated. While lacking a central authority that pre-approves content and still needing to rectifying mistakes − omissions or distortions − a free media ought to resolve this paradox by acting as a self-regulator. Specifically, media content itself can be analyzed by others within the media, leaving the final judgment up to the viewers. Arguably, self-regulation is important because anyone in the media is capable of conveying bias; in lieu of restricting content, a free media would be capable of 'policing' itself.

After examining the UK broadcasting regulations under the Communications Act 2003, governing the BBC and all other traditional TV and radio stations, we will have a look at the main statutory communications regulator Ofcom and how its role and influence have increased in importance over the past decade, especially in relation to the BBC.

We then take a look at how the advertising industry is regulated. This is largely done by self-regulation via the Advertising Standards Authority (ASA) and EU-wide regulation, such as the CAP Code and the Blue Book. The focus will be on the commercial powers of social media advertising, such as Facebook and YouTube, including the advertising power of vloggers and increased product placement in films compared with traditional TV and radio advertising.

Linked to the previous topic of election campaigning, we will take a look at some aggressive online advertising strategies which have become intrusive, targeted at specific audiences. The official Vote Leave campaign, for example, spent more than £2.7m on

See

Chapter 7.7

targeting ads at specific groups of people on Facebook, helping it to win the 2016 EU referendum. Two years later, in July 2018, the US social media giant eventually released these ads to the Digital, Media and Culture Select Committee of MPs, investigating fake news.

The ads, created by Canadian company Aggregate AIQ, often focused on specific issues – such as immigration or animal rights – targeting certain groups of people, based on their age, where they live and other personal data taken from social media, such as Facebook. The 120 pages of Facebook documents appeared to back up the findings of the Electoral Commission (2017–2018), which ruled that Vote Leave broke electoral law by working jointly with another campaign, BeLeave – something denied by both groups. The adverts contained in the Facebook data set were seen more than 169 million times in total.

The BeLeave messages were more closely directed at younger voters, promising a 'brighter future' if the UK could stop 'EU regulators keeping us in the past' and accusing Brussels of regulating ride-sharing apps such as Uber and enforcing quotas on data streaming. Data provided by Facebook suggested some of the most seen images were produced by BeLeave. This image was displayed on the screens of target audience members more than five million times.[1]

Another self-regulatory body is the British Board of Film Classification (BBFC), which has been given statutory recognition to classify and regulate not only cinema films but also music DVDs, videos and games. In January 2019 the BBFC published new Classification Guidelines for age ratings across different platforms. The BBFC's consultation – involving more than 10,000 people – confirmed that people feel a heightened sense of anxiety when it comes to depictions of 'real-world' scenarios, in which audiences – especially young people – are likely to be concerned that it could happen to them. For example, realistic contemporary scenarios showing terrorism, self-harm, suicide and discriminatory behaviour. The regulator's new classification demonstrates that young people and parents want to see an increase in classification guidance, particularly around online content, as well as more consistency across all platforms.

The chapter then turns to the laws governing elections and party political and party election broadcasts. Since 1883, the UK has had legislation on its statute books that limits candidates' spending on political campaigns, corruption and fraud.[2] Broadcasting legislation ensures impartiality and fairness in elections and rationing of air time. As social media and other online services become primary sources of information for many, and campaign advertising spending moves decisively online, the current framework covers a shrinking amount of campaign activity. Campaign regulation aims to ensure that elections are free and fair and not captured by a narrow range of interests.

8.2 Broadcasting regulations: TV and radio

Until the early 1980s, Western European broadcasting was largely state-controlled. For example, advertising 'spots' were either not permitted or strictly controlled by state

---

1   House of Commons (2018) Digital, Culture, Media and Sport Committee, 'Investigation into the use of data analytics for political purposes', paras 31–50.

2   Illegal and Corrupt Practices (Prevention) Act 1883.

regulation, and increasingly by EU Treaty provision and EU Regulations.[3] The UK was one of the first European countries to dismantle this monopoly by the introduction of commercial broadcasting in September 1955 via 'Independent Television' or ITV. ITV came under the regulatory auspices of the Independent Television Authority (ITA) to provide competition to the public service broadcaster the BBC.[4]

See below 8.7

Although this regulatory framework still exists to a certain extent today, it has been frequently challenged by independent broadcasting providers and increasingly by streaming services such as Netflix, Hulu and Amazon Prime. As mentioned before, Amazon is a UK-based service and can therefore be regulated in the UK, whereas Netflix and Hulu are on-demand video and streaming services based in the United States. The Hulu platform differs from Netflix and Amazon Prime in that it allows users earlier access to popular series from multiple traditional networks. Hulu mainly focuses on popular TV series.

Areas covered by any broadcasting or regulatory standards normally include the following guidelines:

- protection of minors;
- offence to human dignity;
- protection against harm, e.g. flashing lights, on-air hypnosis;
- no encouragement of behaviour which is harmful to health or safety;
- no incitement to crime and disorder;
- no incitement to hatred, contempt, racial hatred or hatred on grounds of national or ethnic origin, colour, religion, sex, sexual orientation, age or mental or physical disability;
- rules on advertising and programming.

8.3 Regulation of public service broadcasting

The public service TV broadcasters in the UK include the British Broadcasting Corporation (BBC), Channel 4, Channel 5, BBC Scotland TV[5] and S4C. While all BBC public service television channels are Public Service Broadcast (PSB) channels, only the main channels of each of the other public service broadcasters have this status. The main objective of PSB is to provide a range of public benefits, including high-quality television reflecting UK culture.

The communications regulator Ofcom found in its survey that linear television continues to be an important part of people's viewing, with live TV still accounting for 58 per cent of all TV and audiovisual content viewed (2017).[6] Public service broadcasters can reach large audiences, bring the nation together at key moments, and inform, entertain

---

3   *Commission v Kingdom of Spain (supported by United Kingdom of Great Britain and Northern Ireland)* (2011) (Case C-281/09) Judgment of the Court (First Chamber) of 24 November 2011. The case concerned 'advertising spots' and transmission times on Spanish national TV and the state's failure to fulfil obligations under Directive 89/552/EEC.
4   For further discussion see: Gibbons, T. (2018).
5   The new BBC TV channel commenced broadcasting on 24 February 2019. Ofcom granted the licence in June 2018. Director General of the BBC Tony Hall said he wanted the channel to reflect modern Scotland. BBC Scotland airs about 50 per cent original content and 50 per cent repeats.
6   Ofcom (2017).

and educate society with popular programmes such as *Strictly Come Dancing* (BBC 1) and *Britain's Got Talent* (ITV).

In its Media Nation survey report of 2018, Ofcom found that generally viewers' confidence in public service broadcasting remains high. Of those people who watch channels from the public service broadcasters, three-quarters (75 per cent) said they were satisfied, and 84 per cent of people considered trusted news to be the most important feature of their output.[7] But the regulator's report also underlined the challenges facing the UK's public service broadcasters from changing technology, audience fragmentation and global competition.

As part of the Communications Act 2003 and the Digital Economy Act 2017, the UK Parliament requires that traditional, scheduled television – known as linear channels – that provides PSB programmes (the designated channels) should be given prominence within television guides, known as electronic programme guides (EPG). This ensures that such programmes are easily available and discoverable to audiences, which should encourage more viewing and greater public benefits.

8.3.1 The British Broadcasting Corporation: Royal Charter and governance

The BBC started life as a company, changing to a corporation following a report by the Crawford Committee.[8] The government accepted the Committee's findings and established by Royal Charter[9] the British Broadcasting Corporation (BBC). The Charter set out the way in which the BBC would be governed. The first Charter ran for ten years from 1 January 1927 and recognized the BBC as an instrument of education and entertainment. Subsequent Charters expanded this remit to include the dissemination of information.

During the first 80 years of the BBC's existence there was comparatively little change in the way in which it was governed. The BBC began its daily radio transmissions in September 1922, and 'listening in' to the 'wireless' quickly became a social and cultural phenomenon in Britain. From 1927 – when the BBC was established by Royal Charter to be the monopoly broadcaster in the UK – until 2006 – when the Royal Charter was last reviewed – the BBC had a Board of Governors which acted as 'trustees' of the public interest. The BBC's monopoly lasted until 1955 when Independent Television (ITV) began broadcasting a regional commercial broadcasting service on Channel 3. This heralded the start of an era when a separate regulatory regime was established for commercial television.

Prior to the Royal Charter review in 2016, the BBC governors were constitutionally part of the BBC but were independent of management. Each of the 12 governors, including the Chairman, was appointed by the Secretary of State, and they were responsible for the appointment of the Director General, ensuring that the BBC management implemented its strategy and overseeing complaints from the public. The governors were accountable to Parliament by appearing before parliamentary Select Committees.

---

7 Ofcom (2018).

8 Crawford Committee Report of the Broadcasting Committee (1925).

9 A Royal Charter is an instrument of incorporation, granted by the Queen, which confers independent legal personality on an organization and defines its objectives, constitution and powers to govern its own affairs. Incorporation by Charter is a prestigious way of acquiring legal personality and reflects the high status of that body. The authority for the grant of a Charter comes from the Royal Prerogative, that is to say, the grant is made by the Sovereign on the advice of the Privy Council.

Harold Wilson's Labour Government appointed Lord Hill of Luton in 1967 as Chairman of the Board of Governors and the Thatcher government appointed a succession of governors with the intent of bringing the BBC 'into line' with government policy, such as Marmaduke Hussey (latterly Lord Hussey of North Bradley), appointed Chairman of the Board of Governors in 1986. In January 2004 Gavyn Davies, who had been appointed Chairman by the Labour government in 2001, resigned in the wake of the Hutton Inquiry. Lord Ryder, previously a Conservative Member of Parliament and a member of Margaret Thatcher's personal staff, replaced him as Acting Chairman. It has been claimed that Ryder and other Conservatives on the Board of Governors were effectively responsible for 'forcing out' Director-General Greg Dyke, who had not initially believed that his offer of resignation would be accepted by the Governors following the Hutton Report. In May 2004, Michael Grade took over as permanent Chairman. He was to be the last permanent Chairman of the BBC Board of Governors until November 2006.[10]

The eighth Charter (1 January 2007) charged the BBC with delivering the latest technology to the public and taking a leading role in the switchover to digital television, setting out major changes to the governance of the Corporation. The BBC Trust was established with 12 trustees and a chairman. In technical legal terms it was not a 'trust' at all but a part of the BBC which was both separate and within the BBC as a whole. The main role of the Trust was to be the guardian of the licence fee and the public interest.

It is fair to say that the BBC Trust has been harshly criticized, for example, for its role in investigating the Jimmy Savile historic child abuse scandal or the way it dealt with false allegations against Lord McAlpine (see: Lord McAlpine of West Green v Sally Bercow (2013)[11]). The Trust was condemned by the National Audit Office (NAO) for its over-generous pay-offs for departing executives. The NAO annual report of 2013 revealed that the BBC Trust paid the former BBC Director General, George Entwistle, £475,000 after announcing his resignation and that the former Deputy Director General, Mark Byford, received a pay-off package of £949,000.[12]

See Chapter 3

As the BBC Charter came to an end in 2016, the Conservative government commissioned an inquiry asking for a 'fundamental reform' of how the Corporation should be governed in future. Rona Fairhead was the last Chair of the BBC Trust before its abolition and the first woman to hold the post.

Sir David Clementi led the inquiry into the future governance of the BBC and published his report in March 2016 (the Clementi Report[13]). The Report called the BBC Trust model a 'mistake', and Clementi's recommendations included that regulatory oversight should be overseen by an 'external' body, such as the Office of Communications (Ofcom).

See below 8.4

The most recent Royal Charter was awarded from 1 January 2017 for a period of 11 years. The new, unitary BBC Board is led by a non-executive Chairman, Sir David

10 House of Commons (2004) The Hutton Report.
11 [2013] EWHC 1342 (QB).
12 National Audit Office (2013) 'Severance and wider benefits for senior BBC managers'. 1 July 2013.
13 Clementi, Sir David (2016) 'A Review of the Governance and Regulation of the BBC'. Presented to Parliament by the Secretary of State for Culture, Media and Sport by Command of Her Majesty. March 2016. Cm 9209 ('The Clementi Report'). Sir David Cecil Clementi was former chairman of Virgin Money and Prudential and previously Deputy Governor of the Bank of England.

Clementi, and consists of a majority of non-executive directors alongside executive directors including the BBC's Director-General and Editor-in-Chief, Tony Hall. The Board is responsible for ensuring the BBC fulfils its mission and public purposes as set out in the Royal Charter. It does this by:

- setting the strategic direction for the BBC;
- establishing the creative remit;
- setting the BBC's budget;
- determining the framework for assessing performance.

The Board is accountable for all the BBC's activities including the publicly funded services in the UK and around the world, as well as its commercial activities and all BBC online services. The Director-General, Tony Hall, chairs the Executive Committee, which is responsible for the day-to-day running of the BBC and consists of the senior directors managing large operational areas of the BBC.

How can the traditional public service broadcasters, such as the BBC, Channel 4 or ITV, survive in this competitive streaming and paid-for services world? Ofcom has urged UK broadcasters to collaborate rather than to compete to match online competitors' growing scale. That means UK broadcasters joining forces with each other, or with third parties, to share ideas and pool resources. It is important that public service broadcasters adapt for the digital age by finding new ways to distribute programmes, capture younger audiences and make world-class content that reflects life in the UK – which has not typically been a focus for global internet video streaming companies.

 FOR THOUGHT

You are the legal adviser for the BBC. The newsroom has been sent film footage by an independent news crew of a children's massacre in Syria. The live footage shows a violent death, bombing and gruesome graphic imagery of many dead bodies in the foreground. The video editor asks your advice whether he should filter and edit out some of these child images. The ten o'clock TV news editor wants to show the full video coverage of the massacre. What would your advice be before the news goes out that night on national TV?

8.4 Office of Communications (Ofcom)

Ofcom is the UK's broadcasting, telecommunications and postal regulatory body. Under the BBC's Royal Charter it has responsibility for regulating the BBC. It does this through an Operating Framework and by setting a licence for the BBC that contains the regulatory conditions the BBC is required to meet. Ofcom also assesses performance, ensures fair and effective competition and regulates how the BBC's commercial activities interact with its public services. In addition, it regulates BBC content and output against its Broadcasting Code.

See below 8.4.1

Ofcom was established as a statutory regulator ('a body corporate') by the Office of Communications Act 2002, replacing the Broadcasting Standards Commission (BSC), the Independent Television Commission (ITC) and the Radio Authority, the 'media watchdogs' that previously dealt with complaints against broadcasters. Sharon White was the Chief Executive of Ofcom from 2015 to 2019. Under her watch the regulator oversaw Rupert Murdoch's Sale of Sky, BT's Openreach broadband seperation from BT's main operation and the growing influence of social media and streamed services.

The main statute which covers Ofcom's duties is the Communications Act 2003. Section 3(1) states:

> It shall be the principal duty of Ofcom, in carrying out their functions:
>
> (a) to further the interests of citizens in relation to communications matters; and
> (b) to further the interests of consumers in relevant markets, where appropriate by promoting competition.

Ofcom operates under a number of statutes, including:

- the Broadcasting Act 1996;
- the Broadcasting Act 1990;
- the Competition Act 1998;
- the Enterprise Act 2002;
- the Communications Act 2003;
- the Wireless Telegraphy Act 2006;
- the Digital Economy Act 2010;
- the Digital Economy Act 2017;
- the Enterprise and Regulatory Reform Act 2013;
- the Postal Services Act 2011;
- and EU legislation.

Section 355 of the Communications Act 2003 obliges the regulator to carry out periodic reviews and reallocation of (local) radio licences. Part of the remit involves the character of the service, the quality and range of programming and the amount of local content. Ofcom has other responsibilities, such as shaping public policy in the future of broadcasting and new media. Apart from watching over correct allocation of broadband width and ISP compliance, Ofcom also allocates and administers radio frequencies and bandwidths under its periodic 'spectrum trading process', the relevant legislation being the Wireless Telegraphy Act 2006. In summary, Ofcom's key responsibilities related to content standards regulation include the following:

> ### Ofcom's role in regulating content standards to protect audiences
>
> - Since its inception in 2003, Ofcom has been responsible for ensuring that audiences of broadcast TV are adequately protected, by requiring compliance with the Broadcasting Code. Audience protection has been a long-standing statutory duty in the UK, predating Ofcom, and stemming from legislation in the 1950s.
> - In 2010, following the Audiovisual Media Services Directive of 2007, Ofcom became responsible for the regulation of on-demand content, including broadcaster on-demand services like All4, and subscription services like Amazon Prime. This duty was previously performed jointly with its co-regulator – the Authority for Television on Demand (ATVOD). In 2015, ATVOD was merged with Ofcom.
> - Ofcom's statutory duties evolved in 2017 to include sole oversight of the BBC's output, including its websites and apps – the first time Ofcom had been given a role in relation to written online content.
> - With the Advertising Standards Authority (ASA), Ofcom is responsible for the regulation of broadcast advertising; the ASA also oversees online commercial advertising on a self-regulatory basis. One requirement of the broadcast rules is that TV and radio programmes should be free from political advertising. In addition, Ofcom directly regulates party political and election broadcasts.

8.4.1 The Ofcom Broadcasting Code

Under the Communications Act 2003, Ofcom has a duty to set standards for broadcast content to secure the standards objectives. Ofcom also has a duty to ensure that On Demand Programme Services (ODPS) comply with certain standards requirements set out in the Act. Ofcom reflects these requirements in its codes and rules.

The Ofcom Broadcasting Code[14] applies to radio and television content (with certain exceptions for the BBC[15]). Broadcasters are required by the terms of their Ofcom licence to observe the Standards Code and the Fairness Code. This includes any local TV and radio broadcast services and community digital sound programme services.

The Ofcom Code is divided into ten sections which are primarily drawn from the objectives as set out in section 319(2) Communications Act 2003 and section 107(1) Broadcasting Act 1996, as well as the Representation of the People Act 1983 (as amended). In setting these standards, Ofcom must secure the standards objectives set out in the 2003 Act. This not only involves setting minimum standards but also such other standards as may be appropriate.[16] The Code also gives effect to a number of

---

14 The Ofcom Broadcasting Code (2017) with the Cross-promotion Code and the On-Demand Programme Service Rules.

15 In the case of the BBC, Ofcom's power to impose sanctions is set out in the BBC Charter (2017).

16 Sections 3(1)(a) and (b), (2)(e) and (f) and (4)(b), (g), (h), (j), (k) and (l), 319, 320, 321, 325, 326 and Schedule 11A of the Communications Act 2003 and sections 107(1) of the Broadcasting Act 1996.

requirements relating to television in EC Directive 2010/13/EU ('The Audiovisual Media Services Directive').[17]

The Code has also been drafted in the light of the Human Rights Act 1998 and the European Convention on Human Rights. In particular, the right to freedom of expression, as expressed in Article 10(1) of the Convention, encompasses the audience's right to receive creative material, information and ideas without interference but subject to restrictions prescribed by law and necessary in a democratic society (Article 10(2)). This Article, together with Article 8(1) ECHR regarding the right to a person's private and family life, home and correspondence; Article 9 ECHR, the right to freedom of thought, conscience and religion; and Article 14 ECHR, the right to enjoyment of human rights without discrimination on grounds such as sex, race and religion underpin the principles of the Ofcom Code.

In drafting, reviewing and revising the Code (2017), Ofcom also paid regard to the matters specified in section 149(1) of the Equality Act 2010 ('the public sector equality duty') and section 75 of the Northern Ireland Act 1998.

Broadcasters must ensure that they comply with the rules, as set out in the Code this includes all platforms such as BBC iPlayer and all other 'catch-up' services. The Code is divided into sections which are primarily drawn from the objectives as set out in section 319(2) of the 2003 Act and section 107(1) of the 1996 Act, as well as the Representation of the People Act 1983 (as amended). The main criteria covered by the Code include:

- the degree of harm and offence likely to be caused by the inclusion of any particular sort of material in programmes generally or in programmes of a particular description;
- the likely size and composition of the potential audience for programmes included in television and radio services generally or in television and radio services of a particular description;
- the likely expectation of the audience as to the nature of a programme's content and the extent to which the nature of a programme's content can be brought to the attention of potential members of the audience;
- the likelihood of persons who are unaware of the nature of a programme's content being unintentionally exposed, by their own actions, to that content;
- the desirability of securing that the content of services identifies when there is a change affecting the nature of a service that is being watched or listened to and, in particular, a change that is relevant to the application of the standards set under this section;
- the desirability of maintaining the independence of editorial control over programme content.

---

17 Directive 2010/13/EU on the coordination of certain provisions laid down by law, regulation or administrative action in Member States concerning the provision of audiovisual media services (Audio-Visual Media Services Directive).

The Ofcom broadcasting code

Section 1: Protecting the under-eighteens[18]

Principle: To ensure that people under 18 are protected.

Rules

Scheduling and content information

1.1   Material that might seriously impair the physical, mental or moral development of people under eighteen must not be broadcast.

1.2   In the provision of services, broadcasters must take all reasonable steps to protect people under eighteen. For television services, this is in addition to their obligations resulting from the Audiovisual Media Services Directive (in particular, Article 27).

1.3   Children[19] must also be protected by appropriate scheduling from material that is unsuitable for them. Although scheduling requirements in this section are not relevant to the provision of programmes on demand, the BBC must put in place appropriate measures on BBC On Demand Programme Services (ODPS)[20] that provide equivalent protection for children.

1.4   Television broadcasters must observe the watershed.[21]

1.5   Radio broadcasters must have particular regard to times when children are particularly likely to be listening.[22]

1.6   The transition to more adult material must not be unduly abrupt at the watershed (in the case of television) or after the time when children are particularly likely to be listening (in the case of radio). For television, the strongest material should appear later in the schedule.

1.7   For television programmes broadcast before the watershed, or for radio programmes broadcast when children are particularly likely to be listening, or for BBC ODPS content that is likely to be accessed by children, clear information about content that may distress some children should be given, if appropriate, to the audience (taking into account the context).

The coverage of sexual and other offences in the UK involving under-eighteens

1.8   Where statutory or other legal restrictions apply preventing personal identification, broadcasters should also be particularly careful not to provide clues which may lead to the identification of those who are not yet adult (the defining age may differ in different parts of the UK) and who are, or might be, involved as a victim,

---

18 Relevant legislation includes ss 3(4)(h) and 319(2)(a) and (f) of the Communications Act 2003, Article 27 of the Audiovisual Media Services Directive, Article 10 ECHR and the BBC Charter and Agreement of November 2016 between Her Majesty's Secretary of State for Culture, Media and Sport and the British Broadcasting Corporation (as may be amended from time to time).

19 Meaning of 'children' under 15.

20 Such as the BBC iPlayer and iPlayer Kids (both audiovisual and sound programmes).

21 The watershed only applies to television. The watershed is at 2100. Material unsuitable for children should not, in general, be shown before 2100 or after 0530.

22 This phrase particularly refers to the school run and breakfast time.

witness, defendant or other perpetrator in the case of sexual offences featured in criminal, civil or family court proceedings:

- by reporting limited information which may be pieced together with other information available elsewhere, for example in newspaper reports (the 'jigsaw effect');
- inadvertently, for example by describing an offence as 'incest'; or
- in any other indirect way.

1.9   When covering any pre-trial investigation into an alleged criminal offence in the UK, broadcasters should pay particular regard to the potentially vulnerable position of any person who is not yet adult who is involved as a witness or victim, before broadcasting their name, address, identity of school or other educational establishment, place of work, or any still or moving picture of them. Particular justification is also required for the broadcast of such material relating to the identity of any person who is not yet adult who is involved in the defence as a defendant or potential defendant.

Drugs, smoking, solvents and alcohol

1.10 The use of illegal drugs, the abuse of drugs, smoking, solvent abuse and the misuse of alcohol:

- must not be featured in programmes made primarily for children unless there is strong editorial justification;
- must generally be avoided and in any case must not be condoned, encouraged or glamorized in other programmes broadcast before the watershed (in the case of television), when children are particularly likely to be listening (in the case of radio), or when content is likely to be accessed by children (in the case of BBC ODPS) unless there is editorial justification;
- must not be condoned, encouraged or glamorized in other programmes likely to be widely seen, heard or accessed by under-eighteens unless there is editorial justification.

Violence and dangerous behaviour

1.11 Violence, its after-effects and descriptions of violence, whether verbal or physical, must be appropriately limited in programmes broadcast before the watershed (in the case of television), when children are particularly likely to be listening (in the case of radio) or when content is likely to be accessed by children (in the case of BBC ODPS) and must also be justified by the context.

1.12 Violence, whether verbal or physical, that is easily imitable by children in a manner that is harmful or dangerous:

- must not be featured in programmes made primarily for children unless there is strong editorial justification;
- must not be broadcast before the watershed (in the case of television), when children are particularly likely to be listening (in the case of radio), or when

content is likely to be accessed by children (in the case of BBC ODPS), unless there is editorial justification.

1.13 Dangerous behaviour, or the portrayal of dangerous behaviour, that is likely to be easily imitable by children in a manner that is harmful:

- must not be featured in programmes made primarily for children unless there is strong editorial justification;
- must not be broadcast before the watershed (in the case of television), when children are particularly likely to be listening (in the case of radio), or when content is likely to be accessed by children (in the case of BBC ODPS), unless there is editorial justification.

Offensive language

1.14 The most offensive language must not be broadcast before the watershed (in the case of television), when children are particularly likely to be listening (in the case of radio), or when content is likely to be accessed by children (in the case of BBC ODPS).

1.15 Offensive language must not be used in programmes made for younger children except in the most exceptional circumstances.

1.16 Offensive language must not be broadcast before the watershed (in the case of television), when children are particularly likely to be listening (in the case of radio), or when content is likely to be accessed by children (in the case of BBC ODPS), unless it is justified by the context. In any event, frequent use of such language must be avoided before the watershed.

Sexual material

1.17 Material equivalent to the British Board of Film Classification ('BBFC') R18 – rating must not be broadcast at any time.

1.18 'Adult sex material' – material that contains images and/or language of a strong sexual nature which is broadcast for the primary purpose of sexual arousal or stimulation – must not be broadcast at any time other than between 2200 and 0530 on premium subscription services and pay per view/night services which operate with mandatory restricted access. In addition, measures must be in place to ensure that the subscriber is an adult.

1.19 Broadcasters must ensure that material broadcast after the watershed, or made available on BBC ODPS, which contains images and/or language of a strong or explicit sexual nature, but is not 'adult sex material' as defined in Rule 1.18 above, is justified by the context.

1.20 Representations of sexual intercourse must not occur before the watershed (in the case of television), when children are particularly likely to be listening (in the case of radio), or when content is likely to be accessed by children (in the case of BBC ODPS), unless there is a serious educational purpose.

1.21 Any discussion on, or portrayal of, sexual behaviour must be editorially justified if included before the watershed, when children are particularly likely to be listening, or when content is likely to be accessed by children on BBC ODPS, and must be appropriately limited.

Films, premium subscription film services, pay per view services

1.22 No film refused classification by the British Board of Film Classification (BBFC) may be broadcast, unless it has subsequently been classified or the BBFC has confirmed that it would not be rejected according to the standards currently operating. Also, no film cut as a condition of classification by the BBFC may be transmitted in a version which includes the cut material unless:

- the BBFC has confirmed that the material was cut to allow the film to pass at a lower category; or
- the BBFC has confirmed that the film would not be subject to compulsory cuts according to the standards currently operating.

1.23 BBFC 18-rated films or their equivalent must not be broadcast before 2100, on any service (except for pay per view services), and even then they may be unsuitable for broadcast at that time.

1.24 Premium subscription film services may broadcast up to BBFC 15-rated films or their equivalent, at any time of day provided that mandatory restricted access is in place pre-2000 and post-0530. In addition, those security systems which are in place to protect children must be clearly explained to all subscribers.

See below 8.8

1.25 Pay per view services may broadcast up to BBFC 18-rated films or their equivalent, at any time of day provided that mandatory restricted access is in place pre-2100 and post-0530.

In addition:

- information must be provided about programme content that will assist adults to assess its suitability for children;
- there must be a detailed billing system for subscribers which clearly itemizes all viewing including viewing times and dates; and
- those security systems which are in place to protect children must be clearly explained to all subscribers.

1.26 BBFC R18-rated films must not be broadcast.

Exorcism, the occult and the paranormal

1.27 Demonstrations of exorcisms, occult practices and the paranormal (which purport to be real), must not be shown before the watershed (in the case of television) or when children are particularly likely to be listening (in the case of radio), or when content is likely to be accessed by children (in the case of BBC ODPS). Paranormal practices which are for entertainment purposes must not be broadcast when significant numbers of children may be expected to be watching, or are particularly likely to be listening, or when content is likely to be accessed by children (in the case of BBC ODPS), (This rule does not apply to drama, film or comedy.)

The involvement of people under eighteen in programmes

1.28   Due care must be taken over the physical and emotional welfare and the dignity of people under eighteen who take part or are otherwise involved in programmes. This is irrespective of any consent given by the participant or by a parent, guardian or other person over the age of eighteen in loco parentis.

1.29   People under eighteen must not be caused unnecessary distress or anxiety by their involvement in programmes or by the broadcast of those programmes.

1.30   Prizes aimed at children must be appropriate to the age range of both the target audience and the participants.

Section 2: Harm and offence[23]

Principle: To ensure that generally accepted standards are applied to the content of television and radio services so as to provide adequate protection for members of the public from the inclusion in such services of harmful and/or offensive material.

Rules

2.1   Generally accepted standards must be applied to the contents of television and radio services and BBC ODPS so as to provide adequate protection for members of the public from the inclusion in such services of harmful and/or offensive material.

2.2   Factual programmes or items or portrayals of factual matters must not materially mislead the audience.

2.3   In applying generally accepted standards broadcasters must ensure that material which may cause offence is justified by the context (see meaning of 'context' below). Such material may include, but is not limited to, offensive language, violence, sex, sexual violence, humiliation, distress, violation of human dignity, discriminatory treatment or language (for example on the grounds of age, disability, gender reassignment, pregnancy and maternity, race, religion or belief, sex and sexual orientation, and marriage and civil partnership). Appropriate information should also be broadcast where it would assist in avoiding or minimising offence.

Violence, dangerous behaviour and suicide

2.4   Programmes must not include material (whether in individual programmes or in programmes taken together) which, taking into account the context, condones or glamorises violent, dangerous or seriously antisocial behaviour and is likely to encourage others to copy such behaviour.

2.5   Methods of suicide and self-harm must not be included in programmes except where they are editorially justified and are also justified by the context.

---

23 Relevant legislation includes ss 3(4)(g) and 319(2)(a), (f) and (i) of the Communications Act 2003, Articles 10 and 14 ECHR, and the BBC Charter and Agreement.

Exorcism, the occult and the paranormal

2.6 Demonstrations of exorcism, the occult, the paranormal, divination, or practices related to any of these that purport to be real (as opposed to entertainment) must be treated with due objectivity.

2.7 If a demonstration of exorcism, the occult, the paranormal, divination, or practices related to any of these is for entertainment purposes, this must be made clear to viewers and listeners.

2.8 Demonstrations of exorcism, the occult, the paranormal, divination, or practices related to any of these (whether such demonstrations purport to be real or are for entertainment purposes) must not contain life-changing advice directed at individuals. (Religious programmes are exempt from this rule but must, in any event, comply with the provisions in Section Four: Religion. Films, dramas and fiction generally are not bound by this rule.)

Hypnotic and other techniques, simulated news and photosensitive epilepsy

2.9 When broadcasting material featuring demonstrations of hypnotic techniques, broadcasters must exercise a proper degree of responsibility in order to prevent hypnosis and/or adverse reactions in viewers and listeners. The hypnotist must not broadcast his/her full verbal routine or be shown performing straight to camera.

2.10 Simulated news (for example in drama or in documentaries) must be broadcast in such a way that there is no reasonable possibility of the audience being misled into believing that they are listening to, or watching, actual news.

2.11 Broadcasters must not use techniques which exploit the possibility of conveying a message to viewers or listeners, or of otherwise influencing their minds without their being aware, or fully aware, of what has occurred.

2.12 Television broadcasters must take precautions to maintain a low level of risk to viewers who have photosensitive epilepsy. Where it is not reasonably practicable to follow the Ofcom guidance (see the Ofcom website), and where broadcasters can demonstrate that the broadcasting of flashing lights and/or patterns is editorially justified, viewers should be given an adequate verbal and also, if appropriate, text warning at the start of the programme or programme item.

Broadcast competitions and voting

2.13 Broadcast competitions and voting must be conducted fairly.

2.14 Broadcasters must ensure that viewers and listeners are not materially misled about any broadcast competition or voting.

2.15 Broadcasters must draw up rules for a broadcast competition or vote. These rules must be clear and appropriately made known. In particular, significant conditions that may affect a viewer's or listener's decision to participate must be stated at the time an invitation to participate is broadcast.

2.16 Broadcast competition prizes must be described accurately.

Section 3: Crime, Disorder, Hatred and Abuse

Principle: To ensure that material likely to encourage or incite the commission of crime or to lead to disorder is not included in television or radio services or BBC ODPS.

Rules

Incitement of crime and disorder

3.1   Material likely to encourage or incite the commission of crime or to lead to disorder must not be included in television or radio services or BBC ODPS.

Note: Under Rule 3.1, 'material' may include but is not limited to:

- content which directly or indirectly amounts to a call to criminal action or disorder;
- material promoting or encouraging engagement in terrorism[24] or other forms of criminal activity or disorder; and/or
- hate[25] speech which is likely to encourage criminal[26] activity or lead to disorder.

Hatred and abuse

3.2   Material which contains hate speech must not be included in television and radio programmes or BBC ODPS except where it is justified by the context.

3.3   Material which contains abusive or derogatory treatment of individuals, groups, religions or communities, must not be included in television and radio services or BBC ODPS except where it is justified by the context.

Portrayals of crime and criminal proceedings

3.4   Descriptions or demonstrations of criminal techniques which contain essential details which could enable the commission of crime must not be broadcast unless editorially justified.

3.5   No payment, promise of payment, or payment in kind, may be made to convicted or confessed criminals whether directly or indirectly for a programme contribution by the criminal (or any other person) relating to his/her crime/s. The only exception is where it is in the public interest.

3.6   While criminal proceedings are active, no payment or promise of payment may be made, directly or indirectly, to any witness or any person who may reasonably be expected to be called as a witness. Nor should any payment be suggested or made dependent on the outcome of the trial. Only actual expenditure or loss of earnings necessarily incurred during the making of a programme contribution may be reimbursed.

3.7   Where criminal proceedings are likely and foreseeable, payments should not be made to people who might reasonably be expected to be witnesses unless there is a clear public interest, such as investigating crime or serious wrongdoing, and the payment is necessary to elicit the information. Where such a payment is made

---

24 As defined in s 1 of the Terrorism Act 2000.
25 Meaning all forms of expression which spread, incite, promote or justify hatred based on intolerance on the grounds of disability, ethnicity, gender, gender reassignment, nationality, race, religion or sexual orientation.
26 Meaning any offence under law that is punishable by imprisonment or by a fine.

it will be appropriate to disclose the payment to both defence and prosecution if the person becomes a witness in any subsequent trial.

3.8   Broadcasters must use their best endeavours so as not to broadcast material that could endanger lives or prejudice the success of attempts to deal with a hijack or kidnapping.

Section 4: Religion

Principles:

To ensure that broadcasters exercise the proper degree of responsibility with respect to the content of programmes which are religious programmes.

To ensure that religious programmes do not involve any improper exploitation of any susceptibilities of the audience for such a programme.

To ensure that religious programmes do not involve any abusive treatment of the religious views and beliefs of those belonging to a particular religion or religious denomination.

Rules

4.1   Broadcasters must exercise the proper degree of responsibility with respect to the content of programmes which are religious programmes.

4.2   The religious views and beliefs of those belonging to a particular religion or religious denomination must not be subject to abusive treatment.

4.3   Where a religion or religious denomination is the subject, or one of the subjects, of a religious programme, then the identity of the religion and/or denomination must be clear to the audience.

4.4   Religious programmes must not seek to promote religious views or beliefs by stealth.

4.5   Religious programmes on television services or BBC ODPS must not seek recruits. This does not apply to specialist religious television services. Religious programmes on radio services may seek recruits.

4.6   Religious programmes must not improperly exploit any susceptibilities of the audience.

4.7   Religious programmes that contain claims that a living person (or group) has special powers or abilities must treat such claims with due objectivity and must not broadcast such claims when significant numbers of children may be expected to be watching (in the case of television), or when children are particularly likely to be listening (in the case of radio), or when content is likely to be accessed by children (in the case of BBC ODPS).

Section 5: Due impartiality and due accuracy and undue prominence of views and opinions[27]

Principles:

To ensure that news, in whatever form, is reported with due accuracy and presented with due impartiality.

To ensure that the special impartiality requirements of the Act are complied with.

---

27   Relevant legislation includes ss 319(2)(c) and (d), 319(8) and section 320 of the Communications Act 2003, the BBC Charter and Agreement and Article 10 ECHR.

Rules

Due impartiality and due accuracy in news

5.1   News, in whatever form, must be reported with due accuracy and presented with due impartiality.

5.2   Significant mistakes in news should normally be acknowledged and corrected on air quickly (or, in the case of BBC ODPS, corrected quickly). Corrections should be appropriately scheduled (or, in the case of BBC ODPS, appropriately signaled to viewers).

5.3   No politician may be used as a newsreader, interviewer or reporter in any news programmes unless, exceptionally, it is editorially justified. In that case, the political allegiance of that person must be made clear to the audience.

Special impartiality requirements: news and other programmes

Matters of political or industrial controversy and matters relating to current public policy[28]

The exclusion of views or opinions

5.4   Programmes in the services (listed above) must exclude all expressions of the views and opinions of the person providing the service on matters of political and industrial controversy and matters relating to current public policy (unless that person is speaking in a legislative forum or in a court of law). Views and opinions relating to the provision of programme services are also excluded from this requirement.

The preservation of due impartiality

5.5   Due impartiality on matters of political or industrial controversy and matters relating to current public policy must be preserved on the part of any person providing a service (listed above). This may be achieved within a programme or over a series of programmes taken as a whole.

5.6   The broadcast of editorially linked programmes dealing with the same subject matter (as part of a series in which the broadcaster aims to achieve due impartiality) should normally be made clear to the audience on air.

5.7   Views and facts must not be misrepresented. Views must also be presented with due weight over appropriate timeframes.

5.8   Any personal interest of a reporter or presenter, which would call into question the due impartiality of the programme, must be made clear to the audience.

5.9   Presenters and reporters (with the exception of news presenters and reporters in news programmes), presenters of 'personal view' or 'authored' programmes or items, and chairs of discussion programmes may express their own views on matters of political or industrial controversy or matters relating to current public policy.

---

28 Matters of political or industrial controversy are political or industrial issues on which politicians, industry and/or the media are in debate. Matters relating to current public policy need not be the subject of debate but relate to a policy under discussion or already decided by a local, regional or national government or by bodies mandated by those public bodies to make policy on their behalf, for example non-governmental organizations, relevant European institutions etc.

However, alternative viewpoints must be adequately represented either in the programme, or in a series of programmes taken as a whole. Additionally, presenters must not use the advantage of regular appearances to promote their views in a way that compromises the requirement for due impartiality. Presenter phone-ins must encourage and must not exclude alternative views.

5.10   A personal view or authored programme or item must be clearly signalled to the audience at the outset. This is a minimum requirement and may not be sufficient in all circumstances. (Personality phone-in hosts on radio are exempted from this provision unless their personal view status is unclear.)

Matters of major political or industrial controversy and major matters relating to current public policy

5.11   In addition to the rules above, due impartiality must be preserved on matters of major political and industrial controversy and major matters relating to current public policy by the person providing a service (listed above) in each programme or in clearly linked and timely programmes.

5.12   In dealing with matters of major political and industrial controversy and major matters relating to current public policy an appropriately wide range of significant views must be included and given due weight in each programme or in clearly linked and timely programmes. Views and facts must not be misrepresented.

The prevention of undue prominence of views and opinions on matters of political or industrial controversy and matters relating to current public policy

5.13   Broadcasters should not give undue prominence to the views and opinions of particular persons or bodies on matters of political or industrial controversy and matters relating to current public policy in all the programmes included in any service (listed above) taken as a whole.[29]

Section 6: Elections and referendums[30]

Principle: To ensure that the special impartiality requirements in the Communications Act 2003 and other legislation relating to broadcasting on elections and referendums, are applied at the time of elections and referendums.

Rules

Programmes at the time of elections and referendums

6.1   The rules in Section Five, in particular the rules relating to matters of major political or industrial controversy and major matters relating to current public policy, apply to the coverage of elections and referendums.

---

29 Rule 5.13 applies to local radio services (including community radio services), local digital sound programme services (including community digital sound programme services) and radio licensable content services. For the avoidance of doubt, it does not apply to any BBC services.

30 Relevant legislation includes ss 319(2)(c) and 320 of the Communications Act 2003, the BBC Charter and Agreement, and Article 10 ECHR; the Representation of the People Act 1983 (as amended), in particular sections 66A, 92 and 93 (which is amended by section 144 of the Political Parties, Elections and Referendums Act 2000.

Programmes at the time of elections and referendums[31] in the UK[32]

6.2 Due weight must be given to the coverage of parties and independent candidates during the election period. In determining the appropriate level of coverage to be given to parties and independent candidates broadcasters must take into account evidence of past electoral support and/or current support. Broadcasters must also consider giving appropriate coverage to parties and independent candidates with significant views and perspectives.

See below 8.9

6.3 Due weight must be given to designated organisations in coverage during the referendum period. Broadcasters must also consider giving appropriate coverage to other permitted participants with significant views and perspectives.

6.4 Discussion and analysis of election and referendum issues must finish when the poll opens. (This refers to the opening of actual polling stations. This rule does not apply to any poll conducted entirely by post.) BBC ODPS are not required to remove archive content for the period when the polls are open.

6.5 Broadcasters may not publish the results of any opinion poll on polling day itself until the election or referendum poll closes. (For European Parliamentary elections, this applies until all polls throughout the European Union have closed.)

6.6 Candidates in UK elections, and representatives of permitted participants in UK referendums, must not act as news presenters, interviewers or presenters of any type of programme during the election period. BBC ODPS are not required to remove archive content for the election or referendum period.

6.7 Appearances by candidates (in UK elections) or representatives (of permitted participants in UK referendums) in non-political programmes that were planned or scheduled before the election or referendum period may continue, but no new appearances should be arranged and broadcast during the period. BBC ODPS are not required to remove archive content for the election or referendum period.

Constituency coverage and electoral area coverage in elections

6.8 Due impartiality must be strictly maintained in a constituency report or discussion and in an electoral area report or discussion.

6.9 If a candidate takes part in an item about his/her particular constituency, or electoral area, then broadcasters must offer the opportunity to take part in such items to all candidates within the constituency or electoral area representing parties with previous significant electoral support or where there is evidence of significant current support. This also applies to independent candidates. However, if a candidate refuses or is unable to participate, the item may nevertheless go ahead.

6.10 Any constituency or electoral area report or discussion after the close of nominations must include a list of all candidates standing, giving first names, surnames and the name of the party they represent or, if they are standing independently, the fact that they are an independent candidate. This must be conveyed in sound and/or vision. Where a constituency report on a radio service is repeated on several

---

31 A referendum held under the Northern Ireland Act 1998 (as amended) begins when the draft of an Order is laid before Parliament for approval by each House.
32 This section only applies during the actual election or referendum period.

occasions in the same day, the full list need only be broadcast on one occasion. If, in subsequent repeats on that day, the constituency report does not give the full list of candidates, the audience should be directed to an appropriate website or other information source listing all candidates and giving the information set out above.

6.11 Where a candidate is taking part in a programme on any matter, after the election has been called, s/he must not be given the opportunity to make constituency points, or electoral area points about the constituency or electoral area in which s/he is standing, when no other candidates will be given a similar opportunity.

6.12 If coverage is given to wider election regions, for example in elections to the Scottish Parliament, Welsh Assembly, Northern Ireland Assembly, London Assembly or European Parliament, then Rules 6.8 to 6.12 apply in offering participation to candidates. In these instances, all parties who have a candidate in the appropriate region should be listed in sound and/or vision, but it is not necessary to list candidates individually. However, any independent candidate who is not standing on a party list must be named. Where a report on a radio service is repeated on several occasions in the same day, the full list need only be broadcast on one occasion. If, in subsequent repeats on that day, the constituency report does not give the full list of candidates, the audience should be directed to an appropriate website or other information source listing all candidates and giving the information set out above.

Section 7: Fairness[33]

Principle: To ensure that broadcasters avoid unjust or unfair treatment of individuals or organisations in programmes.

Rule

7.1 Broadcasters must avoid unjust or unfair treatment of individuals or organisations in programmes.

Dealing fairly with contributors and obtaining informed consent

7.2 Broadcasters and programme makers should normally be fair in their dealings with potential contributors to programmes unless, exceptionally, it is justified to do otherwise.

7.3 Where a person is invited to make a contribution to a programme (except when the subject matter is trivial or their participation minor) they should normally, at an appropriate stage:

- be told the nature and purpose of the programme, what the programme is about and be given a clear explanation of why they were asked to contribute and when (if known) and where it is likely to be first broadcast;

---

33 Relevant legislation includes ss 3(2)(f) and 326 of the Communications Act 2003 and sections 107(1) and 130 of the Broadcasting Act 1996 (as amended), Article 28 of the Audiovisual Media Services Directive, Article 10 ECHR and the BBC Charter and Agreement.

- be told what kind of contribution they are expected to make, for example live, pre-recorded, interview, discussion, edited, unedited, etc.;
- be informed about the areas of questioning and, wherever possible, the nature of other likely contributions;
- be made aware of any significant changes to the programme as it develops which might reasonably affect their original consent to participate, and which might cause material unfairness;
- be told the nature of their contractual rights and obligations and those of the programme maker and broadcaster in relation to their contribution; and
- be given clear information, if offered an opportunity to preview the programme, about whether they will be able to effect any changes to it.

Note: Taking these measures is likely to result in the consent that is given being 'informed consent'. It may be fair to withhold all or some of this information where it is justified in the public interest or under other provisions of this section of the Code.

7.4 If a contributor is under sixteen, consent should normally be obtained from a parent or guardian, or other person of eighteen or over in loco parentis. In particular, persons under sixteen should not be asked for views on matters likely to be beyond their capacity to answer properly without such consent.

7.5 In the case of persons over sixteen who are not in a position to give consent, a person of eighteen or over with primary responsibility for their care should normally give it on their behalf. In particular, persons not in a position to give consent should not be asked for views on matters likely to be beyond their capacity to answer properly without such consent.

7.6 When a programme is edited, contributions should be represented fairly.

7.7 Guarantees given to contributors, for example relating to the content of a programme, confidentiality or anonymity, should normally be honoured.

7.8 Broadcasters should ensure that the re-use of material, i.e. use of material originally filmed or recorded for one purpose and then used in a programme for another purpose or used in a later or different programme, does not create unfairness. This applies both to material obtained from others and the broadcaster's own material.

Opportunity to contribute and proper consideration of facts

7.9 Before broadcasting a factual programme, including programmes examining past events, broadcasters should take reasonable care to satisfy themselves that:

- material facts have not been presented, disregarded or omitted in a way that is unfair to an individual or organisation; and
- anyone whose omission could be unfair to an individual or organisation has been offered an opportunity to contribute.

7.10 Programmes – such as dramas and factually-based dramas – should not portray facts, events, individuals or organisations in a way which is unfair to an individual or organisation.

7.11 If a programme alleges wrongdoing or incompetence or makes other significant allegations, those concerned should normally be given an appropriate and timely opportunity to respond.

7.12 Where a person approached to contribute to a programme chooses to make no comment or refuses to appear in a broadcast, the broadcast should make clear that the individual concerned has chosen not to appear and should give their explanation if it would be unfair not to do so.

7.13 Where it is appropriate to represent the views of a person or organisation that is not participating in the programme, this must be done in a fair manner.

Deception, set-ups and 'wind-up' calls

7.14 Broadcasters or programme makers should not normally obtain or seek information, audio, pictures or an agreement to contribute through misrepresentation or deception. (Deception includes surreptitious filming or recording.) However:

- it may be warranted to use material obtained through misrepresentation or deception without consent if it is in the public interest and cannot reasonably be obtained by other means;
- where there is no adequate public interest justification, for example some unsolicited wind-up calls or entertainment set-ups, consent should be obtained from the individual and/or organisation concerned before the material is broadcast;
- material involving celebrities and those in the public eye can be used without consent for broadcast, but it should not be used without a public interest justification if it is likely to result in unjustified public ridicule or personal distress. (Normally, therefore such contributions should be pre-recorded.)

Section 8: Privacy[34]

Principle: To ensure that broadcasters avoid any unwarranted infringement of privacy in programmes and in connection with obtaining material included in programmes.

Rule

8.1 Any infringement of privacy in programmes, or in connection with obtaining material included in programmes, must be warranted.

8.2 Information which discloses the location of a person's home or family should not be revealed without permission, unless it is warranted.

8.3 When people are caught up in events which are covered by the news they still have a right to privacy in both the making and the broadcast of a programme, unless it is warranted to infringe it. This applies both to the time when these events are taking place and to any later programmes that revisit those events.

---

34 Relevant legislation includes ss 3(2)(f) and 326 of the Communications Act 2003, ss 107(1) and 130 of the Broadcasting Act 1996 (as amended), Articles 8 and 10 ECHR and the BBC Charter and Agreement.

8.4   Broadcasters should ensure that words, images or actions filmed or recorded in, or broadcast from, a public place, are not so private that prior consent is required before broadcast from the individual or organisation concerned, unless broadcasting without their consent is warranted.

Consent

8.5   Any infringement of privacy in the making of a programme should be with the person's and/or organisation's consent or be otherwise warranted.

8.6   If the broadcast of a programme would infringe the privacy of a person or organisation, consent should be obtained before the relevant material is broadcast, unless the infringement of privacy is warranted. (Callers to phone-in shows are deemed to have given consent to the broadcast of their contribution.)

8.7   If an individual or organisation's privacy is being infringed, and they ask that the filming, recording or live broadcast be stopped, the broadcaster should do so, unless it is warranted to continue.

8.8   When filming or recording in institutions, organisations or other agencies, permission should be obtained from the relevant authority or management, unless it is warranted to film or record without permission. Individual consent of employees or others whose appearance is incidental or where they are essentially anonymous members of the general public will not normally be required.

- However, in potentially sensitive places such as ambulances, hospitals, schools, prisons or police stations, separate consent should normally be obtained before filming or recording and for broadcast from those in sensitive situations (unless not obtaining consent is warranted). If the individual will not be identifiable in the programme then separate consent for broadcast will not be required.

Gathering information, sound or images and the re-use of material

8.9   The means of obtaining material must be proportionate in all the circumstances and in particular to the subject matter of the programme.

8.10   Broadcasters should ensure that the re-use of material, i.e. use of material originally filmed or recorded for one purpose and then used in a programme for another purpose or used in a later or different programme, does not create an unwarranted infringement of privacy. This applies both to material obtained from others and the broadcaster's own material.

8.11   Doorstepping[35] for factual programmes should not take place unless a request for an interview has been refused or it has not been possible to request an interview, or there is good reason to believe that an investigation will be frustrated if the subject is approached openly, and it is warranted to doorstep. However, normally broadcasters may, without prior warning interview, film or record people in the news when in public places.

---

35 Doorstepping is the filming or recording of an interview or attempted interview with someone, or announcing that a call is being filmed or recorded for broadcast purposes, without any prior warning. It does not, however, include vox-pops (sampling the views of random members of the public).

8.12 Broadcasters can record telephone calls between the broadcaster and the other party if they have, from the outset of the call, identified themselves, explained the purpose of the call and that the call is being recorded for possible broadcast (if that is the case) unless it is warranted not to do one or more of these practices. If at a later stage it becomes clear that a call that has been recorded will be broadcast (but this was not explained to the other party at the time of the call) then the broadcaster must obtain consent before broadcast from the other party, unless it is warranted not to do so.

8.13 Surreptitious filming[36] or recording should only be used where it is warranted. Normally, it will only be warranted if:

- there is *prima facie* evidence of a story in the public interest; and
- there are reasonable grounds to suspect that further material evidence could be obtained; and
- it is necessary to the credibility and authenticity of the programme.

8.14 Material gained by surreptitious filming and recording should only be broadcast when it is warranted.

8.15 Surreptitious filming or recording, doorstepping or recorded 'wind-up' calls to obtain material for entertainment purposes may be warranted if it is intrinsic to the entertainment and does not amount to a significant infringement of privacy such as to cause significant annoyance, distress or embarrassment.

The resulting material should not be broadcast without the consent of those involved. However if the individual and/or organisation is not identifiable in the programme then consent for broadcast will not be required.

Suffering and distress

8.16 Broadcasters should not take or broadcast footage or audio of people caught up in emergencies, victims of accidents or those suffering a personal tragedy, even in a public place, where that results in an infringement of privacy, unless it is warranted or the people concerned have given consent.

8.17 People in a state of distress should not be put under pressure to take part in a programme or provide interviews, unless it is warranted.

8.18 Broadcasters should take care not to reveal the identity of a person who has died or of victims of accidents or violent crimes, unless and until it is clear that the next of kin have been informed of the event or unless it is warranted.

8.19 Broadcasters should try to reduce the potential distress to victims and/or relatives when making or broadcasting programmes intended to examine past events that involve trauma to individuals (including crime) unless it is warranted to do otherwise. This applies to dramatic reconstructions and factual dramas, as well as factual programmes.

---

36 Surreptitious filming or recording includes the use of long lenses or recording devices, as well as leaving an unattended camera or recording device on private property without the full and informed consent of the occupiers or their agent. It may also include recording telephone conversations without the knowledge of the other party or deliberately continuing a recording when the other party thinks that it has come to an end.

- In particular, so far as is reasonably practicable, surviving victims and/or the immediate families of those whose experience is to feature in a programme, should be informed of the plans for the programme and its intended broadcast, even if the events or material to be broadcast have been in the public domain in the past.

People under sixteen and vulnerable people

8.20 Broadcasters should pay particular attention to the privacy of people under sixteen. They do not lose their rights to privacy because, for example, of the fame or notoriety of their parents or because of events in their schools.

8.21 Where a programme features an individual under sixteen or a vulnerable person in a way that infringes privacy, consent must be obtained from:

- a parent, guardian or other person of eighteen or over in loco parentis; and
- wherever possible, the individual concerned;
- unless the subject matter is trivial or uncontroversial and the participation minor, or it is warranted to proceed without consent.

8.22 Persons under sixteen and vulnerable people should not be questioned about private matters without the consent of a parent, guardian or other person of eighteen or over in loco parentis (in the case of persons under sixteen), or a person with primary responsibility for their care (in the case of a vulnerable person), unless it is warranted to proceed without consent.

Section 9: Commercial references in television programming[37]

Principles:

To ensure that broadcasters maintain editorial independence and control over programming (editorial independence).

To ensure that there is distinction between editorial content and advertising (distinction).

To protect audiences from surreptitious advertising (transparency).

To ensure that audiences are protected from the risk of financial harm (consumer protection).

To ensure that unsuitable sponsorship is prevented (unsuitable sponsorship).

Rules

9.1 Broadcasters must maintain independent editorial control over programming.

9.2 Broadcasters must ensure that editorial content is distinct from advertising.

9.3 Surreptitious advertising is prohibited.

9.4 Products, services and trade marks must not be promoted in programming.

---

37 Relevant legislation includes ss 319(2)(f)(a), (i) and (j) and 319(4)(a), (c), (e) and (f), section 321(1) and (4) and section 324(3) of the Communications Act 2003; section 202 of the Broadcasting Act 1990 (paragraph 3 in Part 1 of Schedule 2), Articles 9, 10, 11, and Chapter VII (Articles 19 to 26) of the Audiovisual Media Services Directive; regulation 3(4)(d) of the Consumer Protection From Unfair Trading Regulations 2008; section 21(1) of the Financial Services and Markets Act 2000; paragraph 3 of the Investment Recommendation (Media) Regulations Act 2005; Article 10 ECHR and the BBC Charter and Agreement.

9.5   No undue prominence may be given in programming to a product, service or trade mark. Undue prominence may result from:

●   the presence of, or reference to, a product, service or trade mark in programming where there is no editorial justification; or

●   the manner in which a product, service or trade mark appears or is referred to in programming.

Product placement[38] (and prop placement[39])

9.6   Product placement is prohibited except in the following programme genres:

a)   films;

b)   series made for television (or other audiovisual media services);

c)   sports programmes; and

d)   light entertainment programmes.

9.7   Programmes that fall within the permitted genres must not contain product placement if they are:

a)   news programmes; or

b)   children's programmes.

9.8   Product placement must not influence the content and scheduling of a programme in a way that affects the responsibility and editorial independence of the broadcaster.

9.9   References to placed products, services and trade marks must not be promotional.

9.10 References to placed products, services and trade marks must not be unduly prominent.

9.11 The product placement of the following products, services or trade marks is prohibited:

a)   cigarettes or other tobacco products;

b)   placement by or on behalf of an undertaking whose principal activity is the manufacture or sale of cigarettes or other tobacco products;

c)   prescription-only medicines; or

d)   electronic cigarettes or refill containers.

9.12 Product placement is not permitted in the following:

a)   religious programmes;

---

38 The inclusion in a programme of, or of a reference to, a product, service or trade mark where the inclusion is for a commercial purpose, and is in return for the making of any payment, or the giving of other valuable consideration, to any relevant provider or any person connected with a relevant provider, and is not prop placement.

39 The inclusion in a programme of, or of a reference to, a product, service or trade mark where the provision of the product, service or trade mark has no significant value, and no relevant provider, or person connected with a relevant provider, has received any payment or other valuable consideration in relation to its inclusion in, or the reference to it in, the programme, disregarding the costs saved by including the product, service or trade mark, or a reference to it, in the programme.

b)   consumer advice programmes; or

c)   current affairs programmes.

9.13   The product placement of the following is prohibited:

a)   alcoholic drinks;

b)   foods or drinks high in fat, salt or sugar;

c)   gambling;

d)   infant formula (baby milk), including follow-on formula;

e)   all medicinal products

f)   cigarette lighters, cigarette papers, or pipes intended for smoking; or

g)   any product, service or trade mark that is not allowed to be advertised on television.

9.14   Product placement must be signalled clearly, by means of a universal neutral logo, as follows:

See below 8.7

a)   at the beginning of the programme in which the placement appears;

b)   when the programme recommences after commercial breaks; and

c)   at the end of the programme.

Sponsorship

Content that may not be sponsored

9.15   News and current affairs programmes must not be sponsored.

Prohibited and restricted sponsors

9.16   Programming (including a channel) may not be sponsored by any sponsor that is prohibited from advertising on television. This rule does not apply to electronic cigarettes and refill containers which are subject to Rule 9.16(a).

a)   Sponsored programming with the aim or direct or indirect effect of promoting electronic cigarettes and/or refill containers is prohibited.

9.17   Sponsorship must comply with both the content and scheduling rules that apply to television advertising.

Content of sponsored output

9.18   A sponsor must not influence the content and/or scheduling of a channel or programming in such a way as to impair the responsibility and editorial independence of the broadcaster.

Sponsorship credits

9.19   Sponsorship must be clearly identified by means of sponsorship credits. These must make clear:

a)   the identity of the sponsor by reference to its name or trade mark; and

b)   the association between the sponsor and the sponsored content.

9.20   For sponsored programmes, credits must be broadcast at the beginning and/or during and/or end of the programme.

9.21 Sponsorship credits must be distinct from editorial content.

9.22 Sponsorship credits must be distinct from advertising. In particular:

   a)   Sponsorship credits broadcast *around sponsored programmes* must not contain advertis-
        ing messages or calls to action. Credits must not encourage the purchase or
        rental of the products or services of the sponsor or a third party. The focus of
        the credit must be the sponsorship arrangement itself. Such credits may include
        explicit reference to the sponsor's products, services or trade marks for the sole
        purpose of helping to identify the sponsor and/or the sponsorship
        arrangement.

   b)   Sponsorship credits broadcast *during programmes* must not be unduly prominent.
        Such credits must consist of a brief, neutral visual or verbal statement iden-
        tifying the sponsorship arrangement. This can be accompanied by only a
        graphic of the name, logo, or any other distinctive symbol of the sponsor.
        The content of the graphic must be static and must contain no advertising
        messages, calls to action or any other information about the sponsor, its
        products, services or trade marks.

9.23 Where a sponsor is prohibited from product placing in the programme it is spon-
     soring, sponsorship credits may not be shown during the sponsored
     programme.

9.24 Where a sponsorship credit is included in a programme trail, the credit must
     remain brief and secondary.

9.25 Programme-related material may be sponsored and the sponsor may be credited
     when details of how to obtain the material are given. Any credit must be brief
     and secondary, and must be separate from any credit for the programme
     sponsor.

Use of Controlled Premium Rate Services[40]

9.26 Where a broadcaster invites viewers to take part in or otherwise interact with its
     programmes, it may only charge for such participation or interaction by means
     of controlled premium rate telephone services or other telephony services for
     which the revenue generated is shared between relevant parties.

9.27 Controlled premium rate telephony services will normally be regarded as products
     or services, and must therefore not appear in programmes, except where:

   a)   they enable viewers to participate directly in or otherwise contribute directly
        to the editorial content of the programme; or

   b)   they fall within the meaning of programme-related material.

9.28 Where a controlled premium rate telephony service is featured in a programme,
     the primary purpose of the programme must continue to be clearly editorial.
     Promotion of the featured service must be clearly subsidiary to that primary
     purpose.

9.29 Any use of controlled premium rate telephone numbers must comply with the
     Code of Practice issued by PhonepayPlus.

---

40 Controlled Premium Rate Services are a subset of Premium Rate Services which are regulated by PhonepayPlus.

Non-geographic call costs

9.30 The cost to viewers for using non-geographic telephony services must be made clear to them and broadcast as appropriate.

Programme-related material (PRM)

9.31 Programme-related material may be promoted only during or around the programme from which it is directly derived and only where it is editorially justified.

9.32 The broadcaster must retain responsibility for ensuring the appropriateness of promoting programme-related material.

Charity appeals

9.33 Charity appeals that are broadcast free of charge are allowed in programming provided that the broadcaster has taken reasonable steps to satisfy itself that:

a) the organisation concerned can produce satisfactory evidence of charitable status, or, in the case of an emergency appeal, that a responsible public fund has been set up to deal with it; and

b) the organisation concerned is not prohibited from advertising on television.

9.34 Where possible, the broadcast of charity appeals, either individually or taken together over time, should benefit a wide range of charities.

Financial promotions and investment recommendations

9.35 When broadcasting financial promotions and investment recommendations broadcasters must comply with the relevant provisions in Appendix 4 to this Code.

Appeals for funds for programming or services

9.36 Viewers must be told the purpose of the appeal and how much it raises.

9.37 All donations must be separately accounted for and used for the purpose for which they were donated.

9.38 Broadcasters must not offer any additional benefits or other incentives to donors.

9.39 Appeals for funds for programming or services must not be given undue prominence in relation to the overall output of the service.

Section 10: Commercial communications in radio programming[41]

Principle: To ensure the transparency of commercial communications as a means to secure consumer protection.

---

41 Relevant legislation includes ss 319(2)(f), (i) and (j), 319(4)(e) and (f) and 321 of the Communications Act 2003, regulation 3(4)(d) of the Consumer Protection From Unfair Trading Regulations 2008, section 21(1) of the Financial Services and Markets Act 2000, paragraph 3 of the Investment Recommendation (Media) Regulations Act 2005, Article 10 ECHR and the BBC Charter and Agreement.

Rules

10.1 Programming that is subject to, or associated with, a commercial arrangement must be appropriately signalled, so as to ensure that the commercial arrangement is transparent to listeners.

10.2 Spot advertisements must be clearly separated from programming.

10.3 No commercial reference, or material that implies a commercial arrangement, is permitted in or around news bulletins or news desk presentations.

This rule does not apply to:

- reference to a news supplier for the purpose of identifying that supplier as a news source;
- specialist factual strands that are not news bulletins or news desk presentations, but may be featured in or around such programming;
- the use of premium rate services (e.g. for station/broadcaster surveys); and
- references that promote the station/broadcaster's own products and/or services (e.g. the programme/station/broadcaster's website or a station/broadcaster's event).

10.4 No commercial reference, or material that implies a commercial arrangement, is permitted on radio services primarily aimed at children or in children's programming included in any service.

This rule does not apply to:

- credits for third party association with either programming or broadcast competition prize donation;
- the use of premium rate services (e.g. for broadcast competition entry); and
- references that promote the station/broadcaster's own products and/or services (e.g. the programme/station/broadcaster's website or a station/broadcaster's event).

10.5 No commercial arrangement that involves payment, or the provision of some other valuable consideration, to the broadcaster may influence the selection or rotation of music for broadcast.

10.6 No programming may be subject to a commercial arrangement with a third party that is prohibited from advertising on radio. This rule does not apply to electronic cigarettes and refill containers which are subject to Rule 10.6(a).

(a) Sponsored programming with the aim or direct or indirect effect of promoting electronic cigarettes and/or refill containers is prohibited.

10.7 Commercial references in programming must comply with the advertising content and scheduling rules that apply to radio broadcasting.

10.8 Commercial references that require confirmation or substantiation prior to broadcast must be cleared for broadcast in the same way as advertisements.

Controlled Premium Rate and similar services

10.9 Any use of controlled premium rate telephony services in programming must comply with the Code of Practice and any additional broadcast-related requirements issued by PhonepayPlus.

10.10 The cost to listeners for using controlled premium rate telephony services, or other communications services for which the revenue generated is shared between relevant parties, must be made clear to them and broadcast as appropriate.

Charity appeals

10.11 Fund-raising activity broadcast on behalf of a charity (or emergency appeal) is only permitted if:

- it is broadcast free of charge;
- it does not contain any commercial reference that is subject to a commercial arrangement with the relevant charity (or emergency appeal); and
- the broadcaster has taken reasonable steps to satisfy itself that:
  - the organisation concerned can produce satisfactory evidence of charitable status, or, in the case of an emergency appeal, that a responsible public fund has been set up to deal with it; and
  - the organisation concerned is not prohibited from advertising on radio.

Appeals for funds for programming or services

10.12 Broadcasters may broadcast appeals for donations to make programming or fund their service. Listeners must be told the purpose of the appeal and how much it raises. All donations must be separately accounted for and used for the purpose for which they were donated.

Financial promotions and investment recommendations

10.13 When broadcasting financial promotions and investment recommendations broadcasters must comply with the relevant provisions in Appendix 4 to this Code.

8.4.2 Co-regulation: the BBC, Ofcom and ATVOD

Until the BBC Charter Review in 2016, there existed a degree of uncertainty of overlap of jurisdiction between the BBC Trust and Ofcom. It was unclear whom viewers and listeners could complain to or seek redress from. For example, in cases of 'TV-like' VoD services, complaints about programmes accessed online via BBC iPlayer could be raised with either the BBC or with Ofcom. But, if a BBC iPlayer programme was accessed on another platform (e.g. via Virgin Media or BT Vision), the complaint had to first be raised directly with the BBC. Only once this process had been exhausted could the complainant go directly to the Authority for Video On Demand (ATVOD) since that regulator operated under a 'broadcaster first' system of regulation.[42]

---

42 Section 2, Memorandum of Understanding between the Office of Communications (Ofcom) and the BBC Trust, March 2007.

The Authority for Television on Demand (ATVOD) was an industry body designated by Ofcom as the 'co-regulator' of video-on-demand services (VOD). ATVOD – formerly the Association for Television On-Demand – had originally been created as a self-regulatory industry body with the support and encouragement of the government in 2007. As EU legislation in this sphere increased, ATVOD was founded following the EU Directive on the regulation of audiovisual media ('the Audiovisual Media Services Directive' 2007/65/EU).[43] ATVOD was responsible for regulating on-demand services such as ITV Player and Channel 4's More Four, as well as paid-for content on websites which were deemed to be 'TV-like'. On 31 December 2015 all these regulatory functions were taken over by Ofcom. This arrangement was given legal force when the UK Parliament passed the Audiovisual Media Services Regulations 2010 which came into force on 18 March 2010. The Communications Act 2003 was further revised giving ATVOD greater enforcement powers in relation to VOD services. Minimum editorial and advertising standards were drawn up and published and became part of the Ofcom Code (see above).

However, neither Ofcom nor ATVOD had any jurisdiction over BBC 'non-TV like' online content; so, any complaints made about the BBC website had to be made directly to the BBC. Likewise, complaints about BBC radio programmes listened to online via iPlayer Radio had to be made directly to the BBC and could not be appealed to either Ofcom or ATVOD.

From April 2017 with the new BBC Charter and Agreement, Ofcom became the first independent regulator responsible for the content standards of the BBC's television, radio and on-demand programmes. Ofcom also became responsible for the regulation of the BBC's competitive and commercial services (such as BBC World and BBC Studioworks).

The unitary BBC Board continues to be responsible for governing and running the Corporation, and the BBC also handles complaints about its contents in the first instance, with Ofcom overseeing that process and handling appeals through a transparent process. The National Audit Office is responsible for ensuring the BBC delivers value for money, while the Royal Charter and the BBC licence fee remain matters for government.

8.4.3 Ofcom's statutory enforcement powers

Where the Code has been breached, Ofcom will normally publish a finding and explain why a broadcaster has breached the Code. When a broadcaster breaches the Code deliberately, seriously, repeatedly or recklessly, Ofcom may impose statutory sanctions against the broadcaster; this can include a fine or losing the licence to the service.

As a statutory regulator, Ofcom takes enforcement action across a number of industry sectors and is able to use a range of statutory powers granted by the various statutes mentioned above.

See above 8.4

Section 392(6) of the Communications Act 2003 gives Ofcom the power to punish breaches of the Code and impose penalties as it sees fit. Before determining how to publish, the regulator must consult the Secretary of State.

---

43 Directive 2007/65/EC on the Audiovisual Media Services Directive amended EU Directive 89/552/EEC Television Without Frontiers Directive Directive 1989 (89/552/EEC) and includes the all TV-like and video-on-demand services (VOD).

One such example is that in July 2015, Ofcom imposed a £1m fine on EE, Britain's biggest mobile phone operator at the time, for misleading customers who made complaints. The company which had been bought by BT did not tell some of its 27 million customers that their complaint could be decided by an independent adjudicator. EE, whose brands included Orange and T-Mobile, sent letters to customers that did not inform them of their right to take a complaint to alternative dispute resolution (ADR) after eight weeks. Ofcom's investigation into EE's complaints handling between July 2011 and April 2014 found that EE had failed to give certain dissatisfied customers correct or adequate information about their rights. The fine was Ofcom's largest penalty for poor complaints handling in any industry and the regulator's fifth biggest overall.[44]

8.4.4 Ofcom adjudications and decisions

In 2018, *Celebrity Big Brother* was once again the television programme that attracted most viewer complaints to Ofcom, followed by *Loose Women* and *Sky News*. During 2018, Ofcom received almost 56,000 complaints about programmes from viewers and listeners. Following investigations, the watchdog found that its broadcasting rules had been broken in 80 cases in 2018.[45]

The 'top 10' programmes which attracted the most complaints to Ofcom in 2018 were:

1. Celebrity Big Brother: 27,602
2. Loose Women: 8,002
3. Sky News: 4,251
4. Love Island: 4,192
5. Coronation Street: 1,098
6. Emmerdale: 759
7. Good Morning Britain: 548
8. This Morning: 402
9. I'm a Celebrity . . . Get Me Out of Here!: 335
10. The X Factor: 286

Key issues prompting audience complaints about the top 10 programmes in 2018:

- **Celebrity Big Brother: 27,602 complaints** (of which 25,327 related to the incident involving Roxanne and Ryan (30, 31 Aug and 1 Sept 2018); and 1,101 related to Rodrigo Alves using a racial slur (17 Aug 2018)).
- **Loose Women: 8,002 complaints** (of which 7,912 related to an interview with guest Kim Woodburn which resulted in her walking off set (29 Aug 2018)).

---

44 Source: 'EE fined £1m by Ofcom for misleading customers', by Sean Farrell, *Guardian*, 3 July 2015.
45 Ofcom News Update, 'Most complained about TV programmes of 2018', 27 December 2018: www.ofcom.org. uk/about-ofcom/latest/media/media-releases/2018/most-complained-about-tv-programmes-of-2018.

- *Sky News*: **4,251 complaints** (of which 3,462 alleged bias in the editing of Tommy Robinson in an interview (27 Sept 2018); and 592 related to comments by Kay Burley comparing Simon Weston's injuries to a woman wearing a burqa (7 Aug 2018)).
- *Love Island*: **4,192 complaints** (of which 2,644 related to Dani Dyer's reaction when shown a video of boyfriend Jack reacting to his former partner entering Casa Amour (1 July 2018); 632 raised concerns about the emotional well-being of contestant, Laura Anderson (10 July); and 540 related to perceived unfair editing of contestant, Samira Mighty (12 July 2018)).
- *Coronation Street*: **1,098 complaints** (of which 214 related to the storyline involving the date-rape of David Platt and its aftermath (16,19 March 2018); 211 related to Billy Mayhew taking drugs in a church (26 Feb); and 95 related to Pat Phelan's murder of Luke Britton (5 Jan 2018)).
- *Emmerdale*: **759 complaints** (of which 366 complaints related to an acid attack storyline (8 Feb 2018); and 116 related to the murder of Gerry Roberts (17 May 2018)).
- *Good Morning Britain*: **548 complaints** (of which 86 considered that Piers Morgan displayed bias in favour of President Trump during an interview with Ash Sarkar (12 July 2018); and 74 related to Adil Ray's introduction of the show as 'Good Morning Asian Britain' (13 August 2018)).
- *This Morning*: **402 complaints** (of which 133 raised concerns that a guest who featured in a segment about breastfeeding was not sufficiently expert (12 Sept 2018); and 30 related to a discussion about donor breastmilk which complainants considered did not support breastfeeding and promoted formula milk (12 Apr 2018)).
- *I'm a Celebrity . . . Get Me Out of Here: 335:* The majority of these complaints (180) related to the use of animals in Bushtucker trials.
- *The X Factor*: **286 complaints** (of which 104 related to Cheryl's routine (18 Nov 2018); and 95 related to sound issues affecting the performances of Danny Tetley and Anthony Russell (3 Nov 2018)).

Ofcom is responsible for securing standards on television and radio to protect audiences from harm. Each complaint made to Ofcom is carefully assessed against our broadcasting rules to determine whether further action against the broadcaster might be necessary. Upon the receipt of a complaint, Ofcom will follow a procedure where it investigates cases and applies statutory sanctions to broadcasters where the Code has been breached. When a broadcaster breaches the Code deliberately, seriously or repeatedly, Ofcom may impose statutory sanctions against the broadcaster. Where the Ofcom Broadcasting Code has been breached, the regulator will normally publish a finding and explain why a broadcaster has breached the Code. Here follow a few examples of broadcast standards cases[46] which were in breach (or not) of the Code.

---

46 Note: these are not legally reported cases (i.e. law reports) but are to be found on the Ofcom website under its adjudications.

The George Galloway ruling of January 2019 (below) concerned a live chat show on 'Talk Radio' in which the former MP for Glasgow Hillhead discussed the Salisbury poisoning and attempted murder of Yulia and Sergei Skripal in March 2018 on live radio. The Ofcom ruling followed shortly after the regulator announced in December 2018 that the RT news channel – formerly Russia Today – had not been impartial in seven of its news and current affairs programmes aired in the UK over a six-week period following the Skripals' attack. The seven RT breaches took place over six weeks between 17 March and 26 April.[47]

See below
8.4.6

❖ KEY CASE   George Galloway

Talk Radio, 16 March 2018, 19:00
- ❖ **Breach of Rule 5.11** ('due impartiality must be preserved on matters of major political and industrial controversy')
- ❖ **Breach of Rule 5.12** ('an appropriately wide range of significant views must be included and given due weight in each programme')

Introduction and background
Talk Radio is a national digital speech radio station, the licence for which is held by TalkSport Ltd. The *George Galloway* programme is typically broadcast on Fridays between 19:00 and 22:00. A complainant alleged the programme on 16 March 2018 contained 'biased and unbalanced views' about the response of the UK and Russian governments to the poisoning of Yulia and Sergei Skripal in Salisbury on 4 March 2018.

The three-hour programme aired on 16 March 2018 – 12 days after the for-mer Russian double agent and his daughter were discovered unconscious on a bench in Salisbury, having been poisoned with the nerve agent Novichok. A UK investigation blamed Russia for the attack, and sanctions were placed on the country as a result – with many allies following the UK's lead, including the US. But the Kremlin denied any involvement.

After questioning Russia's culpability and saying the county was 'the least likely suspect of them all', Mr Galloway then spoke to a number of listeners, most of whom agreed with his point of view. When, on three occasions, listeners dis-agreed with his view, Mr Galloway joked that they had sent their messages from Broadmoor psychiatric hospital. During his chat show Mr Galloway acknowl-edged that Russia was capable of committing a crime such as poisoning of Yulia and Sergei Skripal but queried Russia's culpability in this case. At about 19.25 he said:

> And it's not that I'm saying that Russia would not, could not carry out such a crime. Russia has carried out many such crimes. I'm not saying

---

47 Issue 369 of Ofcom's Broadcast and On Demand Bulletin 20 December 2018.

the Russian intelligence services are above such a crime. They have committed many such crimes, just like every other intelligence agency in the world, including – and perhaps particularly – our own. Don't get me started on intelligence services. The question is 'Why?' 'Why would Putin – who is personally, overwhelmingly likely responsible, said the clown Boris Johnson, who is in charge of our foreign affairs – Putin, Why?'

The regulator requested comments from the Licensee (Talk Radio and therein TalkSport) that the programme had not complied with the Ofcom Broadcasting Code Rules 5.11 and 5.12 regarding impartiality.

The Licensee's Response (TalkSport)

TalkSport described Mr Galloway as a 'national figure known for his controversial views which would not come as a surprise to listeners'. It added that the 'majority of listeners are familiar with his reputation as well as the format of his "personal view" phone-in programmes . . . and would be comfortable with adjusting their expectations of due impartiality'. The Licensee also described Mr Galloway as 'famous for holding highly partial opinions that are anything but mainstream and are more often than not at odds with the majority of his fellow presenters on Talk Radio'. TalkSport said it was 'reasonable to suggest the government's view on who was responsible for the Skripal poisoning was universally known to Talk Radio listeners at the time of the broadcast', and 'it was merely the Government's strong opinion of what happened, not a matter of policy'.

The Licensee acknowledged that Mr Galloway's 'introduction against the Government's position on the Skripal-Novichok affair went unchallenged' but considered it 'reasonable to assume that Galloway's colourful critique would be regarded by listeners as a highly opinionated personal-view attack by Galloway that did not require a formal rebuttal'. TalkSport was also of the view that Mr Galloway's comments were largely 'questioning the calibre of those in power and their comments . . . rather than major matters of government policy'. It also considered that, rather than 'attacking government policy or action', Mr Galloway was 'putting forward a number of hypotheses as to who was responsible for the Skripal poisoning'. By way of example of a balanced programme output, TalkSport told Ofcom that the breakfast programme, presented by Julia Hartley-Brewer, broadcast on the same day – 16 March 2018 – included four guests who discussed the Skripal poisoning and expressed support for the government's handling of the crisis.

TalkSport defended Mr Galloway's right to broadcast his opinions without interference, as well as its overall approach to complying with due impartiality requirements across the radio station. However, it accepted that perhaps on this occasion, there had not been enough lively debate provided by either listeners or guests to challenge Mr Galloway's views within the programme itself.

Response from George Galloway

Mr Galloway told Ofcom that he did not merely welcome alternative views to his programme but relished them, and when listeners with alternative views were included in his programme he treated them respectfully and listened to them at length without interruption. In conclusion, Mr Galloway described the regulator's investigation as a 'transparently politically motivated attempt at censorship', which had 'already received its intended result', namely the partial stifling of his 'lone voice on the airwaves'.

Decision

Ofcom considered that this programme had been dealing with a matter of major political controversy and major matter relating to current public policy, namely, the policies and actions of the UK and Russian authorities, concerning the poisoning of Sergei and Yulia Skripal in March 2018. It its ruling, Ofcom said that TalkSport had failed to include and give due weight to an appropriately wide range of significant viewpoints in relation to the relevant matters of major political controversy and major matters relating to current public policy dealt with in the programme.

Ofcom stated that it had taken the broadcaster's right to freedom of expression into account when making its decision, as set out in Article 10(1) ECHR. At the same time, it established the audience's right to receive information and ideas without interference (referring to *Lingens v Austria* (1986)[48]. It applies not only to the content of information but also to the means of transmission or reception (referring to *Autronic v Switzerland* (1990)[49]. The Ofcom ruling further stated that any interference must pursue a legitimate aim and be necessary in a democratic society (i.e. proportionate to the legitimate aim pursued and corresponding to a pressing social need) as outlined in Article 10(2) ECHR. Decisions of the European Court of Human Rights make clear that there is little scope for restrictions on freedom of expression in two fields, namely political speech and on matters of public interest. Accordingly, a high level of protection of freedom of expression will normally be accorded, with the authorities having a particularly narrow margin of appreciation.

Ofcom ruled that George Galloway's radio show seriously breached impartiality rules, namely Rules 5.11 and 5.12 of the Ofcom Code. Ofcom stated that the majority of comments from Mr Galloway and his listeners were highly critical of the government, while the small number of opposite views were treated dismissively.

Analysis

In passing the Communications Act 2003, Parliament set out in legislation the restrictions prescribed by law necessary in a democratic society – these have

---

48 (1986) 8 EHRR 407 (EctHR).
49 12 EHRR 485 (ECtHR).

been adhered to by Ofcom in its Code. The statutory framework set by Parliament specifically assigns an area of judgment, to be exercised by Ofcom, as to how the requirements of the legislation are to be applied to the facts of each case. As envisaged by section 320 of the Act – which is given effect by Rules 5.11 and 5.12 of the Ofcom Code – a broadcaster must maintain an adequate and appropriate level of impartiality in its presentation of matters of major political controversy, including times when it is being critical of a nation state's policies and actions on a major matter. How this is done is an editorial matter for the broadcaster.

The Ofcom Code makes clear that the approach to due impartiality (Section 5) may vary according to the nature of the subject, the type of programme and channel, the likely expectation of the audience as to content and the extent to which the content and approach is signalled to the audience. In addition, context, as set out in Section 2 (Harm and Offence) of the Code is important in preserving due impartiality. Context includes a number of factors such as the editorial content of the programme, the service on which the material is broadcast, the likely size, composition and expectation of the audience and the effect on viewers who may come across the programme unawares.

As highlighted in Ofcom's Guidance on Section 5 of the Code, the broadcasting of highly critical comments concerning the policies and actions of, for example, any one state or institution, is not in itself a breach of due impartiality rules. It is essential that current affairs programmes are able to explore and examine issues and take a position even if that is highly critical.

In order to reach a decision on whether due impartiality was maintained in the *George Galloway* radio programme, Ofcom stated it had careful regard to the Article 10 rights and relevant contextual factors. Given the nature and amount of criticism of it in the programme and taking into account that the programme was dealing with a matter of major political controversy, it could have been reasonably expected that the viewpoint of the UK government on the Skripal incident be appropriately reflected.[50]

Following its ruling, Ofcom was considering whether to impose a statutory sanction over the breach, which could include a fine.

Another Ofcom investigation included the use of offensive language in Jeremy Vine's Channel 5 TV show.[51] Broadcaster Anne Diamond was filling in for Vine on

---

50 Ofcom's Code (2017) explains that 'significant views' can include the viewpoint of nation states whose policies are considered to be 'major matters'.
51 Jeremy Vine, Channel 5, 24 October 2018, 09:15, Issue 371 of Ofcom's Broadcast and On Demand Bulletin 28 January 2019.

24 October 2018 during the morning show, when a caller suddenly used the c-word to verbally attack her live on-air. The word was used by the telephone caller, identified as 'Chris', just after 10.30am. Diamond apologized to viewers twice 'for that creeping in on air'. A viewer alerted Ofcom to offensive language in the programme during a discussion around oversharing on social media.

The regulator considered the material raised potential issues under Rule 1.14 of the Code which states that the most offensive language must not be broadcast before the watershed on television. Ofcom's 2016 research[52] on offensive language clearly indicates that the word 'c**t' is considered by audiences to be amongst the most offensive language. The inclusion of the word in this programme at 10:33 was therefore a clear example of the most offensive language being broadcast before the watershed. Programmes which feature live interaction with viewers carry an increased risk of offensive language being used on air, and broadcasters should have procedures in place to minimise the risk, as far as practicable.

In the Jeremy Vine case Ofcom took into account that the Licensee (ITN) had taken a number of measures in advance to minimize the risk of offensive language being broadcast. While it was unfortunate that the software system did not identify the caller's number, steps had been taken by ITN to minimize further the risk of offensive language being broadcast in future. In light of these factors, Ofcom's decision was that this matter had been resolved.

In the ruling on *Lokkho Praner Sur*,[53] a talent show for young contestants on TV ONE, the licensee, Light Upon Light Media Limited, was found in breach of Rule 9.5: 'No undue prominence may be given in programming to a product, service or trade mark'. TV ONE is a general entertainment channel aimed at the Muslim community in the UK.

Ofcom had received a complaint that the programme on 11 July 2018 had contained several visual references to the fruit juice manufacturer 'Shezan'[54] as the young contestants had performed religious-themed songs for a panel of judges. Logos for Shezan and the product Shezan Mango were situated on the talent judges' desks and in various locations around the stage area. Although sometimes obscured by on-screen graphics, these logos were clearly visible to viewers on many occasions throughout the programme.

Rule 9.5 requires that references to products, services or trade marks in programming must not be unduly prominent. In this case, there were several visual references to Shezan and Shezan Mango during a singing contest. Given the circumstances, there did not appear to be any editorial justification for their inclusion in the programme. Ofcom accepted that the appearance of the logos occurred as a result of human error and acknowledged the Licensee's assurance that the error would not be repeated. However, Ofcom's decision was that the programme gave undue prominence to Shezan and Shezan Mango, in breach of Rule 9.5 of the Code.

---

52 On 30 September 2016, Ofcom published updated research in this area: 'Attitudes to potentially offensive language and gestures on television and on radio' at: www.ofcom.org.uk/__data/assets/pdf_file/0022/91624/OfcomOffensiveLanguage.pdf.

53 *Lokkho Praner Sur*, TV ONE, 11 July 2018, 13:00, Issue 371 of Ofcom's Broadcast and On Demand Bulletin, 28 January 2019.

54 Shezan International Ltd. is a Pakistani beverage manufacturer based in Lahore. It is the largest beverage company in Pakistan, part of Shahnawaz Group.

8.4.5 Judicial review and Ofcom

The ruling in *Ali v Channel 5* (2018)[55] is an important one. Arnold J did not only consider the balance between the programme makers' freedom of expression (Article 10 ECHR) and their advancing the public interest test, but also Mr Ali and Ms Aslam's Article 8 rights as well as the relevant Ofcom broadcasting privacy codes. The defendant broadcast was part of a popular Channel 5 TV series called *Can't Pay? We'll Take It Away*. This particular episode in April 2015 had been watched by 9.65 million viewers. The eviction was filmed by a television production company called Brinkworth Films Ltd which showed a landlord having obtained a High Court writ of possession and enforcement officers (bailiffs) attended the couple's property to evict the claimants. The first claimant, Shakir Ali, who was the voluntary media secretary of a Muslim political party, was awoken as they entered the property. He was given an hour to vacate. The second claimant, Shahida Aslam, had just returned after taking her children to school. The landlord's father, also in attendance during the filming, posted on social media two videos he had recorded of the eviction. The claimants' daughter subsequently suffered bullying at school. The claimants accepted that the writ was a public court order and that the defendant was entitled to broadcast the fact that they had been evicted, but contended that the programme included filming of them in their home, in distress and being taunted by the landlord's father in breach of their right to respect for private and family life under Article 8(1) ECHR.

 **KEY CASE**

Shakir Ali and Shahida Aslam v Channel 5 Broadcast Ltd [2018] EWHC 298 (Ch)

Precedent

- The 'ultimate balancing test' must be between the individuals' right to privacy (Art 8 ECHR) and the general public interest.
- Section 12(4)(b) HRA 1998 requires the court to have regard to any relevant privacy codes (including Ofcom) when Art 10 ECHR is at issue (the broadcaster's right to freedom of expression).
- Rule 8.1 of the Ofcom Code provides that any infringement of privacy in programmes, or in connection with obtaining material included in programmes, must be 'warranted'.

Facts

The legal challenge by the claimants Shakir Ali and Shahida Aslam concerned the Channel 5 TV series and reality show *Can't Pay? We'll Take It Away*. The episode complained of was a one-hour programme, featuring the eviction of the couple from their home they had been renting at 137 Fanshawe Avenue, Barking, Essex on 2 April 2015. The eviction was executed by 'High Court Enforcement Agents' enforcing a 'Writ of Possession' obtained

---

55 *Ali (Shakir) and Aslam (Shahida) v Channel 5 Broadcast Ltd* [2018] EWHC 298 (Ch).

by their landlord Rashid Ahmed. The programme showed shots of Mr Ali having just woken up, wearing pyjama bottoms and a vest, and shots of the couple's bedroom and their two children's rooms and of family possessions stored in bags. It also showed the landlord's son humiliating the couple, and revealed details including that the couple were unemployed and receiving housing benefit. The show was watched 9.6m times on Channel 5 channels over an 18-month period and resulted in the couple's daughter being bullied at school. The couple claimed they had a reasonable expectation of privacy under Art 8 ECHR. Channel 5 defended the filming tactics as in the public interest as the show addressed real-life issues including personal debt and the dependence of tenants on benefits and claimed viewing such scenes 'was the best way to engage the public and stimulate debate'. But the production notes on the 'story synopsis' showed capturing the drama of the eviction scene was the main focus.

Decision

Mr Justice Arnold allowed the claim by the couple and awarded £20,000 in damages (£10,000 each). Arnold J referred to the 'ultimate balancing test' between the individuals' right to privacy and the general public interest:

> I consider that the Claimants did have a reasonable expectation of privacy in respect of the information included in the Programme about which they complain. The justification relied upon by Channel 5 for interfering with the Claimants' Article 8 rights is that the Programme contributed to a debate of general interest. As I have explained, I accept that the Programme did contribute to a debate of general interest, but I consider the inclusion of the Claimants' private information went beyond what was justified for that purpose.[56]

In addition to the couple's right to privacy the judge also referred to the Ofcom Code and Ofcom adjudications.[57] Furthermore that s 12(4)(b) HRA 1998 required the court to have regard to any relevant privacy code when Art 10 ECHR is at issue (the broadcaster's right to freedom of expression). The relevant privacy code in force at the time of the first broadcast of the Programme was s 8 of the Ofcom Broadcasting Code of July 2015. Rule 8.1 of the Code provides that any infringement of privacy in programmes, or in connection with obtaining material included in programmes, must be 'warranted'.

Analysis

The court ruling in *Ali v Channel 5 TV* is an important one. The court found that the focus of the programme was not upon the matters of public interest, but upon the drama of the conflict between the landlord, the eviction agents ('bailiffs') and the claimants, a conflict which had been encouraged by the

---

56 Ibid. at para. 210 (Arnold J).
57 Ibid. at para. 207.

programme makers to make 'good television', resulting in the millions of viewings. The claimants' and their children's faces were not pixelated in the programme. The judge made the point that he did not find the programme in itself was materially unfair or inaccurate in its presentation of what happened during the eviction; but his ruling and justification relied upon by the claimants for restricting Channel 5's Article 10 rights was their right to respect for their private and family life and their home. Mr Justice Arnold awarded the couple £20,000 in damages (£10,000 each) for invasion of privacy.

The judgment in R (Traveller Movement) v Ofcom (2015)[58] contains an important ruling in relation to applications involving regulators and the non-adversarial procedure. In February 2015 Ouseley J dismissed a judicial review application brought against Ofcom by the Traveller Movement (TM), a charity supporting 300,000 gypsies and travellers. The charity had claimed that the Channel 4 broadcasts of Big Fat Gypsy Wedding and Thelma's Gypsy Girls had depicted children in a sexualized way, that the gypsy communities engaged in and endorsed violent sexual assaults of female children and young women and portrayed men and boys as feckless, violent and criminal as a cultural norm.

TM, the claimant charity, had made a complaint to Ofcom about the programmes in November 2013. The gist of the complaint was that the programmes, particularly Big Fat Gypsy Wedding, were unfair and portrayed Irish Traveller, English Traveller, Gypsy and Romany groups in a negative and racially stereotypical way. TM's lawyers argued on grounds of procedural unfairness and irrationality and that the regulator had acted unlawfully. TM specifically complained to Ofcom that the 'Standards' and 'Fairness' Codes had been breached. Ofcom found no breach of either Code.

TM's application for judicial review (at standing stage) included procedural impropriety, that Ofcom should have used its powers to seek further information to enable the regulator to reach a properly considered decision; that Ofcom acted irrationally in not accepting the extended assistance of the Equality and Human Rights Commission in considering the complaint; and that the decision not to accept TM's expert evidence as adequate evidence of harm was irrational. The charity also argued on grounds of unfairness that Ofcom's 'draft decision' had only been visible to one party (the broadcaster) but not to the complainant and that this was manifestly unfair.

Ouseley J rejected each of these grounds and held that it was not necessary in the interests of fairness for parties to have sight of a preliminary or provisional view of an adjudicatory body in order for its decision, or the process as a whole, to be fair. He ruled that a 'standards' complaint could be made by anyone, even by someone who had not seen the programme at all. By contrast, the broadcaster (here Channel 4) was directly affected by the outcome of the complaint and decision, and might face sanctions and financial penalties.

---

58 [2015] EWHC 406 (Admin).

In these circumstances, there was nothing unfair or irrational in the 'standards' complaint by the travellers' representatives nor was the procedure unfair for Ofcom to provide its preliminary view to the broadcaster but not to the complainant. Ofcom's counsel, Dinah Rose QC, told the judge that it was fully aware of the sensitivity of potentially racially negative stereotypes and had conducted a 'careful and painstaking' investigation before concluding that the programmes did not breach the broadcasting code.

The judge then agreed with Ofcom's decision that Channel 4 had not depicted such stereotypes but that the programmes were, in fact, a balanced portrayal which offered considerable insight into those communities, including the challenges they faced when dealing with prejudice.

The *Jon Gaunt* case also questioned an Ofcom decision, and therein challenged the Ofcom Broadcasting Code in relation to harmful and offensive broadcasts (here involving TalkSport radio).[59] Gaunt also argued that the Code breached his Article 10 ECHR right. The *Ken Livingstone* case[60] was cited in this case, where the judge said that Mr Livingstone was not to be regarded as expressing a political opinion, attracting a high level of protection, when he indulged in offensive abuse of an *Evening Standard* journalist outside a City Hall reception.

❖ **KEY CASE**   *R (on the application of Jon Gaunt) v Ofcom* [2011] EWCA Civ 692

Precedent

❖ An interference with a person's Article 10 rights has to be proportionate to the legitimate aim pursued and must be established convincingly.

❖ When deciding whether any interference with freedom of expression falls foul of Article 10, the court will have particular regard to the words used, the context in which they were made public and the case as a whole.

❖ There is a distinction to be drawn between harsh words which constitute a gratuitous personal attack and those which form part of a political debate.

Facts

The case concerned an explosive outburst by radio show host 'shock jock' Jon Gaunt on his *TalkSport* radio programme on 7 November 2008. Around 11am Gaunt interviewed Michael Stark, Cabinet Member for Children's Services for Redbridge London Borough Council, live on radio about the council's controversial proposal to ban smokers from becoming foster parents on the ground that passive smoking has a propensity for harming foster children. Gaunt, himself a foster child, had published a controversial article 'Fags didn't stop my foster mum caring for me', criticizing Redbridge Council as 'health and safety Nazis', referring to a 'master race philosophy' by Redbridge Social Services, whom

---

59 Section 319(2) Broadcasting Act 2003.
60 *Livingstone v Adjudication Panel for England* [2006] HRLR 45.

he called 'the SS', though the High Court did not hold this article to be unduly offensive.[61]

Mr Stark explained the council's stance on the radio show, stating that smoker foster parents would not be used in the future, to which Mr Gaunt responded, 'So you are a Nazi, then?' After Mr Stark protested, Mr Gaunt reiterated, 'No you are, you're a Nazi', with the interview degenerating into an unseemly slanging match. When Mr Stark protested that the insult, as he saw it, was probably actionable, the claimant, Jon Gaunt, replied, 'Take action if you wish', adding, 'You're a health Nazi' and a little later 'you ignorant pig' and 'health fascist' and an 'ignorant idiot'. Gaunt's live broadcast apology an hour later included: 'The councillor wants me to apologize for calling him a Nazi. I'm sorry for calling you a Nazi'. Gaunt was subsequently suspended with his contract terminated immediately.

Ofcom received 53 complaints from listeners and issued its adjudication on 8 June 2009, stating that Mr Gaunt had breached rules 2.1 and 2.3 of the Broadcasting Code.[62]

Jon Gaunt claimed that Ofcom's decision breached his Article 10 right and amounted to an unlawful interference with his freedom of expression. Gaunt was represented by the human rights group Liberty. Mr Millar QC, on behalf of the claimant, submitted there was no pressing social need and that Ofcom's reasons were insufficient to justify the interference with Article 10(2) ECHR[63] (see for this approach: *R v Shayler* (2003);[64] *R (on the application of SB) v Governors of Denbigh High School* (2007);[65] *Belfast City Council v Miss Behavin' Ltd* (2007)[66]).

In July 2010, Mr Gaunt lost his High Court 'freedom of expression' challenge against Ofcom. The High Court ruled that Ofcom's findings did *not* interfere with Mr Gaunt's Article 10 right, but that the 'ignorant pig' comment and the continued bullying and insulting of the Redbridge councillor on live radio amounted to gratuitous and offensive abuse, therefore breaching the Broadcasting Code.

Mr Gaunt's appeal reached the Court of Appeal where he did *not* argue that the Ofcom Code breached his Convention rights. However, Mr Gaunt argued that Ofcom's finding was a breach of his Article 10 rights because it was a

---

61 See: *Gaunt and Liberty v Ofcom* [2010] EWHC 1756 (QBD).
62 Rule 2.1 of the Code provides that generally accepted standards must be applied to the contents of television and radio services so as to provide adequate protection for members of the public from the inclusion in such services of harmful and/or offensive materials. Rule 2.3 provides that, in applying generally accepted standards, broadcasters must ensure that material which may cause offence is justified by the context. Such material may include, among other material, offensive language.
63 [2010] EWHC 1756 at para. 17.
64 [2003] 1 AC 247 at para. 23 (Lord Bingham) and para. 61 (Lord Hope).
65 [2007] 1 AC 100.
66 [2007] 1 WLR 1420.

disproportionate interference and did not meet a pressing social need. The CA dismissed Mr Gaunt's appeal in a judgment given by the Master of the Rolls, Lord Neuberger, endorsing the approach of the Divisional Court (High Court).

The CA emphasized that the freedom of expression, encompassing the right to say what one wants and how one wants, was the 'lifeblood' of democracy. But freedom of expression also carried with it responsibilities, which necessitated certain restrictions (referring to *Handyside v UK* (1976)[67]). Jon Gaunt applied for judicial review on human rights legislation grounds.

Decision
The CA dismissed Mr Gaunt's claim for judicial review. Reasons included that the public interest aspect (i.e. 'standing') was of limited importance when set in the context of the actual contents of the Michael Stark interview. It concluded that the court's task was to decide whether the amended finding *disproportionately* infringed the claimant's Article 10 right. The court found that there was no 'pressing social need' and that Ofcom's adjudication did not constitute an interference with Mr Gaunt's freedom of expression.

The CA held that the claimant's right to freedom of expression did *not* extend to gratuitous offensive insult or abuse, nor to repeated abusive shouting that served to express no real content.

Analysis
Since it was a live broadcast and Jon Gaunt was considered an experienced interviewer, the interview with the Redbridge Councillor could have been stopped by either Mr Gaunt or the *TalkSport* producers, once it had become clear that Jon Gaunt had lost control on live radio. The tone of the interview degenerated from the point where he called Michael Stark a 'Nazi', and the claimant – Mr Gaunt's – conduct of the interview became increasingly abusive, hectoring and out of control. This was followed by the expression 'ignorant pig' which had no contextual justification, said with 'such venom' as to constitute gratuitous offensive abuse.

It was therefore right that the regulator Ofcom found a breach of the Broadcasting Code. The decision of the courts (Divisional Court and CA) acknowledged the adjudication of the statutory regulator was correct. Consequently, there had been no unlawful interference with Mr Gaunt's Article 10 rights. Ofcom was therefore justified in its conclusion, because the offensive and abusive nature of the broadcast was gratuitous, having no factual content or justification, and the 'Amended Finding' constituted no material interference with the claimant's freedom of expression.

---

67 (1976) 1 EHRR 737 at para. 59 (ECHR).

 **FOR THOUGHT**

Compare and contrast the two Ofcom decisions involving Talk Radio (*George Galloway* March 2018) and TalkSport (*Jon Gaunt* June 2009). Do you agree with the regulator's decisions in each case? Why could both broadcasters not avail themselves of Article 10(1) ECHR? Discuss with reference to each ruling, legislation and the Ofcom Code.

8.4.6 Regulating converged media platforms

Who then is editorially responsible for content on media platforms? The answer would seem to be found in the Ofcom ruling in the Vice News 'case'.

Vice News,[68] BuzzFeed[69] and the Canary are online current affairs and social media brands with news services located in the USA and the UK – which is where the problem of regulation lies. Vice News, BuzzFeed and the Canary are primarily targeted at a younger demographic audience.

The Vice Media, Inc. group (Vice) is based in New York, though it has bureaus worldwide. Vice mainstream news covers events that may not be as well covered by other news sources, distributing written articles and video content on its website and YouTube.

BuzzFeed – also American – receives the majority of its traffic by creating content that is shared on social media websites, such as Twitter and Facebook. The site continues to test and track their custom content with an in-house team of data scientists and external-facing 'social dashboard'. Staff writers are ranked by views on an internal leader board.

The UK-based the Canary is a left-wing news website, set up in 2015. The media outlet prides itself of being free from advertising and political parties; at the same time it has been financially struggling. Canary's Editor, Kerry-Anne Mendoza, says of the Canary's ideology that it is 'here to disrupt the status quo of the UK and international journalism, by creating content that compels audiences to view the world differently'.

How are these online services to be regulated? Vice, for example, has several forms of output, including photo galleries, news videos and articles about the writers' personal experiences. The platform covers subjects other traditional media sources do not, in a casual editorial voice others avoid. This 'Gonzo-style' journalistic approach means that the range of subjects its output deals with is exceptionally broad, from neuropsychology to pornography. Examples such as, 'I Went Undercover in America's Toughest Prison' and

---

68 Vice News is American and was created in December 2013 as a division of Vice Media and primarily consists of documentaries. Vice's investors have been Rupert Murdoch's 21st Century Fox, investing some $70m in Vice Media in 2013 with a 5 per cent stake; A&E Networks, in a joint venture with Hearst Corporation and the Walt Disney Company, acquired a 10 per cent share in Vice in 2014 for $250m. According to the *Wall Street Journal*, Vice was in the process of trimming its 3,000-person global headcount by 15 per cent, reporting Vice's losses at more than $50m in 2018. Source: 'Vice Media to Shrink Workforce by as Much as 15% as Growth Stalls', by Keach Hagey, Benjamin Mullin and Alexandra Bruell, *Wall Street Journal*, 7 November 2018.
69 BuzzFeed was founded in 2006 in New York by Jonah Peretti and John S. Johnson III as a 'viral lab'. BuzzFeed's Jonah Peretti told the *New York Times* that there might be a multi-company merger between BuzzFeed, Vice, Vox Media, Group Nine Media, and Refinery29, as a means to rival the Facebook-Google ad duopoly. Source: 'Founder's Big Idea to Revive BuzzFeed's Fortunes? A merger with rivals Jonah Peretti, the chief executive, says his company could eventually merge with other online publishers in order to negotiate better terms with tech platforms like Facebook', by Edmund Lee, *New York Times*, 19 November 2018.

'Making Friends Inside Brooklyn's Last Porno Theatre' give an idea of the sort of content Vice is known for.

Video is central to Vice's output, and Vice has been putting video online longer than most media companies. The main Vice channel is on YouTube, ranging from one-minute comedy videos to half-hour or longer in-depth documentaries on subjects such as Ukraine Fashion Week. Vice News frequently produces 'raw coverage' videos, which are hours of unedited footage from areas of instability streamed live and then uploaded alongside the edited news stories.

The Ofcom ruling ('determination') in the Vice News 'case' means that on-demand video services on Vice's UK website cannot be regulated by the British authorities because the firm's head office is in America, it is outside British jurisdiction. The decision means on-demand video on Vice's UK website will not be subject to the British Communications Act 2003, as its UK-based rivals are. The Vice-Ofcom ruling contradicts an earlier ruling by the Authority for Television On Demand (ATVOD).

❖ KEY CASE   *The Vice News – Ofcom determination* (2015)[70]

Facts and background

The regulator 'The Authority for Television On Demand' (ATVOD) determined in 2013 that Vice's UK news office provided 'on-demand programme services' (ODPS) because the video tab constituted 'a service in its own right, the principal purpose of which is the provision of TV-like programmes'. Vice appealed this decision to Ofcom – the 'umbrella' regulator of ATVOD. In July 2015 Ofcom upheld Vice UK's appeal and quashed ATVOD's determination.[71]

Vice's Appeal to Ofcom

Ofcom made its decision on the basis of new information provided by Vice, which submitted that the person with editorial responsibility for its video tab was established in the United States and therefore outside the jurisdiction of the UK for the purposes of the Communications Act 2003. Ofcom agreed with Vice's submission.

In determining where Vice's service was established, Ofcom considered Article 2(3) of the Audiovisual Media Services Directive (2010/13/EU), which states:

For the purposes of this Directive, a media service provider shall be deemed to be established in a member state in the following cases:

(a) The media service provider has its head office in that member state and the editorial decisions about the audiovisual media service are taken in that member state;

---

70 See: Ofcom Determination of 21 July 2015 'Appeal by Vice UK Ltd against a Notice of Determination that the provider of the service 'Vice (Video)' (www.vice.com/en_uk/video) has contravened ss 368BA ('requirement to notify on-demand programme service') and 368D(3)(ZA) ('requirement to pay a fee') of the Communications Act 2003.

71 This decision overturned the previous determination made by ATVOD on 14 August 2013, which judged the video tab made available on the Vice website to be an ODPS.

(b) If a media service provider has its head office in a member state but decisions on the audiovisual media service are taken in a third country, or vice versa, it shall be deemed to be established in the member state concerned, provided that a significant part of the workforce involved in the pursuit of the audiovisual media service activity operates in that member state.

Decision

Ofcom determined that the entity with editorial responsibility was, for the purposes of Article 2(3)(a) of the Directive, the US-based Vice Media Inc., rather than Vice UK. The decision was based on the following facts:

❖ the UK Vice team had no role in selecting which video content to include;
❖ all US video content had to be included (except if deemed culturally offensive or legally problematic); and
❖ decisions on arranging the content were also made by the team based in the USA.

Ofcom also considered the jurisdiction test at Article 2(3)(c); it found this to be relevant as although Vice's head office was in a third country, some decisions on the audiovisual media service were taken in an EU Member State. Ofcom determined that there was no significant part of the UK workforce involved in the audiovisual media service activity because only an estimated 18 of Vice's 192 staff were based in the UK. In addition, it was determined that the US head office's authority greatly limited the decision-making capacity of the UK-based staff.

Analysis

In the Vice News case, Ofcom made some observations for future regulatory reference. The communications regulator said it is necessary to look at what the website offers as a whole: purely written content or audiovisual material or both? Ofcom noted that a video tab could be an *incidental* part of a text- and photo-based magazine-style website. It also said that faced with similar decisions in future, ATVOD may find it helpful to seek evidence to show how consumers in fact access and use the audiovisual material on the site in question.

Ofcom's decision provides a clear indication that where editorial responsibility for an on demand programme service (ODPS) is established outside the EU, that service will not fall within the definition of an ODPS for the purposes of the UK Communications Act 2003 and so will not be subject to regulation in the UK.[72]

---

72 See: Ofcom Determination of 21 July 2015 'Appeal by Vice UK Ltd', paras 101–102.

8.5 Regulating paid-for services: who controls YouTube, Netflix and Amazon?

The wider media landscape in which the public service broadcasters operate is changing rapidly. In today's market, viewers are no longer bound by the television schedule or watching programmes only on a television set. They have access to a much wider range of content, from a wider selection of providers ranging from the streaming pioneer Netflix to Google's YouTube. This has contributed to a drop in the viewing of live TV. Whilst Netflix has around 151m paid subscribers global subscribers, there is other serious competition from other US media companies, such as Disney and AT&T-owned WarnerMedia who are taking a share of the market. Apple is also getting ready to launch its own video streaming service, and Amazon Prime has taken a fair share of the UK market.

There are now more UK subscriptions to Netflix, Amazon Prime and NOW TV than to 'traditional' pay TV services. We have already highlighted that broadcast TV remains popular, but viewing among 16- to 34-year-olds is moving online as Ofcom's Media Nations UK Report in 2018 pointed out. The report highlights a competitive shift within the UK television industry, driven by the rise of the major global internet companies and the changing habits and preferences of UK audiences. With more choice for viewers than ever before, traditional UK broadcasters are competing for viewers in an increasingly fragmented landscape. Spending by the BBC, ITV, Channel 4 and Channel 5 on new UK-made TV programmes fell to a 20-year low.[73] At the same time, people are spending less time watching television: average daily broadcast viewing on the television set fell by nine minutes in 2017 – and is down 38 minutes since 2012. The amount of revenue generated from pay TV fell for the first time in 2018 after a period of sustained growth.[74] In music, streaming revenues now outstrip physical sales.

See
Chapter 10

The number of UK subscriptions to TV streaming services like Netflix has overtaken those to traditional pay TV, marking a major shift in the UK's viewing habits. The total number of UK subscriptions to the three most popular online streaming services – Netflix, Amazon Prime and Sky's Now TV – reached 15.4 million 2018,[75] overtaking, for the first time, the number of pay TV subscriptions, at 15.1 million.

Ofcom's Media Nations UK Report in 2018[76] confirmed that traditional viewing of broadcast television on a TV set fell for the sixth successive year. Between 2016 and 2017, viewing per person declined by 4.2 per cent to 3 hours 22 minutes, down by nine minutes. The Ofcom report stated that the BBC is facing an existential crisis as a result of its failure to reach younger audiences in the face of competition from commercial rivals and

---

73 The 20-year low is for spend on network first-run originations by BBC1, BBC2, ITV, C4, C5 and the BBC portfolio channels combined, in real terms. This figure does not include S4C, BBC Alba and nations and regions original programming spend. Source: Ofcom (2018).
74 Despite this decline, pay TV revenue remains significantly higher than revenue generated via video-on-demand subscriptions (£6.4bn versus £895m). Source: Ofcom (2018).
75 This figure includes subscriptions to multiple subscription VOD services within one household: 11.1 million households (39.3 per cent) have at least one of either Netflix, Amazon or Now TV. Source: Ofcom (2018).
76 Source: Ofcom (2018).

online services such as YouTube and Netflix. Nearly half (47.5 per cent) of all the decline in TV viewing levels is due to under 25s.

One in eight young Britons currently consumes no BBC content at all in a given week – a worrying figure given the corporation's current funding model is based on convincing the vast majority of the public to pay £154.50 a year for a colour TV licence. The regulator pointed out in its report that the online-only BBC Three channel was reaching only about 8 per cent of people in the 16–34 category each week, despite being specifically designed to appeal to younger viewers.

Young people told Ofcom they felt the BBC focused on older audiences too much. 'Young people also want the BBC to take more risks and felt it was too reliant on conventional formats', the regulator said. For young adults (16–34s), the consumption of non-broadcast sources (across all devices) is now greater than their broadcast-derived consumption. They watch subscription video-on-demand services (SVOD) for half an hour a day on average, but the largest chunk of their time is spent on YouTube, which they watch for an hour a day on average. Audiences are also watching content on a much wider range of devices. This includes tablets, smartphones, internet-connected TVs, set-top boxes and plug-in devices such as Amazon's Fire TV stick.

Radio listening reached a significant milestone in the first quarter of 2018, as, for the first time, more than half of all listening hours (50.9 per cent) were through a digital platform – DAB, online or through digital TV. This is being driven by an increase in the proportion of adults who now have a DAB set (64 per cent) and the greater choice of national commercial stations now available to listeners.[77]

8.5.1 Regulating TV streaming services and pay TV

In 2017 Netflix screened the 13-episode series '13 Reasons Why', aimed at teenagers, based on a novel by Jay Asher. The series depicts Hannah and her graphical account about her own suicide. The Royal College of Psychiatrists warned of potentially tragic consequences of the series. But the creators of the series claimed they were hoping to 'help' young people struggling with the issues shown in the show. The Samaritans reported that '13 Reasons Why' exposed serious failings in the UK's media regulation. It remains of serious concern that a drama series, aimed at young audiences, can be produced outside of the UK and made available to UK audiences and yet not be subject to UK media regulation.

Since there have been increasing calls for streaming services to monitor their harmful content, some have actioned against violent content.

In January 2019 some 45 million Netflix subscribers streamed the thriller Bird Box, starring Sandra Bullock, in its first week of release: a record for original movie content on the platform. Netflix had to issue a public health warning upon release of the film responding to a growing social media fad for 'the Bird Box challenge', in which people emulate characters in the film who must perform every task blindfolded, lest lurking monsters drive them to suicide. Netflix's call for moderation (but not abstention) from

77 Source: Ofcom (2018).

the craze came after thousands of videos posted online showed people stumbling around houses, stairs and woods with scarves wrapped round their eyes.

YouTube also took action against creators who copied or re-enacted scenes from dangerous *Bird Box* challenges, after a wave of incidents prompted by a viral challenge, involved YouTubers who drove blindfolded into oncoming traffic, and trying to imitate online celebrities, such as Jake Paul, walked through blindfolded through traffic. This, in turn, led to a Utah teenager crashing her car into oncoming traffic whilst repeating the stunt. The original, and still the most famous, challenge to hit YouTube was the 'Ice Bucket Challenge' in 2014, attracting over one billion views in one month when ever bigger celebrities jumped on board to support the charitable aims of the challenge. Users who violate the YouTube 'code', having their videos removed from the platform, receive a 'strike' against their account; this means they are limited in what they can do for 90 days, but then all privileges are being restored if they do not receive a second strike in that time. YouTube tightened rules on creators in 2019 and now applies 'strikes' to users' accounts who 'egregiously' violate rules in video thumbnails or links to external content.

More controversially, Netflix took down an episode of the satirical comedy 'The Daily Show' where comedian Indian-American Hasan Minhaj had been critical of the Kingdom of Saudi Arabia and Crown Prince Mohammed bin Salman. In his weekly episode, Minhaj had used his comedic voice questioning the brutal killing of the Saudi dissident and *Washington Post* columnist, Jamal Khashoggi, inside the Saudi consulate in Istanbul in October 2018. US senators had linked Khashoggi's death to the Saudi crown prince. The episode of 'Patriot Act' with Hasan Minhaj was removed on 2 January 2019, following a legal demands from the Saudi Kingdom which reportedly said the episode violated a Saudi anti-cybercrime law.

Currently, there is no statutory regulation of these streaming services in the UK and the Ofcom Code does not apply to television delivered via the internet and on-demand services outside the UK, such as Netflix or YouTube, smart TVs or streaming sticks. The UK Parliament would need to introduce new legislation to extend regulation to online platforms and services. Ofcom does, however, regulate Amazon Prime.

That said, the streaming and online services are beginning to regulate their own inappropriate content. YouTube (Google) announced a clampdown on disturbing and inappropriate children's videos in 2019, following accusations that the site enabled 'infrastructural violence' through the long-run effects of its content recommendation system.[78] Google's new privacy policy provides restrictions which apply to content featuring 'inappropriate use of family entertainment characters', such as unofficial videos depicting Peppa Pig being 'tortured' by a dentist. The company already had a policy that rendered such videos ineligible for advertising revenue, in the hope that doing so would reduce the motivation to create them in the first place.

See
Chapter 10

Age-restricted content is automatically not allowed in YouTube Kids. Age-restricted videos cannot be seen by users who are not logged in, or by those who have entered their age as below 18 on both the site and the app. The Google age-restricted content policy makes clear that their 'review team' may place an age restriction on a video once they are notified of the content. Age-restricted videos are then not visible to users who are logged out, are under

---

78 See: Google Privacy Policy of 22 January 2019.

18 years of age or have the 'restricted mode' enabled. When evaluating whether content is appropriate for all ages, here are some of the things which Google considers:

> **Google/YouTube policy on harmful or dangerous content (2019)**
>
> - *Vulgar language* – such as the use of sexually explicit language or excessive profanity in the video; associated metadata may lead to the age-restriction of the video.
> - *Violence and disturbing imagery* – such as terrorist organizations using YouTube for their purpose, including recruitment and content promoting terrorist acts, inciting violence or celebrating terrorist attacks. Graphic or controversial footage may be subject to age-restrictions or a warning screen.
> - *Nudity and sexually suggestive content* – such as pornography or videos containing fetish content. These will be removed or age-restricted depending on the severity of the act in question. In most cases, violent, graphic, or humiliating fetishes are not allowed to be shown on YouTube. Content that contains nudity or other sexual content may be allowed if the primary purpose is educational, documentary, scientific, or artistic, and it is not gratuitously graphic. For example, a documentary on breast cancer would be appropriate, but posting clips out of context from the same documentary might not be.
> - *Portrayal of harmful or dangerous activities* – such as instructional bomb making, challenges that encourage acts that have an inherent risk of severe physical harm, pranks that make victims believe they are in physical danger, pranks that cause emotional distress to children, hard drug use or any acts that may result in serious injury.

8.5.2 Regulating the watershed

So, how is the watershed regulated on streaming and paid-for services such as Netflix? Broadly speaking, the watershed covers all aspects of unsuitable material, including distressing images, after 9pm, in order to protect children. Ofcom rules state that even after 9pm frequent bad language or violence must be justified by context in all programming, and special care must be taken for shows that children are liable to watch.

See above
8.4.1

The fact that many people now record their viewing and watch at another time presents issues, as does the fact that YouTube services can be freely available online. None of these online services, such as Netflix, Hulu, Rakuten, YouTube TV, HBO Online, Pluto TV, FuboTV and many more, have any watershed restrictions. And how an on-demand service is regulated depends on where the provider is established and the server is situated. Most of these are outside the EU, therefore fall outside the EU's Audio Visual Media Services Directive (AVMS).[79]

---

79 See: Articles 16 and 17 of Directive 2010/13/EU on the coordination of certain provisions laid down by law, regulation or administrative action in Member States concerning the provision of audiovisual media services (Audio-Visual Media Services Directive – AVMS).

European programming no longer allows some programmes partly financed from European sources to be screened after the watershed. In the case of Netflix, it falls within the jurisdiction of the Netherlands, but it still has to abide by the terms of the Directive (AVMS), which dictates standards for on-demand services, particularly covering potential harm to children. But Ofcom has no power to issue sanctions on Netflix, as it is regulated by the Dutch regulator and its server and overall jurisdiction are situated in the USA.

The country of origin principle is therefore at the core of this Directive, as it is regarded essential for the creation of an audiovisual internal market to ensure legal certainty for media service providers as the necessary basis for new business models and the deployment of such services. It is also essential in order to ensure the free flow of information and audiovisual programmes in the internal market.[80] Chapter VI Article 16 AVMS ('Promotion of Distribution and Production of Television Programmes') states:

> 1 In accordance with the Audio Visual Media Services ('AVMS') Directive, television broadcasters shall ensure that, where practicable, and subject to paragraphs 2 and 3:
>
> a) a majority of their Transmission Time is devoted to European programming;
> b) at least 10% of their Transmission Time or programming budget is devoted to European programming created by producers who are independent of broadcasters; and
> c) at least 50% of programming included in their Transmission Time in accordance with (b) above is created no less than five years earlier by producers who are independent of broadcasters.

Ofcom has regulatory procedures in place for the handling and resolution of complaints, or conduct investigations, for potential breaches of rules applying to on-demand programme services (ODPS) such as Amazon Prime. However, these procedures do not apply to BBC UK public broadcasting ODPS, but do apply to the BBC's commercial worldwide services. It is important to note the nature of ODPS (in comparison with linear broadcast) that material will often remain available for viewing on demand, for a long time, meaning a risk of any harm from a breach may be ongoing. Breaches are potentially very serious where the protection of minors is concerned.[81] Complaints under these pro-

---

80 Article 33 AVMS.
81 Part 4A of the Communications Act 2003 makes provision for the regulation of ODPS. Section 368C of the Act imposes various duties on the 'appropriate regulatory authority' which, in the absence of another body being designated under section 368B in relation to programme content, is Ofcom. These include a duty to take steps to secure that every provider of an ODPS complies with requirements in section 368D.

cedures can be made to Ofcom by any person or body who considers that an ODPS provider has failed to comply with the relevant requirements as set out in the Rules. Examples related to the Ofcom Code are cited here:

Making a complaint to Ofcom about an ODPS provider

- Harmful Material: Material Likely to Incite Hatred (Rule 10).
- Harmful Material: Protection of under 18s (Rule 11).
- Sponsorship (Rule 12).
- Product Placement (Rule 13).
- Harmful Material: Prohibited Material (Rule 14).

Ofcom will not normally consider a complaint unless the complainant has sought to follow the ODPS provider's own complaints procedure first.

8.6 Regulating online harmful content

The internet has revolutionized how people communicate and access news, entertainment and other media, creating an increasingly converged communications market, with the major UK communications companies increasingly in the business of telecoms, content and online distribution. Innovation in online services has delivered major benefits to individuals and society. But there is an intensifying, global debate over how to address the various problems that people experience online. Issues include:

- young people's exposure to harmful content and conduct;
- privacy and use of personal data;
- the growth in cybercrime;
- concerns with the ways in which online businesses compete, and the impact of this on innovation, investment and consumer choice; and
- the potential effects on content production, including journalism, and media plurality.

Issues related to harmful content and conduct – including illegal and age-inappropriate content, misleading political advertising, 'fake news' and bullying – are particular areas of focus. The UK government has said it will legislate to improve internet safety. The UK Parliament's Digital, Culture, Media and Sport (DCMS) Committee has published an interim report on disinformation and 'fake news', which includes a recommendation that existing broadcasting standards be used as the basis for new online standards.[82]

---

82 See: House of Commons (2018).

8.6.1 Molly Russell's suicide after Instagram self-harm searches

British schoolgirl, Molly Russell, 14, took her own life in November 2017. When her family looked into her Instagram account they found distressing material about depression and suicide. In a distressing video account, Molly's father, Ian Russell, told the BBC he believed that Instagram was partly responsible for his daughter's death. He said that harmful suicide and self-harm content online 'has the effect of grooming people to take their own lives' and that images are easily found at #suicide or #self-harm. For a year Molly's family tried to get Molly's iPhone and iPod Touch unlocked to see what she was exposed to and what messages she might have received the night she took her life. They were rebuffed by Apple. Yet Ian Russell and his oldest daughter could see some of the sites Molly had accessed on the family computer. They found her Instagram account and saw that among the hundreds of people she followed were 50 or 60 with tags such as 'sad', 'lonely' or 'depressed'. The sites seemed to be completely encouraging of self-harm, linking depression to self-harm and to suicide, making it seem inevitable, normal, graphically showing things such as cutting, biting, burning, bruising, taking pills. Mr Russell told the BBC, 'There's no doubt that Instagram played a part in Molly's death'. When he examined Molly's email account, he was shocked to realise that Pinterest had been sending her automated messages suggesting she look at distressing images.[83]

Mr Russell had asked Apple to help with unlocking Molly's devices, but calls to its call centre proved futile. Only when the inquest into Molly's death opened in north London in January 2019 did Coroner Andrew Walker, presiding over the inquest, write to Apple, WhatsApp, Instagram, Snapchat, YouTube and Pinterest, asking the tech firms to disclose everything they held about Molly's accounts. In a statement, Adam Mosseri of Instagram responded that it did not allow content that promoted or glorified self-harm or suicide and would remove content of this kind. Adam Mosseri, who took over Instagram after the app's founders departed suddenly in 2018, promised a series of changes such as the introduction of 'sensitivity screens' to hide images of self-harm in an attempt to protect young people who use the site. In a commentary for the Daily Telegraph, Mosseri stated that the Facebook-owned app already banned posts that promote or encourage suicide or self-harm, but that Instagram faced challenges in finding those posts to take them down, as well as ensuring that users could still share imagery related to those topics in ways that allow them to express themselves but do not amount to incitement.[84]

The UK government has urged social media companies to take more responsibility for harmful online content which illustrates and promotes methods of suicide and self-harm. The then Digital Minister, Margot James, promised to 'crack down' on many of the social media platforms that had fallen short in their response to online bullying, abuse and misinformation. In a speech at a conference for 'Safer Internet Days' at BT's UK Safer Internet Centre in February 2019, Ms James said: 'We will soon be publishing an Online

---

83 Source: 'Instagram 'helped kill my daughter': a video account by Molly Russell's father Ian Russell, BBC Online, 22 January 2019: www.bbc.co.uk/news/av/uk-46966009/instagram-helped-kill-my-daughter.
84 Source: 'Our commitment to protect the most vulnerable on Instagram', by Adam Mosseri, Daily Telegraph, 4 February 2019.

Harms White Paper which will set out clear expectations for companies to help keep their users, particularly children, safe online. We will introduce laws that force social media platforms to remove illegal content, and to prioritise the protection of users beyond their commercial interests'.[85]

Apart from self-harm and suicide apps children are also using dating apps, lying about their age and thereby being manipulated and groomed by adults. Anne Longfield, the Children's Commissioner for England and Wales, called for a statutory duty of care which would ensure that social media companies take more responsibility for what is happening on their platforms. In a letter to the *Times* she wrote:

> I hope the government and the companies themselves will seize the moment and back measures that would make them do more to protect children from harm. Those who wish to exploit children are always quick to spot opportunities to do so. It is our duty to be equally speedy in preventing them. The era of letting the internet giants write their own rules is coming to an end.[86]

The failure of tech giants to enforce adult age limits on dating apps has placed a generation of children at risk of grooming and sexual exploitation. Lax controls on apps used by millions, such as Tinder and Grindr, are giving sexual predators and paedophiles easy access to children across Britain.

Self-harm, suicide, bullying and sexual content should have no place on social media sites, yet Facebook, YouTube, Twitter, Snapchat and Pinterest have repeatedly failed to enforce their own rules and have failed to protect young people despite repeated promises. They should be forced by law since the tech companies have lost control. Alongside legislation a digital ombudsman could also be introduced.

Since the inquest into Molly Russell's suicide, social media companies have faced increasing demands from the UK government to protect children from harmful online content, amid growing concerns over suicide and self-harm among teenagers. Health Secretary Matt Hancock warned companies including Facebook, Google and Twitter that he would use the law to force them to act should they fail to remove inappropriate content. He warned that the benefits of new technology could be 'lost because of reasonable concerns about its risks'. In an exclusive interview to *The Sun on Sunday* Mr Hancock revealed he would set up a handpicked cyber-squad to oversee the removal of self-harm pictures from Instagram. He declared: 'This is far too important to be left to the whims of social media companies'.[87]

New European legislation is scheduled to extend some protections to activities of video sharing platforms, such as YouTube.

---

85 Source: Margot James speech on Safer Internet Day. Minister for Digital outlines plans to make the UK the safest place on the world to be online. 5 February 2019: www.gov.uk/government/speeches/ margot-james-speech-on-safer-internet-day.

86 Source: Letter to the *Sunday Times*, 17 February 2019 by Children's Commissioner, Anne Longfield. See also her paper 'Growing up Digital' at www.childrenscommissioner.gov.uk/publication/growing-up-digital/.

87 Source: Health Secretary vows to get specialists to 'clean up social media for children' and oversee the removal of self-harm pictures online', by David Wooding, *The Sun on Sunday*, 10 February 2019.

Germany introduced a controversial new law which allows for the deletion of hate speech, defamatory and extreme sexual content that can harm children, teenagers and vulnerable adults from TV, on-demand and paid-for services and social media platforms.

The Network Enforcement Act[88] (NetzDG) came into full effect on 1 January 2018. Though the NetzDG covers mainly social media platforms it applies to all telemedia service providers which, for profit-making purposes, operate internet platforms and pay-TV services which are designed to enable users to share any content with other users or to make such content available to the public (i.e. social networks).[89] Journalistic or editorial content remain the responsibility of the service provider and do not constitute 'social networks' within the meaning of this Act. Online platforms and paid-for TV services face fines of up to €50m (£44m) if they do not remove 'obviously illegal' hate speech and other offensive publications within 24 hours of receiving a notification. A seven-day period is granted for removal of 'illegal' content.[90] But a number of controversial deletions and suspensions in the German law's first few days have bolstered critics who say the statute impacts on free speech, as companies try to avoid fines.

8.6.2 Regulating harmful content in broadcasting

How is harmful content regulated in broadcasting and private streaming services? The Ofcom Broadcasting Code allows for films rated up to '15' by the BBFC to be broadcast during the daytime on premium subscription channels and up to '18' on pay per view film channels, provided that they are protected by a mandatory PIN code – called mandatory daytime protection – that cannot be removed or bypassed by viewers. But these PIN code rules only affect premium pay channels in the UK, such as Sky and Virgin. Technical limitations make it unfeasible for free-to-air services delivered via digital terrestrial television, such as Freeview, to use a mandatory daytime protection system. Ofcom has made it clear that hard core pornography must not be broadcast pre-watershed.

But the NSPCC[91] has raised concerns that PINs are an inadequate form of protection because children often gain knowledge of the PIN, either through parents or older siblings, and may then access potentially harmful content for extended periods of time until a parent opts to change the PIN. The NSPCC also said that children may sometimes be more 'tech savvy' than their parents, particularly older adults, and parents can be dependent on their children to install PINs on devices.[92]

It is of course up to parents and supervising adults to invoke parental controls on subscriptions on all devices; Netflix offers these safeguards for example. The principle of choice was surveyed by Ofcom in 2018, which found that a majority of adults (58 per cent) thought that adults should be able to view post-9pm watershed content on TV channels during the daytime or early evening if a mandatory PIN was in place to prevent

---

88 Network Enforcement Act (Netzdurchsetzunggesetz, NetzDG).
89 Article 1(1) NetzDG.
90 The German Federal Ministry of Justice and Consumer Protection, in agreement with the Federal Ministry of the Interior and the Federal Ministry for Economic Affairs and Energy has issued general administrative guidelines on the exercise of discretion by the regulatory fine authority in initiating regulatory fine proceedings and in calculating the fine. See Art. 4(4) NetzDG ('Provisions on regulatory fines').
91 The National Society for the Prevention of Cruelty to Children is a charity campaigning and working in child protection in the United Kingdom and the Channel Islands.
92 Ofcom (2016).

children from accessing the content. Agreement levels were higher (73 per cent) among those who watched post-9pm watershed content during the day on catch-up and VOD services. However, personal interest was lower (24 per cent), with the main reason cited that they tended not to watch TV during the day or early evening, rather than an objection to being able to view post-9pm watershed programmes behind mandatory daytime protection.[93]

8.6.3 The future of regulating online platforms: summary and analysis

We have discussed experiences by regulators – such as Ofcom – social media platforms and individual challenges, such as by Molly Russell's family, the teenager who committed suicide in 2017 'inspired' by harmful content on Instagram. What then are the specific challenges presented online and in broadcasting and how they might affect future regulation? These include:

- *scale*: the sheer volume of text, audio and video generated or shared by online platforms is far beyond that available on broadcast television and radio;
- *service variety and innovation*: the nature and features of online platform services vary widely, including the level of control over what content users see;
- *multinational nature of online platform operators*: most of the services are US-based and fall outside EU jurisdiction, i.e. fall outside UK and EU law enforcement;
- *role in content creation*: many online platforms do not create or commission the content that is accessed by their users; a great deal is audience- and client-generated; though this should not exonerate social media platforms, such as Facebook (and therein Instagram), YouTube (Google) and Twitter et al.;
- *variety of content types, voices and opinions*: the diversity of types of content available online is much broader than that of traditional broadcast content and includes user-generated content and conversations between people; many will argue that the regulation of such content would infringe freedom of expression;
- *audience expectations and context differ between broadcasting and online*: In some areas, people's expectation of protection online maps closely to the standards that apply to broadcasting – the protection of minors, protection from illegal content and from a range of other harmful content and conduct. There are certain broadcasting standards – such as those for impartiality and accuracy (Ofcom) – that might be undesirable or impractical to introduce online in the same way.

93 Ofcom (2018) Daytime PIN Research, page 8. Kantar Media, 20th February 2018.

Currently, the UK regulates audiovisual media services in line with the requirements of the European-wide Audiovisual Media Services (AVMS) Directive[94] which also includes the regulation of the video sharing platforms such as YouTube.

Harmful content and conduct are now the focus of multiple EU governments' policy initiatives, and each Member State must now impose certain minimum requirements on audiovisual media services regulated according to the legislative principles of the AVMS. The quid pro quo is that a service regulated in any Member State may then be transmitted for reception in other Member States without further regulation (commonly referred to as the 'country of origin principle'). The UK is currently a significant hub for audiovisual services, being the home to a wide variety of audiovisual media services intended for reception both within the UK and elsewhere.

If the UK were to cease to be party to AVMS Directive (after Brexit), there are some benefits in that the UK would no longer have to be bound by the minimum requirements laid out in the AVMS Directive.

That said, current UK regulation leans towards being more, rather than less, restrictive than those minimum requirements, and the UK would still be bound by the European Convention on Transfrontier Television.[95] This Convention was the first international treaty creating a legal framework for the free circulation of transfrontier television programmes in Europe, through minimum common rules, in fields such as programming, advertising, sponsorship and the protection of certain individual rights. It entrusts the transmitting signatory states with the task of ensuring that TV programme services transmitted comply with its provisions. The Convention provides similar rules to the AVMS Directive in terms of freedom of reception of linear services originating from a signatory state. However, not all EU Member States have ratified the Convention, and unlike an EU Directive, the way the Convention has been incorporated in local law will be relevant, meaning that anyone seeking to rely on it will need to seek local advice in each relevant jurisdiction.

See Chapter 6.5

Several countries including Germany and Australia have enacted new legislation in relation to 'fake news' and online harmful content. The General Data Protection Regulation (GDPR) has set common rules within the European Economic Area (EEA) on how organizations and individuals can collect, process and store personal data.

See Chapter 6.4

Regulators in the UK, France, Germany have undertaken enforcement action and investigations around data protection. One example is the UK ICO's investigation into the use of data analytics in political campaigns.

Global policymakers are considering the competitive dynamics of online markets, amid wider concerns from academics and other experts.[96] In the UK, the Cairncross Review (2019) commissioned by the government, looked at commercial relationships between online platforms and news publishers, among other things. Dame Frances Cairncross[97] was appointed chair of the review into the sustainability of high-quality

---

94 Directive 2010/13/EU on the coordination of certain provisions laid down by law, regulation or administrative action in Member States concerning the provision of audiovisual media services (AVMS).

95 European Convention on Transfrontier Television (ETS No. 132). Strasbourg, 05/05/1989 – Treaty open for signature by the Cultural Convention and by the European Union.

96 For further discussion see: Barwise, T. P. and Watkins, L. (2018) at pp. 21–49.

97 Frances Cairncross is the former Rector of Exeter College, Oxford University. Prior to her decade at Oxford, she was a journalist, spending 13 years on *The Guardian* as an economic columnist and 20 years at the *Economist* magazine as a senior editor.

journalism in the UK in March 2018. Its purpose was to examine and make recommendations relating to:

- the overall state of the UK news market;
- threats to financial sustainability of the UK news industry;
- the role and impact of digital search engines and social media platforms;
- and the role of digital advertising.

Cairncross considered ways in which the news industry in the UK could become more sustainable, supporting it whilst it transitioned from print to digital. The report presents an overview of the challenges facing high-quality journalism in the UK, considers where intervention might be focused and puts forward a range of recommendations to help secure its future. The Cairncross Report has wide-ranging implications for the news media market, the threats to the financial sustainability of publishers, the impact of search engines and social media platforms and the role of digital advertising. The aim of the review was to advocate measures that would ensure the market in which journalists and publishers operate today is efficient, and to defend their most democratically significant outputs. In tackling the challenging market facing publishers, the Cairncross Review made the following recommendations:

1 Online platforms should set out codes of conduct for commercial agreements with news publishers, which should be approved and overseen by a regulator 'with powers to insist on compliance'.

2 The UK competition watchdog, the Competition and Markets Authority, should carry out a market study into the online advertising industry, taking a closer look at the different players, their 'roles, costs and profitability' and identify whether the market is working and what remedies are needed, if any.

3 A regulator should supervise online platforms' efforts to improve users' news experience, including expanding efforts to identify reliable and trustworthy sources. 'This task is too important to leave entirely to the judgment of commercial entities'.

4 The Government should develop a media literacy strategy, working with Ofcom, online platforms and news publishers and broadcasters, voluntary groups and academics to 'identify gaps in provision' and opportunities to collaborate further.

5 A new Institute for Public Interest News should be created as a dedicated body, free from political or commercial obligations, that can 'amplify efforts' to ensure the future sustainability of public-interest news.

6 The Government should launch an innovation fund to develop new approaches and tools to improve the supply of public-interest news which would ultimately be run by the Institute for Public Interest News once it is established.

7 The Government should introduce new forms of tax relief, including extending zero-rated VAT to digital newspapers and magazines as well as

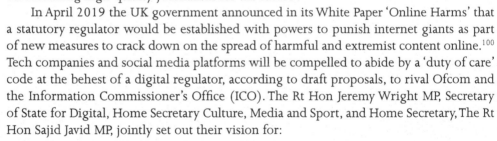

    digital-only publications, and develop a new form of tax relief, under the Charities Act or along the lines of Creative Sector reliefs, to support public interest journalism.

8   The local democracy reporting service, managed by the BBC in partnership with the News Media Association, should be expanded. Eventually the management of this should be passed to Institute for Public Interest News.

9   Ofcom should assess whether BBC News Online is 'striking the right balance' between getting a wide reach for itself and driving traffic to commercial publishers, particularly local ones. The BBC 'should do more to share its technical and digital expertise' to help local publishers.[98]

The Cairncross Review was published at a time when the UK print press were facing declining print and circulation revenues and stiff competition for online advertising revenues from the Duopoly, namely Facebook and Google. In her report, Dame Frances recommended expanding the local democracy reporter scheme (which at that time employed about 140 journalists) set up by the BBC and News Media Association. Regional publishers of local newspapers welcomed this expansion, advocating using the infrastructure already in place in regional newsrooms nationwide. Jonathan Heawood, chief executive of the alternative to IMPRESS, called the Cairncross Review a milestone in the history of journalism. 'Dame Frances has focused not on rebuilding the industry of the past, but on sustaining high-quality journalism for the future'.[99]

See
Chapter 7.3

In April 2019 the UK government announced in its White Paper 'Online Harms' that a statutory regulator would be established with powers to punish internet giants as part of new measures to crack down on the spread of harmful and extremist content online.[100] Tech companies and social media platforms will be compelled to abide by a 'duty of care' code at the behest of a digital regulator, according to draft proposals, to rival Ofcom and the Information Commissioner's Office (ICO). The Rt Hon Jeremy Wright MP, Secretary of State for Digital, Home Secretary Culture, Media and Sport, and Home Secretary, The Rt Hon Sajid Javid MP, jointly set out their vision for:

- a free, open and secure internet;
- freedom of expression online;
- an online environment where companies take effective steps to keep their users safe, and where criminal, terrorist and hostile foreign state activity is not left to contaminate the online space;
- rules and norms for the internet that discourage harmful behaviour;

---

98 The Cairncross Review (2019) Exectuive Summary pp. 5–12: https://assets.publishing.service.gov.uk/government/uploads/system/uploads/attachment_data/file/778021/021119_THE_CAIRNCROSS_REVIEW_A_sustainable_future_for_journalism.pdf.

99 Source: IMPRESS News 12 February 2019: https://impress.press/news/impress-welcomes-milestone-report-press-sustainability.html.

100 House of Commons (2019c).

- the UK as a thriving digital economy, with a prosperous ecosystem of companies developing innovation in online safety;
- citizens who understand the risks of online activity, challenge unacceptable behaviours and know how to access help if they experience harm online, with children receiving extra protection;
- a global coalition of countries all taking coordinated steps to keep their citizens safe online;
- renewed public confidence and trust in online companies and services.[101]

The new regulator (not yet defined at the time of publication) has the power to levy fines against companies for breaching standards. Senior managers will also be subject to these fines and held liable in a criminal context. The new regulatory framework will apply to companies that allow users to share or discover user-generated content or interact with each other online (which is a reminder of the Cambridge Analytica scandal).

See Chapter 6.7

The regulator will take a risk-based and proportionate approach across this broad range of business types. This will mean that the regulator's initial focus will be on those companies that pose the biggest and clearest risk of harm to users, either because of the scale of the platforms or because of known issues with serious harms.

In addition the ICO published proposals on 12 April 2019 on 16 standards that online services, such as Facebook and Instagram, must meet to protect children's privacy (under-18s). Snapchat could be prevented from allowing the age group to build up 'streaks', under the new rules proposed by Information Commissioner Elizabeth Denham. She believes the tools, such as 'likes', encourage users to share more personal data and spend more time on apps than desired. 'Likes' also help build up profiles of users' interests while streaks encourage them to send photos and videos daily. The ICO's 'Age Appropriate Design Code' sets out the standards expected of those responsible for designing, developing or providing online services likely to be accessed by children and which process their data. In addition to calling for restrictions on children being exposed to so-called nudge techniques, the ICO advocates internet firms make the following changes among others for their younger members:

- make privacy settings 'high' by default;
- switch location-tracking off by default after each session and make it obvious when it had been activated;
- give children choices over which elements of the service they want to activate and then collect and retain the minimum amount of personal data;
- provide 'bite-sized' explanations in clear language about how users' personal data is used;
- make it clear if parental controls, such as activity tracking, are being used.

---

101 Ibid. at p. 6.

The ICO suggests that firms that do not comply with the code could face fines of up to €20m (£17.2m) or 4 per cent of their worldwide turnover under the General Data Protection Regulation (GDPR).[102]

See
Chapter 6.4

8.6.4 Does online regulation infringe freedom of expression?

The right to freedom of expression includes freedom to seek and receive information. It is a key component of democratic governance as the promotion of a participatory decision-making process in a modern democratic internet society. While the internet has brought global freedom to communicate and exchange ideas, its growth has introduced difficulties too, for instance, the expression of personal opinion on social media sites bringing with it risk of 'fake news', misinformation, defamation, harassment and invasion of privacy.

Freedom of expression is fundamental to the functioning of democracy. This applies especially to the communication of opinions and includes views and arguments advanced on social media platforms and traditional broadcasts (see: R (*Animal Defenders International v Secretary of State for Culture, Media and Sport* (2008)[103]). Even where a statement amounts to a value judgment, the proportionality of an interference may depend on whether there exists a sufficient factual basis for the impugned statement, since even a value judgment without any factual basis to support it may be excessive (see: *Dichand v Austria* (2002);[104] also: *Monnat v Switzerland* (2006)[105]).

See
Chapter 1

Freedom of expression includes not only the inoffensive, but also the irritating, the contentious, the eccentric, the heretical, the unwelcome and the provocative, provided it does not tend to provoke violence (see: *Redmond-Bate v DPP* (1999)[106]). But in the *Otto-Preminger-Institut v Austria* (1994)[107] case, the ECtHR concluded in relation to the obligations expressed relating to Article 10(2) ECHR, that expressions which are gratuitously offensive to others must be avoided wherever possible. It is then accepted that Strasbourg jurisprudence does not protect gratuitous abuse unrelated to a topic being discussed (on the radio for example), but this is a very limited exception to the broad protection of political expression. For this reason, the regulatory body – Ofcom's – decision in the Jon Gaunt[108] case may well be incompatible with Convention Article 10 if tested in the ECtHR, though to date radio broadcaster Jon Gaunt has not pursued his case in the Strasbourg Court.

See above 8.4

In the CG case (below), the Belfast court granted a right to privacy to a convicted sex offender, including any publications on social media (here: Facebook).

102 Source: ICO launches consultation on Code of Practice to help protect children online 12 April 2019: https://
 ico.org.uk/about-the-ico/news-and-events/news-and-blogs/2019/04/ico-launches-consultation-on-code-of-
 practice-to-help-protect-children-online/.
103 [2008] 1 AC 1312 at para. 27 (Lord Bingham).
104 (2002) (Application No 29271/95) of 26 February 2002 (ECHR).
105 (2006) (Application No 73604/01) of 21 September 2006 (ECHR).
106 [1999] 163 JP 789.
107 [1994] ECHR 26 at para. 49 (ECHR).
108 See: R (*on the application of Gaunt*) *v Ofcom* [2011] EWCA Civ 692.

❖ KEY CASE	*CG v Facebook Ireland Ltd and Joseph McCloskey* [2015] NIQB 11. Queen's Bench Division (Northern Ireland) 20 February 2015

Precedent

- ❖ Every person has an expectation of privacy online (on the internet) in respect of their personal information – including sex offenders.
- ❖ Information which can harm the public interest may also create a risk of re-offending.
- ❖ A social media company (here: Facebook) is a primary publisher and liable for misuse of private information.
- ❖ An ISP must remove any publication (relevant page/s) from its website which exposes the claimant to vilification and the risk of serious harm.
- ❖ Regulation 22 of the Electronic Commerce (EC Directive) Regulations 2002 takes into account all matters which appear to be relevant with postings on social networking sites.

Facts

CG was a convicted sex offender, jailed for five years and released on licence. He lived with his disabled father and had a disabled son with whom he had regular, supervised contact. He had complied with the terms of his licence, had been assessed as not presenting any significant risk to the public and was under supervision by the authorities. Joseph McCloskey operated a page on Facebook's website named 'Keeping our Kids Safe from Predators 2'. McCloskey had posted a newspaper article with a photograph of CG from the time of his conviction on the Facebook page. In response, between 160 and 180 comments appeared on the page containing abusive and violent language as well as expressions of support for acts of violence against CG. There were also postings of his location, abusive language in relation to his family and allegations of other criminal acts.

CG lived in increased fear of violence, worried about his whereabouts being identified. Direct contact with his son was suspended, and relations with other family members were strained. CG told the court that he had been approached and threatened in public as a result of the posts.

Facebook also facilitated a page operated by the father of one of CG's victims, namely RS. The father had posted a photograph of CG and information about his whereabouts which attracted more comments suggesting that CG should be harmed. No proceedings were brought against RS. After receiving letters from CG's lawyers, Facebook refused to investigate the comments until CG provided the URL for each specific comment. Facebook removed the entire series of comments two weeks later.

CG claimed against both defendants that the material posted amounted to a misuse of private information, was in breach of Articles 2, 3 and 8 ECHR and amounted to harassment of him contrary to the Protection from Harassment (Northern Ireland) Order 1997 as actionable negligence. CG further asserted that Facebook was in breach of the Data Protection Act 1998 (DPA). It was further submitted for CG that the case against Facebook was most properly categorized as 'misuse of private information' and against Mr McCloskey as 'misuse of private information and harassment', and it was upon these claims that the judgment was focused.[109]

CG sought damages and injunctions preventing Mr McCloskey from harassing him by publishing any information on Facebook's website and requiring Facebook to terminate McCloskey's page.

Decision

The case against Joseph McCloskey

The High Court in Northern Ireland found that Mr McCloskey's purpose in setting up the profile and Facebook page was to destroy the family life of sex offenders, to expose them to total humiliation and vilification, to drive them from their homes and expose them to the risk of serious harm. Stephens J found that McCloskey knowingly encouraged harassment of sex offenders by other individuals by the comments he made and by the aim and purpose of his page on Facebook.[110]

The court found that Mr McCloskey had engaged in a course of conduct in relation to harassment of CG so that he 'was extremely concerned and lived in increased fear as he anticipated violence being inflicted on him'.[111]

In relation to misuse of private information and the DPA the court found that CG's privacy, data protection and Article 8 rights had been infringed. The data disclosed via social media had been 'sensitive personal data' under the DPA, including information relating to sexual life, the commission of offences and criminal proceedings. Stephens J said that CG had an expectation of privacy in relation to such information after his conviction had been spent. Accordingly, Mr McCloskey was liable for harassment and misuse of private information of CG.

The case against Facebook

Stephens J ruled that Facebook had misused private information in not deleting the information about CG on the 'Keeping our Kids Safe from Predators 2' profile, the content of which was unlawful being a misuse of private information. The page and postings had incited violence and hatred and had placed CG in serious risk of harm. The judge said that this was indiscriminate and could have led to the development of public order situations. Facebook was the primary publisher and was liable for misuse of private information.

---

109 The relevant legislation was the Electronic Commerce (EC Directive) Regulations 2002 and the Protection from Harassment (Northern Ireland) Order 1997 (NI 1997/1180).
110 [2015] NIQB 11 at 74.
111 Ibid. at 35.

The court ruled that Facebook could not claim lack of knowledge under regulation 22 of the Electronic Commerce (EC Directive) Regulations 2002[112] and was therefore liable for the whole period of posting.[113] The court reached the same conclusion in relation to the postings on RS's profile page except that liability only arose from the date of receipt of CG's solicitors' letters in relation to each of the two series of postings.

Stephens J pointed out that regulation 22 also provides that the court 'shall take into account all matters which appear to it in the particular circumstances to be relevant'. The judge was highly critical of demands made by Facebook in correspondence for the provision of the URL for every offending posting and comment, together with an explanation in relation to each as to why it transgressed, before it would take any steps to investigate a complaint. Stephens J commented that regulation 22 is 'not an attempt to be prescriptive as to precisely how notice is to be given to a service provider or as to how actual knowledge is required' and must be seen in the context of a requirement to take into account all matters which appear to be relevant.[114]

The court awarded CG damages totalling £20,000. An anti-harassment injunction was made against Mr McCloskey, and a mandatory injunction was made against Facebook requiring it to terminate the entirety of the 'Keeping our Kids Safe from Predators 2' profile, including all material referring to other sex offenders.[115]

Analysis

The Northern Ireland High Court's decision in *CG* has a number of notable features. First, a mandatory injunction was made against Facebook requiring it to take down an entire page despite the fact that the offending material had been removed from it immediately following receipt of CG's solicitors' letter. Secondly, the mandatory injunction was made not only to protect the privacy rights of CG but of other sex offenders featured on the web page. Thirdly, the judge used the provisions of the Data Protection Act 1998 for the definitions of sensitive personal data and misuse of private information. Fourthly, Stephens J declared Facebook a primary publisher rejecting its argument that the social media provider had no 'actual knowledge' for the purpose of regulation 22 of the Electronic Commerce (EC Directive) Regulations 2002 for each offending post or comment (unless and until it had provided with the URL) (see also: *AB Ltd v Facebook Ireland Ltd* (2013);[116] *XY v Facebook Ireland Ltd* (2012)[117]).

---

112 Regulation 22 sets out the particular matters that the court shall have regard to in determining whether a service provider has been placed on notice and can therefore be held liable. These include 'details of the location of the information' and 'details of the unlawful nature of the activity or information in question'.
113 [2015] NIQB 11 at 102.
114 Ibid. at 95.
115 Ibid. at 105.
116 [2013] NIQB 14 QBD (NI) 06 February 2013.
117 [2012] NIQB 96 QBD (NI) 30 November 2012.

In December 2008, the European Court of Human Rights handed down its judgment in the *Norwegian Pensioner* case.[118] The ECtHR found that a blanket ban on advertising for political parties violated Article 10 ECHR. The background to the case concerned regional elections in Rogaland province where the Pensioner Party (Pensjonistparti – located in Stavanger) broadcast three political advertising slots on TV ('TV Vest') in the spring of 2003 with elections in September that year. Since political advertising is illegal in Norway and contravenes the broadcasting legislation, the Pensioner Party received a warning from the Norwegian Media Authority. Nevertheless, the commercials were broadcast from 14 August to 13 September, and TV Vest was fined NOK 35,000 by the Oslo City Court (Oslo tingrett) for violating the prohibition on political advertising in TV broadcasts.[119]

TV Vest appealed against the decision stating that the prohibitions in the Norwegian Broadcasting Act and Regulations were incompatible with the right to freedom of expression under Article 10 ECHR. The City Court upheld the Media Authority's decision in February 2004, supported by the Norwegian Supreme Court in November of that year. The case progressed to the Strasbourg Human Rights Court where Christos Rozakis, President of the ECtHR (First Section) ruled that there had been a violation of Article 10, because the proportionality aspect had not been addressed; there had not been:

> [a] reasonable relationship of proportionality between the legitimate aim pursued by the prohibition on political advertising and the means deployed to achieve that aim. The restriction which the prohibition and the imposition of the fine entailed on the applicants' exercise of their freedom of expression cannot therefore be regarded as having been necessary in a democratic society, within the meaning of paragraph 2 of Article 10, for the protection of the rights of others, notwithstanding the margin of appreciation available to the national authorities.[120]

The judgment in the *Norwegian Pensioner* case caused great controversy and subsequently had considerable consequences for political advertising in other signature countries to the Convention.

In the light of rather mixed messages from Strasbourg jurisprudence, it is increasingly left to the regulators of a country to strike a balance between the parameters of indecent, obscene and violent material as well as sensitive issues, such as ethics and morals, in broadcasting, media and online platform publications. In this context, it is submitted that the courts should regard rulings or adjudications by a regulatory authority as an additional 'jurisprudence' to assess what are 'generally accepted standards'. Examples are the Ofcom Broadcasting Code or IPSO's Editors' Code.

Where should the line be drawn between regulating indecency, obscenity, invasion of privacy on one hand and freedom of expression and 'freedom to view' and 'freedom to blog and tweet' on the other? Ultimately should this not be left to the autonomy of and freedom to choose of the end-user? While the international community is fast promoting the transfer of technology and information, there appear to be a number of different

---

118 *TV Vest AS & Rogaland Pensjonistparti v Norway* (2008) (Application No 21132/05) Judgment of the 11 December 2008 (ECtHR) (the Norwegian Pensioner case).

119 Under s 10(3) of the Norwegian Broadcasting Act 1992 and reg. 10(2) of the Norwegian Broadcasting Regulations.

120 *Rogaland Pensjonistparti v Norway* (2008) at para. 78 (Christos Rozakis, President, ECHR).

policies and laws in place across Europe, the United States[121] and other international juris-dictions, each attempting to regulate, control and curtail the internet and digital media technology.

In summary, regulation of the internet as far as online activities are concerned poses ongoing challenges to national governments, and the big tech companies should take more responsibility for what is published on their sites.

8.7 Advertising standards

Print media advertising has, in the past, been the most widely used form of advertising. Traditionally advertisements ('ads') appeared in newspapers or magazines and occasion-ally in form of brochures or fliers. With the demise of newspaper publishing, the print media has been losing increasing advertising revenue as people are browsing online. A new way of advertising, especially on social media platforms, has grabbed individu-als' attention. The structure of the online advertising sector and the enormous growth in the digital advertising business brings with it potential harms to young and vulnerable people.

In addition to online advertising, brands use online platforms for other forms of marketing, not generally considered to be online advertising, such as influencer market-ing and product placement. This can involve brands paying social media influencers to mention advertisers' products and services in their social media output. Online display advertising is often targeted to reach the right people at the right time in the right context in order to achieve an advertiser's objectives.

The online advertising market has evolved fast. Emerging online advertising formats include augmented reality (e.g. sponsored AR lenses), virtual reality (e.g. 360 video ads), dynamic content optimization (e.g. creating different ads for each user) and voice adver-tising (e.g. paid search results on voice assistants). Increasingly, trading techniques devel-oped for online advertising are being applied to advertising on other platforms such as television and digital out of home (e.g. digital billboards). The main types of targeting used in online advertising include contextual (e.g. content attributes), demographic (e.g. age, gender), behavioural (e.g. interests inferred from user web browsing), retargeting (e.g. targeting users to recapture interest in products or services after they have browsed away from an e-commerce site) and personalized (e.g. content personalized to an indi-vidual, based on user data) and the use of AI in facial recognition.

A report commissioned by the House of Commons Digital, Culture, Media and Sport Committee ('The Plum Report 2018') found that the UK internet advertising expenditure increased from £3,508m in 2008 to £11,553m in 2017, a compound annual growth rate of 14 per cent. In 2017, internet advertising overtook all other forms of advertising (television, press, radio, cinema and outdoor) combined, to reach 52 per cent share of

---

121 The Digital Millennium Copyright Act ('the Copyright Act') (Title 17 of the US Code) to provide in part cer-tain limitations on the liability of online service providers (OSPs) for copyright infringement. Section 512(c) of the Copyright Act provides limitations on service provider liability for storage, at the direction of a user, of copyrighted material residing on a system or network controlled or operated by or for the service provider, if, among other things, the service provider has designated an agent to receive notifications of claimed infringe-ment by providing contact information to the Copyright Office and by posting such information on the ser-vice provider's website in a location accessible to the public.

total advertising spending. Paid for search has been the largest category of online advertising, accounting for 50 per cent of the UK online advertising market in 2017, compared to 36 per cent for display, 13 per cent for classifieds and 1 per cent other formats. Mobile accounts form an increasing share of the online advertising market, with smartphone expenditure accounting for 45 per cent of total online advertising in 2017, compared to 37 per cent in 2016. Of the internet display advertising market, video (£1.6bn) accounts for the largest share, followed by banners (£1.3bn) and native (£1.0bn). Social media (mainly Facebook and YouTube) accounts for an increasing share of display advertising. In 2017, 57 per cent of online display advertising expenditure was on social media, compared to 49 per cent in 2016.[122]

Advertising is generally self-regulated, though at times some ads are close to bribery so that the police have to get involved.

8.7.1 The Advertising Standards Authority

The Advertising Standards Authority (ASA) is the UK's independent self-regulator of advertising across all media. The ASA applies the Advertising Codes, which are written by the Committees of Advertising Practice (known as 'the CAP Code'). The regulator's work includes acting on complaints and proactively checking the media to take action against misleading, harmful or offensive advertisements. The ASA senior management team is the executive decision-making team responsible for setting the direction for the organization, overseeing the management of core responsibilities and ensuring the delivery of the regulator's objectives. The Chief Executive is Guy Parker.[123]

The ASA Council is the jury that decides whether advertisements have broken the advertising rules. Those ads that break the rules have to be withdrawn or changed. Led by ASA Chairman, David Currie,[124] two-thirds of the 13-strong Council are independent of industry, and the remaining members have a recent or current knowledge of the advertising or media sectors. While it would not be appropriate to publish details of deliberations, the parties to a complaint are made aware of the collective decision of Council, along with detailed reasoning. This information is also made publicly available online by way of detailed weekly rulings.

See below
8.7.6

Unlike a statutory regulator, such as Ofcom, the ASA does not have the power to issue fines. But an adjudication (or ruling) which finds a breach of the CAP code will generally request an immediate amendment of or a withdrawal of the ad. This in itself is costly to the ad agency and often results in a greater deterrent than a fine.[125]

Ofcom acts as a backstop regulator, which means the ASA can refer cases to Ofcom if advertising continues to appear despite an ASA adjudication against it. Ofcom can then

---

122 House of Commons (2019) The Plum Report.

123 Guy Parker has been CEO of the ASA since 2009. From 2013 to 2016, Mr Parker chaired the European Advertising Standards Alliance; he is an Executive Committee member of the International Council for Advertising Standards, a member of the Fundraising Regulator's Standards Committee, a member of the UK government's Consumer Protection Partnership Strategic Group, a member of the International Chamber of Commerce's UK Marketing and Advertising Committee and a Fellow of the Institute of Promotional Marketing.

124 Lord Currie of Marylebone is a cross-bencher in the House of Lords. David Currie is an economist and professor at the University of London, Deputy Dean at London Business School and Dean of Cass Business School. He was the founding Chair of Ofcom and also a member of the Competition and Markets Authority.

125 For further discussion on country-specific advertising regulation see: Jordan, P. (2014).

take immediate action on serious breaches of the ASA rules, for instance by using its statutory powers to order the immediate suspension of an advertisement accompanied by a fine.

See above 8.4

The ASA is funded by advertisers through an arm's length arrangement that guarantees the ASA's independence. Collected by the Advertising Standards Board of Finance (Asbof) and the Broadcast Advertising Standards Board of Finance (Basbof), the 0.1 per cent levy on the cost of buying advertising space and the 0.2 per cent levy on some direct mail ensure the ASA is adequately funded to keep UK advertising standards high. Advertisers can choose to pay the levy, but they cannot choose to comply with the Advertising Codes or the ASA's rulings.

The ASA responds to approximately 31,000 complaints each year. It reviews the advertisement against the CAP Code and, if it decides to uphold the complaint, takes up the matter with the advertiser. In the majority of cases the advertiser amends or withdraws the ad. If it refuses, the ASA has a range of sanctions it can apply (though these are not statutory). The ASA also proactively conducts compliance surveys in various sectors, particularly those of public concern.

8.7.2 Advertising codes: regulating broadcast and non-broadcast advertising

The Code on the Scheduling of Television Advertising (COSTA) contains rules on how much advertising and teleshopping may be scheduled on commercial television, how many breaks are allowed and when they may be taken. The UK Code of Broadcast Advertising is for television and radio services for which Ofcom retains regulatory responsibility. These include:

See above 8.4

- the prohibition on 'political' advertising;
- 'participation TV' advertising, e.g. long-form advertising predicated on premium rate telephone services – notably chat (including 'adult' chat), 'psychic' readings and dedicated quiz TV (Call TV quiz services); and
- gambling, dating and 'message board' material where these are broadcast as advertising.

The UK advertising industry is committed to self-regulation for advertising. The requirement for advertising is that it is 'legal, decent, honest and truthful'. Detailed rules setting out what this means in practice have been drawn up by the Committee of Advertising Practice (CAP) and are known as the Advertising Code or CAP Code. The CAP code deals with non-broadcasting.[126] CAP is primarily concerned with the content of marketing communications and not with terms of business or products themselves. Some rules, however, go beyond content; for example, those that cover the administration of sales promotions, the suitability of promotional items, the delivery of products ordered through an

---

126 CAP Code Edition 12 of 2014. UK Code of Non-broadcast Advertising and Direct & Promotional Marketing (CAP Code) is the rule book for non-broadcast advertisements, sales promotions and direct marketing communications (marketing communications): www.asa.org.uk/uploads/assets/uploaded/7c856612-4a2b-4c89-bd294ab8ff4de0a7.pdf.

advertisement and the use of personal information in direct marketing. Editorial content is specifically excluded from the Code, though it might be a factor in determining the context in which marketing communications are judged. The main aim of the CAP Code is that advertisements must not mislead or be unfair. There are specific rules that cover advertising to children and adverts for alcohol, gambling, motoring, health and financial products.

The CAP non-broadcast code applies to:

1   advertisements in newspapers, magazines, brochures, leaflets, circulars, mailings, emails, text transmissions (including SMS and MMS), fax transmissions, catalogues, follow-up literature and other electronic or printed material;

2   posters and other promotional media in public places, including moving images;

3   cinema, video, Blu-ray advertisements;

4   advertisements in non-broadcast electronic media, including but not limited to: online advertisements in paid-for space (including banner or pop-up advertisements and online video advertisements); paid-for search listings; preferential listings on price comparison sites; viral advertisements; in-game advertisements; commercial classified advertisements; advert-games that feature in display advertisements; advertisements transmitted by Bluetooth; advertisements distributed through web widgets and online sales promotions and prize promotions;

5   marketing databases containing consumers' personal information;

6   sales promotions in non-broadcast media;

7   advertorials;

8   advertisements and other marketing communications by or from companies, organizations or sole traders on their own websites, or in other non-paid-for space online under their control, that are directly connected with the supply or transfer of goods, services, opportunities and gifts, or which consist of direct solicitations of donations as part of their own fund-raising activities.

The Communications Act 2003 sets out provisions for the regulation of broadcasting and television and radio services, including provisions aimed at securing standards for broadcast advertisements. The most relevant sections of the legislation concern the protection of children and young persons:

- section 319(2)(a) that persons under the age of 18 are protected; and
- section 319(2)(h) that the inclusion of advertising which may be misleading, harmful or offensive in television and radio services is prevented.

The BCAP Code applies to broadcast advertising in the UK. The overarching principles of this Code are that advertisements should not mislead or cause serious or widespread offence or harm, especially to children or the vulnerable.[127] Broadcasters are responsible for ensuring that the advertisements they transmit comply with both the spirit and the letter of the Code. All compliance matters (copy clearance, content, scheduling and the like) are the ultimate responsibility of each broadcaster.

8.7.3 Data flows in online advertising: the 'walled garden'

In the open internet market, data collection and processing are fragmented across multiple different publishers and intermediaries. When AOL first started it was essentially a 'walled garden', carefully tended and pruned to encourage users to remain on AOL-owned and affiliated sites. 'Walled garden' is a term for a browsing environment that controls a user's access to content – like Facebook Instant Articles, Snapchat Discover or Twitter Moments. Theoretically, it is more convenient to stay in the proverbial garden than to venture outside. 'Walled gardens' have been the major successes of internet tech giants, such as Google, Facebook (and therein Instagram) and Amazon which are leading the digital market by taking over 65 per cent of the total advertising spend and representing up to 90 per cent of the industry's annual growth. Meanwhile, the rest of the advertising industry is shrinking at about 3 per cent each year.

Increasingly, with the growth of social media platforms, the 'walled garden' approach also includes mobile apps that cannot or will not communicate with each other. All internet tech firms rely on the walled garden approach from large numbers of logged-in users' data sets on their multiple platforms. This log-on data allows them to identify users, based on registration data, across devices and browsers. 'Walled garden' then means they do not share data with third-parties but do allow partners to import data onto their platforms for use in advertising and marketing targeting or to measure attribution.

Data is the lifeblood of the online advertising industry, enabling brands to target advertising and to analyze campaign performance and impact. Data types include user data (demographic, interest, browsing, location, purchasing), device data (browser, operating system), contextual data (ad format, environment) and campaign data. The main sources of data are advertisers (customer data), publishers (browsing data, sign-up data), major internet companies such as Facebook (vast array of data such as location, communications, network of friends, contacts) and specialist data providers. Data may be first-party (collected directly from consumers), second-party (first-party data shared directly with a partner) or third-party data (data sold on via an intermediary). The online advertising market is increasingly divided between the 'walled gardens' of major internet companies and the fragmented open internet.

Collecting data can be problematic and lead to errors. For example, when family members share devices and logons, or consumers lie when they fill in forms. All data may quickly become out of date. Consequently, audience advertising targeting can be imperfect. The Plum Report found although 91 per cent of digital advertising targeted at over 18-year-olds reached this audience, only 50 per cent of advertising aimed at over 18-year-old females was on target in 2016.[128]

---

127 See: The BCAP Code: The UK Code of Broadcast Advertising, 2010: www.asa.org.uk/uploads/assets/
       uploaded/73f1188d-d40a-4453-92c3a6988caa69b1.pdf.
128 The Plum Report (2019) pp. 15–16.

The use of data in advertising has been affected by regulatory developments. The implementation of the General Data Protection Regulation (GDPR) has decreased availability of third-party data in the open internet market and led Google and Facebook to stop third-party access to user IDs. The proposed ePrivacy Regulation (so-called cookies law) by the EU Commission in January 2019 would require the consent of users for the lawful use of cookies and other advertising identifiers.

The Privacy and Electronic Communications Regulations (PECR)[129] sit alongside the Data Protection Act 2018 (DPA) and the GDPR. They give people specific privacy rights in relation to electronic communications, specifically relating to:

- marketing calls, emails, texts and faxes;
- cookies (and similar technologies);
- keeping communications services secure; and
- customer privacy as regards traffic and location data, itemized billing, line identification and directory listings.

In the UK the Information Commissioner is the guardian of all these data protection laws and will commence enforcement action against any organization that persistently ignores their obligations in relation to the DPA, GDPR and PECR. These pieces of UK legislation are derived from the EU 'ePrivacy Directive'[130] which complements the GDPR regime and sets out more specific privacy rights on electronic communications. It recognizes that widespread public access to digital mobile networks and the internet opens up new possibilities for businesses and users, but also new risks to their privacy. PECR have been amended seven times. The more recent changes were made in 2018, to ban cold-calling of claims management services and to introduce director liability for serious breaches of the marketing rules, and in 2019 to ban cold-calling of pensions schemes in certain circumstances. The EU is in the process of replacing the ePrivacy Directive with a new e-Privacy Regulation to sit alongside the GDPR. However, the new Regulation is not yet agreed. For now, PECR continues to apply alongside the GDPR.

For network or service providers, Article 95 of the GDPR says the GDPR does not apply where there are already specific PECR rules. This is to avoid duplication, and means that network or service providers only need to comply with PECR rules (and not the GDPR) on:

- security and security breaches;
- traffic data;
- location data;
- itemized billing; and
- line identification services.

---

129 The Privacy and Electronic Communications (EC Directive) Regulations 2003 (No. 2426).
130 Directive 2002/58/EC of the European Parliament and of the Council of 12 July 2002 concerning the processing of personal data and the protection of privacy in the electronic communications sector (Directive on privacy and electronic communications – 'ePrivacy Directive').

8.7.4 Assessment of potential harms in online advertising: dark ads

The online advertising industry has put in place numerous policies and procedures to quality assure ads and publishers involved in data flows and to prevent fraud. Social media and search platforms generally conduct checks on ads and advertisers involving automated screens and human escalation. The growth and complexity of the online advertising market has generated policy and regulatory debate in the UK and overseas. This debate has included consideration of a number of potential harms to consumers, firms and wider society that could arise as a result of the structure and operation of the sector.

We have by now heard of the dark net. Increasingly, we are made aware of 'dark ads' comprising 'dark posts', targeted ads on social media, which do not appear on the user's timeline. To avoid confusion: this does not mean 'dark social', which refers to traffic to your website from social media that is not detected by analytics tools (dark net). Dark ads are different: they do not show up in the feeds of one's followers. Instead, they show up as sponsored content in the feeds of users you might be specifically targeting. Because these dark ads are not 'published' the same way as organic posts, dark posts are more formally known on Facebook as 'unpublished posts'. This means these ads only exist for the targeted users that see them. Dark ads exist on all major social media platforms; for example, when advertising on Facebook, LinkedIn, Pinterest and Twitter, the poster can select whether to boost organic content or create a dark post. When it comes to Snapchat and Instagram, all advertising is technically 'dark posts' by default.

1 *Precise targeting* – targeted posts on e.g. Facebook can reach users based on several variables, such as age, gender, or areas of interest. The precision factor is much higher since targeted ads use specific keywords.
2 *Optimizing A/B targeting* – targeted headlines for either A or B groups, e.g. a randomly selected half of the users would see headline A, and the other half would see headline B. A/B testing helps optimize future dark posts based on valuable feedback (by way of maximum clicks to one's website), thereby improving one's organic and boosted posts.
3 *Keeping loyal followers' feeds from looking spammy* – the only people who see your dark ads/posts are the people you have carefully selected; they, in turn, are receiving your tailored ads according to their interests.

So, what are the benefit of dark ads on social media? They can boost targeted campaigns and only reach a precise audience. Here are some reasons for using dark ads:

It has become the norm that major tech companies are regulating themselves. However, the challenge for particularly Facebook and YouTube (Google) is the large volume of user-generated content that advertising might be placed against or adjacent to. Facebook has its 'Community Standards', setting out what is and is not allowed on Facebook, covering areas such as violence and criminal behaviour, safety, objectionable content, integrity and authenticity and respecting intellectual property. Facebook uses technology and manual review to enforce these standards. Facebook advertisers need to have a Facebook account in order to place ads. Facebook has advertising policies that prohibit certain content (e.g. illegal products, discriminatory practices, tobacco products, and weapons), restrict certain content (e.g. alcohol, dating, gambling) and restrict targeting practices (e.g. discrimination against users, predatory advertising).[131] Facebook uses automated screening involving artificial intelligence (AI) to check compliance with these policies, with escalation to human review. Google Ads takes a similar approach. Snapchat conducts manual checks on ads before these ads are served. Despite these measures, some bad ads are placed in publisher content or fraud takes place. The potential harms can be thought of in terms of three broad categories:

- *individual harms* – digital advertising fraud and brand risk impacting on individual firms and consumers;
- *societal harms* – practices which may be detrimental to society, such as non-transparent political advertising or discriminating on the basis of race, gender, religion etc.;
- *economic harms* – arise from lack of competition or inefficiencies within the sector, such as the dominance of Google Search advertising.

In January 2019 YouTube suspended adverts on the account of former English Defence League leader Tommy Robinson (whose real name is Stephen Yaxley-Lennon; he left the EDL in 2013). Mr Robinson was found to have broken the site's advertising rules, and YouTube found that his channel covered 'controversial issues and sensitive events'. The decision by the platform meant that the Tommy Robinson channel and account, @TRobinsonNewEra, which had 270,000 subscribers at the time, would no longer earn revenue when people watched his videos. The video posted in January 2019 to the channel showed Mr Robinson punching a migrant on an Italian street and included references to a 'rape jihad phenomenon'. YouTube said it believed in freedom of expression but also stated its platform had a duty to protect viewers from 'derogatory and disparaging' content. The decision came a day after YouTube removed adverts for anti-Islamic group Britain First from its site (16 January 2019), saying they breached its advertising rules prohibiting 'hatred, intolerance or discrimination'.

Mr Robinson's account had already been marked as 'suspended' by Twitter in March 2018 for four months because he had been judged by the US company of breaching their 'hateful conduct' policy when he had posted that '90% of grooming gang convictions are Muslims'. Twitter also acted against another account – @tommysnewspage – which had also been associated with Mr Robinson.

As we have seen above in only a brief snapshot of the current advertising market, data is used extensively within the online advertising market to enhance the targeting and measurement of advertising campaigns. Integrated firms and large platforms, such as Amazon, Facebook and Google, dominate the market with their 'walled garden' approach. This means only they have access to richer and more comprehensive datasets as these platforms operate 'logged in' environments for user services, which generates high-quality

---

131 Facebook policies on advertising: www.facebook.com/policies/ads.

data on user activity. Smaller, non-integrated firms are unlikely to have access to such data and must therefore rely instead on data from third-party data brokers, which does not perform as well. That said, the new data protection legislation – GDPR and PECR rules – has made access to data more challenging for all players, as they must verify user consent for the usage and sharing of their data.

In February 2019 the House of Commons Digital, Culture, Media and Sport Committee reported to Parliament that the era of internet self-regulation must come to an end, and that the likes of Facebook and Google should face statutory fines for failing to remove harmful content on their UK-based platforms. Further that all tech companies should have a compulsory code of ethics enforced by an independent regulator with statutory powers to launch legal action. The new system of regulation would be funded by a levy on tech companies operating in the UK. Social media companies that breach the code by failing to remove such material would face financial penalties. Jeremy Wright QC,[132] Chairman of the Committee, proposed these legislative measures:

- *Establishment of an independent regulator* to monitor technology companies for breaches of a new code of ethics, designed to halt the spread of harmful or illegal content.
- *Information Commissioner's Office (ICO) to investigate* social media platform's practices surrounding the use of users' data.
- *Levy on tech companies* to fund the investigative work of a 'beefed-up' ICO and new regulatory system.
- *Absolute transparency in online political campaigning*, including clear details on source and funding of all political ads on social media.
- *Electoral Commission's maximum fine to be increased* from £20,000 to a fixed percentage of a company's turnover. New powers for the Commission to obtain information from social media companies.[133]

See below 8.9

How is gaming and betting advertising regulated? The Football World Cup 2018 in Russia sent Britain into an unprecedented betting frenzy as England's winning start and a surge of gambling adverts on TV encouraged viewers to bet record amounts. Industry figures showed that up to £2.5bn were wagered on the tournament, an increase of almost 50 per cent on the previous World Cup, with an unprecedented rise in the number of female gamblers. At the previous World Cup only 1 in 10 bets was made by a woman; in 2018 it was 1 in 3. The scale of the increase alarmed anti-gambling campaigners and intensified calls for a crackdown on betting adverts.

---

132 The Rt Hon Jeremy Wright QC MP was appointed Secretary of State for Digital, Culture, Media and Sport on 9 July 2018. He was Attorney General from 15 July 2014 to 9 July 2018. He was elected the Conservative MP for Kenilworth and Southam in 2010.

133 The Rt Hon Jeremy Wright QC MP, Secretary of State for Digital, Culture, Media and Sport spoke at the ISPA UK Parliament and Internet Conference, 20 November 2018; extracts of which were repeated in Parliament on 18 February 2019: www.gov.uk/government/speeches/jeremy-wrights-speech-at-the-parliament-and-internet-conference.

About a fifth of adverts shown during ITV's World Cup coverage were devoted to gambling with many encouraging viewers to bet during matches on their smartphones. Campaigners argued that the adverts normalized betting for young people and encouraged people who had never bet before to start the habit.

While the Gambling Act 2005 was intended to position gambling as an acceptable leisure activity, concern has now been expressed by Gamblers Anonymous that the volume of gambling advertising goes beyond what is socially responsible. Live 'in play' betting has become so popular that more than £4,000 is being wagered per second on average during football or cricket matches. Figures from the Gambling Commission show that in 2018 the amount Britons lost gambling online increased by 10 per cent to £4.68bn. The amount lost online increased by 136 per cent since 2010.

The ASA published new standards and guidelines to protect children and young people from irresponsible gambling ads. The new guidelines came into force on 1 April 2019 and are targeted at advertising gaming and betting and its impact on under-18s. The new standards include:

- prohibit online ads for gambling products being targeted at groups of individuals who are likely to be under 18 based on data about their online interests and browsing behaviour;
- extensively list unacceptable types of content, including certain types of animated characters, licensed characters from movies or TV and sportspeople and celebrities that are likely to be of particular appeal to children and references to youth culture;
- prohibit the use in gambling ads of sportspersons, celebrities or other characters who are or appear to be under 25; and
- add to existing guidance on the responsible targeting of ads, covering all media (including social networks and other online platforms).

👁 FOR THOUGHT

Gambling ads should not be directed to under-18s or vulnerable adults. Consider how you would judge someone as vulnerable. Study the relevant gambling legislation and the CAP Code on the definition of 'vulnerable'. Draft a letter of complaint to the ASA objecting to the following Facebook advertisement. The text reads: 'Addicted to slots?' The Facebook banner ad for a gambling website features a picture of a fruit machine. Further text states: 'Register now on www.666casino & spin. You get a whole year ABSOLUTELY FREE! Get the chance to win every day. No deposit necessary'.

8.7.5 French Sapin Law on digital media advertising

Why would the author of this text single out French advertising laws? The French digital media and advertising market is one of the largest in Europe. France spent £7 bn (pounds sterling) on digital advertising in 2019, proceded by UK spend at £15 bn on push advertising alone.

Following a large-scale sector-specific investigation into online advertising and malpractice, the French Competition Authority (République Française Autorité de la Concurrence – FCA) made public an opinion No. 18-A-03 on 6 March 2018, regarding data exploitation in the online advertising sector. This opinion outlines the necessity to develop a legislative framework that will allow publishers and advertisers to benefit from a high level of transparency in their relations with advertising intermediaries and content distribution platforms.[134] Following the investigation and a finding of a magnitude of abusive practices in the digital advertising sector the French Parliament decided to extend the scope of the Sapin Law (le loi Sapin) to digital media.

The Sapin Decree came into force on 1 January 2018.[135] Loi Sapin is an anti-corruption law that was introduced in France in 1993,[136] in order to make the business of media-buying more transparent. Under the Sapin Law, media-buying agencies are not allowed to work as both the buyer and seller of advertising for their client. In other words, it means they cannot bulk-buy media inventory ahead of time and sell it back to their client at a later date. The law also requires that an agency can only be paid by the advertiser, meaning they cannot receive rebates from a publisher or media owner. The Sapin Law extends the French legislator's fight against the opaque pricing practices to the various intermediaries providing online advertising services. Sapin constitutes a clear step forward in terms of transparency in the statutory regulation of digital advertising sector.

Sellers of advertising space established in France – as well as those established in another EU or EEA Member State – insofar as they are not subject to similar obligations – are now subject to a reporting obligation toward advertisers on the global campaign price and on the unitary price of each advertising space, including the date and place of diffusion of the advertisements. The Sapin requirement includes any previously undisclosed rebates or incentives received by media buying agencies that have previously not been disclosed to advertisers. Sapin's impact has been particularly felt in the interpretation and enforcement of audit clauses in advertiser/media agency agreements requiring transparency across all media platforms. In addition, in the case of digital advertising campaigns that rely on real-time services purchasing methods, the sellers of advertising space are required to provide advertisers with information on the actual implementation and the quality of their advertising services, as well as on the ways and means used in order to provide adequate protection of the image of the advertiser.

However, the FCA noted that the new Sapin Law gave rise to different interpretations between advertisers, publishers and technical intermediaries. The notion of 'publisher' was not clear. Whom did the Sapin decree address, a publisher of a website or an agency? Who – under Sapin – could be considered as a seller of advertising space within

---

134 Opinion no. 18-A-03 of 6 March 2018 on data processing in the online advertising sector. The Autorité de la concurrence (plenary hearing) (translation into English): www.autoritedelaconcurrence.fr/doc/avis18a03_en_.pdf.

135 Sapin Decree (loi Sapin) no. 2017–159 of 9 février 2017, on digital advertising services ('the Sapin Decree') came into force on 1 January 2018 (loi Macron no. 2015-990 of 6 août 2015).

136 The Sapin Decree adapts the rules of the French Sapin Law of 29 January 1993, originally introduced for traditional media (i.e. television, radio and press) to digital media.

the meaning of the decree? If not deemed a 'seller', then the law would not apply. There are also a number of intermediaries that are likely to be involved in a digital advertising campaign, such as platforms, trading desks, demand side platforms (DSP), supply side platforms (SSP) etc. The relations between advertisers and digital media owners are rarely direct, as advertising professionals with varied roles often act as intermediary.

The qualification of these numerous actors under the Sapin Decree remains uncertain and needs to be clarified. The FCA points out that there is still doubt arising out of the aforementioned grey areas and the law calls for clarification. The French government, fully aware of the difficulties, has indicated a willingness to provide further advice in order to clarify several points of the Sapin Decree and to specify the conditions for its implementation.

8.7.6 ASA rulings

Each year, the UK public sees millions of ads, direct marketing and sales promotions about products, services, causes and awareness campaigns. Anyone can complain to the ASA free of charge; its self-regulatory values are founded on the 'Unfair Commercial Practices Directive'[137] and the Copyright Enforcement Directive[138] both relating to misleading and unfair advertising practices.

Adverts featuring a twerking businessman in high heels, a lesbian kissing scene and a mother telling her son about his dead father's favourite McDonald's burger angered viewers the most in 2018. The Moneysupermarket 'dance-off' ads, featuring a man called Dave wearing denim cutoffs and heels received the most complaints – 455 – of any campaign in any medium, with viewers objecting that it was offensive and overtly sexual, possibly homophobic and having the potential to encourage hate crimes. Match.com's ad showing a woman removing her partner's top and passionately kissing her drew the second-highest number of complaints between January and June, at 293.

However, these complaints did not lead to the ASA banning these commercials, ruling that neither was likely to cause serious or widespread offence. McDonald's swiftly pulled its poorly received campaign featuring a mother helping her son grieve for his father while sitting in one of the chain's restaurants, but not before viewers lodged 255 complaints that it exploited child bereavement to sell fast food. The ASA decided an investigation was not needed.

The vast majority of ads comply with the advertising rules. In 2018, the ASA dealt with more than 30,000 complaints, investigating concerns about ads which allegedly breached the rules of the CAP or BCAP codes. As a result, some 7,232 ads were changed or withdrawn (4,161 in 2015). The ASA publishes weekly rulings on its website.

Decisions are subject to independent judicial review by the Administrative Division of the High Court (QBD). One such case was that of *Ex parte Matthias Rath* (2000),[139] where a local health authority, namely Barking and Havering, had made a complaint to the ASA on 8 November 2000 in relation to the contents of a leaflet issued by the company owned

---

137 Directive 2005/29/EC Concerning Unfair Business-to-Consumer Commercial Practices in the Internal Market of 11 May 2005 ('The Unfair Commercial Practices Directive').
138 Directive 2006/11/EC On the Term of Protection of Copyright and Certain Related Rights of Enforcement.
139 *R v Advertising Standards Authority Ltd ex parte Matthias Rath BV* [2000] 12 WLUK 122; [2001] EMLR 22 (Also known as: *R (on the application of Matthias Rath BV) v Advertising Standards Authority Ltd*).

by the claimant, Dr Rath, to various promote health products. The complaint was upheld, and the ASA adjudicated[140] that Dr Rath had to withdraw the promotion literature. The claimant sought to halt publication of the adjudication on the grounds that its publication would be contrary to his right to freedom of expression under Article 10(1) ECHR and would damage his and his company's reputation. Dr Rath further submitted that the adjudication did not fall within the exceptions contained in Article 10(2) since it was not 'prescribed by law'.

The court refused the application and held that the adjudications of the ASA published under the Codes were 'prescribed by law' for the purposes of Article 10(2) ECHR. The Control of Misleading Advertisements Regulations 1988 provided statutory recognition of accepted methods for handling complaints. It was therefore apparent that the ASA Codes were recognized within subordinate legislation. They also satisfied the requirements of accessibility and precision set out in *Barthold v Germany* (1985).[141] Accordingly, whilst not having direct statutory effect, the ASA Codes fell within the meaning of Article 10(2); from this we can deduct that parliamentary delegation is an essential requirement for the ASA rules in question to acquire the force as having been prescribed by law.[142] In summary, in the instant case, the adjudications were, for the purpose of Article 10(2) ECHR, 'necessary for the protection of health'.[143]

The ASA blacklists traders who continue to make claims on their websites that do not comply with the advertising despite repeated requests for changes from the ASA compliance team.[144]

Sexualized imagery remains one of the most complained about areas in advertising, where the brand owners hope to entice consumers to buy their products, such as Wonderbra's billboard, 'Hello Boys' in 1994, voted the most iconic advert image of all time.

Sex sells, such as Calvin Klein's ad-campaign featuring racy images overlaid with 'sexting' messages (#mycalvins). New York shots by Mario Sorrenti feature sultry photos overlaid with sexy text messages about threesomes, nude photos and cheating on one's partner. The tagline is: 'Raw texts, real stories', and fine print says the chats are 'inspired by actual events and people'. Tweeters commented on the ads more than 122,000 times worldwide in one day in 2015. The infamous Protein World 'beach body ready' ads caused public outcries in 2015, but the brand reported £1m additional revenue over the first four days of the advert going 'viral'.

In August 2018 the confectionery company Mars pulled its advertising from YouTube after one of its brands was shown with a drill rap music video. The move was prompted after an advert for Starburst sweets was put at the start of a video by group Moscow17. One of the group's members, Siddique Kamara, also known as Incognito and SK, was stabbed to death in south London in August 2018. Drill music has been linked to violence with lyrics by rappers often talking about stabbings and killings, using gang-related symbols, such as wearing balaclavas. It has also been used to fuel rivalries between gangs.

---

140 Pursuant to the 'British Codes of Advertising and Sales Promotion', 10th edition 1999.
141 (1985) 7 EHRR 383 (ECtHR).
142 Ibid. at paras 45, 46 and 47.
143 *Ex parte Matthias Rath* [2000] at paras 28–30 (Turner J).
144 For a list of non-compliant advertisers in 2019 see: www.asa.org.uk/codes-and-rulings/non-compliant-online-advertisers.html.

> ❖ **KEY CASE** — *ASA ruling Amazon Europe Core Sarl (15 August 2018)*[145]

The advert

Claims on www.amazon.co.uk, promoted their 'one-day delivery' service as part of Amazon Prime membership. In the top right-hand corner of the home page of the website, the ad featured the claim 'One-Day Delivery for Christmas'. Further text on the home page stated, 'get unlimited One-Day Delivery with Amazon Prime', with a link to start a 30-day free trial with Amazon Prime. On a web page titled 'About Amazon Prime', under the heading 'Delivery', text stated 'Unlimited One-Day Delivery on millions of eligible items at no extra cost. Depending on the time of day that you place your order and your delivery address, if in stock it'll be dispatched that same day and delivered the next day'. On a separate web page, text stated 'Start Your Amazon Prime Free Trial Membership. Start a 30-day free trial to also get: Enjoy fast delivery. Unlimited One-Day Delivery on millions of eligible items'. On a product listings page, the web page included a tick-box alongside the text 'Yes, I want a free trial with FREE One-Day Delivery on this order'.

The issue

Two hundred eighty complaints were received. Complainants reported not receiving their delivery by the following day, challenged whether the 'one-day delivery' claims were misleading.

Response by Amazon

Amazon Europe Core Sarl t/a Amazon pointed out that the vast majority of the complaints were received following widespread media coverage of an initial handful of complaints about the issue. Amazon explained that the Prime service included benefits relating to delivery, video and music among other things. They said one of the benefits was the use of the One-Day Delivery service at no additional cost, whereby Prime members were not charged delivery fees when selecting the One-Day Delivery option, whereas non-Prime members had to pay a flat fee.

Amazon said that consumers were likely to understand from the ad that they would not have to pay to use the One-Day Delivery option and that it was available on a selection of items. They said the ads did not promise a particular speed of delivery of a particular product. They believed consumers understood from using the website that individual delivery dates were displayed for each order and that they would have to check each item they were interested in purchasing to find out whether One-Day Delivery was available and what the delivery date was with One-Day Delivery at that particular time to the address to which they wanted the item delivered.

---

145 Amazon Europe Core Sarl, 5 Rue Plaetis, L-2338 Luxembourg, 15 August 2018. Complaint Ref: A17–408329.

Amazon explained that for a delivery to be recorded as on-time, the delivery needed to have been received by the customer one day after it was dispatched. They said that late deliveries could occur for a number of reasons that were specific to each order and often outside of their control such as bad weather, carrier failure and human error. They said they received very few customer complaints relating to late deliveries. Amazon said that their Deliveries in the UK Help page of their website, which was two clicks away from the home page, stated that the delivery time for their One-Day Delivery service was one day after dispatch. They showed that it was also stated on a separate web page 'About One-Day Delivery'. That web page said that the time of day will affect whether or not dispatch occurred on the day of the order.

Assessment

Upheld
The ASA noted that the home page featured the claim 'get unlimited One-Day Delivery with Amazon Prime', with a link to start a 30-day free trial with Amazon Prime. In the absence of information to indicate otherwise, the ASA considered consumers were likely to interpret the claim 'One-Day Delivery' in those contexts to mean that all Prime labelled items were available for delivery by the end of the day after the order was placed, so long as the customer did not order too late in the day or for Sunday delivery.

The ASA noted that text on one web page in the 'Help and Customer Service' section of the website stated that the delivery time for One-Day Delivery was '1 business day after dispatch', while another web page in that section included text which stated 'If you choose One-Day Delivery, your order will be dispatched with the intention that it's delivered one day after dispatch'. But this information was unlikely to be of use to consumers as it did not inform them how soon after their order they would receive their delivery. In any case, many consumers were unlikely to visit those separate web pages (which in some cases were two clicks away) before deciding to make a decision in relation to purchasing Amazon Prime.

The ad breached CAP Code (Edition 12) rules 3.1 (Misleading advertising), 3.7 (Substantiation) and 3.9 (Qualification).

Action
The ad must not appear again in its current form. Amazon had to make it clear that some Prime labelled items were not available to be delivered by the next day.

The smartphone application (app), 'Natural Cycles', promoted itself as a form of non-hormonal, non-intrusive contraception. The Stockholm-based company, founded by Cern physicist Elina Berglund and her husband, Raoul Scherwitzl, claimed to be 93 per cent effective with typical use – and without the side effects that many women experience from hormonal birth control. Women input information about their menstrual cycles and body temperature into the app, and it used algorithms to predict which days they were at risk of getting pregnant in the event of unprotected sex. Natural Cycles' annual subscription in the UK was £39.99 in 2018. The data from the Swedish technology firm suggested that, if used correctly, this method might be more effective than other methods such as the combined pill (9 in 100) or condoms (18 in 100). But the NHS criticized the study's research methods, saying it was based on retrospective data and was not impartial, given that it was paid for by the app's founders. Not only was the Swedish startup company criticized by the ASA in the UK, but Swedish public broadcaster SVT reported in January 2018 that 37 of the 668 women who sought an abortion at one of Stockholm's largest hospitals from September to December 2017 had relied on Natural Cycles for birth control.[146]

❖ KEY CASE   *ASA Ruling on NaturalCycles Nordic AB Sweden t/a Natural Cycles (29 August 2018)[147]*

The advert
A paid-for post on Facebook for Natural Cycles, seen on 20 July 2017, stated 'Natural Cycles is a highly accurate, certified, contraceptive app that adapts to every woman's unique menstrual cycle. Sign up to get to know your body and prevent pregnancies naturally'. A video below the text also stated, 'Natural Cycles officially offers a new, clinically tested alternative to birth control methods'.

Issue
Five complainants challenged whether the following claims were misleading and could be substantiated:

1 'highly accurate contraceptive app'; and
2 'clinically tested alternative to birth control methods'.

Response from Natural Cycles Nordic AB Sweden
1 & 2: Natural Cycles provided copies of their EC medical device certification; a prospective observational study looking at the efficacy of the app using the Pearl Index (number of pregnancies per 100 woman years); two articles on retrospective studies carried out; and a fact sheet that was available on their website. They said that the app was certified and CE marked and had been marketed as a contraceptive since February 2017. They explained that the certification was based on clinical data which demonstrated the effectiveness of the app as a contraceptive, and the clinical claims for the medical device were based on clinical studies that they had carried out. The app was stand-alone software

---

146 Source: '"P-app" anmäls till Läkemedelsverket'. Svt Nyheter, Publicerad 11 januari 2018.
147 NaturalCycles Nordic AB Sweden, Luntmakargatan 26, 111 37 Stockholm, Sweden. 29 August 2018. Complaint Ref: A17–393896.

intended to be used for contraception and fertility monitoring and would inform the user whether and when they could get pregnant.

They stated that based on their clinical evaluation, claims on contraceptive effectiveness were that the app had a method failure rate of 0.5, which was a measurement as to how often the app incorrectly displayed a green day when the user was actually fertile and got pregnant after having unprotected intercourse on that green day. This meant that 5 out of 1,000 women who used the app for one year would become pregnant specifically due to a falsely attributed green day. The app had a perfect-use failure rate of 1.0, which meant that 10 out of 1,000 women who used the app for one year and became pregnant would have done so either because (i) they had unprotected intercourse on a green day that was falsely attributed as non-fertile (method failure) or (ii) the user had protected intercourse on a red day but the chosen method of contraception failed. The app had a typical-use failure rate of 6.8, which meant that in total 68 women out of 1,000 got pregnant during one year of use due to all possible reasons, including wrongly attributed green days, having unprotected intercourse on red days and failure of contraceptive method used on red days.

2. They clarified that the claim 'Clinically tested alternative to birth control methods' was a quote from the news site Business Insider which they considered to be correct as Natural Cycles was clinically tested and intended and certified for contraceptive use and could therefore be used as an alternative to other birth control methods. The claims were backed by scientific evidence, including clinical trials.

Assessment

Upheld

The ASA considered that, in the context of the ad, the claim 'highly accurate contraceptive app' would be understood by consumers to mean that the app had a high degree of accuracy and was therefore very reliable in being able to prevent unwanted pregnancies. The ASA further considered that the claim 'Clinically tested alternative to birth control methods', presented alongside the 'Highly accurate' claim, would be understood to mean that the app was a reliable method of contraception which could be used in place of other established birth control methods, including those that were highly reliable in preventing unwanted pregnancies.

The ASA noted from the studies that the reporting of intercourse was low with only 32 per cent of cycles inputting such data, and that only 9.6 per cent of cycles were considered as perfect-use, where the app had been used precisely as instructed. Given the very low level of perfect-use by users of the app and the significant difference between the effectiveness of the app when in perfect-use and in typical-use, we considered that it would be misleading to base an accuracy claim on the perfect-use results and that the relevant data was the level of effectiveness seen in typical-use. The ASA concluded that the advertisement was misleading to describe the app as 'highly accurate'.

The ad breached CAP Code (Edition 12) rules 3.1 (Misleading advertising), 3.7 (Substantiation), 3.1 (Exaggeration) and 12.1 (Medicines, medical devices, health-related products and beauty products).

Action

The ad must not appear again in the form complained about. Natural Cycles Nordic AB Sweden were told not to state or imply that the app was a highly accurate method of contraception and to take care not to exaggerate the efficacy of the app in preventing pregnancies.

 FOR THOUGHT

A TV ad for Haertel Beanz, seen in September 2019, began with two men standing in an office kitchen. One of them, who was wearing gym clothing, said, 'I've just returned from a high intensity workout. I lifted some seriously heavy weights'. On-screen text stated: 'Protein contributes to a growth in muscle mass'. The microwave pinged, and the other man took out a tub of baked beans. The first man asked, 'What's that?' to which the other replied, 'I'm just having some beans'. On-screen text stated: 'High in protein. High in fibre. Low in fat'. The final scene showed a tin of Haertel Beanz next to a plate of jacket potato and baked beans. Text on the screen stated: 'Good for you, without going on about it'.

Six complainants challenged whether the ad made an implied health claim, that eating Haertel Beanz had similar health benefits to exercise. Their complaint is related to the BCAP Code, stating that Haertel Foods breached rules 13.4 and 13.42 of the code ('Food, supplements and associated health or nutrition claims').

You are acting as lawyer for Haertel Foods UK Ltd. Draft a letter to the Advertising Standards Authority (ASA) citing EU legislation in your response (i.e. Regulation (EC) 1924/2006) on nutrition and health claims made on foods), also reflected in the BCAP Code. In your argument you need to make it clear that the advertisement did not imply any equivalence between Haertel Beanz and exercise.

8.8 Regulating the film and video industry: the British Board of Film Classification

Deciding where to draw the line when regulating sexually explicit and violent material relates to the degree of control exercised by a society. Film, video and games regulators in each country have to decide where to place restrictions on access to these images, who can watch them and what is appropriate for adults. They can then decide for themselves what is appropriate. The means of regulating sexually explicit and violent material has been debated for decades. Arguments over what denotes a masterpiece or an obscenity in film, image or literature abound.

8.8.1 Film censorship in the early twentieth century: the British Board of Film Censors

British film censorship goes back to the early 1900s when the first film regulator, the British Board of Film Censors (BBFC), set up in 1912. It was a self-regulatory body, and by the mid-1920s it became general practice for local authorities to accept the decisions of the board.

When T. P. O'Connor was appointed President of the BBFC in 1916,[148] one of his first tasks was to give evidence to the Cinema Commission of Inquiry, set up by the National Council for Public Morals. He summarized the board's policy by listing 43 grounds for a film's exclusion or rejection. Some of the topics included:

- the irreverent treatment of sacred subjects;
- drunken scenes carried to excess;
- vulgar accessories;
- the *modus operandi* of criminals;
- nude figures;
- indecorous dancing;
- excessively passionate love scenes;
- realistic horrors of warfare including scenes and incidents calculated to afford information to the enemy;
- subjects dealing with India in which British officers are seen in an odious light;
- scenes laid in disorderly houses.

Mrs Mary Whitehouse became the first General Secretary of the National Viewers' and Listeners' Association in 1965. The prominent campaigner for public morality made it her life's quest to highlight public decency and the moral decline of television standards – particularly at the BBC. The first chairman of the subsequent BSC (Broadcasting Standards Council), Lord Rees-Mogg, credited Mrs Whitehouse for her influence on the setting-up of the Council in 1988 and for ensuring that the public view was always taken into account. Mrs Whitehouse threatened legal action a number of times against the BBC, including against programmes such as Monty Python's Flying Circus, The Kenny Everett Television Show – with its skimpily clad dance troupe, Hot Gossip, run by Arlene Phillips – and Doctor Who. Mrs Whitehouse indirectly influenced the BBFC with her quest for public morals and

---

148 President from 11 December 1916 to 18 November 1929. Thomas Power O'Connor (1848–1929), known as T. P. O'Connor, was a journalist and Irish nationalist, as well as a Member of Parliament at Westminster for nearly 50 years.

decency. She also famously took out a private prosecution against the editor of *Gay News*, Denis Lemon, which ultimately bankrupted him and the magazine.[149]

The American film director Stanley Kubrick had moved to England in 1962 to film *Lolita*, his motivation being that the UK would prove to have more relaxed censorship laws than the United States. But he fell afoul of the Obscene Publications Act 1959 and Mrs Mary Whitehouse. He subsequently made a large number of films including *Dr Strangelove* (with Peter Sellers), *2001: A Space Odyssey* and *Eyes Wide Shut. Lolita* was eventually screened in 1997

Kubrick's 1971 film *A Clockwork Orange*, based on an adaptation of Anthony Burgess' novel of 1962, proved to be another controversial film. It worried the government to such an extent that before the film's general release in January 1972, Home Secretary Reginald Maudling arranged a private viewing of the film. *A Clockwork Orange* is a dark satirical film depicting Alex (Malcolm McDowell), a charismatic delinquent who engages in 'ultra-violence', including rape, performed to Beethoven's music. The BBFC had passed the film with an 'X' rating, requiring no cuts (the age bar for an 'X'-rated film had just been raised from 16 to 18). With the film's general release, the BBFC had advised the distributors, Warner Brothers, that the film portrayed 'an unrelieved diet of vicious violence and hooliganism'.

Kubrick became a target for hate mail and abusive phone calls in the UK after a number of rapes and murders in the early 1970s were linked to the film, including a sex attack in Lancashire carried out by a gang chanting the Gene Kelly song *Singin' in the Rain*. This resulted in Kubrick secretly withdrawing the film by arranging with Warners that the film would just be allowed to die off quietly, after further allegations that *A Clockwork Orange* was inspiring young people to copy its scenes of violence. Stanley Kubrick died on 7 March 1999, aged 70, and the director's widow, German-born actress and painter Christiane, retained all consultation rights on the re-released *A Clockwork Orange* in the same year. In the film a large floral oil painting by Christiane can be seen during the famous *Singin' in the Rain* scene.

When the film *The Exorcist* opened in America on 26 December 1973, the response was immediate and extraordinary. It is based on a book by William Peter Blatty, published in 1971, and depicts a demonic possession and subsequent exorcism of a young girl in Washington, DC. Despite much press attention in advance of the film's release, the 'Classification and Ratings Administration' of the Motion Picture Academy of America (MPAA) granted *The Exorcist* an uncut 'R' rating ('for strong language and disturbing images'), allowing minors to view the film if accompanied by an adult. MPAA President Jack Valenti pointed out that *The Exorcist* contained 'no overt sex' and 'no excessive violence', a conclusion echoed by the generally cautious Catholic Conference, which rated the film 'A-IV', an adult classification meaning that the film was 'moral, but may offend some [adult] viewers'. Yet Washington police barred persons under the age of 17 from showings of the movie in spite of the MPAA's 'R' rating. Eventually, Marvin Goldman, head of the KB Theatre chain, which owned the Cinema Theatre in DC where the movie was first shown, told the *Washington Post* that he would comply with the (MPAA) ruling, stating that the movie

---

149 *R v Lemon (Denis); R v Gay News Ltd* [1979] AC 617 ('Gay News case'). The indictment described the offending publication as 'a blasphemous libel concerning the Christian religion, namely an obscene poem and illustration vilifying Christ in his life and in his crucifixion'.

should have been rated X (no one under 17 admitted) in the first place.[150] Walter Cronkite devoted a full ten minutes of his legendary CBS news programme to 'The Exorcist Phenomenon' and the history of demonic possession.

The film struck a unique chord with audiences around the world. In Milan, the crowd at a packed news conference refused to leave a museum where the film's director, William Friedkin, and technical adviser, Father Thomas Bermingham, were answering questions about *The Exorcist*. In Rome, the film made the national news when a sixteenth-century church across the street from a cinema where the film premiered was struck by lightning, causing an ancient cross to plummet from its roof onto the pavement below. At a preview screening in New York, one audience member had to be helped out after becoming dizzy, provoking a wave of press reports of fainting, vomiting and other hysterical reactions. By the time *The Exorcist* came to the UK, rumours of its traumatizing power had grown to such proportions that the St John Ambulance Brigade were standing by for the first showings around London.

But *The Exorcist* was immediately banned by the BBFC, due to Mary Whitehouse's urging them to prohibit it. She called the film 'outright nasty – blasphemous and evil', despite the fact she had never seen a frame of it. She relied purely on adverse media coverage such as Stanley Kaufmann's comment in *New Republic*: 'This is the most scary film I've seen in years – the only scary film I've seen in years . . . If you want to be shaken – and I found out, while the picture was going, that that's what I wanted – then *The Exorcist* will scare the hell out of you'.[151] The British film board eventually granted an 'X' certificate to *The Exorcist* in January 1974, which allowed over-18s to view it without cuts or alterations. At the Golden Globe awards of 1974, *The Exorcist* picked up awards for Best Film, Best Director (William Friedkin), Best Screenplay (William Peter Blatty) and Best Supporting Actress (Linda Blair), while the Oscars that year generated ten nominations including Best Picture, Best Screenplay (Blatty) and Best Sound. In box-office terms, the movie became the biggest-grossing hit in Warner Brothers' history, nearly trebling the $34m gross of the studio's previous record holder, *My Fair Lady*.

Prior to the 1990s it was not an uncommon occurrence that local authorities would ban films in their local cinemas, such as Ken Russell's *The Devils* and Stanley Kubrick's *A Clockwork Orange* in 1971[152] and Monty Python's *Life of Brian* in 1988. In 1996, Westminster Council banned *Crash* by David Cronenberg, a film first premiered at the 1996 London Film Festival. When Westminster Council demanded cuts to certain parts of this sexually violent film – solely for screenings in Westminster – the distributors declined, and the film was therefore banned from screens in the West End, including Leicester Square. However, cinemagoers could easily see the film in neighbouring Camden, where that council allowed the film to play uncut with its BBFC certificate.

Hally (2012) found that more broadminded councils, such as Manchester, were frequently ahead of BBFC policy and practice during the 1950s and 1960s, first in having an adults-only category before the 'X' certificate, then in relaxing the strictures against screen nudity (the naturist films) and over artistic sex and 'bad language' (e.g. *Ulysses*). Generally Conservative-led councils, such as Sale, continued trying to hold back the tide of 'X' films.

---

150 Source: 'The Exorcist: No one under 17 admitted', by Tom Shales, *Washington Post*, 4 January 1974.

151 Kaufmann's quote in *New Republic*, as quoted in Travers, P. and Reiff, S. (1974), pp. 152–154.

152 *A Clockwork Orange* was re-released uncut and passed by the BBFC on 13 February 2019.

Manchester tended to be more liberal-minded than the BBFC on matters of nudity, sex and language but less so on issues of violence and disorder.[153]

The Video Recordings Act 1984 was passed by Parliament to regulate and classify video recordings offered for sale or hire commercially in the UK. The President and Vice Presidents of the BBFC were so designated, and charged with applying the new test of 'suitability for viewing in the home'. At this point the Board's title was changed to the British Board of Film Classification to reflect the fact that classification plays a far larger part in the BBFC's work than censorship.

8.8.2 The British Board of Film Classification and its remit

The British Board of Film Classification (BBFC) is an independent self-regulator and censor of films, videos, DVDs and video games. Its income is from the fees it charges for its services, calculated by measuring the running time of films or games submitted for classification. The BBFC consults the Department of Digital, Culture, Media and Sport before making any changes to its fees. The BBFC rates about 10,000 pieces a year, though traditional classified film content has been steadily falling.

Since 2017 video-on-demand (VOD) and online video subscription services such as Netflix, Amazon and NowTV have been included in the BBFC's remit (though the latter is on a voluntary basis). The BBFC licensing scheme allows Digital Video Services to use existing BBFC home entertainment classifications on their platforms when they make the equivalent digital versions available under the Video Recordings Act 1984. Digital-only classification in 2017 amounted to 3,565 works viewed, representing just under 160,000 minutes of content classified, a 25.3 per cent increase from 2016.

Each of these services has taken a different approach to film content. Amazon UK acquires prestige movies to premiere on their service after a traditional theatrical window for films, such as *Moonlight, The Handmaiden, The Big Sick* and *Manchester by the Sea*. Netflix (USA) streams exclusives on its platform such as *The Crown, House of Cards, The Meyerowitz Stories* and *Mudbound*. NowTV – which does not use BBFC classifications – offers consumers earlier access to cinema films from Sky's premium movie channels without the need for a 12-month contractual commitment, a dish, or to be tied to linear broadcast schedules.

BARB (Broadcasters Audience Research Board) research showed that in 2017 some 9.5 million UK homes had at least one VOD subscription. Although sales of physical media continued to decline, the growth in digital subscriptions and digital transactions helped the UK video market grow by 7.5 per cent, the third consecutive year of growth. The study found that nearly 50 per cent of children in the UK have access to at least one VOD service, with the number rising to 60 per cent for those aged between 16 and 24.[154]

On a best practice, voluntary basis, the BBFC also regulates mobile services and content delivered via mobile networks, such as EE, O2, Three and Vodafone. The BBFC's Classification Guidelines for film and video form the basis of the Mobile Classification Framework, which defines content that is unsuitable for customers under the age of 18. In addition, the BBFC maintains an additional Classification Framework specifically for EE network customers who wish to set filter levels to 'Strict'. This Framework outlines

---

153 Hally, M. (2012).
154 Source: 'Netflix UK subs rate slows as NowTV gains – BARB', by Jesse Whittock, 9 January 2018: https://tbivision.com/2018/01/09/netflix-uk-subs-rate-slows-as-now-tv-gains-barb/.

content that is unsuitable for children under the age of 12 and is based on BBFC Classification Guidelines for PG.

In 2017, the BBFC adjudicated in relation to 21 cases on whether filters had been appropriately applied to websites. These requests came from website owners, members of the public and the Mobile Network Operators (MNOs).

BBFC age ratings are used by VOD platforms, content producers, film studios and airlines. These include:

- Amazon Instant Video/Prime Instant Video
- BFI Player
- British Airways
- British Airways High Life
- BT TV
- Curzon Home Cinema
- DisneyLife
- Find Any Film
- Google – Including Google Play Store, YouTube Movies, Google Web Search
- iTunes Film Store
- Joybear
- Microsoft Film & TV Store
- Netflix
- Rakuten TV
- Sky Store
- Soho Theatre On Demand
- Sony Entertainment Network
- Virgin Media
- Virgin Atlantic

8.8.3 Legislation covering film, video and games censorship

The BBFC is governed by several pieces of legislation, the most significant being the Video Recordings Acts (VRA) of 1984 and 2010, which particularly affect classification standards. The 1984 Act requires all 'video works' (films, TV programmes, video games etc.) which are supplied on a disc, tape or any other device capable of storing data electronically to be classified by the BBFC, unless they fall within the definition of an exempted work.

The Video Recordings Act 2010 repealed and then brought back into force parts of the Video Recordings Act 1984.[155] The reintroduction of the 1984 Act was deemed necessary after Parliament forgot to notify the European Commission in August 2009 of the (original) existence of the 1984 Act.[156] This meant neither the 1984 nor the 2010 VRA were initially in accordance with Directive 98/34/EC.[157]

---

155 Section 1 VRA 2010 ('Repeal and revival of provisions of the Video Recordings Act 1984'): ss 1 to 17, 19, 21 and 22 of the VRA 1984 ceased to be in force.
156 House of Commons, Parliamentary debate of 6 January 2010, Hansard, cc 181–209.
157 EC Directive 98/34/EC laying down a procedure for the provision of information in the field of technical standards and regulations and of rules on Information Society services of 22 June 1998.

Section 4A of the 1984 VRA requires 'special regard' to be given to the likelihood of video works being viewed in the home and to any harm that may be caused to potential viewers or, through their behaviour, to society by the manner in which the work deals with:

- criminal behaviour;
- illegal drugs;
- violent behaviour or incidents;
- horrific behaviour or incidents; or
- human sexual activity.

Section 4A(1) of the Video Recordings Act 1984 (VRA) came under judicial review scrutiny when the administrative court was asked to examine the meaning of the phrase 'harm that may be caused'. In BBFC v Video Appeals Committee (2008)[158] the BBFC had declined to classify the video game 'Manhunt 2' marketed by Rockstar Games Inc, having described it as depicting brutal and unremitting violence towards humans.

Rockstar appealed to the Video Appeals Committee (VAC) which in turn allowed Rockstar's appeal. The committee stated that the game could be classified as one suitable only for those over the age of 18. They made reference to an introductory statement made by a Home Office Minister in respect of section 4A(1) VRA. The statement said that that there might be some works that the BBFC believed would have such a devastating effect on individuals or on society if they were released that there should be the possibility of their being refused classification altogether. The VAC also made clear its interpretation of the reference to the phrase 'harm that may be caused' in section 4A(1) of the Act. It held that there must be *actual* harm as opposed to potential harm.

Granting the application, Mr Justice Mitting said that it was not and had never been a legal requirement that the BBFC or the Video Appeals Committee should determine that a video game would have a devastating effect on individuals or on society before refusing certification. The judge then turned to the Committee's interpretation of 'harm'. The words in section 4A(1) of the Act were plainly directed to harm that *might* be caused. If Parliament had intended it to be necessary to demonstrate that harm had been caused, then the words 'that may be' could have been omitted. The judge said that it was self-evident that, in respect of video games that had yet to be released, the Committee would have to judge their impact if they were to be released.

The task of both the BBFC and the VAC was to have special regard to any harm that might, in the future, be caused to potential viewers. If the final conclusions of the committee had stood alone, it would be difficult to challenge them on the ground of legal error. The committee had misinterpreted Parliamentary comments and the interpretation of the words 'harm that may be caused'. In those circumstances, the only just method of

---

158 R (on the application of British Board of Film Classification) v Video Appeals Committee [2008] EWHC 203 (Admin); [2008] 1 WLR 1658 (sub nom. 'BBFC v Video Appeals Committee').

disposing of the case was to quash the committee's decision and to have the matter remitted back to the BBFC for classification of the work.

The Obscene Publications Acts 1959 and 1964 made it illegal to publish a work in the UK which is regarded as 'obscene' in content (as a whole). The film, DVD, game etc. must have the tendency to 'deprave and corrupt', unless the 'publication' can be justified as being for the 'public good' on the grounds that it is in the interests of science, art, literature or learning or other objects of general concern.

Section 22 of the Public Order Act 1986 makes it illegal to distribute or play to the public a recording of images or sounds which are threatening, abusive or insulting if the intention is to stir up racial hatred or hatred on the grounds of sexual orientation.

There are two Acts which cover animal welfare issues in films. The Cinematograph Films (Animals) Act 1937 renders it illegal to show any scene 'organised or directed' for the purposes of a film that involves the cruel treatment of any animal. The Animal Welfare Act 2006 makes it illegal to show or publish a recording of an animal fight which has taken place in the UK since 6 April 2007. This is to combat illegal dog fighting and the breeding of dangerous dogs for fights, habitually filmed and uploaded by criminals on to YouTube.

Trading standards and law enforcement officers have the power to seize illegal video works including, but not limited to, DVDs, Blu-rays and video games The BBFC is designated by the government (the Department of Digital, Culture, Media and Sport) to provide evidence to help secure convictions under the terms of the Video Recordings Act (VRA) 1984 for copyright infringement. The BBFC will issue a Certificate of Evidence under the VRA 1984 or the Criminal Procedure (Scotland) Act 1995. This evidence is admissible in court as 'standalone' evidence and does not require anyone from the BBFC to attend as a witness.

8.8.4 BBFC classifications

In February 2019 new BBFC Classification Guidelines came into force which now cover age-ratings across different platforms. Following a wide consultation of some 10,000 participants (2018), the BBFC found that demand for age classification has never been higher, with 97 per cent of people saying they benefitted from age ratings being in place. Ninety-one per cent of people (and 95 per cent of teenagers) wanted consistent age ratings that they recognized from the cinema and DVD to apply to content accessed through streaming services. The BBFC's consultation confirmed that people felt a heightened sense of anxiety when it came to depictions of 'real world' scenarios, in which audiences – especially young people – are likely to be concerned that it could happen to them. For example, realistic contemporary scenarios showing terrorism, self-harm, suicide and discriminatory behaviour.

The large-scale research also found that attitudes towards sexual threat and sexual violence had moved on since 2013–2014. Although the BBFC already classifies such content restrictively, the respondents said that certain depictions of rape in particular should receive a higher rating. For this reason, the BBFC adjusted its Classification Guidelines in these areas. Strongest sex references, in particular those that use the language of pornography, are now classified as 18. The survey found that film classification checking is most evident among parents of children under the age of 12, finding that 87 per cent check all or most of the time, and a further 9 per cent check occasionally. Interestingly, there has been a marked increase in the level of claimed classification checking by parents of children aged 12–14 years – up from 90 per cent ever checking in 2013 to 97 per cent in 2018.[159]

The BBFC examines each film (DVD, video, game etc.) for its overall tone, making an overall assessment on classification. A 'U' ('Universal') film should be suitable for audiences aged 4 years and over, allowing very mild bad language, such as 'damn' and 'hell'. The 1964 Walt Disney version of *Mary Poppins*, featuring Julie Andrews and Dick van Dyke, and the 2018 *Mary Poppins Returns*, with Emily Blunt and Ben Whishaw both received a U-rating, and so does *Peppa Pig: Festival of Fun* (2019).

A 'PG' (Parental Guidance) film should not disturb a child aged 8. There may be mild bad language, such as 'shit' or 'son of a bitch', and violence is only acceptable in a historical or fantasy setting. An example would be the 2007 film, *Mr Bean's Holiday*, starring Rowan Atkinson, or Michael Jackson's *This Is It*, released following the legendary pop singer's death in June 2009, or *The Boy Who Harnessed the Wind* (2019).

The 12A classification requires an adult to accompany any child under 12 seeing a 12A film at the cinema. This ought to be strictly enforced by cinema staff, and a cinema may lose its licence if adult accompaniment is not enforced. In 2019 the documentary *Jimi Hendrix: Electric Church*, received a 12A rating. The film is about Jimi Hendrix's historic performance at the 1970 Atlanta Pop Festival. There is infrequent use of strong language ('f**k') as well as uses of 'hell', 'crap', 'screwed' and 'freaking'. There is footage of a stall at a music festival selling marijuana plants, in addition to brief sight of a man smoking hash from a pipe. The film also shows some natural nudity, when men and women take off their clothes at the music festival. Additionally, there are verbal references to campus killings at Kent State University, as well as brief sight of a newspaper featuring a black-and-white photo of a dead body.

No one under 15 is legally allowed to see, buy or rent a certificate '15'-rated film, DVD or video games. This classification generally includes strong violence, frequent strong language such as 'f***k', and brief scenes of sexual activity or violence are permitted – so are discriminatory language and drug-taking.

A Northern Soul is a UK documentary classified 15 for cinema release for around 20 uses of strong language. Prior to its submission to the BBFC in early 2018, Sheffield City Council classified the film 12A, for its premiere, as did Hull City Council. The film's director complained in the media about the BBFC's decision. A letter co-signed by three Hull MPs was sent to the BBFC requesting that the 15 classification be reviewed, to which David Austin, the Chief Executive of the BBFC, responded. The film was re-classified 12A by seven local authorities (Sheffield, Hull, Leeds, Liverpool, Halifax, Southampton and Lambeth).[160] 15 remains the most common classification.

No one younger than 18 may see an 18-rated film in a cinema, rent or buy an 18-rated video work. Adults should be free to choose their own entertainment, and this includes 'sex works', i.e. for the purpose of sexual arousal or stimulation. Sex works containing clear images of real sex, strong fetish material, sexually explicit animated images or other

159 Source: BBFC Press release 16 January 2019: www.bbfc.co.uk/about-bbfc/media-centre/bbfc-launches-new-classification-guidelines-and-calls-greater-age-rating.
160 Source: Minutes of the BBFC Board meeting No. 204 Classification Meeting. Friday 14 September 2018.

very strong sexual images are confined to the R18 category. In the 18 category are *Now Apocalypse* and *The Downward Spiral* (both 2019), both containing strong sex and sexual references. *A Clockwork Orange* remains 18 under the re-release of 2019 (and used to be an 'X' rating under the old categorization in 1971). Classification exceptions in this category include:

- where the material is in breach of the criminal law;
- where material or treatment appears to harm individuals through their behaviour or to society. For example, the detailed portrayal of violent or dangerous acts, or of illegal drug use, which may cause harm to public health or morals. This may include portrayals of sadistic violence, rape or other non-consensual sexually violent behaviour which make this violence look appealing; reinforce the suggestion that victims enjoy rape or other non-consensual sexually violent behaviour; or which invite viewer complicity in rape, other non-consensual sexually violent behaviour or other harmful violent activities;
- where there are more explicit images of sexual activity in the context of a sex work. In the case of video works, which may be more accessible to younger viewers, intervention may be more frequent than for cinema films.

The BBFC has, from time to time, rejected foreign films even though they were openly released in their countries of origin, with sexual topics generally being the norm for rejection.

Reinventing Marvin (*Marvin ou la belle éducation*) is a French drama, classified in France for the 15 age group, released in 2017. The film follows a boy's path through an abusive childhood to a theatrical career in Paris. The film contains one scene, featuring the central character being subjected to a sexual assault by an older boy at school. There is use of strong language ('f**k', 'motherf**ker'), as well as milder terms such as 'bitch' and 'Jesus'. There is also use of discriminatory language ('nigger', 'faggot'), and there are strong sex scenes with rear nudity.

When the BBFC board viewed the film, the Head of Compliance requested proofs of age for the actors involved, which confirmed the central character was played by an actor who was 15 at the time of filming while the older boy was played by an actor who was 18. The board concluded that the scene included a potentially indecent image of a child within the meaning of the Protection of Children Act 1978. Accordingly, a cut was required.

The company, Peccadillo Pictures, appealed against the proposed cut, submitting documentary proof that included parental consent and information about the child protection steps taken on set. The scene was viewed again by the President, Chief Executive, Head of Compliance and Compliance Manager of the BBFC. However, it was concluded that the fact the film makers did not intend to create an indecent image did not alter the fact of the indecency of the image in question. The cut was upheld and the cut version received a 15 rating.[161]

---

161 Ibid.

8.8.5 Public complaints and BBFC decisions

The BBFC generally receives a relatively small number of complaints about its classification decisions, In 2017, for example, there were only 262 complaints received compared to 371 the previous year.[162] Here follow some examples which received public feedback or complaints in 2017–2018:

Logan generated the largest amount of public feedback in 2017, with 20 complaints received. It is a superhero film in the X-Men series, starring Hugh Jackman as Wolverine. The number of complaints was relatively small, compared with previous years, some of which attracted between 40 and 50 complaints. This time complainants felt that the film's violence was too strong for a 15 classification and would have been more appropriately placed at 18. However, the BBFC Classification Guidelines permit strong violence at 15 provided it does not dwell on the infliction of pain or injury. The Board expressed the view, while the violence in *Logan* is strong and frequently bloody, it is also rapidly edited with a focus on action rather than sadism. The film's fantastical setting and super-powered central character further distances the violence from reality, allowing the issue to be acceptable at 15.

Padmaavat is a Hindi-language epic period drama in which a Sultan leads an invasion to capture a Rajput queen, directed by Sanjay Leela Bhansali. With a production budget of ₹2.15bn ($30m), *Padmaavat* is one of the most expensive Indian films ever made. Initially scheduled for release on 1 December 2017, *Padmaavat* faced numerous controversies in the UK and India. It received the 12A classification. Amid violent protests, its release was indefinitely delayed. Following media and public feedback to the distributor of the film, a new version was submitted for classification in January 2018, also classified 12A. Ten people complained to the BBFC that the film misrepresented a revered figure in ancient India, namely Padmavati, a thirteenth-century Indian queen (Rani) (the original title of the film was to be *Padmavati*). The film was regarded as potentially harmful to a young audience since it promotes the 'walking into fire' by women whose husbands die. The film ends with the Khilji army succeeding in defeating the Rajputs but unable to capture the Rajput women who perform the ancient Hindi custom of *jauhar* (mass self-immolation) by walking into a large fire to avoid capture, enslavement and rape by the foreign invading army. In spite of the complaints the BBFC kept the 12A category finding that there was nothing in *Padmaavat* that was unacceptable.

---

162 BBFC Annual Report 2018.

Atomic Blonde attracted eight complaints highlighting the film's violence and to a lesser extent its sexual content and language. *Atomic Blonde*, an American action thriller, revolves around a spy who has to find a list of double agents who are being smuggled into the West, on the eve of the collapse of the Berlin Wall in 1989. The film, directed by David Leitch, starring Charlize Theron, James McAvoy and Til Schweiger was given a 15 rating. The board concluded that the film rating should remain at the lower end of the 15 classification, though there are frequent scenes of strong violence in the film, including people being shot, resulting in large spurts of blood into the air or onto walls, and gruelling fist fights. However, the violence is presented in a stylized manner, without dwelling on the infliction of pain or violence in a manner that would demand an 18 classification. Very strong language is permitted at 15 depending on the manner in which it is used, who is using the language, its frequency within the work as a whole, and any special contextual justification. Very strong language ('c**t') is used just once in *Atomic Blonde*, and it was therefore held acceptable at 15.

Kingsman: The Golden Circle attracted eight complaints in 2017, most focused on the film's sexual content. The film classified as 15 is an action spy comedy film, a sequel to *Kingsman: The Secret Service* (2014). The film features Colin Firth, Julianne Moore, Halle Berry and Elton John amongst others and was premiered in London on 18 September 2017. Complainants thought the sexual behaviour in the film breached the BBFC guidelines for a 15 rated film, since there were very strong verbal references to sexual behaviour and one complainant took issue with a scene of cannibalism in which a man is required to eat a burger as part of an initiation. Before he does so the camera pans to a pair of clothed legs sticking out from the top of a mincing machine, and then to a pile of minced meat. The board felt that this content was acceptable at 15.

 FOR THOUGHT

How far should film, games and music DVD censorship go – given the fact that anything can now be viewed in private by video-on-demand and streaming services? Discuss with reference to BBFC adjudications in the light of statutory legislation.

8.9 Party political, elections and referendum broadcast legislation and regulation

All broadcasts must observe the law already mentioned in this book, such as libel, privacy, contempt, obscenity, incitement to violence or to racial or religious hatred and copyright. See Chapter 9

See above 8.3

See above
8.4.1

Whilst political parties are responsible for the content of their own broadcasts, they are required to observe strict broadcasting legislation and guidelines, designed to cover compliance issues and production requirements agreed by all public service broadcasters, equally to all parties.

All broadcasts must comply with the Ofcom Broadcasting Code, in particular in relation to harm and offence (Section 2) and to fairness and privacy (Sections 7 and 8).

Parties should also refer to the BBC Editorial Guidelines that relate to harm and offence (Chapter 5) and fairness and privacy (Chapters 6 and 7).[163] Impartiality on the part of the broadcaster is achieved by the allocation of broadcasts or a series of broadcasts to different parties. Broadcasters may inform parties if they reasonably believe any content in the broadcast does not comply with the law, the Ofcom Broadcasting Code or in respect of the BBC, its Editorial Guidelines.

It is the responsibility of the political party to ensure that all permissions and third party rights (such as for music and archive footage) required for broadcast and online publication have been secured prior to transmission. Broadcasters may seek written confirmation of these rights clearances before transmission, following the delivery of the broadcast.

8.9.1 History of party political broadcast legislation

Sir John (later Lord) Reith (1889–1971), founder and first general manager of the BBC in 1922, envisaged that part of the public broadcaster's remit ought to be that broadcasting time should be offered to qualified political parties. Reith fought off the politicians' attempts to influence the BBC, while offering the British people programmes to educate, inform and entertain. The principle that political parties should be able to freely publicize their platforms and policies to voters, and that voters should be able to receive such information, was extended to the broadcast media as their audience and influence developed.

See above
8.3.1

Following the reconstitution of the BBC in 1926 under a Royal Charter, arrangements for the future allocation of broadcasting time between the parties were left solely to the BBC. In May 1926, Conservative Prime Minister, Stanley Baldwin, made the first prime ministerial broadcast outside a general election, addressing the nation during the general strike. At the 1929 general election the parties could not agree about party political broadcasting time and 'order of play', and Reith himself allocated broadcasting time on behalf of the BBC. The government was given the same number of broadcasts as the opposition parties combined and was given the first broadcast, while an opposition party was given the final broadcast. Minor parties were given access dependent on the number of candidates they fielded at the election. From 1947 the process of allocating party political broadcasts became more structured. A Committee on Party Political Broadcasting was established as an informal body to facilitate discussion between the BBC and the political parties (Conservative, Labour and Liberal) and to help secure agreement on allocation arrangements.

The first election-night television broadcast in the UK was the BBC's 1950 Election Results (including a black, white and grey electoral map). The first televised Party Election Broadcasts (PEBs) went out in 1951 during the General Election campaign. The Conservative, Labour and Liberal parties each made a 15-minute broadcast, which was transmitted in addition to their radio broadcasts.

---

163 BBC Editorial Guidelines: www.bbc.co.uk/editorialguidelines/guidelines.

Clement Attlee's Labour Government was on its last legs. Most of the promises set out by the Labour Party in its 1945 manifesto had been put into practice, leaving the party directionless. The General Election of 1950 had slashed Attlee's majority to just five seats. Attlee's Cabinet was also suffering from long years in office. Sir Stafford Cripps, the Chancellor, resigned due to illness in 1950, and Ernest Bevin, the Foreign Secretary, died in 1951. This left the ageing Conservative leader Winston Churchill to win the 1951 election with a comfortable majority. The Conservatives were back in power once more, but they did little to alter the welfare state created by the previous Labour government.[164]

In 1955, Richard Dimbleby hosted a more ambitious Election Results programme. Constituencies rushed to get their results out, and 357 (out of 630) declared on the night. But concerns about the Representation of the People Act 1948 meant coverage was sober, with little commentary.

ITV (Independent Television) and therein ITN (Independent Television News) came on air in 1955, and in 1956 began simultaneous transmission of party political broadcasts. Broadcasts on commercial television were, and have since been, scheduled within programming time rather than advertising time. The arrival of ITN and the spread of television ownership spurred the BBC into a more user-friendly approach for the 1959 election. Around 13 million viewers watched the BBC's election night coverage that year.

Debates on how party finance and campaign spending should be regulated recurred through the 1970s and '80s following the Houghton Report (1976).[165]

Election broadcast legislation developed slowly and piecemeal. For example, section 93 of the Representation of the People Act 1983 prohibited broadcasting about a parliamentary or local election where one or more of the candidates did not give his or her consent. This section still applies at constituency level for parliamentary elections but does not affect coverage of elections nationally. If the candidate participates and consents, there are further restrictions. The programme cannot be aired until nominations have closed, and even then, all the candidates must consent to the programme. Originally, the provision was conceived as an attempt to protect the rights of minority candidates, but effectively, this means that every candidate for a particular constituency can insist on taking part and so has a veto on the broadcast. For parliamentary elections the restrictions came into force when the intention to dissolve Parliament is announced. This provision has been seen as unnecessarily inhibiting coverage of local issues and has been opposed by a number of broadcasters. The case of *Marshall v BBC* (1979)[166] is relevant in this context. Here the court held that a candidate, James Marshall, had not 'taken part' since there had only been pictures of his canvassing. The programme did not, therefore, require consent before being broadcast.

8.9.2 Broadcasting legislation from 1990 to date: party political and election broadcasts

The principles of fairness and due impartiality are enshrined in various pieces of legislation and broadcasting rules, covering all party political and party election broadcasts in the UK (e.g. s 333 Communications Act 2003 regarding party election broadcasts (PEBs),

---

164 For further discussion see: Freedman, D. (2003).
165 Houghton Committee on Financial Aid to Political Parties (1976).
166 [1979] 3 All ER 80.

party political broadcasts (PPBs) and referendum campaign broadcasts). The statutory provisions then regulate the special responsibility to audiences who are about to and entitled to vote. The closer to the election or referendum date, the greater the need for care not to appear biased towards one particular party or forum.

The 1990 Broadcasting Act put party political broadcasting on a statutory footing for the first time. Section 36 of the Act requires that holders of any Channel 3, 4 or 5 television licence must include party political broadcasting in the service and must observe the rules devised by the Independent Television Commission (ITC)[167] in relation to the allocation of PPBs and PEBs. The 1990 ITC programme code (revised in 1998 and 1999) provided that airtime on ITV would be made available each year to UK parties represented in the House of Commons and to the SNP in Scotland and Plaid Cymru in Wales. The unofficial formula for the allocation of PPBs agreed by the Committee on Party Political Broadcasting was formalized in the ITC code. When Channel 5 came on air in March 1997, it was required by the ITC code to carry general election and European election broadcasts.

Similarly, section 107 of the 1990 Act required national radio licence holders to observe rules determined by the 'Radio Authority' (established in 1991) in relation to PPBs and PEBs. Licences for the national commercial radio stations, Classic FM, Talk Radio (now TalkSport) and Virgin Radio, were awarded in 1997, and all three stations carried PPBs and PEBs from September 1997. The Radio Authority's programme code provided similar rules for the allocation of PPBs and PEBs to those set out in the ITC programme code.[168] These requirements of the 1990 Act did not affect the BBC, which continued to operate under its own Charter and Licence until 2017 (now also regulated under the Ofcom Code on elections).

See 8.4.1

The Broadcasting Act 1990 banned any paid political advertising. Anybody whose objects were wholly or mainly of a political nature was not permitted to advertise on radio or television.[169] The Neill Committee's Report on Standards in Public Life (1998) included detailed discussion regarding the extent to which this ban constituted a restriction on the right of free expression under Article 10(1) ECHR. While the Neill Committee recommended that the ban on political advertising should be maintained, it acknowledged that the legal position had not been properly tested in the European Court of Human Rights and that the introduction of the Human Rights Act 1998 would open up the possibility for direct challenge in the UK courts. The Neill Report noted that 'the advent of satellite and cable television and of digital broadcasting means that the current arrangements governing political broadcasting may soon no longer be relevant'[170]. It soon became clear that the broadcasting industry had expanded and would enter extraordinary times of change as it entered the digital age.

In *Verein gegen Tierfabriken v Switzerland* (2001)[171] (the applicant being an animal rights pressure group), the ECtHR held that a blanket prohibition on political advertising does constitute an interference with the right to freedom of expression under Article 10(1) of the Convention. While the Court stated that it 'cannot exclude that a prohibition of

167 The Independent Television Commission (ITC) licensed and regulated commercial television services in
      the UK (except S4C in Wales) between 1 January 1991 and 28 December 2003. It was then replaced by Ofcom.
168 The Radio Authority subsumed into Ofcom in 2003.
169 Sections 8(2)(a) and s92(2)(a) Broadcasting Act 1990.
170 *The Neill Report* (1998) pp. 174–176, sections 13.8–13.11.
171 *Verein gegen Tierfabriken Schweiz (VgT) v Switzerland* (No.2) (Application no. 32772/02) [2009] ECHR (ECtHR).

political advertising may be compatible with the requirements of Article 10 of the Convention in certain situations', any interference has to be 'necessary in a democratic society' which means that there has to be a 'pressing social need'. Significantly, the Court did not see how that test could be applied only to one form of media and not to others. However, the full implications of this judgment for the current prohibition on paid political advertising in the UK broadcast media never became clear.[172]

The Broadcasting Act 1996 set up the Broadcasting Standards Commission (BSC). Under section 108 the BSC had a duty to draw up a code giving guidance as to the portrayal of sex and violence and 'standards of taste and decency for such programmes generally'. It was then the duty of each broadcasting or regulatory body (including the BBC), when drawing up any code relating to 'standards and practice for programmes', to reflect the general effect of the BSC's code. The ITC Programme Code and the BBC Producers' Guidelines were revised to comply with this requirement.

A further revision to the broadcasters' allocation arrangements for elections was made for the 2001 General Election PEBs. Wherever it was possible to split broadcasts, PEBs were allocated to parties in each of the four devolved nations on the basis of those parties fielding candidates in one-sixth of the seats in each nation, rather than applying the threshold across the UK as a whole. In addition to the main political parties with Parliamentary representation, eight minor parties were allocated one or more broadcasts on television or radio in England, Scotland or Wales, while a further two parties were allocated broadcasts in Northern Ireland. The major parties were allocated separate series of broadcasts in each nation. The numbers of broadcasts allocated to the major parties were determined, for England, in line with the allocations made at the previous general and local elections, and for Wales and Scotland, in line with allocations made in those nations for devolved elections and the previous European Parliamentary elections.

Prior to the general election, the Pro-Life Alliance launched a High Court action against the BBC.[173] In May 2001 the Pro-Life Alliance had fielded enough candidates for the June 2001 general election to entitle it to make one PEB in Wales. The BBC Wales transmission was scheduled for a little under five minutes. The major part of the proposed programme was devoted to explaining the processes involved in different forms of abortion, with prolonged and graphic images of the product of suction abortion: aborted foetuses in a mangled and mutilated state, tiny limbs, a separated head and the like. The BBC declined to show the PEB in full on the grounds that it would breach its own codes on taste and decency.[174] The Alliance applied for judicial review of the decision not to broadcast. The application was dismissed at first instance, but the Alliance was successful in the Court of Appeal. The BBC appealed to the HL. The majority of the House of Lords criticized the CA for failing to recognize the legislative framework and the ITC Code. The CA had essentially suggested the BBC should simply have ignored their obligations under the legislative codes and have permitted the broadcast. The Broadcasting Act 1990 required broadcasters to consider whether the proposed PPB complied with the relevant

---

172 For further discussion see: Holtz-Bacha, C. and Kaid, L.L. (2006).

173 R (on the application of Pro-Life Alliance) v BBC & Others [2004] 1 AC 185 (HL).

174 Section 6(1)(a) Broadcasting Act 1990. The BBC was subject to a comparable, non-statutory obligation under paragraph 5.1(d) of its agreement with the Secretary of State for National Heritage under Royal Charter.

codes for taste and decency set by the ITC.[175] The HL held that the broadcaster's application of the statutory criteria could not be faulted, and the Alliance had not made out a case for interfering with the decision. The BBC's appeal was allowed.

8.9.3 Why do we need so much legislation to regulate election and campaign broadcasts?

Under electoral legislation, television and radio broadcasters have to follow legislation and various codes of practice in their coverage of candidates during election periods. Ofcom is responsible for the code regulating independent broadcasters; the BBC and S4C have to draw up (and observe) their own. Though broadcasters should achieve an appropriate balance they are not required to give exactly the same amount of coverage to each candidate but are required to have regard to the relative electoral strength of the candidates and their parties.

See below
8.9.8

If it is considered that a programme could have an undue and unfair influence on an election or referendum, then it is up to the Electoral Commission to either ask the broadcast to delay transmission until after polling or to prosecute a party or broadcaster (together with Ofcom) if the law has been breached. Furthermore Article 10 ECHR enshrines freedom of expression relevant to party political and referendum broadcasts, and further rules are enshrined in the Ofcom Rules on Party Political and Referendum Broadcasts.

Section 333 of the Communications Act 2003[176] requires Ofcom to ensure that Party Political Broadcasts (PPBs), Party Election Broadcasts (PEBs) and Referendum Campaign Broadcasts (RCBs) on behalf of registered political parties and designated referendum organizations[177] are included in every licensed public service television channel (regional Channel 33, Channel 4, Channel 5), every local digital television programme service, and every national (i.e. UK-wide, commercial) analogue radio service and their digital simulcast services (Classic FM, TalkSport and Absolute Radio AM).[178] The BBC Agreement requires Ofcom to ensure that PPBs and RCBs are included in such of the BBC's UK Public Services as Ofcom consider appropriate.[179]

See above
8.4.1

Section Six of Ofcom's Broadcasting Code provides that broadcasts under these Rules are required to comply with the relevant provisions of the Code (for example, the provisions regarding harm and offence) notwithstanding that the content of broadcasts is normally the responsibility of the relevant political parties (or designated referendum organizations). Licensees should apply these Rules in accordance with relevant provisions of the Code.

---

175 The ITC published a Programme Code (revised from time to time) and made it a condition of every licence that the broadcaster must comply with the Code. Section 1 dealt with, among other things, offence to good taste and decency.

176 Under Schedule 12, paragraph 18 of the Act, the Welsh Authority must prepare and publish a policy with respect to party political and referendum broadcasts and their inclusion in S4C. In doing so it must have regard to (a) any views expressed by the Electoral Commission, and (b) any rules made by Ofcom with respect to party political and referendum broadcasts.

177 Section 333(3) of the Act, and ss 37 and 127 of the Political Parties, Elections and Referendums Act 2000.

178 This section does not apply to the Channel Islands.

179 These rules also apply to the following BBC services in accordance with the BBC Agreement: BBC One; BBC Two; BBC Radio Two; BBC Radio Four; BBC London Radio; BBC Radio Scotland; BBC Radio Nan Gaidheal; BBC ALBA; BBC Radio Wales; BBC Radio Cymru; BBC Radio Foyle; and BBC Radio Ulster.

Extracts in sound or vision featuring members not of the party making the broadcast require the consent of the member and the other party concerned. Wide shots of the chambers of the National Assembly of Wales, Scottish Parliament and Northern Ireland Assembly are allowed, but wide shots of Westminster chambers during sittings are not. Extracts from party conference speeches of the party allocated the broadcast may be used, and can be licensed in the normal way from broadcasters.

News footage featuring the party's own leader and politicians can also be licensed from broadcasters. But clips that identify the programme source (via on screen logos, theme music or the inclusion of presenters or reporters) will not be allowed. Visual and audio material (e.g. archive and news clips) of political figures from other UK political parties should not be included without the consent of the individual concerned. Undistorted stills that have been lawfully published previously can normally be used without the individuals' or their party's consent. Archive footage or undistorted stills of international public figures can normally be used without such individuals' consent, where such use does not imply the support of that figure for the party making the broadcast. Written consent from a parent or guardian must be obtained for the appearance of any child (i.e. someone under the age of 16).

Candidates can take part in party election broadcasts, but there should be no explicit visual or verbal reference to the candidate's own constituency, ward or electoral area, such as a clearly identifiable landmark. This does not apply in the European elections to images or general references to Scotland, Wales and Northern Ireland, or, similarly, in the GLA election to the London-wide list. It also does not apply to images of the Houses of Parliament, the Scottish Parliament, the Senedd or Stormont, which can be used in broadcasts featuring candidates for the constituencies in which those buildings are located, provided there is no reference to issues within the constituency or electoral area.

See below
8.9.6

Direct appeals for funds are not allowed, and no revenue-generating telephone or text numbers can be used in political broadcasts. Appeals for members of the audience to contact the party are allowed at the end of the broadcast via nonrevenue generating telephone or text numbers, email, website or social media addresses.

The length of broadcasts is precisely measured by stop watch. Parties and designated organizations may choose a length of 2'40", 3'40" or 4'40" on TV. For BBC Radio, broadcasts should be 1'30". For commercial radio, broadcasts can be any duration up to 2'30", but the preferred length is 1'00". Broadcasters should be informed of the selected duration at least 14 days prior to the transmission date. Party broadcasts will not be transmitted unless a form of words agreed with the broadcaster is used.

Delivery broadcasts should be delivered via digital file using common technical standards agreed by the BBC, Channel 4, Channel 5, STV and ITV. Delivery to S4C should be on HDCam. Broadcasts should be in widescreen format (16x9 full height anamorphic). The sound can be in mono or stereo. The broadcast master material should be delivered together with two DVD copies to each broadcaster carrying the broadcast. Details of delivery requirements and addresses should be checked directly with each of the broadcasters individually. The digital files or tapes, transcripts and details of any music used must be delivered by 10am at least three working days before the date of transmission.[180]

---

180 BBC Editorial Guidelines Section 10: Politics, Public Policy and Polls: www.bbc.co.uk/editorialguidelines/guidelines/politics/political-broadcasts.

Broadcasters reserve the right to cancel and reschedule the broadcast of any material that is not delivered on time, or where compliance issues are identified by the broadcaster on delivery, requiring amendments prior to broadcast. Broadcasters reserve the right to charge for any costs incurred due to late delivery.

8.9.4 European elections

Since 1999, Members of the European Parliament for England, Scotland and Wales (MEPs) have been elected using a regional list system. The three members for the Northern Ireland region are elected using the STV system. At the 1999 election, PEBs were offered to Labour, Conservatives and Liberal Democrats, and also to SNP in Scotland and Plaid Cymru in Wales. Other parties which put forward a full list of candidates in each of the regions in any nation were offered one broadcast in that nation. Six other parties qualified for a single broadcast in England, four in Wales and five in Scotland. Of those broadcasters unable to split their signal between nations, Channel 4 did not carry any PEBs, while Channel 5 allocated UK-wide broadcasts to Labour, Conservatives, Liberal Democrats, Plaid Cymru and SNP. Under revised allocation arrangements, any party fielding one or more candidates which could point to prior electoral support – defined as either gaining more than 2.5 per cent of first preference votes at the previous European election or sufficient support at the most recent election (the Assembly elections in 1998) to gain one or more seats – would be offered a broadcast. Two other parties qualified for a single broadcast in Northern Ireland on this basis.

New election and party political guidance was issued by Ofcom ahead of the local and EU elections in May 2019 as Brexit uncertainty continued.[181]

8.9.5 Devolution

With the establishment of devolved legislatures in Northern Ireland in 1998 and in Scotland and Wales the following year, arrangements were established for the allocation of PEBs to contesting parties. Members of both the Scottish Parliament and the Welsh Assembly were elected by the Additional Member System (AMS), with a top-up vote from a regional party list in addition to single-member constituencies. While the larger parties fielded candidates in both the constituency seats and regional top-up lists, smaller parties concentrated their efforts on the regional lists alone, and some parties fielded only the number of candidates realistically electable on each regional list, rather than the maximum possible.

In each nation of the UK, parties are offered one or more PPBs over a 12-month period if:

- a party holds one seat or more in that nation in any relevant parliament or assembly; and
- evidence of their past electoral support and/or current support at a particular election or in that nation means it would be appropriate to do so.

---

181 Ofcom (2019) Evidence of past electoral support and evidence of current support ahead of the various elections taking place on 2 May 2019: www.ofcom.org.uk/__data/assets/pdf_file/0017/112094/evidence-past-current-electoral-support-may-elections-2019.pdf.

Parties in Great Britain are offered one PPB per season: autumn, winter and spring. Parties in Northern Ireland are offered one or two PPBs in the period 1 September to 30 March (excluding December). No PPBs should be broadcast during election or referendum periods. Each designated referendum organization is allocated a series of RCBs before each referendum. The allocation should be equal for each referendum organization.

At the Scottish Parliament and Welsh Assembly elections in 1999, PEBs were allocated to Labour, Conservatives and Liberal Democrats, and also to SNP in Scotland and Plaid Cymru in Wales. Parties fielding a slate of sufficient candidates to match the number of seats available on half or more of the regional top-up lists were also offered one PEB on this basis. A further five parties qualified for a broadcast in Scotland, while four qualified in Wales.

Members of the Northern Ireland Assembly were elected by the STV system. The first elections to the Assembly were held in 1998, following the broadcasters' decision formally to allocate a series of PEBs to parties in Northern Ireland. Five parties – the Alliance Party, Democratic Unionist Party, Sinn Fein, Social Democratic and Labour Party and the Ulster Unionists – were each offered two TV and two radio broadcasts. Other parties fielding one or more candidates in at least one-sixth of the constituencies contested (in practice, a minimum total of three candidates across three different constituencies) qualified for a single broadcast. Six other parties qualified on this basis.

8.9.6 Greater London elections

The first contests for a directly elected Mayor of London and the Greater London Assembly were held in May 2000. The broadcasting authorities faced some difficulty in allocating PEBs for the mayoral election in which 11 candidates stood for one post. The qualifying criteria determined by the broadcasters stated that candidates must demonstrate both previous electoral support (in the three most recent elections in London: the 1999 European election, 1998 borough elections and the 1997 general election), and current electoral support, taking into account opinion polls or other evidence of widespread support.

Of the 11 mayoral candidates, 5 were offered PEBs: Frank Dobson (Labour), Steven Norris (Conservative), Susan Kramer (Liberal Democrat), Darren Johnson (Green Party) and Ken Livingstone the independent candidate. The Mayoral and Assembly contests were held at the same time as local elections elsewhere in England, and no separate broadcasts for the Assembly elections were allocated in addition to the series of local government broadcasts. Ken Livingstone became the first elected Mayor of London in May 2000.

8.9.7 Referendums

Under the provisions of the Political Parties, Elections and Referendums Act 2000 (PPERA), referendum campaign broadcasts at a UK-wide, national or regional referendum are allocated to each of the umbrella campaign organizations designated by the Electoral Commission. Detailed allocation arrangements are made by the broadcasters at the time of any referendum, and the Commission must be formally consulted on any such rules before they are adopted.

8.9.8 The Electoral Commission

The Electoral Commission is the regulator overseeing elections in the UK and ensuring that UK laws on spending by political parties are followed. The Commission was established under the Political Parties, Elections and Referendums Act 2000 (PPERA) (section 1). Sections 5–13A PPERA set out the general functions of the Commission in overseeing elections and referendum. The main functions include:

- make sure people understand the rules and try to prevent people breaking the rules;
- investigate and impose sanctions when people do break the rules;
- publish data on political funding and spending by political parties;
- ensure how much parties can spend on campaigning at certain elections;
- ensure transparency in our political system;
- receive, analyze and publish information about party donations and campaign spending and monitor how well the rules are being followed (Part IV and Chapter II);
- advise governments on changes to the rules and make recommendations for change;
- investigate malpractice and ask companies to disclose party funding (Schedule 19B 'investigatory powers of the commission');
- deal with possible breaches of the rules (civil monetary penalties Schedule 19C; criminal penalties and fines Schedule 20).

There are limits on candidate spending at elections and controls on the sources of funding for that spending. After the election, candidates' agents must account for the costs of campaigning and donations to the campaign in a spending return. Returning Officers must receive spending returns from all candidates by a certain date, which varies depending on the election. The Returning Officer is then responsible for making the returns available for public inspection.

8.9.9 The Brexit referendum and election fraud

On 23 June 2016 a referendum was held across the United Kingdom and Gibraltar about whether the UK should remain a member of the European Union or leave the European Union. This became known as 'Brexit' (or 'Britain exiting the European Union'). The UK government was responsible for the detailed legislation for this referendum. The European Union Referendum Bill was introduced to Parliament on 28 May 2015 and passed into law on 17 December 2015.[182]

The Electoral Commission had a number of specific responsibilities and functions in relation to the Brexit referendum (under secondary legislation), which included former Chairman, Jenny Watson, acting as Chief Counting Officer (CCO) with overall responsibility for the administration of the poll. The Commission was also responsible for overseeing and accounting to the UK Parliament for the payment of fees to RCOs and COs for

---

182 European Referendum Act 2015.

running the referendum and the reimbursement of the costs they incurred in doing so. The total cost of the conduct of the Brexit referendum was £129.128m.[183]

The Vote Leave campaign, fronted by Conservative MPs, Boris Johnson and Michael Gove, won the contest to be the official 'Leave Campaign' in the 2016 referendum on whether Britain should stay in the European Union. The result of the referendum is by now well known, namely 51.9 per cent of the population voted 'Leave' and 48.1 per cent voted 'Remain'. A number of companies and individuals were referred to the National Crime Agency for suspected criminal offences committed during the EU referendum.

In 2017 the Electoral Commission began an investigation into the funding and possible breaches of electoral legislation in relation to the Vote Leave campaign. Bob Posner, legal counsel for the regulator, said on 1 November in a press release:

> We have reasonable grounds to suspect a number of offences under electoral law may have been committed. Further offences are not within the regulatory remit of the Commission. For those offences where we may impose civil sanctions, our sanctions are limited at £20,000.[184]

Because of limitations in the law, the regulator referred a number of companies supporting the EU 'Leave' Brexit referendum campaign to the UK National Crime Agency.[185] The Electoral Commission's investigation focused specifically on £2m reported to have been loaned to the Vote Leave organization by Arron Banks, a British businessman and political donor and co-founder of the 'Leave.EU' campaign, to whom he had donated a further reported £6m (his organization 'Better for the Country' ran the 'Leave.EU' referendum campaign).

The Electoral Commission's investigations found that financial transactions for 'Vote Leave' were complex and complicated, including offshore companies incorporated in Gibraltar and the Isle of Man. These jurisdictions were beyond the reach of the Electoral Commission's legal remit, and the sums of money involved were significant: electoral funding amounting to approximately £8m, which included loans of £6m to Leave.EU and Arron Banks, a registered campaigner in the EU Referendum.[186]

In July 2018, 'Vote Leave' was fined £61,000 for breaching electoral law. The Electoral Commission announced that Vote Leave had exceeded its £7m spending limit in 2016 by funnelling £675,315 through pro-Brexit youth group 'BeLeave' during the Brexit Campaign in advance of the referendum on 23 June 2016. The founder of BeLeave, Darren Grimes, was also fined £20,000 and referred to the Metropolitan Police, along with Vote Leave official David Halsall. The regulator's findings were that Mr Grimes had 'wrongly'

---

183 Electoral Commission (2017).
184 Source: Electoral Commission statement regarding 'Better for the Country Limited and Mr Arron Banks', 1 November 2017: www.electoralcommission.org.uk/i-am-a/journalist/electoral-commission-media-centre/party-and-election-finance-to-keep/electoral-commission-statement-regarding-better-for-the-country-limited-and-mr-arron-banks.
185 s 123(4) of the Political Parties, Elections and Referendums Act 2000.
186 Source: Electoral Commission statement regarding 'Better for the Country Limited and Mr Arron Banks', 1 November 2017: www.electoralcommission.org.uk/i-am-a/journalist/electoral-commission-media-centre/party-and-election-finance-to-keep/electoral-commission-statement-regarding-better-for-the-country-limited-and-mr-arron-banks.

reported the electoral spending as his own. This meant that, including this amount, the Electoral Commission found that Vote Leave spent £7,449,079, breaching its £7m spending limit.

In March 2019 the Electoral Commission announced its intention that it would like a change in legislation in order to prosecute political parties and referendum campaign groups in future, rather than having to pass on all potentially criminal cases to the police of the NCA. The watchdog urged ministers to advance legislation, by altering its enforcement policy in the face of another EU referendum in case Parliament could not agree on a suitable Brexit strategy (i.e. 'hard Brexit' or another referendum).

In February 2019 the House of Commons Digital, Culture, Media and Sport Committee (DCMSC) published its report on disinformation, 'fake news' and breaches of electoral law.[187] The report concluded *inter alia* that ex-UKIP funder Arron Banks and his associate Andy Wigmore had shown complete disregard and disdain for the parliamentary process, when they appeared as witnesses before the committee in 2017. The DCMS report (2019) recommended that the National Crime Agency (NCA) should investigate election fraud and urged a review of self-regulation for the strategic communications industry on whether new regulation is necessary to curb bad behaviour in the industry when it comes to dark ads during elections and referendums.

The report concluded that current electoral laws are not fit for the digital age, stating that 'gone are the days of billboard advertising and leaflet-dropping during election campaigns'. Now all parties micro-targeted online campaigning. The report called for absolute transparency of political campaigning, with clear banners on all paid-for political advertisements and videos, identifying the source and the advertiser. There should be statutory definition of digital campaigning and online political advertising. New laws should take the impact of social media into account when it comes to elections or referendums.

8.9.10 Are broadcasting laws sufficient to control social media campaigning? Discussion and analysis

A significant proportion of political campaigning has now moved online. The June 2017 General Election was largely conducted online by the opposition Labour Party which not only outspent but also outscored Theresa May's Conservative Party with a strategy that harnessed Facebook and YouTube to bolster the opposition Labour Leader, Jeremy Corbyn's, immense support. The Conservatives' digital campaign was described by media commentators as unprepared and unresponsive. On polling day, 8 June, Labour spent considerably more than the Conservatives promoting its hashtag #forthemany on Twitter.

Whilst traditional party election or political broadcasts are fast becoming out of date, campaigners now largely use digital platforms to campaign during an election or referendum, such as the United States, France, Germany, the UK, Ireland and so forth. Legislators are trying to keep in step with fast evolving unregulated platforms as campaigners range from registered political parties to individual campaigners to

---

187 House of Commons (2019b).

non-registered campaigners. In the UK, non-party campaigners must register with the Electoral Commission if they intend to spend more than £20,000 in England or £10,000 in Scotland, Wales or Northern Ireland at a UK parliamentary General Election. Campaigners at the 2016 EU referendum had to register if they wanted to spend more than £10,000. Political parties must register with the regulator to stand candidates in any elections.

The rise of digital campaigning raises important issues for a number of regulators and organizations. The UK Information Commissioner has been investigating the use of personal data and analytics by political campaigns, parties, social media companies and other commercial organizations since the Brexit Referendum in June 2016.

Academic researchers are increasingly concerned about a number of problems that have emerged as a result, which could undermine democratic processes. Key problems include the fact that the impact of broadcasting regulation is lessened, and campaigning is carried out on platforms that are closed and – for the most part – beyond scrutiny. As a result, it is becoming difficult to ensure fairness and transparency and guard against corruption. Online and social media also undermine the spending regime. Invoices do not detail how and where money is being spent, so it is hard to track how much is being spent on what, where, and by whom. Major pre-campaign expenses, such as the development of detailed databases of voters, may not be included, even though they have a substantive impact during the campaign itself. Digital campaigns can also target voters far more precisely compared than analogue campaigns, which raises questions about transparency, privacy and equal access to information. Commentators have raised concerns about the impact of targeting on the integrity and honesty of campaigns. It is also increasingly difficult to monitor spending and support-in-kind from third parties and unofficial media.

The last decade has seen an explosion in the use of digital tools in political campaigning. Perceptions have also changed in that time. The use of social media was first heralded as a positive revolution in the mass engagement of voters. More recently we have seen serious allegations of misinformation, misuse of personal data, and overseas interference. Concerns that our democracy may be under threat have emerged. Currently with the British electoral laws very much out of date and the power of law enforcement and fines by the Electoral Commission relatively weak, it can be argued that democracy is at risk from the malicious and relentless targeting of British and EU citizens with disinformation and personalized 'dark adverts' from unidentifiable sources, delivered through the major social media platforms used every day. Much of this is directed from agencies working in foreign countries, including Russia. The big tech companies are failing in the duty of care they owe to their users to act against harmful content, and to respect their data privacy rights. It is clear that self-regulation is not working and there needs to be statutory intervention which requires the tech companies to adhere to electoral codes of conduct, possibly overseen by an independent regulator.

If it is accepted that British electoral regulations and legislation are out of date and not fit for the digital age, there should be legislation which requires major donors to clearly establish the source of their funds. The Electoral Commission conducted its own research into digital campaigning and the future of election broadcasting. The Commission's recommendations are summarized below:

- Each of the UK's governments and legislatures should change the law so that digital material must have an imprint saying who is behind the campaign and who created it.
- Each of the UK's governments and legislatures should amend the rules for reporting spending. They should make campaigners sub-divide their spending returns into different types of spending. These categories should give more information about the money spent on digital campaigns.
- Campaigners should be required to provide more detailed and meaningful invoices from their digital suppliers to improve transparency.
- Social media companies should work with the Electoral Commission to improve their policies on campaign material and advertising for elections and referendums in the UK.
- UK election and referendum adverts on social media platforms should be labelled to make the source clear. Their online databases of political adverts should follow the UK's rules for elections and referendums.
- Each of the UK's governments and legislatures should clarify that spending on election or referendum campaigns by foreign organizations or individuals is not allowed. They would need to consider how it could be enforced and the impact on free speech.
- Each of the UK's governments and legislatures should increase the maximum fine the Commission can sanction campaigners for breaking the rules, and strengthen the regulator's powers to obtain information outside of an investigation.[188]

The House of Commons Digital, Culture, Media and Sport Committee called on the Government to launch an independent investigation in 2019. One of the recommendations included an independent review of campaign regulation and possibly a new regulator altogether with enhanced statutory powers to 'punish' and issue more wide-ranging fines. It is a modern-day fact that digital campaign tools can make it easier and cheaper for legitimate campaigners to communicate with voters. It is a sign of a healthy democracy when campaigners tell voters about their policies and political views via Facebook or Twitter.

However, these (new) techniques for reaching voters may well reduce confidence in the integrity of elections and referendums if they are not regulated and conducted properly. Broadcasting and spending regulation need to be investigated including the impact of disinformation and fake news on voter manipulation.

---

188 Electoral Commission (2018).

8.10 Further reading

Barwise, T. P. and Watkins, L. (2018) 'The evolution of digital dominance: how and why we got to GAFA [Google, Apple, Facebook, Amazon]'. In: Moore, M. and Tambini, D., *Digital Dominance: The Power of Google, Amazon, Facebook, and Apple*. New York: Oxford University Press, 21–49. https://lbsresearch.london. edu/914/1/9780190845124_Barwise_Chapter%201.pdf

Google, Apple, Facebook and Amazon (GAFA) are now the most valuable public companies in the world by market capitalization. The authors argue that these tech companies have dominated the stock market since the mid-1990s and dominate our daily lives. They wield enormous power, raising difficult questions about their governance, regulation and accountability. Increasingly, these companies also operate in multiple product markets, often with products and services offered free or below cost as part of a wider strategy to protect and extend. Examples include Amazon's Kindle and Google's Maps and Gmail. Barwise and Watkins discuss these distinctive winner-take-all characteristics of digital markets under four headings: direct network effects; indirect network effects ('multisided markets'); big data and machine learning; and switching costs and lock-in. The authors conclude that GAFA's market dominance brings many benefits to consumers and other businesses. Current competition regulation is designed to prevent firms from using their market power to charge higher prices, or offer lower quality, than would prevail in a competitive market. It is unsuited to a platform context where, in Google's case, consumers pay nothing and advertisers have a highly effective tool that did not exist 20 years ago and for which they pay a competitive, auction-based market price. Of course, incumbent industries disrupted by tech-based platforms (hotels by Airbnb, taxis by Uber, etc.) complain and highlight their real and imagined negative impacts. But much of this is just a normal part of disruptive innovation: the victims of creative destruction do not like it. On this basis, the authors advance some positive arguments for light-touch, perhaps technology-specific, regulation of platform businesses but not, in their view, for no regulation at all.

Mueller, B. (2017) *Dynamics of International Advertising: Theoretical and Practical Perspectives*. 3rd ed. New York: Peter Lang.

Barbara Mueller's textbook provides excellent and comprehensive coverage of current issues affecting global advertisers. The book provides rich conceptual frameworks and detailed, relevant examples. It is exceptionally strong in providing deep cultural insights for the reader. The book takes a holistic corporate view, making it appropriate for those working in advertising, marketing and international legal practices in this field.

Stanford, B. (2018) 'Compulsory voter identification, disenfranchisement and human rights: electoral reform in Great Britain', *European Human Rights Law Review*, 1, 57–66.

Ben Stanford examines the human rights implications of the British government's proposals to reform the electoral process in Great Britain. The author looks in particular at pilot study of May 2018 during the local elections in England, which required eligible voters to produce some form of identification when voting in polling stations. Whilst the European Court of Human Rights has granted a wide margin of appreciation to states when it comes to the organizing and running of electoral systems, the Court has made it clear that any conditions that restrict the right to vote must satisfy a number of requirements, not least that the free expression of the people to choose the legislature must not be thwarted. In contrast, Stanford looks at the compulsory identification laws in Northern Ireland which have been received relatively well. He proposes that any electoral reform in the UK ought to take into account and comply with the requirements of Article 3 of the First Protocol to the ECHR. Stanford notes of importance that voters in Great Britain should be allowed to cast a provisional vote, subject to verification, should they forget to bring an acceptable form of identification on the day of the election. Ultimately, at a time when voter apathy amongst the electorate is consistently highlighted as a real cause for concern, the author recommends that the British government should not be considering such fundamental reforms, however well-intentioned the rationale may be, in response to what is a relatively insignificant problem and in a way that may in fact discourage or even thwart the free expression of the people to choose the legislature.

Wring, D., Mortimore, R. and Atkinson, S. (eds) (2016) *Political Communication in Britain: Polling, Campaigning and Media in the 2015 General Election.* **London: Palgrave Macmillan.**
This book offers a unique exploration of the 2015 UK General Election from the perspectives of those most intimately involved as strategists, journalists and analysts. It features contributions from the rival parties, news and polling organizations as well as academic experts who examine all aspects of the campaign. A common theme that emerges is the increasing complexity of the democratic process given the development of a more multifaceted party system and a growing fragmentation in mass media audiences. The UK electoral landscape has changed: in 2015 six parties received more than a million votes whereas in the 2010 General Election it was only three. This book provides invaluable insights into contemporary British politics and its relation with the media through analysis of an election whose outcome, an outright Conservative victory, surprised many commentators. The various authors explain, *inter alia*, electoral regulation, media and communication legislation and appeals to a wider readership – not just lawyers.

Chapter 9

Intellectual property law

Key points

This chapter will cover the following questions:

- What is intellectual property law?
- What amounts to 'passing off'?
- What constitutes copyright under the Copyright, Designs and Patents Act 1988 (CDPA)?
- How do durations of copyright differ?
- What are the remedies for copyright infringement?

9.1 Overview

This chapter focuses primarily on copyright law – though the concept of IP law will be explained, and a general overview will be given, including trade marks, patents and design rights. For the purpose of studying basic copyright law, we are then still treating the traditional perspective as British copyright law, where the Copyright, Designs and Patents Act 1988 (CDPA) treats the creation of works as separate elements, such as artistic, musical, literary and dramatic works.

It could be argued that UK copyright law is convoluted and outdated, and the rights enshrined in the CDPA are no longer sufficient in the digital age. The statute has been frequently amended, and a large number of new sections and subsections have been added, making the CDPA cumbersome and difficult to navigate. Additionally, EU harmonization legislation and a number of international conventions (particularly in the entertainment industry) have expanded this area of IP law to the point that infringement remains easy and law enforcement in both civil and criminal procedure rather challenging.

Since authors' works are now held mostly in digital format the concept of 'originality' becomes at times difficult to prove and assert. Though originality is enshrined in section 1(1) CDPA there exists an extensive body of case law with increasing reliance on judicial reasoning and interpretation where the initial statute is no longer sufficient. We will reflect whether current copyright laws still reflect commercial reality.

This chapter should be jointly read with Chapter 10 where examples from the entertainment industry are introduced.

9.2 Introduction to copyright law

Copyright law has two basic functions, a property function and an authenticity function, both seeking to establish who is the author of a work. This means that a person who creates, produces or invests in an original creative work should be the one who receives the rewards in the form of accreditation, payment or royalties; in other words, that this person be recognized as the original rights or copyright owner. Copyright provides that the rights holder determines whether and how copying, distributing, broadcasting and other uses of his work takes place.

Much of what businesses are often seeking to protect is not covered by IP rights, but is instead a concept, idea or know-how. The only way to protect such information is through the law of confidentiality, often by using a non-disclosure agreement (NDA) or contract. But once information is in the public domain (for example once a business has launched and its concept is revealed), an NDA will prove very difficult to enforce.

IP rights also contain rights to freedom of expression as well as reputational and moral rights which need to be protected by robust legislation in order for law enforcement agencies to adequately act on copyright theft, piracy and trade mark infringement.

A person will usually not own the IP right for something he has created as part of his work while being employed by someone else (though this tends to be a cause for dispute). IP can have more than one owner or belong to more than one person or business and can be sold ('assigned') or transferred ('licensed').

9.2.1 Brief history of English copyright law

Unfortunately, the history of English copyright law is itself quite complicated. The original legislative purpose of laws on literary copyright was the protection of the commercial interests of stationers or Stationers' Company – the early publishers and booksellers – and the control of unlicensed publications, rather than the vindication of the legal and moral rights of authors.

The 'right to copy' introduced by the Statute of Anne (Copyright Act 1709)[1] came after nearly three centuries of copyright monopoly by the monarchs and the Stationers' Company who also had the right to censor radical or subversive literature. The Statute of Anne introduced the principle of a fixed term of protection.[2] The 1709 Act protected literary works, books and other writings. During the eighteenth century protection was extended by statute to engravings and (by a liberal interpretation of the 1709 Act) to musical and dramatic compositions. The Statute of Anne provided the conceptual skeleton for copyright law for centuries to come, with economic consequences, affirmed by the House of Lords in *Donaldson v Becket* (1774).[3]

Three-dimensional works of art were brought within the scope of copyright by the Copyright Act 1798, but it was very badly drafted and offered little practical protection – as Lord Ellenborough pointed out in *Gahagan v Cooper* (1811) that 'the statute seems to have been framed with a view to defeat its own object'.[4] The 1798 Act was replaced by the Sculpture Copyright Act 1814. The class of protected works was described in discursive and detailed terms. The sculpture was required to bear the maker's name and the date when it was made.

Paintings, drawings and photographs were not protected until the Fine Arts Copyright Act 1862. The 1862 Act required registration as a condition of protection.

The Scottish case of *Caird v Sime* (1887)[5] established the right of a professor to restrain the publication of lectures orally delivered in his classroom. This case established that the law of property exists in intangible works, such as literature, songs or lectures, irrespective of implied contract or breach of duty.

The HL held in *Walter v Lane* (1900)[6] that copyright subsisted in reports prepared by shorthand writers of The Times of public speeches as 'original literary' works.[7] A speech and

---

1 Its full title reads: 'An Act for the Encouragement of Learning, by vesting the Copies of Printed Books in the Authors or purchasers of such Copies, during the times therein mentioned'.
2 For further discussion see: Baloch, T.A. (2007).
3 (1774) 2 Bro PC 129 (HL).
4 (1811) 3 Camp 111 at para. 113 (Lord Ellenborough).
5 (1887) LR 12 App Cas 326 (HL).
6 [1900] AC 539 (HL).
7 For further discussion see: Gravells, N.P. (2007).

a report of a speech were therefore held to be two different things. Lord Rosebery was the author of his speeches. The shorthand reporters were the authors of their reports of Rosebery's speeches, because they spent effort, skill and time in writing up their reports of these speeches that they themselves had not written. This is still known as the 'sweat of the brow' doctrine in copyright law, meaning that an author gains rights through simple diligence during the creation of a work. *Walter v Lane* is still good law and was confirmed in *Express Newspapers v News (UK)* (1990)[8] and *Sawkins v Hyperion Records Ltd* (2005).[9]

See Chapter 10.4.2

The Copyright Act 1911 was 'the first attempt to provide a comprehensive code of copyright protection'.[10] The introduction by the 1911 Act of full copyright protection for 'a work of artistic craftsmanship' was mainly influenced by the arts and crafts movement inspired by William Morris and John Ruskin.

Section 1(1) of the 1911 Act was in terms similar to those of section 1(1)(a) of the Copyright, Designs and Patents Act 1988 (CDPA) still in use today (see below), except that the words 'irrespective of artistic quality' did not appear in the 1911 Act.[11]

The Copyright Act 1956 introduced no substantive amendments to the 1911 Act, but was significant for the development of the phonogram (record) industry. Most importantly, the 1956 Act extended copyright to sound recordings, cinematographic works (films) and broadcasts. As well as record producers, there were other entrepreneur investors in the phonogram, entertainment and film industry who were now going to be protected under the 1956 Act.[12]

See Chapter 10.2

9.2.2 Categories of IP protection

The importance of intellectual property (IP) was first recognized internationally in the Paris Convention for the Protection of Industrial Property (1883) and the Berne Convention for the Protection of Literary and Artistic Works (1886).

Under the Berne Convention the copyright owner has the following exclusive rights and none of the actions below can be carried out without permission:

- the right to authorize translations of the work;
- the exclusive right to reproduce the work, though some provisions are made under national laws which typically allow limited private and educational use without infringement;
- the right to authorize public performance or broadcast and the communication of broadcasts and public performances;
- the right to authorize arrangements or other types of adaptation to the work;
- recitation of the work (or of a translation of the work);
- the exclusive right to adapt or alter the work.

---

8 [1990] 1 WLR 1320 (Sir Nicolas Browne-Wilkinson VC).
9 [2005] EWCA Civ 565.
10 As Lord Bridge observed in *British Leyland Motor Company v Armstrong Patents* [1986] AC 577 at para. 619.
11 For further discussion see: *Copinger and Skone James on Copyright* (2010) at paras 2–08 to 2–42.
12 For further discussion see: Cornish, W., Llewelyn, D. and Aplin, T. (2019).

Owning IP means:

- *it is created* (and it meets the requirements for copyright, a patent or design);
- *you have acquired IP rights* from the creator or a previous owner;
- *you have a brand* that could be a trade mark, such as a well-known product name.

The type of protection depends on what has been created. Some IP rights are automatically protected the minute they are created, written down or recorded in physical form – under UK copyright law (CDPA); others have to be applied for or registered, such as a trade mark or patent. There is no register of copyright works in the UK (unlike in the United States) – though some authors simply use the copyright symbol (©) to mark their work together with their name and the year of creation. Copyright is also automatically protected in most countries since copyright is territorial in nature.

Table 9.1 Examples of intellectual property law

Automatic protection	
Type of protection	*Examples of intellectual property*
Copyright	Writing and literary works, art, photography, films, TV, music, web content, sound recordings
Design right	Shapes of objects
Protection you have to apply for	
Type of protection	*Examples of intellectual property (time to allow for application)*
Trade marks	Product names, logos, jingles (four months)
Registered designs	Appearance of a product including shape, packaging, patterns, colours, decoration (one month)
Patents	Inventions and products, e.g. machines and machine parts, tools, medicines (approx. five years)

9.3 The Copyright, Designs and Patents Act 1988

The purpose of the Copyright, Designs and Patents Act 1988 (CDPA – also known as the 'UK Copyright Act') – frequently amended by EU legislation – is to protect the rights of creators to be paid for, and to control the use of, their works and to address the needs of users who want access to material protected by copyright. The creator's statutory rights are limited by 'exceptions' for the benefit of certain users (e.g. educational establishments, libraries, braille copies or copying for private use).

Copyright law is concerned primarily with authorship, ownership and originality. These fundamental principles are summarized in the following sections of the CDPA:

Section 1(1): Copyright is a property right which subsists in accordance with this Part in the following descriptions of work –

(a) original literary, dramatic, musical or artistic works . . .

Section 2(1): The owner of a copyright in a work of any description has the exclusive right to do the acts specified in Chapter II as the acts restricted by the copyright in a work of that description.
Section 4(1): In this part 'Artistic work' means (a) graphic work, photograph, sculpture or collage, irrespective of artistic quality.
Section 9(1): In this part 'author' in relation to a work means the person who creates it.

When using and working with the CDPA it is important to consult secondary legislation, such as the Copyright and Related Rights Regulations 2003, relating to the prevention of unauthorized use, extraction of contents of databases and the use of works published online.

9.3.1 Categories covered by the Copyright, Designs and Patents Act 1988

Section 1 of the CDPA introduces an immediate copyright which exists automatically in original literary, dramatic, musical or artistic works.

'Literary work' means any work, other than a dramatic or musical work, which is written, spoken or sung, and accordingly includes tables, compilations, computer programmes and databases.[13] 'Dramatic work' includes dance or mime, and 'musical work' means a work consisting of music, exclusive of any words or action intended to be sung, spoken or performed with the music.

The basic rights of copyright include:

- the right to copy the work;
- the right to issue copies of it to the public;
- the right to rent or lend copies to the public;
- the right to perform, show or play the work in public;
- the right to communicate the work to the public, which includes the broadcasting right;
- the right to make an adaptation, which includes the translation right, of the work.

---

13 s 3(1) CDPA.

Copyright does not subsist in a literary, dramatic or musical work *unless* and until it is recorded, in writing or otherwise,[14] though not necessarily by the author – a recording of an extempore jazz performance at a pub if recorded by a drinker would vest musical copyright in members of the jazz band. 'Recorded' includes the digital medium, storage on a computer hard drive or memory stick, as well as digital music recordings.

See
Chapter 10

Section 4(1)(a) CDPA provides that artistic works, including photographs, are protected as copyright works 'irrespective of artistic quality'.

A copyright-protected work can have more than one copyright, or another intellectual property right, connected to it. For example, an album of music can have separate copyrights for individual songs, sound recordings, artwork, and so on. While copyright can protect the artwork of the album's logo, it could also be registered as a trade mark.

Immediate copyright subsists in:

- *Literary works*, including novels, instruction manuals, computer programs, song lyrics, newspaper articles.
- *Dramatic works*, including theatrical performances such as plays, pantomimes, musical scores used, scripts, stage directions, set design and ballet. In ballet, for instance, if the choreography of the dance has been recorded in writing or filmed, the dramatic performance of the dance itself can be entitled to copyright.
- *Musical works*, including compositions, opera, musicals. With a song there will usually be more than one copyright associated with it, i.e. the composer of the music is the 'author of the musical work' and has copyright in that music. The lyrics of a song are protected separately by copyright as a literary work. The person who writes the lyrics will own the copyright in the words. If the work is subsequently recorded, the sound recording will also have copyright protection: the producer of the recording will own the copyright in the sound recording. Composers of music may also have moral rights in their work.
- *Artistic works*, including paintings, engravings, photographs, sculptures, cartoons, collages, architecture, technical drawings, diagrams and maps.
- *Typographical arrangements or layouts* used to publish a work, such as a book.
- *Recordings* of a work, including sound and film.
- *Broadcasts, TV and films*, including the original screenplay, the music score of a film and cable, wireless and satellite broadcasts. Films do not have to be original, but they will not be new copyright works if they have been copied from existing films. Broadcasts do not have to be original, but there

---

14 s 3(2) CDPA.

will be no copyright, if, or to the extent that, they infringe copyright[15] in another broadcast.

- *Databases and software*, e.g. computer programs and games; computer languages and codes; databases are usually collections of copyright works, such as a database of poetry.
- *Websites*, copyright applies to the internet in the same way as material in other media; e.g. any photographs posted on the internet are protected in the same way as other artistic works; any original written work will be protected as a 'literary' work.

Moral rights include that an author of a work has the right not to have his work subjected to derogatory treatment[16] or to have the work falsely attributed to him.[17]

Software for computer games and the PlayStation are protected on the same basis as literary works under UK and EU copyright legislation. Many games developers have tried to establish generic copyrights for their games, some of which have succeeded, such as the Guildford-based studio, Wonderstruck, developers for PS4 and PC creation of *Boundless*, a multiplayer open-world game (2018).

9.3.2 The protection of literary, dramatic, musical and artistic works and internet ownership

See
Chapter 10.2

Can a recording artist or publishing author protect his name, a song or title by copyright? It depends. Copyright may or may not be available for titles, slogans or logos, depending on whether they contain sufficient authorship. In most circumstances copyright does not protect names.

Does an artist or performer need to register his work or sound recording to be protected? Not really, because copyright protection is formality-free in countries party to the Berne Convention, which means that protection does not depend on compliance with any formalities such as registration or deposit of copies.

Under the CDPA 1988, a literary work is defined as 'any work, other than a dramatic or musical work, which is written, spoken or sung'.

'Artistic works' can mean graphic work, a painting, drawing, map, engraving, etching, lithograph, woodcut or similar work, a photograph, sculpture or collage, a work of architecture, such as either a building or a model of a building, or a work of artistic craftsmanship – irrespective of artistic quality.[18] It is not an infringement of the copyright in a work to draw, take a photograph or make a film of buildings or sculptures or works of artistic craftsmanship which are located in a public place or in premises open to the public. Copyright is not infringed in any material when it is used in legal proceedings.

In the landmark case of *Grisbrook* (2010),[19] the courts examined how far licence terms can be implied when technology has moved on beyond what the legislators of the CDPA

---

15 s 27 CDPA ('Meaning of "infringing copy"').
16 s 80(1) CDPA.
17 s 84(1) CDPA.
18 s 4 CDPA.
19 *Mirror Group Newspapers & Ors v Grisbrook (Alan)* [2010] EWCA Civ 1399 (CA).

initially intended or even imagined. Celebrity photographer Alan Grisbrook's work was first commissioned by the *Daily Mirror* in 1981 to provide photographs for the Mirror's 'Diary' page. For the next 16 years 'snapper' Grisbrook supplied Mirror Group Newspapers (MGN) with hundreds of photographs, such as Ali MacGraw, Alan Bates and Sarah Miles, many of which made the front page.

In his court action Mr Grisbrook claimed £161,238 in respect of the use of his photographs without his permission between 1982 and October 1997. The newspaper publishers had put his exclusive photos on the paper's website.

| ❖ KEY CASE | *Mirror Group Newspapers & Ors v Grisbrook (Alan)* [2010] EWCA Civ 1399 (CA) |

Precedent

❖ Whether a licence agreement extends to subsequent forms of (new) technology (such as online publication and archiving of photos) depends on the form of words used in the contract.

❖ A copyright licence should be limited to what is in the joint contemplation of the parties *at the time* the agreement was made (in Grisbrook's case, prior to the internet).

Facts

In 1998, Alan Grisbrook commenced proceedings against Mirror Group Newspapers (MGN) to recover unpaid licence fees of £161,238 for photos of his available on various MGN websites for sale (mydailymirror.com, mirrorarchive.co.uk and arcitext.com). By 1998 MGN's website FastFoto held about 350,000 images. As part of the licence fee settlement in 2002, MGN agreed to delete all electronic copies of Mr Grisbrook's photos from the digital photo library. But he discovered in 2008 that MGN were making available back copies of their image library online to paying customers.[20] Alan Grisbrook commenced proceedings for breach of copyright, arguing that the publication of his photographic material on the newspaper's online photo archive amounted to copyright infringement and a breach of undertaking given by MGN. He sought an order for imprisonment of the officers of MGN, and sequestration of MGN's assets. MGN argued that the licence originally granted verbally by Grisbrook permitting publication in the newspaper also extended to subsequent reproduction of the published material, including archiving on the internet. MGN relied on the defence of public interest under section 171(3) CDPA.

---

20 The MGN archive websites included: mydailymirror.com, launched in June 2006 enabling users to buy *Daily Mirror* front pages in the form of posters, T-shirts or greetings cards; www.arcitext.com, launched in February 2006 allowing subscribers to access the *Mirror*'s archives as pdf documents which reproduce part of the newspaper as it was printed; and www.mirrorarchive.co.uk, launched as a test site in April 2007 but intended to be the commercial equivalent of arcitext.com.

Decision

The CA[21] found that the implied licence did *not* extend to the exploitation of Mr Grisbrook's photos on back-issue websites and databases and therefore amounted to breach of copyright (though perhaps not deliberate on the *Mirror*'s part). Leveson LJ said that though permission to store pictures for possible future use or for archiving could be an 'implied term' of the oral contract, the same could not be said for the presentation of the archived material to the public for a fee.

The court found that on the facts the licence granted by Mr Grisbrook did *not* allow MGN to publish the images on the websites because this form of commercial exploitation had simply not been in the contemplation of the parties at the time the licence was granted and because this term was not otherwise necessary. MGN had therefore infringed Mr Grisbrook's copyright in the images. Mr Grisbrook was awarded the full amount owed plus costs.

Analysis

Mr Grisbrook and other freelance paparazzi were obviously aware that MGN, like any other newspaper publisher, would retain an archive of published editions. But this was before the existence of the World Wide Web, and photographs were stored in the form of hard copies and microfiche by the newspaper publishers.

The only real issue in this case was whether the verbal licence also extended to making the back numbers database more widely available to members of the public via the internet. The CA held that Mr Grisbrook's photographs on the newspaper's websites were 'a different kind of operation'.[22] In effect the exploitation of the photographs of Mr Grisbrook by inclusion in the websites, from which copies could be downloaded and printed at will, was a 'new method of exploitation' which, by reference to the conditions prevailing in the period from 1981 to 1997, was wholly outside anything the parties could have contemplated at the time the photographs were first submitted to MGN.

In the light of the *Grisbrook* judgment, authors of creative works ought to study their licence agreements with media and newspaper publishers carefully. If they have granted licensed images to a newspaper, which, like MGN, is making back copies of their editions available online to paid subscribers, they may well have a claim in copyright infringement if their licence agreement does not clearly allow such 'extended' use (i.e. archives online).

9.3.3 Copyrights in film

Copyright in the film sector is particularly complex because of the many IP layers involved and the fact that there is no single 'creator' of a film.[23] Each year when the Oscars are

---

21 The case was heard before the Chancellor of the High Court, Leveson LJ and Etherton LJ.
22 [2010] EWCA Civ 1399 at para. 65.
23 Sections 5A and 5B CDPA cover 'film'. Sections 5A and 5B have been substituted by reg. 9(1) (with Pt III) the Performances (Moral Rights, etc.) Regulations 2006 (S.I. 2006/18); s 5B(3)(b)–(d) substituted by s 5B(3)(b) Performances (Moral Rights, etc.) Regulations 2006 (S.I. 2006/18), reg. 2, Sch.

awarded in Hollywood, some of the categories below will be awarded an Oscar individually within the same film. *Bohemian Rhapsody* did not just win the best male actor's award (Rami Malek) in the 91st Academy Awards in February 2019, but also an Oscar for each category: film editing, sound editing and sound mixing.

Copyright law makes the producer and the principal director of a film joint first owners of copyright,[24] although in practice the director will often assign his interest in the copyright to the production company (or financiers or both jointly). The producer must ensure that all underlying rights in the film, including in the screenplay itself, have been acquired by assignment before they will be able to raise finance for the film. Assignments of rights must be in writing, signed by both parties (although technically they only have to be signed by the assignor) and should include rights to exploit the film (or underlying material) in every imaginable manner, including in ways that have not yet been invented at the time of the assignment.

See
Chapter 10.3

While an idea for a film cannot be protected by copyright, the title of a film might be protected in limited circumstances. Titles most certainly qualify for trade mark registration and may therefore be protected. It is worth mentioning that not all films are commercial productions; home movies, mobile phone pictures, camcorder images and so on can also constitute 'film', but have a shorter period of protection of 50 years from when they are made.[25] For instance, if a bystander films an important or traumatic event – such as the assassination of US President John F. Kennedy in Dallas in 1963 – and a news agency wants to use that film footage, they may not be able simply to use the whole film without the 'cameraman's' consent. The following box shows that various copyrights can exist in each 'strata' of a film.

Copyrights existing in film

- *artistic* – i.e. the set designs used in the film;
- *dramatic* – if the film is based on a dramatic work, dance or mime material;
- *literary* – within the source material and the original screenplay;
- *musical* – the soundtrack of the film, including both musical score and any lyrics;
- *film* – the images in the 'first fixation' of the film;
- *sound recordings* – the physical recording of the soundtrack;
- *broadcasts* – for sale of the underlying material and film for other exploitation;
- *performance* – any live interpretation of the film;
- *published editions* – within the typographical layout of the page for any published versions of the screenplay.

In *Norowzian Nr 2 (2000)*,[26] filmmaker Mehdi Norowzian launched an unsuccessful lawsuit in the High Court Chancery Division in 1998, seeking remuneration for the use

---

24 s 9(2)(a) CDPA now substituted by s 9(2)(aa), (bb) in relation to films made on or after 1 July 1994 (S.I. 1996/2967, regs 18(1), 36).
25 s 13 CDPA.
26 *Norowzian (Mehdi) v Arks Ltd and Guinness Brewing Worldwide Limited (No 2)* [1999] EWCA Civ 3018 (CA).

of techniques and style from his short film which he made in 1992, called *Joy*. The background to this case was that drinks giant Diageo had launched a successful Guinness advertising campaign in 1994, promoting the stout with a film clip called *Anticipation*. Mr Norowzian claimed that *Anticipation* was a copy of his *Joy* dance sequence clip and that the makers of the Guinness advert had breached his copyright. *Anticipation* portrayed a man who, having been served by a barman with a pint of Guinness, waits for the frothing liquid in his glass to settle, and, while he waits, carries out a series of dance movements.

Was *Anticipation* a copy of *Joy* under section 17(2) CDPA? Mr Justice Rattee had to first decide whether the *Joy* sequence constituted a 'dramatic work' within the meaning of section 1(1) CDPA in order to decide whether an advertising clip for Guinness stout breached Mr Norowzian's copyright.[27] Mr Norowzian claimed that his film clip of *Joy* fell under section 3 CDPA, as a 'work of dance or mime', which entitled him to be regarded as the maker of it and therefore the 'author' within the meaning of sections 9 and 11 of the 1988 Act. Rattee J concluded that *Joy* was neither a dramatic work nor a recording of a dramatic work; therefore *Anticipation* did not infringe copyright.

The Court of Appeal in *Norowzian No 2* (1999)[28] clarified the earlier judgment in the first *Norowzian* action (1998) and held that a film might be purely protected as a film (i.e. a dramatic work) and be subject to copyright law, but not the artistic techniques demonstrated in the film, somewhat similar to the French idea of treating the film director as 'the author' (l'auteur). While the justices did not criticize the original trial judge, they stated that the standards applied by the law in different contexts vary a great deal in precision and by applying different standards and factors when weighing up what constitutes a 'dramatic' work in a film.[29] In any case section 5(1) CDPA did not specifically define 'film' – it merely stated that it is a 'recording on any medium from which a moving image may by any means be produced'.

Concerns have been raised when dealing with adaptations of plays or books in the making of a film. With either original or adapted works, the film producer needs to ensure that all *ancillary rights* are acquired, for example to adapt the work for television or to copy the work in the form of a remake, sequel or prequel to the film or to acquire merchandizing rights.[30]

9.3.4 Copyright in artistic works

The exploitation of artistic works used in films was addressed in the *StarWars* case, *Lucasfilm Ltd v Ainsworth* (2011).[31] The first *StarWars* film (later renamed *StarWars Episode IV – A New Hope* in order to provide for 'prequels' as well as sequels) was released in the United States in 1977. It was an enormous commercial success. It won an Oscar for best costume design. This appeal was concerned with IP rights in various artefacts made for use in the film. The most important of these was the Imperial Stormtrooper helmet.

The film's storyline and characters were conceived by Mr George Lucas. Between 1974 and 1976 Mr Lucas' concept of the Darth Vader's foot soldiers, the Imperial Stormtroopers, as threatening characters in 'fascist white-armoured suits' was given visual

---

27 *Norowzian Nr 1* [1998] EWHC 315 (Ch) (Rattee J).
28 *Norowzian No 2* [1999] EWCA Civ 3018 (CA).
29 Ibid. (Buxton, Nourse, Brooke LJJ).
30 s 21 CDPA ('Infringement by making adaptation or act done in relation to adaptation').
31 [2011] UKSC 39 ('the *StarWars* case').

expression in drawings and paintings by an artist, Ralph McQuarrie, and three-dimensional form by Nick Pemberton (a freelance scenic artist and prop-maker) and industrial designer, Andrew Ainsworth. Between 1976 and 1977 Mr Ainsworth produced some 50 prototype vacuum-moulded helmets for use in the film in England. Although Mr Lucas and his companies were based in California he had come to live in England while the film was made at Elstree Studios near London.

Mr Ainsworth subsequently sold some of the goods that he had produced online to the value of at least $8,000 but not more than $30,000 in the United States. In 2005 Lucasfilm (and Mr George Lucas) sued Mr Ainsworth for breach of copyright and trade mark laws in the United States District Court, Central District of California, and in 2006 they obtained a default judgment for $20m, $10m of which represented triple damages under the Lanham Act.[32] Mr Ainsworth counterclaimed to enforce his own copyright in the Imperial Stormtrooper helmet. The whole judgment remains unsatisfactory.

Lucasfilm also commenced proceedings in the Chancery Division of the English High Court. The re-amended particulars of claim put forward a variety of claims under English law, including infringement of copyright, a claim for enforcement of the United States judgment to the extent of $10m and claims under US copyright law.[33] The complex case did not only centre on whether the three-dimensional object was a 'sculpture' for the purposes of section 4(2) CPDA, but also on the conflict between the UK, the US and EU law as to the forum conveniens for legal action. Lucasfilm sued for $20m, arguing Mr Ainsworth did not hold the IP rights and had no right to sell them – a point upheld by a US court.

The trial at the High Court in London occupied 17 days during April and May 2008. In his judgment delivered on 31 July 2008 Mann J dismissed all Lucasfilm's claims based on English copyright law. He held that the helmet made by Mr Ainsworth was a substantial reproduction of original work carried out by Mr McQuarrie and other persons working for Lucasfilm. But the English copyright claims failed because the helmet was not a work of sculpture, and Mr Ainsworth had defences (to a claim that he was reproducing Mr McQuarrie's work) under sections 51 and 52 CDPA. The judge also dismissed Mr Ainsworth's counterclaim based on his own claim to copyright in the helmet.

In July 2011 the Star Wars case reached the Supreme Court which centred on the meaning of 'sculpture' in UK copyright law. Their Lordships held that the Star Wars film itself was 'a work of art' and that the helmet was utilitarian in the sense that it was an element in the process of production of the film. Most importantly, the justices ruled that the helmet was not a sculpture.[34] Lords Walker and Collins held that the helmet was not a sculpture. They said that the helmets were 'a mixture of costume and prop' in order to contribute to the artistic effect of the Star Wars film as a film (Mr Justice Mann had said as much in his High Court ruling). They were part of the production process (here, the making of a full-length film). It would not accord with the normal use of language to apply the term 'sculpture' to a twentieth-century military helmet used in the making of a film, whether it was the real thing or a replica made in different material, however great

---

32 The Lanham Act – also known as the US Trademark Act of 1946 – is the federal statute that governs trade marks, service marks and unfair competition. It was passed by the US Congress on 5 July 1946 and signed into law by President Harry Truman.

33 Lucasfilm Ltd v Ainsworth [2008] EWHC 1878 (Ch) at paras 1–17.

34 Lucasfilm Ltd and Another v Ainsworth and Another [2011] UKSC 39 (Lord Phillips, President, Lord Walker, Lady Hale, Lord Mance, Lord Collins) judgment on 27 July 2011.

its contribution to the artistic effect of the finished film. It was the *Star Wars* film that was the work of art that Mr Lucas and his companies created. The helmet was *utilitarian* in the sense that it was an element in the process of production of the film. Their Lordships ruled that Mann J had not erred in law or reached an obviously untenable conclusion, and the Court of Appeal was right to uphold his decision on this point. Together with Lucasfilm's acceptance that the section 51 defence therefore applied, it meant that Mr Ainsworth had not infringed Lucasfilm's UK copyright through his activities in selling 'Stormtrooper' helmets made from the original moulds he produced.

9.4 Duration of copyright

National copyright laws stipulate the duration of copyright, and the actual duration will vary between nation states. The Copyright, Designs and Patents Act 1988 (CDPA) provides for copyright protection in the UK, i.e. musical, literary, dramatic and artistic works have a 70-year duration of copyright *after* the author's death (enhanced by the Berne Convention and EU harmonization law).[35]

An author from any country that is a signatory of the Berne Convention is awarded the same rights in *all* other countries that are signatories to the Convention as they allow their own nationals, as well as any rights granted by the Convention. The Convention also sets out a minimum duration that copyright will apply in various types of work.

When the term of copyright protection has expired, the work falls into the public domain. This means that the work has effectively become public property and may be used freely.

See
Chapter 10

Sound recordings will have an individual copyright separate to the underlying composition. If the underlying composition is in the public domain, it does not follow that a sound recording is.

A summary of duration of copyrights is given below.

9.4.1 How long does a copyright last?

i. Literary, dramatic, musical or artistic works
70 years from the end of the calendar year in which the last remaining author of the work dies. If the author is unknown, copyright will last for 70 years from the end of the calendar year in which the work was created, although if it is made available to the public during that time (by publication, authorized performance, broadcast, exhibition etc.), then the duration will be 70 years from the end of the year that the work was first made available.

ii. Sound recordings
70 years.[36] The 70-year period runs from the date of first lawful publication or (if none) first lawful communication to the public (if the publication or, as the case may be, communication occurs within 50 years of the date of recording). If neither occurs within

---

35 s 12 CDPA, as amended by the Duration of Copyright and Rights in Performances Regulations 1995 (S.I. 1995/3297).
36 Extended from 50 to 70 years by Directive 2006/116/EC ('EU Copyright Term Directive').

50 years of the date of recording, the term of copyright will expire at that point. The extension will have prospective and retrospective effect. For existing copyrights, the new legislation applies only to sound recordings that are less than 50 years old as at the date falling two years after the date of the amending Directive (2011). In other words, no copyrights will be 'revived' under the new law.

iii. Films

70 years from the end of the calendar year in which the last principal director, producer, author or composer dies. If the work is of unknown authorship: 70 years from the end of the calendar year of creation or, if made available to the public in that time, 70 years from the end of the year the film was first made available.

iv. Typographical arrangement of published editions

25 years from the end of the calendar year in which the work was first published.[37] Typographical arrangement covers the style, composition, design, layout and general appearance of a page of a published work. In a typical book publication, copyright subsists both in the content of a work and also in the typographical arrangement and design elements of the work. Copyright in the typographical arrangement of a published edition rests with the publisher of that published work (in accordance with sections 9(2)(d) and 11 CDPA).

v. Broadcasts and cable programmes

50 years from the end of the calendar year in which the broadcast was made.[38]

vi. Crown copyright[39]

50 years if the work has been published from the end of the year in which the work was published. **125 years** for unpublished works from the end of the year in which the work was made or until 31 December 2039 (which is 50 years from the year in which the CDPA 1988 came into force).

These include copyrighted works, produced by civil servants and owned by the Crown, which means government departments do not own copyright in their own right. Copyright can also come into Crown ownership by means of assignment or transfer of the copyright from the legal owner of the copyright to the Crown. This often happens where a government department commissions a person or organization to produce a report on its behalf and arranges for the copyright to be assigned to the Crown. The responsibility for the management and licensing of copyright and database rights owned by the Crown rests with the National Archives.

vii. Parliamentary copyright

50 years from the end of the calendar year in which the work was made, i.e. material produced by the Westminster Parliament is protected by Parliamentary copyright. Most of the information produced by Parliament can be reused under the Open Parliament

---

37 s 15 CDPA.
38 s 14 CDPA.
39 s 163 CDPA.

Licence (e.g. the printing of Acts of Parliament or copies of *Hansard*).[40] Material produced by the Scottish Parliament is the copyright of the Scottish Parliamentary Corporate Body.[41]

viii. The creation of artistic works which have been industrially manufactured

See below 9.7

Following the *Flos*[42] judgment, the UK government repealed section 52 CDPA. This now means that the period of copyright protection for an *artistic work*, which has been *industrially manufactured*, has been extended from **25 years** to the life of the artist plus **70 years** (the same as all other artistic works).[43]

Table 9.2 Copyright lifetimes: overview

Literary works	Written works. Includes lyrics, tables, compilations, computer programs, letters, memoranda, email and web pages.	Author's life plus 70 years after death. Anonymous corporation authors: 70 years from year of publication (see above for special rules for unpublished works).
Dramatic works	Plays, works of dance and mime, and also the libretto of an opera.	Author's life plus 70 years after death.
Crown copyright	All works made by Her Majesty or by an officer or servant of the Crown in the course of his or her duties.	Published by HM Stationery Office: 50 years from the end of the year when first published. Unpublished work: 125 years beyond the year it was created.
Parliamentary copyright	All works made by or under the direction or control of the House of Commons or House of Lords.	Mostly 50 years beyond year it was created. Exceptions include bills of Parliament.
Musical compositions and lyrics	Musical composition (music scores) and the lyrics.	This term of protection will (as long as the music and lyrics were specifically created for the relevant work) expire 70 years after the death of the last of the composers of the musical composition and the authors of the lyrics (whether or not those persons are designated as co-authors).

---

40 Open Parliament Licence at www.parliament.uk/site-information/copyright-parliament/open-parliament-licence/.

41 Scottish Parliament Copyright Licence and Re-Use of Public Sector Information Regulations 2015 at: www.parliament.scot/abouttheparliament/13591.aspx.

42 *Flos Spa v Semeraro Casa e Famiglia Spa* (2011) (Case C-168/09) (CJEU).

43 s 74 Enterprise and Regulatory Reform Act 2013.

Artistic works	Graphic works (painting, drawing, diagram, map, chart, plan, engraving, etching, lithograph, woodcut), photographs (not part of a moving film), sculpture, collage, works of architecture (buildings and models for buildings) and artistic craftsmanship (e.g. jewellery).	Author's/creator's life plus 70 years after death.
Computer-generated works	Literary, dramatic and musical works.	50 years from first creation or 50 years from creation if unpublished during that time.
Databases	Collections of independent works, data or other materials which (a) are arranged in a systematic or methodical way, or (b) are individually accessible by electronic or other means.	Full term of other relevant copyrights in the material protected. Also, there is a database right for 15 years (this can roll forward).
Performers and sound recordings	Regardless of medium or the device on which they are played.	The copyright term for live performances and sound recordings is 70 years. The 70-year period runs from the date of first lawful recording or live performance or (if none) first lawful communication to the public.
Films	Any medium from which a moving image may be reproduced.	70 years from death of whoever is the last to survive from: principal director, producer, author of dialogue, composer of film music.
Broadcasts	Transmissions via wireless telegraphy through the air (not via cable or wires), includes satellite transmissions.	50 years from when broadcast first made.
Cable programmes	Services via cable.	50 years from when broadcast first made.

(Continued)

Table 9.2 (Continued)

Published editions	The typography and layout of a literary, dramatic or musical work.	25 years from first publication.
Orphan works	Copyrighted works for which the owner of the copyright is unknown or cannot be found.	70 years from the year in which the work was created or first made available or until 2039.

 FOR THOUGHT – PROBLEM QUESTION

Brigitte, an author of legal textbooks, asks her sister Daniella to type up her handwritten manuscript of 'Media Law' and proof read the manuscript. Daniella does so, as a favour to her sister Brigitte; she types out the whole manuscript of 1,000 pages on a word processor and corrects obvious grammatical errors and eliminates any spelling mistakes. Shortly afterwards Brigitte dies in a car crash. Her husband Mick succeeds to Brigitte's estate, including all of Brigitte's authored works and copyright rights (including the 'Media Law' book). Mick is not interested in any of the works and asks Daniella to destroy the recent manuscript of 'Media Law'. Daniella does not do this; she, in turn, makes 'Media Law' available on a legal website which provides teaching assistance to law students. Daniella receives a small 'killer fee' of £200 for the manuscript. Mick finds out about this and – suddenly interested in the published copy of 'Media Law' on the 'LawTeach' website – brings an action against Daniella and a separate action against LawTeach for copyright infringement. Daniella uses in her defence the ground that she is the author of 'Media Law' claiming joint copyright (authorship), and by making the online text available to all law students, claims fair use. Discuss and evaluate all the issues in this litigation.

9.4.2 Moral and related rights

Linked to UK copyright legislation are 'moral' rights, covered by Chapter IV of the CDPA 1988 ('Right to be identified as author or director'). Moral rights are distinct from any economic rights tied to copyrights. Even if an artist has assigned his or her copyright rights to a work to a third party, he or she still maintains the moral rights to the work. These rights protect non-economic interests, for example the right to claim authorship of a work, to protect the work from harm and distortion and ultimately to protect the creator's reputation.[44] Moral rights may be waived but cannot be assigned or passed on after the author's death.[45]

---

44 s 80 CDPA.
45 s 86 CDPA.

Moral rights do not extend to computer programs, the design of a typeface or any computer-generated work.[46] Furthermore, the right does not apply to publications in a newspaper, magazine or periodical, or an encyclopaedia, dictionary, yearbook or other collective work of reference, or a work in which Crown copyright or parliamentary copyright subsists (such as *Hansard*).[47]

Related rights are a term in copyright law and have developed alongside copyright. They include those of performing artists in their performances, producers of phonograms in their recordings and those of broadcasters in their radio and television programmes. Related rights tend to be of a more limited nature. They are usually of shorter duration and are used in opposition to the term 'author's rights'. Related rights are primarily a result of technological development and generally concern the exploitation of works. The first organized support for the protection of related rights came from the phonogram industry, which sought (and gained, at least in countries following the common law tradition) protection under copyright law against unauthorized copying of phonograms (i.e. records, CDs etc.) under copyright. Here follows a summary:

See chapter 10.2

1   *Moral rights* of the author and creator of work include the right of attribution (e.g. name of the author), the right to have a work published anonymously or by pseudonym and the right of integrity of the work. This means that the work is barred from alteration, distortion or mutilation. Anything else that may detract from the artist's relationship with the work even after it leaves the artist's possession or ownership may bring these moral rights into play.

2   *Related rights* (or 'neighbouring rights' – from the French *droits voisins*) are the rights of a creative work *not* connected with the work's actual copyright (such as fine art, sculpture, paintings, film making, musical composition, literature). The term is used in opposition to the term 'author's rights'. Related rights vary much more widely in scope between different countries than authors' rights. The rights of performers, phonogram producers and broadcasting organizations are covered by the CDPA, the Rome Convention for the Protection of Performers, Producers of Phonograms and Broadcasting Organizations of 1961.

Section 103 CDPA deals with remedies for infringement of moral rights under section 80 CDPA, actionable as a breach of statutory duty owed to the person entitled to the right.

9.5 Passing off

Passing off is a common law tort and available remedies include injunctive relief, delivery up of the offensive goods and damages to the owner of the rights or an accounting of profits by the offender.

---

46 s 79 CDPA.
47 s 79(6) and (7) CDPA.

The most common type of passing off involves the defendant selling goods that purport to be those of the claimant. Most commonly this occurs where a famous trade mark (brand) is copied, where packaging or 'get up' is copied and where websites become 'look-alikes'. There is also 'reverse passing off', where a third party without authorization takes your trade mark or brand name and presents it as theirs.

See below 9.7.3

Graphic designs are potentially covered also by the passing off area of the law, which has been shown by decisions of the courts to be a strong form of protection in cases where a reputation has been clearly established.

To establish this right of action, the claimant must show three elements, sometimes referred to as the 'classic trinity', first established by Lord Oliver of Aylmerton in the House of Lords' decision of *Reckitt & Colman Products Ltd v Borden Inc.* (1990) (the *Jif Lemon* case).[48] In this case the HL issued a permanent injunction preventing Borden from marketing a lemon-shaped container to sell 'squeezy' lemon juice, which the US firm had done since 1985, branded as 'ReaLemon'. Reckitt & Colman had been selling 'squeezy Jif Lemon' juice since 1956. Reckitt sued Borden for passing off their product. Had 'Jif Lemon' been a registered trade mark, the case would have been much simpler to prove. Reckitt succeeded in the House of Lords which established.

> The 'classic trinity' test (the *Jif Lemon* principle) for all passing off actions involves
>
> 1   misrepresentation;
> 2   goodwill;
> 3   damage.

In detail this means:

1   The defendant misrepresents his goods or services, either intentionally or unintentionally, so that the public believe or are led to believe that the offered goods or services are those of the claimant.
2   Since the claimant supplies his goods or services under a distinctive 'get-up' (e.g. brand or packaging), his goods or services have acquired goodwill and/or reputation in the marketplace that distinguishes the claimant's goods or services from its competitors'.
3   The claimant suffers damage because of the misrepresentation.[49]

In 2007 the frontman of the 1980s pop band Frankie Goes to Hollywood, Holly Johnson, attempted to register the mark 'Frankie Goes to Hollywood' as a community trade mark. The main issue in *Frankie Goes to Hollywood*[50] centred on the law of passing off in relation to a non-registered trade mark. Though Holly Johnson had invented the name, the Office of

---

48 [1990] 1 WLR 491.
49 Ibid. at para. 880 (Lord Oliver).
50 *Gill v Frankie Goes to Hollywood Ltd* [2008] ETMR 4 (Case B 849 069) (OHIM) 27 July 2007.

Harmonization in the Internal Market (OHIM) ruled that the mere act of inventing a name did not, in itself, bring the 'inventor' any rights. It then followed that the use of the non-registered trade mark 'Frankie Goes to Hollywood' was 'of more than mere local significance', in that the original band members could show that the original band name 'Frankie Goes to Hollywood' was very successful both in the UK and in other European countries between 1984 and 1987; moreover, that the band's music continues to be very popular. It was for this reason that the OHIM prevented the registration of a new trade mark in the very same name.[51]

See below
9.7.1

The result then was that Holly Johnson's application was successfully opposed by the four other band members, Peter Gill (in whose name the action was brought), Paul Rutherford, Brian Nash and Mark O'Toole. Relying on Lord Oliver's classic trinity test to establish 'passing off', both the UK Intellectual Property Office (UK-IPO)[52] and OHIM[53] (parallel UK and European actions) decided the rights to the name were owned equally by all five original band members, and no one band member had the right to claim exclusivity to that name.

In *Moroccanoil Israel Ltd v Aldi Stores Ltd* (2014),[54] the court applied the *Jif Lemon* principle. Moroccanoil Israel Ltd (MIL) sold its argan oil products worldwide from 2009, the star product being the hair oil, sold in a brown bottle with a blue label. In March 2012, German supermarket giant Aldi started selling a new hair oil product called 'Miracle Oil', sold in a similarly shaped bottle with a blue label. MIL alleged customer confusion and in addition to passing off also alleged misrepresentation.[55] MIL enjoyed considerable goodwill in the UK, both in the brand and get-up (shape, colour, packaging etc.). The company further argued that the misrepresentation had caused damage to MIL's goodwill. Aldi admitted in court its willingness to 'live dangerously' by marketing products with similar get-up and packaging to their expensive equivalents but argued that this alone did not constitute passing off.

The Intellectual Property Enterprise Court (IPEC) then applied the classic trinity test (Jif Lemon principle) in *Moroccanoil*:

(a) goodwill in MIL's business in the sale of Moroccanoil in the UK, which goodwill is associated with the get-up and name of the product such that they are in combination recognized by the public as distinctive of MIL's product;

(b) a misrepresentation on the part of Aldi (whether or not intentional) in relation to the source of Aldi's Miracle Oil product; and

(c) damage to the goodwill by reason of the misrepresentation.[56]

Additionally, His Honour Judge Hacon considered the observations of Morritt LJ in the *Interflora* case.[57] He found that the important point to be taken from this case was that passing off might be established even though most people were not deceived.

---

51 Ibid. at 97–99.
52 UK-IPO 'Frankie Goes to Hollywood', O/140/07 dated 25 May 2007.
53 OHIM Opposition No B849 069 *Gill v Frankie Goes to Hollywood Ltd* [2008] ETMR 4.
54 [2014] EWHC 1686 (IPEC).
55 As per s 10 Trade Marks Act 1994, the provision by which Article 5 of Directive 2008/95 was transposed into UK law.
56 *Moroccanoil* [2014] at para. 4 (Hacon HHJ).
57 *Interflora Inc. v Marks and Spencer plc* [2012] EWCA Civ 1501 at para. 30 (Morritt LJ).

The court dismissed MIL's action and concluded that the evidence submitted did not show that members of the public were likely to assume that Aldi's Miracle Oil and Moroccanoil were the same product; that there was no misrepresentation.

Cases like *Moroccanoil* demonstrate the importance of formally protecting the distinctive elements of a product, particularly in relation to its get-up and packaging. It then makes absolute business sense to register a sign or brand as trade mark in order to seek more effective redress (rather than a passing-off action). While the two actions of passing off and trade mark infringement share many similarities, the fact remains that they are both separate doctrines (see also: *United Biscuits (UK) Ltd v Asda Stores Ltd* (1997)[58] – 'the Penguin and Puffin' case; also: *Specsavers International Healthcare Ltd v Asda Ltd* (2012)[59]).

See below
9.7.1

In early 2006, authors Michael Baigent and Richard Leigh filed a copyright suit against publishers Random House.[60] The claimants (two of three authors) alleged that significant portions of best seller *The Da Vinci Code* by Dan Brown had been plagiarized from their text, *The Holy Blood and the Holy Grail*. Whilst Brown admitted that he had referred to *The Holy Blood* text in the course of his research, he denied copyright infringement. Lloyd LJ in the CA agreed with the trial judge's decision on the issue of 'substantiality' in that there had been no 'central theme' to copy and accordingly no breach of copyright was found. The claimants were ordered to pay 85 per cent of Random House's legal costs, estimated at £1.3m.[61]

Blythe (2015) argues that the tests for passing off and trade mark infringement have essentially been the same, based on the confusion rationale. This is where the defendant sells goods under a sign that is identical or similar to a registered trade mark, the goods being identical or similar to those for which the mark is registered, and where the average consumer encounters those goods there exists a likelihood of confusion whereby the consumer mistakenly thinks that the defendant's goods are the claimant's goods, or mistakenly believes that there exists an economic link between the two undertakings[62] (see: *Reed Executive plc v Reed Business Information Ltd* (2004)[63]).

9.6 Copyright infringement, general defences and remedies

Infringement of IP laws can amount to criminal offences as well as being actionable in civil law. Unfortunately, copyright infringements go undetected at times and organized crime, including copying and counterfeiting goods, is now one of the most widespread offences, particularly with auction sales on the internet (e.g. eBay).

9.6.1 Primary infringement

Primary infringement of IP rights amounts to a strict liability action. This means the claimant does not have to prove intention, recklessness or carelessness, and purely innocent breaches may be actionable.

---

58 [1997] RPC 513.
59 [2012] EWCA Civ 24.
60 *Baigent and Leigh v The Random House Group Ltd* [2007] EWCA Civ 247 (CA) (the *Da Vinci Code* case).
61 For further discussion see: Kirk, E. (2006).
62 Blythe, A. (2015), pp. 484–489.
63 [2004] EWCA Civ 159.

> **Examples of IP infringement include when someone:**
>
> - uses all or some of your work under copyright without your permission;
> - uses, sells or imports your patented product or process;
> - makes, offers or sells your registered design for commercial gain;
> - uses a trade mark that is identical or similar to one you have registered.

If the owner of a copyright believes that his work has been copied or pirated, he can enforce these rights in the Patents County Court or the Chancery Division (if the amount sought, i.e. damages, is under £500,000) or similarly in the Sheriff Court in Scotland or the local County Court in Northern Ireland. The Chancery Division of the High Court of Northern Ireland deals with complex or valuable claims. For EU disputes there will be the Unified Patent Court.

See below 9.7.4

The Intellectual Property Enterprise Court (IPEC) is a specialist court in London, part of the Business and Property Court of the High Court of Justice, based in the Rolls Building. It hears cases relating to intellectual property disputes, including:

> - registered designs;
> - patents;
> - registered trade marks;
> - copyrights;
> - other intellectual property rights.

IPEC hears cases where the claim is under £500k. The Patents Court or the Chancery Division will hear cases where the amount sought is over £500,000 (unless all parties agree, then the IPEC may hear it). Certain intellectual property disputes where the amount sought is £10,000 or less will be handled by the 'small claims track' and will be heard at the Thomas More Building in the Royal Courts of Justice.

The courts usually use equitable remedies such as 'specific performance' or injunctions to remedy IP infringement. A decree of specific performance is a court order directed to someone to perform specific obligations, for example, to 'deliver up' the copied manuscript or disclose to the court any royalties already received for a hit single. In addition, the High Court can issue a warrant for an inspection of the copiers' premises for evidence of production or possession of the copied or 'pirated' goods ('Anton Piller order').[64] The IP owner can also apply for an interim injunction (or *interdict* in Scotland) to stop the illegal activities. There are no limits to legal costs or damages you can claim.

See below 9.6.3

When assessing breach of copyright courts will look in detail at how much of the work has been copied. If the court believes that a 'substantial part' of your work has been copied or broadcast, this will still constitute an infringement of the work. A 'substantial

---

64 *Anton Piller KG v Manufacturing Processes Ltd and Bernard Preston Wallace and Alfred Henry Stephen Baker* [1976] Ch 55.

part' is assessed qualitatively and could be a very small part of the work if that part was 'distinctive' and 'substantial'.

9.6.2 Secondary infringement of copyright

'Secondary infringement' includes selling, importing, providing premises for primary infringed goods or equipment.[65] In other words, where a person, without a licence agreement from the copyright owner, sells or hires out an article or makes copies of that work, knowing that it is to be used in the course of a business – it amounts to secondary infringement of copyright.[66]

The Privacy and Electronic Communications Regulations 2003[67] introduced the ability for copyright owners (and certain licensees) to take infringement proceedings against anyone who circumvents technological measures – such as copy control devices which have been applied to a work – or who removes or alters electronic rights management information associated with a work or imports or sells devices for these acts to be done. This became a challenging issue in the *Karen Murphy (Pub Landlady)*[68] case(s).

The cases related to pubs in the UK which, in order to screen Football Association Premier League (FAPL) football matches, were purchasing foreign decoder cards rather than buying the more expensive authorized BSkyB subscription. The foreign decoder cards enabled the pubs – such as Karen Murphy's 'Red, White and Blue' pub in Portsmouth – to show the Saturday matches, which no UK broadcaster was permitted to show live. Instead of paying for a Sky subscription, landlady Murphy used the Greek TV station Nova to show Premier League matches. She was convicted under section 297(1) CDPA ('Offence of fraudulently receiving programmes').[69]

The CJEU ruled that the FAPL could not stop individuals from seeking better deals for TV sports subscriptions than that offered by BskyB (now 'Sky') at the time. The broadcaster was paying more than £1bn at the time for broadcast rights for Premier League matches from foreign broadcasters.

The *Karen Murphy* ruling is complex and concerns the applicability of the section 72(1) CDPA (as amended)[70] defence to acts of communication to the public. The defence provides where someone plays or shows a broadcast in public, to an audience which has not paid for admission to their premises, this does not infringe any copyright in the broadcast or any film included in the broadcast. The Murphy ruling found that the pubs in question could rely on that defence stating that the transmission in a pub is a 'communication to the public', which means that without the permission of the Premier League Murphy would be in breach of the EU Copyright Directive (Directive 93/83/EEC). But this Directive does not stop individuals from buying foreign decoder cards for domestic use.

The Court of Justice ruled that live match coverage itself was not covered by copyright protection, although the Premier League could claim ownership of FAPL-branded

---

65 ss 22 to 27 CDPA.
66 s 24(2) Copyright and Related Rights Regulations 2003 (EC Regulation 2003/2498) (replacing s 23 CDPA).
67 EU Regulation 2003/2426.
68 *Karen Murphy v Media Protection Services Ltd* (C-429/08) and *Football Association Premier League Ltd and Others v QC Leisure and Others* (C-403/08) Judgment of the European Court of Justice – Grand Chamber of 4 October 2011.
69 Note: the words in s 297(1) were repealed and substituted by reg. 2(2), Sch. 2 of the Copyright and Related Rights Regulations 2003.
70 Note: the words in s 72 were repealed and substituted by reg. 2(2), Sch. 2, regs 31–40 of the Copyright and Related Rights Regulations 2003.

opening video sequences, theme music, on-screen graphics and highlights of previous matches. This means that as long as the FAPL and BSkyB ensure that match coverage includes enough copyright elements pubs will not be allowed to show foreign broadcasts.

Aside from the CDPA, the TRIPS Agreement[71] describes in some detail how law enforcement measures in IP infringement should be handled, including rules for obtaining evidence, provisional measures, injunctions, damages and other penalties. It states that courts have the right, under certain conditions, to order the disposal or destruction of pirated or counterfeit goods, covering wilful trade mark counterfeiting or copyright piracy on a commercial level. All governments that have signed up to TRIPS have agreed to ensure that owners' IP rights must receive the assistance of police, trading standards and customs authorities to prevent imports of counterfeit and pirated goods.

The following legislation creates specific IP offences

- **Section 2(1) CDPA** 'Criminal liability for making or dealing with infringing articles etc.' (six months and/or a £50,000 fine, on indictment ten years and/or unlimited fine).[72]
- **Section 2(2) CDPA** 'Criminal liability for making, dealing with or using illicit recordings' (six months and/or a £50,000 fine, on indictment ten years and/or unlimited fine).[73]
- **Section 2(3) CDPA** 'Devices and services designed to circumvent technological measures' (three months and/or a £5,000 fine, on indictment two years and/or unlimited fine).[74]
- **Section 2(4) CDPA** 'Offence of fraudulently receiving programmes', i.e. a broadcasting service provided from a place in the UK with intent to avoid payment of any charge applicable to the reception of the programme (£5,000 fine).[75]
- **Section 2(5) CDPA** 'Unauthorised decoders', i.e. making or exposing for sale, importing, distributing, any unauthorized decoder (six months and/or a £5,000 fine, on indictment ten years and/or unlimited fine).[76]
- **Section 1(1) Trade Mark Act 1994** 'Unauthorised use of a trade mark offence' (six months and/or a £5,000 fine, on indictment ten years and/or unlimited fine).[77]
- **Section 3(1) Registered Designs Act 1949** 'Offence of unauthorised copying etc. of design in course of business', i.e. intentionally copying a registered

---

71 The Agreement on Trade-Related Aspects of Intellectual Property Rights (TRIPS) is an international agreement administered by the World Trade Organization (WTO) that sets down minimum standards for many forms of intellectual property (IP) regulation as applied to nationals of other WTO members.
72 Also s 107(1), (2), (3) CDPA.
73 Also s 198(1), (2) CDPA.
74 Also s 296ZB CDPA.
75 Also s 297 CDPA.
76 Also s 297A.
77 Also ss 92(1)–(3) Trade Mark Act 1994.

design exactly in the course of a business, with features that differ only in immaterial details from that design, knowing, or having reason to believe, that the design is a registered design (in England, Wales or Northern Ireland maximum six months' imprisonment or a fine not exceeding the statutory maximum or to both; in Scotland, to imprisonment for a term not exceeding 12 months or to a fine not exceeding the statutory maximum or to both).[78]

- Section 4(1) Video Recordings Act 2010[79] 'Supplying video recording of unclassified work', i.e. a person who supplies or offers to supply a video recording containing a video work in respect of which no classification certificate has been issued is guilty of an offence (six months and/or a £20,000 fine, on indictment two years and/or unlimited fine).[80]

- Section 4(2) Video Recordings Act 2010 'Possession of video recording of unclassified work for purposes of supply' (six months and/or a £20,000 fine, on indictment two years and/or unlimited fine).[81]

- Section 4(3) Video Recordings Act 2010 'Supplying of video recording of classified work for purposes of supply' (six months and/or maximum £5,000 fine).[82]

- Section 4(4) Video Recordings Act 2010 'Supply of video recording not complying with requirements as to labels' (maximum £5,000 fine).[83]

- Section 5(1) Fraud Act 2006 'Fraud by false representation' (maximum 12 months and/or a £5,000 fine, on indictment ten years and/or a fine)

- Section 5(2) Fraud Act 2006 'Possession of any article(s) for use in the course of or in connection with any fraud' (maximum 12 months and/or a £5,000 fine, on indictment five years and/or unlimited fine).

- Section 5(3) Fraud Act 2006 'Making or supplying articles for use in fraud' (maximum 12 months and/or a £5,000 fine, on indictment ten years and/or unlimited fine).[84]

- Section 5(4) Consumer Protection from Unfair Trading Regulations Act 2008[85] The Regulations introduce a general duty not to trade unfairly and seek to ensure that traders act honestly and fairly towards their customers. They apply primarily to business to consumer practices (but elements of business to business practices are also covered where they affect, or are likely to affect, consumers). When deciding which offence(s) are appropriate the date of the offence will be an important factor.

---

78 Also ss 35ZA (1), (3) Registered Designs Act 1949.
79 The 2010 Act repealed and revived provision of the 1984 Act.
80 Also s 9 Video Recordings Act (VRA) 2010.
81 Also s 10 VRA 2010.
82 Also s 11 VRA 2010.
83 Also s 13 VRA 2010.
84 Also ss 2, 6 and 7 Fraud Act 2006.
85 These regulations implemented the Unfair Commercial Practices Directive (UCPD) in UK law and replaced several pieces of consumer protection legislation that were in force prior to 26 May 2008, including the Trade Descriptions Act 1968.

9.6.3 *Anton Piller* orders

An *Anton Piller* order is a type of injunction and amounts to a search order which is now frequently used in IP infringement, granted by a High Court prior to trial.[86] It is an *ex parte* (i.e. one-sided) application with the main purpose to preserve evidence for fear that the other party may destroy (copied or counterfeited) material if the search is not conducted immediately.

Anton Piller orders developed in the 1970s, established in *Anton Piller KG v Manufacturing Processes Ltd and Others* (1975).[87] The CA case concerned the copyright infringement and misuse of confidential information by the defendants to competitors, which the defendants had obtained from German manufacturers Anton Piller KG in relation to electrical equipment, computer parts and frequency converters.

The defendants were agents in the UK, called Manufacturing Processes Ltd (MPL). Pillers had supplied MPL with extensive confidential information, including technical drawings and manuals, all of which were subject to copyright. Pillers claimed that MPL were in secret talks with Canadian and US firms, disclosing the confidential, copyrighted information and thereby damaging Pillers' business.

Pillers applied for an *ex parte* interim injunction to enter MPL's premises to inspect all documents on the site and, if necessary, remove them if they concerned Piller's copyrights. The defendants appealed but Lord Denning MR granted the search and confiscation order with the proviso that such an order must remain 'extremely rare' and should be made only when there was no alternative way of ensuring that justice was done.

Anton Piller orders are not without criticism because therein lies an underlying suggestion that a person (the defendant) cannot be trusted and is likely to destroy evidence if challenged. The order is not simply a search warrant (conducted by the police) – it is an order which is made without the permission of or notice to the defendant (*ex parte*) and will not be granted easily by the courts. The argument against *Anton Piller* orders (and *Mareva* orders)[88] was highlighted by Hoffmann J in *Lock International*[89] where such an order was wrongfully granted, implying dishonesty of the defendant, which, in turn could damage his reputation and business.

9.6.4 General defences

The CDPA allows 'permitted acts' to copy a work without the permission of the copyright owner.[90]

There are two distinct types of permitted acts:

- fair dealing;
- exceptions.

---

86 s 109 CDPA.
87 [1975] EWCA 12 (Civ Div).
88 *Mareva Compania Naviera SA v International Bulkcarriers SA* [1975] 2 Lloyd's Rep. 509. Mareva injunctions, also known as 'asset freezing orders', are court orders that negate the banker's duty to pay or transfer funds as per the instructions of the customer.
89 *Lock International plc v Beswick* [1989] 1 WLR 1268.
90 Chapter III CDPA 'Acts Permitted in relation to Copyright Works', ss 28–76 CDPA.

9.6.5 Fair dealing and exceptions to copyright infringement

One emerging problem for schools, colleges and universities has been the expansion of plagiarism where students make use of copying from websites to write essays and complete their coursework. Such action can be criminally prosecuted under section 84 CDPA ('False attribution of work'); alternatively, the tort of 'passing off' can be used in a civil action against the student when the true identity of the author of a work has not been attributed.

The fair dealing (or fair use) exceptions are fairly limited, such as 'research and private study'[91] and the 'public interest'.[92] The reason is, if copyright laws are too restrictive, it may stifle free speech and news reporting, or result in disproportionate penalties for inconsequential or accidental inclusion.

> **Fair dealing acts include**
>
> - private and research study purposes;
> - performance, copies or lending for educational purposes;
> - reviews and news reporting (see: *Time Warner v Channel 4* (1994)[93]);
> - incidental inclusion;
> - parody or pastiche;
> - copies and lending by librarians;
> - acts for the purposes of royal commissions, statutory enquiries, judicial proceedings and parliamentary purposes;
> - recording of broadcasts for the purposes of listening to or viewing at a more convenient time ('time-shifting'), including podcasts and the BBC iPlayer;
> - producing a backup copy for personal use of a computer program;
> - playing a sound recording for a non-profit-making organization, club or society.

The courts usually ask these questions: first, is the person really using the work for the stated purpose? For example, if an entire work has been used and it is followed by two lines of vague review, this will not constitute the criticism and review defence. Secondly, has the (alleged) copyright infringer availed himself of the 'fair dealing' exception? And, if so, has he provided a sufficient acknowledgement alongside his work? Has he demonstrated a visible and prominent notice which amounts to a sufficient acknowledgement to the copyright owner? So, it could well be within the scope of 'fair dealing' to make single copies of short extracts of a copyrighted work for non-commercial research or private study, criticism or review or reporting current events.

---

91 s 30 CDPA ('Criticism, review, quotation and news reporting').
92 s 171(3) CDPA.
93 [1994] EMLR 1 of 22 October 1993 (CA).

From 1 October 2014, a number of changes to UK rules on copyright exceptions were introduced. The Copyright and Rights in Performances (Quotation and Parody) Regulations 2014 introduced the parody exception, creating a new 'fair dealing' right to use copyrighted material in works of caricature, parody or pastiche. UK courts have determined a number of factors for determining whether the use of a copyrighted work is 'fair', including an assessment of whether use of the copied material affects the market for the original work and whether the amount of the material copied is reasonable and appropriate.

Two additional exceptions to copyright infringement entered into force on 1 October 2014 with additional subsections to the CDPA, taking account of the digital age:

1   private copying (section 28B CDPA);
2   caricature, parody and pastiche (section 30A CDPA).

The new quotation right allows copyrighted material to be quoted provided that

the work has been made available to the public, the use of the quotation is fair dealing with the work, the extent of the quotation is no more than is required by the specific purpose for which it is used, and the quotation is accompanied by a suffi cient acknowledgement (unless this would be impossible for reasons of practicality or otherwise).

Quoting from a copyrighted performance or recording is also now permitted so long as

the performance or recording has been made available to the public, the use of the quotation is fair dealing with the performance or recording, and the extent of the quotation is no more than is required by the specific purpose for which it is used.

Previously using extracts of copyrighted material in the UK without rights holders' permission was restricted to defined purposes, including for use within news reports.

Section 30 1 ZA CDPA allows quotation ('whether for criticism, review or otherwise'):

Specifically s 30 1ZA provides:

Copyright in a work is not infringed by the use of a quotation from the work (whether for criticism or review or otherwise) provided that –

(a) the work has been *made available to the public*,
(b) the use of the quotation is *fair dealing* with the work,
(c) the extent of the quotation is *no more than is required* by the specific purpose for which it is used, and
(d) the quotation is accompanied by a *sufficient acknowledgement* (unless this would be impossible for reasons of practicality or otherwise).

Quotation is then allowed for the purposes of a work which has been made available to the public, including:

- the issue of copies to the public;
- making the work available by means of an electronic retrieval system;
- the rental or lending of copies of the work to the public;
- the performance, exhibition, playing or showing of the work in public;
- the communication to the public of the work.

9.6.6 Parody and pastiche

See chapter
10.5

Section 30A CDPA now permits the use of copyright material for the purpose of 'caricature, parody or pastiche'. The use has to amount to 'fair dealing' to benefit from the exception. Under Article 5(3)(k) of Directive 2001/29 ('Copyright' or 'Infosoc Directive'), the concept of 'parody' has to be linked to and evoke an existing work, while being noticeably different from it, and to constitute an expression of humour or mockery. It is then for domestic courts to strike a fair balance between the rights in a protected work and the freedom of expression of the user under Article 10(1) ECHR of that work who is relying on the exception for parody. Neither EU nor UK law define the meanings of caricature, parody or pastiche.

In the past, 'parody' and 'caricature' in common law meant an imitation of the style of a particular writer with deliberate exaggeration for comic effect. The leading case is that of political sketch writer and former Conservative MP Alan Clark (1928–1999).[94]

During the General Election of 1997, *Evening Standard* columnist, Peter Bradshaw, wrote a weekly column titled 'Alan Clark's Secret Election Diary' and 'Alan Clark's Secret Political Diary', next to a photograph of the claimant. To most people 'in the know' these were clearly parodies; however (the real) Mr Clark argued that the 'diaries' deceived a substantial number of *Evening Standard* readers into attributing their authorship to him. In the *Alan Clark's Diaries* case (1998),[95] Mr Clark invoked his statutory right under section 84 CDPA 1988 ('false attribution of work'[96]) and his common law right of 'passing off'.

Lightman J found that the claimant had a substantial reputation as a diarist, and his identity as author of the articles would plainly be of importance to readers of the London evening newspaper with a substantial readership. The High Court judge held that the consequent identification of the claimant as author was not sufficiently neutralized to prevent a substantial number of readers being deceived. Lightman J held that it was highly likely that the readership had been misled 'more than momentarily and inconsequentially' into believing that the claimant, Alan Clark, was the author of these articles and that he had suffered reputational damage.

Lightman J concluded that the defendants, Associated Newspapers, the editor Max Hastings and Peter Bradshaw had been in clear breach of section 84 CDPA and had

---

94 Clark (1993). Alan Clark's published diaries cover the period 1983 to 1992 after he left the House of Commons, describing the government (and downfall) of Prime Minister Margaret Thatcher.
95 *Clark v Associated Newspapers Ltd* [1998] All ER 6 (Ch D).
96 Note: the words in s 84(3)(a), (b) now substituted by regs 31–40 of the Copyright and Related Rights Regulations 2003 reg. 2(1), Sch. 1 para. 10(2) to include 'databases'.

additionally committed the common law tort of passing off. The *Alan Clark* case set the precedent for the meaning of 'parody': whether a rational reader had been deceived.

> **Essential characteristics of a parody in common law are:**
>
> - to evoke an existing work while being noticeably different from it; and
> - to constitute an expression of humour or mockery.

The case of *Deckmyn* (2014)[97] provides helpful guidance in respect of parody. In this case the CJEU held that to fall within the parody exception, a work must:

> fulfil a critical purpose; ... show originality; display humorous traits; seek to ridicule the original work; and not borrow a greater number of formal elements from the original work than is strictly necessary in order to produce the parody.[98]

In 2011 Mr Deckmyn, a Flemish nationalist and a member of the Vlaams Belang political party (sponsored by Vrijheidsfonds VZW, a non-profit association) edited and distributed a calendar which had as its front cover a drawing that resembled a cartoon appearing on the cover of a comic book *Suske en Wiske* (*Spike and Suzy*), titled 'De Wilde Weldoener' ('The Compulsive Benefactor'). The original drawing of 1961 by Mr Vandersteen had been altered so as to show money being distributed by the Mayor of Ghent, whose image replaced that of the original character, and the persons shown collecting the money had dark-coloured skin and were wearing scarves. No permission had been given by Mr Vandersteen to use the original drawing on the cover.

Mr Vandersteen's heirs brought the action against Mr Deckmyn and the Vrijheidsfonds VZW, alleging copyright infringement. Mr Deckmyn argued that 'a child could see it [the drawing] was a parody' of the original drawing and that he only intended to make a political point regarding the distribution of taxpayers' money in Ghent. He said that this political cartoon fell within the scope of 'parody' in Belgian law.[99] The CJEU held that national courts must strike a 'fair balance' when applying the parody exception between domestic copyright law and freedom of expression rights of individuals.[100]

Jongsma argues that the CJEU decision is not without defects. By leaving it to the 'margin of appreciation' of Member States, the law remains unclear which other rights and interests the CJEU meant to 'balance'.[101] Arguably, *Deckmyn* provides a too flexible framework for humorous, parody and pastiche uses of copyright-protected works.[102]

Following the ruling in *Deckmyn* there are then circumstances in which copyrighted material *may* be used without rights holders' permission under the parody exception,

---

97 *Deckmyn (Johan),Vrijheidsfonds VZW v Vandersteen* (2014) (C-201/13) Judgment of the Court of Justice (Grand Chamber) 3 September 2014 (CJEU).
98 Ibid. at para. 12 (Advocate General P. Cruz Villalón).
99 Article 22(1) of Belgian Copyright Law of 30 June 1994.
100 Ibid. at paras 26–28.
101 Jongsma, D. (2017) at pp. 652–682.
102 For a detailed discussion see: Arrowsmith, S. (2015), pp. 55–59.

which also enables material to be used for the purposes of pastiche and caricature. In broad terms: parody imitates a work for humorous or satirical effect. It evokes an existing work while being noticeably different from it. Whilst parody does involve an expression of humour or mockery, it does not have to comment on the original work or its author. It can be used to comment on any theme or target. *Deckmyn* makes clear, however, that use of copyrighted material in line with the parody exception will not be a defence against defamation caused by the parody works.

How are parody and pastiche treated in the music business? Until recent changes in the law, parodies amounted to 'copying'. Pastiche is musical or other composition made up of selections from various sources or one that imitates the style of another artist or period. A caricature portrays its subject in a simplified or exaggerated way, which may be insulting or complimentary and may serve a political purpose or be solely for entertainment.

One early example was that of MJ (Morgan Jane) Delaney who – in July 2010 – availed herself of the 'viral marketing' medium YouTube, when she released her title 'Newport (Ymerodraeth State of Mind)'. EMI records said that her 'spoof' unashamedly breached copyright law (s 84 CDPA) and served YouTube (Google) with a take-down notice. MJ claimed that her short video clip, promoting the Welsh city of Newport, was a parody, merely an in-joke of Alicia Keys' and Jay-Z's 'Empire State of Mind', and that she had never contemplated obtaining a music rights licence.

The 'Newport' music video clip attracted more than 100,000 people within the first 48 hours because it was littered with witty one-liners, among them the city's twinning with Guangxi Province in China ('there's no province finer'). Instead of the Manhattan skyline as a backdrop to their video, scenes from the Welsh town were featured, including Newport rapper Alex Warren and singer Terema Wainwright. The video was later permitted to reappear including viral marketing advertising ('virals').[103]

9.6.7 Private copying

Section 28B CDPA introduced the exception of 'private copying' in October 2014 which permits individuals to make personal copies of *any* copyright works (other than computer programs) for private, non-commercial use, provided the original was acquired lawfully and permanently. Under the private copying exception, individuals in the UK received a new right to make a copy of copyrighted material they have lawfully and permanently acquired for their own private use, provided it is not for commercial ends. Section 28B then makes the making of a private copy of the material in these circumstances no longer an act of copyright infringement. This change also allowed copying for purposes such as format shifting (e.g. digital storage of music purchased on CDs), backups and storage on a private cloud, provided the copier owns the original. Making a private copy of a computer program is still prohibited under the new framework.[104]

The introduction of the private copying exception proved immediately controversial and was challenged in the *BASCA* (2015)[105] case. The applicants argued that section 28B CDPA was incompatible with European law, which requires that if an exemption to allow

103 See: 'Jay-Z and Keys spoof is YouTube hit', YouTube, 30 July 2010, available at www.youtube.com/watch?v=maNgAxUnJ8I.
104 For further discussion see: Jacques, S. (2015), pp. 699–706.
105 R (on the application of British Academy of Songwriters, Composers and Authors and others) v Secretary of State for Business, Innovation and Skills (The Incorporated Society of Musicians Ltd intervening) (Nos 1 and 2) [2015] EWHC 2041 (Admin) (QBD) 17 July 2015 (sub nom. 'the BASCA case').

copying for private use causes any harm then that harm must either be zero or minimal, or be compensated for by a fair and adequate compensation scheme for rights holders.[106] The Secretary of State had introduced the provision on the basis that any harm caused to right holders would be zero or minimal; however that was not justified by the evidence. The High Court held that an individual cannot transfer a personal copy to anyone else, except on a private and temporary basis, or give away the original whilst retaining any personal copies. And the section was held to be unlawful.

KEY CASE

R (on the application of British Academy of Songwriters, Composers and Authors and others) v Secretary of State for Business, Innovation and Skills (The Incorporated Society of Musicians Ltd intervening) (Nos 1 and 2) [2015] EWHC 2041 (Admin) (QBD) 17 July 2015 (the BASCA case)

Precedent

❖ The copyright exception under s 28B CDPA no longer permits personal copies to be made for private use.

❖ There is (currently) no exception to copyright in fringement for private copying in the UK.

❖ It is (Currently) unlawful to copy lawfully downloaded music on to a CD intended for personal use.

❖ Copyright of a work is infringed if the copier transfer a personal copy of the work to another person.

Facts

The British Academy of Songwriters, Composers and Authors (BASCA), the Musicians' Union (MU) and UK Music sought judicial review of the section 28B exception arguing it was unlawful because it failed to provide fair compensation to rights holders in line with European law. The applicants estimated that the introduction of the exception, without the introduction of any mechanism for fair compensation for rights holders, would cause a loss of £58m per year for rights owners of the various intellectual property rights falling under the legislation. The Secretary of State for Business, Innovation and Skills, when implementing the Copyright Directive in national law, was required to consider the competing interests of consumers, rights holders and manufacturers of copying devices to gain evidence that the harm would be minimal.

The evidence asserted by the Secretary of State was found by the High Court to show that the harm caused by the private copying exception was not minimal, and this was the only reason for which the Secretary of State could avoid the introduction of a fair compensation scheme. Its justification for not introducing the scheme was:

1   the only harm that would need to be compensated for was the risk to rights holders of a loss of duplicate sales. The Secretary of State did not feel there

---

106 Article 5(2)(b) Directive 2001/29/EC (the Copyright Directive).

was a direct correlation between the ability to make private copies and a loss of sales and therefore did not predict an impact on duplicate sales;

2   sellers included an amount to take account of consumers making private copies in the price of first sale (the 'Pricing-in Principle') regardless of the legislation in place. The Secretary of State concluded that any harm would in future be compensated for by Sellers extending this principle to cover for any lost duplicate sales.

Decision

The High Court ruled that the new copyright exception under s 28B CDPA that permits personal copies to be made for private use without a compensation scheme for rights holders is unlawful. The High Court found that, whilst there was reasonable literature to support the Secretary of State's position in relation to the Pricing-in-Principle, it still needed to provide evidence that the harm caused by the introduction of the exception would be none or minimal. The High Court found that the evidence relied upon by the Secretary of State did not support its conclusions, and therefore the introduction of the exception without the compensation mechanism was unlawful.

In a follow-up decision, the High Court quashed the Copyright and Rights in Performances (Personal Copies for Private Use) Regulations 2014 in their entirety in light of its previous decision that they were unlawful. The court ruled that the quashing had prospective effect but declined to make any ruling as to whether or not the Regulations were void *ex tunc*.

Analysis

The Copyright and Rights in Performances (Personal Copies for Private use) Regulation 2014 were quashed. Any private copying of copyright works does not benefit from the exception contained *in* sections 28B CDPA. The High Court decided that it would not be appropriate to make a reference to the CJEU in this case, for example concerning a consideration of the meaning of 'harm'.

The scope and impact of these exceptions (parody, pastiche, private copying) will ultimately be decided by the courts and how they interpret the fair dealing proviso. As with the other fair dealing exceptions, an attempt will be made to strike a fair balance between the rights of the copyright owner and those seeking to make use of their work.

In 2015, global collections in the entertainment sector of private copying levies represented almost €310m (£277m), with CISAC estimating that, if properly managed and executed, private copying levies could yield significantly greater earnings for rights holders. This study was the first global analysis of private copying systems that existed around the world and covered music copyright laws of 191 countries on five continents.[107] The report showed that the creative sector is worth over $10bn and paying royalties to millions

---

107 CISAC (International Confederation of Societies of Authors and Composers) (2017).

of creators worldwide. Creators around the world still depend on a diverse range of revenue streams to earn a living. These are led by broadcasting (TV and radio) and live music, which generate billions in royalties. One vital element of this mixed income portfolio is private copying levies – a much under-exploited area of collections in both the physical and online worlds.

EU laws now allow countries that introduce a private copying exception into national laws to do so without an associated mechanism for compensating rights holders where only minimal harm to rights holders would arise as a result of private copying activities. The interesting question for businesses wanting to make use of third party works is the extent to which it can be considered 'fair dealing' when the use is for commercial purposes, particularly in cases where reliance on the exception deprives the rights holder of an income stream.

9.6.8 Photographs and online images

Whether you are blogging, creating a presentation, writing for publication or designing a poster, you are likely to want to illustrate your material with other people's images. Though we can freely view all kinds of images and photographs online all photos are copyright protected even if they are uncredited or not water marked. If the creator of the image or photograph has not stated that they allow further use of the image, you must ask for permission to reproduce it. If you do not you are breaching the author's copyright.

There is one exception: if you intend to reproduce an image in order to critique or review it, you may not need permission. UK copyright law permits you to 'quote' from copyright material, including images, providing your use is 'fair dealing'.[108] Essentially, this means your copy must have no impact on the market for the original image (e.g. a lower resolution or a cropped version), and you must credit the rights holder.

Most commercial online image libraries allow you to use advance filters, resulting in 'free-to-use images' (such as Google, Alamy or Getty Images). The platform will then find images or videos which you have permission to use ('usage rights'). You ought to know, however, that these image providers do not accept responsibility for the reliability of these results, and it is always worth checking the terms of use. Be aware that all professional image libraries, such as Getty Images, actively pursue unlicensed copying of their images and will invoice the website owner. Corporate logos can be particularly problematic, as they are likely to be trade marked as well as protected by copyright. Ensure that any logo which you reproduce for the purpose of 'instruction' does not leave the (physical or virtual) classroom if used for educational purposes. If in doubt, it is best to contact the company for permission to use their logo in any educational material. A reproduction of work by a long-deceased artist may still be protected by copyright – the creators of the digital image may claim the right to license its use.

In 2005 the *Daily Mail* cropped and published a now notorious picture of Prince Harry wearing a Nazi uniform at a party, complete with swastika, 'lifted' from *The Sun* which led to a copyright dispute.

---

108 s 30 CDPA ('Criticism, review, quotation and news reporting').

In British *Satellite Broadcasting Ltd* (1991),[109] the BBC's copyright action against British Satellite Broadcasting was dismissed by Scott J. The dispute was over the use of highlights from the BBC's exclusive coverage of the 1990 Football World Cup finals in a sports programme on the satellite channel. Since the BBC had bought exclusive rights, it was found that the use of short clips (all accompanied by a BBC credit line) was protected by the defence of fair dealing. In the BBC case, Scott J referred to Lord Denning's comments in *Hubbard v Vosper* (1972),[110] stating that:

> It is impossible to define what is 'fair dealing' . . . but, short extracts and long comments may be fair . . . after all is said and done, it must be a matter of impression . . . the quality and quantity of BBC copyright material used in each programme seemed . . . consistent with the nature of a news report and to be no more than was reasonably requisite for a television news report.

British Satellite Broadcasting was not ordered to pay damages because they were found to be reporting current news events.

In the *Jason Fraser* case (2005),[111] (below) the High Court (Chancery Division) provided further guidance on the application of the fair dealing defence for review and criticism.

❖ KEY CASE	***Fraser-Woodward Limited v (1) British Broadcasting Corporation (2) Brighter Pictures Ltd* [2005] EWHC 472 (Ch) (*sub nom. the Jason Fraser case*)**

Precedent

❖ Fair dealing for the purpose of criticism or review is an established exclusion in the CDPA – providing only a *reasonable* amount of the work is used.

❖ The section 30 CDPA defence is relied on for day-to-day journalistic practices by all media organizations.[112]

❖ The key requirement for the defence of fair dealing to apply is that the author/s of the allegedly infringing material must demonstrate a genuine intention to criticize or review, rather than a desire to compete with the copyright work or to reproduce the copyright work simply to advance or promote their own product or service.

Facts

The case concerned the use by the BBC and Brighter Pictures of 14 'off-guard' photos of the Beckham family, taken by celebrity photographer Jason Fraser, during the making of a TV programme, *Tabloid Tales*, presented by Piers Morgan. Fraser-Woodward Ltd and its owner Jason Fraser sued for copyright

---

109 *British Broadcasting Corporation v The British Satellite Broadcasting Ltd* [1991] 3 All ER 833.

110 [1972] 2 QB 84 (Lord Denning). This was a Scientology case where Lord Denning defined the defence of fair dealing under s 6(2) Copyright Act 1956.

111 *Fraser-Woodward Limited v* (1) British Broadcasting Corporation (2) Brighter Pictures Ltd [2005] EWHC 472 (Ch).

112 s 30 CDPA 'Criticism, review and news reporting'.

infringement seeking flagrancy damages. The BBC and Brighter Pictures argued that the photos fell within the 'fair dealing' defence of section 30 CDPA 1988. The defendants argued that the programme included criticism of the photos and the tabloid press in general. Mr Fraser argued at first instance that there was no fair dealing and that there was no sufficient acknowledgement. This was rejected and Fraser appealed.

Decision

Mr Fraser's appeal was dismissed. The CA held that all but one of the photographs had been used for the purposes of criticism and review. This meant that the BBC could use his photographs of the Beckhams without his permission and without paying for them because the programme *Tabloid Tales* amounted to a 'review' of the press coverage of the high-profile couple.

Mann J referred to Walker LJ's judgment in the *Pro Sieben* case,[113] that the defence of fair dealing should be interpreted liberally. Mann J also confirmed *Hubbard v Vosper* (1972) that there could be no limitations on the extent of commentary capable of amounting to 'criticism' for the purpose of the defence.

Analysis

Fair dealing for the purpose of criticism or review is an established exclusion in the CDPA 1988. It is relied on for day-to-day journalistic practices by all media organizations, not just the BBC. The important outcome of the *Jason Fraser* case was that any review or criticism should be considered in its context. The fact that Mr Fraser on occasion licensed his photographs for use in television programmes, and without apparently significantly undermining his ability to license the pictures elsewhere, contradicted his evidence that undue damage to their value was inevitable from their use in the BBC show. Overall, Mann J held that there was not 'excessive use' of the material in question.

Some lawyers have argued that the fair dealing provisions in UK copyright law are too restrictive and that they are asphyxiating the copyright system, calling into question both its credibility and efficacy. The ruling in respect of 'fair dealing' in the *Jason Fraser* case extended the scope of the defence, which now stretches not only to criticism and review of other copyrighted works, but will also cover criticism of works that may not be protected by copyright at all or are unpublished or not identified with any specificity, such as the tabloid press in general. The case also provides guidance as to the meaning of sufficient acknowledgement, in respect of which there is very little case law (see also: *IPC Media Ltd v News Group Newspapers Ltd* (2005);[114] see also: *Ashdown v Telegraph Group Ltd* (2001)[115]).

---

113 *Pro Sieben Media AG v Carlton UK TV Ltd* [1999] FSR 160 at p. 162 (Walker LJ) (CA).
114 [2005] EWHC 317 (Ch).
115 [2001] Ch 685 (Ch).

9.6.9 Citizen journalism

Citizen journalism is not new. When dressmaker Abraham Zapruder took his movie camera to Dealey Plaza in Dallas, Texas on 22 November 1963, he had no idea he would capture the most iconic example of citizen journalism. It has been called the most important 26 seconds of film in history: the 486 frames of 8-millimeter Bell + Howell home movie footage shot in the midday sun, capturing the assassination of President Kennedy. Zapruder had no doubt about the exclusivity and value of his film. It was sold to *Life Magazine* for $150,000 three days later.

The watershed of street photography with mobile phone cameras during disasters and life tragedies really started in the UK with the London 7/7 bombings (7 July 2005). It was of course a terrible and profoundly shocking event. But for the BBC's newsgathering team at the relatively new BBC News Online it marked the point where their news gathering operation began to include 'accidental' or 'citizen' journalism, that is obtaining images and video footage from people who had witnessed the event and including these in online (and indeed print) news coverage. Within 24 hours, the BBC had received 1,000 stills and videos, 3,000 texts and 20,000 emails.

News agencies now frequently use street or citizen journalists' images particularly during disasters, street riots or terrorist attacks. These images will carry copyright, and the author should be remunerated.[116]

The evolution of photographic technology brings with it all sorts of challenges which bring with them some critical issues around editorial control. The inventor of the World Wide Web, Tim Berners-Lee, warned about the misuse of information and that credible information worldwide could be destroyed, when he said about images from the internet:

'The medium can be perverted, giving you what seems to be the world, but in fact is a tilted and twisted version'.[117]

Helen Boaden, former Director of BBC News, comments that mainstream journalism must guard against running the same risk to take any material offered by citizen journalists, not only because of issues of copyright but also that the sources can be trusted to avoid fake news and hoaxes, warning that

> most news organisations have been duped at some point, despite the strict controls we have in place. We must guard against mindless interactivity replacing genuinely useful debate and insights. We must careful not to encourage citizen journalists to take risks in dangerous situations. And we must continue to consider the motivation of contributors and ask why they are telling us this.[118]

9.6.10 Remedies

The court will order remedies for infringement of copyright depending on the circumstances, such as how flagrant the infringement was and what benefit the defendant gained

---

116 For further discussion see: Council of Europe (2013) – Expert paper by McGonagle, T.: 'How to address current threats to journalism?"

117 Source: 'I was devastated: Tim Berners-Lee, the man who created the World Wide Web, has some regrets. Berners-Lee has seen his creation debased by everything from fake news to mass surveillance'. In an interview with Katarian Brooker for *Vanity Fair*, 1 July 2018.

118 Source: The role of citizen journalism in modern democracy – Helen Boaden, former Director of BBC News, BBC Online, 13 November 2008: www.bbc.co.uk/blogs/theeditors/2008/11/the_role_of_citizen_journalism.html.

from the infringement. Did that person carry out one of the restricted acts without the copyright owner's permission? Is there a possible defence or an exemption under the CDPA?

Most commonly, damages are awarded for loss of royalties or loss of profit. The calculation is usually based on royalties or licence fee, or alternatively on the equitable remedy of an account for profits which focuses on the illegal gains of the defendant as opposed to the damages suffered by the claimant. Section 97(2) CDPA provides some forms of damages for 'flagrant' copyright infringement depending on the 'benefit' accrued to the defendant rights infringer.

Exemplary (or punitive) damages can be made, though they are rarely awarded in the UK. These are compensation awards in excess of actual damages – a form of punishment awarded in cases of malicious or wilful misconduct or breach of copyright.

 FOR THOUGHT

When reporting on the Oslo attacks by mass killer, Anders Behring Breivik, in August 2012, killing 77 people, the BBC included photographs in its broadcast and online coverage from Twitter, taken by other photographers, whom the BBC did not name. Was the public broadcasting company right in availing itself of the 'fair dealing' defence when Challenged by some citizen journalist photographers? Discuss.

9.7 Trade marks, patents and designs

So far, we have covered the principles of copyright law. We will now look at some of the other basic rules and forms of IP law, namely trade marks, patents and designs. For each area you will learn the basics: eligibility, scope of protection, exceptions, infringement and enforcement.

Most of the famous trade marks originated during the nineteenth century with increased industrialization, communications technologies and the creation of global markets. Some of the oldest trade marks include the Czech beer trade mark 'PILSNER URQUELL' from 1859 and the British trade mark registered by the brewery 'Bass' (BASS & CO. PALE ALE). Until relatively recently, however, trade marks remained unregistered, and some of the defining and distinctive rights could be easily copied. Countries subsequently created their own trade mark legislation and registration offices, recognizing that trade mark law and registers would facilitate trade by defining rights, limiting monopolies and clarifying the boundaries between marks.

The Paris Convention for the Protection of Industrial Property of 20 March 1883 ('the Paris Convention')[119] established basic levels of protection and reciprocal recognition for so-called industrial property. This international agreement was the first major

---

119 The Paris Convention has been revised many times: at Brussels on 14 December 1900; at Washington on 2 June 1911; at The Hague on 6 November 1925; at London on 2 June 1934; at Lisbon on 31 October 1958; at Stockholm on 14 July 1967 and 28 September 1979. Summary at: www.wipo.int/treaties/en/ip/paris/summary_paris.html.

step taken to help inventors ensure that their intellectual works were protected in other countries and at some of the great world exhibitions, such as the Weltausstellung in Wien 1873 (Vienna World Exhibition) and the Exposition Universelle in Paris in 1900. The Paris Convention applies to industrial property in the widest sense, including patents, trade marks, industrial designs, utility models, service marks, trade names, geographical indications[120] and the repression of unfair competition.

This inherently territorial and geographical limitation of trade mark laws and registration was then subsumed in various intellectual property treaties. Many countries then protected their unregistered well-known marks in accordance with their international obligations under the Paris Convention for the Protection of Industrial Property and the Agreement on Trade-Related Aspects of Intellectual Property Rights (the TRIPS Agreement). TRIPS established legal compatibility between member jurisdictions by requiring the harmonization of applicable laws. For example, Article 15(1) of TRIPS provides a definition for 'sign' which is used as or forms part of the definition of 'trade mark' in the trade mark legislation of many jurisdictions around the world.

9.7.1 Trade marks

A trade mark (or brand) is a badge of origin of goods or services and is usually a name, logo or strap line. Under the Trade Marks Act 1994 a trade mark may be a word, or a symbol, or a combination of the two; a shape (of goods or their packaging); or for example an advertising slogan. The fundamental requirement is that the design is distinctive and functions as a distinguishing mark. It is possible to register logotypes by this means. Marks which distinguish the goods or services of one trader from those of others in the same line of business may be registered as trade marks. Trade marks last initially for ten years and may be renewed every ten years thereafter. Provided they remain in use and are carefully managed, trade marks last indefinitely.

The UK unregistered design right, created by the CDPA 1988, protects shape and configuration, but leaves the protection of surface decoration and ornamentation to the remit of copyright.

 FOR THOUGHT

In the light of Arnold J's ruling in the *Cartier* decision (2014),[121] there have been a number of these section 97A CDPA orders granted over recent years. Find out about similar cases where the courts granted 'blocking' injunctions to a number of record companies, for example for breach of copyright in respect of illegal music downloads and music trade mark infringement.

---

120 A geographical indication (GI) is a sign used on products that have a specific geographical origin and possess qualities or a reputation that are due to that origin. In order to function as a GI, a sign must identify a product as originating in a given place, such as Switzerland's Gruyère cheese, Mexico's tequila and Roquefort cheese from the French Roquefort-sur-Soulzon region.
121 *Cartier International AG v British Sky Broadcasting Ltd* [2014] EWHC 3354 (Ch).

9.7.2 Registered trade marks

A trade mark or brand is the symbol your customers use to pick you out. It distinguishes you from your competitors. The only condition imposed on a registered trade mark is that it must be clearly defined; otherwise neither you nor your competitors will be certain of what it covers. Trade marks are signs that distinguish goods or services from one business from those of other businesses. Unlike copyright which cannot be registered in the UK, trade marks should (or even must) be registered to ensure that no one else has registered a mark which is the same or similar to the one which is proposed for goods or services.

Peppa Pig is a global brand and a registered trade mark.[122] The character is owned by Entertainment One, which makes and distributes TV and films including *Grey's Anatomy*, *Spotlight* and *The Hunger Games*. The Peppa Pig–brand merchandise brought in more than $1.1bn in retail sales in 2015–2016, added to which came 500 new or renewed licence deals with TV companies around the world.[123] The company behind the cartoon character has faced increasing trade mark infringement in China, although the British production company has said it is in a better position to fight those actions, largely due to the improved legal system that helps Western brands fight against intellectual property rights (IPR) infringement. Niall Trainor, who led the brand protection team at the Family & Brands division of Entertainment One told the *Global Times* in September 2018 that the infringement faced by Peppa Pig has worsened in China:

> Before 2015, when Peppa Pig was introduced into the Chinese market, there were already some infringing trade mark applications in China, but the problem has got bigger recently with the increasing popularity of Peppa Pig.[124]

Originally the new trade mark registers were designed to enhance business confidence and provide businesses with a fast and efficient way of resolving disputes. Trade mark registration was not mandatory (and still is not), but for companies who wanted to expand, a registered trade mark became an indispensable way of guaranteeing quality and building brands.

Trade mark registration in the UK is by application to the government's Intellectual Property Office (IPO). This means you can put the ® symbol next to your brand. Most importantly, the trade mark must be unique. These marks then provide business exclusivity for a brand, goods or services. However, a mark which simply describes what a business does may not be registered.

Section 1 of the Trade Marks Act 1994 defines a 'trade mark' as:

(1)   any sign capable of being represented graphically which is capable of distinguishing goods or services of one undertaking from those of other undertakings.

---

122 The trade mark for Peppa Pig was filed by Astley Baker Davies Ltd, London, W1B 5TB on 9 June 2015. The PEPPA PIG trade mark serial number is 78647159.

123 Source: 'Peppa Pig on track to be $2bn brand after making splash in US and Asia', by Mark Sweney, *Guardian*, 24 May 2016.

124 Source: 'Chinese legal enforcement of trade marks improving: Peppa Pig production company', by Xie Jun Source, *Global Times*, 18 September 2018.

A trade mark may, in particular, consist of words (including personal names), designs, letters, numerals or the shape of goods or their packaging.

Section 2 Trade Marks Act 1994 defines a 'registered trade mark' as:

(2) a property right obtained by the registration of the trade mark under this Act and the proprietor of a registered trade mark has the rights and remedies provided by this Act.

Trade marks can include

- words;
- sounds;
- logos;
- colours;
- a combination of any of these.

A trade mark cannot

- be offensive (e.g. contain swear words or pornographic images);
- describe the goods or services it will relate to (e.g. the word 'cotton' cannot be a trade mark for a cotton textile company);
- be misleading (e.g. the word 'organic' for goods that are not organic);
- be a three-dimensional shape associated with a brand (e.g. use the shape of an egg for eggs);
- be too common and non-distinctive (e.g. a simple statement, such as 'we lead the way').

The Community Design Regulation 2005 created a unitary right which provided a minimum level of consistent protection across all EU Member States, but with each having the ability to impose different local or national design right protection. Further EU legislation on Trade Marks and Designs came into force on 23 March 2016 (Regulation (EU) No 2015/2424 – European Trade Mark Regulation – EUTMR), making EU-wide registration easier. Trade mark registration is now facilitated by the European Union Intellectual Property Office (EUIPO) located in Alicante, Spain, and registration costs on average €900.[125] The EUIPO registers about 135,000 marks each year. The EU certification allows a certifying institution or organization to use the mark as a sign for goods and services complying with the certification requirements (Article 74b EUTMR). In addition, TRIPS defines what types of signs can be eligible for protection as trade marks and what the minimum rights conferred on their owners must be.

You can register the following:

- word mark – e.g. Volvo; Adidas; Levi's;
- figurative mark – Jaguar cars; Fujitsu; Gore-Tex;

---

125 European Union Intellectual Property Office at: https://euipo.europa.eu/ohimportal/en.

- shape mark – e.g. the Toblerone bar; the LEGO brick; the Coca-Cola bottle;
- pattern mark – e.g. Burberry scarf pattern; Louis Vuitton (LV) luggage;
- sound mark – with the abolition of the graphical representation requirement from 1 October 2017, EUTM applications for sound marks can only be an audio file reproducing the sound or an accurate representation of the sound in musical notation;
- multimedia mark – The EUIPO Office accepts the following file format: MP4 (video), JPEG (for series of still sequential images);
- hologram marks.

9.7.3 Graphic designs and shapes

There is substantial case law in this area, and definitions of 'design' have been shaped by domestic and CJEU jurisprudence over recent years. Article 1 (a–c) of the Directive 98/71/EC on the legal protection of designs defines a 'design' as meaning the appearance of the whole or a part of a product resulting from the features of, in particular, the lines, contours, colours, shape, texture and/or materials of the product itself and/or its ornamentation. This includes 'graphic symbols'.

The definition also includes 'visual disclaimers', indicating that protection is not being sought for, and registration has not been granted for, certain features of the design (this will be shown in the visual representation which must accompany the design registration).

The landmark *Louboutin red soled shoed case* (2018)[126] centred on European trade mark law that forbids the registration of shapes where they add substantial value to goods. Louboutin high heeled shoes, starting at £500, have become staple footwear for the world's most famous women, such as Kendall Jenner, Rihanna and Melania Trump. The eponymous brand's scarlet soles date back to 1992, when the French fashion designer, Christian Louboutin, painted a sole red with nail varnish borrowed from an assistant.

In 2010 Louboutin registered the trade mark in Benelux for 'footwear' and separately for 'high-heeled shoes' in 2013:

the mark consists of the colour red (Pantone 18-1663TP) applied to the sole of a shoe as shown (the contour of the shoe is not part of the trade mark but is intended to show the positioning of the mark.

Figure 9.1 The EU Trade Mark Directive 2008/95 EC[127] sets out a number of grounds on which registration of a mark may be refused or declared invalid, particularly in relation to *signs* that consist exclusively of a shape that gives substantial value to the goods.

---

126 *Christian Louboutin and Christian Louboutin SAS v Van Haren Schoenen BV* (2018) (Case C-163/16) Luxembourg, 12 June 2018 (CJEU).
127 Article 3(1)(e)(iii) of Directive 2008/95/EC of the European Parliament and of the Council of 22 October 2008 to approximate the laws of the Member States relating to trade marks (OJ 2008 L 299, p. 25).

The Dutch Van Haren company, operating shoe retail outlets in the Netherlands, sold high-heeled women's shoes with red soles in 2012. Mr Louboutin and his company brought proceedings before the District Court in The Hague (*Rechtbank Den Haag*), seeking a finding of trade mark infringement by Van Haren. The latter claimed that the mark at issue was invalid.[128] The referring Dutch court considered that the mark at issue was inextricably linked to a shoe sole, and it raised the question as to whether the concept of 'shape', within the meaning of the directive, was limited solely to three-dimensional properties of a product, such as its contours, measurements and volume, or whether that concept also covers other characteristics, such as colours.

In July 2018, the CJEU stated that a sign such as the Louboutin's trade mark of red-soled shoes was intended purely to show the positioning of the red colour covered by the registration and its not consisting 'exclusively' of a shape. The CJEU found that a mark consisting of a colour applied to the sole of a shoe is not covered by the prohibition of the registration of shapes. Such a mark did not consist 'exclusively of the shape', within the meaning of the Trade Mark Directive 2008/95 EC. The court took the view that, since the Trade Mark Directive provides no definition of the concept of 'shape', the meaning of that concept must be determined by considering its usual meaning in everyday language. The court pointed out that it did not follow from the usual meaning of that concept that a colour per se, without an outline, may constitute a 'shape'. The Court also held that a sign, such as that at issue, could not, in any event, be regarded as consisting 'exclusively' of a shape, where the main element of that sign was a specific colour designated by an internationally recognized identification code (Pantone 18-1663TP).

In the present instance, the mark did not relate to a specific shape of sole for high-heeled shoes since the description of that mark explicitly states that the contour of the shoe does not form part of the mark and is intended purely to show the positioning of the red colour covered by the registration. In short, a mark consisting of a colour applied to the sole of a shoe is not covered by the prohibition of registration of shapes as trade marks – which must have come as a welcome judgment for Christian Louboutin. The case was then referred back to the Dutch court for a decision on the validity and infringement claim. Christian Louboutin's signature red soles are seemingly saved from copycats.

In the case of *Textilis Ltd* (2018),[129] the CJEU ruled on two questions, concerning absolute grounds of refusal of a European Trade Mark (EUTM), submitted by the Court of Appeal of Stockholm applying the ruling in *Louboutin*.

Textilis is a UK company in Preston, founded by Özgür Keskin, in 2013. They sell textile products not protected by any IP laws in the UK. Svenskt Tenn is an interior design company with a webshop and a store located on Strandvägen in Stockholm, founded in 1924 by Estrid Ericson. Svenskt Tenn's registered the pattern 'Manhatten' as a figurative trade mark (EUTM registration No 10 540 268 'Manhattan')[130] consisting of the pattern of a furnishing fabric also sold on the company's website.

---

128 Based on an absolute ground for invalidation according to national trade mark legislation as well as Article 3(1)(e)(iii) of the European Trade Mark Directive (2008/95/EC).
129 *Textilis Ltd and Özgür Keskin v Svenskt Tenn Aktiebolag* (2018) (Case C-21/18) (2018/C 094/16) 11 January 2018 (CJEU).
130 Article 7(1)(b) Community Trade Mark Regulation 207/2009 EC (CTMR) and consisted of a shape which gives substantial value to the goods.

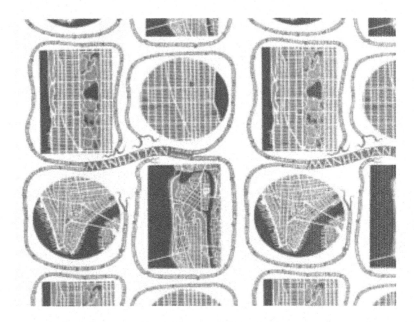

Figure 9.2 Svenskt Tenn filed a lawsuit in the Swedish courts against Textilis and its owner Mr Özgür, arguing copyright and trade mark infringement. The Swedish company asked the court to prohibit Textilis from offering the infringing goods for sale. Textilis in turn filed a counterclaim arguing for the invalidation of the EUTM. Textilis argued that the trade mark lacked distinctiveness under Article 7(1)(e)(iii) of Reg. 207/2009 (the original or amended version) and its interpretation with respect to two-dimensional marks.

On 22 March 2016 the Stockholm District Court found that Textilis was guilty of trade mark and copyright infringement. The court emphasized that the Community Trade Mark Regulation 207/2009 EC (CTMR) allows for the registration of *any* sign capable of being represented *graphically* if it is distinctive. As there were no reasons to cancel the trade mark the court assessed the infringement. The Swedish Court of Appeal (Patents and Trade Marks) requested a preliminary ruling from the CJEU following its decision of 14 December 2017.[131]

The Swedish court specifically requested whether the new wording (of the new Directive) after the entry into force on or after 23 March 2016 was *immediately* applicable in a court's assessment of invalidity, even if the action was initiated *before* that date and thus also concerned a trade mark registered *before* that date.

The CJEU noted that Textilis had not furnished any evidence showing that the trade mark in question lacked distinctiveness. In relation to the new Article 7(1)(e)(iii), the court dismissed Textilis' claim simply based on the fact that the contested trade mark did

---

131 Request for a preliminary ruling under Article 267 TFEU from the Svea hovrätt, Patent- och marknadsöver-domstolen (Svea Court of Appeal, Patents and Market Court of Appeal, Stockholm, Sweden), made by decision of 14 December 2017, received at the Court on 11 January 2018, in the proceedings.

not consist of a shape. The court held that the figurative mark 'Manhatten' was a work protected by copyright (unlike the mark which gave rise to the *Louboutin* judgment of 12 June 2018,[132] which consisted of a colour applied to the sole of a shoe). It was held that Textilis using the design pattern 'Manhattan' risked causing harm to at least the origin function of the EUTM and had infringed the trade mark of the Swedish Company in its 'Manhatten' shape and pattern.

The court could therefore not find any valid reason to cancel the (original) trade mark. In particular, the CJEU took into consideration the following elements:

- the definition of 'shape' provided in the *Louboutin* judgment;
- in the context of trade mark law, the concept of 'shape' is usually understood as a set of lines or contours that outline the product concerned;
- the presence of decorative elements which were situated both inside and outside the external outline of the graphic drawings; and
- the inclusion of words, namely the word 'Manhattan'.

Furthermore, the CJEU affirmed that:

> it cannot be held that a sign consisting of two-dimensional decorative motifs is indissociable from the shape of the goods where that sign is affixed to goods, such as fabric or paper, the form of which differs from those decorative motifs.[133]

This case is highly interesting because it concerned the implementation of the amending Regulation on 23 March 2016. The CJEU in *Textilis* applied a very strict approach to Article 7(1)(e)(iii) CTMR, as this was then limited to the shape of the goods alone. In light of the above, the CJEU held that:

> Article 7(1)(e)(iii) of Regulation No 207/2009 must be interpreted as meaning that a sign such as that at issue in the main proceedings, consisting of two-dimensional decorative motifs, which are affixed to goods, such as fabric or paper, does not 'consist exclusively of the shape', within the meaning of that provision.[134]

The CJEU judgment in *Textilis* of 14 March 2019[135] noted that Özgür Keskin and his company Textilis Ltd had violated a figurative EUTM consisting of a textile design inspired by the map of Manhattan and including the word 'Manhatten' which had been registered (albeit before the entry into force of the new EUTM regulation). The CJEU made clear that the EUTMR No. 2015/2424, as well as the Directive No. 2015/2436, introduced various changes to EU and national trade mark laws.

However, the court noted *inter alia* that both directives failed to provide transitory rules determining what was the applicable law for trade marks registered *before* the entry into force of the new law. In its appeal Textilis had asked whether the wording 'other

---

132 Louboutin and Christian Louboutin (C-163/16, EU:C:2018:423) (CJEU).

133 Textilis Ltd, at para. 42 (Advocate General G. Pitruzzella).

134 Ibid. at para. 25.

135 *Textilis Ltd and Özgür Keskin v Svenskt Tenn Aktiebolag* (2019) (C-21/18) Judgment of the Court, 5th Chamber, Luxembourg, 14 March 2019 (CJEU).

characteristics' of the new Article 7(1)(e)(iii) Regulation 2015/2424 could or could not be applied retroactively.

The court held in *Textilis* (2019) that the new Article 7(1)(e)(iii) was (and is) *immediately* applicable to all trade mark applications as at 23 March 2016 (and the same applied to national marks pending at the various dates of entry to force of the national laws implementing the Recast Directive No. 2015/2436). The ruling then is confusing and somewhat inconsistent and does not provide legal certainty (compared with the CJEU's decision in the *Lambretta* case (2017)[136]). This means that certain kind of trade marks which were granted registrations immediately before 23 March 2016 are valid as a matter of law, while the same kind of marks simply because they were pending on 23 March 2016 could be refused as a matter of law.

L'Oréal v Bellure (2010)[137] marked two complex landmark rulings, first in 2007 and then in 2010, concerning counterfeit 'smell-alike' perfumes. The CA had to determine whether the Belgian defendants Bellure had contravened Article 5(1)(a) Trade Marks Directive ('use of an identical sign for identical goods'[138]) for trading online in 'smell-alike' perfumes ('Stitch', 'Création Lamis' and 'Dorrall'). Each 'creation' smelt like a famous luxury branded perfume with a registered trade mark. All smell-alike products were manufactured in Dubai by Bellure, who, in turn, claimed that the articles were not imitations in the sense of being counterfeits. Bellure argued that the use of trade marks was used only for 'comparative advertising'; L'Oréal had to show that there was detriment to any of the functions of their brands. Lewison J (Chancery Division) found Bellure to have infringed L'Oréal's and other brands' trade marks, and that Bellure had taken unfair advantage of L'Oréal et al.'s reputation in the UK: that is, trying to *pass off* its own brand as that of L'Oréal (see also: *L'Oréal SA v eBay International AG* (2009)[139] and the French judgment in *L'Oréal SA v eBay France SA* (2009)[140]).

The *L'Oréal SA v Bellure* case[141] reached the Court of Justice (CJEU) for a preliminary ruling on trade mark offences. In its decision the court gave guidance on many issues regarding trade mark law, providing a synthesis of several earlier decisions. The decision stresses the wide-reaching protection under Article 5(2) of the Trade Marks Directive in that the Directive protects trade marks which have a reputation and protects the brand against the use of unfair advantage and detriment to the brand which is of distinctive character (including its trade mark). The Court of Justice stressed that *any* comparative advertising which would not meet the requirements of the Directive, while using the trade mark, would constitute a trade mark infringement: for example, if the goods in question are presented as an imitation or replica (which had been the case in *L'Oréal v Bellure*). The Court

---

136 *Brandconcern BV v European Union Intellectual Property Office (EUIPO) and Scooters India Ltd.* (2017) (case C-577/14) (ECLI:EU:C:2017:122) Judgment of the Court (Fifth Chamber) of 16 February 2017 (CJEU) (sub nom. 'Lambretta case'). The CJEU held in favor of Scooters India.

137 *L'Oréal SA; Lancôme Parfums et Beauté & CIE; Laboratoire Garnier & CIE v Bellure NV Malaika Investments Ltd (t/a Honeypot Cosmetic & Perfumery Sales); Starion International Ltd* [2010] EWCA Civ 535; See also: *L'Oréal SA; Lancôme Parfums et Beauté & CIE; Laboratoire Garnier & CIE v Bellure NV; NorthWest Cosmetics Ltd, HMC Cosmetics Ltd; Malaika Investments Ltd, Sveonmakeup. co.uk; Starion International Ltd* [2007] EWCA Civ 968 (Ch).

138 Directive 2008/95/EC to approximate the laws of the Member States relating to trade marks ('the Trade Marks Directive').

139 [2009] EWHC 1094 (Ch).

140 (2009) (RG 07/11365) Tribunal de grande instance, Paris, judgment of 13 May 2009 (unreported).

141 *L'Oréal SA v Bellure NV* (2010) (Case C-487/07) Court of Justice (First Chamber) 10 February 2009 (CJEU); [2010] RPC 1.

of Justice stressed that actual detriment or actual unfair advantage need not be shown, but that it suffices that the use *would* take unfair advantage of or *would* be detrimental to the distinctive character or the trade mark reputation.

Helpfully, the CJEU supplemented the term 'trade mark infringement' with alternative terms, such as 'tarnishment' and 'degradation' to a brand. And the term 'gaining of unfair advantage' was broadly defined with alternative terms such as 'parasitism' and 'free-riding'. These concepts relate not only to the detriment caused to the trade mark but to the unfair advantage taken by the infringer as a result of the use of the identical or similar signs.

Companies which specialize in 'rip-off' (counterfeit) goods have experienced lawyers who advise them on a daily basis on how close to the copyright infringement line they can get without crossing it. However, the *L'Oréal v Bellure* ruling (both in the UK Court of Appeal and the CJEU) is seen by the fashion and cosmetics industries as ground-breaking in deterring future copying and trade mark infringements of genuine brands (see also other trade mark cases: the *Saxon Trade Mark* case (2003);[142] *Harrods Ltd v Harrodian School* (1996);[143] *Barlow Clowes International Ltd (In Liquidation) v Eurotrust International Ltd* (2005)[144]).

In *Interflora Inc. v Marks & Spencer plc* (2015),[145] the claimants, Interflora, brought trade mark infringement proceedings against Marks and Spencer (M & S). Interflora claimed infringement of their UK and Community-registered trade marks for the word 'interflora' and that M & S's activities in the flower delivery market amounted to an infringement of their marks under Article 5(1)(a) and (2) of First Council Directive 89/104 EEC of 21 December 1988 and Article 9(1)(a) and (c) of Council Regulation 40/94 of 20 December 1993 on the Community trade mark.[146] The CJEU had already granted ISPs a common carrier status similar to the post office, by taking action against platform providers like Google, eBay and Amazon etc. in relation to claims for trade mark infringement or passing off (see: *Google France SARL v Louis Vuitton Malletier SA* (2011)[147]).

The long-drawn-out *Interflora v M & S* action did not come to a satisfactory conclusion. The CA referred to the complex commercial network of Interflora: as trade mark proprietor it is also composed of a large number of retailers which vary greatly in terms of size and commercial profile. And in such circumstances, it may be particularly difficult for the reasonably well-informed and reasonably observant internet user to determine whose advertisement is displayed in response to a search using that trade mark as a search term.[148] Whilst finding in favour of Interflora, the CA remitted the case back for retrial.

The two key issues that arose in the CA were firstly the issue of the burden of proof and, secondly, the introduction of the controversial initial interest doctrine into the case, i.e. the concept of the 'average consumer' using the internet. Perhaps the *Interflora* case might still be referred to the CJEU for a definitive ruling in the 'initial interest' doctrine.

---

142 *Byford v Oliver & Dawson* [2003] EWHC 295 (Saxon Trade Mark case) (Ch).
143 [1996] RPC 697.
144 [2005] UKPC 37.
145 [2015] EWHC 675 (Ch) 9 March 2015.
146 Now Directive 2008/99/EC of 22 October 2008 and CTM Regulation 207/2009 of 26 February 2009.
147 (C-236/08) [2011] Bus LR 1 (CJEU).
148 *Interflora v M & S* [2015] at paras 51 and 52.

The *Glee Club*[149] ruling in the Court of Appeal in February 2016 ended the long-running legal battle between a small comedy club in the UK and the US giant corporation, Twentieth Century Fox. The case centred on the popular TV show *Glee* – a fictional school singing club and a small UK comedy club concern. Legal action began in 2009 when Comic Enterprises Ltd found that the TV show *Glee* was causing damage to its comedy clubs across the UK, since customers were associating them with the US TV show, which, the comedy club alleged, discouraged customers from attending their clubs. Comic Enterprises registered the name 'The Glee Club' as a trade mark in 2001.

The CA upheld the earlier judgment in the Patents County Court (PCC).[150] Given the similarities between the marks, the Court of Appeal found that the average consumer would consider that the producer of the TV show was also responsible for, or connected with, the UK comedy club. This is known as 'wrong way round' confusion, where a consumer familiar with the accused sign was confused upon seeing the mark, rather than vice versa and therefore it was held a trade mark infringement under section 10(2)(b) Trade Marks Act 1994. In addition, the CA ruled that the broadcast and distribution of a television show are activities that are similar to the provision of venues for live comedy and music shows. The court suggested, for example, that comedy shows could be televised and that a television series could give rise to live tours. The claim for passing off was rejected.

The *Glee* decision demonstrates the importance of registering a brand. The fact that even a Goliath with the financial might of Twentieth Century Fox could be found to infringe a trade mark (and was ordered by the court to pay £100,000 on account of damages that could run into millions) shows that trade marks can have a major impact on businesses of any size (see also: *Associated Newspapers Ltd v Bauer Radio Ltd* (2015)[151] – a case concerning the brand *Metro* newspaper and *Metro Radio*).[152]

Disputes over shapes are complex in trade mark law. It can be more straightforward to protect a word as a trade mark rather than a shape, such as the KitKat chocolate bar. Marks like KitKat or LEGO are inherently distinctive, though distinctiveness may need to be acquired through commercial use and the average consumer associating the shape with the brand. So, with the KitKat shape, the court considered whether the use was proved to acquire distinctiveness.

The KitKat chocolate bar action was a long-drawn-out legal action whereby the Swiss company Nestlé tried to convince European judges to let it trade mark the shape of the four-finger version of a KitKat in the UK.[153] The action started in 2011 with a number of rulings. For example, the CJEU ruled in September 2015 that the KitKat's shape was not distinctive enough for consumers in the UK to associate it with the chocolate covered

149 *Comic Enterprises Ltd v Twentieth Century Fox Film Corp.* [2016] EWCA Civ 41 (CA Civ Div), 8 February 2016 (sub nom. the Glee Club case).
150 *Comic Enterprises Ltd v Twentieth Century Fox Film Corp.* [2012] EWPCC 13 (Patents County Court), 22 March 2012) (the Glee Club case).
151 *Associated Newspapers Ltd v Bauer Radio* (2015) in the matter of Application No 2233378 by Associated Newspapers Ltd to register the trade marks metro. co.uk and metro.com (A SERIES) in classes 9, 16, 35, 36, 38, 39, 41 and 42 Trade Marks Act 1994 and the opposition thereto under No 97043 by Bauer Radio Ltd. (O-241–13) (2015) WL 3750864 (Metro v Metro Radio).
152 For further discussion see: Lundie Smith, R. and Kendall-Palmer, C. (2016), pp. 165–168.
153 Article 3(1)(e)(ii) of Directive 2008/95, under which registration may be refused of signs consisting exclusively of the shape of goods which is necessary to obtain a technical result, must be interpreted as referring only to the manner in which the goods at issue function, and it does not apply to the manner in which the goods are manufactured.

wafer.[154] Three years later, in July 2018, Nestlé, Mondelez UK Holdings & Services Ltd (formerly Cadbury) and the European Union Intellectual Property Office (EUIPO)[155] asked the CJEU to set aside the judgment of the General Court of the European Union of 15 December 2016,[156] by which the General Court had annulled the decision of the Second Board of Appeal of EUIPO of 11 December 2012.[157]

The CJEU ruling of July 2018 meant that KitKat shape is no longer a valid trade mark across the EU. It is now only valid in Member States where Nestlé has made a successful application as a national trade mark, and KitKat's EU shape trade mark was annulled.

Image rights have become a tricky field for IP lawyers concerning the branding (i.e. trade marking) of celebrities' and famous artists' reputations. It has to be said that the notion of protecting a person's 'image rights' from unauthorized exploitation is not a new one. We first met this in the form of breach of confidence in the Prince Albert case in the nineteenth century when Queen Victoria's husband actioned in breach of confidence and 'copyright' against publishers Strange concerned to protect private etchings of the royal family from unsanctioned distribution.[158]

Rihanna v Topshop (2015)[159] is such a case where in January 2015, global pop star Rihanna narrowly won her trade mark battle against the British high street fashion store Topshop. Topshop (Arcadia Group) had sold RiRi's 'tank' sleeveless T-shirt without her permission. Kitchin LJ held that the use of her image was damaging to the star's 'goodwill' and represented loss of control over her reputation in the 'fashion sphere'.[160]

It is worth mentioning that Rihanna almost lost her goodwill for the purpose of celebrity endorsement when she reconciled with her former boyfriend, musician Chris Brown, after he assaulted her.

 FOR THOUGHT

> What advice would you give a new brand that wants to register its new name 'JamTart'? Discuss relevant legislation and the practicalities.

9.7.4 Patents

A patent protects an invention with a practical application, which is new. Provided it has some practical use, it covers an underlying idea or concept, although it does not mean the holder has a monopoly on a given process, idea or invention.

---

154 *Société des produits Nestlé SA v Mondelez UK Holdings & Services Ltd (formerly Cadbury Holdings Ltd UK)* (Case C-215/14) 16 September 2015 (CJEU, First Chamber) (sub nom. 'KitKat – Shape of a chocolate bar case').

155 *Mondelez UK Holdings & Services v EUIPO v Société des produits Nestlé* (2018) (in joined Cases C-84/17 P, C-85/17 P and C-95/17 P) Judgment of the Court (Third Chamber) 25 July 2018 (sub nom. 'KitKat – Shape of a chocolate bar case').

156 *Mondelez UK Holdings & Services v European Union Intellectual Property Office (EUIPO) v Société des produits Nestlé (Shape of a chocolate bar)* (T-112/13, not published, EU:T:2016:735; 'the judgment under appeal').

157 (Case R 513/2011–2) relating to invalidity proceedings between Cadbury Holdings and Nestlé ('the decision at issue').

158 *Albert (Prince) v Strange* [1849] 1 Macnaghten & Gordon 25.

159 (1) *Robyn Rihanna Fenty; (2) Roraj Trade LLC; (3) Combermere Entertainment Properties, LLC v (1) Arcadia Group Brands Limited; (2) Topshop/Topman Limited* [2015] EWCA Civ 3 (Ch) ('Rihanna v Topshop' case).

160 For further discussion see: Fletcher, S. and Mitchell, J. (2015) at pp. 394–405.

The right to own a patent derives initially from the inventor or inventors of the invention to be protected by the patent under section 7 Patents Act 1977. However, the inventor may not be entitled to own the patent, for example, because there is a contract or confidentiality agreement which entitles another person to the ownership in preference to the inventor.

A patent application takes a long time and only applies for specific territories. A patent is a title granted by the state to the creator or owner of an invention, which entitles the inventor to prevent others from manufacturing, using, selling and, in some cases, importing the technology without his permission for a specified period of years (TRIPS states 20 years for inventions). Patent protection must be available for both products and processes, in almost all fields of technology.

The European Patent Register and European Patent Office (EPO) is in Munich, Germany, and contains all the publicly available procedural information on European patent applications as they pass through each stage of the granting process.[161] The 16th edition of the European Patent Convention (2016) contains:

- the Convention on the Grant of European Patents (EPC) as in force since 13 December 2007;
- the EPC Implementing Regulations as in force since 1 May 2016 but also including an amendment that entered into force on 1 November 2016;
- the rules of procedure of the EPO boards of appeal and Enlarged Board of Appeal, included for the first time in an edition of the EPC;
- the protocols forming integral parts of the EPC (Protocol on the Interpretation of Article 69 EPC, Protocol on Centralisation, Protocol on Recognition, Protocol on Privileges and Immunities, Protocol on the Staff Complement);
- an extract from the EPC Revision Act of 29 November 2000;
- the Administrative Council's decision of 28 June 2001 on the transitional provisions under Article 7 of the Revision Act;
- the Rules relating to Fees.[162]

To stop a patent owner from abusing his rights – for example by failing to supply the product on the market – governments can issue 'compulsory licences', allowing a competitor to produce the product or use the process under licence. If a patent is issued for a production process, then the rights must extend to the product directly obtained from the process.

Under certain conditions, alleged infringers may be ordered by a court to prove that they have not used the patented process. However, only the inventors or their successors in title are entitled to the grant of a patent. Before a patent is granted, an indication of how the inventor derived the rights to the invention from the inventor(s) must be filed at the patent office. Employers automatically derive the rights to an invention made by an employee during the course of carrying out the duties of their employment.

---

161 European Patent Office at: www.epo.org/index.html.
162 The EPC also contains an index of decisions and opinions of the Enlarged Board of Appeal published in the EPO's Official Journal (Annex I), a list cross-referencing the EPC 2000 provisions with their EPC 1973 equivalents (Annex II) and an alphabetical keyword index.

The HL decision in *Rhone-Poulenc Rorer International Holdings Inc. v Yeda Research & Development Co. Ltd* (2007)[163] restated that the rights to an invention arise from the inventor, and no complexities or uncertainties usually arise in cases where patent rights are claimed under the entitlement provisions. Such proceedings are generally determined simply on the facts of the case.

9.7.5 Forum shopping and the Unified Patent Court project

Forum shopping has become inevitable as parties now try to take advantage of differences in national courts' interpretation of harmonized EU patent law and in procedural laws of other countries, as well as differences in speed (between 'slow' and 'quick' courts) and in the level of damages awarded. One such example is the famous *Star Wars* action concerning the Stormtrooper helmet.[164]

The action concerned the design and possible copyright infringement Stormtrooper helmet. Lucasfilm commenced proceedings for copyright infringement in the United States, obtaining a default judgment against Mr Ainsworth who had not engaged in the US proceedings save as to challenge jurisdiction of the court. Lucasfilm then commenced proceedings in the UK where Mr Ainsworth was domiciled under UK copyright law. At the same time Lucasfilm sought to enforce the US judgment in the British court to determine its claims under US copyright law. Mr Justice Mann in the High Court Chancery Division dismissed almost every part of Lucasfilm's action holding that the helmets were not protected by copyright but decided there was no absolute bar against the English court hearing an action to enforce copyright in respect of infringements that took place abroad.[165]

See above
9.3.4

The Court held that under the twofold rule in *Moçambique*[166] and for policy reasons, the supposed international jurisdiction over copyright infringement claims did not exist and that it was not for judges to assume such a jurisdiction. In *Moçambique* the House of Lords held that the English courts had no jurisdiction to entertain an action to recover damages for trespass to land situated abroad. Lord Hershell LC accepted a distinction between matters which are 'transitory or personal' in their nature and matters which are 'local' in their nature and held that the English courts would not exercise jurisdiction in relation to the latter where the matters occurred outside the territorial limits of the English courts. A trespass to foreign land was local for these purposes and was not justiciable in these courts.

The grant of a patent for example involves a positive act by an organ of the state, and a copyright can arise without that in the UK and in the United States. However, that distinction is not always relied on. An Australian decision, found in the authority of *Def Lepp Music v Stuart-Brown* (1986),[167] stated that:

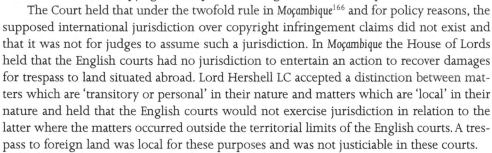

a claim that acts done outside the United Kingdom constitute an infringement of the copyright law of a foreign country is not justiciable in English courts.[168]

---

163 [2007] UKHL 43.
164 *Lucasfilm Ltd and Another v Ainsworth and Another* [2011] UKSC 39.
165 *Lucasfilm Ltd v Ainsworth* [2008] EWHC 1878 at paras 235–277 (Mann J) (Ch).
166 *British South Africa Co v Compania De Moçambique* [1893] AC 602 ('the Moçambique rule').
167 [1986] RPC 273.
168 Ibid. at p. 87B.

And concluding that

> therefore the question whether the defendant is entitled to copyright under the law of the United States of America or of any of the states of the United States of America is not justiciable in the English court.[169]

National courts and authorities of the contracting states of the European Patent Convention (EPC) have long been competent to decide on the infringement and validity of European patents. However, this has risen to a number of difficulties when a patent proprietor wishes to enforce a European patent – or when a third party seeks the revocation of a European patent – in several countries. It means high costs, risk of diverging decisions and a lack of legal certainty.

The Unified Patent Court (UPC)[170] project commenced in 2016–2017, and the Unified Patent Court Agreement (16351/12)[171] seeks to addresses the above problems by creating a specialized patent court. Only EU Member States can be signatory to the Agreement and the UPC. In 2018 two more signatory states ratified the Agreement, namely Latvia and the UK, and at the point of going to print of this book, 25 EU Member States, except Spain Croatia and Poland, had signed the Agreement.

The UPC is a court common to the contracting EU Member States and thus part of their judicial system, comprising a Court of First Instance, a Court of Appeal and a Registry. The court is has exclusive competence in respect of European patents and European patents with unitary effect. The UPC's rulings have effect in the territory of those contracting Member States, having ratified the UPC Agreement. The UPC does not have any competence with regard to national patents. Presently, the UPC's divisions and locations are:

- the Court of Appeal in Luxembourg;
- central and local divisions in Germany (Munich); Italy (Milan); Luxembourg; Sweden (Stockholm); and UK (London).

9.7.6 Design rights

The protection of designs has presented the legislature and judiciary with challenges for over 400 years. During this time, the duration, exclusions, scope and definition and the minimum requirements for protection of designs have oscillated between extremes, responding to changes in industry and economic pressures.

The Industrial Revolutions of the nineteenth and twentieth centuries heralded a new era in which designs were applied to utilitarian objects, whose mass production was facilitated by new technologies. Whilst there was a desire to continue to protect creative designs, there was concern about fettering the development of functionality. This concern was compounded during the early twentieth century as the United States emerged as a

---

169 Ibid. at p. 88D.
170 For updates: The Unified Patent Court at: www.unified-patent-court.org/.
171 Regulation (EU) No 1257/2012 of the European Parliament and of the Council of 17 December 2012 implementing enhanced co-operation in the area of the creation of unitary patent protection including any subsequent amendments. OJEU L 361, 31.12.2012, p. 1.

major international player, and designs became an integral part of many utilitarian objects rather than merely being applied to them.

The Patents and Designs Act 1919 amended the 1907 Act by substituting for the definition in section 93 of the 1907 Act a new definition of 'design' which referred to features applied 'by any industrial process' and did not make an express exception for a design for a sculpture for example. Because of the way that section 22 of the Copyright Act 1911 was framed, this had the effect of withdrawing from works of sculpture their specially privileged position in relation to mass-production of copies.

Its effect was illustrated by *Pytram Ltd v Models (Leicester) Ltd* (1930).[172] The Boy Scouts Association had commissioned a model of a wolf-cub's head which was to be used to produce a permanent mould for the production of large numbers of papier-maché models to be attached to the top of wooden poles. Clauson J dismissed the plaintiff's claim to copyright in the original model. He accepted that the model was a work of sculpture, but it was not automatically exempt from registration under the 1907 Act as amended, and it did not come within the exception in section 22(1) because, 'the whole point in the preparation of this model was to enable the plaintiffs to supply totem poles in large quantities'.[173]

After the Second World War there was a legislative shift back again. In 1947 the Swan Committee recommended that works of sculpture should again be excluded from registrable designs. The Registered Designs Act 1949 provided for exclusions from registration of articles which were primarily literary or artistic in character.[174]

Today, design rights protect aesthetic and visual qualities for shapes and 3D designs (which are not covered by copyright). Design right only applies to the shape and configuration (how different parts of a design are arranged together) of objects. There now exists a unified EU design right which automatically protects your design for ten years after it was first sold or fifteen years after it was created – whichever is earliest.[175] However, a registered design right has to be renewed every five years.

The look of a design right includes the

- appearance;
- physical shape;
- configuration (or how different parts of a design are arranged together);
- decoration.

A registered design right (Community Design Registrations (CDR))

- protects any aspect of a design, e.g. both the product's shape and decoration;
- prevents others from using it for up to 25 years;

---

172 [1930] 1 Ch 639.
173 Ibid. at para. 647 (Clauson J).
174 s 1(3) and (4).
175 Council Regulation 6/2002/EC on Community Designs ('the Community Design Right').

- makes taking legal action against infringement and copying more straightforward;
- once registered the registration number of the design can be displayed on the design.

What you can or cannot register

To register your design, it must:

- be new;
- not be offensive (e.g. feature graphic images or words);
- not make use of protected emblems or flags (e.g. the Olympic rings; the European flag; the Royal Crown, etc.);
- not be an invention or relate to how a product works (this would be a patent);
- not concern the functionality of a design – e.g. a chair that folds down more quickly than others of the same kind.

The case which ultimately lead to the repeal of section 52 CDPA is that of Flos.[176] This case concerned the design of the famous 'Arco' lamp,[177] created by the Italian designers Achilles and Pier Giacomo Castiglioni. The Italian lighting manufacturing company Flos held the IP rights in the lamp since the early 1960s. There were a number of cheap copies made in China on the market. Importers Semeraro were marketing the 'Fluida' lamp design in Italy, an imitation copy of the Arco lamp. In 2006 Flos brought an action against Semeraro, claiming that the importer had infringed the IP right in the industrial design for the Arco lamp and that the Fluida lamp 'slavishly imitated all [its] stylistic and aesthetic features'.[178]

The case reached the CJEU in 2011. The court's preliminary ruling concerned the interpretation of Article 17 of the Directive 98/71 in proceedings for breach of copyright between a manufacturer of lamps (Flos) and an importer of lamps (Semeraro).

The CJEU (Second Chamber) ruled that:

1   Article 17 of Directive 98/71/EC ('on the legal protection of designs') must be interpreted as precluding legislation of a Member State which excludes from copyright protection in that Member State designs which were protected by a design right registered in or in respect of a Member State and which entered the public domain before the date of entry into force of that legislation, although they meet all the requirements to be eligible for copyright protection.

2   Article 17 must be interpreted as precluding legislation of a Member State which – either for a substantial period of ten years or completely – excludes from copyright

---

176   *Flos Spa v Semeraro Casa e Famiglia Spa* (2011) (Case C-168/09) Judgment of the Court of Justice (Second Chamber) of 27 January 2011 (CJEU).

177   The Arco Lamp was created in 1962 and entered the public domain before 19 April 2001 and was eligible for copyright protection as an industrial design under Law No 633/1941, as amended by Legislative Decree No 95/2001.

178   *Flos* judgment (2011) at paras 20–24 (as per judgment of Advocate General Y. Bot) (CJEU).

protection designs which, although they meet all the requirements to be eligible for copyright protection, entered the public domain before the date of entry into force of that legislation, that being the case with regard to any third party who has manufactured or marketed products based on such designs in that State – irrespective of the date on which those acts were performed.[179]

The CJEU's preliminary ruling in Flos means that a national law cannot refuse copyright protection to industrial designs that are eligible for this protection, even if they have entered into the public domain. The Italian government then amended Article 239 of the Italian Industrial Property Code ('the IPC')[180] in order to expressly recognize copyright protection to industrial designs which bear 'inherent artistic value'.

Following the Flos decision, the UK Parliament repealed section 52 CDPA, and from 2020 onwards it is a criminal offence to sell replica goods unless 70 years have passed from the date the item originally went on sale which means the end of buying cheap designer furniture replicas in the UK, such as the Eames Lounge Chair (designed by Charles and Ray Eames), the Egg chair (by Arne Jacobsen) or the Barcelona Chair (by Mies van der Rohe) – all of which had been sold for less than £500 instead of £5,000.

It is not clear from the CJEU judgment in Flos whether or not industrial designs which were created before 2001 benefit from full IP protection. That said, the creative and design industry welcomed the Flos ruling.

Design rights are particularly useful for creative industries in sectors such as furniture, home wares, packaging, footwear, architectural features and other 3D objects. Any small business that has developed, or is promoting, a 3D design should think about design right protection, and the long-running Trunki case[181] is such an example.

In this case, Bristol-based company Magmatic, which makes the Trunki case – a ride-on suitcase for children which looks like an animal – argued that 'Kiddee' suitcases, made in Hong Kong by PMS, infringed its registered design rights. Kiddee cases are, like Trunki cases, decorated to look like animals. Robert Law's company, Magmatic, was first granted a judgment in their favour by the High Court in July 2013.[182] However, the ruling was overturned by the CA in March 2014, stating that the Kiddee case looked sufficiently different in design to the Trunki one.[183] Magmatic appealed.

In March 2016, five Supreme Court justices unanimously dismissed Magmatic's appeal, ruling in favour of PMS. Lord Neuberger in his leading judgment centred on the 'Community Design Right'. This provides that a design shall be protected to the extent that it is new and has individual character. What then mattered in this case was the overall impression created by the design (i.e. a ride-on children's suitcase) and that potential customers would appreciate it on the basis of its distinctiveness.[184]

---

179 Ibid. at paras 48–50, 53–56, 61–65.
180 Legislative Decree no 30/2005 ('IPC').
181 PMS International Group Plc v Magmatic Limited [2016] UKSC 12 ('the Trunki case').
182 Magmatic Ltd v PMS International Group plc [2013] EWHC 1925, High Court of Justice Chancery Div (Patents Court).
183 Magmatic Ltd v PMS International Group plc [2014] EWCA Civ 181 (CA).
184 [2016] UKSC 12 at paras 6–10 (Lord Neuberger).

PMS (i.e. 'Kiddee case') claimed that its distinctive design was that of either an insect with antennae or an animal with ears. The Supreme Court justices said that – to the end-user – the overall impression given by the cases' design was that of a horned animal and that a Community Design Registration (CDR) does not merely register a shape, but – in this case – a shape in two contrasting colours. Their Lordships stated that the original judge had been wrong in holding that the design right simply covers a shape.[185] Lord Neuberger expressed sympathy for Magmatic and Mr Law, as the idea of the Trunki case was a clever one; but he stressed that a CDR is intended to protect designs not ideas.[186]

The Trunki ruling had far-reaching consequences for the design industry and was seen as disastrous for those who had sought to protect their designs with CDR. The judgment called the legal scope of protection into question.

Following Professor Ian Hargreaves' Report (2011)[187] – an independent review of UK copyright legislation – the Intellectual Property Act 2014 ('IPA' or 'IP Act')[188] was passed and introduced changes to:

1 **copyright** regarding home copying, quotation, parody and fair dealing;
2 **designs** regarding copying a registered design, first owner, the good faith defence to infringement and unregistered design rights; and
3 **patents** regarding the Unified Patent Court, patent notices and patent opinions.

The IPA 2014 modernized intellectual property law to help UK businesses better protect their IP rights. The Act deals mainly with design rights. One of the main objectives of Parliament was to make the design rights system more user-friendly as well as improving design right protection. The 2014 Act introduced a number of new measures, making the law simpler, clearer and more robust.

Key changes in design law include

- a new criminal offence for the copying of registered designs;[189]
- changes to design ownership in relation to commissioned designs;[190]
- private use of unregistered designs;[191]
- scope of an unregistered design right;[192]
- introduction of a design opinions service.[193]

---

185 Ibid. at paras 51–56.
186 Ibid. at para. 57.
187 Hargreaves, I. (2011) Digital Opportunity (The Hargreaves Report).
188 The Intellectual Property Bill 2013–14 was introduced in May 2013 by Lord Younger in the House of Lords; it received Royal Assent on 14 May 2014.
189 s 13 IPA 2014 ('Offence of unauthorised copying etc. of design in course of business').
190 s 2 IPA 2014 ('Ownership of design').
191 ss 2 and 6 IPA 2014; 249A CDPA.
192 s 1 IPA 2014.
193 s 11 IPA 2014 ('Opinions service'); 28A Registered Designs Act 1949 ('Opinions on designs').

Key changes to patent law include

- marking patented products with a web address;[194]
- expansion of the patent opinions service;[195]
- patents worksharing.[196]

Infringement of a registered design is now a criminal offence, bringing design rights into parity with copyright and trade marks. A small business that has a registered design will be able to report those who are producing or selling 'knock-off' designs to the police, as well as pursuing its own action.

Another important change, and one that may set a trap for some businesses, is that when a business commissions a design from a third party, the designer will own the design right intellectual property (IP) rather than the business that has commissioned the work. A business that pays a designer (who is not an employee) to develop a product will not actually own the design unless this is specifically agreed.

9.8 Disputes about IP rights in the virtual world

See above
9.6.4

Is material on the internet protected by copyright? Yes. Under UK law copyright material sent over the internet or stored on web servers will usually be protected in the same way as material recorded on other media. So, if you want to put copyright material on the internet or distribute or download copyright material that others have put on the internet, you will need to make sure that you have permission from the people who own the rights in the material – similar to photographs.

9.8.1 The use of hyperlinks

There has been much controversy regarding whether hypertext links between websites, which allow users to surf from one site to another, infringe copyright under section 20 CDPA. However, the section was amended by the substitution of the words 'communication right' which now protects works distributed on the internet.[197] For this reason, the Shetland Times case is now purely of historical value but still worth mentioning. Shetland Times v Wills (1997),[198] involved the use of hyperlinks between two rival newspapers on the Shetland islands of Scotland. Dr Jonathan Wills, former editor of the Shetland Times, began to publish the Shetland News after falling out with Robert Wishart, owner of the Shetland Times. Dr Wills also operated a website for his newspaper, Shetland News, using news headlines as the means of access to its stories. From 14 October 1996, Shetland News incorporated in its website certain news headlines copied verbatim from the Shetland Times site. The Shetland News page included Shetland Times headlines as hypertext links, and by clicking on these a person would be directed to the relevant stories on the Shetland Times website, bypassing the front page of that site altogether.

The Shetland Times owner objected primarily because the hyperlinks enabled browsers to bypass the front pages which contained advertising. He feared that the paper's advertising

---

194 s 15 IPA 2014 ('Infringement: marking product with internet link').
195 s 16 IPA 2014.
196 s 18 IPA 2014 ('Sharing information with overseas patent offices').
197 s 20 has been substituted by the Copyright and Related Rights Regulations 2003 reg. 6(1).
198 [1997] SLT 669.

revenue would accordingly be reduced and instigated a copyright infringement action against Dr Wills under sections 7 ('cable programmes') and 17 CDPA ('Infringement of copyright by copying').

The Scottish Court of Session accepted that linking to another website does not involve copying material but simply provides a means of access to the other site. The only material which had been copied was the text of the various headlines. The court held that there was an arguable case for the subsistence of both copyrights in question. Its decision that a website is a 'cable programme service' was to have far-reaching consequences (beyond copyright law) for the regulation and development of the internet. But the court also ruled that the headlines could in fact attract copyright protection despite the *de minimis* rules. On these findings Lord Hamilton granted an interim *interdict* (injunction) – but the case was settled before a full proof could be heard on the facts.

The law in this area evolved rapidly, and ten years later the jurisprudential authority by the Court of Justice of the European Union (CJEU) had developed. In *Svensson* (2014)[199] the CJEU determined that there would be no infringement where the work is made available on a publicly available website with the authorization of the right holder.

Svensson was a case brought by the film industry concerning hyperlinks against four websites (www.viooz.co; www.megashare.info; www.1.zmovie.tw and www. watch32.com). Hoy (2015) concludes that the decision in *Svensson* focused specifically on the identification of the 'relevant public', which was, in fact, the same public as that to which the material had originally been lawfully communicated. Where the websites simply collated users' links to torrent files the website operators were communicating to the public and therefore infringing copyright because that public was not the public originally contemplated by the copyright holders, but a 'new' public able to download the uploaded files without authorization and without making any payment.

In summary, where a right holder authorizes his work to appear on a website which is freely available to all via hyperlinks, it will be treated as having authorized all internet users so that linking to the content on the authorized website will not infringe copyright. There will be infringement, however, where the link constitutes availability to a 'new public'. The court in *Svensson* specifically distinguished the situation where a link circumvents measures on the host site which were designed to restrict public access – such as a subscription paywall, which would then constitute a communication to a new public not contemplated by the right holder.

There are now many 'third-party' websites, whose sole purpose is to link to copyright-infringing content. The so-called *Playboy hyperlink* case (2016)[200] judgment by the CJEU leads the field. The case involved hyperlinked pornographic photos of Dutch model Britt Dekker and *Playboy Magazine* publishers Sanoma Media. The case caused quite a stir (not only in the Netherlands) when Advocate General Wathelet opined that posting a link to a third-party website that contains 'freely accessible' copyright infringing content does not itself amount to copyright infringement.

---

199 *Svensson v Retriever Sverige AB* (C-466/12) (2014) Bus LR 259 (4th Chamber) (CJEU).

200 *GS Media BV v Sanoma Media Netherlands BV, Playboy Enterprises International Inc., Britt Geertruida Dekker* (2016) (Case C-160/15) (CJEU). Request for a preliminary ruling by the CJEU from the Hoge Raad der Nederlanden (Supreme Court of the Netherlands). Opinion of Advocated General Wathelet, delivered on 7 April 2016. OJ 2001 L 167, p. 10 ('Playboy hyperlink case').

❖ KEY CASE

GS Media BV v Sanoma Media (2016) (Case C-160/15) Netherlands BV (*Playboy hyperlink case*) (Case C 160/15) (CJEU)[201]

Precedent

❖ Copyright holders in the EU have the exclusive right to control the communication to the public of their works.

❖ Hyperlinking to unauthorized (third party) content does not itself constitute copyright infringement.

Facts

In October 2011, Sanoma Media commissioned a *Playboy* photo shoot of Britt Dekker, a popular figure in the Dutch media. GS Media, which operates the Dutch news-and-scandal website, *GeenStijl*,[202] posted a hyperlink to a third-party website where users could download the commissioned pictures. By clicking on a hyperlink on the *GeenStijl* story ('Nude photos . . . Dekker' click: 'HERE'), readers were directed to an Australian data-storage website called Filefactory.com. Readers were then able to open a zip file containing 11 pdf files of Ms Dekker's porn photo shoot.

GS Media repeatedly refused Sanoma's requests to remove the hyperlink from its website and even posted links to alternative websites, where the photographs could also be downloaded. As a result of this, the publisher issued a claim in the Amsterdam District Court for copyright infringement against GS Media. The District Court ruled in Sanoma's and Ms Dekker's favour; however, this ruling was overturned by the Dutch CA.

Eventually the case was referred by the Supreme Court of the Netherlands to the CJEU for a preliminary ruling on certain questions regarding the interpretation of Directive 2001/29/EC of the European Parliament and of the Council of 22 May 2001 on the harmonization of certain aspects of copyright and related rights in the information society (Article 3(1) of the InfoSoc Directive) in respect of hyperlinking to works, which are *freely accessible* on another (third party) website, but which have been posted without the copyright owner's consent. The Advocate General was asked to give a preliminary opinion on whether this amounted to copyright infringement under the InfoSoc Directive.

Decision (non-binding legal opinion by the CJEU)

The Advocate General Melchior Wathelet (Belgium) opined that copyright holders (in EU law) have the *exclusive* right to control the communication to the

---

201 *GS Media BV v Sanoma Media Netherlands BV, Playboy Enterprises International Inc., Britt Geertruida Dekker* (2016) (Case C-160/15) (CJEU). Request for a preliminary ruling by the ECJ from the Hoge Raad der Nederlanden (Supreme Court of the Netherlands). Opinion of Advocated General Wathelet, delivered on 7 April 2016. OJ 2001 L 167, p. 10 ('Playboy hyperlink case').

202 'Geen stijl' roughly translates as 'having no class or style'.

public of their works. An internet user posting a hyperlink to infringing content does not constitute an act of communication to the public within the meaning of the InfoSoc Directive, where the hyperlink is not indispensable to the making available of the infringing works in question, for example where no security measures have been bypassed by using the hyperlink.

In the absence of an 'act of communication to the public', the fact that the person or website posting the link is or ought to be aware that the copyright holder has not authorized the placement of the works in question on that other website was irrelevant. Wathelet said that internet users in general do not have the means to verify whether the initial communication to the public of a protected work freely accessible on the internet is with or without the copyright holder's consent. The Advocate General felt that this would impede the proper functioning of the internet and limit the development of the information society in Europe, one of the principal objectives of the InfoSoc Directive.[203]

Analysis
Advocate General Wathelet provided the CJEU legal opinion that posting a link to a website that contains 'freely accessible' copyright infringing content does not in itself amount to copyright infringement. This meant he did not have to consider whether it was necessary for the right holder to have already consented to the work being made available.

The AG's opinion may well shut down the argument that a hyperlink infringes copyright if it links to a site on which the copyright work has been posted without the copyright owner's consent. The result could mean serious damage to the creative community's efforts to restrict infringement of their copyrighted content. *GS Media* is good news for ISPs who generate income by (knowingly) hyperlinking to infringing material. But if internet users risked liability for copyright infringement every time they posted a link they would be much more reluctant to do so.

 FOR THOUGHT

Many businesses in the publishing world employ press cutting agencies to scan international, national and regional newspapers which then provide their clients with cuttings of articles that would be of interest to them. Most of the 'cuttings' are taken from online news gathering agencies such as the Press Association (PA). Do the new typographical arrangements attract separate copyright within the meaning of the doctrine 'sweat of the brow'? Discuss in the light of the *Infopaq* judgment by the CJEU (2009).[204]

---

203 Ibid. at paras 32–47 (Advocate General Wathelet).
204 *Infopaq International A/S v Danske Dagblades Forening* (C-5/08) [2009] ECR I-6569 (CJEU) (4th Chamber)).

9.8.2 Website blocking orders of copyrighted works

In *Scarlet v SABAM* (2011),[205] the Belgian collecting society SABAM obtained an injunction against the ISP Scarlet. Scarlet's service was being used by internet users for the illegal P2P filesharing of copyright works administered by SABAM, and the injunction required Scarlet to install and implement a system to filter all communications carried over its service in order to identify files containing works in SABAM's catalogue, which would then be blocked.

Scarlet appealed, arguing (successfully) that the injunction was contrary to Article 15 of the E-Commerce Directive and Article 3 of the IP Enforcement Directive.[206] The Court of Justice recognized that national courts must weigh up competing rights and strike a fair balance between users' rights to freedom of expression and privacy rights (e.g. in IP protection). In *Scarlet* the injunction sought failed to strike a fair balance, not least because it could lead to legitimate content being blocked, particularly since copyright exceptions and other provisions for lawful use of copyright material vary from one Member State to another.

Regulations 17, 18 and 19 of the E-Commerce Regulations apply where an ISP is a 'mere conduit' or where it is 'caching' or 'hosting' information. In summary, the defences apply to:

> *Mere conduit*: An ISP is acting as a 'mere conduit' if its services consist of transmitting information or providing network access, which includes the 'automatic, intermediate and transient' storage of information, where the sole purpose of the storage is to carry out the transmission and the information is not stored for longer than reasonably necessary (regulation 17).
>
> *Caching*: Caching is the local storage of information in frequent demand, to enable quicker access to that information by avoiding making repeated requests to the information's source (regulation 18).
>
> *Hosting*: Hosting is the storage of information e.g. the provision of space to internet users; this may be for websites, blogs, discussion boards etc. (regulation 19).

In *Google France SARL v Louis Vuitton Malletier SA* (2011)[207] the CJEU held that an ISP could rely on the hosting defence only if it,

> has not played an active role of such a kind as to give it knowledge of, or control over, the data stored.

Section 97A CDPA provides injunctions against service providers which means that the High Court in England and Wales (in Scotland, the Court of Session) has the power to

---

205 *Scarlet Extended SA v Societe Belge des Auteurs, Compositeurs et Editeurs SCRL (SABAM)* (C-70/10) [2011] ECR I-1195 (CJEU).
206 Directive 2004/48/EC of the European Parliament and of the Council of 29 April 2004 on the enforcement of intellectual property rights ('the IP Enforcement Directive'). Official Journal L 157, 30/04/2004 p. 45.
207 (C-236/08) [2011] Bus LR 1 (CJEU).

grant relief in form of a 'blocking order' against a service provider, where that ISP has actual knowledge of another person using their service to infringe copyright.[208]

In determining whether an ISP has *actual knowledge*, a court will have to take into account all 'matters which appear to it in the particular circumstances to be relevant' (section 97A (2)), such as:

- whether a service provider has received a notice through a means of contact made available in accordance with regulation 6(1)(c) of the Electronic Commerce Regulations 2002; and
- the extent to which any notice includes the full name and address of the sender of the notice; and
- details of the infringement in question.

The leading case is *Cartier v BskyB* (2014),[209] where the High Court granted relief ordering five defendant ISPs (namely BskyB [now Sky], BT, EE, Talk Talk and Virgin) who together have a market share of approximately 95 per cent of UK broadband users to block access to a number of counterfeiting websites.

❖ KEY CASE	*Cartier International and Others v British Sky Broadcasting Ltd and Others* [2014] EWHC 3354 (Ch)

Precedent
In order to be granted an injunction for website-blocking, the following conditions must be met. The relief must:

- ❖ be effective;
- ❖ be dissuasive;
- ❖ not be unnecessarily complicated or costly;
- ❖ avoid barriers to legitimate trade;
- ❖ be fair and equitable and strike a 'fair balance' between the applicable fundamental rights;
- ❖ be proportionate.

Furthermore:
- ❖ the target website must have infringed the trade mark/s, even where they state that the goods are replicas, as this can still lead to customer and post-sale confusion;
- ❖ the target website's operators used the ISPs' services to infringe the trade marks;
- ❖ the ISPs had actual knowledge of the infringement.

Facts
The claimants were all companies within the Richemont Group, owners of a portfolio of luxury brands, such as Cartier and Montblanc. Richemont sought

---

208 Hoy, R. (2015), pp. 44–47.
209 *Cartier International and Others v BSkyB and Others* [2014] EWHC 3354 (Ch) 17 October 2014 (the Cartier case).

injunctions pursuant to section 97A CDPA requiring the ISPs BSkyB et al. to block access to six websites that infringed its trade marks by advertising and selling counterfeit goods, target websites such as e.g. www.cartierloveonline.com. Each had targeted UK customers offering for sale replicas of products bearing one of the trade marks.

The key EU provisions which allow right holders to apply for injunctions against intermediaries are:

❖ Article 8(3) of the InfoSoc Directive;[210]
❖ Article 11 of the IP Enforcement Directive.[211]

The main problem was that the UK Parliament implemented Article 8(3) of the InfoSoc Directive (concerning copyright infringement) by inserting section 97A into the CDPA. However, the government did not think it necessary to implement the relevant sentence within Article 11 of the Enforcement Directive, therefore providing no specific statutory provision equivalent to section 97A in relation to trade marks.

The question before the High Court was: could the court order such an injunction? Arnold J consulted section 37(1) Senior Courts Act 1981 and interpreted it in light of Article 11 of the IP Enforcement Directive which requires that:

Member States must ensure that right holders are in a position to apply for an injunction against intermediaries whose services are used by a third party to infringe an intellectual property right, without prejudice to Article 8 (3) of the [InfoSoc Directive].[212]

Decision

Arnold J granted the orders, finding the likely costs burden on the ISPs was justified and the orders were proportionate. He also acknowledged that ISP costs might be significant in future if applications for such blocking orders grew rapidly in number. On the proportionality aspect in particular, the judge held that the threshold conditions were met.

The Court granted orders substantially in the form sought but with two modifications: (i) a requirement that the notice on the blocked page should identify

---

210 Directive 2001/29/EC of the European Parliament and of the Council of 22 May 2001 on the harmonization of certain aspects of copyright and related rights in the information society, transposed into UK law by the Copyright and Related Rights Regulations 2003, S.I. 2003/2498 ('the InfoSoc Directive').

211 Directive 2004/48/EC of 29 April 2004 on the enforcement of intellectual property rights, transposed into UK law by the Intellectual Property (Enforcement, etc.) Regulations 2006, S.I. 2006/1028 ('the IP Enforcement Directive').

212 The Court also considered: Article 5 of Directive 2008/95/EC of October 2008, Articles 5(1)(a) and (3), which were implemented in the UK by s 10(1) and (4) Trade Marks Act 1994; Directive 2000/31/EC of June 2000, which was transposed into UK law by the Electronic Commerce (EC Directive) Regulations 2002 and the Charter of Fundamental Rights of the European Union.

the party who applied for it to be blocked; and (ii) the orders should contain a 'sunset clause' such that they cease to apply at the expiry of a defined period.

Analysis

The *Cartier* decision marks an important development in the protection of brands online, i.e. as a new option for trade mark holders seeking to limit the online sale of counterfeit goods. The problem had been until then, that there was no specific statutory provision concerning trade marks and blocking websites that sold counterfeit goods.

The 'sunset clause' means that ISPs and operators of websites can now apply to the High Court to discharge or vary such 'blocking' orders following a change in circumstances. The orders will cease to have effect after a defined period (provisionally set at two years) unless either the ISPs consent or the court orders that they should be continued.

Arnold J's additional comments about the effectiveness of alternative measures and the proportionality of imposing the obligation on ISPs may well encourage rights holders to seek site-blocking injunctions.

The public interest in preventing the sale of counterfeit goods was definitely a significant factor in the *Cartier* decision whether to make the blocking order or not. It is fair to say that the case has raised concerns about the impact on online businesses and possible restrictions on freedom of expression on the internet as a market place.

In *L'Oreal v eBay* (2012)[213] the Court of Justice held that eBay would have provided an active role if it provided assistance including:

optimising the presentation of the offers for sale . . . or promoting those offers.

In this case the internet auction site eBay was not able to rely on the 'hosting' exemption. (See below)

 FOR THOUGHT

Are internet blocking injunctions the right way forward? Would it not be simpler to prosecute the company selling fake goods on the internet via eBay or Amazon for 'counterfeiting'? Discuss.

---

213 *L'Oréal SA and Ors v eBay International AG and Ors* (2012) (Case C-324/09) Judgment of the Court of Justice Grand Chamber, 12 July 2011 (CJEU); [2012] Bus LR 1369.

9.8.3 ISP liability in relation to online auction houses

See above
9.7.1

Are online auction 'houses' such as eBay or Gumtree liable for IP infringements committed by their users and dealers? This was the question raised by the Chancery Court with reference to the CJEU in the landmark case of *L'Oréal v eBay* (2012).[214] The claimants were all cosmetics companies bringing claims for trade mark infringement against three defendant companies which facilitated the online auction and sale of goods, as well as seven individual sellers of cosmetic products which, the claimants maintained, infringed a number of Community trade marks and UK trade marks of which they were the proprietors.[215]

The central questions in this case were: did eBay (Europe) itself commit infringements by using trade marks in relation to infringing goods? Or was eBay simply a 'host' and therefore not liable for copyright infringement as a mere auction site?

Furthermore the court raised the important point of sponsored hyperlinks and 'link marks' – a further question referred by the Court of Chancery to the CJEU – this point focusing on the scope of infringement of Article 5(1) of EC Directive 89/104, which approximated the laws of the Member States relating to trade marks. The problem was that this Directive did not specifically define the use of a trade mark by third parties; it only covered the use of a trade mark sign in relation to the proprietor's goods.

In this action the CJEU had to determine whether the sellers had sold goods which infringed the claimants' trade marks in that they were:

1   counterfeit;
2   non-European Economic Area (EEA) goods;
3   tester products that were not intended for resale; or
4   products which, being unboxed, would have damaged the reputation of claimants' trade marks.

See above
9.8.1

L'Oréal further argued that hyperlinks at the top of the sponsored link led to a page from the eBay Express site showing a search for 'matrix hair' and 'magie noire' which brought up 48 items from international sellers and that all of these were to infringing goods. The basis of this allegation was that the country or region stated was the United States in all cases, and the items were priced in sterling. L'Oréal contended that, so far as the auction-style listings were concerned, eBay did in fact conduct an auction. eBay disputed this and L'Oréal accepted at least that eBay's activities differed from those of traditional auctioneers. L'Oréal claimed that each of the fourth to tenth defendants infringed one or more of the trade marks by using signs identical to the

---

214 *L'Oréal SA and Ors v eBay International AG and Ors* (2012) (Case C-324/09) Judgment of the Court of Justice Grand Chamber, 12 July 2011 (CJEU) (by reference from the High Court Chancery Division in L'Oréal SA v eBay International AG [2009] EWHC 1094 (Ch).

215 L'Oréal divided the trade marks into two groups for the purposes of their claims. The first group, referred to as 'the Lancôme Marks', consisted of Lancôme, Renergie, Definicils and Amor Amor. The second group, referred to as 'the Link Marks', consisted of Definicils together with the remaining trade marks not included in the first group.

trade marks of goods to those for which the trade marks are registered. These claims all concerned the Lancôme marks.[216]

In their defence, eBay argued that they had set up systems and policies which discouraged the sale of infringing products and which enabled trade mark owners, by notifying them, to have taken down the webpages on which allegedly infringing products were sold.[217] eBay also argued that they were merely fulfilling the function of an ISP ('hosting site') and were not involved in the sale of infringing goods, relying on Article 14 of Directive 2000/1 (the E-Commerce Directive). eBay submitted that, as a matter of law, eBay Europe was under no duty or obligation to prevent third parties from infringing L'Oréal's (or anyone else's) registered trade marks. The online trading house also argued that it attempted to prevent or at least minimize infringements, in particular through the VeRO programme which filtered infringing goods, such as counterfeit watches by Rolex. Counsel for eBay Europe submitted that in reality L'Oréal's claim of joint tortfeasorship was a thinly disguised attack on eBay's business model.

In this respect, the CJEU did not come to a conclusive decision. It held that EU trade mark law had not been completely harmonized in respect of copyright and trade mark infringement via hyperlinks and link marks. Since Article 11 of the EC Enforcement Directive is not clear on third-party obligation with regard to future infringements as a result of online auction site operation, there is, as yet, no liability for past infringements on the ground of joint tortfeasorship. In view of the current uncertainty over this area of law, the CJEU's response to the L'Oréal case does not provide a clear message.

What then was really at the heart of the L'Oréal case? Was it not – as counsel for eBay Europe argued – an attack on eBay's business model? That said, copyright and industrial property rights are at increased risk, and it could be argued that the high profits which eBay (and others) make from their sites oblige them to ensure that IP rights are not infringed. The answer lies partly in the Cartier[218] ruling which followed on from the L'Oréal action, resulting in website blocking orders.

9.8.4 Harmonization of copyright laws: the EU copyright *acquis*

There has been significant harmonization of the substantive copyright law in Europe to reduce barriers to trade and to adjust the framework to new forms of exploitation. The result has been the so-called EU copyright *acquis*, a French term (*acquis communautaire*) meaning 'the EU as it is'. Accepting the *acquis* on copyright means taking legislation as you find it, that is 'autonomous and uniform' throughout the European Union. This then includes the terms of the copyright directives.

---

216 The complaint against the fourth defendant concerned advertisements and offers for sale for 'Lancôme Maqui-complet Concealer Light Buff RRP £18.50', sold on 23 November 2006; 'Lancôme Renergie Microlift Active Redefining Treatment', sold on 23 November 2006; and 'Lancôme Definicils Full Size Black Mascara Waterproof', sold on 5 December 2006.
217 eBay Europe pleaded defences under ss 10(6) and 11(2) Trade Marks Act 1994 (though these were not pursued at trial).
218 *Cartier International and Others v BSkyB and Others* [2014] EWHC 3354 (Ch) 17 October 2014 (the Cartier case).

Under the EU copyright *acquis* and the WIPO treaties, copyright protection is created automatically when you create

- original literary, dramatic, musical and artistic work, including illustration and photography;
- original non-literary written work, e.g. software, web content and databases;
- sound and music recordings;
- film and television recordings;
- broadcasts;
- the layout of published editions of written, dramatic and musical works.

The overarching test for whether a work is protected by copyright is now governed by EU law: a work is protected only if it is *original* in the sense that it is the author's own intellectual creation. This was established in the CJEU case of *Infopaq*.[219] This case, referred to the Court of Justice by the Danish Supreme Court (Højesteret), resulted from an eight-year dispute between Infopaq International A/S (now Infomedia) and Danske Dagblades Forening (DDF),[220] concerning the use ('copying') of extracts from daily newspapers, magazines, broadcasting and social networking sites in order to reproduce short text extract summaries for subscribers. The Danish Supreme Court had ruled that extracts of newspaper articles comprising no more than 11 words *can* be works protected by copyright. The CJEU considered two actions *Infopaq* I and *Infopaq* II: whether short reproductions of extracts from newspaper articles infringed copyright.

The ECJ ruled in favour of Danske Dagblades Forening, in that the process of data capture was copyright protected and that even 11 printed words were not exempt under Article 5(1) of the Infosoc Directive.[221]

Lucas (2010) argues that international copyright litigation nowadays centres on the question of whether the 'reproduction' constitutes an 'expression of the intellectual creation of the author'? This question is now left to the national courts to decide following the *Infopaq* ruling.[222]

So, where copyright work is copied by an unlicensed third party, it will qualify as a substantial part within the meaning of section 16(1) CDPA ('The acts restricted by copyright in a work'), specifically under section 16(3)(a) – and thus there will be an infringement of the copyright if the part in question contains elements which are the expression of the intellectual creation of the author of the work (see: *SAS Institute Inc v World Programming Ltd* (2013)[223].

---

219 *Infopaq International A/S v Danske Dagblades Forening* (C-5/08) [2009] ECR I-6569 (ECJ (4th Chamber)).
220 The professional association of Danish daily newspapers; its function is, *inter alia*, to offer advice on copyright issues.
221 For further discussion see: Rosati, E. (2011), pp. 746–755.
222 Lucas, A. (2010), pp. 277–282.
223 [2013] EWCA Civ 1482.

Further preliminary rulings by the CJEU in this area of harmonized IP laws have set out the terms of international treaties, such as TRIPS (see: *Anheuser-Busch Inc. v Budejovicky Budvar Narodni Podnik* (2004)[224]).

However, Handig (2013) argues that the CJEU's interpretations in relation to 'copyright work' are not that straightforward, as there are definitions only for three categories of works – namely computer programs,[225] databases[226] and photographs.[227] He doubts that the term 'copyright work' can (and indeed should) be interpreted uniformly across all copyrighted works in the Member States – as the EU *copyright acquis* suggests. Handig points out that in the recent IP directives there are no more definitions because the Member States could not agree on an 'implantation' to avoid harmonization.[228]

Since the *Karen Murphy* case[229] a considerable number of changes have been made to protect and harmonize copyright law across Europe. As the numerous footnotes in this chapter indicate, this has had considerable impact on UK copyright law (i.e. the CDPA).

 FOR THOUGHT

Is current UK IP legislation creaking at the seams, and are attempts by legislators to update legislation working or simply confusing matters? Discuss.

9.8.5 Orphan works

What if you cannot find out the identity or address of the copyright holder? Orphan works are works, such as books, newspaper and magazine articles and films that are still protected by copyright but whose authors or other right holders are not known or cannot be located or contacted to obtain copyright permissions.

Under the Enterprise and Regulatory Reform Act 2013, the UK government has powers to enable licensing of orphan works in the UK for commercial and non-commercial use (via the IPO).[230] The licensing scheme has been implemented through the Copyright and Rights in Performances (Licensing of Orphan Works) Regulations 2014 which state that a diligent search must comprise a reasonable search of the relevant sources to identify and locate the right holder.[231]

---

224 (C-245/02) [2004] ECR I-10989; [2005] ETMR 27 (CJEU).
225 Directive 2009/24 on the legal protection of computer programs [2009] OJ L111/16 Article 1(3); originally, Directive 91/250 on the legal protection of computer programs [1991] OJ L122/42.
226 Directive 96/9 on the legal protection of databases [1996] OJ L 77/20 Article 3(1).
227 Directive 2006/116 on the term of protection of copyright and certain related rights (codified version) Article 6, [2006] OJ L372/12 Article 6; originally, Directive 93/98 harmonizing the term of protection of copyright and certain related rights, [1993] OJ L 290/9. The directive is sometimes also called the 'Duration Directive'.
228 Handig, C. (2013), pp. 334–340.
229 *Football Association Premier League Ltd v QC Leisure* (C-403/08) [2012] All ER (EC) 629 (Karen Murphy pub landlady case).
230 s 77 Enterprise and Regulatory Reform Act 2013 (ERRA) ('Orphan Works licensing and extended collective licensing'), added new ss 116A 'Power to provide for licensing of orphan works' and 116B 'Extended collective licensing' to the CDPA 1988.
231 Implementing Directive 2012/28/EU On certain permitted uses of orphan works sets out common rules on the digitization and online display of so-called orphan works.

A licensing scheme on orphan works is now in place, providing greater access to about 91 million culturally valuable creative works – including diaries, photographs, oral history recordings and documentary films. You can obtain a licence from the Intellectual Property Office (IPO) so that these works can be reproduced on websites, in books and on a video without breaking the law, while protecting the rights of owners so they can be remunerated if they come forward.

Many museums and art collections now rely on orphan works licences, such as Leeds Museums and Galleries (LMG), the largest local authority-run museum service in England. LMG cares for 1.3 million objects, including a fine art collection of national significance. Shortly after the new orphan licensing scheme was introduced, the LMG wanted to include works by Charles Ginner in its British Art collection 1900–1920. Ginner had strong connections with Leeds, having worked, exhibited and lectured there.[232] Ginner died in 1952, so his artworks were still in copyright until 2022 and could not generally be reproduced without permission from the holder/s of the copyright, most likely his heirs. By contacting the IPO and therein conducting a diligent search, no right holders could be found. The IPO then issued an orphan works licence to the Leeds Museum to allow the works to be used. Had the legitimate right holders come forward within seven years of the licence issue, any claims for recompense would have been dealt with by the IPO.

A 'diligent search'[233] means a search of:

- the orphan works register maintained by the IPO;
- the orphan works register maintained by the Office for Harmonization in the Internal Market (OHIM);[234]
- the sources listed under Part 2 of Schedule ZA1 CDPA ('Certain permitted uses of orphan works by relevant bodies'). For visual works, these include books, newspapers and periodicals; journals and magazines; the databases of relevant collecting societies and picture agency databases.

If your diligent search fails to identify the owner, or the owner is identifiable but cannot be contacted, you can apply to the IPO for an orphan work licence to use the image on a non-exclusive basis. These licences can be given for commercial or non-commercial use. An application fee and a licence fee are payable; the licence fee will be handed over to the copyright holder if their identity becomes known.

You can have hours of fun searching the UK Government Orphan Works Register[235] in the following categories:

---

232 Drawing by Charles Ginner, 'University Buildings in Leeds', 1915: https://explore.library.leeds.ac.uk/special-collections-explore/256/university_buildings_leeds.

233 Reg. 4(3) The Copyright and Rights in Performances (Licensing of Orphan Works) Regulations 2014.

234 The Office for Harmonization in the Internal Market (OHIM) is the European Union agency responsible for managing Community trade marks and designs. Based in Alicante, Spain since 1994, OHIM was created as a decentralized agency of the European Union to offer IP rights protection to businesses and innovators across the EU at: www.inta.org/2015TMAP/Information/Pages/About-OHIM.aspx.

235 UK Orphan Works Register: www.orphanworkslicensing.service.gov.uk/view-register/search?workCategory=All&filter=0.

- moving images;
- music notation;
- script and choreography;
- sound recordings;
- still visual art;
- written works.

9.9 The EU Copyright Directive 2019

As we have seen in this chapter, many of the existing rules governing copyright originated in an era when the most powerful tools for piracy were the photocopier and the tape recorder rather than Google or Safari's search engines. The EU copyright reform is an attempt to make these laws fit for the digital age.

In March 2019 Members of the European Parliament voted in favour of a controversial directive which introduced sweeping changes to copyright enforcement across all EU Member States, despite ferocious campaigning led by Google and internet freedom activists.[236]

This Directive is based on and complements the rules laid down in the directives currently in force in this area of law, in particular Directives 96/9/EC,[237] 2000/31/EC,[238] 2001/29/EC,[239] 2006/115/EC,[240] 2009/24/EC,[241] 2012/28/EU[242] and 2014/26/EU.[243] These directives that have been adopted in the area of copyright and related rights contribute to the functioning of the internal market, provide for a high level of protection for right holders, facilitate the clearance of rights, and create a framework in which the exploitation of works and other protected subject matter can take place.

The idea was to harmonize the legal framework under one directive in order to contribute to the proper functioning of the internal market, stimulating innovation, creativity, investment and production of new content, particularly in the digital environment, in order to avoid the fragmentation of the EU internal market. The protection provided by that legal framework also contributes to the EU's objective of respecting and

---

236 348 MEPs voted in favour and 274 against.
237 Directive 96/9/EC of the European Parliament and of the Council of 11 March 1996 on the legal protection of databases (OJ L 77, 27.3.1996, p. 20) (Database Directive).
238 Directive 2000/31/EC of the European Parliament and of the Council of 8 June 2000 on certain legal aspects of information society services, in particular electronic commerce, in the Internal Market (OJ L 178, 17.7.2000, p. 1) (E-Commerce Directive).
239 Directive 2001/29/EC of the European Parliament and of the Council of 22 May 2001 on the harmonization of certain aspects of copyright and related rights in the information society (the Copyright – or InfoSoc Directive) (OJ L 167, 22.6.2001, p. 10).
240 Directive 2006/115/EC of the European Parliament and of the Council of 12 December 2006 on rental right and lending right and on certain rights related to copyright in the field of intellectual property (OJ L 376, 27.12.2006, p. 28).
241 Directive 2009/24/EC of the European Parliament and of the Council of 23 April 2009 on the legal protection of computer programs (OJ L 111, 5.5.2009, p. 16).
242 Directive 2012/28/EU of the European Parliament and of the Council of 25 October 2012 on certain permitted uses of orphan works (OJ L 299, 27.10.2012, p. 5).
243 Directive 2014/26/EU of the European Parliament and of the Council of 26 February 2014 on collective management of copyright and related rights and multi-territorial licensing of rights in musical works for online use in the internal market (OJ L 84, 20.3.2014, p. 72).

promoting cultural diversity while at the same time bringing European common cultural heritage to the fore.[244]

The new directive covers everything from the digitization of medieval manuscripts to the distribution of television sitcoms, but at its heart is an intent to strengthen the hand of those who create videos, images, games, music, articles and other material against the technology companies that profit from reusing these creations. Most of the 24 articles of the directive are uncontroversial, but two are regarded as quite divisive. The European Copyright Directive 2019 is best known for two provisions: Articles 11 and 13, referred to as the 'link tax' and 'upload filter', respectively, by its opponents. Tim Berners-Lee, the British inventor of the World Wide Web, campaigned against Article 13 as 'an unprecedented step towards the transformation of the internet . . . into a tool for the automated surveillance and control of its users'.[245] Where Article 13 makes it harder for tech companies to release user-generated content, Article 11 relates specifically to the sharing of news articles.

- *Article 11*: gives news outlets the power to charge tech companies for 20-year licences to use parts of their articles, such as the snippets of text that appear below links on Facebook and Twitter ('link tax').

Publishers have long argued it is increasingly difficult for news organizations to continue funding quality journalism, and that technology firms which monetize the sharing of news should pay their share. Against a backdrop of dwindling revenues from advertising and free online news, publishers hope this source of income could turn out to be a lifeline for professional journalism. Internet users in the EU will notice changes to the way news is distributed on social media and may be blocked from sharing protected text, pictures, videos or clips of audio.

- *Article 13*: makes tech companies liable for policing their users' posts for signs of copyright violation ('upload filters').

This means that copyright holders should in theory find it easier to make money when their material is recycled online. For example, a YouTube user uploads a video that illicitly includes someone else's copyrighted photographs. YouTube must actively find the video and take it down rather than simply wait for the photographer to complain. Tech companies have argued that the only way the 'upload filters' can realistically be done is to use algorithms that automatically recognize and reject suspicious material before their users can publish it. This has prompted fears of clumsy and industrial-grade censorship by machine and AI (Artificial Intelligence).

---

244 Article 167(4) TFEU requires the EU to take cultural aspects into account in its action.
245 https://twitter.com/timberners_lee: The #CopyrightDirective would hurt small-scale creatives and startups who would be unable to comply with a regulatory model designed for the era of the printing press. #EU reps must stand up for our digital future #SaveYourInternet, 30 November 2018.

Much internet culture is now based on the 'remixing' of existing material into new forms such as memes.[246] A key argument against the directive is that it could serve as a 'meme ban', given the strong rules against uploading copyrighted material without permission, and the fact that much shareable content depends on things like TV and movie scenes. But technology companies say the new copyright protection is impossible to uphold, since no automatic filter can usefully determine whether a given upload is parody, pastiche, criticism, review, caricature or for purposes of quotation.

The new legislation emphasizes that you will still be able to upload content, but technology firms, including Google (and YouTube) and Facebook, have warned they will have to remove vastly more content automatically. These companies already remove music and videos that are copyrighted. For example, YouTube scans uploads and matches them up to a database of files submitted by content owners, giving the original creator of the work the option to block, monetize or simply track it. Under the new legislation, tech companies are more liable for any copyrighted content uploaded on to their platforms, particularly if they already run automated scans. The claim most commonly raised by protesters is that the reforms are a muzzle on their freedom of expression.

While there are plenty of exemptions under the EU regime for purposes such as satire or education, the new era of EU copyright law and its boundaries have yet to be properly tested in the courts.

 ## 9.10 Further reading

Booton, D. (2018) 'How to be bad: the importance of standpoint in intellectual property disputes', *Intellectual Property Quarterly*, 4, 279–304.
This article analyzes and evaluates legal determinations of the scope of IP rights. It compares and contrasts the origins and use of the standpoint of the person skilled in the relevant art in the determination of patent scope with that of the average consumer as used in trade mark law. David Booton points out that in IP cases the courts are often called upon to make value judgments involving matters of impression, making them vulnerable to the criticism that they are acting unfairly, such as the comments of Lord Neuberger in the *Trunki* case.[247] Booton states that the Supreme Court's decision in the case 'was not well received by many in the design community'. The article sets out to show how the adoption of a standpoint contributes to the perception of fairness in judicial decision making and how this in turn informs a critical consideration of the standpoint of the informed user as deployed in deciding the scope of registered designs.

Davis, P. S. (2017) 'Costs of blocking injunctions', *Intellectual Property Quarterly*, 4, 330–345.
The author explains the UK courts' jurisdiction to grant blocking injunctions. Whilst these are now well established in the IP field Davis wonders how prevalent they might also be in defamation actions (though most of these actions are now settled

---

246 A meme is an idea, behavior or style that spreads from person to person within a culture, often with the aim of conveying a particular phenomenon, theme or meaning represented by the meme.
247 *PMS International Group Plc v Magmatic Limited* [2016] UKSC 12 at para. 24.

out of court). He questions whether such injunction are proportionate, and whether alternative measures may be equally effective and less burdensome. The article examines a number of interesting judgments in the IP field, such as *Cartier v BskyB* (2016) and *McFadden v Sony Music* (2014), where the CJEU held that the safe harbour defences did not prevent intermediaries having to pay money as costs, emphasizing that costs were a matter for the national courts.

Fletcher, S. and Mitchell, J. (2015) 'Court of Appeal found no love for Topshop tank: the image right that dare not speak its name', *European Intellectual Property Review*, 37(6), 394–405.

Susan Fletcher and Justine Mitchell present an extremely readable article on the notion of protecting a person's image from unauthorized exploitation citing a number of authorities. Starting with confidentiality and early 'image rights' issues starting with the *Prince Albert* case of 1849 then moving on to privacy issues in the *Douglas v Hello!* (2001) case, concerning the unauthorized publication of the celebrity couples' wedding photographs, then moving on to confidence and privacy issues in the *John Terry (LNS)* (2010) super injunction. The authors balance the 'harm' suffered by the famous claimants in terms of their privacy invasion and the commercial information concerned including trade marks, brands and their image rights. Tugendhat J famously dismissed the footballer John Terry's application, partly on the basis that the 'nub' of the applicant's complaint was damage to his commercial reputation rather than safeguarding his family's privacy. The authors argue that subsequent development of image rights per se has been 'stunningly slow' in the jurisdiction of the UK, compared with other countries such as the US, France and Germany – and they then discuss the issues in the *Rihanna v Topshop* case (2015). Privacy and commercial exploitation have been reconciled in over half the states of the US which recognize a well-developed, sui generis 'publicity right'.

Handig, C. (2013) 'The "sweat of the brow" is not enough! – more than a blueprint of the European copyright term "work" ', *European Intellectual Property Review*, 35(6), 334–340.

Christian Handig examines EU intellectual property legislation and jurisprudence in relation to the term 'copyright work' to receive copyright protection and the importance of EU harmonization in this field. Given that the European Union established the first copyright provisions more than two decades ago, it comes rather as a surprise that the first substantial decisions on this issue were brought before the Court of Justice of the European Union (CJEU) only fairly recently. The author discusses a small bundle of CJEU decisions that gave the Court of Justice the opportunity to do more than just to lay a foundation in this field (e.g. *Painer v Standard Verlags GmbH* (2012);[248] *Football Association Premier League Ltd v QC Leisure* (2012)[249]).

Ullrich, H., Hilty, R. M., Lamping, M. and Drexl, J. (eds) (2015) *TRIPS plus 20: From Trade Rules to Market Principles.* MPI Studies on Intellectual Property and Competition Law. Heidelberg: Springer-Verlag.

This book examines the impact and shortcomings of the TRIPS Agreement. The authors argue that the framework conditions of TRIPS have fundamentally changed over the past 20 years. New technologies have emerged, markets have expanded

---

248 (C-145/10) [2012] ECDR6 (3rd Chamber) (CJEU).
249 (C-403/08) [2012] All ER (EC) 629; Times, November 23, 2011 (Grand Chamber) (CJEU) (the Karen Murphy pub landlady case).

beyond national borders, some developing states have become global players, the terms of international competition have changed and the intellectual property system faces increasing friction with public policies. The contributors to this text, including the leading academic, Professor William Cornish, inquire whether the TRIPS Agreement should still be seen only as part of an international trade regulation, or whether it needs to be understood – or even reconceptualized – as a framework regulation for the international protection of intellectual property. Various contributors to this text suggest not to define the terms of an outright revision of TRIPS but rather to discuss the framework conditions for an interpretative evolution that could make the agreement better suited to the expectations and needs of today's global economy.

Chapter 10

Entertainment law

Chapter contents

10.1 Overview

Copyright is the foundation upon which the music and entertainment business is built. Copyright is essential in the music business to ensure that songwriters, artists and producers are adequately protected and compensated for the use and sale of their creative works in the form of royalties (or 'economic rights').

This chapter picks up from the previous chapter, discussing the development and advancement of online technology and the impact on authors' and creators' intellectual property (IP) rights. The main focus will be on the music and entertainment industries and how copyright legislation is protecting artists' and performers' economic rights in the form of royalty payments. It is fair to say that neither civil and nor criminal remedies available to the UK courts have been completely adequate to protect artists from piracy and copying of their works via the internet. We have seen that the law on copying for personal use and the meaning of parody or pastiche (as explained in Chapter 9) have not been completely satisfactory when challenged in the courts.

There will be quite a lengthy discussion regarding sampling in the *Kraftwerk* case[1] in this respect with the recent judgment from the CJEU.

The chapter ends with the rather complex arrangements for music licensing, playing music in public and obtaining a music licence from one of the many performing rights and music collection societies. As the chapter closes, we take a final look at the notion of intellectual property law which can be seen as a protection of a fundamental right to property. It will be concluded that it is necessary for the courts to strike a balance between an individual's right to his intellectual property and its protection and the freedom of expression and the arts when work is copied (such as a two second sample of a song) – when, in principle, neither right is superior to the other. Copyright law itself achieves the author's IP right through the provision of a number of limitations and exceptions which will be highlighted in this final chapter.

---

1   *Pelham GmbH, Moses Pelham, Martin Haas v Hütter [Ralf Hütter, Florian Schneider-Esleben* (2019) (Case C-476/17) The Court (Grand Chamber) 29 July 2019 (Pelham v Hütter; 'the Kraftwerk case') (CJEU).

10.2 Phonograms and musical works

The main objective of copyright and related rights is to promote the development of the arts by ensuring artists receive revenue from their works, so that they are not dependent on patrons and are free to pursue their creative activity.

The music industry is a complicated business with a number of representative sectors and components interacting to make it work. The UK music industry grew by 2 per cent in 2017 to contribute a record £4.5bn to the economy – up by £100m on 2016, according to a report by UK Music (2018).[2] Among the big success stories were the record music sector which saw a rise of 9 per cent to £700m and music publishing which grew by 7 per cent to £505m in 2017.

Successful British acts including Ed Sheeran, Dua Lipa, Rag'N'Bone Man, Stormzy, Harry Styles and Depeche Mode helped exports of UK music soar in 2017 by 7 per cent to £2.6bn. This makes the UK Europe's largest music market and the world's third largest contributor. Millions of fans who poured into concerts ranging from giant festivals to grassroots music venues generated a contribution of live music to the UK's economy of around £1bn (£991m).[3]

The global recorded music market grew by 8.1 per cent in 2017, its third consecutive year of growth since the International Federation of the Phonographic Industry (IFPI)[4] began tracking the market in 1997. Figures released by IFPI's Global Music Report 2018 showed total revenues for 2017 were $17.3bn.

Streaming remains the main driver of recovering revenues and, for the first time in 2017, became the single largest revenue source with 176 million users of paid streaming services contributing to year-on-year streaming growth of 41.1 per cent. Streaming now accounts for 38.4 per cent of total recorded music revenue, and its growth has more than offset a 5.4 per cent decline in physical revenue and a 20.5 per cent decline in download revenue. Total digital income in 2017 accounted for more than half of all revenue (54 per cent) for the first time. The industry's third consecutive year of growth follows 15 years of significant revenue decline. Despite the recent uplift, revenues for 2017 are still only 68.4 per cent of the market's peak in 1999.[5]

Article 3 of the WIPO Convention defines the following terms:

(a) 'performers' means actors, singers, musicians, dancers, and other persons who act, sing, deliver, declaim, play in, or otherwise perform literary or artistic works;

---

2   UK Music is an industry-funded body established in October 2008 to represent the collective interests of the recorded, published and live arms of the British music industry: www.ukmusic.org/research/.
3   Source: UK Music (2018) Measuring Music: Methodology 2018 Report. 81,153 professional full-time musicians based in the UK were surveyed and the respondents gave their average earnings: www.ukmusic.org/assets/general/Measuring_Music_2018_Methodology.pdf.
4   IFPI is the organization that represents the interests of the recording industry worldwide. It is a non-profit members' organization registered in Switzerland and founded in Italy in 1933.
5   IFPI Global Music Report 2018: www.ifpi.org/news/IFPI-GLOBAL-MUSIC-REPORT-2018.

> (b) 'phonogram' means any exclusively aural fixation of sounds of a performance or of other sounds;
>
> (c) 'producer of phonograms' means the person who, or the legal entity which, first fixes the sounds of a performance or other sounds;
>
> (d) 'publication' means the offering of copies of a phonogram to the public in reasonable quantity;
>
> (e) 'reproduction' means the making of a copy or copies of a fixation;
>
> (f) 'broadcasting' means the transmission by wireless means for public reception of sounds or of images and sounds;
>
> (g) 'rebroadcasting' means the simultaneous broadcasting by one broadcasting organisation of the broadcast of another broadcasting organisation.

10.2.1 Phonograms

'Phonogram' should not be confused with 'phonograph' (sound writer), originally used for Thomas Edison's invention of the 'cylinder player' in 1877, also known as the 'gramophone' (letter voice), trade marked in 1887. Whilst the US tends to use the word 'phonograph' for the music playback device, the UK uses the term 'gramophone'.

One of the earliest phonogram producers was *The Gramophone Company Limited*, founded in 1898, founded on behalf of Emil Berliner (1851–1929), inventor of the gramophone record. Most of the company's early records were made in Hannover, Berliner's birthplace. *The Gramophone Company Limited* was one of the early UK recording companies, the parent organization for the *His Master's Voice* (HMV) label, and the European affiliate of the American *Victor Talking Machine Company*. Although the company merged with the *Columbia Graphophone Company* in 1931 to form *Electric and Musical Industries Limited* (EMI), its name 'The Gramophone Company Limited' continued in the UK into the 1970s. When Emil Berliner emigrated to the United States, he founded the *Deutsche Grammophon Gesellschaft* in 1898 as the German branch of his UK *Gramophone Company* (see above). Though no longer connected to the British Gramophone Company, *Deutsche Grammophon* continued to use the HMV trade mark featuring the dog Nipper in Germany until the late 1940s.

Phonogram producers are the entities or individuals who finance the creation of the sound recording and are therefore the owners of the sound recordings and therein the copyright – usually the record company or record label. Phonogram producers ('record producers' or 'record labels') will normally own a sound recording copyright and a recording right in relation to the performers used, in the sense that they may provide finance and recording studio facilities.[6]

For example, George Martin (1926–2016) (later Sir George Martin CBE), often referred to as the 'the Fifth Beatle', was the phonogram producer of the Beatles, producing 30 number-one hit singles in the UK and 23 number-one hits in the United States.

---

6 Sections 185–188 CDPA.

The phonogram producer is usually responsible for the following:

- hire and pay sessions musicians;
- pay for studio time;
- hire and pay for the services of the recording engineer;
- hire and pay for the services of the mixing and mastering engineer(s);
- payment of mechanical royalty licence to the songwriters/publishers (the owner of the song for use of the song).

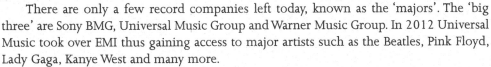

See below
10.9

Each record label or phonogram will try to secure an exclusive contract with the artist or group. For example, the Beatles recorded their albums at Abbey Road Studios exclusively with EMI. Tom Jones also used to record with EMI (*What's New Pussycat?* and *Delilah*), and then left for the Island record label (*Praise and Blame*); Decca Records have their own classical, jazz and crossover artists, like Wynton Marsalis (blues trumpet), Rolando Vilazón (tenor) and the Three Tenors: José Carreras, Plácido Domingo and Luciano Pavarotti.

There are only a few record companies left today, known as the 'majors'. The 'big three' are Sony BMG, Universal Music Group and Warner Music Group. In 2012 Universal Music took over EMI thus gaining access to major artists such as the Beatles, Pink Floyd, Lady Gaga, Kanye West and many more.

Today, digital music services (such as iTunes or Amazon) involve a combination of mechanical rights (storage of the digital musical work on a hard disk) and performing rights (the musical work is made available to the public on a website). So, a performing artist needs to obtain several licences from several entities, each holding either the performing or the mechanical rights if he or she wants to perform a 'cover' song. The mechanical licence is usually limited to one configuration, such as a physical CD or album, as opposed to a digital download, which is different again from a mobile phone ringtone. Almost all publishers require a separate licence for each use.

10.2.2 Music publishing

Music publishing generates over a quarter of the UK music industry's £2.6bn in export revenue. In 2017 music publishing in the UK contributes £505m to the UK economy. As well as safeguarding and championing the interests of its members, the British Music Publishers Association (MPA)[7] promotes the value of publishing to the wider music industry, creative industry, government and the general public.

The UK is the world's fourth-largest music publishing market, providing 10 per cent of worldwide revenues, and is second only to the United States as a source of repertoire. The MPA also owns and operates two commercial businesses:

- *Mechanical-Copyright Protection Society* – MCPS is the UK collection society that licenses mechanical (or reproduction) copyrights on behalf of over 26,000 music publisher and composer members.

---

7   The MPA is the UK's largest and most established music publishers' organization, acting for independent labels and start-ups. See: www.mpaonline.org.uk.

- *Printed Music Licensing Ltd* – PMLL represents music publishers to allow UK educational establishments and amateur societies to make copies of printed music.

The MPA offers a number of other commercial functions for music publishers, including template contracts and blanket industry licensing agreements.

That said, does an artist or performer need to register his or her work or sound recording to be protected? Not really. Though the UK Copyright Acts of 1911, 1956 and 1988 generally safeguarded the artist's rights in the UK, international law does not grant automatic copyright to the author in another country, such as America. The minimum protection guaranteed by the Rome Convention 1961 to performers is to sanction performances without their consent. It is important to remember that the performer of the song has rights as well as the writer of the song (note: a performer's rights ought not to be confused with the performance right in copyright law).

Under the Rome Convention, record producers ('producers of phonograms') have the right to authorize or prohibit the direct or indirect reproduction of their recordings ('phonograms'). The Convention also provides for the payment of equitable remuneration for broadcasting and communication to the public of phonograms.[8]

Copyright protection today is formality-free in countries party to the Berne Convention, which means that protection does not depend on compliance with any formalities such as registration or deposit of copies. It exists immediately once it is created. However, the various performance rights and collecting agencies and the Musicians' Union (MU) tend to differ.

See below
10.8

10.2.3 Sound recordings

Sound recordings and film soundtracks are covered by sections 5A and 5B CDPA.[9] Chapter II CDPA deals with rights conferred on performers and persons having recording rights. The copyright in a sound recording now runs for 70 years from the year of recording, or 70 years from date of release if released in that time.[10]

> **Every record track has two rights:**
>
> 1 a copyright in the individual musical and lyrical composition; and
> 2 a separate copyright in the total sound recording.

Live performances are often recorded or transmitted and may be sold for a profit, for example a live recording of a comedy act or classical performance. It is then perfectly acceptable to make your own recording of your own performance of, say, Mozart's Piano Concerto No 21 (because the composer has been dead for more than 70 years). Provided you performed and recorded the work yourself, then no infringement would have occurred.

---

8 Article 10 Rome Convention.
9 Substituted by reg. 9(1) (with Pt III) The Duration of Copyright and Rights in Performances Regulations 1995.
10 For further discussion see: Yeoh, F. (2015), pp. 119–129.

The reproduction of the recorded materials began on vinyl and, later, on CDs. Authors, performers and producers are each given 'performers' rights' for their creative works (related rights).

The record label, by way of licence, will then be able to control the exploitation of the works. Indirect copyright holders comprise the music publishers, who are not directly involved in the creative process of the works. Their task is to support the authors and ensure that the musical works and scores are exploited by making sure that the repertoires are provided to the public and that the rights holders are granted their copyright; this includes all productions such as musicals or operettas performed by amateur societies.

Though American singer Taylor Swift announced in August 2019 that she was going to rerecord all six albums with her first record label Big Machine it is doubtful whether the label which owns the copright in the master recordings would agree.

10.2.4 Derivative works

A derivative work is a work that is based on (or 'derived from') another work; for example a painting based on a photograph, a collage, a musical work based on an existing piece or samples, or a screenplay based on a book. Sound recordings of, for instance, films, are known as 'derivative works', that is they derive from works which themselves are copyrighted (film soundtracks). Generally, one needs the permission of the copyright owner before making a derivative work. If copyright has expired (i.e. under present legislation this means the author died over 70 years ago), the work will be in the public domain and may be used as a basis for a derivative work without permission.

A higher standard is applied by the courts where derivative works are concerned, particularly in the digital age of so-called recreative works. These are works that have been derived from, and which purport to be perfectly accurate copies of, antecedent works that were created at an earlier point in history. They can comprise, for example, ancient religious scholarly works, old compositions or music scores and paintings. The recreative author engages in reproducing the work, and it is this process which may or may not be defined as 'copying'. This will depend on what raw materials he has to copy from, what sources of information are available to him to help him accurately identify all the expressive contents of the antecedent work that need to be faithfully reproduced and what tools and resources are at his disposal to facilitate the execution of his recreative enterprise.

In what form that copying takes place will vary significantly in each case. Recreative derivative works are then identical to the antecedent works from which they were copied. The test for breach of copyright will depend on whether there is a material difference between the original works and the derivative work.[11] Legally, only the copyright owner has the right to authorize adaptations and reproductions of their work – this includes the making of a derivative work. The copyright owner is generally the creator of the original work, or it may be someone the creator has given copyright to (e.g. next of kin).

The Court of Appeal's judgment in the *Dr Sawkins* case[12] caused disquiet in the recording industry. The case centred on musical scholar, Dr Lionel Sawkins, the world's

---

11 For further discussion see: Pila, J. (2010).
12 *Sawkins v Hyperion Records* [2005] EWCA Civ 565 (CA Civ Div).

leading authority on Lalande's musical works,[13] and Hyperion Records, an independent classical label. The copyright battle focussed on an acclaimed recording of the French baroque composer Michel-Richard de Lalande for the court of the Sun King, Louis XIV. Dr Sawkins had been commissioned by Hyperion to edit the scores. Dr Sawkins regarded his endeavour as amounting to a new musical work, entitling him to copyright and royalties.

Hyperion Records then produced a compilation CD of early French music, including recordings of performances of Lalande's compositions using the Sawkins' scores. The record label had paid Dr Sawkins a one-off ('killer') fee for providing the performing editions, but refused to pay him any subsequent royalties on the basis that an editor was not entitled to copyright in a performing edition of non-copyright music. Dr Sawkins claimed that his performance editions were original musical works with a separate copyright under section 3 CDPA.[14]

The first question before the CA was whether copyright could subsist in modern performing editions, such as those produced by Dr Sawkins. The second question concerned the meaning of 'music' in copyright terms. The problem was that the CDPA does not specifically define 'music'. Was it the sound or the scores from which music was played? Hyperion's counter-argument was that Sawkins' works were merely transcriptions of Lalande's music, and the company continued to deny Dr Sawkins any royalties because they claimed that he had not created *original* musical works within the meaning of the CDPA.

The CA held that there had been a breach of section 77 CDPA, because the Hyperion CD did not identify Dr Sawkins as the author of the performing editions. The court held that Dr Sawkins had spent hundreds of 'sweat of the brow' hours making the performing editions, which therefore satisfied the requirement of an 'original' work in the copyright sense, following the *Walter v Lane* doctrine.[15]

Mummery LJ summarized his reasons why Dr Sawkins' editions were original musical works and therefore entitled to copyright protection in their own right:

(a) Dr Sawkins originated the performing editions by his own expert and scholarly exertions.
(b) The editions did not previously exist in that form.
(c) The contents of his editions affected the combination of sounds produced by the performers.
(d) The resulting combination of sounds embodied in the CD was music.[16]

The court awarded damages to Dr Sawkins both for infringement of his copyright and for infringement of his 'moral rights' (referring to: *Ladbroke v William Hill* (1964)[17]).

---

13 Michel-Richard de Lalande (1657–1726) was the principal court composer of two French kings during the seventeenth and eighteenth centuries. Few of Lalande's original manuscripts survived.
14 Dr Sawkins completed three modern performance editions of Lalande's original works in 2001. The editions covered *Te Deum Laudamus* (1684), *La Grande Piece Royale* (1695) and *Venite Exultemus* (1701).
15 *Walter v Lane* [1900] AC 539.
16 *Sawkins* [2005] EWCA Civ 565 at para. 32 (Mummery LJ).
17 [1964] 1 WLR 273.

10.3 Joint authorship of copyright

Let us remind ourselves again of the meaning 'first owner of copyright': in the case of literary, dramatic, musical or artistic works, the author or creator of the work is usually the first owner of any copyright in it.

Until the end of the nineteenth century, the concept of 'joint copyright' (or 'authorship') only existed in common law. The Literary Copyright Act 1842 contained no concept of joint authorship, and the concept only emerged for the first time in the Copyright Act 1911. However, the 1911 Act on joint authorship reflected the law as it had previously existed under the 1842 Act. This meant that section 16(3) of the 1911 Act was effectively the same as the current section 10(1) CDPA (see also: *Beckingham v Hodgens* (2003)[18]).

In *Tate v Thomas* (1921),[19] Mr Peterman commissioned the claimant to write the music of a play, and it was agreed that two others should write the libretto. This was done. Peterman devised the name of the play and the leading characters; he arranged the scenic effects and supplied certain catch lines in the dialogue. He claimed all this entitled him to be a joint author in copyright. Eve J held that the scenic effects were not in themselves subject to copyright protection under the Copyright Act 1911, and therefore to be disregarded, and his other contributions were too insignificant to make him a joint author.

Wiseman v George Weidenfeld & Nicholson Ltd (1985)[20] concerned a play called *The English Way of Doing Things*, written by the second defendant, William Donaldson, who based it on his novel of the same name. Donaldson was an established novelist but had never written a play. The idea for transforming the novel into a play came from the claimant, Wiseman, an aspiring stage producer, who provided Donaldson with advice and criticism during the writing of the play and who claimed to be a joint author. Whitford J found as a fact that Wiseman had written no part of the play. The judge went on to consider whether the contribution Wiseman had qualified him as a joint author. It did not.

Where two or more people have created a *single* work protected by copyright and the contribution of each author is not distinct from that of the other(s), those people may be considered joint owners. There are slightly different rules for what are referred to as 'co-written works' (see below).

Joint ownership might arise, for example, if a person was commissioned to create a website together with one of the company's employees. It is likely that both the person being commissioned and the company would be joint first owners of copyright in the website. If someone wanted to copy or use a work of joint ownership in some way, all of the owners would have to agree to such a request, otherwise an infringement of copyright could still occur.

On the other hand, where individual contributions are distinct or separate, each person would be the author of the part they created (for instance where the music and lyrics of a song are created by two different people). In these circumstances, if you wished to use just the lyrics you would only need the permission of the copyright owner of the lyrics.

---

18 [2003] EWCA Civ 143.
19 [1921] 1 Ch 503.
20 [1985] FSR 525.

Today statute and common law are quite clear on the meaning of 'collaboration': where two or more people *collaborate* in creating a work and their individual contributions are not distinct, they are 'joint authors' of that work (or joint owners of copyright). However, where two or more persons collaborate but it is possible to determine the separate parts attributable to each author, it will not be a work of joint authorship.

The test for joint authorship falls under section 10(1) CDPA which states:

In this Part a 'work of joint authorship' means a work produced by the collaboration of two or more authors in which the contribution of each author is not distinct from that of the other author or authors.

1A)   A film shall be treated as a work of joint authorship unless the producer and the principal director are the same person.

2)   A broadcast shall be treated as a work of joint authorship in any case where more than one person is to be taken as making the broadcast.

This means, there must be *collaboration* between two or more authors; the contribution of each author *must not be distinct* from that of the other author/authors, and the contribution must be *sufficient* for an individual to qualify as a joint author, given that the author must still be an author within the meaning of section 9(1) CDPA and therefore have contributed a significant part of the skill and labour protected by copyright.

Where the music and the lyrics in a musical work with words are written specifically for each other by different people (a co-written song from a musical, for example), the term of copyright will last until 70 years following the death of the last surviving composer or lyricist. The music and lyrics will still be separate copyright works but will have the same length of protection.

Ownership of copyright can be transferred, so where something is produced that has involved contributions from more than one person, it would be possible for copyright in all the material to be owned by a single person as a result of appropriate transfers. Indeed, collaborators can agree in advance that copyright in what is to be produced should be owned by a single person or body. This could be helpful when permission needs to be given in the future. However, alternative solutions that might be equally helpful could involve all parties agreeing licensing arrangements in advance.

See below 10.6

10.3.1 When does a contribution amount to joint copyright?

In *Ray v Classic FM* (1998),[21] Robin Ray (1934–1998) brought an action against the radio station Classic FM, alleging infringement of his copyright in the playlists which he had created between 1991 and 1997. He had undertaken the mammoth task of drawing up a list of 50,000 pieces of classical music and rating them for popular appeal, which became the basis for the Classic FM playlist. Classic FM claimed joint authorship of these works on the basis that Mr Ray had simply put into writing ideas initiated by the radio station's representatives at a series of meetings concerning the contents of the catalogue and its categories.

---

21 [1998] ECC 488 (Ch D).

The Chancery Division upheld Mr Ray's claim, not granting joint authorship to Classic FM. The court ruled that, in order to be a joint author for the purposes of section 10 CDPA, a *significant creative contribution* as an author had to be made to the production of the work which was not distinct from that of the other author with whom there was a collaboration. The contribution had to be something which was incorporated into the finished work and protected by copyright. The court observed that Mr Ray was solely responsible for five documents, i.e. the catalogue, playlists and ideas contained in these, and duly awarded Robin Ray the sole copyright in these works.

In the *Spandau Ballet* case,[22] the court ruled that to be a joint owner of copyright the parties must have substantially contributed to the song's creation, not just to its interpretation. As per Park J:

> There is a vital distinction between composition or creation of a musical work on the one hand and performance or interpretation of it on the other.[23]

So, if a drummer just adds a short drum loop, this would not make any material difference to the song and would not justify the claim that the song was co-written, attracting joint copyright under section 10 CDPA. However, one could argue that the performable arrangement produced by a group would constitute a separate copyright for the new arrangement.

In the landmark case of *Fisher v Brooker* (2009),[24] Matthew Fisher managed to assert joint ownership of copyright (retrospectively) in the famous song 'A Whiter Shade of Pale' (1967)[25]. The song achieved sales in the millions and is still regarded as one of the greatest songs ever written. Fisher had been the Hammond organist of the pop group Procol Harum. The claimant, Fisher, had composed the familiar organ solo at the beginning of the song and had left the band in 1969. Crucial in this case was that Mr Fisher made his claim some 40 years after the song's release.

 KEY CASE   *Fisher v Brooker* [2009] UKHL 41 (HL)

Precedent

- A claimant cannot be denied the opportunity of exercising his right of intellectual property even after an extensive time period has passed (here nearly 40 years).
- A claimant of copyright cannot be estopped from asserting his copyright interest on equitable grounds, to declare that the right existed (under the equitable doctrine of proprietary estoppel).

22 *Hadley v Kemp* [1999] EMLR 589 (the Spandau Ballet case).
23 Ibid. at para. 589 (Park J).
24 [2009] UKHL 41 (HL).
25 'A Whiter Shade of Pale' can be heard here: https://www.youtube.com/watch?v=Mb3iPP-tHdA

Facts

On 7 March 1967, the original band members of Procol Harum, namely Gary Brooker, Bobby Harrison, Ray Royer and Dave Knight, entered into a recording contract with Essex Music Ltd. Shortly after, Matthew Fisher ('the claimant') joined the band as Hammond organist. 'A Whiter Shade of Pale' ('the song') became an instant worldwide hit after the recording was released as a single by the Decca label on 12 May 1967. Around 1993, Essex's recording rights were assigned to Onward Music Ltd, who were registered with PRS-MCPS as owner of the copyright in the song. There were 770 versions of the song performed by other groups, and the introductory bars were used commonly as mobile phone ring tones.

During April 2005, the claimant, Mr Fisher (then aged 61 and working as a computer programmer in Croydon) launched his claim against the lead singer of Procol Harum, Gary Brooker, and Essex and Onward Music. The main claim was that Mr Fisher wanted a share of the musical copyright in the song. After his claim was rejected, Mr Fisher began legal proceedings on 31 May 2005. At the High Court, the respondents argued that the claimant was far too late – nearly 40 years – in claiming the copyright for joint authorship in the song. They asked the court for laches and to strike out the claim under the doctrine of estoppel.[26]

The judge held that the claimant was entitled to declarations (1) that he was a joint author of the work, (2) that he was a joint owner of the copyright to the extent of 40 per cent, and (3) that the defendants' implied licence had been revoked from the date of issue of proceedings. After a number of cross-appeals, the case reached the House of Lords in 2009.

Decision

The HL declared that Matthew Fisher was joint owner and author of copyright under section 10 CDPA. The reasons being that, 'Mr Fisher's instrumental introduction – the organ solo – is sufficiently different from what Mr Brooker had composed on the piano to qualify in law, and by quite a wide margin, as an original contribution to the work'.[27]

Their Lordships held that it did not matter that the claimant had not asserted his joint authorship for such a long time. His claim was still valid even after 40 years, and they awarded Mr Fisher a 40 per cent share in royalties, backdated to the date of his original claim in 2005. Baroness Hale (one of five Law Lords) commented: 'As one of those people who do remember the Sixties, I am glad that the author of that memorable organ part has at last achieved the recognition he deserves'.

Analysis

It might strike us as extraordinary that Matthew Fisher had waited some 38 years before he brought his joint authorship action, fully in the knowledge,

---

26 Fisher v Brooker and another [2006] EWHC 3239 (Ch).
27 Ibid. at 42.

and without reasonable excuse, that the other band members of Procol Harum, in particular Gary Brooker, had exploited the work for so many years.

Fisher v Brooker set the precedent for any future claims of this kind where an artist wishes to assert his (joint authorship) rights in a song or recording during his lifetime, even if the claim is more than 40 years old. The court ruling meant that Matthew Fisher (and his heirs) could receive royalties in 'A Whiter Shade of Pale' for years to come. For the various royalty collecting societies, such as the PRS and the MCPS, it meant that they had to amend their records and backdate the royalties payable to Mr Fisher to the start of his legal action.

Where more than one person has created a work, the work may be classed as a work of joint authorship if the contribution of each author is not distinct from that of the other authors.[28] If it is distinct, two or more separate works will exist. In general, each joint author has the same rights as a sole author. However, one joint author may sue any of his other joint authors who does any of the acts restricted by copyright (including reproduction) without his consent.[29]

The HL ruling in *Fisher v Brooker* (confirming the decision by the High Court Chancery Div) has meant an ongoing music copyright headache for major artists, musicians and their lawyers, who will have all lined up for similar claims for their contributions to successful songs following the HL ruling – sometimes decades after the band split up.

In the *Florence Foster Jenkins* film case (2017) ('Florence'),[30] Julia Kogan was unsuccessful in claiming joint authorship of the copyright in a screenplay for the film, starring Meryl Streep and Hugh Grant, premiered on 12 April 2016 in London. The film is based on the latter part of the life of Florence Foster Jenkins, a New York heiress and socialite who died in 1944. Florence became famous for her striking soprano voice. The comedy drama was directed by Stephen Frears.

The film's credits identified the first Claimant, Nicholas Martin, as the sole author of the screenplay; however Ms Kogan had claimed joint copyright since April 2014 and had sought a proportion of royalties from Mr Martin's income from the film. Mr Martin and Ms Kogan had lived together as partners during the period in which the idea of a film based on *Florence* arose and when early drafts of the screenplay were written. Mr Martin is a professional writer of film and television scripts. Ms Kogan is principally a professional opera singer.

Just like we have seen the principles developed by the court in *Fisher v Brooker*, *Florence* established the principles of joint authorship in a film. In assessing the contribution of the supposed joint author in the film, the judge introduced a consideration of whether the contribution was due to 'primary' or 'secondary' skills, some skills being more likely to give rise to a claim for joint authorship than other skills. Mr Martin sought a declaration that he was the *sole* author of the screenplay. Ms Kogan disagreed and filed a counterclaim

---

28 s 10(1) CDPA.
29 s 173(2) CDPA.
30 *Nicholas Martin, Big Hat Stories Ltd. v Julia Kogan and (1) Florence Film Ltd. (2) Pathé Productions Ltd (3) Qwerty Films Ltd.* [2017] EWHC 2927 (IPEC).

for a declaration that she had joint authorship, and also joined the production and financing companies for the film in her lawsuit.

The court considered section 10 CDPA, where it must be established that collaboration and a 'common design' must take place at the time of the screenplay's creation, i.e. the parties must work on the script together. The court found that the final draft of the screenplay was written *after* Mr Martin and Ms Kogan had split up. Mr Justice Hacon rejected Ms Kogan's submissions that her consent to the use of her material in the early drafts of the final screenplay was sufficient to establish her as a collaborator.[31]

Citing the precedent set in *Levy v Rutley* (1871),[32] the judge in the *Florence* case stated that the concept of 'collaboration' established in this old case was still good law, reflected in section 10(1) CDPA. *Levy* concerned a claim of joint authorship in a play, titled *The King's Wager, or The Camp, the Cottage and the Court.*

Whilst consent is necessary for collaboration, it is not sufficient: there must be *common design* which there could not have been given that she was not present for the screenplay's creation.[33] Hacon J set out the guiding principles from UK case law and harmonized EU copyright law under the *Infopaq* test:[34] to be protected by copyright, a work must be *original* being an expression of the author's own intellectual creation, which constitutes a 'substantial part'.[35]

As we have previously established: an idea can never be copyrighted nor establish joint authorship: the collaborator must constitute an author, and there must be common design and a shared responsibility regarding the necessary decisions as to the work (as per the *Robin Ray* case – see above). See Chapter 9.8.4

To summarise the law on joint authorship of copyright:

1   A party will be joint owner of the copyright in a work only if they (or in the case of a company, its employees) *collaborated* in the creation of the work. The collaboration must be by way of a *common design*, i.e. co-operative acts by the authors, at the time the copyright work in issue was created, which led to its creation.

2   The contribution of each author must *not* be distinct from that of the other author or authors. Contributions by an alleged joint author which formed no part of the creation of the work are to be disregarded in the assessment of joint authorship.

3   No distinction is to be drawn between types of contribution that did form part of the creation of the work. In particular, there is no distinction which depends on the kind of skill involved in making the contribution.

4   The contribution, assuming it is relevant to the assessment of joint authorship, must be sufficient. This depends on whether the contribution constitutes a *substantial part* of the whole of the work in issue.

5   If the contribution alone were copied by an unlicensed third party and such copying would result in an infringement of the copyright, the contribution constitutes a substantial part of the whole.

---

31 For further discussion see: Goodbody, S. (2018) at pp. 77–82.
32 (1871) L.R. 6 C.P.
33 *Florence* [2017] EWHC 2927 at paras 21–25.
34 *Infopaq International A/S v Danske Dagblades Forening* (C-5/08) [2009] ECR I-6569 (ECJ (4th Chamber)).
35 *Florence* [2017] EWHC 2927 at para. 38 (Hacon J).

6   The test of *substantiality* in the context of joint authorship of copyright, as in the context of infringement, involves a qualitative as well as quantitative assessment.

7   Suggestions from an alleged joint author as to how the main author should exercise their skill – for instance by way of criticism or editing of a literary work or song – will not lead to joint authorship where the main author has the final decision as to the form and content of the work.

8   If joint authorship is established, the court may apportion ownership of the copyright.

See below
10.6

If a work is a joint venture, then it may be difficult to establish exactly who owns what. It is then useful from the start to clarify by way of contract or licence agreement who is contributing what to a work. This will avoid unnecessary disputes and animosity later.

10.4 Performers' rights

At the start of the creative process there is the person who is responsible for writing the music: the composer of the music and the lyricist of musical works (remember that there are two separate copyrights here – musical in the notes and literary in the words). Copyright law recognizes them as the 'authors'.

While separate copyright subsists in the recording of the performer, the performance itself is also IP protected. The performance then gives rise to performers' rights which – in turn – are covered by the term 'dramatic performances', which include dance and mime, musical performances, readings and recitations of literary works and variety acts. Circus acts can also be included as well as certain sporting events, such as ice dancing.

10.4.1 Classifications of performers

Traditionally there are a number of categories of 'performers' involved in the process of music composition and exploitation. Some are direct copyright holders, others indirect. The sound recording owner is usually the record company which released the original recording (or 'single') for a public performance and airplay. In recordings, the phonogram producers ('record producers' or 'record labels') finance the performance and will normally own a sound recording copyright and a recording right in relation to the performers used, in the sense that they may provide finance and recording studio facilities.[36]

Does an artist or performer need to register his work or sound recording to be protected? Not really. Copyright protection is formality-free in countries party to the Berne Convention, which means that protection does not depend on compliance with any formalities such as registration or deposit of copies. It exists immediately once it is created. The minimum protection guaranteed by the Rome Convention 1961 to performers is to sanction performances without their consent.[37] It is important to remember that the performer of the song has rights as well as the writer of the song (note: a performer's rights ought not to be confused with the performance right in copyright law).

---

36 ss 185–188 CDPA.
37 Article 10 Rome Convention.

This expression was used in order to allow IFPI[38] countries like the UK to continue to protect performers by virtue of penal statutes, determining offences and penal sanctions under public law, such as the Copyright Acts of 1911 and 1956. Under the Rome Convention, record producers ('producers of phonograms') have the right to authorize or prohibit the direct or indirect reproduction of their recordings ('phonograms'). The Convention also provides for the payment of equitable remuneration for broadcasting and communication to the public of phonograms.

A copyright owner or performer's rights are infringed by a person who, without his consent:

- makes a copy or recording of the whole or any substantial part of a qualifying work or performance (directly from the live performance);
- broadcasts live the whole or any substantial part of a qualifying performance; or
- makes a copy or recording of the whole or any substantial part of a qualifying work or performance (e.g. directly from a broadcast of the live performance).[39]

10.4.2 Extended duration of performers' rights

The Copyright and Duration of Rights in Performances Regulations 2013 implemented the EU Copyright Term Directive[40] into UK law. Sir Paul McCartney and Sir Cliff Richard (and several other famous artists) had lobbied the EU Commission since April 2006 to extend copyright law in sound recordings since most of their performance rights were approaching the 50-year limit which meant any label could 'grab' their past musical performances and reissue these 'royalty free'. Many of the most popular songs recorded in the 1960s were due to come out of copyright, including popular songs by Tom Jones, the Beatles, the Rolling Stones and many other bands and recording artists from the 1960s.

With the new extended duration in performance copyright their hit singles would now not expire until at least 2033, since the Regulation extended music performers' and sound recordings' rights to 70 years. The implementation of the Europe-wide legislation (known as 'Cliff's law') meant that thousands of music performers, from little-known session musicians to Dame Shirley Bassey, would now receive royalties from songs released in the 1960s for an extra 20 years. Session musicians originally involved in the acts would also benefit from the change in legislation.

10.5 Music piracy: bootlegging, sampling and parody

EU (harmonized) copyright law takes account of various rights and interests which could conflict with the exclusive rights of authors and other right holders, in particular the

---

38 The International Federation of the Phonographic Industry (IFPI) represents the interests of the recording industry worldwide. It is a not-for-profit organization registered in Switzerland, with a secretariat in London and regional offices in Brussels, Hong Kong and Miami at: http://ifpi.org.
39 ss 183, 184, 187, 188 CDPA.
40 Directive 2011/77/EU of the European Parliament and of the Council of 27 September 2011 amending Directive 2006/116/EC on the term of protection of copyright and certain related rights ('the EU Copyright Term Directive').

See Chapter
9.6.6.

freedom of the arts. Exceptions to the exclusive rights such as the quotation, and caricature, parody and pastiche exceptions facilitate dialogue and artistic confrontation through references to pre-existing works. Within the framework of the current rules, that confrontation may occur, in particular, in the following three ways. First, by the creation of works which, while drawing on pre-existing works, do not directly reproduce protected elements; second, in the context of existing limitations and exceptions to exclusive rights and finally, third, by obtaining the necessary authorization (see: *Deckmyn v Vandersteen* (2013)[41]).

Running a record label today is not easy, and there are only a few large labels that have survived. Gone are the days when record executives ruled the musical world, serving as the chief gatekeepers of what music would ever see the light of day. Thirty years ago, the record industry was dominated by the Big Six: Warner Music, CBS, MCA, BMG, Capitol-EMI and PolyGram. A series of mergers and acquisitions in 2016 reduced that to the 'Big Three' (all British labels) – Sony, Universal and Warner – accounting for three-quarters of the global recorded music market.

Revenue reached an all-time high in 1999, the year that 18-year-old college dropout Shawn Fanning launched Napster, the file-sharing software that taught a generation that music could – and even should – be free. Through a combination of technological inevitability and terrible decisions, CD sales halved between 2000 and 2008, and digital stores such as iTunes could not plug the gap because they unbundled songs from albums. Between 1999 and 2014, the industry lost almost 40 per cent of its revenue, even without adjusting for inflation. Due to ever declining physical CD sales, meagre revenue from streaming, changing technologies, illegal downloads and artists going completely independent by releasing their records free of charge on YouTube – the recording business today is a tough and competitive one. Still, some labels continue talent-spotting, thereby discovering and developing great new artists each year.

Record labels enable artists, through advances in royalties, sales and marketing support, to be able to have a musical career. If one purchases sheet music of, for instance, Elton John's 'Song for Guy', this gives the right to use each single copy purchased, but it does not grant the right to photocopy additional copies, nor to perform the work in a live public performance, nor to record the work, nor to broadcast a recording or live performance. The process is covered by mechanical copyright protection and licensing, whereby the cost of the sheet music is expected to cover approximately half of the total licensing expenses required to put on a public performance.

10.5.1 What is music piracy?

The commonly used term 'piracy' describes the deliberate infringement of copyright on a commercial scale, including activities that cause economic harm. In relation to the music industry it refers to unauthorized copying. Piracy falls into four categories, namely:

- physical piracy;
- counterfeits;
- bootlegs;
- internet piracy.

---

41 (C 201/13) EU:C:2014:2132 (CJEU).

Physical music piracy is the making or distribution of copies of sound recordings on physical carriers without the permission of the rights owner whereby the packaging of pirate copies may or may not be different from the original. Pirate copies are often compilations, such as the 'Greatest Hits' or 'Best of' a specific artist or group, or a compilation of a specific genre, such as '400 Best Running Songs' or '40 Best R & B songs'; this extends to music videos, films and games.[42]

Music piracy platforms became increasingly popular and difficult to control from the year 2000 onwards. Napster was the first online song-swapping peer-to-peer (P2P) file-share service, based in the United States, attracting more than 60 million users in July 2000. Created by Shawn Fanning in 1999 while studying at Northeastern University in Boston, the service was named after Fanning's unusual hairstyle. Napster's technology allowed people to share their MP3 music files with other internet users, thereby bypassing the commercial music licensing market and avoiding buying physical CDs.

In 2000, Napster was accused of violating US copyright law, the Digital Millennium Copyright Act of 1998 (DMCA). The lawsuit was filed jointly by the Recording Industry Association of America (RIAA), AOL, Time Warner, Bertelsmann, EMI, Vivendi Universal and Sony. Heavy metal band Metallica and rap artist Dr Dre sued in separate legal actions, demanding, *inter alia*, that some 60,000 pages be removed from Napster containing the artists' names. In May 2000, San Francisco Judge, Marilyn Hall Patel, ruled that Napster was guilty of online copyright infringement and trading copyrighted music without permission. Napster was not entitled to claim protection under the DMCA, because the company did not transmit, route or provide connections for infringing material through its system. Napster was ordered to pay damages, and the service was shut down.[43]

While appealing against the court's decision, Napster's chief executive, Konrad Hilbers, tried to reach an amicable settlement with the companies concerned, by suggesting various licensing agreements. This resulted in Napster's brand and logo being registered as trade marks in January 2002. Napster then launched a legal file-swapping service as a free beta test version to a selected 20,000 users with more than 100,000 music files on a subscription basis. Shawn Fanning assured the courts that 98 per cent of the code behind the program had been rewritten, adding a music player, chat rooms and instant messaging to the service.[44] There is no doubt that Napster paved the way for decentralized P2P file-sharing and distribution programs.

The next P2P copyright case was that of The Pirate Bay. On 17 April 2009, the Stockholm district court (Tingsrätt) found the four men behind TPB guilty of internet piracy, i.e. facilitating illegal downloads of copyrighted material.[45] After a 13-day trial, judge Tomas Norström and three namndeman (a jury with extended powers) found Peter Sunde, Gottfrid Svartholm Warg, Fredrik Neij and Carl Lundström guilty of 'assisting in making copyright content available', that is, having made 33 copyright-protected files

---

42 For further discussion see: Parsons, K. (2000).
43 The movie documentary *Downloaded* (2013) tells the story of Napster.
44 The new service offered standard MP3 music files and 'nap' files, which are MP3s with the addition of a protective layer that prevented them being copied off the host computer or burned onto CDs. There was also a 'buy' button, linking the service to the music retail site CDNow, owned by Bertelsmann.
45 Source: Internationella åklagarkammaren Stockholm, 31 January 2008 (Swedish Criminal Court).

accessible for illegal file-sharing via the TPB website. The Pirate Bay's founders and owners were imprisoned for one year.[46]

Resulting from a parallel civil legal action, the four TPB defendants were fined SEK 30m (€2.7m or £3m) in damages to copyright holders for lost sales, including 17 media and record companies such as Warners, MGM Pictures, Columbia Pictures, Twentieth Century Fox Film, Sony BMG, Universal and EMI. The Pirate Bay website was shut down by a court order. The TPB appellants demanded a retrial on the grounds that the Stockholm Tingsrätt judge had been biased in that he was a member of several copyright protection agencies in Sweden, but their appeal was dismissed by the Swedish Court of Appeal.

By March 2013, The Pirate Bay had regrouped and set up 'shop' in North Korea. To coincide with celebrations of its tenth anniversary, TBP released the 'PirateBrowser', a bundle of Firefox add-ons that helped users 'dodge' ISP filters.[47] The Pirate Bay is still accessible on the Tor network, as traffic goes through a separate server to the regular version.

See below
10.6

Google and Apple Music then jumped on the music-streaming bandwagon and launched their own streaming services to compete with Spotify and Deezer. Amazon Music too has a music streaming platform and online music store; it became the first music store to sell music without digital rights management from the four major music labels, as well as many independents. All the music on these streaming services has been licensed from and delivered by labels or other rights holders. If an artist asks the server how their music ended up on iTunes or Soundcloud, it often turns out that the artist's music has been licensed and delivered by their label or aggregator without the artist knowing about this. Streaming services are either advertisement-supported or subscription based.

So, are music-streaming services legal? Seemingly so, though songwriter and producer Pete Waterman remarked in 2010 that streamed music services online were 'scandalous', stating that 'these streaming business models are a disgrace, they devalue our artists, they damage this country economically, culturally and morally'.[48]

There is no doubt that music streaming services offer great convenience to fans. But artists are getting a raw deal. The average listening to streaming services amounts to around 32 hours per week (and rising). Spotify pays its artists about $0.006 to $0.0084 per stream to the holder of music rights. And the 'holder' can be split among the record label, producers, artists, and songwriters. For example, Taylor Swift, one of the world's leading pop stars, earned between $280,000 and $390,000 for her song 'Shake It Off' in 2017, resulting from 46.3 million streams. Most musicians will not generate that many streams in their lifetime, and therefore their royalties are small. One million plays on Spotify translates to around $7,000, and one million plays on Pandora generates $1,650. Taylor Swift and other well-known artists have long campaigned that music streaming services such as Spotify and Apple Music should raise rates considerably, so that artists can make more money from their IP.[49]

---

46 Source: 'Artist hoppar av Pirate bay-åtalet', Svenska Dagbladet, publicerad Tobias Brandel, 17 April 2009.
47 PirateBrowser also supplies an index of bookmarked torrent sites including Kickass Torrents, Bitsnoop and H33T.
48 Source: 'A bum note for rock 'n' roll', by Justin Stoneman, *Sunday Times*, Culture Supplement, 3 January 2010, p. 27.
49 For further discussion see: Passman, D.S. (2019).

10.5.2 Bootlegs

Bootlegs are unauthorized audio or video recordings of live performances, not officially released by the artist. The process of making and distributing such recordings is known as bootlegging. The first bootlegged live recording of a Bob Dylan concert, 'Live at the Albert Hall', part of his first UK tour, can be traced back to 1965, with songs including 'The Times They Are a-Changin' and 'Mr Tambourine Man'. 'Dylan Bootlegs' were then duplicated and sold without the artist's permission. A great many such recordings were then simply copied and traded among Dylan fans without any financial reward in the form of royalties to the artist.

By the early 1980s the bootleg industry in Germany and the Netherlands was thriving. Music industry experts claim that there were about 30,000 illegal Dylan bootleg recordings in Italy alone, claiming that the bootleg industry was the most serious form of piracy at that time.[50] Bob Dylan subsequently released his own official edition of a 'bootleg' series in several volumes. Volume 9 (2010), for example, features the legend's studio recordings from 1962 to 1964, also known as the 'Witmark' and 'Leeds' demos in mono format, never previously released on CD; just one way to extend copyright in his recordings and thereby increase royalties (see also: the *Bob Dylan* case).[51]

It could, however, be argued that in some cases bootlegging serves a useful cultural service. Some of the early recordings of the great opera singer Maria Callas, for example, in her live performances at La Scala Opera House in Milan only exist – and are now sold 'officially' by record companies – because of the illicit activities of members of the audience and technicians. Today, some bootlegged records are sold as rarities for profit, sometimes by adding professional-quality sound engineering and packaging to the raw material.[52]

 FOR THOUGHT

> Many people at festivals (e.g. Glastonbury or Isle of Wight) make amateur video recordings of events at the festival, such as impromptu performances of an 'unknown' artist's original songs that do not take place on one of the main stages. If you make bootleg recordings and subsequently compile them for sale on YouTube, who has copyright in which aspects of the performance and the recording?

10.5.3 Sampling: the *Kraftwerk case*

Sampling ('sample of a phonogram') is a technique consisting in taking, by means of electronic equipment or digital means, extracts from a phonogram in order to use those elements for a new composition in another phonogram. Although the concept of composers reusing motifs from earlier works is probably as old as music itself, sampling is

---

50 Heylin, C. (1994).

51 *Sony Music Entertainment (Germany) GmbH v Falcon Neue Medien Vertrieb GmbH* (C-240/07) [2009] ECDR 12.

52 Hildebrand, L. (2009).

a new phenomenon made possible by modern recording and sound modification techniques, at first analogue, but now digital. Unlike the use of a fragment of another musical work in the composition of a new work, the idea behind sampling is to take the sounds fixed in the phonogram, that is to say the work performed and recorded, directly in order to incorporate them into the phonogram that contains the new work. Consequently, sampling is a phenomenon specific to the reality of music recorded in the form of phonograms. In other words, copying fragments from the score of a musical work to be incorporated into the score of a new work and subsequently performing that score does not constitute sampling.

Sampling is therefore a multifaceted phenomenon, thus making its legal characterization difficult. Sampling is different from 'covering' (or 'covers'), where typically one artist sings the song of another artist (the Beatles were covered 3,376 times).

The technique of sampling dates back to the 1970s, when a Jamaican-born DJ in the Bronx, named Kool DJ Herc, began playing the 'break' in a rock, soul, funk or even Latin song over and over by switching between records, while MCs would 'rap' over the beat they created. Rap and hip hop music is rooted in the practice of disc jockeys ('DJs') who splice, manipulate and mix sounds from music tracks recorded on vinyl. That practice has resulted in genuine compositions derived therefrom. Accordingly, sampling forms the basis of those musical genres. Some works may even consist only of a mix of samples.[53]

From rap's inception to the present day, many rap beats contain parts of recognizable songs, such as Run DMC's 1986 hit, 'Walk This Way', which borrows a guitar riff, drum beat and chorus from rock band Aerosmith. Although sampling can be used in any musical genre, it is particularly important in rap and hip hop music.[54]

With the release of De La Soul's debut album, 3 Feet High and Risin, in March 1989, hip hop sampling changed considerably. At a time when samples of James Brown and various other breakbeat staples ruled supreme, De La Soul and long-time production partner Prince Paul cast the net far wider, sampling snippets of vintage soul, rock'n roll, disco, spoken word albums and children's records to create a collage the likes of which had not been heard before and would not be heard again until the release of Beastie Boys' similarly eclectic Paul's Boutique several months later. Today, The Prodigy repeatedly hits the top sampling spot; most sampled overall remain James Brown (6,519 times) and Public Enemy (2,507 times), and Michael Jackson's songs have been sampled 1,629 times and covered 867 times with 291 remixes.[55]

Sampling artists are at the mercy of large record labels, music publishers and collecting societies and lawsuits abound, particularly in the UK and the United States, because a sample infringes copyright. Firstly, on the underlying composition, secondly, on the sound recording copyrights of the original song. In addition to breach of copyright, sampling may also fall foul of the composer's moral rights if it distorts his work in the sample.[56]

Sampling has become a genuine legal issue, especially since hip hop left the streets of the Bronx to enter the mainstream and became a significant source of revenue for

---

53 For further discussion see: Evans, T.M. (2011) at p. 843.
54 Sanjek, D. (1992).
55 Who Sampled Whom: www.whosampled.com/.
56 ss 79–82 CDPA.

its authors, performers and producers (see: *Grand Upright Music Ltd v Warner Bros. Records Inc.* (1991)[57]).

The difficulty in the legal assessment of that phenomenon lies in the fact that it is not a question of the classic relationship between works under copyright law, but between phonogram, a commercial product, and work, an artistic creation. By sampling, the artist not only draws inspiration from the creations of others, but also appropriates the results of that effort and editorial investment in the form of the phonogram. That set-up, which is new in copyright law, concerns issues such as the related rights of producers of phonograms, on the one hand, and the creative freedom of samplers, on the other.

Ideally, what the sampler should do is either ask the original artist for permission to use extracts of the song and/or the lyrics or obtain a licence from the collection societies or the record labels (see Chapter 10.8). If this is not done, sampling in phonograms may involve the risk of legal action as the Kraftwerk case demonstrates (see below). There may be the defence of 'fair use' of the original depending how recognizable the sample is in the new song or recording. Alternatively, the defendant MC or DJ could claim that the sampling was done in parody, which also amounts to 'fair use' (see: *Twentieth Century Music Corp. v Aiken* (1975)[58]). The CJEU ruled in Kraftwerk's favour in July 2019.[59]

See below
10.8

German techno-pop group Kraftwerk brought an action against hip-hop producers Moses Pelham and Martin Haas which began over a decade ago at the Landgericht Hamburg (federal city court) in 1999 over the Sabrina Setlur song 'Nur Mir' ('Only Me'). The *Kraftwerk case* (2019) (*Pelham v Hütter*) comprises a lengthy legal saga initially at German domestic level where two of the highest German courts gave two differing and confusing rulings, followed by a lengthy opinion at EU level by Advocate General Szpunar, resulting in the final preliminary ruling by the Grand Chamber of the CJEU in July 2019 where Kraftwerk's Ralf Hütter, Florian Schneider-Esleben eventually won thweir case on a narrow ruling. The request for a preliminary ruling by the German Federal Court (*Bundesgerichtshof - BGH*) from the CJEU in the *Kraftwerk case* brought the complex legal issue of sampling without authorization to the forefront of the music copyright debate.

The CJEU ruled in July 2019 that sampling without authorization *can* infringe a phonogram producer's rights. However, the use of a sound sample taken from a phonogram in a modified form *unrecognizable* to the ear does *not* infringe those rights, even without such authorization. The Advocate General's opinion of 12 December 2018 contributed to the debate about artistic freedom in relation to copyright infringement claims.

❖ KEY CASE   *Pelham v Hütter (CJEU) (2019)*

Precedent
❖ Phonogram producers have the exclusive right to authorize or prohibit reproduction in whole or in part of their phonograms.
❖ Sampling without authorization can infringe a phonogram producer's rights.

---

57 (1991) 780 F. Supp. 182 (US District Court for the Southern District of New York). This was one of the first cases concerning sampling.
58 [1975] 422 U.S. 151.
59 Hampel, S. (1992), p. 559.

❖ However, the use of a sound sample taken from a phonogram in a modified form *unrecognizable* to the ear does not infringe those rights, even without such authorization.

Facts

In 1977, the German techno pop group *Kraftwerk* published an LP (phonogram) 'Trans Europa Express' featuring the song 'Metall auf Metall' ('Metal on Metal'). In 1997 Moses Pelham and Martin Haas composed the song 'Nur mir' ('Only mine'), which was released on phonograms recorded by Pelham GmbH performed by German Rapper Sabrina Setlur. Two founder members of Kraftwerk, Ralf Hütter and Florian Schneider-Esleben, claimed that Pelham had copied, by means of the technique known as sampling, approximately 2 seconds of a rhythm sequence from the song 'Metall auf Metall' and used that sequence in a continuous loop in the song 'Nur mir'. On the basis that their related right as the producers of the phonogram in question was infringed, Hütter and Schneider-Esleben sought, inter alia, a prohibitory injunction, damages and the surrender of the phonograms featuring the song 'Nur Mir' for the purposes of their destruction.

In the earlier actions in the German Federal Court (*Bundesgerichtshof - BGH*) (1999–2012), Hütter and Schneider-Esleben won their copyright infringement action against Pelham and Haas when the German court ruled that 'Nur Mir' should no longer be promoted, and that it was copyright infringement. The Kraftwerk duo were awarded damages and were granted an injunction against 'Nur mir'. Pelham and Haas appealed and in May 2016 eight federal constitutional judges of the First Senate of the German Constitutional Court (*Bundesverfassungsgericht*) overturned the injunction on Pelham's song-sample. The justices ruled that the BGH had not sufficiently considered whether the impact of the sample on Kraftwerk might be 'negligible'. German Constitutional Court also commented that the lower court had not taken the fundamental right of 'artistic freedom' ('Kunstfreiheit') into account when making its decision. It ruled that the detrimental impact of the sample on Kraftwerk did not outweigh the 'artistic freedom' of the sampling producers. Pelham had successfully argued on a point of law that sampling was now common practice in the hip-hop genre and that,

. . . artistic freedom overrides the interest of the owner of the copyright.

In 2016 the Bundesgerichtshof (BGH) referred the matter to the CJEU for a preliminary ruling, concerning the two-second sampling of Kraftwerk's 1977 release 'Metall auf Metall'. In particular, the German Federal Court asked the Court of Justice (CJEU) whether the non-authorized inclusion of a sound sample in a song (phonogram) by means of sampling taken from another phonogram constitutes, in the light of EU copyright and related rights law and of the fundamental rights enshrined in the Charter of Fundamental Rights of the European Union, an infringement of the rights of the producer of the phonogram from which the sample in question was taken. The Federal German Court (BGH) also sought clarification on the exceptions and limitations set out in EU law to the rights of rightholders. On that basis, the Bundesgerichtshof wished to know whether the German legislation, which allows an independent work created in free use of a protected work to be published and exploited *without* the consent of rightholders, is compatible in EU law? In addition, the court wished to know whether sampling was capable of falling with the 'quotation exception', which exempts a user from the need to seek the authorization of the appropriate phonogram producer?

Decision (CJEU)

In its judgment (preliminary ruling), the Court of Justice stated, firstly that phonogram producers have the exclusive right to authorize or prohibit reproduction in whole or in part of their phonograms. Consequently, the reproduction by a user of a sound sample, even if very short, taken from a phonogram must, in principle, be regarded as a reproduction 'in part' of that phonogram so that such a reproduction falls within the exclusive right granted to the phonogram producer.

However, the CJEU noted that, where a producer of phonograms, in exercising the *freedom of the* takes a sound sample from a phonogram in order to embody it, in a modified form and *unrecognizable* to the ear in another phonogram, that is *not* a 'reproduction' *arts* ('die Verwendung von Samples zur künstlerischen Gestaltung'). In that context, the Court of Jsutice underlined that to regard such use of a sound sample taken from a phonogram as a reproduction subject to the authorization of the phonogram producer would run counter to the requirement to strike a fair balance between, on the one hand, the interests of the holders of copyright and related rights in the protection of their intellectual property rights guaranteed by the Charter and, on the other hand, the protection of the interests and fundamental rights of users of protected subject matter, which are covered by the freedom of the arts, also enshrined in the Charter, as well as the public interest.

Secondly, the Court found that a song ('an article') which reproduces all or a substantial part of the sounds fixed in a phonogram (record) amounts to a copy of that phonogram, in relation to which the phonogram producer enjoys an exclusive right of distribution. However, the CJEU added that an article which merely embodies sound samples, where relevant in a modified form, transferred from that phonogram for the purposes of creating a *new and distinct work* from that phonogram does *not* amount to such a copy. The Court also considered that the exceptions and limitations to the rights of rightholders provided for in EU law already reflected the fact that the EU legislature had taken into account the interests of the producers and users of protected subject matter and the public interest. Furthermore, those exceptions and limitations were determined exhaustively in order to ensure the proper functioning of the internal market for copyright and related rights. The Court reminded the German legal representatives that EU law (i.e. copyright and related rights regulations) already provides sufficient 'exhaustive' exceptions and limitations, allowing a distinct work, created in the free use of a protected work, in principle, to be published and exploited without the consent of the rightholders. Consequently, the CJEU held that the German legislation was not in conformity with EU law.

In relation to quotations from a protected work, the Court found that the use of a sound sample taken from a phonogram allowing the work from which that sample was taken to be identified *may* amount to a quotation, provided that such use is aimed at entering into a 'dialogue' with the work in question. However, use of that sample if it is not possible to identify the work in question is not a quotation.

Lastly, where the action of the Member States is not entirely determined by EU law, the Member States may, in applying EU law, apply national standards for the protection of fundamental rights, provided, in particular, that the application of such fundamental rights does not compromise the level of protection laid down in the Charter. However, the substantive law relating to a phonogram producer's exclusive right of reproduction had been the subject of full harmonization so that such national standards were inapplicable.

Analysis

The *Kraftwerk* case highlights that in today's musical creations and with the enhancement of digital technology, the majority of songs (or phonograms) are no longer created from scratch. Music is not mere noise, as was held in the *Dr Sawkins' case* (2005), (see above 10.2.4), which was addressed, inter alia, by the Advocate General's opinion and eventually in the preliminary ruling of the Grand Chamber: did Pelham's 'Nur mir' song sample breach the copyright of the 2-second rhythm sequence phonogram 'Metal auf Metal' by Kraftwerk? The short answer is 'yes'. In this case Moses Pelham's and Martin Haas' 'Nur mir' song did not amount to a *separate composition*; it did therefore not amount to a completely new song which could stand on its own. Therefore the 'Nur mir' sample breached Kraftwerk's copyright. Arguably, the CJEU ruling remains narrow and to a certain extent non-committal, merely stating that Article 2(c) of Directive (EC) 2001/29 ('the Copyright Directive' or also: 'InfoSoc Directive') should, in the light of the Charter of Fundamental Rights of the European Union ('freedom of the arts), be interpreted as meaning that the final word lies with the phonogram producer's exclusive right (here Kraftwerk's Hütter). Under that provision the phonogram producer can allow or prevent another person (here Pelham) from taking a sound sample of his phonogram for the purposes of including that sample in another phonogram, to reproduce or distribute his phonogram. The CJEU added the rider: *unless* that sample included in the (new) phonogram is modified in such a form that it is *unrecognizable* to the ear.

In his opinion in December 2018 (in advance of the Grand Chamber ruling in July 2019), Advocate General Szpunar had taken a different view to the German Federal Court (BGH) on the issue of 'freedom of the arts', as enshrined in Article 13 of the Charter of Fundamental Rights of the European Union. The AG had opined that the exclusive right of phonogram producers under Article 2(c) of the Copyright Directive to authorize or prohibit reproduction of their phonogram in the event of its use for sampling purposes was *not* contrary to the fundamental right of freedom of the arts. The CJEU held that a 'freedom of the arts' exemption would only apply where the sample is modified to make it unrecognizable to the ear. Is it fair or in the interest of justice – in the context of sampling and the advancement of digital technology – that the test is then whether the sampled song, recognizable to the human ear, should be held as either a completely new phonogram or a ripped off copy of the original?

Summary of the CJEU's preliminary ruling in *Pelham v Hütter* (*Kraftwerk case*)

1. Article 2(c) of Directive 2001/29/EC of the European Parliament and of the Council of 22 May 2001 on the harmonisation of certain aspects of copyright and related rights in the information society, must, in the light of the Charter of Fundamental Rights of the European Union, be interpreted as meaning that the phonogram producer's exclusive right under that provision to reproduce and distribute his or her phonogram allows him to prevent another person from taking a sound sample, even if very short, of his or her phonogram for the purposes of including that sample in another phonogram, unless that sample is included in the phonogram in a modified form unrecognisable to the ear.
2. Article 9(1)(b) of Directive 2006/115/EC of the European Parliament and of the Council of 12 December 2006 on rental right and lending right and on certain rights related to copyright in the field of intellectual property must be interpreted as meaning that a phonogram which contains sound samples transferred from another phonogram does not constitute a 'copy', within the meaning of that provision, of that phonogram, since it does not reproduce all or a substantial part of that phonogram.
3. A Member State cannot, in its national law, lay down an exception or limitation, other than those provided for in Article 5 of Directive 2001/29, to the phonogram producer's right provided for in Article 2(c) of that directive.
4. Article 5(3)(d) of Directive 2001/29 must be interpreted as meaning that the concept of 'quotations', referred to in that provision, does not extend to a situation in which it is not possible to identify the work concerned by the quotation in question.
5. Article 2(c) of Directive 2001/29 must be interpreted as constituting a measure of full harmonisation of the corresponding substantive law.[60]

---

60 For further discussion see: Adeney, E. (2018) at pp. 91–106.

CJEU *Kraftwerk* ruling has provided a welcome clarification for rights owners but may well have a chilling effect on artistic expression in an increasingly hip hop, sampling and remix culture. Rights holders can now enforce their rights against unauthorized copying which in turn protects the value of music from those who 'sample' songs without permission to use it. We now await the German court's (Bundesgerichtshof) final ruling in the *Kraftwerk* case: does Kraftwerk's 'Metall auf Metall' form the *Leitmotiv* in Pelham's 'Nur mir' song or is it merely a 2 second sound bite snippet in an otherwise completely new creation in the rap hip hop song, sung by Sabrina Setlur? The reader will have to find out for themselves as this book went to print before the German final judgment in this case.

10.6 Licensing agreements and assignments

The music industry is a complicated business with a number of representative sectors and components interacting to make it work. Despite a shrinking market and slumping sales, there are now more pop artists than ever. Nothing is absolutely legally clear in this area of music licensing law. One reason that copyright law is the subject of such contention worldwide today is that it does not accurately reflect the contemporary tradition of musical creation. Most music today, sampled or 'originated', is an amalgamation of previous – mostly classical – works, such as Bach and Händel, Stravinski or Dvorak's Symphony No 9 'From the New World', which in itself 'samples' 'Swing Low Sweet Chariot'.

In 2014, according to the Official Charts Company, 47,751 albums were sold for the first time. The comparable figure in 1994 was 11,654. The quantity of recordings has multiplied – and so too have listening figures. Although one million-selling albums are in danger of extinction, the rise of music-streaming services such as Spotify and Apple Music has introduced a whole new order of superlatives.

The most streamed artists in 2018 were hip hop artists Drake and Post Malone, with over 8.2 billion streams. Ariana Grande was the most streamed female artist, followed closely by Dua Lipa, Taylor Swift and Camila Cabello.

See above
10.3

10.6.1 Licensing agreements in the music business

We have seen that complications can arise in joint authorship and joint copyright cases, particularly where a work is commissioned or there is a collaboration on a work.

Typical examples of where this may be appropriate are:

- books that are written by more than one author;
- musical compositions written as a group effort;
- speculative business projects, such as start-ups, where there is no employment contract in place.

Setting out the ground rules will help you avoid problems later if things do not work out or one member of the team leaves. Joint authors or co-writers of a script, some lyrics or a song should then draw up an agreement to describe what they have jointly decided. This should be signed by each member (author) to signify their agreement. This agreement does not need a lawyer but would be handled by a solicitor in a business or commercial environment. This is what such an agreement (or indeed licence with a company) should bear in mind:

> ● What happens if someone leaves. Can they use the work in their own right? Can the collective still use the work of the person that left?
> ● Is it worth treating this joint ownership as a separate entity – such as a limited company, which can hold assets in its own right?
> ● What happens to royalties and commissions if any work is later published or sold? Will they be split evenly, or should you work out a percentage based on input?

In recording contracts, each record label will try to secure an *exclusive* contract with the artist or group. For example, the Beatles recorded their albums at Abbey Road Studios exclusively with EMI. Tom Jones also used to record with EMI (*What's New Pussycat?* and *Delilah*), and then left for the Island record label (*Praise and Blame*); Deutsche Grammophon have their own classical, jazz and crossover artists like Rolando Vilazón (tenor) and the Three Tenors: José Carreras, Plácido Domingo and Luciano Pavarotti. The Decca label looks after Wynton Marsalis (blues trumpet) and so on.

Several countries have different forms of royalty collection. Some record labels and their artists have exclusive rights of reproduction ('private copying') and reprographic reproduction and therefore different rights to remuneration covered by EU legislation.[61] Since there is now a great deal of cross-border representation of artists and performers, collecting societies have created different categories of rights (to existing copyright) under one umbrella, referred to in the industry as the GEMA categories (Gesellschaft für musikalische Aufführungs- und mechanische Vervielfältigungsrechte: Society for musical performing and mechanical reproduction rights). GEMA is the society for musical performing and mechanical reproduction rights which originated in Germany.[62] GEMA, in turn, is a member of the BIEM (Bureau International des Sociétés Gérant les Droits d'Enregistrement et de Reproduction Mécanique: International bureau of societies administering the rights of mechanical recording and reproduction).

See below
10.8

The record label, by way of licence, will then be able to control the exploitation of the works. Licensing schemes for public performances of sound recordings are firmly grounded in conventional contract law, particularly in relation to 'related rights'. Indirect copyright holders comprise the music publishers, who are not directly involved in the creative process of the works. Their task is to support the authors and ensure that the musical works and scores are exploited by making sure that the repertoires are provided to the public and that the rights holders are granted their copyright; this includes all productions such as musicals or operettas performed by amateur societies.

---

61 Directive 92/100/EEC On Rental Rights and Lending Rights and on Certain Rights Related to Copyright in the Field of Intellectual Property which introduced such a right in favour of the authors and performers – the 'unwaivable right to equitable remuneration' in respect of the rental of phonograms and audiovisual works into which their works or, respectively, performances have been incorporated.
62 The reference to the GEMA categories was notably relied on by the EU Commission in its 1971 GEMA Decision. See Decision of 2 June 1971 (IV/26 760 – GEMA) [2971] OJ L134/15.

Musicians and record labels are constantly asking the question: how can we preserve our copyright in response of streaming platforms such as Pandora, Spotify, Tidal, Apple Music and Amazon? And what about the evolution in the music industry of blockchain? The digital era has made music easier to record and edit where thousands of songs can now be stored on a single device, and the P2P sharing and piracy have become blurred. Protective music licensing is now continuously under threat from blatant copiers.[63]

Licensing schemes and assignments of copyright are stated to be within the scope of the UK Copyright Act, namely Chapter V of the CDPA 1988. Assignments tend to be more popular in the United States, whereby artists will assign their copyright to a publishing company. An assignment is an outright transfer of ownership of rights by the copyright owner (e.g. the songwriter) to someone else, which usually covers the life of the copyright: 70 years from the end of the year in which the original author and owner of copyright dies.

Royalties in the music industry tend to be a percentage ownership of future production or revenues from a given licence agreement. These include moral rights, that is, the right to be identified as performer.[64] If recordings are made without the consent of the recording company or that of the performer, this creates an action relating to the use of illicit recordings.[65] Performers' moral rights include the right to object to derogatory treatment of their performance.[66]

The golden rule of music licensing for an artist and producer begins with the knowledge as to which licences exist and how to obtain them. Is the work in the public domain? Is the artist using a composition or a sound recording or both? Is he creating a cover song? Is he sampling an existing recording? Or is the work out of copyright? Knowing the difference between compositions and sound recordings is key to determining the necessary licence and can be a headache for any budding artist, who may incur high legal costs from copyright violations. The short answer is: unless the artist or producer controls the composition or sound recording, he will need a licence to use it.

The requirements for a valid express assignment are set out in section 90 CDPA;[67] but fortunately for many the law recognizes in addition to express statutory assignments equitable implied assignments based on the circumstances or conduct of the parties: for example, in university research collaboration agreements where the contracted sponsor may wish to own the IP created by the university research assistants or professors. Then the IP needs to be formally transferred, i.e. assigned to the sponsor. The assignment will then give 'full title guarantee' to the sponsor in the 'research collaboration agreement'. If indeed the university agrees to such an assignment, this will have to be formalized in a contract with guarantees and warranties (e.g. promising that it has the right to dispose of the IP); the IP is free from all charges and encumbrances, such as a mortgage, and rights of third parties; licensing back the IP and so forth – J.K. Rowling, for instance, assigned rights to her entire *Harry Potter* series at the start of her enterprise in 1993 to Bloomsbury Publishing.

---

63 For a more detailed discussion see: Finck, M. and Moscon, V. (2019) at pp. 77–108.

64 ss 205A – F CDPA ('rights in performances' and 'moral rights') plus the Performances (Moral Rights, etc.) Regulations 2006. Rights are also conferred on a performer by Chapter 3 of the Regulations (moral rights) and s 205C CDPA ('right to be identified') and s 205F CDPA ('right to object to derogatory treatment of performance').

65 s 191(i) and (j) CDPA.

66 s 205F CDPA.

67 Section 90(1) CDPA states that copyright is transmissible by assignment, by 'testamentary disposition' or by operation of law, as personal or moveable property.

It is possible to license a right instead of assigning it. In granting a licence, the copyright owner merely gives another person permission to use that right for the particular purpose as agreed in the licence terms, such as publishing the book from a given manuscript or making a CD from a particular sound recording or live performance. Licensing tends to be more flexible than an assignment as it is possible to license multiple copyrights to many people simultaneously, such as multiple music publishers. This is known as a non-exclusive licence. Usually licences permit sub-licences but generally the 'head licensee' cannot grant more rights to any sub-licensee than were granted to him.

A licence granted by a copyright owner is binding on every successor in title to his interest in the copyright, except a purchaser in good faith for valuable consideration and without notice (actual or constructive) of the licence or a person deriving title from such a purchaser. The licensor can then do anything with the work as he sees fit.[68] This practically means that a music publisher, for example, may do anything with a composer's script, such as issue an abridged or electronic version, subject of course to non-assignable moral rights, though these may be waived by the author. The same is true of book manuscripts. A principle of *de minimis* will be presumed in respect of licensing requirements and that an entitlement would be intended for such an arrangement. The scope of the licence ought to be limited in respect of those opportunities as envisaged by the parties at the time of the agreement. New exploitation and/or unexpected opportunities will not be considered to be included within such scope.

What about implied assignments and licences? Given the often hurly burly world of real commercial practice, parties do not always enter into the appropriate statutory written assignment, which can cause injustice later and frustrate the real intentions of the parties. In certain circumstances English law recognizes an implied assignment or licence. Nowadays, record labels try to persuade recording artists to sign '360-degree' licence deals so that they can exploit the artists' recordings commercially, including touring and merchandise. Record labels traditionally pay for the recording and mixing of albums and tend to underwrite new acts' touring costs to help raise their profile and sales. In addition, they fund the manufacturing, packaging and distribution of the recordings, plus all the branded merchandise that goes with live performances.

In a fast-changing digital world where music can be 'packaged' in a range of different formats, it can be difficult to identify and verify whether the use of the musical composition is licensed, by whom and for what kind of use. The record industry eventually came up with an identification system, the International Standard Recording Code (ISRC) and the Information System Work Code (ISWC), to identify composers, authors and music publishers to support the sales, licensing and tracking needs of artists and record labels, crucial to the successful operation of online commerce.

10.6.2 Music Modernization Act: a new deal for online music licensing (USA)

Providing a music download or streaming service requires that at least two different types of copyright-relevant acts be considered: the act of reproduction ('mechanical right') and the act of performing. This is true for Digital Music Providers (DMP) all over the world.

---

68 s 90(4) CDPA.

In the United States, it has been decided that a permanent download of a sound recording only exploited the mechanical rights of the underlying song,[69] while it was agreed as a matter of industry consensus that a personalized non-interactive radio service like Pandora or iHeartRadio only exploited the performing rights of that song. However, with on-demand streaming, it has generally been accepted that both the mechanical and performing rights are being exploited.

Licensing DMPs schematically works as follows: the performing right is licensed by performing rights societies (PROs). In the United States these are the American Society of Composers, Authors and Publishers (ASCAP)[70], internationally the BMI.[71] They act collectively on behalf of music publishers and rights holders in accordance with a collective licensing scheme provided for by the US Copyright Act. Mechanicals, on the other hand, are licensed directly by music publishers.

The US Music Modernization Act (MMA) is seen as the most sweeping reform of music licensing in 40 years, and was signed into law on 11 October 2018 following its unanimous passage through the US House and Senate. Officially named the *Orrin G. Hatch-Bob Goodlatte Music Modernization Act*, the MMA brings licensing and royalty collection into the digital age, combining three pieces of legislation into a single piece of legislation:

- The *Music Licensing Modernization Act* of 2018[72], which updates several key features of music licensing;
- The *Classics Protection and Access Act*,[73] which ensures that artists receive royalties on pre-1972 recordings;
- The *Allocation for Music Producers Act* (AMP), which codifies into law, for the first time, a producer's right to collect royalties from non-interactive digital services.

The MMA updates licensing and mechanical royalties related to streaming, setting rates via a 'willing buyer/willing seller' standard that is also expected to put performing rights organizations in a stronger negotiating position for the future. The Mechanical Licensing Collective (MLC) now collects and administers those royalties on behalf of songwriters and publishers.

A second part, the CLASSICS Act (Compensating Legacy Artists for their Songs, Service and Important Contributions to Society Act), was introduced in February 2018, and closes the so-called pre-1972 loophole, which enabled digital services to avoid paying royalties to legacy artists and led to extensive litigation in the courts over recent years

The MMA rectifies the existing mechanical licensing system in two main ways:

---

69 See: (i) The Report Of The Working Group On Intellectual Property Rights 71 (1995), available at: www.uspto.gov/about-us/organizational-offices and (ii) US Copyright Office, DMCA Section 104 Report, at 140 (2001), available at: www.copyright.gov/reports/studies/dmca/dmca_study.html.

70 www.ascap.com.

71 www.bmi.com.

72 Section 2334.

73 The Classics Protection and Access Act, Title II of the Orrin G. Hatch–Bob Goodlatte Music Modernization Act, brings pre-1972 sound recordings partially into the federal copyright. The legislation created a new chapter 14 of the copyright law, title 17 United States Code, which, among other things, extends remedies for copyright infringement to owners of sound recordings fixed before February 15, 1972 ('Pre-1972 Sound Recordings') when the recordings are used without authorization. The new chapter includes several limitations and exceptions to the eligibility for these remedies and related administrative procedures.

1   Creation of a Mechanical Licensing Collective ('the Collective'): the MMA creates a centralized entity, akin to a collecting society, responsible for the collection and distribution of mechanical royalties. The Collective establishes and maintains a publicly available database embodying information on the identity and location of copyright owners of musical works. The DSPs can obtain blanket licences from the Collective for their downloading and interactive streaming activities by filing a notice of licence.

2   Blanket Licensing: from 1 January 2020, DMPs can obtain blanket licences from the Collective to use musical works for downloading and interactive streaming. The DMPs are required to submit a notice of licence to the Collective, submit monthly usage reports and make royalty payments. The Collective then distributes the royalties to the correct copyright holders by matching the information provided by the usage reports and the information contained in the database. The Collective will also distribute unclaimed royalties, where it has been unable to identify the owner of songs for three years, further to the decision of a committee created for that purpose.

The option to enter into voluntary licences with music publishers remains. However, DMPs entering into direct licenses with music publishers will still be required to notify the Collective of their existence and to also help pay for its operations.

The MMA has produced a great deal of support in the music industry. There is now of course the obligation for copyright holders to register their copyright directly with the Collective regardless of where they live or their nationality. Non-registration will risk rights holders' royalties being treated as 'unclaimed' and being distributed in accordance with the three years scheme created by the act. Time will tell whether this may become a significant issue where unclaimed royalties may be the result of a failure by the Collective to properly identify the music tracks in spite of a successful registration by a publisher or phonogram producer.

The Collective is then a new entity with the composition of the board of directors and the governance of this newly created body. How will the Collective handle a considerable amount of confidential information about the US licensing market? Might they give unfair competitive advantage to the Collective's board of directors, which consists primarily of representatives of music publishers?

In February 2019 the National Music Publishers' Association, the Nashville Songwriters Association International and the Songwriters of North America unveiled the board members and endorsements for their Mechanical Licensing Collective submission to the US Copyright Office. Members of the various boards and committees include representatives from most major music publishers and performing-rights organizations, as well as several songwriters and artists who have been outspoken about creators' rights, including Camper Van Beethoven/Cracker frontman David Lowery, former Letters to Cleo singer Kay Hanley and former 'American Idol' judge Kara DioGuardi.[74]

---

74 Source: 'Music Modernization Act's Mechanical Licensing Collective Takes Shape', Variety, 5 February 2019: https://variety.com/2019/biz/news/music-modernization-acts-mechanical-licensing-collective-takes-shape-1203127834/.

 **FOR THOUGHT**

Is it right to say 'all recordings must be licensed'? If your friends sing 'Happy Birthday' to you in a pub and video-record the 'performance' on their mobile phones, and one of the 'group members' uploads the recording on to Facebook or YouTube, should she obtain a licence? Discuss.

10.7 Copyright claims in the entertainment industry

Over the past few decades there have been a number of high-profile copyright actions involving musicians and performing artists. Most of these cases involve international artists and laws.

To determine infringement in the music business, courts have relied on the following two-pronged test:

1 copying of a prior work; and
2 a substantial similarity to the prior work sufficient to constitute improper appropriation.

10.7.1 International cases

In 2016 the iconic 1970s rock group, Led Zeppelin. Led Zeppelin were, wasbeing sued in a Californian court by the estate of the 1960s psychedelic rock band Spirit's late guitarist, Randy 'California' Wolfe (who died in 1997). A trustee for the late Randy Wolfe, Michael Skidmore, demanded, as part of the lawsuit, that Led Zeppelin would give credit to Wolfe on their 1971 album, *Led Zeppelin IV*, which contains 'Stairway To Heaven'. Randy Wolfe composed the song 'Taurus', which it was alleged was 'ripped off' by Led Zeppelin. Wolfe's lawyers also claimed substantial backdated royalties. Guitarist Jimmy Page, 72, and his co-defendant, singer Robert Plant, 67, were relying on the *Mary Poppins* defence. Led Zeppelin's defence pressed the argument that the descending chromatic scale in 'Taurus', which they were accused of having copied, is exceedingly common in popular music and is not subject to copyright protection. Page explained, by playing 'Stairway to Heaven' on his guitar to the jury, that the song shared its musical DNA with the *Mary Poppins* song 'Chim Chim Cher-ee', and that the chord sequence in both songs was similar. Page explained that the descending musical motif of the *Mary Poppins* song was common to both 'Taurus' and 'Stairway to Heaven' and 'had been around forever'.[75]

On 23 June 2016, a Los Angeles jury found Robert Plant and Jimmy Page not guilty of stealing the famous passage from the 1971 anthem from the band Spirit. Francis Malofiy,

75 Source: 'Led Zeppelin's "Stairway to Heaven" Trial, Day 3: The "Mary Poppins" Connection', by Matt Diehl, *Rolling Stone*, 16 June 2016.

the estate's attorney, said he was sad and disappointed by the jury's decision. 'Stairway to Heaven' remains one of the most played songs on radio and is estimated to have generated more than $500m over the decades. Damages, however, can extend back only three years and into the future.[76]

Led Zeppelin's victory in the United States over allegations the band stole the opening chords of 'Stairway to Heaven' may reverse the surge in copyright infringement lawsuits over pop songs that followed the 'Blurred Lines' verdict in the same court in the case of *Williams v Gaye* (2018).[77]

The background to this US copyright infringement case goes back to 2013, when Pharrell Williams and Robin Thicke wrote and recorded 'Blurred Lines'. Marvin Gaye's estate alleged breach of copyright in the Marvin Gaye 1976 hit 'Got To Give It Up'. The Gaye family (Frankie Christian Gaye, Nona Marvisa Gaye and Marvin Gaye III) duly filed a copyright infringement suit in a California federal court. Any negotiations failed among the parties, and Williams and Thicke, along with Clifford Harris Jr, who separately wrote and recorded a rap verse for 'Blurred Lines', filed for a declaratory judgment of non-infringement. The Gayes counterclaimed. The Gayes added UMG Recordings Inc., its subsidiaries and other publishing companies and record labels as third-party defendants, asserting that they were liable for their manufacture and distribution of the song.

The US Court of Appeal for the Ninth Circuit affirmed in part and reversed in part the district court's judgment. The panel held that 'Got To Give It Up' was entitled to broad copyright protection because musical compositions were not confined to a narrow range of expression; the panel accepted, without deciding, the merits of the district court's ruling that the scope of the defendants' copyright was limited, under the US Copyright Act of 1909, to the sheet music deposited with the US Copyright Office, and did not extend to sound recordings; the district court's order denying summary judgment was not reviewable after a full trial on the merits. The district court did not err in denying a new trial. Furthermore, the district court did not constitute an abuse its discretion in admitting portions of expert testimony, namely the issue of copyright a musical style'. According to the dissent, the two songs were not objectively similar, and the similarities presented by the Gayes involved unprotectable elements, so the lack of substantial similarity meant that judgment should have been given as a matter of law. In Circuit Judge, Jacqueline Nguyen's view, the two works were not objectively similar as a matter of law under the extrinsic test because they differed in melody, harmony and rhythm – according to the expert opinion of the musicologist in court. The Appeal Court also held that the verdict was not against the clear weight of the evidence; the awards of actual damages and profits and the district court's running royalty were properly awarded. The district court did not abuse its discretion in apportioning costs among the parties. In summary, the US Appeal court affirmed in part and reversed in part the district court's judgment after a jury trial, ruling that plaintiffs' song 'Blurred Lines' infringed defendants' copyright in Marvin Gaye's song 'Got To Give It Up.' The

---

76 Source: 'Led Zeppelin cleared of stealing riff for Stairway to Heaven', by Rory Carroll, *Guardian*, 23 June 2016 with a link to a musical comparison.
77 *Williams v Gaye* (case No. 15–56880 D.C. No. 2:13-cv-06004-JAK-AGR) Ninth Circuit, California, 21 March 2018.

panel held that 'Got To Give It Up' was entitled to broad copyright protection because musical compositions are not confined to a narrow range of expression.

Benassi concludes that the decision in Williams v Gaye does not herald the 'end of musical creativity as we know it', rather it serves as a cautionary tale for future phonogram copyright cases.[78]

To avoid having to expend time, money and resources engaging in a protracted legal dispute, as well as exposure to the possibility of liability for monetary damages and/or injunctive relief as part of an adverse ruling, the most likely conclusion to these kind of disputes is a confidential settlement agreement involving a payment or series of payments to the original artist and composer.

That is precisely how Led Zeppelin resolved prior claims of copyright infringement brought by third-party artists regarding other Led Zeppelin songs including 'Whole Lotta Love', 'Babe I'm Gonna Leave You', 'The Lemon Song' and 'Dazed and Confused'.

In January 2015, three-times Grammy-nominated pop singer, Sam Smith, settled a copyright lawsuit with American singer-songwriter Tom Petty over the likeness between Smith's hit 'Stay With Me' and Petty's hit 'I Won't Back Down', co-written with ELO's Jeff Lynne. Smith agreed to a 12.5 per cent writing credit and royalties to Petty and his joint singer-composers Jeff Lynne and Jimmy Napes.[79]

It was even claimed that the world's most popular song, 'Happy Birthday', is under copyright. Music publishers Warner Chappell have earned an estimated $2m a year from the song by claiming copyright. In 2013, film director Jennifer Nelson filed a lawsuit claiming the song should not be under copyright. Nelson and Good Morning to You Productions were sued by Warner Chappell's for royalties of $1,500 for the use of the song in a documentary. Nelson claimed she had found a songbook from 1927, containing 'Happy Birthday', with no copyright notice – predating Warner Chappell's copyright claim by eight years.[80]

10.8 Performing rights and music collecting societies

Every time a musical work is downloaded via the internet (e.g. via iTunes) – or in the old days a CD, audio cassette or LP is played on the radio for example – the phonogram producers require a licence from the owner of the works, and they must pay royalties for each song (or copy).

Collective rights management is the practice by which organizations, which were founded by and represent creators and authors, look after the enforcement of the authors' rights (i.e. collect royalties and make sure their music is not copied or sampled).

---

78 Benassi, J. (2018) at pp. 220–221.
79 Source: 'Sam Smith on Tom Petty Settlement: "Similarities" But "Complete Coincidence"', by Daniel Kreps, *Rolling Stone*, 26 January 2015.
80 Source: 'World's most popular song is not under copyright, according to lawsuit', by Michael Hann, *Guardian*, 28 July 2015.

10.8.1 Music publishing, mechanical licensing and reproduction rights

The distinctions between mechanical and performing rights are not easily understood. They arose at a time when the exploitation of musical works occurred mainly in the public arena – that is in live performances – from the mid-nineteenth century onwards.

For example, Gilbert and Sullivan's works were shamelessly copied in the United States during live performances since there was no international copyright protection until the late 1890s.[81] Whilst the duo's operettas provided hours of fun to the New York audiences, their true artistic talents did not generate the profits they deserved since American theatricians frequently copied them.[82] Gilbert and Sullivan's transatlantic 'hits' in 1879 motivated not only new songs but also closely imitated Gilbert's patter songs and some distinctive Sullivanesque musical elements which nowadays would amount to sampling or at least parody.[83]

Two early US cases imply that the size of the borrowed portion could determine whether or not copyright infringement occurred. In *Boosey v Empire Music Co.* (1915),[84] the Southern District Court of New York ruled that six similar notes or more constituted copyright infringement while in *Northern Music Corp. v King Record Distribution Co.* (1952),[85] the same court indicated that the use of more than four bars constituted an infringement.

It is then important to distinguish ownership of a physical product from the ownership of the copyright embodied within it. For example, the purchase of a pop music CD or downloading a track via iTunes does not mean that the purchaser owns the copyright in the musical work within it or the copyright in the sound recording. Therefore, purchasing a music track or album via Amazon does not entitle the purchaser to copy the work or do any other acts which are restricted to the copyright owner (the original artist, producer and/or songwriter). The same goes for the purchase of a book – it does not mean that the purchaser owns the copyright of the manuscript.

The UK is the world's fourth-largest music publishing market, providing 10 per cent of worldwide revenues, and is second only to the United States as a source of repertoire. Music publishing generates over a quarter of the UK music industry's £2.6 billion in export revenue. In 2017 music publishing in the UK contributed £505m to the UK economy; this has increased by 7 per cent since 2016.[86]

The Music Publishers Association (MPA) has a worldwide catalogue of printed music and links to publishers (digitally and in hard copy). The MPA acts on behalf of over 200 members ranging from the UK's largest and most established music publishers to independents and start-ups. Apart from music publishing across all genres, the MPA participates in policymaking and is founder of UK Music. They lobby government on behalf

---

81 'Gilbert and Sullivan' refers to the Victorian-era theatrical partnership of the dramatist W.S. Gilbert and the composer Arthur Sullivan and to the works they jointly created. Librettist W.S. Gilbert wrote the words and composer Sir Arthur Sullivan wrote the score for their 14 operas (or operettas) in a collaboration that lasted 25 years. Their quarter of a century long partnership began in 1871, when the pair were brought together by theatre manager Richard D'Oyly Carte. Gilbert and Sullivan are perhaps best known for their comic operas: *The Mikado, H.M.S. Pinafore, The Pirates of Penzance* and *Iolanthe.*
82 Kislan, R. (1995); see also: vor der Bruegge, A. (2011).
83 For further discussion see: Allen, R. (1979).
84 [1915] 224 F. 646 (S.D.N.Y. 1915).
85 (1952) 105 F. Supp. 393 (S.D.N.Y. 1952).
86 Source: UK Music Measuring Music Report 2018: www.ukmusic.org/research/measuring-music-2018/.

of the wider music business.[87] The MPA has long argued that all recordings should be licensed, even non-commercial recordings.

The MPA also owns and operates two commercial businesses:

- Mechanical-Copyright Protection Society (MCPS) – the UK collection society that licenses mechanical (or reproduction) copyrights on behalf of over 26,000 music publisher and composer members;
- Printed Music Licensing Ltd (PMLL) – represents music publishers to allow UK schools to make copies of printed music.

Collectively, these subsidiary businesses are known as the MPA Group. The MPA offers a number of other commercial functions for music publishers – including a range of widely used template contracts and blanket industry agreements – and is the national agent for the dissemination of ISMNs.[88]

'Mechanicals' are publishing rights. Any time an artist or producer produces a recording of a composition which they do not control, they need a mechanical licence. Mechanical rights royalties are different and are paid to the songwriter, composer or publisher when music is reproduced as a physical product (such as sheet music) or for broadcast or online downloads such as iTunes. A mechanical licence is a broad term that refers to the reproduction for distribution or sale of musical compositions in the form of sound recordings. The mechanical licence royalties are collected by the MCPS.

Mechanical royalties are usually based on the amount of 'phonorecords' sold: that is, sales based on sound recordings determined by the record companies through 'Sound Scan' and other reporting systems. While US mechanical royalties are calculated on a 'penny basis' per song, other countries might base mechanical royalties on percentages or 'needle time'.[89]

Performing rights royalties are paid to a songwriter, composer or publisher whenever their music is played or performed in any public space or place. This includes TV, radio, online, in a shop, an office, pub or restaurant, at a concert, a sporting event and thousands of other places. Mechanical rights royalties are different and are paid to the songwriter, composer or publisher when music is reproduced as a physical product or for broadcast or online. These royalties are collected by the MCPS (Mechanical Copyright Protection Society – now part of the PRS). The MCPS is now covered by the broader 'PRS for Music' brand, and licenses the mechanical (reproduction) rights and pays mechanical royalties to the original author (music copyright holder).[90] The PRS-MCPS system grants a mechanical licence for the entire record based on a percentage of the wholesale or retail price, regardless of the number of songs. Public performance monies collected by the organization depend on their survey and consensus of how many times the song is played, when, where and at what time of day, and on what type of medium

---

87 See: https://mpaonline.org.uk/104
88 International Standard Music Numbers (ISMNs) are an international system created in 1993 specifically for printed music publications. ISMNs are to printed music what ISBNs are to books.
89 The term 'needle time' comes from the use of gramophone record players using a gramophone needle.
90 MCPS-PRS collects royalties whenever a piece of music is reproduced for broadcast or online.

10.8.2 What do collecting societies do?

Having established that the works of the dynamic operatic duo Gilbert and Sullivan's music was shamelessly copied – and most likely other composer's musical works in general until the late nineteenth century – some collecting societies began to establish themselves mainly in France where composers realized the benefits of operating collectively when licensing public places to use their music. The first collective was the Propriété Littéraire et Artistique, which signed the Berne Convention of 9 September 1886.

The *Confédération Internationale des Sociétés d'Auteurs et de Compositeurs* – or CISAC (International Confederation of Societies of Authors and Composers) was founded in 1926. It is an international non-governmental, not-for-profit organization that aims to protect the rights and promote the interests of musical creators worldwide. It advocates for strong legal protection of copyright and authors' rights. CISAC is now the world's largest collective rights management organization comprising an international network of authors' and collecting societies. The current president is French electronic music composer Jean Michel Jarre, appointed in June 2013, replacing US singer-songwriter Robin Gibb of the Bee Gees, who died in 2012. CISAC's membership in 2019 extends to nearly 900 authors' collection societies in more than 120 countries.[91]

Collecting societies act as intermediaries between right holders ('authors') – and they do not only exist in the music business but also generally in publishing. The *Authors' Licensing and Collecting Society* (ALCS) collects royalties on behalf of writers, for example.

All collecting societies have one thing in common: they have licensing rights, collect royalty rights on behalf of authors, and redistribute revenue to the right holders in circumstances where individually negotiating licences with individual creators would be impractical and entail high transaction costs.[92] Each collecting society has its own unique monitoring systems and detection techniques based on random survey, census, sampling, or digital detection methods.

Collecting societies in the music and entertainment business enjoy considerable market power since their collective practice is largely standardized, such as using the same tariffs, licensing conditions and distribution rights in the repertoire. This system guarantees a certain level of solidarity among rights holders and strengthens the rights of relatively unknown or niche authors and artists, who can expect the same level of protection as popular performers or songwriters. In general, fees are charged to the authors, composers or performers in return for 'collection' services ('collection fee') and allocating such revenues to the rights holder ('allocation fee').

The difficulty for authors and creators remains how the various layers of collecting organizations track all of the music samples, covers or remixes, etc. accurately so that royalty monies are correctly paid to songwriters, performing artists, session musicians and publishers, because each of the organizations uses slightly different systems and methods for calculations.

10.8.3 Playing music in public: PPL licences

Any person or business wishing to play copyrighted music in public must obtain a 'public performance' licence from either the copyright owner or the collecting society to do so. If

---

91 Global Collections Report 2019: www.cisac.org
92 Koempel, F. (2007), pp. 371–376.

the person or business does not obtain the required licence, they run the risk of infringing copyright (a criminal offence).

Under section 16 CDPA the following acts, by way of an example, constitute primary infringement, if performed without the copyright owner's consent:

- copying the work (section 16(1));
- communicating the work to the public (section 16(1)); and
- authorizing another to do any of the above acts (section 16(2)).

Communication to the 'public' is construed broadly, and case law suggests that only domestic or family circles will be deemed not to constitute a 'public' gathering. Section 16 CDPA then deals with the rights of an owner of copyright ('acts restricted by copyright in a work'), namely:

16 (1) The owner of the copyright in a work has, in accordance with the following provisions of this Chapter, the exclusive right to do the following acts in the United Kingdom—

   (a) to copy the work (see section 17);
   (b) to issue copies of the work to the public (see section 18);
   (ba) to rent or lend the work to the public (see section 18A);
   (c) to perform, show or play the work in public (see section 19);
   (d) to communicate the work to the public (see section 20);
   (e) to make an adaptation of the work or do any of the above in relation to an adaptation (see section 21);

   and those acts are referred to in this Part as the "acts restricted by the copyright".

  (2) Copyright in a work is infringed by a person who without the licence of the copyright owner does, or authorises another to do, any of the acts restricted by the copyright.

A 'public performance' occurs whenever sound recordings are played outside the domestic or private circle. There is no statutory definition of 'playing in public', but the UK courts have given guidance on its meaning and ruled that it is any playing of music outside a domestic setting – so, for example, playing recorded music at a workplace, public event or in the course of any business activities is considered to be 'playing in public'.

A 'qualifying performance' relating to a performers' right means it is given by a 'qualifying individual' or takes place in a 'qualifying country' (under the Berne Convention).[93] Public performance rights may be licensed directly from the copyright owner by way of a direct request or from the collection society directly. Previously, businesses and organizations had to obtain separate music licences from PPL and PRS for Music. They have now

---

93 ss 181–184 CDPA.

joined under one organization PPL PRS Ltd and now issue one licence, known as 'The Music Licence' in the UK.[94] In the USA this is the Broadcast Music, Inc. (BMI).[95]

A PPL (Phonographic Performance Ltd) licence is required when recorded music, including radio and TV, is played in public. In contrast, any recorded music being played as part of domestic home life or when there is an audience entirely composed of friends and/or family (such as at a private family party) does not require a PPL licence. Each business must register with and pay a fee to PPL, otherwise they risk criminal prosecution under copyright law.

Phonographic Performance Ltd (PPL) was formed by EMI and Decca records in May 1934 following its successful action in the *Stephen Carwardine* case.[96] Here, restaurant proprietors were playing music recordings by Auber, played by the LSO, in its tea and coffee rooms. The record label 'The Gramophone Company' (later EMI) argued it was against the law to play the recordings in public without first receiving the permission of the copyright owners. The judge agreed. The case established the principle that owners of sound recordings should be paid for the broadcasting and public performance of their works.

That said, there will be those artists who prefer to manage their own conditions and royalties. With music mostly digitized now, the distinction between the two rights (mechanical and performance) has become blurred, and performing artists are often not sure whether they need an MCPS or PRS licence.

So, how many licences does a business need and for which type of music? This has been an ongoing issue for businesses over many years and the courts have sent different and confusing messages over recent years. Typically, music licences include fitness clubs, cinemas, shopping centres, funeral parlours, providers of wedding functions and medical premises.

This issue was addressed in *Re Phonographic Performance Ltd (Re PPL)* (2009),[97] where an action was brought by the British Beer and Pub Association (BBPA) jointly with the British Hospitality Association (BHA) against PPL for charging additional fees for background music, effectively asking each pub and bar restaurant for two licences: one for public performances (PRS) and another for phonographic playback (PPL). This had brought in additional subscription fee revenue of about £20m for PPL.

In *Re PPL*, Kitchin J held that the PPL could not charge a separate licence fee for playing background music of sound recordings because the businesses in question had already paid their PRS fees; a second music licence was therefore not necessary. Based on the Chancery Court's decision, Kitchin J stated that there was nothing in sections 125–128 CDPA to suggest that separate royalties ought to be charged for playing background music, since that was covered by 'public performances'. Kitchin J further ruled that PPL had to pay back all over-charged licence fees to the hoteliers and pub landlords. The case became a landmark victory for the hospitality industry. The PPL ruling meant that pubs could now play background music with just one music licence.

As of February 2018, the PRS and PPL formed a joint venture, namely PPL PRS for Music.[98] Any businesses playing music in public can now obtain a single licence, named 'The Music Licence', potentially making compliance more straightforward and

94   PPL PRS United for Music: https://pplprs.co.uk/.
95   See: www.bmi.com.
96   *Gramophone Co., Ltd v Stephen Carwardine Co.* [1934] 1 Ch 450 – involving the Copyright Act 1911.
97   *Phonographic Performance Ltd v The British Hospitality Association* [2009] EWHC 175 (Ch) ('Re PPL').
98   For 'The Music Licence' for playing music in public see: https://pplprs.co.uk/.

bringing an end to the requirement to obtain separate music licences from PRS and PPL.

In the *Mama Africa* restaurant case (2018),[99] restaurant owner defendant, Mr Balgun, applied to have the summary judgment set aside.[100] A summary judgment application (here by the claimants PPL) is normally made at a relatively early stage in litigation where the court determines the case without a trial being required. When deciding whether to grant summary judgment, the court has to consider that the defendant has no real prospect of successfully defending the claim and that there is no other compelling reason why the case should be dealt with at trial. As Mr Balgun failed to attend the summary judgment without telling the court the reasons, summary judgment was granted against him.

❖ **KEY CASE**   *Phonographic Performance Ltd v Abimbola Balgun t/a Mama Africa [2018] EWHC 1327 (Ch).*

Precedent
❖ The playing of recorded music in any business premises for employees or customers is lawful only if the relevant licences are obtained (namely Performing Right Society Limited [PRS] and Phonographic Performance Limited [PPL]).

❖ The granting of such licences constitutes authorization by the artist to perform their music and lyrics and to play their sound recordings in public without the need for further consent.

❖ The Master had not erred in law in refusing to set aside summary judgment concerning the restoring of proceedings after a failure by the defendant to attend trial. The reasons for the defendant's non-attendance and his prospects of success at trial were all relevant considerations.

Facts
The defendant, Mr Abimbola Balgun, a restaurant owner, let his premises to a third party for a function. The third party hired DJs who played recorded music on the premises. The claimant, Phonographic Performance Ltd [PPL], brought a claim against the defendant for infringement of copyright laws. PPL claimed that Mr Balgun had played a sound recording at his restaurant known as 'Mama Africa' which infringed the Claimant's copyright it held in relation to two songs. The restaurant owner-defendant, Mr Balgun, argued that the act of booking DJs to play at his premises did not constitute copyright infringement and that he had no control over the specific music the DJs chose to play.

The defendant was served with the application for summary judgment by PPL but did not attend the hearing on 20 September 2017. Mr Balgun was then served with the summary judgment order the following day. He did not bring an application to set aside the summary judgment until enforcement proceedings

---

99 *Phonographic Performance Ltd v Abimbola Balgun t/a Mama Africa* [2018] EWHC 1327 (Ch).
100 See Rule 24.2 CPR.

were brought on 3 November 2017. The judge, Master Price, stated at the summary judgment hearing that:

> As it seems to me, that is a risk he took and that, in fact, by reason of allowing these events to take place on his premises he, in effect, is authorising what took place in relation to the playing of music and that music has proven to be played in infringement of the claimant's rights.[101]

Mr Balgun acting in person filed a defence stating that he had no idea about the claim and denied playing any of the songs. Master Price gave directions in the matter, including directing consideration of a summary judgment application under CPR 24 which the claimant, PPL, ultimately brought.

Decision

Miss Penelope Reed QC held the copyright infringement arose from the music being played in public without the necessary consent and whether the owner had an input in selecting the songs was irrelevant; Mr Balgun was responsible for booking DJs to perform in public and absent possession of the relevant licences had infringed copyright under section 16(2) of the CDPA. The Judge agreed with the Master at the earlier hearing that playing sound recordings at the restaurant 'Mama Africa' without a PPL licence, infringed copyright in relation to two songs. On the facts, Miss Reed QC found that the Master had been correct to find that Mr Balgun had not acted promptly. She also found that Master Price had not erred in his approach as the decision was a discretionary one, and he had not applied CPR 39.3(5) too rigidly.

Mr Balgun had argued that the earlier decision by the Master was at odds with the decision in *CBS Songs Ltd v Amstrad Consumer Electronics Plc* (1988);[102] but Miss Reed QC said that Amstrad in that case had no control over the use to which its equipment was put. Mr Balgun, on the other hand, had complete control over the playing of music in his premises. There were therefore no real prospects that Mr Balgun's defence would succeed.

Analysis

The *Mama Africa* case has both procedural and substantive significance regarding copyright infringement. Firstly, the court had to deal with the question of non-attendance in an application to set aside a summary judgment. Secondly there was the question of law as to the consideration of the possible breadth of liability for copyright infringement. Miss Reed QC observed that whether the claim had real prospects of success was a 'vitally important factor', whatever test was applied.[103] Importantly, she concluded that the court should take into

---

101 *Mama Africa* [2018] EWHC 1327 at para. 7 (Miss Penelope Reed QC).
102 [1988] 1 AC 1013.
103 *Mama Africa* [2018] EWHC 1327 at para. 21.

account that the defence could be amended. Thus, rather than focussing on the defence as presently pleaded, she considered whether there was *in fact* a defence (relying on *Tubelike Ltd v Visitjourneys.com Ltd* (2016)[104]).

This case should come as a warning to restaurant owners to act with caution when letting their premises out for functions and the importance of retaining a degree of control over the events. It seems that the judgment turns on theoretical, rather than actual, control over the playing of music. The result is that the risk of copyright infringement is placed almost entirely, and perhaps unfairly, upon the owners of premises. Owners of premises, where music is played, are required to have licences from the relevant collecting societies in order to avoid liability for music and public performance copyright infringement (see also: *PPL & PRS v CGK Ltd and others* (2016)[105]).

This judgment leaves a number of questions unanswered. Where should the line be drawn between playing music in public and at a private party? Would a party held at an individual's home for a child's birthday party constitute playing music in public? Beyond that, would an individual owner have to physically turn the music off should an individual party-goer request a track for which the DJ does not hold the licence? To mitigate that risk, an individual owner of premises may well have to seek contractual assurances from the DJ that they have the appropriate licences for the music being played.

 FOR THOUGHT

The High Court has found a nightclub manager liable for authorizing and procuring acts infringing copyright, namely the playing of sound recordings at the club without licences from the collecting societies, Performing Rights Society Ltd (PRS) and Phonographic Performance Ltd (PPL). Advise your client, the owner of the nightclub, as to the setting aside of a summary judgment, applied for by PRS and PPL. Draft a statement to the court, articulating your client's witness evidence and assessing the real prospects of your client's success at trial.

10.9 Artistic freedom of expression: concluding thoughts

Modern copyright law is characterized by a growing awareness of the tension between the protection of the right to intellectual property and other fundamental rights, such as

---

104 [2016] EWHC 43 (CH).
105 [2016] EWHC 2642.

artistic freedom[106] When legal action is taken against 'copiers' of music or illegal downloads, the courts' discussions invariably turn to fundamental rights, such as freedom of expression (in the case of parody) and the undisputed rights of various interested parties involved in a production and performance of a recording (phonogram).

Legal disputes are then not simply between an artist and a phonogram producer, but the courts have to balance all these different interests and take these into account when striking a balance between artistic freedom (say of the sampler) and intellectual property rights of the creator and phonogram producer.

We have seen the debate in the German and EU courts in Kraftwerk that copyright and related rights in the music and entertainment business may amount to a restriction of freedom of expression and freedom of the arts. There are some CJEU judgments which send conflicting and at times, confusing 'copyright' messages in relation to the scope of copyright exceptions (e.g. fair dealing or quotation), limitations and enforcement (such as the rule in *Deckmyn v Vandersteen* (2013)[107]) (see also: *Productores de Música de España (Promusicae) v Telefónica de España SAU* (2008);[108] *Scarlet Extended SA v Société Belge des Auteurs, Compositeurs et Éditeurs SCRL (SABAM)* (2011);[109] *UPC Telekabel Wien GmbH v Constantin Film Verleih GmbH* (2014);[110] *McFadden v Sony Music Entertainment Germany GmbH* (2017)[111]).

Freedom of expression, from which the freedom of the arts emanates, concerns above all obtaining and disseminating ideas and information and, consequently, as regards phonograms, the content of works – as was held in the opinion by Advocate General Maciej Szpunar in the long-running Kraftwerk dispute.[112] He opined that freedom of (musical) artists is less extensive when they acquire (copy) samples of other works for the means of their creations (phonograms). Freedom of the arts does not free artists from the constraints of copyright law.

It is clear that in today's musical genres such as hip hop or rap, sampling plays an essential role which provides not only the means of creation but also an artistic process in itself. However, artistic freedom cannot become a 'free for all' and the interpretation of CJEU rulings in the area of EU copyright law must be the same for all for all Member States. The message in Kraftwerk is that generally, sampling requires either the permission of the original rights holder (artist and/ or phonogram producer) or a licence for such use from the relevant music licensing or collecting agencies. This legitimate practice does not restrict the freedom of the arts beyond normal market constraints, especially since those new works often generate significant revenue for their authors and producers.

Freedom of the arts cannot guarantee the possibility of free use of whatever is wanted for creative purposes. It seems fair that artists and phonogram producers should share in the revenue derived from the exploitation of works created using their phonogram in samples or covers. In balancing fundamental rights, it is necessary to take account of the rights and material interests of phonogram producers, as well as the rights of performers

---

106 Article 13 of the EU Charter of Fundamental Rights ('freedom of the arts and sciences').
107 (C 201/13) EU:C:2014:2132 (CJEU).
108 (Case C-275/06) 29 January 2008 (OJ C64/9 2008) EU:C:2008:54 [2008] 2 C.M.L.R. 17 (CJEU).
109 (C-70/10) EU:C:2011:771 [2011] E.C.R. I-11959; [2012] E.C.D.R. 4).
110 (C-314/12) EU:C:2014:192 [2014] Bus. L.R. 541.
111 (C-484/14) EU:C:2016:689 [2017] Bus. L.R. 430.
112 *Pelham v Hütter* [2019] E.C.D.R. 3 (Case C-476/17) at para. AG 92 (Szpunar AG).

See

Chapter 9.6

and artists, including moral rights, particularly the integrity right, which may legitimately preclude use of the original creation, even where that use is covered by an exception as we saw in *Deckmyn*.

10.10 Further reading

Adeney, E. (2018) 'How much is too much? The gradual coalescence of the law on sampling'. *Intellectual Property Quarterly* (2018) 2, 91–106.
Elizabeth Adeney discusses the development in the law in an international context on sampling, favourable to derivative creators. Australia courts, for instance, have indicated that they will look at the principle of substantiality in relation to 'subject matter other than works' in a way that is akin to their reading of substantiality in relation to 'works', despite the manifest differences between the interests involved. The author argues that the 'potency' of the material taken (sampled) will play a leading role in the determination. The author then looks at the determination by the German courts in the *Kraftwerk* case (2016) and the (then expected) CJEU judgment in the case, particularly regarding the fundamental rights and freedoms of the derivative creator in relation of small samples.

Harding, T. (2013) 'BitTorrent tracking as a means of detecting illegal file-sharing'. *E-Commerce Law & Policy*, 15(2), 8–9.
The article discusses the legal issues for copyright proprietors who use specialized software to track users of the BitTorrent file-sharing system, detect copyright infringement and apply to the court for disclosure of the names and addresses of the alleged infringers. Harding discusses two cases in this area of copyright infringement and licensing: *Golden Eye v Telefonica* (2012) and *Media CAT Ltd v Adams* (2011). He also considers, *inter alia*, the study by Chothia and Cova, 'The Unbearable Lightness of Monitoring', on the technical aspects of monitoring BitTorrent. An examination of (complex) case law suggests that there are problems with this sort of evidence and its probative value.

Husovec, M. and Peguera, M. (2015) 'Much ado about little – privately litigated internet disconnection injunctions'. *International Review of Intellectual Property and Competition Law*, 46(1), 10–37.
Martin Husovec and Miguel Peguera examine the legal framework of the European Union for injunctions against intermediaries (i.e. private internet injunctions) whose services are used by third parties to infringe an IP right (as per the InfoSoc Directive and the Enforcement Directive[113]) and how the CJEU has construed the conditions. The authors then look at the types of injunctions that right holders may apply for against intermediaries on the basis of Article 8(3) of the InfoSoc Directive, namely those that would consist of enjoining an ISP from providing internet access to one of its users allegedly engaging in copyright infringement. Relevant case law is discussed. The authors then argue that these injunctions raise serious issues regarding their compatibility

---

113 Directive 2001/29 on the harmonization of certain aspects of copyright and related rights in the information society [2001] OJ L167/10; Article 8 Directive 2004/48 on the enforcement of intellectual property rights [2004] OJ L157/45.

with the EU Charter of Fundamental Rights[114] and come to the conclusion that these Directives' provisions 'promise much, but if applied correctly, they deliver little'.

Litman, J. (2018) 'What we don't see when we see copyright as property'. *Cambridge Law Journal,* **77(3), 536–558.**
In this article Jessica Litman argues that copyright law and licensing rules are a byzantine concept in today's digital world. Twentieth-century copyright law as we have it presently is a complex system with a bunch of interlocking and sometimes inconsistent purposes. Litman uses a turn of phrase popularized by Amazon. com's vice president Russ Grandinetti, who said that the only essential players in the copyright system are the author and the audience. There appears to be little point in 'throwing more copyright rights at copyright owners', unless and until we understand more of the dynamic that results in their getting such a small share of the proceeds from their creations. The author suggests that the law should be adjusted to enhance the bargaining power of publishers over platforms or platforms over publishers. Any recent efforts to revise and modernize copyright law face obstacles that seem insurmountable. The author concludes that the firm hold that copyright intermediaries have on national and international law-making processes, and their current preoccupation with marshalling all available resources to vanquish each other, suggest that realistic opportunities for authors empowering copyright reforms may be scant.

Yeoh, F. (2015) 'Adaptations in music theatre: confronting copyright'. *Entertainment Law Review,* **26(4), 119–129.**
Francis Yeoh provides an extensive overview of music copyright in the UK dating back to the Statute of Anne 1710 and examples of musical and dramatic works and compositions dating back to the nineteenth century, such as the works by Gilbert and Sullivan. For example, *HMS Pinafore* (1878) was widely pirated and copied particularly in the United States. G & S's predicament was due to the fact that copyright established in the United Kingdom was not recognized in the United States at the time. The author then raises awareness as to music adaptations and the acquiring of copyright. He discusses the concept of copyright as 'property' and the 'economic' approach to copyright. Yeoh's criticism of current copyright law is the proposition that the increases in authorial rights have been exploited to destroy the delicate balance between authorial rights and the public interest. He compares international copyright legislation (e.g. Berne Convention) with UK provisions and investigates how these have encroached on the freedom of expression. Yeoh argues the shortcomings of harmonized copyright law in the context of the adaptor/author's rights as owner and user in the context of UK and US copyright legislation.

Yin Harn Lee (2018) 'United Kingdom copyright decisions 2017'. *International Review of Intellectual Property and Competition Law,* **49(3), 324–330.**
This extensive report highlights the main UK copyright decisions in 2017, citing and discussing the rulings in substantial case law, marvellously summarized by the author, including *Banner Universal Motion Pictures Ltd v Endemol Shine Group Ltd*

---

114 Article 11 Charter of Fundamental Rights of the European Union [2000] OJ C364/1.

(2017);[115] *Martin v Kogan* (2017);[116] *Football Association Premier League Ltd v British Telecommunications Plc* (2017)[117] and *R v Evans (Wayne)* (2017).[118] The article deals with copyright protection of dramatic formats, the subsistence of copyright and *sui generis* database right in a database, joint authorship, blocking injunctions and the sentencing in the context of copyright-related offences.

---

115 [2017] EWHC 2600 (Ch).
116 [2017] EWHC 2927 (IPEC).
117 [2017] EWHC 480 (Ch).
118 [2017] EWCA Crim 139.

Bibliography

Adeney, E. (2018) 'How much is too much? The gradual coalescence of the law on sampling', *Intellectual Property Quarterly*, 2, 91–106.

Akdeniz, Y. (2008) *Internet Child Pornography and the Law: National and International Responses*. Aldershot: Ashgate.

Allan, S. and Zelizer, B.(eds) (2004) *Reporting War: Journalism in Wartime*. Abingdon, Oxon: Routledge.

Allen, R. (1979) *Gilbert and Sullivan in America: The Story of the First D'Oyly Carte Company American Tour*. New York: Gallery Association of New York State.

Allcott, H. and Gentzkow, M. (2017) 'Social Media and Fake News in the 2016 Election', *Journal of Economic Perspectives*, 31(2), 211–236.

Andrew, C. (2009) *The Defence of the Realm: The Authorized History of MI5*. London: Allen Lane.

Arrowsmith, S. (2015) 'What is a parody? Deckmyn v Vanderstee'. Case Comment, *European Intellectual Property Review*, 37(1), 55–59.

Benaim, G. and Oakley, J. (2014) 'Reporting, the courts and young people: time to reconsider?' *Entertainment Law Review*, 25(6), 221–223.

Baloch, T.A. (2007) 'Law booksellers and printers as agents of unchange', *Cambridge Law Journal*, 66(2), 389–421.

Barber, N.W. (2003) 'A right to privacy?', *Public Law*, Winter, 602–610.

Barendt, E. (1989) 'Spycatcher and freedom of speech', *Public Law*, PO 204.

Barendt, E. (2016) *Anonymous Speech: Literature, Law and Politics*. Oxford: Hart.

Barnum, D.G. (2006) 'Indirect incitement and freedom of speech in Anglo-American law', *European Human Rights Law Review*, 3, 258–280.

Barron, A. (2012) 'Kant, copyright and communicative freedom', *Law & Philosophy*, 31(1), 1–48.

Barwise, T.P. and Watkins, L. (2018) 'The evolution of digital dominance: how and why we got to GAFA [Google, Apple, Facebook, Amazon]'. In: Moore, M. and Tambini, D., *Digital Dominance: The Power of Google, Amazon, Facebook, and Apple*. New York: Oxford University Press, pp. 21–49. https://lbsresearch.london.edu/914/1/9780190845124_Barwise_Chapter%201.pdf.

Bedat, A. (2015) 'Tim Yeo MP v Times Newspapers Ltd – discretion to order trial by jury under Defamation Act 2013', *Entertainment Law Review*, 26(1), 31–33.

Benassi, J. (2018) '"Blurred Lines" songwriters have got to give it up for the Gaye family'. *Entertainment Law Review*, 29(7), 220–221.

Bennett, T.D.C. (2010) 'Horizontality's new horizons – re-examining horizontal effect: privacy defamation and the Human Rights Act (Part 2)', *Entertainment Law Review*, 21(4), 145–149.

Benson, V. and Turksen, U. (2017) 'Privacy, security and politics: current issues and future prospects', *Communications Law*, 22(4), 124–131.

Bessant, B. (2018) 'Sharenting: balancing the conflicting rights of parents and children', *Communications Law*, 23(1), 7–24.

Bindman, G. (1989) 'Spycatcher: judging the judges', *New Law Journal*, 139, 94.

Blair, A. (2010) *A Journey*. London: Hutchinson/Random House.

Blom-Cooper, L. (2008) 'Press freedom: constitutional right or cultural assumption?', *Public Law*, Summer, 260–276.

Blythe, A. (2015) 'Misrepresentation, confusion and the average consumer: to what extent are the tests for passing off and likelihood of confusion within trade mark law identical?', *European Intellectual Property Review*, 37(8), 484–489.

Blythe, A. (2017) 'Website blocking orders post-*Cartier v B Sky B*: an analysis of the legal basis for these injunctions and the potential scope of this remedy against other tortious acts', *European Intellectual Property Review*, 39(12), 770–777.

Booton, D. (2018) 'How to be bad: the importance of standpoint in intellectual property disputes', *Intellectual Property Quarterly*, 4, 279–304.

Brooke, H. (2011) *The Silent State: Secrets, Surveillance and the Myth of British Democracy*. London: William Heinemann.

Brown, J. (2018) '"Revenge porn" and the actio iniuriarum: using "old law" to solve "new problems"', *Legal Studies*, 38(3), 396–410.

Bryden, C. and Salter, M. (2017) 'Posting hate online. Legal Update Social Media/ Harassment', *New Law Journal*, 167, 7755, p. 11.

Burchill, R., White, N. D. and Morris, J. (eds) (2005) *International Conflict and Security Law: Essays in Memory of Hilaire McCoubrey*. Cambridge: Cambridge University Press.

Cabinet Office (2018) Freedom of Information Code of Practice. 4 July 2018 (minor amendments): https://assets.publishing.service.gov.uk/government/uploads/system/uploads/attachment_data/file/744071/CoP_FOI_Code_of_Practice_-_Minor_Amendments_20180926_.pdf

Caddick, N., Gwilym Harbottle, G. and Davies, G. (eds) (2010) *Copinger and Skone James on Copyright* 16th edition. London: Sweet & Maxwell.

Cairncross Review (2019) 'A sustainable future for journalism', 12 February. Department for Digital, Culture, Media and Sport: https://assets.publishing.service.gov.uk/government/uploads/system/uploads/attachment_data/file/778021/021119_THE_CAIRNCROSS_REVIEW_A_sustainable_future_for_journalism.pdf

Campbell, W. J. (2001) *Yellow Journalism: Puncturing the Myths, Defining the Legacies*. Opa-Locka, FL: Praeger.

Carney, D. (2017) 'Up to standard? A critique of IPSO's Editors' Code of Practice and IMPRESS' Standards Code', Communications Law, 22(4), 112–123.

Carter-Ruck, P. F. (1990) *Memoirs of a Libel Lawyer*. London: Weidenfeld & Nicolson.

Carter-Silk, A. and Cartwright-Hignett, C. (2009) 'A child's right to privacy: "Out of a parent's hands"', *Entertainment Law Review*, 20(6), 212–217.

Carty, H. (2007) 'The common law and the quest for the IP effect', *Intellectual Property Quarterly*, 3, 237–266.

CISAC (International Confederation of Societies of Authors and Composers) (2017) *Private Copying Global Study*. Legal and Policy Department.

Clark, A. (1993) *Diaries*. London: Weidenfeld & Nicolson.

Clementi, Sir David 'A Review of the Governance and Regulation of the BBC'. Presented to Parliament by the Secretary of State for Culture, Media and Sport by Command of Her Majesty. March 2016. Cm 9209 ('The Clementi Report').

Cobbe, J. (2018) 'Casting the dragnet: communications data retention under the Investigatory Powers Act', *Public Law*, January, 10–22.

Cooley T. M. (McIntyre) (1888) *Law of Torts: A Treatise on the Law of Torts, or the Wrongs which Arise Independent of Contract*. 2nd ed. Chicago: Callaghan & Co.

Cornish, W. (2009) 'Conserving culture and copyright: A partial history', Edinburgh Law Review, 13(1), 8–26.

Cornish, W., Llewelyn, D. and Aplin, T. (2019) Intellectual Property: Patents, Copyrights, Trademarks & Allied Rights 9th edition. London: Sweet & Maxwell.

Council of Europe. 'How to address current threats to journalism?: The role of the Council of Europe in protecting journalists and other media actors'. Expert paper by Dr. Tarlach McGonagle, presented at the Congress in Belgrade, 7 November 2013: Conference of Ministers responsible for Media and Information Society on 'Freedom of Expression and Democracy in the Digital Age – Opportunities, Rights, Responsibilities', MCM(2013)009. https://rm.coe.int/1680484e67

Council of Europe (2016) European Ministerial Conferences on Mass Media Policy & Council of Europe Conferences of Ministers responsible for Media and new Communication Services. Media and Internet Directorate General of Human Rights and Rule of Law Strasbourg. https://rm.coe.int/16806461fb

Crawford Committee Report of the Broadcasting Committee Appointed 20 July 1925. Report published 2 March 1926.

Crespi, S. (2018) 'The applicability of Schrems principles to the Member States: national security and data protection within the EU context', European Law Review, 43(5), 669–686.

Crossman, R.H.S. (1976a) The Diaries of a Cabinet Minister, 1964–1966. Volume I. New York: Holt, Rinehart & Winston.

Crossman, R.H.S. (1976b) The Diaries of a Cabinet Minister: Lord President of the Council, 1966–68. Volume II. London: Hamish Hamilton.

Crossman, R.H.S. (1977) The Diaries of a Cabinet Minister: Secretary of State for Social Services, 1968–70. Volume III. London: Penguin.

Davis, P.S. (2017) 'Costs of blocking injunctions', Intellectual Property Quarterly, 4, 330–345.

Davis, R., St Quintin, T. and Tritton, G. (eds) (2018) Tritton on Intellectual Property Law 5th ed. London: Sweet & Maxwell.

Department of Digital, Culture, Media and Sport. Government response to the consultation on the Leveson Inquiry and its implementation section 40 of the Crime and Courts Act 2013 and part 2 of the Leveson Inquiry. 1 March 2018. https://assets.publishing.service.gov.uk/government/uploads/system/uploads/attachment_data/file/684678/GOVERNMENT_RESPONSE_TO_THE_CONSULTATION_ON_THE_LEVESON_INQUIRY_AND_ITS_IMPLEMENTATION_.pdf

Descheemaeker, E. (2009) 'Protecting reputation: defamation and negligence', Oxford Journal of Legal Studies, 29(4), 603–641.

Electoral Commission. Report on the regulation of campaigners at the referendum on the UK's membership of the European Union held on 23 June 2016. March 2017. www.electoralcommission.org.uk/__data/assets/pdf_file/0004/223267/Report-on-the-regulation-of-campaigners-at-the-EU-referendum.pdf

Electoral Commission. 'Digital campaignin: increasing transparency for voters'. Report. June 2018. www.electoralcommission.org.uk/__data/assets/pdf_file/0010/244594/Digital-campaigning-improving-transparency-for-voters.pdf

Evans, T.M. (2011) 'Sampling, Looping, and Mashing . . . Oh My!: How Hip Hop Music is Scratching More Than the Surface of Copyright Law', Fordham Intellectual Property, Media and Entertainment Law Journal, 21(4), 843.

Finck, M. and Moscon, V. (2019) 'Copyright law on blockchains: between new forms of rights administration and digital rights management 2.0', International Review of Intellectual Property and Competition Law, 50(1), 77–108.

Fischer, P. (2018) 'From the safe harbour to the privacy shield: selected aspects of the EU-US privacy shield', *International Business Law Journal*, 2, 143–153.

Fischman Afori, O. (2014) 'Proportionality – A New Mega Standard in European Copyright Law', *International Review of Industrial Property and Copyright Law*, 45(8), 889–914.

Fletcher, S. and Mitchell, J. (2015) 'Court of Appeal found no love for Topshop tank: the image right that dare not speak its name', *European Intellectual Property Review*, 37(6), 394–405.

Foster, S. (2010) 'Possession of extreme pornographic images, public protection and human rights', *Coventry Law Journal*, 15(1), 21–27.

Fox, Sir John C. (1927) *The History of Contempt of Court: The Form of Trial and the Mode of Punishment*. Oxford: The Clarendon Press.

Freedman, D. (2003) *Television Policies of the Labour Party 1951–2001*. Oxford: Routledge.

Frosio, G. F. (2018) 'Why keep a dog and bark yourself? From intermediary liability to responsibility', *International Journal of Law and IT*, 26 (1), 1.

Gatley, J.C.C. (2017) *Gatley on Libel and Slander* 12th ed. Parkes, R., Mullis, A., Busuttil, G., Speaker, A., Scott, A. and Strong, C. (eds). London: Sweet & Maxwell.

Geddis, A. (2010) 'What we cannot talk about we must pass over in silence: judicial orders and reporting Parliamentary speech', *Public Law*, July, 443–451.

Gelfert, A. (2018) 'Fake News: A Definition', *Informal Logic*, 38(1), 84–117.

Gibbons, T. (1996) 'Defamation reconsidered', *Oxford Journal of Legal Studies*, 16(4), 587–615.

Gibbons, T. (2018) *Media Law in the United Kingdom*. 3rd ed. Alphen aan den Rijn, Netherlands: Kluwer Law International B.V.

Goodbody, S. (2018) 'Florence Foster Jenkins: joint authorship, costs and 'the world's worst opera singer', *Entertainment Law Review*, 29(3), 77–82.

Grant, H. and Round, N. (2012) 'Recent decisions of the Commissioner and tribunal', *Freedom of Information*, 9(2), 8–12.

Gravells, N. P. (2007) 'Authorship and originality: The persistent influence of *Walter v Lane*', *Intellectual Property Quarterly*, 3, 267–293.

Green, W. (ed) (2018) *Understanding Scots Law*, 3rd ed. London: Sweet & Maxwell.

Habermas, J. (1962, translation 1989) *The Structural Transformation of the Public Sphere: An Inquiry into a Category of Bourgeois Society* (original in German Strukturwandel der Öffentlichkeit. Untersuchungen zu einer Kategorie der bürgerlichen Gesellschaft). Cambridge: Polity Press.

Habermas, J. (1992, translation 1996) *Between Facts and Norms: Contributions to a Discourse Theory of Law and Democracy* (original in German Faktizität und Geltung). Cambridge: Polity Press.

Habermas, J. (1994) 'Three normative models of democracy', *Constellations: An International Journal of Critical and Democratic Theory*, 1(1) (December), 10.

Hally, M. (2012) 'Local authorities and film censorship: a historical account of the "Naughty Pictures Committees" in Sale and Manchester', *Entertainment and Sports Law Journal*, 11.

Hampel, S. (1992) 'Note: Are Samplers Getting a Bum Rap? Copyright infringement of technological creativity?', *University of Illinois Law Review*, 559.

Handig, C. (2013) 'The "sweat of the brow" is not enough! – more than a blueprint of the European copyright term "work"', *European Intellectual Property Review*, 35(6), 334–340.

Harding, T. (2013) 'BitTorrent tracking as a means of detecting illegal file-sharing', *E-Commerce Law & Policy*, 15(2), 8–9.

Hargreaves, I. (2011) *Digital Opportunity: A Review of Intellectual Property and Growth* ('The Hargreaves Review'). Newport: Intellectual Property Office.

Harrison, A. (2017) *Music: The Business. The essential guide to the law and the deals* 7th ed. Chatham: Virgin Books.

Hauch, J.M. (1994) 'Protecting private facts in France: The Warren and Brandeis tort is alive and well and flourishing in Paris', *Tulane Law Review*, 68, 1219.

Heistie, R. and Pennington, N. (1996) 'The O.J. Simpson Stories: Behavioral Scientists' Reflections on the *People of the State of California v. Orenthal James Simpson*', *University of Colorado Law Review*, 67(4), 957–976.

Henderson, G. (2009) 'A new form of libel tourist? *Ewing v Times Newspapers Ltd.* Case Comment', *Scots Law Times*, 20, 116–118.

Heylin, C. (1994) *The Great White Wonders: A History of Rock Bootlegs*. London: Viking.

Hildebrand, L. (2009) *Inherent Vice: Bootleg Histories of Videotape and Copyright*. Durham, NC: Duke University Press.

Hixson, R. (1987) *Privacy in a Public Society: Human Rights in Conflict*. Oxford: Oxford University Press.

HM Government. *Consultation on Copyright. Summary of Responses*. June 2012 ('The Hargreaves Review').

HM Government. *EU Exit. Legal position on the Withdrawal Agreement*. December 2018. Cm 9747.

Hodes, W.W. (1996) 'Lord Brougham, the Dream Team, and Jury Nullification of the Third Kind', *University of Colorado Law Review*, 67, 1075–1108.

Hollingsworth, M. and Fielding, N. (1999) *Defending the Realm: MI5 and the David Shayler Affair*. London: Andre Deutsch Ltd.

Holtz-Bacha, C. and Kaid, L.L. (2006). *Advertising in International Comparison: The Sage Handbook of Political Advertising*. Thousand Oaks, CA: Sage.

Home Office (1975) *Report of the Advisory Group on the Law of Rape* ('the Heilbron Report'), Cmnd 6352, December. London: HMSO.

Home Office (1987) *The Byford Report*. Home Office papers 1981–86. London: HMSO.

Hooper, D., Waite, K. and Murphy, O. (2013) 'Defamation Act 2013 – what difference will it really make?', *Entertainment Law Review*, 24(6), 199–206.

House of Commons (1973) *The Committee on Privacy Report* (chaired by the Rt. Hon. Kenneth Younger (The Younger Report). Cmnd. 5012.

House of Commons (1990) *Report of the Committee on Privacy and Related Matters* (The Calcutt Report). Cm 1102.

House of Commons (1994) *First Report of the Committee on Standards in Public Life: The Nolan Report*. Volume 1: Report, Cm 2850-I; Volume 2: Transcripts of Oral Evidence, Cm 2850-II. London: HMSO.

House of Commons (1995) 'Privacy and media intrusion'. HC Debate 17 July, Hansard, vol. 263: cc 132–139.

House of Commons – Department of Culture, Media and Sport (2003) *Privacy and Media Intrusion. Select Committee Report*. Session 2002–03. 16 June. HC 458-I. London: The Stationery Office.

House of Commons (2004) Report of the Inquiry into the Circumstances sourrounding the Death of Dr David Kelly C.M.G. by Lord Hutton ('The Hutton Report'). 28 January. HC 247. London: The Stationery Office.

House of Commons – Department of Culture, Media and Sport (2007) *Report by the Select Committee on 'Self-Regulation of the Press'*, 7th Report, 3 July. Session 2006–07, HC 375. London: The Stationery Office.

House of Commons – Department for Culture, Media and Sports (DCMS) and Department for Innovation, Business and Skills (BIS) (2009) *Digital Britain*. Presented to Parliament by The Secretary of State for Culture, Media and Sport and the Minister for Communications, Technology and Broadcasting. June. Cm 7650. London: The Stationery Office.

House of Commons – Department of Culture, Media and Sport Select Committee (2010a) *Second Report on 'Press standards, privacy and libel'*, 9 February. London: The Stationery Office.

House of Commons (2010b) *The Government's Response to the Culture, Media and Sport Select Committee on Press Standards, Privacy and Libel*. April. Cm 7851. London: The Stationery Office.

House of Commons – Department of Culture, Media and Sport Select Committee (2010c) *Press Standards, Privacy and Libel*, Session 2009–10, HC 362. London: The Stationery Office.

House of Commons – Department of Culture, Media and Sport Committee (2012a) *News International and Phonehacking*. Eleventh Report of Session 2010–12 Volume I: Report, together with formal minutes; Volume II: Oral and written evidence. 1 May. HC 903-I. London

House of Commons (2012b) *The Report of the Hillsborough Independent Panel*. September. HC 581. London: The Stationery Office.

House of Commons (2014) Home Affairs Committee. 'Police, the media, and high-profile criminal investigations: Government Response to the Committee's Fifth Report of Session 2014–15'. Sixth Special Report of Session 2014–15. 3 December. HC 867.

House of Commons (2015) Home Affairs Committee Oral evidence: Policing in London, HC 929 Tuesday 10 March.

House of Commons (2016) Chilcot Inquiry Report. Number CBP 6215, 1 July.

House of Commons (2017) The Official Secrets Acts and Official Secrecy. HC briefing papers by Gail Bartlett and Michael Everett. Number CBP07422. 2 May.

House of Commons (2019a) Digital, Culture, Media and Sport Committee. 'Online advertising in the UK'. A report commissioned by the Department for Digital, Culture, Media and Sport, January. Plum Consulting: Adshead, S., Forsyth, G., Wood, S. and Wilkinson, L. ('The Plum Report').

House of Commons (2019b) Digital, Culture, Media and Sport Committee. Disinformation and 'fake news'. 18 February.

House of Commons (2019c) Department of Culture, Digital Media and Sport 'Online Harms White Paper'. Presented to Parliament by the Secretary of State for Digital, Culture, Media & Sport and the Secretary of State for the Home Department by Command of Her Majesty. April. CP 57.

House of Lords and House of Commons (2010) *Human Rights Joint Committee. Counter-Terrorism Policy and Human Rights*. 16th Report. Annual Renewal of Control Orders.

Houghton Committee on Financial Aid to Political Parties. 10 March 1976 (CAB 164/1318).

Hoy, R. (2015) 'Internet blocking injunctions are alive and well in the post Svensson world', *Entertainment Law Review*, 26(2), 44–47.

Information Commissioner's Office (ICO) (2006a) *What Price Privacy? The unlawful trade in confidential personal information*, presented by the Information Commissioner to Parliament pursuant to section 52(2) of the Data Protection Act 1998. 10 May. HC 1056. London: The Stationery Office.

Information Commissioner's Office (ICO) (2006b) *A Report on the Surveillance Society*, for the Information Commissioner by the Surveillance Studies Network. September.

Isocrates (1980) *Isocrates: with an English Translation in three volumes*, by George Norlin, PhD, LLD. Cambridge, MA: Harvard University Press; London: William Heinemann Ltd.

Israel, J. (2006) *Enlightenment Contested: Philosophy, Modernity, and the Emancipation of Man 1670–1752*. Oxford: Oxford University Press.

Jacques, S. (2015) 'Are the new "fair dealing" provisions an improvement on the previous UK law, and why?', *Journal of Intellectual Property Law & Practice*, 10(9), 699–706.

Johnson, H. (2008a) 'Freedom of information – confidence and journalism exemptions from Disclosure', *Communications Law*, 13(5), 174–176.

Johnson, H. (2008b) 'Defamation: the media on the defensive?', *Communications Law*, 13(4), 126–131.

Jongsma, D. (2017) 'Parody after Deckmyn: a comparative overview of the approach to parody under copyright law in Belgium, France, Germany and the Netherlands', *International Review of Intellectual Property and Competition Law*, 48(6), 652–682.

Jordan, P. (ed.) (2014) *International Advertising Law. Practical Global Guide*. Llandysul: Globe Business Publishing.

Judicial College (2015) Reporting Restrictions in the Criminal Courts, 3rd ed (revised 2016). www.judiciary.uk/wp-content/uploads/2015/07/reporting-restrictions-guide-may-2016-2.pdf

Kant, I. (1784) 'What is Enlightenment?' Königsberg, Prussia.

Kant, I. (1787) *Kritik der reinen Vernunft*. Derived from HTML files at 'Projekt Gutenberg – DE', prepared by Gerd Bouillon. www.gutenberg2000.de/kant/krvb/krvb.htm

Keays, S. (1985) *A Question of Judgement*. London: Quintessential Press Ltd.

Kilbrandon, Lord (1964) *Report of the Committee on Children and Young Persons, Scotland* ('The Kilbrandon Report'). Cmnd 2306, London: HMSO.

Kilbrandon, Lord (1971) 'The Law of Privacy in Scotland', 2 *Cambrian Law Review*, 35, 128.

Kirk, E. (2006) 'The *Da Vinci Code* case – *Baigent & Leigh v Random House*: ideas v expression revisited', *Intellectual Property & Information Law*, 11(3), 4–6.

Kislan, R. (1995) *The Musical: A Look at the American Musical Theater*. Revised ed. New York: Applause Books.

Koempel, F. (2007) 'If the kids are united', *Journal of Intellectual Property Law & Practice*, 2(6), 371–376.

Lawrence, D.H. (1928; first UK publication 1960) *Lady Chatterley's Lover*. London: Penguin Classics.

Ledward, J. and Agate, J. (2017) 'Revenge porn and Section 33: the story so far', *Entertainment Law Review*, 28(2), 40–42.

Leigh, I. (1992) 'Spycatcher in Strasbourg', *Public Law*, 200.

Lennon, C. (1978) *A Twist of Lennon*. London: Avon/Harper Collins.

Lester, A. (Lord Lester of Herne Hill) (2016) *Five Ideas to Fight For: How Our Freedom Is Under Threat and Why It Matters*. Bloomsbury, London: One World Publications.

Leveson, Lord, LJ (2012) *An Inquiry into the Culture, Practices and Ethics of the Press. Report by The Right Honourable Lord Justice Leveson in 4 Volumes*. Volume I 'The Inquiry', Volume II 'The Culture, Practices and Ethics of the Press', Volume III 'The Press and Data Protection', Volume IV 'Aspects of Regulation: the Law and the Press Complaints Commission'. November. London: The Stationery Office.

Lindsay, R. (ed) (2016) *Ad Law: The Essential Guide to Advertising Law and Regulation*. London: Institute of Practitioners in Advertising (IPA) Publication.

Lipstadt, D.E. (1994) *Denying the Holocaust: The Growing Assault on Truth and Memory*. London: Penguin.

Lipstadt, D.E. (2006) *History on Trial: My Day in Court with David Irving*. New York: Harper Collins.

Litman, J. (2018) 'What we don't see when we see copyright as property', *Cambridge Law Journal*, 77(3), 536–558.

Litvinenko Inquiry, The (2016) Report into the death of Alexander Litvinenko. By Sir Robert Owen. https://assets.publishing.service.gov.uk/government/uploads/system/uploads/attachment_data/file/493860/The-Litvinenko-Inquiry-H-C-695-web.pdf

Lord Chief Justice of England and Wales (2018) The Right Hon. The Lord Burnett of Maldon, 'Becoming Stronger Together'. Speech given to the Commonwealth Judges and Magistrates' Association Annual Conference, Brisbane, Australia, 10 September. www.judiciary.uk/wp-content/uploads/2018/09/lcj-speech-brisbane-lecture-20180910.pdf

Lord Neill of Bladen QC Fifth Report of the Committee on Standards in Public Life: 'The Funding of Political Parties in the United Kingdom'. Presented to Parliament by the Prime Minister by Command of Her Majesty October 1998 (Cm 4057 Vol I and II) ('The Neill Report').

Lovelace, L. (Linda Susan Boreman) (1976) *Inside Linda Lovelace*. London: Pinnacle Books.

Lucas, A. (2010) 'For a reasonable interpretation of the three-step test', *European Intellectual Property Review*, 32(6), 277–282.

Lundie Smith, R. and Kendall-Palmer, C. (2016) 'No Glee in the United Kingdom with reverse confusion: *Comic Enterprises Ltd v Twentieth Century Fox Film Corp.*', *Entertainment Law Review*, 25(4), 165–168.

Mahoney, P. (1997) 'Universality versus subsidiarity in the Strasbourg case law on free speech: Explaining some recent judgments', *European Human Rights Law Review*, 4, 364–379.

Markesinis, B.S. (ed) (1999) *Protecting Privacy*. Oxford: Oxford University Press.

Markesinis, B.S. and Unberath, H. (2002) *The German Law of Torts: A Comparative Treatise*. London: Hart.

McEvedy, V. (2013) 'Defamation and intermediaries: ISP defences', *Computer and Telecommunications Law Review*, 19(4), 108–112.

McGartland, M. (2009) *Fifty Dead Men Walking*. London: John Blake Publishing Ltd.

McInnes, R. (2009a) 'Footballers' faces: Photographs, identification and publication contempt', *Scots Law Times*, 21, 123–126.

McInnes, R. (2009b) 'The ones which got away? Reporting of criminal trials', *Scots Law Times*, 25, 149–152.

McInnes, R. (2016) *Scots Law for Journalists* 9th ed. Edinburgh: W Green/Sweet & Maxwell.

Mill, J.S. (1859) *On Liberty* 4th ed. London: Longmans, Green, Reader and Dyer.

Milton, J. (1644 reprinted 1915) *Areopagitica: A Speech for the Liberty of Unlicensed Printing to the Parliament of England*. London: Macmillan and Co. Limited.

Mindell, R. (2012) 'Rewriting privacy: the impact of online social networks', *Entertainment Law Review*, 23(3), 52–58.

Ministry of Justice (2010b) *Review of Civil Litigation Costs*. Final Report by Rupert Jackson J, December 2009. P002341871 c7 01/10 860 19585 ('The Jackson Report') London: HMSO.

Ministry of Justice (2010c) *Providing Anonymity to Those Accused of Rape: An Assessment of Evidence*. Ministry of Justice Research Series 20/10, November.

Ministry of Justice (2012c) *The Government's Response to the Report of the Joint Committee on the Draft Defamation Bill*. Cm 8295. London: Stationery Office.

Ministry of Justice (2013) *Implementing the Coroner Reforms in Part 1 of the Coroners and Justice Act 2009. Consultation on Rules, Regulations, Coroner Areas and Statutory Guidance*. Consultation Paper CP2/2013, 12 April.

Ministry of Justice (2017) Report of the Chief Coroner to the Lord Chancellor Fourth Annual Report: 2016–2017. (CCS0817752928 09/17). London: Stationery Office.

Moore, B. (1984) *Privacy: Studies in Social and Cultural History*. Armonk, NY: M.E. Sharpe Publishing.

Mueller, B. (2017) *Dynamics of International Advertising: Theoretical and Practical Perspectives*. 3rd ed. New York: Peter Lang.

Mulligan, A. (2016) 'Constitutional aspects of international data transfer and mass surveillance', *Irish Jurist*, 55, 199–208.

Mulvihill, D. (2000) 'Irving v. Penguin: Historians on Trial and the Determination of Truth Under English Libel Law'. In *Fordham Intellectual Property, Media and Entertainment Law Journal* Volume 11, Volume XI Number 1, Volume XI Book 1 Article 6. https://ir.lawnet.fordham.edu/cgi/viewcontent.cgi?article=1211&context=iplj

Neill, B. (1999) 'Privacy: a challenge for the next century' in *Protecting Privacy*, B. Markesinis, ed. Oxford: Oxford University Press.

Nelson, L.S. (2018) *Social Media and Morality: Losing Our Self Control*. Cambridge: Cambridge University Press.

Normand, the Right Hon Lord (1938) 'The Law of Defamation in Scotland', *The Cambridge Law Journal*, 6, 327–338.

Ofcom (2016) Review of the rules for mandatory daytime PIN protections Call for Inputs. www.ofcom.org.uk/__data/assets/pdf_file/0031/79861/pin_call_for_inputs.pdf

Ofcom (2017) Review of rules for prominence of public service broadcasters and local TV consultation on proposed changes to the linear EPG Code and future of the regime. 27 July.

Ofcom (2018) Media Nations Report 2018. www.ofcom.org.uk/__data/assets/pdf_file/0014/116006/media-nations-2018-uk.pdf

O'Leary, S. (2018) 'Balancing rights in a digital age', *Irish Jurist*, 59–92.

Palmer, T. (1971 reprinted 2014) *Trials of Oz*. London: Gonzo Media.

Parsons, K. (2000) 'Pirates' web', *European Lawyer*, 1(1), 38–39, 41–42.

Passman, D.S. (2019) *All You Need to Know about the Music Business* 9th ed. London/New York: Viking.

Phillipson, G. (2003) 'Breach of confidence, celebrities, freedom of expression, legal reasoning, newspapers, privacy, public interest, right to respect for private and family life', *European Human Rights Law Review* (Special Issue 'Privacy'), 54–72.

Pila, J. (2010) 'Copyright and its categories of original works', *Oxford Journal of Legal Studies*, 30(2), 229–254.

Prosser, W.L. (1971) *The Law of Torts*. 4th ed. Eagan, MN: West Publishing Co.

Rachels, J. (1975) 'Why privacy is important', *Philosophy and Public Affairs*, 4, 323.

Rampal, K.R. (1981) 'The concept of the Press Council', *International Communication Gazette*, 28, 91–103.

Raymond, J. (1998) 'The newspaper, public opinion, and the public sphere in the seventeenth century', *Prose Studies*, 21(2) (August), 109–136.

Richardson, M. and Thomas, J. (2012) *Fashioning Intellectual Property: Exhibition, Advertising and the Press 1789–1918*. Cambridge: Cambridge University Press.

Rosati, E. (2011) 'Originality in a work, or a work of originality: the effects of the Infopaq decision', *European Intellectual Property Review*, 33(12), 746–755.

Rowbottom, J. (2012) 'To rant, vent and converse: protecting low level digital speech', *Cambridge Law Review*, 71(2), 355–383.

Rushdie, S. (1989 reprinted 1998) *The Satanic Verses*. Minneapolis, MN and London: Consortium Press.

Rushdie, S. (2012) *Joseph Anton*. London: Jonathan Cape/Random House.

Sanders, K (2003) *Ethics and Journalism*. London: Sage.

Sanjek, D. (1992) ' "Don't have to DJ no more": Sampling and the "autonomous" creator', *Cardozo Arts and Entertainment Law Journal*, 10(2), 612–615.

Scaife, L. (2013) 'Social media and injunctions: can *contra mundum* apply when stories develop wings?', *Communications Law*, 18(2), 42–44.

Scanlon, T.M. (1972) '*A theory of freedom of expression*', *Philosophy and Public Affairs*, 1(2), Winter, 204–226.

Schwiddessen, S., Clark, B., Defaux, T. and Groom, J. (2018) 'Germany's Network Enforcement Act – closing the net on fake news?' *European Intellectual Property Review*, 40(8), 539–546.

Scottish Information Commissioner. 'Annual Report and Accounts 2017/18: Opening the door to meaningful participation.' Laid before the Scottish Parliament in September 2018 in pursuance of section 46 of the Freedom of Information (Scotland) Act 2002 and section 22(5) of the Public Finance and Accountability (Scotland) Act 2000. SG laying number – SG/2018/149.

Scottish Law Commission. 'Defamation Law: Time for change?' A Discussion Paper, issued on behalf of the Scottish Law Commission on 17 March 2016.

Scottish Law Commission. Report on Defamation Laid before the Scottish Parliament by the Scottish Ministers under section 3(2) of the Law Commissions Act 1965 December 2017. Scot Law Com No 248 (SG/2017/263).

Sereny, G. (1998) *Cries Unheard: The Story of Mary Bell*. London: Macmillan.

Smartt, U. (2007) 'Who still observes the law of contempt?', *Justice of the Peace Journal*, 171 (3 February), 76–83.

Smartt, U. (2011) 'Twitter undermines super injunctions', *Communications Law*, 16(4), 135–140.

Smartt, U. (2012) 'Safety first: the Ryan Giggs super injunction Part 2 of March 2012', *Communications Law*, 17(2), 50–52.

Smartt, U. (2014) 'Internet libel: will the new Defamation Act 2013 make a real difference?' *Criminal Law and Justice Weekly*, 174(42), 645–647.

Smartt, U. (2015a) 'Prince Charles "black spider memos": how a *Guardian* journalist succeeded in his 10-year quest under the Freedom of Information Act 2000', *European Intellectual Property Review*, 37(8), 529–538.

Smartt, U. (2015b) 'Why I was right to name the teacher's teen killer: naming teenagers in criminal trials and law reform in the internet age', *Communications Law*, 20(1), 5–13.

Smartt, U. (2018) The three Rs: Remorse, Rehabilitation, Right to be forgotten: how de-listing is left up to the courts in NT1 & NT2 and *AR v Chief Constable of Greater Manchester*, *European Intellectual Property Review*, 40, 804–811.

Smith, A. (1776 reprint 2008) *An Inquiry into the Nature and Causes of the Wealth of Nations K. Sutherland, ed.* Oxford: Oxford Classics.

Solzhenitsyn, A. (1962) *One Day in the Life of Ivan Denisovich*. London: Penguin (reprinted in 1996. London: Bantam Press).

Spencer, J.R. (1989) *Jackson's Machinery of Justice* 8th ed. (Original publication by Professor R.M. Jackson in 1903). Cambridge: Cambridge University Press.

Spurrier, M. (2012) '*Gillberg v Sweden* : towards a right of access to information under Article 10?', *European Human Rights Law Review*, 5, 551–558.

Stanford, B. (2018) 'Compulsory voter identification, disenfranchisement and human rights: electoral reform in Great Britain', *European Human Rights Law Review*, 1, 57–66.

Stein, E. (2000) *Thoughts from a Bridge. A retrospective of writings on new Europe and American federalism*. Ann Arbor: University of Michigan Press.

Taylor, The Rt Hon Lord Justice (1989) *The Hillsborough Stadium Disaster, 15 April 1989, Interim Report*. Cm 765, London: Her Majesty's Stationery Office.

Thornton, S. (2009) *Seven Days in the Art World*. London: Granta Books.

Thurlbeck, N. (2015) *Tabloid Secrets: The Stories Behind the Headlines at the World's Most Famous Newspaper*. London: Biteback Publishing

Travers, P. and Reiff, S. (1974) *The Story Behind 'The Exorcist'*. New York: Signet Books.

Varotto, S. (2016) 'The Schrems decision, the EU-US Privacy Shield and the necessity to rethink how to approach cross border personal data transfers at global level', *Communications Law*, 21(3), 78–87.

Vor der Bruegge, A. (2011) *A Dull Engima: Historians' Analysis of Gilbert and Sullivan 's Impact on the Development of the American Musical Theatre*. Winthrop University.

Wacks, R. (2013) *Privacy and Media Freedom*. Oxford: Oxford University Press.

Waisbord, S. (2018) 'Truth is What Happens to News: On journalism, fake news, and post-truth', *Journalism Studies*, 19, 1866–1878.

Warby, M., Mareham, N. and Christie. I. (eds) (2016) *The Law of Privacy and The Media* 3rd ed. Oxford: Oxford University Press.

Warren, S.D. and Brandeis, L.D. (1890) 'The right to privacy', *Harvard Law Review*, 4(5) (15 December), 193–220.

Watson, R., Roldan, R. and Faza, A. (2017) 'Toward Normalization of Defamation Law: The U.K. Defamation Act of 2013 and the U.S. SPEECH Act of 2010 as Responses to the Issue of Libel Tourism', *Communication Law and Policy*, 1.

Whitty, N.R. and Zimmermann, R. (eds) (2009) *Rights of Personality in Scots Law: A Comparative Perspective*. Dundee: Dundee University Press.

Wilkinson, N. (2015) *Secrecy and the Media: the Official History of the United Kingdom's D-Notice System*. Abingdon, Oxon: Routledge

Williams, A.T. (2012) *A Very British Killing: The Death of Baha Mousa*. London: Jonathan Cape.

Wilmshurst, P. (2011) 'The regulation of medical devices', *British Medical Journal*, 342, 1093–1094.

Wilmshurst, P. (2012) 'CLOSURE 1 seen through the MIST', *British Medical Journal*, 344, 51.

Winfield, P.H. (1937) *A Textbook of the Law of Tort*. London: Sweet & Maxwell.

Witzleb, N. (2009) 'Justifying gain-based remedies for invasions of privacy', *Oxford Journal of Legal Studies*, 29, 325.

Wood, H. (2018) 'From Judge Judy to Judge Rinder and Judge Geordie: humour, emotion and "televisual legal consciousness"', *International Journal of Law in Context*, 14(4), 581–595.

Wragg, P. (2015) 'The legitimacy of press regulation', *Public Law*, April, 290–307.

Wright, P. (1987) *Spycatcher: The Candid Autobiography of a Secret Intelligence Officer*. Australia: William Heinemann and Viking Press.

Wring, D., Mortimore, R. and Atkinson, S. (eds) (2016) *Political Communication in Britain: Polling, Campaigning and Media in the 2015 General Election*. London: Palgrave Macmillan.

Yeoh, F. (2015) 'Adaptations in music theatre: confronting copyright', *Entertainment Law Review*, 26(4), 119–129.

Yin Harn Lee (2018) 'United Kingdom copyright decisions 2017', *International Review of Intellectual Property and Competition Law*, 49(3), 324–330.

Internet sources and useful websites

Advertising Standards Authority (ASA): www.asa.org.uk
Associated Press (AP) (Global News Network): www.ap.org
Association for Television on Demand (ATVOD): http://atvod.co.uk
Attorney General's Office (England & Wales): www.attorneygeneral.gov.uk
Authors' Licensing and Collecting Society (ALCS): www.alcs.co.uk
BMI – Broadcast Music, Inc.: www.bmi.com
British Board of Film Classification (BBFC): www.bbfc.co.uk
British Phonographic Industry (BPI): www.bpi.co.uk
Cabinet Office (UK): www.gov.uk/government/organisations/cabinet-office
CISAC (Confédération Internationale des Sociétés d'Auteurs et Compositeurs – the
Competition and Markets Authority: www.cisac.org
Court martial (the military court service): www.gov.uk/the-military-court-service
Court of Justice of the European Union (CJEU): www.curia.eu
Department for Digital, Culture, Media and Sport: www.gov.uk/government/
    organisations/department-for-digital-culture-media-sport
European Advertising Standards Alliance (EASA): www.easa-alliance.org
European Commission: https://ec.europa.eu/commission/index_en
European Court of Human Rights: www.echr.coe.int
European Parliament: www.europarl.eu
European Patent Office (Munich): www.epo.org
European Union Intellectual Property Office (Office for Harmonization in the
    Internal Market – OHIM) (EU Trademark Office): http://oami.europa.eu
Featured Artists Coalition (FAC): www.featuredartistscoalition.com
Federation Against Copyright Theft (FACT): www.fact-uk.org.uk
Freedom of Information Advocates (global network): www.freedominfo.org
GEMA (Gesellschaft für musikalische Aufführungs- und mechanische
    Vervielfältigungsrechte – Musical copyright association): www.gema.de
Hansard: https://hansard.parliament.uk
HUDOC (database for case law of the European Court of Human Rights): http://
    hudoc.echr.coe.int/eng
IMPRESS (independent press regulator): http://impress.press
Independent Press Standards Organisation (IPSO): www.ipso.co.uk
Information Commissioner for Northern Ireland: https://ico.org.uk/about-the-ico/
    who-we-are/northern-ireland-office
Information Commissioner's Office (ICO): https://ico.org.uk
Intellectual Property Office UK: www.ipo.gov.uk
International Federation of Journalists: www.ifj.org
International Federation of the Phonographic Industry (IFPI): www.ifpi.org
International Press Institute (IPI): https://ipi.media
Internet Corporation for Assigned Names and Numbers (ICANN): www.icann.org
Internet Watch Foundation (IWF): www.iwf.org.uk

Investigatory Powers Commissioner's Office: www.ipco.org.uk
Irish Department of Justice and Law Reform: www.justice.ie
Irish Parliament for the Dáil – Houses of the Oireachtas: www.oireachtas.ie
Judiciary (England & Wales – courts & tribunals): www.judiciary.gov.uk
Mechanical Copyright Protection Society (MCPS) – see: PRS
Music Publishers Association (for sheet/printed music): www.mpaonline.org.uk
Musicians' Union (MU): www.musiciansunion.org.uk
National Archives: www.nationalarchives.gov.uk
National Council for the Training of Journalists (NCTJ): www.nctj.com
National Union of Journalists (NUJ): www.nuj.org.uk
Northern Ireland Assembly: www.niassembly.gov.uk
Northern Ireland Courts and Tribunal Service: www.courtsni.gov.uk
Northern Ireland Law Commission: www.nilawcommission.gov.uk
Ofcom (Office of Communications): www.ofcom.org.uk
Office of National Statistics (UK): www.statistics.gov.uk
Office of Public Sector Information: www.opsi.gov.uk/psi
Parliament, UK: www.parliament.uk
Performing Right Society (PRS): www.prsformusic.com
PhonepayPlus (regulates phone-paid services in the UK): www.phonepayplus.org.uk
Phonographic Performance Ltd (PPL): https://pplprs.co.uk
Press Association: www.pressassociation.com
Press Council of Ireland: www.presscouncil.ie
Press Recognition Panel (PRP): https://pressrecognitionpanel.org.uk
Scots Law Online: www.scottishlaw.org.uk
Scottish Court Service: www.scotcourts.gov.uk
Scottish Information Commissioner: www.itspublicknowledge.info/home/
    ScottishInformationCommissioner.aspx
Scottish Law Commission: www.scotlawcom.gov.uk
Scottish Parliament: www.scottish.parliament.uk
Society of Authors: www.societyofauthors.net
Society of Editors: www.societyofeditors.co.uk
Trading Standards: www.nationaltradingstandards.uk
Unified Patent Court (EU): www.unified-patent-court.org
US Patent Office (Patents & Trademarks): www.uspto.gov
Video Standards Council (VSC) and Games Regulator: www.videostandards.org.uk
Welsh Assembly: www.assembly.wales
World Intellectual Property Organization (WIPO): www.wipo.int/portal/en
World Trade Organization (WTO): www.wto.org

Index

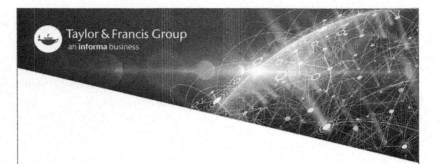